Using Microsoft® Office, Special Edition

Que Development Group

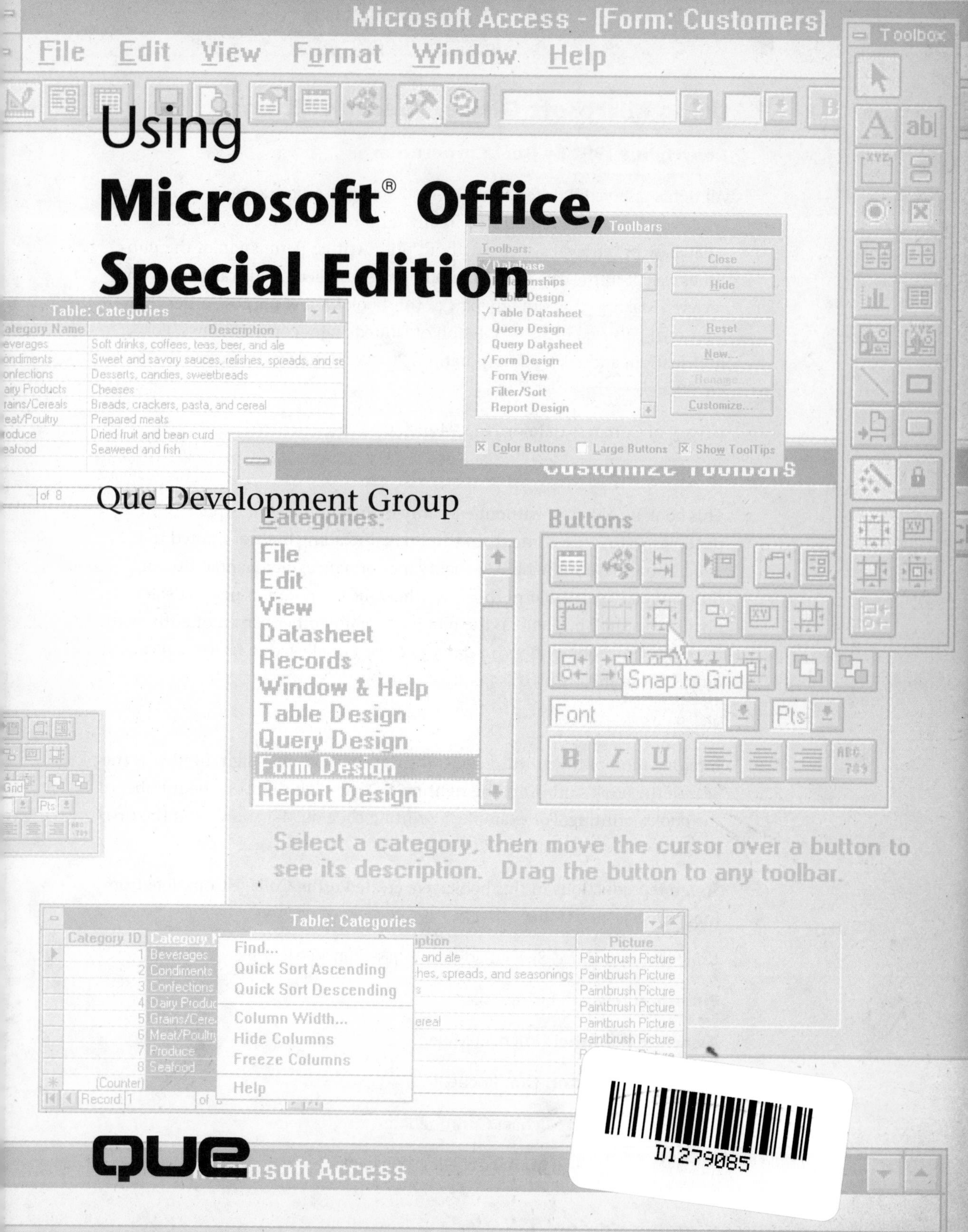

QUE

Using Microsoft Office, Special Edition

Library of Congress Catalog No.: 94-65880

ISBN: 1-56529-721-0

96 95 94 5

Interpretation of the printing code: the rightmost double-digit number is the year of the book's printing; the rightmost single-digit number, the number of the book's printing. For example, a printing code of 94-1 shows that the first printing of the book occurred in 1994.

Screen reproductions in this book were created using Collage Complete from Inner Media, Inc., Hollis, NH.

Using Microsoft Office, Special Edition is based on Version 4.2.

Publisher: David P. Ewing

Associate Publisher: Michael Miller

Publishing Director: Don Roche, Jr.

Managing Editor: Michael Cunningham

Product Marketing Manager: Greg Wiegand

Credits

Publishing Manager
Charles O. Stewart III

Acquisitions Editor
Nancy Stevenson

Product Director
Jim Minatel

Product Development Specialists
Kathie-Jo Arnoff
Joyce J. Nielsen
Lisa Wagner

Production Editor
Lori A. Lyons

Editors
Noelle Gasco
Kathy Simpson
Barb Colter
Danielle Bird
Lori Cates
Patrick Kanouse
Diana R. Moore
Lynn Northrup
Joy Preacher
Brad Sullivan

Technical Editors
Patrick Irwin
Jonathan Ruffing
Janice A. Snyder
Michael Watson

Figure Specialist
Wilfred R. Thebodeau

Book Designer
Paula Carroll

Editorial Assistants
Jill Stanley
Michelle Williams

Production Team
Stephen Adams
Angela Bannan
Cameron Booker
Jodie Cantwell
Anne Dickerson
Karen Dodson
Bob LaRoche
Joy Dean Lee
Jay Lesandrini
Elizabeth Lewis
G. Alan Palmore
Nanci Sears Perry
Linda Quigley
Caroline Roop
Linda Seifert
Michael Thomas
Becky Tapley
Mary Beth Wakefield

Indexers
Charlotte Clapp
Greg Eldred

Composed in *Stone Serif* and *MCPdigital* by Que Corporation

About the Authors

Cathy Kenny is an assistant editor for a computer magazine in Boston, Massachusetts. She is the author of Que's *1-2-3 VisiRef* and a contributing author of *Using 1-2-3 Release 4.0 for Windows,* Special Edition, *Using Excel 5.0,* Special Edition, and *Excel Version 5 for Windows QuickStart.* She has also served as technical editor on more than 15 books for both Que and Howard W. Sams.

William J. Orvis is an electronics engineer at the University of California's Lawrence Livermore National Laboratory, where he is involved in the large-scale numerical modeling of solid-state devices, development of micron-sized vacuum microelectronic devices, and computer security research. (He describes himself as a computer virus smasher.) He is a member of CIAC, the Department of Energy's computer incident response team. Orvis received both his B.S. and M.S. degrees in Physics and Astronomy at the University of Denver in Colorado. He is the author of several computer books and has written for magazines.

Susan Plumley owns Humble Opinions, a consulting firm that offers training in popular software programs and system connectivity. In addition, Sue is the author of several Que books, including *Windows 3.1 SureSteps, Crystal Clear DOS, Crystal Clear Word,* and *Easy PowerPoint.* Sue is also a contributing author to *Using WordPerfect Version 6 for DOS,* Special Edition, *Using OS/2 2.1,* and *Using WordPerfect Version 6 for Windows,* Special Edition.

Stephen A. Swope is a programmer analyst and trainer for Blue Chip Computers in Dayton, Ohio. Steve has published several technical articles in USAF computer journals. He has an M.A. in Rhetoric and Communication from the University of Pittsburgh.

Diane Tinney is proprietor of The Software Professional, a business that provides education, development support, and consulting on a variety of Windows and DOS applications. Diane specializes in the integration of Windows products, and specifically, database implementation and integration. Most recently, Diane authored Que's *Paradox for Windows Programming By Example* and contributed to *Using Paradox 4.5 fo DOS,* Special Edition. Diane's background includes creating corporate tax systems, international tax consulting, and accounting. Diane can be reached on Compuserve at 72074,2525 or via MCI address DTinney.

Debbie Walkowski has worked in the computer industry since 1981 writing documentation, designing user interfaces, and teaching computer courses. Her company, The Writing Works, specializes in writing computer self-help books and providing writing services to companies such as Microsoft Corporation and Digital Equipment Corporation. Debbie has a degree in scientific and technical communication and has authored and coauthored 12 books on popular computer software including Microsoft Excel, WordPerfect, Microsoft PowerPoint, Lotus 1-2-3, Microsoft Works, Microsoft Project, Quicken, and Professional Write Plus.

Rick Winter is a Senior Partner at PRW Computer Services. He has trained over 2,800 adults on personal computers. He is the coauthor of Que's *Excel for Windows SureSteps, Look Your Best with Excel*, and *Q&A QueCards*. He is also the revision author for Que's *1-2-3 QuickStart Release 3.4* and *1-2-3 QuickStart Release 2.4, MicroRef Quick Reference Guide to Lotus 1-2-3 Release 3.0*, and *MicroRef Quick Reference Guide to Lotus 1-2-3 Release 2.2*. Rick is a contributing author for Que's *Using Excel 5 for Windows, Using WordPerfect 6 for Windows*, and *Using PC Tools 8*. He is the revision script writer for Video Professor *Lotus 1-2-3 Version 2.2 and 3.0 Level I* and *Lotus 1-2-3 Version 2.2 and 3.0 Level II* and script writer for Video Professor *Lotus 1-2-3 Version 2.2 and 3.0 Level III.*

Patty Winter is a Senior Partner at PRW Computer Services. She has trained over 1,500 adults in the art of using personal computers. She is the coauthor of *Excel for Windows SureSteps* and *Look Your Best with Excel*, and *Que's Q&A QueCards*. Patty established, and is President of, Colorado Q&A User Group.

Trademarks

Contents at a Glance

Contents

VI Working Together with Microsoft Office Applications 735

43 Using Visual Basic for Applications 895

Introduction

Using Microsoft Office, Special Edition, pools the talents of a diverse collection of software experts. The members of this team were chosen for their proven ability to write clear instructional text as well as their expertise with Microsoft Office Professional and the individual Windows applications that make up the suite: Excel, PowerPoint, Word, and Access.

This collaborative approach gives you the best information about the individual suite applications as well as expert advice on how to get the most out of integrating them. We chose experts in Word, Excel, Access, and PowerPoint to write about those programs. For the integration part of this book, we chose an authoring team with much experience in using Word, Access, Excel, PowerPoint, and Mail together to combine information in ways nearly impossible or very difficult before Microsoft Office.

Microsoft has designed the Office applications to work extremely well together to allow you to create documents that rely on information from multiple applications, and to accomplish this feat nearly seamlessly. The applications are designed to act and look alike to reduce your "learning curve." Office includes all the tools to help you get your work done so that you can concentrate on the task without worrying about the application. Office includes shared programs, such as WordArt, ClipArt Gallery, Microsoft Query, and Microsoft Chart, and many common interface features that point the way beyond what columnist Jeff Raskin has called the "walled cities" of traditional applications.

Most industry experts believe that suites are the wave of the future. According to data from Microsoft, nearly 50 percent of Word for Windows and Excel sales are driven by sales of the Microsoft Office suite, with sales of 75 percent predicted for 1994. Corporate America is witnessing an increasing emphasis on Windows integration, especially in settings where support and productivity are critical. *Using Microsoft Office,* Special Edition, helps you take advantage of this new way of working with software.

Who Should Use This Book?

Using Microsoft Office, Special Edition, is the right choice for home-office workers, corporate personnel, students, teachers, consultants, computer support staff—anyone using two or more of the Office suite applications. *Using Microsoft Office*, Special Edition, also is useful for anyone new to the Microsoft suite of applications and wishing to get up to speed quickly on the Office applications.

This book assumes that you are familiar with Microsoft Windows but not familiar with all the applications in the Office suite.

If you want to integrate two or more of the Office applications and exchange information, *Using Microsoft Office*, Special Edition, is designed to meet your needs. If you are sharing data across a workgroup, this book shows you how Office helps you and others collaborate effectively on a project.

Using Microsoft Office, Special Edition, is the ideal companion volume to *Using Word Version 6 for Windows*, *Using Windows 3.1*, *Using Excel Version 5 for Windows*, *Using Access 2 for Windows*, and *Using PowerPoint 4 for Windows*—all from Que.

How This Book Is Organized

Using Microsoft Office, Special Edition, is designed to complement the documentation that comes with Microsoft Office. Beginners will find the step-by-step information in this book helpful; experienced users will appreciate the comprehensive coverage and expert advice. After you become proficient with one of more of the applications within Office, you can use this book as a desktop reference.

Using Microsoft Office, Special Edition, is divided into eight parts:

Part I: Learning a New Way To Work

Part II: Using Word

Part III: Using Excel

Part IV: Using PowerPoint

Part V: Using Access

Part VI: Working Together with Microsoft Office Applications

Part VII: Customizing Microsoft Office

Part VIII: Appendixes

Part I introduces you to Microsoft Office and describes the "new way of working" the suite represents, whether you work alone or collaborate with others in an office. In chapters 1 and 2, you learn about the features shared by all the Office applications that enable you to move from program to program and share data effortlessly. The final chapter in Part I deals with managing files and work areas across the applications. Part I helps prepare you for Part VI, which deals with using the Office applications together to create a range of documents. If you are unfamiliar with Office and need to work with one or more of the applications, you should read Part I.

Parts II-V cover the essentials of Word 6, Excel 5, PowerPoint 4, and Access 2, respectively. Chapters 4-11 cover the essentials of Word, chapters 12-18 cover the essentials of Excel, chapters 19-26 cover the essentials of PowerPoint, and chapters 27-34 cover the essentials of working with Access. If you know one of the Office applications and need to get up to speed quickly on one or more of the other suite applications, you should work through these focused presentations. Even if you haven't used any of the Office applications, you can get up to speed quickly by working through this part of the book. Parts II-V are designed to prepare you for the integration section that follows.

Part VI is the heart and soul of *Using Microsoft Office*, Special Edition, dealing as it does with how these suite applications work in concert. Chapter 35 begins with a simple application that involves creating a document directory, organizing files, moving and organizing multiple windows, and searching for information to answer phone calls.

Chapter 36 builds a few notes by using cut, copy, and paste to bring information from various sources into a letter and memo. Chapter 37 allows you to link information between different applications, which means that when you change information in the source document, the target document will change. The target document in this case is a business report.

Chapter 38 shows you how to use embedding, or combining actual documents, to create electronic mail messages and produce product information. Chapter 39 builds on the preceding chapters in Part VI by using a variety of data sources to create a personalized mailing to a list of clients.

In Chapter 40, you learn how to create a database while linking and embedding information from other applications.

Chapter 41 is the grand finale of Part VI. To create a presentation, you switch between windows; look up information; cut, copy, and paste text and data;

and link and embed information. You create an outline in Word, grab data from Access, summarize data and create charts in Excel, and pull all this together into a PowerPoint and Word presentation.

Part VII deals with customizing Microsoft Office. Chapter 42 shows you how to customize toolbars and menus in all the Office applications. In Chapter 43, you learn how to create macros and use Visual Basic for Applications (VBA) to automate tasks across applications in the suite.

Conventions Used in This Book

Office enables you to use both the keyboard and the mouse to select menu and dialog box items: you can press a letter or you can select an item by clicking it with the mouse. Letters you press to activate menus, choose commands in menus, and select options in dialog boxes are printed in boldface type: **F**ile **O**pen.

Names of dialog boxes and dialog box options are written with initial capital letters. Messages that appear on-screen are printed in a special font: `Document 1`. New terms are introduced in *italic* type. Text that you are to type appears in **boldface**.

The following example shows typical command sequences:

> Choose the **F**ile **O**pen command, or press Ctrl+O.

Uppercase letters are used to distinguish file and directory names.

The programs included with Office provide toolbars for your convenience. By clicking a button in the toolbar, you can execute a command or access a dialog box. Chapters in this book often contain button icons in the margins, indicating which button you can click to perform a task.

Tip

This paragraph format suggests easier or alternative methods of executing a procedure.

Note

This paragraph format indicates additional information that may help you avoid problems or that should be considered in using the described features.

Caution

This paragraph format warns the reader of hazardous procedures (for example, activities that delete files).

Troubleshooting

This paragraph format provides guidance on how to find solutions to common problems.

Using Microsoft Office, Special Edition, uses margin cross-references to help you access related information in other parts of the book.

► "Section title," p. xx

Right-facing triangles point you to related information in later chapters. Left-facing triangles point you to information in previous chapters.

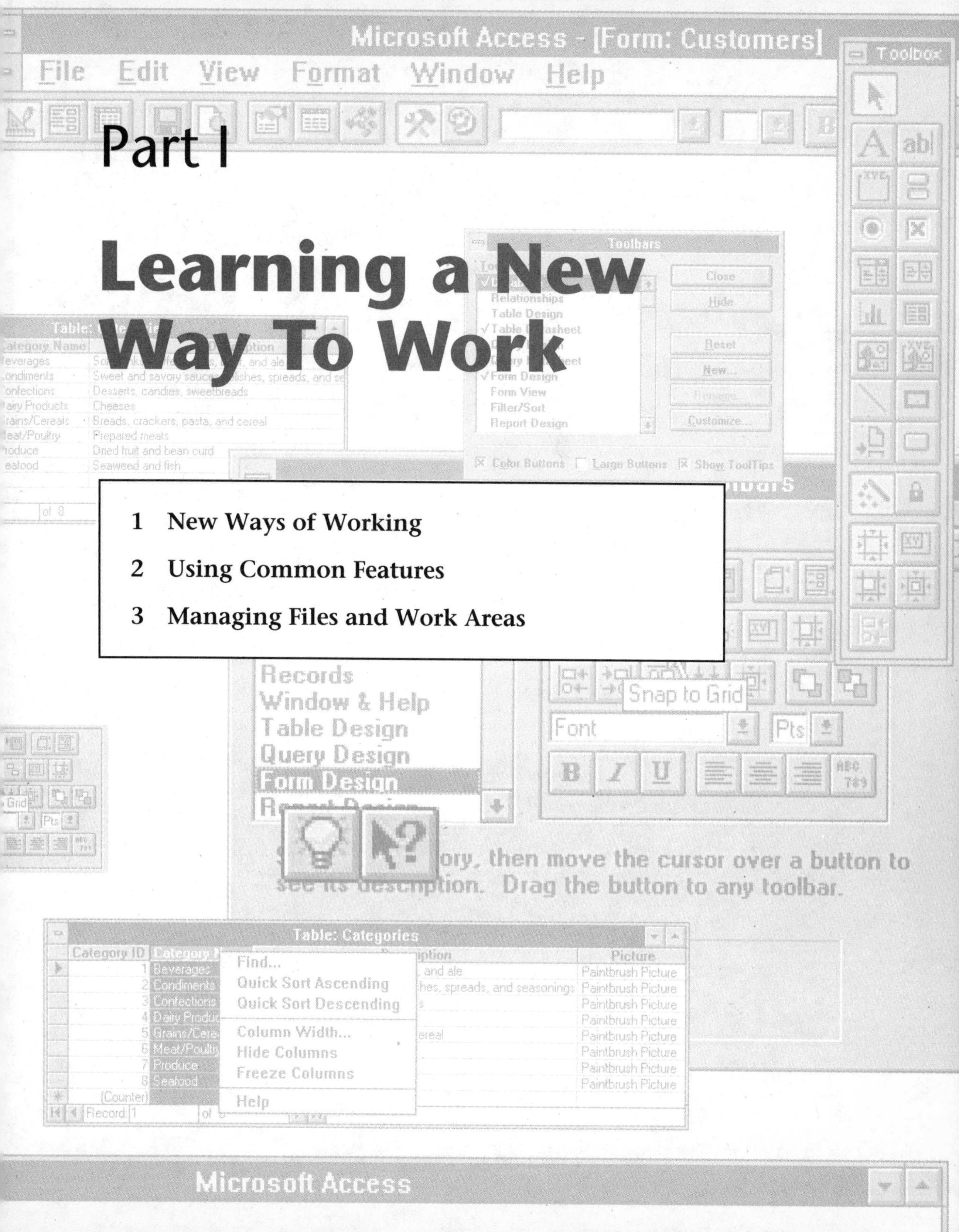

Part I

Learning a New Way To Work

1 New Ways of Working

2 Using Common Features

3 Managing Files and Work Areas

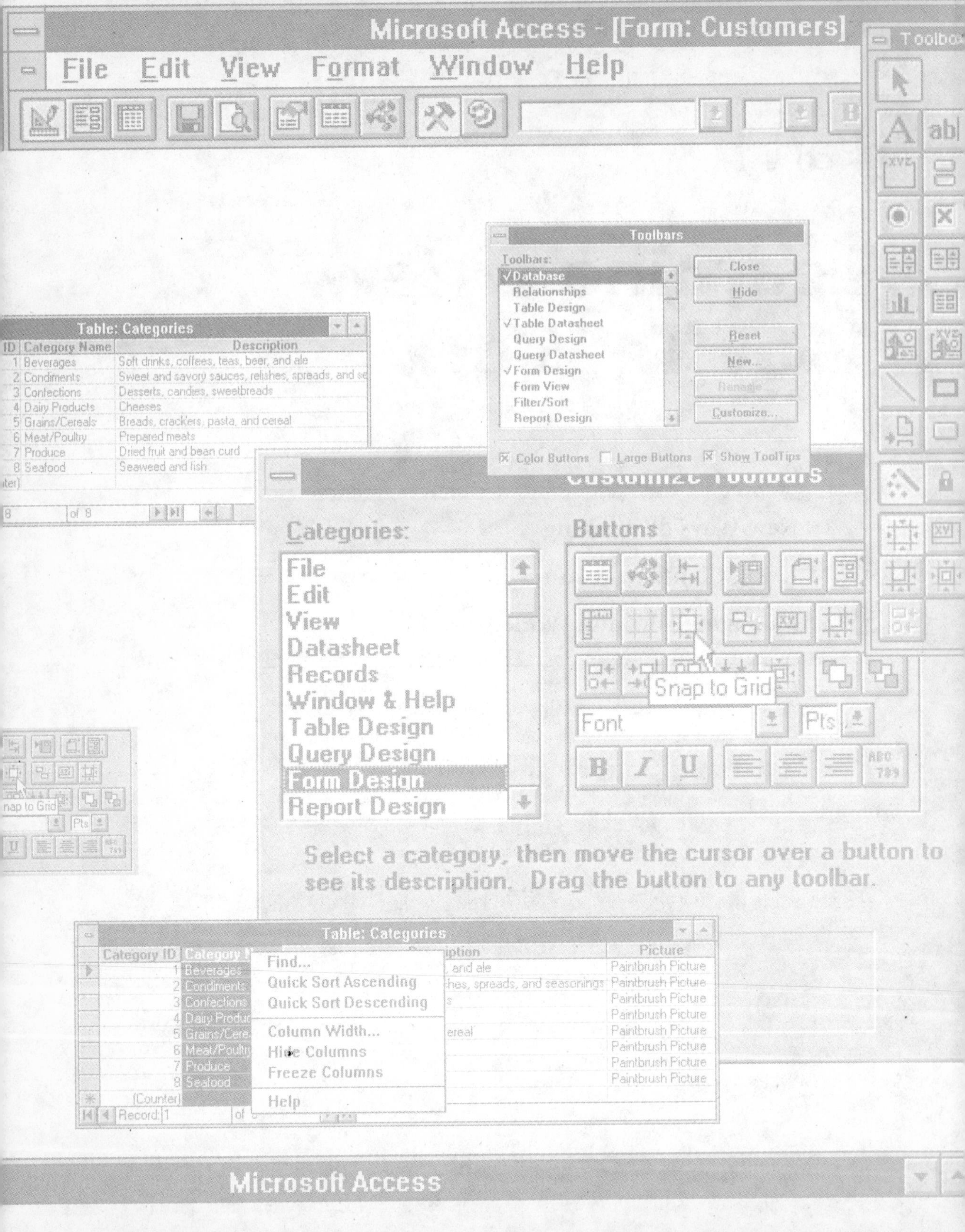

Microsoft Access - [Form: Customers]
File Edit View Format Window Help
Toolbox
Toolbars
Toolbars:
Database
Relationships
Table Design
Table Datasheet
Query Design
Query Datasheet
Form Design
Form View
Filter/Sort
Report Design
Close
Hide
Reset
New...
Rename...
Customize...
Color Buttons
Large Buttons
Show ToolTips
Table: Categories
Category Name
Description
Beverages
Soft drinks, coffees, teas, beer, and ale
Condiments
Confections
Desserts, candies, sweetbreads
Dairy Products
Cheeses
Grains/Cereals
Breads, crackers, pasta, and cereal
Meat/Poultry
Prepared meats
Produce
Dried fruit and bean curd
Seafood
Seaweed and fish
Customize Toolbars
Categories:
File
Edit
View
Datasheet
Records
Window & Help
Table Design
Query Design
Form Design
Report Design
Buttons
Snap to Grid
Font
Pts
Select a category, then move the cursor over a button to see its description. Drag the button to any toolbar.
Table: Categories
Category ID
Picture
Paintbrush Picture
Find...
Quick Sort Ascending
Quick Sort Descending
Column Width...
Hide Columns
Freeze Columns
Help
(Counter)
Record: 1
Microsoft Access

Chapter 1

New Ways of Working

by Diane Tinney

Combining a vendor's software products to sell them as one unit is not new. Software bundles have been around for years. However, what is new is the full integration of these software products. Integration no longer means just switching between applications or one application that attempts but fails to do the work of four applications.

In what is termed the *office suite*, leading software vendors provide core office applications such as word processing, spreadsheet, database, and presentation graphics. The core products are the award-winning applications in their categories. Vendors add to this core some auxiliary applications such as electronic mail, graphing, personal information management, and organization charting, offering the entire suite of products for as much as 50 percent less than the sum of the individual product purchase prices.

Microsoft Office leads the way with key applications that work together and offer a common user interface. The applications look alike and work alike—thus reducing the learning curve and improving productivity. Microsoft Office makes it easier for users to share data, documents, and graphics across applications.

In this chapter, you learn

- What's included in Microsoft Office
- The design goals of Microsoft Office
- How to determine which application to use

What's Included in Microsoft Office

The standard edition of Microsoft Office includes the following applications:

- Microsoft Word for Windows, Version 6.0
- Microsoft Excel, Version 5.0
- Microsoft PowerPoint, Version 4.0

The professional edition of Microsoft Office adds to the basic suite a powerful database, Microsoft Access, Version 2.0.

Design Goals of Microsoft Office

The goal of Microsoft Office is to provide users with the following:

- A common user interface (standardized operation of menus, toolbars, and dialog boxes)
- Quick access to one office suite application from another
- Data shared across applications
- Resources shared across applications
- In the future, a common task automation language

Microsoft strives to meet these goals. Many of the core applications underwent (and continue to undergo) revisions to meet these goals. To some longtime users of a core product, the resulting menu or toolbar changes may be annoying. In the long run, however, a common user interface across applications increases efficient and effective use of all applications.

Providing a Common User Interface

A clear benefit of a common user interface across applications is that by learning one application in the suite, you know the operational basics of the other applications. Figure 1.1 illustrates the similarity between Excel and Word menu bars and toolbars. Notice that Word has a Table menu option, but Excel has a Data menu option. Although the goal is to provide one common user interface, some degree of uniqueness will remain in each application. However, key common features such as the File Open and Edit Find commands can be found in exactly the same place in each application.

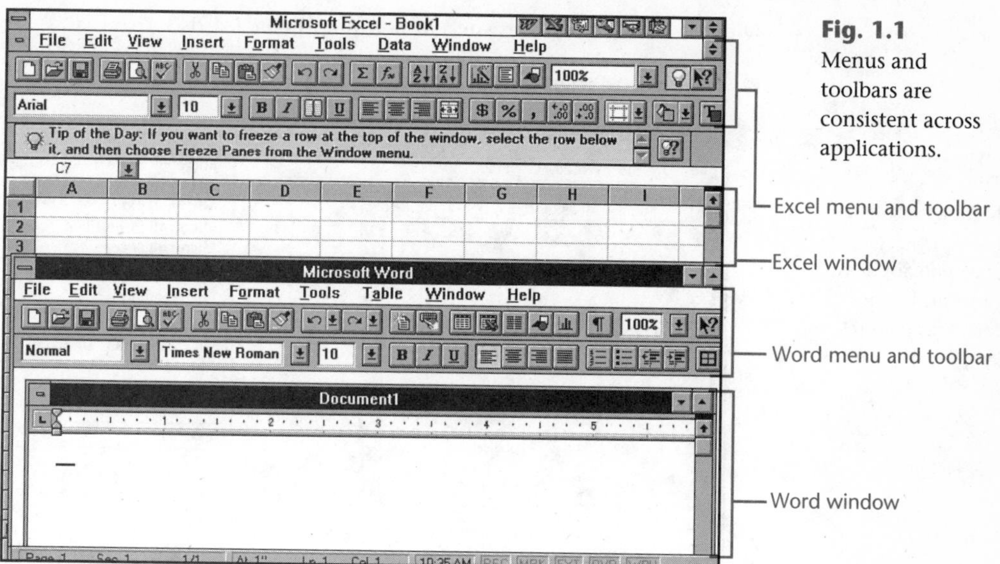

Fig. 1.1
Menus and toolbars are consistent across applications.

Microsoft Office applications provide consistency in more than just similar toolbars and menus. Dialog boxes, customizable features, and operational features are similar too. On-line help is available in several forms in all applications:

- Help Application
- Cue Cards
- Wizards
- Tip of the Day

► "On-Line Help," p. 62

► "'How To' Windows and Cue Cards," p. 66

► "Wizards," p. 68

► "Tip of the Day," p. 65

Quick Access to Other Applications

Microsoft Office provides a shell program called Microsoft Office Manager (MOM). Office Manager appears as a toolbar that, by default, appears in the upper-right corner of the current application's title bar (see fig. 1.2). You can use Office Manager to do the following:

- Switch between Microsoft Office applications
- Launch Microsoft Office applications
- Add other applications to the Office Manager toolbar

- Access Office features such as Setup and Cue Cards
- Work with Program Manager and File Manager

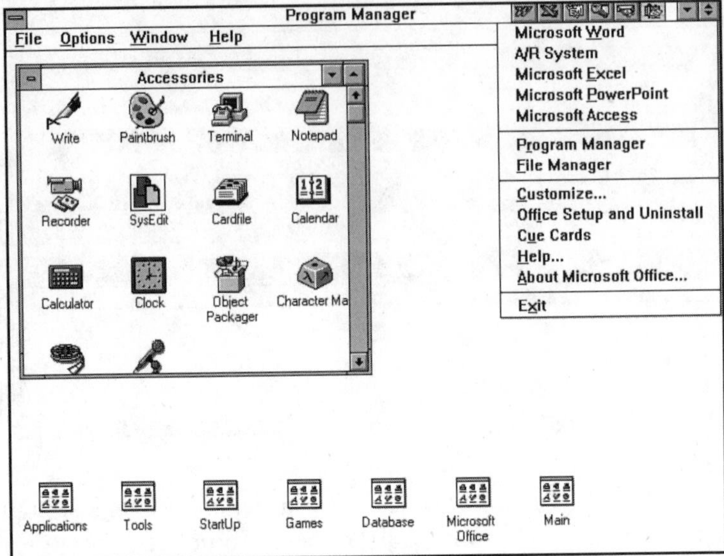

Fig. 1.2
The Office Manager toolbar provides easy access to applications and Office Manager features.

Note

Microsoft Office is an application that runs concurrently with the other applications. Thus, when you press Alt+Tab to switch between running applications, Microsoft Office is listed.

Office Manager is just one way that Microsoft Office provides quick access to applications. In each Microsoft Office application, the application toolbar provides direct access to pertinent features of other applications. For example, in Word you can insert an Excel Worksheet into a document by simply clicking a toolbar button. Doing so launches Excel and provides the full features of Excel for that embedded worksheet (see fig. 1.3). Note that, without your having to leave Word, the menu and toolbars change to Excel's when you edit the worksheet. Microsoft Office Manager 4.2 must be modified to work with Access 2.0. A workaround is to deselect the Access menu option that is available by default and add Access manually.

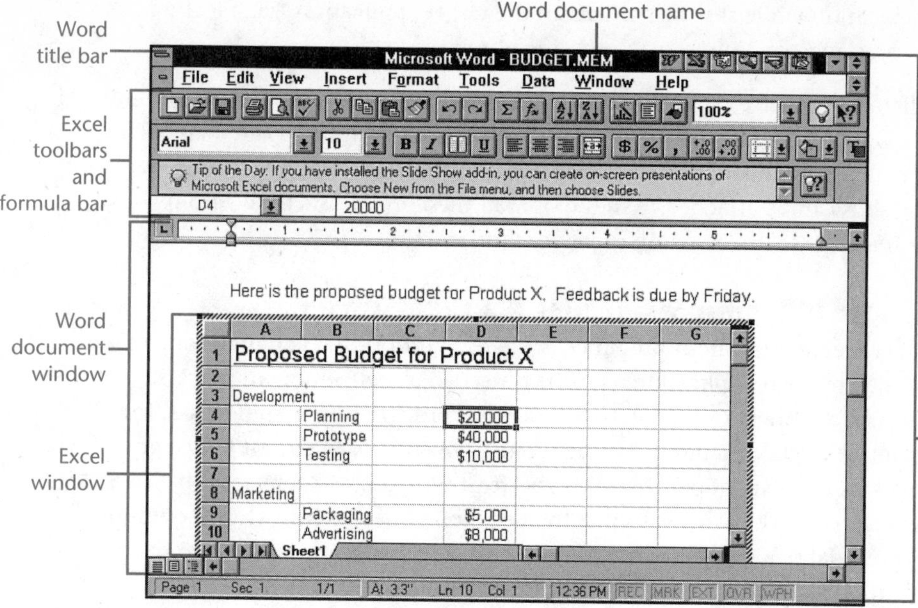

Fig. 1.3 Connectivity between applications allows you to insert an Excel worksheet into a Word document and edit the worksheet using Excel menu and toolbars without leaving Word.

Sharing Data across Applications

Microsoft Office products provide several methods of sharing data between applications:

► "Switching Between Documents," p. 89

► "Switching Between Applications," p. 93

Method	Description
Copying	Copies the data from the source application to the target application using the Clipboard
Linking	Links a copy of the data to the original document (saves data with the original document)
Embedding	Embeds data from the source document into the target document (saves data with the target document)

The Microsoft Office applications share data effortlessly. When you copy a table from Excel to Word, for example, you get a Word table which retains all the font and formats from Excel. You do not need to reformat your table, as you might with some other products.

Linking and embedding features take advantage of the new Microsoft Windows OLE 2.0 specifications. Linked documents automatically update when a source document changes. Embedded documents provide access to the source

▶ "Copying Spreadsheet Information" p. 772

▶ "Using Comon Steps to Link Documents." p. 789

▶ "Importing Excel Spreadsheet Information into Access," p. 855

▶ "Inserting Clip Art Pictures," p. 467

application while storing the data in the target application. Each feature has its pros and cons and serves a specific purpose.

Microsoft Office extends the data sharing beyond application integration by providing workgroup integration with Microsoft Mail. Users can mail documents, spreadsheets, and data files from within the source application. Routing slips can be attached to files that Mail then broadcasts to the group—or routes to each person, in sequence, one at a time.

Sharing Resources across Applications

A key element in Microsoft Office is the recognition that certain resources are needed by each application. Clip art is needed to perform word processing tasks, spreadsheet tasks, database tasks, and presentation graphic tasks, for example. Rather than duplicating program overhead, Microsoft Office provides an auxiliary application, Microsoft ClipArt Gallery, for use with all applications. The same is true of the need for a query engine (to ask questions of your data), a graphing tool (see fig. 1.4), and an organization chart drawing tool.

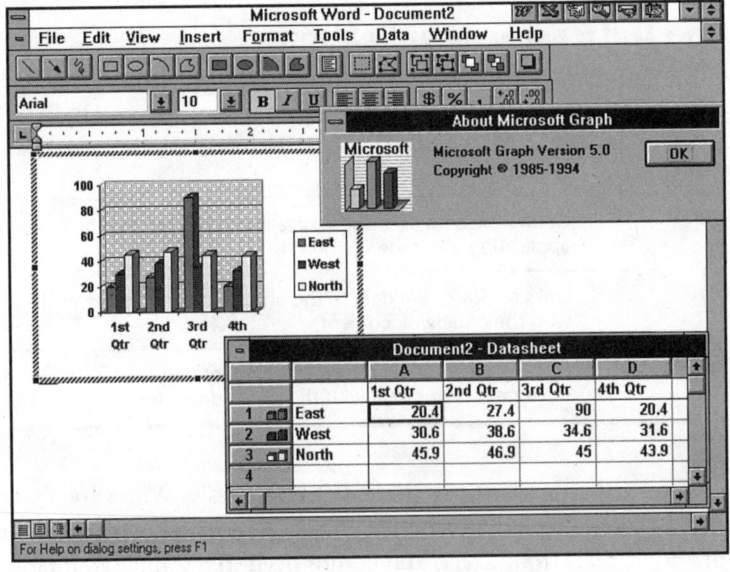

Fig. 1.4
Microsoft Graph, one of the auxiliary applications that ship with Microsoft Office, is used by all applications to draw graphs.

Providing a Common Language

Providing a common language across applications is the most challenging goal of Microsoft Office. In the past, each product has had a different programming and/or macro language. Excel Version 5.0 is the first Microsoft Office suite product to provide what will be the common language of the Office products: Visual Basic, Applications Edition (VBA). VBA uses OLE 2.0 and can send keystrokes to other applications (making it possible for VBA to run a cross-application process).

Until VBA is added to the other suite products, users will have to learn WordBasic, Access Basic, and VBA to automate common office tasks.

► "Using Macros," p. 226

► "Using the Macro Recorder To Automate a Task," p. 408

► "Understanding Visual Basic for Applications," p. 895

Determining Which Application To Use

The following table lists some common office tasks and suggested application tools to accomplish the task.

Task	Application	Comments
Mailing lists	Access Word	Maintain data in Access, optionally print labels from Access Merge data into Word to print personalized cover letters, brochures, and labels
Table of financial data to be used in a presentation	Excel Powerpoint	Create a table in Excel Embed table into PowerPoint slide
Send a document to a group of people for feedback, and receive a response	Word, Excel, Access Mail	Create the document, spreadsheet, database, or presentation in the desired application(s) Send the file(s) using Mail's routing feature
Track client contacts, log phone support, and follow up with form letters	Access Word	Create a contact database in Access with related tables for clients, phone calls, projects, and correspondence. Create forms for data entry. Optionally print letters (reports) directly from Access. Optionally merge client contact data into Word and print follow-up form letters from Word

(continues)

Task	Application	Comments
Provide audit trail between supporting spreadsheet data and annual report document	Excel Word	Create the supporting schedules needed in Excel. Create the annual report document in Word. Use OLE to link the data from Excel to the Word document. Whenever the spreadsheet data changes, the annual report document is updated automatically.
Create, print and distribute department newsletter	Word Mail	Create newsletter in Word. Distribute newsletter electronically using Mail's Send feature.

With four or five new software applications so tightly integrated, deciding on which product to use for which task could be difficult. Experience with each application is the best guide on how to combine the powers of each application to meet your needs. The rest of this book is dedicated to helping you in this endeavor. The next few chapters review the common features found in all suite applications and point out any digressions. Parts II through V guide you through the features and capabilities of each product. Part VI provides business scenarios to illustrate how Microsoft Office products work together. Part VII teaches you how to customize Microsoft Office with your own toolbars, menus, and automation (macros and VBA).

Sit back and enjoy the new way of working that Microsoft Office provides.

From Here...

Now that you are familiar with the new way of working that Microsoft Office offers, you are ready to begin learning the common features of Microsoft Office.

- Chapter 2, "Using Common Features," teaches you how to start Microsoft Office, use menus, toolbars, dialog boxes and Help, and how to navigate the windows.
- Chapter 3, "Managing Files and Work Areas," teaches you how to work with files and print documents and guides you through the work areas of each application.

Chapter 2

Using Common Features

by Rick & Patty Winter

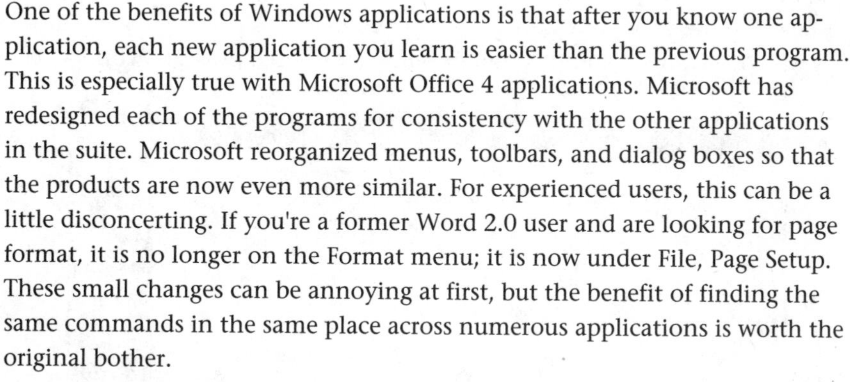

One of the benefits of Windows applications is that after you know one application, each new application you learn is easier than the previous program. This is especially true with Microsoft Office 4 applications. Microsoft has redesigned each of the programs for consistency with the other applications in the suite. Microsoft reorganized menus, toolbars, and dialog boxes so that the products are now even more similar. For experienced users, this can be a little disconcerting. If you're a former Word 2.0 user and are looking for page format, it is no longer on the Format menu; it is now under File, Page Setup. These small changes can be annoying at first, but the benefit of finding the same commands in the same place across numerous applications is worth the original bother.

In this chapter, you learn to

- Start and exit programs and files
- Move between programs
- Move around the screen
- Use menus and dialog boxes
- Type, edit, copy, and move text
- Use help

Launching Programs

Just as with other Windows procedures, you can launch an application in several different ways. Windows applications allow for users coming from different platforms and different skills. You can use the keyboard or the mouse or both together. You can use the Program Manager or File Manager. Windows NT allows you to launch Windows programs by typing their name at the command prompt. Microsoft Office 4 even adds a new way to launch programs through the Office Toolbar.

Launching a Program from a Group

The standard way to begin any application is to double-click the group icon where the application is located and then to double-click the program icon for the application you want to start. If you installed your applications individually or if you have earlier versions of the programs, each program may be in a different group. You may need to open the Excel group to launch Excel and the Word group to launch Microsoft Word (see figs. 2.1 and 2.2). If you installed all the applications in one group, double-click the group icon (usually Microsoft Office) and then double-click the desired program icon.

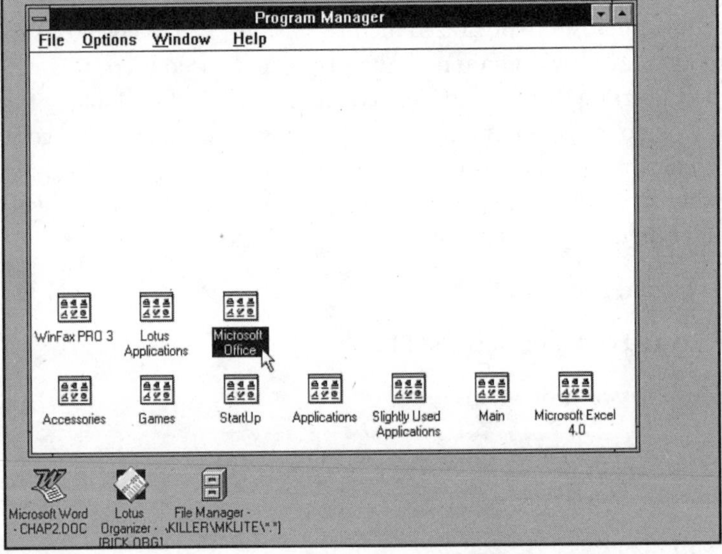

Fig. 2.1
Double-click the Microsoft Office group to open the group. Alternatively, click the group icon once and press Enter.

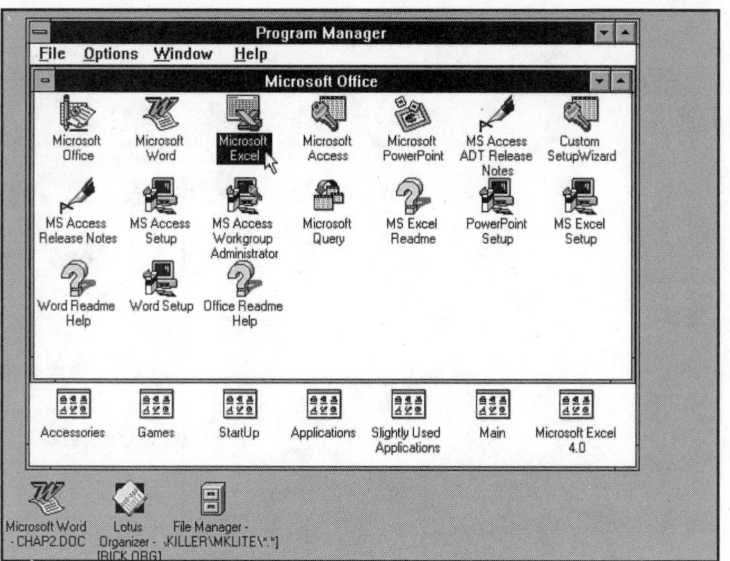

Fig. 2.2
Double-click the Microsoft Excel program icon to start Excel. Alternatively, click the program icon once and press Enter.

Caution

Be careful when you open an application. If the application is already open, you may launch another version of the same application (see fig. 2.3). This may cause unnecessary use of memory or may make it more difficult to find a document. If you cannot see the applications that are open, press Ctrl+Esc to bring up the Task List, which shows you all applications. From the Task List you can close an application (End Task) or go to an open program (Switch To).

Opening Up a File from File Manager

If you use different applications like Word and Excel for one project, you may want to save all documents related to the same project in one directory. You can use the File Manager to create the directory, copy the document files into the directory, and then open the file without worrying about opening its application. To work with the File Manager, double-click the Main group icon, and then double-click the File Manager program icon. For more information on the File Manager, see "Using the File Manager" later in this chapter.

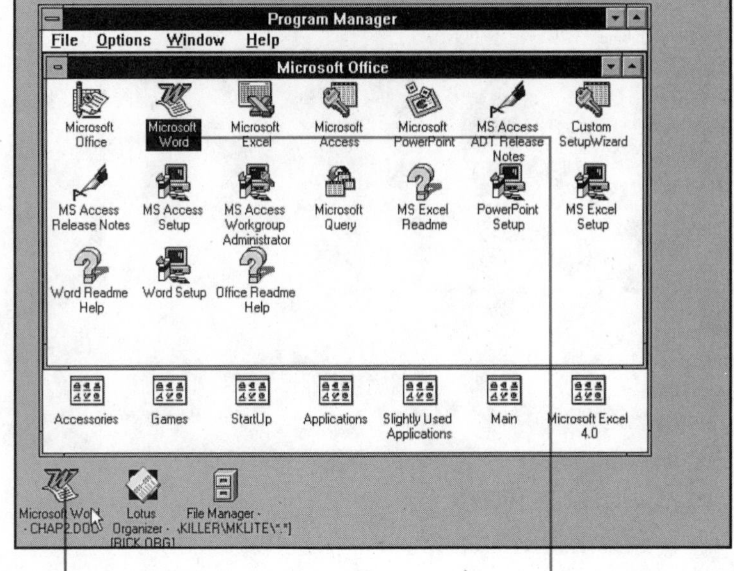

Fig. 2.3 Because you already have Microsoft Word running (as shown by this application icon outside the Program Manager) avoid opening up Word again by clicking on the program icon inside the Program Manager.

Word application icon indicates that program is running. Double-click this icon to reopen Word.

Do not launch Word again by clicking on this program icon.

Launching Files from File Manager

After you have all your files in your project directory, you can double-click a file name to launch the program associated with the file and open the file at the same time. You can tell which files have associated programs because a document icon that looks like it has small horizontal lines is next to the file name (see fig. 2.4). If an icon is blank, the file is not associated with a program and it will not open.

File Manager is able to identify the program for the file because of the files extension. The extensions for the Microsoft Office applications are as follows:

Microsoft Word	DOC
Microsoft Excel	XLS
Microsoft PowerPoint	PPT
Microsoft Access	MDB

Because File Manager uses extensions, do not change the default extension of a file when you save the file.

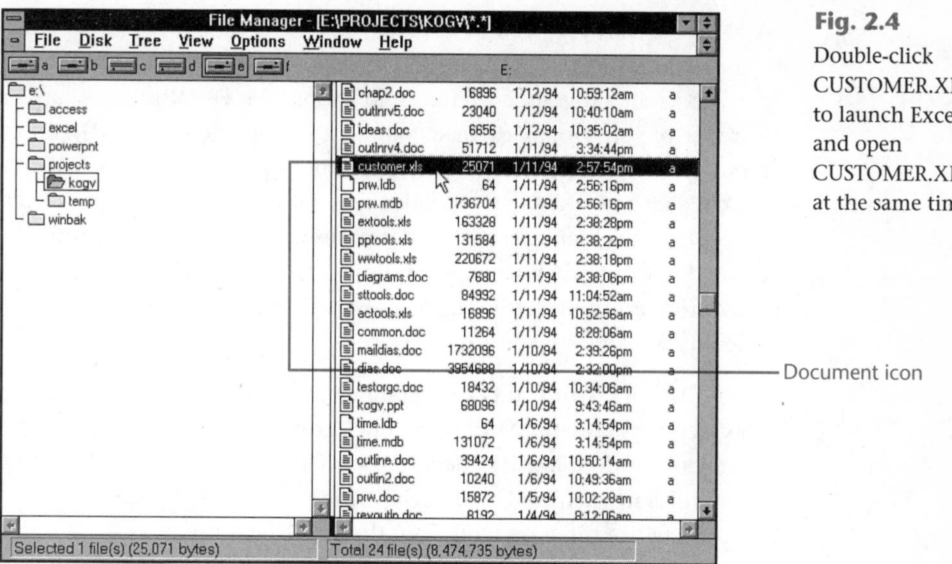

Fig. 2.4
Double-click CUSTOMER.XLS to launch Excel and open CUSTOMER.XLS at the same time.

Looking at Microsoft Office

Microsoft Office 4 has added a neat new toolbar that makes it much easier to start programs and move between them when they're open (see fig. 2.5). You can choose the location of the toolbar. The default toolbar with small icons fits on the title bar of any maximized application. You can customize Microsoft Office to include additional applications on the toolbar or its drop-down menu.

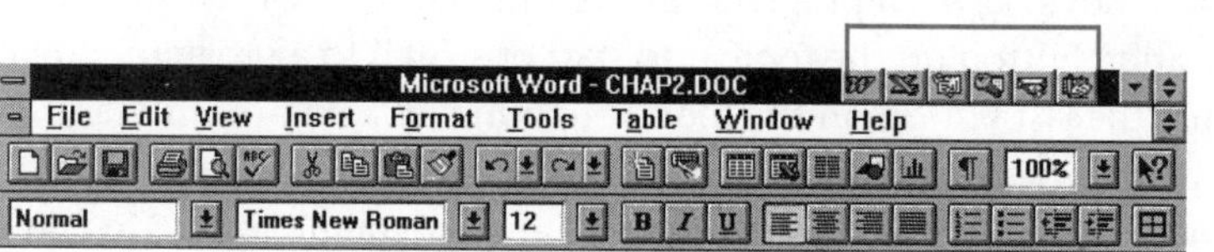

Fig. 2.5
The default location for the Microsoft Office toolbar is on the title bar of a maximized window.

Starting Microsoft Office

If you have not installed Microsoft Office, insert Disk 1 into your floppy drive, go to the Program Manager, and choose the **F**ile **R**un command. Type the name of your floppy drive, a colon, and setup and choose OK; for example, type **a:setup**. Choose the Add/Remove button on the Microsoft Office dialog box. On the next dialog box with the list of options, check the Microsoft Office Manager box (and if necessary, unselect all the other boxes). Choose the Continue button and follow the instructions on-screen. For more information on setting up Microsoft Office and the applications, see Appendix A.

Microsoft Office Setup adds a program icon for Microsoft Office in the group you specify (usually the Microsoft Office group). To display the Microsoft Office toolbar, double-click the Microsoft Office program icon. Microsoft Office will start each time you begin Windows, unless you delete the Microsoft Office program icon from the StartUp group.

Note

When you have any application icons in the StartUp group, the application will launch when you start Windows. To copy an application into the StartUp group, hold Ctrl down and drag the application icon from another group to the StartUp group.

For more information about installing Microsoft Office and the StartUp group, see Appendix A.

Moving between Programs

► "Switching between Applications," p. 89

► "Using File Manager To Organize Files," p. 738

► "Moving between Window Programs," p. 753

You can move between programs in two different ways. You can click the application button on the toolbar to start or switch to a program. You can also use the last button on the toolbar to bring up a pull-down menu to select a program, as shown in figure 2.6. Click the application name. Notice that the menu also includes the File Manager and Program Manager in addition to Microsoft applications.

Closing Microsoft Office

If you no longer want to see the Microsoft Office toolbar, choose the last button on the toolbar, and choose E**x**it on the drop-down menu. If you do not want Microsoft Office to run every time you start Windows, open to the StartUp group, select the Microsoft Office program icon, and press the Delete key (see fig. 2.7). When prompted, choose **Y**es to indicate that you are sure you want to delete the item.

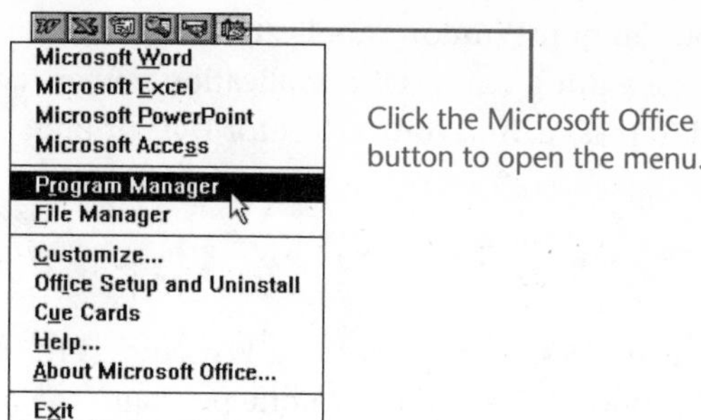

Fig. 2.6
The Microsoft Office pull-down menu allows you to also go to Program Manager and File Manager.

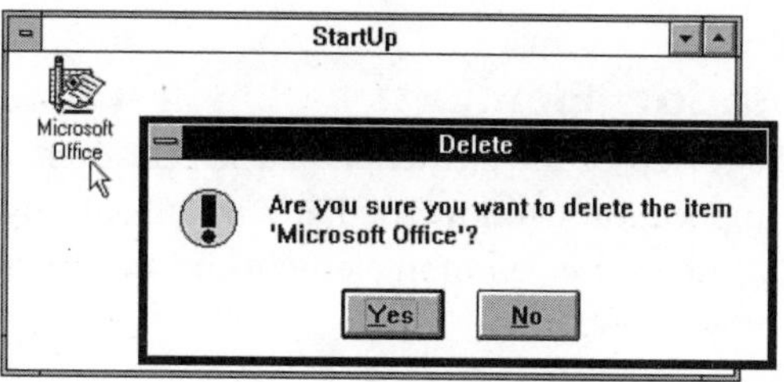

Fig. 2.7
Go to the StartUp group and delete the Microsoft Office program icon if you do not want Office to start up every time you start Windows.

Closing Programs

After you've worked in an application and no longer need to use its features, you will probably want to close the application. You will want to close applications especially if you have limited memory. All Windows programs close the same way. Do one of the following:

- Double-click the program Control-menu box in the upper left corner of the application window.
- On the menu bar, choose the **F**ile **E**xit command.
- Press Alt+F4.
- Bring up the task list with Ctrl+Esc, choose the program, and choose the **E**nd Task button.

If you have not saved changes to your documents, you will see a dialog box asking if you want to save changes to each of your open documents. You will probably want to save your documents. If prompted, fill in the File Save As dialog box. For more information on saving files, see the section "Saving, Opening, and Closing Files" in Chapter 3.

► "Using the Word Screen," p. 104

► "Defining Excel Terms," p. 243

► "Getting Familiar with the PowerPoint Window," p. 424

If you run non-Windows applications, you need to exit through the procedure for exiting the specific application you are running. For example, you need to press F7 in WordPerfect for DOS or press / **Q** in Lotus 123 for DOS.

Viewing Parts of the Window

One of the best parts of learning Windows is the similarity between different applications. When you learn one program, the next and subsequent programs are easier to learn. This is especially true because parts of the window are similar.

Common Window Elements

Figure 2.8 shows a review of the elements on a screen. Each application usually displays the application window itself and usually at least one document window. Table 2.1 shows the common elements on the application window and the document window.

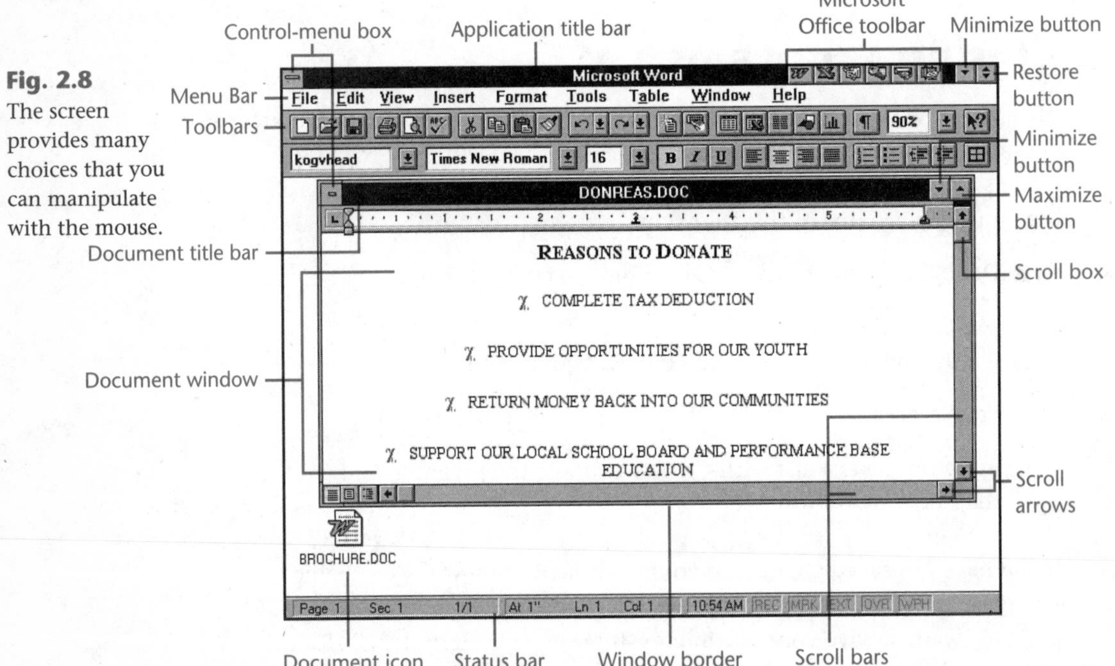

Fig. 2.8 The screen provides many choices that you can manipulate with the mouse.

Table 2.1 Window Features Common to Application and Document Windows

Feature	Description	Use
Control-menu box	Minus sign in upper left corner of window. If the document window is maximized, the minus in the document Control-menu box is smaller and directly below the program Control-menu box.	Double-click to close the application or the document. Single-click to open up the Control menu and choose **R**estore, Mi**n**imize, Ma**x**imize, **C**lose window or to switch to commands. Single-click the document Control-menu box to switch between windows.
Title bar	On top of window. Dark if active window. White if other window is active.	Shows name of program or document. If document window maximized, program title bar shows name of application and name of document. Double-click to toggle back and forth between maximize and restore. If a window is restored (not full screen), drag title bar to move window.
Restore button	Double up/down arrow in upper right corner of window.	Click to change window to partial screen. Action will cause change to Maximize button.
Maximize button	Single up arrow in upper right corner of window.	Click to change window to largest possible size. Action will cause change to Restore button.
Minimize button	Down arrow button in upper right corner of window.	Click to shrink window to icon. Program button will shrink program to icon outside of Program Manager on desktop. Document button will shrink document to icon in work area above status bar (and possibly behind another document).

(continues)

Table 2.1 Continued

Feature	Description	Use
Menu Bar	Line below title bar starting with File.	Click to select menu or press Alt and then type underlined letter on menus.
Window border and corner	Thin gray line surrounding a window that is not maximized.	Move mouse pointer until double arrow appears and drag to change size of window.

Some items generally occur just on application windows but are common to most applications. Table 2.2 discusses these items. Microsoft Word, Excel, PowerPoint, Access, and Mail call the pictorial strip of buttons toolbars.

Table 2.2 Window Features Common to Application Windows

Feature	Description	Use
Toolbar(s)	Picture buttons below menu bar or other places on-screen.	Click button for the most used commands. Sometimes the button only gives you one feature for a command. Use the menu for more options on a feature.
Status bar	Bottom line of application window.	May tell information about insertion point location on document and status of some toggle keys on the keyboard such as the Insert/Overwrite or Num Lock key. In some programs, describes menu or toolbar choice in more detail. In some programs, can double-click status bar to accomplish tasks.
Document window	Area between toolbars and status bar.	Shows open document, scroll bars, and possible title of document in title bar.
Document icon	Icon on bottom of screen above status bar visible if document window is not maximized.	Document is minimized. Double-click to open into a document window.

Most document windows also have features common to each other. Table 2.3 shows some of the features common to document windows across applications.

Table 2.3 Window Features Common to Document Windows

Feature	Description	Use
Scroll bar	Gray area between scroll arrows on right and bottom of the document window.	Click above or below scroll box on vertical scroll bar or to the left or right of scroll box on horizontal scroll bar to move view of document a full screen up, down, left, or right.
Scroll box	Gray square box inside scroll bars.	Drag scroll box to position view of document.
Scroll arrows	Arrows on either side of scroll bar.	Click arrow to move view one line in the direction of the arrow. Hold down mouse cursor on arrow to scroll quickly.
Document window	Area inside the window	Location where document resides and where editing takes place.

Microsoft Applications Toolbars

One of the improvements Microsoft made with the upgrades from Word 2 to Word 6, Excel 4 to Excel 5, PowerPoint 3 to PowerPoint 4, and Access 1 to Access 2 is to reorganize and improve the toolbars so that the tools are more consistent across the Microsoft Office applications. Although many buttons are unique to each application, many buttons are also common to all or some of the applications. Microsoft also changed the name of the ribbon in Word 2. It is now the Formatting toolbar. You can now choose from more than one toolbar in all of the applications. You can also customize the toolbars (add or remove buttons).

► "Customizing Application Toolbars," p. 887

To turn on or off a toolbar, follow these steps:

1. Click the right mouse button on an active toolbar.

2. A pull-down menu shows a list of the potential toolbars. Microsoft displays those toolbars with a check mark to the left of the name. Figure 2.14 shows a list of the toolbars for each application later in this chapter.

3. Click the toolbar you want to turn on or off. If the toolbar is floating, you can click the toolbar's Control box.

> **Note**
>
> If the program does not show any toolbar, choose **V**iew, **T**oolbars, and choose the toolbar(s) you want to display.

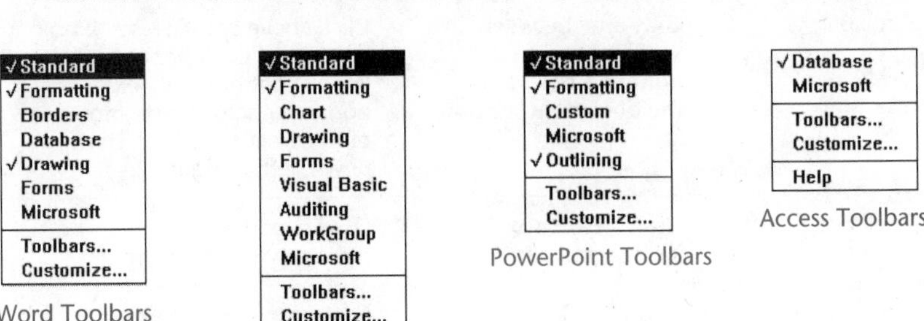

Fig. 2.9 When you click the right mouse button on a toolbar, a menu appears, showing the active and available toolbars.

Some buttons change on toolbars when you change the view. For example, Word adds an outline toolbar when you change to outline view. Access changes toolbars depending on what part of the database you look at (table, query, form) and whether you are viewing the object or designing the object. For a complete list of toolbars in Access, choose the **V**iew Tool**b**ars command. To avoid confusion, however, you should let Access change the toolbars for you.

Standard Toolbars

Figure 2.10 shows the standard toolbar for each Microsoft Office application. Notice how many of the buttons are the same. Table 2.4 shows the common buttons and their purpose.

Microsoft Word Standard Toolbar

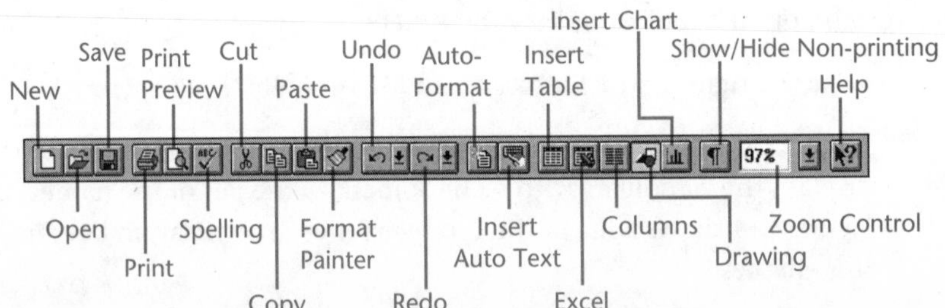

Fig. 2.10 The standard toolbars for Word, Excel, PowerPoint, and the Access database toolbar show many similarities.

Microsoft Excel Standard Toolbar

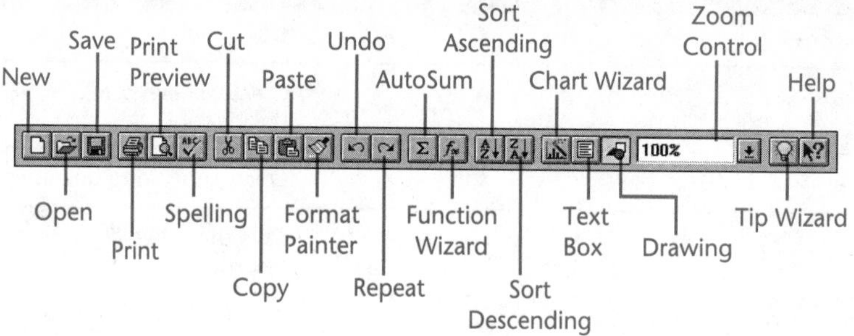

Microsoft PowerPoint Standard Toolbar

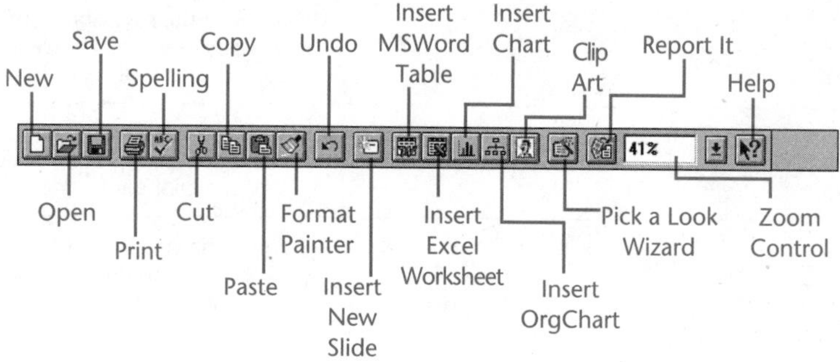

Microsoft Access Database Toolbar

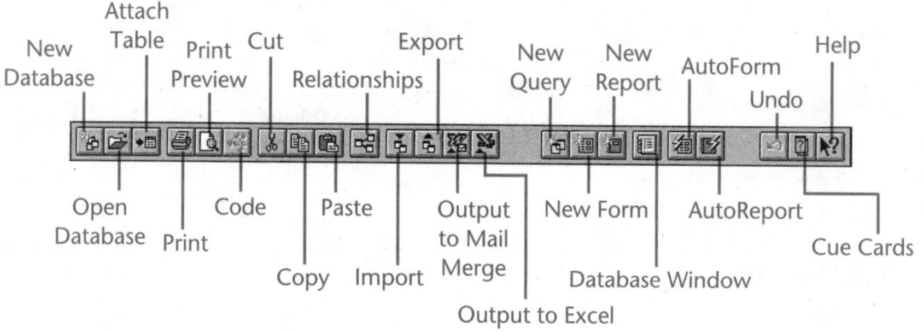

Table 2.4 Common Buttons on the Standard Toolbars

Button	W	E	P	A	Use
New	X	X	X		Create a new, blank document.
Open	X	X	X	X	Open an existing document.
Save	X	X	X		Save the active document on screen.
Print	X	X	X	X	Print the document.
Print Preview	X	X		X	Preview what printing the document will look like.
Cut	X	X	X	X	Remove the selection from the document and place a copy into the clipboard.
Copy	X	X	X	X	Copy the selection from the document and place a copy into the clipboard.
Paste	X	X	X	X	Copy the contents of the clipboard into the document at the location of the insertion point.
Format Painter	X	X	X		Copy the formatting from the selected items to the next selection.
Undo	X	X	X	X	Reverse your last action.
Insert Chart	X		X		Insert a chart into the document.
Zoom Control	X	X	X		Change the size of your display (does not affect printing).
Help	X	X	X	X	Click toolbar button, or menu choice for help on that choice. Double-click to search for help on a topic you type.

W, E, P columns are for the Word, Excel, and PowerPoint standard toolbars, and A is for the Access Database toolbar.

Formatting Toolbars

Many of the buttons are also similar on the formatting toolbars. Figure 2.11 shows the Formatting toolbars for Word, Excel, and PowerPoint, and the Report Design Toolbar for Access. Table 2.5 shows the common buttons and their purpose.

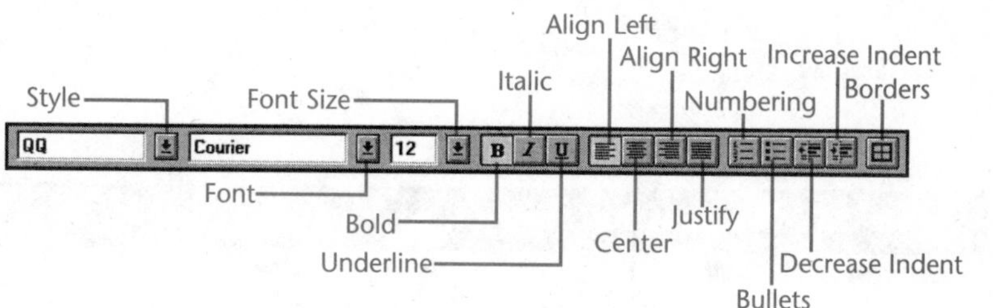

Fig. 2.11
The formatting toolbars for Word, Excel, PowerPoint, and the Access report design toolbar show many similarities.

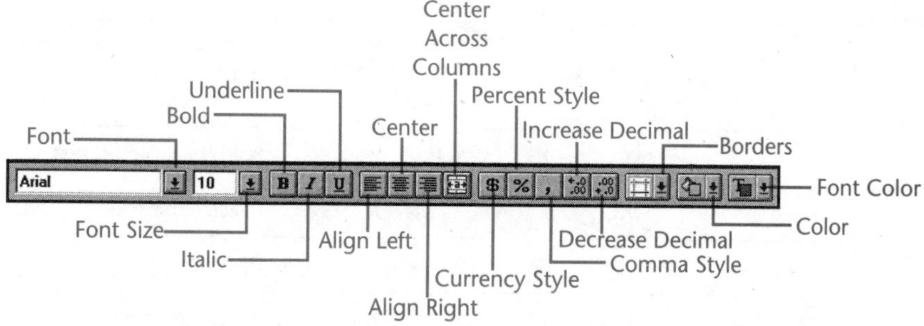

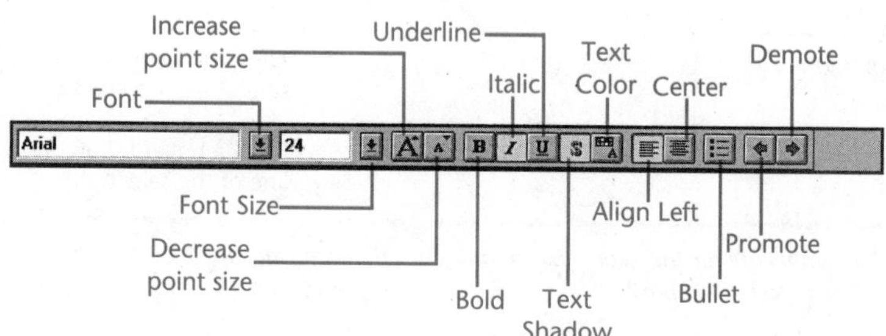

Microsoft Access Report Design Toolbar

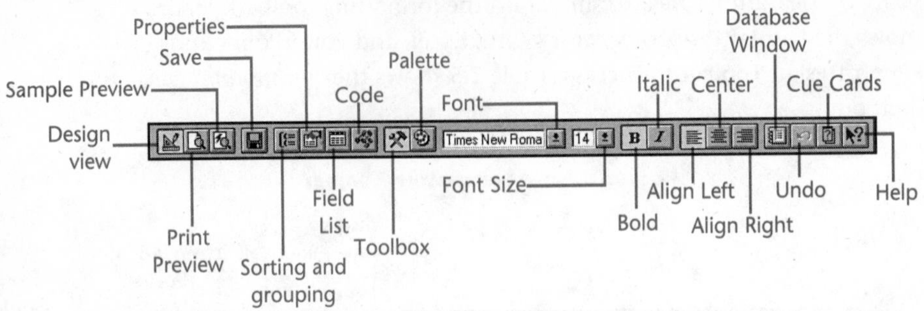

Table 2.5 Common Buttons on the Formatting Toolbars

Button	W	E	P	A	Use
Font	X	X	X	X	Click pull-down arrow to right of font name to display a list of typefaces. Click the desired font.
Font Size	X	X	X	X	Click pull-down arrow to display and choose desired size for text.
Bold	X	X	X	X	Bold the selected text.
Italic	X	X	X	X	Italicize the selected text.
Underline	X	X	X		Underline the selected text.
Align Left	X	X	X	X	Align the items so the left side of each is lined up.
Center	X	X	X	X	Align the items so each is centered.
Align Right	X	X		X	Align the items so the right side of each is lined up.
Bullet	X		X		Place a bullet before each line of the selected text.

W, E, P columns are for the Word, Excel, and PowerPoint formatting toolbars, and A is for the Access Report Design toolbar.

Drawing Toolbars

The Drawing toolbars for Word, Excel, and PowerPoint also have common buttons, as shown in figure 2.12. Table 2.6 shows the common buttons and their purpose. The similar buttons on Access are called the Toolbox. Figure 2.12 and table 2.6 also show these Access buttons.

Microsoft Word Drawing Toolbar

Format Callout
Bring to Front
Snap to Grid
Text box
Line Color
Bring in front of text
Create Picture
Rectangle
Arc
Ungroup Objects
Line
Ellipse
Freeform
Line Style
Send to Back
Group Objects
Reshape
Insert Frame
Rotate Right
Callout
Fill Color
Send behind text
Flip Vertical
Save
Select Drawing Objects
Flip Horizontal
Align Drawing Objects

Microsoft Excel Drawing Toolbar

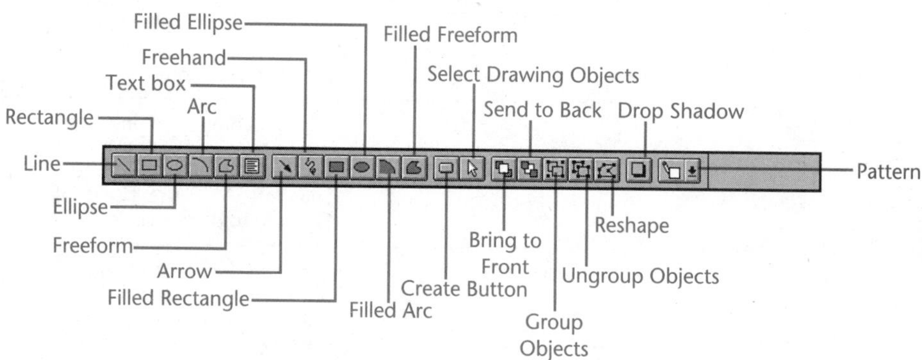

Microsoft PowerPoint Drawing Toolbar

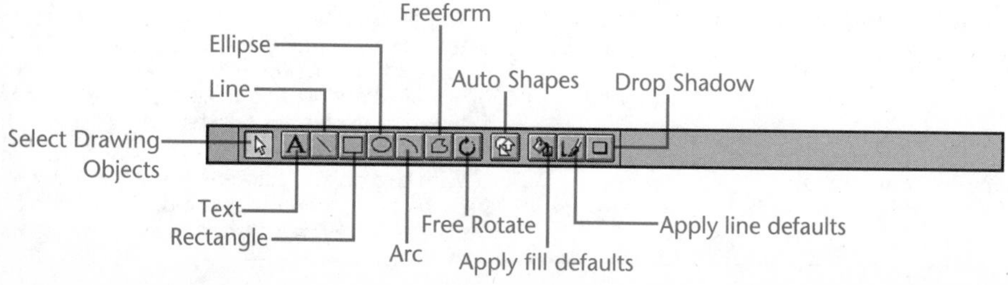

Fig. 2.12
The drawing toolbars for Word, Excel, PowerPoint, and the Access Toolbox show many similarities.

Microsoft Access Toolbox

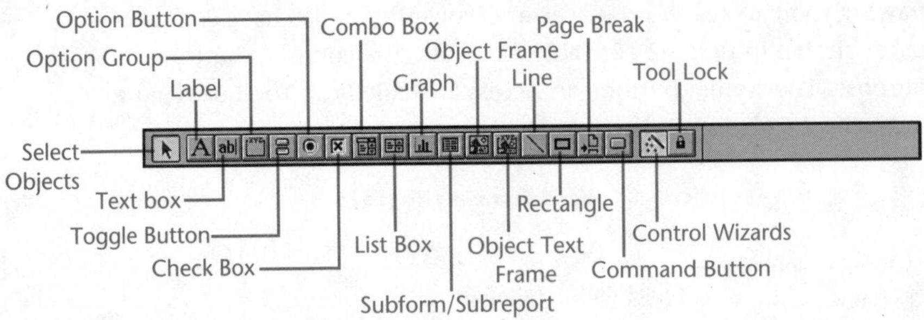

Table 2.6 Common Buttons on the Drawing Toolbars

Button	W	E	P	A	Use
Line	X	X	X	X	Click and drag to start and draw the line. Release the mouse button to end the line. Use the Shift key to draw lines at 30, 45, and 60 degree angles.
Rectangle	X	X	X	X	Click and drag from one corner to the opposite corner. Release the mouse button to complete the rectangle. Use the Shift key to draw a square.
Ellipse	X	X	X		Click and drag from one corner to the opposite corner. Release the mouse button to complete the ellipse. Use the Shift key to draw a circle.
Arc	X	X	X		Click and drag to start and draw the arc. Release the mouse button to end the arc.
Freeform	X	X	X		Drag the mouse to draw. Double-click to end the drawing.
Selection Tool	X	X	X	X	To select multiple objects, drag mouse from upper left corner to bottom right and release mouse. Black binding boxes tell you the object is selected.
Bring to Front	X	X			With two objects stacked on each other, bring the selected object to the top (or front).

Button	W	E	P	A	Use
Send to Back	X	X			With two objects stacked on each other, send the selected object to the bottom (or back).
Group Objects	X	X			Combine more than one drawn object into a single object for editing and moving.
Ungroup Objects	X	X			Uncombine grouped objects back into their original drawings.
Reshape	X	X			Drag black binding boxes to reshape freeform object.
Drop Shadow		X	X		Apply a shadow to the bottom and right of the object.

W, E, P columns are for the Word, Excel, and PowerPoint drawing toolbars.
A is for Access Toolbox.

Using Menus

In addition to common toolbars, Microsoft has also reworked the menus on the applications within Microsoft Office in order to come up with similar placement for commands.

General Description of Menus

Directly below the title bar in all applications is the menu bar. In all Microsoft Office applications and most Windows applications, the menu bar begins with the File, Edit, and View menus and ends with the Window and Help menus. When the mouse pointer is on a menu, the pointer changes to a white arrow. To pull down a menu, click the mouse button on the menu. If you want to use the keyboard, press Alt and the underlined letter on the menu. When you open a menu, a list of commands appears. Click the command or type the letter of the underlined character. As you select menu choices, the status bar on the bottom of the screen shows a description of the menu or command.

If you accidentally go into the wrong menu, you can do any of the following:

- Click another menu.
- Click in the document to turn off the menu.

- Press Alt or click the menu again to get out of the menu.
- Press Esc to keep the menu word highlighted and see the description of the menu on the status bar. Press Esc a second time to get out of the menu.

Menus throughout Windows applications have common symbols that help you know what will happen when you select the command and that give you shortcuts to do the commands. The symbols include ellipses, keyboard shortcuts, arrows, check marks, and option bullets. Each menu is also divided into sections by horizontal lines. The sections generally group similar commands together (such as Save, Save As, and Save All) or group commands that are mutually exclusive (see option bullet below). The following list describes common menu symbols:

- Three dots, or an ellipsis, after a command indicates that a dialog box appears after you select the command. For example, the command File Print occurs in all four applications and an ellipsis indicates that the Print dialog box follows the selection of this command. For more information on dialog boxes, see "Using Dialog Boxes" later in this chapter.
- To the right of some commands are keyboard shortcuts. Instead of using the menu, you can press the shortcut key or key combination to choose the command. Most shortcuts begin with holding the Ctrl key down in combination with a letter. For example, to undo your latest action, press Ctrl+Z in all applications. Shortcut keys also include function keys (for example, F7 for Spelling), and editing keys (for example, Delete to erase the selection).
- Some Microsoft Office applications (all except Word) have arrows on the right side of some menus indicating that another drop-down menu will appear. After you choose the command with an arrow, you choose another command on the resulting menu. Figure 2.13 shows that in Excel if you choose **F**ormat **R**ow, you get another menu that begins with H**e**ight.
- Another character on some menus is a check mark to the left of the menu choice. A check mark indicates that this choice is selected and that the choice can be on or off. For example, the Window menu of all Microsoft Office applications shows a list of open documents on the bottom of each menu. The active open document is indicated by a check mark.

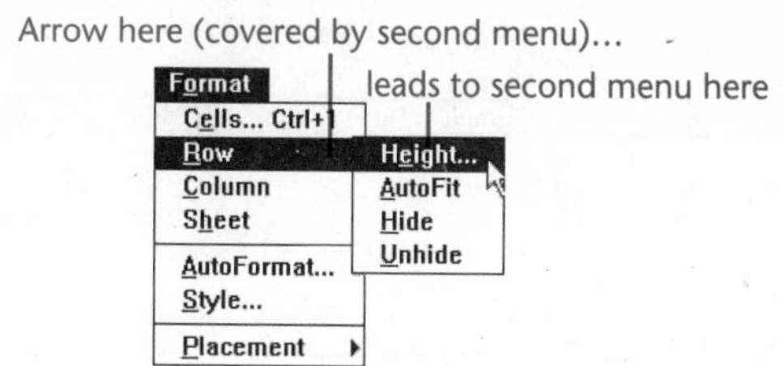

Fig. 2.13
An arrow on the right side of a command indicates another menu follows.

- Another on or off indicator on some applications (Word and PowerPoint) is an option bullet to the left of a menu item. The bullet indicates that only one item in a menu section (the area between two horizontal lines) can be selected at a time. If you choose any other command in the same section, the bullet moves to the selected item. For example, the View menu of Word in figure 2.14 indicates that you can only choose Normal, Outline, Page Layout, or Master Document at one time and that Normal is currently selected.

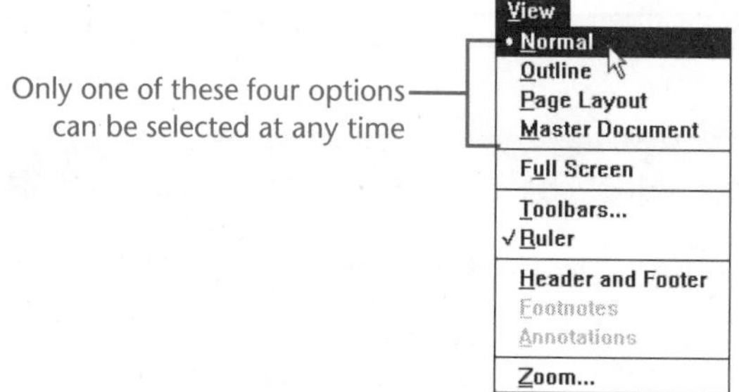

Fig. 2.14
Normal is the exclusive choice in this menu section.

Menu Similarities in Microsoft Office Suite

In addition to the common symbols on menus, Microsoft has also repositioned menu commands to appear on the same menus within each application as much as possible. Figure 2.15 shows a diagram with the menu bars for each application. Although Microsoft Access changes depending on your current screen (no database, database, table), you can see the menu bar similarities between the different applications. Table 2.7 lists the menus and their general functions.

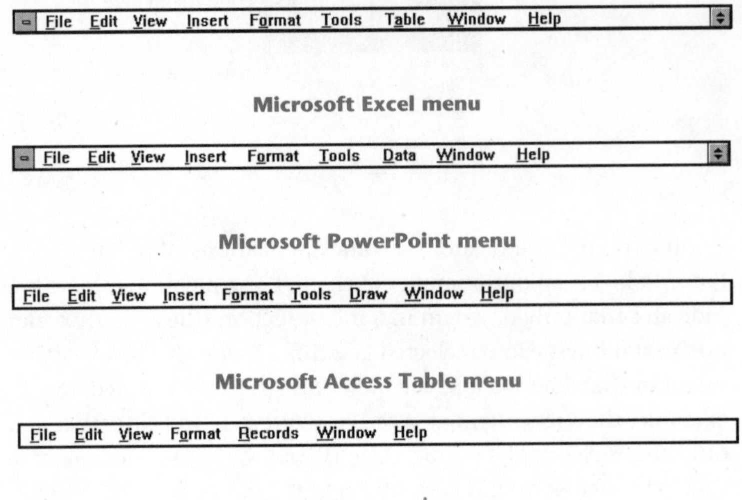

Fig. 2.15
The Microsoft Office applications have similar menu names on their menu bars.

Table 2.7 Common Menus on the Microsoft Office Applications

Menu	W	E	P	A	M	Similar command functions
File	X	X	X	X	X	Open, create new, save, close, print files and exit program.
Edit	X	X	X	X	X	Copy, move, paste from other applications, delete selections; undo last command, search and replace text.
View	X	X	X	X	X	Change the way the document and screen items such as toolbars display on-screen.
Insert	X	X	X			Insert objects into the document.
Format	X	X	X	X		Change font, line spacing or row height, add lines, have program pick out a "look" for your document with pre-determined formatting.
Tools	X	X	X			Check spelling, create macros, customize the way the keyboard, menus, and toolbars look.

Menu	W	E	P	A	M	Similar command functions
Window	X	X	X	X	X	Arrange document windows on the screen; switch between documents.
Help	X	X	X	X	X	Show step-by-step procedures, definitions, and examples. Do on-screen tutorials, list Microsoft technical support phone numbers and procedures.

W, E, P columns are for the Word, Excel, and PowerPoint menu bars, and A is for the Access Table menu bar. M is for Mail menu bar.

Shortcut Menus

Microsoft has also added shortcut menus to Word, Excel, PowerPoint, and Access. To access a shortcut menu, select the item you want to change and click the *right* mouse button in the selected area. The menu that appears gives you options for only the selection. You don't have to wade through the menu bar to figure out what menu items go with what you are doing.

In addition to shortcut menus for toolbars, there are shortcut menus for selected text, drawing and graphics objects, rows, columns, and others depending on your application. Figure 2.16 shows an example of the shortcut menus for selected text in each of the applications. Notice that each of the shortcut menus has Cut, Copy, and Paste, but also has menu items specific to the application.

Word

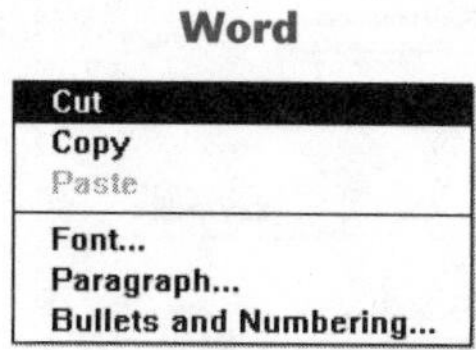

Excel

Fig. 2.16
The shortcut menus for selected text contain similar and different menu items for each application.

Fig. 2.16
continued

PowerPoint

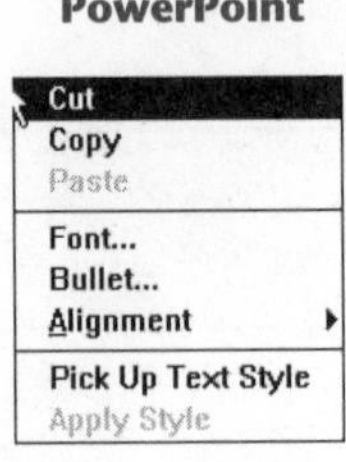

Access

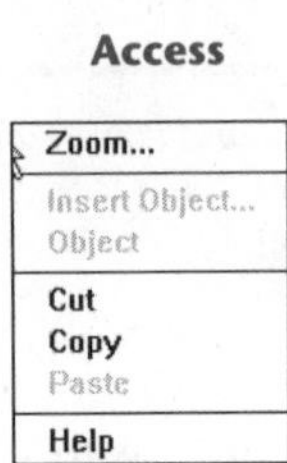

Using Dialog Boxes

When you choose a command with an ellipsis, a dialog box appears. The dialog box can be very simple with only one button (such as OK), or the dialog box can have many choices. Just as the menus have common symbols, so do the dialog boxes. Figure 2.17 shows examples of two dialog boxes.

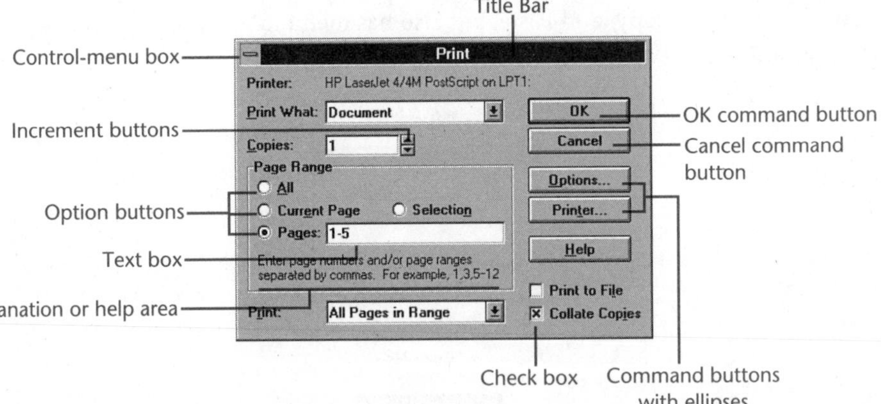

Fig. 2.17
The Print dialog box of Word and Format Cells dialog box of Excel show features of all dialog boxes.

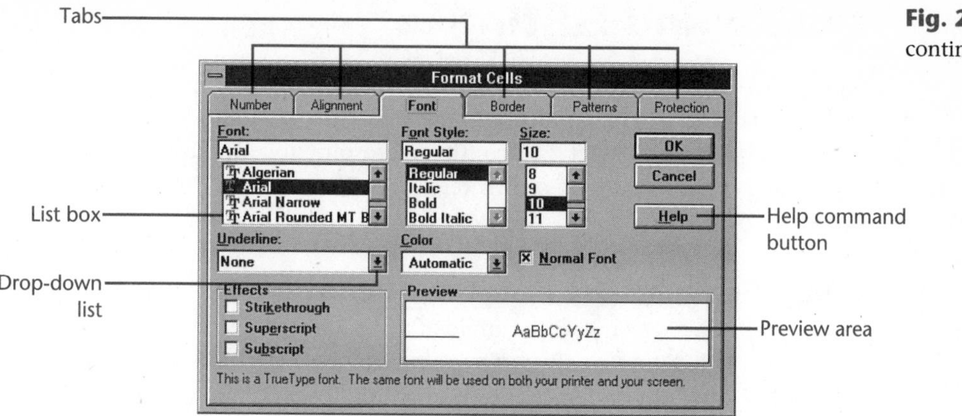

Fig. 2.17
continued

Dialog boxes allow you to see all the current settings for a command as well as change them. On the newer applications, Microsoft added tabs (the Font tab shows in the Format Cells dialog box shown in fig. 2.17). Click a tab to go to that area of the dialog box. Sometimes, you may need to see your underlying document to make a choice on the dialog box. Drag the title bar of the dialog box to move the dialog box out of the way. Within a dialog box you click an object to select or change the value. For example, on the Font Style list box, click italic to select italic. Within a dialog box you generally click an object, type a value, or select from a list. For more detail, see figure 2.17.

In addition to using the mouse to make selections within a dialog box, you can also use the keyboard. Press Tab to move to each section of a dialog box or press Shift+Tab to move backward through the dialog box. When you get to a list, click the up or down arrow to make a selection. When you get to a check box, press the space bar to select or unselect the choice. You can also press Alt+any underlined letter on a choice on the dialog box to move to that choice.

To get out of a dialog box without selecting any of the settings, choose the Cancel command button or press Esc. To use the settings, choose the OK command button. In some cases, choose the Close command button to finish your selections. Notice that some command buttons have ellipses (Options and Printer in fig. 2.17). This indicates that another dialog box will appear when you choose this button.

Typing and Editing

Typing and editing within different Windows applications is similar. When you're working within an application, there are three different kinds of modes: text, cell, and object. Each of the Microsoft Office applications can include any of these modes. Editing items are different depending on the mode.

Text, I-Beam Mouse Pointer, and Insertion Point

▶ "Editing Text," p. 110

▶ "Editing Worksheet Data," p. 263

The normal Word screen is an example of text mode. When you come to the margin, text will automatically wrap to the next line. As you type, a blinking vertical line called the cursor or insertion point moves. When you move the mouse across an area in text mode, the mouse pointer becomes an I-beam as shown in figure 2.18. Click the I-beam mouse pointer to position the insertion point. As you type, the insertion point pushes existing text after the insertion point. If you want to replace text, drag the I-beam mouse pointer to select the text to replace. When you begin typing, the new text replaces any selected text.

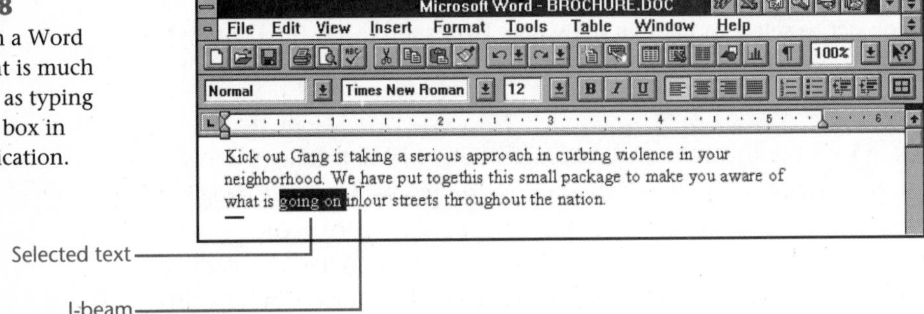

Fig. 2.18
Typing in a Word document is much the same as typing in a Text box in any application.

Moving the mouse pointer across a document within word shows the I-beam mouse pointer. While you work in a table or form in Access, the mouse pointer is an I-beam when you position the mouse pointer over text (see fig. 2.19). Click the I-beam mouse pointer to position the insertion point and type, or drag the I-beam mouse pointer across text to select it and type to replace the selected text.

This method of editing works the same in a text box within a dialog box, such as the File Name text box in the Save As dialog box shown in figure 2.20. In a dialog box, the I-beam replaces the arrow when the mouse pointer enters a text box. Drag the mouse pointer across text to select the text and type the new entry. In this example, text was selected and the letter *b* was pressed. The selected text was replaced with *b*.

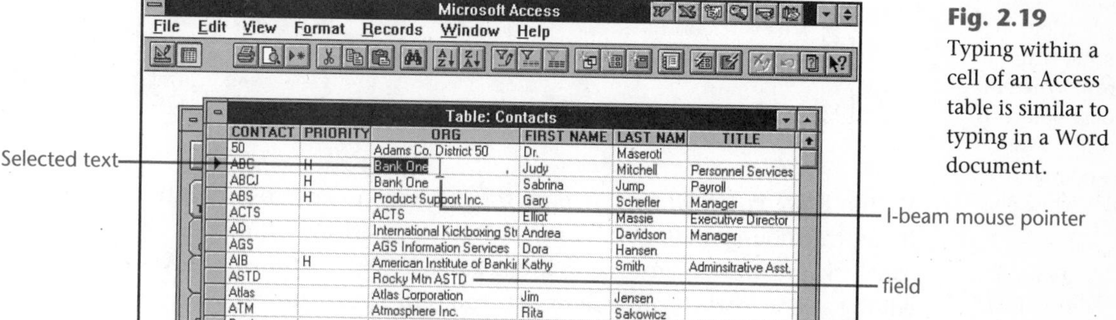

Fig. 2.19
Typing within a cell of an Access table is similar to typing in a Word document.

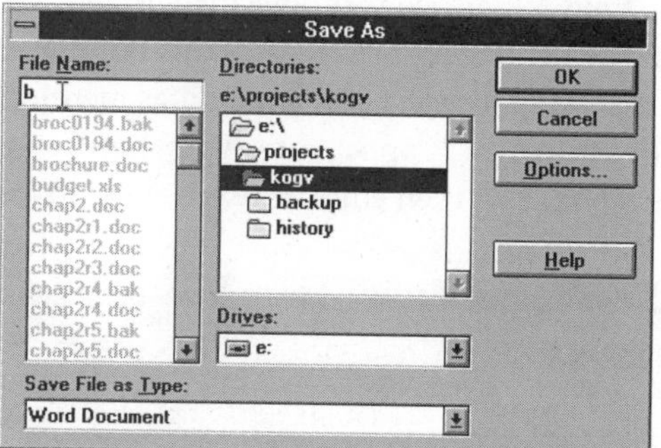

Fig. 2.20
Typing within a text box of a dialog box is similar to typing in an Access cell.

Within Excel, the mouse pointer is normally a thick white plus as you move the mouse pointer across the screen. When your cursor enters the formula bar at the top of the screen, however, the mouse pointer changes to an I-beam and you can drag across to select text or click to position the insertion point (see fig. 2.21). You can also accomplish in-cell editing if you move the thick white plus to the cell and double-click. The mouse pointer changes to an I-beam while you are in the cell and the blinking insertion point appears. This is called edit mode in Excel.

► "Selecting Cells and Ranges," p. 251

► "Entering and Editing Text," p. 459

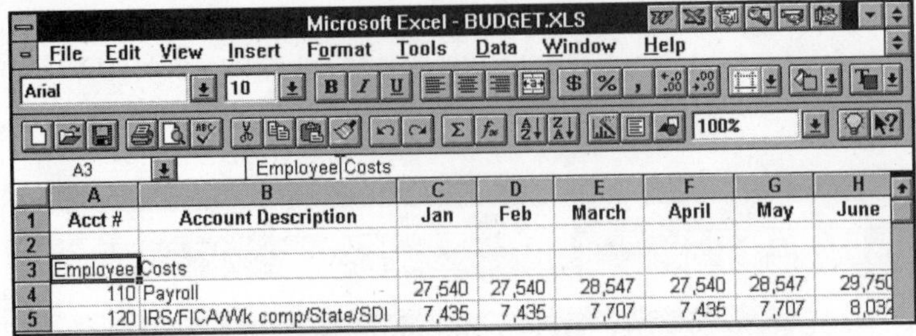

Fig. 2.21
When the mouse pointer is in a menu or on a toolbar for any application, the pointer is an arrow. When the mouse pointer is in the worksheet, the pointer is a thick white plus.

▶ "Entering and Editing Text," p. 459

Within PowerPoint, when you move the mouse pointer across most text items, the mouse pointer is an I-beam. While you are in outline view, you can click and drag on any text as if you are in a Word document. However, editing a slide works slightly different. You cannot drag to select text within a text object (title, bullet item, or added text) until you click the object. When you click, you position the insertion point within the text and select the text object at the same time. When the text object is selected, a hatched outline appears around the object (see fig. 2.22). After this outline and insertion point appear, you can drag to select text and edit as mentioned previously. If you include text boxes in other applications, you also need to first select the text object (the text box) and then edit the text as you do for PowerPoint.

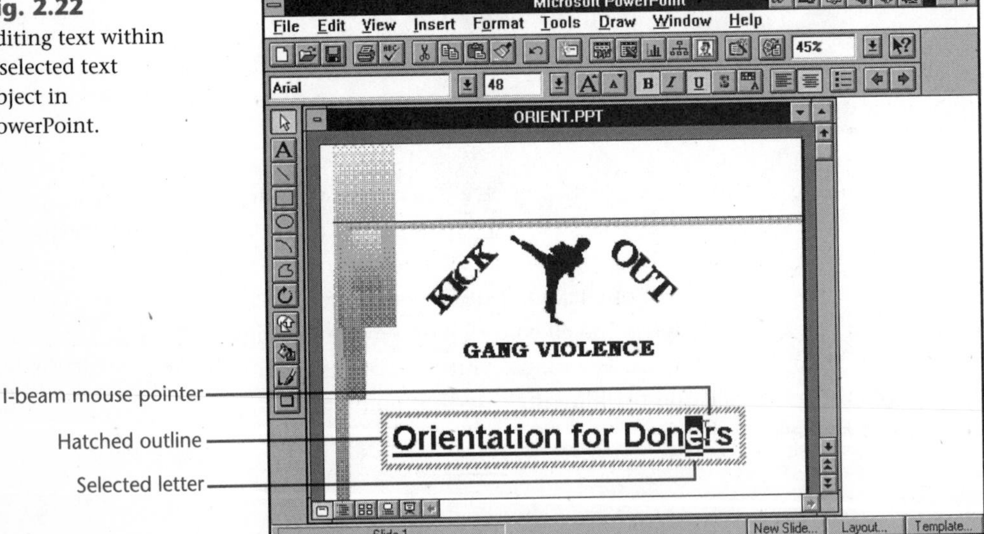

Fig. 2.22
Editing text within a selected text object in PowerPoint.

Cells, Text Boxes, and Fields

Excel worksheets, Word tables, and Access tables and queries are organized in rows and columns (see fig. 2.23). The intersection of a row and column is called a *cell*. When you press Tab, you move to the next cell. If you press Shift+Tab, you move to the previous cell. When you move to a cell with Tab or Shift+Tab in Word and Access, the text within the cell is highlighted. When you type, new text replaces the existing text within a cell. In Excel, when you press Tab or Shift+Tab, the text is not highlighted in a cell. Type the new entry for the cell and press Enter or Tab to replace the entry.

▶ "Defining Excel Terms," p. 243

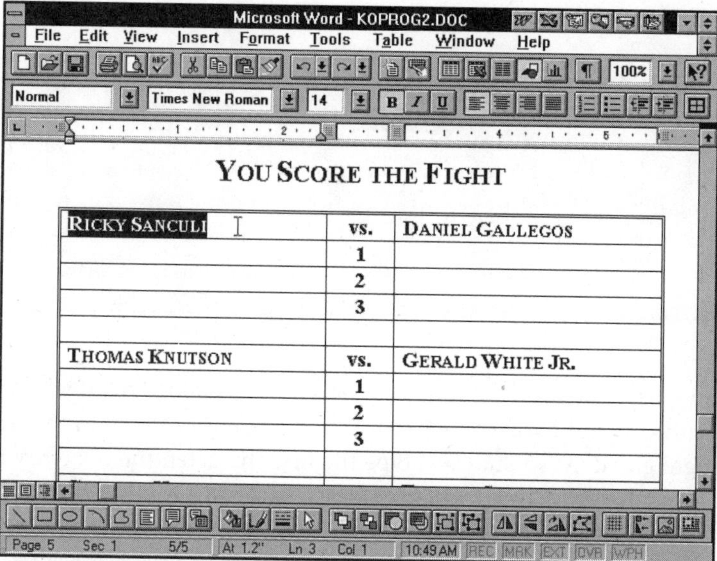

YOU SCORE THE FIGHT

RICKY SANCULI	VS.	DANIEL GALLEGOS
	1	
	2	
	3	
THOMAS KNUTSON	VS.	GERALD WHITE JR.
	1	
	2	
	3	

Microsoft Excel - BUD94.XLS

File Edit View Insert Format Tools Data Window Help

Arial 10 100%

A1 Budget 1994

	A	B	C	D	E	F	G	H
1	Budget 1994							
2		Jan	Feb	Mar	Apr	May	Jun	
3	Payroll	$ 100.00	$ 800.00	$ 800.00	$ 800.00	$ 800.00	$ 800.00	$ 800
4	Marketing	200.00	200.00	200.00	200.00	200.00	200.00	200
5	Supplies	500.00	50.00	50.00	50.00	50.00	50.00	50
6	Equipment	1,500.00	250.00					
7	Travel	50.00	500.00	50.00	50.00	500.00	50.00	50
8	Lease & Rental		400.00	450.00	450.00	450.00	450.00	450
9	Other			50.00	100.00	100.00	100.00	100
10	Scholarships		10,000.00		20,000.00		20,000.00	
11	Totals	$2,350.00	$12,200.00	$1,600.00	$21,650.00	$2,100.00	$21,650.00	$1,650
12								
13								
14								
15								
16								
17								
18								

Budget / Actual / YTD / Budget-Yr / Sheet5 / Sheet6

Ready NUM

Fig. 2.23
These three tables from Word, Excel, and Access use rows, columns, and cells (fields).

▶ "Moving Around in a Worksheet," p. 244

▶ "Working with Tables," p. 210

▶ "Inserting a Word Table or Excel Spreadsheet," p. 469

▶ "Navigating in Datasheet View," p. 612

Fig. 2.23
continued

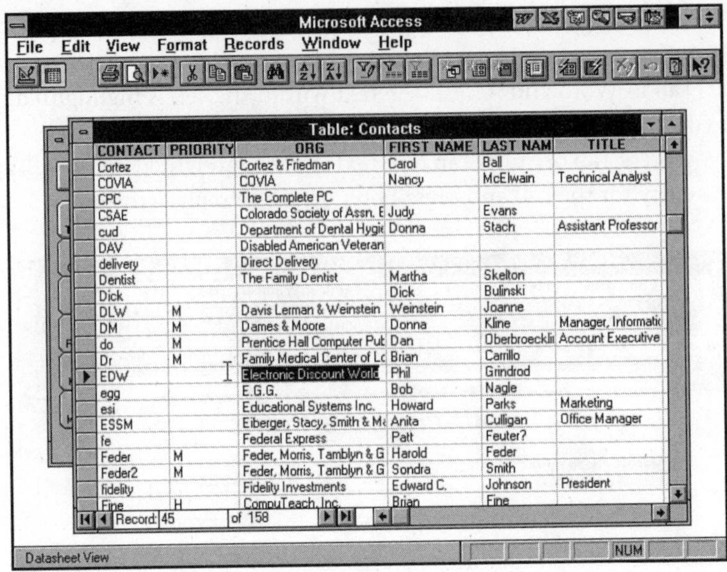

CONTACT	PRIORITY	ORG	FIRST NAME	LAST NAM	TITLE
Cortez		Cortez & Friedman	Carol	Ball	
COVIA		COVIA	Nancy	McElwain	Technical Analyst
CPC		The Complete PC			
CSAE		Colorado Society of Assn. E	Judy	Evans	
cud		Department of Dental Hygi	Donna	Stach	Assistant Professor
DAV		Disabled American Veteran			
delivery		Direct Delivery			
Dentist		The Family Dentist	Martha	Skelton	
Dick			Dick	Bulinski	
DLW	M	Davis Lerman & Weinstein	Weinstein	Joanne	
DM	M	Dames & Moore	Donna	Kline	Manager, Informatic
do	M	Prentice Hall Computer Pub	Dan	Oberbroeckli	Account Executive
Dr	M	Family Medical Center of Lc	Brian	Carrillo	
EDW		Electronic Discount World	Phil	Grindrod	
egg		E.G.G.	Bob	Nagle	
esi		Educational Systems Inc.	Howard	Parks	Marketing
ESSM		Eiberger, Stacy, Smith & Ma	Anita	Culligan	Office Manager
fe		Federal Express	Patt	Feuter?	
Feder	M	Feder, Morris, Tamblyn & G	Harold	Feder	
Feder2	M	Feder, Morris, Tamblyn & G	Sondra	Smith	
fidelity		Fidelity Investments	Edward C.	Johnson	President
Fine	H	CompuTeach, Inc.	Brian	Fine	

▶ "Navigating Form Design View," p. 645

Forms and dialog boxes work similar to tables. On a dialog box, if you press Tab or Shift+Tab until you come to a text box, the current item in the text box is highlighted. As soon as you type the first character, the old entry is erased. Access forms, Word data-entry forms, Excel data forms, and the upper part of a Mail message contain fields for entering or editing information (see fig. 2.24). When you press Tab or Shift+Tab to move to a field, the entry within a field is highlighted. When you type, the old entry is replaced with the new entry. If you want to edit an entry instead, click the I-beam mouse pointer to position the insertion point.

Objects

▶ "Working with Charts," p. 215

In some cases, you will have objects attached to your document. Objects can include charts, pictures, clip art, WordArt, and other documents. If you click an object, an outline appears around the object with small square binding boxes at each corner and halfway between each corner on each line surrounding the object. You can perform any of the following actions:

▶ "Working with Graphics," p. 219

- To delete the object, press Delete.
- To move the object, move into the object (or on the border surrounding the object) until the mouse pointer changes to a white arrow, and drag the mouse to the new position on the document.

- To change the size, stretch, or flatten the object, move the mouse pointer on top of one of the binding boxes until the pointer changes to a small, black, double arrow (see fig. 2.25). Drag the double arrow to make the object smaller or larger.

- To edit the object, you can usually double-click the object. You may enter the program that created the object, or the menu and toolbar of your current program change to the menu and toolbar of the source object. Figure 2.26 shows an example of an Excel worksheet object within a Word document. If you go into the source program, finish editing by choosing **F**ile E**x**it and Return to Document. If you remain in the target document and the menu and toolbar change, click outside the object and in the target document to finish editing.

► "Linking an Excel Worksheet to a Word Document," p. 795

► "Selecting and Grouping Objects," p. 479

Note

Orgchart 1.0 is provided as an applet (small program) with PowerPoint. Even if you don't use PowerPoint, you can use Orgchart to create organization charts within your documents.

► "Database Objects," p. 582

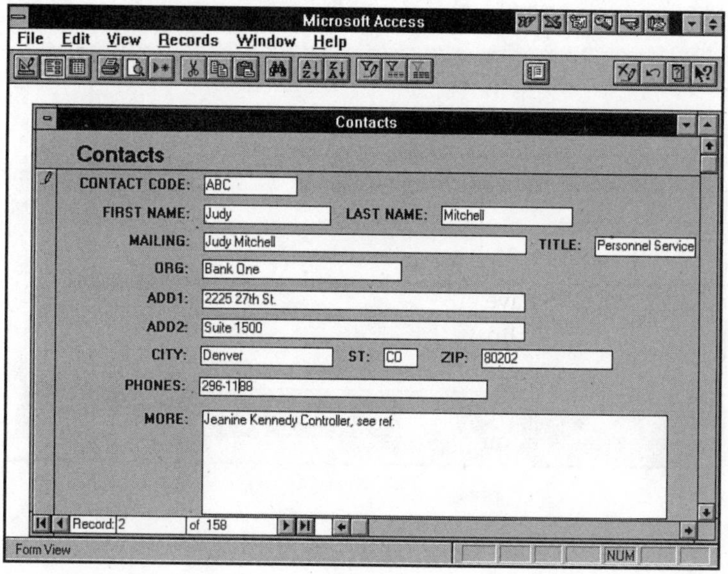

Fig. 2.24
The Access form and Excel data-entry form have fields for data input.

Fig. 2.24
continued

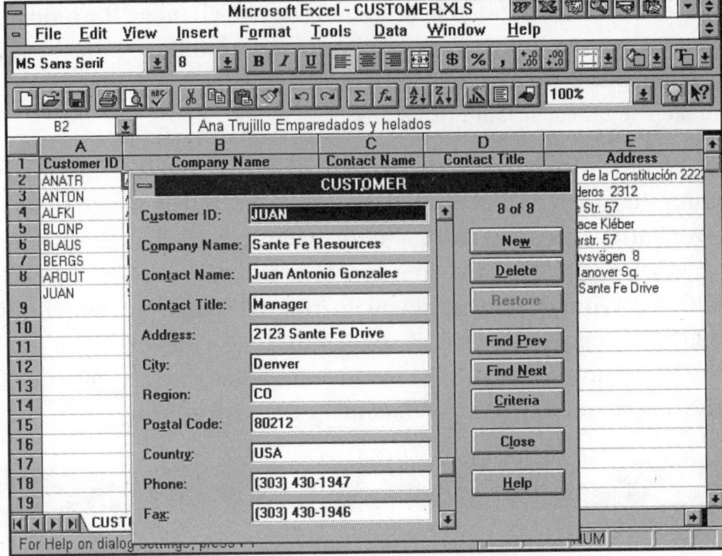

Fig. 2.25
This organization chart was created with Insert, Object, Orgchart 1.0. Notice the binding boxes and the note on the status bar.

You can size with the black double-arrow mouse cursor

Status bar

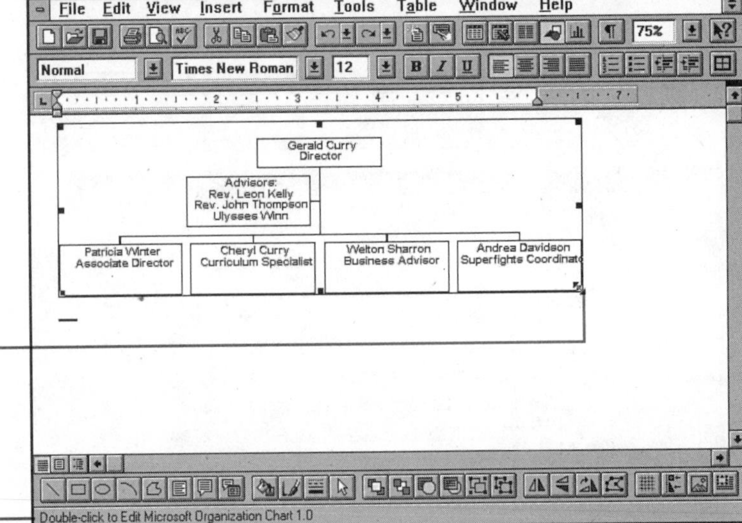

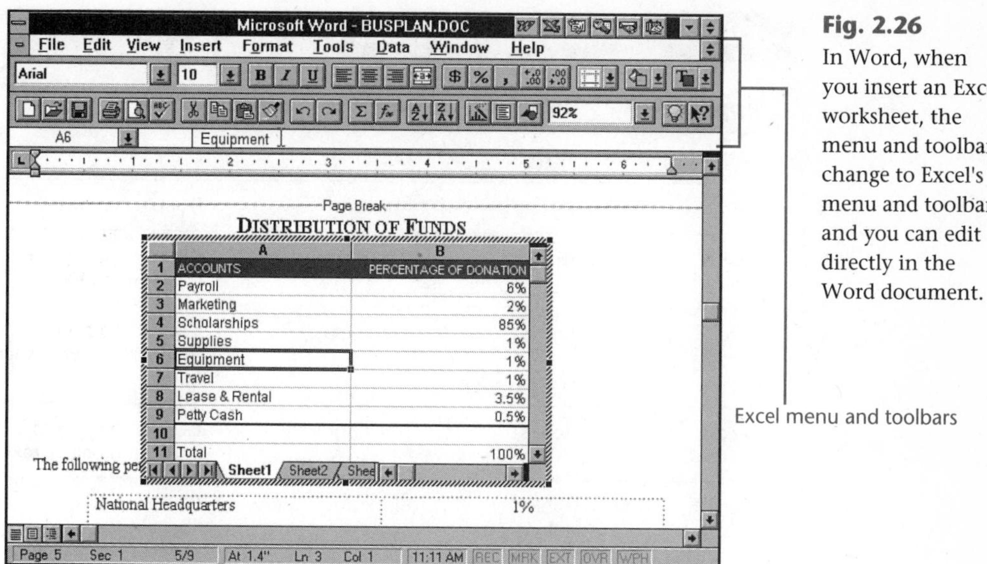

Fig. 2.26
In Word, when you insert an Excel worksheet, the menu and toolbar change to Excel's menu and toolbar, and you can edit directly in the Word document.

Most products work by clicking the object once to bring up the binding box. In PowerPoint, if you click a text object once, you get a cross-hatched outline around the text that allows you to select text within the box. Move to the cross-hatched outline and click a second time to bring up the binding box.

Selecting Text

As mentioned in the preceding section, to select an object, click it. However, you have much more flexibility when you want to select text. To edit, change the appearance, copy, or move text, you first need to select the text, and then do the procedure to make the change. There are some similarities between the applications. For example, you can always drag across the area with the I-beam mouse pointer. You can also hold down the Shift key and use your movement keys to expand the selection or click the mouse at the end of the selection. There are also some differences between the applications, as shown in Table 2.8. For example, to select a row in Word, Excel, and Access, position the mouse pointer before the row and click. However, in Word the mouse pointer changes to a right-pointing arrow, in Excel the pointer is a white cross, and in Access the pointer is a black right arrow.

► "Selecting Text," p. 108

► "Selecting Cells and Ranges," p. 251

► "Selecting Cells, Rows, and Columns," p. 538

Table 2.8 Selecting with the Mouse

Application	To select	Use mouse pointer	And...
All	Text	I-beam	Drag
All	Word	I-beam	Double-click word
Word	Line(s)	White arrow	Click or drag before text (in left margin)
Excel	Row(s)	White cross	Click or drag on number(s) in worksheet frame
Access	Row(s)	Black right arrow	Click or drag on row selector(s) before text
Word	Table column(s)	Black down arrow	Click or drag above first row of table
Excel	Column(s)	White cross	Click or drag on column letter(s) in worksheet frame
Access	Columns(s)	Black down arrow	Click or drag on field name(s)
Word	Entire document	White arrow	Hold down Ctrl and click in left margin
Excel	Entire worksheet	White cross	Click Select All button above row numbers and to left of column letters
Access	Entire table	White arrow	Click button above row selectors and to left of field names

Moving around the Document

► "Moving Around in a Worksheet," p. 244

To move throughout the document, you can use both the mouse and the keyboard. Moving around a document is similar in each application. To position the insertion point or cell pointer, click a visible area on-screen.

Scroll Bars

Scroll bars enable you to scroll the view of the document. Be careful when using the scroll bar, however; the cursor remains in the location before the scroll took place and may not be visible on-screen. You may start typing in the wrong place. To avoid typing in the wrong place, make sure that the cursor is visible by clicking where you want to begin typing.

► "Moving through a Presentation," p. 447

The scroll bars are divided into three parts: the scroll arrows, the scroll box, and the scroll bar. Use each part as follows:

► "Navigating in Datasheet View," p. 612

- *Down or Up Scroll Arrow*. Click to move one line at a time. This is true except in PowerPoint. Although this works in outline view, clicking on the scroll arrows in slide view moves you one slide at a time.
- *Scroll Box*. Drag the scroll box in the scroll bar. When you drag the box all the way to the bottom, you are at the bottom of the document, no matter how many pages there are.
- *Scroll Bar*. Click between the scroll box and a scroll arrow to move one screen-full at a time.
- *Horizontal Scroll Bar*. Drag to move left and right on wide documents.
- *Double Arrows*. In Word page layout view and PowerPoint slide view, you have two double arrows at the bottom of the vertical scroll bar. Click the double arrows to move down or up a page at a time.

Movement Keys

The movement keys on the keyboard are similar, depending on which mode you are working in. Movement keys do the following:

- Left- and right-arrow keys move one character to the left or right in text mode or one column to the left or right in cell mode.
- Up- and down-arrow keys move one line or row up or down.
- PgUp and PgDn keys move one screenful up or down.
- Ctrl+Home moves to the top of the document.
- Ctrl+End moves to the bottom of the document. In Excel, this moves to the last cell containing data.
- Home moves to the beginning of the line in Word. In Excel or Access, Home takes you to the first column in cell mode or the beginning of entry in edit (text) mode.

- End moves to the end of the line in Word or end of entry in Excel or Access edit mode. End moves to the end of the row in Access cell mode. End works differently in Excel. You press End followed by an arrow to move to the end of a continuous range of cells.
- Ctrl+Right and Ctrl+Left in text mode move you one word at a time.
- Ctrl+Up and Ctrl+Down in text mode move you one paragraph at a time.
- F5 is the Go To key. Press F5 in Word and then type the page number to go to. Press F5 in Excel and type the cell reference. Press F5 in Access table mode and go to the record number.

Copying and Moving

▶ "Editing Text," p. 110

▶ "Copying Worksheet Data," p. 266

▶ "Moving Worksheet Data," p. 270

▶ "Moving and Copying Objects," p. 483

▶ "Cutting, Copying, and Pasting Data," p. 623

▶ "Copying Text between Word Documents," p. 767

The procedure for copying and moving is generally the same for all Microsoft Office applications. The procedure works for copying information from one area of a document to a different place on the document, as well as copying information from one document to a different document. This same procedure even works for copying information from a document in one application (such as Excel) to a document in another application (such as Word). The item that you are copying can be text, numbers, a chart, a picture, or any other Windows object.

Using the Clipboard

The reason the procedure for copying and moving is the same is because of the Clipboard. This Windows accessory holds a copy of the item when you cut or copy. When you use cut, the item is removed from the source application and goes into the Clipboard. When you use copy, the item remains in the source application and goes into the Clipboard. When you use paste, a copy of the item you cut or copied goes from the Clipboard into the active application. Because all Windows applications share the Clipboard, you can easily copy information between applications.

Using Cut, Copy, and Paste

The procedure for copying or moving is as follows:

1. Select the item you want to copy or move. If the item is text, this usually involves dragging the I-beam mouse pointer or some other shortcut. If the item is a picture, chart, or object created in another application, this usually involves clicking on the object to show the binding box.

2. Do one of the following:

   - To move the selected item, choose the **E**dit Cu**t** command, or press Ctrl+X.

   - To copy the selected item, choose the **E**dit **C**opy command, or press Ctrl+C.

3. Use the scroll bars and movement keys to position the cursor in the document.

4. Choose the **E**dit **P**aste command, or press Crtl+V.

All Office applications have the Edit menu from which you can choose Cut, Copy, or Paste. In some minor cases, you may not even be able to use the menu (such as editing within a field such as To or Cc in Mail). In these cases, you can use the keyboard shortcuts.

► "Moving between Windows Programs," p. 753

Troubleshooting

If you did not use cut or copy at the right time and then click the paste button, you get a copy of whatever is in the clipboard.

Click the Undo button immediately or choose the **E**dit **U**ndo command to remove any unwanted copy.

Tip

To go to another open application to paste the selection, use Ctrl+Esc to list the open applications and double-click the application name. To go to another open document, choose **W**indow from the menu bar and select the open document.

Moving with Drag and Drop

Microsoft Word, Excel, and PowerPoint have another capability that makes moving even easier. This feature is called drag and drop. You first select the text or cells to move and then drag the selection to the new location. In some cases, this new location can be on a different document or even in a different application.

The drag-and-drop mouse pointer changes to a left-facing arrow when you position the mouse pointer in the selected text (the normal mouse pointer points to the right). In Word and PowerPoint, you position the mouse pointer anywhere within the selected area. In Excel, you point to the outline surrounding the selected cells. When you drag the mouse in Word and PowerPoint, two additional shapes are added to the left-arrow mouse pointer. A small rectangle appears under the mouse pointer and a dashed vertical line (ghost cursor) appears where the new text will be inserted when you release the mouse button. In Excel, a gray outline appears where the new text will appear when you release the mouse button.

Tip
Right-click in the selected area to bring up the shortcut menu to cut or copy. To use the shortcut menu to paste, right-click in the document where you want to paste. Most Office applications have these on the shortcut menu.

The drag-and-drop feature is limited in PowerPoint. You can move text only from one area of the current text object to another area of the same text object on the slide. In Excel, you can drag and drop items from one area of a spreadsheet to another area of the same spreadsheet. You can even drag the selection into a document in an open Word or PowerPoint window. However, you cannot drag the selection between two open documents in the same Excel program window. Figure 2.27 shows the drag-and-drop feature between Excel and Word. With Word, you can drag the selection to another place on the same document, to another open document window within the Word program window, and to an Excel worksheet or PowerPoint slide. Table 2.9 summarizes these relationships.

Table 2.9 Whether Drag and Drop Works between Two Different Applications or Two Different Document Windows within the Same Application

From	To				
	Word	**Excel**	**PowerPoint**	**Access**	**Mail**
Word 6	Yes	Yes	Yes	No	No
Excel 5	Yes	No	Yes	No	No
PowerPoint 4	No	No	No	No	No
Access 2	No	No	No	No	No
Mail 3.1	No	No	No	No	No

If you want to copy instead of move the selected item, hold down Ctrl, then begin to drag. The mouse pointer adds a small plus. First release the mouse button and then release Ctrl to perform the copy.

Troubleshooting

The drag and drop does not leave the original when you try to copy.

The operation of the Ctrl key is essential. Hold down Ctrl before you start the drag, and release Ctrl after you release the mouse button. If you need to restore the source application, return to the source application and click the Undo button or choose **E**dit **U**ndo.

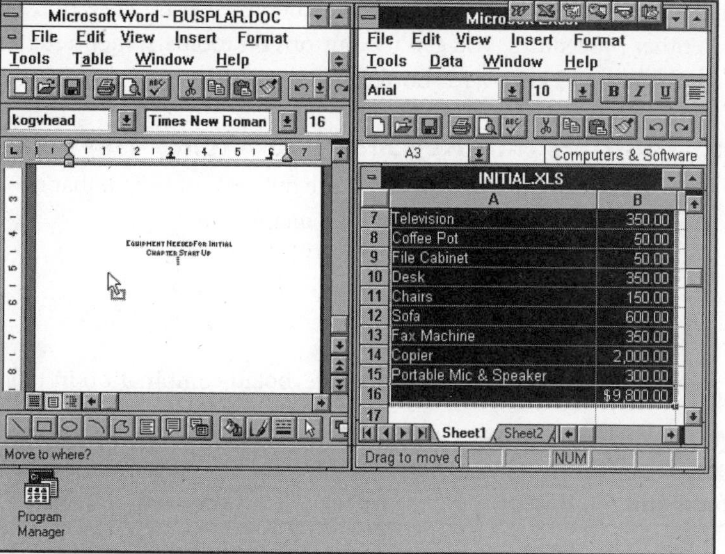

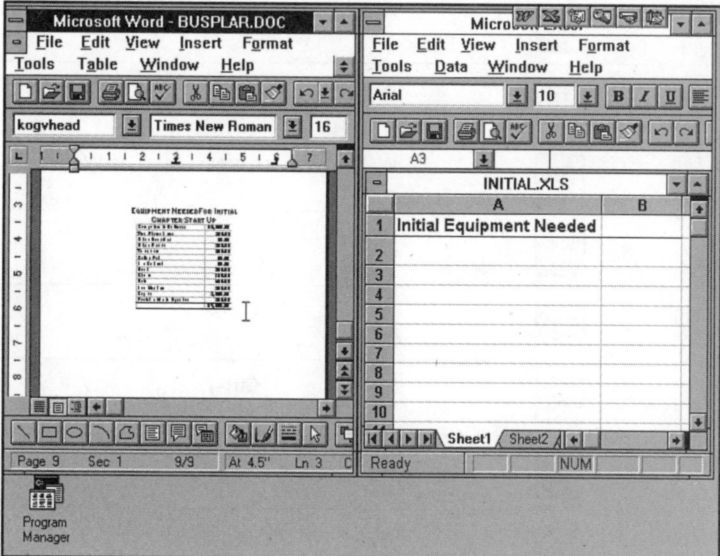

Fig. 2.27
Excel and Word were tiled using the Task List (Ctrl+Esc). The status bar in each application provides help about the task you are performing.

Formatting Documents

Formatting text involves changing the font (typeface), font size, font characteristics (such as bold, italic, and underline), and alignment of text. The general procedure to format text is the same in the different applications. First you select the text to format, and then you do the formatting. If nothing is

▶ "Formatting Text," p. 124

selected, formatting applies only to new text entered at the insertion point. As with other procedures, you can use buttons on toolbars, menu items, shortcut menus, and keyboard shortcuts.

Using Toolbars and Keyboard Shortcuts To Format

▶ "Changing Fonts, Sizes, and Styles," p. 295

Formatting is usually quicker when you use buttons on the toolbar or keyboard shortcuts compared to using the menu.

The procedure for formatting is as follows:

1. Select text to format.

▶ "Enhancing Text," p. 513

2. Choose one of buttons or press the keyboard combination in table 2.10.

Table 2.10 Formatting Buttons and Keyboard Shortcuts

Command	Buttons	Notes	Keyboard	Notes
Bold	B	W, E, P, A*	Ctrl+B	W, E, P
Italic	I	W, E, P, A*	Ctrl+I	W, E, P
Underline	U	W, E, P	Ctrl+U	W, E, P
Align Left		W, E, P, A*	Ctrl+L	W, P
Center		W, E, P, A*	Ctrl+E	W, P
Align Right		W, E, A*	Ctrl+R	W, P
Justify		W	Ctrl+J	W, P
Font	A	W, E, P, A*		
Font Size	A	W, E, P, A*		

*In the notes columns, W, E, P, and A represent Word, Excel, PowerPoint, and Access. An * indicates that the format buttons are available on the Access Report and Form Design toolbars.*

To use the Format Painter button, select the text with the formatting you want to copy. The mouse pointer changes to include a paintbrush icon. Select the text to receive the format. When you release the mouse, the target range receives the formatting of the source range.

Using Undo

If you want to undo the formatting or the last procedure, you can immediately choose the **E**dit **U**ndo command or press Ctrl+Z.

Word has a multiple level undo that lets you do more than the last procedure. To use Word's undo feature, click the Undo button to undo the last procedure. Click the pull-down arrow portion of the button to show a list of procedures and select the procedure you want to undo.

Word also has a Redo button that lets you repeat the last action you did. For example, you can apply the same formatting you did on the last selection. The Redo button also reverses an undo. If you want to undo your undo, use redo. The Redo button also has a pull-down arrow that shows a list of procedures you can redo.

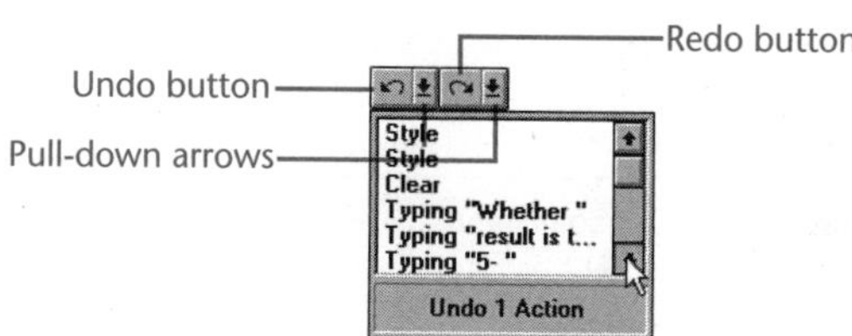

Fig. 2.28
Word Undo and Redo buttons.

Using Menus To Format

The formatting toolbars give you the most-used choices for formatting. If you want more complete choices, use the menu bar. Word, Excel, and PowerPoint have Format menus. Access displays the Format menu during report and form design. Word, PowerPoint, and Access display different formatting categories on the Format menu itself. Excel displays the formatting categories on tabs on the Format Cells dialog box, as shown on figure 2.29. Table 2.11 summarizes some of the formatting possible on the Format menu of Word, PowerPoint, and Access and the Format Cells dialog box of Excel. As with the toolbar and shortcut keys, you first need to select the text to format. When you finish with a dialog box, choose OK.

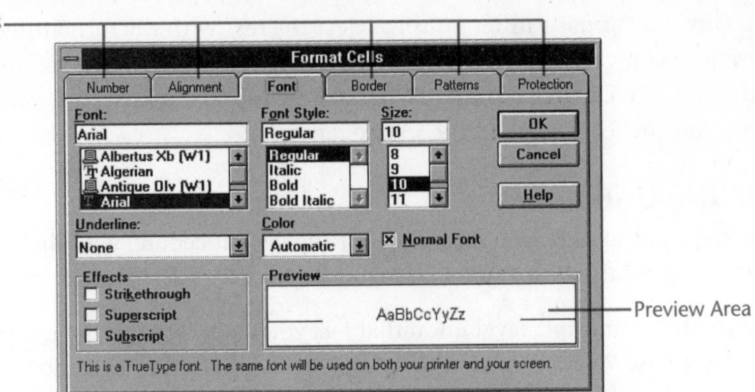

Fig. 2.29
This Excel dialog box allows you to change many characteristics of the font.

▶ "Modifying a Table," p. 212

▶ "Changing Column Width and Row Height," p. 288

▶ "Changing the Datasheet Layout," p. 632

▶ "Using AutoFormat," p. 200

Table 2.11 Formatting Commands

Command	Word	PowerPoint	Access	Excel
	*F**o**rmat then menu item*	*F**o**rmat then menu item*	*F**o**rmat then menu item*	*F**o**rmat C**e**lls then tab*
Font,	**F**ont	**F**ont	**F**ont	Font
Font size, Font color, Underline				
Border (lines)	**B**orders and Shading	Colors and **L**ines	Add with Toolbox	Border
Shading (patterns)	**B**orders and Shading	Colors and **L**ines	Not available	Patterns
Alignment	**P**aragraph	**A**lignment	**A**lign	Alignment
Line spacing	**P**aragraph	Line **S**pacing	Hori**z**ontal Spacing	Use F**o**rmat, **R**ows, He**i**ght

Troubleshooting

When you play with formatting, you may accidentally use the wrong format.

Immediately choose Undo. If you've waited too long, you can sometimes click the same button to undo the format or another button to change the format. For example, click the Bold button to bold or unbold. You can also click Align Left to change from any other alignment.

Changing Column Width

▶ "Formatting with Styles," p. 196

Changing the column width of tables in Word, spreadsheets in Excel, or tables in Access is essentially the same. You move above the document to the column marker until the mouse pointer changes to a double black arrow, and drag the mouse to the desired width. In Word, the area you change is called the *ruler* and the insertion point must be inside the table. In Excel, the area you change is called the *worksheet frame* and the mouse pointer is between the column letters. In Access, the mouse pointer is between field names. Figure 2.30 shows the three applications.

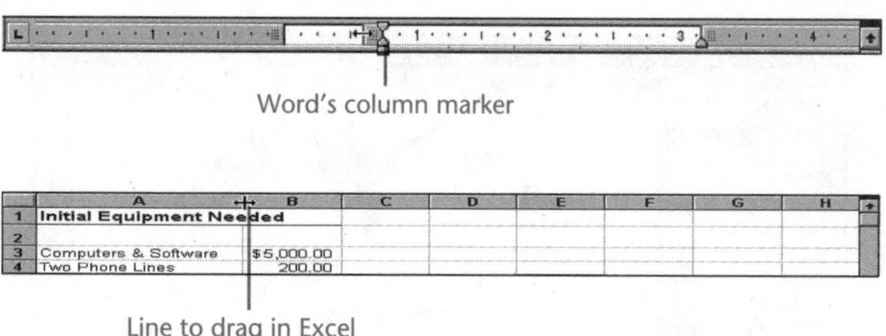

Table: Contacts

CONTACT	PI	ORG	FIRST NA	LAST NAM	MAILING	PHONES
50		Adams Co. District 50	Dr.	Maseroti	Dr. Maseroti	428-3511
ABC	H	Bank One	Judy	Mitchell	Judy Mitchell	296-7788
ABCJ	H	Bank One	Sabrina	Jump	Sabrina Jump	296-7788 x391
ABS	H	Product Support Inc.	Gary	Schefler	Gary Schefler	935-1302; 800

Line to drag in Access

Fig. 2.30
Changing the column width of tables in Word, Excel, and Access.

Letting the Application Do the Formatting for You

▶ "Using Template Wizards," p. 204

▶ "Creating and Applying a Style," p. 300

▶ "Using Form Wizards," p. 640

▶ "Creating a Presentation Using a Wizard," p. 440

Although formatting is fun, you can spend a lot of time and still not get a professional look for your effort. The Microsoft Office suite of applications is starting to give you choices of a series of formats that will automatically format the document for you. These will automatically add fonts, shading, colors, and borders for you. If you want to maintain a consistent image with your documents, using the predefined formats is worth your while.

To apply automatic formatting to your document, do the following:

- For a Word document, choose the F**o**rmat **A**utoFormat command. On the AutoFormat dialog box, choose OK. After Word formats the document, you can accept or reject the changes or choose the **S**tyle Gallery command button and choose from displayed examples (see fig. 2.31).

▶ "Creating a Presentation Using a Template," p. 444

- For Excel, position the cell pointer within the area to format and choose the F**o**rmat **A**utoFormat command. Choose from a list of examples in the **T**able Format list box (see fig. 2.32).
- For PowerPoint, choose the F**o**rmat **P**resentation Template command and select from the File **N**ame list of file templates in one of the template subdirectories (see fig. 2.33).

You can also use professionally designed formats through Wizards. See the next section, "Using Help."

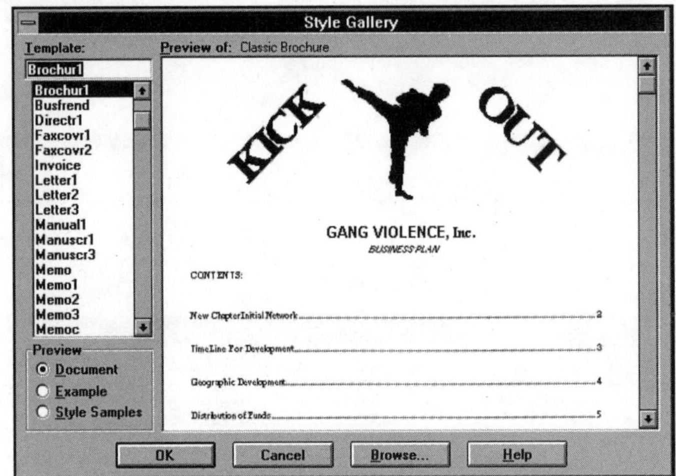

Fig. 2.31
Choose the Style Gallery to change the automatic formatting that Word created for you.

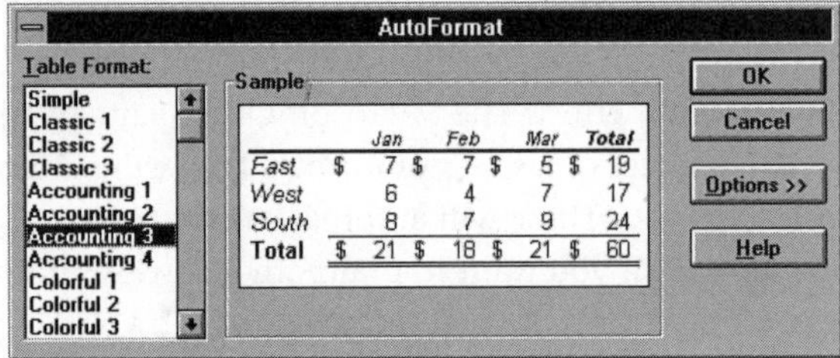

	Jan	Feb	Mar	Total
East	$ 7	$ 7	$ 5	$ 19
West	6	4	7	17
South	8	7	9	24
Total	$ 21	$ 18	$ 21	$ 60

Fig. 2.32
Choose from a list of table formats provided by Excel on the AutoFormat dialog box.

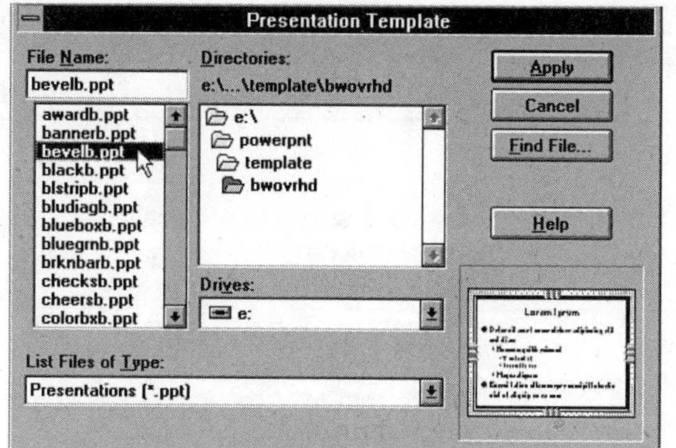

Fig. 2.33
On PowerPoint's Presentation Template, choose the file template that has the formatting features you want to apply to your presentation.

Using Help

Microsoft has significantly added tools to help you become more productive quicker. In addition to the standard on-screen help, table 2.12 shows which features are available to each of the products.

▶ "Report Wizards," p. 683

▶ "Learning More with On-Line Help," p. 898

Table 2.12 Help Features Available for Microsoft Office Applications

Feature	Description	Applications
On-line help	Allows you to look up help on a topic by searching through an index or searching for a specific help topic.	W, E, P, A
Help Pointer	Allows you to point to an item on the screen for a description of the item.	W, E, P, A
Tips of the Day	When you first start the program, a helpful hint appears.	W, P
Quick Preview	Shows you an overview of the basics of the program, what's new, and possible tips for users of competing software products.	W, E, P
Examples and Demos	A computer-based demonstration that illustrates features of the product as you watch.	W, E

(continues)

Table 2.12 Continued

Feature	Description	Applications
Cue Cards	An open window that you use along with your document that shows you the steps to perform.	P, A
How To Window	An open window that you use along with your document that shows you the steps to perform.	W, E
Wizards	Dialog boxes that take you step by step through a process. You are prompted for choices throughout the process that are required to build your document.	W, E, P, A

W = Word, E = Excel, P = PowerPoint, A = Access.

On-line Help

You can find help on a topic in a number of ways. Table 2.13 describes some of the ways to enter a help topic.

Table 2.13 Finding Help on a Topic

To find help on options on a dialog box	Press F1 while you are in the dialog box or click the Help command button if available.
To find help on a button on a toolbar	Click the help button on the Standard toolbar and then click the button.
To find help on a menu item	Open the menu, move to item on menu and press F1, or click Help button and then menu item.
To search for help on a topic	Choose **H**elp, **S**earch for Help, or from within a Help window, click the Search button. See the steps that follow to use the Search window.
To display a list of help topics	On the Help menu, choose Contents to see a list of topics organized by procedures or Index to see an alphabetical list.

If you are searching for a topic, a Search window appears similar to the one shown in figure 2.34. Begin typing the topic name in the first text box. As you type, the list of topics scrolls down to the characters you type. When you see your topic, click the topic and choose the **S**how Topics button. The second list box shows the related topics. Select one of the topics and choose the **G**o To button.

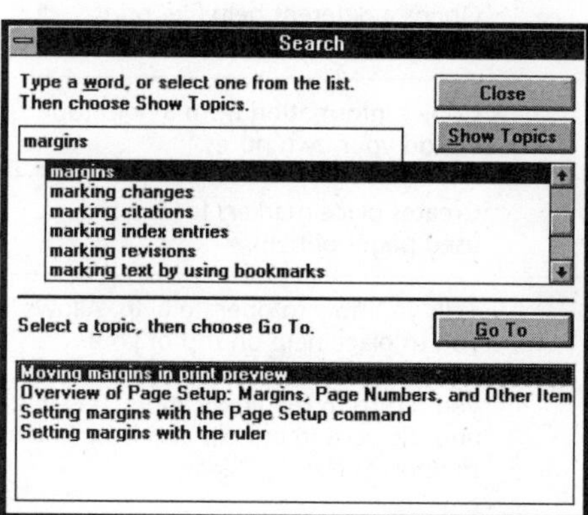

Fig. 2.34
The Search window.

After you choose help in one of the methods mentioned above, you enter a Help window with its own menu, buttons, and scroll bar (see fig. 2.35). To see more of the Help window, use the scroll bar or maximize the Help window. Table 2.14 describes the features in the Help window.

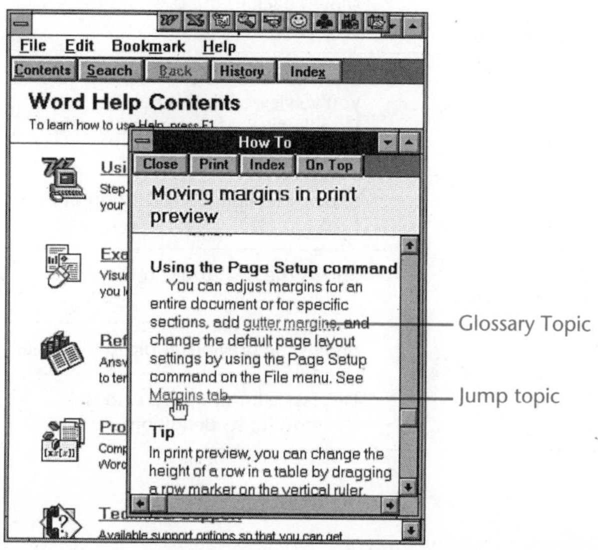

Fig. 2.35
This help window brought up both the normal Help window and the How To Help window.

Table 2.14 Items on Help Windows

Help item	Description	Applications (All unless indicated)
Menus		
File	Opens a different help file, print the help topic, exit help.	
Edit	Copies information from a help topic or add your own notes.	
Book**m**ark	Creates place markers for the most used pages of help.	
Help	Tells you how to operate help. Allows you to place help on top of your window so it doesn't disappear when you return to the application. Tells you the version of help and how much memory is free.	
Buttons		
Contents	Goes to the help table of contents of topics organized by procedure.	
Search	Allows you to search for a help topic by typing the name of the topic.	
Back	Moves back to the previous page you viewed in help.	
His**t**ory	Shows a list of all the help topics you've viewed in this help session. Double-click a topic name to return to that topic.	
Inde**x**	Shows the alphabetical listing of help topics.	W, E, P
>>	Shows the next topic in the series.	P, A
<<	Shows the previous topic in the series.	P, A
Glossary	Displays a list of terms. Choose the term for its definition.	A

Help item	Description	Applications (All unless indicated)
Screen elements		
Solid green underline	Jumps topic—choose to move to a different page in help.	
Dotted green underline	Glossary topic—choose to see pop-up definition of highlighted term. Click in the help window to turn off the definition.	
Examples and Practice buttons	Goes to a demonstration of the help topic.	W, E

W = Word, E = Excel, P = PowerPoint, A = Access.

Tip of the Day

Word and PowerPoint display a dialog box with a helpful tip when you start the program (see fig. 2.36). To remove the tips, uncheck the **S**how Tips At Startup check box. To see additional tips, choose the **M**ore Tips button and choose one of the topics in the help window. You can also display the Tip of the Day dialog box by choosing **H**elp, Ti**p** of the Day.

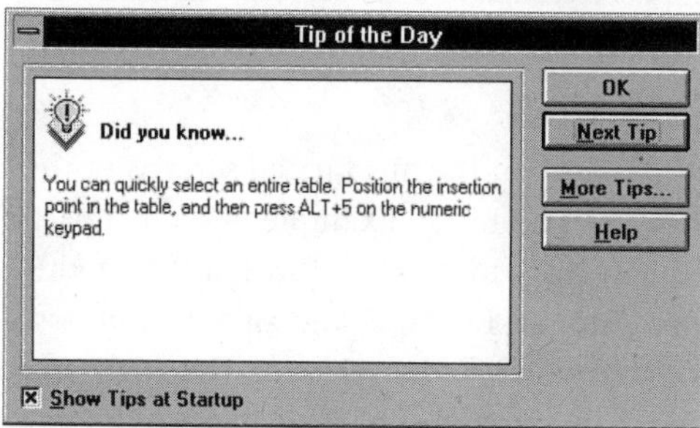

Fig. 2.36
The Tip of the Day shows when you start the program or when you choose the Help menu item.

Quick Preview

When you first use Word, Excel, or PowerPoint, a Quick Preview screen appears similar to the one in figure 2.37. The Quick Preview displays a series of automated screens showing features of the application. This preview screen will show a couple of times after you start your application. If you want to see the preview screen, you can also choose the **H**elp **Q**uick Preview command.

Topic buttons on the screen allow you to choose getting started, new features of the current release, and tips for other users. Choose one of the topics or click the **R**eturn button to return to the application. If you choose a topic, the application loads the demonstration and then prompts you after each screen. Choose the **N**ext button. If you want to return to the opening screen, choose the Cancel or Close button.

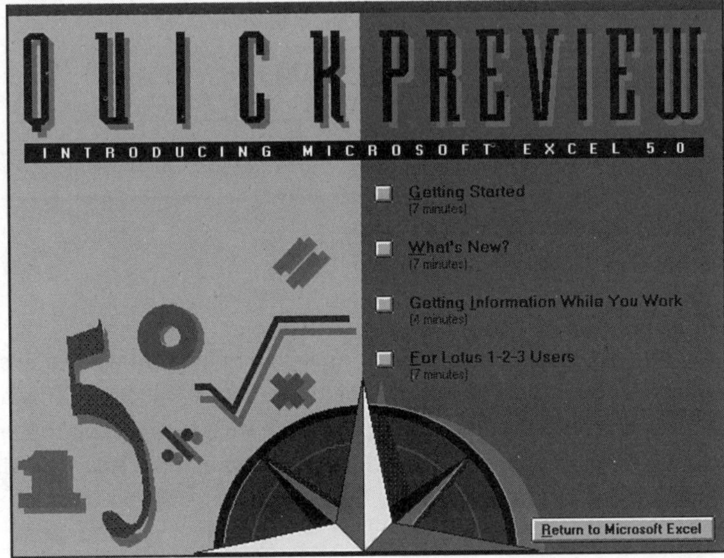

Fig. 2.37
Quick Preview allows you to get a jump start on the program and see what's new.

Examples and Demos

Examples and Demos expand on the automated screens of the Quick Preview. They are available in Word and Excel. Examples and Demos are also automated screens, but they show you more features of the product, as shown in figure 2.38. You can enter an Example and Demo by choosing the **H**elp **E**xamples and Demos command, or by selecting the Examples and Demos button that displays on some help topics. You then see a series of pictures illustrating the topic. Click a balloon topic to move to that area in the demo. Choose the **C**lose button to turn off the demo.

"How To" Windows and Cue Cards

As you go through help in Word and Excel, sometimes you get a separate help window with a How To title bar. Click the On Top button to keep this window displayed as you work in your document. A How To window describes a series of steps for a process. You can work in your document at the same time you scroll through the How To window. To close the How To window, click the Close button.

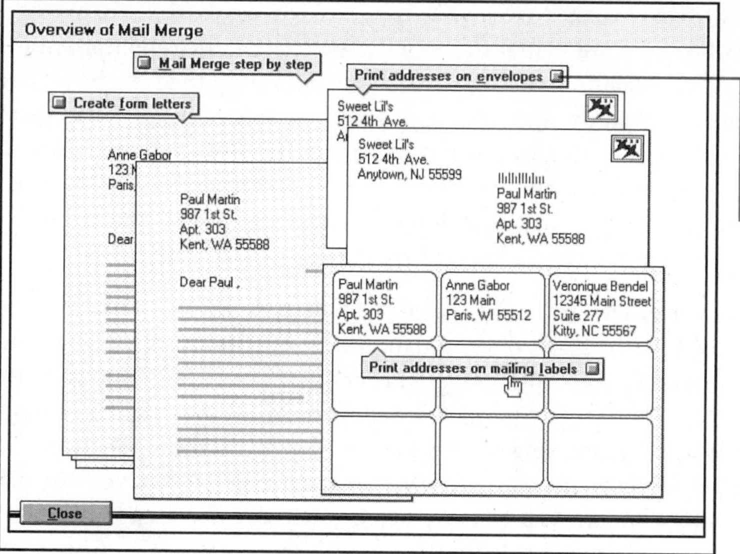

Fig. 2.38
Example and demo screens show detail of difficult procedures.

Access and PowerPoint have Cue Cards instead of a How To window (see fig. 2.39). Cue Cards and the How To window are similar in that they display step-by-step instructions. (On Cue cards, click the Next button to go to the next step.) Cue Cards also have more background information, such as defining what is a database. Cue Cards differ from How To windows because they automatically appear on top of your application. To see the application window, you need to minimize the Cue Card window (and the icon remains on top of the application) or close the Cue Card window by double-clicking on the Control-menu box.

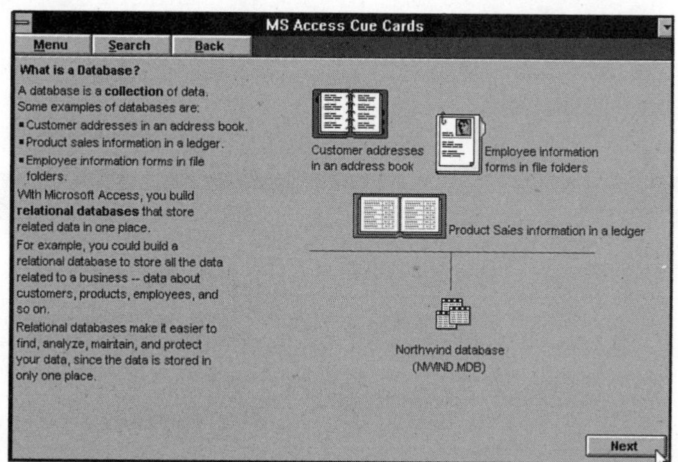

Fig. 2.39
Cue Cards give you an overview and step-by-step instructions on tasks.

Wizards

▶ "Using Template Wizards," p. 204

▶ "Creating a Presentation Using a Wizard," p. 440

▶ "Using Form Wizards," p. 640

One of the greatest help features in the Microsoft Office applications is not really a help feature at all. Wizards do not appear on the Help menu but appear throughout the applications. Wizards are special dialog boxes that ask you questions about the document you want to create and then use your answers to layout and format the document. Excel started with the Chart wizard in Release 4, and now all the applications have wizards to help you build documents.

When you enter a wizard as shown in figure 2.40, the wizard asks you to enter text in text boxes or choose from a list of options. When you finish filling in one step of the wizard, you choose the **N**ext button to go to the next step. You can skip to the last step if you know the default settings for your wizard by choosing the **F**inish button. If you want to cancel the wizard, click the Cancel button or press Esc. On some dialog boxes, you also have the capability to return to a previous step by choosing the **B**ack button.

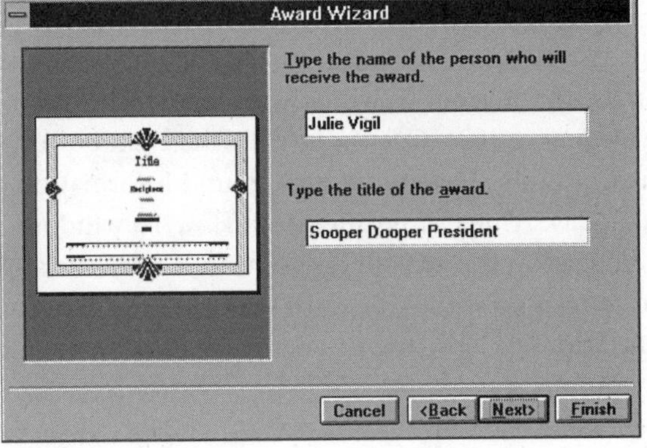

Fig. 2.40
Word's Award Wizard prompts you for a name and a title as well as other options.

▶ "Report Wizards," p. 683

You activate a wizard by different means in the programs. Table 2.15 lists some of the wizards.

Table 2.15 Wizards Available To Make Your Work Easier

Program and Wizard	How to start	What it does
Word Agenda Wizard	**F**ile, **N**ew Agenda Wizard	Creates a meeting agenda.
Word Award Wizard	**F**ile, **N**ew Award Wizard	Creates an award certificate.
Word Calendar Wizard	**F**ile, **N**ew Calendar Wizard	Creates a monthly calendar.

Program and Wizard	How to start	What it does
Word Fax Wizard	**F**ile, **N**ew Fax Wizard	Creates a fax cover sheet.
Word Letter Wizard	**F**ile, **N**ew Letter Wizard	Creates a business or personal letter.
Word Memo Wizard	**F**ile, **N**ew Memo Wizard	Creates a memo.
Word Newsletter Wizard	**F**ile, **N**ew Newsletter Wizard	Creates a newsletter with formatting and table of contents.
Word Resume Wizard	**F**ile, **N**ew Resume Wizard	Creates a resume.
Word Table Wizard	**F**ile, **N**ew Table Wizard or T**a**ble, **I**nsert Table, Wi**z**ard	Creates or inserts a formatted table.
Excel Chart Wizard	Click Chart Wizard button and drag mouse area where chart will appear.	Creates a chart. 
Excel Pivot Table Wizard	**D**ata, **P**ivotTable	Analyzes and summarizes a list of data.
Excel Text Import Wizard	**F**ile, **O**pen and choose Text **T**ype	Separates data into columns.
Excel Text Wizard	**D**ata, T**e**xt to Columns	Separates (parses) data from a long line of text into columns.
PowerPoint AutoContent Wizard	Click AutoContent Wizard button.	Allows you to choose from a series of presentation types and helps you create the title and supporting slides. 
PowerPoint Pick a Look Wizard	Click Pick a Look Wizard button.	Helps you format your slides. 
Access Table Wizard	Click Table database tab and choose New button and then Table Wizard button.	Creates names of fields and relationships in a database table.
Access Query Wizard	Click Query database tab and choose New button and then Query Wizard button.	Chooses type of query, tables, fields, and relation-ships for a database query.
Access Form Wizard	Click Form database tab and choose New button and then Form Wizard button.	Creates formatting and layout for a database form.

(continues)

Table 2.15 Continued

Program and Wizard	How to start	What it does
Access Report Wizard	Click Report database tab and choose New buttonand then Report Wizard button.	Creates formatting and layout for a database report.

From Here...

To continue your introduction to working with the applications, you may want to review the following chapters:

- Chapter 3, "Managing Files and Work Areas." You learn how to save, open, print, and close files, work with drives and directories, and switch among your applications.
- Chapter 4, "Creating and Editing Documents," gives you the basics for creating a Word document.
- Chapter 12, "Creating Worksheets," gives you the fundamentals of creating an Excel worksheet.
- Chapter 20, "Creating, Saving, and Opening Presentations," gives you the basics on how to create a slide presentation.
- Chapter 27, "Creating a Database," tells you about database terminology and how to start a new database.

Chapter 3

Managing Files and Work Areas

by Rick and Patty Winter

As you learned in Chapter 2, "Using Common Features," many features are common to the Microsoft Office suite of applications. In addition to starting the programs, typing and editing text, and using help, these features enable you to manage your files similarly across applications. The procedures for saving, closing, opening, and printing documents are much the same. You also use similar steps to find a document, attach a summary, and move between applications.

In this chapter, you learn to

- Open, save, and close documents
- Work with disk drives and directories
- Attach summary information to a file
- Find a file by name, contents, or summary info
- Switch to different documents and applications
- Compare work areas of the applications

Working with Files

For most applications, when you are working on-screen, the work you do is only in the computer's memory. If the power fails or some other accident happens, you could lose all or part of your work. The process of *saving* a file copies the information from memory to a file on disk (floppy disk or hard disk). You can manually save the file or set up the program to save the file automatically.

When you close a file, you are removing the information only from the computer's memory or from your screen. During the close process, the program prompts you to save the file if you have made any changes since the last save or if you have not yet saved the file. *Opening* a file involves copying the information from a disk into memory. When you create a new file, a new document window opens.

Saving, Opening, and Closing Files

► "Saving, Closing, and Opening a Document," p. 114

► "Saving Workbooks," p. 259

► "Saving a Presentation," p. 455

The procedures for saving, opening, and closing files are similar. You choose the necessary commands by using a button, menu item, or shortcut key. In most cases, a dialog box opens, requesting information about the file name, location (drive and directory), and type of file you are using. Sometimes, this dialog box does not open. When you save a file after naming it, the program assumes that you want to use the default choices in the File dialog box for the name, location, and file type. You can rename the file with the Save As command.

Table 3.1 shows the different methods of saving, opening, and closing files.

Table 3.1 Saving, Closing, and Opening Files

Action	Button	Menu Command	Shortcut Key
Save		File Save	Ctrl+S
Save As		File Save As	
Open		File Open	Ctrl+O
New		File New	Ctrl+N
Close	Double-click document's Control-menu box	File Close	Ctrl+F4

You also can easily find one of the last files you worked with. At the bottom of the File menu is a list of your most recent files (see fig. 3.1). Choose the file name to open the file.

If you have not saved the latest changes to your file and you close a file by using any method, including exiting the application, you are asked whether you want to save your changes. If you choose Yes, the Save As dialog box appears.

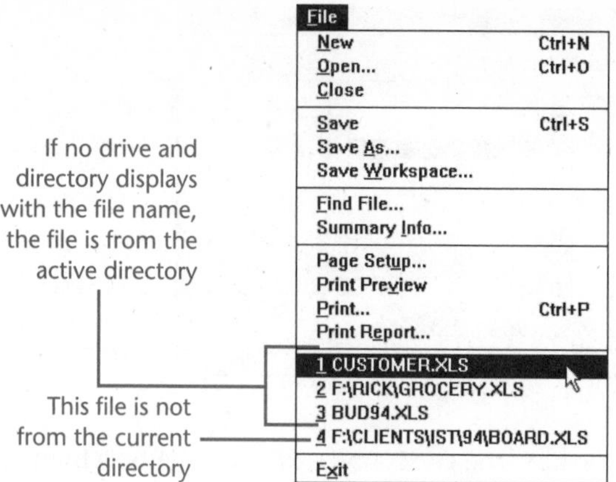

Fig. 3.1
The last few files you opened appear at the bottom of the File menu.

When you click the New button or press Ctrl+N, a new blank file window opens. If you use the menu command File New, you may be prompted for a template or wizard. *Templates* are files that may have stored formatting, macros, styles, text, and different menus and toolbars. After you open a template with the File New command, you still need to give the document a name to save it. *Wizards* are a series of dialog boxes that lead you through the steps of creating a document or performing function.

▶ "Using Template Wizards," p. 204

▶ "Understanding Masters and Templates," p. 433

▶ "Creating a Presentation Using a Wizard," p. 440

▶ "Using Form Wizards," p. 640

▶ "Report Wizards," p. 683

▶ "Maintaining an Access Database," p. 586

Note

Access works slightly different from other Microsoft Office applications. When you create a new database, the first thing you do is give the database a name in a file dialog box. When you make changes to a record in a table, query, or form, the changes are saved to disk as soon as you go to the next record; you do not have to use a file-save procedure. You cannot turn this automatic-save feature on or off. However, when you change the design of a form, record, query, or report, you can manually save the changes (or the program will ask whether you want to save the changes when you try to exit that object). The File Save As command is available only in some cases, and then you give an object (form or report) a name only within the database file itself; you do not go to a file dialog box, as in the other applications.

Using File Dialog Boxes

When you save a file for the first time, change the file name, or open a file, the program you are using displays a dialog box similar to the one shown in figure 3.2, asking you the name of the file and its location. The file name consists of up to eight characters, a period, and a three-letter extension. The extension generally tells Windows what program created the application. The location of the file is defined as the drive and directory where it is stored.

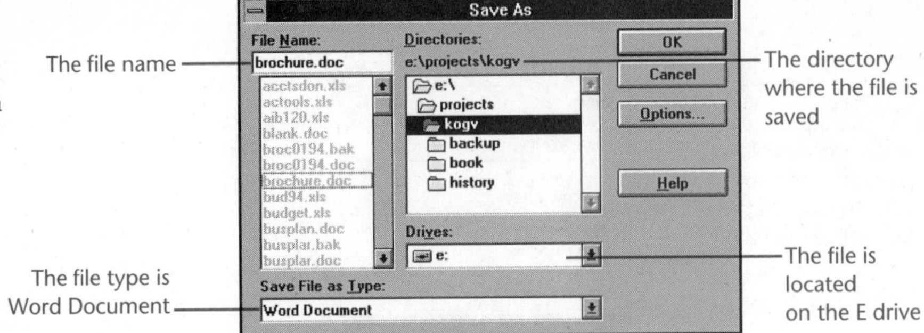

Fig. 3.2
This Word File Save As dialog box shows information about the file.

When you open a File dialog box, the File Name text box usually is highlighted. In most cases, you can type a letter, and the file name list box will scroll down to files beginning with that letter. To choose a file, you can type the entire file name in the File Name text box, move to a file name by using the up or down scroll bars, or click the file name. If your file name is not listed, you may have to change the drive, directory, or file type.

In addition to the save and open commands that bring up a dialog box, table 3.2 shows more commands that bring up a file dialog box.

Table 3.2 Commands That Bring Up a File Dialog Box

Command	Description	Application
Insert File	Places an existing document inside the current document.	W
Insert Picture	Inserts a graphic file into the document.	W, E, P
Insert Database	Inserts a table into the document.	W
Insert Object	Inserts a file into your document so you can later edit the object with the application that created the source file.	W, E
Insert Clip Art	Inserts a picture from the clip-art library.	P
Insert Microsoft Word Table	Inserts a Word table object that can be formatted like Word tables.	P

Command	Description	Application
Insert Microsoft Graph	Inserts a graph (chart) into the document.	P

W = Word, E = Excel, P = PowerPoint

Troubleshooting

When I look for a file, the file name does not appear in the file list box.

The file name may not appear in a file list box for several reasons. First, you may have to use the scroll bars to display more files in the list. Second, the file may not have the correct extension. In the List Files of Type list box, select All Files, and see whether your file is listed. Third, you may have to change the drive and directory. Finally, if all else fails, use the Find File feature, discussed in "Finding Files" later in this chapter.

Working with Disks and Drives

When you save a file, the file goes to a disk somewhere. In the simplest case, you may have a hard disk inside your computer and one floppy disk drive. In this case, the floppy drive is indicated by an A, and the hard drive is indicated by a C. However, your personal computer may have additional floppy and hard drives, removable disk cartridges and optical drives, and a CD-ROM. Your computer also could be connected to a network, giving you access to computer drives that are not directly attached to your personal computer. In this case, many more drive letters will be available. Generally, A and B are reserved for floppy drives, and C is reserved for the first hard drive. To change the drive, click the Drives arrow in the File Open dialog box, and then select the new drive (see fig. 3.3).

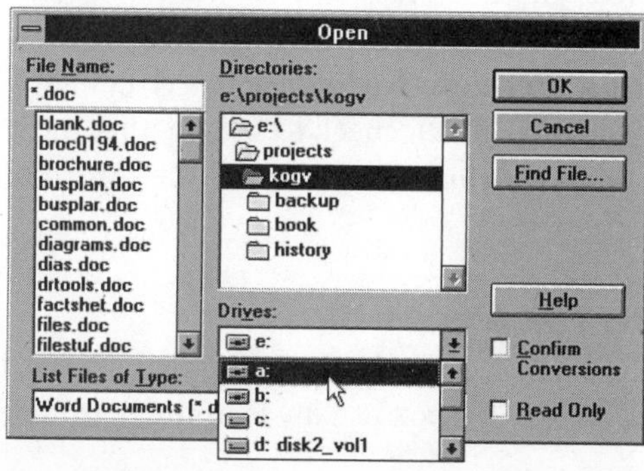

Fig. 3.3
To change the drive, click the Drives arrow.

Working with Directories

Larger drives are organized with directories. An analogy is a file cabinet. The drive is divided into directories (file drawers) and subdivided into subdirectories (hanging folders), which can be further subdivided (file folders and files). To change to different directories, you use the Directories part of the file dialog box (see fig. 3.4). The name of the current directory appears below the word *Directories*. Below the current directory is a list that identifies the drive, directory, and subdirectories. Each entry is indicated by a yellow file folder. The relationships among directories are indicated by indents. All directories on the same level have the same amount of indentation. Open directories are indicated by an open file folder. Directories you can open are indicated by a closed file folder.

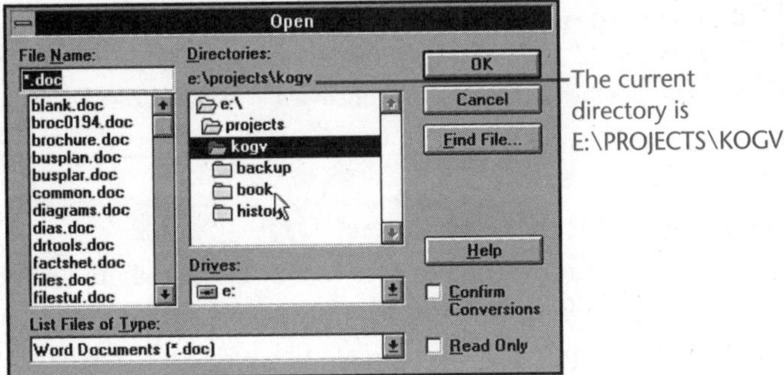

Fig. 3.4
To open a file, you need to identify the location (drive and directory) as well as the file name.

To show all directories on the same level as PROJECTS, double-click e:\. Double-click PROJECTS to show all the directories on the same level as KOGV. BACKUP, BOOK, and HISTORY are subdirectories of KOGV. To open one of the directories, double-click the directory name.

To move back up the chain of subdirectory, directory, and drive, double-click the level to which you want to move. To see all directories on the C drive, for example, double-click the c:\ icon in the Directories list box. To open a closed directory (indicated by a closed file folder), double-click the file folder. Because a double-click isn't always a double-click (you may click too slowly or move the mouse when you click), check to see whether the correct directory is listed under the word *Directories* and whether the correct file folders are open.

Working with File Types

In dialog boxes relating to files, you see a pull-down list box that says something about Files of Type. This box usually is in the bottom left corner of the dialog box. The default choice for this list box is the file type for the program in which you are working. If you are creating a Word document, for example, this box displays `Word Documents (*.doc)`. The `*.doc` file name is important, because all files with a DOC extension will appear in the File Name list box. When you save a file, you could add a period and a three-letter extension; however, this practice is not recommended. If you change the extension of a Word document to LET (for a letter), for example, you would have to list all files the next time you tried to open the document. Also, if you later wanted to launch the file from the File Manager, Windows would not know the application associated with the file.

Note

In the List Files of Type drop-down list, asterisks are part of the entries (for example, *.DOC or *.*). The asterisk is a *wild card*, which means that it can replace any character in the file name and the extension. To list all files, use an asterisk on each side of the period (*.*). To display any file with a DOC extension, use an asterisk in the filename area. An asterisk in the extension area (94REV.*) displays all extensions with file names of 94REV. You can type your own entry in the File Name text box and press Enter to limit the number of files that display in the file list box. For example, you could type **d*.doc** to display all files that begin with *d* and have the extension DOC (DIAS.DOC, DTOOLS.DOC).

The Microsoft Office applications use the following extensions:

Word	DOC
Excel	XLS
PowerPoint	PPT
Access	MDB
Backup files	BAK

In some cases, you will want to change the file type. For example, if you want to convert a Lotus file to Excel, follow these steps:

1. Choose the **F**ile **O**pen command.

2. Click the arrow next to the Files of Type box. A list of file types appears.

Note

If the Files of Type list has more choices than you can see, an up and down scroll bar appears, enabling you to scroll to other items in the list and select the file type you want.

3. For this example, select `Lotus 1-2-3 Files (*.wk*)`. The names in the File Name list box change to show only those files that include the extensions of the file type you chose.
4. Select the file name in the list box, and then choose OK to open the file.

You also can use the Files of Type pull-down list to save files in a different format (see fig. 3.5). When you change the Files of Type entry for one file dialog box (Open, Save, and others), that choice remains in effect in every file dialog box until you change the Files of Type setting or exit the application.

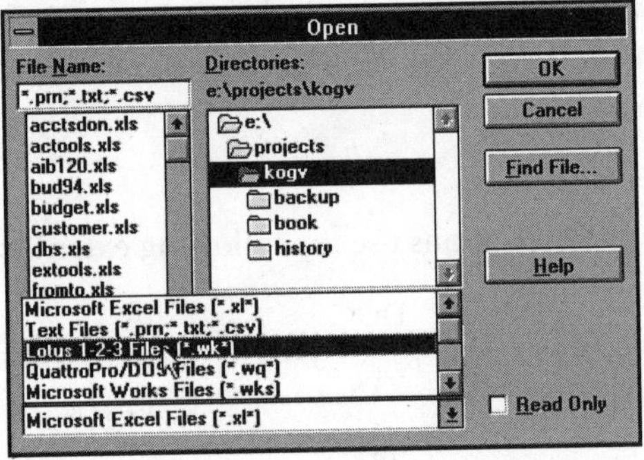

Fig. 3.5
Use List Files of Type to open or save files that are not the default type for your application.

If the file you want to open has an extension that is not on the list, select `All Files (*.*)`, which shows all files in the selected directory. You can limit the number of files listed in the File Name list box by changing the wild cards `(*.*)`. Each asterisk means "use any number of characters." If you edited the File Name entry to J*.LET, all files beginning with the letter *j* and that have the LET extension would be listed—for example, JDW.LET, JEFF.LET, and JOURNAL.LET. If the entry is *.W*, the file list would include ANY.WP, ALL.WK4, and 91REV.WK1.

You usually change the file type when you want to convert a file from one kind of worksheet (Lotus 1-2-3 to Excel), word processing document (WordPerfect to Word), or database (dBASE to Access) to another. You also can change the file type when you change the extension of a file (from DOC to LET, for example). In some cases, however, you may want to open a different kind of file. For example, you can open an Excel worksheet file in a Word document. Table 3.3 shows some possibilities for opening different kinds of files.

Table 3.3 File Types You Can Open in a Different Application

Application Opening File	File Type Opened in Application	Result
Word	*.XLS (Excel worksheet)	Word table (can be a merge data document)
PowerPoint	*.DOC (Word [outline])	Heading 1 = slide title, Heading 2, 3 = points and subpoints
PowerPoint	*.XLS (Excel worksheet)	Each row becomes the title of the slide

If your application cannot convert the file type, an error message appears, stating that the file format is not valid, or a dialog box appears, asking you to convert the file.

Using Save Options

Although most applications require that you save files, Word and Excel enable you to create backup files and set up automatic saving. You still should use the Save button, the menu command, or the shortcut key to save often, especially after you spend a significant amount of effort to make the document look the way you want or before you perform a major procedure on your file (such spell checking, sorting, replacing, automatic formatting, or importing). You may want to use the Save As feature to save different revisions of the same file until your project is complete.

A backup file has the extension BAK instead of the normal extension (such as DOC or XLS). You create a backup file after you have saved the file at least once. When you save a file the second time and all subsequent times, the backup procedure renames the old file on disk with the same file name, but with a BAK extension, and saves the document on-screen with the normal extension. If you need to use your backup file, change the file type to *.BAK. To start the backup procedure, choose the **F**ile Save **A**s command, and then choose **O**ptions Always Create **B**ackup.

▶ "Backing Up Your Database," p. 586

In Word and Excel, you can set up the automatic-save feature so that the program saves your work at time intervals that you specify. In Word, automatic save places a temporary copy of your document in the temp directory of your AUTOEXEC.BAT file. The file name starts with a tilde (~). When you restart Word after a crash, the file may automatically appear on-screen. In Excel, the program prompts you for a file name if you have not already saved the file.

Using Summary Info

► "Creating Summary Info Records," p. 155

As mentioned earlier, when you name a file, you are limited to eight characters, a period, and a three-character extension (which you should reserve for the file type). Eight characters have limited capability to describe a file, however. Word, Excel, and PowerPoint feature a Summary Info dialog box that enables you to use a longer title and to add a subject, the author's name, keywords, and comments to your file.

To save summary information with a file, follow these steps:

1. From your document, choose the **F**ile Summary **I**nfo command. The Summary Info dialog box appears, as shown in figure 3.6.

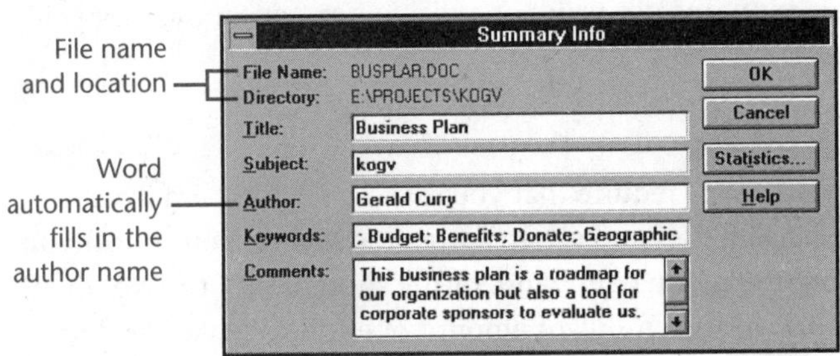

Fig. 3.6 Use Summary Info to help you remember the file so you can find it later if you forget the name.

2. Type a longer description in the **T**itle text box. (You can include spaces.)

3. If desired, type a subject, author name, keywords, or comments. To move between fields, press Tab or click the field.

   Word automatically fills in the author name, based on the User Info. To change the author, type a new name in the text box. To change the User Info, choose the **T**ools **O**ptions command, select the User Info tab, and change the name in the **N**ame box.

4. In Word, if you want to see the number of words or other document statistics, click the Stat**i**stics button.

5. When you finish, choose OK.

Finding Files

Have you ever tried to find a file when you forgot where you put it or what you called it? Life can be difficult when you cannot find a file and have to re-create it. Word, Excel, and PowerPoint now have a Find File feature that enables you to search for a file based on the file name, summary information, file contents, or file dates. You can look for a file in either of two ways: use the Search dialog box or use the Advanced Search dialog box. After you search for files, they appear in the Find File dialog box.

▶ "Working in Find File," p. 168

Using the Search Dialog Box

To find files through the Search dialog box, follow these steps:

1. Choose **F**ile **F**ind File. The Search dialog box appears (see fig. 3.7).

> **Note**
>
> You may see the Search dialog box or the Find File dialog box, depending on your last search. If the Find File dialog box appears, click the Search button to go to step 2.

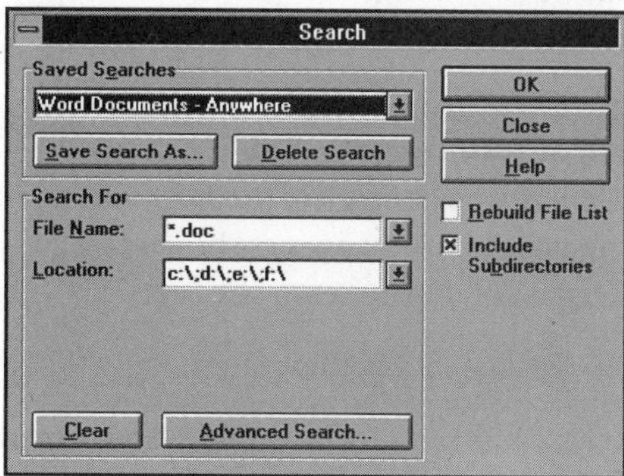

Fig. 3.7
The Search dialog box.

2. Enter the file criteria in the File **N**ame text box. Use asterisks (*) for wild cards.

3. Enter the drive and/or directories in the **L**ocation text box. You can separate multiple locations with semicolons.

4. Check the Include Subdirectories check box if you want to see files in the directory and any of its subdirectories.

5. To start the search, choose the OK command button.

The results of your search appear in the Find File dialog box (see "Using the Find File Dialog Box" later in this chapter).

Using the Advanced Search Dialog Box

The Advanced Search dialog box enables you to go beyond searching for file names. You also can search for text within the file, look for the file by date, or look for the file based on other information in the Summary Info dialog box. The Advanced Search dialog box has three tabs, which are described in the following sections.

To find a file by using the Advanced Search dialog box, follow these steps:

1. Choose **F**ile **F**ind File. The Search dialog box appears. (If the Find File dialog box appears instead, choose the **S**earch command button.)

2. In the Search dialog box, choose the **A**dvanced Search command button. The Advanced Search dialog box appears, with three tabs. To move to a tab, click it or press the shortcut key.

3. Select options in any or all of the tabs to define your search criteria.

4. When you finish selecting options in the tabs, choose OK. The Find File dialog box appears (see "Using the Find File Dialog Box" later in this chapter).

Tip

You can select multiple adjacent directories by clicking the first file, holding down the Shift key, and then clicking the last file. You also can select nonadjacent directories by holding down the Ctrl key and clicking each directory.

Using the Advanced Search Location Tab

In the Advanced Search dialog box, select the **L**ocation tab to display the location options. The dialog box changes as shown in figure 3.8. The purpose of this tab is to build a list of directories in the S**e**arch In list box.

To change the search criteria, follow these steps:

1. If you want to clear the existing directory search criteria, choose the Re**m**ove All command button.

2. If you want to remove one directory from the search criteria, select the directory in the S**e**arch In list box and then choose the **R**emove command button.

3. In the Dri**v**es list, select the drive where the files are located.

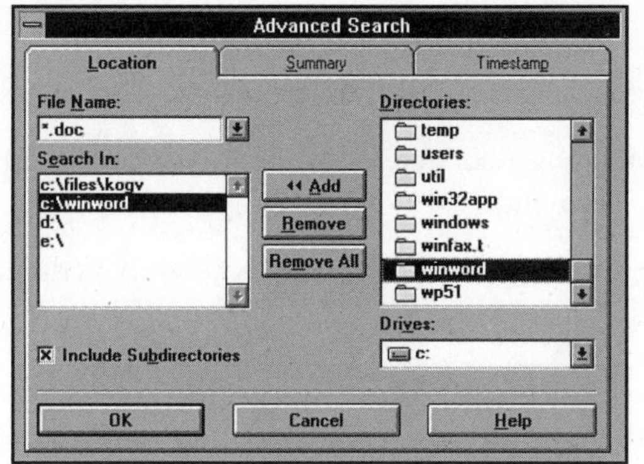

Fig. 3.8
The Location tab of the Advanced Search dialog box enables you to select drives and directories in lists.

4. In the **D**irectories list box, select a subdirectory to search. If the directory is not visible, double-click the higher-level directory. To display all the subdirectories of the root directory of drive D, for example, double-click the d:\ icon in the **D**irectories list.

5. To add a directory to the search list, choose the **A**dd command button. The directory appears in the S**e**arch In list box.

6. To include additional directories, repeat steps 3–5.

7. To search within the subdirectories of the selected directories in the S**e**arch In list box, select the Include Su**b**directories option.

8. To choose specific application files, select a file type in the File **N**ame pull-down list.

9. Select another tab to add more search criteria, or choose OK to return to the Search dialog box.

Using the Advanced Search Summary Tab

Use the Summary tab to change the search criteria to include information from the Summary Info dialog box, or text within the file.

In the Search dialog box, select the **S**ummary tab. The dialog box changes as shown in figure 3.9.

Do any of the following things:

- Type the title of the document (from the Summary Info dialog box) in the **T**itle text box.

- Type the author's name in the **A**uthor text box.

- Type a keyword in the **K**eywords text box.
- Type a word or phrase in the S**u**bject text box.
- In the **C**ontaining Text area, type a word or phrase that is in the file you want to find.
- If you want the capitalization to match the search criteria, select **M**atch Case.

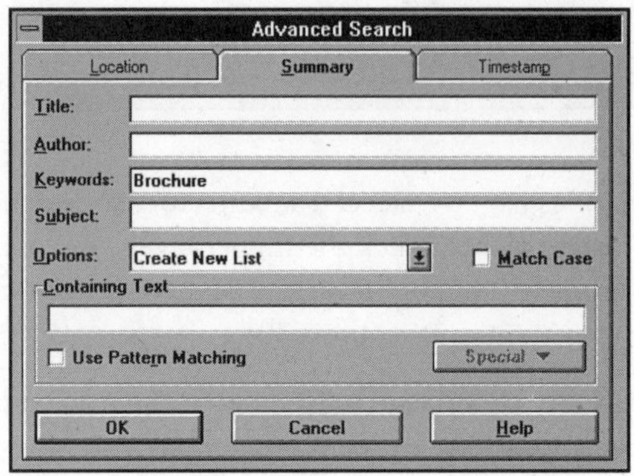

Fig. 3.9
The Summary tab of the Advanced Search dialog box enables you to search for any information you entered in the Summary Info dialog box.

When you finish with the Summary tab, choose OK to return to the Search dialog box, or select another tab.

Using the Advanced Search Timestamp Tab

In the Advanced Search dialog box, select the Timesta**p** tab to display the Location portion. The dialog box changes as shown in figure 3.10.

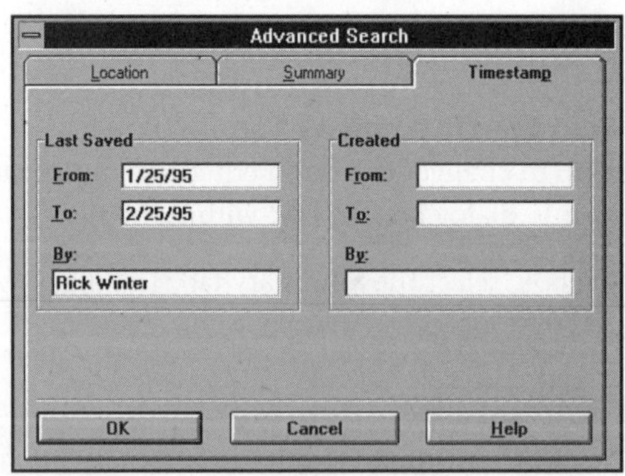

Fig. 3.10
The Timestamp tab of the Advanced Search dialog box enables you to look for files based on when they were saved or created or by whom they were created.

The Timestamp tab contains two sections. Use the Last Saved section to search for the file based on when the file was last saved (with the File Save or

Save As command). Use the Created section to search for the file based on when the file was created (with the File Save command). In either section, type the starting and ending dates for which you want to search. The file date must fall between those two dates. In the **B**y text box in either section, type the name of the user. This name is the user's name, as defined in User Info, and does not have to be the author's name, as shown in the Summary tab (although these names usually match).

When you finish with the Timestamp tab, choose OK to return to the Search dialog box, or select another tab.

Saving and Using Saved Search Criteria

After you identify the file name, location, summary information, text, or dates, you can save these settings. Follow these steps:

1. If you are in the Advanced Search dialog box, choose OK to return to the Search dialog box.
2. Choose the **S**ave Search As button.
3. Type the name of the search.

When you want to use a named search, select the search from the Saved S**e**arches pull-down list. To delete the search, choose the **D**elete Search command button. Figure 3.11 shows a list of saved searches.

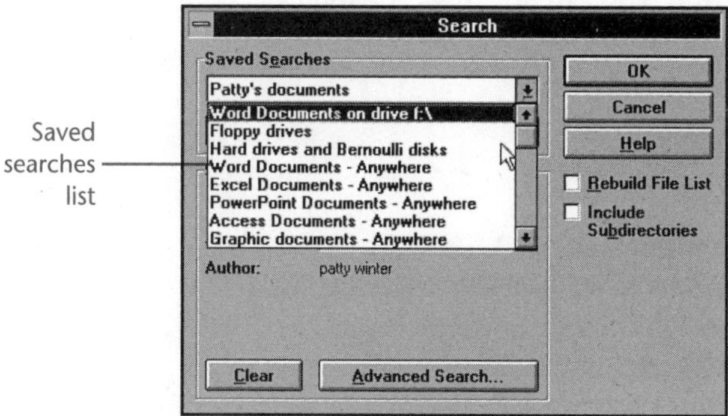

Fig. 3.11
Select saved searches in the Saved Searches pull-down list.

Using the Find File Dialog Box

After you choose OK in the Search dialog box, the program builds a list and displays the files in the Find File dialog box (see fig. 3.12). The left side of the dialog box shows the list of files within drives and directories that match your criteria. The right side of the dialog box can show files in any of three views.

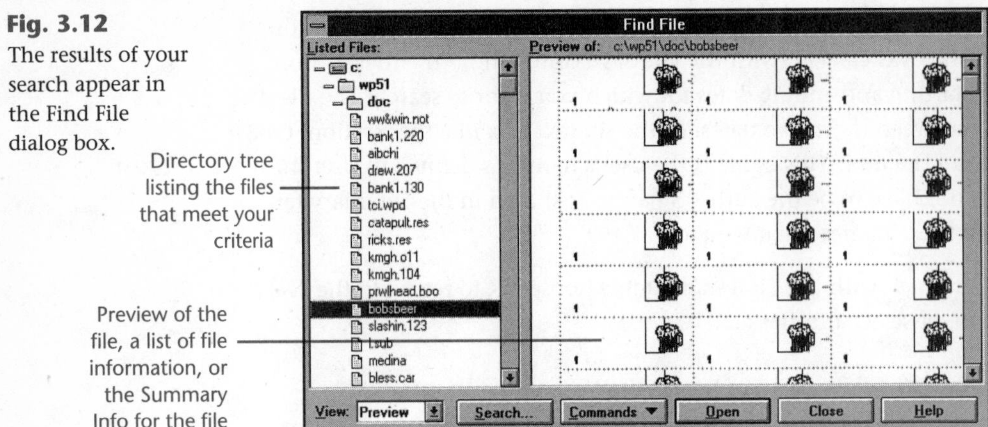

Fig. 3.12
The results of your search appear in the Find File dialog box.

You can select the following views in the **V**iew pull-down list:

- *Preview*. Shows an image of the file.
- *File Info*. Shows the file name, title, size, author, and date and time saved.
- *Summary*. Shows the title, author, keywords, comments, date, time, and statistics.

You can open the file by choosing the **O**pen command button. If you choose the **C**ommands button, you can do any of the following things:

- Open a read-only copy of the file. When you try to save the file, you are asked for another name.
- Print the file.
- Display the summary.
- Delete the file.
- Copy the file.
- Sort the list by name, date, title, author, or size.

As in the File Manager, you can select multiple files. When you select multiple files, you also can open, print, delete, or copy them.

Printing Documents

As mentioned in the preceding section, you can print one or more files by selecting the Commands Print option in the Find File dialog box. To print or preview the current document, you can use menu commands, toolbar buttons, or shortcut keys.

Printing All or Part of the Document

To print the document, choose the **F**ile **P**rint command or press Ctrl+P.

When you use the Print button or shortcut key, the entire document prints. If you use the menu command, a dialog box similar to figure 3.13 appears, displaying more choices.

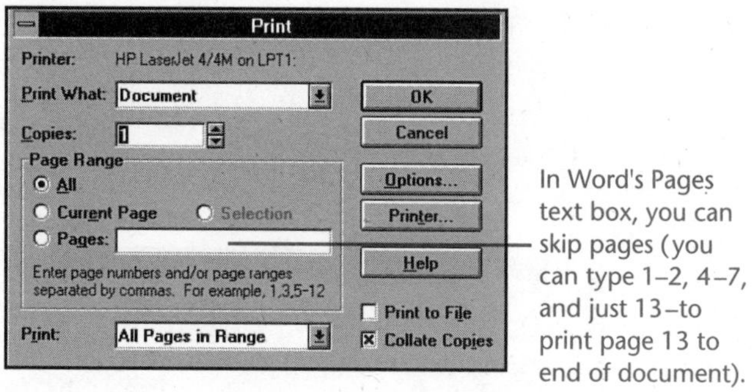

In Word's Pages text box, you can skip pages (you can type 1–2, 4–7, and just 13–to print page 13 to end of document).

Fig. 3.13
The Print dialog box enables you to specify what you want to print in more detail.

Options in the different applications' Print dialog boxes enable you to print the entire document, the current page, specific pages, or selected text. You also can specify the number of copies to print.

Changing Printing Options

If you want to make additional printing choices, use the Page Setup and Print Setup dialog boxes, shown in figures 3.14 and 3.15. The options in these dialog boxes enable you to set margins, print headers and footers, specify the print orientation, and change the printer settings.

To change margins, paper size, and other features, use the following commands:

Application	Menu Command	Button in Print Dialog Box
Word	**F**ile Page Set**u**p	None
Excel	**F**ile Page Set**u**p	Page Set**u**p

(continues)

Application	Menu Command	Button in Print Dialog Box
PowerPoint	**F**ile Slide Set**u**p	None
Access	**F**ile P**r**int Setup	**S**etup

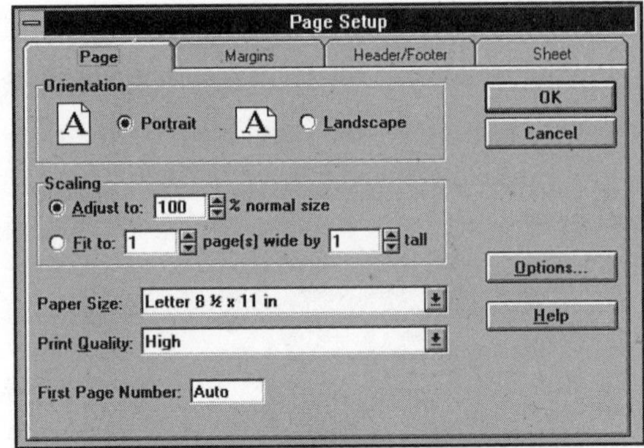

Fig. 3.14
The Excel Page Setup dialog box.

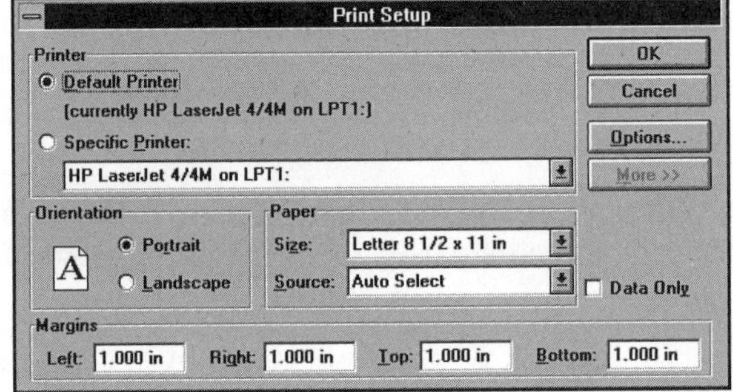

Fig. 3.15
The Access Print Setup dialog box has fewer options than the Word or Excel dialog boxes.

To change the printer, choose the following buttons:

Application	Button in Print Dialog Box
Word	Prin**t**er
Excel	P**r**inter Setup
PowerPoint	Prin**t**er
Access	**S**etup

Using Print Preview

Although your screen shows what you will see on the printed page, Word, Excel, and Access have a Print Preview option that enables you to see the entire page (or more than one page), including headers and footers, page numbers, and margins. You enter the preview by choosing the **F**ile Print Pre**v**iew command. Table 3.4 shows the features available while you are in preview mode.

Table 3.4 Features Available in Print Preview

Feature	W	E	A
Change margins	X	X	
Magnify	X	X	X
Zoom to different sizes	X		
Multiple pages	X		
Shrink to fit	X	X	
Print	X	X	X
Edit	X		

W = Word, E = Excel, A = Access

Figure 3.16 shows Print Preview for Word, and figure 3.17 shows Print Preview for Excel.

To change margins, click the Margins button, move the mouse pointer to the top or side until the pointer changes to a double black arrow, and drag the margin. To magnify, click the Magnify button, and click the document where you want magnification. To turn magnification off, click the document again. In Word, to edit the document, click the Magnify button to turn magnification off and editing on.

Switching between Documents

When you open more than one file at a time, you have a window for each file. You can switch between open documents in the following ways:

- Choose the open document from the bottom of the **W**indow menu.
- Press Ctrl+F6 to cycle through the open documents.

- If parts of documents are visible on-screen, click them. If a document is minimized, as shown in figure 3.18, double-click its icon.

Fig. 3.16
The Word Print Preview can show more than one page at a time.

Use the ruler to change the margins

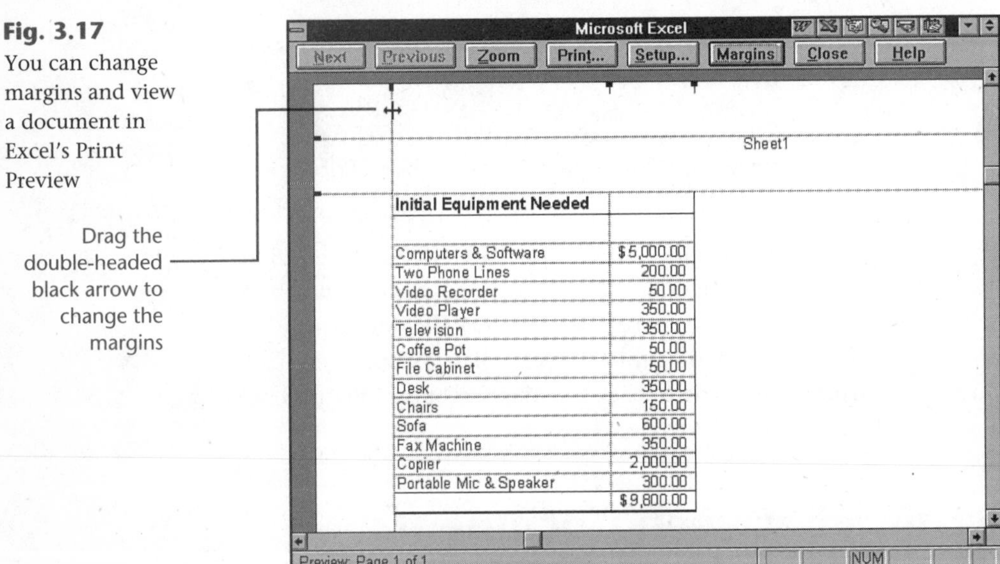

Initial Equipment Needed	
Computers & Software	$5,000.00
Two Phone Lines	200.00
Video Recorder	50.00
Video Player	350.00
Television	350.00
Coffee Pot	50.00
File Cabinet	50.00
Desk	350.00
Chairs	150.00
Sofa	600.00
Fax Machine	350.00
Copier	2,000.00
Portable Mic & Speaker	300.00
	$9,800.00

Fig. 3.17
You can change margins and view a document in Excel's Print Preview

Drag the double-headed black arrow to change the margins

If you want to copy information between documents, you may want to display two or more windows, as follows:

■ In Word, choose the **W**indow **A**rrange All command to display the documents as shown in figure 3.19.

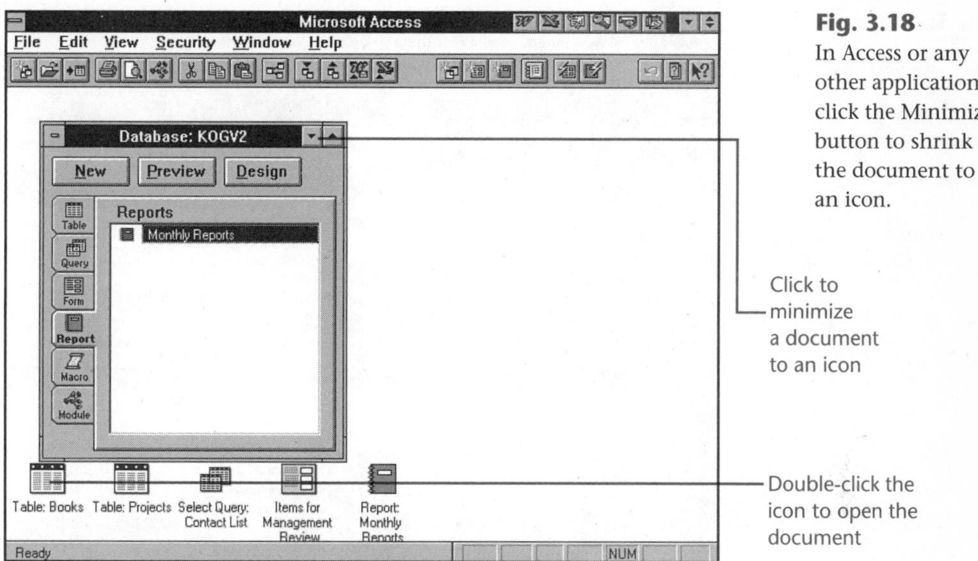

Fig. 3.18 In Access or any other application, click the Minimize button to shrink the document to an icon.

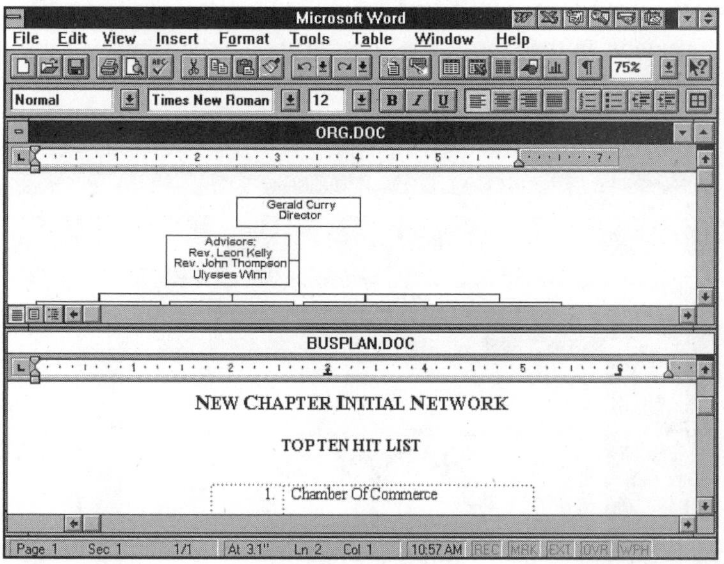

Fig. 3.19 In Word, choose **W**indow **A**rrange All to arrange the document windows horizontally.

■ In Excel, choose the **W**indow **A**rrange command. A dialog box appears, asking how you want to arrange the windows. The **T**iled option displays the windows in small rectangles (see fig. 3.20). H**o**rizontal displays the windows in rows across the screen (like Word). **V**ertical displays the windows in columns across the screen. **C**ascade stacks the windows, with the title bar of each window showing.

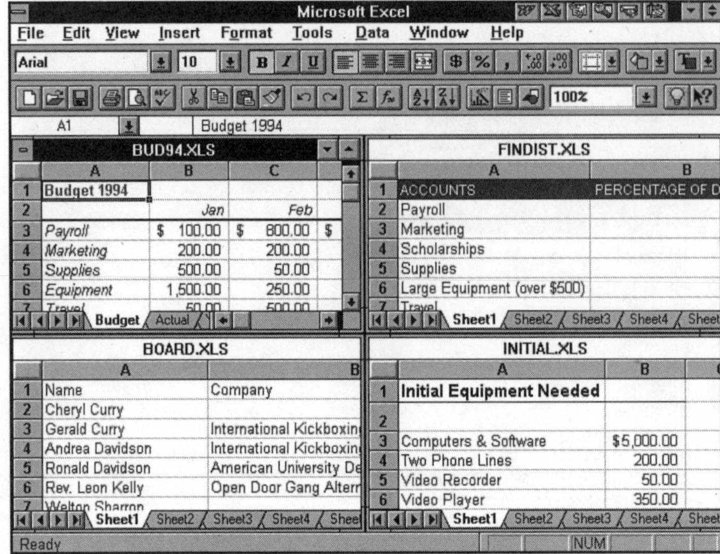

Fig. 3.20
In Excel, choose Window Arrange, and then select Tiled to display the document windows in equal-size squares.

- In PowerPoint, choose the **W**indow **A**rrange All command to show the documents in tiled form. You also can choose the **W**indow **C**ascade command to stack the windows, with the title bar of each window showing (see fig. 3.21).

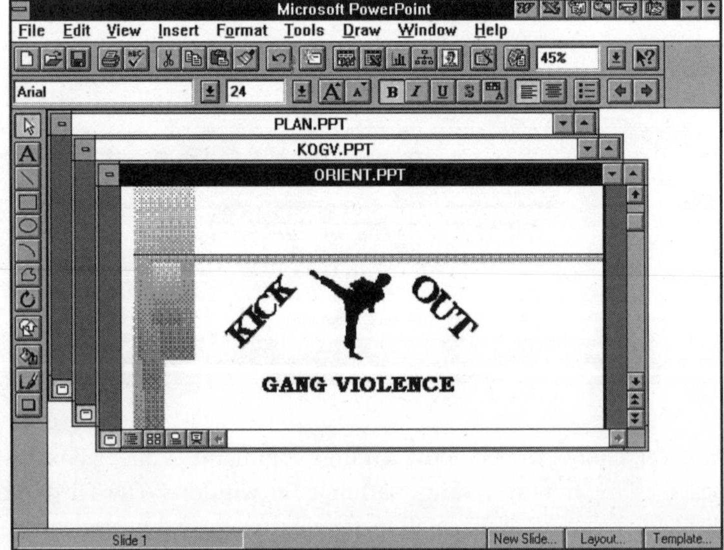

Fig. 3.21
In PowerPoint, choose Window Cascade to stack the document windows.

- In Access, choose the **W**indow **T**iled command to show the documents in tiled form, or choose the **W**indow **C**ascade command to stack the windows, with the title bar of each window showing. You also can minimize the documents to icons and then double-click an icon when you need a document (refer to fig. 3.18).

When several documents are visible, a dark title bar indicates which window is active. To make another window active, click that window. To show one of the windows full-screen, click the Maximize button or double-click the title bar. In Word, you can use the drag-and-drop feature to move between document windows.

Switching between Applications

In addition to switching between documents within an application, you can switch between applications. You can switch between open applications in the following ways:

- Click an application button in the Microsoft Office toolbar.
- Press Alt+Tab to scroll between the open applications.
- If part of the application window is visible, click it, or double-click the minimized icon.
- Press Ctrl+Esc to bring up the Task List. Double-click the application in the list, or highlight the application and then choose the **S**witch To button.

The Task List has added features that make it valuable for work with multiple applications (see fig. 3.22):

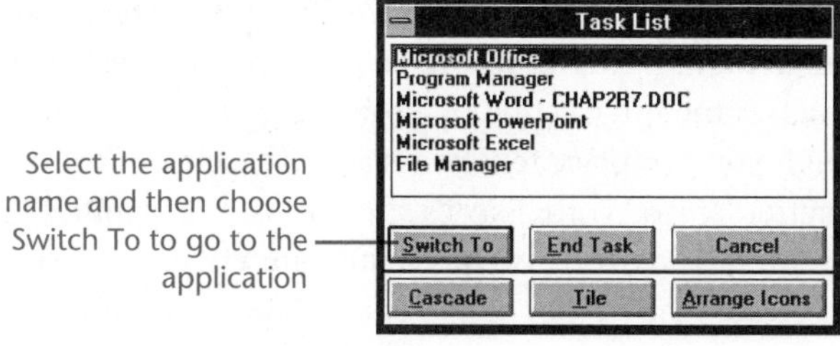

Fig. 3.22
Open the Task List with Ctrl+Esc and double-click an application name to switch to the application.

- Choose **E**nd Task to close a Windows application. (You must exit a DOS application through its normal exit procedure.)

- Choose **T**ile to display the applications in small rectangles.
- Choose **C**ascade to stack the applications, with the title bar of each window showing.

Tip
A fast way to exit Windows is to bring up the Task List, select Program Manager, and choose **E**nd Task. If you made changes in any documents, you are prompted to save the files.

When several applications are visible, a dark title bar indicates which window is active. To make another window active, click that window. To show one of the windows full-screen, click the Maximize button. You can use the drag-and-drop feature to go from Excel and PowerPoint to a Word document. You also can use drag-and-drop to go from Word and Excel to PowerPoint and from Word to Excel.

Looking at the Work Areas of the Different Applications

The Microsoft Office applications have many similarities—for example, all applications have at least one document window, a menu bar, toolbars, and status bars. Because the Microsoft Office applications are different, however, each application has a different focus and a different kind of work area.

Word Document

The work area of Word is the document (see fig. 3.23). The document window is like a blank sheet of paper on which you can type. When your typing reaches the margin, the text automatically wraps to the next line. The focus of Word is text. Although you can place numbers and data in Word documents, the strength of Word is its capability to format text documents, such as letters, memos, and reports. The length of your document is virtually unlimited.

Excel Worksheet

The work area of Excel is a grid of columns and rows (see fig. 3.24). The Excel document is called a *worksheet* and is similar to a table in Word or Access. The focus of Excel is a *cell*, which is the intersection of a row and column. All data must go into cells. Although you can place text boxes across a range of cells; long sections of text are better left to Word; Excel's strength is its capability to summarize and analyze numbers. Excel also has significant charting capabilities that enable you to create many types of pie, bar, column, and line charts.

An Excel worksheet has 256 columns (indicated by letters A to IV) and 16,384 numbered rows. Each cell is indicated by the column letter and the row number. E6, for example, is the cell in the fifth column and sixth row. An Excel worksheet can have several sheets. Each sheet has 255 columns and 16,384 rows.

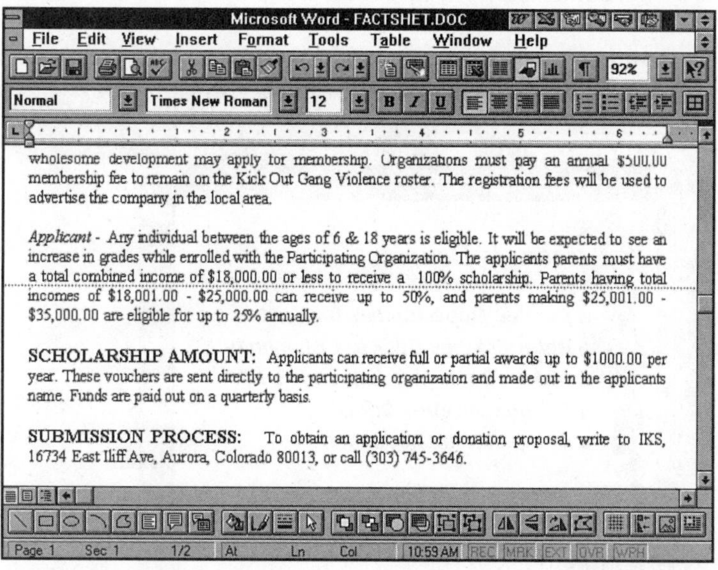

Fig. 3.23
Text automatically wraps in a Word document.

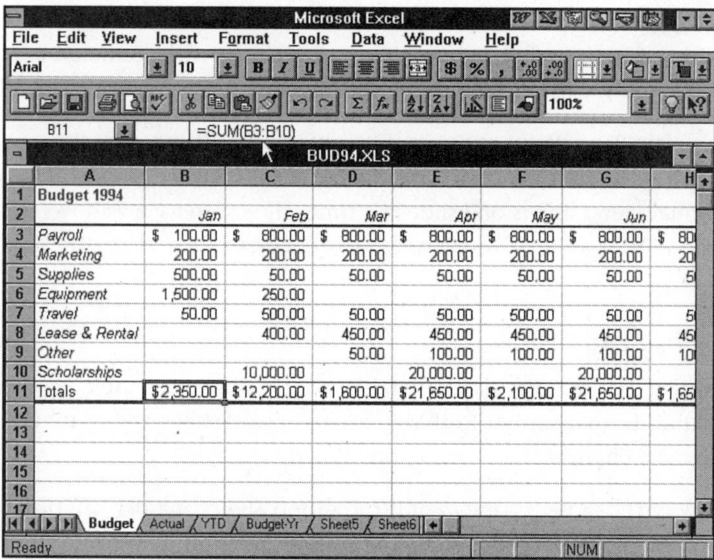

	A	B	C	D	E	F	G	H
1	Budget 1994							
2		Jan	Feb	Mar	Apr	May	Jun	
3	Payroll	$ 100.00	$ 800.00	$ 800.00	$ 800.00	$ 800.00	$ 800.00	$ 80
4	Marketing	200.00	200.00	200.00	200.00	200.00	200.00	20
5	Supplies	500.00	50.00	50.00	50.00	50.00	50.00	5
6	Equipment	1,500.00	250.00					
7	Travel	50.00	500.00	50.00	50.00	500.00	50.00	5
8	Lease & Rental		400.00	450.00	450.00	450.00	450.00	45
9	Other			50.00	100.00	100.00	100.00	10
10	Scholarships		10,000.00		20,000.00		20,000.00	
11	Totals	$2,350.00	$12,200.00	$1,600.00	$21,650.00	$2,100.00	$21,650.00	$1,65
12								
13								
14								
15								
16								
17								

Fig. 3.24
The focus of Excel is the cell.

PowerPoint Slide

The focus of PowerPoint is the slide (see fig. 3.25). PowerPoint is used primarily to make presentations. You can create slides for uses such as overhead transparencies, 35mm slides, or on-screen presentations.

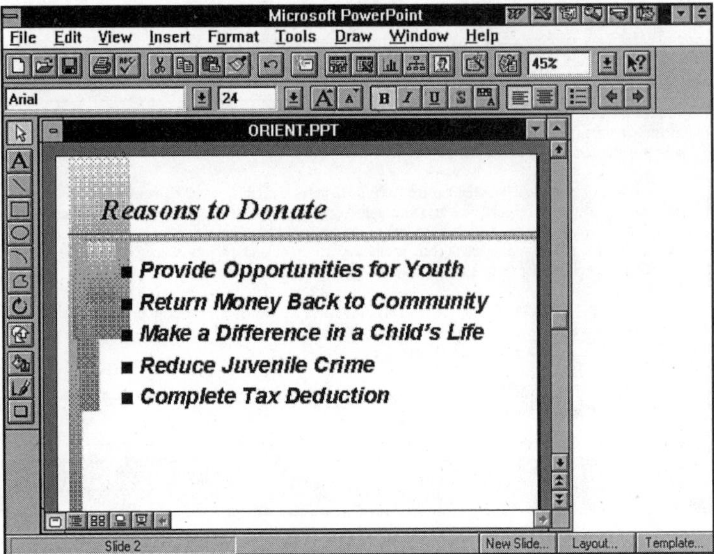

Fig. 3.25
The focus of PowerPoint is the slide.

Each slide has attached objects, which may include a title, bulleted items, other text, and graphics. To edit an object, you first have to select the object.

You can view PowerPoint slides in different ways. Outline view shows the titles of all slides in list format with their attached bulleted items. Slide view (the normal view) shows one slide at a time. Slide sorter view shows more than one slide at a time. Notes pages view enables you to type notes for each slide.

Access Table

The focus of Access is the database table (see fig. 3.26). The table is in a row-and-column format similar to that of an Excel worksheet; the number of rows and columns changes, however, depending on the table.

Each row in the table is a *record* of information about one person, place, or thing. Each column in the table is a *field* that shows an item of information about the record—for example, last name, phone number, quantity, or price. Because Access is a relational database, you can connect multiple tables through a related field.

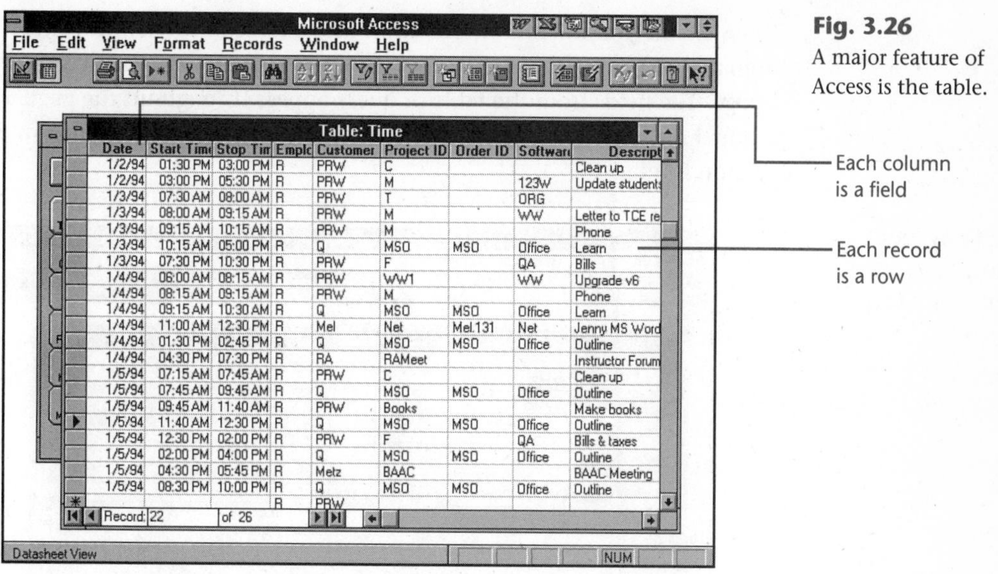

Date	Start Time	Stop Tim	Emplc	Customer	Project ID	Order ID	Softwarı	Descript
1/2/94	01:30 PM	03:00 PM	R	PRW	C			Clean up
1/2/94	03:00 PM	05:30 PM	R	PRW	M		123W	Update students
1/3/94	07:30 AM	08:00 AM	R	PRW	T		ORG	
1/3/94	08:00 AM	09:15 AM	R	PRW	M		WW	Letter to TCE re
1/3/94	09:15 AM	10:15 AM	R	PRW	M			Phone
1/3/94	10:15 AM	05:00 PM	R	Q	MSO	MSO	Office	Learn
1/3/94	07:30 PM	10:30 PM	R	PRW	F		QA	Bills
1/4/94	06:00 AM	08:15 AM	R	PRW	WW1		WW	Upgrade v6
1/4/94	08:15 AM	09:15 AM	R	PRW	M			Phone
1/4/94	09:15 AM	10:30 AM	R	Q	MSO	MSO	Office	Learn
1/4/94	11:00 AM	12:30 PM	R	Mel	Net	Mel.131	Net	Jenny MS Word
1/4/94	01:30 PM	02:45 PM	R	Q	MSO	MSO	Office	Outline
1/4/94	04:30 PM	07:30 PM	R	RA	RAMeet			Instructor Forum
1/5/94	07:15 AM	07:45 AM	R	PRW	C			Clean up
1/5/94	07:45 AM	09:45 AM	R	Q	MSO	MSO	Office	Outline
1/5/94	09:45 AM	11:40 AM	R	PRW	Books			Make books
1/5/94	11:40 AM	12:30 PM	R	Q	MSO	MSO	Office	Outline
1/5/94	12:30 PM	02:00 PM	R	PRW	F		QA	Bills & taxes
1/5/94	02:00 PM	04:00 PM	R	Q	MSO	MSO	Office	Outline
1/5/94	04:30 PM	05:45 PM	R	Metz	BAAC			BAAC Meeting
1/5/94	08:30 PM	10:00 PM	R	Q	MSO	MSO	Office	Outline
			R	PRW				

Fig. 3.26
A major feature of Access is the table.

As you do in Excel, you enter information in the intersection of a row and column or in a specific field within a record.

Queries enable you to see a portion of a table or related tables (see fig. 3.27). Queries are organized in rows and columns, and include the same information as a table (or summaries and calculations based on data in a table). You could use a query to link a customer table with an order table or to find the total sales for each salesperson.

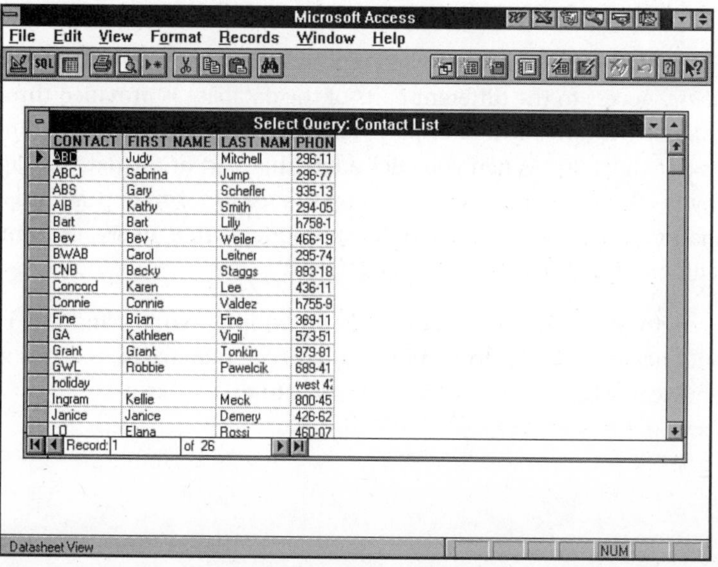

CONTACT	FIRST NAME	LAST NAM	PHON
ABC	Judy	Mitchell	296-11
ABCJ	Sabrina	Jump	296-77
ABS	Gary	Schefler	935-13
AIB	Kathy	Smith	294-05
Bart	Bart	Lilly	h758-1
Bev	Bev	Weiler	466-19
BWAB	Carol	Leitner	295-74
CNB	Becky	Staggs	893-18
Concord	Karen	Lee	436-11
Connie	Connie	Valdez	h755-9
Fine	Brian	Fine	369-11
GA	Kathleen	Vigil	573-51
Grant	Grant	Tonkin	979-81
GWL	Robbie	Pawelcik	689-41
holiday			west 4:
Ingram	Kellie	Meck	800-45
Janice	Janice	Demery	426-62
LO	Elana	Rossi	460-07

Fig. 3.27
An Access query can show only the fields and records you want to see, or it can link different database tables.

I

A New Way To Work

Forms enable you to enter information into a table or to view information from a table or query (see fig. 3.28). A form usually is organized one record to a page. The fields from the table or query appear throughout the page. Forms can include more than one table or query and can be organized in row-and-column format.

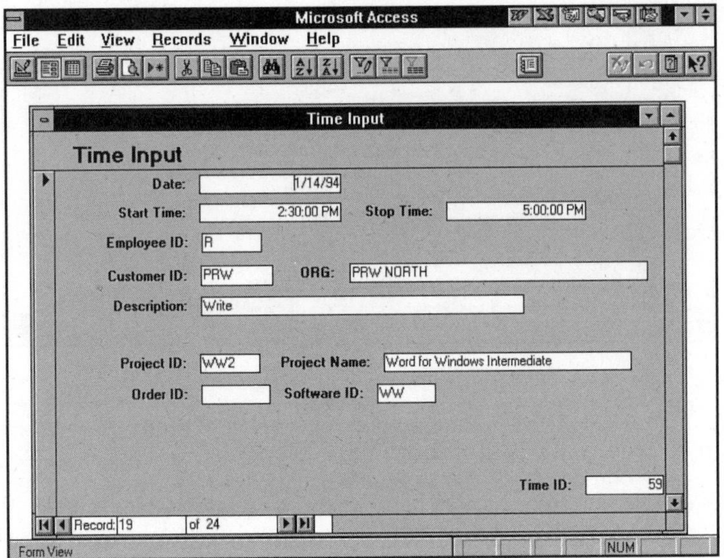

Fig. 3.28 An Access form makes data entry easy.

Reports are used to print a list or summary of information in tables and queries (see fig. 3.29). Reports usually are in table form, but can include subtotal and total lines. In some cases, reports can be output as labels.

All related tables, queries, forms, and reports are organized into one file called a *database*. Access to the different parts of the database is provided through the database window , which displays tabs for tables, queries, forms, and reports (see fig. 3.30). When you click a tab, that part of the database appears. When you click the Forms tab, for example, a list of forms appears. To edit information in the database, go to the appropriate table, query, or form and then edit or add information in a field.

The strength of Access is its capability to find, input, output, and link information. The amount of information that you can manage in Access is greater than in Excel, which has its own database feature.

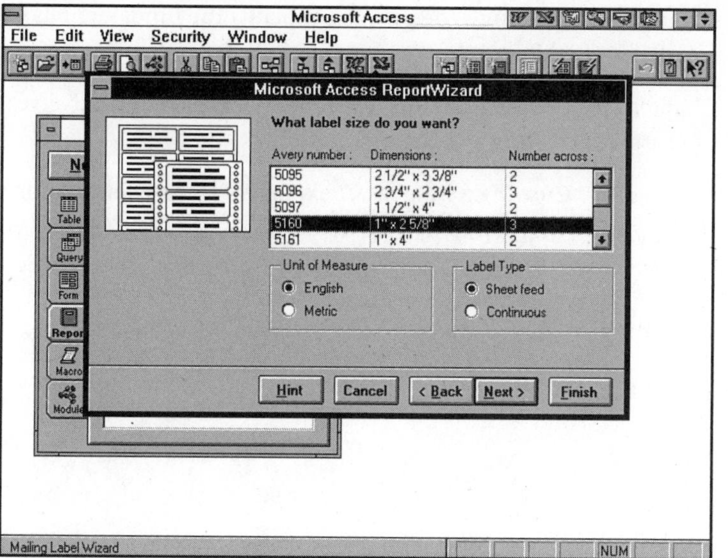

Fig. 3.29
You can design reports with the Report Wizard. Report types include mailing labels.

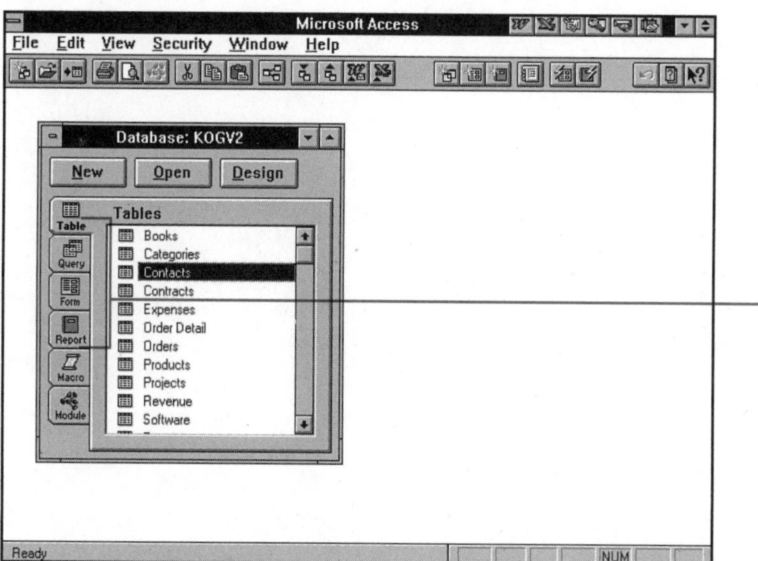

Fig. 3.30
The Database window is the "control panel" of the database, enabling you to go to any object.

Click the Table, Query, Form, or Report tab to display a list of database objects

From Here...

To continue your introduction to the Microsoft Office applications, you may want to review the following chapters:

- Chapter 4, "Creating and Editing Documents," covers the basics of creating a Word document.

- Chapter 12, "Creating Worksheets," explains the fundamentals of creating an Excel worksheet.
- Chapter 20, "Creating, Saving, and Opening Presentations," gives you the basics of creating a slide presentation.
- Chapter 27, "Creating a Database," explains database terminology and shows you how to start a new database.

Part II

Using Word

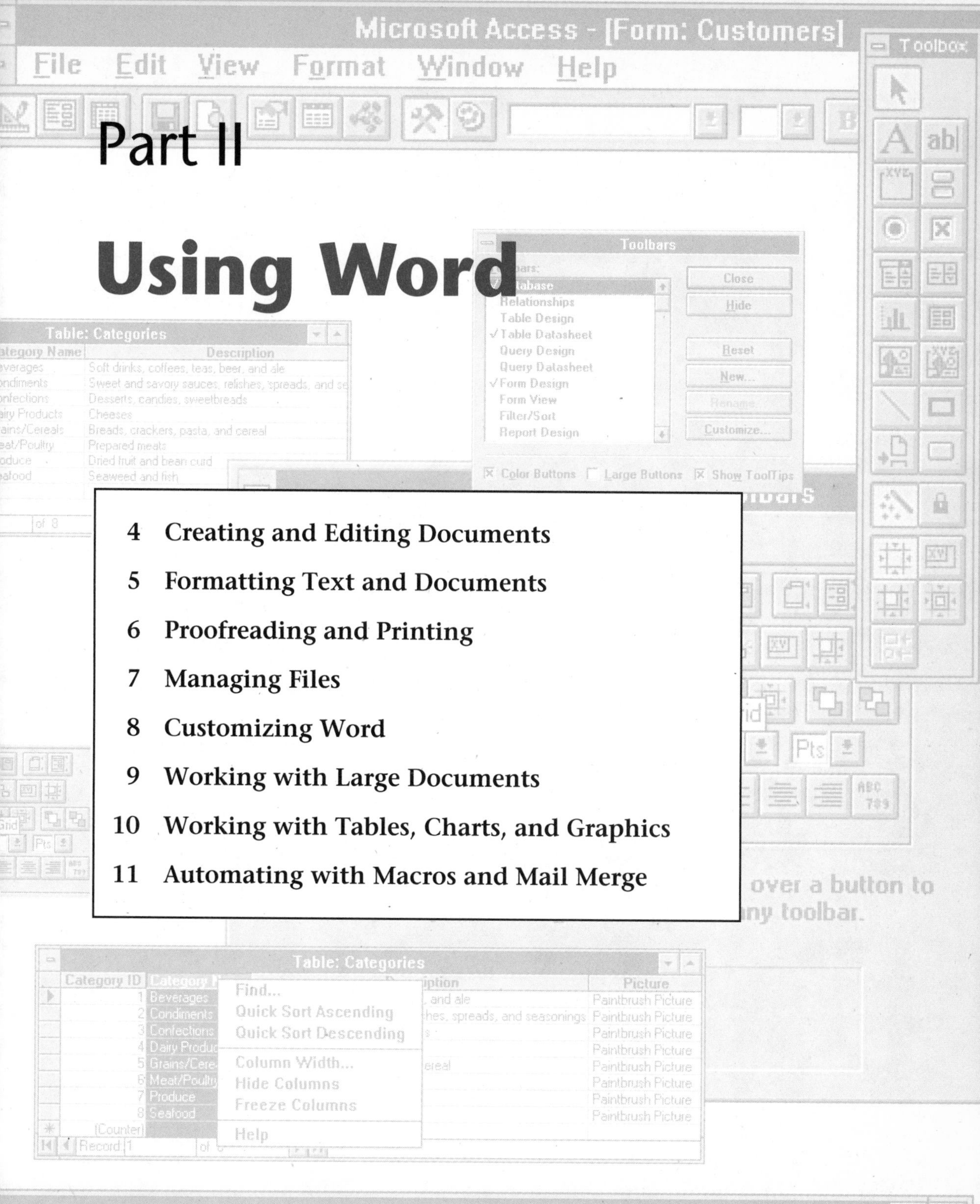

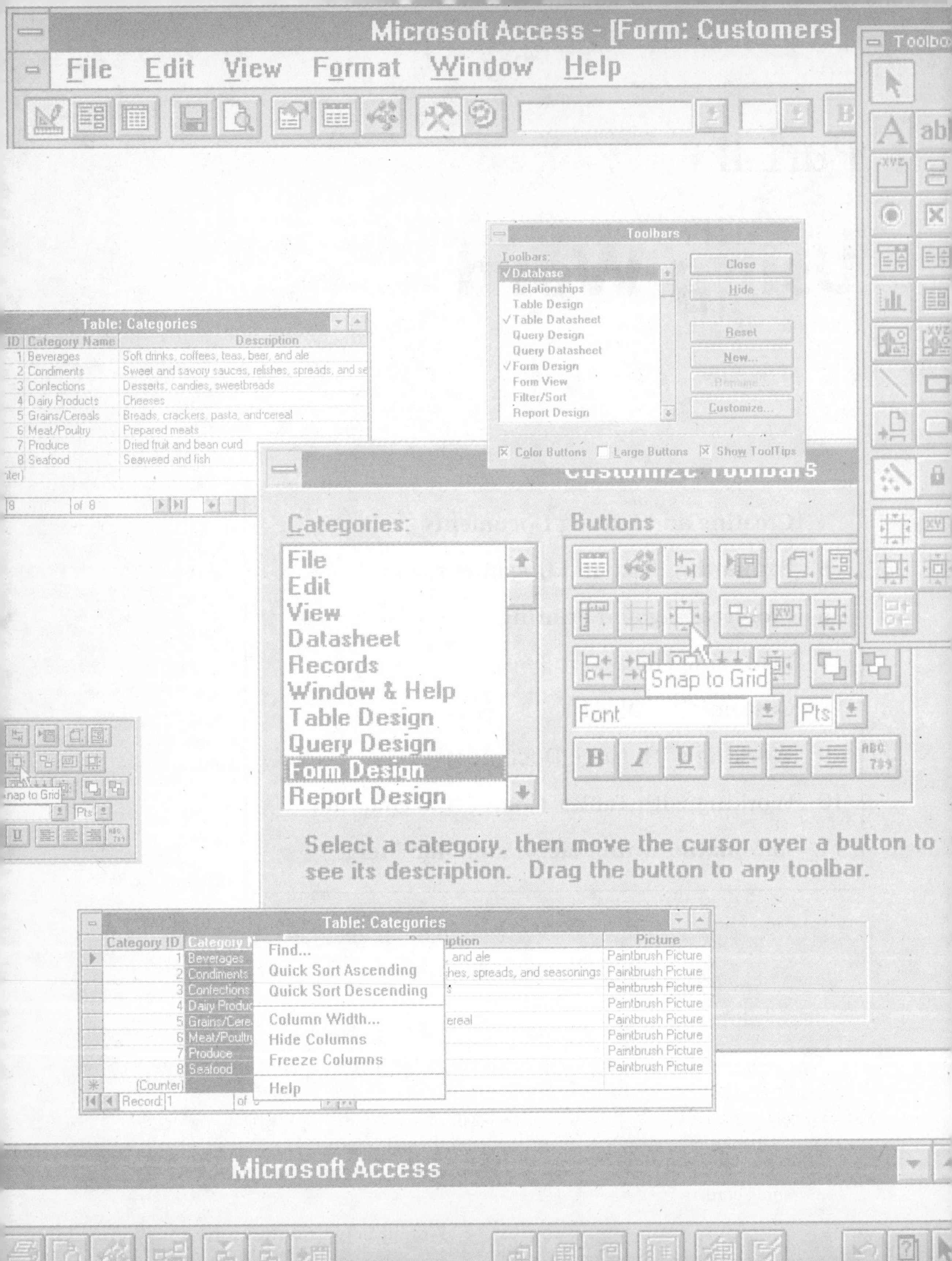
Microsoft Access - [Form: Customers]
File Edit View Format Window Help
Toolbox
Toolbars
Toolbars:
Database
Relationships
Table Design
Table Datasheet
Query Design
Query Datasheet
Form Design
Form View
Filter/Sort
Report Design
Close
Hide
Reset
New...
Rename...
Customize...
Color Buttons
Large Buttons
Show ToolTips
Table: Categories
ID
Category Name
Description
1 Beverages
Soft drinks, coffees, teas, beer, and ale
2 Condiments
Sweet and savory sauces, relishes, spreads, and se
3 Confections
Desserts, candies, sweetbreads
4 Dairy Products
Cheeses
5 Grains/Cereals
Breads, crackers, pasta, and cereal
6 Meat/Poultry
Prepared meats
7 Produce
Dried fruit and bean curd
8 Seafood
Seaweed and fish
Customize Toolbars
Categories:
File
Edit
View
Datasheet
Records
Window & Help
Table Design
Query Design
Form Design
Report Design
Buttons
Snap to Grid
Font
Pts
Select a category, then move the cursor over a button to see its description. Drag the button to any toolbar.
Table: Categories
Category ID
Category Name
Description
Picture
Find...
Quick Sort Ascending
Quick Sort Descending
Column Width...
Hide Columns
Freeze Columns
Help
Paintbrush Picture
(Counter)
Record: 1
Microsoft Access

Chapter 4

Creating and Editing Documents

by Susan Plumley

Of all the applications included with Microsoft Office, Word 6 may be the one you use most. You probably need a word processor to produce letters, envelopes, and so on in your everyday work. Using Word, you also can create memos, fax cover sheets, reports, newsletters, mailing labels, brochures, and many other business documents.

In this chapter, you learn to

- Identify the parts of the screen and the toolbar buttons
- Enter text
- Select text
- Edit text
- Reverse the last editing action
- Start a new document
- Save a document
- Close and open documents

Word offers many commands and features that help you complete your work quickly and easily. Word provides easy graphics handling, outlining, calculations of data in tables, the capability to create a mailing list, list sorting, and efficient file management. In addition, you can perform many desktop publishing tasks, such as formatting fonts, creating display type, aligning text, adding graphic borders, and adding shading.

Microsoft Office offers another advantage of using Word as your day-to-day word processor. When you use Word with Office and a Windows application, you have flexibility and control of data shared with Excel, PowerPoint, Access, Mail, and any other Windows application you may use.

Understanding Word Basics

◄ "Using Help," p. 61

Word is an excellent program offering many features that help you perform your word processing tasks efficiently. If you are familiar with Windows applications, you already know quite a bit about operating Word. You know, for example, how to use such features as the Control menu, the Window menu, and Help. Additionally, you understand the use of the mouse, scroll bars, dialog boxes, and other features of a Windows application. For more information about Word for Windows, refer to Que's book, *Using Word Version 6 for Windows,* Special Edition.

This section shows you how to use some features and screen elements that are particular to the Word program, including the toolbar, scroll bars, and status bar.

Using the Word Screen

◄ "Viewing Parts of the Window," p. 24

◄ "Using Menus," p. 35

When you start the program, Word displays specific screen elements as defaults, including the title bar, menu bar, two toolbars, a ruler, and scroll bars. You can, of course, hide these elements or show different components, at any time, by choosing a command from the View menu. Suppose that you want to hide the ruler. Choose the View **R**uler command to hide it; choose **V**iew **R**uler again to display the ruler.

Figure 4.1 illustrates the default Word screen and indicates the components of the screen.

The following list describes the screen elements. The toolbars are covered in more detail in the next chapter.

- *Title bar.* The title bar contains the name of the program and the document, the Control-menu box, and the Maximize, Minimize, and Restore buttons. Additionally, the title bar contains the Microsoft Office toolbar.

- *Menu bar.* The menu bar contains specialized menus containing related commands. Choose commands from the Format menu, for example, to change fonts, set tabs, add a border, and so on.

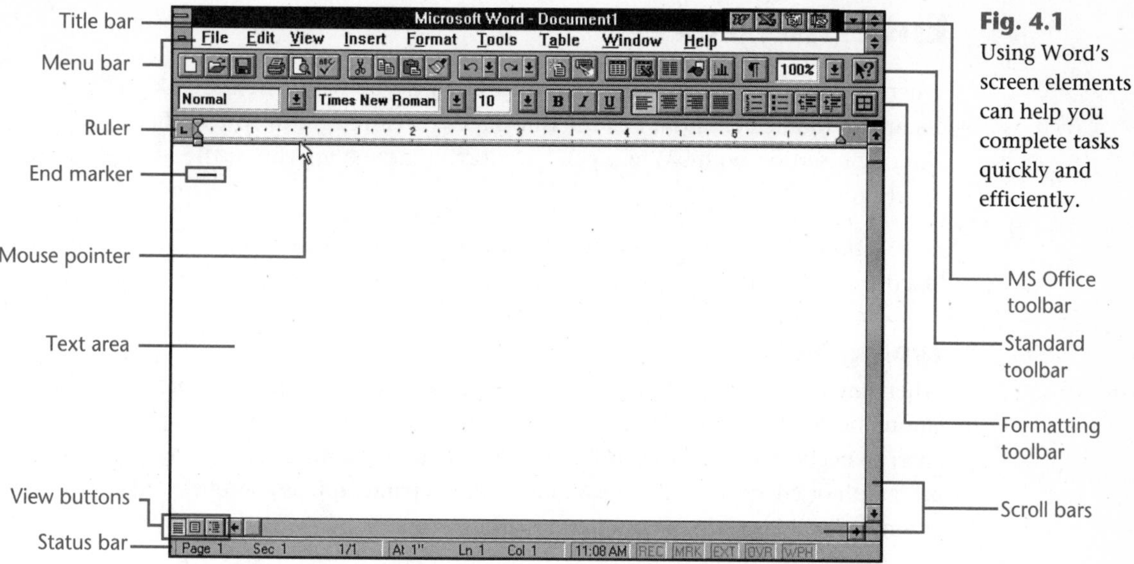

Fig. 4.1
Using Word's screen elements can help you complete tasks quickly and efficiently.

II

Using Word

- *Standard toolbar.* This toolbar contains buttons you click to perform common tasks, such as starting a new document, saving a document, checking spelling, and undoing an action. The buttons in the Standard toolbar provide shortcuts for menu commands.

- *Formatting toolbar.* The buttons in the Formatting toolbar provide shortcuts for choosing fonts, font sizes, styles, alignments, and so on. Use this toolbar to format text quickly as you work.

► "Formatting Paragraphs," p. 127

- *Ruler.* The ruler provides a quick and easy method of setting tabs and indents in your text. For more information about the ruler, see Chapter 5, "Formatting Text and Documents."

- *Text area.* The text area consists of a blank "page" in which you enter text or place pictures, graphics, and so on.

◄ "Viewing Parts of the Window," p. 24

- *Scroll bars.* Use the scroll bars to move quickly to another area of the document.

◄ "Moving Around the Document," p. 50

- *Status bar.* The status bar lists information and displays messages as you work in Word. When you position the mouse pointer on a toolbar button, for example, a description of that button's function appears in the status bar.

Entering Text

When you start the Word program, Word supplies you with a new, blank document (named `Document1` in the title bar). You can begin to type at the blinking insertion point. When you enter text, that text appears at the insertion point.

This section describes the basic techniques of entering text, moving around in a document, and selecting text for editing.

Typing Text

When entering text, you type as you would in any word processor. Word automatically wraps the text at the end of a line, so you do not have to press Enter to begin a new line. Press Enter only when you want to start a new paragraph or create a blank line. Word defines a paragraph as a letter, word, or sentence ending with a paragraph mark.

A paragraph mark is a nonprinting character inserted whenever you press Enter. You can view paragraph marks by clicking the Show/Hide ¶ button in the Standard toolbar. To hide the paragraph marks, click the Show/Hide ¶ button again. Figure 4.2 illustrates paragraph marks and the Show/Hide ¶ button in the Standard toolbar. In addition, the right margin in the figure is set at 4 1/2 inches so you can see the automatic word wrap.

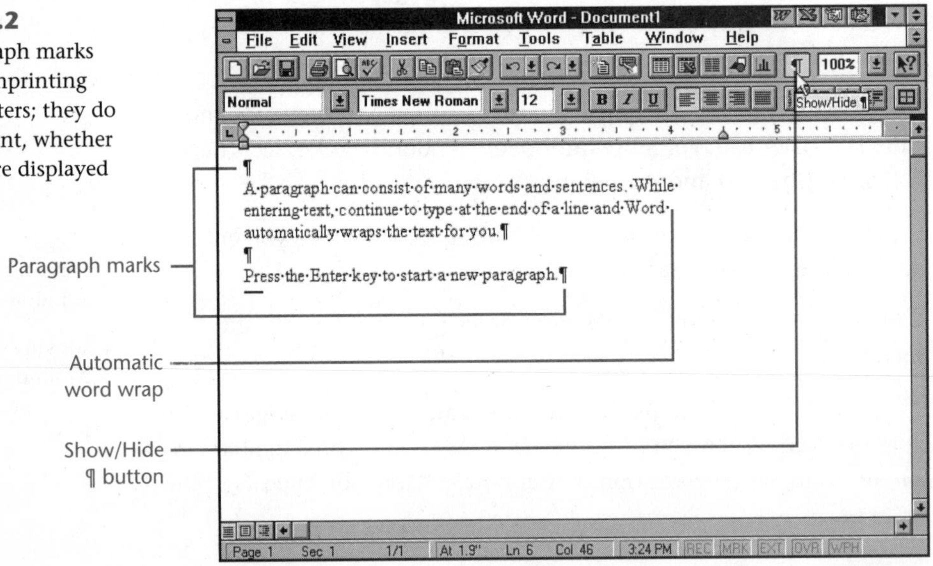

Fig. 4.2
Paragraph marks are nonprinting characters; they do not print, whether they are displayed or not.

Paragraph marks

Automatic word wrap

Show/Hide ¶ button

Following are some useful shortcuts and features you can use when entering text in Word:

- If you make a mistake while typing, press the Backspace key to erase a character to the left of the insertion point.
- Press the Del key to remove characters to the right of the insertion point.
- To repeat the text you just typed, choose **E**dit **R**epeat Typing or press Ctrl+Y.
- To erase the text you just typed, choose **E**dit **U**ndo Typing or press Ctrl+Z. You also can click the Undo button in the Standard toolbar.

- To start a new line without inserting a paragraph mark, press Shift+Enter. Word inserts a line-break character.
- Double-click the OVR indicator in the status bar to use overtype mode, in which the text you enter replaces existing text. Double-click the indicator again to turn off overtype mode.

II

Using Word

Positioning the Insertion Point

To move the insertion point, move the I-beam mouse pointer to the new location and click the left mouse button. You can position the insertion point anywhere in the text area except below the end marker, which is the short horizontal line displayed in the text area. You can move the end marker by inserting paragraph returns (pressing Enter) before the marker.

If you want to move the insertion point to a location that doesn't appear in the current window, you can use the horizontal or vertical scroll bar to move to the new location. When the new location is displayed in the window, place the I-beam pointer where you want to position the insertion point and click the left mouse button.

Tip
The insertion point always stays within the page margins. If you click outside the margin, Word places the insertion point in the nearest text.

Additionally, you can press some of the keys on the keyboard to move the insertion point quickly to a new location. Sometimes, using the keyboard to move around in a document is faster and easier than using the mouse. The following table lists common keys you can use to move around in your documents:

Key	Moves Insertion Point
Arrow keys	One character up, down, left, or right
PgUp/PgDn	One screen up or down

(continues)

Key	Moves Insertion Point
Ctrl+←/→	One word to the left or right
Home/End	Beginning or end of a line
Ctrl+Home/End	Beginning or end of the document
Ctrl+PgUp/PgDn	Top or bottom of screen

Selecting Text

After entering text, you may want to delete or move a word, sentence, or paragraph. In addition, you may want to format the text by changing the font or font size, indenting text, and so on. Before you can perform one of these actions on the text in your document, you must select the text. *Selecting*, or highlighting, the text shows Word where to perform the action.

You can select text by using the mouse, the keyboard, or a combination of methods, depending on how much text you want to select. The following list describes the methods of text selection:

- To select one word, position the I-beam pointer anywhere in a word and double-click. The word and the space following the word are selected.
- To select a sentence, hold down the Ctrl key while clicking anywhere in the sentence. Word selects all words in the sentence to the ending punctuation mark, plus the blank space following the punctuation mark.
- To select a paragraph, triple-click the paragraph.
- To select specific text, click and drag the I-beam pointer over one character, one word, or the entire screen.
- To select one line of text, place the mouse pointer in the selection bar and click. The *selection bar* is a vertical band to the left of the text area. When you point the mouse in the selection bar, the I-beam pointer changes to an arrow (see fig. 4.3).
- To select the entire document, hold down the Ctrl key while clicking the selection bar. Alternatively, press Ctrl+A to select the entire document.

- To select a vertical block of text—the first letters of words in a list, for example—hold down the Alt key and then click and drag the mouse pointer across the text. Figure 4.4 shows a vertical block of selected text.

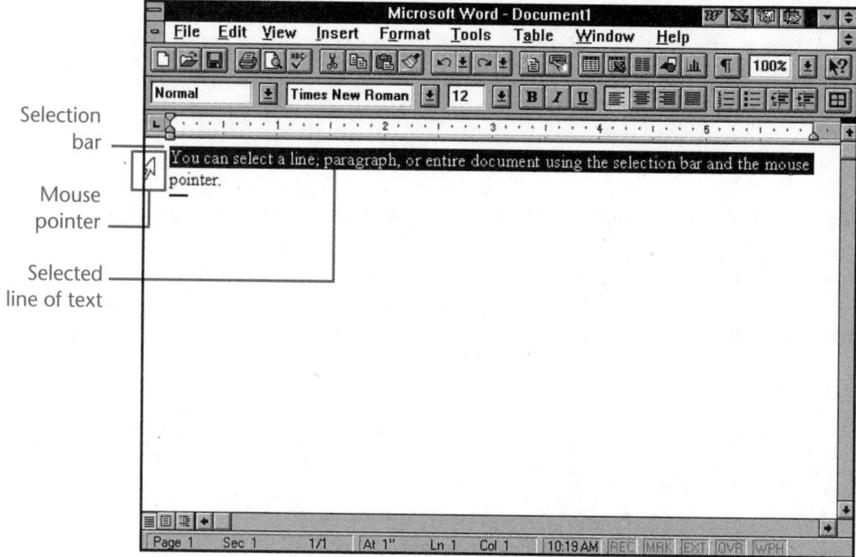

Fig. 4.3
Use the selection bar to select one line quickly; select more than one line by dragging the mouse pointer in the selection bar.

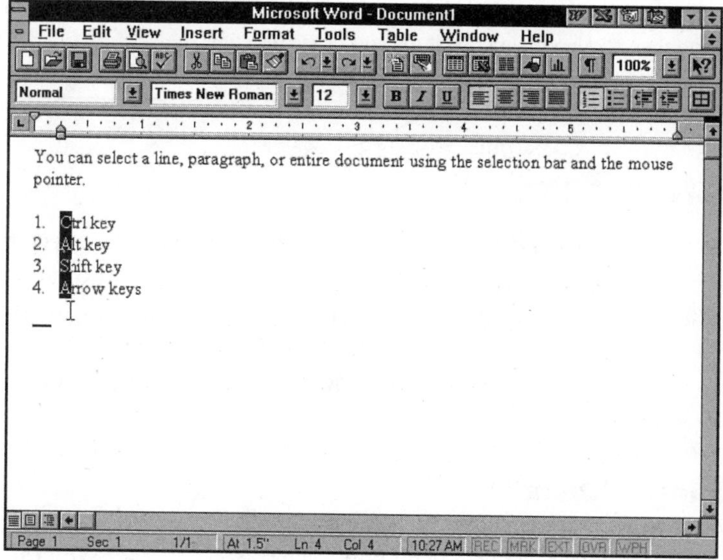

Fig. 4.4
Select one, two, or more characters vertically by holding down the Alt key while dragging the mouse pointer.

- To select text with the keyboard arrow keys, position the insertion point where you want to start selecting, press and hold down the Shift key, and then press the appropriate arrow key to move up, down, left, or right.
- To select to the end of a line of text with the keyboard, position the insertion point where you want to start selecting and then press Shift+End. Alternatively, select to the beginning of the line of text by pressing Shift+Home.

To deselect text, click the mouse anywhere in the document or text area, or press any of the arrow keys.

Troubleshooting

I began typing the text, but nothing changed on-screen.

You must click the mouse to position the insertion point before you begin typing the text. A blinking vertical line indicates the insertion point.

I tried to select text with the mouse, but I had trouble controlling the selection.

It takes practice to control the mouse when you select text. Try one of the alternative methods of selecting text that were described in this section. For example, try positioning the insertion point at the beginning of the selection, holding down the Shift key, and then clicking the mouse at the end of the selection.

Editing Text

◄ "Typing and Editing," p. 42

With Word, changes and corrections are easy to make. You can select any text in your document and delete it, copy it, or move it. You also can make other changes easily. How many times have you typed text, only to discover that the Caps Lock feature was on? Don't type the text again; use Word's Change Case command. This section shows you how to edit your document quickly and easily.

Undoing a Mistake

Many mistakes can be reversed by using the Undo command. Suppose that you type a sentence and decide you don't like the way it reads. You can delete it by choosing **E**dit **U**ndo, or by pressing either of the shortcut keys: Ctrl+Z or Alt+Backspace. If you make a correction and change your mind, you can use the Undo command to reverse the action.

Word also provides a Redo command (Edit menu) that you can use to reverse the last Undo. The keyboard shortcut for the Redo command is Ctrl+Y. Both the Undo and Redo commands describe the action you just performed: for example, Undo Typing, Redo Clear, and so on.

The Edit Undo or Redo command only works on the last task you performed. If, for instance, you delete a sentence and decide that you want it back, you must choose the Undo command before carrying out another task. However, Word supplies Undo and Redo buttons in the Standard toolbar that enable you to undo or redo other recent actions. Figure 4.5 shows the Undo drop-down list displaying six of the most recent actions.

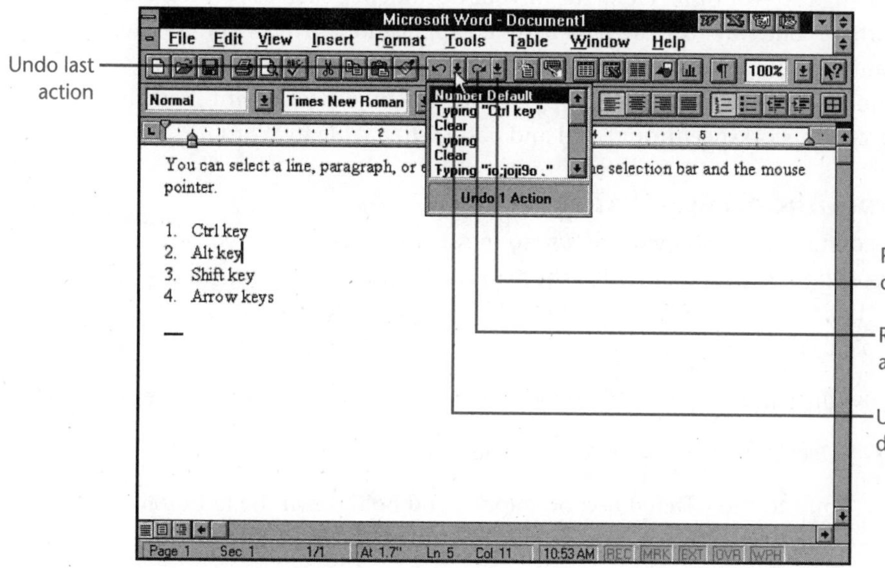

Fig. 4.5
Use the Undo and Redo drop-down lists to reverse any of the last several actions performed.

Deleting and Moving Text

To delete any amount of text, select the text and then press the Del key. When you press Del, the text is erased; the only way to recall the text is to choose the Undo command. Alternatively, you can delete text by selecting it and then choosing **E**dit Cle**a**r. The Edit Clear command deletes the text just as the Del key does.

Tip
If you make a mistake while typing text, or if you discover a misspelled word or misplaced punctuation, you can press Backspace or Del to delete the mistake.

You also can use the **E**dit Cu**t** command to remove the text. Edit Cut moves the selected text from the document to the Windows Clipboard. The text remains on the Clipboard until you use the Edit Cut command again.

II

Using Word

Tip
The shortcut key for Cut is Ctrl+X; the shortcut key for Paste is Ctrl+V. You can also use the Cut and Paste buttons in the Standard toolbar.

To move text that you cut to another location in the same document or to another document, position the insertion point where you want the text to appear, and then choose **E**dit **P**aste. The cut text reappears at the insertion point. You can paste this text again and again until you cut or copy new text.

Copying Text

To copy text, select the text and then choose the **E**dit **C**opy command or press the shortcut key Ctrl+C. Word copies the text to the Clipboard. You then can paste the copied text in a new location or document by positioning the insertion point and then choosing **E**dit **P**aste or pressing Ctrl+V.

Copying text—or other elements in your documents, such as pictures and charts—is one way to share data between applications. The Windows Clipboard is common to all the Microsoft Office applications. You can, for example, create text in Word, copy it, and paste it in PowerPoint. You also can copy a worksheet from Excel and paste it to a table in Word.

Drag-and-Drop Editing

An additional method you can use to move or copy text is called *drag-and-drop editing*. Word supplies this shortcut for moving or copying selected text a short distance—one screen at a time, for example. You also can use drag-and-drop editing to copy or move graphics.

Tip
To copy the text or graphic instead of moving it, hold down the Ctrl key as you point to the selected text or graphic and drag the dotted insertion point to a new location.

To use drag-and-drop editing to move text or graphics, follow these steps:

1. Select the text or graphics that you want to move.
2. Point to the selected text or graphic, and hold down the left mouse button. The drag-and-drop pointer appears (see fig. 4.6).
3. Drag the pointer and the dotted insertion point that appears to the new location, and then release the mouse button.

Note

The drag-and-drop editing option is activated by default. If you do not want to use drag-and-drop editing, you can turn the feature off by choosing the **T**ools **O**ptions command. In the Edit tab, select **D**rag-and-Drop Text Editing to turn the option off.

Converting Case

Word includes a handy command you can use to convert the case of text that you entered earlier. Suppose that you decide you do not want a heading to appear in all caps. You can use the Change Case command to make the change.

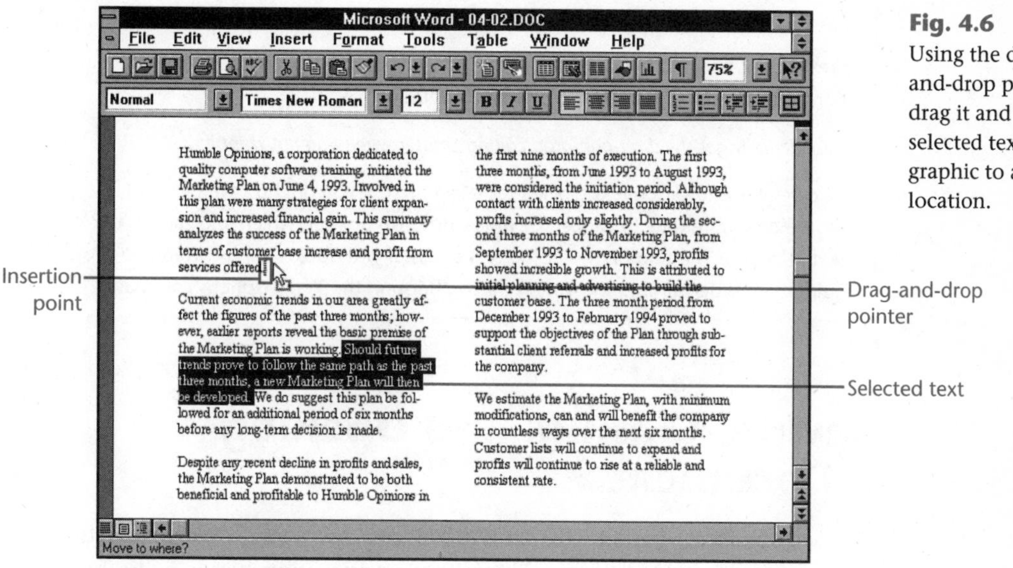

Fig. 4.6
Using the drag-and-drop pointer, drag it and the selected text or graphic to a new location.

To change the case of text, choose the F**o**rmat Change Cas**e** command. The Change Case dialog box appears. Select any of the following options:

- ***S****entence Case.* Capitalizes the first letter only in selected sentences.
- ***L****owercase.* Changes all selected text to lowercase.
- ***U****ppercase.* Converts all selected text to all caps.
- ***T****itle Case.* Changes each word of selected text to initial caps.
- *To**g**gle Case.* Changes uppercase to lowercase and lowercase to uppercase in all selected text.

Tip
You also can use the shortcut key to change case. Select the text, and then press Shift+F3. Each time you press the shortcut key, Word toggles the case from lowercase to uppercase to title case.

Troubleshooting

I accidentally deleted or cleared text that I did not mean to delete.

Click the Undo button in the Standard toolbar, and select Clear in the drop-down list to reverse that action.

(continues)

(continued)

I pasted selected text in the wrong place.

Press Ctrl+Z to undo the paste. Then position the insertion point in the correct location and choose the **E**dit **P**aste command again.

I accidentally get the drag-and-drop editing pointer when I do not want it.

Be careful not to click a text block after selecting it. If you do, however, click the mouse one more time to cancel the drag-and-drop pointer, which also cancels the text selection. Then simply select the text again. If you do not use the drag-and-drop pointer, consider turning the option off by choosing the **T**ools **O**ptions command.

Saving, Closing, and Opening a Document

◀ "Working with Files," p. 71

This section shows you how to save and close a document, open an existing document and start a new one. The following discussion is specific to the Word program; for information about basic file management, refer to Chapter 3, "Managing Files and Work Areas."

Saving a Document

Tip
Save your documents early in their creation, and then save often as you work on them. If a power failure occurs while you are working on your document and you have not saved it as a file, you will lose the document.

As in other Microsoft Office programs, you save a Word document by assigning it a name and a location in your drive and directory list. After naming the file, you can save changes made in that document without renaming the file by pressing a shortcut key or clicking a button in the Standard toolbar.

Naming a Document

The first time you save a document, choose the **F**ile Save **A**s command. Word displays the Save As dialog box, shown in figure 4.7.

When you save a document, Word places the file in the C:\WINWORD directory on your hard drive, unless you specified a different directory for Word when you installed Microsoft Office. In addition, Word's default file type is Word Document (DOC extension). Word also suggests a file name for the document; you can either accept the suggested name or rename the document to suit yourself by typing a new name in the File Name text box.

You can save a file to a hard drive, floppy drive, network drive, and so on; available drives are in the Drives list. Next, select a directory. Finally, in the

Save File as Type box, you can select a format other than Word in case you want to use the file in another application, such as WordPerfect, Ami Pro, or Word for Macintosh.

Tip
You also can customize settings for saving your documents. See Chapter 8, "Customizing Word," for more information.

To save a document, follow these steps:

1. Choose the **F**ile Save **A**s command. The Save As dialog box appears.
2. Select the drive, directory, and file type, if you do not want to save with Word's defaults.
3. Enter the name of the file in the File **N**ame text box, or accept Word's suggested file name.
4. Choose OK to save the document.

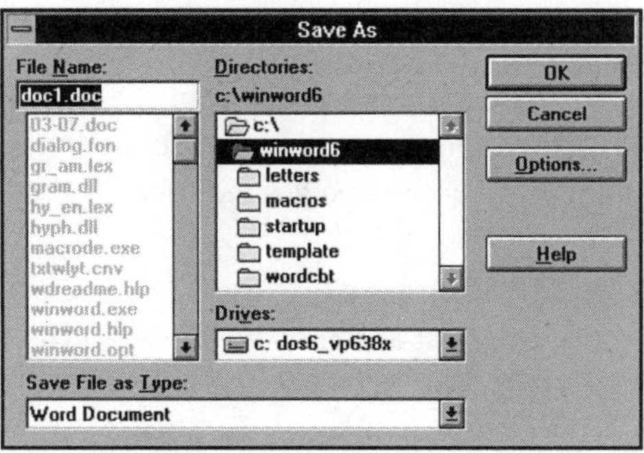

Fig. 4.7
Enter the name of the document in the File Name text box, or accept Word's default name.

Saving Changes to a Named Document

After you have saved your document by assigning it a name and location on the disk, you can continue to work on it. The changes you make are not saved, however, unless you tell Word to save them. You do not have to rename the document file to save changes; you can simply use the Save command.

After modifying or editing an already-named document, choose **F**ile **S**ave or press Ctrl+S. Word saves the changes in a few seconds, and you are ready to proceed.

Saving All

The File Save All command saves all open documents. Additionally, using this command saves any open templates, macros, and AutoText entries. When you use the Save All command, Word displays a message box, asking you to confirm that you want to save each open document. If you have not named a document, Word displays the Save As dialog box.

Opening a Document

To open a saved document in Word, choose the **F**ile **O**pen command or press Ctrl+O. Word displays the Open dialog box (see fig. 4.8).

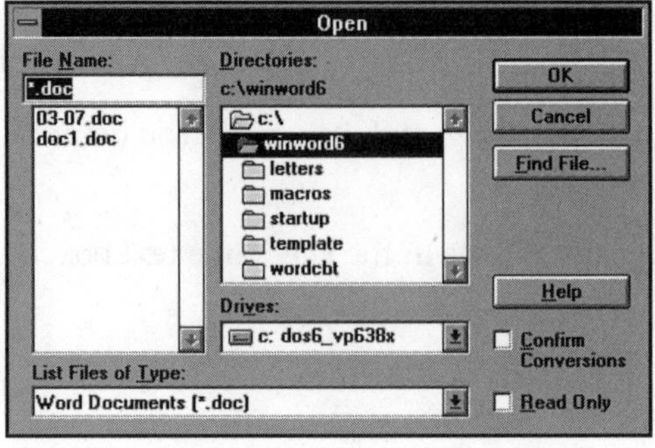

Fig. 4.8
Select the file from the list of files, and then choose OK to open the document.

Tip
If you click the New button on the Standard toolbar, the New dialog box does not appear. Instead, a new document based on the default Normal template appears.

In the Open dialog box, select the file name from the list of files, if you saved in Word's default directory. Otherwise, you can change the drive and directory, or even the file type, to access the desired file.

Starting a New Document

You can start a new document at any time by choosing the **F**ile **N**ew command or by pressing Ctrl+N. The New dialog box appears, as shown in figure 4.9.

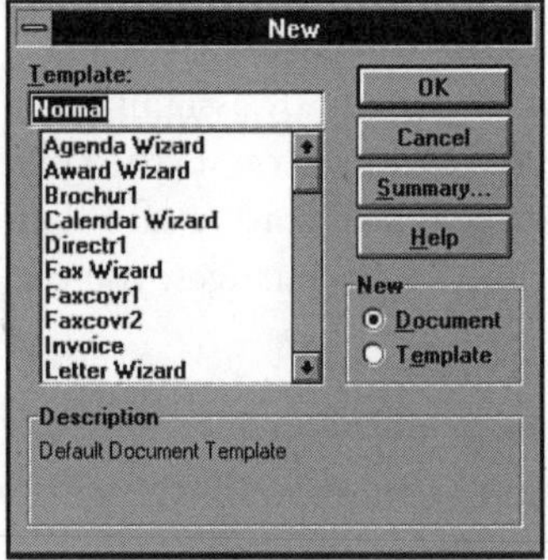

Fig. 4.9
In the New dialog box, select the template on which you want to base the new document.

The New dialog box lists several templates. A *template* is a basic document design, including page size and orientation, font sizes, fonts, tab settings, page margins, and columns. For more information about templates, see Chapter 9, "Working with Large Documents."

The Normal template is Word's default. The Normal template has the following characteristics:

- Uses an 8 1/2-by-11-inch portrait-oriented page.
- Includes 1-inch top and bottom margins and 1 1/4-inch left and right margins.
- Uses Times New Roman 10-point body text.
- Supplies three headings: Arial 14-point bold, Arial 12-point bold italic, and Times New Roman 12-point bold. All three headings are left-aligned and use single line spacing.

▶ "Formatting Text," p. 124

▶ "Formatting Paragraphs," p. 127

▶ "Formatting with Styles," p. 196

▶ "Using Template Wizards," p. 204

To accept the Normal template, choose OK. Word displays a new, blank document.

Troubleshooting

I wanted to save a file in a different file format, but that format is not listed in the file types.

You did not install that file converter when you installed Word. See Appendix A, "Installing Microsoft Office," for more information about installing the file converters.

I opened a document that was created in another file format, and now I want to save it.

Click the Save button in the toolbar or choose the **File Save** command. Word displays the Save Format dialog box, in which you can select the correct file format.

From Here...

In this chapter, you learned to create text in a document and then edit that text by copying, moving, deleting, and so on. Additionally, you learned to save the document in Word and then open that document for further editing. For more information about working in the Word application, see the following chapters:

- Chapter 5, "Formatting Text and Documents," covers how to change the views of your document; how to format such items as the font, type size, and style; how to adjust spacing between lines and paragraphs, indent text, and set tabs; and how to change margins and page orientation.

- Chapter 6, "Proofreading and Printing," covers using the Spelling Checker and Grammar Checker to proofread your documents, and provides information about previewing and printing documents.
- Chapter 9, "Working with Large Documents," covers formatting with styles and using template wizards.

Chapter 5

Formatting Text and Documents

by Susan Plumley

Many of Word's distinctive features and commands pertain to formatting documents. Formatting a document includes assigning fonts and font sizes, adjusting the spacing between lines and paragraphs, aligning text, dividing text into columns, and setting page margins. Many of these tasks are considered to be part of *desktop publishing*—designing and formatting a document so that it is attractive and professional-looking. Word provides many desktop publishing features and commands you can use to enhance your business documents.

In this chapter, you learn to

- View the document in the way that best fits the task
- Change font, font size, and format styles
- Adjust line and paragraph spacing
- Set tabs and indents
- Left-align, right-align, center, or justify text
- Create columns and set page margins
- Change page size and orientation

Word not only supplies methods for improving the look of your documents, but also makes formatting quick and easy. You can use menu commands and toolbar buttons to transform an ordinary business document into an eye-catching piece.

This chapter shows you how to format text, paragraphs, and pages, using the easiest and fastest methods.

Understanding Views

Word enables you to view your document in a variety of ways. Each view—normal, outline, page layout, and master document—offers advantages for text editing, formatting, organizing, and similar tasks. You may prefer one view, but you also will use the other views while formatting documents. This section covers the two most commonly used views: normal and page layout.

Tip
No matter what view or magnification you use, the insertion point remains where it was in the preceding view.

In addition, Word provides various magnification options for viewing a document. You can magnify the view to 200 percent, for example, or reduce it to fit the entire page (or even the entire document) on-screen. Finally, you can remove or display the various screen elements to produce a better view. This section describes the views and their advantages and disadvantages.

Viewing the Document

The two most common views are normal and page layout. Normal view is mainly for entering and editing text; page layout view is perfect for formatting the text and page.

► "Previewing a Document," p. 147

► "Outlining a Document," p. 190

Two other views—outline and master document—are more specialized views. Outline view is covered in detail in Chapter 9, "Working with Large Documents." Master document view is a method of viewing and organizing several files at one time; this view is not discussed in this book. Finally, print preview is discussed in detail in Chapter 6, "Proofreading and Printing."

Normal View

Normal view, which is the default view in Word, shows the basic document and text. Although you can view various fonts and font sizes, tabs, indents, alignments, and so on, you cannot view formatted columns, page margins, or the appearance of the formatted text on the page (see fig. 5.1).

Use normal view for entering and editing text or for formatting text. Figure 5.1 shows the Normal View button. You learn about the other view buttons in the following sections. You can use the view buttons in the horizontal scroll bar to switch between views quickly.

Page Layout View

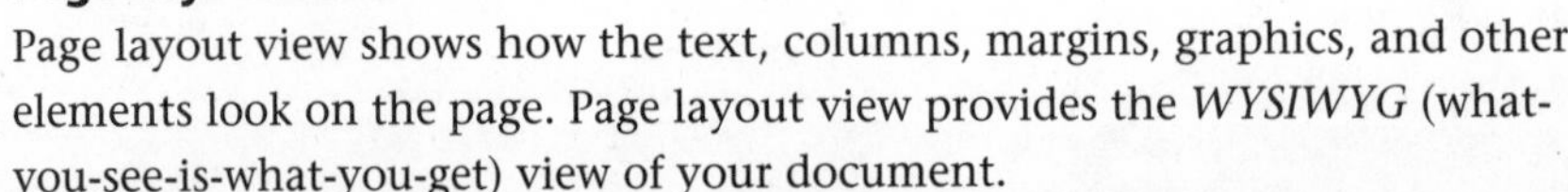

Page layout view shows how the text, columns, margins, graphics, and other elements look on the page. Page layout view provides the *WYSIWYG* (what-you-see-is-what-you-get) view of your document.

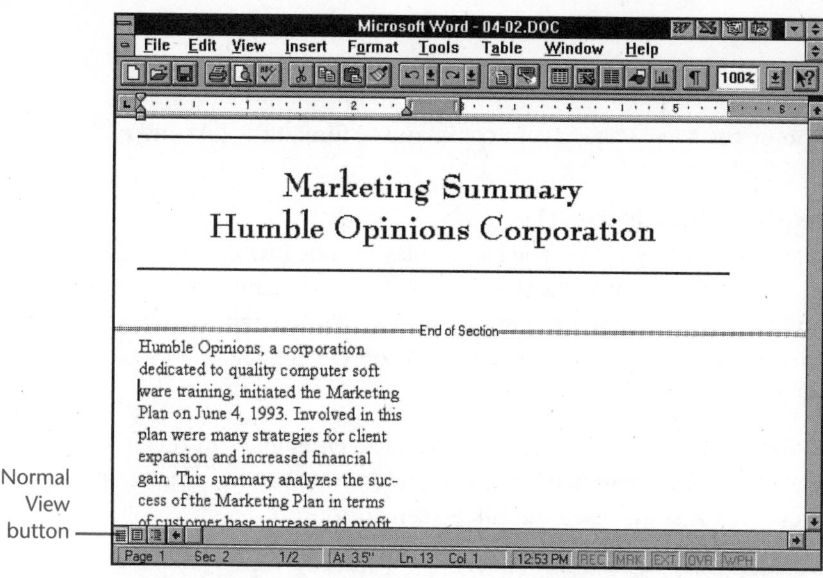

Fig. 5.1 The text in columns appears one column per page in normal view.

Editing and formatting may be slower in page layout, but you can get a better idea of how your document looks as you format and when you finish formatting. Figure 5.2 shows the same document as in figure 5.1, but in page layout view.

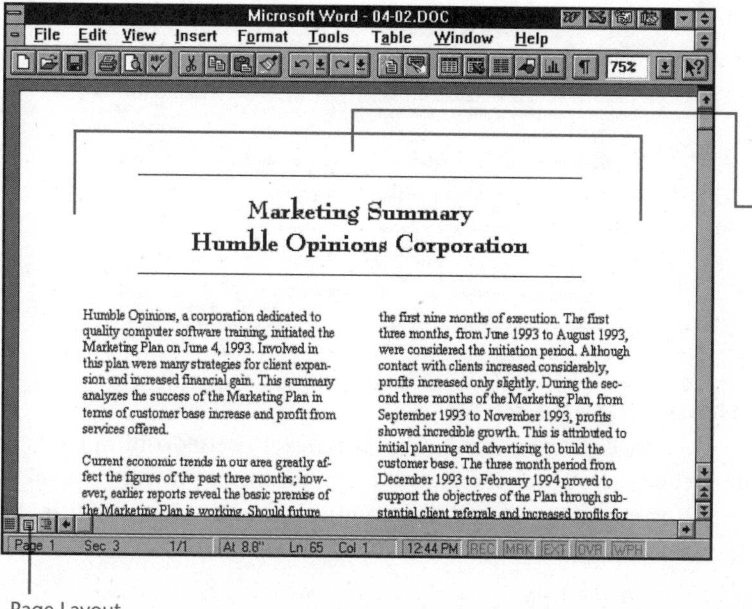

Fig. 5.2 You can view columns and page margins in page layout view.

To change views by using the **View** menu, follow these steps:

1. Choose the **V**iew **N**ormal command for text editing and entering.

2. Choose the **V**iew **P**age Layout command to format the text and page.

Hiding Screen Elements

▶ "Modifying Viewing Options," p. 175

In addition to changing views, you can display or hide the screen elements so you can see the document design better. Use the **V**iew menu to remove the rulers and toolbars. You also can choose the **V**iew F**u**ll Screen command to view a document with nothing but the Microsoft Office toolbar on-screen with the document.

Figure 5.3 illustrates the full screen view. You can enter and edit text in this view as well as move pictures and objects. To return to normal or page layout view, press the Esc key or click the Full Screen button.

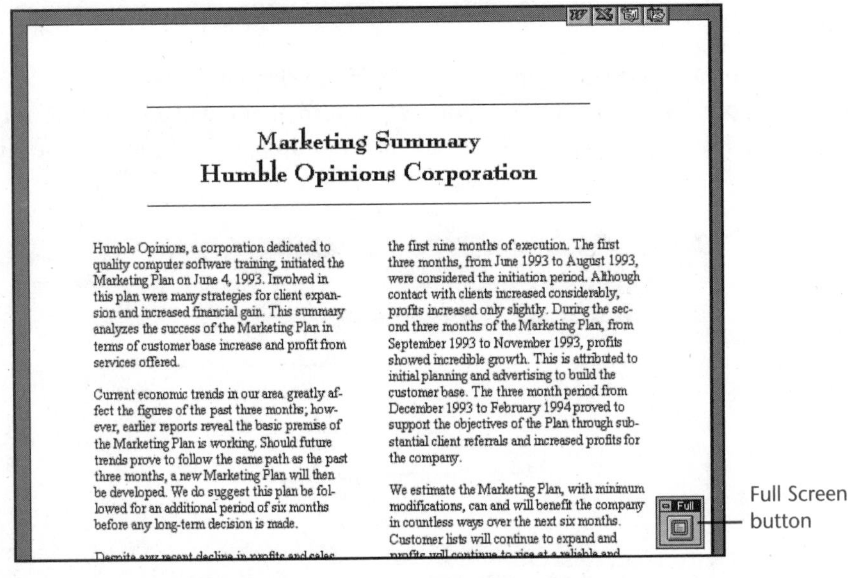

Marketing Summary
Humble Opinions Corporation

Humble Opinions, a corporation dedicated to quality computer software training, initiated the Marketing Plan on June 4, 1993. Involved in this plan were many strategies for client expansion and increased financial gain. This summary analyzes the success of the Marketing Plan in terms of customer base increase and profit from services offered.

Current economic trends in our area greatly affect the figures of the past three months; however, earlier reports reveal the basic premise of the Marketing Plan is working. Should future trends prove to follow the same path as the past three months, a new Marketing Plan will then be developed. We do suggest this plan be followed for an additional period of six months before any long-term decision is made.

the first nine months of execution. The first three months, from June 1993 to August 1993, were considered the initiation period. Although contact with clients increased considerably, profits increased only slightly. During the second three months of the Marketing Plan, from September 1993 to November 1993, profits showed incredible growth. This is attributed to initial planning and advertising to build the customer base. The three month period from December 1993 to February 1994 proved to support the objectives of the Plan through substantial client referrals and increased profits for the company.

We estimate the Marketing Plan, with minimum modifications, can and will benefit the company in countless ways over the next six months. Customer lists will continue to expand and

Fig. 5.3
Full screen view enables you to see your document with no screen elements or obstructions.

Tip
To set your own magnification, click the down arrow next to the Zoom Control box, and then select a percentage, or enter any number between 10 and 200.

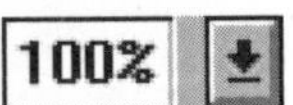

Magnifying the View

You can change the magnification of the view to better control how much of your document you see on-screen at any time. Word provides two methods of changing views: the **V**iew **Z**oom command and the Zoom Control button in the Standard toolbar.

Figure 5.4 illustrates the whole page view. The document also is in page layout view.

To change magnifications by using the Zoom dialog box, follow these steps:

1. Choose the **V**iew **Z**oom command. The Zoom dialog box appears.

2. In the Zoom To area, select the magnification you want or enter a percentage in the P**e**rcent box.

3. Choose OK to close the dialog box.

Tip

The Zoom dialog box enables you to view more than two pages at a time in page layout view.

Troubleshooting

My document is in landscape view, but I cannot see enough of it to edit the text.

Use the Zoom Control button in the Standard toolbar to change the view to Page Width or Whole Page.

I formatted two columns, but I see only one column on the page.

You are in normal view. Choose the **V**iew **P**age Layout command.

My page is formatted with many fonts, font sizes, and graphics, and screen redraw is slow.

Choose the **V**iew **N**ormal command to view the less-formatted version of the document and speed screen redraw.

Tip

The Zoom dialog box also offers the Many Pages option, in page layout view only, in which you click the monitor button and select the number of pages you want to view at one time (1 to 6).

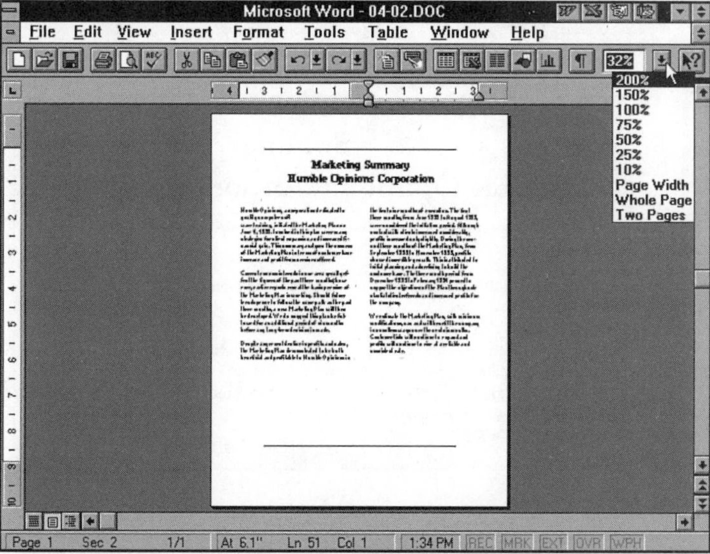

Fig. 5.4
You can format the text and document at any view magnification.

Formatting Text

Tip
To display the Formatting toolbar, choose **V**iew **T**oolbars, select Formatting, and then choose OK.

Word provides many options for formatting text; you can select a variety of fonts, sizes, and styles to enhance your documents. In addition, Word provides a Formatting toolbar that makes text formatting easy. Alternatively, you can use the Font dialog box, which is described later in this section.

You can format text by first selecting the text and then making the formatting changes. Alternatively, you can position the insertion point, make the formatting changes, and then enter the text. All text entered from that point on will be formatted according to your specifications until you change the formatting again.

Tip
When you are formatting documents, you may find it easier to see the results of your changes if you view the document in page layout view.

Changing Font

Font is the typeface of the text. A typeface can, for example, be Times New Roman or Helvetica. The font you choose helps create an impression or set the mood for the document. Suppose that you want to create an informal flyer for a sale. You can use a light italic font, such as Brush, Cooper, or Univers italic. A formal, sophisticated font could be Shelley, Old English, or Caslon Openface.

Select the font you want to use from the Formatting toolbar's Font drop-down list, shown in figure 5.5.

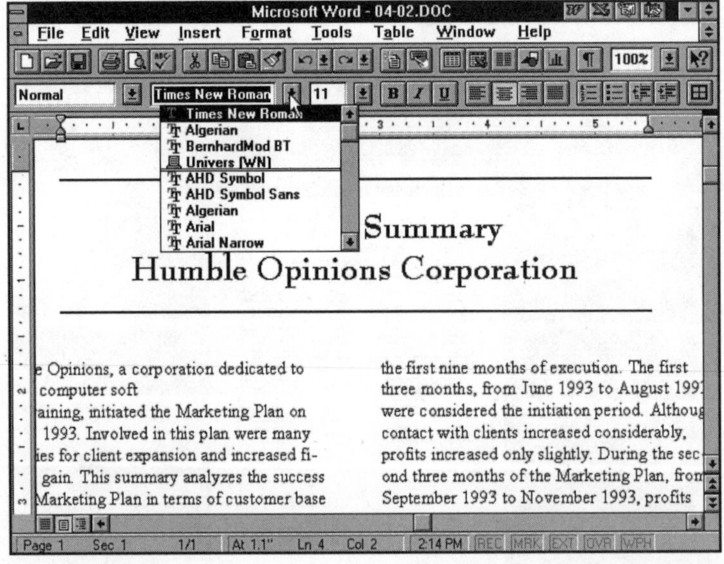

Fig. 5.5
Word lists the most recently used fonts at the top of the list so you can find them quickly. The rest of the available fonts are listed in alphabetical order.

Changing Font Size

Font size is measured in *points*. Points and *picas* are typesetter's measurements used for measuring spacing, line thickness, and so on. There are 12 points to a pica and 6 picas to an inch; therefore, there are 72 points to an inch.

All text you enter in a new, Normal template document is 10-point Times New Roman by default. You can, of course, change the type size. Use the drop-down Font Size list in the Formatting toolbar to select the size you want.

► "Using Template Wizards," p. 204

The font sizes available in the Font Size drop-down list depend on your printer. If you know that your printer can print a size that is not listed in the box—126 point, for example—type the number in the Font Size text box and then press Enter.

Choosing Font Styles

Type *styles*, also called type *attributes* and *character formats*, are characteristics applied to text. The Formatting toolbar supplies buttons for three type styles: Bold, Italic, and Underline. To apply any of these attributes, simply click the B, I, or U button. You can apply one, two, or all three attributes at the same time.

Besides these three type styles, Word supplies several effects—including strikethrough, superscript, subscript, and all caps—in the Font dialog box.

Using the Font Dialog Box

You can use the F**o**rmat **F**ont command to display the Font dialog box. Use this dialog box to format the text all at once; for example, you can use the dialog-box options to change the font, size, and style of the selected text. Figure 5.6 shows the Font tab of the Font dialog box.

► "Formatting with Styles," p. 196

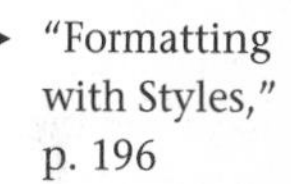

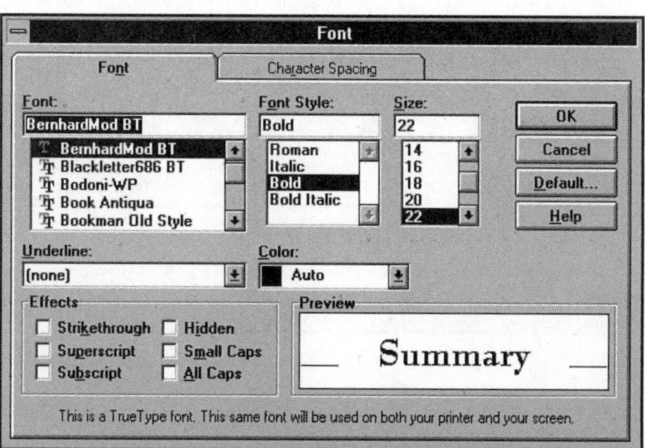

Fig. 5.6
Use the Font dialog box to perform many changes at one time to the selected text.

Tip
Another possibility for formatting text is to use Word's styles and your own to format the same style of text over and over. For more information about styles, see Chapter 9.

Using the Font tab of the Font dialog box, you can select a font and style, and see the results in the Preview box. You also can choose among more styles than in the Formatting toolbar, including single, double, or dotted underlines and colors. After you select the options you want, choose OK to close the dialog box.

Copying Formats

Word makes formatting text easy with the Format Painter feature, which enables you to format an entire document quickly and easily.

When you format text—such as a heading, complicated tabs, or indents—and need to format other text in the document the same way, you can save time and energy by copying the formatting of the original text. Suppose that you formatted a heading as 18-point Univers, bold and italic, center-aligned, and with 5 points spacing below the head. Rather than select and format each head in your document separately, you can use the Format Painter to copy the format to another head.

First, select the formatted text—the text with the format you want to copy—and then click the Format Painter button in the Standard toolbar. The pointer changes to a paintbrush and I-beam (see fig. 5.7). Select the text to be formatted, and that text automatically changes to the copied text format.

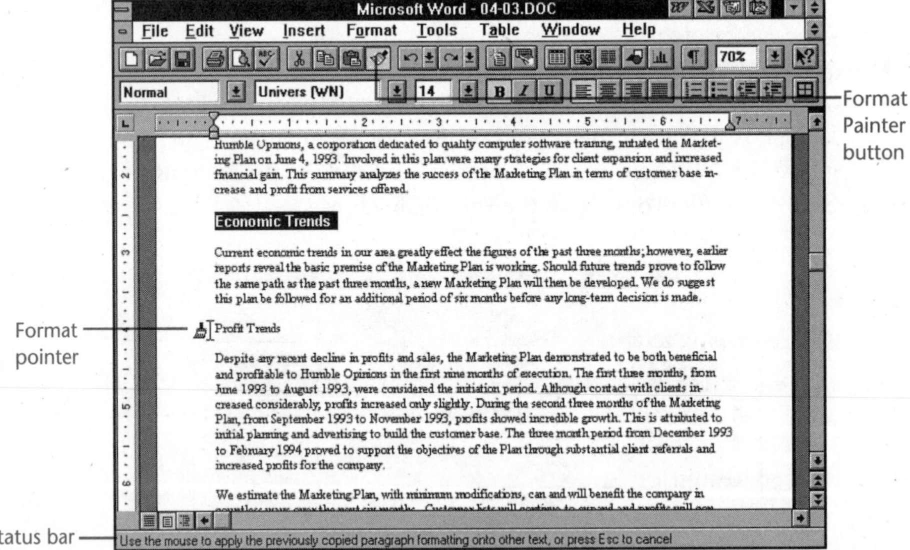

Fig. 5.7
The status bar explains the next step in copying the format of the selected text.

Troubleshooting

I have changed the font, font size, font style, and alignment of the selected text, and now I want to change the text back to its original formatting.

Undo the formatting, using the Undo drop-down list in the Standard toolbar.

I just formatted some text with the Format Font command, and I want to use the same formatting for text on the next page of my document.

Select the text, and then choose **E**dit **R**epeat or press Ctrl+Y. Word repeats the last formatting command you used.

Formatting Paragraphs

A large part of formatting a page of text occurs when you format the paragraphs of body text, headings, lists, and so on. When producing an attractive, professional-looking document, you want to present a unified arrangement of the text elements. You can accomplish this by specifying line, word, and paragraph spacing; aligning the text; setting tabs and indents; and specifying how the text flows on the page.

Note

Word's definition of a paragraph is any amount of text—one character or 10 sentences—ending with a paragraph mark.

Word enables you to select a paragraph of text and change its arrangement by choosing commands or clicking buttons in the Formatting toolbar. This section shows you how to format paragraphs of text.

Tip

You can enter text, select it, and then format it, or you can specify the formatting before you enter the text.

Adjusting Spacing

You can use spacing to change the design and readability of your text. For the most part, Word's default spacing will work quite well for most of your documents, but you may want to apply specific spacing sometimes. This section shows you how to change line and paragraph spacing, and gives you a few tips on when to adjust spacing.

Line Spacing

Line spacing, also called *leading* (pronounced LED-ing), is the space that separates a line of text from the text above and below it. Without line spacing, uppercase letters, ascenders (the top strokes of *t, b, d,* and so on), and descenders (the bottom strokes of *g, j, y,* and so on) in one line would touch those in the next line.

Word's default line spacing is single. Word measures spacing in points or in lines. 10-point text uses approximately 12-point spacing, or one line (single). 12-point text uses 14-point spacing, which still is one line. The "line" spacing depends on the size of the type. The larger the type size, the greater the line spacing: 24-point text, for example, would use about 27-point line spacing. Typesetting guidelines generally call for leading to be about 120 percent of the point size of the text.

Tip
Never use different line spacings in one document, as in figure 5.8. Different spacings confuse the reader and make the text hard to read.

Word enables you to change the line spacing in your text. You can set spacing to single, double, or one and a half lines, or you can set a specific measurement in points. Figure 5.8 shows three paragraphs of text with different line spacings. The top paragraph is Word's default: single spacing, or 12-point text on 14-point spacing. The second paragraph is 12 on 16, and the third paragraph is 12 on 20.

To set line spacing, follow these steps:

1. Choose the F**o**rmat **P**aragraph command. The Paragraph dialog box appears, as shown in figure 5.9.

2. Select the **I**ndents and Spacing tab.

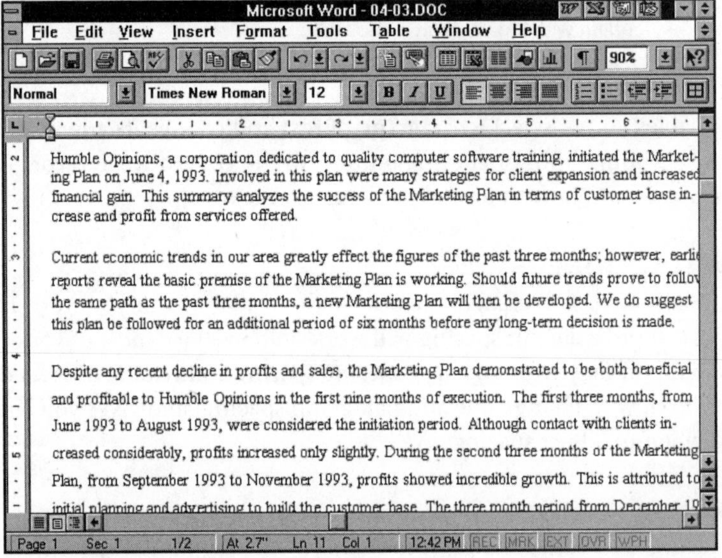

Fig. 5.8
Line spacing affects readability and page design.

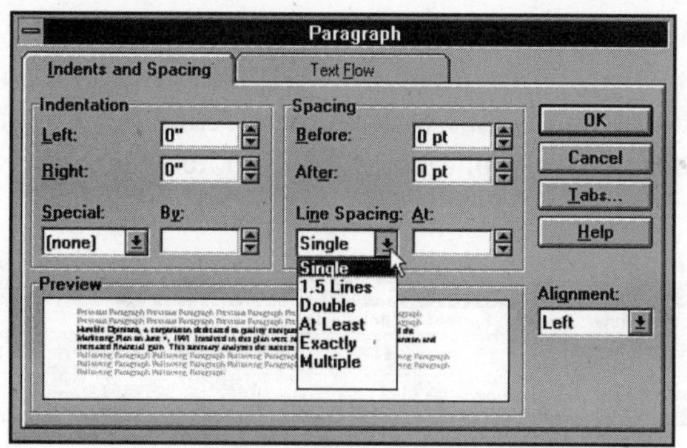

Fig. 5.9
The Paragraph dialog box, with the Indents and Spacing tab displayed. Use the Spacing area to control line spacing.

3. In the Li**n**e Spacing drop-down list, select the option you want; enter a value in the **A**t box, if necessary. These options are described in the table that follows these steps.

4. Choose OK to close the dialog box.

Option	Result
Single	Default line spacing (2 to 5 points larger than text size).
1.5 Lines	Spacing that is one and a half times the size of the text. For 12-point text, the spacing would be 18 points.
Double	Spacing that is twice the size of the text. For 12-point text, the spacing would be 24 points.
At Least	Accommodates larger font sizes within a line of text. In the **A**t box, enter an amount that Word can use as minimum spacing.
Exactly	Limits Word to a certain amount of spacing, which you enter in the **A**t box.
Multiple	Decreases or increases line spacing by the percentage you enter in the At box. To increase spacing by 20 percent, for example, enter 1.2; to decrease spacing by 20 percent, enter .8.

Paragraph Spacing

You can add extra space between paragraphs to improve readability in your documents and to add valuable white space. *White space*, or areas of a page that contain no text or graphics, provides rest for the reader's eyes and prevents the page from being too crowded. Readability often is improved when you add space between paragraphs.

Use extra paragraph spacing instead of a first-line indent when you use left-aligned body text, as shown in figure 5.10. The reader's eyes can find the beginning of a paragraph easily without the indent. You also can add more spacing after headings or subheadings, between items in a list, within tables, and in outlines.

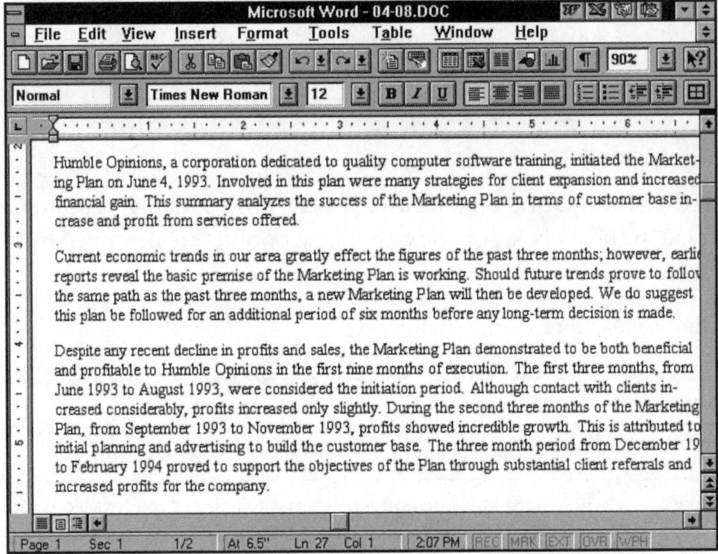

Fig. 5.10
Extra spacing makes the beginning of each paragraph easy to find and provides valuable white space.

To add extra paragraph spacing, follow these steps:

1. Choose the F**o**rmat **P**aragraph command. The Paragraph dialog box appears (refer to fig. 5.9).

2. Select the **I**ndents and Spacing tab.

3. In the Spacing area, enter a value in the **B**efore box, the Aft**e**r box, or in both boxes. You can enter the measurement in either lines (li) or points (pt).

4. Choose OK to close the dialog box.

Tip
If you want to use leaders with your tabs, first choose F**o**rmat **T**abs, and then select tab position, alignment, and leader options in the Tabs dialog box.

Setting Tabs

You can set tabs in a document by using either the Tabs dialog box or the ruler. This section describes using the ruler to set tabs because it is a quick and easy method for the task. The ruler also is handy for other kinds of paragraph formatting, such as indenting text and changing margins.

Note

Whether you use the ruler or the Tabs dialog box, you can select the text and then set the tabs, or set the tabs and then enter the text.

To use the ruler to set tabs in your text, first choose the tab alignment. The horizontal ruler contains a Tab alignment button, shown in figure 5.11. Click the Tab alignment button until the type of tab you want appears. Then click the place in the ruler where you want to set the tab.

You can reposition any tab in the ruler by clicking and dragging it to a new location. To remove a tab, drag it off the ruler.

Tip
When you position the insertion point in any paragraph of text, tab and indent settings for that paragraph appear in the ruler.

Indenting Text

You can use the ruler or the Paragraph dialog box to set indents for text. Using the ruler, you can indent the left side, the right side, or only the first line of a paragraph. Figure 5.12 shows indents for selected text.

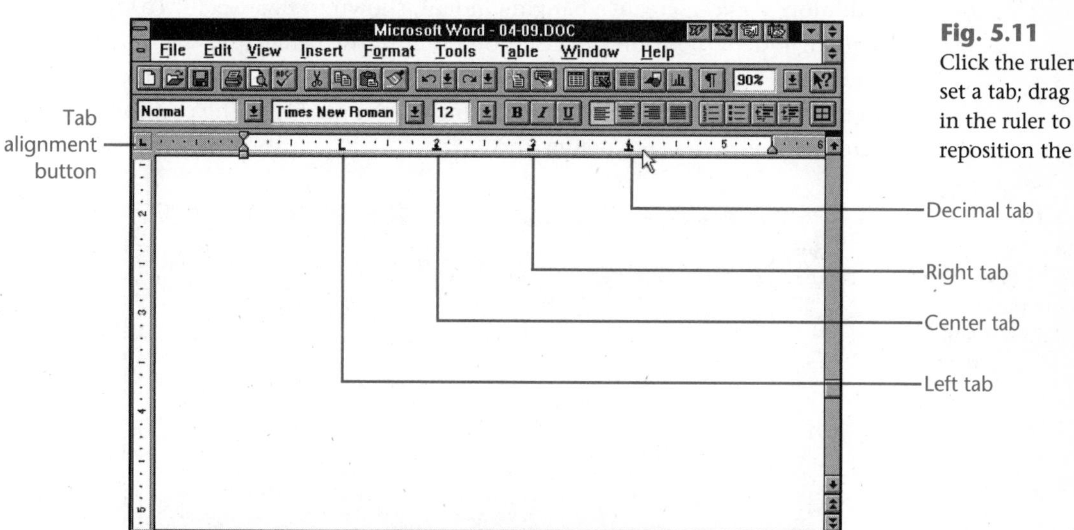

Fig. 5.11
Click the ruler to set a tab; drag a tab in the ruler to reposition the tab.

Word also supplies an Increase Indent and a Decrease Indent button in the Formatting toolbar. Each time you click one of these buttons, you increase an indent of the selected text to the next tab stop or decrease the indent to the preceding tab stop. (You can set the tab stops or use the default half-inch tabs.)

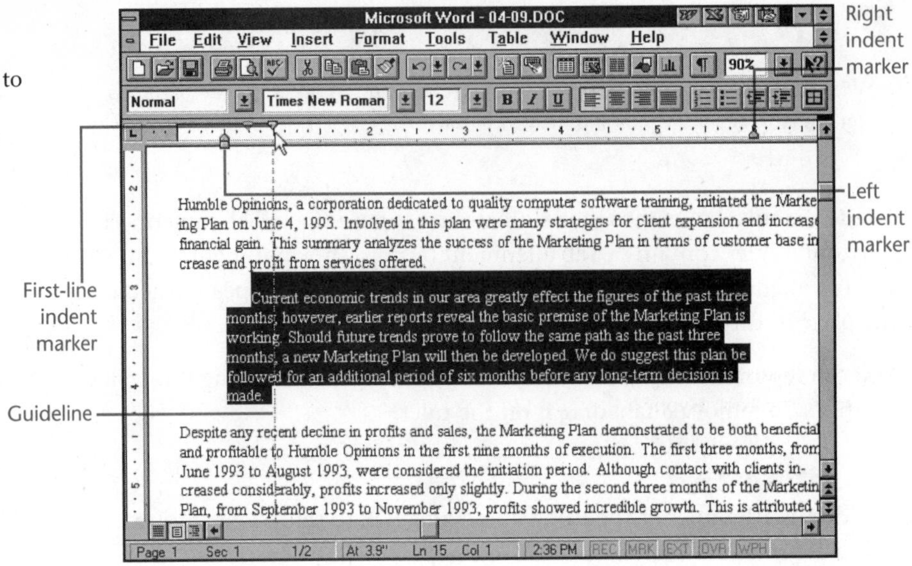

Fig. 5.12
Word supplies a dotted guideline to help you align indents and tabs when using the ruler.

Right indent marker

Left indent marker

First-line indent marker

Guideline

In addition, you can create a hanging indent, shown in figure 5.13. To create a hanging indent, position the insertion point in the paragraph, and drag the left indent marker to the position where you want lines 2, 3, and so on of the paragraph to begin. Then drag the first-line indent marker to the position where you want the overhanging line to start.

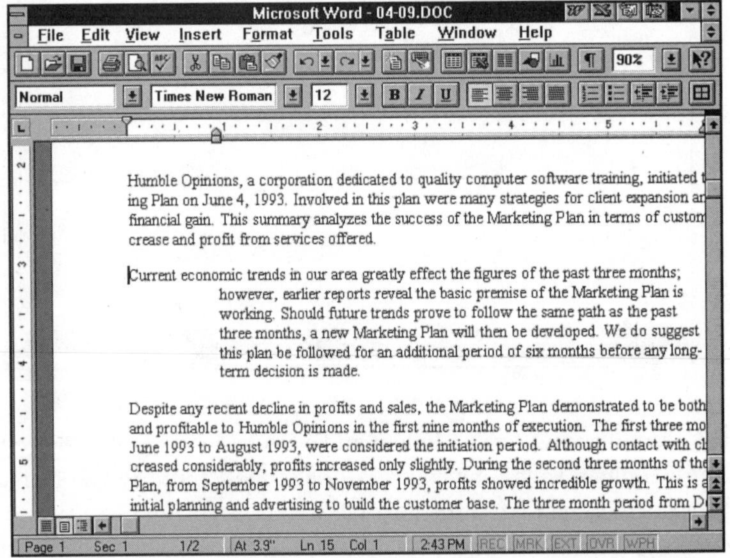

Fig. 5.13
Create a hanging indent by first dragging the left indent marker and then dragging the first-line marker into position.

Adjusting Alignment

Alignment is a way of organizing your text. The way you align the text in a document makes the text easy to read, decorative, eye-catching, formal and sophisticated, or casual and flexible. Word enables you to left-align, right-align, center, or justify the text in your documents.

Figure 5.14 illustrates the four alignments and the corresponding toolbar buttons.

Tip

You can select existing text and then align it, or you can select an alignment and then enter the text.

Note

When you use justified text, be sure you turn on the hyphenation feature. To do so, choose the **T**ools **H**yphenation command. In the Hyphenation dialog box, select **A**utomatically Hyphenate Document, and then choose OK.

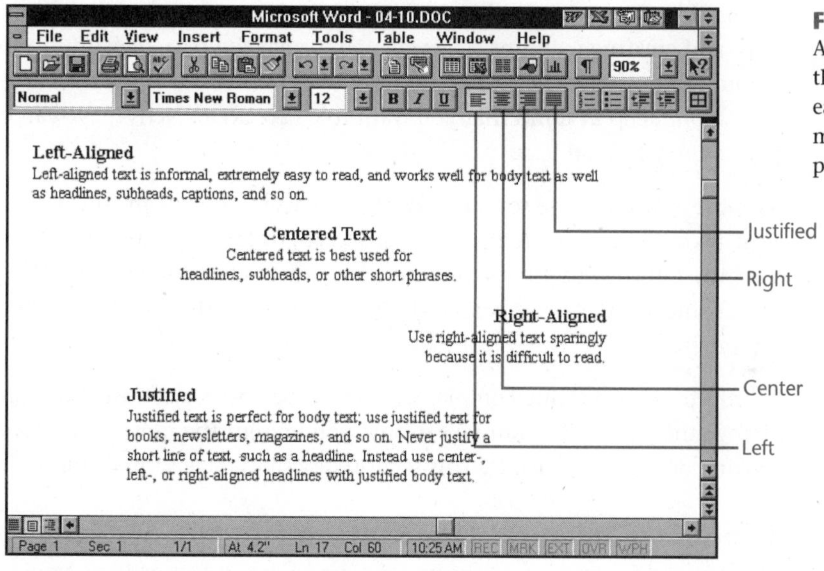

Fig. 5.14
Align your text so the reader can easily follow the message and so the page is attractive.

II

Using Word

Troubleshooting

I set the line and paragraph spacing in the Paragraph dialog box, and I don't like the results. I want to change the line spacing back to the way it was, but I don't want to change the paragraph spacing.

Choose the F**o**rmat **P**aragraph command, and then select the **I**ndents and Spacing tab. In the Li**n**e Spacing list, select Single. Then choose OK to close the dialog box.

(continues)

(continued)

I want to see how the tabs or indents are set in a specific paragraph of text.

Position the insertion point in the paragraph, and view the indent and tab markers in the ruler. (To display the ruler, choose the **V**iew **R**uler command.)

I justified the text in a paragraph, and now there are large gaps between the words.

Turn on the hyphenation feature by choosing the **T**ools **H**yphenation command and then selecting **A**utomatically Hyphenate Document. Choose OK to close the dialog box.

Formatting the Page

Formatting the page includes changing page size, orientation, setting margins, and creating columns. The way you format the page depends on the amount of text, the size and orientation of graphics, the type of document, and so on. Keep in mind that you want to create an attractive, eye-catching page of easy-to-read text.

Suppose that you have several drawings of cars to go into an ad with very little text. You can create the ad in *landscape* (wide) orientation with 1-inch margins. On the other hand, if your text contains two long lists of items and no graphics, you can use *portrait* (tall) orientation with two columns and half-inch margins.

Word's page-formatting commands are flexible and easy to use. You can change the page to fit your text so that you present the most professional-looking document possible. This section describes page formatting.

Changing Size and Orientation

The size and orientation of the paper you use depends mostly on your printer. Some printers take 8 1/2- by 11-inch sheets only; others can print sheets ranging from small envelopes to legal-size paper. Most laser and inkjet printers can print in either orientation. Check your printer manual before changing paper size and orientation.

To change page size and orientation, use the Page Setup dialog box. Figure 5.15 shows the Paper Size tab in the Page Setup dialog box.

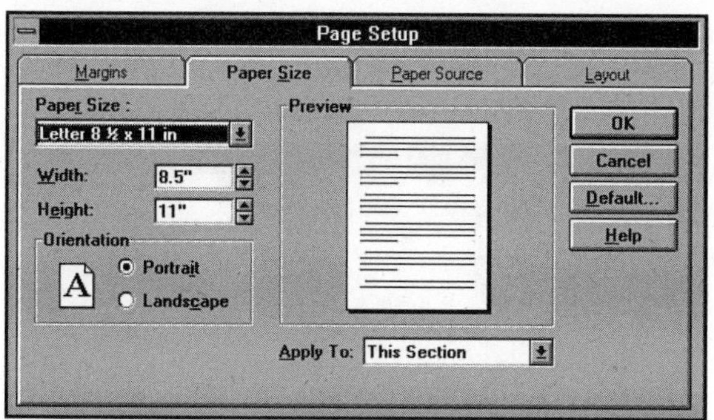

Fig. 5.15
Choose paper size and orientation, and then view the change in the Preview box.

To change paper size and orientation, follow these steps:

1. Choose the **F**ile Page Set**u**p command. The Page Setup dialog box appears.
2. Select the Paper **S**ize tab.
3. Select a size in the drop-down Pape**r** Size list.
4. In the Orientation area, select Portra**i**t or Lands**c**ape.
5. Choose OK to close the dialog box.

Setting Margins

You can change the margins of your document from the default settings to any margin you want. Word's Normal template uses 1-inch top and bottom margins and 1 1/2-inch left and right margins. You can set the margins by using the Page Setup dialog box, shown in figure 5.16.

Tip
When you set margins, Word applies those measurements to all pages in the document, unless you divide your document into sections.

To change the margins of your document, follow these steps:

1. Choose the **F**ile Page Set**u**p command. The Page Setup dialog box appears.
2. Select the **M**argins tab.
3. Enter measurements in the **T**op, **B**ottom, Le**f**t, and Ri**g**ht boxes.
4. Choose OK to close the dialog box.

Creating Columns

You can divide the page into one, two, three, or more columns to make the text well organized and easy to read. Documents such as books, magazines, catalogs, newsletters, brochures, and even advertisements often are divided into columns. Word makes dividing your documents into columns easy.

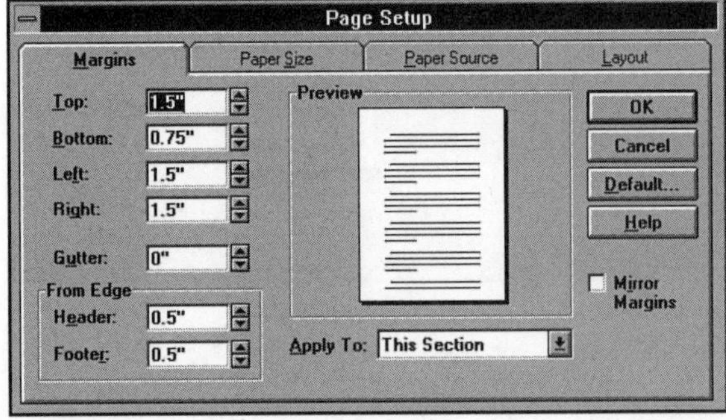

Fig. 5.16
You can change the margins to shorten the line length and to add valuable white space.

Note

Normally, divide an 8 1/2- by 11-inch portrait-oriented page into no more than three columns; divide the same-size landscape-oriented page into no more than five columns. When you use too many columns on a page, the lines of text become too short and are hard to read.

You divide a document into columns by using the Columns dialog box (see figure 5.17). You can select a preset number of columns and designs or enter a number of columns and each column width, if you prefer. When you enter your own column width, you must specify spacing, called *gutter space,* between the columns.

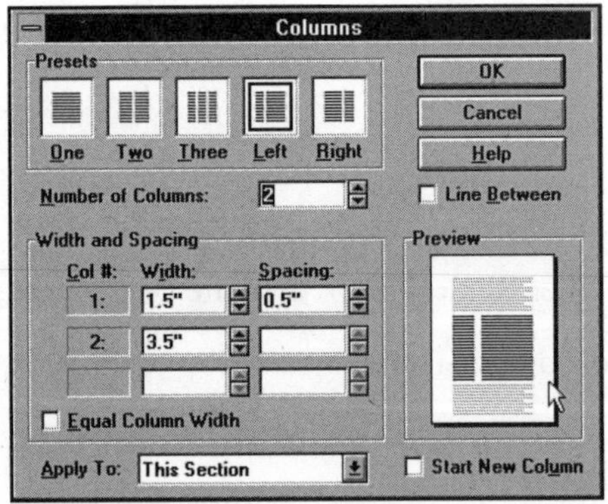

Fig. 5.17
Use equally wide columns or, in this case, make one column wider than the other for an interesting effect. View the result in the Preview box before choosing OK.

If you like, you can add a line between the columns by selecting the Line **B**etween option. Word even enables you to start a new column at the insertion point by selecting the Start New Col**u**mn option. Preview your column choices in the Preview box before accepting or rejecting the changes in the dialog box.

To format the columns in your document, follow these steps:

1. Choose the F**o**rmat **C**olumns command. The Columns dialog box appears.
2. In the Presets area, select the number and type of columns you want.
3. Use the other options in the dialog box to customize columns.
4. Choose OK to accept the changes and close the dialog box.

Tip

For best results in creating columns, use no less than 1/4 inch of gutter space and no more than 1/2 inch. Too little gutter space makes the text in the columns run together; too much space creates wide gaps and makes the text hard to follow.

Troubleshooting

I created an 8 1/2- by 14-inch document, and now I can't print it.

Check your printer manual. You may have changed the page to a size larger than your printer can print.

I made my margins narrower than 1/4 inch, and now some of the edges of the text will not print.

Most printers have a required margin—usually 1/4 or 3/8 inch—because they cannot print to the edge of the page. Check your printer manual. Make it a habit to allow at least 3/8 inch of margin space in all your documents.

From Here...

In this chapter, you learned to format text, paragraphs, and pages by using Word's commands and toolbars. You now can change the font, font size, and font style; align text; adjust spacing, indents, and tabs; and set page size, page orientation, and margins. For more information about creating documents in Word, see the following chapters:

- Chapter 6, "Proofreading and Printing," covers checking the spelling and grammar in a document, using the thesaurus, previewing and editing a document in Print Preview, and printing a document.
- Chapter 7, "Managing Files," covers using Word's Find File feature to display summary information; view file information; and preview, sort, select, and delete files.

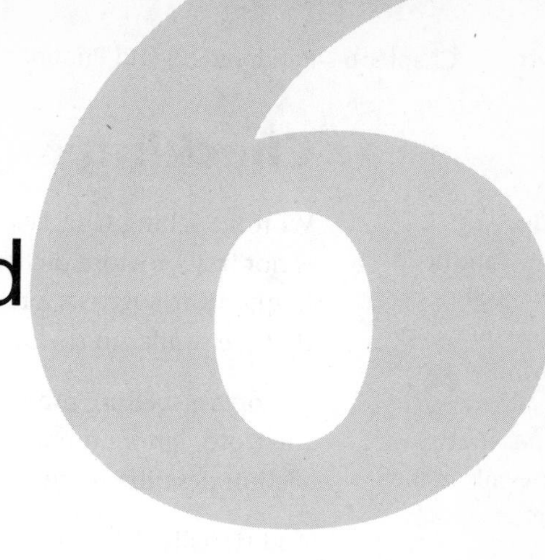

Chapter 6

Proofreading and Printing

by Susan Plumley

After you finish entering and editing text, you will want to proofread and then print your documents. Word supplies three tools that make proofreading easy. You can use Word's Spelling Checker, Thesaurus, and Grammar Checker to proofread your documents and supply suggestions for improvement.

No matter how long or short a document is, using the Spelling Checker is well worth the time it takes. Word quickly reviews the text and alerts you if it finds a misspelled word. Additionally, you can use Word's Thesaurus to find alternative words so that your text is not monotonous and repetitive. Finally, Word supplies a Grammar Checker that critiques your writing and offers suggestions for improvement.

After your document is complete, you can print it. Word has a special print preview mode in which you can view the document and make last-minute changes in the design before printing. Finally, you can print your document by using Windows defaults or by setting options in Word.

In this chapter, you learn to

- Use the Spelling Checker
- Use the Thesaurus
- Use the Grammar Checker
- Preview a document before you print it
- Print a document

Checking Spelling

Tip
You can check the spelling of the entire document, or you can select text and check spelling only in the selected text.

Word's Spelling Checker reads text and notifies you when it finds a word that is not in its custom dictionary. The Spelling dialog box shows you the word in question, suggests a replacement word, and displays a list of other words that are similar in spelling, as possible replacements.

To solve a spelling problem, you can use a variety of options. You can change the word, ignore the word, add the word to the dictionary, and so on. This section describes each of these options.

Additionally, Word includes a feature called AutoCorrect. Using AutoCorrect, you can instruct Word to correct spelling mistakes as you make them. If, for example, you often type **teh** rather than **the**, AutoCorrect can fix the error immediately after you make it. This section also discusses how to use the AutoCorrect feature.

Using the Spelling Checker

Tip
You also can start the Spelling Checker by clicking the Spelling button in the Standard toolbar or by pressing F7.

The Spelling Checker looks for words that are not in Word's dictionary. In addition, it alerts you to punctuation and capitalization problems. You can choose to change the spelling or ignore the problem; you even can add the word to the dictionary for later use.

To use Word's Spelling Checker, choose **T**ools **S**pelling. The Spelling dialog box appears (see fig. 6.1).

The following table describes each option in the Spelling dialog box.

Option	Description
Not in Dictiona**r**y	Displays the word in question.
Change **T**o	Suggests an alternative spelling; you can enter your own new spelling in this text box.
Delete	If the Change To text box is empty, the Change button becomes Delete, which deletes the word.
Delete A**l**l	If the Change To text box is empty, the Change All button becomes Delete All, which deletes all occurrences of the word in the document.
Suggestio**n**s	Select a word in the Suggestio**n**s list box to replace the misspelled word.
Ignore	Skips this word.

► "Changing Spelling Options," p. 184

Option	Description
Start	The Ignore button changes to Start when you click outside the Spelling dialog box to edit your document. The dialog box remains on-screen; choose the Start button to resume the spelling check.
Ignore All	Skips all occurrences of this word in the document.
Change	Substitutes the selected or entered word for misspelled word.
Change All	Substitutes the selected or entered word for all occurrences of this word in the document.
Add	Updates the dictionary to include a word that you often type. The added word must appear in the Not in Dictionary text box.
Suggest	If the Always Suggest option in the Options dialog box is deactivated, choose Suggest to list suggestions for correcting the misspelled word.
Add Words To	If you installed more than one dictionary, select the dictionary to which you want to add from the drop-down list.
AutoCorrect	Adds frequently misspelled words to the AutoCorrect list. See the following section, "Using AutoCorrect," for more information.
Options	Enables you to choose default settings or customize the Spelling Checker. For more information on spelling options, see Chapter 8, "Customizing Word."
Undo Last	Choose Undo Last to change your mind about the last spelling change.
Close/Cancel	Cancel ends the spelling check and cancels any changes; Close ends the spelling check and saves any changes. The Cancel button changes to Close after you make a change in the document.
Help	Choose this button for detailed help on the Spelling dialog box options.

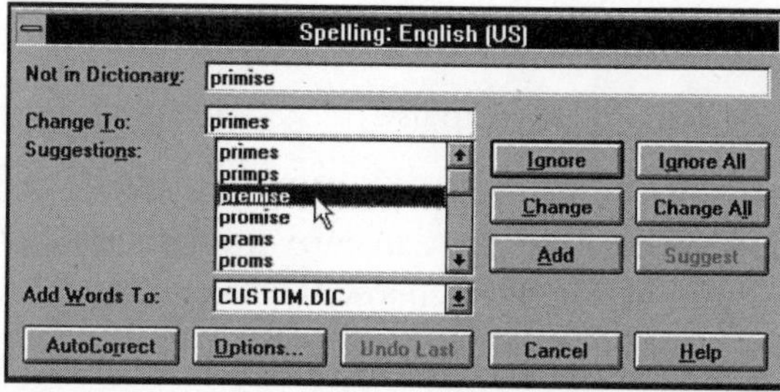

Fig. 6.1
Select a word in the Suggestions box or enter the correct word in the Change To text box to correct the mistake in the text.

Using AutoCorrect

The AutoCorrect feature automatically corrects spelling mistakes and formatting errors, or replaces characters you enter with specific words or phrases. Using this feature saves you time. Suppose that you consistently type **anohter** instead of **another** or **WHen** instead of **When**. You can enter these common mistakes into AutoCorrect, and the next time you make the mistake, Word corrects it automatically.

To set options and make entries for AutoCorrect, choose the **T**ools **A**utoCorrect command. Figure 6.2 shows the AutoCorrect dialog box with a new entry.

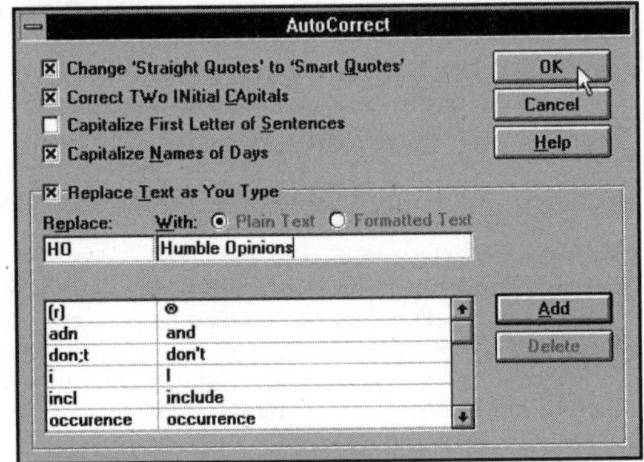

Fig. 6.2
You can add shortcuts to the AutoCorrect entry list. For example, enter two letters to represent a name or company name that you often type.

The AutoCorrect dialog box lists five options—including converting quote marks and correcting capitalization problems—that you can choose to turn on or off. The Replace and With text boxes enable you to enter your own items, and the list at the bottom of the AutoCorrect dialog box displays Word's default list plus any items you add. You can add or delete items at any time. For related information, see Chapter 8, "Customizing Word."

To use the AutoCorrect feature, follow these steps:

1. Choose **T**ools **A**utoCorrect. The AutoCorrect dialog box appears.
2. Select the options you want to use.
3. If you enter items in the R**e**place and **W**ith text boxes, choose **A**dd to add them to the list. To remove an entry from the list, highlight the item in the list box, and then choose **D**elete.
4. Choose OK to close the dialog box.

Troubleshooting

I have a lot of words that contain numbers, such as measurements, in my document, and I want Word to ignore those words.

Choose the **T**ools **O**ptions command, and select the Spelling tab. In the Ignore area, select Words with Num**b**ers. Choose OK to close the dialog box.

I want to edit some of the words in a custom dictionary.

Choose the **T**ools **O**ptions command, and select the Spelling tab. In the dictionaries area, select the dictionary you want to modify, and then choose the **E**dit button.

I want to add an AutoCorrect entry without opening the Spelling Checker.

Choose the **T**ools **A**utoCorrect command. In the R**e**place text box, type the misspelled word. In the **W**ith text box, type the correct spelling of the word. Choose OK to close the dialog box.

Using the Thesaurus

The Thesaurus supplies a variety of synonyms you can use to replace the word you are looking up. To use the Thesaurus, position the insertion point in the word you want to look up, and choose the **T**ools **T**hesaurus command. Word automatically highlights the word, and the Thesaurus dialog box appears.

Suppose that you want to find a synonym for the word *second*. Using the words in the Meanings list box, you can look up either *next* or *moment* (see fig. 6.3). Selecting a word in the Meanings list on the left displays several synonyms in the Replace with Synonym list on the right. Additionally, you can look up new words, either related to the original word or not, or go back to a word you looked up earlier. If you want to look up a word that is different from the original word, position the insertion point in the Replace with Synonym text box, type a new word, and then choose **L**ook Up.

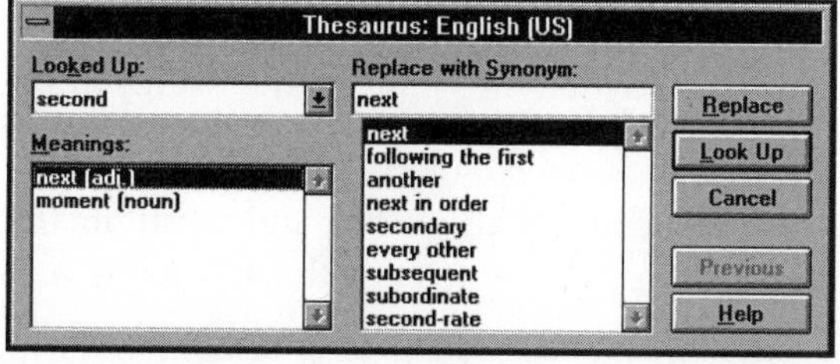

Fig. 6.3
Replace the selected word with any of the displayed synonyms, or continue to look up words until you find the correct meaning.

The following table describes the options in the Thesaurus dialog box:

Option	Description
Looked Up/Not Found	A drop-down list of all the words you have looked up since you opened the Thesaurus dialog box; the list disappears when you close the dialog box. The text-box name changes to Not Found if the word is not in the Thesaurus.
Meanings/Alphabetical List	Definition and part of speech of selected word; selecting a different meaning results in a new list of synonyms. Alphabetical List appears if the word is not in the Thesaurus.
Replace with Synonym	The word in the text box is the selected word that you can Look Up or Replace when you choose either of those command buttons. The list of words below the text box is a list of synonyms you can select.
Replace with Antonym	If Antonyms is available in the Meanings list box, you can highlight it and then select an antonym from this list box.
Replace	Choose this button to substitute the selected word (in the Replace with Synonym text box) for the original word in the text.
Look Up	Displays meanings and synonyms for the selected word (in the Replace with Synonym text box).
Cancel	Closes the dialog box.
Previous	Displays the last word you looked up. Works only in the current Thesaurus dialog box.

To use the Thesaurus, follow these steps:

1. Position the insertion point in the word you want to look up.
2. Choose the **T**ools **T**hesaurus command or press Shift+F7. Word automatically highlights the word, and the Thesaurus dialog box appears.
3. In the **M**eanings list, select the meaning you want.
4. In the Replace with **S**ynonym list, select the word you want to use as a replacement.
5. Choose **R**eplace to close the dialog box and substitute the new word for the old one, or choose Cancel to close the dialog box without replacing the word.

Tip
Double-click a synonym or meaning to display more synonyms.

Troubleshooting

I looked up several meanings, and now I want to go back to the original word I looked up in the Thesaurus.

Choose Loo**k**ed Up or click the down arrow to the right of that option. A drop-down list of the words you looked up during this session appears. Select the original word.

I want to go back to the last word I looked up.

Choose the **P**revious command button.

Checking Grammar

If you have problems with your writing, Word may be able to help you. Word's Grammar Checker reviews text in your document and reports possible problems, such as passive verbs, pronoun errors, punctuation errors, jargon, and double negatives. You can review the error and suggestion, and then decide whether to change the text. You even can ask for a further explanation of the grammar rule.

Tip
You can set grammar rules and styles by using the Customize Grammar Settings dialog box. For more information, see Chapter 8.

► "Customizing Options," p. 171

To check the grammar in a document, choose the **T**ools **G**rammar command. The Grammar dialog box appears (see fig. 6.4).

Note

You must read the suggestions carefully. You may find that the suggestion is not valid and that the problem, as the Grammar Checker sees it, is not really a problem.

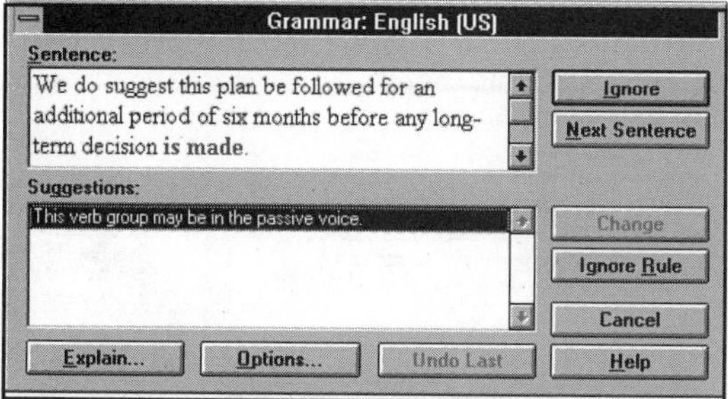

Fig. 6.4
You can choose to ignore or change the problem, ignore the rule for this document, or ask for an explanation of the problem.

The following table describes the options in the Grammar dialog box:

Option	Explanation
Sentence	The sentence in question appears in this text box, where you can edit the sentence.
Su**g**gestions	Word defines the problem and may suggest alternative solutions.
Ignore	Choose this command button if you want to ignore the problem.
Next Sentence	Moves to the next grammar problem, ignoring the current one.
Change	Changes the sentence if an alternative suggestion was made in the Su**g**gestions box.
Ignore **R**ule	Choose this button if you want to ignore a specific rule for the rest of the document.
Cancel/Close	Cancel closes the dialog box without making a change; after you make a change, the Cancel button changes to Close. Choose Close to return to your document.
Explain	Displays a message box that further explains the rule and often offers examples (see fig. 6.5).
Options	Enables you to customize rules and style for the Grammar Checker. For more information, see Chapter 8, "Customizing Word."
Undo **L**ast	Choose this button if you change your mind about the last grammar change you made.
Help	Choose this button for more information about the Grammar dialog box.
Start	Appears in place of the Ignore command button when you click the document. The Grammar dialog box remains on-screen while you edit your document; choose **S**tart to continue the grammar check.

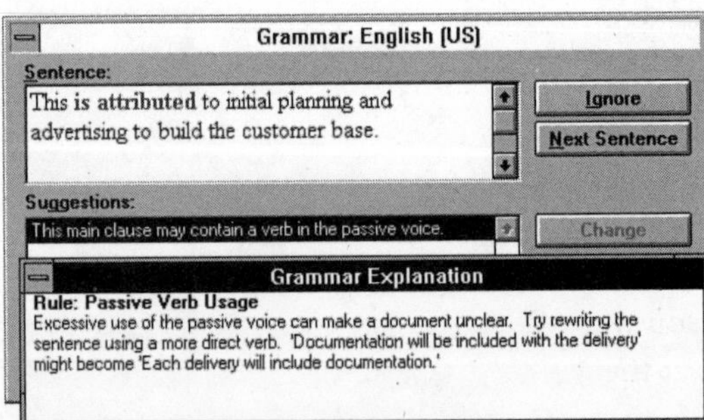

Fig. 6.5
Choose Explain to learn more about the grammar rule in question; double-click the Control-menu box to close the message box.

Troubleshooting

I don't want to check the spelling at the same time I check the grammar.

Choose the **T**ools **O**ptions command, and select the Grammar tab. Click the Check **S**pelling option to deactivate it. Then choose OK.

I changed my mind about the last change I applied in the Grammar dialog box.

Choose the Undo **L**ast button in the dialog box.

Previewing a Document

After you enter, edit, format, and proofread your text, you are ready to print your document. Sometimes, when you format a page of text in normal view, problems are revealed when you print the document. The margins may be too wide, a headline may break in an odd place, a paragraph may be indented by mistake, and so on. You can save time, effort, and paper if you view your document in Print Preview before you print it.

◄ "Printing Documents," p. 87

Note

You do not have to use Print Preview before you print a document. If you want to print without first previewing a document, choose the **F**ile **P**rint command. For more information, see "Printing a Document" later in this chapter.

Tip

You can edit and format your document in Print Preview, just as you can in page layout or normal view. Use the menus and commands, or display any of the toolbars to use as shortcuts.

Figure 6.6, which shows a document in Print Preview, reveals a problem with graphic lines that are too short to extend from the left edge of the body text to the right edge. You can quickly fix the problem, in this view, before you print; drag the margin markers in the rulers to set new margins for the lines and the text.

Using the Rulers

By default, Word does not display the rulers in Print Preview (File menu). You can, however, choose the **V**iew **R**ulers command to display both the horizontal and vertical rulers. Use the rulers as you would in any other view: set tabs, adjust indents, and change the margins.

Tip

The default view in Print Preview is Whole Page view, which is best for adjusting margins.

To adjust the margins by using the ruler, position the insertion point at the point you want to change. Any margin changes occur from the insertion point on; so if you want to change margins in the entire page, position the insertion point at the top of the page.

Move the mouse pointer over the margin marker on the ruler until you see the double-headed arrow (at the point where the white ruler meets the gray arrow). Click and drag the arrow left or right (in the horizontal ruler) or up or down (in the vertical ruler) to change the margin. A dotted guideline appears across the page as you drag the margin; use the guideline to align elements on the page.

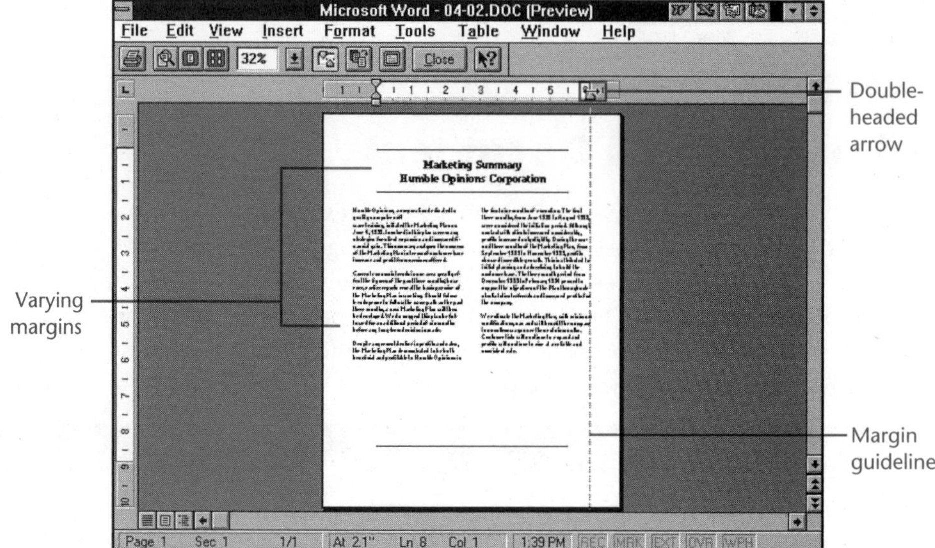

Fig. 6.6
Drag the left and right margin markers (in the horizontal ruler) or the top and bottom margins (in the vertical ruler).

Tip
Choose **E**dit **U**ndo to reverse the Shrink to Fit operation. Because the Print Preview toolbar does not include an Undo button, you must choose **E**dit **U**ndo.

Using the Preview Toolbar

Print Preview includes a special toolbar you can use to edit your document. The Preview toolbar works in much the same way as the other toolbars. You can place the mouse pointer on a toolbar button to view the ToolTip and the description of the button in the status bar.

You can use a toolbar button to print your document, view one page or multiple pages, display or hide the ruler, view the full screen (without screen elements such as the title bar, scroll bars, and so on), exit Print Preview, and get help on a specific topic. Two toolbar buttons are particularly useful: Shrink to Fit and the Magnifier.

The Shrink to Fit button adjusts elements in a document, such as line and paragraph spacing and margins, so you can fit a little bit more on the page. Suppose that your document fills one page, and one or two sentences overflow to a second page. Try clicking the Shrink to Fit button to squeeze all the text onto the first page.

The Magnifier enables you to toggle between the normal mouse pointer and the magnifier pointer. When the magnifier pointer contains a plus sign (+), you can magnify the document to 100 percent. When the magnifier pointer contains a minus sign (–), as shown in figure 6.7, clicking the page reduces the view to whole page view (32 percent). To change the magnifier pointer back to the normal pointer, click the Magnifier button again.

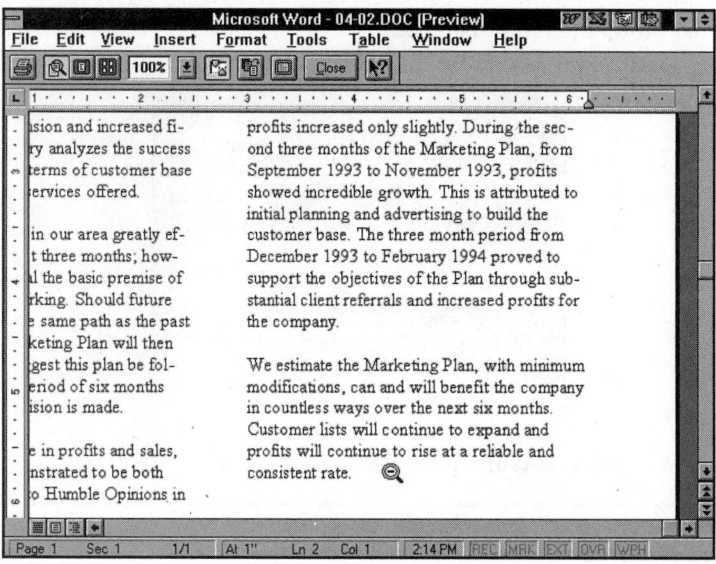

Fig. 6.7
Reduce a specific area of the document by clicking the pointer on that area.

Using the Print button on the Preview toolbar prints the document using the default options in the Print dialog box. If you want to make changes to any printing options, see the following section, "Printing a Document."

Troubleshooting

I have several lines of text that overflow to the second page of my document, but I would like them to be on the first page.

Click the Shrink to Fit button in the Print Preview toolbar. Magnify the document, and look carefully at the changes in the text spacing and sizing. You may prefer to undo the change if the text appears to be too crowded on one page.

I have trouble setting the margins for the document with the ruler in Print Preview.

Choose the **F**ile Page Set**u**p command, and select the **M**argins tab.

Printing a Document

▶ "Customizing Printing," p. 178

When you print from Word, you generally use the defaults set up in Windows. You can, however, change these defaults in the Print dialog box. Most often, however, you will print with the default options in the Print dialog box.

The default options print one copy of all the pages in the document. Figure 6.8 shows the Print dialog box.

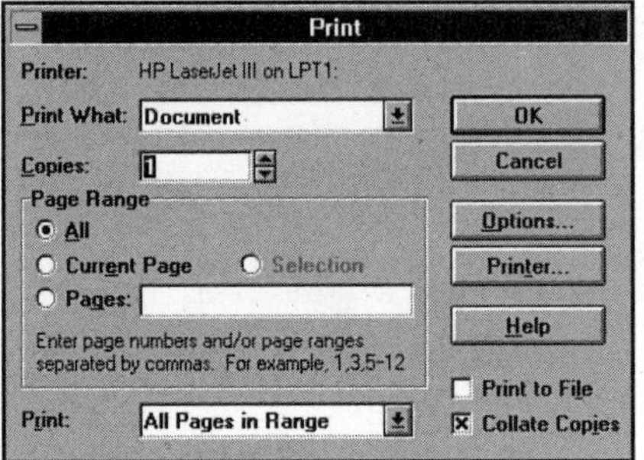

Fig. 6.8
To print using the default options in the Print dialog box, choose OK.

The following table describes the options in the Print dialog box:

Option	Description
Print What	Specify what to print: the document, summary sheet, a list of styles, key assignments, annotations, or auto text assignments associated with the document.
Copies	Enter the number of copies to be printed.
All	Prints all pages in the document.
Current Page	Prints only the page in which the insertion point is located.
Pages	Enter a page range in the text box. Separate individual pages with commas (1,4,5); separate a page range with a hyphen (1-5).
Selection	Select text in the document before choosing to print; choose Selection to print only selected text.
Print	Specify which pages to print: all pages, even pages, or odd pages in the page range.
Print to File	Prints the document to a file on disk so you can transport it to another computer or service bureau.

Option	Description
Collate Cop**i**es	Select this option to print copies in order. Print pages 1 to 5 in the first copy, for example, before printing pages 1 to 5 in the second copy.
Options	Choose this button to customize printing options. For more information, see Chapter 8, "Customizing Word."
Prin**t**er	Choose this button to select another printer on which to print this document. If you change the default printer in the Print Setup dialog box, you change the default printer for all Windows programs.
Help	Choose this button for more information about printing options.
Cancel	Choose this button to cancel all changes and close the dialog box without printing the document.
OK	Choose this button to send the selected pages to the printer.

Troubleshooting

I created a form, and I want to print the data in my form without printing the table lines and fill.

Choose the **O**ptions button in the Print dialog box. In the Print tab, select **P**rint Data Only for Forms.

I want to change to a different printer before printing a document.

Choose the Prin**t**er button in the Print dialog box. Select a printer from the list of **P**rinters, and choose OK.

Printing Envelopes

You can print envelopes in Word quickly and easily by choosing the **T**ools **E**nvelopes and Labels command. Word makes it easy to enter the delivery and return addresses, choose an envelope size and method of feed, and then print an envelope.

Figure 6.9 shows the Envelopes and Labels dialog box.

Tip

You can change the default return address. For more information, see Chapter 8.

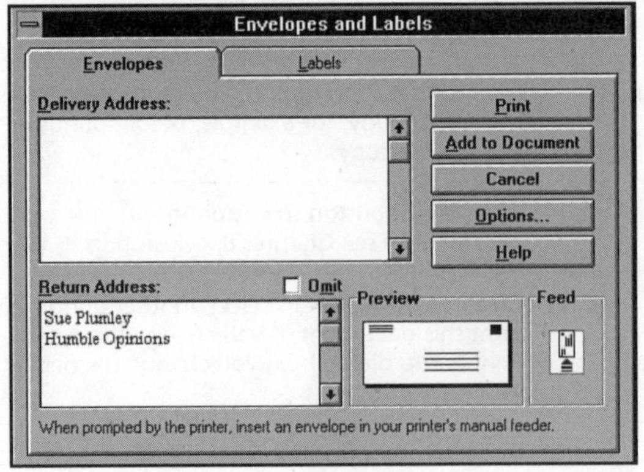

Fig. 6.9
Enter the delivery and return addresses, and then choose OK to print the envelope.

► "Customizing Options," p. 171

The following table describes the options in the Envelopes and Labels dialog box:

Option	Description
Delivery Address	Enter the name and address to which the envelope will be mailed.
Return Address	Enter your name and address.
O**m**it	Choose this option to exclude the return address.
Preview	Click the envelope in the Preview box to display the Envelope Options dialog box (**E**nvelope Options tab). Select the size, bar code, placement, and font for the addresses in this dialog box.
Feed	Click the Feed box to display the Envelope Options dialog box and the Printing Options tab. Select the method of feeding envelopes that best fits your printer.
Options	Displays the Envelope Options dialog box.
Add to Document	Adds the envelope style and contents to the document so you can save it for later use.
Help	Choose this button to see more information about the dialog box and envelope options.
Print	Choose this button to send the envelope to the printer.
Cancel	Choose this button to cancel your choices and close the dialog box without printing the envelope.

To print an envelope in Word, follow these steps:

1. Insert an envelope into the printer.
2. Choose the **T**ools **E**nvelopes and Labels command. The Envelopes and Labels dialog box appears.
3. Select the **E**nvelopes tab.
4. Enter a **D**elivery Address and **R**eturn Address.
5. Select envelope and feed options, if necessary.
6. Choose OK.

From Here...

After your document is complete, you can print it. Use Word's Print Preview feature to view the document and make last-minute changes in the design before you print it. Then print your document by using Windows defaults or by setting options in Word.

For more information about working in Word, see the following chapters:

- Chapter 7, "Managing Files," covers creating summary information for your documents. It also includes information about Find File, ways of viewing file information, how to organize and search for specific files or documents, and how to sort and select files.
- Chapter 8, "Customizing Word," covers options that you can change or modify to better suit your working style, including options for viewing, printing, saving, spelling, and grammar.

Chapter 7

Managing Files

by Susan Plumley

After you work with any program for a significant amount of time, the files you have saved start piling up. Locating the file you need in a disk that contains tens, hundreds, even thousands of files becomes harder and harder. All you want is to open, edit, and print one letter you wrote last week; but you cannot find it. Word supplies a file manager, similar to Windows File Manager, that you can use to search for and find files.

In addition to the never-ending file search, you need to clean your disk periodically by copying some files to floppies and perhaps deleting others. Instead of switching to Windows File Manager, you can use Word's File Manager, called Find File, to copy, delete, sort, and print files.

In this chapter, you learn to

- Create records to help identify and sort document files by title, keywords, author, and other criteria
- Set and save search criteria for finding files
- Find any file by using different types of information
- Select one or more files
- Copy files to other drives and directories
- Delete one or more files without leaving Word

Creating Summary Info Records

A *Summary Info* record helps you keep track of your documents. Suppose that you type 20 letters each day: letters to advertisers, clients, employees, and others. When you need to look up one specific letter or a group of related

► "Changing Save Options," p. 182

letters, how can you find it? Summary Info records help you organize, manage, and find the documents you need quickly and easily.

Note

You also can organize your files by directory (JANUARY, FEBRUARY, MARCH), by file name (LETSMITH.DOC, LETJONES.DOC, LETROBIN.DOC), or by extension (LETSMITH.001, LETSMITH.002, LETSMITH.003).

Summary information includes the document's title, subject, author, any keywords that would help identify the document, and comments about the document. You can use any or all of these supplied categories.

One of the best uses for Summary Info records is *Find File,* a file-management program included with Word that enables you to search for files by using any of the data you enter as summary information. For more information about this program, see "Using Find File" later in this chapter.

Displaying Summary Info

Word's default is to prompt for summary information each time you save a document. When you choose the **F**ile Save **A**s command, name a document, and choose OK to close the dialog box, Word displays the Summary Info dialog box, shown in figure 7.1. Alternatively, you can choose the **F**ile Summary **I**nfo command to display the dialog box any time you are working on a document.

Tip
To determine whether Word automatically prompts you for summary information, use the **T**ools menu. For more information, see Chapter 8.

Entering Summary Info

In the Summary Info dialog box, enter any text that will help you recognize the document later. Suppose that you write a letter to a client named David Walkup. You quote six hours of consulting for installation of a peer-to-peer network to four computers. This is the third quote on the same subject, but with different configurations.

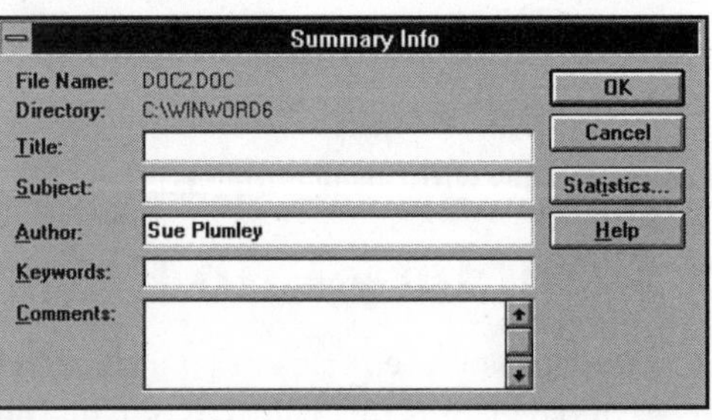

Fig. 7.1
Use the Summary Info dialog box to enter information about your document. You can enter text in any or all of the text boxes.

Because you already have two other letters dealing with this client and this same consulting job, use Summary Info records to help distinguish this letter from the others. Figure 7.2 shows a suggested Summary Info dialog box for this letter to David Walkup.

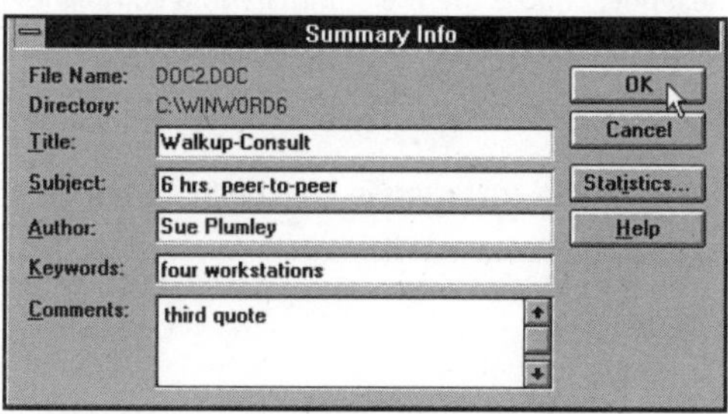

Fig. 7.2
When entering summary information, use keywords, a title, comments, and other items that you will easily recognize months from now.

Viewing Statistics

Within the Summary Info dialog box is a command button labeled Statistics. When you choose this button, Word displays information about your document, including its location, creation and last-saved date, file size, total editing time, and so on. Review this information when you want to know more about a file or document.

Figure 7.3 shows the Document Statistics dialog box.

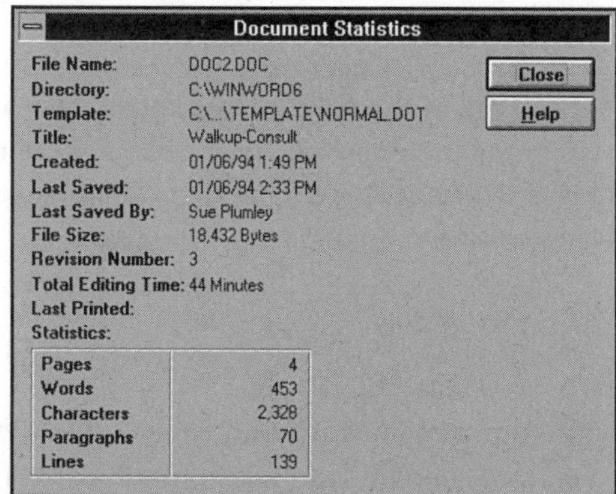

Fig. 7.3
View Document Statistics when you need to know the last-saved or last-printed date, the number of pages or words, or even the template used for a document.

Note

You can print the summary information by choosing the **F**ile **P**rint **O**ptions command. For more information, refer to Chapter 6, "Proofreading and Printing."

Troubleshooting

I didn't enter a title in the Summary Info dialog box, but Word shows a title.

Word displays the first several words of a document as a title unless you create your own title. To create a title, choose the **F**ile Summary **I**nfo command. In the **T**itle box, enter the proper title. Then choose OK to close the dialog box.

I want to add several keywords, but I'm not sure how many Word accepts.

Word accepts a maximum 255 characters in each of the Summary Info text boxes.

Using Find File

◀ "Working with Files," p. 71

To locate specific files, Find File enables you to search directories on your computer's hard drive, network drives, floppy drives, and so on. You can search for a file with a particular extension, creation date, author, type of summary information, or other search criteria.

In addition, Find File enables you to select, copy, delete, and sort files. You even can view a document before opening it to make sure that the file is the right one. This section shows you how to use Find File.

Caution

Any time you choose to delete a file or files, make sure that you are deleting the correct files. Use Find File features to help you distinguish the files you want to delete from the ones you want to keep. Additionally, Word displays a confirmation box when you attempt to delete a file or files. Choose **Y**es to delete the selected file(s); choose **N**o to cancel the command.

Locating Files

Find File is a mini-program within Word that enables you to find and manage files. When you choose the **F**ile **F**ind File command, Word displays the Search dialog box, which enables you to designate search criteria. Search criteria can include the following:

- Location of file, such as the drive, directory, extension, or file type
- Summary information, such as the title, author, keywords, and subject
- Time stamp for last date and time saved or created, and by whom

You must specify search criteria before you open Find File. After you specify search criteria the first time, Find File uses the same criteria the next time you open Find File. You then can change the criteria, if you want.

Figure 7.4 shows the Search dialog box.

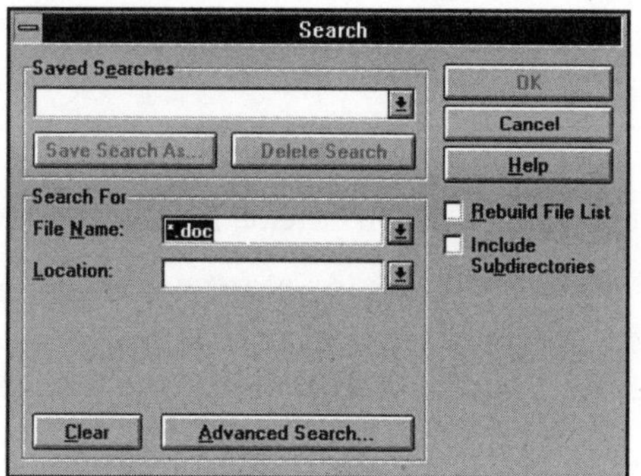

Fig. 7.4
Use the Search dialog box to specify the drive, directory, and other criteria that describe the missing file.

Search Criteria

The following table describes the options in the Search dialog box:

Option	Description
Saved S**e**arches	After selecting the search criteria, save them for quick reference and later use. You also can delete or modify the saved search criteria.
Save Search As	Choose this button to enter a name for the defined search criteria. You can create search criteria that display the directory (C:\WORD\DOCS*.*, for example) and save the criteria as a saved search. The next time you want to search the directory, you can select it in a list instead of describing it in the Search dialog box.
Delete Search	Erases the saved search criteria.
File **N**ame	In the Search For area, select an extension from the list, or enter your own in the text box. Extension examples are DOC, DOT, BMP, WMF, and *.* (all files). You can search for one extension or several. For example, type ***.DOC,*.BAT** to search for all documents with either extension.
Location	Select the drive for the search in this drop-down list, or type the drive and directory in the text box.
Rebuild File List	Replaces previously found files with files that meet the new search criteria.

(continues)

Option	Description
Include Su**b**directories	Select this option to search all subdirectories within the specified directory.
Clear	Removes the preceding search criteria from the text boxes.
Advanced Search	Choose this button to set more-specific search criteria. For details, see the following section, "Advanced Search Criteria."

To search for a file by using location criteria, follow these steps:

1. Choose the **F**ile **F**ind File command. The Search dialog box appears if there were no previous search criteria. If the Find File dialog box appears, click the **S**earch button to display the Search dialog box.
2. In the File **N**ame box, select or enter the file extension(s).
3. In the **L**ocation box, select or enter the drive and/or directory.
4. Choose the **S**ave Search As button. The Save Search As dialog box appears (see fig. 7.5).
5. Choose OK to close the Save Search As dialog box and return to the Search dialog box. Figure 7.6 shows sample search criteria in the Search dialog box.

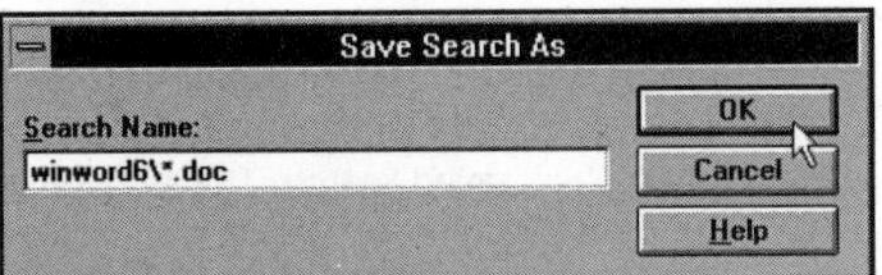

Fig. 7.5
Use this dialog box to save the search criteria for later use. This example searches for all DOC files in the WINWORD6 directory.

6. Choose OK to close the dialog box. The Find File dialog box appears. For further instructions on using Find File, see "Viewing Files" later in this chapter.

Advanced Search Criteria

You can specify additional or different search criteria before closing the Search dialog box, by choosing the **A**dvanced Search button. In the Advanced

Search dialog box, you can specify location, summary info, or time-stamp criteria for use in your search.

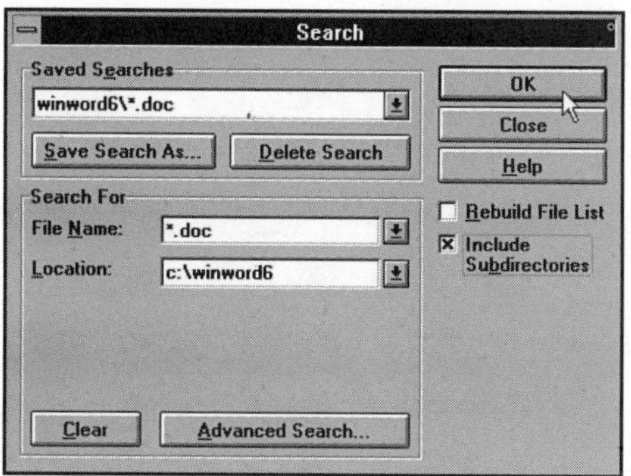

Fig. 7.6
Enter the search criteria and choose OK to close the dialog box and display Find File.

> **Caution**
>
> The more search criteria you use, the longer it takes Find File to complete the search. On the other hand, the more search criteria, the more accurate the search.

Figure 7.7 shows the Advanced Search dialog box, which has three tabs; select the **L**ocation tab.

Fig. 7.7
Use the Location tab to select the drive, directory, and even subdirectories for the search.

Figure 7.8 shows the **S**ummary tab. Enter any or all of the information used in the Summary Info sheet for the specific document or a group of documents. Enter only the author's name, for example, to search for all documents created by that author, or narrow the search by entering the author's name, the title, and the subject.

Note

You must use the exact wording and spelling you entered in the Summary Info sheet for such categories as Subject, Author, and Title. Otherwise, Find File cannot match the correct Summary Info.

Fig. 7.8
Enter search criteria in the Summary tab as well as the Location and Timestamp tab for very specific searches.

Figure 7.9 shows the Timestam**p** tab. If you know the approximate date and/or time the file was last saved or created, you can enter the information in this tab as search criteria.

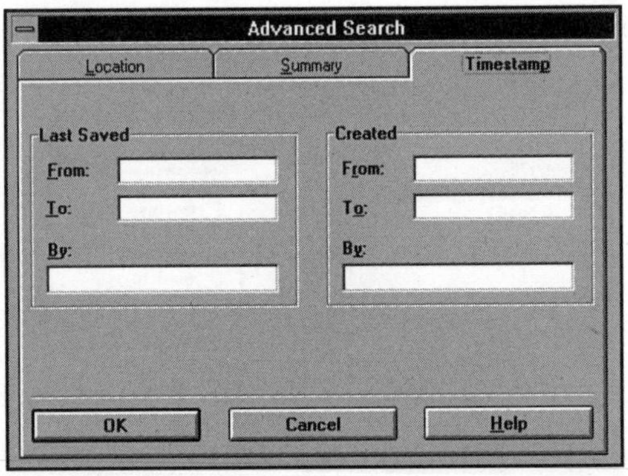

Fig. 7.9
Enter a range of dates—such as From 2-9-94 To 2-21-94—and, optionally, the author's name as additional search criteria.

Note

To use a saved search, select it in the Saved S**e**arches drop-down list in the Search dialog box. If you want to change any of the search criteria in the saved search, select any of the search options and then choose the **R**ebuild File List command. Choose the **S**ave Search As command if you want to save the new list.

Troubleshooting

I'm having trouble locating a specific file with the search criteria I have chosen.

Widen the search. If your search criteria are too narrow, you may not have included enough information for Find File to target the correct file. Try searching two or three subdirectories, or include subdirectories in the search.

I want to search for specific text within a document, such as computer programming.

Choose the **A**dvanced Search button in the Search dialog box, and select the **S**ummary tab. In the **C**ontaining Text box, enter the text for which you are searching. You also can use wild cards in your search, such as a question mark—for this example, you could enter **computer ?**. Using this wild card includes in the search such phrases as *computer programming* and *computer software*.

Viewing Files

After you enter the search criteria in the Search dialog box and choose OK to begin the search, the Find File dialog box appears, displaying a list of files described by the search criteria. Figure 7.10 shows the Find File dialog box in preview view.

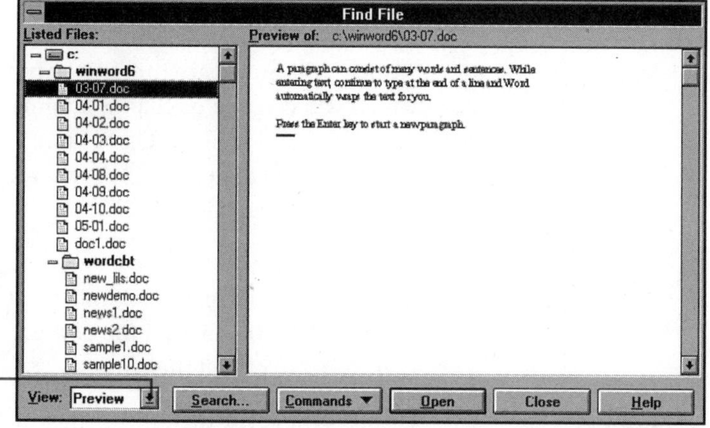

Fig. 7.10
The Find File default view is preview. A list of files appears on the left, and a preview of the selected file appears on the right.

Tip
To change views in Find File at any time, select a different view in the **V**iew drop-down list.

Find File provides three modes in which you can view files and file information: preview, file info, and summary. Each view provides specific information about the selected files, and you can change views at any time to get more information about the files. Additionally, each view uses the same command buttons at the bottom of the dialog box. This section describes the command buttons, the three views, and how to make the best use of each view.

Using the Command Buttons

Tip
You can select several files in the **L**isted Files box and then print, delete, or copy those files by selecting a command in the **C**ommands drop-down list.

The command buttons at the bottom of the Find File dialog box are the same for all three views. You can choose a command button and perform a command at any time while in Find File. The following list describes each command button and drop-down list:

- *View*. Choose the **V**iew command to display preview, summary, or file info view, each of which uses file information in a different way.
- *Search*. Displays the Search dialog box, in which you can specify new search criteria to display different directories and files.
- *Commands*. Displays a drop-down menu containing six commands that you can perform in any selected file. The commands are as follows:

Open **R**ead Only	Opens a file so you can read it but not edit or modify it in any way.
Print	Opens the Print dialog box so you can print the selected file or files. When you choose OK to print the file, Word returns to the Word screen, thus closing Find File.
Summary	Displays the Summary Info dialog box, in which you can add or change summary data. When you choose OK to close the Summary Info dialog box, Word returns to the Find File dialog box.
Delete	Deletes the selected file or files. This command displays a confirmation box. Choose **Y**es to delete the selected file or files; choose **N**o to cancel the request.
Copy	Displays the Copy dialog box, in which you can enter a location to copy the file to; alternatively, you can create a new directory to copy to. When you choose OK to close the Copy dialog box, Word returns to the Find File dialog box.

Sor**t**ing	Displays the Options dialog box, in which you can select various methods of sorting the files in the file list. When you choose OK to close the Options dialog box, Word returns to the Find File dialog box.

- ***O**pen.* Opens the selected file.
- *Close.* Closes the Find File dialog box.
- ***H**elp.* Displays help information about using Find File.

Using Preview View

Preview view enables you to select a file in the **L**isted Files list box and view it in the **P**review Of box. The **L**isted Files list box includes only the drive and directory or directories specified in the search criteria. You can scroll through the list of files and select any file to preview.

The **P**review Of list box displays the formatted document selected in the list of files. You can scroll through the previewed document, but you cannot edit or alter the previewed document.

If the selected file is not a Word document, Find File displays the Convert File dialog box (see fig. 7.11). Word can convert files from other programs—including Excel, WordPerfect, Word for Macintosh, Word for DOS, and earlier versions of Word for Windows—by using one of the displayed file filters.

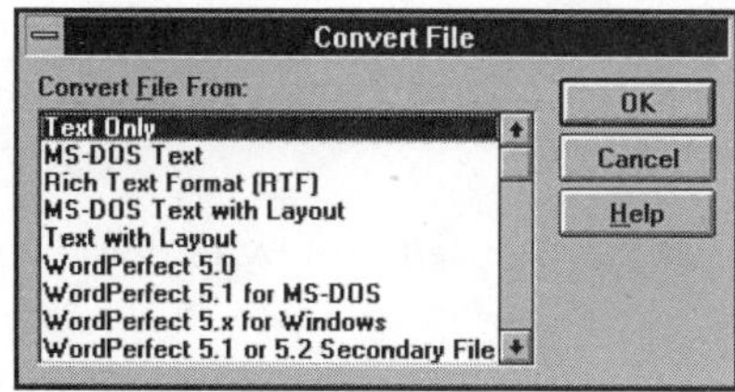

Fig. 7.11
Select the file filter to convert the file to a Word document so you can preview and/or open the document in Word.

Using File Info View

File info view lists information about the specified files in the search criteria, including the file name, size, and last-saved date. Figure 7.12 shows the file info view of the WINWORD6 directory.

Note

Word normally is installed in the WINWORD directory; in this example, Word was installed in the WINWORD6 directory. Word 2.0 still is intact in the WINWORD directory on this computer.

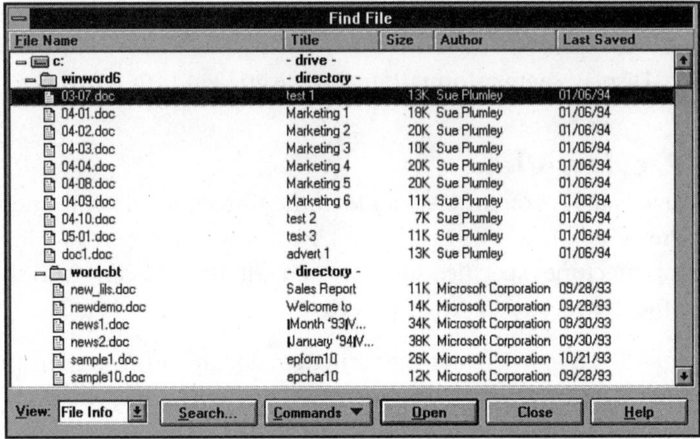

Fig. 7.12
Use file info view to identify files by location, title, size, and other criteria.

Tip
Use file info view when you want to sort files by file name, extension, title, size, and so on. For more information, see "Sorting Files" later in this chapter.

The following list describes the information displayed in file info view:

- *File Name.* Lists the drive, directory, and file names that fit the search criteria.
- *Title.* Lists the title assigned in the Summary Info sheet. If no summary sheet was completed for the file, Word lists the first 10 or 11 characters in the document as a title.
- *Size.* Lists the file size in thousands of bytes (kilobytes), such as 13K or 18K.
- *Author.* Lists the author according to the Summary Info sheet. If no summary sheet was completed for the file, Word displays the name in the User Info text box. For more information, see Chapter 8, "Customizing Word."
- *Last Saved.* Lists the date when the file was last saved.
- *Created.* Lists the date when the file was created.

► "Changing Save Options," p. 182

Using Summary View

If you completed Summary Info sheets for your documents, you can use that information to search for files. When you display a file in summary view, Find File shows summary information as well as date saved, number of revisions, document size, and so on. Figure 7.13 shows a document in summary view.

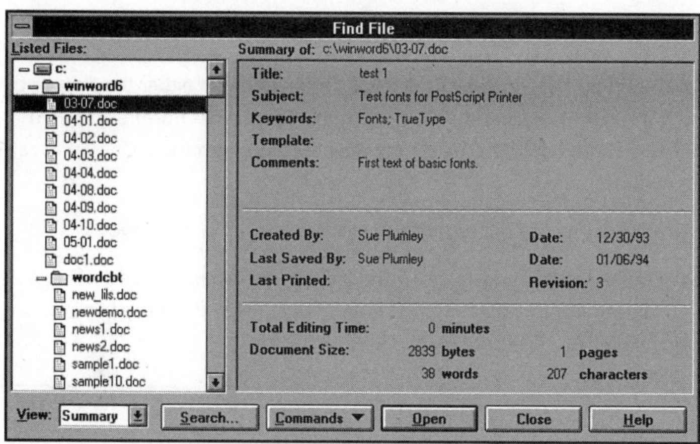

Fig. 7.13
You can review Summary Info to see whether the file is the one you want before you open it.

The **L**isted Files list box in summary view is the same as in preview view. The drive, directory, and files fit the search criteria. When you select a file, information about that file appears in the Summary Of area. The name and location of the file follow Summary Of. The following list describes the information shown in the Summary Of area:

- *Summary Info.* The first section lists the title, subject, keywords, template, and comments entered in the Summary Info sheet. Only information in the Summary Info sheet appears in this section; if you did not fill out the sheet, only a title appears in this area.
- *Creation.* The second section lists the author and creation date, the person who last revised the document and the revision date, the last date when the file was printed, and the number of revisions in the file.
- *Editing and Size.* The third section lists the total editing time and the document size in bytes, words, pages, and characters.

Tip
If you need to add or edit summary information, select the file in summary view and then choose **C**ommands **S**ummary. Enter any summary information you want to save to your document.

Troubleshooting

In the top right corner of the Find File dialog box, I see a small icon that looks like a floppy disk drive containing a spinning disk. What is it?

This icon appears while Word is updating information in the Find File dialog box. When the icon disappears, the information is up to date, and you can continue your work.

I want to copy or delete several files at one time.

Select the files you want to copy or delete by holding down either the Shift or the Ctrl key as you click the various files. Choose the **C**ommands button, and then choose either the **C**opy or the **D**elete command, to perform the action on all selected files at one time.

I want to print several files at one time without opening and printing each file.

Select the files by holding down either the Shift or the Ctrl key while clicking each file. Then choose **C**ommands **P**rint. Find File prints the documents while you continue your work.

Working in Find File

Find File provides quick, easy file management within the Word program. Using the command buttons in the Find File dialog box, you can manage and organize files as well as find the file you want to open. When you manage files with Find File, you can delete and copy files without the hassle of switching to Program Manager and then to Windows File Manager or DOS.

This section describes some of the intricacies of managing files in Find File.

Sorting Files

When you use the Sor**t**ing command, you can sort and display files by author, creation or revision date, file name, or file size. In addition, you can display either the file name or the title of the file as the file list.

Figure 7.14 shows the Options dialog box that appears when you use the Sor**t**ing command.

To use the Sor**t**ing command while in the Find File dialog box, follow these steps:

1. In the **V**iew drop-down list, choose **V**iew File Info.

2. Choose **C**ommands Sor**t**ing. The Options dialog box appears.

3. In the Sort Files By area, select an option. Alternatively, you can choose to list files by **T**itle; the default is **F**ilename.

4. Choose OK to close the dialog box and return to the Find File dialog box.

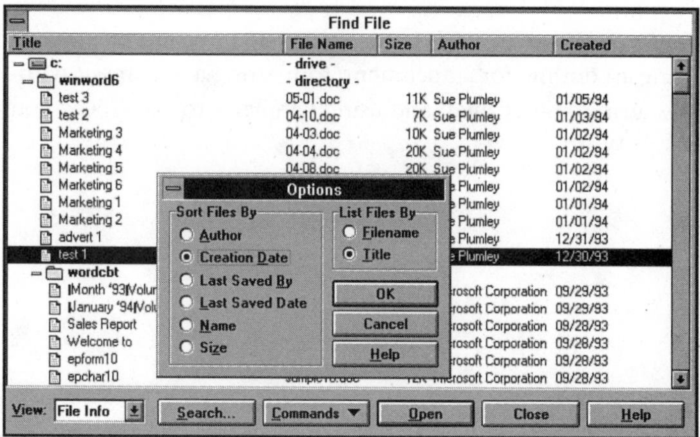

Fig. 7.14
Use this dialog box to sort and list files in any way that makes it easier for you to find the file you want.

Tip
The files remain sorted in this manner each time you open the Find File dialog box until you choose the **C**ommands **S**orting command and change the sort order.

Selecting Files

No matter which view you use in the Find File dialog box, you must select files before you can delete, print, or copy them. Use the mouse to select one or several files. You can perform an action on several files by selecting them, choosing the **C**ommands button, and then choosing the command from the drop-down menu.

To select several files in a row, click the first file, press and hold down the Shift key, and then click the last file. To select several files that are not in sequence, click the first file, press and hold down the Ctrl key, and then click the other files individually.

After you select the files, choose the **C**ommands command button and then choose **C**opy, **D**elete, or **P**rint.

From Here...

You can use Word's Find File program to organize and manage your files without the inconvenience of leaving Word to use Windows' File Manager.

Find File enables you to search for specific files; sort a list of files; and delete, copy, or print one or several files without leaving Find File.

For related information, see the following chapters:

- Chapter 8, "Customizing Word," covers how to modify and alter Word's default settings to better suit your working style, including viewing, editing, printing, and spelling and grammar options.
- Chapter 9, "Working with Large Documents," covers creating and editing an outline for a document, formatting a document with styles, using AutoFormat, and using templates to help speed your work in Word.

Chapter 8

Customizing Word

by Susan Plumley

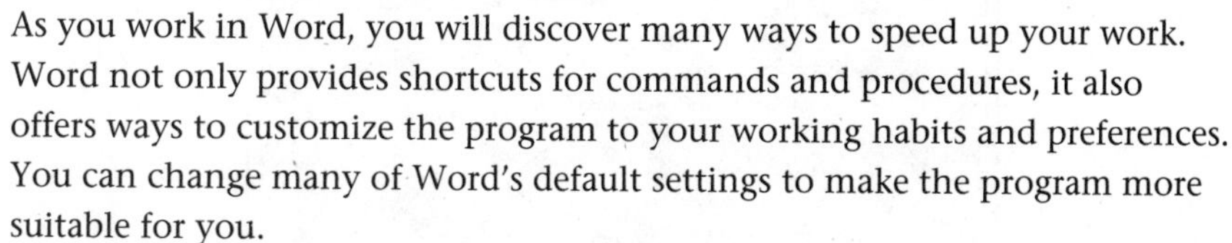

As you work in Word, you will discover many ways to speed up your work. Word not only provides shortcuts for commands and procedures, it also offers ways to customize the program to your working habits and preferences. You can change many of Word's default settings to make the program more suitable for you.

Ways of customizing Word include changing measurement units, selecting various grammar and style rules for the grammar checker, instructing Word to create backup copies automatically, and prompting for summary information. In addition, you can change the default file locations, such as the location of documents, clip art, and templates.

In this chapter, you learn to

- Change the default location to a directory you create for document files
- Modify User Info to place your company's name and address automatically in the return-address area of envelopes
- Set save options
- Establish spelling- and grammar-checking options
- Select printing options
- Establish editing options

Customizing Options

Word provides various methods for customizing the program to meet your needs. Using the **T**ools **O**ptions command, you can modify Word's default settings—the predetermined selections Word makes when you install the program. When you install Word, for example, the program automatically displays the status bar and the scroll bars on-screen. You can change this default setting. When you change any option in the Options dialog box, that option then applies to all documents and incidences until you change the option again.

You can change Word's default settings in two ways. One way is to choose the **T**ools **O**ptions command, which displays 12 tabs containing options for customizing. Figure 8.1 shows the Options dialog box.

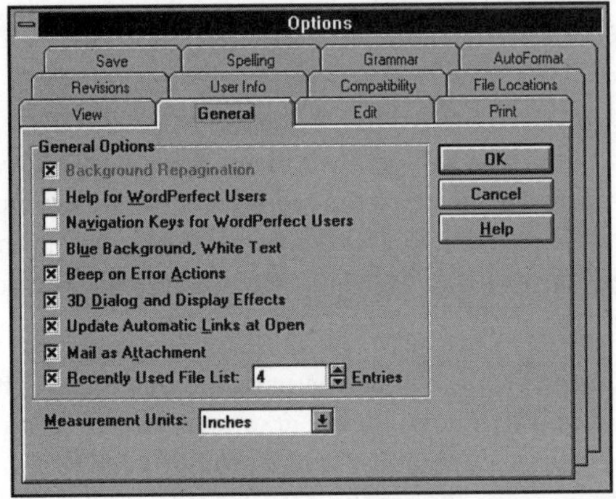

Fig. 8.1
The Options dialog box enables you to modify several options at one time.

Tip
Other dialog boxes that include the **O**ptions command button include Print, Spelling, and Grammar.

Alternatively, you can customize specific options in certain dialog boxes. The Save As dialog box, for example, includes the **O**ptions command button, shown in figure 8.2. When you choose the **O**ptions command button in any dialog box, the Options dialog box appears; all tabs except the applicable one are dimmed and, thus, unavailable.

To customize various options in Word, follow these steps:

1. Choose **T**ools **O**ptions. The Options dialog box appears.
2. Select the tab or tabs representing the options you want to modify.
3. Make your changes.
4. When you finish, choose OK to close the dialog box.

To customize specific options from a dialog box, follow these steps:

1. Choose the **O**ptions command button in the dialog box. The Options dialog box appears, with only one tab available.

2. Make your changes.

3. When you finish, choose OK to close the Options dialog box and return to the preceding dialog box.

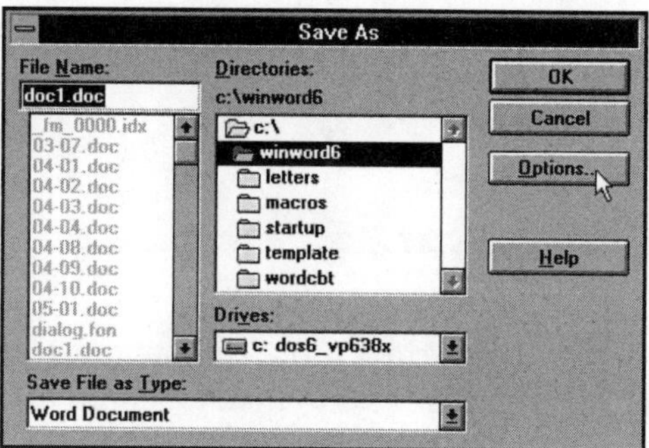

Fig. 8.2
You can modify options in a dialog box before you complete the command.

> **Note**
>
> Options that show an X in the check box are activated. If you select an option with an X in the check box, you deactivate that option. Selecting an option with no X in the check box activates that option and places an X in the box.

The following section briefly describes each option in the General tab.

Changing General Settings

The General tab in the Options dialog box includes options that affect the common operations of Word. You can select one, several, or all the options in the General Options area. The following list describes these options:

- ***B**ackground Repagination.* Background Repagination governs how Word deals with page breaks as you enter or edit text. When the option is on, Word automatically adjusts the text on each page as you type. **B**ackground Repagination is on all the time in page layout view and print preview; you cannot turn it off in either view. You can turn this option off in normal and outline views, however.

- *Help for **W**ordPerfect Users.* When you select this option, Word helps you make the shift from WordPerfect for DOS to Word for Windows. Each time you press a WordPerfect key combination, Word displays information or demonstrates a command. Figure 8.3 shows a Help dialog box that appears when you press Shift+F7, for example.

Tip
When you turn **B**ackground Repagination off, you may notice a slight increase in the program's speed and efficiency.

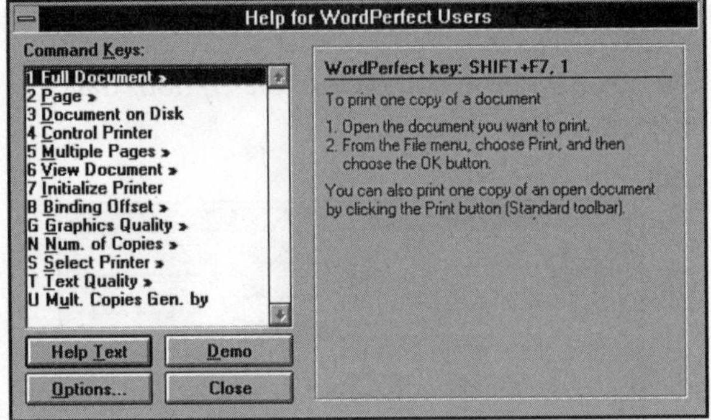

Fig. 8.3
In WordPerfect, Shift+F7 prints a document. This Help dialog box describes how to print in Word, and offers options, more help, and a demonstration.

- *Na**v**igation Keys for WordPerfect Users.* This option modifies the PgUp, PgDn, Home, End, and Esc keys to their functions in WordPerfect.

- *Bl**u**e Background, White Text.* This option changes the Word screen's background to blue and the text to white.

- *Beep On Error **A**ctions.* By default, Word beeps when you make an error or perform a wrong action, such as clicking outside a dialog box. This option governs whether the program beeps to warn you of an error.

- *3-D **D**ialog and Display Effects.* Changes the display from the default—gray dialog boxes with a three-dimensional appearance—to plain white dialog boxes.

▶ "Using Common Steps To Link Documents," p. 789

- *Update Automatic **L**inks at Open.* If you have included links in your document, using object linking and embedding (OLE), this option automatically updates data added to other files when you open your document in Word. It's a good idea to keep the Update Automatic **L**inks at Open option activated if you use Microsoft Office to its full capacity.

▶ "Starting Mail and Addressing the Message," p. 814

- *Mail as A**t**tachment.* This option connects a document to a message that is to be sent via a mail program, such as Microsoft Mail. This option works only if a mail program is installed.

- ***R**ecently Used File List.* This option enables Word to display the most recently used files at the end of the **F**ile menu. You must enter the number of files (0 to 9) to be displayed in the **E**ntries text box. Figure 8.4 shows the **F**ile menu listing the last four files opened.

- ***M**easurement Units.* This option governs the default unit of measurement in Word. The unit you specify—inches, picas, points, or centimeters—is the unit of measurement that appears in dialog boxes and in the rulers.

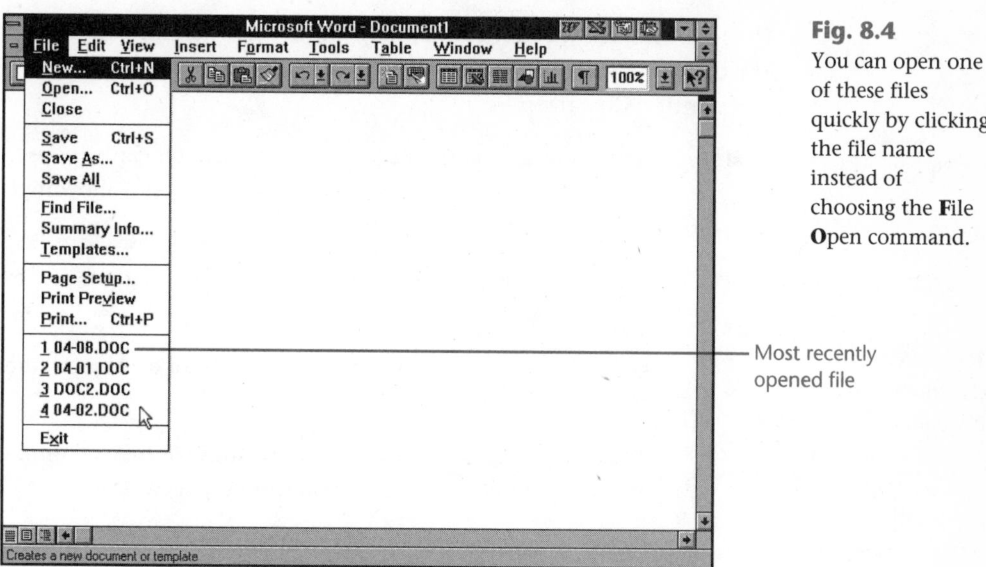

Fig. 8.4
You can open one of these files quickly by clicking the file name instead of choosing the **F**ile **O**pen command.

Modifying Viewing Options

View options represent another tab in the Options dialog box. Using the View tab, you can specify whether to show or hide Window elements, nonprinting characters, and various other components of Word.

◄ "Viewing the Document," p. 120

The options you can customize vary slightly from view to view. For example, you can hide or show the vertical ruler in page layout view; but, because there is no vertical ruler in normal view, that option is available only in page layout view. To set the options for a certain view, change to that view before opening the Options dialog box. Figure 8.5 shows the View tab for page layout view.

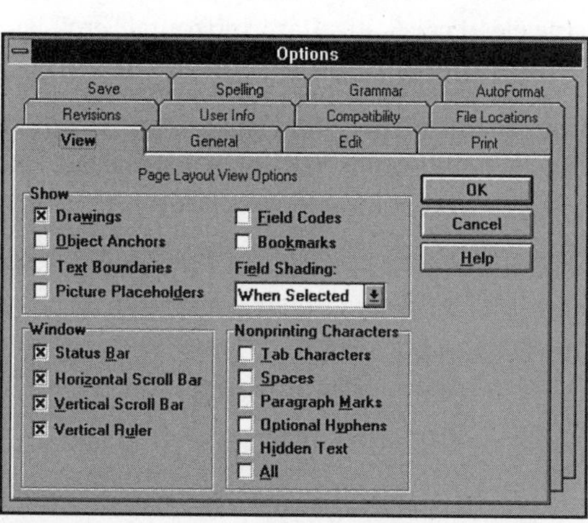

Fig. 8.5
Use the View tab of the Options dialog box to select the screen and window elements you want to view.

The following list describes the options in the View tab for page layout view. The options are divided into three categories: Show, Window, and Nonprinting Characters.

- *Show*. The Show area contains several elements you can choose to hide (no X in the check box) or show (X in the check box). Following is a brief description of each option:

  Drawings. Drawings include clip art, imported art, or pictures you create in Word.

  Object Anchors. Show or hide the anchors for all objects, including spreadsheets, charts, and graphs.

  Text Boundaries. Select this option to show or hide column guides and section marks that help you format pages.

  Picture Placeholders. If selected, this option displays empty frames that show picture placement to save memory and speed scrolling throughout the document.

  Field Codes. Shows or hides the field-code names when a field is inserted into the document.

  Bookmarks. Select this option to view bookmarks in the document; it's especially useful to show bookmarks when you want to edit them.

  Field Shading. Select this option to add shading to a field. Shading makes fields easier to find in a large document.

Tip
Use the Picture Placeholder option to quickly print a proof without pictures or to speed up screen redraw.

▶ "Adding Field Names to Your Letter," p. 836

- *Window*. This area enables you to specify which window elements appear on-screen and which elements are hidden. You can hide or show the following elements: Status **B**ar, Hori**z**ontal Scroll Bar, **V**ertical Scroll Bar, and Vertical R**u**ler (in page layout view).
- *Nonprinting Characters*. This option enables you to show or hide any of the following nonprinting characters: **T**ab Characters, **S**paces, Paragraph **M**arks, Optional H**y**phens, H**i**dden Text, or **A**ll.
- *Draft Font* (outline and normal views). This option displays character formatting—such as 24-point Times Roman—as 12-point, underlined, and bold. Graphics are displayed as empty boxes for fast screen redraw.
- *Wrap To Windows* (outline and normal views). This option wraps the text from one line to the next within the document window for easier viewing.

- *Style Area Width* (outline and normal views). This option shows or hides the area at the left side of the document that lists the applied styles.

▶ "Formatting with Styles," p. 196

Changing Editing Options

The Edit tab of the Options dialog box enables you to change such options as use of the Ins key, how overtype mode works, and whether typing replaces selection. Figure 8.6 shows the Edit tab in the Options dialog box.

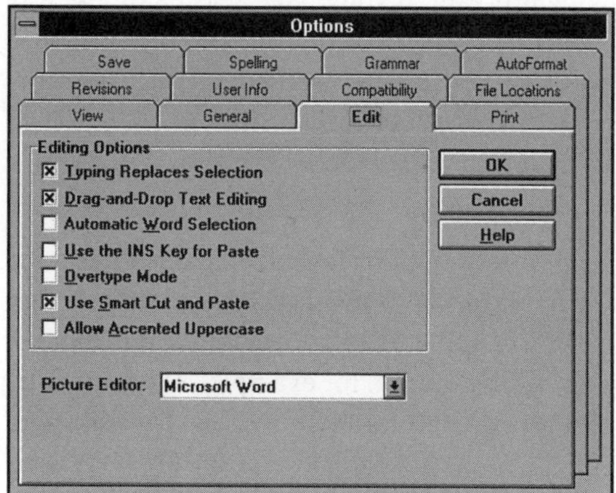

Fig. 8.6
Modify the editing settings by specifying whether to use drag-and-drop editing and whether to remove spaces during a cut-and-paste procedure.

The following list describes the Edit tab's options:

- *Typing Replaces Selection.* If selected, this option deletes the selected text as you type new text.
- *Drag-and-Drop Text Editing.* Drag-and-drop is a method of editing text without cutting, copying, or pasting. When this option is activated, you can select the text and then click and drag the selection to another location in the document.
- *Automatic Word Selection.* This option selects the entire word when you select part of it. If this option is activated, you cannot drag the I-beam pointer across one character in a word and select only that character: the whole word is selected.
- *Use the INS Key for Paste.* This option enables you to paste items from the Clipboard by pressing the Ins key.
- *Overtype Mode.* When selected, this option replaces existing text as you type, one character at a time.

- *Use **S**mart Cut and Paste.* This option removes unneeded spaces when you delete text and adds spaces when you add text.

- *Allow **A**ccented Uppercase.* This option suggests that Word add an accent mark to uppercase letters formatted as French.

▶ "Working with Graphics," p. 219

- ***P**icture Editor.* Use the drop-down list to specify the program Word displays when you edit a picture. If, for example, you double-click an imported clip-art graphic, Word's default Picture Editor selection is the Word drawing program. If you prefer, select a different program in the drop-down list, such as PowerPoint Presentation or PowerPoint Slide. For more information about PowerPoint, see Chapter 19, "Getting Acquainted with PowerPoint."

Customizing Printing

◀ "Printing Documents," p. 87

◀ "Printing a Document," p. 150

The Print tab offers various options for printing documents, including how the documents print and what elements print. As with any option in this dialog box, your choices apply to all documents and instances. If you select **D**raft Output as a printing option, for example, all documents printed from this point on will print in draft form.

Figure 8.7 shows the Print tab of the Options dialog box.

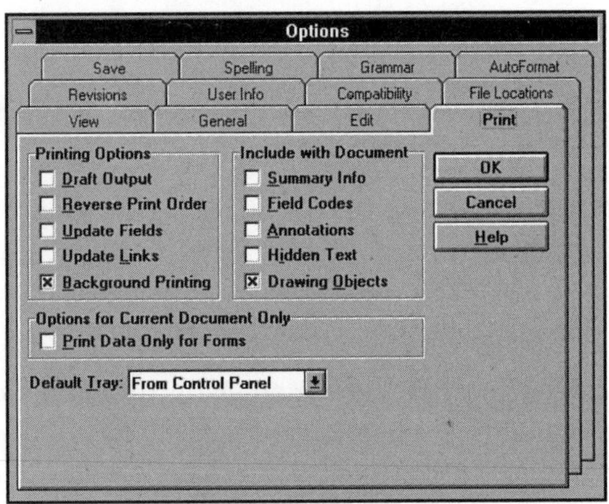

Fig. 8.7
In the Print tab, select options that affect all documents you print.

The following list describes the options in the Print tab:

- *Printing Options.* Offers various choices for printing:

  ***D**raft Output.* Prints a copy of your document for proofreading. Depending on your printer, graphics and pictures may not print.

***R**everse Print Order.* Changes the page-printing order—3, 2, 1 instead of 1, 2, 3, for example.

Update Fields. Revises fields (codes that instruct Word to insert elements into the document automatically) in the document before printing.

► "Adding Field Names to Your Letter," p. 836

*Update **L**inks.* Brings links (information created in another document and connected with the Word document) up to date before printing.

► "Embedding and Linking Objects," p. 713

***B**ackground Printing.* Documents print in the background so you can continue your work.

- *Include with Document.* Prints additional information with your document: **S**ummary Info, **F**ield Codes in place of field results, **A**nnotations on a separate page, H**i**dden Text, and Drawing **O**bjects.
- *Options for Current Document Only.* Contains only one option: **P**rint Data Only for Forms. This option applies only to the active document and pertains only to an on-line or preprinted form. If you select **P**rint Data Only for Forms, Word prints only the input for a form instead of the input and the actual form lines and text.
- *Default **T**ray.* Identifies the paper source (tray).

Changing Revisions Options

The Revisions tab governs the display of revision marks. You can select different options for inserted text, deleted text, and revised lines. *Inserted text* is text that has been added to the original text; *deleted text* has been erased from the original; and *revised lines* describes how Word will mark all lines of text that have been modified in any way.

Tip
You usually use revision marks when more than one person works on a document and you need to see what has been added, deleted, and modified.

Each area offers similar options (but with different hot keys) and shows the results in the Preview box. Figure 8.8 shows the Revisions tab of the Option dialog box.

The following list describes the Revisions options:

- *Inserted Text.* This area enables you to specify the **M**ark Word uses to identify added text: no mark, underline, bold, italic, or double underline. Additionally, you can specify a C**o**lor to help identify the added text.

Fig. 8.8
Select different marks for each area so you can tell inserted text from deleted or revised text.

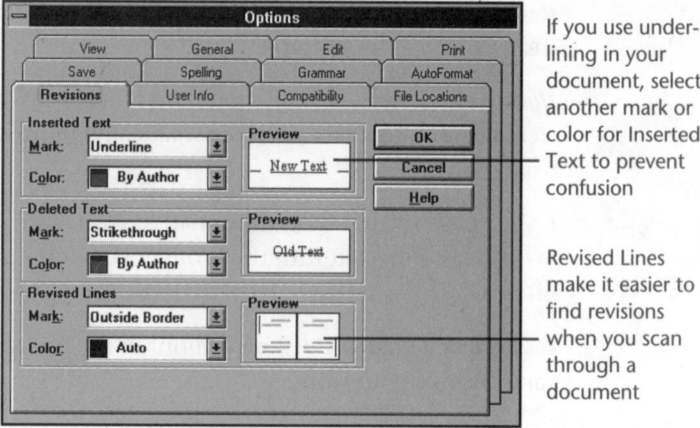

Tip
If you choose to mark deleted text as hidden text, use the View tab of the Options dialog box to show the hidden text.

- *Deleted Text.* You can M**a**rk text that has been deleted from the document with either Strikethrough or Hidden Text format. Additionally, you can choose a Co**l**or to mark the text.
- *Revised Lines.* You can Mar**k** lines of text that have been altered with a vertical border at the left margin, right margin, or (for odd and even pages) outside margin. You also can specify a Colo**r** for the border.
- *Preview.* A Preview box appears beside each area so you can see the results of your choices before closing the dialog box.

Modifying User Info

◀ "Printing Envelopes," p. 151

▶ "Attaching Word, Excel, or PowerPoint Files to Your Message," p. 827

The User Info tab of the Options dialog box lists the name that was entered when Word was installed. The name may be yours, the name of the person who installed the program, and/or your company's name. The name entered when Word was installed also is the name that appears in the **M**ailing Address text box. The information in the **M**ailing Address text box is inserted automatically into the Return Address text box in the Envelopes tab of the Envelopes and Labels dialog box.

Other information in the User Info tab is used elsewhere in Word. Name is used as the author in Summary Info records, and Initials are used to identify the person who entered annotation marks.

You easily can change the **N**ame, **I**nitials, and **M**ailing Address text boxes in the User Info tab. Figure 8.9 shows the User Info tab.

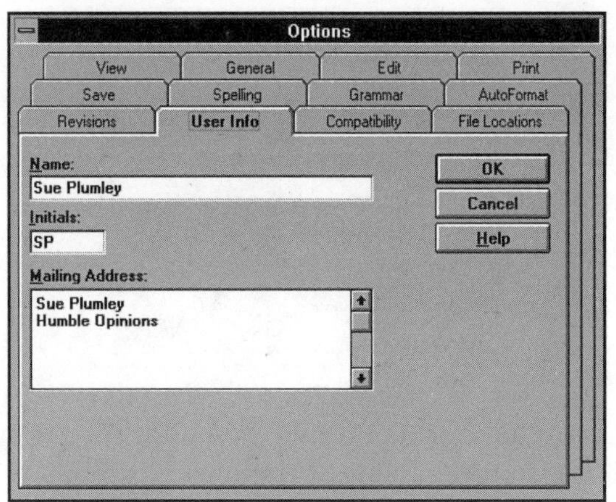

Fig. 8.9
Enter a name and address in the Mailing Address text box, and that address appears as the return address any time you use the Envelopes and Labels dialog box in Word.

Changing File Locations

To change the location of document files, clip-art files, templates and so on, use the File Locations tab of the Options dialog box. Suppose that you want to create a Document directory within the WINWORD directory so you can save specific documents in one place. Use this tab to direct saved documents to the new directory automatically. Figure 8.10 shows the File Locations tab.

◄ "Saving, Closing, and Opening a Document," p. 114

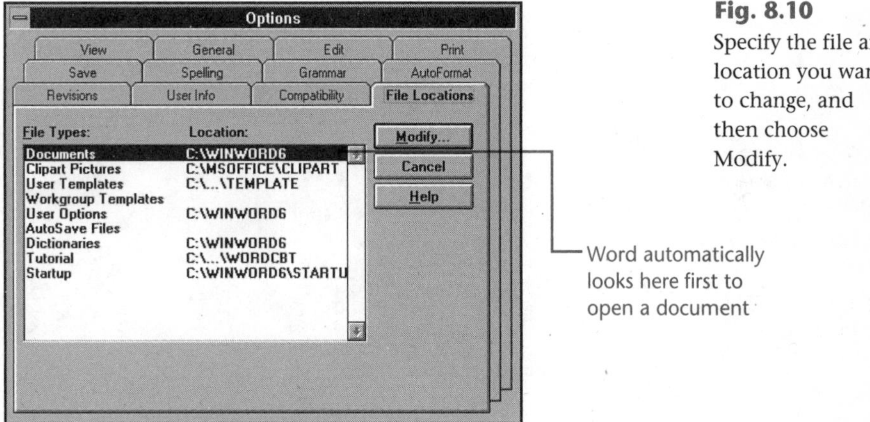

Fig. 8.10
Specify the file and location you want to change, and then choose Modify.

To change the location for specific files, follow these steps:

1. In the File Locations tab, select the **F**ile Types you want to relocate.

2. Choose the **M**odify button. The Modify Location dialog box appears (see fig. 8.11).

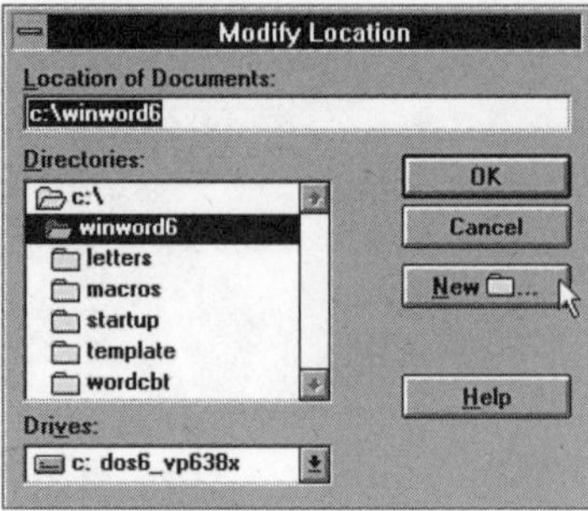

Fig. 8.11
Enter a new location for the documents in the Location of Documents text box, or select a new location from the Directories list; you can even add a new directory, if need be.

3. Select the new directory in the **D**irectories list, enter the path of the new directory in the **L**ocation of Documents text box, or choose the **N**ew button to create a new directory.

4. Choose OK to close the Modify Location dialog box and return to the File Locations tab.

Changing Save Options

◀ "Saving, Opening, and Closing Files," p. 72

The options available in the Save tab affect how and when Word saves your document. In addition, you can add a protection device, such as a password, to specific documents.

Figure 8.12 shows the Save tab of the Options dialog box.

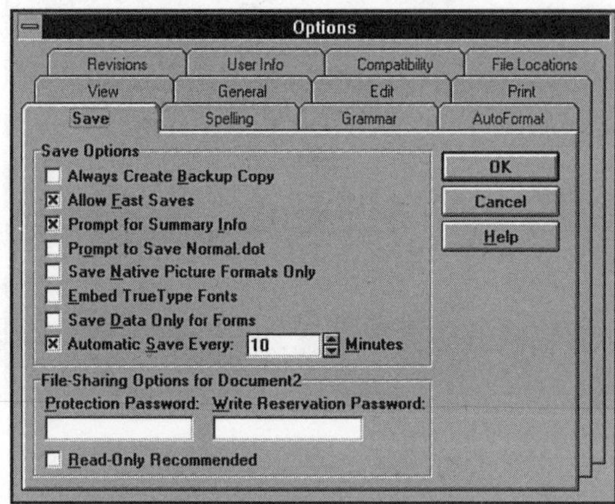

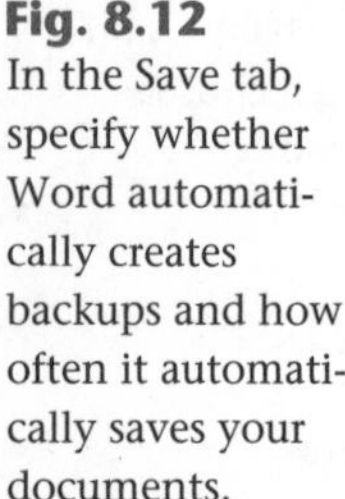

Fig. 8.12
In the Save tab, specify whether Word automatically creates backups and how often it automatically saves your documents.

The following list describes the options in the Save tab:

- *Save Options*. This area provides options for saving your documents and certain elements of those documents:

*Always Create **B**ackup Copy*. Select this option to tell Word to create a copy of each document you create.

*Allow **F**ast Saves*. Activate this option to save only the changes to your document.

*Prompt for Summary **I**nfo*. Select this option to display the Summary Info dialog box each time you save a new document.

*Pr**o**mpt To Save Normal.dot*. When activated, this option warns you when you have changed the Normal template by displaying a message to save changes. You may want to save the changes to the template; if you do not, however, selecting this option gives you an out.

◀ "Creating Summary Info Records," p. 155

*Save **N**ative Picture Formats Only*. This option saves imported graphics in the Windows version only. If you import a graphic from a Macintosh program, for example, you can save disk space by saving the graphic only in the native picture format (Windows version) instead of in the Macintosh format.

***E**mbed TrueType Fonts*. This option implants TrueType fonts in the document so that the fonts display correctly, even if the document is being used on a computer that does not support TrueType fonts.

*Save **D**ata Only for Forms*. This option saves the data in a form as a single record for use in a database.

*Automatic **S**ave Every*. Select this option to tell Word to save your document automatically; set the interval in the **M**inutes text box.

Note

Use the Automatic **S**ave Every option all the time so that if a power failure occurs, Word recovers the document when you restart the program. Word then prompts you to save, delete, or continue to work on the saved version of your document. The amount of time you set for automatic save depends on how critical the document is and on personal preference.

- *File-Sharing Options for Document1*. Select the following protection options for the current document:

Protection Password. Enter a password (up to 12 characters) to keep other users from opening the document. Word displays an asterisk for each character you enter; so *you* must remember your password; you cannot open a password-protected file without the password.

Write Reservation Password. This option permits anyone to open the document, but only users who know the password can modify or edit the document. Enter a password, and then choose OK. Word prompts you for confirmation; enter the password and choose OK again.

- *Read-Only Recommended.* This option means that when the document is opened, Word suggests that the document be opened as read-only. The reader can open the document either way. If the document is opened as read-only, no changes can be made in the document; the document is available only for reading, not for alteration.

◄ "Checking Spelling," p. 140

Changing Spelling Options

Although Word's spelling dictionary is sufficient for most documents, you may have a special need for a medical, legal, or foreign-language dictionary. You can add a third-party dictionary for use with Word by using the Spelling tab in the Options dialog box. Additionally, you can customize other options that handle the spelling checker.

Figure 8.13 shows the Spelling tab with Word's custom dictionary and a third-party Spanish dictionary added.

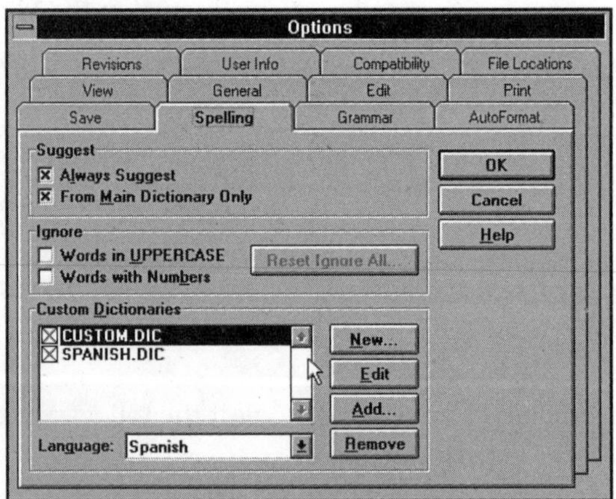

Fig. 8.13
You can add a custom dictionary—even a foreign-language dictionary—in the Spelling tab.

The following list describes the options in the Spelling tab:

- *Suggest.* This area handles the suggestions Word offers for misspelled words during a spelling check. You can select either or both options:

  Always Suggest. If this option is selected, Word displays a list of likely candidates to replace the misspelled word.

  From Main Dictionary Only. This option limits Word's suggestions to the main dictionary. If you have another dictionary in which the word may appear, such as a legal dictionary, do not select this option.

- *Ignore.* You can ignore all Words in UPPERCASE and/or Words with Numbers. A third option in this area—Reset Ignore All—returns the Ignore All list to its original state. Thereafter, Word again questions any words for which you used the Ignore All command earlier in the session.

- *Custom Dictionaries.* This option displays all installed dictionaries; you can select up to 10 for use during any session. Within this area are several more options:

  New. This option creates a new custom dictionary.

  Edit. This option opens the selected dictionary so you can edit it.

  Add. This option adds a third-party dictionary from another location.

  Remove. This option deletes a dictionary from the list, but not from your disk.

  Language. When you are using a custom dictionary, select the language in the drop-down list to apply special formatting for that language. Make sure that the correct custom dictionary is selected.

Customizing Grammar Options

Word enables you to select various grammar rules and styles of writing for checking the grammar in your documents. The default style is business writing. You also can choose a stricter style or an informal writing style, or create your own custom styles. Additionally, you can review the grammar rules used with a specific style and even deactivate some of those rules.

◄ "Checking Grammar," p. 145

Figure 8.14 shows the Grammar tab of the Options dialog box.

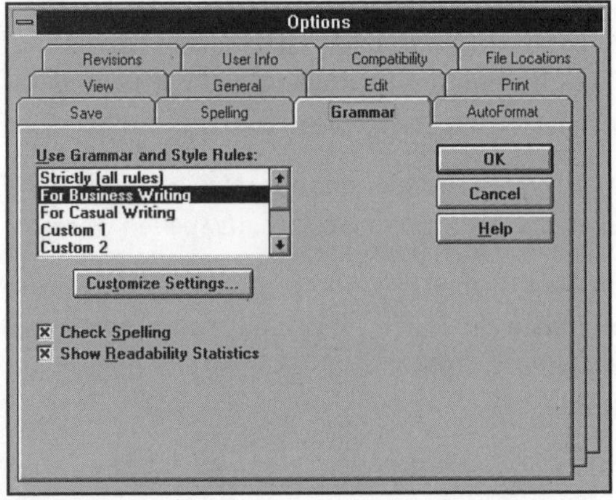

Fig. 8.14 Select the style you want the Grammar Checker to use when checking your documents, or customize the settings by selecting your own rules.

Note

To view all grammar and style rules attached to the highlighted item in the **U**se Grammar and Style rules list box, choose the Cus**t**omize Settings button. In the Customize Grammar Settings dialog box, choose either the **G**rammar button or the **S**tyle button, and scroll through the list of rules. You can choose the **E**xplain button for further information about any rule. Choose OK to exit the dialog box.

When you specify grammar and style rules, you can select options from the following categories in the **U**se Grammar and Style Rules drop-down list:

- *Strictly (All Rules).* This option applies all grammar and style rules, including checking for clichés and checking for quoted text, homonyms, jargon, pretentious words, redundant expressions, and so on.
- *For Business Writing.* This option includes all grammar rules, but leaves out the style rules mentioned for Strictly, plus a few more.
- *For Casual Writing.* This option, which is informal in both grammar and style rules, leaves out three grammar rules: format errors, informal usage, and jargon words. In addition, this option leaves out about half the style rules.
- *Custom 1, Custom 2,* or *Custom 3.* You can create your own set of rules by selecting one of these options and then choosing the Cus**t**omize Settings button. The Customize Grammar Settings dialog box appears (see fig. 8.15). All the check boxes are marked when this dialog box opens; you uncheck the rules you do not want to use. When you finish, choose OK to close the dialog box and return to the Grammar tab.

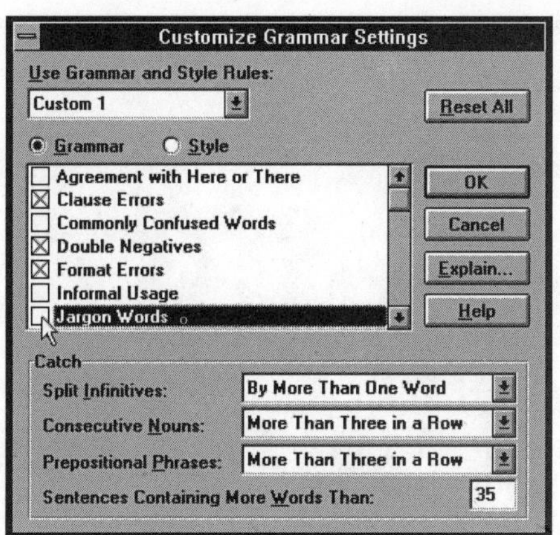

Fig. 8.15
Specify which grammar and style rules you want the Grammar Checker to follow by creating your own custom options in the Customize Grammar Settings dialog box.

In addition to choosing grammar and style rules, you can specify whether you want Word to Check Spelling while checking the grammar and whether to Show Readability Statistics. The Readability Statistics dialog box displays the number of words, characters, paragraphs, and sentences in the document and the average number of sentences per paragraph, words per sentence, and characters per word. In addition, the dialog box shows readability indexes based on the average number of syllables per word and average number of words per sentence. These readability indexes are Reading Ease and Grade Level values.

Additionally, the Catch area of the Customize Grammar Settings dialog box enables you to specify when Word should catch (alert you to) split infinitives, consecutive nouns, prepositional phrases, and long sentences. You can select options for each of these settings; for example, you can catch split infinitives always, by more than one word, two words, three words, or never. Also, you can limit the number of words a sentence can contain—15, 30, or 40, for example.

Changing AutoFormat Options

AutoFormat is a formatting tool within Word that automatically applies built-in styles and a template to your document. You can select various options for AutoFormat to apply. Figure 8.16 shows the AutoFormat tab of the Options dialog box.

▶ "Formatting with Styles," p. 196

The following list describes the options in the AutoFormat tab:

- *Preserve*. This area has only one option: Previously Applied **S**tyles. Select this option to keep any styles you have already assigned within your document.

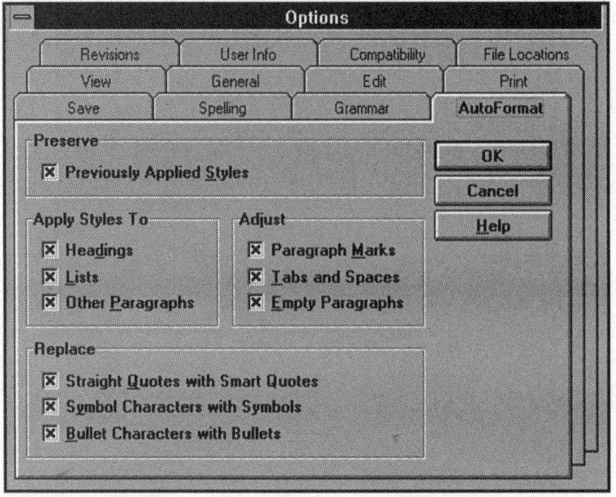

Fig. 8.16
Select the options you want AutoFormat to apply when formatting your documents.

Tip
To use AutoFormat, choose the F**o**rmat **A**utoFormat command. For more information, see Chapter 9, "Working with Large Documents."

- *Apply Styles To.* Select the types of text to which you want to assign the styles: Hea**d**ings, **L**ists, and Other **P**aragraphs (such as subheads, tabs, and indented text).
- *Adjust.* Select the elements you want Word to fit to the style: Paragraph **M**arks, **T**abs and Spaces, and **E**mpty Paragraphs. When adjusting these elements, Word may take extra spaces or tabs out, remove extra blank lines, and so on.
- *Replace.* Select the elements you want to substitute: Straight **Q**uotes with Smart Quotes (also called open and closed quotes), S**y**mbol Characters with Symbols (replaces *TM*, for example, with ™), and **B**ullet Characters with Bullets (replaces the plus sign or asterisk with bullets that your printer can print).

From Here...

You can customize many Word settings to speed up your work and increase efficiency. You can change spelling and grammar options, file locations, editing choices, and more. Setting the options to suit your preferences and work habits makes the program all the more beneficial and useful.

You learn even more about the Word program in the following chapters:

- Chapter 9, "Working with Large Documents," covers outlining documents and editing the outline, formatting text with styles, using AutoFormat to speed up your work, and using templates.
- Chapter 10, "Working with Tables, Charts, and Graphics," covers creating and editing tables, producing and modifying charts, and adding lines, borders, and pictures to your documents.

Chapter 9

Working with Large Documents

by Susan Plumley

When you are producing a document that contains many pages—from ten or fifteen to hundreds—you need special organizational and managerial techniques. Word provides several features that help you manage long documents. (You can use these features for short documents as well.)

In this chapter, you learn to

- Create an outline by using Word's outline view and Outline toolbar
- Edit an outline by rearranging text and headings
- Use Word's built-in styles to format the text in a document
- Use AutoFormat and Style Gallery to have Word format a document for you
- Create and edit your own styles
- Use template wizards to format your documents

One organizational feature you can use in a large document is *outlining*. Word provides special outlining features, including an outline view that helps you order your text. You can arrange headings and text, move headings to new positions in the outline, and print the outline as you work on it.

Word also provides document-formatting methods that make your work easier. You can use *styles*—preformatted fonts and paragraph attributes—to format your documents quickly and to guarantee consistency within the document.

Word offers a variety of techniques and processes to help you work with large documents. This chapter introduces many of those techniques.

Outlining a Document

When creating a large document, use an outline and outline view to get an overview of how the document is put together. You can also easily rearrange headings and text to better suit the flow of information. Finally, use outlining in long documents to quickly move to a specific location and then view the text.

To outline a document, you assign headings to the text to signify different levels of topic development. You can create up to nine different levels of text, including body text. Word formats and indents each level so you can organize the text quickly. The headings remain formatted in other views as well, although the indents appear.

Figure 9.1 shows an initial outline for a document. This sample outline contains three levels of headings. As you enter more headings and body text, you can format the text, arrange the headings, and move text around to better organize the document.

Word provides an outline view in which you can organize your documents. Outline view provides an Outline toolbar (see fig. 9.1) that enables you to assign headings to your text, hide body text or headings, and rearrange your outline. You can outline an existing document or create a new document in outline view.

Following is a brief description of each of the tools in the Outline toolbar:

- *Promote.* Elevates a heading to a higher level.
- *Demote.* Reduces a heading to a lower level.
- *Demote to Body Text.* Reduces the heading to body text.
- *Move Up.* Repositions the selected heading up one line in the outline.
- *Move Down.* Repositions the selected heading down one line in the outline.
- *Expand.* Shows subheadings and body text under selected heading.
- *Collapse.* Hides subheadings and body text under selected heading.

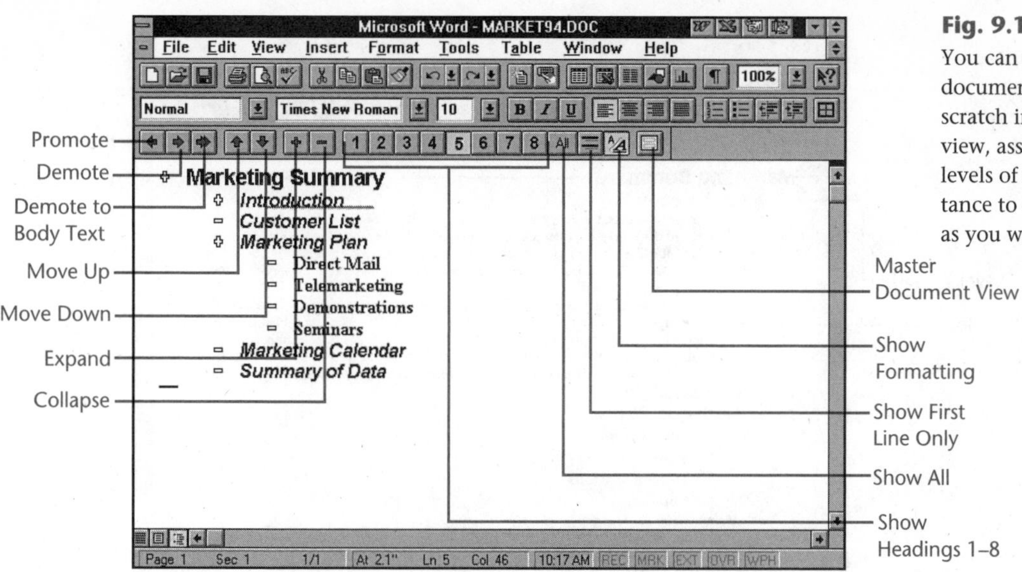

Fig. 9.1
You can plan a document from scratch in outline view, assigning levels of importance to headings as you write.

- *Show Headings 1 through 8.* Expands or collapses the outline to a specific level.
- *Show All.* Expands or collapses the entire outline.
- *Show First Line Only.* Shows all body text or only the first line.
- *Show Formatting.* Shows or hides character formatting.

Creating an Outline

You create an outline by entering, formatting, and assigning headings in Word's outline view. The view provides helpful features that you use as you organize your document. After creating your outline, you easily can change heading levels, add text, and otherwise edit your document by using the Outline toolbar and other features of outline view.

Tip
To change to outline view, simply click the third page button from the left in the horizontal scroll bar.

Viewing the Outline

To start the outline, choose the **V**iew **O**utline command. In outline view, use the Outline toolbar to specify various levels of headings and body text. Word indents each heading and its text, and formats the text for you. Outline view also includes the Outline toolbar (see fig. 9.2).

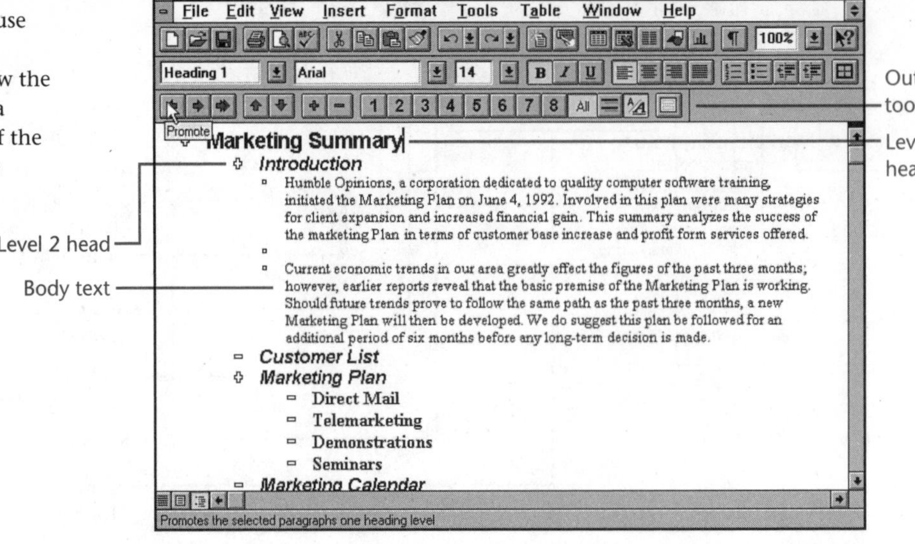

Fig. 9.2
Place the mouse pointer on a button to view the ToolTip and a description of the button in the status bar.

Note

You can reformat any text formats easily by using styles. For more information, see "Formatting with Styles" later in this chapter.

Entering Text

◄ "Viewing the Document," p. 120

◄ "Entering Text," p. 106

◄ "Formatting Text," p. 124

You can enter text as you normally would by typing paragraphs, heading text, and so on in normal, page layout, or outline view. You can assign Heading styles to existing text by using the Formatting toolbar.

The Formatting toolbar includes a drop-down list of styles (see fig. 9.3). Heading 1 style is used for the broadest topics; Heading 2 is used for the subdivisions of Heading 1 topics; and so on.

Alternatively, you can designate outline levels as you enter text. Simply select a style from the drop-down list and type the heading. Then change the style, if necessary, and type the next heading or body text (Normal is the same as the body text style; see the section "Formatting with Styles," later in this chapter).

Selecting Text

Outline view provides a slightly different method of selecting text than do the other views. Each paragraph of text, whether that text is a heading or body text, is preceded by a plus sign (+) or a minus sign (–). If you position the mouse pointer on one of these symbols, the pointer changes to a four-headed arrow. When the pointer changes shape, simply click the plus sign or minus sign to select the associated paragraph and any lower-level headings and body text below it.

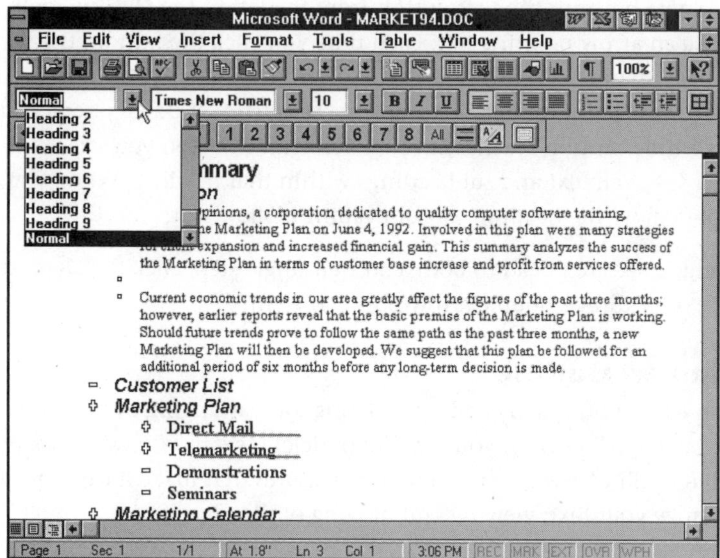

Fig. 9.3
You can assign heading styles by using the Formatting toolbar.

Note

The plus and minus signs also indicate whether more text has been entered under that level of the outline. A plus sign next to a Heading 1 entry, for example, means that other headings and/or body text have been entered under that heading. A minus sign always appears next to body text, which is the lowest level.

Suppose that you click the plus sign preceding the *Marketing Summary* heading (refer to fig. 9.2). By doing so, you select all text from that point to the next Level 1 heading. (In this case, all the text would be selected.) Similarly, if you click the plus sign preceding the Level 2 head *Introduction*, you select all text from that point to the next Level 2 heading (*Customer List*). You also can select text by clicking the selection bar, which is to the left of the text area, or by dragging the I-beam pointer across specific text. After you select the text, you can then choose the level of the heading you want to assign. See the next section "Promoting and Demoting Heads."

Promoting and Demoting Heads

After assigning various heading levels to your text, you might decide to change those levels. You can do so by using the Promote and Demote buttons in the Outline toolbar. Simply select the text and then click the Promote or Demote button.

The Promote button—the first button from the left in the Outline toolbar—looks like an arrow pointing left. Each time you click the button, the selected text moves up one level (until it reaches Level 1). Similarly, the Demote button—an arrow pointing right—bumps the selected text down one heading level at a time (until it reaches Level 9). Remember, when you select a heading, you select all text and subheadings within that heading. When you promote or demote the heading, all subheadings follow suit.

To change a selected head to body text in a single step, click the Demote to Body Text button—a double arrow pointing right.

Editing an Outline

Tip
Double-click the plus sign that precedes a heading to display all of the text below that heading. Double-click again to hide all the text.

You can edit an outline by adding, deleting, or rearranging body text and headings. In outline view, you can add or delete text as you would in any view. But outline view also provides two features that make it easier for you to rearrange your text: viewing and moving outline levels.

You can use the Outline toolbar to view specific levels of the outline. In addition, you can rearrange topics easily without cutting and pasting text.

Collapsing and Expanding Outlines

You can view various levels of an outline by using the Show Heading buttons—the buttons numbered 1 through 8 in the Outline toolbar. If you click the Show Heading 1 button, for example, only Heading 1 text appears onscreen. If you click the Show Heading 2 button, you see only Heading 1 and Heading 2 text.

If you show only headings with no body text, you are *collapsing* the outline. *Expanding* the outline means just the opposite. If only Heading 2 text is showing, for example, click the Show Heading 3, Show Heading 4, or Show All button to expand the outline.

Figure 9.4 shows a collapsed outline. The plus sign next to each heading indicates that more text levels exist within that heading. If a minus sign appears next to a heading, the heading contains no further text levels.

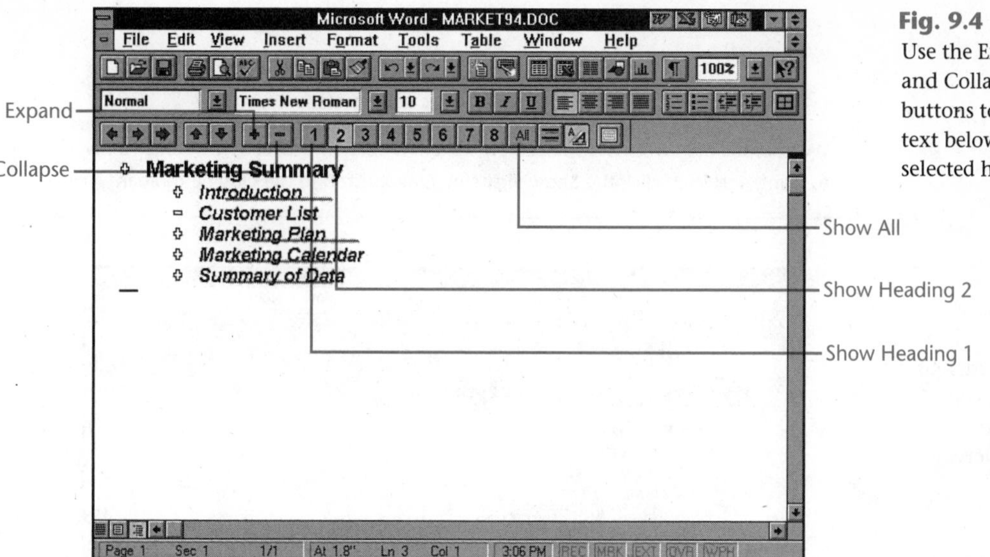

Fig. 9.4
Use the Expand and Collapse buttons to reveal text below the selected head.

II

Using Word

Rearranging Heads and Text

You can rearrange topics in your document by selecting and moving headings in outline view. The easiest method is to collapse the outline to the level to be moved, select the heading you want to move, and drag the heading to its new position. Subheads and body text move with the selected heading.

Caution

If you do not collapse the outline before moving the text, you might leave some body text behind. Be sure to select *all* text to be moved.

Figure 9.5 illustrates moving a head, plus its subheads and body text, to a new position. The mouse pointer changes to a double-headed arrow, and a guideline moves with the mouse to help you position the heading.

Tip
To print the outline at any level, choose the **F**ile **P**rint command or click the Print button.

Troubleshooting

I collapsed the outline so I could focus on the headings while scrolling through the document, but I want to remind myself about the contents of the body text below each heading.

Click the Show First Line Only button in the Outline toolbar to display the first line of body text below each heading.

(continues)

(continued)

I want to print only the headings and first lines of body text.

Word prints only what is displayed on-screen. Display the level of headings you want to print, and then click the Show First Line Only button in the Outline toolbar.

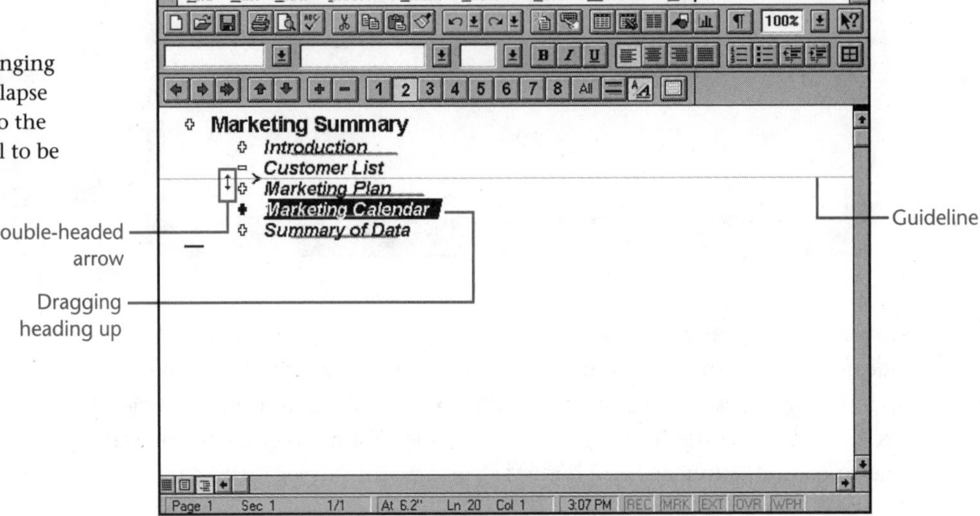

Fig. 9.5 For the most efficient and easiest rearranging of topics, collapse the outline to the heading level to be moved.

Formatting with Styles

A *style* is a collection of text attributes that you can assign to selected text in a document. Each style includes attributes such as font, type size and style, spacing, leading, alignment, indents, and tabs. Styles enable you to format your documents quickly and consistently. Word provides a large number of ready-to-use styles; you also can create your own styles as you work.

One of Word's styles, for example, is the Heading 1 style used to outline a document. Heading 1 text initially appears in the 14-point Arial font, bold and left-aligned. You can assign this style, or any other style, as often as necessary in your documents.

Word's styles are associated with its *templates*, which are a preset collection of page, paragraph, and text formatting styles that you can use to develop a particular type of document. Each time you start a new document, the New dialog box lists many different templates. The Normal template

(Word's default) offers three heading formats and a body-text format. Other templates, such as the Invoice, Letter, and Memo templates, provide different styles for your use.

Styles are particularly useful when you are working on a large document. Rather than moving from page to page and formatting each head, list, tab setting, and so on, you can format a style one time and then assign the style to all occurrences within the text.

Note

Examine some of Word's templates by choosing the **F**ile **N**ew command. In the New dialog box, select any template and then choose OK. Open the Style drop-down list in the Formatting toolbar to view the available styles for that template. Enter some text on the page, assigning different styles to the text to see how each style is formatted. When you finish, choose the **F**ile **C**lose command; when you are prompted to save changes, choose No.

This section shows you how to use Word's styles and how to create and assign your own styles.

Using Word's Styles

To apply a style, first select the text you want to format. Then open the Style drop-down list in the Formatting toolbar and select the style you want to apply (see fig. 9.6).

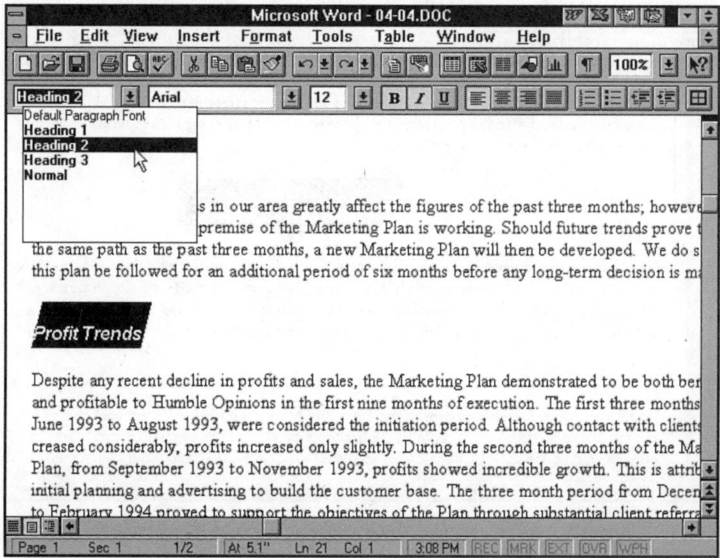

Fig. 9.6
The Heading 2 style is 12-point Arial, bold italic, left-aligned, with spacing set at 12 points before and 3 points after the paragraph.

You can change the format of text after applying a style. You could, for example, change the *Profit Trends* heading shown in the figure to 14-point or center-aligned. Changing a particular heading, however, does not change the style itself or other headings to which you applied that style. For more information about changing the attributes of styles, see "Editing a Style" later in this chapter.

Creating a Style

Creating your own styles in Word is easy. Suppose that you want to create a heading style for use throughout your document. This style is 18-point Times New Roman, bold and center-aligned. You can create this style, add it to the drop-down list, and use it as you would any other Word style.

To create your own style, follow these steps:

1. Select the text on which you want to base your style, and apply the desired formatting.
2. With the text still selected, position the insertion point in the Style box in the Formatting toolbar.
3. Delete the style name in the text box, and enter your own name for the style (see fig. 9.7).
4. Press Enter to add the name to the Styles list.

Fig. 9.7
When you enter a new name in the Style box, you do not actually delete the original style; you are just adding a new style to the list.

Click here to name the new style

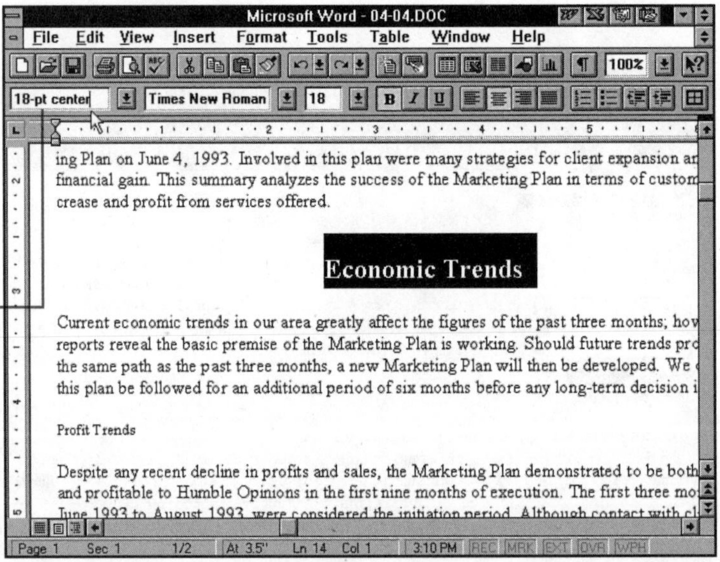

Editing a Style

You can edit any style (changing font, size, alignment, tab stops, and so on), whether it is a preset style provided with Word or a style you created. To edit a style, follow these steps:

1. Choose the F**o**rmat **S**tyle command. The Style dialog box appears (see fig. 9.8).

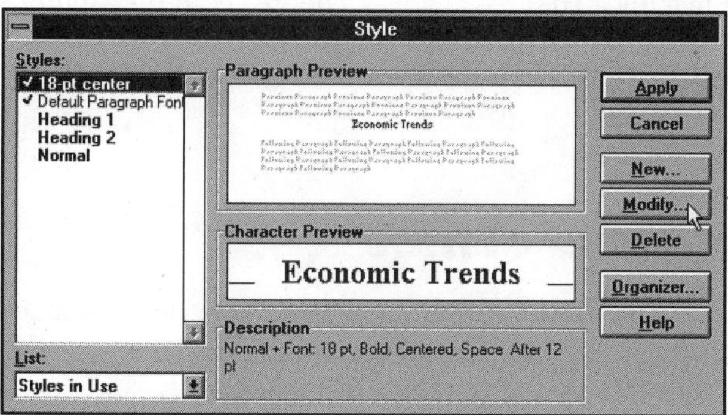

Fig. 9.8
You can view the attributes of a style in the Description area at the bottom of the dialog box.

2. In the **S**tyles list box, select the style you want to modify. Samples of the text as it is now formatted appear in the Paragraph Preview and Character Preview boxes.

3. Choose **M**odify to edit the style. The Modify Style dialog box appears (see fig. 9.9).

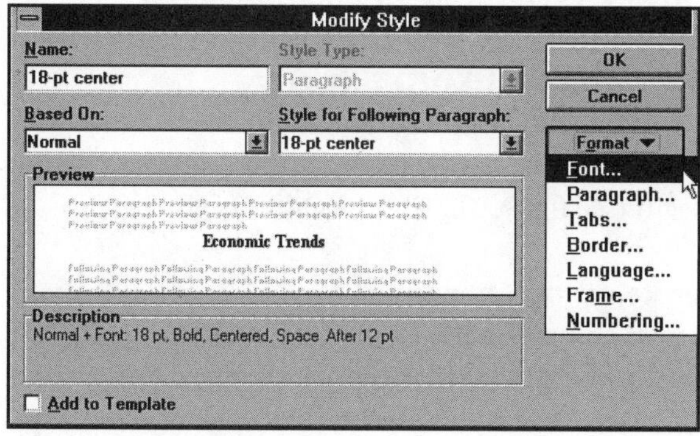

Fig. 9.9
Modify a style by selecting an option in the F**o**rmat drop-down list.

◄ "Formatting Text," p. 124

◄ "Formatting Paragraphs," p. 127

4. Click F**o**rmat to display a drop-down list of the style attributes you can edit.

Tip
To save the styles you create or edit in a document, save the document. After that, the styles will always be available with that document.

5. Select an attribute—**F**ont, **P**aragraph, **T**abs, and so on—in the list, and then make the desired changes in the dialog box that appears. (This dialog box is exactly like the one that appears when you choose the corresponding command from the F**o**rmat menu.) Choose OK to return to the Modify Style dialog box.
6. Repeat step 5 as often as necessary to modify additional style attributes.
7. After making all desired changes, choose OK in the Modify Style dialog box. You return to the Style dialog box.
8. Choose **A**pply to apply the style changes.

Using AutoFormat

AutoFormat is a feature of Word that analyzes your document and automatically applies styles (such as headings, subheads, bulleted lists, and tabs) to your document. Then you can review AutoFormat's choices and accept or reject them. Using AutoFormat can save you time because Word assigns styles for you. The formatting may not be exactly what you want, but you can still change fonts, styles, sizes, and so on after using AutoFormat.

You can use AutoFormat with unformatted text, or you can begin formatting (by creating and applying a few styles) and then let AutoFormat complete the process. AutoFormat finds similar text and assigns the same styles. If you choose the latter method, you have more control over which styles AutoFormat uses. Experiment with both methods and see which you prefer.

Formatting Text Automatically

◄ "Changing AutoFormat Options," p. 187

To start AutoFormat, choose the F**o**rmat **A**utoFormat command. A message box—the first AutoFormat dialog box—appears, announcing that formatting is about to begin (see fig. 9.10). Choose OK to begin formatting.

Accepting or Rejecting Changes

After AutoFormat completes the formatting, another dialog box appears (see fig. 9.11). Choose **A**ccept to accept all changes. If you choose **A**ccept too hastily, you can reverse your decision by clicking the Undo button in the Standard toolbar. If you do not like the changes you see behind the AutoFormat dialog box, choose **R**eject All. Alternatively, choose Review Changes or **S**tyle Gallery.

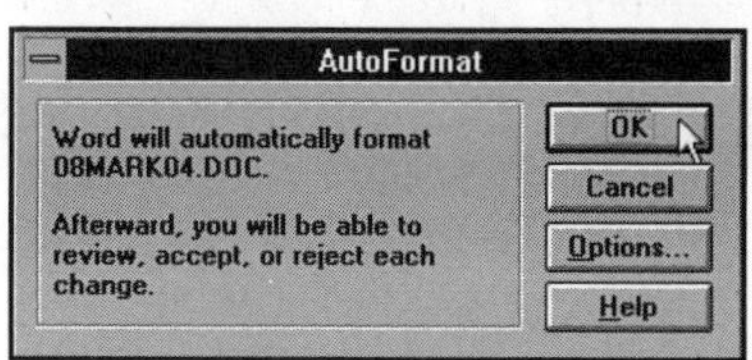

Fig. 9.10
Choose OK to begin formatting, Cancel to cancel the command, Help to get help, or Options to customize formatting.

Fig. 9.11
You can choose to review changes, reject changes, or accept changes.

If you choose to Review Changes, Word shows you each change to the formatting by highlighting the change and displaying a dialog box with a description of the change. You can choose to accept or reject individual changes. If you choose the Style Gallery, you can apply different templates and styles to the document to see what they look like.

Reviewing Changes

If you choose to review the changes, Word takes you through the document step by step, enabling you to examine each change that AutoFormat made. Figure 9.12 shows the Review AutoFormat Changes dialog box.

The Review AutoFormat Changes dialog box enables you to accept or reject changes. To accept a change, choose one of the Find buttons. F**i**nd with a left arrow moves to the previous change; **F**ind with a right arrow moves to the next change. If you do not like the formatting, choose the **R**eject command button. Word changes the selection back to its original formatting.

Choose Close after reviewing the changes, or at any time, and Word displays the initial AutoFormat dialog box again. You can choose to accept or reject all changes.

Note

You can click the mouse outside the Review AutoFormat Changes dialog box to work in your document. The dialog box remains on-screen. This way, you can scroll through the document to compare changes, format text, and add or edit text.

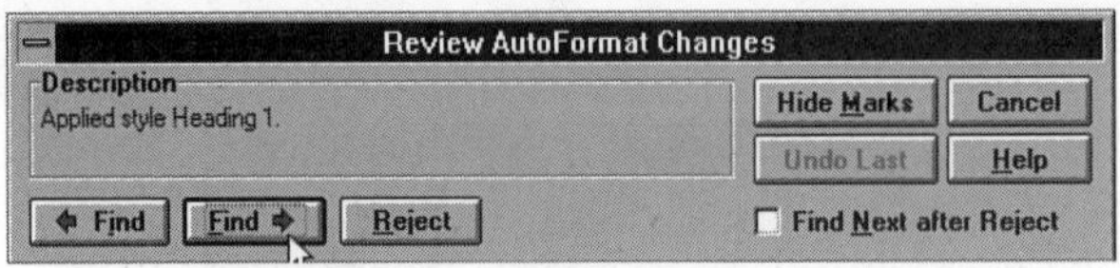

Fig. 9.12
In this dialog box, examine each change and decide whether to keep or reject the changes.

Using Style Gallery

Tip
You can also choose **S**tyle Gallery in the AutoFormat dialog box to choose a different template and style for the document.

◄ "Changing AutoFormat Options," p. 187

Style Gallery is a special dialog box that contains Word's various templates. Each template contains preset page formatting and preset styles. You can use Style Gallery to apply various templates and styles to your document, and view an example in the dialog box before choosing to accept the style.

You can use the Style Gallery with or without AutoFormat. When you use AutoFormat, Word automatically applies a template and style sheet. If you do not like Word's choice, you can choose the Style Gallery command button and choose a different template and style for your document. On the other hand, you may format your document yourself, by applying styles to the text and paragraphs, and then decide to look at the document with various templates applied. Style Gallery gives a formatted document a different look using various styles of fonts, indents, type sizes, and so on.

To open Style Gallery from the AutoFormat dialog box, choose **S**tyle Gallery. Figure 9.13 shows the Style Gallery dialog box with the Report2 template displayed.

Note

Before you can apply a template from Style Gallery to a document, the document must contain styles such as Heading, Index, and List. Therefore, you must have formatted the document with Word's styles or your own.

To use the Style Gallery, follow these steps:

1. In the second AutoFormat dialog box, choose **S**tyle Gallery. The Style Gallery dialog box appears.

2. Select a template in the **T**emplate list. A sample appears in the **P**review Of box.

3. If you find a template and style you like, choose OK. If you do not find a template you like, choose Cancel. Word returns to the AutoFormat dialog box.

4. Choose to **A**ccept or **R**eject All changes. The dialog box closes, and you return to the document.

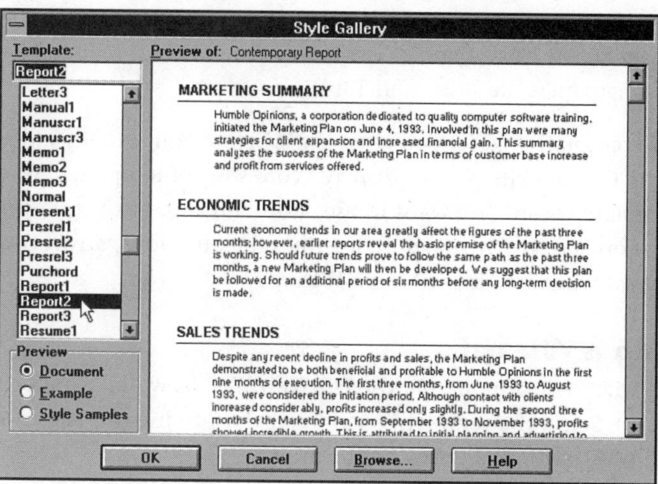

Fig. 9.13
Apply any of the templates and styles to your document, or choose to preview examples of the template.

Troubleshooting

I want to use the styles with a particular template, but I can't find the style names.

Choose the **V**iew **T**oolbars command and display the Formatting toolbar; then choose OK. The Style box is the first box at the left end of the toolbar. In addition, change the view from normal or outline to page layout (View menu) to display all formatting in the document.

AutoFormat does not seem to change the formatting of my document.

AutoFormat assigns styles only to paragraphs formatted in Normal or Body Text style. If you have selected some text and applied a style, or if you used commands in the Format menu to format some text, AutoFormat will not change any of the styles.

I want to format only a section of a document.

Select the text you want to format, and then choose **F**ormat **A**utoFormat.

Using Template Wizards

A *template wizard* is a special template that asks questions and uses your answers to format a document automatically. The available template wizards include Agenda, Award, Calendar, Fax Cover sheet, Letter, Memo, Newsletter, Legal pleading papers, Resume, and Table.

If you use a template wizard, you must use it before you actually enter text in a document. Choose **F**ile **N**ew to display Word's list of templates. Select the type of template wizard you want to use, and then answer the questions as they appear on-screen. This section describes the questions, answers, and formatting associated with the Memo Wizard.

Choosing a Wizard

To begin a wizard document, choose **F**ile **N**ew. The New dialog box appears (see fig. 9.14). Select the template wizard you want to use (for this example, select Memo Wizard), and then choose OK.

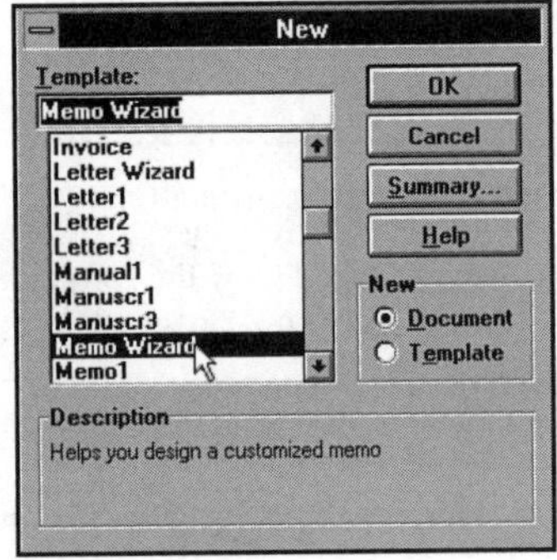

Fig. 9.14
Select a template wizard, and view a brief description in the Description area. Choose OK to accept the template wizard.

Choosing Text Options

Word displays the Memo Wizard dialog box (see fig. 9.15). The dialog box shows you an example of the memo the wizard will format for you. Each dialog box that appears asks you questions about the text and formatting of the document. You choose general text, such as the headings "Interoffice Memo," "To," "From," and so on, from these dialog boxes and Word will apply them to the final memo. You fill in specific text—such as the name, date, and subject—after the memo is created. Additionally, Word asks about other formatting concerns, such as the addition of page numbers, graphics lines, and so on.

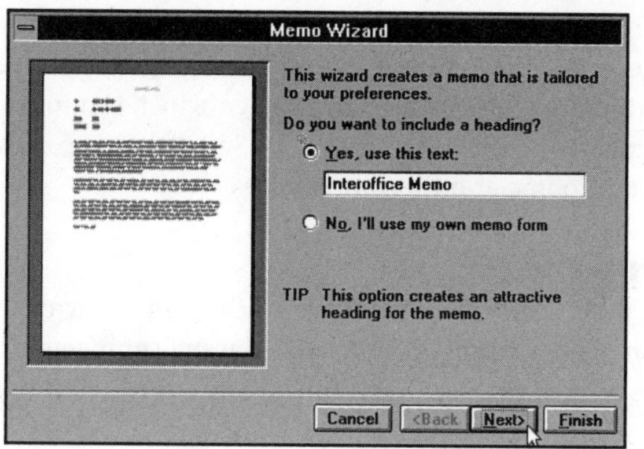

Fig. 9.15
Answer the questions and choose Next to continue creating the memo with the Memo Wizard template.

The first dialog box asks if you want to use a heading and what text you want to use as a heading. After making your decision, choose **N**ext to continue formatting the memo.

Word displays a second dialog box, asking whether you want a separate page for your distribution list. Choose **Y**es if you are sending the memo to several people; choose **N**o if you are sending the memo to only one or two people. Choose **N**ext to move to the next dialog box (see fig. 9.16).

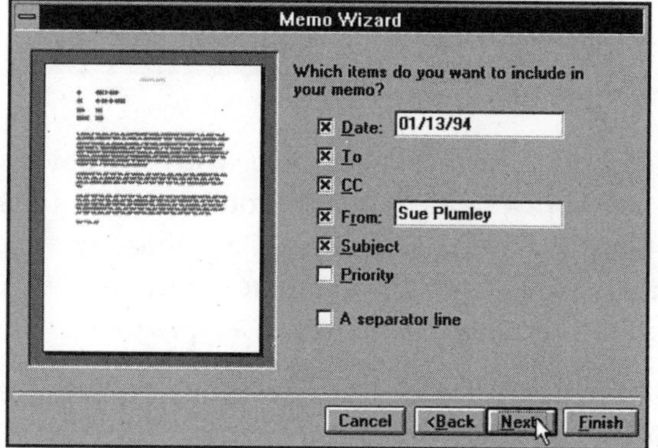

Fig. 9.16
Select the options you want to include, and enter text in the appropriate text boxes.

In this dialog box, select the options you want to use: **D**ate, **T**o, **C**C, F**r**om, **S**ubject, **P**riority, and Separator **L**ine. Enter text in the **D**ate and F**r**om text boxes, replacing the date if it is incorrect.

After you select options, choose **B**ack to return to the preceding dialog box or **N**ext to continue. The next dialog box asks whether you want to include the **W**riter's and **T**ypist's Initials, **E**nclosures, and/or **A**ttachments. Select the options you want and then choose **N**ext.

Next, you can select a *header*, or title, for your memo. The header can contain a **T**opic, D**a**te, and/or Page Numbe**r**; select one, two, or all three to include as a header. Additionally, you can select a footer, which can include the **D**ate, the **P**age Number, or the word **C***onfidential*. Select one, two, or all three of the options for your footer, and then choose **N**ext.

Formatting the Memo

The next Memo Wizard dialog box governs the formatting of the document. Figure 9.17 shows the wizard's prompt for the style of memo to be used. The style Word assigns to the document includes margins, text formatting, tab settings, graphics lines, and so on.

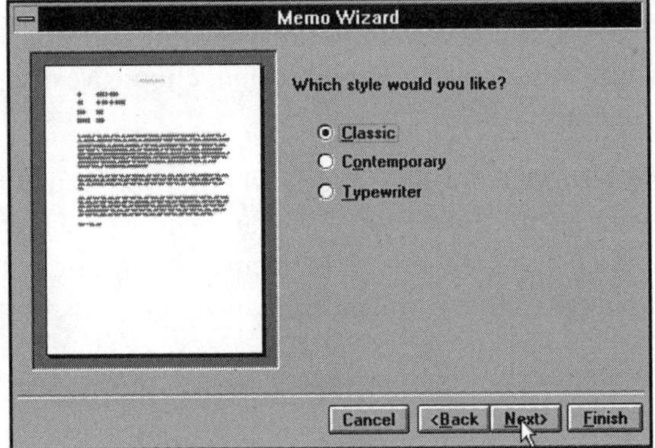

Fig. 9.17
Select a style that best suits your needs; you can modify the style later, if you want.

You can select **C**lassic, C**o**ntemporary, or **T**ypewriter style. Most of the wizards ask this style question about the formatting of documents. **C**lassic usually is plain, formal-looking, and straightforward. C**o**ntemporary, which often contains various fonts and graphics lines, is more modern in design. **T**ypewriter looks as though the document was typed on a typewriter.

When you select one of the styles, an example displays in the dialog box. Select the style that best suits your memo or document. After selecting the style, choose **F**inish to close the dialog box.

Word then creates the memo document for you, adding text and formatting the style with the choices you made. Word displays the memo, as shown in figure 9.18. This memo was created in the Contemporary style. Fill in the specific text and your memo is complete.

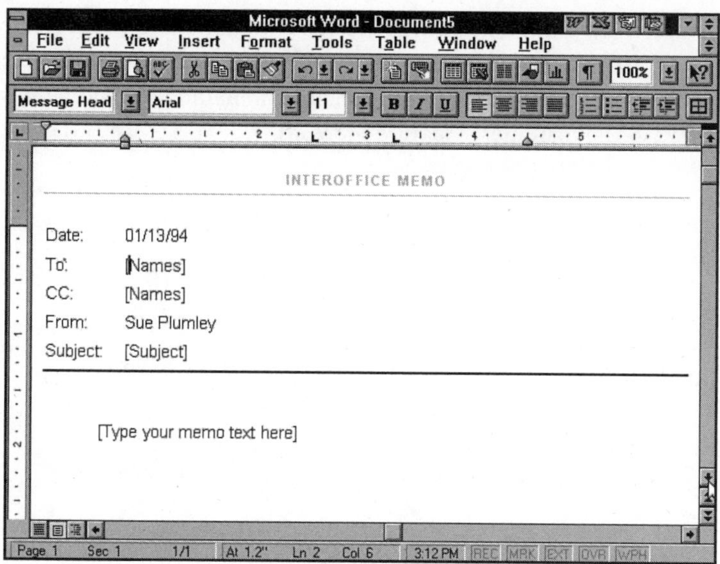

Fig. 9.18
Fill in the text to complete your memo. You can select and format the text, just as you can in any other Word document.

Troubleshooting

I want to use a wizard that is not listed in the New dialog box.

Make sure that you are in the Template directory in the Word program directory. If you installed the templates to another directory, change to that directory. Alternatively, you may need to run Word Setup and install the templates, if you did not install them with the original program. See Appendix A, "Installing Microsoft Office," for more information.

From Here...

Word offers several features that make organizing and managing large documents easier. In addition, you can use Word's features to format a large document quickly, easily, and professionally. The next chapters show you some advanced techniques for working with Word for Windows.

- Chapter 10, "Working with Tables, Charts, and Graphics," covers inserting a table, entering text in a table, and modifying the text and table attributes. Additionally, this chapter covers creating and editing charts, as well as adding borders, lines, shading, and pictures to your documents.

- Chapter 11, "Automating with Macros and Mail Merge," covers how to use Word's built-in macros, record your own macros, and run macros. Additionally, this chapter covers creating a mailing list and letter for use with the mail merge feature in Word.

Chapter 10

Working with Tables, Charts, and Graphics

by Susan Plumley

In this chapter, you learn to

- Insert a table into a document
- Enter, edit, and format the text in a table
- Modify row height and column width
- Create and edit data for charts
- Add lines, borders, and shading to a document
- Insert pictures, such as Microsoft Office's clip art

You can enhance and illustrate your documents by adding tables, charts, and graphics. Added elements, such as these, illustrate, define, and explain the text in your documents.

Create tables to organize columns of numbers, produce forms, or add spreadsheets to your documents. Word enables you to enter and format text in a table, as well as to format the table itself. You can add rows and columns, adjust spacing, add borders, adjust row height, and more.

Additionally, you can create charts to add to your documents. Word includes an *applet*, or mini-application, called Graph that enables you to create charts and embed them in your document. *Embedding* is an efficient method of placing the product of another application into Word. This chapter shows you how to use Graph and how to embed the chart in your documents.

Finally, Word enables you to add graphics such as lines, borders, shading, and even pictures to your documents to illustrate them and to add interest.

Working with Tables

A table is a convenient method of organizing text. You can use a table to create forms, reports, spreadsheets, and columns of numbers. You even can use tables to produce side-by-side paragraphs, such as those in a résumé.

Tables consist of columns and rows. Columns are the vertical divisions of the table; rows are the horizontal divisions. The box formed by the intersection of a column and row is called a *cell*. You can fill cells with text and graphics. When you type text into a cell, the text wraps from one line to the next, enlarging the cell as you enter more text.

When you insert a table, you enter the number of columns and rows for the table. After the table is inserted, you can modify the table and its contents by adding borders and shading, formatting the text, adjusting column width and row height, and so on. This section introduces table basics. For information about adding borders and shading to a table, see "Working with Graphics" later in this chapter.

Inserting a Table

You can insert a table by using the T**a**ble menu or the Insert Table button in the Standard toolbar. To use the menu, choose the T**a**ble **I**nsert Table command. The Insert Table dialog box appears (see fig. 10.1).

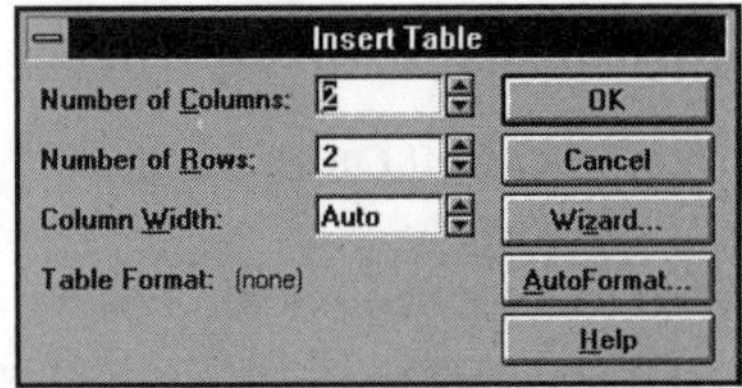

Fig. 10.1
Enter the number of columns and rows in the Insert Table dialog box.

The following list describes the options in the Insert Table dialog box:

- *Number of Columns.* Enter the number of columns for the table.
- *Number of Rows.* Enter the number of rows for the table.
- *Column Width.* Set a specific column width for all columns, or leave the option at Auto. Auto column width divides the space between the left and right margins. You can adjust the width of any column at any time.
- *Table Format.* If you used AutoFormat to format the table, this option displays the predefined format.

- *Wizard.* Starts the Table Wizard; you answer the wizard's questions and choose options for formatting the table.
- *AutoFormat.* Displays the Table AutoFormat dialog box, in which you choose styles, borders, fonts, and so on. AutoFormat is very much like the Style Gallery. For more information, see Chapter 9, "Working with Large Documents."
- *Help.* Displays help on inserting a table.

◄ "Using AutoFormat," p. 200

◄ "Using Template Wizards," p. 204

When you insert a table, Word displays table grid lines. If you do not see any grid lines, choose the T**a**ble Grid**l**ines command to display the nonprinting guides.

Tip

You always can add or delete rows and columns by choosing the T**a**ble **I**nsert Rows/Columns or T**a**ble **D**elete Rows/Columns commands.

To insert a table, follow these steps:

1. Position the insertion point where you want to insert the table.
2. Choose the T**a**ble **I**nsert Table command. The Insert Table dialog box appears.
3. Enter the Number of **C**olumns and the Number of **R**ows.
4. Optionally, enter a value in the Column **W**idth box.
5. If you choose Wi**z**ard or **A**utoFormat, answer all queries in the dialog boxes.
6. Choose OK to insert the table and close the Insert Table dialog box.

Note

If you click the Insert Table button in the Standard toolbar, a grid appears. Drag the mouse pointer across the grid to specify the number of columns and down the grid to specify the number of rows. When you release the mouse button, Word inserts a table with the specified number of columns and rows.

Adding Text to a Table

After you insert the table, you can add text. You enter text in a table much the same way that you enter text in any document. Moving around in a table, however, is a bit different. You also edit the text in a table as you would any text. After you enter the text, you can select it to apply various types of formatting, such as type sizes and alignments.

◄ "Formatting Paragraphs," p. 127

◄ "Formatting Text," p. 124

Entering Text

To enter text in a table, first position the insertion point in a cell, and then type the text. To move to another cell in the table, use the arrow keys. The arrow keys move from cell to cell and from row to row. If a cell contains text, an arrow key first moves one character at a time and then moves from cell to cell.

Pressing the Tab key moves the insertion point to the right from one cell to another, skipping any text in a cell. Press Shift+Tab to move one cell to the left. To actually insert a tab in a cell, press Ctrl+Tab and then set the tab as you normally would.

Selecting Text in a Table

Selecting text in a table is similar to selecting text in any document. You can drag the I-beam pointer over the text to highlight it, or click the selection bar to select an entire row. In addition, you can use some techniques that are specific to selecting text in a table. Following is a list of those techniques:

- To select one cell, triple-click that cell or click the left inside edge of the cell.
- To select an entire column, drag the mouse down the column. Alternatively, place the mouse pointer at the top of the column; the pointer changes to a black down arrow. Then click to select the column, or click and drag across columns to select more than one column.
- Select an entire row by clicking the selection area to the left of the table; drag up or down to select more than one row.
- To select the entire table, position the cursor in the table and press Shift+Alt+5 (on the numeric keypad). Alternatively, place the insertion point in the table and choose the T**a**ble Select T**a**ble command.

Tip
Use the ruler to adjust text indents. For more information, see Chapter 5.

After selecting the text, you can format it as you would any other text by applying various fonts, font sizes, alignments, and so on. Figure 10.2 shows a selected column, centered and bold headings, and right-aligned numbers.

Modifying a Table

You use commands in the Table menu to insert or delete rows and columns, change cell height and width, and make other modifications. When you modify a table element, you first must select that element. You select a row, column, or cell the same way you select text in a table; refer to the preceding section for more information.

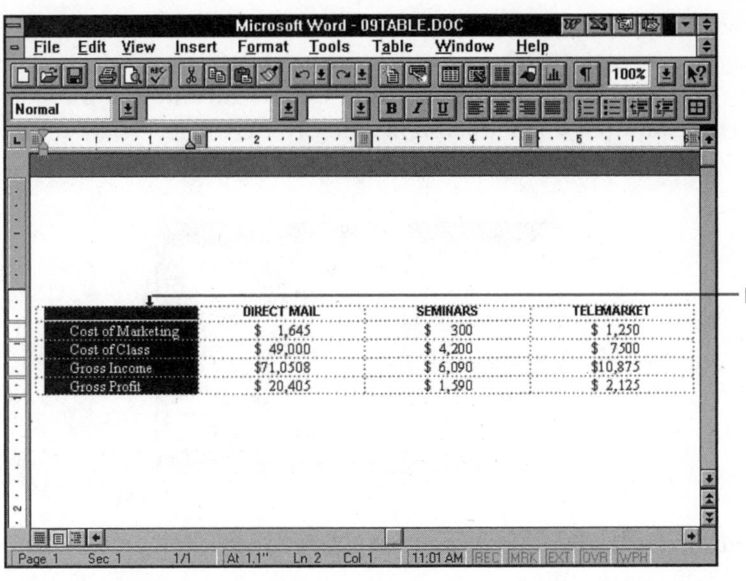

Fig. 10.2
Select text in a table to format it.

Inserting and Deleting Columns and Rows

Inserting columns and rows is relatively simple, once you understand how Word does it. To insert one row, select a row in the table and choose the T**a**ble **I**nsert Rows command. Word inserts one row *before* the selected row. To insert two or more rows, select two or more rows in the table and then choose the Table **I**nsert Rows command. Word inserts as many rows as you selected *before* the selected rows.

Tip
The Table menu commands change, depending on what you select in the table. When you select a column, for example, the Table menu contains the Insert Columns and Delete Columns commands. If you select a cell, the command reads Insert Cells and Delete Cells.

Similarly, to insert one column, select one column and then choose the T**a**ble **I**nsert Columns command. Word inserts one column to the left of, or before, the selected column. Select two or more columns to insert two or more rows before the selected columns.

To delete a row or column, select it and then choose T**a**ble **D**elete Rows or T**a**ble **D**elete Columns.

To insert or delete a column or row, follow these steps:

1. Select the column or row to be deleted, or select the column or row adjacent to the place where you want to add a column or row.

2. Pointing the mouse at the column or row, press the right mouse button to display the quick menu.

3. Select Insert Columns/Rows or Delete Columns/Rows.

Adjusting Cell Height

You can change the height of a cell or the height of a row in the Cell Height and Width dialog box. Choose the T**a**ble Cell Height and **W**idth command. Select the **R**ow tab. Figure 10.3 shows the Cell Height and Width dialog box with the **R**ow tab displayed.

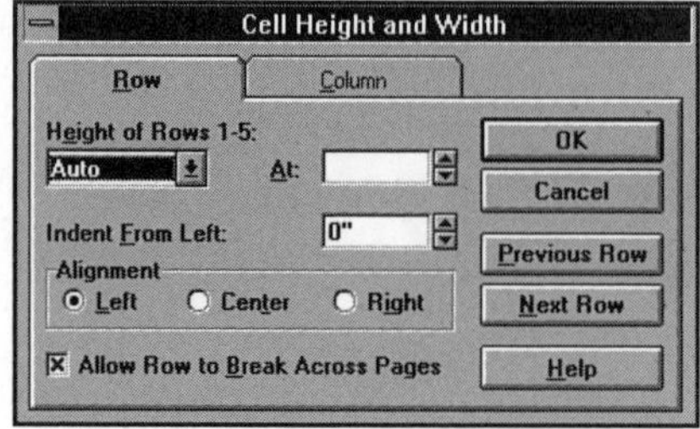

Fig. 10.3
Adjust the height of the rows and indent or align one row in the Row tab of the Cell Height and Width dialog box.

To adjust the height of the row, select one of the following options in the H**e**ight of Row drop-down list:

- *Auto.* Word adjusts the height of the row to the tallest cell.
- *At Least.* Enter the minimum row height in the **A**t box. Word adjusts the height of the rows to the contents of the cells.
- *Exactly.* Enter a row height in the **A**t box. If the cell contents exceed the height you entered, Word prints only what fits in the cell.

To adjust either the previous row or the next row, choose **P**revious Row or **N**ext Row. Choose either command button to move from row to row as you adjust the height of the rows. Click OK when you are finished adjusting the rows, or proceed with adjusting columns.

Note

If no row is selected when you open the Cell Height and Width dialog box, the Height of Row option applies to all rows in the table. When you select a row, Height of Row applies only to that row.

Tip
Choose the **P**revious Column and **N**ext Column command buttons to move from column to column as you adjust the width.

Adjusting Column and Cell Width

You also can adjust column and cell width in the Cell Height and Width dialog box. Choose the T**a**ble Cell Height and **W**idth command. Select the Column tab (see fig. 10.4).

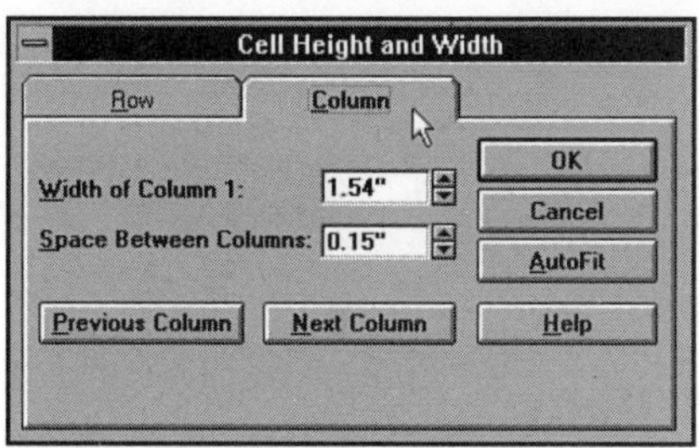

Fig. 10.4
Use the Column tab to specify each column's width and to add space between columns.

To adjust the column width, enter a new width in the Width of Column box. Space Between Columns is the amount of blank space between column boundaries and cell contents. AutoFit automatically resizes all columns in the table to fit the contents of the cells.

> **Troubleshooting**
>
> *I inserted several rows or columns in the wrong place.*
>
> Click the Undo button in the Standard toolbar or choose the **E**dit **U**ndo command. Then select the rows or columns, keeping in mind that the new rows or columns are inserted before the selected ones.
>
> *I want to add a column to the right of a table.*
>
> Position the insertion point just outside the last column and choose the T**a**ble Select **C**olumn command. Then click the Insert Columns button in the Standard toolbar.

Working with Charts

Word includes an applet, or mini-application, called Graph that enables you to create a chart and insert that chart into your Word document. You can use data from a table or spreadsheet in your Word document, or you can enter data directly into the Graph program's worksheet.

After creating the data, you choose chart type, add labels, and otherwise format the chart. When the chart is finished, you embed the chart in your Word document by using *object linking and embedding (OLE)*, a feature that enables Windows programs to share information.

Embedding a chart means that the chart is part of the document; you can resize and move the chart. You also can double-click the chart at any time to open the Graph applet and edit the chart information.

► "Linking an Excel Chart to a Word Document," p. 798

Note

For information about OLE and embedding objects, see Chapter 37, "Sharing Data between Applications with Linking and Embedding."

Creating Chart Data

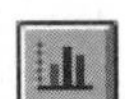

Tip
Alternatively, you can click the Insert Chart button in the Standard toolbar. The Graph applet opens, ready to receive data.

You can create a chart quickly by selecting data in a table or spreadsheet in your Word document and copying it to paste in the Graph data sheet. Alternatively, you can start the Graph applet and enter data in the Graph data sheet. Entering data in a Graph data sheet is similar to entering and editing data in an Excel worksheet.

Note

For more information about using data sheets—entering and editing data, getting around in a data sheet, and so on—see Chapter 12, "Creating Worksheets."

Tip
You can select the Datasheet window at any time and edit the data. Any changes you make are reflected in the Chart window immediately.

To use existing data from a table or spreadsheet, select the data (including headings and labels), and then start the Graph applet.

Starting Graph

To start the Graph applet, choose the **I**nsert **O**bject command. The Object dialog box appears. Select the **C**reate New tab, and then select Microsoft Graph (see fig. 10.5). Choose OK to start the Microsoft Graph applet.

The Microsoft Graph applet opens, as shown in figure 10.6, with a data sheet containing the selected data in a window and a chart with data and labels already in place in another window. Both windows appear in the Microsoft Graph work area. As with any window, if the title bar is in reverse video, that window is active.

Note

If you did not select data before opening Graph, you see the same windows for the datasheet and the chart; however, the data in the windows is sample data. You must delete the sample data and enter your own.

Modifying the Chart

You can select the Chart window and use menu commands to modify the chart—change chart types, labels, titles, axes, and so on.

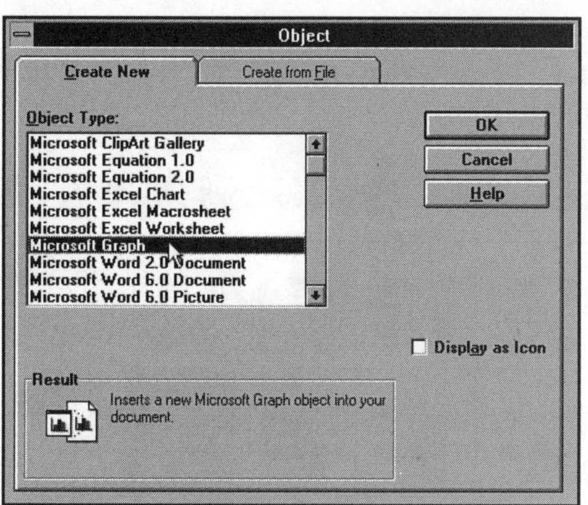

Fig. 10.5 Select Microsoft Graph in the list of Object Types to open the Graph applet.

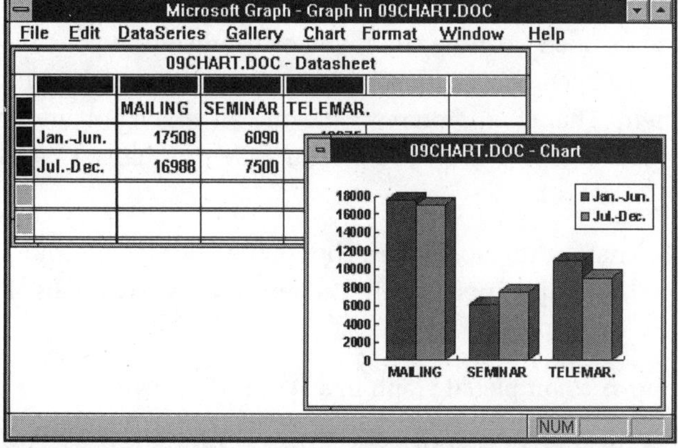

Fig. 10.6 The Graph applet opens with a data sheet and a chart containing the selected information.

Note

Microsoft Graph offers superb techniques for presenting data in chart form. This section presents only the basics of creating a chart. Look at all the Graph menus and experiment with all the commands, including the Gridlines command in the Chart menu and the 3-D View and Chart commands in the Format menu.

To change the chart type, choose an option from the **G**allery menu, which lists various chart types: **A**rea, **B**ar, **C**olumn, **L**ine, **P**ie, **S**catter, Co**m**bination, 3-D Ar**e**a, 3-D Ba**r**, 3-D C**o**lumn, 3-D Li**n**e, and 3-D P**i**e. When you choose an option from the Gallery menu, Word displays the Chart Gallery dialog box.

The Chart Gallery dialog box contains anywhere from five to eight examples of chart variations. For example, figure 10.7 shows the Chart Gallery for 3-D Column charts.

Choose the chart type in the Gallery menu, and then select the chart variation you want in the Chart Gallery dialog box. Choose OK to close the dialog box and apply the variation.

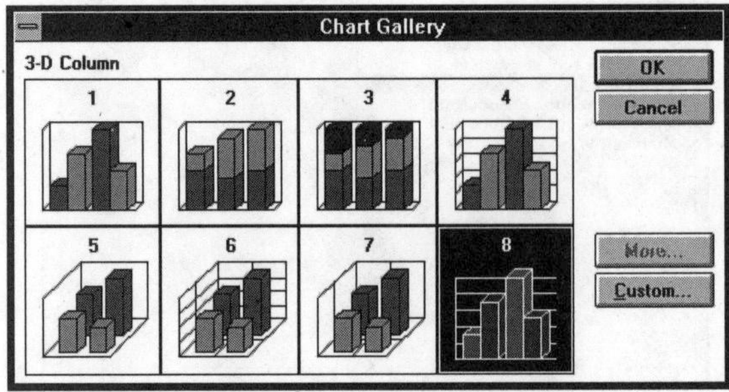

Fig. 10.7
Select a 3-D Column chart in the Chart Gallery dialog box.

Embedding the Chart

When you are satisfied with the chart, you can embed it in your Word document. When you open Graph, the Graph program inserts a chart into your Word document. That chart represents the one on which you are working. Before closing the Graph applet, you must update the chart in Word with any changes you have made.

To update the chart in the document, choose the **F**ile **U**pdate command. Then, to close the Graph applet safely and return to Word, choose **F**ile E**x**it and Return.

Figure 10.8 shows a completed graph in a Word document.

Note

If you choose not to update the chart before exiting the Graph applet, Graph displays a message box, asking whether you want to update. Choose **Y**es to update or **N**o to close the applet without updating the chart.

Troubleshooting

I have data in Excel, Works, and Lotus 1-2-3, and I want to use it in a Word chart.

To import data from another application, open the Graph program and click the worksheet. Choose the **F**ile **I**mport Data command, and select the file you want to import. Choose OK to import the data.

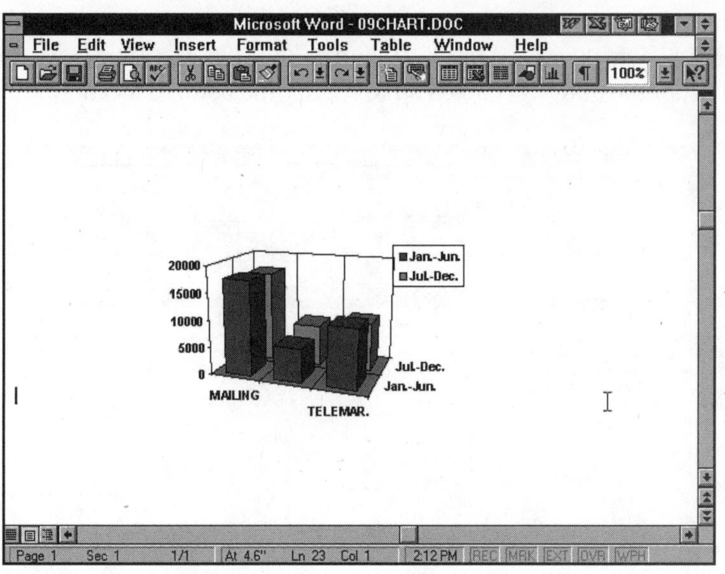

Fig. 10.8
When you want to edit the graph, double-click anywhere in the chart and the Graph program opens.

Working with Graphics

Word includes many graphic elements that you can add to your documents, including lines, borders, shading, and pictures. Use graphics to attract attention to your document, break the monotony of straight text, emphasize text, and pique the reader's interest.

You can add a line above headings to make them stand out or add lines to a table to help divide the data. Create a shaded border to attract attention to text, or add clip art to a newsletter to make it more interesting.

You can add borders and shading to text, tables, charts, and other elements by using the Borders toolbar. To add pictures, you use commands in the Insert menu. This section introduces adding graphics to your documents.

Tip
Alternatively, you can click the Borders button in the Formatting toolbar to display the Borders toolbar. If you click the Borders button again, Word hides the Borders toolbar.

Adding Lines, Borders, and Shading

Word enables you to add graphic lines and borders with the Borders toolbar or menu commands. The toolbar method is by far the easier method.

Displaying the Borders Toolbar

To display the Borders toolbar, place the mouse pointer on any toolbar that currently appears on-screen, and click the right mouse button. The Toolbar quick menu appears. Choose Borders, and the Borders menu appears.

Figure 10.9 shows the Borders toolbar. Drop-down lists contain options for various line thicknesses (Line Style) and various fills and screens (Shading). The rest of the buttons enable you to specify the border's location.

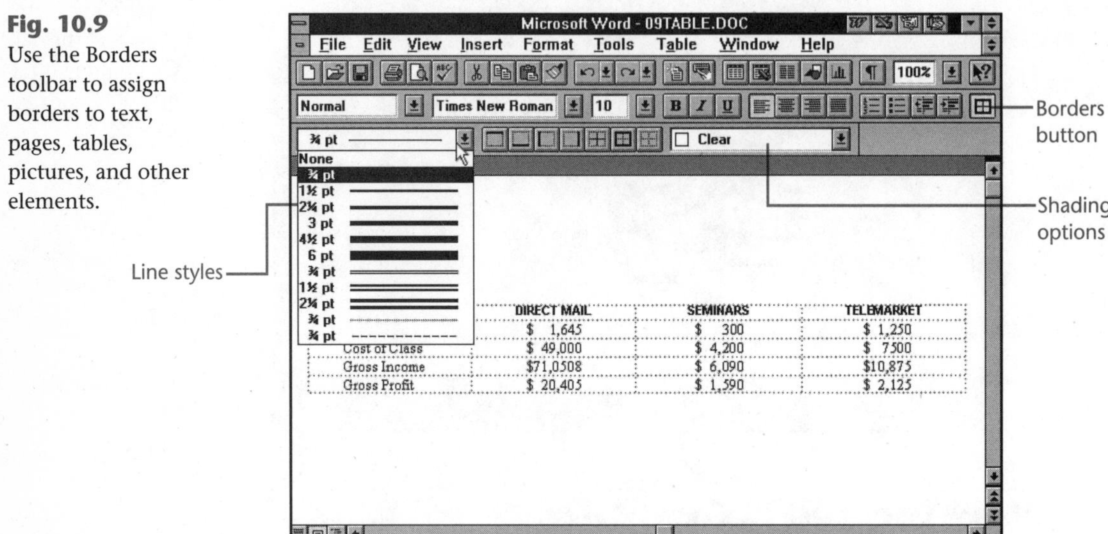

Fig. 10.9
Use the Borders toolbar to assign borders to text, pages, tables, pictures, and other elements.

Applying a Border

To apply a border, place the insertion point where you want the line or border to appear, or select the table, picture, or frame. Choose the Line Style drop-down list from the Borders toolbar; select a line style. Then click the Border button, in the Border toolbar, that you want to use. When you click a Border button, Word inserts the border from margin to margin or side to side (for objects). If you click the Border button again, Word removes the border.

Following is a list of the Border buttons:

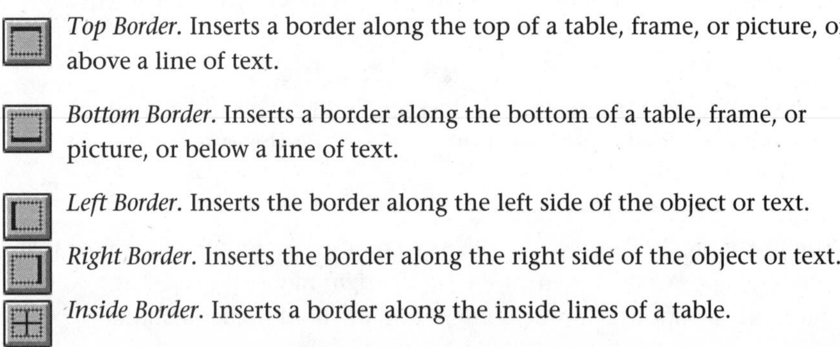

Top Border. Inserts a border along the top of a table, frame, or picture, or above a line of text.

Bottom Border. Inserts a border along the bottom of a table, frame, or picture, or below a line of text.

Left Border. Inserts the border along the left side of the object or text.

Right Border. Inserts the border along the right side of the object or text.

Inside Border. Inserts a border along the inside lines of a table.

Outside Border. Applies a border to the outside of any object or frame.

No Border. Before you use this button to remove a border, select the bordered text or object.

You can apply more than one border to an object or text. You can, for example, apply a 3/4-point top border and a 6-point bottom border. To that, you can add a 3-point left and right border, creating a somewhat strange box around the object or text. You can also apply a shading to the same text or object to which you have applied one or more borders.

Tip
Adjust the length of a line by selecting it and moving the indent markers in the ruler.

You can apply various shading and patterns by selecting the object or the text, or by positioning the insertion point. Choose a shading from the drop-down Shading list in the Borders toolbar. The list provides shading that is stepped in percentages from 5 percent to 100 percent (or solid). Additionally, Word displays a variety of patterns you can apply to text or objects. The pattern list follows the shading list.

Figure 10.10 shows a table with a double 3/4-point outside border, a single 3/4-point inside border, and 20 percent shading for the heading row.

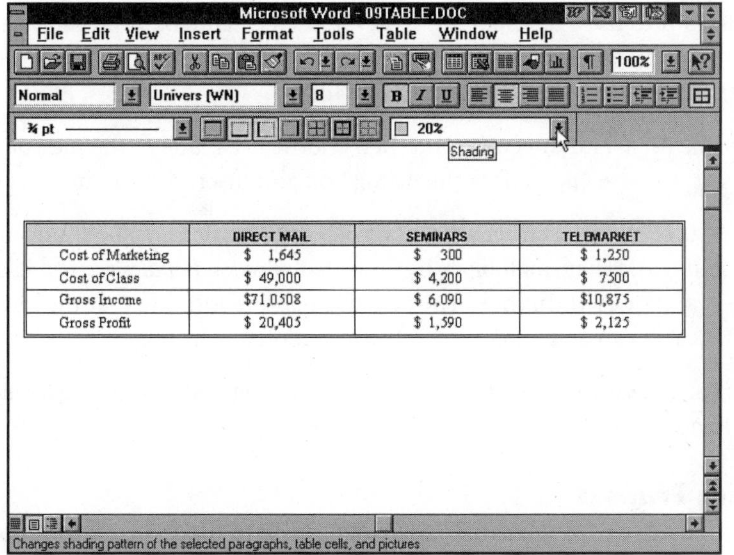

	DIRECT MAIL	SEMINARS	TELEMARKET
Cost of Marketing	$ 1,645	$ 300	$ 1,250
Cost of Class	$ 49,000	$ 4,200	$ 7500
Gross Income	$71,0508	$ 6,090	$10,875
Gross Profit	$ 20,405	$ 1,590	$ 2,125

Fig. 10.10
You can choose different borders for the inside and outside of a table, and add shading to specific areas of the table.

Inserting Pictures and Objects

In the preceding section, you learned to insert an object from another application: Microsoft Graph. You also can insert other objects, including clip art and pictures. Pictures you can add include files from other programs, such as Adobe Illustrator or CorelDRAW!, and clip art from the MSOFFICE directory.

To add a picture to your document, choose the **I**nsert **P**icture command. The Insert Picture dialog box appears (see fig. 10.11).

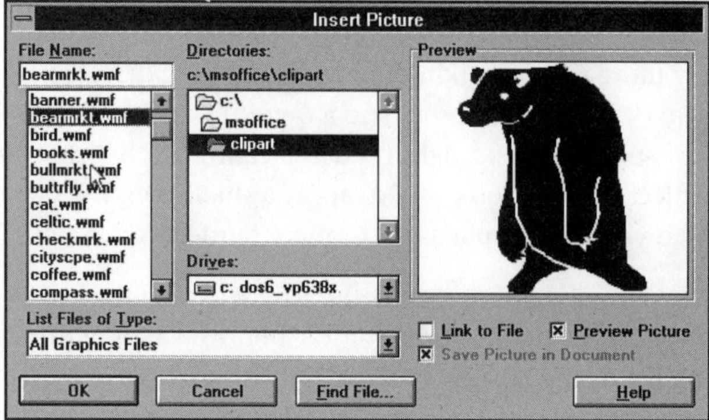

Fig. 10.11
Choose any compatible picture file from any directory or from a floppy drive.

If you want to insert clip art, the Insert Picture dialog box opens, by default, to the Microsoft Office clip-art directory. You can select one of the files in the File Name list. Additionally, select the **P**review Picture check box to see what the picture looks like before you add it.

If you want to use a different file type, choose List Files of **T**ype and select the file type you want to add. Your choices include DrawPerfect, PC Paintbrush, TIFFs, and Encapsulated PostScript (EPS) files.

Select the drive and directory, and then choose the name of the file you want to insert. Choose OK to close the dialog box and insert the picture.

Figure 10.12 shows an inserted clip-art picture. Notice that a box surrounds the picture and that small black boxes called *selection handles* appear at the corners and sides of this box. The box and handles indicate that the picture is selected. You can add borders to any selected picture or object.

Additionally, you can resize the picture by clicking and dragging any selection handle.

Using Frames

Word includes a special feature that enables you to move a picture, object, or text around on the page freely. This feature is a *frame*. You can insert an empty frame anywhere on the page and then fill the frame with text or a picture or object. Alternatively, you can insert a picture or object, select it, and then put it in a frame.

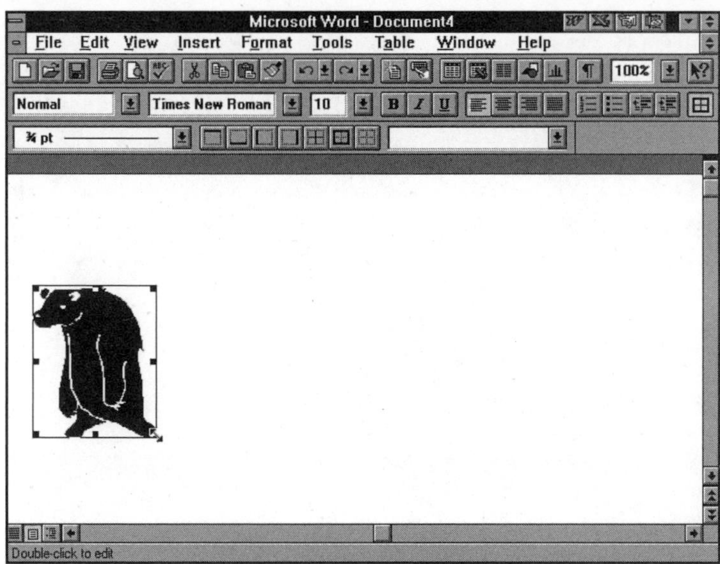

Fig. 10.12 Insert a picture or other object into a frame so you can easily move the object around on the page.

> **Note**
>
> If you choose to insert a frame without selecting a picture or object, the insertion point changes to a crosshair. Position the crosshair and drag it diagonally to draw the frame. Release the mouse button when the frame is the right size.

After inserting the frame, you can move the frame and its contents around on the page. You also can apply borders and shading to a frame. You can move an object, such as a picture or graph, around the page even if you do not use a frame, but it is difficult because the object is linked to the text. Therefore, if the object moves, the text also moves. When you insert the object in a frame, you have much more flexibility.

Figure 10.13 shows a chart with a frame inserted. The gray border indicates the frame. You can select a handle and resize the frame and its contents. You also can move the frame around on the page.

To insert a frame, first select the text, object, or picture. Choose the **I**nsert **F**rame command. If you select an object, Word inserts a frame around the object. If you did not select an object, the pointer changes to a crosshair. You can then use the mouse to draw the frame.

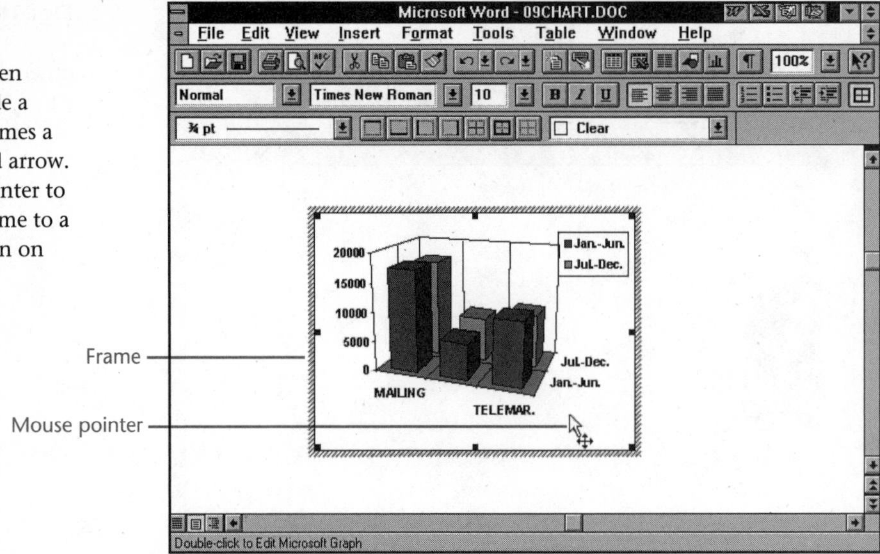

Fig. 10.13
The mouse pointer, when placed inside a frame, becomes a four-headed arrow. Use this pointer to drag the frame to a new position on the page.

From Here...

Add interest to your documents and illustrate the text by using tables, charts, and graphic lines, borders, shading, and pictures. The next chapters introduce more advanced techniques for working in Word:

- Chapter 11, "Automating with Macros and Mail Merge," covers the use of Word's built-in macros, creating and running your own macros, and creating an address list and a letter for use with Word's mail merge feature.

- Part III, "Using Excel," covers how to use the Microsoft Office spreadsheet program. The first chapter in Part III, Chapter 12, introduces you to some Excel terms and explains how to move around in a worksheet, enter data, select cells and ranges, and save a file.

Chapter 11

Automating with Macros and Mail Merge

by Susan Plumley

Word supplies many features that enable you to complete your work quickly and efficiently. Two of these features are macros and mail merge. Both of these features save you time by automating your work; you define parameters one time, and Word takes care of your commands time after time.

You can automate your work with *macros*, or mini-programs, by recording several commands, saving the recording, and then playing it back any time you want to perform those commands. Instead of choosing the menus and commands yourself, the macro automatically performs the task for you with a click of the mouse.

Word's mail merge feature also saves you time and energy. The Mail Merge Helper guides you to create an address list and the letter or document to merge. The Mail Merge Helper then helps you print your merged documents easily. Because this feature is so intuitive, you should never have to dread mail merge again.

In this chapter, you learn to

- Use Word's prerecorded macros for tables, page and text layout, and converting files
- Create your own macros by recording, saving, and testing the macros
- Create and edit a form letter for use with mail merge
- Create the *data source*—address list or database—that you will merge with the letter or other document
- Print the merged documents or save them to a file for later use

Using Macros

Tip
Word records macros in the WordBasic language. If you know programming, you can write your macros in Word. See "Programming with Microsoft Word" in Word Help for more information.

Macros can speed your work by performing everyday tasks automatically. A macro is a mini-program—a series of commands recorded to work as one command. You can, for example, create a macro to assign a specific font, font size, and alignment to selected text by pressing a shortcut key, instead of accessing the F**o**rmat menu and the **F**ont and **P**aragraph commands.

Word supplies several macros you can use; you also can create macros to fit your personal needs. You can use macros to speed regular editing and formatting, automate an elaborate set of tasks, or combine several commands into one. You can even assign a macro to a shortcut key, menu, or button in the toolbar so that it's easier to use. This section introduces Word's macros and explains how to record and run your own macros.

Using Word's Macros

Tip
If your Word directory does not have a Macros subdirectory, you will have to run the Word Setup program to install the templates.

Word provides many macros that you can use with your documents, including macros that speed formatting, create an organizational chart, or find and replace symbols in a document. Word stores these macros in templates that are installed in the Macros subdirectory.

Before you can use Word's macros, you must add them as a global template. *Global templates* are templates available for use with all documents. Adding the macros as a global template, therefore, enables you to use them with any open document.

Choosing Macro Templates

Word supplies four templates containing macros you can use as global templates: LAYOUT.DOT, MACRO60.DOT, TABLES.DOT, and CONVERT.DOT. Each template includes macros related to the template name. Following is a description of each template's contents:

- *LAYOUT.DOT.* This template contains more than 15 macros that deal with text, paragraph, and page layout. Some macros increase or decrease paragraph indents, character spacing, line spacing, or type size. Other macros arrange open windows on-screen by tiling or cascading them.
- *MACRO60.DOT.* This template contains more than 10 macros that govern file commands, such as saving all documents when exiting Word, generating a sample of all printable fonts, and presenting all the information about a document in one dialog box.

- *TABLES.DOT.* This template contains five macros that automate your work with tables. One macro, for example, exports a table from Word to a Microsoft Access database; another macro numbers the cells in a table.
- *CONVERT.DOT.* This template automates conversions from other programs. For example, one macro exports outline information from Word to Microsoft PowerPoint.

Note

You can easily view the macro names and their descriptions in the Macro dialog box; see "Running Predefined Macros" later in this chapter for more information.

Adding Word's Macros

To add Word's macro templates as global templates, choose the **F**ile **T**emplates command. The Templates and Add-ins dialog box appears (see fig. 11.1).

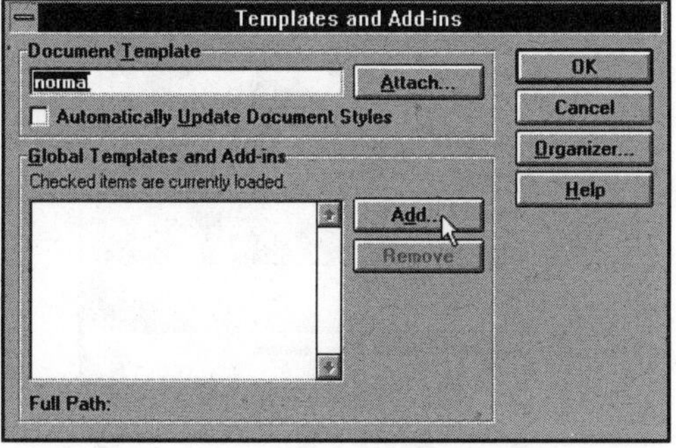

Fig. 11.1
Choose Add in the Templates and Add-ins dialog box to select the macro templates you want to add as global templates.

Choose A**d**d; the Add Template dialog box appears. Change directories to the MACROS subdirectory in the WINWORD directory and select one of the macro templates, as shown in figure 11.2. Choose OK. The templates are added to the **G**lobal Templates and Add-ins list in the Templates and Add-ins dialog box.

Note

Templates in the Global Templates and Add-ins list box that are checked with an X are loaded for use in all documents. To prevent a template from loading into all documents, deselect that template to remove the X from its check box.

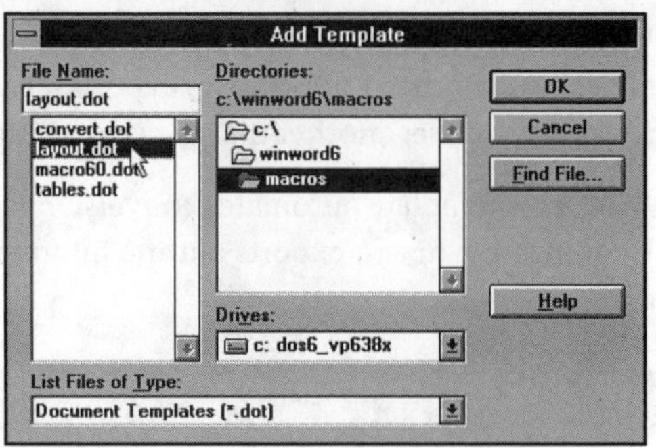

Fig. 11.2
Select the template containing the macros you want to use. The LAYOUT.DOT and MACRO60.DOT templates may be the most useful to you.

Running Predefined Macros

You can view each template and the macros it contains in the Macro dialog box. Choose the **T**ools **M**acro command to display the Macro dialog box, shown in figure 11.3.

Fig. 11.3
To view a description of a macro, select the macro in the list and view the Description box.

To display macro names, select the macro template in the Macros **A**vailable In drop-down list; all macros contained in that template appear in the **M**acro Name list box. Select any macro, view the description, and choose the **R**un button to start the macro.

Creating Your Own Macros

As handy as Word's macros are, you probably will want to create your own macros to perform commands you use repeatedly. You can record a macro, for example, that automatically switches from normal to page layout view, shows the ruler, displays the Formatting and Borders toolbars, and zooms to 100 percent. After recording the macro, you can assign a keyboard shortcut to it. Any time you want to perform these commands, press the shortcut keys; Word performs the commands.

To create your own macros, you first name the macro and assign a shortcut key. Then turn on the macro recorder. Using the mouse, the keyboard, or a combination of both, perform the commands you want to include in the macro. Then just turn the recorder off.

Tip
You can use up to 36 characters in a macro name; however, the shorter and more concise the macro name is, the more easily you can remember it.

Naming the Macro

You use the **T**ools **M**acro command to access the Macro dialog box, shown in figure 11.4.

Choose the Rec**o**rd button. Word displays the Record Macro dialog box (see fig. 11.5). You can assign the macro to a toolbar, the menu, or the keyboard. For more information about customizing the toolbars and menus, see Chapter 42, "Changing Toolbars and Menus."

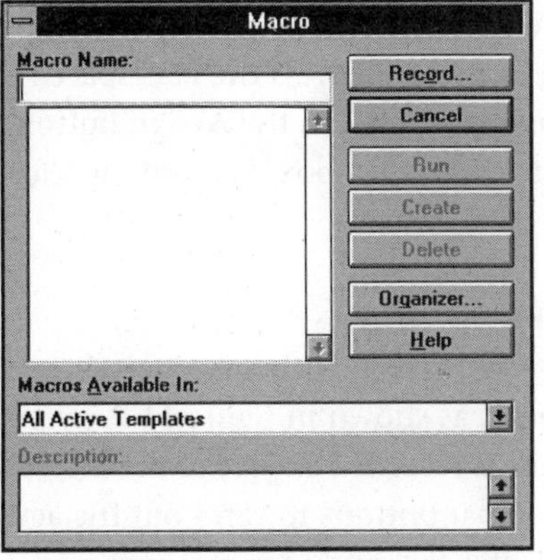

Fig. 11.4
Name the macro by entering a name in the **M**acro Name text box. Word considers spaces, commas, or symbols in the macro name to be illegal characters.

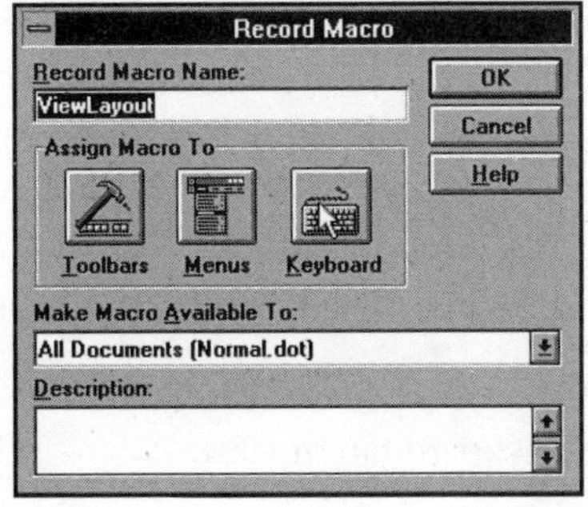

Fig. 11.5
If you plan to use many macros, don't clutter the toolbars and menus. Instead, choose to assign the macro to the **K**eyboard.

II

Using Word

Assigning Keys

When you choose **K**eyboard, for example, the Customize dialog box appears with the **K**eyboard tab in view (see fig. 11.6). The insertion point is already in the Press **N**ew Shortcut Key text box; press a key combination to use as the shortcut.

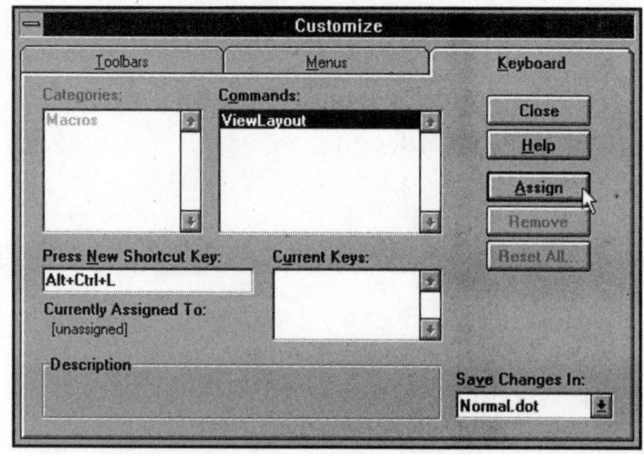

Fig. 11.6
Press a key combination to assign to the macro; don't use a key combination that is already in use.

Tip
To find an unused key combination, try using one that starts with Ctrl+Alt or Ctrl+Shift.

If the key combination is already assigned, Word displays its current use in the Currently Assigned To area below the Press **N**ew Shortcut **K**ey text box. If the key combination is assigned, press the Backspace key and try again. If the combination is not assigned, choose the **A**ssign button. Word adds the assignment to the C**u**rrent Keys list box. Choose the Close button to begin recording the macro.

Tip
You can start and stop recording a macro by double-clicking the REC indicator in the status bar.

Recording the Macro

Word returns to the Word screen with the Macro Recording toolbar and the modified mouse pointer, as shown in figure 11.7. Everything you do with the mouse or the keyboard is recorded as part of the macro. Choose menus and commands or click toolbar buttons to carry out the actions you want to record. You also can enter text and format it, open or close files, and arrange windows with macros; the possibilities are endless.

Tip
If you accidentally choose a command or enter something you do not want to record, choose the **E**dit **U**ndo command. During playback, the macro skips anything you undo.

To record a macro, follow these steps:

1. Choose the **T**ools **M**acro command. The Macro dialog box appears.
2. Enter a name in the **M**acro Name text box.
3. Choose the Rec**o**rd button. The Record Macro dialog box appears.
4. Choose to assign the macro to the **K**eyboard. The Customize dialog box appears with the Keyboard tab in view.
5. Press the key combination you want to represent the macro; the key combination appears in the Press **N**ew Shortcut Key text box.
6. Click the **A**ssign button and then the Close button. The dialog box closes, and Word returns to the screen.

7. Using the mouse or the keyboard, record the commands for the macro.

8. Click the Stop Recording button in the Macro Recording toolbar.

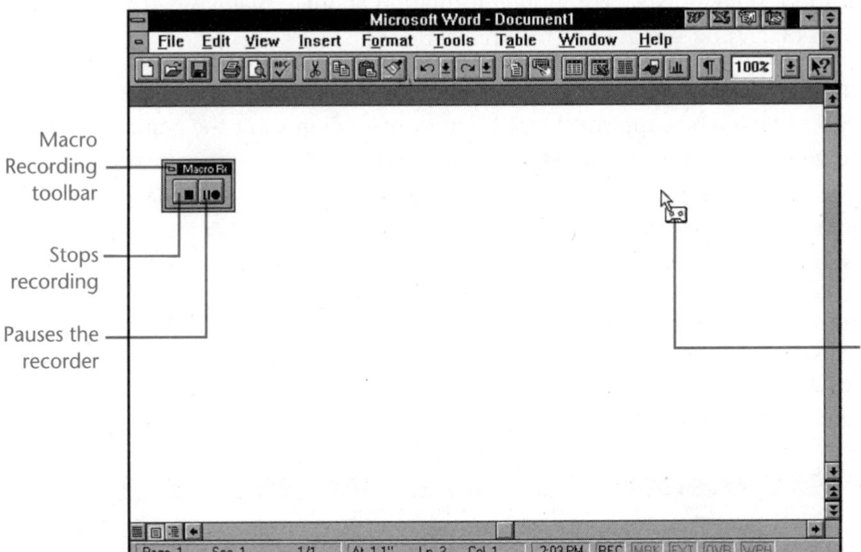

Fig. 11.7
Choose the commands you want to record; click the Stop Recording button in the Macro Recording toolbar when you finish.

Running the Macro

After recording a macro, run the macro to test it. To test and run the macro, press the shortcut key combination or choose the **T**ools **M**acro command, select the macro name, and choose **R**un. Word runs the macro.

If you do not get the results you want, delete the macro and re-record it. To delete the macro, select the macro in the Macro dialog box and choose the **D**elete button. Word displays a confirmation dialog box; choose **Y**es to delete the macro.

> **Note**
>
> Consider the position of the insertion point when creating a macro. If, for example, the macro will check spelling, press Ctrl+Home before choosing the **T**ools **S**pelling command so your insertion point will be at the top of the document.

Writing Your Own Macros

If you are familiar with Basic programming, you can write your own macros in Word. Word's programming capability is known as WordBasic. Although WordBasic is not the same as Visual Basic, which is used in Excel, Word is compatible with Visual Basic for Applications. Visual Basic for Applications is based on the Visual Basic for Windows programming language. The advantage is that because Word is compatible, it can be controlled by another application, such as Excel. For more information about Visual Basic, see Chapter 43, "Using Visual Basic for Applications."

To write your own macro while in the Word program, choose **T**ools **M**acro. The Macro dialog box appears. Enter the new macro name, or the name of a macro you want to edit, in the **M**acro Name text box. Choose the Cr**e**ate/**E**dit button. The button reads Cr**e**ate if you entered a new name in the **M**acro Name text box and **E**dit if you entered the name of a macro that already exists. If the macro already exists, its contents appear in the macro-editing window.

The macro-editing window appears, with the Macro toolbar, as shown in figure 11.8. You can write the entire macro in the text area, or you can use a combination of recording and writing by using the Macro toolbar.

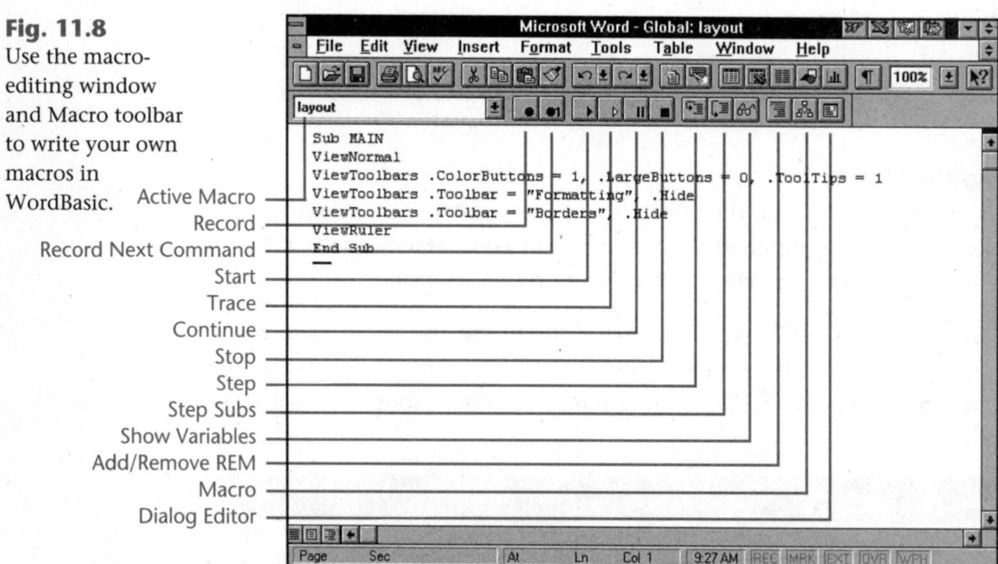

Fig. 11.8
Use the macro-editing window and Macro toolbar to write your own macros in WordBasic.

Note

Word includes extensive help on programming with WordBasic. Choose **H**elp **S**earch for help information. In the Type a **W**ord text box, type **macros**. In the Select a **T**opic text box, select WordBasic Help. Then choose OK.

When you finish writing the macro, save both the macro and the template by choosing **F**ile **S**ave Template or by pressing Ctrl+S. Word displays a dialog box, asking whether you want to keep the changes in the macro. Choose **Y**es. Choose **F**ile **C**lose to close the macro-editing window and return to the document window.

Troubleshooting

I'm recording a macro to move the insertion point and select text; however, I cannot use the mouse to move the cursor within the text.

The macro recorder cannot record mouse actions within document text, such as moving the cursor, creating an insertion point, or selecting text. Use the keyboard to record any actions within the text. You can, however, use the mouse to choose menus and commands.

I want to load Word's macros, but I cannot find the Macros directory.

The templates may not have been installed when you installed the program. Run the Word Setup program to install the directory and the templates. See Appendix A, "Installing Microsoft Office," for more information.

I want to move a macro from the Normal template to another template for use in a specific document.

Choose **T**ools **M**acro Or**g**anizer. In the **M**acros tab, copy any macros from the current template to the selected template. Choose Close when you finish. Run the macro to test your edits.

Using Mail Merge

Using Word's mail merge feature, you can personalize letters—such as announcements, change of address, advertising, and so on—so each letter contains a different name, address, and company name. In addition, you can include the addressee's title, phone number, and other personal information. You can even position the information in the address, salutation, or anywhere within the text.

To perform a mail merge in Word, you must complete several steps. You identify the type of document you want to create, such as a letter. Then you create or open a file containing the address list. You can create the address list in Word or use an existing list from another program—Access, for example.

Next, you create the letter containing general text that is common to all recipients; you also enter fields that represent information specific to each recipient. Finally, you merge the address list with the letters to produce the completed letters.

Identifying the Document

The first step in creating a mail merge is to identify the document type in Word's Mail Merge Helper. Mail Merge Helper is an assistant of sorts that leads you step by step through the merging process. To use the Mail Merge Helper, choose the **T**ools Mail Me**r**ge command. The Mail Merge Helper dialog box appears, as shown in figure 11.9.

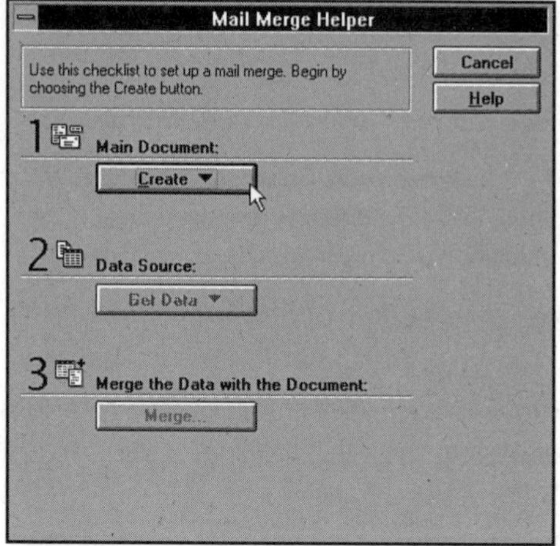

Fig. 11.9
Follow the step-by-step instructions in Mail Merge Helper; choose Create to identify the document type.

Select the first option in the Mail Merge Helper dialog box: Main Document. Then choose the **C**reate button; a drop-down list appears. You can create Form **L**etters, **M**ailing Labels, **E**nvelopes, or a Catalog. Select Form **L**etters to begin the mail merge process.

Word displays a message box, stating that you can use the active document window to create your letter or start a new document. If you already have a letter typed, or if you just started a new document, you can choose to use the active document window. Otherwise, you can start a new document for the letter. Choose the appropriate response, and Word returns to the Mail Merge Helper. You will create the actual letter later.

Choosing a Data Source

The next step is to choose option number 2: Data Source. The Data Source is the address list. Choose the **G**et Data button; a drop-down list appears. If you already have a database of names and addresses—in Access, for example—select **O**pen Data Source. If you do not have a data source, select **C**reate Data Source to enter names and addresses into Word.

Opening a Data Source

If you choose to open a data source, the Open Data Source dialog box appears (see fig. 11.10). Select the drive, directory, and file name; then choose OK to open the data source.

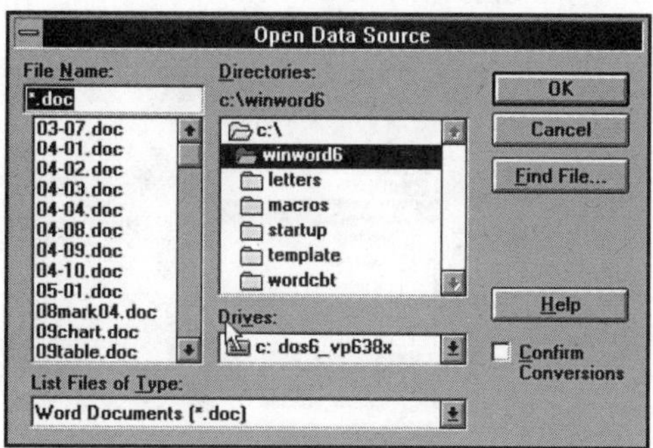

Fig. 11.10
The Open Data Source dialog box enables you to open a data source from another program to use as your address list.

Word displays a message, asking whether you want to add fields to your main document. Choose Edit **M**ain Document. Word returns to the document screen but adds the Merge toolbar for you to use. To continue from this point, skip to "Creating the Letter" later in this chapter.

Creating a Data Source

If you do not have an existing data source, choose **C**reate Data Source to enter the names and addresses in Word. The Create Data Source dialog box appears, as shown in figure 11.11.

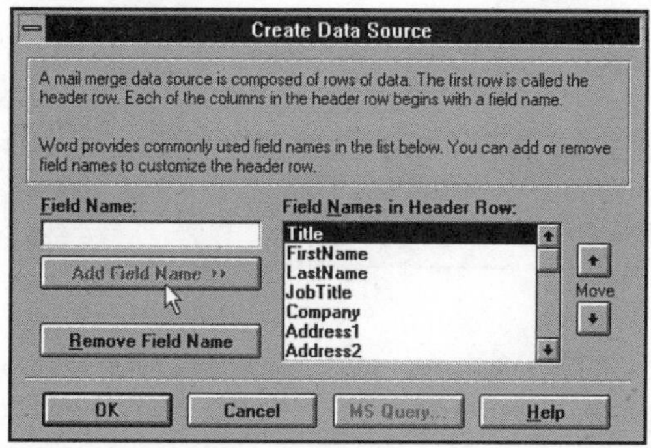

Fig. 11.11
You must name the fields you will use in the document to be merged; you can select Word's fields or enter your own.

Tip
If you have problems adding a field name, make sure that the name contains no spaces, symbols, or punctuation.

To accept all the field names in the Field **N**ames in Header Row list, choose OK. Probably, however, you will want to remove some of Word's fields and enter some of your own. To add your own fields, type the new names in the **F**ield Name text box, and then choose **A**dd Field Name. To remove fields from the Field **N**ames in Header Row list, select the fields, and then choose **R**emove Field Name. You might choose, for example, to keep Title, FirstName, LastName, Company, Address1, City, State, and PostalCode. Choose OK when you're satisfied with the field names. Word displays the Save Data Source dialog box (see fig. 11.12).

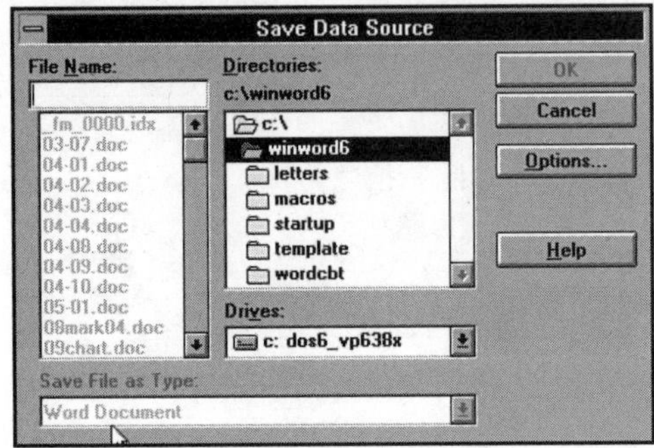

Fig. 11.12
Name the new data source file; you may want to use the file again later for more letters, envelopes, mailing labels, and so on.

Select a drive and directory, and enter the file name of the data source you are about to create. Word displays a message box, asking whether you want to enter the records in the data source or work on the main document (the letter). Choose to Edit **D**ata Source; Word displays the Data Form dialog box (see fig. 11.13).

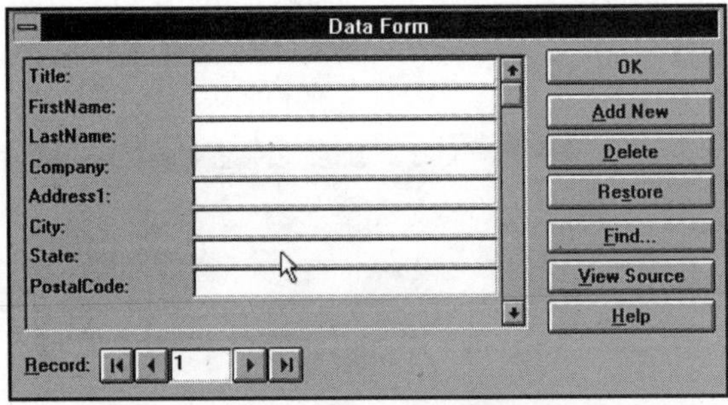

Fig. 11.13
Enter the data in the fields for the first record; choose **A**dd New to continue.

As you enter the data for each record, you can review records by choosing **R**ecord and entering the record number. Additionally, you can delete records by choosing **D**elete. Choose **H**elp if you need more information about the data form. When you finish entering records, choose OK to close the Data Form dialog box. Word displays the document screen and the Merge toolbar.

Creating the Letter

When you finish entering data, or when you have opened a data source file, Word displays the editing screen and the Merge toolbar, as shown in figure 11.14.

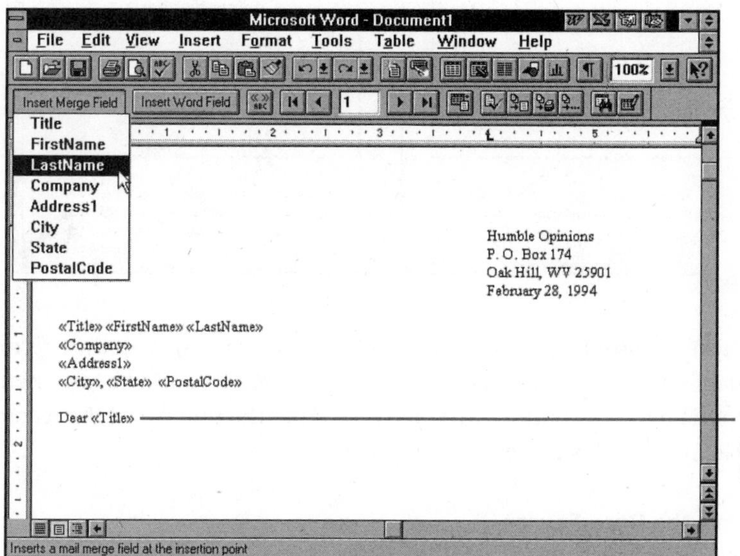

The LastName field will be inserted here

Fig. 11.14
To insert personalized information into the document, select the field you want to place from the Insert Merge Field list.

Type and format the letter as you normally would, with one exception: insert a merge field wherever you want to insert personalized information. Position the insertion point, and then click the Insert Merge Field button in the Merge toolbar. Select the field from the drop-down list.

Be sure to add spaces, paragraph returns, and punctuation before, between, and after the fields. Between <<City>> and <<State>> fields, for example, enter a comma and a space; after the <<State>> field, enter a space or two to separate the state and the ZIP code.

When you finish entering the letter and the merge fields, save the document.

Viewing Data

Use the Merge toolbar to view the data in place of the merge fields by clicking the View Merged Data button, as shown in figure 11.15.

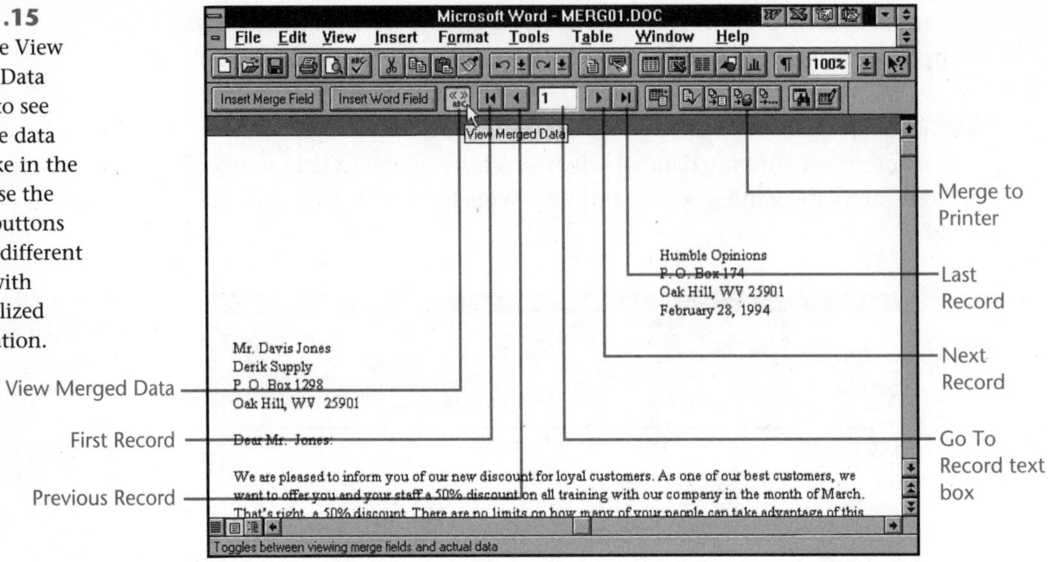

Fig. 11.15
Click the View Merged Data button to see what the data looks like in the letter; use the record buttons to view different letters with personalized information.

View Merged Data
First Record
Previous Record
Merge to Printer
Last Record
Next Record
Go To Record text box

You also can use the Record buttons to view each record or specific records in the data source. View the first, last, next, or previous record by clicking the appropriate toolbar button. Alternatively, enter the number of the record in the Go To Record text box in the toolbar.

Editing the Data Source

If you find that you need to edit the data source, add a record, or delete a record, click the Edit Data Source button (the last button on the right in the toolbar). Clicking this button displays the Data Form dialog box, with your records in view. Make any editing changes, and choose OK to close the dialog box. Word returns to the document.

Merging the Data and the Document

You can merge the data and the document to a new document or to the printer by clicking buttons in the Merge toolbar. Most of the time, you will merge your files to the printer.

Merging the files to the printer prints each letter with its personalized information. The letter file remains separate from the data source file, but the information is merged just before printing.

If you click the Merge to New Document button, Word creates a document containing one letter for each record in the data source. The reasons you would merge the data to a new document are to check each letter (and perhaps add personal comments to some of the letters) and to start printing where you left off if your printer jams.

Caution

If you have many records in your data source—hundreds or even thousands—a merged file may be unmanageable; it could slow your system considerably.

To merge the files to the printer, click the Merge to Printer button in the Merge toolbar.

From Here...

Learning to use macros and mail merge can save you time and energy. You can automate your work with macros by recording several commands, saving the recording, and then playing it back any time you want to perform those commands. Additionally, you can use Word's Mail Merge Helper to create an address list and a letter, and then print your merged documents. For related information on these topics, see the following chapters:

- Chapter 12, "Creating Worksheets," covers common terms used in Excel, moving around a worksheet, entering data, selecting cells and ranges, entering series data, and saving and naming a file.
- Chapter 13, "Editing Worksheets," covers editing, copying, and moving worksheet data; inserting and deleting columns, rows, and cells; inserting and deleting worksheets; finding and replacing data; and spell-checking text in a worksheet.

Part III

Using Excel

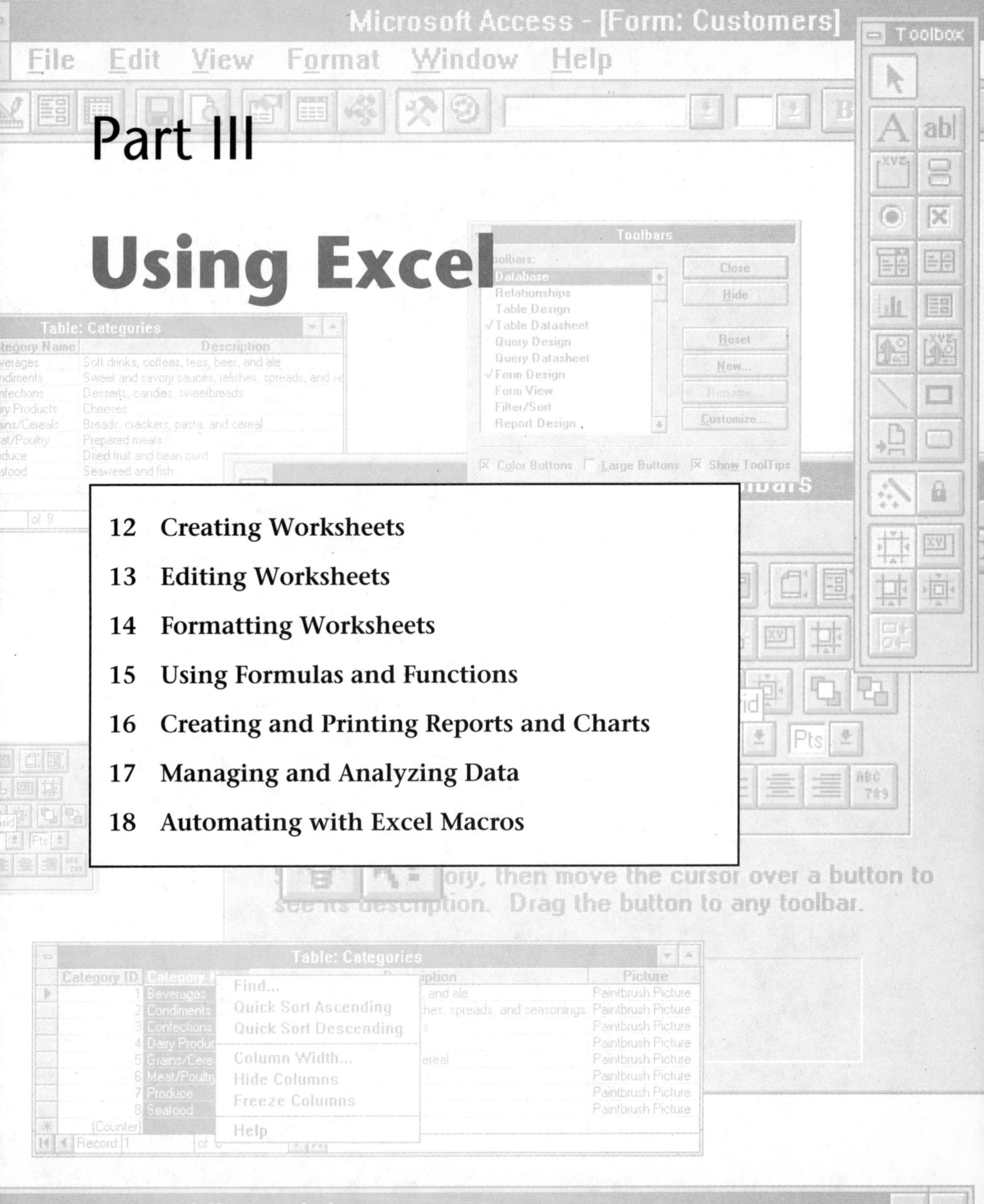

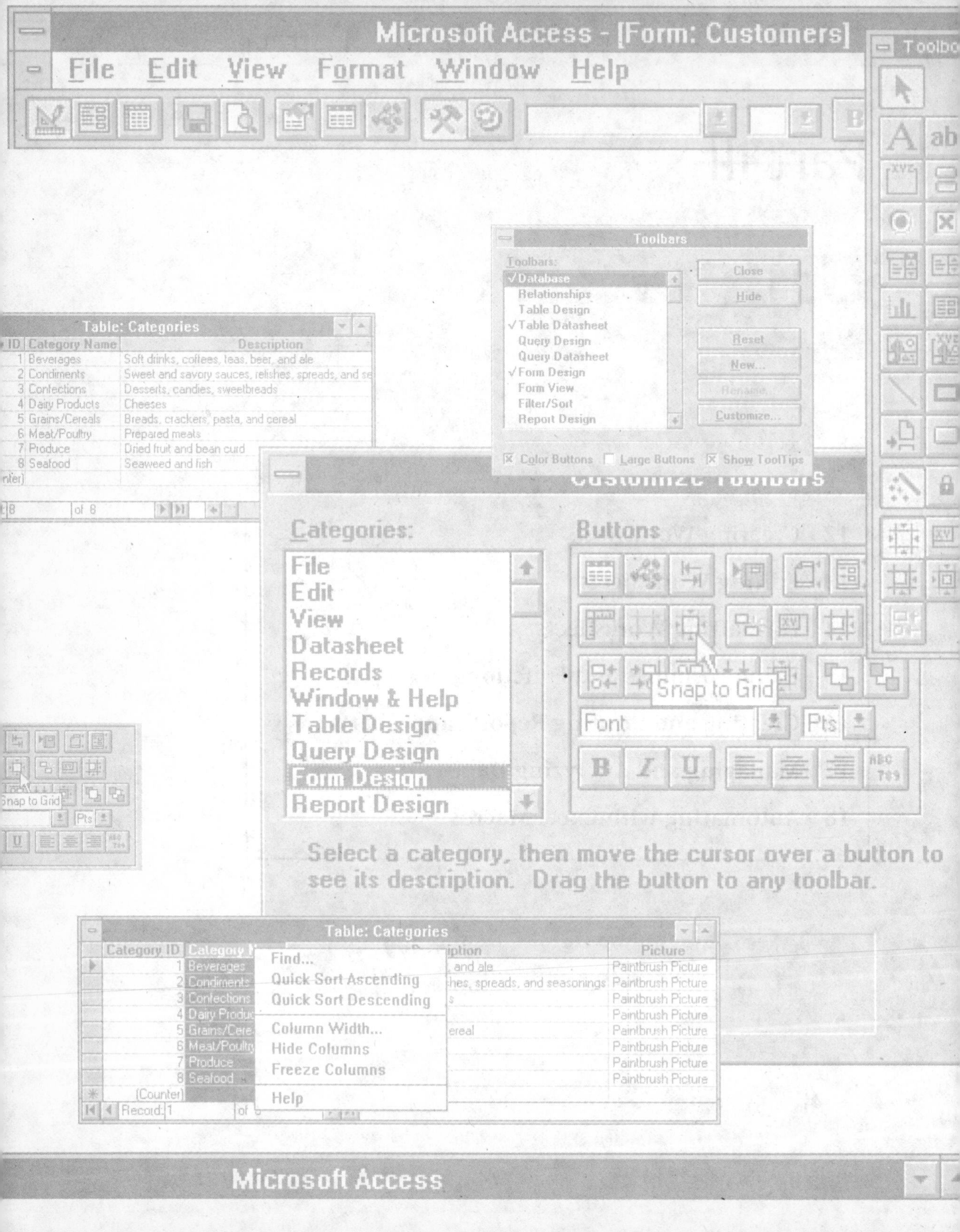
Microsoft Access - [Form: Customers]
File Edit View Format Window Help
Toolbars
Toolbars:
√Database
Relationships
Table Design
√Table Datasheet
Query Design
Query Datasheet
√Form Design
Form View
Filter/Sort
Report Design
Close
Hide
Reset
New...
Rename...
Customize...
Color Buttons
Large Buttons
Show ToolTips
Table: Categories
Category Name
Description
1 Beverages
Soft drinks, coffees, teas, beer, and ale
2 Condiments
Sweet and savory sauces, relishes, spreads, and se
3 Confections
Desserts, candies, sweetbreads
4 Dairy Products
Cheeses
5 Grains/Cereals
Breads, crackers, pasta, and cereal
6 Meat/Poultry
Prepared meats
7 Produce
Dried fruit and bean curd
8 Seafood
Seaweed and fish
Customize Toolbars
Categories:
File
Edit
View
Datasheet
Records
Window & Help
Table Design
Query Design
Form Design
Report Design
Buttons
Snap to Grid
Font
Pts
Select a category, then move the cursor over a button to see its description. Drag the button to any toolbar.
Category ID
Picture
Find...
Quick Sort Ascending
Quick Sort Descending
Column Width...
Hide Columns
Freeze Columns
Help
Paintbrush Picture
(Counter)
Record: 1
Microsoft Access

Chapter 12

Creating Worksheets

by Cathy Kenny

In this chapter, you learn the basic techniques for creating worksheets in Excel. The chapter begins with an introduction to fundamental Excel terms and concepts. You then learn how to enter data, move to other areas in the worksheet, and select cells and ranges. Once you've mastered these skills, you'll have the confidence to create nearly any type of worksheet.

In this chapter, you learn to

- Move around the worksheet
- Enter text, numbers, and formulas
- Select cells and ranges
- Repeat and undo Excel commands
- Save a worksheet

Defining Excel Terms

When you start Excel, a blank workbook appears in the document window. The *workbook* is the main document used in Excel for storing and manipulating data. A workbook consists of individual worksheets, each of which can contain data. Initially, each new workbook you create contains 16 worksheets; you can add more worksheets.

Each worksheet is made up of 256 columns and 16,384 rows. The columns are lettered across the top of the document window, beginning with A through Z and continuing with AA through AZ, BA through BZ, and so on through column IV. The rows are numbered from 1 to 16,384 down the left side of the document window.

The intersections of rows and columns form *cells*, which are the basic units for storing data. Each cell takes its name from this intersection and is referred to as a *cell address*. The address of the cell at the intersection of column C and row 5, for example, is referred to as cell C5.

At the bottom of each worksheet is a series of *sheet tabs*, which enable you to identify each worksheet in the workbook. The tabs initially are labeled Sheet1, Sheet2, and so on, as shown at the bottom of the screen in figure 12.1.

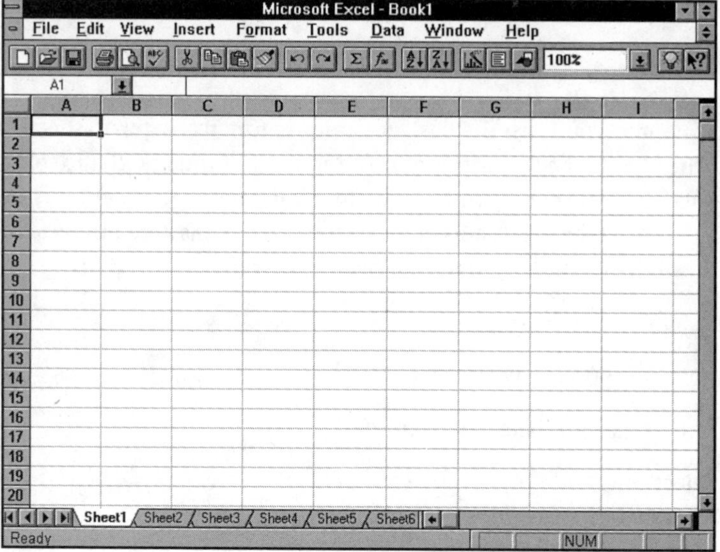

Fig. 12.1
An Excel workbook is made up of columns, rows, cells, and worksheets.

Each workbook can contain as many as 255 sheets. In Excel you can create up to six different types of sheets. You can create a worksheet, chart sheet, visual basic module, dialog, Microsoft Excel 4.0 macro sheet,and a Microsoft Excel 4.0 international macro sheet.

Moving Around in a Worksheet

In a new worksheet, the cell at the intersection of column A and row 1 is highlighted, indicating that cell A1 is the active cell. When you start typing, the data appears in the active cell. To enter data in another cell, first make that cell active by moving the cell pointer to it, using either the mouse or keyboard.

Mouse Movements

Using the mouse, you can activate a cell quickly by placing the cell pointer on the cell and clicking the left mouse button. Figure 12.2 shows the cell pointer highlighting the active cell.

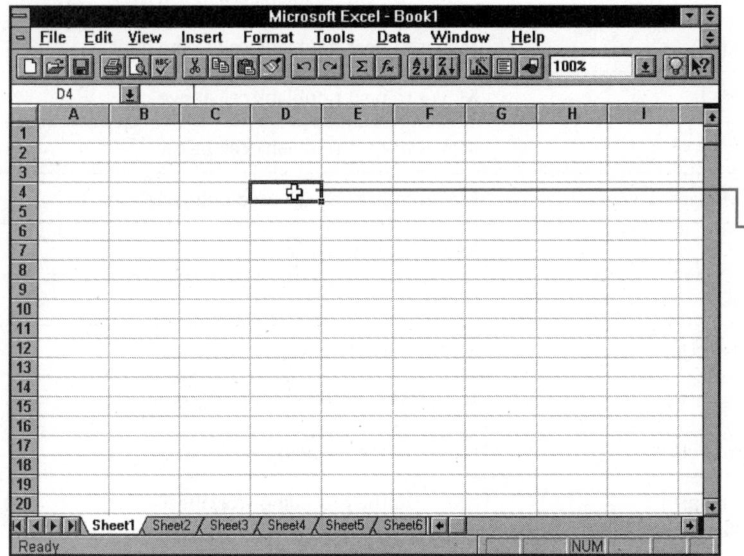

Fig. 12.2
To activate a cell, place the cell pointer on that cell and click the mouse.

Keyboard Movements

You can use the arrow, PgUp, and PgDn keys on your keyboard, or various key combinations, to move to another cell. The keys that you use to move to new locations are listed in table 12.1.

Table 12.1 Using the Keyboard to Move among Cells

Keys	Description
←,→,↑,↓	Moves one cell to the left, right, up, or down, respectively
Ctrl+←, →, ↑, ↓	Moves to the next cell of data separated by a blank cell
Tab	Moves one cell to the right
Enter	Moves one cell down
Shift+Tab	Moves one cell to the left
Home	Moves to column A of the active row

(continues)

Table 12.1 Continued

Keys	Description
Ctrl+Home	Moves to cell A1 of the worksheet
End+←	Moves to next nonblank cell to the left
End+→	Moves to next nonblank cell to the right
End+↑	Moves to next nonblank cell above
End+↓	Moves to next nonblank cell below
Ctrl+End	Moves to the last cell used in the worksheet
PgUp	Moves up one screen
PgDn	Moves down one screen
Alt+PgUp	Moves one screen width to the left
Alt+PgDn	Moves one screen width to the right
Ctrl+PgUp	Moves to the following worksheet
Ctrl+PgDn	Moves to the preceding worksheet

Use the Go To command to move to a specific cell. Choose the **E**dit **G**o To command or press the F5 function key to display the Go To dialog box (see fig. 12.3).

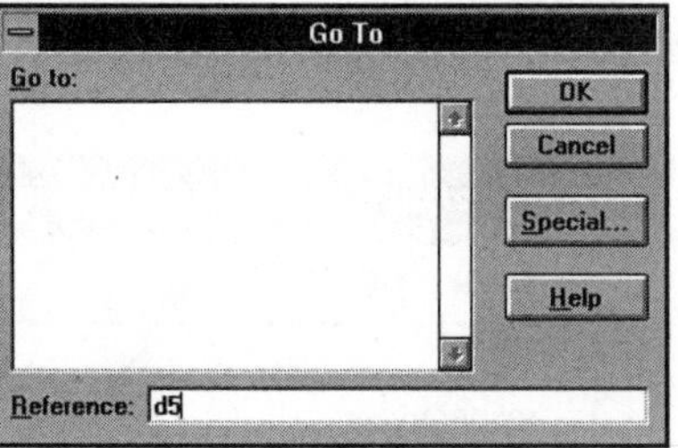

Fig. 12.3
The Go To dialog box enables you to move to a specific cell.

When the Go To dialog box appears, type the address of the cell you want to move to in the **R**eference text box, and then press Enter. To move to cell D5, for example, type **D5** and then press Enter or click the OK button. The cell pointer moves to cell D5, which becomes the active cell.

You also can move to a specific cell by using the *name box*, located at the left end of the formula bar. Click the box, type the address of the cell to which you want to move, and then press Enter. (The formula bar is discussed in "Entering Data" later in this chapter.)

Moving Around by Scrolling

To view another section of the worksheet without moving the active cell, use the vertical and horizontal scroll bars to reposition the screen. Using the mouse, click the up or down scroll arrow to scroll line by line. You also can scroll the screen by dragging the scroll box up and down the scroll bar. If you click the scroll bar above the scroll box, the screen scrolls up one page. If you click the scroll bar below the scroll box, the screen scrolls down one page.

Tip
If you want to see the active cell when it is not visible in the current window, press Ctrl+Backspace. The window scrolls to display the active cell and selected ranges remain selected.

To scroll through a worksheet by using the keyboard, press the Scroll Lock key on your keyboard, and use the arrow keys to scroll to the section of the worksheet you want to view. Scrolling moves the screen but does not change the active cell.

Entering Data

After you activate the cell in which you want to enter data, you can type text, numbers, dates, times, or formulas in the cell. As you type, the data appears in the active cell and in the area above the worksheet called the *formula bar* (see fig. 12.4). The formula bar displays the *insertion point*, a blinking bar that indicates where the next character you type will appear.

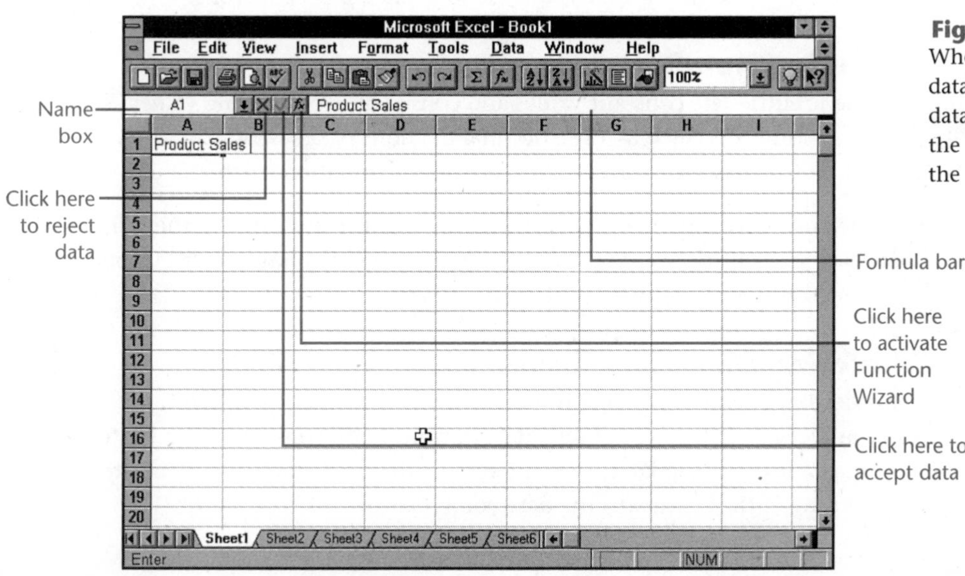

Fig. 12.4
When you enter data in a cell, the data appears in the cell and in the formula bar.

Three small boxes appear between the scroll arrow for the name box and the insertion point in the formula bar. The first two boxes enable you to reject or accept the data you entered. To reject your entry, click the X box or press Esc. To accept your entry, click the check box or press Enter. The third box in the formula bar activates the Function Wizard, a dialog box that enables you to build formulas by using Excel's built-in functions. Chapter 15, "Using Formulas and Functions," describes how to enter formulas with the Function Wizard.

Entering Text

Text entries consist of alphanumeric characters such as letters, numbers, and symbols. You can enter up to 255 characters in a single cell, although Excel may not be able to display all the characters if the cell is not wide enough or if an entry appears in the cell to its right. When you enter text in a cell, Excel stores that entry as text and aligns it to the left edge of the cell.

When you enter data that consists of numbers and text, Excel evaluates the entry to determine its value. If you type an entry such as **1098 Adams Street**, for example, Excel automatically determines that it is a text entry because of the letters.

If you want to enter a number as text, such as a ZIP code, precede the entry with an apostrophe. Excel uses the apostrophe label prefix to denote a text entry. You can use the apostrophe when you want to enter a number but do not want Excel to interpret it as a value to be used in calculations.

Entering Numbers

▶ "Changing Column Width and Row Height," p. 288

▶ "Formatting Numbers," p. 281

Numeric entries are constant values and consist only of numeric values. You can enter integers (such as 124), decimal fractions (such as 14.426), integer fractions (such as 1 1/5), and values in scientific notation (such as 1.23E+08).

If you enter a long number in a cell and the cell displays ##### or the number appears in scientific notation (1.23E+08), the current column width is too small to display the number in its entirety.

Entering Dates and Times

In addition to entering text and numbers, you can enter dates and times in a worksheet cell. When you enter a date or time, Excel converts the entry to a serial number. This serial number represents the number of days from the beginning of the century to the date you type.

Because Excel converts dates and times to serial numbers, you can perform calculations on these values as you would with any number. For example, you could determine the number of days that have passed between two dates.

To enter a date, type the date, using any of these formats:

3/12/94
12-Mar-94
12-Mar
Mar-12

Tip
To enter the current date in a cell quickly, press Ctrl+; (semicolon). To enter the current time, press Ctrl+: (colon).

To enter a time, use any of these formats:

14:25
14:25:09
2:25 PM
2:25:09 PM

Entering Formulas

One of the most valuable features of Excel is its capability to calculate values by using formulas. Excel formulas can range from the simple, such as adding a range of values, to the complex, such as calculating the future value of a stream of cash flows.

You can calculate values based on numbers that you type directly into the formula. For example, you can enter the formula **=4+5+7** to add the values 4, 5, and 7. However, the power of Excel's formula capability lies in the fact that formulas also can refer to data in other cells in the worksheet. The formula =B2+B3+B4, for example, adds the values in cells B2, B3, and B4. When the values in these cells change, Excel automatically updates and recalculates the formula, using the new data in these cells.

▶ "Creating Formulas," p. 309

Excel recognizes a formula in a cell if the entry starts with an equal sign (=) or a plus sign (+). To enter a formula, first type = and then type the formula. The active cell and the formula bar display the formula as you enter it. After the formula is complete, press Enter; the active cell displays the result of the formula (see fig. 12.5). The formula bar continues to show the formula when the cell is the active cell.

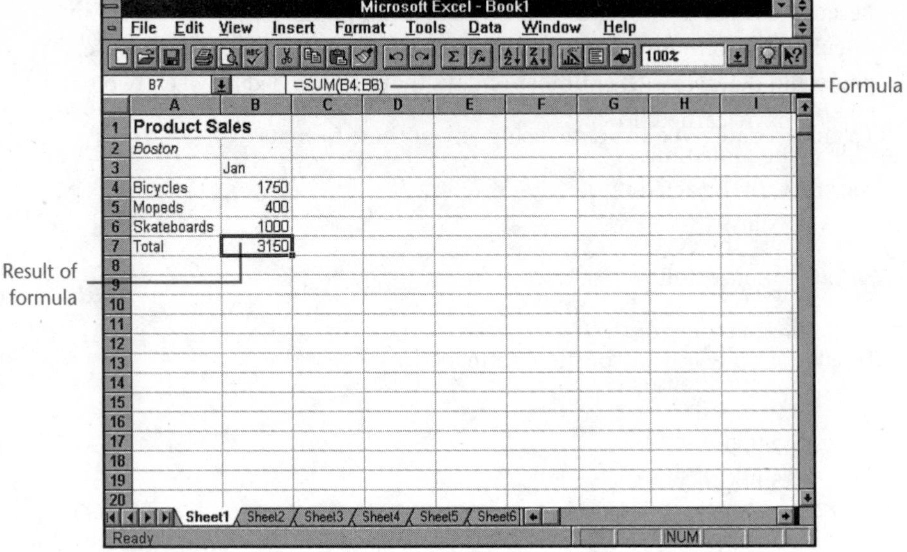

Fig. 12.5
When you enter a formula in a cell, Excel displays the result.

Troubleshooting

A formula used to calculate a range of cells does not calculate properly.

Make sure that values in the range have not been entered as text. To do so, highlight each cell in the range, and check for the appearance of an apostrophe at the beginning of the entry. If an apostrophe appears, press F2 to enter edit mode, press the Home key to move to the beginning of the entry, press the Delete key to remove the apostrophe, and press Enter. Continue with these steps until all cell entries have been checked.

Excel converted a date to a number.

You must enter dates in a format that Excel recognizes—for example, 3/12/94 or 12-Mar-94. Other characters may not produce a valid date. Sometimes a cell in which you enter a date may already contain a numeric format. Use the Format Cells command to assign a different format.

A formula appears as a label in a cell.

If you neglect to enter an equal sign or plus sign in front of a cell reference, Excel interprets the entry as a label. To fix this problem, highlight the cell and press F2. Then press the Home key, type the equal sign, and press Enter.

Selecting Cells and Ranges

Many commands in Excel require that you select a cell or range of cells. You already have learned how to select a single cell. You also can select several cells at the same time. A group of cells is called a *range*. A range is a group of cells that can be acted upon with Excel commands.

You can use the keyboard or the mouse to select a range. To select a range with the mouse, follow these steps:

1. Click a corner of the range you want to select.
2. Drag the mouse over the range.
3. When you reach the end of the selection range, release the mouse button.

To select a range with the keyboard, follow these steps:

1. Move to a cell at a corner of the range you want to select.
2. Press and hold down the Shift key, and then press the arrow keys to select the range.

Figure 12.6 shows a selected range.

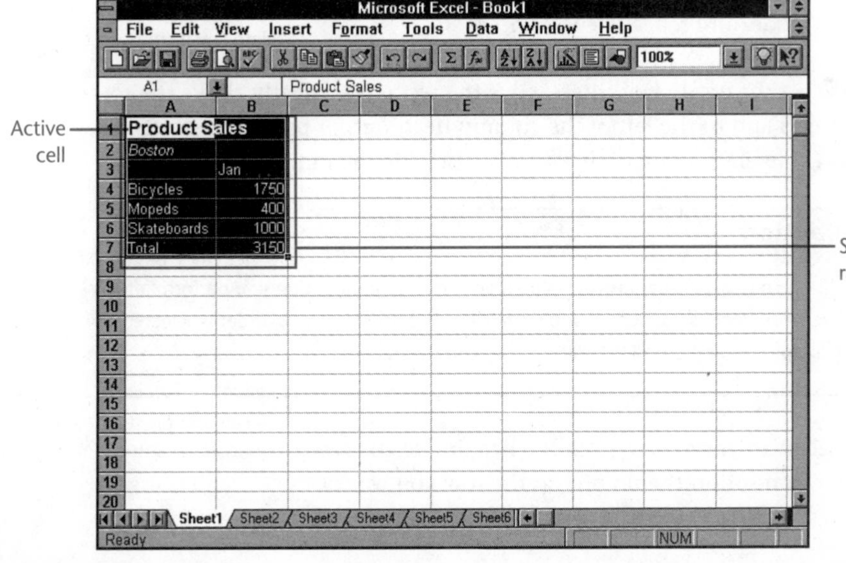

Fig. 12.6
The first cell of the selected range is the active cell and has a white background.

Note

If you select a range of cells and then move the cell pointer, the range is deselected. If this happens, just select the range again.

Excel also enables you to select more than one range of cells at a time with the same ease as selecting a single range.

To select multiple ranges with the mouse, follow these steps:

1. Click and drag the mouse over the first range you want to select.

2. Press and hold down the Ctrl key, and continue selecting other ranges.

To select multiple ranges with the keyboard, follow these steps:

1. Press and hold down the Shift key, and use the arrow keys to select the first range.

2. Press Shift+F8. The indicator ADD appears in the status bar at the bottom of the screen indicating that you can extend a selection.

3. Move to a cell at a corner of the next range you want to select.

4. Press Shift and an arrow key to select the range. ADD disappears from the status bar. To add another range, press Shift+F8 to go back to add mode, and repeat steps 3 and 4.

To select the entire worksheet, click the rectangle directly above the row numbers and to the left of the column headings, or press Ctrl+Shift+space bar. To deselect a range, click any cell outside the range.

Caution

When you select an entire worksheet, any command or action you perform affects the worksheet as a whole. If you press Del while an entire worksheet is selected, for example, you delete all the data in the worksheet.

To select an entire row, click the heading of the row you want to select. You also can position the pointer in the row you want to select and press Shift+space bar. Figure 12.7 shows two ranges selected in a worksheet.

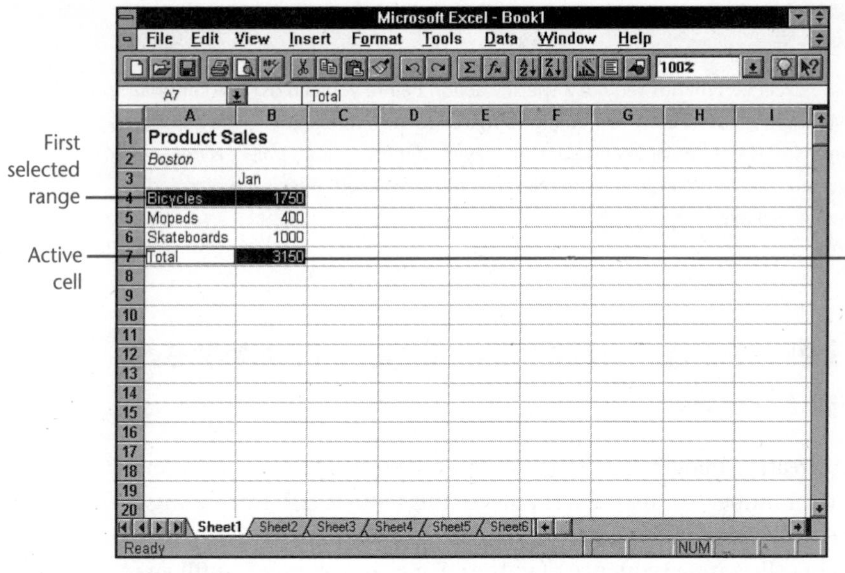

Fig. 12.7
Two nonadjacent ranges are selected at the same time.

To select an entire column, click the heading of the column you want to select. You also can position the pointer in the column you want to select and press Ctrl+space bar (see fig. 12.8).

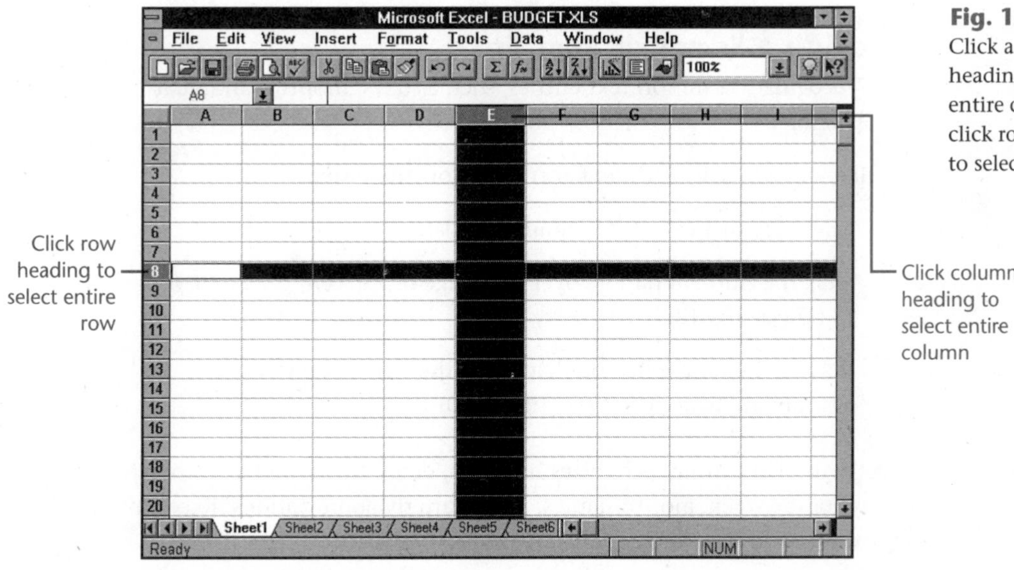

Fig. 12.8
Click a column heading to select entire column; click row heading to select entire row.

III

Using Excel

Note

Some Excel commands require a specific action before you can use the command. If you do not cut or copy something to the Clipboard, for example, the **E**dit **P**aste command is not available and appears grayed (dimmed). If an object is not selected, the commands that are relevant only to selected objects are dimmed and unavailable.

Entering a Series of Text, Numbers, and Dates

When creating budgets and forecasts, you often need to include a series of dates, numbers, or text. Excel relieves this tedious task by offering the AutoFill feature, which enables you to create a worksheet quickly by filling a range of cells with a sequence of entries. For example, you can fill a range of cells with consecutive dates or create a series of column headings.

You can create a series of entries in two ways: use the mouse to drag the *AutoFill handle* (the small square at the bottom right corner of the active cell), or choose the **E**dit F**i**ll **S**eries command.

Creating a Series of Text Entries

Excel recognizes common text entries, such as days, months, and quarterly abbreviations.

To fill a range of cells with text entries, follow these steps:

1. Select the first cell that contains the data.
2. Drag the AutoFill handle over the range of adjacent cells that you want to fill (see fig. 12.9).
3. Release the mouse button. Excel fills the range of selected cells with the appropriate text entries (see fig. 12.10).

Excel's AutoFill feature recognizes numbers, dates, times, and key words, such as days of the week, month names, and quarterly abbreviations. Excel knows how these series run and extends the series to repeat correctly. Table 12.2 shows examples of series that Excel can use with AutoFill.

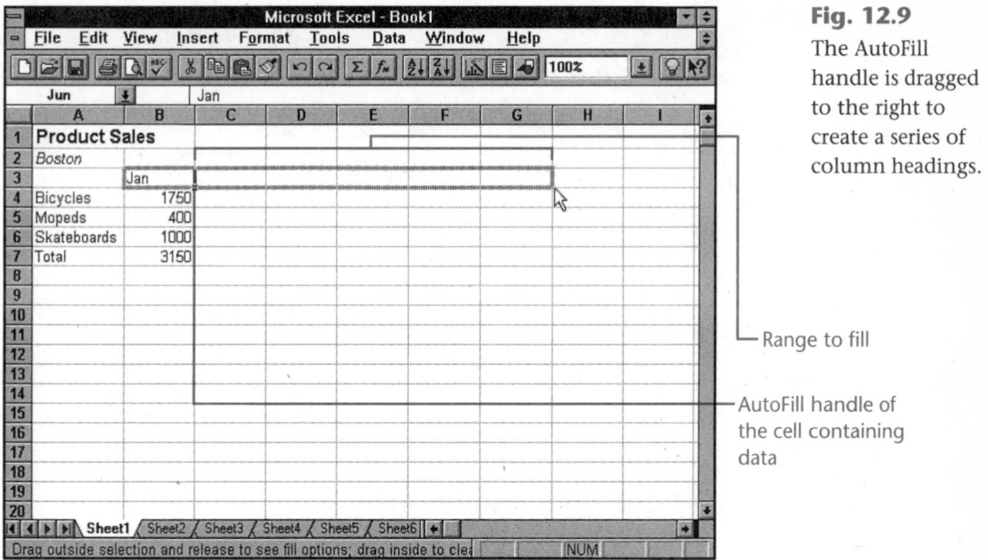

Fig. 12.9
The AutoFill handle is dragged to the right to create a series of column headings.

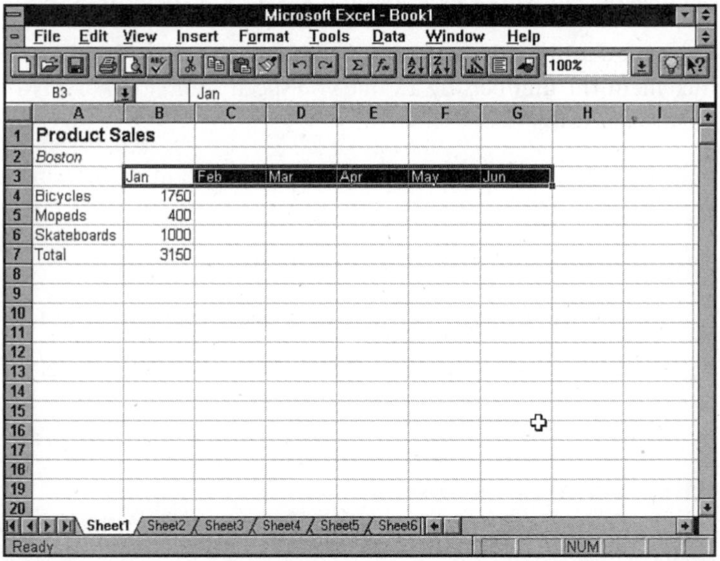

Fig. 12.10
Excel fills the selected range of cells with a series of column headings.

Table 12.2 Fill Sequences	
Data You Enter	**Sequence Returned**
Qtr 1	Qtr 2, Qtr 3, Qtr 4
Product 1	Product 2, Product 3, Product 4

(continues)

Table 12.2 Continued

Data You Enter	Sequence Returned
1993	1994, 1995, 1996
Jan	Jan, Feb, Mar
Jan 93	Jan 94, Jan 95, Jan 96
Mon	Tue, Wed, Thu
North	South, East, West
2, 4	6, 8, 10...

Creating a Series of Numbers

You can enter a series of numbers that increment by 1 or that increment by values that you specify.

Tip
To prevent a series from incrementing, hold down the Ctrl key as you drag the Auto-Fill handle.

To fill a range of cells with a series of numbers, follow these steps:

1. Enter the starting number in the first cell of the range. If you want to increment the numbers by a value you specify, enter the first two values in adjacent cells.

   Excel uses these two values to determine the amount to increment in each step.

2. Select the range containing the numbers.
3. Drag the fill handle over the range of adjacent cells you want to fill.
4. Release the mouse button. Excel fills the range of selected cells with the appropriate numeric entries (see fig. 12.11).

Creating a Series of Dates

You can fill a range of cells with a series of consecutive dates that increment by a specific value.

To fill a range of cells with dates, follow these steps:

1. Enter the starting date in the first cell in the range. If you want to increment the date by a specific value, enter the appropriate date in the next cell in the range.
2. Select the range containing the dates.

3. Drag the AutoFill handle over the range of adjacent cells you want to fill.

4. Release the mouse button. Excel fills the range of selected cells with the appropriate dates (see fig. 12.12).

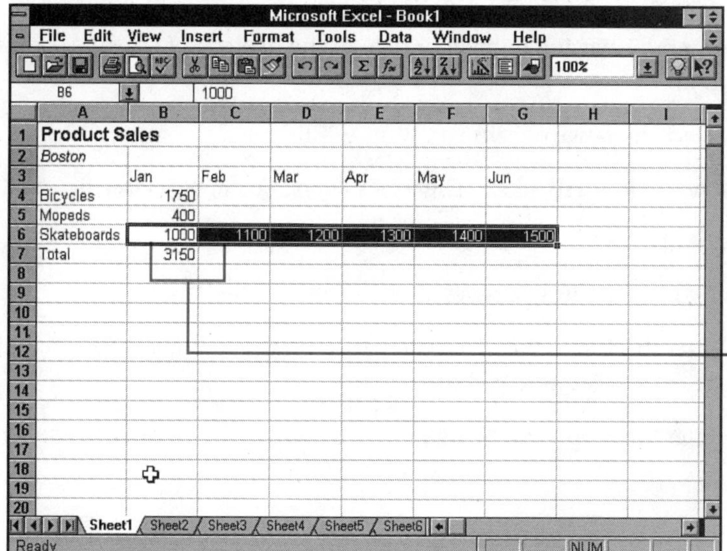

To increment by a value other than 1, enter desired values in the first two cells of the range

Fig. 12.11
The AutoFill handle creates this series of numbers in increments of 100.

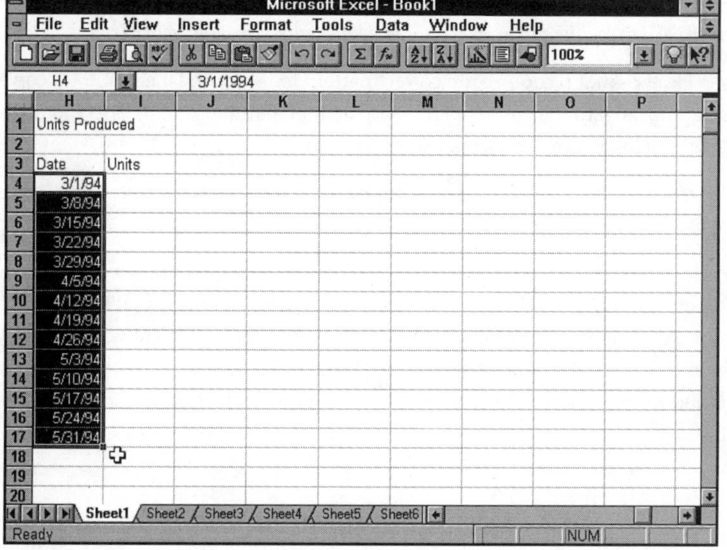

Fig. 12.12
The AutoFill handle created this series of dates in increments of one week.

Entering a Series with the Edit Fill Series Command

The **E**dit F**i**ll **S**eries command enables you to fill a range of cells with greater precision than with the AutoFill handle. For example, when you choose **E**dit F**i**ll **S**eries, you can specify a stop value as well as a start value.

To fill a range of cells with the **E**dit F**i**ll **S**eries command, follow these steps:

1. Enter the starting number or date in the first cell of the range you want to fill.
2. Select the range of cells you want to fill.
3. Choose **E**dit F**i**ll **S**eries. The Series dialog box appears (see fig. 12.13).
4. Specify the Type of series you want to create.
5. If you are creating a series of dates, specify the Date Unit.
6. Enter the **S**tep Value. This value represents the amount by which the series changes from cell to cell.
7. Enter the St**o**p Value. This value represents the last value in the series.
8. Choose OK.

Troubleshooting

AutoFill filled the entire range with the same label entered in the first cell of the range.

When Excel cannot recognize the correct pattern for entering labels, AutoFill copies the starting label to the entire range. Make certain that the starting label is one that AutoFill can recognize. For example, Qtr 1 or January.

I tried to use AutoFill to extend a series, but numbers were not incremented by the difference of the first two numbers of my series.

If the increment in the AutoFill range was 1, you probably did not select the first two cells before using AutoFill. Be sure to select the two cells because that is what Excel uses to determine the increment or it defaults to 1. If the increment was not the difference between your first two cells or 1, you probably selected more than two cells and Excel averaged the difference to determine the increment. Again, be sure to just select two cells.

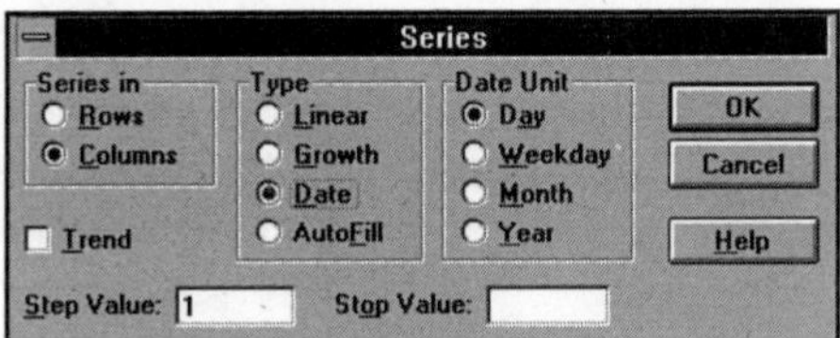

Fig. 12.13
In the Series dialog box, select the type of series and the step and stop values.

Repeating and Undoing a Command

Excel has a built-in safety net that enables you to reverse many commands or actions. The **E**dit **U**ndo command reverses the last command you selected or the last action you performed. To undo a command or action, choose **E**dit **U**ndo or press Ctrl+Z.

Note

Excel retains only the last action or command. You must choose the **E**dit **U**ndo command immediately after the command or action.

Undo is not available for all commands. If you choose **E**dit De**l**ete Sheet and delete a worksheet from a workbook, for example, the **E**dit menu shows `Can't Undo` as a dimmed command. Although **U**ndo can reverse many actions, you still must use certain commands with caution.

To reverse the **U**ndo command, choose **E**dit **U**ndo again or press Ctrl+Z.

Excel also enables you to repeat the last command or action you performed. To repeat a command or action, choose **E**dit **R**epeat or press F4.

Saving Workbooks

When you create a new workbook, Excel assigns to it the name Book1. You must save the file to disk to make the workbook permanent. To save a file in Excel, choose **F**ile **S**ave or press Ctrl+S. Enter a name for the file and specify the location to which the workbook should be saved.

◄ "Working with Files," p. 71

In addition to saving new workbooks, you can also save files to other file formats, such as Excel 4.0 and Lotus 1-2-3. Excel also enables you to save workbook settings in a worskspace file.

Saving Files to Other File Formats

When you save a file, Excel automatically assigns an extension to the file. If you are saving a workbook, the extension is XLS; the extension for a template is XLT; and the extension for a workspace is XLW.

You can use the Save File as **T**ype drop-down list to save an Excel file in another file format. To save an Excel file for use in Lotus 1-2-3, for example, drop down the Save File as **T**ype list, and then select the 1-2-3 Lotus file format you want (see fig. 12.14). Excel supports 1-2-3 Releases 1 (WKS), 2 (WK1), and 3 (WK3).

Fig. 12.14
You can save an Excel file in a 1-2-3 file format.

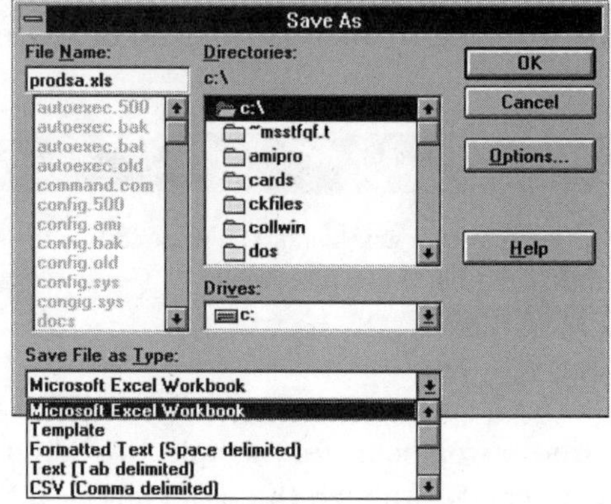

If you use a worksheet feature that is not supported by earlier versions of Excel or other spreadsheets, the value result of that feature is calculated and saved with the worksheet.

Saving a Workspace File

If you work with the same set of workbooks on a daily basis, Excel enables you to save information about what workbooks are open and how they are arranged on-screen. The next time you want to work with these workbooks, you only need to open the workspace file, and all the workbooks are opened and arranged as they were when you saved the file.

The **F**ile Save **W**orkspace command creates a workspace file that contains the name and location of each workbook in the workspace and the position of each workbook when the workspace was saved.

To create a workspace file, follow these steps:

1. Open and arrange the workbooks as you want them to be saved in the workspace.

2. Choose the **F**ile Save **W**orkspace command. Figure 12.15 shows the Save Workspace dialog box that is displayed.

3. Type a name for the file in the File **N**ame text box.

4. Choose OK.

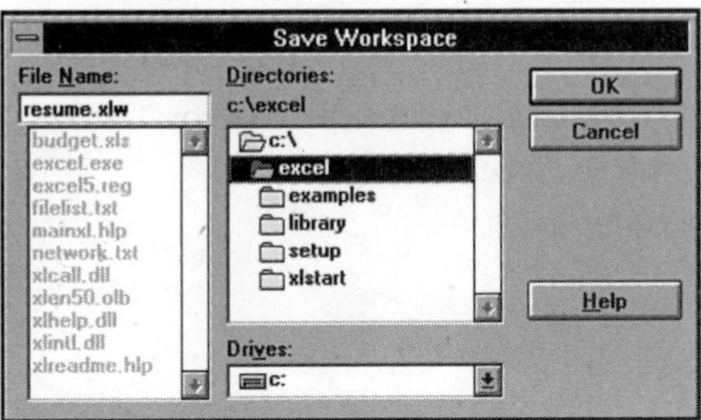

Fig. 12.15
Type a name for the workspace file in the Save Workspace dialog box.

> **Note**
>
> When you create a workspace file, do not move any of the workbook files to a new location. If you do, Excel will not be able to locate the files when you open the workspace file.

You can open a workspace file just as you would any other Excel file. After you have opened the file, you can save and close the individual workbooks in the workspace as you normally would. When you make changes to a workbook in the workspace, you must save the file using the **F**ile **S**ave command. The **F**ile Save **W**orkspace command saves only information on which workbooks are open and how they are arranged on-screen.

From Here...

In this chapter, you learned the basic skills for creating and working with Excel worksheets. For more information about working with worksheets and data, see the following chapters:

- Chapter 13, "Editing Worksheets," shows you how to edit worksheet data.

- Chapter 14, "Formatting Worksheets," presents the formatting features of Excel that enable you to improve the appearance of data in the worksheet.

- Chapter 15, "Using Formulas and Functions," teaches you how to create formulas and use Excel's built-in functions to calculate values.
- Chapter 16, "Creating and Printing Reports and Charts," shows you how to print Excel worksheets and how to present worksheet data in graphs.
- Chapter 17, "Managing and Analyzing Data," explains how to manage lists of information and how to analyze worksheet data.
- Chapter 18, "Automating with Excel Macros," shows you how to create macros to automate Excel features.

Chapter 13

Editing Worksheets

by Cathy Kenny

After creating a worksheet, you will spend the majority of your time editing the work you have done. You may need to move data from one area of the worksheet to another, or you may want to copy a range of data. This chapter presents the basics for editing a worksheet in Excel.

In this chapter, you learn to

- Edit the contents of a cell
- Clear the contents of a cell
- Copy, cut, and paste worksheet data
- Insert and delete columns, rows, and worksheets
- Find and replace worksheet data
- Spell-check your worksheet

Editing Worksheet Data

After you enter data in a cell, you can edit the contents of the cell. You can edit the contents using the formula bar, or you can use the in-cell editing feature of Excel to edit the contents directly in the cell.

Note

To use the in-cell editing feature of Excel, you must make sure that the feature has been enabled. To double-check, choose the **T**ools **O**ptions command, and select the Edit tab. The **E**dit Directly in Cell option should be selected. If it isn't, click the check box to the left of the option. Choose OK when you finish.

Editing an Existing Cell Entry

▶ "Formatting Numbers," p. 281

To edit the contents of a cell, first select the cell you want to edit, and then click the formula bar or press F2. The contents of the cell appear in the formula bar.

To edit the contents of a cell directly in the cell, double-click the cell.

To edit the entry, use the left and right arrow keys to reposition the insertion point in the formula bar, or move the mouse and use the on-screen I-beam to reposition the insertion point in the formula bar. The vertical blinking bar appears where the I-beam is positioned when you click the mouse (see fig. 13.1). Then press Del or Backspace to delete characters to the left or right of the insertion point, respectively.

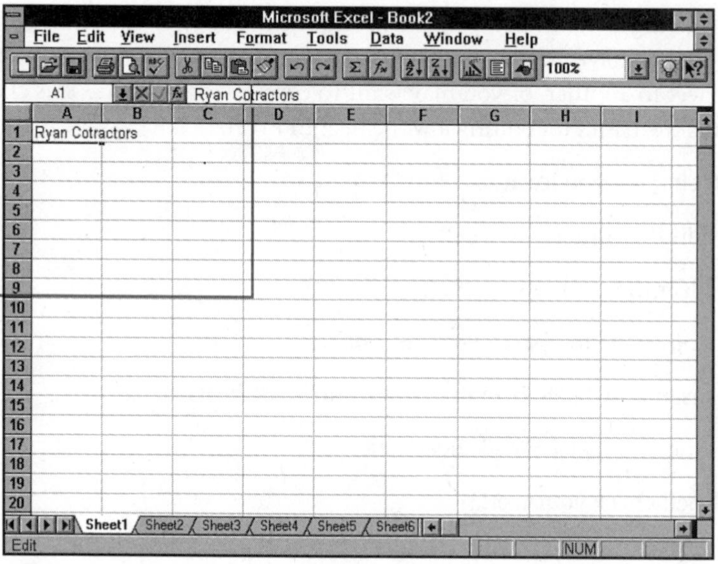

Fig. 13.1 The insertion point shows where the next character you type will appear.

Insertion point

When editing a cell, you can reposition the insertion point by using the mouse or the keyboard. Table 13.1 lists the editing keys on the keyboard.

Table 13.1 Editing Keys

Key	Action
←	Moves one character to the left.
→	Moves one character to the right.

Key	Action
Ctrl+→	Moves to the next word.
Ctrl+←	Moves to the preceding word.
End	Moves to the end of the cell entry.
Home	Moves to the beginning of the cell entry.
Del	Deletes next character to the right.
Backspace	Deletes preceding character.

Deleting Worksheet Data

In addition to editing the contents of a cell, you can delete the data in a cell. To replace an existing cell entry, select the cell and type the new entry. When you do, the new entry replaces the current contents of the cell. If you want to delete the contents of a cell or range altogether, the easiest way to do it is to select the cell or range of cells and then press the Del key. When you do, Excel clears the contents of the cell or range.

Clearing Cell Contents

When you use the Del key to clear a cell, Excel clears all data from the cell, including cell formatting. The **E**dit Cle**a**r command, on the other hand, enables you to choose what you want to clear from the cell.

To clear the contents of a cell or range, select the cell or range and then choose the **E**dit Cle**a**r command. Select from the Edit Clear cascading menu the command that represents the data you want to clear.

Choose **A**ll to clear everything from the cell, including cell formatting and cell notes. Choose **F**ormats to clear only cell formatting from the cell. To clear the contents of a cell, but leave formatting and cell notes intact, choose **C**ontents. To remove only cell notes from a selected range of cells, choose **N**otes.

Caution

A common error many new users make when clearing cells is selecting the cell and then pressing the space bar. Although the cell may appear to be blank, Excel actually is storing the space in the cell. Spaces can cause problems in worksheet calculations. Do not press the space bar to clear a cell. Instead, use the methods outlined in this section.

Tip

To clear the contents of a cell or range quickly, highlight the range and click the right mouse button. Then choose the Clear Contents command from the shortcut menu.

► "Changing Fonts, Sizes, and Styles" p. 295

► "Annotating Worksheets," p. 402

Copying Worksheet Data

Excel provides several options for copying worksheet data. You can copy data by using the drag-and-drop method, copy data to the Clipboard, or copy data to adjacent cells by using the AutoFill feature.

Copying Data with Drag-and-Drop

The quickest way to copy worksheet data is to use the drag-and-drop method. As its name implies, you simply drag the data you want to copy to another area of the worksheet.

◄ "Copying and Moving," p. 52

► "Copying Formulas," p. 322

To copy data with drag-and-drop, follow these steps:

1. Select the range of cells you want to copy.
2. Position the mouse pointer on the border of the selected data.
3. Hold down the Ctrl key, and click and drag the selection to the new location.

   As you move the mouse pointer, Excel displays an outline indicating the size and location of the copied data (see fig. 13.2).
4. Release the mouse button to drop the copied data in its new location.

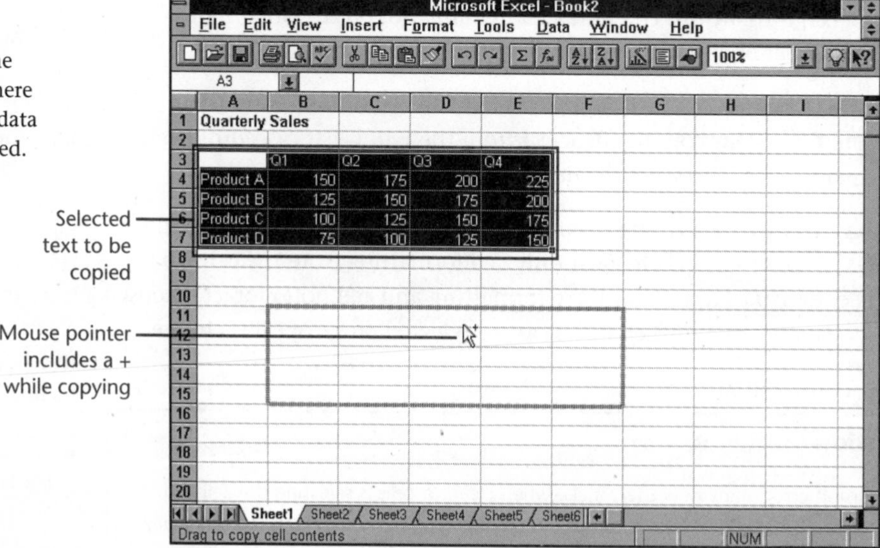

Fig. 13.2 An outline indicates the location where the copied data will be placed.

Copying Data with Copy and Paste

When you need to make multiple copies of worksheet data, the easiest way to accomplish this is to use the Edit Copy and Edit Paste commands. When you use the Edit Copy command, a copy of the selected data is stored on the Clipboard. You then can paste as many copies in the worksheet as you need.

◀ "Copying and Moving," p. 52

To copy data by using Edit Copy and Edit Paste, follow these steps:

1. Select the range of data you want to copy.

2. Choose the **E**dit **C**opy command, or press Ctrl+C. Alternatively, click the right mouse button and then choose Copy from the resulting shortcut menu.

   A marquee surrounds the selection you copied, and the status bar at the bottom of the screen prompts you to select the location to which to copy the data (see fig. 13.3).

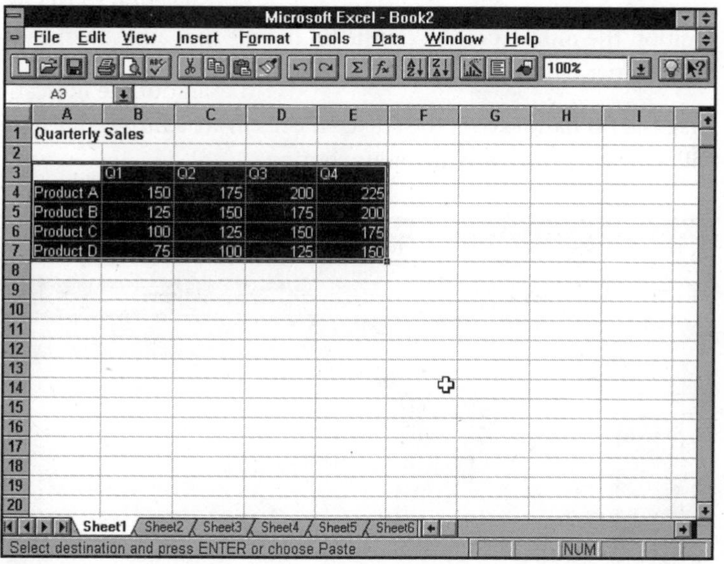

Fig. 13.3
A marquee surrounds the copied data.

3. Select the cell in which you want to paste a copy of the data.

4. Choose the **E**dit **P**aste command, or press Ctrl+V. Alternatively, click the right mouse button and then choose Paste from the resulting shortcut menu. If you want to paste a single copy of the selection, press Enter.

Note

As long as the marquee surrounds the copied data, you can continue to use the Edit Paste command to paste copies of the data in the worksheet. If you press Enter to paste a copy of the data in the worksheet, Excel clears the copied data from the Clipboard.

Copying Data with AutoFill

The AutoFill command enables you to copy cell contents to adjacent cells quickly. As a bonus, if the entry consists of a date, day of the week, or alphanumeric item such as Product 1, Excel automatically extends the series in the selected cells (see fig. 13.4).

◀ "Entering a Series of Text, Numbers, and Dates," p. 254

To use the AutoFill command to copy data, follow these steps:

1. Select the cell that contains the data you want to copy.

2. Position the mouse pointer on the fill handle that appears in the lower right corner of the cell.

3. Drag the fill handle over the adjacent cells in which the copied data will appear, and release the mouse button.

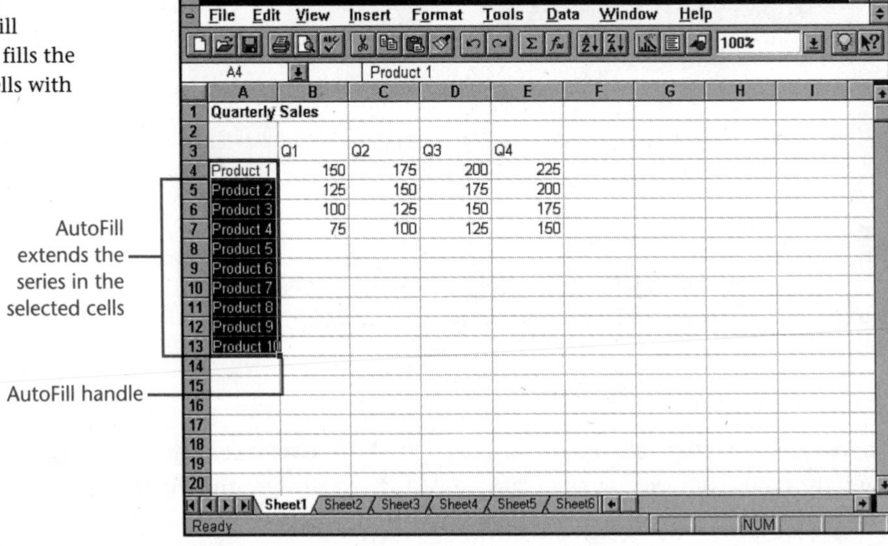

Fig. 13.4
The AutoFill command fills the selected cells with a series.

Copying and Applying Formats

Another option for copying data in your worksheet is to copy cell formatting from one range to another. This feature is handy if you want to apply formatting to a range of cells but don't want to create a style.

► "Creating and Applying a Style," p. 300

To copy formatting from one range to another, follow these steps:

1. Select the range of cells that contains the formatting you want to copy.
2. Click the Format Painter button, or double-click the button if you want to apply the formatting to more than one range. Figure 13.5 shows the result of using the Format Painter.

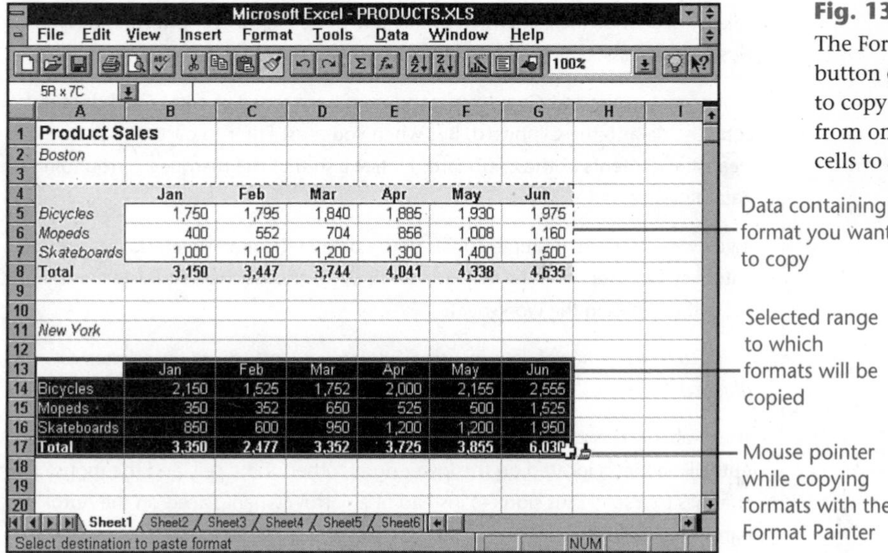

Fig. 13.5
The Format Painter button enables you to copy formatting from one range of cells to another.

3. Select the cell or range of cells where you want to apply the formatting. When you release the mouse button, Excel applies the formatting.
4. Continue selecting each additional range of cells. If you double-clicked the Format Painter button, click the button again to turn off the feature.

Troubleshooting

I tried to copy data, using drag-and-drop, but it wasn't working. Excel would just select the range of cells rather than copy the data

The cell drag-and-drop feature is probably turned off. To check, choose the **T**ools **O**ptions command, and select the Edit tab. Make sure that the Allow Cell Drag and Drop check box is selected (if it is, an X appears in the check box). Choose OK.

If the drag-and-drop feature is enabled, remember that you must click the outer edge of the selected range and then drag the selection.

I used the Edit Copy and Edit Paste commands to copy a range of data in my worksheet. I pressed Enter to paste the data in the new location, and it worked without a hitch. But when I tried to use the Edit Paste command to paste another copy, the Paste command was unavailable.

When you use the Edit Copy command to move a range of data, Excel does indeed copy the data to the Clipboard. But when you press Enter to paste the data, Excel clears the contents of the Clipboard. Notice also that the marquee surrounding the data disappears.

If you want to paste multiple copies of the data in the worksheet, do not press the Enter key to paste the data. Instead, continue to choose the **E**dit **P**aste command to paste the copies in the worksheet.

I tried to copy a range of data by using AutoFill, but I just moved the selected cell when I dragged it.

You probably dragged the edge of the cell rather than the AutoFill handle. The AutoFill handle is located on the lower right corner of the cell, and the mouse pointer changes to a solid plus sign (+) instead of an arrow when placed on the AutoFill handle.

Moving Worksheet Data

As with copying, you can move worksheet data from one area of the worksheet to another. You can use the drag-and-drop method to move a range of data quickly, or you can use the Edit Cut and Edit Paste commands to cut a range of data and paste it in another location.

Moving Data with Drag-and-Drop

Unlike copying data, which enables you to copy a range of data while keeping the source data intact, when you use the drag-and-drop method to move data, you are physically moving the range of data from one area to another.

To move a range of data with drag-and-drop, follow these steps:

1. Select the range that contains the data you want to move.
2. Position the mouse pointer on the border of the selected data.
3. Click and drag the selection to the new location. As you move the mouse, a border appears in the worksheet, indicating the location in which the data will appear.
4. Release the mouse button to drop the selected data in the new location.

Note

Excel does not allow you to overwrite existing data automatically when you use drag-and-drop. An error message appears, warning you that you are about to overwrite existing data. Choose Cancel and indicate a new position, or choose OK if you want to overwrite cells.

Moving Data with Cut and Paste

When you use the Edit Cut (Ctrl+X) command to move worksheet data, a copy of the data is stored on the Windows Clipboard. You then can paste the data in another area of the worksheet.

To move data by using the Edit Cut command, follow these steps:

1. Select the range of data you want to move.
2. Choose the **E**dit Cu**t** command, or press Ctrl+X. Alternatively, click the right mouse button and then choose Cut from the resulting shortcut menu.

   A marquee surrounds the selection you cut, and the status bar at the bottom of the screen prompts you to select the location where you want to paste the data.
3. Select the cell in which you want the data to appear, and then choose the **E**dit **P**aste command or press Ctrl+V. Alternatively, click the right mouse button and choose Paste from the resulting shortcut menu. You also can press Enter.

Note

When using the Edit Paste command to paste data from the Clipboard, indicate a single cell, rather than a range of cells, in which to paste the data. If you select a range of cells, the range you select must be the same size as the range you placed on the Clipboard.

Troubleshooting

I tried to move a range of data by using drag-and-drop, but the data I was trying to move was instead copied to the range of cells I wanted it to move to.

You probably dragged the AutoFill handle rather than the edge of the cell. The AutoFill handle is located on the lower right corner of the cell and is used to quickly fill a range of cells with the data. When the mouse is positioned on the AutoFill handle, the mouse pointer changes to a solid plus sign (+) instead of an arrow.

To move the data, position the mouse pointer on an edge of the cell, and then drag the mouse to move the data.

When I used the Edit Paste command to move a range of data, Excel pasted only a portion of the data in the selected range.

When pasting data, make sure that you select a single cell in which to paste the data. When you do, Excel pastes the entire range. If you select more than one cell, and the selected range is smaller than the original range of cells, Excel pastes only the data that will fit in the selected range.

Note

When copying and moving formulas, keep in mind that Excel may adjust cell references in the formula to reflect the new location. When you copy a formula, Excel adjusts the cell references. When you move a formula, Excel will not adjust cell references. See Chapter 15, "Using Formulas and Functions," for more information.

Inserting and Deleting Columns, Rows, and Cells

Another area of editing you'll perform in Excel is that of inserting and deleting columns, rows, and cells. Sometimes, restructuring a worksheet entails more than moving data to another location. For example, if you add another sales region to your sales tracking worksheet, you can insert a new column to hold the data. Likewise, if you remove a product from your product line, you can delete the rows that contain the data.

Inserting Columns, Rows, and Cells

When you need to insert additional space in your worksheet, you can insert columns, rows, and cells in the middle of existing data. When you insert columns, rows, and cells, existing data shifts to accommodate the insertion.

To insert a column, follow these steps:

1. Position the cell pointer in the column where the new column should appear.

2. Choose the **I**nsert **C**olumns command, or click the right mouse button and then choose the Insert command from the shortcut menu. Excel inserts a new column, and existing columns shift to the right.

To insert a row, follow these steps:

1. Select a cell in the row below where the new row should appear.

2. Choose the **I**nsert **R**ows command, or click the right mouse button and then choose the Insert command from the shortcut menu. Excel inserts a new row, and existing rows move down.

To insert a cell or range, follow these steps:

1. Select the cell or range where the new cells should appear.

2. Choose the **I**nsert C**e**lls command, or click the right mouse button and then choose Insert from the shortcut menu. The Insert dialog box appears (see fig. 13.6).

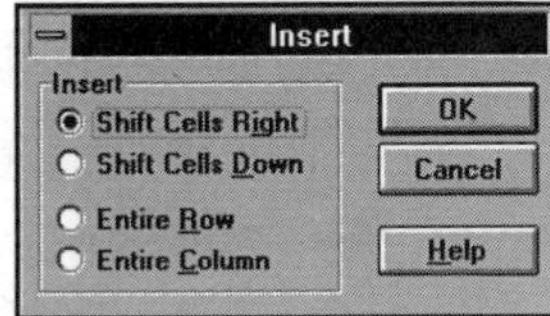

Fig. 13.6
The Insert dialog box prompts you to specify the direction in which the existing cells should move.

3. Select Shift Cells **R**ight to insert the new cells to the left of the selection. Select Shift Cells **D**own to insert the new cells above the selection.

4. Choose OK. The selected cells move in the direction you specified.

Deleting Columns, Rows, and Cells

You can delete columns, rows, and cells from your worksheet when they contain data that is no longer needed. When you delete columns, rows, and cells, existing data moves to close the space.

To delete a column, follow these steps:

1. Click the letter of the column you want to delete. To delete multiple columns, highlight each additional column.

2. Choose the **E**dit **D**elete command, or click the right mouse button and then choose the Delete command from the shortcut menu. The selected column is removed from the worksheet, and existing columns move to the left.

To delete a row, follow these steps:

1. Click the number of the row you want to delete. To delete multiple rows, highlight each additional row.

2. Choose the **E**dit **D**elete command, or click the right mouse button and then choose the Delete command from the shortcut menu. The selected row is removed from the worksheet, and existing rows move up.

> **Caution**
>
> Use care when using the Edit Insert and Delete commands in your worksheets. When you use the Edit Insert and Delete commands, the entire worksheet is affected by your action. If a formula refers to a cell that is deleted, for example, the cell containing the formula returns the #REF! error value. If this occurs, choose the **E**dit **U**ndo command immediately after making a deletion.

To delete a cell or range of cells, follow these steps:

1. Select the range of cells that you want to delete.

2. Choose the **E**dit **D**elete command, or click the right mouse button and then choose the Delete command from the shortcut menu. The Delete dialog box appears (see fig. 13.7).

3. Select Shift Cells **L**eft, and the existing data will move to the left. Choose Shift Cells **U**p, and the existing data will move up.

4. Choose OK after you make your selection.

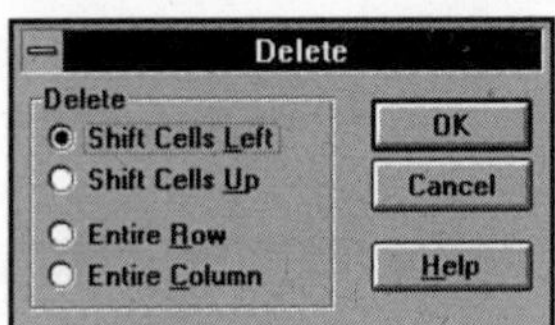

Fig. 13.7
In the Delete dialog box, specify the direction in which the existing cells should move.

Inserting and Deleting Sheets

Excel 5.0 provides true 3-D functionality, which enables you to create workbooks that contain multiple sheets of data. Each new workbook you create contains 16 worksheets; but you can insert up to 255 additional worksheets, as well as delete worksheets that you no longer need.

Inserting Sheets

When you insert a worksheet, Excel inserts the sheet before the current worksheet. To insert a worksheet, select the sheet to the right of where the new worksheet should appear, and choose the **I**nsert **W**orksheet command. Excel inserts a sheet and assigns a name to the sheet.

Deleting Sheets

To delete a sheet, move to the sheet you want to delete, and then choose the **D**elete **W**orksheet command. Excel deletes the sheet.

Moving Sheets

In addition to inserting and deleting sheets, you can rearrange worksheets in the workbook by moving them to a new location.

Excel employs the drag-and-drop method for moving sheets. To move a sheet, click the tab of the sheet you want to move. Hold down the mouse button, and drag the sheet to the new position in the workbook. When you release the mouse button, the sheet is dropped in its new location.

Naming Sheets

Initially, Excel names each worksheet in the workbook Sheet1, Sheet2, and so on, right on up to Sheet255. You can, however, easily rename a sheet to reflect the data it contains. In a Monthly Sales worksheet, for example, you can use a separate sheet for each sales region. You then could name each sheet North, South, East, and West. Thereafter, anyone else who uses the worksheet will be able to tell what the worksheet contains just by looking at the name.

To rename a worksheet, double-click the sheet tab of the worksheet you want to rename. The Rename Sheet dialog box appears (see fig. 13.8).

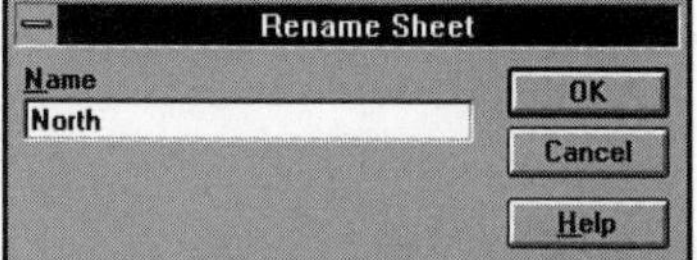

Fig. 13.8
Type a name for the worksheet in the Rename Sheet dialog box.

Enter a name for the worksheet in the text box, and choose OK. Excel displays the name in the selected sheet's tab.

Finding and Replacing Worksheet Data

Excel provides the capability to find and (optionally) replace specific data in your worksheet. You can, for example, search for all occurrences of the value 1993 and replace it with 1994.

Finding Worksheet Data

Tip
If the Search dialog box is obstructing your view of the worksheet, click and drag the title bar of the dialog box until you can see the active cell in the worksheet.

You can search the entire workbook, or you can search only a selected worksheet range. To search the entire workbook, select a single cell. To search a specified range, select the range that you want to search.

1. Choose the **E**dit **F**ind command (Ctrl+F). The Find dialog box appears (see fig. 13.9).

2. In the Fi**n**d What text box, type the data you want to find. Then specify the search options, described in table 13.2 (which follows these steps).

3. Choose **F**ind Next to begin the search. When Excel locates the characters, choose **F**ind Next to find the next occurrence, or choose **R**eplace to access the Replace dialog box (this option is discussed in the next section).

4. Choose Close to end the search and close the dialog box.

Note

If you're not sure of the specific string you are looking for, you can specify wild-card characters in the search string to locate data that contains some or all of the characters. You can use an asterisk (*) to search for any group of characters and a question mark (?) to search for any single character.

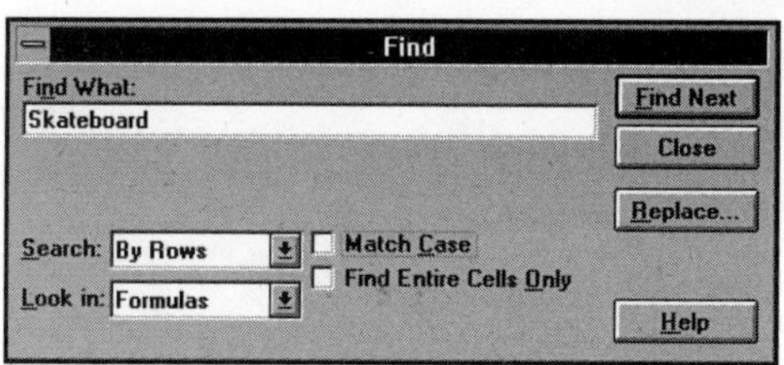

Fig. 13.9
The Find command enables you to locate specific data in your worksheets.

Table 13.2 Find Options

Option	Action
Search	Specify whether to search across rows or down columns.
Look In	Select the location of the data: cell formulas, cell values, or cell notes.
Find Entire Cells **O**nly	Searches for an exact match of the characters you specified. It does not find partial occurrences.
Match **C**ase	Finds only characters that match the case of the characters you specified.
Find Next	Finds the next occurrence of the search string.
Close	Ends the search and returns to the worksheet.
Replace	Opens the Replace dialog box (discussed in the next section).

Replacing Worksheet Data

The Replace command (Ctrl+H) is similar to the Find command in that it enables you to locate specific characters in your worksheet. The Replace command then enables you to replace the characters with new data.

To replace worksheet data, follow these steps:

1. To search the entire workbook, select a single cell. To search a specified range, select the range you want to search.

2. Choose the **E**dit R**e**place command. The Replace dialog box appears (see fig. 13.10).

3. In the Fi**n**d What text box, type the data you want to replace. In the R**e**place With text box, type the data with which you want to replace the current data.

4. Specify the replace options, as described in table 13.3 (which follows these steps).

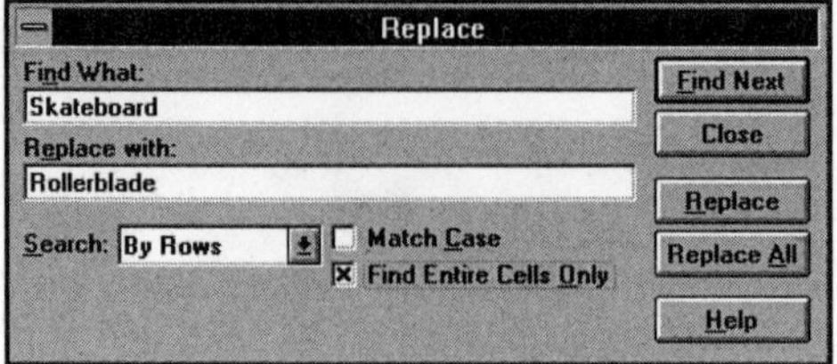

Fig. 13.10
You can use the Edit Replace command to replace formulas, text, or values.

> **Caution**
>
> Make sure that Find Entire Cells Only is activated if you are replacing values or formulas. If it is not selected, Excel will replace characters even if they are inside other strings. For example, replacing 20 with 30 will also make 2000 become 3000.

5. Choose **F**ind Next to begin the search. When Excel locates the first occurrence of the characters, choose the appropriate replace option (see table 13.3).

6. Choose Close to close the dialog box.

Tip
If you make a mistake when replacing data, close the dialog box, and choose the **E**dit **U**ndo command (Ctrl+Z) immediately to reverse the replacement.

Table 13.3 Replace Options

Option	Action
Search	Specifies whether to search across rows or down columns.
Find Entire Cells **O**nly	Searches for an exact match of the characters you specified. It does not find partial occurrences.
Match **C**ase	Finds only characters that match the case of the characters you specified.
Find Next	Finds the next occurrence.
Replace	Replaces the characters in the active cell with those specified in the R**e**place With text box.
Replace **A**ll	Replaces all occurrences of the characters with those specified in the R**e**place With text box.
Close	Closes the Replace dialog box.

> **Caution**
>
> When replacing data in your worksheet, use Replace All with care, because the results may not be what you expect. Whenever you use the Replace command, it's a good idea to first locate the data you want to replace to make sure that the data is correct.

Spell-Checking the Worksheet

Excel's Spelling command enables you to check worksheets, macro sheets, and charts for misspellings and to correct the errors quickly. The spelling checker offers a standard dictionary and also enables you to create an alternate customized dictionary to store frequently used words not found in the standard dictionary. When you run the spelling checker, Excel then looks in the standard dictionary and the custom dictionary for the correct spelling.

In addition to finding spelling errors, Excel finds repeating words and words that might not be properly capitalized. You can check spelling in the entire workbook, a single cell, or a selected range.

To check the spelling of data in your worksheet, follow these steps:

1. Specify the worksheet range you want to check. To check the entire workbook, select cell A1. Excel starts checking from the active cell and moves forward to the end of the workbook. To check a specific word or range, select the cell containing the word, or select the range.

2. Choose the **T**ools **S**pelling command, or press F7. When Excel finds a spelling error, the Spelling dialog box appears (see fig. 13.11).

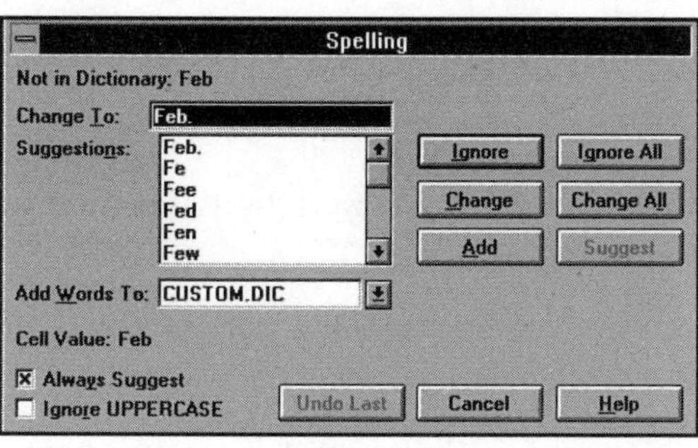

Fig. 13.11
The Spelling dialog box appears when Excel finds a spelling error in the worksheet.

The following options are available to correct a spelling error:

Table 13.4 Spelling Dialog Box Options

Option	Action
Change **T**o	Type a replacement for the word.
Suggestio**n**s	Select a replacement word from a list of suggested words.
Add **W**ords To	Select the dictionary to which you want to add words that are spelled correctly but not found in the standard dictionary.
Ignore	Ignore the word and continue the spell check.
I**g**nore All	Ignore all occurrences of the word.
Change	Change the selected word to the word displayed in the Change **T**o box.
Change A**l**l	Change all occurrences of the word to the word displayed in the Change **T**o box.
Add	Add the selected word to the custom dictionary.
Suggest	Display a list of proposed suggestions.
Alwa**y**s Suggest	Excel automatically displays a list of proposed suggestions whenever a word is not found in the dictionary.
Igno**r**e UPPERCASE	To skip words that are all uppercase.
Undo Last	To undo the last spelling change.
Cancel/Close	Close the dialog box (the Cancel button changes to Close when you change a word or add a word to the dictionary).

From Here...

For additional information on editing worksheets, you may want to review the following chapters:

- Chapter 2, "Using Common Features," provides more information on copying and moving data.
- Chapter 14, "Formatting Worksheets," shows you how to format worksheets.
- Chapter 15, "Using Formulas and Functions," discusses copying and moving Excel formulas.

Chapter 14

Formatting Worksheets

by Cathy Kenny

After you create a worksheet, the next step is to change the appearance of data in your worksheet to make it more visually appealing. Excel provides many features and functions that enable you to produce high-quality worksheets. You can include such formatting options as applying different fonts, and you can add graphics, colors, and patterns to worksheet elements.

In this chapter, you learn to

- Format numbers
- Change column widths and row heights
- Align text
- Change fonts, sizes, and styles
- Apply patterns and borders
- Create and apply a style
- Create and work with graphic objects

Formatting Numbers

When you enter numbers in the worksheet, don't be concerned with the way they look. You can change the appearance of numbers by applying a numeric format.

Excel provides many common numeric formats; you can create your own as well. For example, you can apply a predefined currency format that uses two decimal places or create a currency format that uses an international currency symbol.

To apply a numeric format, follow these steps:

Tip
As you format worksheets in Excel, keep the Formatting toolbar handy so you can access Excel's formatting commands quickly. For details, see the following section, "Applying Number Formats Using the Toolbar."

1. Select the cells containing the numbers you want to format.

2. Choose the F**o**rmat C**e**lls command or press Ctrl+1. Alternatively, click the right mouse button and choose the Format Cells command from the resulting shortcut menu. The Format Cells dialog box appears (see fig. 14.1).

3. Select the type of number format you want to apply from the **C**ategory list. A listing of numeric formats for the corresponding Category list is displayed in the **F**ormat Codes list box. Some common symbols used in these formats are listed in table 14.1 (following these steps).

4. Select the number format you want to use from the **F**ormat Codes list. A sample of the selected format appears in the Sample area of the dialog box.

5. Choose OK. Excel applies the selected number format to the selected cells in your worksheet.

◄ "Microsoft Applications Toolbars," p. 27

Table 14.1 Numeric Formatting Codes

Code	Description
#	Placeholder for digits.
0	Placeholder for digits. Same as #, except that zeros on either side of the decimal point force the numbers to match the selected format.
$	Currency symbol is displayed with the number.
,	Placeholder for thousands separator.
.	Placeholder for decimal point.
%	Multiplies number by 100 and displays number with a percent sign.

Applying Number Formats Using the Toolbar

You can quickly apply commonly used number formats—such as Currency, Comma, and Percentage—by using the Formatting toolbar (see fig. 14.2). Use either the number format buttons that appear in the toolbar by default or the Style menu that you manually add to the toolbar.

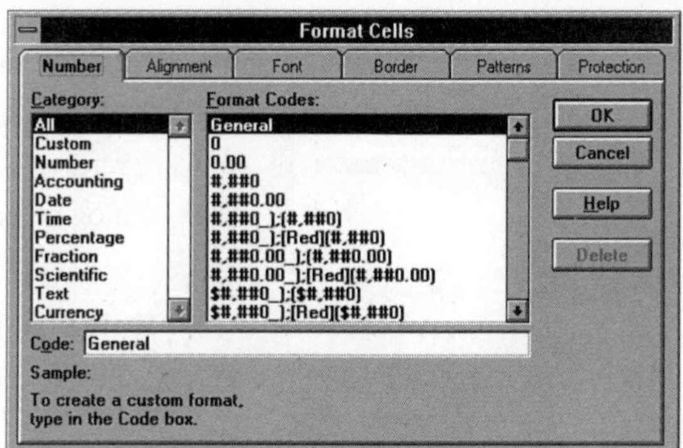

Fig. 14.1
The Format Cells dialog box displays a list of predefined number formats.

To display the Formatting toolbar, choose the **V**iew **T**oolbars command, select Formatting from the list of toolbars, and choose OK; or place the mouse pointer on the Standard toolbar, click the right mouse button, and choose Formatting from the resulting shortcut menu.

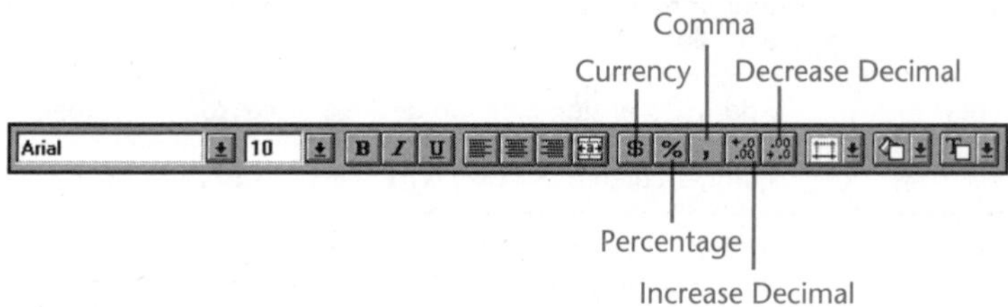

Fig. 14.2
The Formatting toolbar contains five buttons that enable you to apply common number formats quickly.

To apply a number format by using the Formatting toolbar, select the cells containing the numbers you want to format and then click the appropriate button in the toolbar.

Formatting Numbers Using the Style Menu

You also can format numbers by using styles. To apply one of the predefined number formats listed as a style, select the cells containing the numbers you want to format and then choose the F**o**rmat **S**tyle command. The Style dialog box appears (see fig. 14.3). Select the desired style in the **S**tyle Name drop-down list, and then choose OK.

Table 14.2 describes the formatting choices.

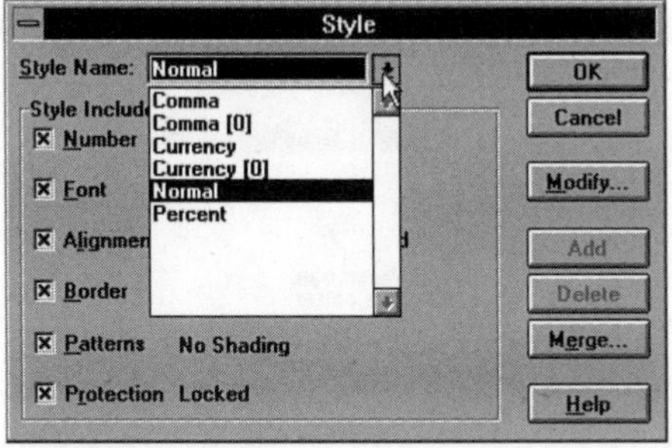

Fig. 14.3
Format numbers using the predefined styles in the Style dialog box.

Table 14.2 Number Formats in the Style Menu

Format	Description
Comma	Adds two decimal places to the number, and adds commas to numbers that contain four or more digits. A number entered as **1000** is formatted as `1,000.00`.
Comma (0)	Rounds decimals and adds commas to numbers that contain four or more digits. A number entered as **1000.55** is formatted as `1,001`.
Currency	Adds a dollar sign and two decimal places to the number. Also adds a comma to numbers that contain four or more digits. A number entered as **1000** is formatted as `$1,000.00`.
Currency (0)	Adds a dollar sign to the number and rounds decimals. Also adds a comma to numbers that contain four or more digits. A number entered as **1000.55** is formatted as `$1,001`.
Normal	Applies the style that defines normal or default character formatting. A number entered as **1000** is formatted as `1000`.
Percent	Multiplies the number by 100 and adds a percentage symbol to the number. A number entered as **.15** is formatted as `15%`.

Tip
To add the Styles box to the Formatting toolbar, choose **V**iews **T**oolbars, and then choose **C**ustomize. Select Formatting from the Categories list. In the Buttons section of the dialog box, click and drag the Style button to the Formatting toolbar, and choose Close.

You also can use the following shortcut keys to format numbers:

Key	Format
Ctrl+Shift+~	General format
Ctrl+Shift+!	Comma format with two decimal places
Ctrl+Shift+$	Currency format with two decimal places
Ctrl+Shift+%	Percent format
Ctrl+Shift+^	Scientific notation format

▶ "Customizing Application Toolbars," p. 887

Creating a Custom Number Format

Although Excel provides most of the common number formats, at times you may need a specific number format that the program does not provide. For example, you may want to create additional numeric formats that use various international currency symbols. Excel enables you to create custom number formats. In most cases, you can base your custom format on one of Excel's predefined formats.

To create a custom number format, follow these steps:

1. Choose the F**o**rmat C**e**lls command or press Ctrl+1. Alternatively, click the right mouse button and choose Format Cells from the resulting shortcut menu. If necessary, select the Number tab in the Format Cells dialog box.

2. Select the category from the **C**ategory list that contains the format you want to modify. Then select the predefined format in the **F**ormat Codes list. The formatting symbols appear in the C**o**de text box, and a sample appears below the text box (see fig. 14.4).

3. Select the C**o**de text box, and edit the selected format.

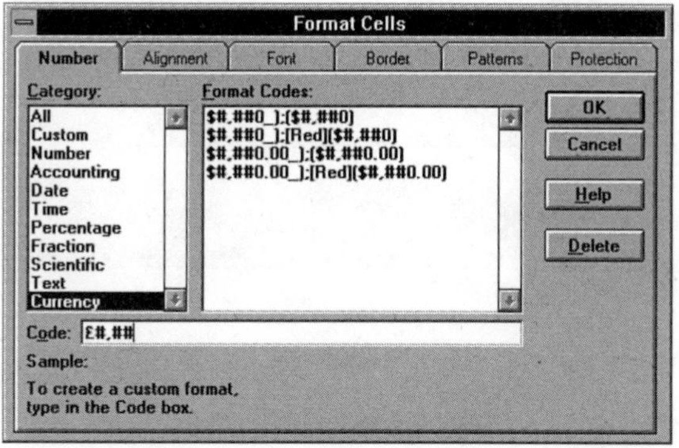

Fig. 14.4
The custom format in the Code text box is defined to display the pound symbol in the Currency format.

4. Choose OK. The custom format appears at the end of the **F**ormat Codes list.

Note

You can select and delete custom formats from the list; however, you cannot delete any of Excel's predefined number formats.

Changing Date and Time Formats

◄ "Entering Dates and Times," p. 248

Excel recognizes most dates and times entered in a worksheet cell. If you enter **1-1-94** in a cell, for example, Excel assumes that you are entering a date and displays the number in a date format. (The default date format is 1/1/94.) If you enter **9:45**, Excel assumes that you are referring to a time and displays the entry in a time format. You can change to another date or time format.

To apply a date or time format, follow these steps:

1. Select the cell or range containing the data you want to format.
2. Choose the **F**ormat C**e**lls command, or press Ctrl+1. Alternatively, click the right mouse button and choose Format Cells from the resulting shortcut menu.
3. Select Date from the **C**ategory list to display the list of date formats (see fig. 14.5). To apply a time format, select Time from the **C**ategory list.

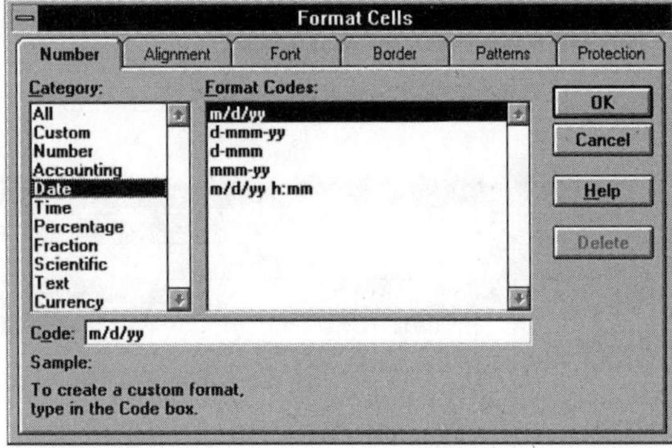

Fig. 14.5 A list of predefined date formats appears in the Date section of the Format Cells dialog box.

4. Select the format you want to use from the **F**ormat Codes list box.
5. Choose OK. Excel applies the format to the data.

You also can use the following shortcut keys to enter and format the current date and time:

Key	Format
Ctrl+;	Current date (entering)
Ctrl+:	Current time (entering)
Ctrl+#	Date format d-mmm-yy (formatting)
Ctrl+@	Time format h:mm AM/PM (formatting)

Use the same procedure to create custom date and time formats as custom number formats; the only difference is that you use date and time format codes. Table 14.3 lists these codes.

Table 14.3 Date and Time Format Codes

Code	Description
m	Month as a number with no leading zero
mm	Month as a number with leading zero
mmm	Month as a three-letter abbreviation
mmmm	Month as a full name
d	Day of week with no leading zero
dd	Day of week with leading zero
ddd	Day of week as a three-letter abbreviation
dddd	Day of week as a full name
yy	Year as a two-digit number
yyyy	Year as a four-digit number
h	Hour with no leading zero
hh	Hour with leading zero
m	Minute with no leading zero
mm	Minute with leading zero

Troubleshooting

Excel fills a cell with ##### when I apply a numeric format to a number in my worksheet.

When a cell is not wide enough to accommodate a formatted number, Excel displays the number as #####. To display the complete number in the cell, you must adjust the column width of the cell. When you widen the column sufficiently, Excel displays the fully formatted number in the cell.

A few methods for changing the width of a column are available. You can adjust the width to a precise amount, using the F**o**rmat **C**olumn **W**idth command, or you can use the mouse to drag the column border until the column is the appropriate width.

(continues)

(continued)

To adjust the width of a column to a precise amount, position the cell pointer in the column and choose the **F**ormat **C**olumn **W**idth command, or click the right mouse button and choose Column Width from the resulting shortcut menu. In the Column Width dialog box, enter the desired column width; then choose OK. To adjust the width of a column by using the mouse, position the mouse pointer on the right border of the column heading whose width you want to change. The mouse pointer changes to a two-headed horizontal arrow when positioned properly. Drag the arrow to the right or left to increase or decrease the column width. A dotted line in the worksheet indicates the column width. Release the mouse button when the column is the width you want. For more information on changing column widths, see the following section, "Changing Column Width and Row Height."

I want to create a numeric format that uses an international currency symbol. I changed the International setting in the Windows Control Panel to reflect the country I wanted to use, but that changed the symbol for all currency formats. How can I use an international symbol in my custom format without changing the others?

To create a custom numeric format with an international currency symbol, choose the F**o**rmat C**e**lls command, and select the Number tab. In the **C**ategory list, select Currency; then select the format that closely resembles the format you want to use from the **F**ormat Codes list box. Select the C**o**de text box, highlight the currency symbol used by that format, and press Del to delete the symbol. You then can enter special characters to display the currency symbols. To use the pound symbol (£), press the Num Lock key, hold down the Alt key, and—using the numeric keypad—type **0163**, which is the ANSI character for that symbol. To use the yen symbol (¥), hold down the Alt key and type **0165** in the numeric keypad. The appropriate currency symbols are inserted into the Code text box. Choose OK to save the custom numeric format.

Changing Column Width and Row Height

When you enter data in a cell, the data often appears truncated because the column is not wide enough to display the entire entry. If a cell cannot display an entire number or date, Excel fills the cell with pound signs or displays the value in scientific notation (for example, 4.51E+08). After you adjust the width of the cell, the entire number or date appears.

You can change the column width by using the mouse or menu commands. When you use the mouse to change the column width, you drag the column border to reflect the approximate size of the column. When you use the Format Column Width command, you can specify an exact column width.

Using the Mouse To Change Column Width

To change the column width by using the mouse, follow these steps:

1. Position the mouse pointer on the right border of the heading of the column whose width you want to change. The mouse pointer changes to a double-headed horizontal arrow when positioned properly. To change the width of multiple columns, select the columns by dragging the mouse over the additional column headings.

2. Drag the arrow to the right or left to increase or decrease the column width, respectively. A dotted line indicates the column width (see fig. 14.6).

3. Release the mouse button when the column is the width you want.

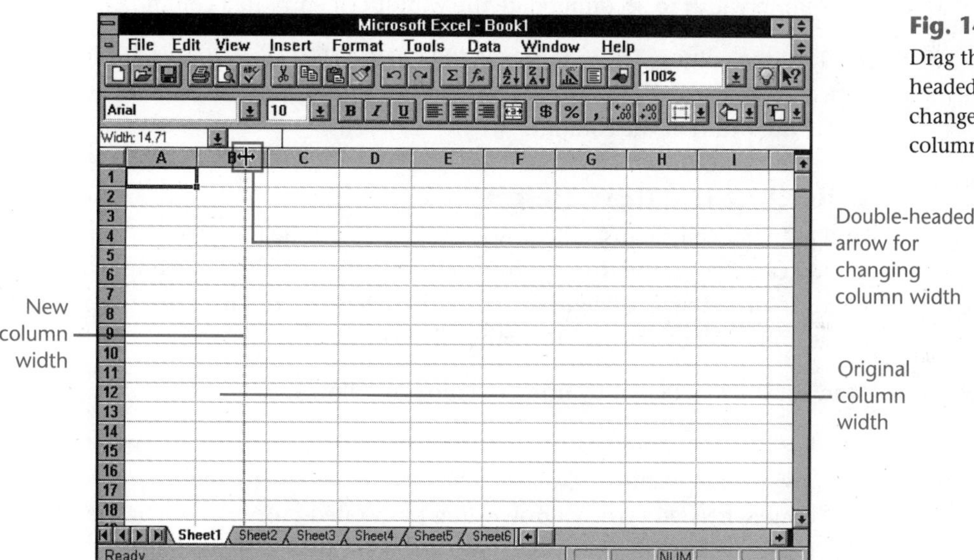

Fig. 14.6 Drag the double-headed arrow to change the column width.

Using the Column Width Command To Change Column Width

To change the column width by using the Column Width command, follow these steps:

1. Click the heading of the column whose width you want to change. To change the width of multiple columns, drag the mouse pointer over each additional column.

2. Choose the **F**ormat **C**olumn **W**idth command. Alternatively, click the right mouse button, and choose Column Width from the shortcut menu. The Column Width dialog box appears (see fig. 14.7).

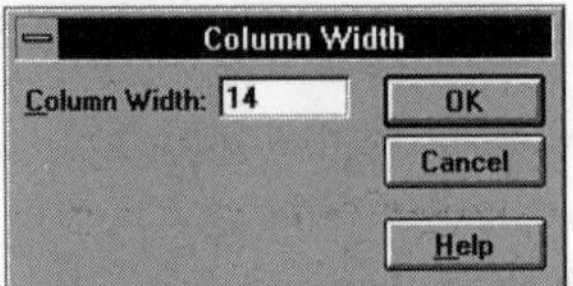

Fig. 14.7
Enter a specific column width in the Column Width dialog box.

3. Enter the column width in the **C**olumn Width text box.

4. Choose OK. Excel adjusts the width of the selected columns.

Adjusting Column Width Automatically

In addition to changing column width manually, Excel enables you to adjust the column width to accommodate the widest cell entry in a column.

Tip
To quickly change the column width to fit the widest entry, position the mouse pointer on the right border of the column heading and then double-click the mouse.

To adjust the column width to the widest entry, select the cell containing the widest entry, and then choose F**o**rmat **C**olumn **A**utoFit Selection. Excel adjusts the width of the column.

Adjusting the Row Height

Excel automatically adjusts the row height based on the font you are using, but you can change the row height to accommodate additional white space or to minimize the row height in your worksheet. You can use both the mouse and Excel commands to change the row height.

To adjust the row height by using the mouse, follow these steps:

1. Position the mouse pointer on the bottom border of the heading of the row whose height you want to change. The mouse pointer changes to a double-headed vertical arrow when positioned properly. To change the height of multiple rows, drag over the additional row headings.

2. Drag the arrow down or up to increase or decrease the row height, respectively. A dotted line indicates the row height (see fig. 14.8).

3. Release the mouse button when the row is the height you want.

To adjust the row height by using the Row Height command, follow these steps:

1. Click the heading of the row whose height you want to change. To change the width of multiple rows, drag the mouse pointer over each additional row.

2. Choose the **F**ormat **R**ow H**e**ight command. Alternatively, click the right mouse button and choose Row Height from the shortcut menu. The Row Height dialog box appears (see fig. 14.9).

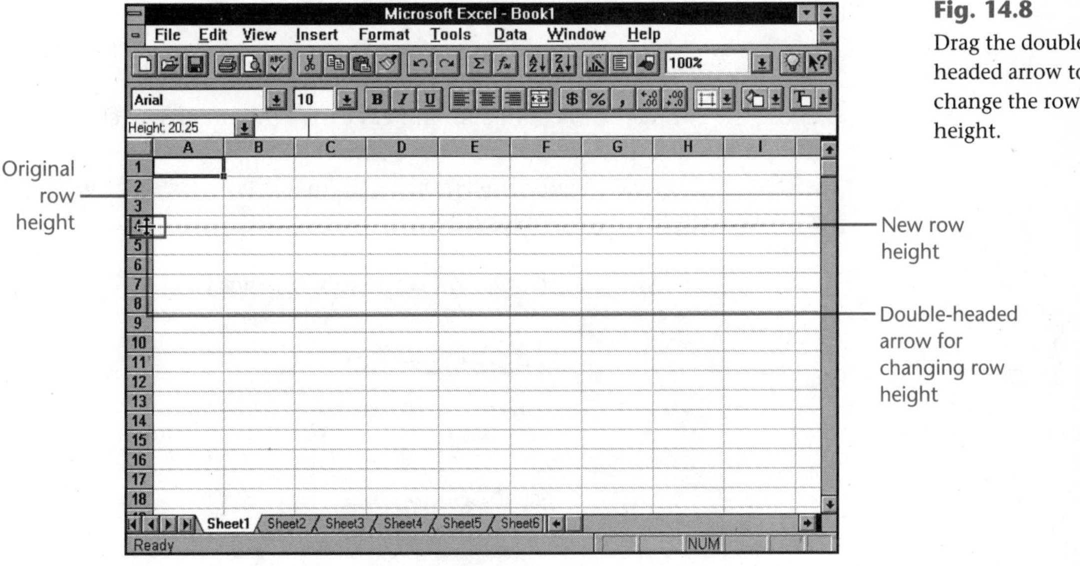

Fig. 14.8
Drag the double-headed arrow to change the row height.

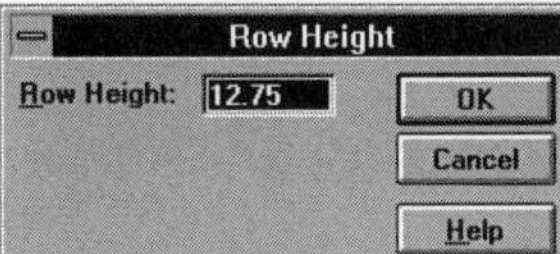

Fig. 14.9
Enter a specific row height in the Column Width dialog box.

Note

The row height is measured in points and is based on the size of the default font used in the worksheet. The default font used by Excel is 12-point Arial.

3. Enter the row height in the **R**ow Height text box.

4. Choose OK. Excel adjusts the height of the selected rows.

Aligning Data

Excel provides several formatting options for changing the appearance of data in the worksheet. For example, you can change the alignment of text or numbers within a cell so that they appear left-aligned, right-aligned, or centered. You also can format lengthy text to wrap within a cell, center text across a range of columns, or align text vertically within a cell.

To align data, follow these steps:

1. Select the cell or range that contains the data you want to align.
2. Choose the Format Cells command or press Ctrl+1. Alternatively, click the right mouse button and choose the Format Cells command from the resulting shortcut menu. The Format Cells dialog box appears (see fig. 14.10). Select the Alignment tab.

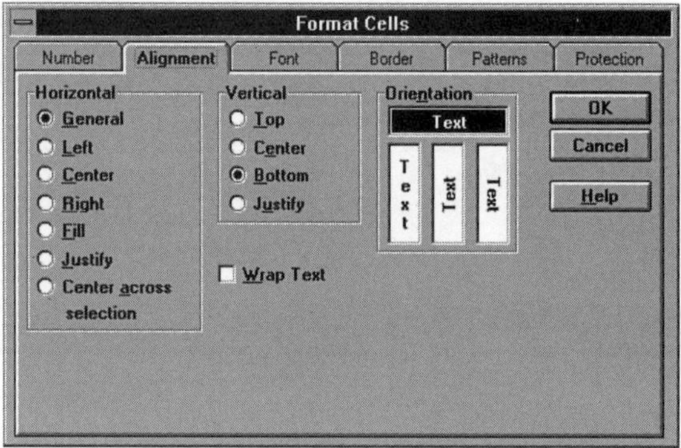

Fig. 14.10
Change the alignment of data in the Alignment section in the Format Cells dialog box.

3. Specify the alignment you want to use. See table 14.4 for descriptions of alignment options.
4. Choose OK.

Table 14.4 Alignment Options

Option	Description
General	Aligns text to the left and numbers to the right
Left	Aligns text and numbers to the left edge of the cell
Center	Centers text and numbers within a cell
Right	Aligns text and numbers to the right edge of the cell

Option	Description
Fill	Repeats the contents until the cell is full
Justify	When text is wrapped within a cell, aligns text evenly between the cell borders

Wrapping Text within a Cell

You can align text entries to wrap within a single cell or a range of cells. To wrap text within a cell or range, select the cell or range of cells containing the entry, and then choose F**o**rmat C**e**lls or press Ctrl+1. You also can click the right mouse button and choose the Format Cells command from the shortcut menu. In the Format Cells dialog box, select the Alignment tab. Then select **W**rap Text and choose OK. Excel wraps the text (see fig. 14.11).

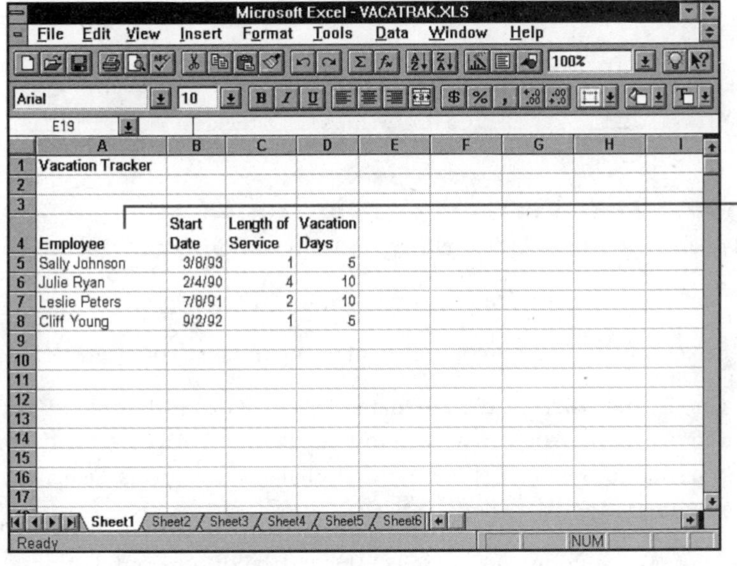

Fig. 14.11 Column headings are wrapped within each cell.

Centering Text across Columns

To center text over multiple columns, first select the cell that contains the text and the range of columns across which you want to center the text. Selected cells defining the range of columns must be blank.

Choose the F**o**rmat C**e**lls command or press Ctrl+1. Alternatively, click the right mouse button and choose the Format Cells command from the shortcut menu. The Format Cells dialog box appears. Select the Alignment tab. Then select Center **A**cross Selection and choose OK. Excel centers the text across the specified columns (see fig. 14.12).

Fig. 14.12
Text is centered across the selected columns.

Text centered across columns A–D

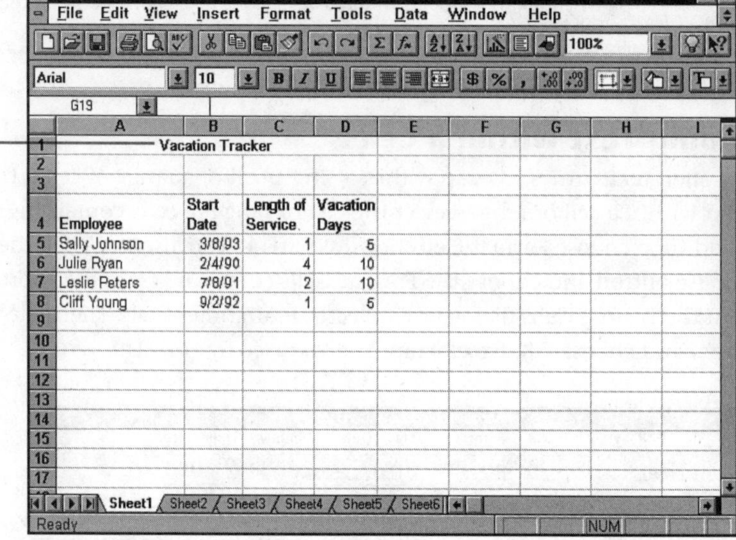

Aligning Text Vertically or Horizontally

Excel enables you to align text either vertically or horizontally in a cell.

To format text vertically or horizontally, follow these steps:

1. Select the cell or range of cells containing the text you want to format.

2. Choose the F**o**rmat C**e**lls command or press Ctrl+1. Alternatively, click the right mouse button and choose the Format Cells command from the shortcut menu. The Format Cells dialog box appears. Select the Alignment tab.

3. In the Orientation section, select the vertical or horizontal orientation. If you select a vertical orientation, you also must select a specific vertical alignment (**T**op, C**e**nter, or **B**ottom) in the Vertical box.

4. Choose OK. Excel aligns the text (see fig. 14.13).

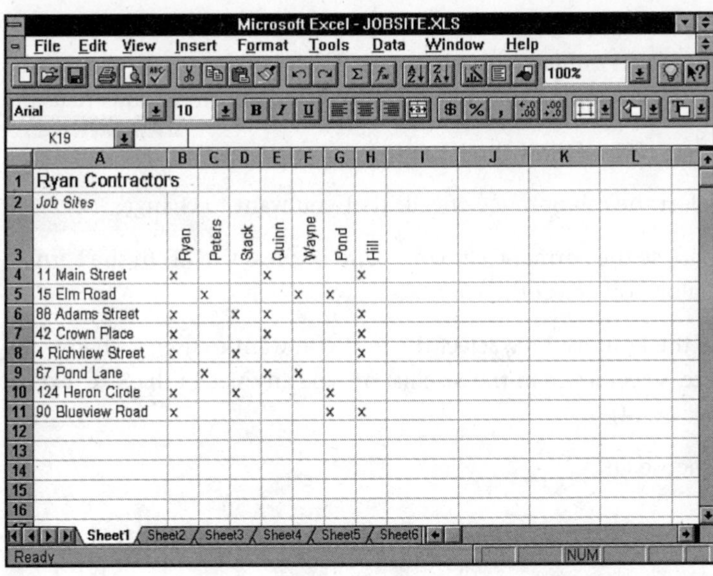

Fig. 14.13
Text is aligned vertically in row 3.

Tip

When aligning text vertically or horizontally, use Excel's F**o**rmat **C**olumn **A**utoFit Selection and F**o**rmat **R**ow **A**utoFit command to adjust the column width or row height quickly.

Troubleshooting

I used the Center Across Selection command to center a text entry across a range of columns, but the entry would not center.

One of the cells in the selection probably contains a space character or some other entry. To remove these characters, select the range of cells (except for the cell containing the entry you want to center) and then press Del. The entry should be selected.

After I aligned text vertically in a cell, some of the characters did not display.

When a row height is set to the default row height, only a few characters of vertically rotated text display. To display the entire contents, position the mouse pointer on the bottom border of the row and double-click the left mouse button, or click the row heading and choose the F**o**rmat **R**ow **A**utoFit command to adjust the height to best fit the row's contents.

Changing Fonts, Sizes, and Styles

Excel provides several formatting options for changing the appearance of text in your worksheets. You can, for example, choose a different font, change the size of the selected font, and apply a font style to cells in your worksheet.

Changing Fonts

The list of fonts available in the Font dialog box depends on the type of Windows fonts you have installed and the type of printer you are using.

To change a font, follow these steps:

1. Select the cell or range of cells that you want to change.

2. Choose the F**o**rmat C**e**lls command or press Ctrl+1. In the Format Cells dialog box, select the Font tab.

3. In the **F**ont list box, select the font you want to use; to change the text size, select a size in the **S**ize list or type any size in the **S**ize text box (see fig. 14.14).

4. Choose OK.

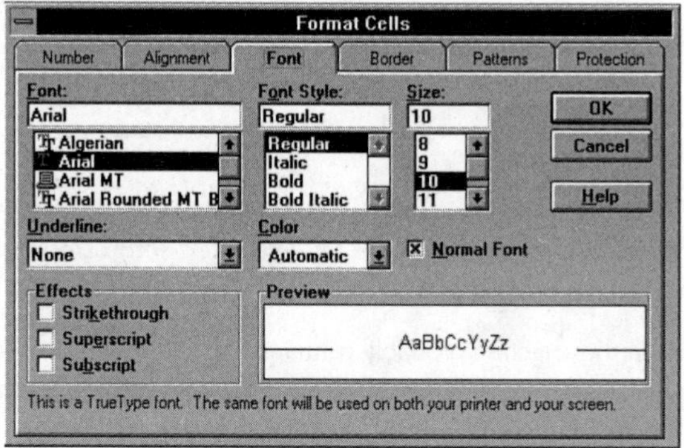

Fig. 14.14
The Font section of the Format Cells dialog box displays the currently installed Windows and printer fonts.

Applying Text Formats

In addition to changing the font and size of data in your worksheets, you can apply text attributes to the data. For example, you can assign such attributes as bold, italic, and underline, and change the color of text.

To apply a formatting attribute, follow these steps:

1. Select the cell or range of cells you want to format.

2. Choose the F**o**rmat C**e**lls command or press Ctrl+1. In the Format Cells dialog box, select the Font tab.

> **Note**
>
> As you make changes in the dialog box, Excel applies the selections to the text in the Preview box. The changes aren't made to the selected cells until you choose OK.

3. Select the style you want to apply in the F**o**nt Style list box. Use the **U**nderline drop-down list to select an underline style. To change the color of the data, click the **C**olor drop-down list and select a color. Select Stri**k**ethrough, Su**b**script, or Sup**e**rscript, if you want.
4. When you finish, choose OK.

Formatting Characters in a Cell

You can apply formatting to individual characters in a text entry. For example, you can assign the Bold format to a single character in a cell.

Tip
When formatting characters in a cell, you also can use the formatting buttons in the Formatting toolbar to change the appearance of text.

To format characters in a cell, follow these steps:

1. Double-click the cell containing the data you want to format, or select the cell and then press F2.
2. In the cell or formula bar, select the characters you want to format.
3. Choose the F**o**rmat C**e**lls command or press Ctrl+1. In the Format Cells dialog box, select the Font tab.
4. Select the attributes you want, and then choose OK.

Applying Patterns and Borders

In addition to formatting numbers or text, you can format cells. For example, you can add a border to a cell or range of cells and fill a cell with a color or pattern.

Applying a Border

Borders enhance a worksheet's appearance by providing visual separations between areas of the worksheet. Borders also improve the appearance of printed reports.

To apply a border, follow these steps:

1. Select the cell or range you want to format.
2. Choose the F**o**rmat C**e**lls command or press Ctrl+1. Alternatively, click the right mouse button and choose the Format Cells command from the shortcut menu. In the Format Cells dialog box, select the Border tab (see fig. 14.15).

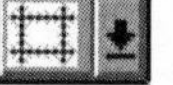

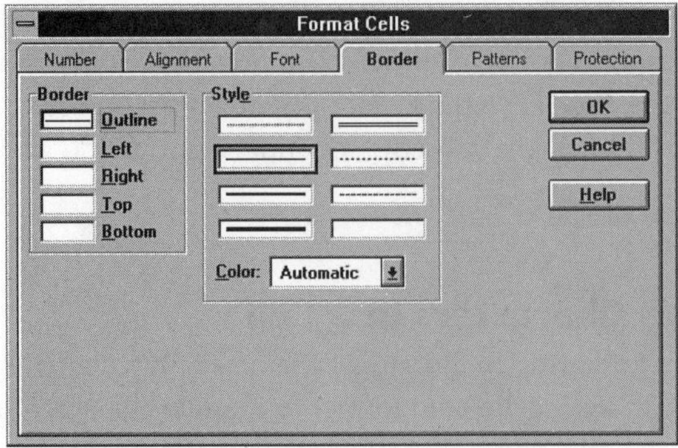

Fig. 14.15
In the Format Cells dialog box, select a border to add to a cell.

Tip
Use the Formatting toolbar to apply borders quickly. Select the cell or range you want to format, and then click the arrow next to the Borders button to display the Border buttons.

3. Choose the placement of the border by selecting **O**utline, **L**eft, **R**ight, **T**op, or **B**ottom in the Border box. The Outline option puts a border around the outer edges of the selection. The Left, Right, Top, and Bottom options place a border along the specified edges of each cell in the selection.

4. In the Styl**e** area, select the type of border you want. To change the color of the border, select the color from the **C**olor drop-down list.

5. When you finish, choose OK.

Applying Patterns

You can enhance a cell with patterns and colors. The F**o**rmat C**e**lls Patterns command enables you to choose foreground and background colors as well as a pattern.

To format a cell with colors and patterns, follow these steps:

1. Select the cell or range you want to format.

2. Choose the F**o**rmat C**e**lls command or press Ctrl+1. Alternatively, click the right mouse button and choose the Format Cells command from the shortcut menu. In the Format Cells dialog box, select the Patterns tab (see fig. 14.16).

3. Select a background color for the cell in the **C**olor section. The Sample box in the bottom right corner of the dialog box shows you what the color looks like.

4. Select a pattern in the **P**attern drop-down list by clicking the down arrow. To specify a background color for the pattern, select a pattern color from the **P**attern pull-down list. If the foreground and

background colors are the same, the cell displays a solid color. The Sample box shows you what the formatting looks like.

5. Choose OK.

Tip

To apply the same formatting to a different area, select the new area and then click the Repeat button or press F4 immediately after you apply the formatting.

Using Automatic Range Formatting

If you aren't sure which colors and formats work well together, Excel's AutoFormat feature can eliminate much of the guesswork. AutoFormat enables you to make choices from a list of predefined formatting templates. These formats are a combination of number formats, cell alignments, column widths, row heights, fonts, borders, and other formatting options.

◀ "Letting the Application Do the Formatting for You," p. 59

To use the AutoFormat feature, follow these steps:

1. Select the range you want to format.

2. Choose the F**o**rmat **A**utoFormat command. The AutoFormat dialog box appears (see fig. 14.17).

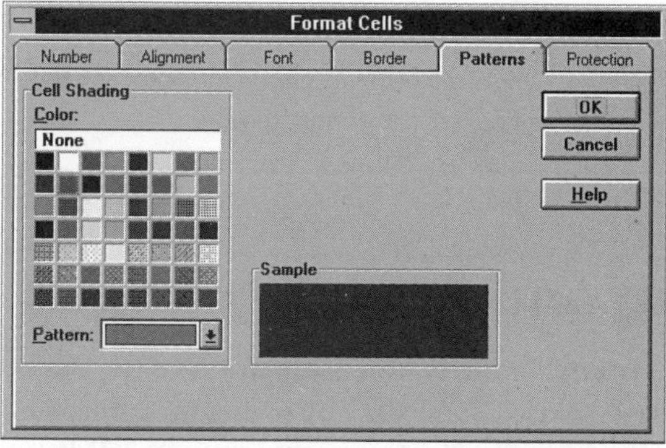

Fig. 14.16
Apply patterns and colors to a cell with the Format Cells dialog box.

AutoFormat

Table Format:

Simple
Classic 1
Classic 2
Classic 3
Accounting 1
Accounting 2
Accounting 3
Accounting 4
Colorful 1
Colorful 2
Colorful 3

Sample

	Jan	Feb	Mar	Total
East	7	7	5	19
West	6	4	7	17
South	8	7	9	24
Total	21	18	21	60

OK
Cancel
Options >>
Help

Fig. 14.17
The AutoFormat dialog box displays formatting templates.

3. Select one of the format types in the **T**able Format list box. Excel displays the selected format in the Sample box.

4. Choose OK to apply the format.

Note

To copy the formats from a range of cells to another range in the worksheet, select the range of cells containing the formats and click the Format Painter button in the Standard toolbar. Then, using the mouse, highlight the range of cells to which you want to copy the formats. When you release the mouse button, Excel applies the formats to the selected range.

Troubleshooting

After I changed the color of a cell, the entry was no longer displayed.

When the background color of a cell is the same color used by the cell entry, you will not see the entry. To change the color of the cell entry, select the cell and choose the F**o**rmat **C**ells command. Select the Font tab, select a color from the **C**olor drop-down menu, and choose OK.

After I choose the AutoFormat command, Excel displays an error message, stating that it cannot detect a table around the active cell.

You probably selected a single cell before choosing the AutoFormat command. You must select more than one cell for AutoFormat to work.

Creating and Applying a Style

When you find yourself applying the same worksheet formats over and over, you can save yourself some time by saving the formats in a style. Then, when you want to use the formats, you can apply all of them with a single command.

You can create a style based on cell formats that already appear in the worksheet, or you can create a new style by using the options in the Style dialog box.

Creating a Style by Example

You can define a style based on existing formats in your worksheet. When you create a style by example, Excel uses the formats of the selected cell to create the style.

To create a style by example, follow these steps:

1. Select the cell that contains the formats you want to name as a style.

2. Choose the F**o**rmat **S**tyle command. The Style dialog box appears (see fig. 14.18).

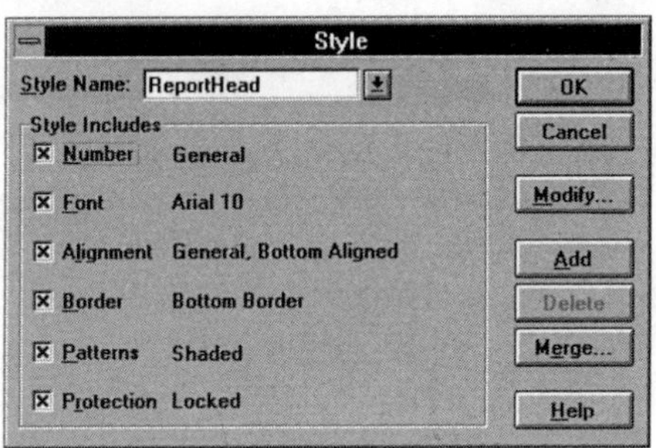

Fig. 14.18
The Style dialog box displays the options you can use to define a style.

3. Type a name for your new style in the **S**tyle Name box, and then choose **A**dd. The style appears in the **S**tyle Name drop-down list.

4. Choose OK.

Defining a Style

To create a new style, follow these steps:

1. Choose the F**o**rmat **S**tyle command to display the Style dialog box.

2. Type a name for the style in the **S**tyle Name text box. (Normal is the default style.) The current format appears in the Style Includes box.

3. Choose the **M**odify button. The Format Cells dialog box appears.

4. Select the tab for the attribute you want to change. The dialog box for the selected attribute appears.

5. Enter the changes you want to make. Choose OK to return to the Style dialog box.

6. After you make all the necessary style changes, choose OK. The dialog box closes, and Excel applies the style to any selected cells in the worksheet.

Applying a Style

To apply a style, follow these steps:

1. Select the cell or range to which you want to apply the style.

2. Choose the F**o**rmat **S**tyle command to display the Style dialog box.

3. Select the name of the style you want to apply in the **S**tyle Name list.

4. Choose OK. Excel applies the style to the selected cell or range.

Note

You also can use the Styles box in the Formatting toolbar to apply styles to cells in the worksheet. To add the Styles box, choose the **V**iews **T**oolbars command, select Formatting from the **T**oolbars list, and choose **C**ustomize. Select Formatting from the **C**ategories list, click and drag the Style box from the Buttons section of the dialog box to the Formatting toolbar, and choose Close.

Creating and Working with Graphic Objects

Excel makes it easy to enhance your worksheets with graphic objects by providing a full set of drawing tools. You can create such objects as circles, squares, and rectangles and add them to your worksheet.

Creating an Object

To create a drawn object, click the Drawing button in the Standard toolbar to display the Drawing toolbar. Select the Drawing tool that represents the object you want to create.

Position the mouse pointer in the area of the worksheet where you want to start drawing (the mouse pointer changes to a small cross when you position it in the worksheet area). Click and hold down the left mouse button, and drag the mouse until the object is the size you want. Then release the mouse button. Excel adds the drawing to the worksheet (see fig. 14.19).

Selecting, Moving, and Resizing Objects

After placing an object in the worksheet, you can move that object to a new location or resize it.

To Select an Object

Before you can move or resize an object, first select it by placing the mouse pointer next to the object and clicking the left mouse button. The mouse pointer becomes an arrow when positioned on the border of the object. Handles appear around the object, indicating that it is selected (see fig. 14.20).

To Move an Object

Select the object you want to move, and then position the mouse pointer inside the boundaries of the object. When the mouse pointer becomes an arrow, click and hold down the left mouse button, drag the selected object to the desired location, and release the mouse button.

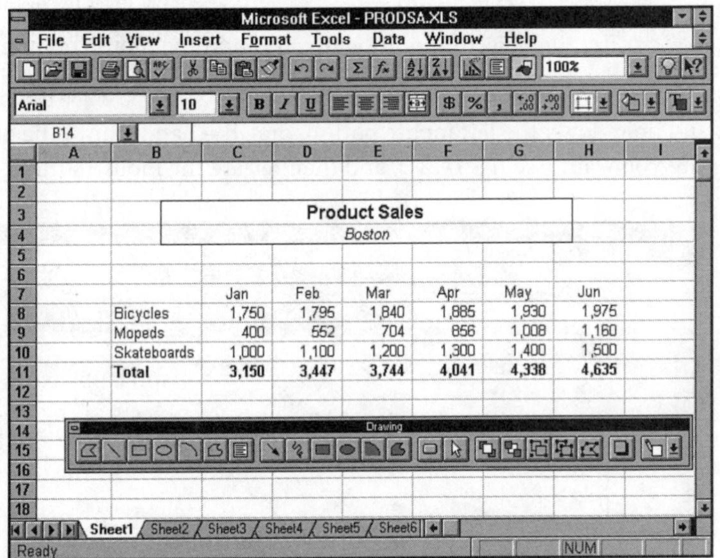

Fig. 14.19
A rectangle is added to the worksheet.

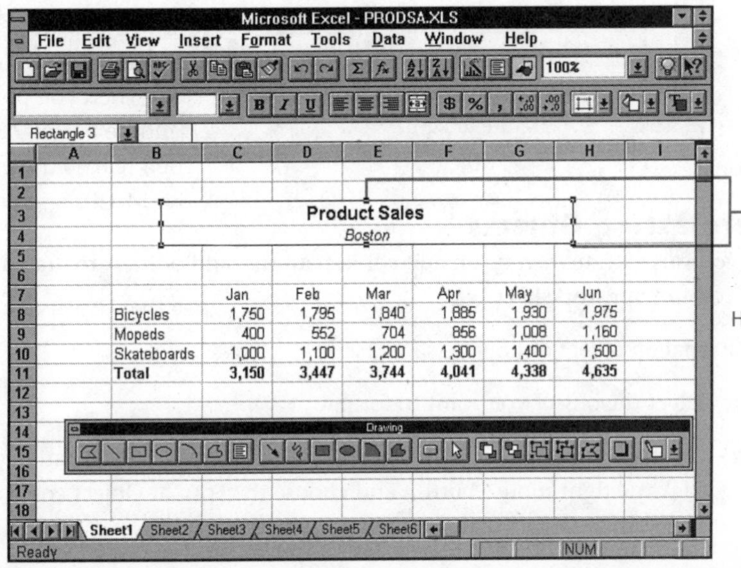

Fig. 14.20
Handles appear around this object, indicating that it is selected and can be moved or resized.

To Resize an Object

Select the object you want to resize. Handles appear around the object; these handles enable you to resize the selected object.

Position the mouse pointer on one of the black handles. The mouse pointer changes to a double-headed arrow when properly positioned. To make the object wider or longer, position the mouse pointer on one of the middle handles. To resize the object proportionally, position the mouse pointer on one of the corner handles.

Click and hold down the left mouse button, drag the handle until the object is the size you want (see fig. 14.21), and then release the mouse button.

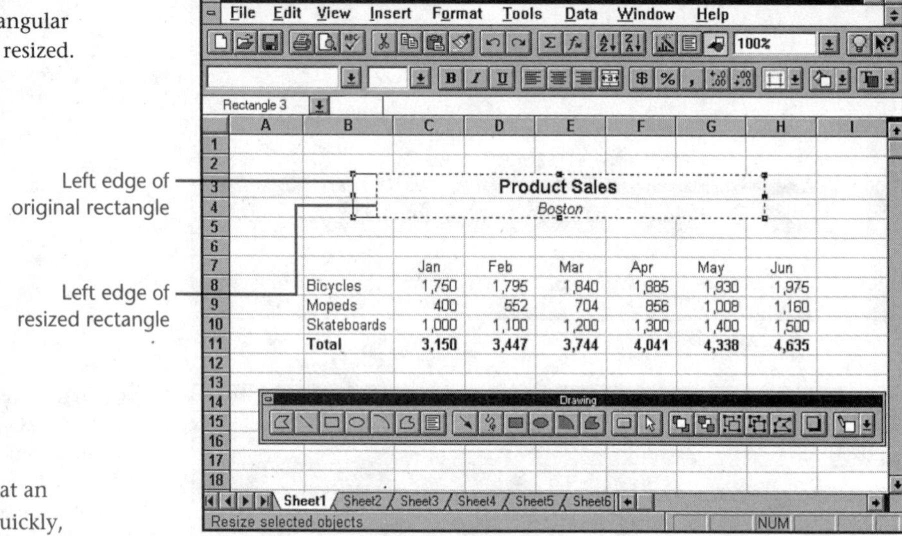

Fig. 14.21
The rectangular object is resized.

Tip
To format an object quickly, position the mouse pointer on the object you want to format. When the pointer changes to an arrow, double-click the object to display the Format Object dialog box.

Formatting Objects

As you can with text, you can add color, patterns, and borders to drawn objects in your worksheet.

To format an object, follow these steps:

1. Select the object you want to format.

2. Choose the F**o**rmat Obj**e**ct command or press Ctrl+1. Alternatively, click the right mouse button and choose the Format Object command. The Format Object dialog box appears (see fig. 14.22).

Fig. 14.22 Change the appearance of a drawn object with the Format Object dialog box.

3. Select a border style in the Border section of the dialog box. Select a color and pattern in the Fill section of the dialog box. The Sample area in the bottom right corner of the dialog box shows what the formatting will look like.

4. Choose OK to close the dialog box and apply the selected formats.

Grouping Objects

In creating a graphic or picture, you might draw several separate objects. If you want to work with multiple objects at the same time—for example, if you want to move the object to another area in the worksheet or want to create a copy of the drawing—you can group the objects to form a single object.

To group objects, first select the objects. (You can use the Selection button in the Drawing toolbar or hold down the Shift key as you click each object.) Choose the F**o**rmat **P**lacement **G**roup command. Excel groups the objects together. A single set of selection handles appears around the grouped object (see fig. 14.23).

To break a grouped object back into multiple objects, select the grouped object, and then choose F**o**rmat **P**lacement **U**ngroup. Individual objects appear, with handles surrounding each object.

Creating a Text Box

Excel enables you to create text boxes in your worksheets for adding paragraphs of text.

To create a text box, select the Text Box button and position the mouse pointer in the worksheet (the mouse pointer becomes a small cross). Click the left mouse button, and drag the pointer in the worksheet area. After you release the mouse button, the insertion point appears in the top left corner of the text box, ready to accept the text you type. The text wraps according to the size of the box (see fig. 14.24).

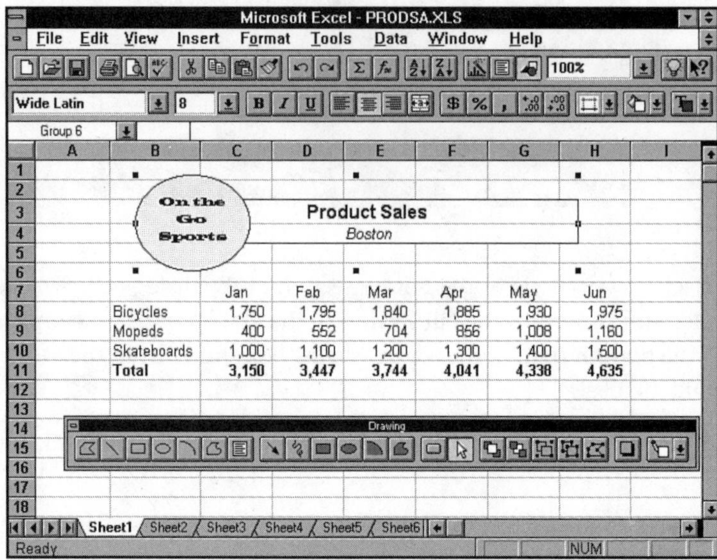

Fig. 14.23
All selected objects appear as one object, with handles outlining the area of the single grouped object.

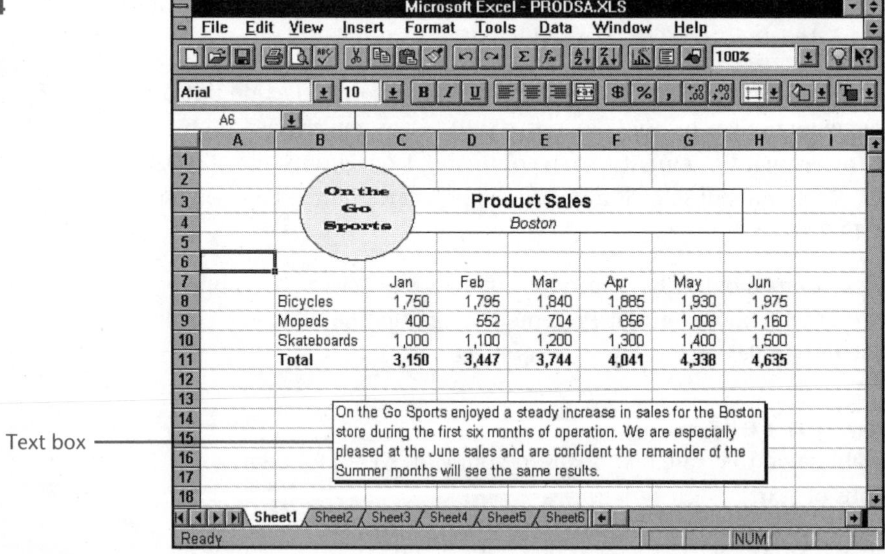

Fig. 14.24
Text wraps within this text box.

You can format, move, and resize a text box as you can any other object in a worksheet. When you resize a text box, the text automatically wraps to fit the new size of the box. You can apply formats to all the text in the text box or only to individual words. To make the entire text bold, for example, select the text box and click the Bold button in the Formatting toolbar. To make a single word of the text bold, place the mouse pointer inside the text box. The mouse pointer changes to an I-beam. Select the text you want to format by clicking and dragging the I-beam over the text. Then use standard formatting commands, tools, or shortcuts to format the selected text. As long as the insertion point appears inside the text box, you can use normal formatting and editing procedures. For information on formatting, refer to sections "Formatting Numbers," "Aligning Text Vertically or Horizontally," and "Changing Fonts, Sizes, and Styles," earlier in this chapter.

B

To select and move a text box, position the mouse pointer (arrow) on the border of the text box and then click the left mouse button.

From Here...

For additional information on formatting documents, you may want to review the following chapters:

- Chapter 2, "Using Common Features," contains additional information on applying document formatting.
- Chapter 13, "Editing Worksheets," shows you how to copy and move document formatting.
- Chapter 16, "Creating and Printing Reports and Charts," provides information on printing Excel worksheets.
- Chapter 42, "Changing Toolbars and Menus," teaches you how to customize the Excel toolbar.

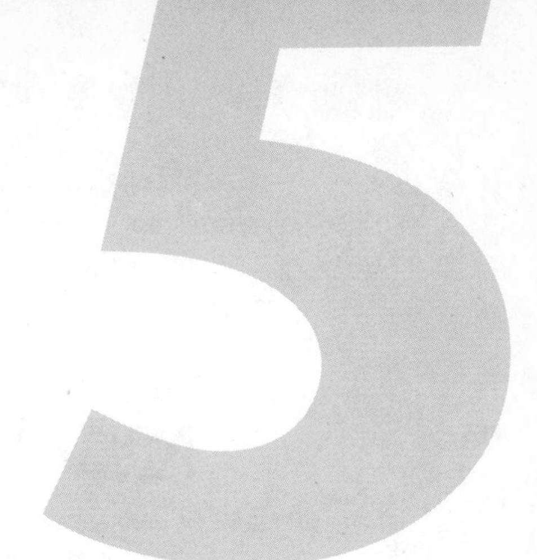

Chapter 15

Using Formulas and Functions

by Cathy Kenny

The greatest benefit in using an electronic spreadsheet program, such as Excel, is the program's power to calculate formulas based on values in the worksheet. You can, for example, create a formula that calculates the difference between sales figures on a quarterly basis. In addition, you can use Excel's built-in functions to calculate the average of a range of values or the monthly payment on a loan.

In this chapter, you learn to

- Create a formula
- Create a formula by using Excel's built-in functions
- Use the Function Wizard to enter a function
- Copy formulas
- Name cells used in formulas

Creating Formulas

You can create formulas in Excel in two ways: type the formula directly in the cell, or point to the cells that you want the formula to compute.

Creating a Formula by Typing

◄ "Entering Data," p. 247

To create a formula by entering the cell addresses and numeric operators in a cell, follow these steps:

1. Select the cell in which you want to enter a formula.
2. Type = (equal sign) to start the formula.

Note

You can enter a plus sign (+) or minus sign (–) to begin a formula; Excel will convert the formula to the appropriate format. If you enter **+B4+B5**, for example, Excel will convert the formula to =+B4+B5.

3. Type the cell addresses containing the values to be computed, entering the appropriate operator. To find the difference between the two values in cells B5 and B11, for example, enter **=B5–B11** in cell B14.
4. Press Enter. Excel displays the result of the formula in the active cell, and the formula appears in the formula bar.

Tip

To display formulas in a worksheet instead of their calculated values, select any blank cell in the worksheet and press Ctrl+` (accent grave). Press Ctrl+` a second time to display the formula result.

Creating a Formula by Pointing

You can, unfortunately, make errors when typing cell addresses in a formula. To minimize errors that occur when you use cell addresses in formulas, build a formula by pointing to cells rather than by typing the cell addresses.

Pointing to Cells with the Mouse

◄ "Moving Around in a Worksheet," p. 244

Suppose that you want to enter, in cell B14, a formula that subtracts the total in cell B5 from the total in cell B11. To build a formula by pointing to cells with the mouse, follow these steps:

1. Select the cell in which you want to enter a formula.
2. Type = (equal sign) to start the formula. For this example, type = in cell B14.
3. Click the cell whose address you want to add to the formula. For this example, click cell B5 to add the cell address in the formula bar.
4. Type – (minus sign).
5. Click the next cell address you want to add to the formula. For this example, click cell B11.
6. Click the check box in the formula bar or press Enter to complete the formula entry (see fig. 15.1).

Microsoft Excel - PSALES2.XLS

File Edit View Insert Format Tools Data Window Help

B14 =B5-B11

	A	B	C	D	E	F	G	H
1	**Product Sales**	Jan	Feb	Mar	Apr	May	Jun	
2	Bicycles	1,750	1,795	1,840	1,885	1,930	1,975	
3	Skateboards	400	552	704	856	1,008	1,160	
4	Rollerblades	1,000	1,100	1,200	1,300	1,400	1,500	
5	**Total Sales**	3,150	3,447	3,744	4,041	4,338	4,635	
6								
7	**Overhead**							
8	Rent	1,100	1,100	1,100	1,100	1,100	1,100	
9	Utilities	250	250	275	300	290	300	
10	Payroll	450	375	400	425	550	575	
11	**Total Expenses**	1,800	1,725	1,775	1,825	1,940	1,975	
12								
13								
14	**Total Revenue**	1,350						
15								
16								
17								
18								
19								
20								

Boston / New York / San Francisco

Ready NUM

Fig. 15.1
The result of the formula appears in cell B14. The formula appears in the formula bar.

Entering Cell References with the Keyboard

Suppose that you want to build, in cell D9, a formula that finds the difference between the totals in cells B9 and C9. To enter cell references with the keyboard, follow these steps:

1. Select the cell in which you want to enter a formula.
2. Type = (equal sign) to start the formula. For this example, type = in cell D9.
3. Use the arrow keys to highlight the cell that contains the data you want to use. For this example, press ← twice to select cell B9. Notice that the marquee is positioned in cell B9. Cell B9 is added to the formula.
4. Type – (minus sign).
5. Use the arrow keys to highlight the next cell you want to use. For this example, press → to select cell C9. Cell C9 is added to the formula.
6. Press Enter to complete the entry.

Using Mathematical Operators

In addition to using Excel's built-in functions to perform calculations, you can use mathematical operators to perform a calculation on worksheet data. Following are the mathematical operators used in basic calculations:

Operator	Purpose
+	Addition
–	Subtraction
*	Multiplication
/	Division
%	Percentage
^	Exponentiation

Most formula errors occur when the mathematical operators are not entered in the proper *order of precedence*—the order in which Excel performs mathematical operations. Following is the order of precedence for mathematical operations in a formula:

^	Exponentiation
*, /	Multiplication, division
+, –	Addition, subtraction

Exponentiation occurs before multiplication or division in a formula, and multiplication and division occur before addition or subtraction. For example, Excel calculates the formula =4+10*2 by first multiplying 10 by 2 and then adding the product to 4, which returns 24. That order remains constant whether the formula is written as =4+10*2 or 10*2+4.

If a formula includes mathematical operators that are at the same level, the calculations are evaluated sequentially from left to right.

You can change the order of precedence by enclosing segments of the formula in parentheses. Excel first performs all operations within the parentheses and then performs the rest of the operations in the appropriate order. For example, by adding parentheses to the formula =4+10*2 to create =(4+10)*2, you can force Excel first to add 4 and 10 and then multiply the sum by 2 to return 28.

Note

Each open parenthesis must be matched by a closed parenthesis, or Excel will not accept the formula. The program displays a message stating that the parentheses don't match. When you use parentheses in a formula, compare the total number of open parentheses with the total number of closed parentheses.

In addition to performing mathematical calculations with formulas, you can manipulate text, perform comparisons, and refer to several different ranges in the worksheet with references.

By using text operators, you can concatenate (join) text contained in quotation marks or text in other cells. For example, entering the formula ="Total Sales: "&B4 returns Total Sales: 28 when cell B4 contains the value 28.

To compare results, you can create formulas with comparative operators, which return TRUE or FALSE, depending on how the formula evaluates the condition. For example, the formula =A4>30 returns TRUE if the value in cell A4 is greater than 30; otherwise, it returns FALSE.

Following are the comparative operators you can use in a formula:

Operator	Purpose
=	Equal to
<	Less than
>	Greater than
<=	Less than or equal to
>=	Greater than or equal to
<>	Not equal to

Reference operators enable you to refer to several different ranges in a single formula. For example, entering the formula SUM(A4:A24) sums the values located in ranges A4 through A24.

Entering Dates and Times in Formulas

You also can create formulas to calculate values by using dates and times. When you use a date or time in a formula, you must enter the date or time in a format that Excel recognizes, and you must enclose the entry in double quotation marks. Excel then converts the entry to its appropriate value. To find the number of days that elapsed between two dates, for example, you would enter a formula such as ="4/2/94"–"3/27/94". In this example, Excel returns 6, the number of days between March 27, 1994 and April 2, 1994.

◄ "Entering Dates and Times," p. 248

If Excel does not recognize a date or time, it stores the entry as text and displays the #VALUE! error value.

Note

You can reduce the time you spend entering repetitive formulas by using arrays. *Arrays* are rectangular ranges of formulas or values that Excel treats as a single group.

Debugging Formulas

Several errors can occur when you enter formulas in Excel. In many cases, Excel displays an error value that enables you to debug your formulas based on that value. Following are the error values and their possible causes:

Error	Meaning
#DIV/0!	The formula is trying to divide by zero
#N/A	The formula refers to a value that is not available
#NAME?	The formula uses a name that Excel does not recognize
#NUL!	The formula contains a reference that specifies an invalid intersection of cells
#NUM!	The formula uses a number incorrectly
#REF!	The formula refers to a cell that is not valid
#VALUE!	The formula uses an incorrect argument or operator

Tip
When an error value appears in the worksheet, click the Tip Wizard button to see a description of the error value.

To access Excel's error-values Help screens, choose the **H**elp **S**earch For Help On command. In the top text box, enter **Error Values**; then choose **S**how Topics. Select Overview of Error Values from the list, and choose **G**o To. Excel displays a Help screen with the list of error values (see fig. 15.2).

Converting Formulas to Values

In many cases, after you create the formula, you need only the result rather than the formula itself. After you calculate your monthly mortgage payment, for example, you no longer need the formula. In such a situation, you can convert the formula to its actual value.

To convert a single formula to a value, follow these steps:

1. Select the cell that contains the formula.

2. Press the F2 function key, or double-click the cell.

3. Press the F9 function key. Excel replaces the formula with the value.

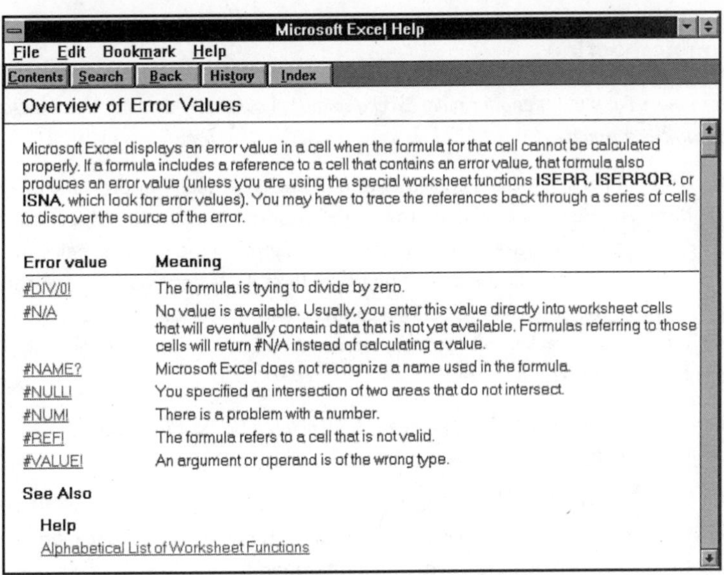

Fig. 15.2
The Help screen displays the list of error values and their causes.

To convert a range of formulas to values, follow these steps:

1. Select the range that contains the formulas you want to convert.

2. Choose the **E**dit **C**opy command, or click the right mouse button and choose Copy from the shortcut menu. A marquee surrounds the selected range.

3. Choose the **E**dit Paste **S**pecial command. The Paste Special dialog box appears (see fig. 15.3).

Fig. 15.3
Select the Values option in the Paste Special dialog box to convert formulas to values.

4. Choose the **V**alues option.

5. Choose OK. Excel replaces the formulas in the selected range with values.

Troubleshooting

After I press Enter to enter a formula, Excel displays an alert box, warning that an error exists in the formula.

When this happens, choose the **H**elp button (if one is available) or press the F1 key. Excel displays a Help window that displays the error message and a possible cause. If, after reading the Help screen, you cannot find the error in the formula, delete the equal sign that appears at the beginning of the formula. When you do, Excel enters the formula in the cell as text. You then can return to the formula later and work on it. To turn the text back into a formula, reenter the equal sign at the beginning of the formula, and press Enter.

After I enter a formula that uses parentheses, Excel displays the error message `Parentheses do not match.`

When you use parentheses in formulas, remember that for every open parenthesis, there must be a closed parenthesis. In many cases, Excel highlights matching pairs of parentheses as you move the insertion point through the formula. As you move the insertion point across an open parenthesis, watch for the closed parenthesis to appear highlighted. If the highlighted parenthesis does not enclose the correct term, you have found the term that requires another parenthesis.

Using Built-In Functions

If you could not calculate complex formulas in Excel, creating worksheets would be quite difficult. Fortunately, Excel provides more than 200 built-in *functions*, or predefined formulas, that enable you to create formulas easily for a wide range of applications, including business, scientific, and engineering applications.

Each function consists of the equal sign (=), the function name, and the *argument* (cells used for carrying out the calculation). The SUM function, for example, adds the numbers in a specified range of cells (see fig. 15.4). The addresses of the specified cells make up the argument portion of the function. The active cell shows the result of the function.

Excel comes with a large number of built-in worksheet functions, including mathematical, database, financial, and statistical functions. The program also includes date, time, information, logical, lookup, reference, text, and trigonometric functions.

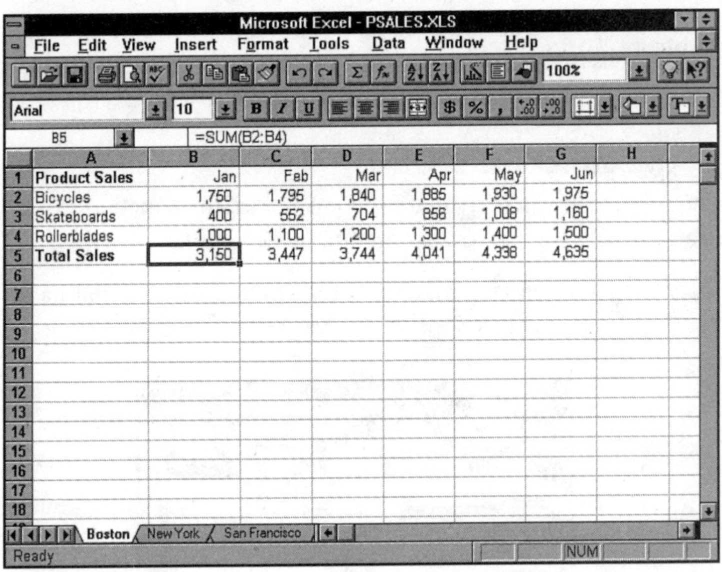

Microsoft Excel - PSALES.XLS
File Edit View Insert Format Tools Data Window Help
100%
Arial 10
B5 =SUM(B2:B4)
A B C D E F G H
1 Product Sales Jan Feb Mar Apr May Jun
2 Bicycles 1,750 1,795 1,840 1,885 1,930 1,975
3 Skateboards 400 552 704 856 1,008 1,160
4 Rollerblades 1,000 1,100 1,200 1,300 1,400 1,500
5 Total Sales 3,150 3,447 3,744 4,041 4,338 4,635
Boston New York San Francisco
Ready NUM

Fig. 15.4
This formula uses the SUM function to total the entries in cells B2, B3, and B4.

Entering Functions

To enter a function in the active cell, type = (equal sign), followed by the function name (for example, **SUM**), followed by an open parenthesis. Then specify the cell or range of cells you want the function to use, followed by a closed parenthesis. When you press Enter to enter the function in the cell, Excel displays the result of the formula in the cell.

Tip
If you're a Lotus 1-2-3 user, you can enter a 1-2-3 function, such as @SUM(A1..A4), and Excel will convert it to the appropriate Excel function.

> **Note**
>
> You do not need to enter the last parenthesis if you are creating a formula with Excel's built-in functions. Excel automatically adds the last parenthesis when you press Enter.

Using the AutoSum Button To Sum Ranges

You can use the AutoSum button, located in the Standard toolbar, to sum a range of cells quickly. You can, for example, use the AutoSum button to total the values in adjacent columns or rows. To do so, select a cell adjacent to the range you want to sum, and then click the AutoSum button. Excel inserts the SUM function and selects the cells in the column above the selected cell or in the row to the left of the selected cell.

You also can highlight the range of cells you want to sum. To do so, select the range of cells (including blank cells) to the right of or below the range, and then click the AutoSum button. Excel fills in the totals.

Using the Function Wizard

If you're not sure how a particular function works, the Function Wizard can guide you through the process of entering the function.

To display the Function Wizard, choose the **I**nsert **F**unction command. The Function Wizard dialog box appears (see fig. 15.5).

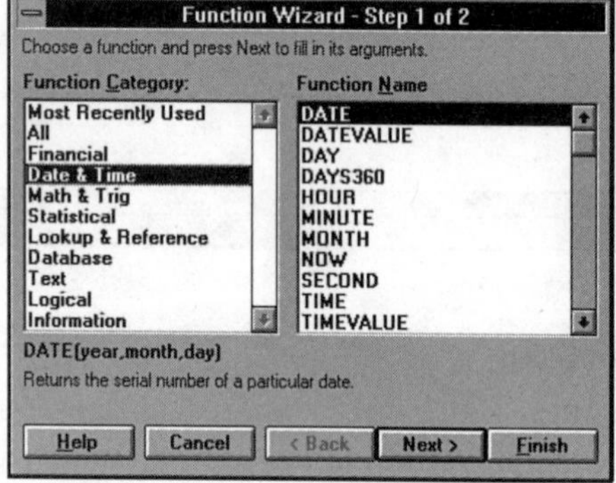

Fig. 15.5
In the Function Wizard dialog box, select the function you want to use.

Tip
If you know how to use the function, choose the **F**inish button. The function and its arguments appear in the formula. Type the required arguments, and then press Enter or click the check-mark button in the formula bar to enter the function in the cell.

The Function Category list displays Excel's built-in functions, and the Function Name list shows an alphabetized list of functions available for the highlighted category. To access the DATE function, for example, select Date & Time in the Function **C**ategory list, and then select DATE in the Function **N**ame list. When you select a function, the function appears in the formula bar, and the formula bar is activated.

After you select the function you want, choose Next or press Enter to display the next Function Wizard dialog box. The Step 2 dialog box prompts you to enter the arguments required for the function (see fig. 15.6). An argument can be a single cell reference, a group of cells, a number, or another function. Some functions require a single argument; others require multiple arguments. Function arguments are enclosed in parentheses, and arguments are separated by commas.

Each of the argument text boxes must contain a cell address or data. If an argument is required, the label to the left of the text box is bold.

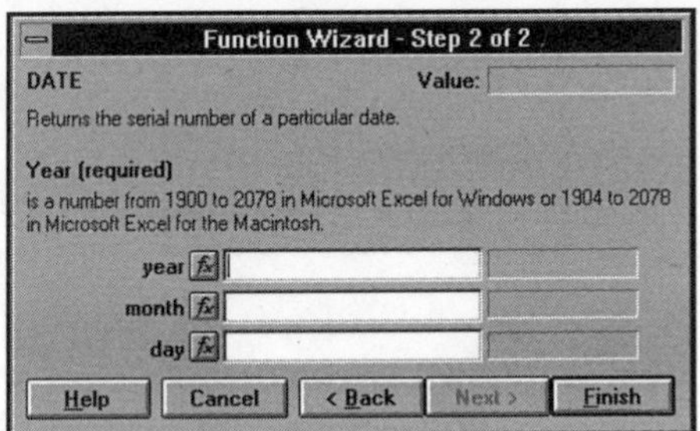

Fig. 15.6
Enter the required arguments for the function in the Function Wizard dialog box.

To enter the argument data, click the mouse or press Tab to position the insertion point in the first argument text box. The Function Wizard displays a description of the argument in the display area above the text boxes. Enter the values to be used for the arguments, use the mouse to select the cell(s) in the worksheet to be used for the argument, or use the keyboard to enter the cell address(es). The Function Wizard displays the value to the right of the text box (see fig. 15.7).

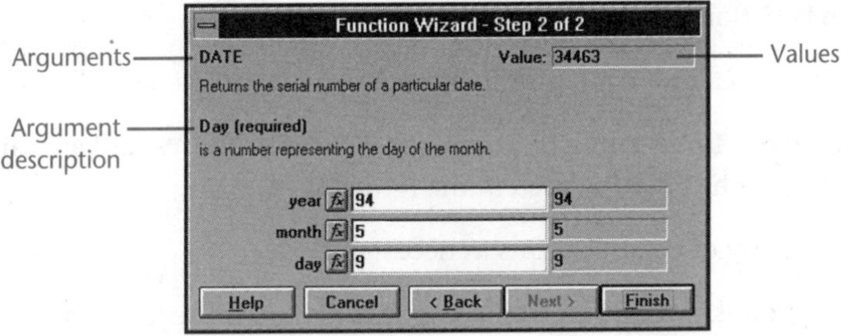

Fig. 15.7
This dialog box contains multiple arguments for the Date function.

To enter the first argument for the function, select the cell that contains the data you want to use. To indicate a range of cells, select the range you want to use in the formula. You also can enter the cell addresses from the keyboard. If, for example, you want to sum the numbers in cells B1, B2, and B3, enter **B1:B3** or **B1,B2,B3** in the argument text box. Each argument appears between the parentheses in the formula bar.

Tip
If the Function Wizard dialog box is in the way, move the dialog box by clicking and dragging its title bar.

When you finish entering the arguments required by the function, the result of the formula appears in the Value box in the top right corner of the Function Wizard dialog box. Choose **F**inish to enter the function in the cell. The dialog box disappears, and the result of the formula appears in the cell. If the formula contains an error, an alert box appears (see fig. 15.8).

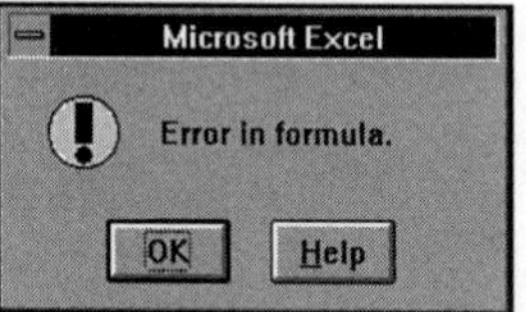

Fig. 15.8
This alert box appears if your formula contains an error.

Choose the **H**elp button in the alert box to find out more about the function error. A help window appears, displaying possible reasons for the error. To clear the error message, choose OK.

In some cases, Excel highlights the part of the function that contains the error. Edit the function in the formula bar, and when the formula is corrected or complete, click the check-mark button or press Enter.

Editing Functions

◄ "Editing Worksheet Data," p. 263

After entering a function, you can edit it. You can use the Function Wizard to edit a function, or you can edit the formula and function directly in the cell.

To use the Function Wizard to edit a formula, follow these steps:

1. Select the cell that contains the function you want to edit.

2. Choose the **I**nsert **F**unction command. The Function Wizard appears, displaying the function used in the formula.
3. Change any of the arguments as necessary.
4. Choose **F**inish when you complete the function. If the formula contains another function, choose Next.
5. Repeat steps 3 and 4 for each function you want to edit.

To edit a function manually, follow these steps:

1. Select the cell that contains the function you want to edit.
2. Double-click the cell or click the formula bar.
3. Select the argument you want to change.
4. Enter the new argument.
5. Press Enter or click the check-mark button in the formula bar.

Getting Help with Functions

As you are using Excel's functions, you can use Excel's context-sensitive help system for assistance. To get help while you are entering a function with the Function Wizard, choose the **H**elp button.

◄ "Using Help," p. 61

To access Excel's on-line help for functions, choose the **H**elp **S**earch for Help on command. Enter **Functions** in the top text box, and then choose **S**how Topics. Select Alphabetized List of Functions from the list, and choose the **G**oto button. Excel displays a Help window with an alphabetized list of functions (see fig. 15.9). Choose the **F**ile E**x**it command when you finish viewing the Help window.

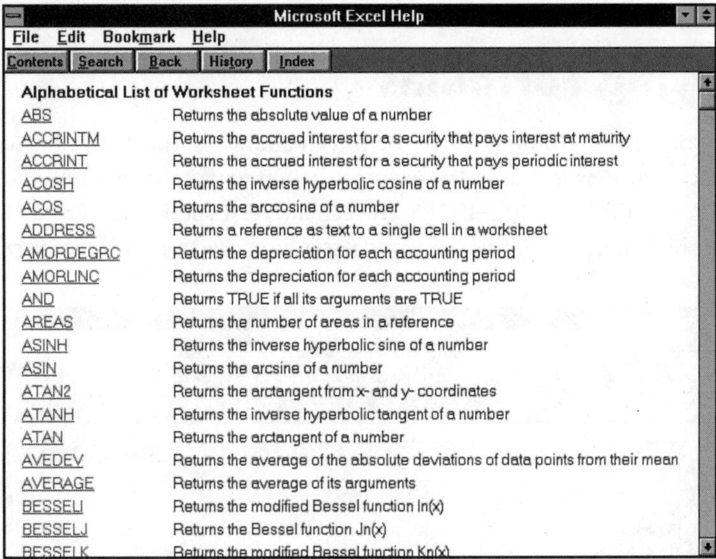

Fig. 15.9

Select the function for which you want help.

Troubleshooting

After I click the AutoSum button, Excel does not produce a total amount.

If you click the AutoSum button and there are no surrounding cells with numbers to add, the SUM function does not recognize a range address to sum. Select the range of cells you want to sum; the range address appears within the parentheses. Remember that to use the AutoSum button, you must select a cell adjacent to the values you want to sum, or you must select the range of cells (including any blank cells) and then click the AutoSum button.

(continues)

(continued)

After I enter a function, Excel displays the error value #NAME? *in the cell.*

There are two possible causes: you specified a range name that does not exist, or you misspelled the function name. To check, press the F2 function key, and remove the equal sign (=) from the beginning of the formula. Then double-check the spelling of the function. If this spelling is incorrect, correct it, and then enter the equal sign. If the function name is spelled correctly, the next step is to make sure that the range to which you referred exists in the worksheet. To do this, click the arrow at the left end of the formula bar, and check the range names in the drop-down list. If the name does not appear in this list, use the Insert Name Define command to create the range name. When you do, the formula will return the correct result.

Copying Formulas

When you copy a formula that contains cell addresses, the cell addresses adjust to their new location. For example, when you copy the formula =B5–B12 from cell B15 to cell C15, the cell addresses adjust to =C5–C12 (see fig. 15.10). In Excel, these cell addresses are called *relative cell references.*

Fig. 15.10 When copied, relative cell references adjust to their new location.

◄ "Copying Worksheet Data," p. 266

◄ "Moving Worksheet Data," p. 270

Microsoft Excel - PSALES.XLS

File Edit View Insert Format Tools Data Window Help

C15 =C5-C12

	A	B	C	D	E	F	G	H
1	**Product Sales**	Jan	Feb	Mar	Apr	May	Jun	
2	Bicycles	1,750	1,795	1,840	1,885	1,930	1,975	
3	Skateboards	400	552	704	856	1,008	1,160	
4	Rollerblades	1,000	1,100	1,200	1,300	1,400	1,500	
5	**Total Sales**	3,150	3,447	3,744	4,041	4,338	4,635	
6								
7								
8	**Overhead**							
9	Rent	1,100	1,100	1,100	1,100	1,100	1,100	
10	Utilities	250	260	270	280	290	300	
11	Payroll	450	475	500	525	550	575	
12	**Total Expenses**	1,800	1,835	1,870	1,905	1,940	1,975	
13								
14								
15	**Total Revenue**	1,350	1,612					
16								
17								
18								

Boston / New York / San Francisco

Ready NUM

If you want the cell addresses to remain the same when copied, use *absolute cell references* in the formula. In an absolute cell reference, a dollar sign appears to the left of the column and/or row address—for example, F6 (see fig. 15.11).

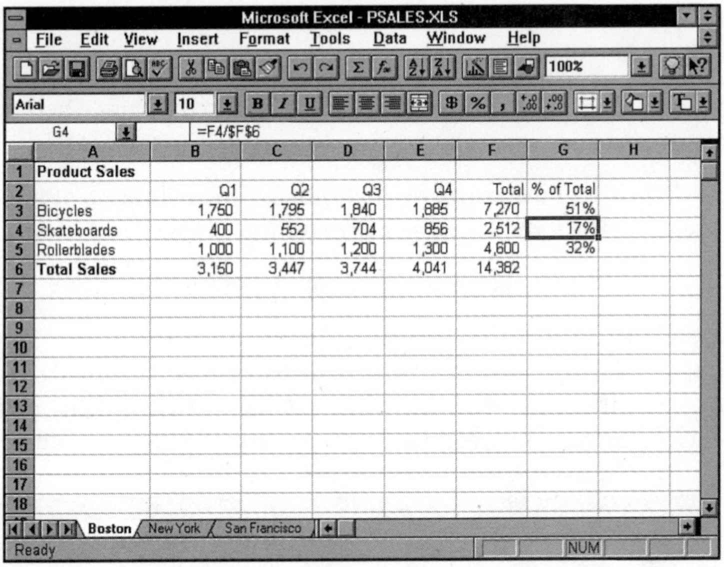

Fig. 15.11
Absolute cell references remain the same when copied.

Create a *mixed cell reference* when you want either the column or row reference to be absolute and the other reference to be relative. $C9 is an example of a mixed cell reference. When you copy a formula that contains this type of cell reference, the column reference remains the same, and the row reference changes. Alternatively, when you copy a formula that includes a reference such as C$9, the column reference changes, and the row reference remains the same.

Before you copy the formula that contains the cell reference, make the cell reference absolute. Follow these steps:

1. Select the cell that contains the formula.
2. Press F2, or double-click the cell.
3. Use the left- or right-arrow key or the mouse to position the insertion point to the left of the cell or row reference, and then press F4. When you do, Excel inserts the dollar sign ($).

Linking Formulas

When you use multiple worksheets in Excel, your formulas may need to refer to cells in other worksheets. For example, if each sheet in your worksheet contains sales data for each sales region, you can create a total worksheet and sum the values for each region by linking formulas.

Creating Linking Formulas

To link formulas, follow these steps:

1. Enter the formula as you normally would, up to the point where you want to reference the cell.

2. Click the tab of the worksheet that contains the cell you want to reference. The formula displays the worksheet name.

3. Select the cell or range of cells you want to reference.

4. Press Enter, or click the check-mark button in the formula bar. Excel displays the worksheet name and cell references in the formula. For example, the SUM function in cell B4 of figure 15.12 contains a reference to the sheet named Boston and appears as =SUM(Boston!B4:E4).

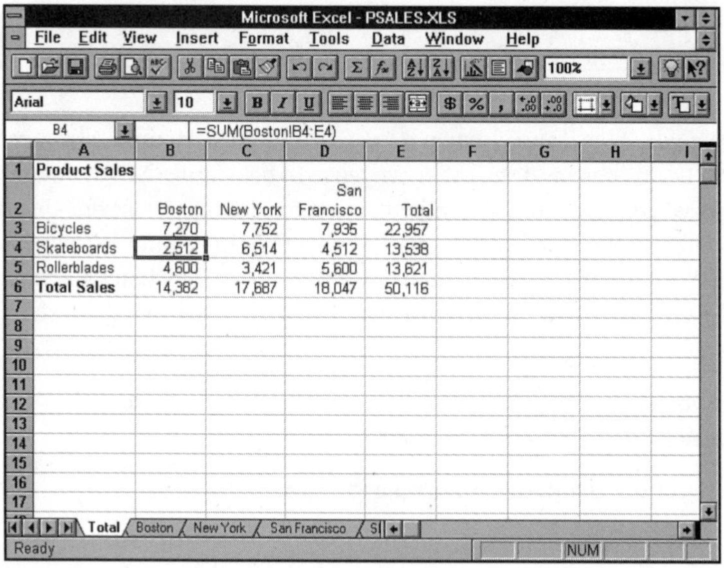

Fig. 15.12
This formula contains a reference to another sheet in the workbook.

Product Sales	Boston	New York	San Francisco	Total
Bicycles	7,270	7,752	7,935	22,957
Skateboards	2,512	6,514	4,512	13,538
Rollerblades	4,600	3,421	5,600	13,621
Total Sales	14,382	17,687	18,047	50,116

Creating Formulas That Link Workbooks

In addition to referring to cells in other worksheets, a formula can refer to cells in other workbooks. Before you can link a formula to another workbook, that workbook must be open.

To link to another workbook, follow these steps:

1. Enter the formula up to the point of reference.

2. From the **W**indow menu, choose the workbook that contains the data you want to reference.

3. If necessary, select the worksheet sheet that contains the data you want to reference. Then select the cell that contains the data you want to reference.

4. Press Enter, or click the check-mark button in the formula bar.

Working with Range Names

As you become more proficient in writing formulas, you will find that cell references are sorely lacking in describing the data that is being calculated. If you saw the formula =B9–C9 in a worksheet, it wouldn't be clear which data is being used.

By assigning a name to a cell or range of cells, you can describe the data in your worksheets. The formula +Total_Sales–Total_Expenses, for example, instantly tells you what data the formula uses.

Tip
To display the cells to which a formula refers select the formula in the worksheet and then click the Trace Precedents button in the Auditing toolbar.

Creating a Range Name

To create a range name, follow these steps:

1. Select the cell or range of cells you want to name.

2. Click the Name box located at the left end of the formula bar.

3. Enter the name you want to assign to the selected range.

4. Press Enter.

To create a range name by using an alternative method, follow these steps:

1. Choose the **I**nsert **N**ame **D**efine command. The Define Name dialog box appears.

2. Type a name in the Names in **W**orkbook text box.

3. Choose OK.

To display a list of range names in the active worksheet, click the arrow next to the Name box in the formula bar. The drop-down list displays all range names in the worksheet (see fig. 15.13).

Tip
To move to a range quickly, type the range to which you want to go to in the Name box.

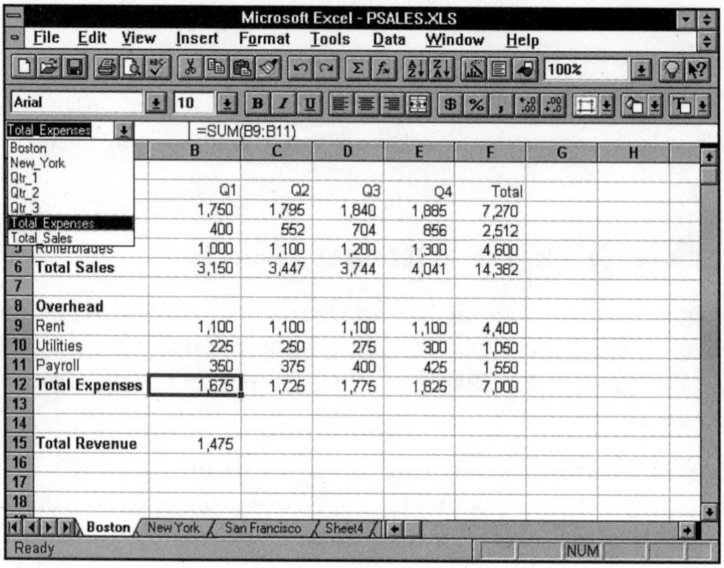

Fig. 15.13
This drop-down list displays all range names in the worksheet.

Tip
You also can use the Name box to insert a name into a formula. Click the drop-down arrow next to the Name box, and select the range name you want to use.

Inserting Names

After you assign a range name, you can refer to that range name the way you refer to cell addresses.

To insert a name into a formula, follow these steps:

1. To create a formula that uses range names, type = (equal sign) to start the formula.

2. Choose the **I**nsert **N**ame **P**aste command. The Paste Name dialog box appears (see fig. 15.14).

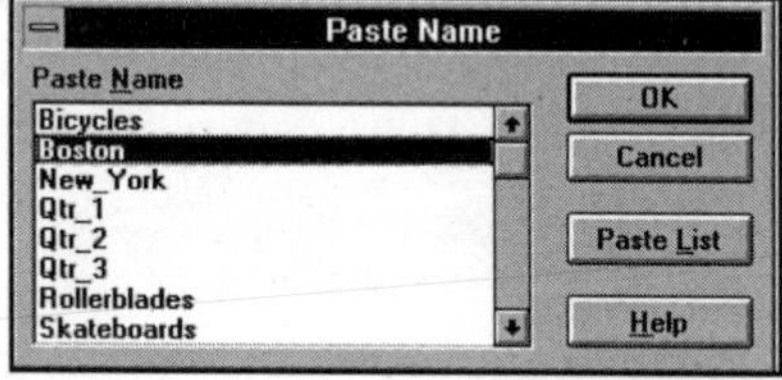

Fig. 15.14
Insert a name into a formula by using the Paste Name dialog box.

3. In the Paste Name list, select the name you want to insert.

4. Choose OK to close the dialog box.

5. Type the rest of the formula, and press Enter or click the check-mark button in the formula bar when you finish (see fig. 15.15).

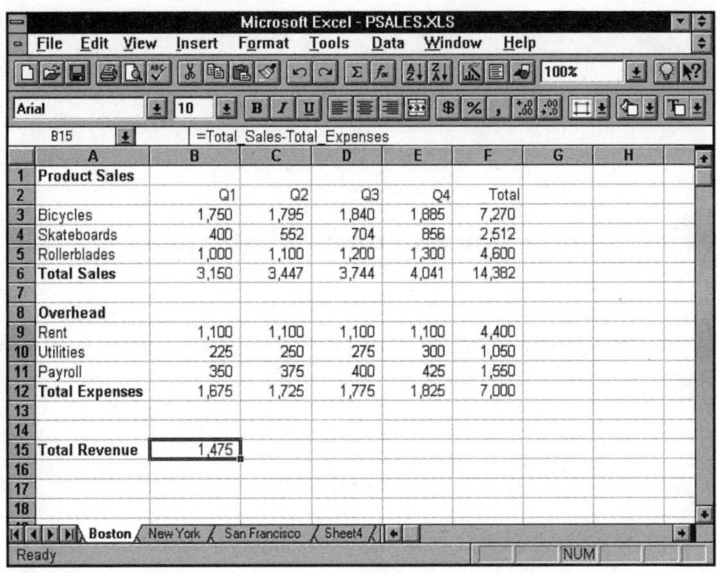

Fig. 15.15
This formula refers to two range names in the worksheet.

Deleting Range Names

To delete a range name, follow these steps:

1. Choose the **I**nsert **N**ame **D**efine command. The Define Name dialog box appears (see fig. 15.16).

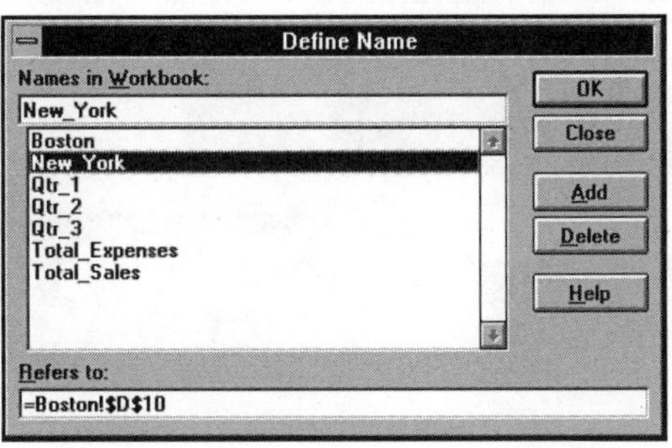

Fig. 15.16
You can delete range names in the Define Name dialog box.

2. In the Names in **W**orkbook list, select the range name you want to delete.

3. Choose the **D**elete button.

4. Choose OK.

> **Note**
>
> When you define names in the Define Name dialog box, use the **A**dd and **D**elete buttons to make multiple changes. Choose OK when you finish making changes.

Creating Range Names from Existing Text

Excel enables you to create range names by using existing text from a worksheet. You can, for example, use text that appears in a column to name the cells to the immediate right. Naming cells from existing data enables you to create many range names at one time.

To create range names from existing text, follow these steps:

1. Select the range of cells that contains the text and the cells to be named.

2. Choose the **I**nsert **N**ame **C**reate command. The Create Names dialog box appears (see fig. 15.17).

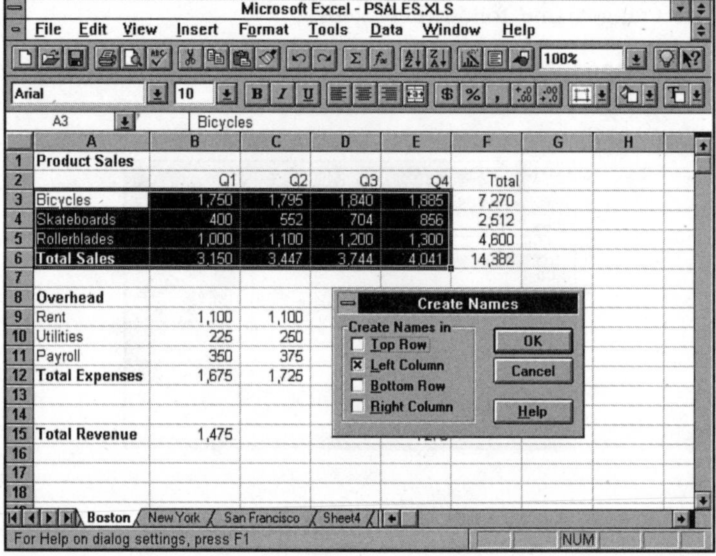

Fig. 15.17 Names will be created from the text that appears in the first column of the selected range.

3. Select the check box that shows the location of the cells containing the text you want to use for range names.

4. Choose OK.

Troubleshooting

After I deleted a range name, Excel replaced some of the formulas in the worksheet with the value #NAME?.

When you delete a range name, any formula that refers to the range name returns #NAME?. To correct a formula that refers to a deleted range name, replace the #NAME? reference with the appropriate cell address, or use the **I**nsert **N**ame **D**efine command to re-create the deleted range name.

After I create a formula that uses a name, Excel interprets the formula as a text entry.

When you use a range name as the first item in a formula, you must begin the formula with an equal sign (=), as in =SALES*4.05. Otherwise, Excel thinks that you are entering a text label.

From Here...

For additional information on using formulas and functions in Excel, see the following chapters:

- Chapter 12, "Creating Worksheets," introduces basic techniques such as selecting cells and entering data.
- Chapter 13, "Editing Worksheets," shows you how to edit worksheet data.
- Chapter 14, "Formatting Worksheets," teaches you how to format numeric entries.
- Chapter 17, "Managing and Analyzing Data," presents the Excel commands.

Chapter 16

Creating and Printing Reports and Charts

by Cathy Kenny

Excel provides sophisticated charting capabilities that enable you to display your worksheet data in graphical form. When you create a chart, you can embed the chart in a worksheet, alongside the data on which it is based, or you can create a separate chart sheet. When you're ready to print worksheet data and charts, you can create reports that consist of multiple worksheet areas.

In this chapter, you learn to

- Define the area to be printed
- Define page settings
- Preview and print worksheet data
- Create and print reports
- Create a chart
- Enhance a chart
- Print a chart

Printing Worksheet Data

Excel provides many options that enable you to control the printed output of your worksheets and charts. You can use the Print Preview command to preview worksheet data before printing. The Page Setup command enables you to define margin settings and to create headers and footers.

Printing a Particular Area

You can print the entire workbook, a specific worksheet in the workbook, or a selected range of data. By default, Excel automatically selects and prints the current worksheet. You can, however, define a portion of the worksheet to be printed.

Printing a Specific Range

To print a specific range in the worksheet, follow these steps:

1. Select the range to be printed, using the mouse or the keyboard.

2. Choose the **F**ile **P**rint command or press Ctrl+P. The Print dialog box appears, as shown in figure 16.1.

Fig. 16.1
The Print dialog box enables you to specify the data you want to print.

3. In the Print What section of the dialog box, choose the Selectio**n** option.

4. Choose OK. Excel prints the selected worksheet range.

Defining a Print Area

If you are printing the same range in a worksheet over and over, you can define that range as the print area so that you no longer need to specify the range each time you print the worksheet.

To define the print area, follow these steps:

1. Choose the **F**ile Page Set**u**p command. The Page Setup dialog box appears, as shown in figure 16.2.

2. Select the Sheet tab, if it is not already selected.

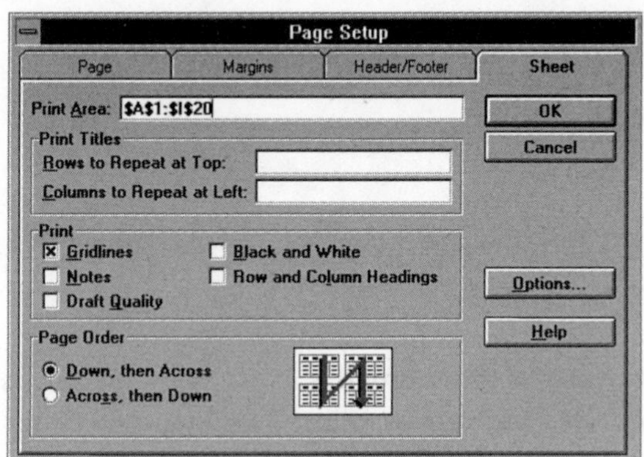

Fig. 16.2
You can define a specific range of the worksheet to be printed.

3. Click the Print **A**rea text box, and define the area to be printed by selecting the range in the worksheet or by typing the range address. A dashed border appears around the defined print area. Excel assigns the name Print_Area to the selected worksheet range.

4. Choose OK when you finish.

Tip
To set the print area quickly, select the range of cells and then click the Set Print Area button.

Removing a Defined Print Area

To remove a defined print area, choose **F**ile Page Set**u**p, and click the Sheet tab, if necessary. Delete the reference in the Print **A**rea text box, and then choose OK. Alternatively, choose the **I**nsert **N**ame **D**efine command, select the name Print_Area from the Names in **W**orkbook list, choose **D**elete, and click OK.

Inserting and Removing Page Breaks

When you define a print area, Excel inserts automatic page breaks into the worksheet. Automatic page breaks, which appear as dashed lines in the worksheet, control the data that appears on each printed page. Excel also inserts automatic page breaks when a selected print range cannot fit on a single page. If you aren't satisfied with the location of the automatic page breaks, you can insert manual page breaks.

You can insert two types of page breaks: vertical page breaks, which break the print range at the current column, and horizontal page breaks, which break the page at the current row.

Inserting a Vertical Page Break

To insert a vertical page break, follow these steps:

1. Click the heading of the column to the left of where the page break should occur.

2. Choose the **I**nsert Page **B**reak command. A dashed line appears in the worksheet, indicating the page break.

Inserting a Horizontal Page Break

To insert a horizontal page break, follow these steps:

1. Click the heading of the row above where the page break should occur.

2. Choose the **I**nsert Page **B**reak command. Excel adds the page break.

Figure 16.3 shows a horizontal page break added to a worksheet.

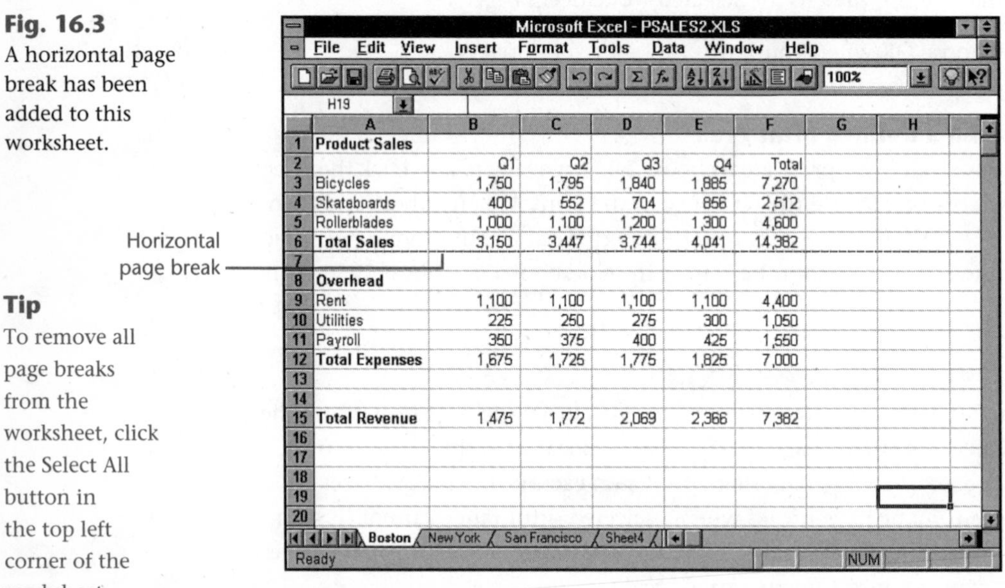

Fig. 16.3
A horizontal page break has been added to this worksheet.

Tip
To remove all page breaks from the worksheet, click the Select All button in the top left corner of the worksheet frame, and then choose **I**nsert Remove Page **B**reak.

Removing Page Breaks

To remove a page break, position the cell pointer below or to the right of the page-break intersection, and then choose **I**nsert Remove Page **B**reak.

Fitting the Print Range to a Single Page

If the specified print range is a few lines too long to print on a single page, you can fit the worksheet to the page. When you use this method, Excel scales the worksheet so that it fits on a single page.

To fit the print range on a single page, follow these steps:

1. Choose the **F**ile Page Set**u**p command.
2. If necessary, select the Page tab.
3. Select the **F**it To option. By default, the **F**it To option is one page wide by one page tall.
4. Choose OK. When you print, Excel scales the worksheet range to a single page.

Modifying the Page Setup

The Page Setup command enables you to define the page settings for the printed output. You can change the orientation of the page, change the margins and text alignment, and set print titles.

Changing the Page Orientation

The default setting for printed output arranges the data in *portrait* orientation—that is, the data is arranged vertically on the page. You may, however, want the data to print in *landscape* orientation—arranged horizontally on the page. If the data range is wide, for example, you may want to print it in landscape orientation, across the width of the page.

To change the page orientation, follow these steps:

1. Choose the **F**ile Page Set**u**p command.
2. Select the Page tab.
3. Select the **L**andscape option to print the range across the width of the page.
4. Choose OK.

Changing Margins

The margins define the distance between the printed output and the edge of the page. Excel enables you to change the top, bottom, left, and right margin

Tip

You also can change the margins from within print preview by dragging the margin borders. For more information, see "Changing Margins and Other Settings in Print Preview" later in this chapter.

settings. In addition, you can specify margins for the headers and footers, as well as center the print range between the margins, either horizontally or vertically.

To change the margins, follow these steps:

1. Choose the **F**ile Page Set**u**p command.
2. Select the Margins tab.
3. Enter the measurements, in inches, in the appropriate text boxes. You also can click the up and down arrows to change the margin settings by increments. Figure 16.4 shows the margins for the current print range.
4. To indicate the header and footer margins, specify the measurement in the From Edge section of the dialog box.

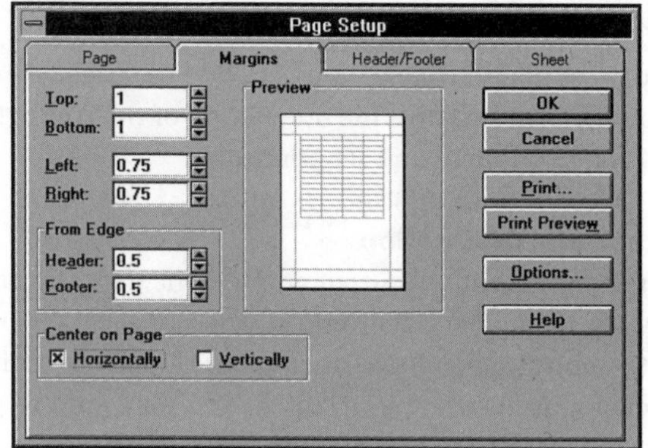

Fig. 16.4

Use the Margins tab of the Page Setup dialog box to change the margins and the alignment of data on a page.

5. To center the data between the top and bottom margins on the page, select the **V**ertically option. To center the data between the left and right margins, select the **H**orizontally option. To center the text both horizontally and vertically on the page, select both options.
6. Choose OK.

Setting and Removing Print Titles

When you print large worksheets, you can set print titles so that information, such as worksheet titles, column headings, and row headings, appears on each page in the printout.

To create print titles, follow these steps:

1. Choose the **F**ile Page Set**u**p command.
2. Select the Sheet tab, if necessary.
3. If you want to define titles across the top of each page, select the **R**ows To Repeat At Top box. If you want to define titles down the left side of each page, select the **C**olumns To Repeat At Left box (see fig. 16.5).

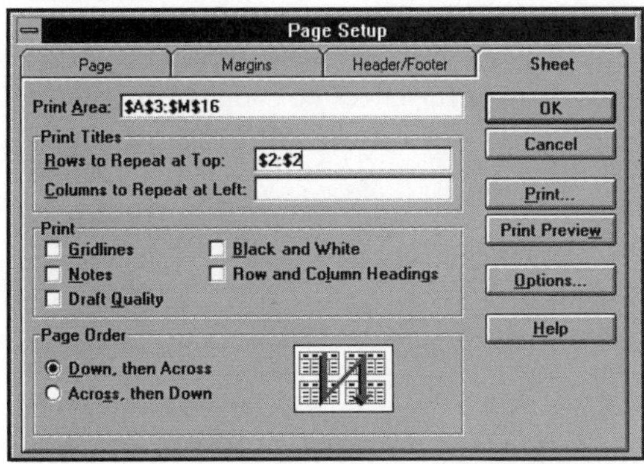

Fig. 16.5
In the Page Setup dialog box, define the area to be used as the print title.

4. If you are defining titles to appear across the top of each page, select the row headings containing the data you want to use as titles, or enter the row addresses.

   If you are defining titles to appear down the left side of the page, select the column headings containing the data you want to use as titles, or enter the column addresses.

   Note

   When you print a worksheet that contains print titles, do not select the range containing the titles when you define the print area. Otherwise, the titles will appear twice on the first page of the printout.

5. Choose OK.

To remove print titles, follow these steps:

1. Choose the **F**ile Page Set**u**p command.
2. Select the Sheet tab, if necessary.

3. Delete the cell references in the Print Titles section of the dialog box.

4. Choose OK.

Setting Other Print Options

You can define additional print settings in the Page Setup dialog box. You can include the worksheet grid lines in the printout; print notes that have been added to cells; print the data in black and white, even if color has been applied to the worksheet; and include the row and column headings.

Choose **F**ile Page Set**u**p, and select the Sheet tab. In the Print section of the dialog box, select or deselect the check box adjacent to the appropriate print option. Figure 16.6 shows the Sheet tab of the Page Setup dialog box.

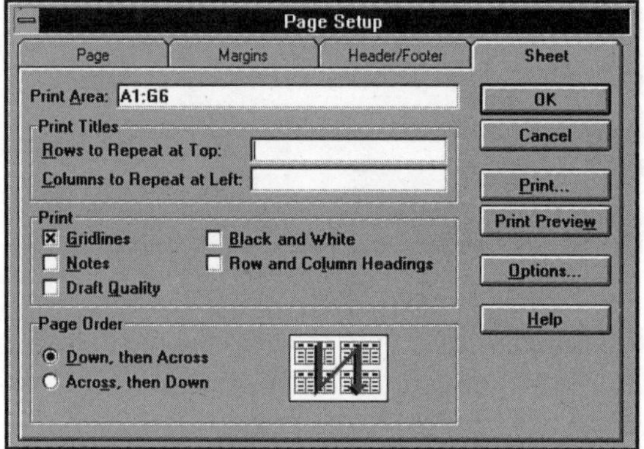

Fig. 16.6
Select the appropriate print options in the Sheet tab of the Page Setup dialog box.

Creating Headers and Footers

Headers and footers enable you to add text—such as the current date, page number, and file name—to the top and bottom of the printed page. Excel provides default header and footer information (the name of the current sheet is centered in the header, and the current page number is centered in the footer). You also can select additional options, and define your own header and footer information.

Using Predefined Headers and Footers

To select one of Excel's predefined header and footer options, follow these steps:

1. Choose the **F**ile Page Set**u**p command.

2. Select the Header/Footer tab. Figure 16.7 shows the predefined header and footer options.

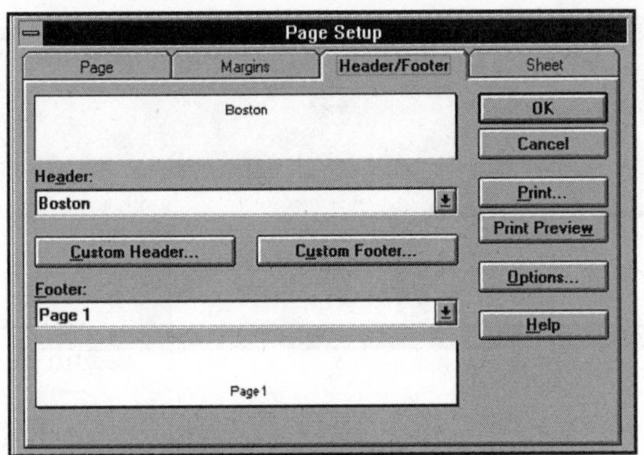

Fig. 16.7
Select the text you want to use in the header and footer area of the printed page.

3. Click the arrow next to the He**a**der box, and select a header from the drop-down list.

4. Select the data you want to use as a footer from the **F**ooter list.

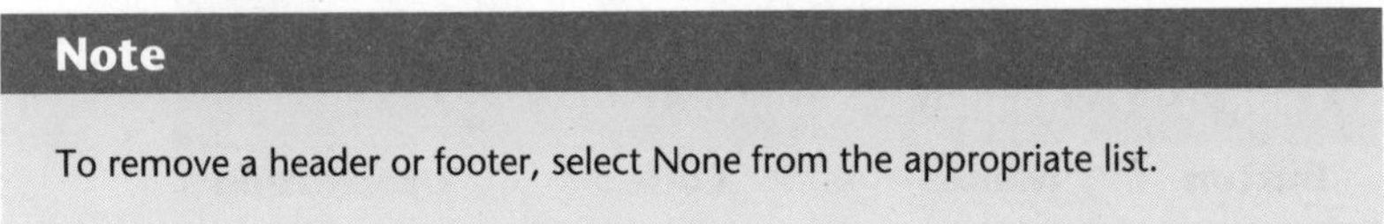

Note

To remove a header or footer, select None from the appropriate list.

5. Choose OK.

Creating Custom Headers and Footers

Instead of using a predefined header and footer, you can define your own custom header and footer. Follow these steps:

1. Choose the **F**ile Page Set**u**p command.

2. Select the Header/Footer tab, if necessary.

3. If appropriate, select an existing header or footer that resembles the header or footer you want to create.

4. Select the **C**ustom Header or C**u**stom Footer option to display a new dialog box. Figure 16.8 shows the Custom Header dialog box.

   Each text box that appears in the dialog box controls, the alignment of the text in the header or footer. Data can be left-aligned, centered, or right-aligned. Excel uses codes to create certain types of text in the headers and footers. The Page Number code, for example, is used to insert page numbering. The buttons that appear above the text boxes are used to insert the codes. Table 16.1, which follows these steps, describes the code buttons you can use in the header and footer.

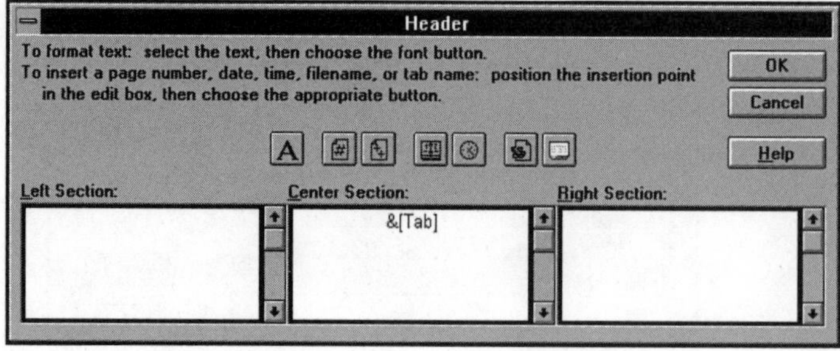

Fig. 16.8
Create custom headers and footers by using the text boxes and buttons that appear in this dialog box.

5. Select one of the three text boxes, and then type the header or footer text, or choose a button to enter a header or footer code. To apply text formatting to the header or footer information, choose the Font button to display the Font dialog box, and select the appropriate options.

6. Choose OK.

Table 16.1 Header and Footer Codes

Button	Name	Code	Description
A	Font	None	Displays the Font dialog box
	Page Number	&[Page]	Inserts the page number
	Total Pages	&[Pages]	Inserts the total number of pages
	Date	&[Date]	Inserts the current date
	Time	&[Time]	Inserts the current time
	Filename	&[File]	Inserts the file name
	Sheet Name	&[Tab]	Inserts the name of the active sheet

Previewing a Worksheet

You can preview the data, before you print the worksheet, to make sure that the data appears the way you want. You also can change the margin settings and column widths, if necessary.

To preview the data, follow these steps:

1. Choose the **F**ile Print Pre**v**iew command. Excel switches to Print Preview and displays the print range, as shown in figure 16.9.

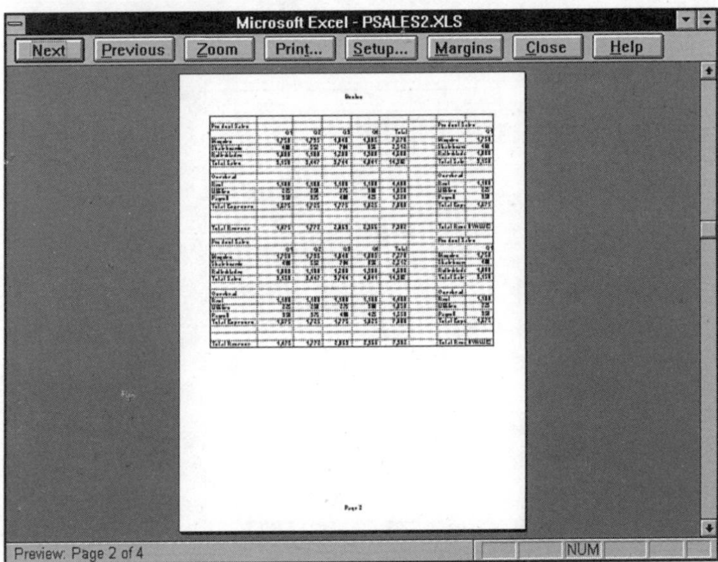

Fig. 16.9
Print Preview shows what the worksheet will look like when printed.

2. Choose the **N**ext and **P**revious buttons to move from page to page. Notice that these buttons appear dimmed if the data you are previewing fits on a single page.

Tip
You also can press the PgUp and PgDn keys to display each page in the document. Press the Home key to move to the first page; press the End key to move to the last page.

Zooming In and Out

For a closer look at data, you can zoom in and view an enlarged display; when you want to see more of the data, you can zoom out.

To zoom in on the worksheet, choose the **Z**oom button, or position the mouse pointer over the section you want to view, and then click the left mouse button. The mouse pointer changes to a magnifying glass when positioned over the page. To view other areas of the page, use the vertical and horizontal scroll bars. To zoom out, choose the **Z**oom button again, or click the left mouse button.

Changing Margins and Other Settings in Print Preview

If, while previewing the worksheet, you find that the current margins or column widths are not adequate, you can change them in Print Preview. When you choose the **M**argins button, light-gray boundaries appear around the page, indicating the margins. Black handles also appear, indicating the top, bottom, left, and right margins. Square handles appear along the top of the page, with lines indicating the width of each column. Figure 16.10 shows margin and column markers in print preview.

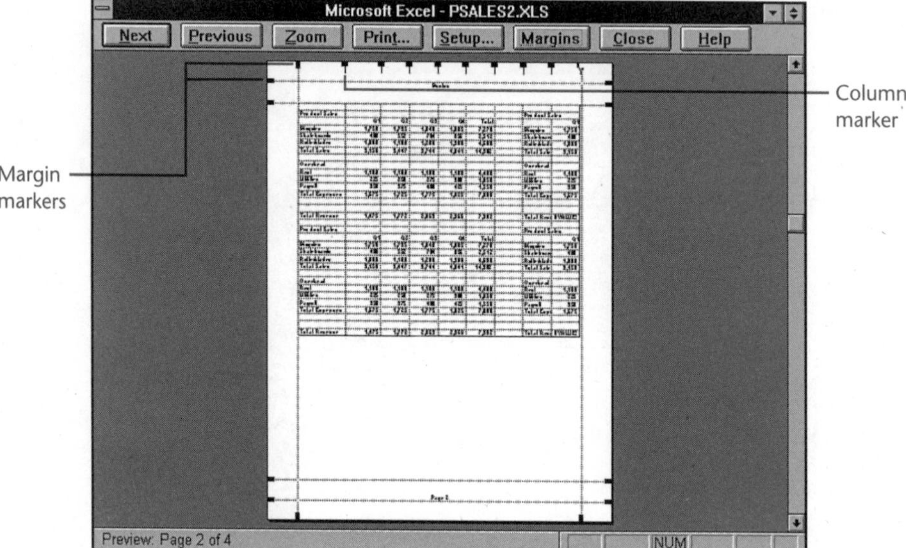

Fig. 16.10 You can change the margins and column widths by dragging the markers.

To adjust the margins, click the handle that represents the margin you want to change. When you do, the mouse pointer changes to a crossbar, and the status bar shows the actual margin setting. Drag the handle to the appropriate location. When you release the mouse button, the margin adjusts, and the data is repositioned on the page.

◄ "Changing Column Width and Row Height," p. 288

To change a column width, click the square handle that indicates the column width you want to change. The status bar displays the current column width. Drag the marker to increase or decrease the column width. When you release the mouse button, the column width and data adjust to fit the new size.

When you're satisfied with the way the data appears, choose the Prin**t** button to print the worksheet. To return to the worksheet, choose the **C**lose button.

Printing the Worksheet

After you define the print settings and preview the data, you're ready to print the worksheet. The File Print command enables you to specify the number of copies you want to print, as well as the number of pages (if the print range spans multiple pages). You also can specify the data you want to print, if you have not already defined a print area.

Tip
Click the Print button in the Standard toolbar to bypass the Print dialog box and send the output directly to the printer with the default print settings.

To print the worksheet, follow these steps:

1. Choose the **F**ile **P**rint command or press Ctrl+P. The Print dialog box appears.

2. If you have not defined a print area, you can specify the data you want to print by selecting options in the Print What section of the dialog box (see fig. 16.11).

Fig. 16.11
The Print dialog box contains options that enable you to specify what you want to print.

3. Choose the Selectio**n** option to print the selected range of cells; choose the Selecte**d** Sheet(s) option to print the selected worksheets in the workbook; or choose the **E**ntire Workbook option to print every worksheet in the current workbook.

4. To specify the number of copies to be printed, enter the amount in the **C**opies box.

5. To specify a specific range of pages to be printed, enter the range in the Page Range section of the dialog box.

6. When you're ready to print the worksheet, choose OK.

Note

The Print dialog box also includes buttons that enable you to access the Page Set**u**p command, Print Preview, and the Printer Setup dialog box. To change any of these settings, click the appropriate button and make the necessary selections.

Troubleshooting

While attempting to remove a page break, I chose the Insert menu, but the Remove Page Break command was not displayed in the menu.

To remove a manual page break, you first must select the cell that contains the manual page-break setting. When the cell pointer is correctly positioned, the Remove Page **B**reak command appears in the **I**nsert menu. To minimize the chance for error, select a range of cells surrounding the page break. When you open the **I**nsert menu, the Remove Page **B**reak command should appear.

*After selecting the entire worksheet, I chose the **I**nsert Remove Page **B**reak command, but Excel removed only some of the page breaks.*

A print area must be defined for the worksheet. When you define a print area, Excel automatically inserts page breaks into the worksheet. Although these page breaks appear similar to the manual page breaks that you insert into the document, you cannot use the Remove Page Break command to delete them; instead, you must delete the defined print area.

To delete a defined print area, choose **F**ile Page Set**u**p, and select the Sheet tab. Delete the range address in the Print **A**rea text box, and choose OK. When you return to the worksheet, the page breaks no longer appear.

Using Views and Reports

Excel provides two add-ins that enable you to create and generate printed reports: the View add-in enables you to assign names to worksheet ranges and to include the print settings and display options for the ranges; the Report Manager add-in enables you to create a report consisting of named views and scenarios.

Installing the View and Report Manager Add-Ins

Before you can define a named view or create a report, you must install the View Manager and Report Manager add-ins.

To install the add-ins, follow these steps:

► "Creating a Scenario," p. 395

1. Choose the **T**ools Add-**I**ns command. The Add-Ins dialog box appears (see fig. 16.12).

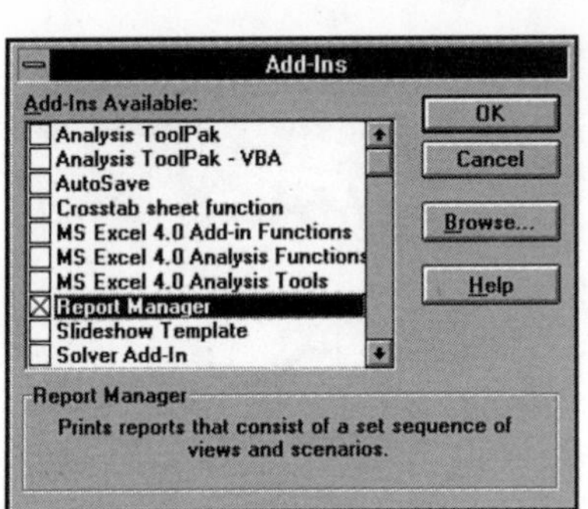

Fig. 16.12
Use the Add-Ins dialog box to install Excel add-ins.

2. Select the Report Manager add-in and the View Manager add-in from the **A**dd-Ins Available list.

3. Choose OK. The Print R**e**port command is added to the **F**ile menu; the **V**iew Manager command is added to the **V**iew menu.

Creating a View

The **V**iew **V**iew Manager command enables you to define multiple print ranges, with different display and page-setup characteristics, in a single worksheet. Normally, every print area of a worksheet must contain the same display characteristics. By using named views, however, you can print multiple ranges with different print settings at the same time.

To create a view, follow these steps:

1. Select the range of cells you want to define as a view.

2. Choose the **V**iew **V**iew Manager command. The View Manager dialog box appears (see fig. 16.13).

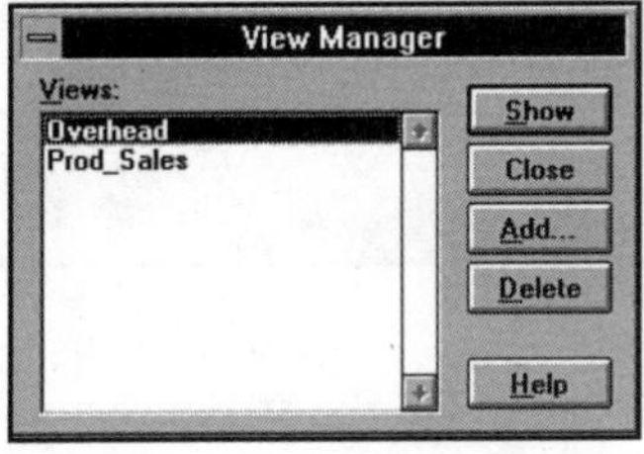

Fig. 16.13
Create multiple views of worksheet data in the View Manager dialog box.

3. Choose the **A**dd button. The Add View dialog box appears (see fig. 16.14).

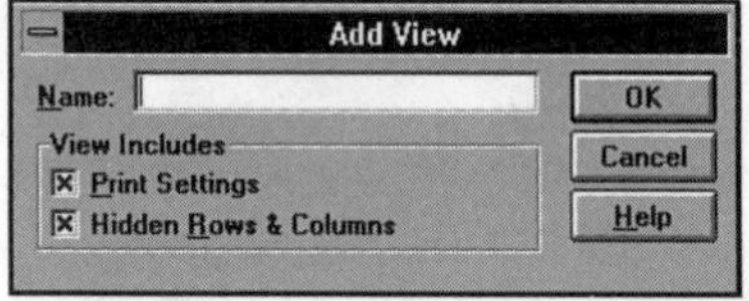

Fig. 16.14
Enter a name for the view in the Add View dialog box.

4. Enter a name for the view in the **N**ame text box.

5. Choose OK.

Creating a Report

If your worksheet consists of multiple views of your worksheet, or scenarios of data, you can print those different views and scenarios as a report.

To create a report, follow these steps:

1. Choose the **F**ile Print R**e**port command. The Print Report dialog box appears.

2. Choose the **A**dd button to create the report. The Add Report dialog box appears (see fig. 16.15).

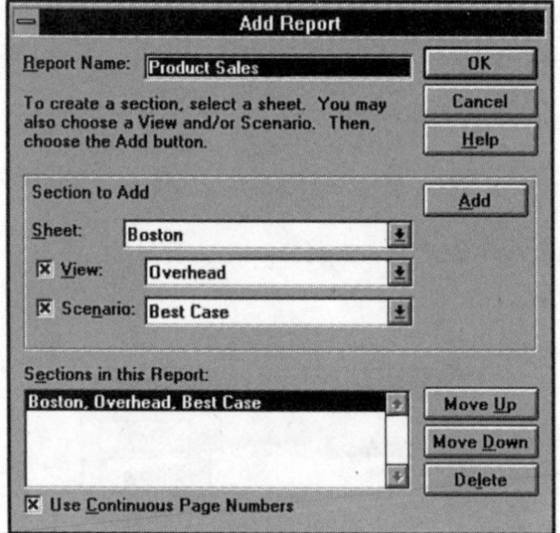

Fig. 16.15
Select the views and scenarios to be added to the report.

3. Enter a name for the report in the **R**eport Name text box.

4. Select the view you want to add to the report from the View drop-down list, and then choose Add. The view you added appears in the Sections in This Report list.

5. Select the scenario you want to add to the report from the Sce**n**ario drop-down list, and then choose **A**dd. The scenario you added appears in the S**e**ctions in This Report list.
6. To change the order of the views and scenarios in the S**e**ctions in This Report list, select a view or scenario, and then choose the Move **U**p or Move **D**own button to rearrange the order.
7. Repeat steps 4-6 until you finish adding views and scenarios to the report.
8. Select Use **C**ontinuous Page Numbers to number the pages consecutively.
9. Choose OK. You return to the Print Report dialog box.
10. Choose **P**rint to print the report, or choose **C**lose to close the dialog box without printing the report.

Editing and Printing a Report

If you want to change the contents of a report or print a report, you can use the File Print Report command to do so.

To edit a report, follow these steps:

1. Choose the **F**ile Print R**e**port command. The Print Report dialog box appears.
2. Select the name of the report you want to edit from the **R**eports list, and then choose **E**dit.
3. Change the views and scenarios, as outlined in the preceding section.
4. Choose OK.

To print a report, follow these steps:

1. Choose the **F**ile Print R**e**port command. The Print Report dialog box appears.
2. Select the report you want to print from the **R**eports list.
3. Choose the **P**rint button. The Print dialog box appears.
4. Specify the number of copies to be printed.
5. Choose OK to print the report.

Troubleshooting

I want to create a report, but the Print Report command does not appear in the File menu.

When the Print Report command does not appear in the File menu, it means that the Report Manager add-in has not been installed. To install the Report Manager add-in, choose the Tools Add-Ins command. In the Add-Ins Available list, check marks appear next to the names of the add-ins that are currently installed. Select Report Manager to add a check mark to the left of the name, and choose OK. The Print Report command now appears in the File menu.

When I print a report, Excel numbers each page in the report page 1.

To use consecutive page numbers in the report, choose the File Print Report command, select the name of the report from the Reports list, and choose Edit. Select the Use Continuous Page Numbers option, and choose OK. The next time you print the report, Excel will number the pages consecutively.

Using Charts

Charts enable you to present worksheet data in graphical form. When you create a chart, the worksheet data used to create the chart is linked to the chart. When the worksheet data changes, the chart is updated to reflect those changes. In Excel, you can create an embedded chart, which is added directly to a worksheet. You also can create a chart in a *chart sheet*, which is a separate sheet in the workbook. After creating a chart, you can add titles and grid lines. Use autoformats to change the format of a chart and to edit the data used in the chart.

Creating a Chart with the ChartWizard

To create an embedded chart with the ChartWizard, follow these steps:

1. Select the data you want to chart.

2. Click the ChartWizard button. The mouse pointer changes to a chart with a plus sign.

3. Position the mouse pointer in the worksheet where you want the chart to appear; then, click and drag the mouse to draw the boundaries.

4. Release the mouse button when the chart is the size you want. The Step 1 ChartWizard dialog box appears (see fig. 16.16).

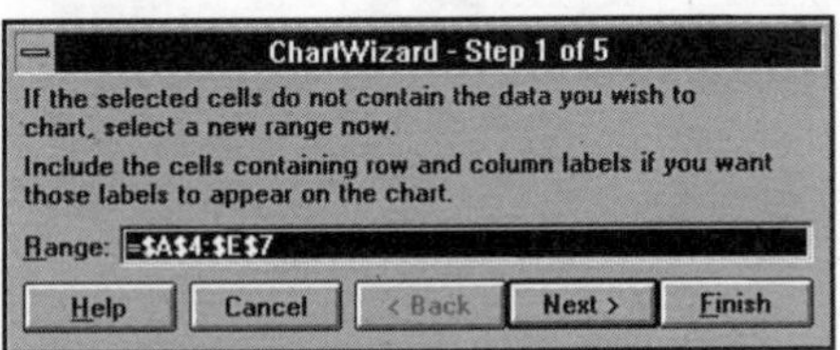

Fig. 16.16 Indicate the range of cells to be charted in this dialog box.

5. If the selected range address that appears in the **R**ange text box is correct, choose Next. Otherwise, select the range of cells in the worksheet that you want to chart or enter the range address; then choose Next. The Step 2 dialog box appears.

Tip
To create a square chart area, hold down the Shift key while you drag the mouse.

Note

The chart is linked to the cells you indicate in the Step 1 ChartWizard dialog box. When the data in the selected range changes, the chart is updated to reflect the changes.

6. Select a chart type (see fig. 16.17).

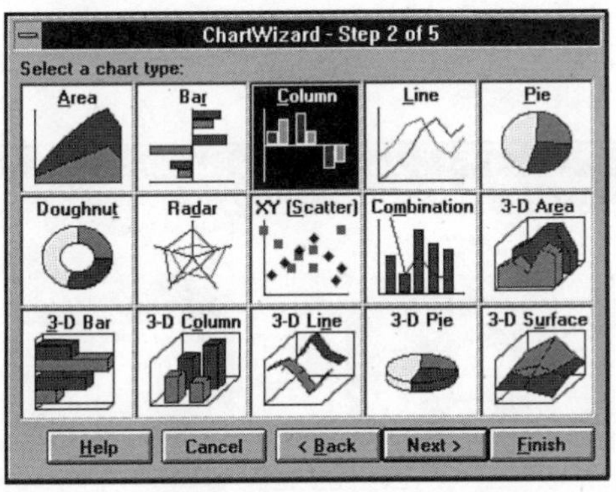

Fig. 16.17 Select the chart type in this dialog box.

7. Choose Next. The Step 3 dialog box appears.
8. Select a chart format (see fig. 16.18).
9. Choose Next. The Step 4 dialog box appears, displaying a sample of the chart in the Sample Chart area (see fig. 16.19).

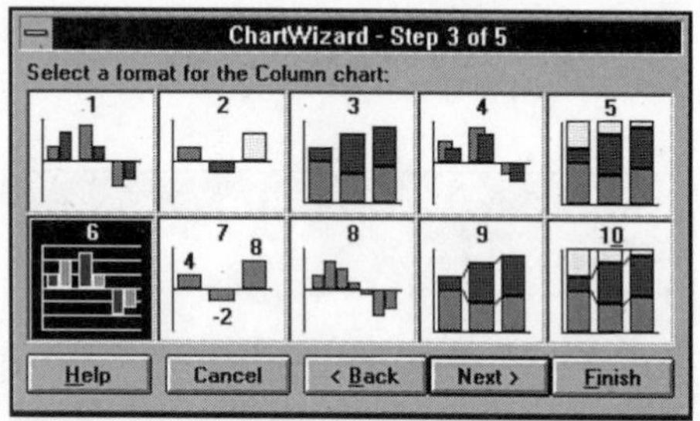

Fig. 16.18
Select the chart format in this dialog box.

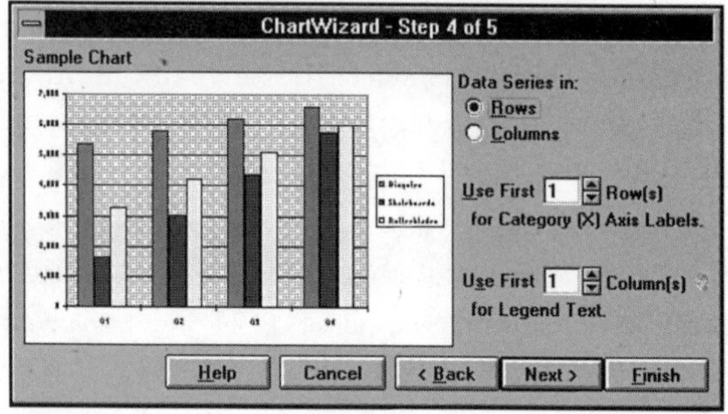

Fig. 16.19
A sample of the chart appears in this dialog box.

10. If the sample chart is incorrect, select other options, and then choose Next. The Step 5 ChartWizard dialog box appears.

11. If you want to add titles to the chart, enter them in the **C**hart Title and Axis Titles text boxes (see fig. 16.20).

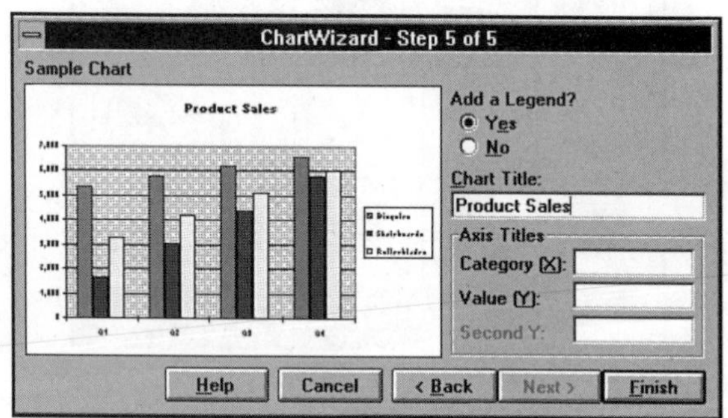

Fig. 16.20
Enter titles for the chart in this dialog box.

12. Choose the **F**inish button. The chart appears in the worksheet (see fig. 16.21).

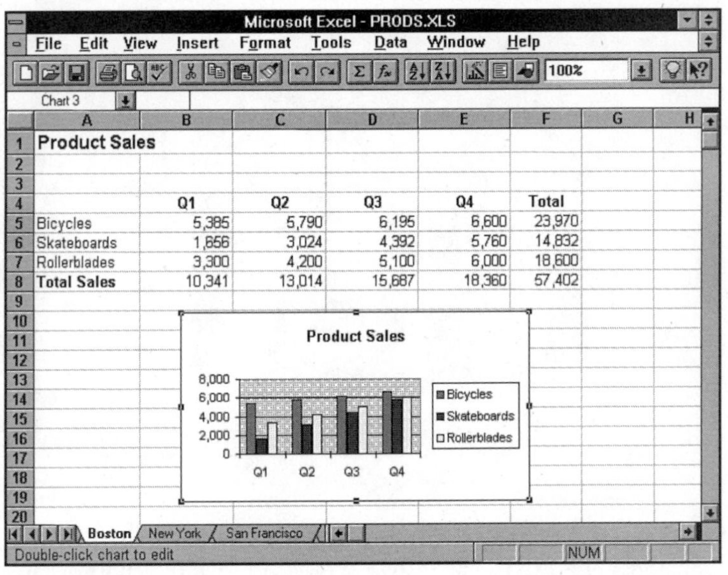

Fig. 16.21
The completed chart is added to the worksheet.

Note

If you need to return to the preceding ChartWizard dialog box, choose **B**ack. You can close the ChartWizard during any step by choosing **F**inish. When you choose **F**inish, the ChartWizard makes the selections for you.

To create a chart sheet, follow these steps:

1. Select the cells that contain the data you want to chart.

2. Choose the **I**nsert C**h**art **A**s New Sheet command, or press F11. The Step 1 ChartWizard dialog box appears. (Refer to the preceding section for instructions on how to use the ChartWizard.)

3. Press the F11 function key. Excel bypasses the ChartWizard and creates a chart based on the default chart settings (see fig. 16.22).

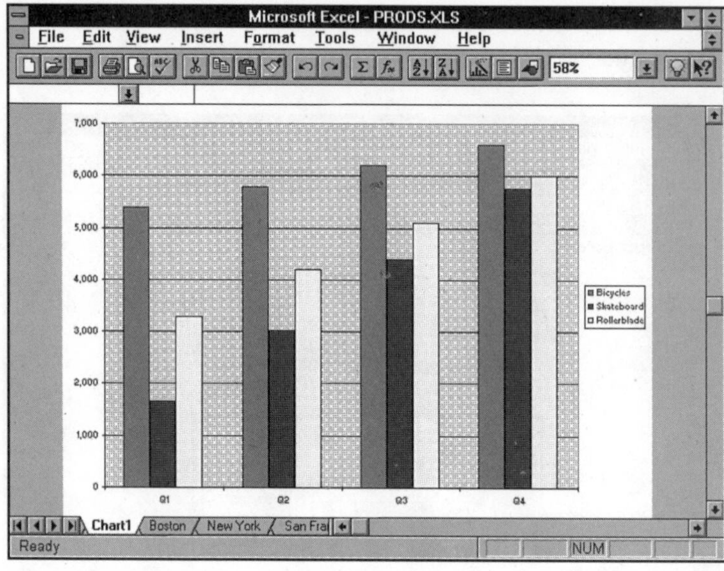

Fig. 16.22
A new chart sheet is added to the workbook.

Tip
You can copy a chart, created in a separate sheet, to another worksheet by using the **E**dit **C**opy and **E**dit **P**aste commands.

Moving and Sizing a Chart Object

After you add a chart to the worksheet, you can resize the chart or move it to another location. Before you can move or resize a chart, you must select the chart.

To select a chart, position the mouse pointer in the chart area and click the left mouse button. Small black squares called *handles* appear on the boundaries of the chart, indicating that it is selected (see fig. 16.23).

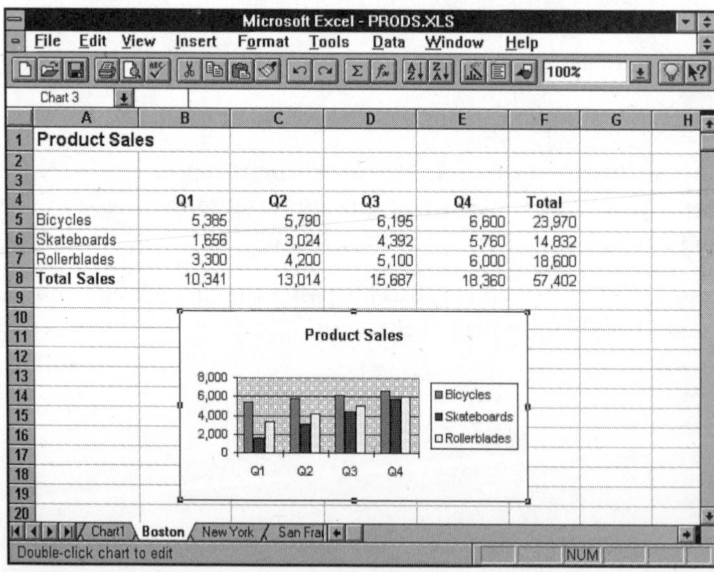

Fig. 16.23
Handles appear on the chart boundaries when a chart is selected.

To resize a chart, follow these steps:

1. Select the chart.
2. Drag a handle until the chart reaches the desired size (see fig 16.24).

   To size the object proportionally, drag one of the corner handles. To increase or decrease the chart either horizontally or vertically, drag one of the middle handles.

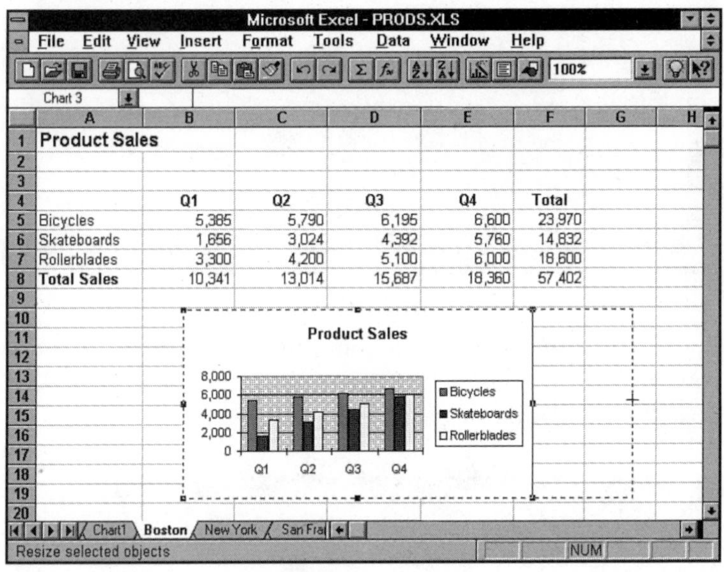

Fig. 16.24
Drag one of the handles to resize the chart.

To move a chart, follow these steps:

1. Select the chart.
2. Click and drag the chart to a new location.

Tip
Keep the Chart toolbar displayed while you work with charts. To display this toolbar, place the mouse pointer on any displayed toolbar, click the right mouse button, and then choose Chart from the shortcut menu.

Changing the Chart Type

You can change the type and format of a chart at any time. When you change a chart type, Excel redraws the chart to reflect the new type.

To change the chart type, follow these steps:

1. Double-click the chart whose type you want to change. A dashed border outlines the chart (see fig. 16.25).

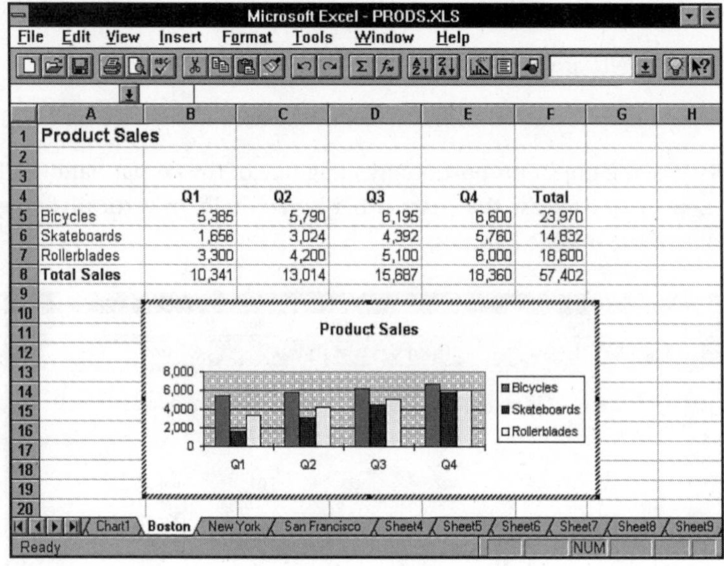

Fig. 16.25
The dashed border indicates that the chart can be edited.

2. Choose the F**o**rmat Chart **T**ype command, or click the right mouse button and then choose Chart Type from the shortcut menu. The Chart Type dialog box appears (see fig. 16.26).

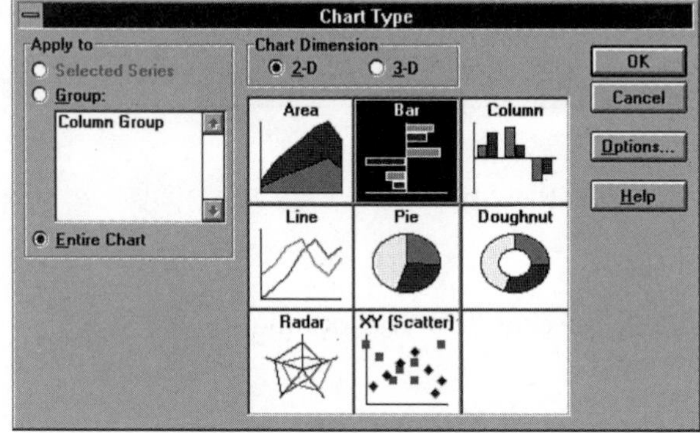

Fig. 16.26
Use the Chart Type dialog box to change a chart to another forma.

3. Select the type of chart you want to use.

4. Choose OK. Excel displays the chart in the new chart type (see fig. 16.27).

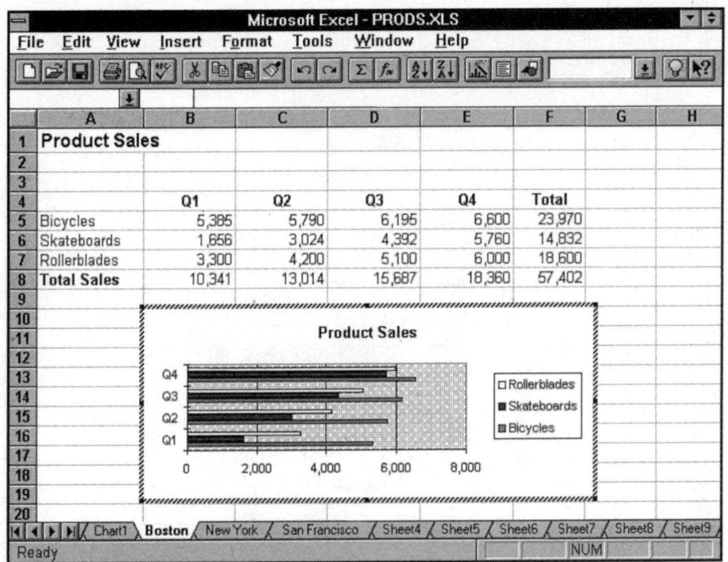

Fig. 16.27
In this figure, a column chart is displayed as a bar chart.

Enhancing a Chart

Excel provides many commands that enable you to enhance your charts. You can, for example, add data labels to a chart to annotate the chart elements. You also can add grid lines and titles to a chart.

To add data labels to a chart, follow these steps:

1. Double-click the chart you want to enhance, or activate the chart sheet.

2. Choose the **I**nsert **D**ata Labels command, or click the right mouse button and then choose Insert Data Labels from the shortcut menu. The Data Labels dialog box appears (see fig. 16.28).

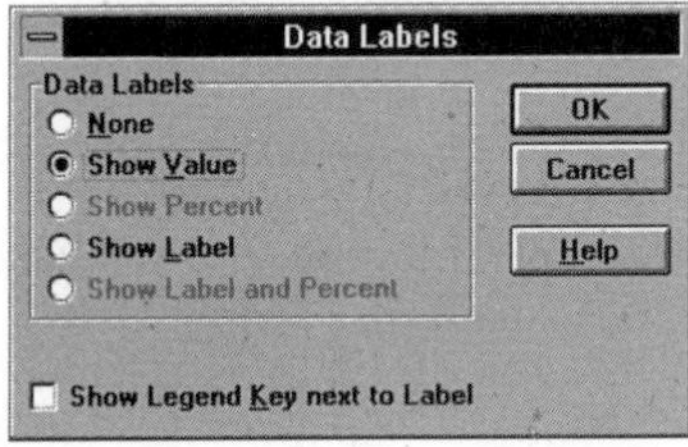

Fig. 16.28
Use the options in the Data Labels dialog box to annotate the chart elements.

3. Select the type of data labels you want to display.

4. Choose OK. Excel adds the data labels to each data series in the chart (see fig. 16.29).

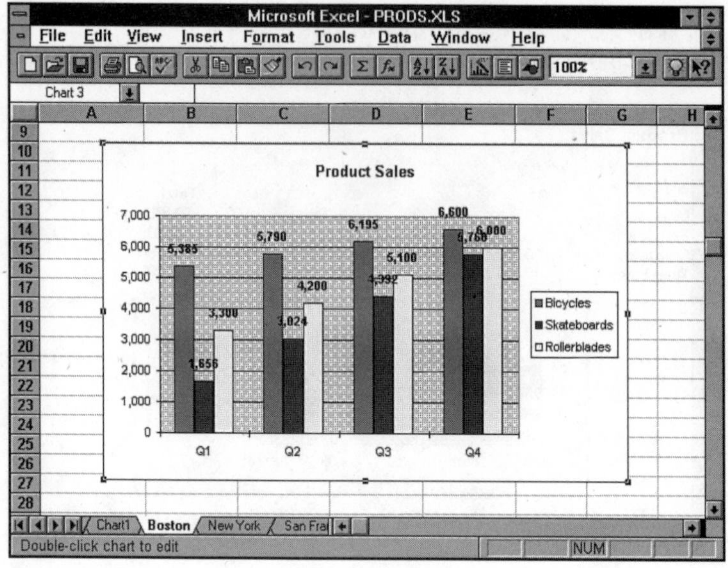

Fig. 16.29
In this figure, the actual data values appear next to each graphic marker.

To add grid lines to a chart, follow these steps:

1. Double-click the chart you want to enhance, or activate the chart sheet.

2. Choose the **I**nsert **G**ridlines command, or click the right mouse button and then choose the Insert Gridlines command from the shortcut menu. The Gridlines dialog box appears (see fig. 16.30).

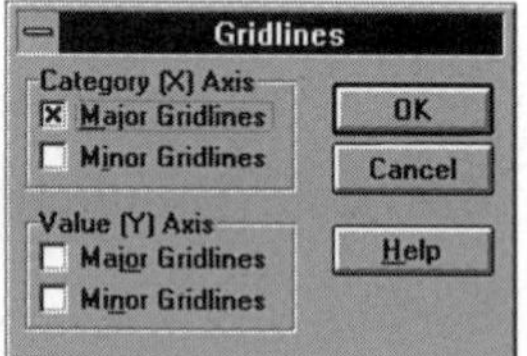

Fig. 16.30
Use this dialog box to add major and minor grid lines to a chart.

3. Select the type of grid lines you want to display.

4. Choose OK. Excel adds the grid lines to the chart (see fig. 16.31).

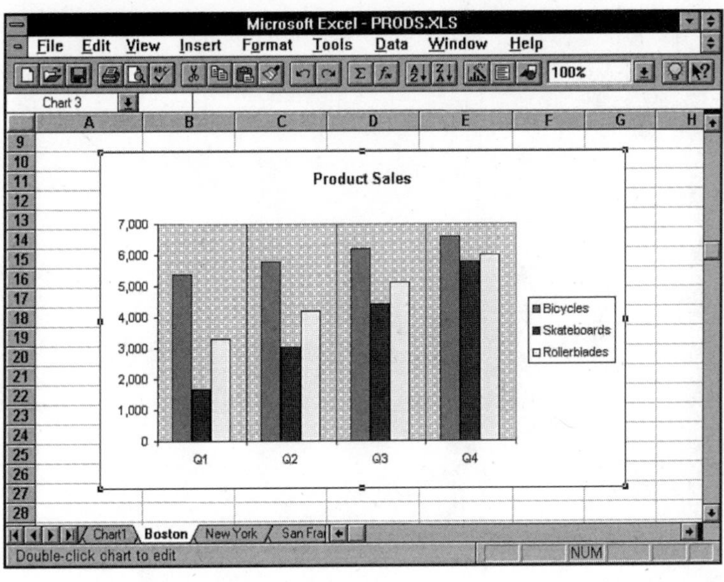

Fig. 16.31 In this figure, major grid lines have been added to the x-axis.

Tip

To add horizontal grid lines to a chart quickly, click the Horizontal Gridline button. Click this button again to remove the grid lines.

To add titles to a chart, follow these steps:

1. Double-click the chart to which you want to add titles, or activate the chart sheet.
2. Choose the **I**nsert **T**itles command, or click the right mouse button and then choose Insert Titles from the shortcut menu. The Titles dialog box appears (see fig. 16.32).

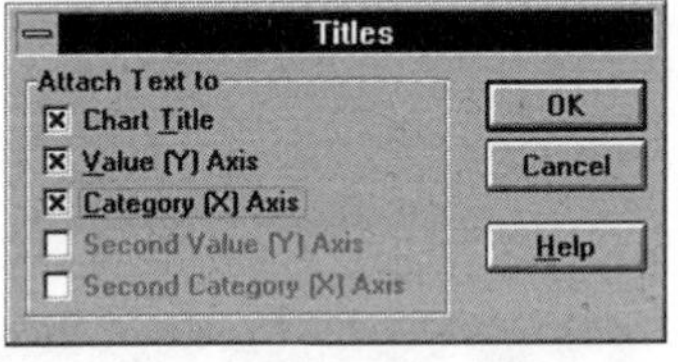

Fig. 16.32 Use the Titles dialog box to select titles.

3. Select the type of titles you want to add, and then choose OK. The dialog box closes, and you return to the chart, in which the title objects now appear.
4. Type the title text, and then press Enter. The titles appear in the chart (see fig. 16.33).
5. Press Esc to deselect the title objects.

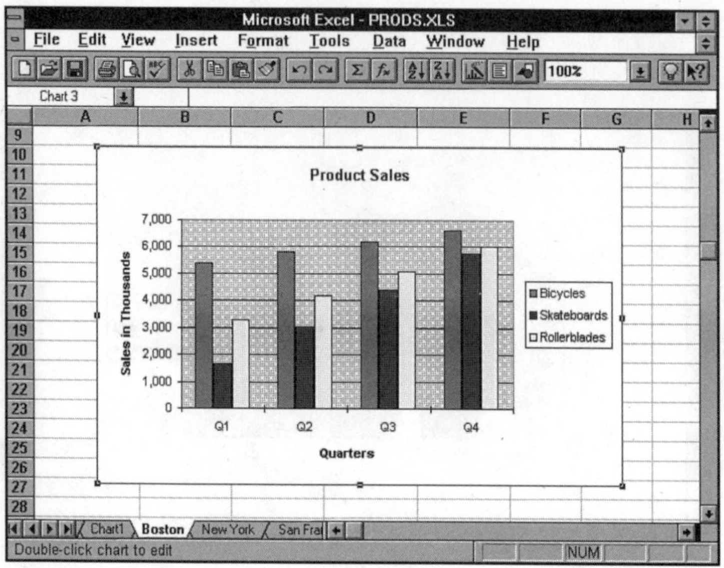

Fig. 16.33
In this figure, titles have been added to the chart.

Using Autoformats

Excel provides several built-in chart formats that you can use to format your charts. For each chart type, there are several autoformats that you can apply. In addition, you can create your own autoformats based on existing charts that you created.

To apply an autoformat to a chart, follow these steps:

1. Double-click the chart you want to format.

2. Choose the F**o**rmat **A**utoFormat command, or click the right mouse button and then choose AutoFormat from the shortcut menu. The AutoFormat dialog box appears (see fig. 16.34).

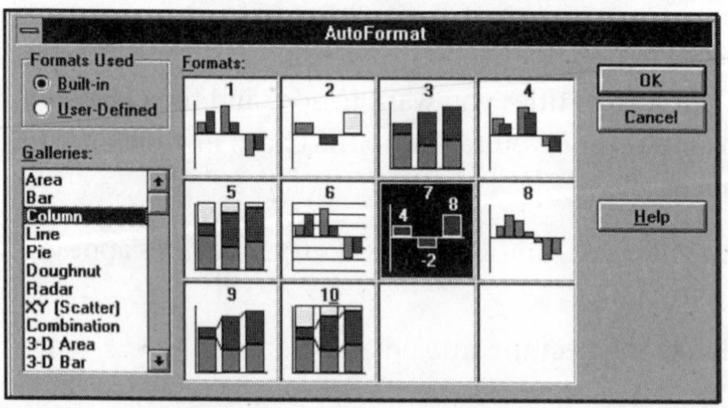

Fig. 16.34
Select a built-in autoformat to apply to a chart.

3. Choose the **B**uilt-in option, if necessary.
4. Select the type of chart you want from the **G**alleries list.
5. Select the format you want to use from the **F**ormats area.
6. Choose OK. Excel applies the autoformat to the chart.

To create a custom chart format, follow these steps:

1. Double-click the chart that contains the formats you want to define as a custom chart format, or activate the chart sheet.
2. Choose the F**o**rmat **A**utoFormat command, or click the right mouse button and then choose AutoFormat from the shortcut menu. The AutoFormat dialog box appears.
3. Select the **U**ser-Defined option. After you select that option, the buttons in the dialog box change.
4. Choose the Custo**m**ize button. The User-Defined AutoFormats dialog box appears (see fig. 16.35).
5. Choose the **A**dd button. The Add Custom AutoFormat dialog box appears (see fig. 16.36).

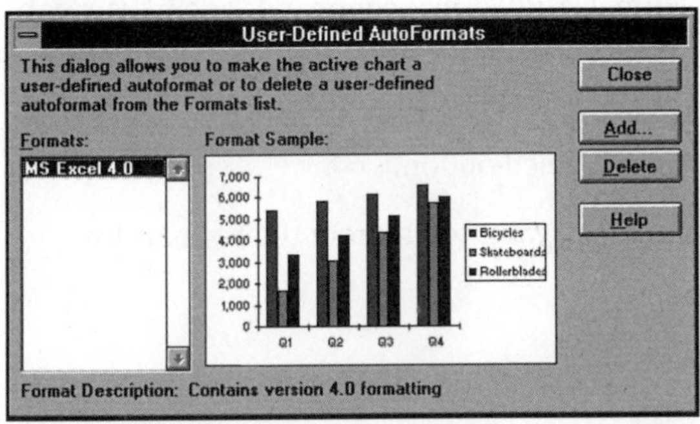

Fig. 16.35
Customized chart formats appear in the Format Sample area.

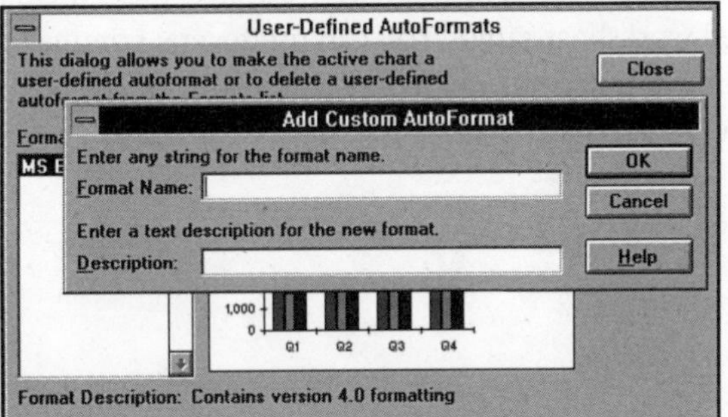

Fig. 16.36
Enter a name and description for the custom autoformat.

6. Enter a name for the autoformat in the **F**ormat Name text box and a description in the **D**escription text box.

7. Choose OK. You return to the User-Defined AutoFormats dialog box, where the custom autoformat now appears in the **F**ormats list (see fig. 16.37).

8. Choose Close.

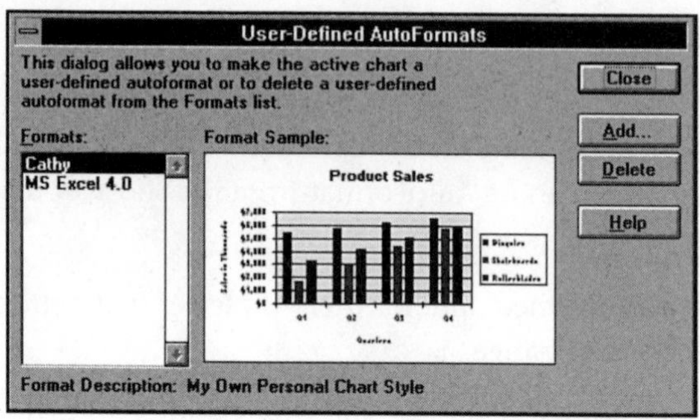

Fig. 16.37
The custom autoformat has been added to the Formats list.

To apply a custom autoformat, follow these steps:

1. Double-click the chart you want to format, or activate the chart sheet.

2. Choose the F**o**rmat **A**utoFormat command, or click the right mouse button and then choose AutoFormat from the shortcut menu. The AutoFormat dialog box appears.

3. Choose the **U**ser-Defined option.

4. Select the format you want to use from the **F**ormats list.

5. Choose Close.

Tip
To remove an autoformat and return to the default chart format, click the Default Chart button.

Editing a Chart

When you use the ChartWizard to create charts, Excel plots the data according to the selected worksheet range. You can use several commands to edit an existing chart. For example, you can delete a data series from a chart, add a new data series to a chart, and change the order in which the data series appears.

To delete a data series from a chart, select the data series you want to remove, and then press the Del key. Excel removes the data series and redraws the chart to reflect the deletion.

To add a data series, follow these steps:

1. Double-click the chart to which you want to add new data, or switch to the chart sheet that contains the chart.

2. Choose the **I**nsert **N**ew Data command. The New Data dialog box appears (see fig. 16.38).

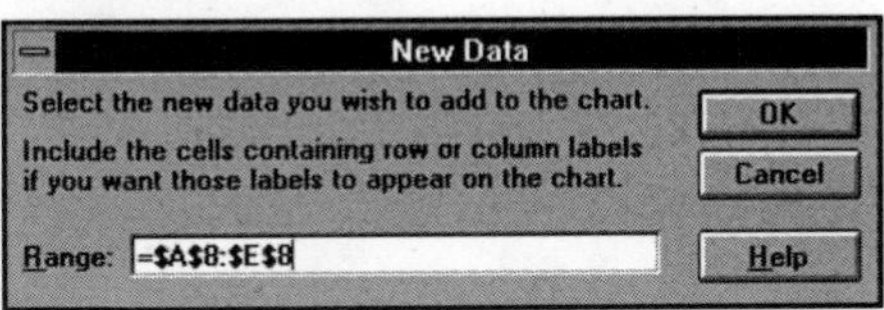

Fig. 16.38
Indicate the range that contains the data you want to add.

3. Enter the range in the worksheet that contains the data you want to add.

4. Choose OK. Excel adds the data series to the chart.

To change the order of the data series, follow these steps:

1. Double-click the chart you want to modify, or switch to the chart sheet.

2. Choose the F**o**rmat Chart **T**ype command, or click the right mouse button and then choose Chart Type from the shortcut menu. The Chart Type dialog box appears.

3. Choose the **O**ptions button.

4. Select the Series Order tab.

5. Select the series you want to change, and then choose the Move **U**p or Move **D**own button until the series are listed in the order you want (see fig. 16.39).

6. Choose OK.

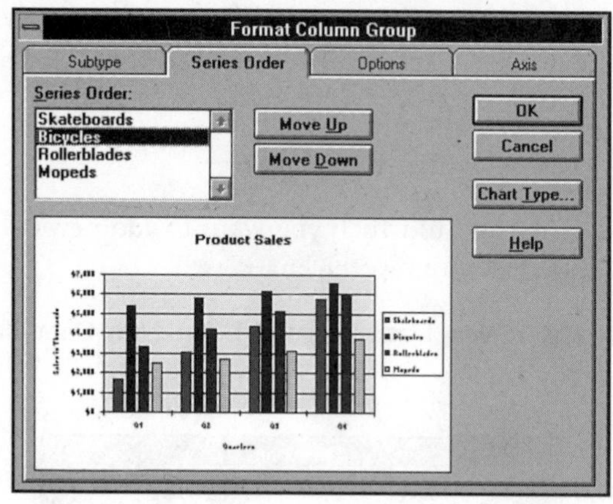

Fig. 16.39 Change the order of the data series markers as they appear in the chart.

Printing Charts

Printing charts in Excel is no different from printing any worksheet range. You can specify print options for charts in much the same way that you do for data that appears in the worksheet. You can, for example, specify the size of the chart and the printing quality, and preview the chart before printing.

Tip
To print the chart with the default print settings, click the Print button in the Standard toolbar.

Before you print a chart, you need to specify the chart print settings. Follow these steps:

1. Double-click the chart you want to print, or move to the chart sheet that contains the chart you want to print.
2. Choose the **F**ile Page Set**u**p command.
3. Select the Chart tab, if necessary. Figure 16.40 shows the printing options that are available for a chart.

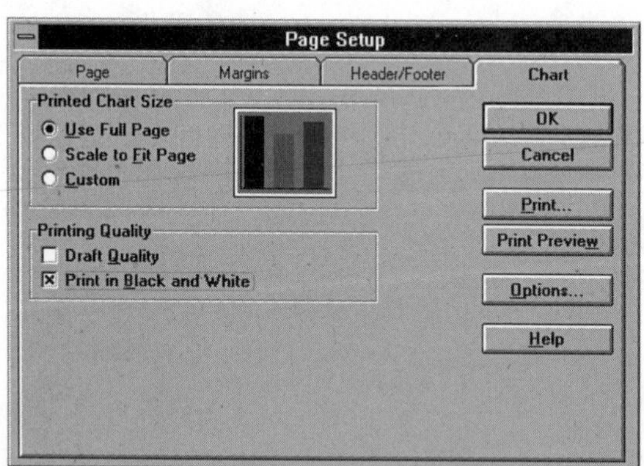

Fig. 16.40 The Chart tab of the Page Setup dialog box includes options for printing charts.

4. Select the appropriate chart size in the Printed Chart Size area of the dialog box.

5. To print the chart in black and white, select the Print in **B**lack and White option in the Printing Quality area.

6. When you finish specifying the print settings, you can print the chart. Choose the **P**rint button in the Page Setup dialog box. The Print dialog box appears.

7. Choose OK to accept the print settings and begin printing the chart.

Troubleshooting

I want to access the chart commands when I embed a chart in my worksheet.

To access the chart commands for an embedded chart, you must double-click the chart you want to edit. When you do, Excel changes the menu commands in the Format and Insert menus to reflect commands for editing charts. When you create a chart in a separate chart sheet, the Insert and Format menus automatically contain these commands.

When I use the AutoFormat command to change the chart type, I lose some of the formats from my chart.

When you use the F**o**rmat AutoFormat command in a chart that has already been custom formatted, you lose some or all of the chart's formatting. To change the chart type of an existing chart, yet retain the custom formatting, choose the F**o**rmat Chart **T**ype command, or select a chart type from the Chart Type list.

My chart has only one data series, so I do not want to display the legend with the chart.

To remove the legend box from a chart, select the chart and then click the Legend button in the Chart toolbar. Excel removes the legend box from the chart.

*I want to print a chart that is embedded in a worksheet. But when I select the chart and choose **F**ile **P**rint, Excel prints the entire worksheet.*

To print an embedded chart, first double-click the chart to select it, and then choose **F**ile **P**rint. Excel will print only the selected chart. To print an embedded chart along with a selected range of cells, you must highlight the range of worksheet cells that contain the data and the chart.

From Here...

In this chapter, you learned the basic techniques for printing data and charts in your worksheets. You may want to explore the following chapters for additional information:

- Chapter 17, "Managing and Analyzing Data," shows you how to use the Scenario Manager and other features to analyze worksheet data.

- Chapter 25, "Creating Charts," teaches you how to create graphs with Microsoft PowerPoint.

- Chapter 37, "Sharing Data between Applications with Linking and Embedding," shows you how to link a chart to a Word document.

- Chapter 38, "Using Mail with Other Microsoft Office Products," explains how to distribute worksheet information electronically.

- Chapter 41, "Using Office Applications To Create a Presentation," shows you how to create a presentation with charts created in Excel.

Chapter 17

Managing and Analyzing Data

by Cathy Kenny

With Excel, you easily can manage data by creating a list. After information is organized into a list format, you can find and extract data that meets certain criteria. In addition, you can sort information in a list to put data into a specific order, and you can extract, summarize, and compare data. You also can create a Pivot Table to summarize information in an Excel list.

Excel 5.0 provides many tools that enable you to analyze and perform more complex calculations than the typical worksheet formula allows. The Goal Seeker command and Solver add-in enable you to calculate an answer based on one or more calculations. When you need to generate different answers for what-if analysis, the Scenario Manager enables you to do just that. Annotating worksheet cells helps both you and others that use your spreadsheet to understand formulas and logic.

In this chapter, you learn to

- Create a list
- Use a data form to enter and edit records
- Sort and filter data in a list
- Generate subtotals and grand totals
- Create pivot tables
- Use the Goal Seeker to calculate a defined result
- Find answers to problems using the Solver
- Annotate formulas with notes

Creating and Editing a List

A *list* is information in worksheet cells that contain similar sets of data. When information is organized in a list, you can sort, filter, and summarize data with subtotals. Each *column* in a list represents a category and determines the type of information required for each entry in the list. Each row in a list forms a *record*.

To create a list, enter a column heading in each column in the section of the worksheet where you want to start the list. You can create a list in any area of the worksheet. Just make sure that the area below the list is clear of any data so that the list can expand without interfering with other data in the worksheet.

You enter data in the rows immediately following the column heading to form a record. Every record must have the same fields, but you do not have to enter data into all fields. Figure 17.1 illustrates a sample list.

Microsoft Excel - PRODS.XLS

File Edit View Insert Format Tools Data Window Help

Product Sales

Product	Store	Region	Month	Amount
Book	Boston	North	Jan	125
Video	Miami	South	Mar	450
Video	Boston	North	Mar	325
CBT	Dallas	South	Feb	225
Book	Boston	North	Apr	325
Video	Boston	North	Jan	100
Book	Dallas	South	May	500
Audio	Dallas	South	Apr	325
CBT	Dallas	South	Jan	375
Audio	New York	North	Jan	250
Video	New York	North	Feb	290
Audio	Miami	South	Apr	150
Book	New York	North	Feb	405
CBT	New York	North	Mar	250

Sales / Sheet2 / Sheet3 / Sheet4 / Sheet5 / Sheet6

Ready NUM

Fig. 17.1
In this sample list, Product sales are tracked by product, store, region, month, and amount.

To facilitate entering and editing records in a list, Excel provides a data form that presents an organized view of the data and makes data entry easier and more accurate. The form displays field names, text boxes for data entry, and buttons for adding, deleting, and finding records. You can enter new records, edit existing records, find records, and delete records using the data form.

Adding Records with the Data Form

The data form provides text boxes, using the column headings or the field names from your list. You enter the data for each field in each text box on the form.

To add a record and enter data using the data form, follow these steps:

1. Position the cell pointer in any cell in your list.

2. Choose the **D**ata **F**orm command. The data form dialog box appears, as shown in figure 17.2.

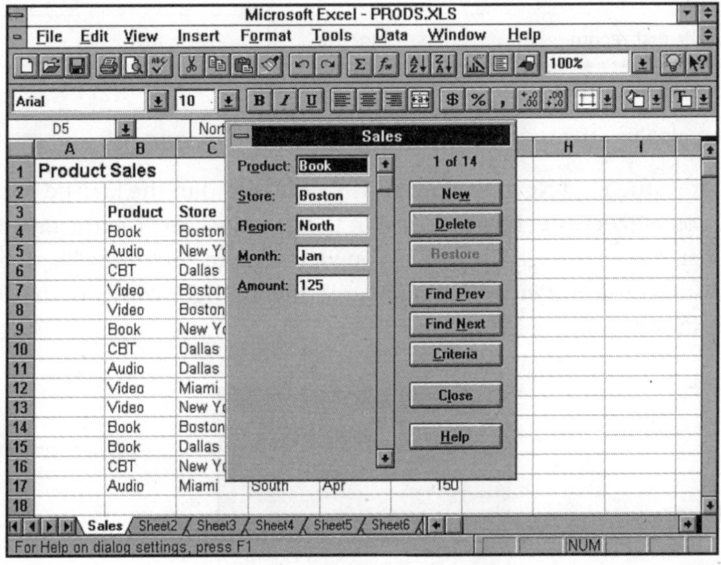

Fig. 17.2
The data form displays the field names and text box to the right of each field name.

3. To add a new record to the list, choose the Ne**w** button. A new blank form appears.

4. Enter the appropriate data in each text box on the form.

   Press Tab to move forward to the next text box. Press Shift+Tab to move to the previous text box.

5. When you have finished entering data for the record, press Enter to add the new record to the list. Another blank form appears, enabling you to enter another new record.

6. Choose the C**l**ose button to return to the worksheet.

Tip
If you type data for a new record in the list and then decide you don't want to add the record, choose the **R**estore button to erase the entry from the form. You must choose **R**estore before pressing Enter to save the record.

Viewing Records with the Data Form

You can use the data form to view records in your list. Position the cell pointer in a cell in your list, and choose the **D**ata **F**orm command.

Use the following procedures to view records in a list:

To	Do this
View the next record	Choose Find **N**ext or press down arrow
View the previous record	Choose Find **P**rev or press up arrow
Move to a new record form	Press Ctrl+Page Down
View the first record	Press Page Up

You can also use the scroll bars to view each record in your list.

If you press the Find **N**ext key to view the next record in the list and Excel beeps, you are viewing the last record in the database. To view the first record in the list, press the Page Up key. As you view each record in the list, the data form displays the current record number in the top right corner of the dialog box, as shown in figure 17.3.

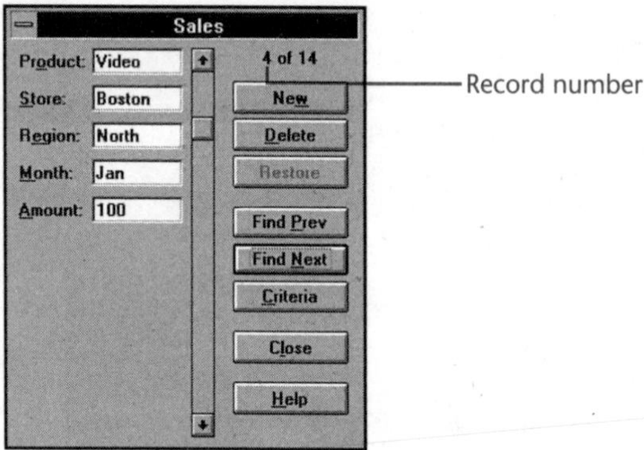

Fig. 17.3
This screen displays the fourth record in a list of 14 records.

Deleting Records with the Data Form

The data form can also be used to delete records from your list. When you use the form to delete records, you are able to delete only one record at a time.

To delete a record from the data form, follow these steps:

1. Position the cell pointer in any cell in your list.
2. Choose the **D**ata F**o**rm command. The data form appears.

3. Choose the Find **N**ext or Find **P**rev button, or press the up arrow or the down arrow to move to the record you want to delete.

4. When the record you want to delete appears in the form, choose the **D**elete button to delete the record.

   The records below the deleted record will be renumbered to account for the deleted record. Excel prompts you with the dialog box shown in figure 17.4 to verify that you want to delete the record.

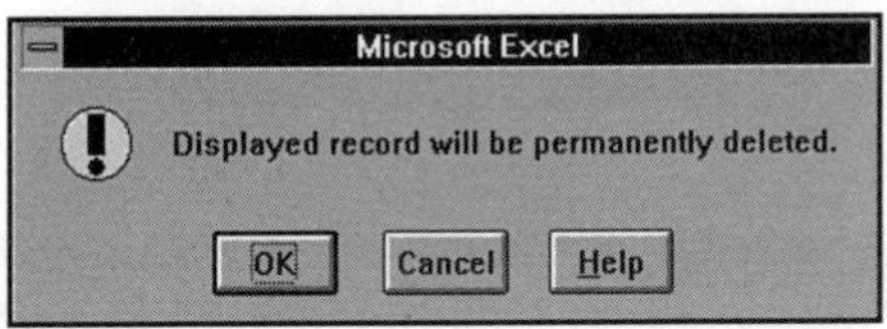

Fig. 17.4
A message box appears reminding you that the record will be permanently deleted.

5. Choose OK or press Enter to delete the record, or click Cancel to keep the record.

6. Choose the C**l**ose button to return to the worksheet.

Finding Records with the Data Form

You can use the data form to find particular records in your database. When you use the data form, you can view only one found record at a time.

To find records from the data form, follow these steps:

1. Select a cell in the list.

2. Choose the **D**ata F**o**rm command.

3. Choose the **C**riteria button.

4. Select a text box and enter the criteria or pattern for which you want to search, as shown in figure 17.5.

5. Choose the Find **N**ext command or press the down arrow after you have entered the criteria. If no matches exist, you hear a beep. Choose the Find **P**rev button or press the up arrow if you want to search backward through the database to find a match.

6. Choose the **C**lose button to clear the dialog box.

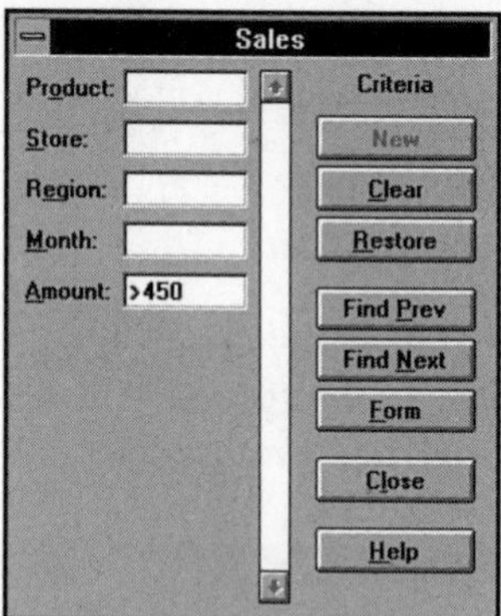

Fig. 17.5
In this example, the search criterion is an amount greater than 450.

Note

You can use multiple criteria when searching for records. To do so, enter the criteria values in the appropriate text boxes.

Troubleshooting

After I choose the Data Form command, Excel displays an error message stating that no list was found.

Select any cell within the list on your worksheet, and choose the Data Form command again. In order to use the Data Form command to manage information in your list, you must first select the list you want to modify before you choose the command.

When I choose New to add a new record to the list in the data form, Excel displays the message `Cannot extend list or database`*, and I can't enter a new record.*

The data form will not allow you to add new records to the list if there are not enough blank rows below the current list range. Choose OK to close the dialog box, and then choose C**l**ose to close the data form. If any data is below the list range, use the **E**dit Cu**t** and **E**dit **P**aste commands to move the data to a new location. When you create a list, remember to select a location in the worksheet with enough room to expand the list.

Sorting and Filtering Data in a List

An Excel list provides you with flexibility so that you can organize data to meet your needs. You can sort the list to display data in a certain order. You can also filter the list so that it only displays certain records.

Sorting Data in a List

Excel sorts lists based on fields. Any field name you have created in the list can be used as a sort field for reorganizing the list.

To sort a list, follow these steps:

1. Position the cell pointer in the list you want to sort. Or, if you want to sort only selected records in a list, highlight the records you want to sort.

2. Choose the **D**ata **S**ort command. The Sort dialog box appears, as shown in figure 17.6.

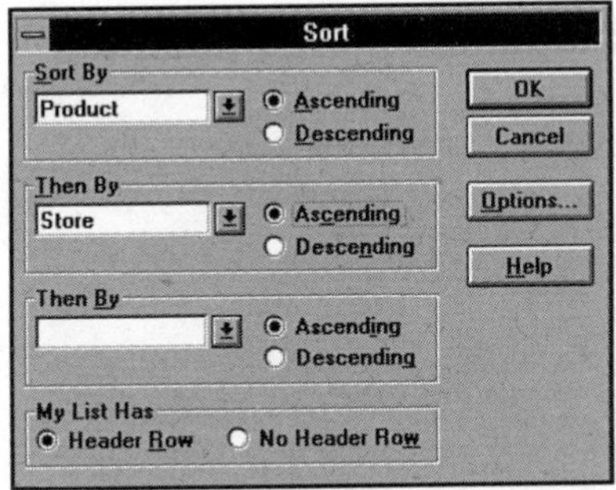

Fig. 17.6
You can sort a list based on multiple field names.

3. To prevent the column labels from being sorted with the rest of the list, select Header **R**ow in the My List Has section of the dialog box.

4. The **S**ort By text box is selected and displays the first field name from the list. Use the drop-down list box to replace the field name in this text box with the field name by which you want to sort. Select the **A**scending or **D**escending option for the order in which you want to sort the selected records.

5. To sort records using additional fields, press Tab or select the **T**hen By text box and specify the field. Select the Then **B**y text box if you want to sort by a third field.

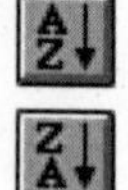

6. Choose OK or press Enter. Excel sorts the data in the list, as shown in figure 17.7.

Tip
To quickly sort a list, select a cell in the column by which you want to sort, then choose the Sort Ascending or the Sort Descending button.

Filtering Data in a List

When you need to work with a subset of data within the list, you can filter the list so that only certain records appear. After you have filtered a list, you can modify the records; generate subtotals and grand totals; and copy the data to another area of the worksheet.

When you filter a list, Excel displays only those records that meet the criteria, while hiding the other records from view. Two methods are available for filtering the records in a list. You can use the AutoFilter command to quickly filter data in a list. To filter data using additional criteria, you can use a custom AutoFilter.

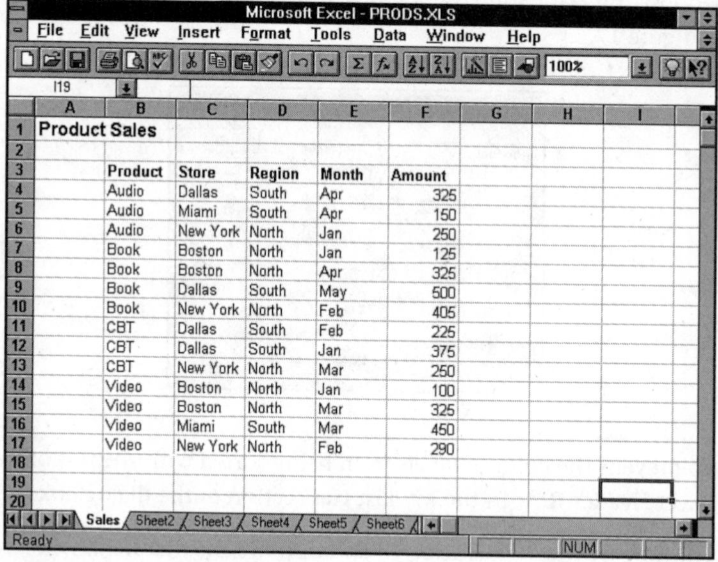

Fig. 17.7
The selected records are sorted according to the options in the Sort dialog box.

Tip
If you perform a sort that is incorrect, choose **E**dit **U**ndo Sort or press Ctrl+Z immediately to reverse the sort and return to the original list.

Using AutoFilter To Filter Records

To filter a list with the AutoFilter command, follow these steps:

1. Select a cell in the list you want to filter.

2. Choose the **D**ata **F**ilter Auto**F**ilter command. Excel inserts drop-down arrows next to each column heading in your list, as illustrated in figure 17.8.

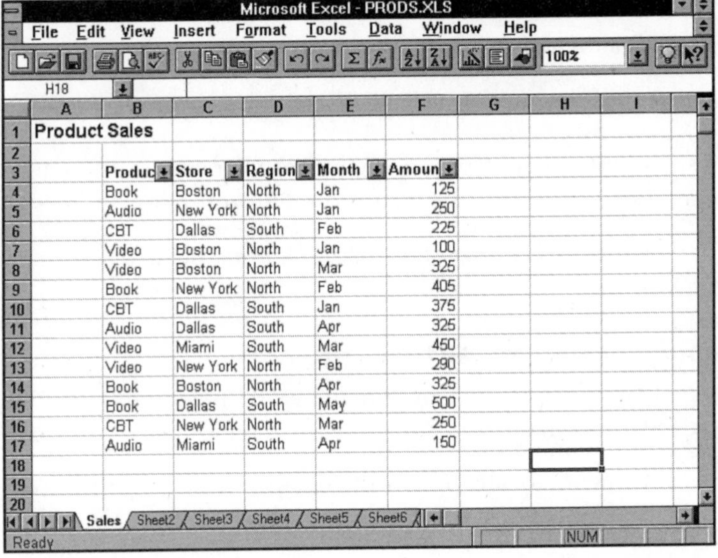

Product	Store	Region	Month	Amount
Book	Boston	North	Jan	125
Audio	New York	North	Jan	250
CBT	Dallas	South	Feb	225
Video	Boston	North	Jan	100
Video	Boston	North	Mar	325
Book	New York	North	Feb	405
CBT	Dallas	South	Jan	375
Audio	Dallas	South	Apr	325
Video	Miami	South	Mar	450
Video	New York	North	Feb	290
Book	Boston	North	Apr	325
Book	Dallas	South	May	500
CBT	New York	North	Mar	250
Audio	Miami	South	Apr	150

Fig. 17.8
Drop-down arrows appear next to each column label.

3. Click the drop-down arrow in the column that contains the data you want to display. Excel displays a menu listing all the unique items in the column, as shown in figure 17.9.

Product	Store	Region	Month	Amount
	Boston	North	Jan	125
	New York	North	Jan	250
	Dallas	South	Feb	225
	Boston	North	Jan	100
	Boston	North	Mar	325
	New York	North	Feb	405
CBT	Dallas	South	Jan	375
Audio	Dallas	South	Apr	325
Video	Miami	South	Mar	450
Video	New York	North	Feb	290
Book	Boston	North	Apr	325
Book	Dallas	South	May	500
CBT	New York	North	Mar	250
Audio	Miami	South	Apr	150

Fig. 17.9
Select the item you want to display from the drop-down list.

III

Using Excel

4. Select the item you want to display. Select Blanks to display empty cells or NonBlanks to display cells that have value.

5. Repeat steps 3 and 4 for each additional column you want to filter.

Tip
To remove the AutoFilter drop-down arrows from your list, choose the **D**ata **F**ilter Auto**F**ilter command again.

Excel displays only those records that meet the filter criteria. Excel displays the row headings of records that match in a different color.

To return the list to its original state, select All from the drop-down menu of each column.

Creating a Custom AutoFilter

You can define a custom AutoFilter when the data you want to filter must meet a specified criteria.

To create a custom AutoFilter, follow these steps:

1. Select a cell in the list you want to filter.

2. Choose the **D**ata **F**ilter Auto**F**ilter command.

3. Click the drop-down arrow in the column that contains the data you want to filter, and choose Custom. Excel displays the Custom AutoFilter dialog box, shown in figure 17.10.

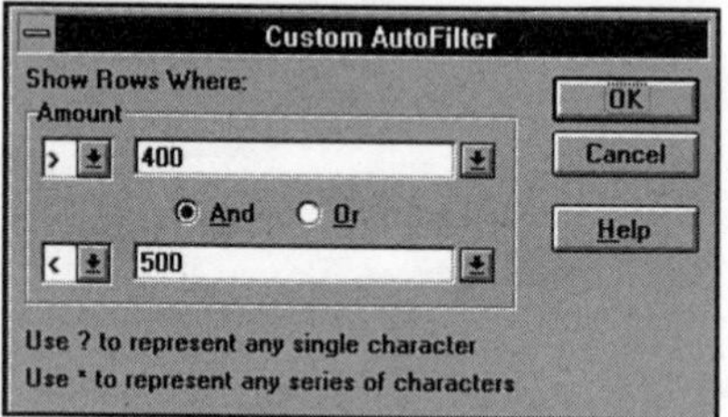

Fig. 17.10
Define a custom filter in the Custom AutoFilter dialog box.

4. Click the arrow in the drop-down list of comparative operators, and select the comparative operator with which you want to compare the data. Enter the data you want to compare in the text box, or click the arrow to display a list of items and select an item.

5. To add a second set of criteria, select **A**nd to indicate that the records must meet both sets of criteria. Select **O**r to indicate that the records must match either set of criteria. Define the second set of criteria.

6. Choose OK or press Enter.

   Excel filters the list and displays those records that match the criteria (see fig. 17.11).

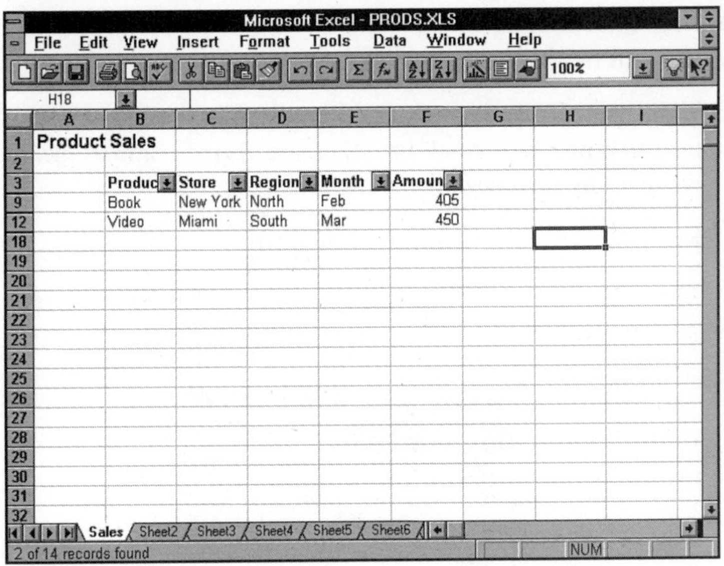

Fig. 17.11
The filtered list displaying records where Amount is greater than 400 but less than 500.

Troubleshooting

After sorting the database, Excel sorts the column headings along with the data in the list.

To prevent the column headings from being sorted with the rest of the list, select Header **R**ow in the My List Has section of the Sort dialog box.

I selected multiple filters, but my list doesn't display any records.

Select All from the AutoFilter drop-down menu to redisplay the records. When you use multiple filters, each record in the list must contain each of the specified criteria. If a record contains one of the specified criteria but not the other, that record will not be displayed. To remove the AutoFilter drop-downs from the list, choose the **D**ata **F**ilter **A**utoFilter command.

Adding and Removing Subtotals

When you sort data in a list, Excel allows you to summarize the data with subtotals. When you summarize a list, Excel calculates subtotals based on subsets of the data and also calculates a grand total.

Creating Subtotals

To add subtotals to a list, follow these steps:

1. Sort the data according to the order in which you want to create subtotals. To generate subtotals based on sales region, for example, first sort the list by Sales Region.

2. Select a cell in the list you want to summarize.

3. Choose the Data Subtotals command. The Subtotal dialog box appears, as shown in figure 17.12.

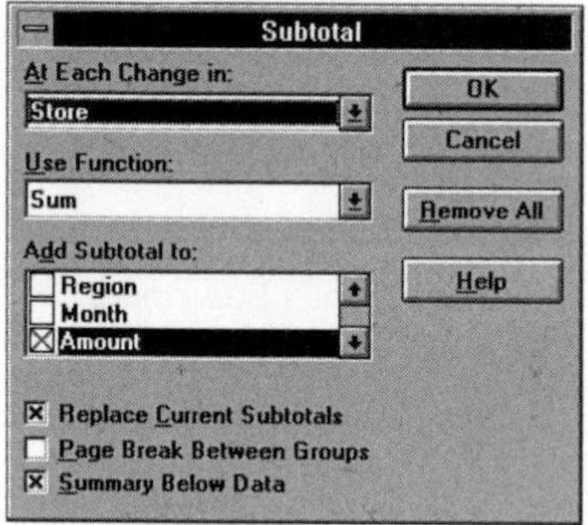

Fig. 17.12
You can generate subtotals for a list in the Subtotal dialog box.

4. Select the group to define the subtotals. To generate automatic subtotals by store, for example, select the Store field from the **A**t Each Change In drop-down list.

5. Select the Subtotal function from the **U**se Function drop-down list. To create subtotals, make sure that Sum is selected.

6. Choose the data you want to subtotal in the Add Subtotal To box. To subtotal the data found in the Amount field, for example, select Amount.

7. Press Enter or choose OK to add the subtotals to your list, as shown in figure 17.13.

Note

If your list is not sorted prior to selecting the Subtotal command, Excel creates a subtotal for each entry in the list. To prevent this from occurring, sort the list before you choose the command.

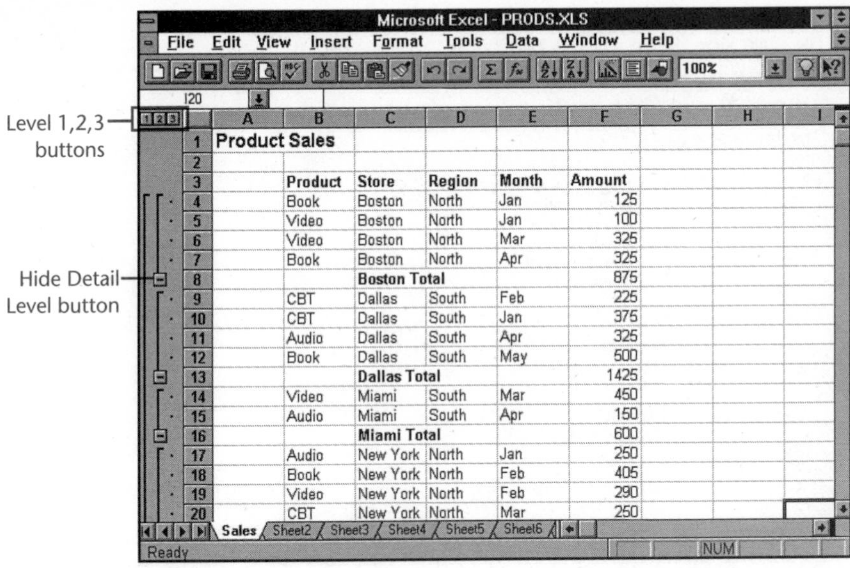

	A	B	C	D	E	F
1	Product Sales					
2						
3		Product	Store	Region	Month	Amount
4		Book	Boston	North	Jan	125
5		Video	Boston	North	Jan	100
6		Video	Boston	North	Mar	325
7		Book	Boston	North	Apr	325
8			Boston Total			875
9		CBT	Dallas	South	Feb	225
10		CBT	Dallas	South	Jan	375
11		Audio	Dallas	South	Apr	325
12		Book	Dallas	South	May	500
13			Dallas Total			1425
14		Video	Miami	South	Mar	450
15		Audio	Miami	South	Apr	150
16			Miami Total			600
17		Audio	New York	North	Jan	250
18		Book	New York	North	Feb	405
19		Video	New York	North	Feb	290
20		CBT	New York	North	Mar	250

Fig. 17.13
Subtotals have been added to the list.

Hiding and Displaying Data in a Subtotaled List

When you add automatic subtotals to a list, Excel displays the list in Outline view. You can expand and contract the level of detail in the list to display only the subtotals and grand totals of data.

Figure 17.13 shows the list displayed in Outline view. The icons that appear along the left edge of the worksheet window enable you to expand and contract the level of detail.

To hide detail level, select a subtotal cell and click the Hide Detail Level button. Excel contracts the list to display the subtotal detail only (see fig. 17.14).

To display a detail level, select a subtotal cell and click the Show Detail Level button. Excel expands the list to show the detail Level.

Removing Subtotals from a List

To remove subtotal data from a list, select a cell in the subtotaled list and choose the **D**ata Su**b**totals command. Choose the **R**emove All button from the Subtotals dialog box.

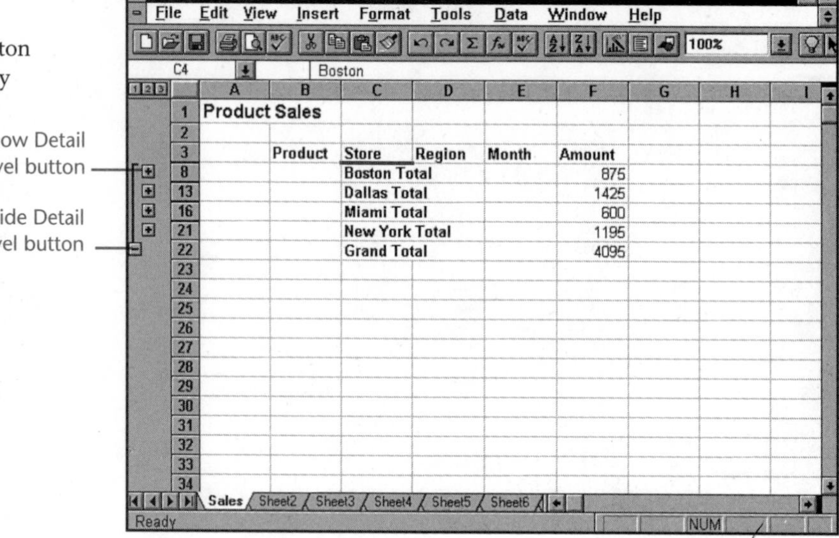

Fig. 17.14
Click the Hide Detail Level button to hide summary detail.

Summarizing Data with Pivot Tables

Tip
Position the cell pointer in a list in your worksheet prior to choosing PivotTable. Excel pastes the range of the list in the Range text box. Click Next if that's the list you want to use.

Excel 5.0 includes a new capability called the *pivot table* that enables you to quickly and easily summarize and compare data found within a list. When you want to summarize your data in another way, you only need to drag and drop fields to create a whole new report, without changing the structure of the data in your worksheets.

You use the automated PivotTable Wizard to create pivot tables in Excel. The PivotTable Wizard guides you step by step through the process of creating a pivot table. The PivotTable Wizard prompts you to define the pivot table information, using the fields defined in a list.

Creating a Pivot Table with the PivotTable Wizard

When you create a pivot table from a list, the column headings in the list are used as Row, Column, and Page fields. The data in the columns become items in the pivot table. When the data in your list contains numeric items, Excel automatically uses the Sum function to calculate the values in the pivot table. If the data in your list contains text items, Excel uses the Count function to calculate a count of the source items in the pivot table.

To create a pivot table from a list in your worksheet, follow these steps:

1. Choose the **D**ata **P**ivotTable command. Step 1 of the PivotTable Wizard appears, as shown in figure 17.15.

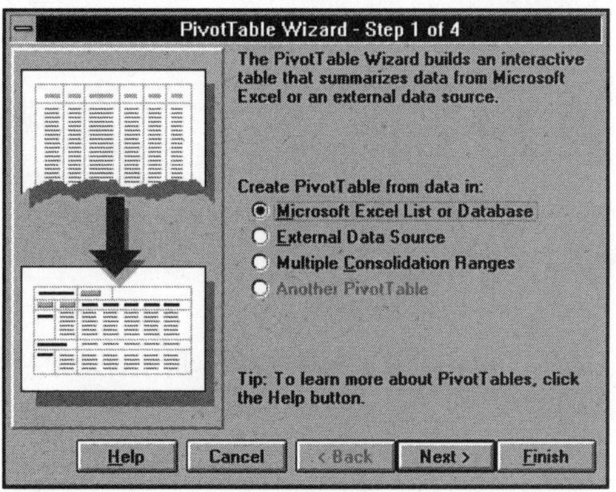

Fig. 17.15
Specify the data to use for the pivot table in Step 1 of the PivotTable Wizard.

2. Specify the data you will be using in the Pivot Table. Select **M**icrosoft Excel List or Database, and click the Next button. Step 2 of the PivotTable Wizard appears, as shown in figure 17.16.

Fig. 17.16
Specify the range of data in Step 2 of the PivotTable Wizard.

3. Specify the location of the list in the **R**ange text box (by typing the range address or by highlighting the range with the mouse), and then click Next. Step 3 of the PivotTable Wizard appears, as shown in figure 17.17.

4. Define the layout of the pivot table by dragging the field names displayed on the right side of the dialog box to the Row, Column, or Page area. Fields placed in the **R**ow area appear in each row in the pivot table. Fields placed in the **C**olumn area appear in each column of the pivot table. Fields placed in the **P**age area filter the data shown in the pivot table.

Tip
Don't spend too much time deciding where to place the fields. You can always rearrange the fields after you have added the pivot table to your worksheet.

PivotTable Wizard - Step 3 of 4
Drag Field Buttons to the following areas to layout your PivotTable
- ROW To show items in the field as row labels.
- COLUMN To show items in the field as column labels.
- DATA To summarize values in the body of the table.
- PAGE To show data for one item at a time in the table.
Store
Month COLUMN
Product
Sum of Amount
ROW
DATA
Product
Store
Region
Month
Amount
You can double click field buttons to customize fields.
Help Cancel < Back Next > Finish

Fig. 17.17
Define the pivot table layout in Step 3 of the PivotTable Wizard.

5. Click Next to display the final step in the PivotTable Wizard (see fig. 17.18).

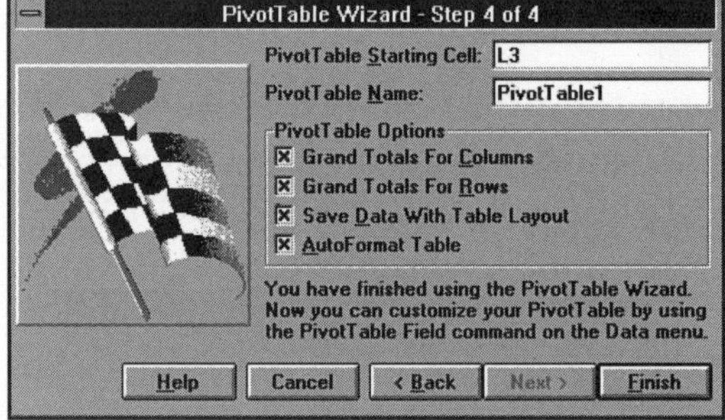

Fig. 17.18
Specify the location of the pivot table in Step 4 of the PivotTable Wizard.

6. Enter a cell address in the PivotTable Starting Cell text box. If you leave this text box empty, Excel creates a new worksheet and adds the pivot table to it. Choose **F**inish. The PivotTable Wizard displays the results in a table on the worksheet (see fig. 17.19).

When you add a pivot table to the worksheet, Excel automatically displays the Query and Pivot toolbar. The toolbar contains buttons for the most frequently used pivot table commands (refer to fig. 17.19.)

Editing and Updating a Pivot Table

After you have added a pivot table to your worksheet, you can quickly rearrange the fields in the pivot table to display an entirely different view of your data. Each field in the list is represented by a shaded cell in the pivot table. Figure 17.20 shows the fields. You change the view of the data by dragging the fields to other areas in the pivot table.

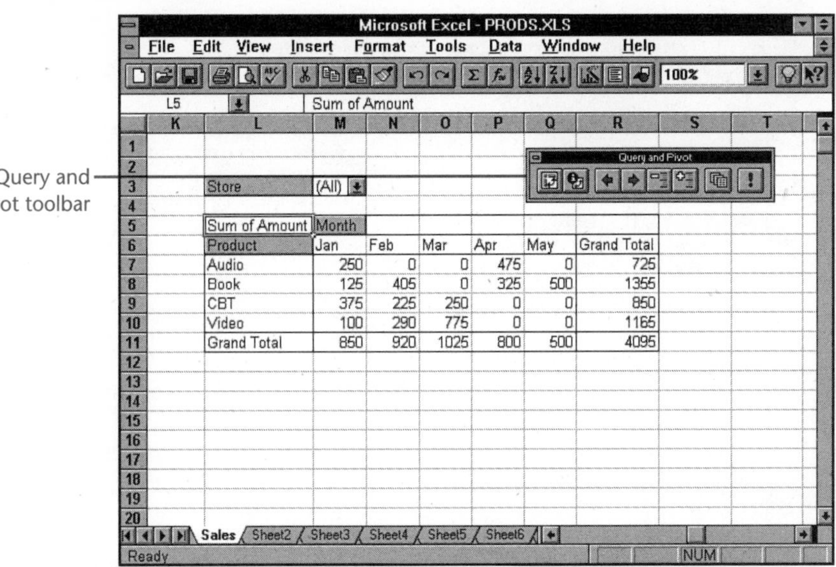

Sum of Amount	Month					
Product	Jan	Feb	Mar	Apr	May	Grand Total
Audio	250	0	0	475	0	725
Book	125	405	0	325	500	1355
CBT	375	225	250	0	0	850
Video	100	290	775	0	0	1165
Grand Total	850	920	1025	800	500	4095

Fig. 17.19
This pivot table summarizes sales by Product, Store, and Month.

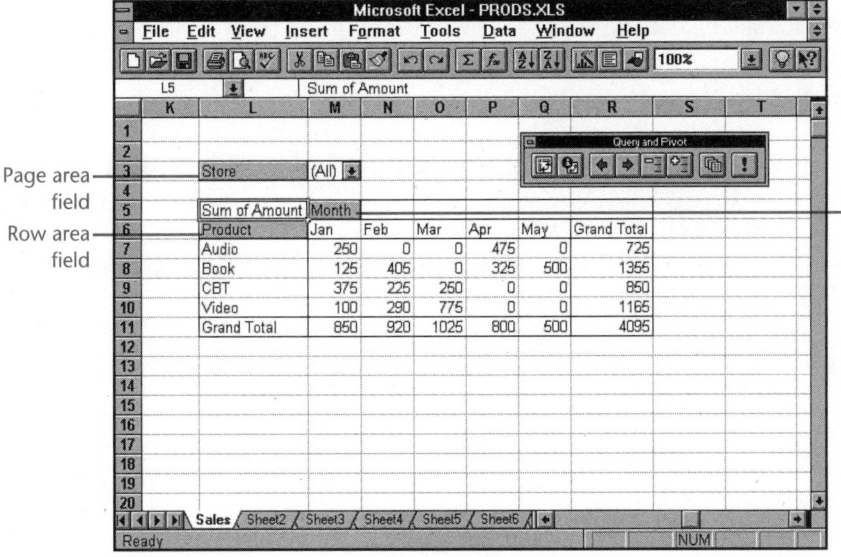

Sum of Amount	Month					
Product	Jan	Feb	Mar	Apr	May	Grand Total
Audio	250	0	0	475	0	725
Book	125	405	0	325	500	1355
CBT	375	225	250	0	0	850
Video	100	290	775	0	0	1165
Grand Total	850	920	1025	800	500	4095

Fig. 17.20
Change the view in a pivot table by dragging fields to the row, column, and page areas.

Tip
To display each page in the data table on a separate worksheet in the workbook, choose the Display Each Page button.

Rearranging a Pivot Table

To change the data displayed on the current page, click the drop-down arrow displayed in the Page area of the pivot table. A list of items for the current field appears. Select an item from the list to filter the data in the pivot table to display data for that item only (see fig. 17.21).

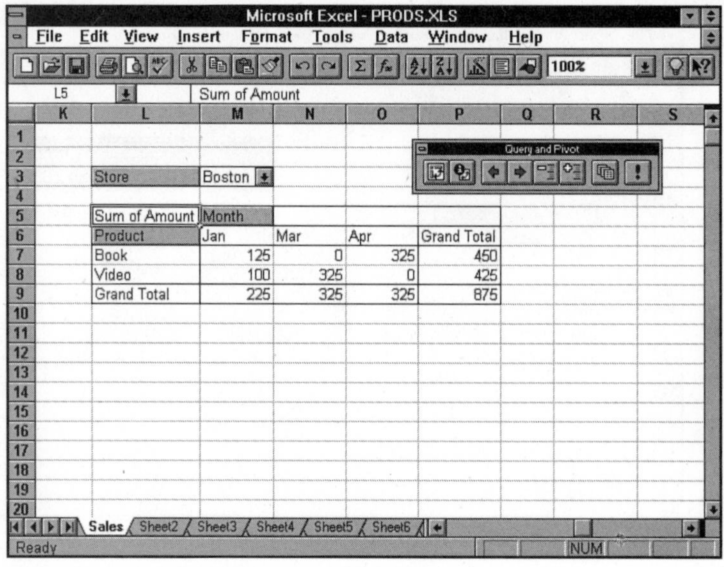

Store	Boston			
Sum of Amount	Month			
Product	Jan	Mar	Apr	Grand Total
Book	125	0	325	450
Video	100	325	0	425
Grand Total	225	325	325	875

Fig. 17.21
The pivot table displays sales data for Boston sales only.

To change the data displayed in the columns of the pivot table, drag a row or page field to the column area of the pivot table. When you do, the pivot table displays a columnar view of the data (see fig. 17.22).

Sum of Amount		Month					
Store	Product	Jan	Feb	Mar	Apr	May	Grand Total
Boston	Book	125	0	0	325	0	450
	Video	100	0	325	0	0	425
Boston Total		225	0	325	325	0	875
Dallas	Audio	0	0	0	325	0	325
	Book	0	0	0	0	500	500
	CBT	375	225	0	0	0	600
Dallas Total		375	225	0	325	500	1425
Miami	Audio	0	0	0	150	0	150
	Video	0	0	450	0	0	450
Miami Total		0	0	450	150	0	600
New York	Audio	250	0	0	0	0	250
	Book	0	405	0	0	0	405
	CBT	0	0	250	0	0	250
	Video	0	290	0	0	0	290
New York Total		250	695	250	0	0	1195
Grand Total		850	920	1025	800	500	4095

Fig. 17.22
The columns in the pivot table show sales by Store and Month.

To change the data displayed in the rows of the pivot table, drag a page or column field to the row area of the pivot table. The pivot table displays data in a row field in each row (see fig. 17.23).

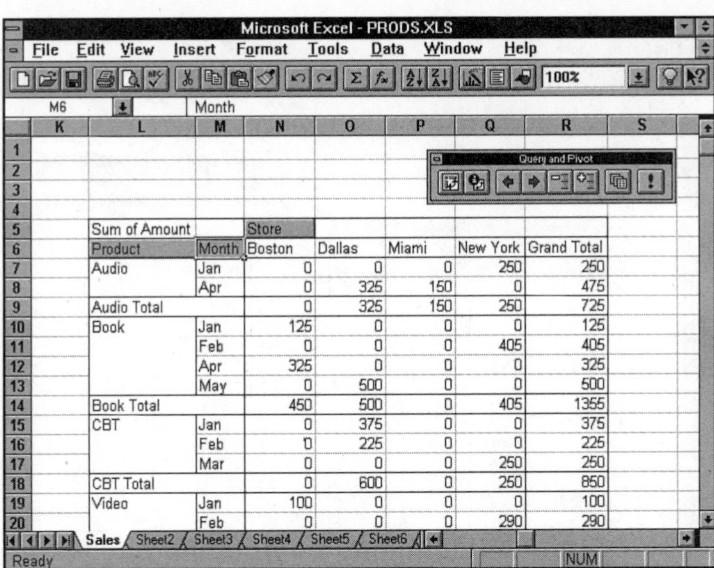

Sum of Amount		Store				
Product	Month	Boston	Dallas	Miami	New York	Grand Total
Audio	Jan	0	0	0	250	250
	Apr	0	325	150	0	475
Audio Total		0	325	150	250	725
Book	Jan	125	0	0	0	125
	Feb	0	0	0	405	405
	Apr	325	0	0	0	325
	May	0	500	0	0	500
Book Total		450	500	0	405	1355
CBT	Jan	0	375	0	0	375
	Feb	0	225	0	0	225
	Mar	0	0	0	250	250
CBT Total		0	600	0	250	850
Video	Jan	100	0	0	0	100
	Feb	0	0	0	290	290

Fig. 17.23
The rows in the pivot table show sales by Product and Month.

Adding and Removing Fields in a Pivot Table

You can change the data used in a pivot table by adding new fields to the pivot table or by removing fields from the pivot table that you no longer need. When you add a new field to the pivot table or delete an existing field, Excel automatically updates the pivot table.

> **Note**
>
> When you add and remove data from a pivot table, the action has no effect on the source data in the list.

To add a field to the pivot table, follow these steps:

1. Position the cell pointer in the area of the pivot table where you want to add a field. To add a field to the row area, for example, select a cell in the row area of the pivot table.

2. Click the right mouse button to display the PivotTable shortcut menu. Choose the Add Row Field command from the shortcut menu.

3. The fields in the list used to generate the pivot table appear in a cascade menu. Select the field you want to add to the pivot table.

   Figure 17.24 shows the pivot table when an additional field has been added.

Tip
You can remove a pivot table field directly from the pivot table in the worksheet. To remove a field, drag it outside the pivot table area. Excel then removes the data from the table.

Fig. 17.24
The Region field has been added to the pivot table layout.

Sum of Amount		Region	Store					
		North		North Total	South		South Total	Grand T
Product	Month	Boston	New York		Dallas	Miami		
Audio	Jan	0	250	250	0	0	0	
	Apr	0	0	0	325	150	475	
Audio Total		0	250	250	325	150	475	
Book	Jan	125	0	125	0	0	0	
	Feb	0	405	405	0	0	0	
	Apr	325	0	325	0	0	0	
	May	0	0	0	500	0	500	
Book Total		450	405	855	500	0	500	1
CBT	Jan	0	0	0	375	0	375	
	Feb	0	0	0	225	0	225	
	Mar	0	250	250	0	0	0	
CBT Total		0	250	250	600	0	600	
Video	Jan	100	0	100	0	0	0	

Modifying a Pivot Table

Excel provides special formatting commands for modifying the appearance of a pivot table. When you use these commands, Excel retains the format, even when you reorganize and recalculate the data in the pivot table.

You can change the numeric format of the data displayed in the data area, format an entire pivot table, and rename fields and items in the table.

Note

When you update a pivot table, Excel recalculates and reformats the data in the table. Because of this, you should avoid manually formatting the table.

Applying a Numeric Format

To change the numeric formatting in the data area of the pivot table, follow these steps:

1. Select a cell in the pivot table.

2. Choose the **D**ata PivotTable F**i**eld command, or click the right mouse button and choose PivotTable Field from the shortcut menu. The PivotTable Field dialog box appears (see fig. 17.25).

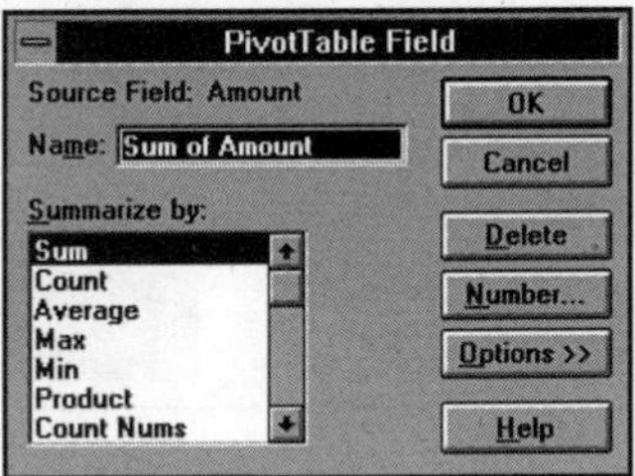

Fig. 17.25
The PivotTable Field dialog box.

3. Choose the **N**umber command from the PivotTable Field dialog box. The Format Cells dialog box then appears (see fig. 17.26).

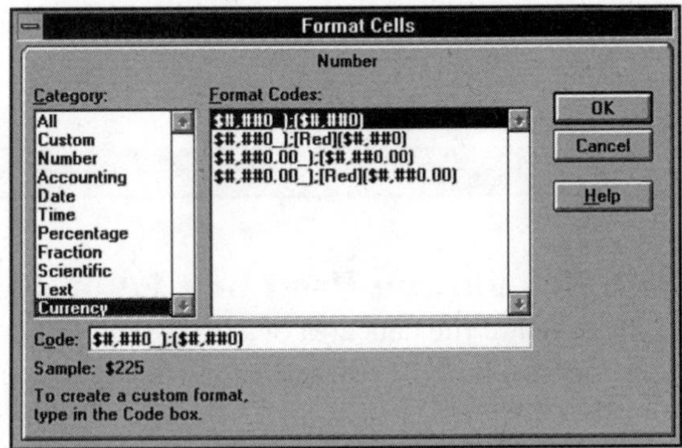

Fig. 17.26
Change the numeric format of cells in the Format Cells dialog box.

4. Select the numeric format you want to apply to the data area.

5. Choose OK twice to return to the worksheet.

Formatting the Pivot Table

When you create a pivot table and select the **A**utoFormat Table check box in the PivotTable Wizard, Excel automatically formats the table for you. To use another format, select a cell in the pivot table and choose F**o**rmat **A**utoFormat. Select the format you want to use from the AutoFormat dialog box, and choose OK (see fig. 17.27).

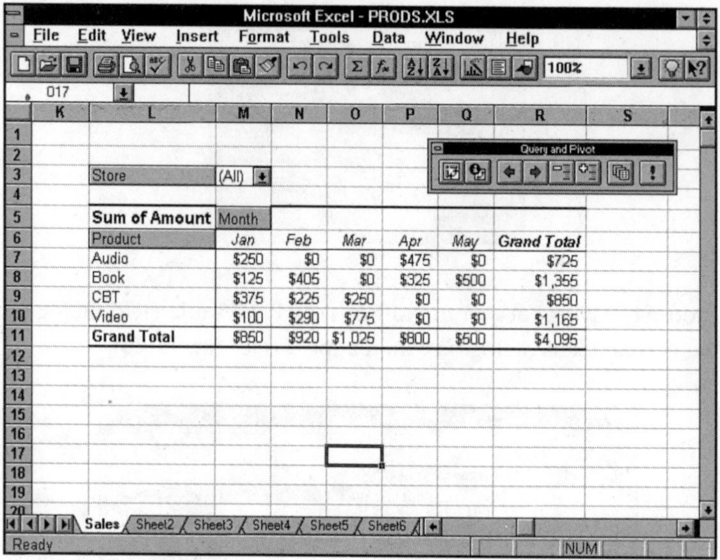

Store	(All)					
Sum of Amount	Month					
Product	*Jan*	*Feb*	*Mar*	*Apr*	*May*	***Grand Total***
Audio	$250	$0	$0	$475	$0	$725
Book	$125	$405	$0	$325	$500	$1,355
CBT	$375	$225	$250	$0	$0	$850
Video	$100	$290	$775	$0	$0	$1,165
Grand Total	$850	$920	$1,025	$800	$500	$4,095

Fig. 17.27
The pivot table has been formatted with the Classic 1 AutoFormat.

Changing the Calculation Used in a Pivot Table

When the items displayed in the data area of a pivot table are numeric, Excel automatically uses the Sum function to summarize the data in the list. When the items are text, the Count function is used to summarize the text items. You can change the summary function used by a data field, for example, to calculate an average or maximum value. You can also change the calculation type used in the data area.

Changing the Summary Function

To change the summary function used by the pivot table, follow these steps:

1. Select a cell in the data area of the pivot table.

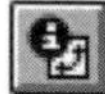

2. Choose the **D**ata PivotTable F**i**eld command, or click the right mouse button and choose the PivotTable Field command from the shortcut menu.

3. In the **S**ummarize By list box, select the function you want to use to summarize the data.

4 Choose OK or press Enter.

The results are shown in figure 17.28.

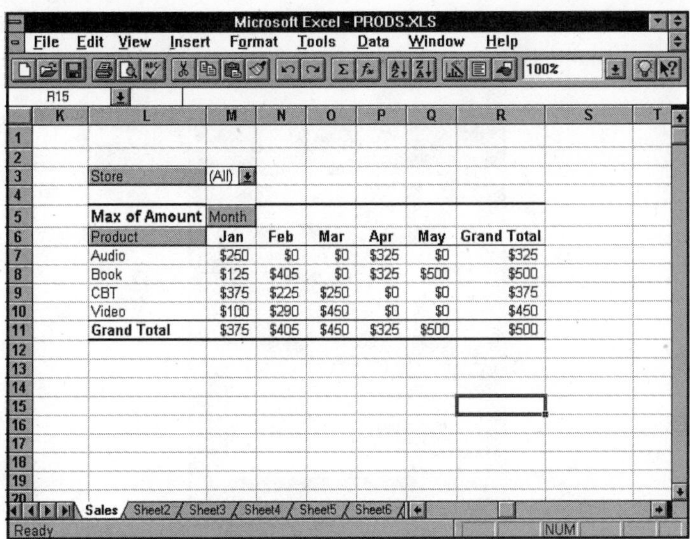

Fig. 17.28
The data area displays the maximum price.

Changing the Summary Type

Excel can calculate values used in the data area based on the values of other cells. You can calculate the difference between items in a field, for example, or calculate the items as percentages of the total.

To change the summary type used by the data field in the pivot table, follow these steps:

1. Select a cell in the data area of the pivot table.
2. Choose the Data PivotTable F**i**eld command, or click the right mouse button and choose the PivotTable Field command.

3. Choose the **O**ptions button in the PivotTable field dialog box (see fig. 17.29).

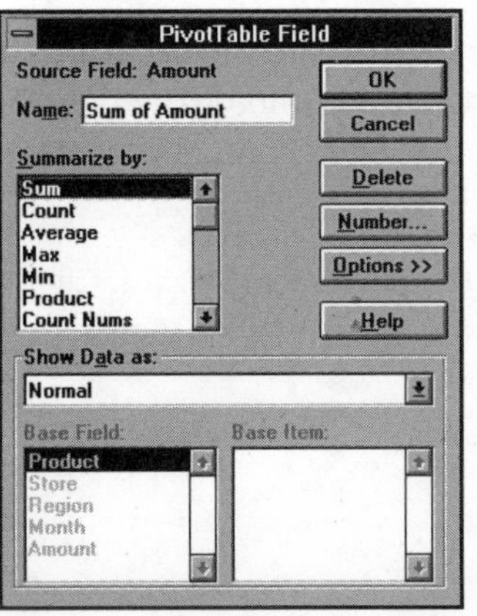

Fig. 17.29
The PivotTable Field dialog box expands to display the summary type options.

III

Using Excel

4. Click the arrow in the Show D**a**ta as text box to display the calculation types available (see fig. 17.30).

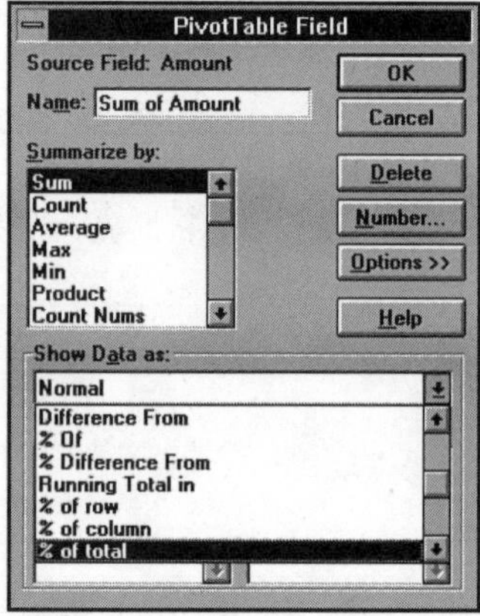

Fig. 17.30
The PivotTable Field dialog box displays the calculations type options.

5. Select the calculation type you want to use from the **S**ummarize By list box, and then select the fields and items you want to use.

6. Choose OK or press Enter.

Refreshing Data in a Pivot Table

When you update the data in the source list in your worksheet, you must refresh the pivot table to include the new information. To refresh data in the pivot table, select any cell in the pivot table and choose the **D**ata **R**efresh Data command or click the right mouse button and choose the Refresh Data command from the shortcut menu.

If you add new records to your source list, you must redefine the source range used to create the pivot table, using the PivotTable Wizard.

To extend the source range to include additional records in the pivot table, select a cell in the pivot table and choose the **D**ata **P**ivotTable command, or click the right mouse button and choose the PivotTable command from the shortcut menu.

Excel displays Step 3 of the PivotTable Wizard. Click **B**ack to display Step 2. Respecify the source data range, and click **F**inish. Excel adds the new records to the pivot table.

Forecasting with the Goal Seeker

Excel's Goal Seek command enables you to perform simple forecasting in your worksheets. You can find a specific value for a defined result by adjusting the value of other cells in the worksheet. For example, you can find out how many houses need to be sold to generate a total sales figure of $1,600,000. The benefit of using the Goal Seek command is that Excel uses the data known—in this case, the total sales amount and the amount per product—and performs the calculation instantaneously, without your having to calculate multiple iterations to come up with the answer.

To use the Goal Seeker, begin by setting up the problem and entering the known variable in the worksheet. The worksheet shown in figure 17.31 contains the data variable for a sales forecasting worksheet.

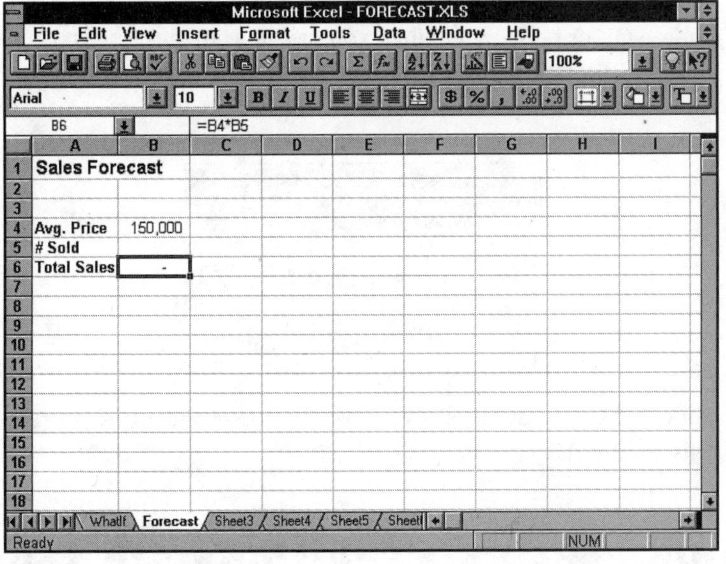

Fig. 17.31 Goal Seek adjusts the amount in cell B4 to meet the proposed sales amount.

To use the Goal Seeker, the variable you want to adjust must be a formula, and the formula must refer to the other cells in the worksheet. You specify the cell containing the formula as the Set Cell. Then the cell to adjust must be referred to by the formula in the set cell. In the worksheet in figure 17.30, the Total Sales cell contains the formula =B4*B5. In this case, we know the average price of a house is $150,000. So, we want to see how many houses must be sold.

Tip

To proceed through the Goal Seek by one calculation at a time, click the Pause button and then click the Step button until you are finished.

To forecast with Goal Seek, follow these steps:

1. Choose the **T**ools **G**oal Seek command. The Goal Seek dialog box appears, as illustrated in figure 17.32.

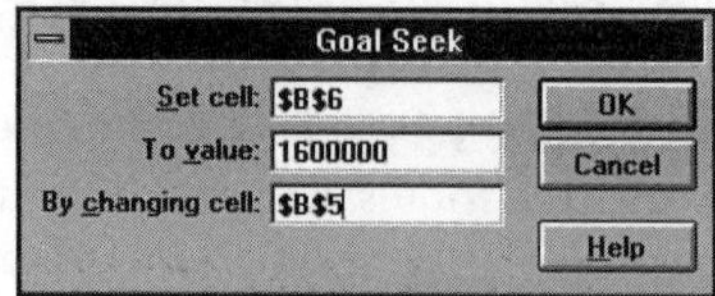

Fig. 17.32
You indicate three input cells in the Goal Seek dialog box: the cell containing the formula, the goal you wish to seek, and the cell that is to be adjusted.

2. Specify the cell containing the formula as the **S**et Cell.
3. In the To **V**alue text box, enter the value the cell must reach.
4. Specify the cell to adjust in the By **c**hanging cell text box.
5. Choose OK or press Enter when you have specified the cells. Figure 17.33 shows the Goal Seek Status dialog box that informs you of the status of the operation.

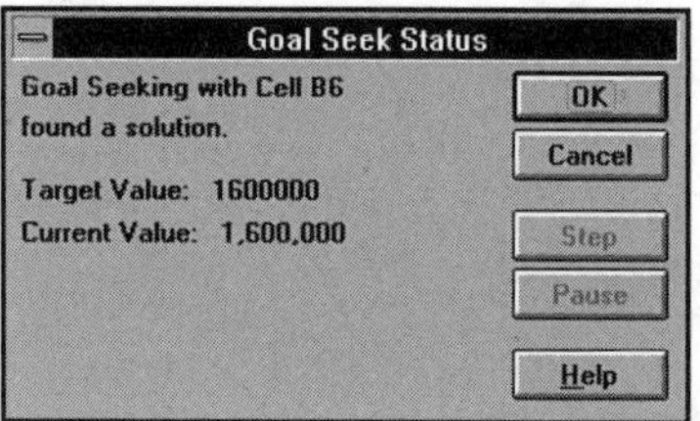

Fig. 17.33
The Goal Seek Status dialog box shows the status of the problem.

6. Choose OK or press Enter. Excel displays the results in the worksheet cells (see fig. 17.34).

Finding the Best Solution with Solver

The Goal Seek command enables you to generate values based on a single input cell. By contrast, the Solver add-in enables you to calculate the values needed to reach a particular result by adjusting the value of one or more cells. Furthermore, you can define constraints, which Solver must meet when generating the optimum solution.

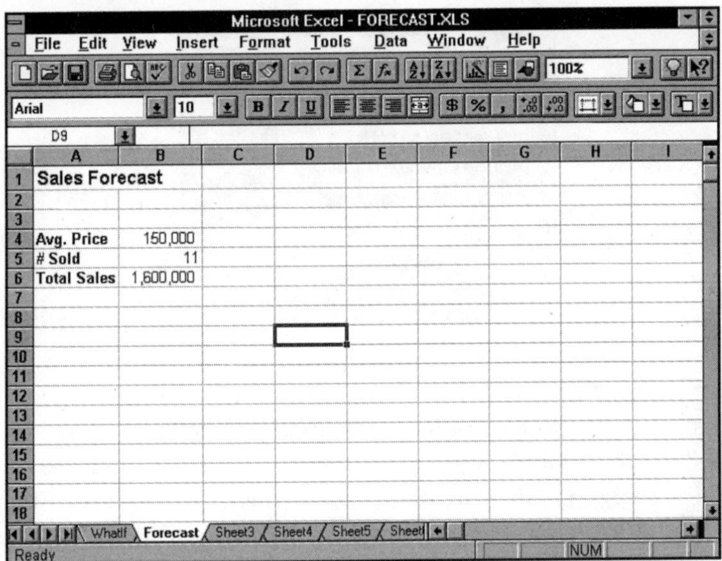

Fig. 17.34
The Goal Seek returns the result, indicating that 11 houses must be sold to reach a value of 1.6 million in sales.

In the case of the real estate agency determining the number of houses that must be sold in order to meet its annual sales forecast, for example, you must take other considerations into account besides the average price of the house and the goal that must be met.

Loading the Solver Add-In

Before you can use the Solver, you must first load the Solver add-in into memory. When you installed Excel, you were given the option of installing the add-ins that ship with Excel. If you chose to install the add-ins, you can use the Tools Add-In command to load Solver into memory. If you did not install the add-ins, you must do so before you can use Solver.

To load Solver into memory, follow these steps:

1. Choose the **T**ools Add-**I**n command. Figure 17.35 shows the currently installed Add-ins.

2. From the list of installed add-ins, select Solver Add-In.

3. Choose OK or press Enter. The Sol**v**er command appears in the **T**ools menu.

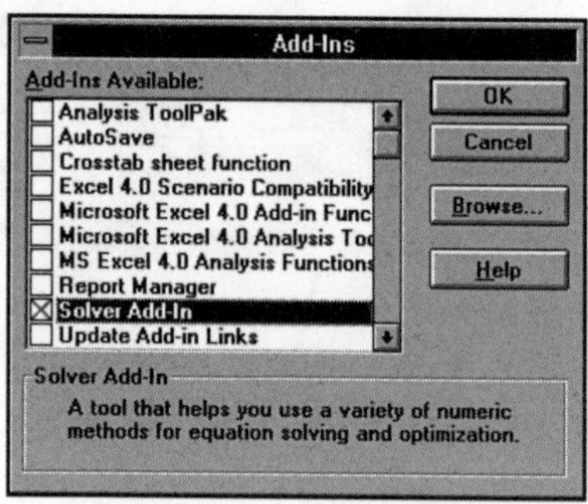

Fig. 17.35
The currently installed add-ins appear in the Add-In dialog box.

Setting Up the Problem

To use the Solver in your worksheets, you must first define the problem that you need to solve. With Solver, each of the constraint cells are based on formulas. The changing values are the values to which each of the constraint cells refer. Therefore, to set up the problem, determine which of the cells will be used as the constraints and make sure that they contain formulas. The worksheet shown in figure 17.36 illustrates a problem that the Solver will help solve.

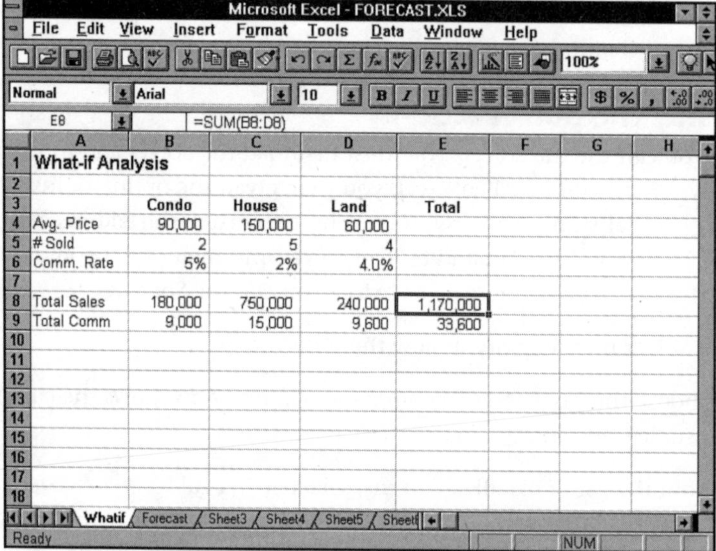

Fig. 17.36
Solver will adjust the data in range B5:D5 until the total sales value in cell E8 equals 1.6 million.

Running Solver

After you have set up the worksheet and located the cells to use, follow these steps to run Solver:

1. Choose the **T**ools Sol**v**er command to start the Solver add-in. Figure 17.37 displays the Solver Parameters dialog box.

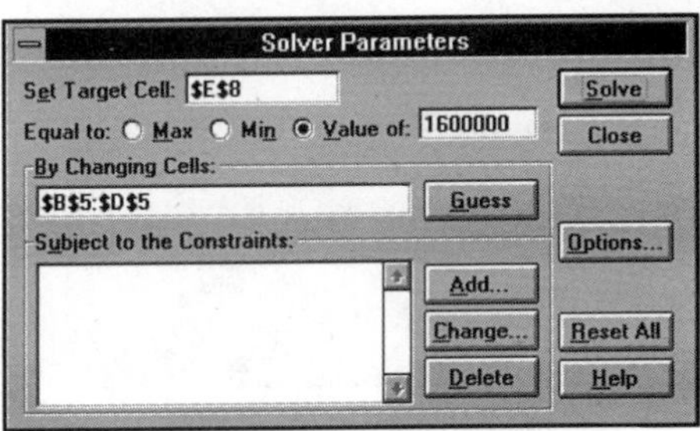

Fig. 17.37
Use the Solver Parameters dialog box to define the optimal cell, the cells to adjust, and the constraints.

2. Indicate the cell that contains the formula you want to solve for in the S**e**t Target Cell text box.

3. Use the Equal To section of the dialog box to indicate the optimum value for the cell: either the Maximum value, Minimum value, or a specific value. To meet a specific value, select the **V**alue of options and then enter the value in the text box.

4. In the **B**y Changing Cells text box, indicate the cell or range of cells that the Solver will need to adjust to reach the optimum value.

5. To specify constraints, choose the **A**dd button to add each constraint to the problem. Figure 17.38 shows the Add Constraint dialog box.

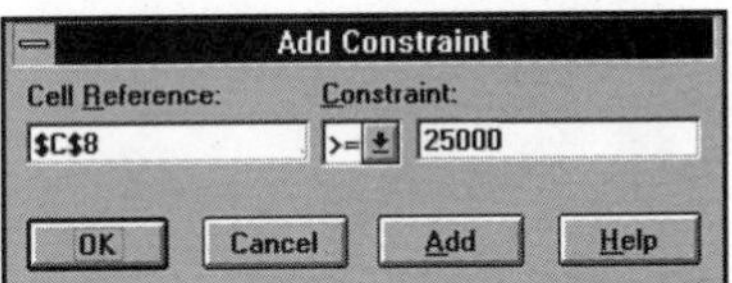

Fig. 17.38
Specify the constraint to use for the problem in the Add Constraints dialog box.

6. To create a constraint, specify the cell containing the formula on which the constraint is based in the Cell **R**eference text box. Click the drop-down arrow to display the list of constraint operators, and select the appropriate operator. In the final text box, enter the value the constraint must meet. Choose the **A**dd command to add the current constraint to the problem and create another, or choose OK to add the constraint and return to the Solver Parameters dialog box.

7. The constraints you have defined appear in the Subject to the Constraints list box. Choose **S**olve to start the Solver. The Solver begins calculating the optimal solutions. When Solver finds a solution, the Solver Results dialog box appears, as shown in figure 17.39.

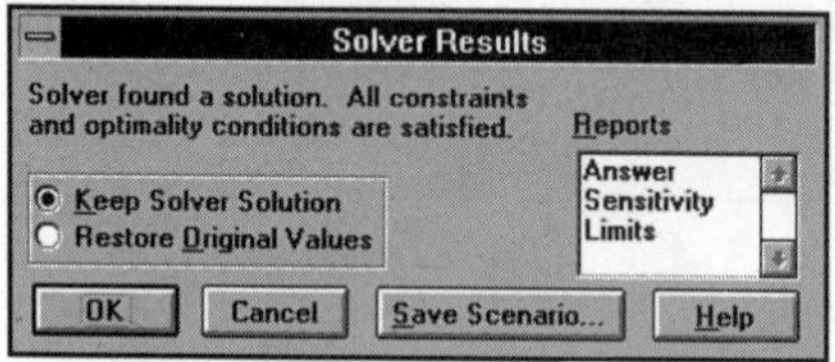

Fig. 17.39
The Solver Results dialog box gives you options for using the solution that has been found.

8. Excel adds the solutions to the worksheet. Select **K**eep Solver Solution to use the offered solutions. Select Restore **O**riginal Values to return to the original worksheet values. Figure 17.40 shows the worksheet after the Solver has found the solutions for the problem.

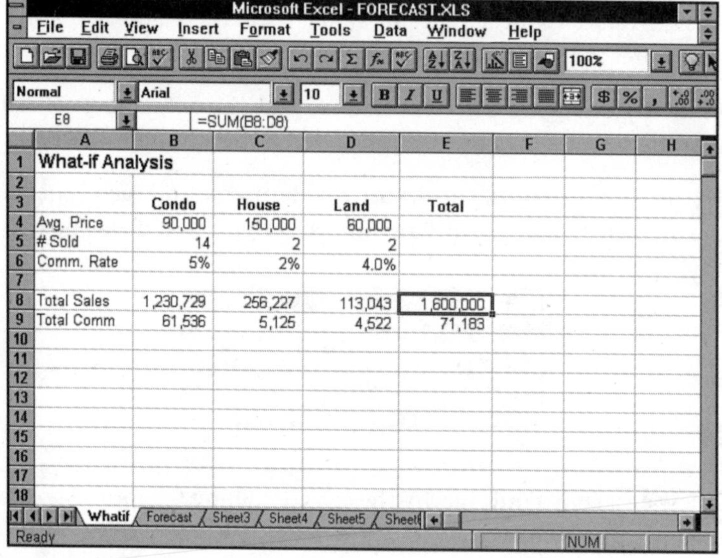

Fig. 17.40
The results produced by Solver show that 14 condos, 2 houses, and 2 plots of land must be sold to generate $1.6 million in sales and about $70,000 of commission.

Creating Solver Reports

Solver enables you to generate reports summarizing the results of its solutions. You can create three types of reports: Answer, Sensitivity, and Limit reports. An answer report shows the original and final values for the target cell and the adjustable cells, as well as the status of each constraint. The sensitivity report shows the sensitivity of each element of the solution to changes in input cells or constraints. A limit report shows the upper and lower values of the adjustable cells within the specified constraints.

Tip
You can create more than one Solver report by pressing Ctrl while you select the report names.

To create a report, select the report from the list that appears in the Solver Results dialog box, and choose OK. Excel creates the report in a separate sheet.

Performing What-If Analysis with Scenarios

For most spreadsheet users, a large portion of analysis involves performing what-if analysis. What effect does changing the average price of home sales have on my forecast? If I sell more condos than houses, will that have a negative impact on total sales?

◀ "Working with Range Names," p. 325

The solution to each of these questions requires that input values in the worksheet change. When these values change, however, the original results are also changed, making it difficult to compare one outcome with another. To account for these changing variables, many users construct multiple data tables to test the outcome of each variable. This allows them to compare the original result to the new result.

One of the pitfalls in creating various solution tables is that it becomes increasingly difficult to monitor the difference between the tables. When the worksheet is used by multiple people, keeping track of the ranges proves to be an exercise in frustration. Finally, as each additional table is created to test a scenario, the worksheet grows larger and more unwieldy with each addition.

Excel 5.0 provides a tool that enables you to track these scenarios with ease. The Scenario Manager feature provides a mechanism that saves each iteration of a problem and then enables you to view one solution at a time.

Creating a Scenario

Before you create a scenario, you must first identify the worksheet range that contains the data, as well as the input cells that will change for each scenario. The worksheet shown in figure 17.41 illustrates a sales worksheet that enables you to track the change in Total Sales and Total Commission, based on the number of properties sold.

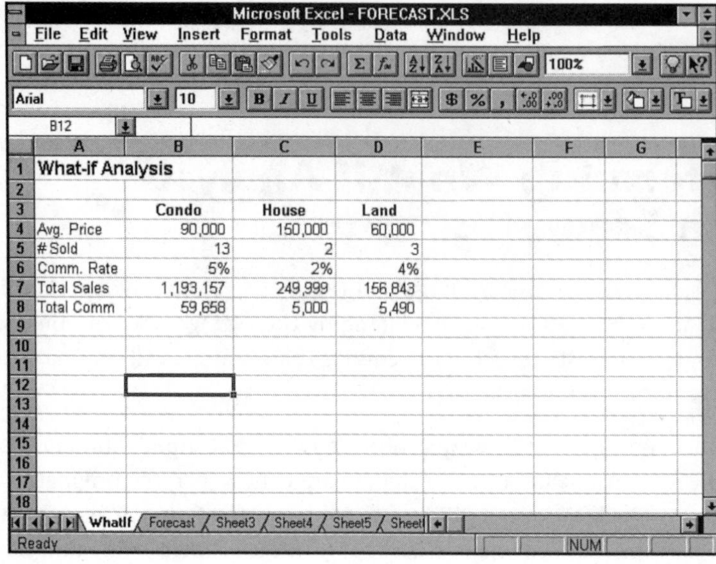

Fig. 17.41
The Sales worksheet lets you perform what-if analysis using the # Sold cells.

After you have identified the data, follow these steps to create a scenario:

1. Choose the **T**ools S**c**enarios command. The Scenario Manager dialog box appears, as shown in figure 17.42.

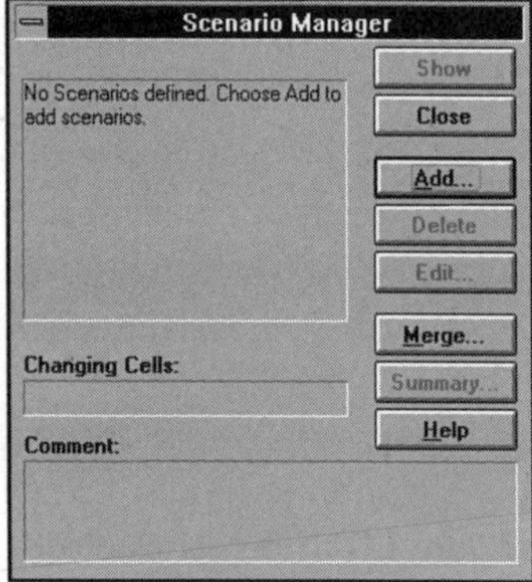

Fig. 17.42
The Scenario Manager dialog box is used to create scenarios.

2. Choose the **A**dd command to display the Add Scenario dialog box, as shown in figure 17.43.

3. Enter a name for the scenario in the Scenario **N**ame text box.

4. In the Changing **C**ells text box, indicate the cell or range of cells that will change for each scenario.

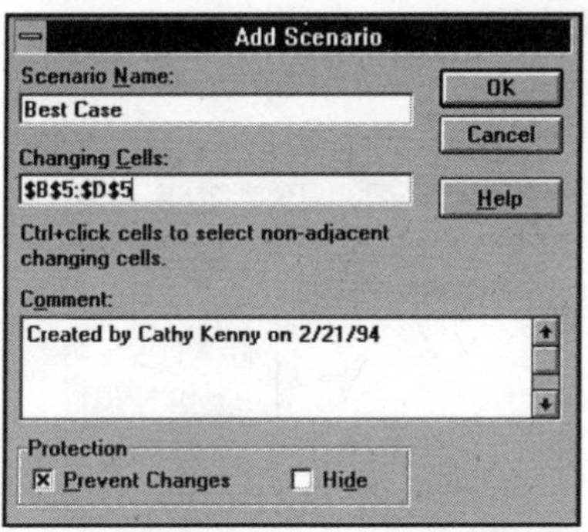

Fig. 17.43
The Add Scenario dialog box enables you to name the scenario and define the cells that will change.

5. In the C**o**mment field, Excel has automatically entered your name and the date the scenario was created. Enter additional information in the text box as necessary.

6. To prevent changes from being made to the cells in the worksheet, select the **P**revent Changes option in the Protection section of the dialog box. To hide the cell data from view, select the **H**ide option.

7. Choose OK when you have finished defining the Scenario. Figure 17.44 shows the Scenario Values dialog box, in which you enter the data for each of the cells in the scenario.

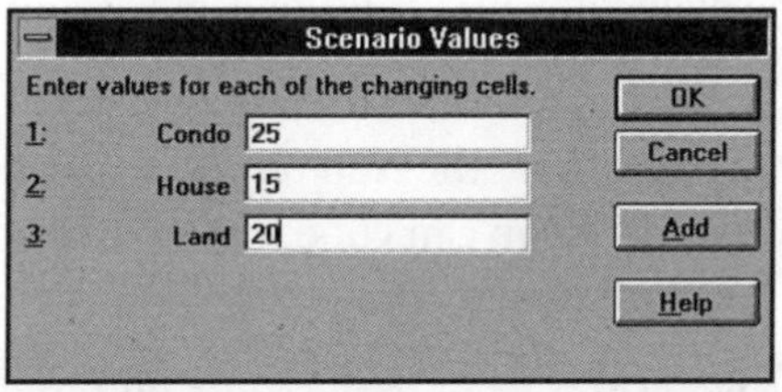

Fig. 17.44
Enter the data for each of the cells in the Scenario Values dialog box.

> **Note**
>
> When creating scenarios, use the **I**nsert **N**ame **D**efine command to assign a name to each of the cells in the scenario. When you do, Excel uses those names in the Scenario Values dialog box and in scenario reports.

Each of the displayed text boxes relates to each of the specified cells for the scenario. The cell address of each cell is displayed for reference.

8. Enter the data that represents the data to be used for the scenario.

9. When you're finished, choose OK or press Enter. The Scenario Manager dialog box reappears, as shown in figure 17.45.

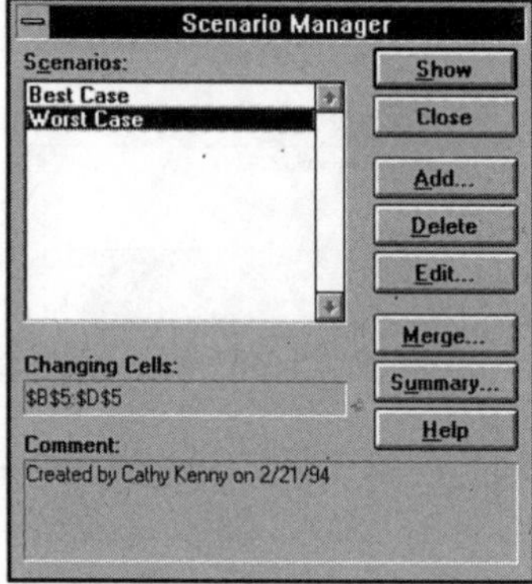

Fig. 17.45
The Scenario Manager dialog box displays each of the defined scenarios.

The name of the newly defined scenario appears in the S**c**enarios list box. When you select a scenario from the list, the Changing Cells field displays the cell addresses of the scenario. The Comments field displays the comments you entered to describe or annotate the scenario.

10. To view the scenario, select the scenario name from the list and choose the **S**how button. Excel displays the values in each of the cells in the worksheet. If the dialog box prevents you from seeing the data, click and drag the title bar of the dialog box to move it out of the way.

11. At this point, you can choose the **A**dd button to define a new range of values as a scenario, or you can choose the **E**dit button to edit the values used by the current scenario.

12. To return to the worksheet, choose the Close button. Excel displays the values defined by the scenario in the worksheet.

Note

Use the Scenario button found in the Workgroup toolbar to quickly switch between scenarios in the worksheet. To display the Workgroup toolbar, choose the **V**iew **T**oolbars command, select Workgroup from the **T**oolbars list, and choose OK. To display a scenario, click the drop-down arrow in the Scenario button, and select the scenario you want to view.

Editing and Deleting Scenarios

You can edit an existing scenario or delete a scenario altogether. When you edit a scenario, you can rename the scenario, specify other worksheet cells as the changing cells, and edit the comment. Furthermore, you can change the values defined by the scenario.

To edit a scenario, follow these steps:

1. Choose **T**ools S**c**enarios to display the Scenario Manager dialog box. Select the scenario you want to edit from the Scenarios list box, and choose the **E**dit button. Excel displays the Edit Scenario dialog box, as shown in figure 17.46.

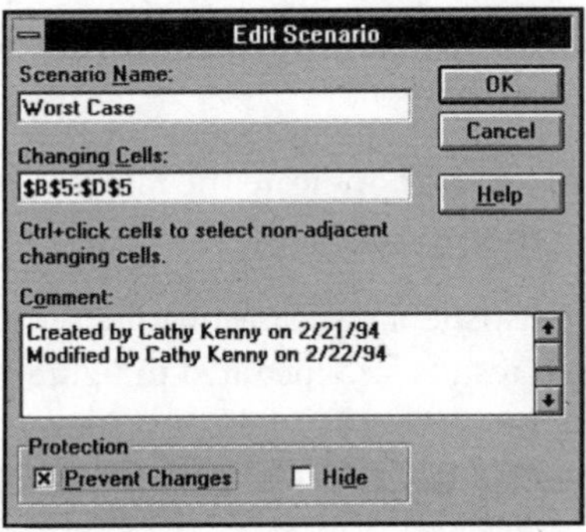

Fig. 17.46
Excel automatically adds the modification date to the Comment field.

2. Make any modifications necessary to the data shown in the text boxes, and choose OK. The Scenario Values dialog box is displayed.

3. Enter the new values, and choose OK.

To delete a scenario, select the scenario you want to delete and choose the **D**elete button. Excel removes the scenario from the Scenario listing.

Summarizing Scenarios with Reports

Excel provides two methods of displaying scenarios in a concise report. The Scenario Summary creates a simple report in table form, showing the data for each of the changing cells and their effect on the results of formulas in a range. You can also generate a Pivot Table Summary from a multiple scenario set.

Creating a Summary Report

To create a summary report, follow these steps:

1. Choose the **T**ools Sc**e**narios command.
2. Choose the Summary button to display the Scenario Summary dialog box, as shown in figure 17.47.

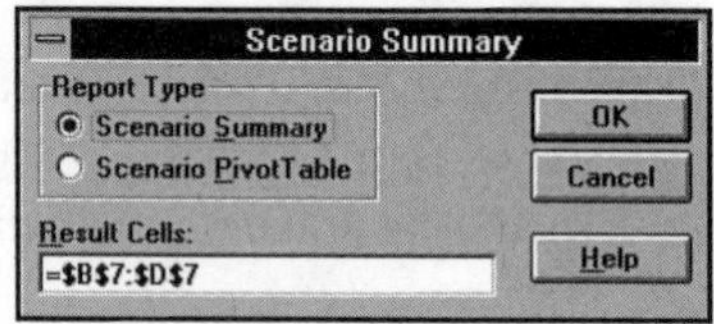

Fig. 17.47
Choose the type of summary report to create.

3. Choose Scenario **S**ummary, if it is not already selected, from the Report Type area of the dialog box.
4. In the **R**esult Cells text box, indicate the range of cells that contain formulas based on the input cells.
5. Choose OK. Excel displays a new sheet with a summary table of the scenario inputs and results, as illustrated in figure 17.48.

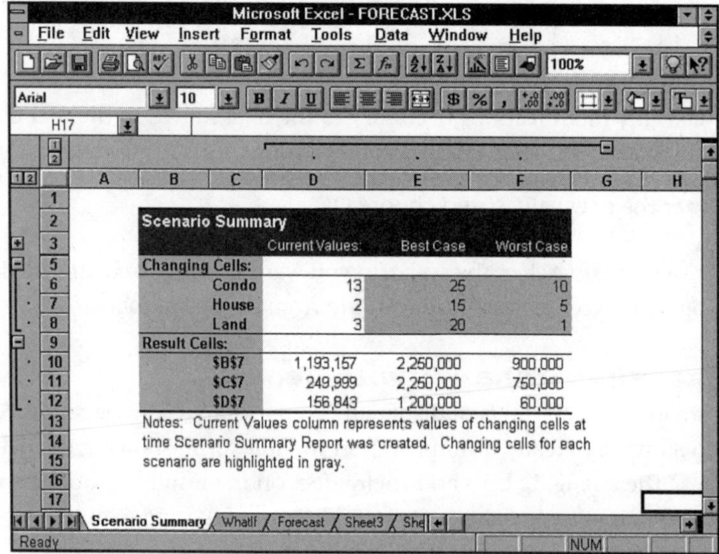

Fig. 17.48
A summary report showing the Best Case and Worst case scenarios, and the results.

Creating a Scenario PivotTable Report

To create a pivot table from the scenarios in your worksheet, follow these steps:

1. Choose the **T**ools S**c**enarios command.
2. Choose the S**u**mmary button.
3. In the Scenario Summary dialog box, choose the Scenario **P**ivotTable option.
4. In the **R**esult Cells text box, indicate the range of cells that contain formulas based on the input cells.
5. Choose OK. Excel displays a new sheet with a pivot table of the scenario inputs and results, as illustrated in figure 17.49.

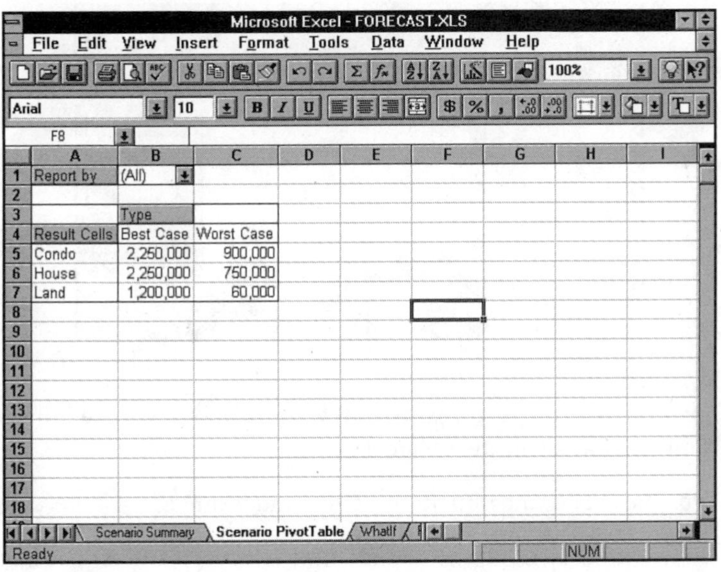

Fig. 17.49
A summary pivot table report showing scenarios by creator, Best Case and Worst case scenarios, and results.

You can manipulate the pivot table summary report as you would any pivot table. If you change a scenario, however, the pivot table is not updated. You must create a new pivot table to account for the changes.

Annotating Worksheets

When you use many formulas and functions for analysis in your worksheets, it can become difficult to remember exactly what each formula is calculating and what data it is using in its calculations. Excel enables you to annotate cells with notes so that you can enter descriptive data about a formula. When you share your worksheets with other users, the notes provide a handy mechanism for describing the contents of a cell or for additional information.

Adding a Note

To annotate a cell, follow these steps:

1. Select the cell, and choose the **I**nsert No**t**e command. The Cell Note dialog box appears, as shown in figure 17.50.

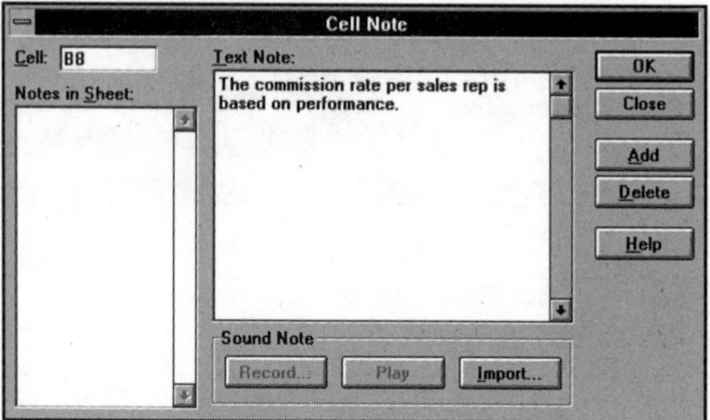

Fig. 17.50 Annotate formulas and other data in your worksheets with notes.

2. Enter the cell address (or point to it with the mouse) of the cell you want to annotate in the **C**ell text box.

3. Type the data of the note in the **T**ext Note text box.

4. Choose the **A**dd button to add the note to the worksheet. The Notes in **S**heet list box displays the cell address, as well as the first few words of the note.

5. Choose OK to return to the worksheet.

Viewing a Note

When a cell in the worksheet has a note attached to it, a small red box appears in the upper right corner of the cell. To display the contents of the note, select the cell and choose the **I**nsert No**t**e command. The text of the note appears in the **T**ext Note text box, as shown in figure 17.51. Choose OK when you have finished viewing the note.

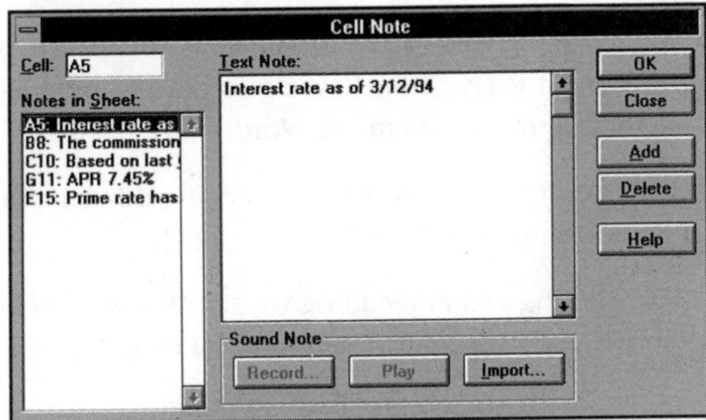

Fig. 17.51
The note attached to the current cell appears in the Text Note text box.

Tip
You also can view the contents of a note by double-clicking the cell with the mouse. To do so, you must first turn off in-cell editing. Choose **T**ools **O**ptions, select the Edit tab, uncheck **E**dit directly in cell, and choose OK.

Note

If the note indicators do not appear in the worksheet, choose the **T**ools **O**ptions command, select the View tab, select the **N**ote Indicator option in the Show portion of the dialog box, and choose OK.

Removing a Note

To remove a note from a worksheet cell, select the cell, and choose the **E**dit C**l**ear command. Choose the **N**otes command from the cascade menu to delete the note from the cell.

From Here...

This chapter presented working with lists to organize and summarize data in your worksheets. In this chapter, you also learned how to use Excel commands to analyze the data in your worksheets. You may want to read the following chapters for additional information, as well as to learn how to use list information with other applications in Microsoft Office:

- Chapter 36, "Working with Wizards, Multiple Documents, and Cut, Copy, and Paste," discusses how to use information from a list in Excel to generate form letters in Microsoft Word.
- Chapter 39, "Sending a Mass Mailing," provides information on creating mailings and using Excel data in Microsoft Word.
- Chapter 40, "Linking and Embedding within Access To Manage Information," shows you how to link data in Excel to an Access database.
- Chapter 15, "Using Formulas and Functions," discusses how to create formulas and use Excel's built-in functions to perform calculations, using data in the worksheet.
- Chapter 16, "Creating and Printing Reports and Charts," explains how to print worksheet data.

Chapter 18

Automating with Excel Macros

by Diane Tinney

A key feature of any serious application today is the capability to help users automate repetitive tasks. Since the introduction of macros (originally termed the "typing alternative") over 10 years ago, users have pushed macro languages farther than ever imagined. Vendors responded by enhancing their macro languages, adding more and more features usually only found in higher-level programming languages, such as BASIC, FORTRAN, and C. Macros have evolved into complex programs that create and display custom menus, prompt users for input, and perform complex analysis of data.

Excel provides the power of an advanced macro language without requiring you to learn a complex programming language. Using the macro recorder, you can record your keystrokes and mouse clicks in macros. Then, when you need to repeat that process, just run the macro and let Excel do the work for you!

In this chapter, you learn to

- Record a macro
- Run a macro
- Change macro options
- Attach a macro to a toolbar button
- Attach a macro to the Tools menu
- Use the Personal Macro Workbook

Recording a Macro

When you find that you are repeating the same set of keystrokes and mouse clicks over and over again, it's time to automate the process by recording a macro. A *macro* is a list of instructions that you want Excel to run. The macro recorder captures your keystrokes and mouse clicks, translates them into the macro language instructions that Excel understands, and writes them on a module sheet in your workbook. You then can run the macro instead of pressing the same keys and mouse buttons over and over again.

The macro recorder can record the process of selecting ranges, menu commands, or dialog-box options. Some common tasks to record include the following:

- Setting up a new worksheet
- Importing or exporting data
- Applying a common set of formats to a specified range
- Changing data in a specified column
- Setting up for a certain printer and printing a specified range
- Opening workbooks and selecting a certain view
- Performing a query
- Selecting cells and playing sound notes

► "Understanding Visual Basic for Applications" p. 895

► "Understanding Why Objects Are Special" p. 896

► "Learning More with On-Line Help," p. 898

Note

Excel Version 5.0 is the first Microsoft Office product to implement the common macro language called Visual Basic, Applications Edition (VBA). Microsoft plans to incorporate this powerful application language across Microsoft Office products so that there is only one programming language to learn.

The old Excel macro language of Excel Version 4.0 can be used in Excel Version 5.0. In fact, you can choose to record a macro in Excel Version 4.0 language. However, Microsoft does not plan to make many future enhancements to the Excel Version 4.0 macro language.

In this chapter, macros will be recorded in VBA format. This chapter covers the basics of recording and playing a macro, along with some tips on using macros. Chapter 43, "Using Visual Basic for Applications," introduces you to the language of Visual Basic, Applications Edition.

Planning the Macro

Before starting to record a macro, you should take some time to plan the task that you want to record. Although you can edit recorded macros, it is always easier to do it right the first time. Verify that all files you need in your macro are where they should be. Write down file names and paths that you might need to type. Walk through the process a few times manually, so that your recording session produces the desired result. Consider other methods to accomplish the same task. Wherever possible, make macros generic so that they can be used on other worksheets or in other areas of the same worksheet.

Starting the Macro Recorder

To start the macro recorder, follow these steps:

1. Click the Record Macro button on the Visual Basic toolbar, or choose the **T**ools **R**ecord Macro **R**ecord New Macro command. Excel displays the Record New Macro dialog box (see fig. 18.1).

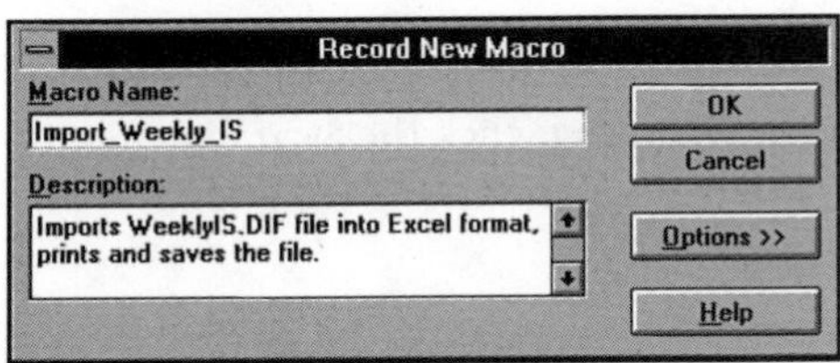

Fig. 18.1
The Record New Macro dialog box prompts you to name and describe your macro.

2. Enter a name for the macro in the **M**acro Name text box. When naming your macro, keep these guidelines in mind:

   - Begin the macro name with a letter.
   - The name can contain letters, numbers, or underscores.
   - Do not include spaces or punctuation marks.
   - Names can be up to 255 characters long.

3. (Optional) Enter a description for the macro in the **D**escription text box.

4. Click OK or press Enter. Excel opens a Stop Macro button in its own toolbar, returns to the worksheet, and displays `Recording` in the status bar (see fig. 18.2).

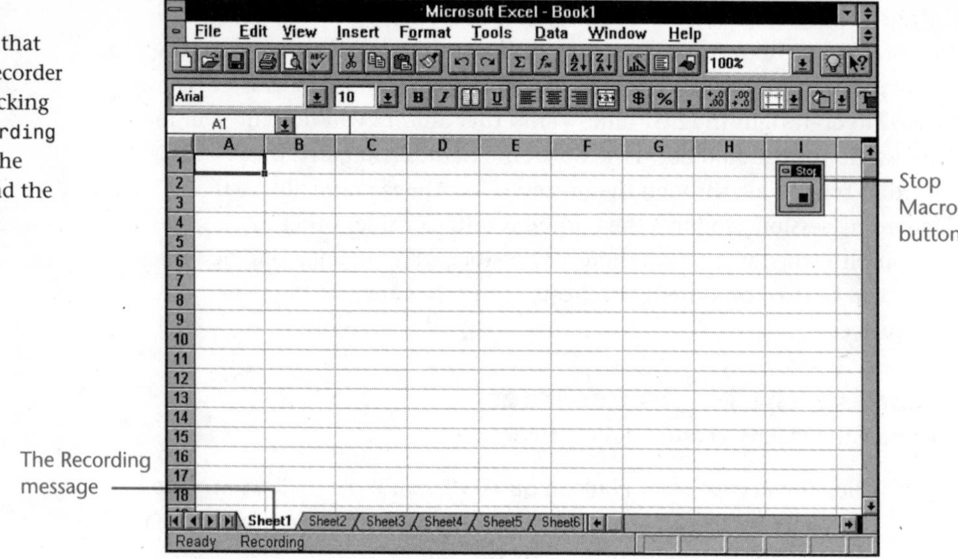

Fig. 18.2
You can tell that the macro recorder is on by checking for the `Recording` message in the status bar and the Stop Macro button.

5. Perform the actions you need to record.

6. When you finish recording, click the Stop Macro button or choose the **T**ools **R**ecord Macro **S**top Recording command.

Using the Macro Recorder To Automate a Task

Suppose that you receive an income statement, downloaded from a mainframe, each week in a DIF file. Each week you need to do the following:

1. Open the file in Excel.
2. Set column widths.
3. Add a report title.
4. Print the income statement.
5. Save the file in Excel XLS format.

Rather than baby-sit the computer each week, you could record a macro and let Excel handle the entire task for you. Figures 18.3 through 18.6 illustrate the recording of this process as a macro named Import_Weekly_IS. Note that dialog-box selections, mouse drags, and file-save settings are recorded.

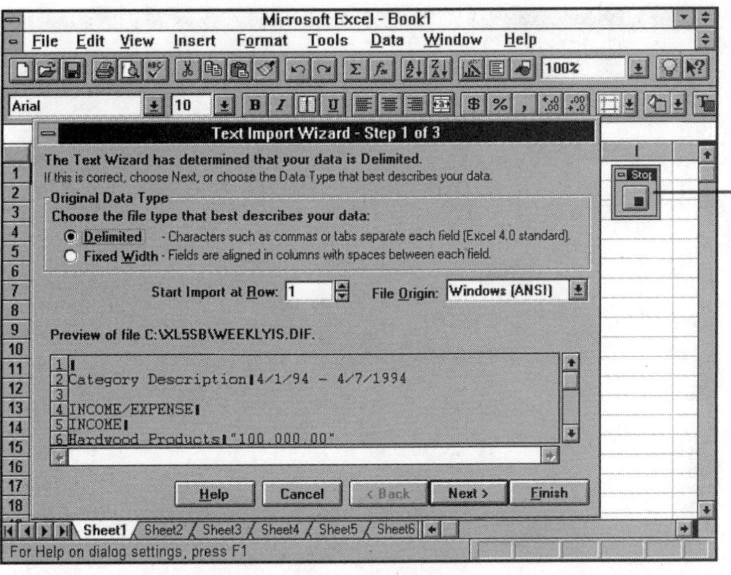

Fig. 18.3
Recording the opening of a DIF file, complete with Text Import Wizard selections.

The presence of the Stop button indicates this action is being recorded.

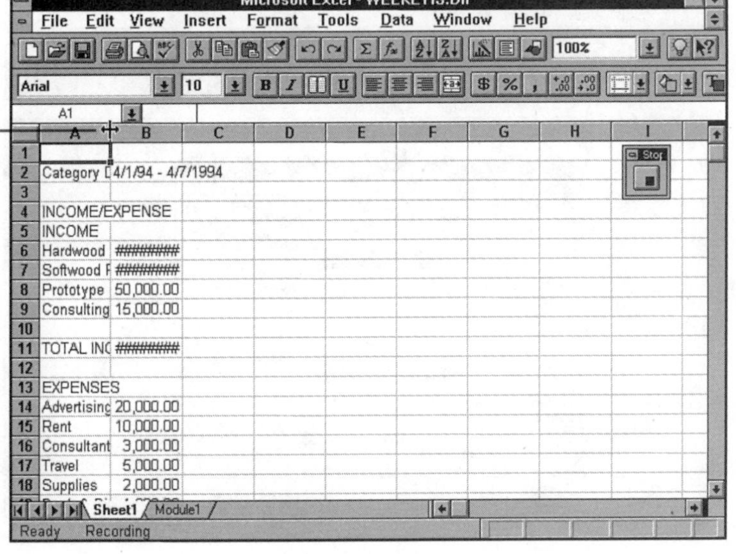

Resizing column

Fig. 18.4
Recording can also capture the dragging of a column divider line to record a new column width.

III

Using Excel

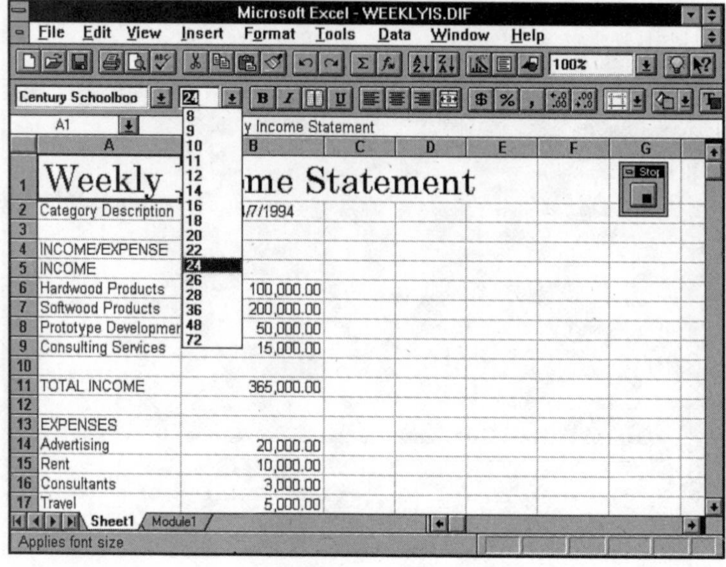

Fig. 18.5
You can automate the process of changing format settings, such as fonts, and entering data, such as a report header.

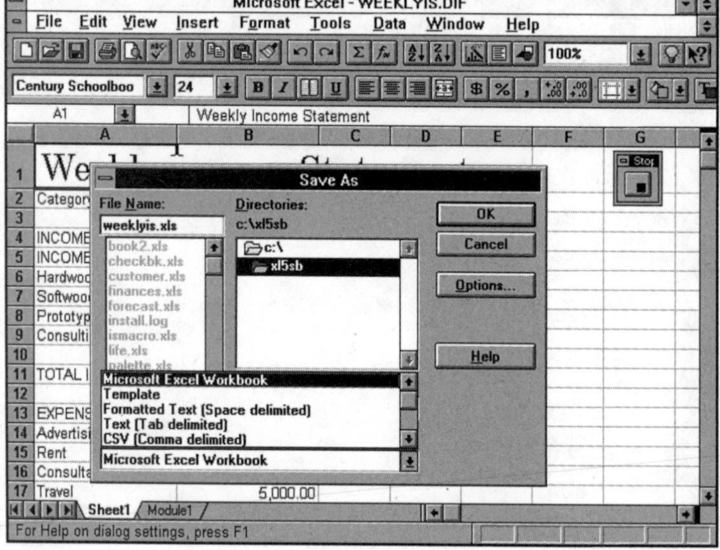

Fig. 18.6
Dialog-box settings, such as the Save As dialog box file name and type, are automatically recorded in the macro.

Troubleshooting

When I recorded the macro, I chose some incorrect menu commands and painted the wrong area. The macro works, but each time it runs, the mistakes are repeated.

You can edit the mistakes out. Excel records the macros on the Module pages of your workbook. You can view and edit the macros on these pages. See Chapter 43, "Using Visual Basic for Applications," for more information on how to safely edit your recorded macro.

I need to record more steps in an existing macro.

To record new steps in an existing macro, choose the Tools Macro command and select the desired macro. Excel displays the macro module page. Place the insertion point where you want to start recording. Choose the Tools Record Macro Mark Position for Recording command. Then choose the Tools Record Macro Record at Mark command to begin recording new steps.

While recording my macro, I pressed the undo key. Now each time the macro runs, the data changes are discarded.

You need to remove the undo command from your recorded macro. See Chapter 43, "Using Visual Basic for Applications," for more information on how to safely edit your recorded macro.

▶ "Starting the Recorder," p. 899

▶ "Recording a Procedure," p. 899

▶ "Stopping the Recorder," p. 900

Running a Macro

After you have recorded a macro, the next step is to test the macro. Before testing the macro, make backups of any worksheets on which the macro operates.

▶ "Running the Procedure," p. 902

To run a macro, follow these steps:

1. Choose the **T**ools **M**acro command, or click the Run button on the Visual Basic toolbar. Excel opens the Macro dialog box (see fig. 18.7).

2. Select or type the name of the macro you want to run.
3. Click Run. Excel runs the macro.

Press Esc to stop running a macro at any time, or choose Pause or Stop on the Visual Basic toolbar.

▶ "Understanding the Procedure," p. 903

▶ "Using the Debugging Tools," p. 940

After you run the Import_Weekly_IS macro, the worksheet looks like figure 18.8. The macro runs uninterrupted, except for one pause to ask for confirmation on saving the file, since the file name previously existed. The final step in the macro prints the worksheet.

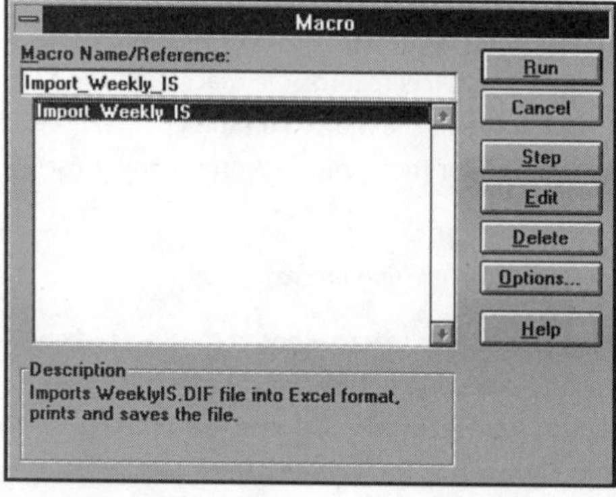

Fig. 18.7 To run a macro, open the Macro dialog box and click Run.

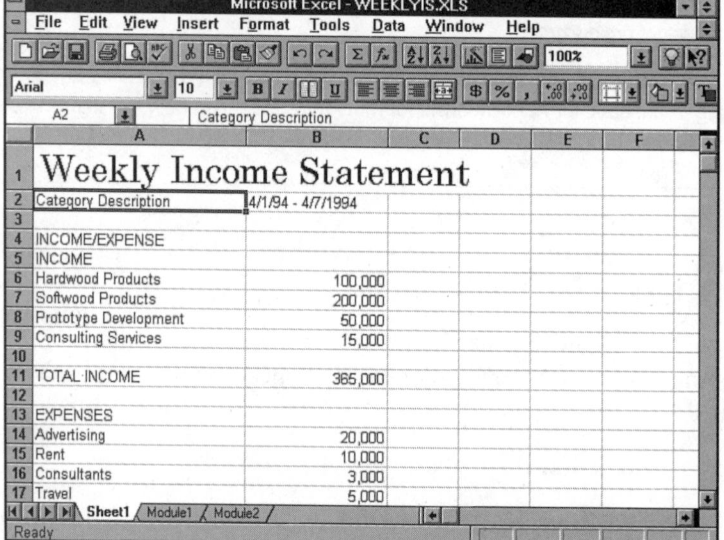

Fig. 18.8 The Import_Weekly_IS macro produces this Excel worksheet.

Changing Macro Options

When you record a new macro, you can set various macro options by using the **O**ptions button in the Record New Macro dialog box (see fig. 18.9). Following is a description of the options available:

- *Assign to Men**u** Item on **T**ools Menu.* Select this box and enter a macro name to be listed on the Tools menu (see fig. 18.10).

- *Assign to Shortcut **K**ey.* Select this box to assign a shortcut key of Ctrl+ a letter that you designate. If a Ctrl+ shortcut key exists for that letter, Excel uses Ctrl+Shift+ the letter.
- *Store in **P**ersonal Macro Workbook.* Select this radio button to save the macro to the Personal Macro Workbook. For more information, see "Using the Personal Macro Workbook" later in this chapter.
- *Store in This **W**orkbook.* Select this radio button to save the macro in the current workbook.
- *Store in **N**ew Workbook.* Select this radio button to save the macro in another workbook.
- *Language **V**isual Basic.* Select this radio button to record the macro using Visual Basic for Applications (VBA).
- *Language MS **E**xcel 4.0 Macro.* Select this radio button to record the macro using the old macro language in Microsoft Excel Version 4.0.

Fig. 18.9
The Options button in the Record New Macro dialog box allows you to determine where the macro is stored, assign a macro to the Tools menu, assign a shortcut key, and select the macro language in which to record.

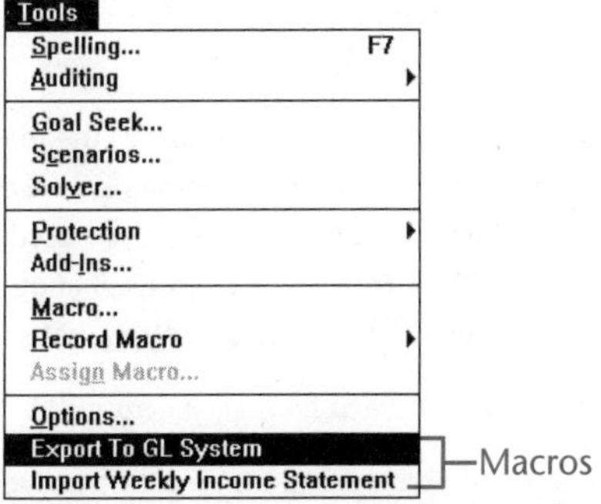

Fig. 18.10
You can add the macros you use most often to the Tools menu.

For existing macros, use the **O**ptions button in the Macro dialog box to access different options. Now the Macro Options dialog box contains a Help Information section, instead of the Store In and Language sections (see fig. 18.11). The Help Information section includes the following options:

- ***F**unction Category*. Select the function category.
- ***S**tatus Bar Text.* Enter text to display in the status bar when the macro runs.
- *Help **C**ontext ID.* Enter the text ID (number) to make the help context-sensitive.
- *Help File **N**ame.* Enter the name of the file that contains the Help Information.

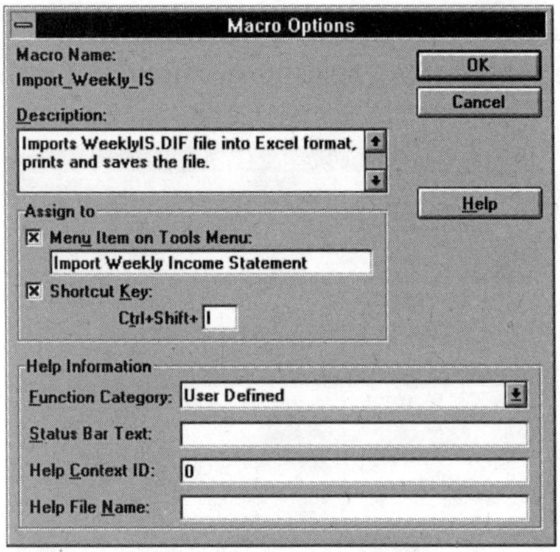

Fig. 18.11
For an existing macro, the Macro Options dialog box allows you to assign the macro to the Tools menu, assign a shortcut key, and provide Help text.

Troubleshooting

I assigned a shortcut key to my macro, but it doesn't work.

Check to make sure that the workbook containing the macro is open. Then choose the Tools Macro command, select the macro name, and click the Options button. Verify the shortcut key assigned and note that if you used a capital letter, Ctrl+A is not the same as Ctrl+Shift+A. Finally, check to see if another macro is using the same shortcut key. Excel will run the first macro that has that shortcut key.

I get a Macro Error dialog box when I run my macro.

The worksheet that the macro operates on must be active for the macro to run.

The macro I recorded is on a worksheet tab called Macro1, and the commands all start with an equal sign.

You have recorded an Excel 4.0 macro. If you meant to record a Visual Basic macro, click the Options button in the Record New Macro dialog box and select the Visual Basic language option. Then rerecord the macro.

Adding Macros to Sheet Buttons and Toolbars

In the last section, you learned how to add a macro to the Tools menu to make a macro more accessible. You also can assign macros to a button object on your sheet or to a toolbar to make them even more accessible.

To assign a macro to a sheet button, follow these steps:

1. Display the Drawing toolbar.
2. Click the Create Button button on the Drawing toolbar.
3. Position the mouse pointer where you want to create the button, click, and drag until the button is the desired size.
4. Excel displays the Assign Macro dialog box (see fig. 18.12).

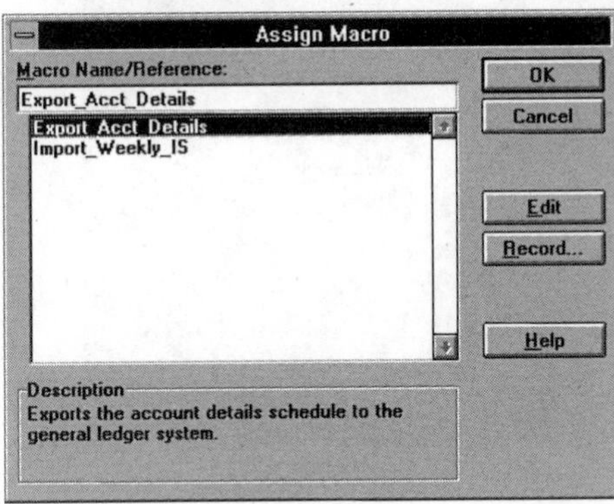

Fig. 18.12
You can assign a macro to a button object on a sheet.

Tip

To add a macro to a custom toolbar button, select the Custom category and drag the desired button icon to the toolbar.

5. Select an existing macro and click OK, or click **R**ecord to create a new macro that will automatically be assigned to the button.

6. With the button still selected, click the label and type an appropriate name for the button.

7. Click anywhere on the sheet, or press Esc to deselect the button.

8. Test the button.

To assign a macro to a button on a toolbar, follow these steps:

1. Choose the **V**iew **T**oolbars command, and click the **C**ustomize button. Excel displays the Customize dialog box (see fig. 18.13).

2. At this point, all displayed toolbars are inactive. If the desired toolbar and button is visible on-screen, select the button and choose the **T**ools **A**ssign Macro command (see fig. 18.14).

3. If the desired button is not visible, select the appropriate category from the **C**ategories list box (see fig. 18.15) and drag the button to a toolbar. Excel opens the Assign Macro dialog box.

4. Select or record the desired macro to assign to the toolbar button. Click OK.

5. Close the Customize dialog box.

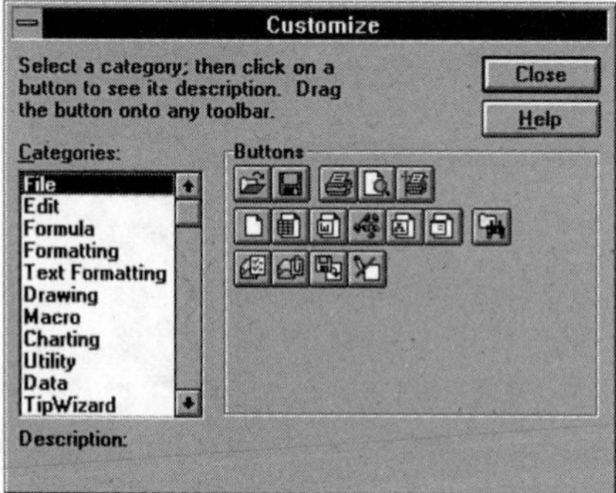

Fig. 18.13
Use the Customize dialog box to select a button to which to assign a macro.

Note

You can access the Assign Macro dialog box for an existing button object from the shortcut menu, by clicking the right mouse button, while pointing at the button, and selecting Assign Macro.

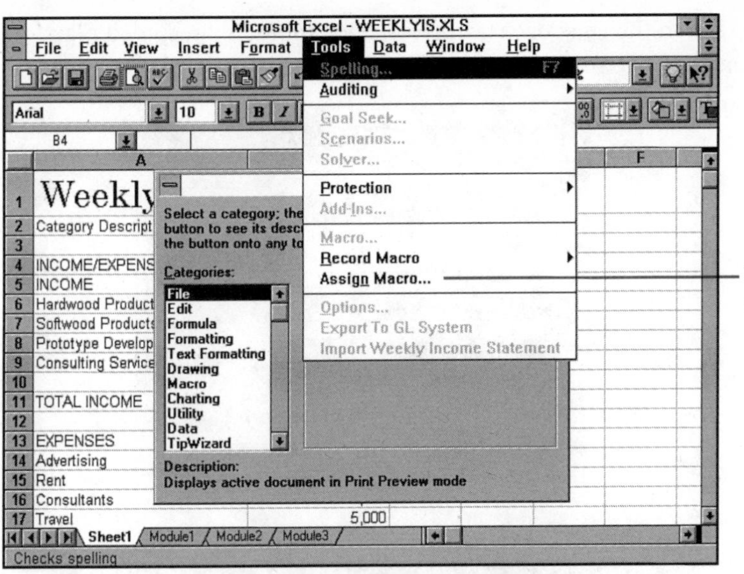

Fig. 18.14 As you select toolbar buttons, Excel describes the button in the Customize dialog box.

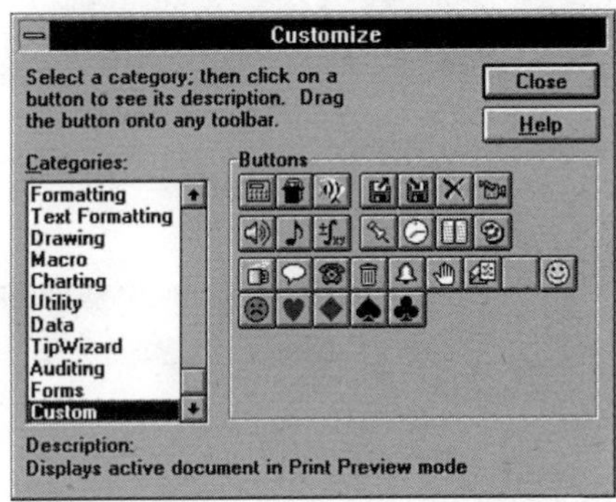

Fig. 18.15 The Custom category provides many buttons you can use to create a custom toolbar. Just drag the desired button to a toolbar.

III

Using Excel

Using the Personal Macro Workbook

Sometimes you need to use the same macro in different workbooks. Excel provides a special workbook, called the Personal Macro Workbook, which stores macros that can be used by many workbooks. Excel automatically creates the Personal Macro Workbook the first time you record a macro and select the macro recorder option, *Store in **P**ersonal Macro Workbook* (see fig. 18.16). Excel saves the Personal Macro Workbook in the startup directory (XLSTART), under the file name PERSONAL.XLS. Once created, the Personal Macro Workbook stays on the desktop as a hidden window. You can show the Personal Macro Workbook by choosing the **W**indow **U**nhide command and selecting the PERSONAL.XLS window. Figure 18.17 shows a macro

► "Customizing Predefined Toolbars," p. 887

► "Creating a Custom Toolbar," p. 889

recorded in the Personal Macro Workbook (note that recorded macros are automatically translated into Visual Basic commands).

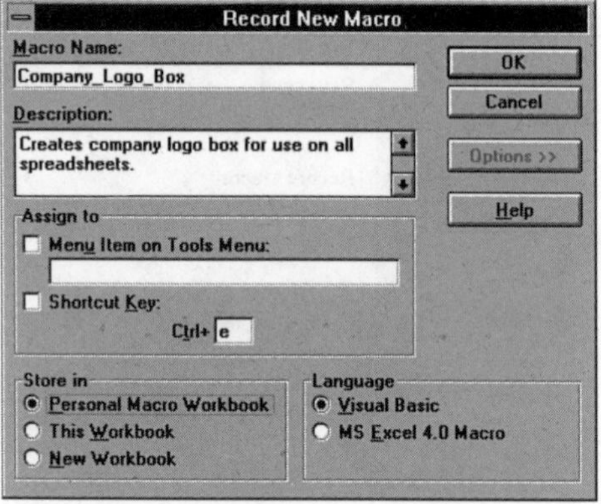

Fig. 18.16
To create global macros, record them in the Personal Macro Workbook.

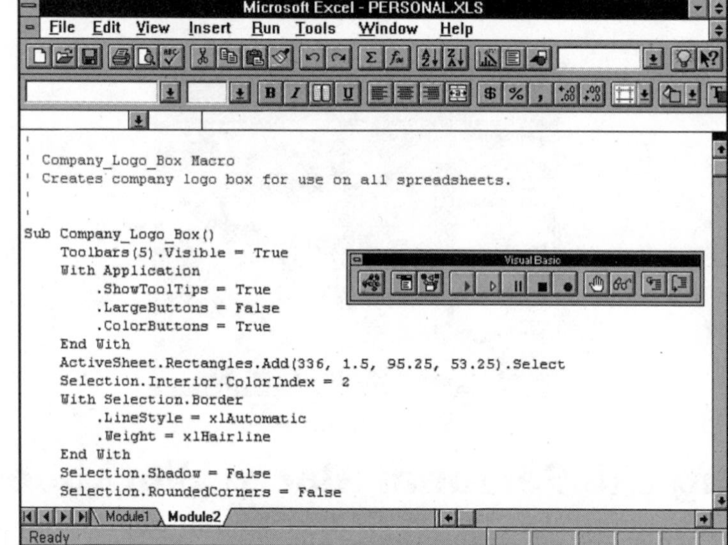

Fig. 18.17
To display the Personal Macro Workbook, choose the Window Unhide command.

► "Examining the Procedure," p. 900

► "Understanding the Procedure," p. 903

► "Understanding Functions and Procedures," p. 912

The ability to record and store global macros allows you to create a toolbox of handy macros. You can also use global macros and the Personal Macro Workbook to help standardize spreadsheet development in your organization. By providing everyone with the same macro toolbox, you will enhance productivity and efficiency for everyone using Excel.

From Here...

Now that you are familiar with working with Excel, you are ready to use Excel with some of the other Microsoft Office applications. To learn more about using Excel with other Microsoft Office applications, refer to the following chapters:

- Chapters 35 to 41 in Part VI, "Working Together with Microsoft Office Applications," provide real life business scenarios that illustrate how to use the Microsoft Office programs together to accomplish various business tasks.
- Chapter 42, "Changing Toolbars and Menus," shows how to customize toolbars and menus.
- Chapter 43, "Using Visual Basic for Applications," teaches you the Visual Basic for Applications (VBA) language in Excel 5.0.

Part IV

Using PowerPoint

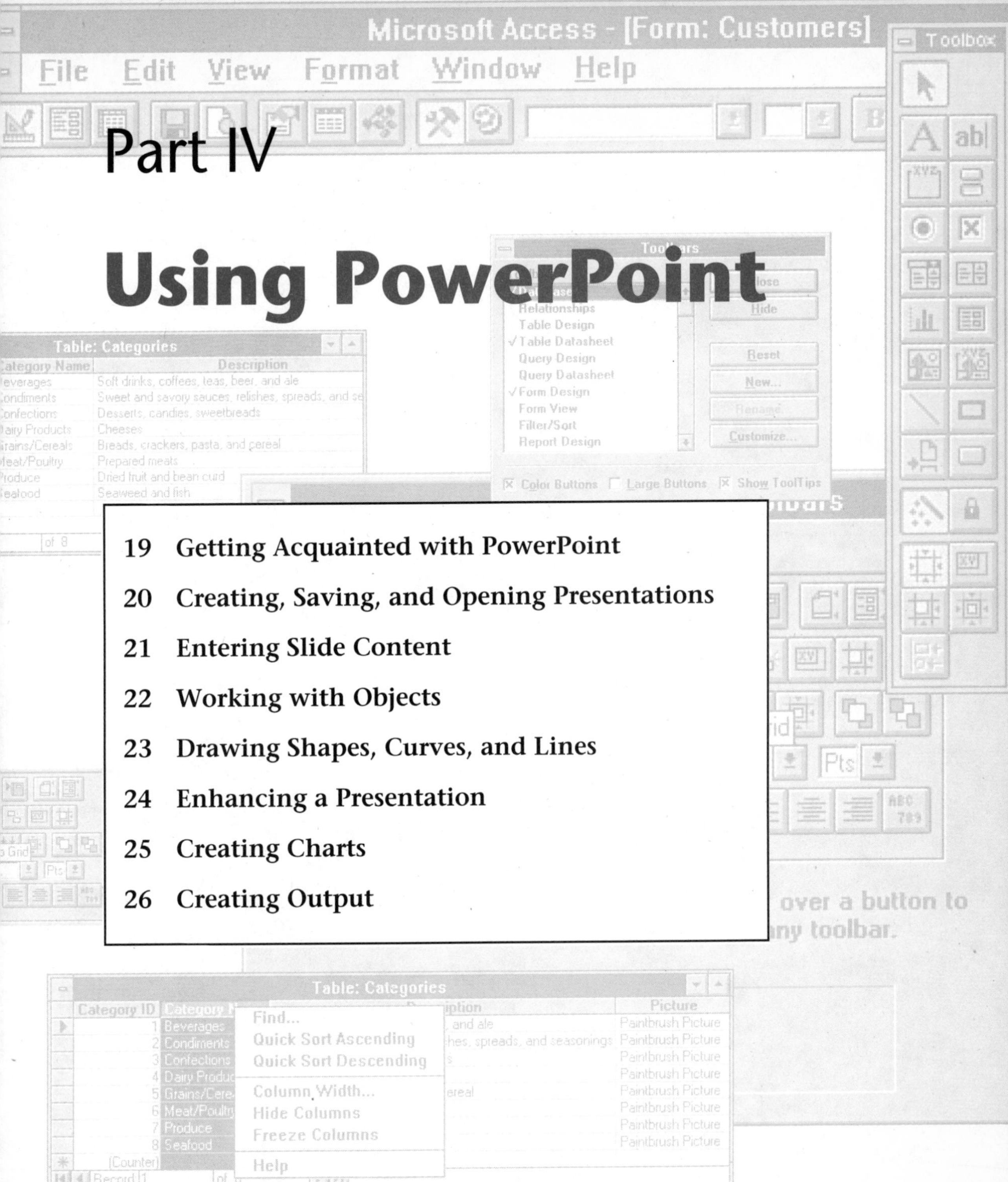

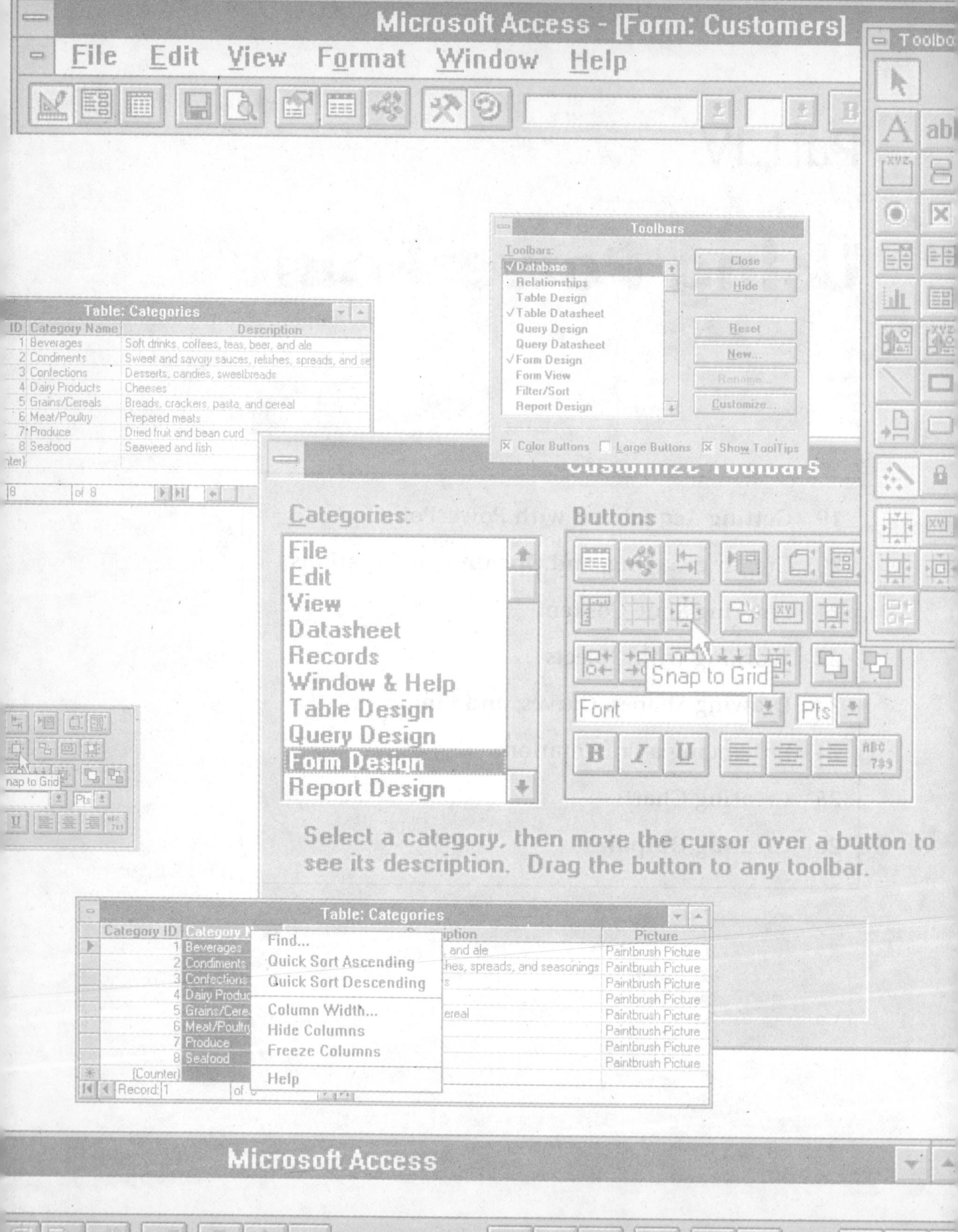

Microsoft Access - [Form: Customers]
File Edit View Format Window Help
Toolbars
Toolbars:
√Database
Relationships
Table Design
√Table Datasheet
Query Design
Query Datasheet
√Form Design
Form View
Filter/Sort
Report Design
Close
Hide
Reset
New...
Rename...
Customize...
Color Buttons
Large Buttons
Show ToolTips
Table: Categories
Customize Toolbars
Categories:
File
Edit
View
Datasheet
Records
Window & Help
Table Design
Query Design
Form Design
Report Design
Buttons
Snap to Grid
Font
Pts
Select a category, then move the cursor over a button to see its description. Drag the button to any toolbar.
Find...
Quick Sort Ascending
Quick Sort Descending
Column Width...
Hide Columns
Freeze Columns
Help
Microsoft Access

Chapter 19

Getting Acquainted with PowerPoint

by Debbie Walkowski

PowerPoint is the component of Microsoft Office that helps you create professional quality overhead, paper, 35mm slide, photoprint, or on-screen presentations. Before working with PowerPoint, you need to familiarize yourself with the PowerPoint window and understand the "theory and process" behind how PowerPoint creates presentations.

In this chapter, look for the following topics:

- Starting and exiting PowerPoint
- Looking at PowerPoint window elements
- Examining components of PowerPoint presentations
- Understanding templates, masters, objects, and layouts
- Adding visuals to PowerPoint slides

Starting and Exiting PowerPoint

You start and exit PowerPoint just like you start and exit any of the applications in Microsoft Office. Click the PowerPoint button in the Microsoft Office toolbar or double-click the PowerPoint button in the Microsoft Office program group. After a few seconds, the PowerPoint window appears. Like other Microsoft Office applications, PowerPoint displays the Tip of the Day dialog box, which contains a new tip each time you start PowerPoint. If you don't want to see the Tip of the Day each time you start PowerPoint, select the Show Tips at Startup check box, in the Tip of the Day dialog box, to

Tip
If you don't see the Microsoft Office toolbar on-screen, return to the Windows Program Manager and double-click the Microsoft Office program button in the Microsoft Office group.

remove the X from the box, then click OK. (You can display tips at any time by choosing the **H**elp Ti**p** of the Day command.)

When you finish using PowerPoint, choose the E**x**it command on the **F**ile menu, or double-click the Control-menu box for the PowerPoint window. If the current file is unsaved, PowerPoint displays a dialog box asking if you want to save the changes you made to the current file. Choose **Y**es if you want to save, **N**o if you don't want to save, or Cancel to return to your file without saving.

Getting Familiar with the PowerPoint Window

After you close the Tip of the Day, PowerPoint automatically displays the dialog box shown in figure 19.1. This dialog box lets you choose how you want to create a presentation. PowerPoint offers a variety of methods for creating presentations, which you learn about in Chapter 20.

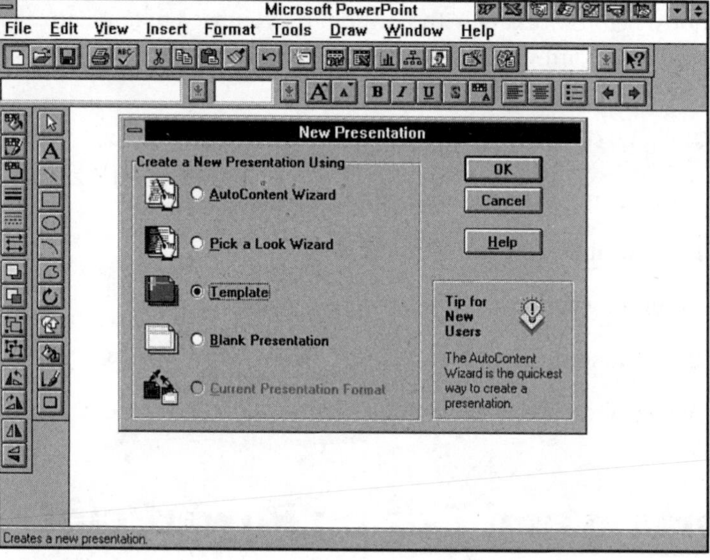

Fig. 19.1
The opening window in PowerPoint.

Tip
If the slide is not full screen, double-click the Slide Window title bar or click the Maximize button.

Figure 19.2 shows what a typical PowerPoint presentation screen might look like after you begin working. The Microsoft Office toolbar appears at the upper right corner of the window. PowerPoint's standard toolbar and menu bar are shown below the window's title bar. Two special drawing toolbars are displayed down the left side of the window. Surrounded by a gray border, the first slide in the presentation is represented by the white area in the middle of the screen (slides are the individual "pages" in a presentation that become overheads, 35mm slides, or an on-screen slide show). Notice that vertical and horizontal scroll bars are now visible on-screen (compare to fig. 19.1). At the left end of the horizontal scroll bar are view tools, used for displaying different views of your presentation. You learn about displaying different views in PowerPoint in Chapter 20, "Creating, Saving, and Opening Presentations."

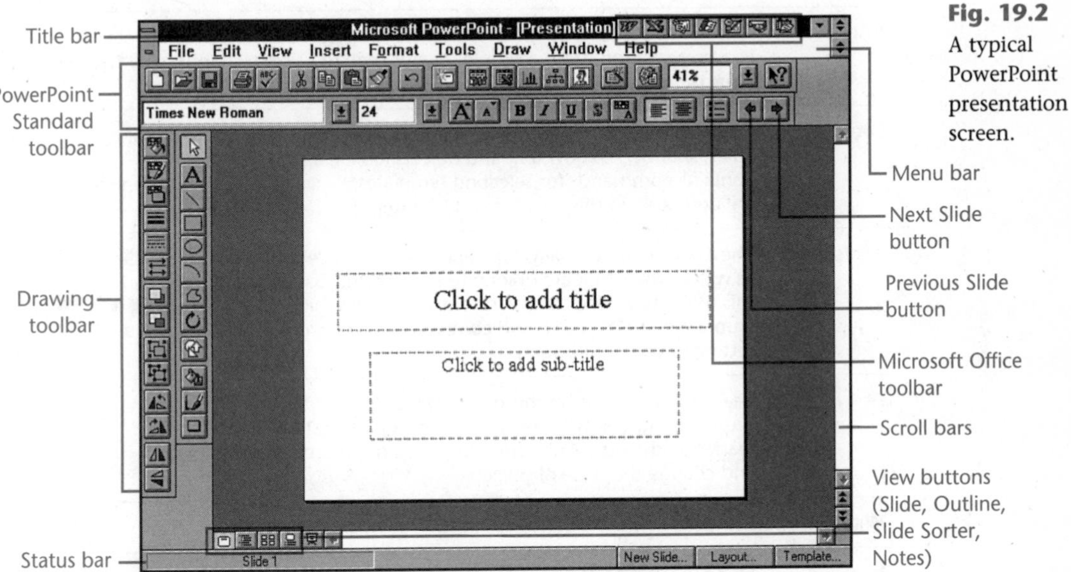

Fig. 19.2 A typical PowerPoint presentation screen.

Window Elements

The menus in PowerPoint are similar to the menus in other Microsoft Office applications. Menus such as File, Window, and Help are standard across all applications. PowerPoint's menus are most similar to Word's, with the Draw menu being unique to PowerPoint. Table 19.1 describes each PowerPoint menu and the types of commands that you find on each.

◄ "Using Menus," p. 35

Table 19.1 PowerPoint Menus

Menu	Description
File	Standard Microsoft Office application File menu.
Edit	Contains commands for undoing, cutting, copying, and pasting. Find (Ctrl+F) and Replace (Ctrl+R) commands are also located on this menu, along with commands for creating links to other files and editing objects.

(continues)

Table 19.1 Continued

Menu	Description
View	Use the View menu to choose the presentation view you want to display on your screen or to display masters. This menu also contains commands for turning on and off the display of toolbars, rulers, and guides (you learn about rulers and guides in the "Displaying Rulers and Guides" section of this chapter). Use this menu also to control the zoom percentage used in a particular view.
Insert	This menu contains commands that let you insert a variety of elements in a presentation, from a simple date or time to ClipArt, graphs, or other objects.
F**o**rmat	Contains commands for changing all aspects (font, alignment, spacing, color, shadow) of how text and objects look in a presentation. Also contains commands for selecting templates, wizards, and layouts, which are described in this chapter and Chapter 20.
Tools	The Tools menu contains typical Microsoft Office tools (such as Spelling) as well as tools that are unique to PowerPoint. Use the commands on this menu to create transitions between slides, hide slides, or recolor or crop a picture. You also find commands for customizing toolbars and setting PowerPoint options.
Draw	Use the commands on this menu to manipulate drawn objects in a presentation. For instance, you can group several objects as one; rearrange the "stacking order" or layers of objects; and rotate, flip, and change the scale of objects.
Window	Standard Microsoft Office application Window menu.
Help	Standard Microsoft Office application Help menu.

► "Viewing a Presentation," p. 449

Along the lower edge of the PowerPoint window is the status bar, which displays the number of the current slide, Slide Master, Outline Master, Handout Master, or Notes Master at the left end; the right end contains three buttons. The New Slide button makes it easy for you to add a new slide to your presentation without choosing the Insert New Slide command (or Ctrl+M). When you click the Layout button, the Slide Layout dialog box appears, from which you can choose a specially designed slide layout. The Template button is used to display the Presentation Template dialog box. You can choose a new template for your presentation at any time by clicking this button. Layouts and templates are described in detail in the "Understanding Masters and Templates" and "Understanding Objects and Layouts" sections later in this chapter.

► "Using PowerPoint's Drawing Tools," p. 495

Above the status bar is the horizontal scroll bar. At the left end are four view buttons. Each button displays a different view of the current presentation. The four buttons are pointed out in figure 19.2 and described in the section "Components of a PowerPoint Presentation" later in this chapter.

PowerPoint's Standard Toolbar

Table 19.2 describes each of the buttons on PowerPoint's Standard toolbar. Each button represents a PowerPoint menu command. You learn how to use most of these buttons in subsequent chapters. Refer to Chapter 23, "Drawing Shapes, Curves, and Lines," for an explanation of the tools on the Drawing toolbar.

Tip
Several non-standard toolbars are available in PowerPoint, which you can display on-screen at any time by using the **V**iew **T**oolbars command. You can also customize toolbars using this command.

Table 19.2 Buttons on PowerPoint's Standard Toolbar

Button	Description
	Displays the New Presentation dialog box.
	Displays the Open dialog box, from which you can choose a presentation file to open.
	Saves the current presentation under the current name and file type. If the presentation has not yet been saved, displays the Save As dialog box.
	Displays the Print dialog box.
	Checks the spelling in the current presentation. Displays the Spelling dialog box if errors are found.
	Removes the selected text or object from the slide and places it on the Windows Clipboard.
	Places a copy of the selected text or object on the Windows Clipboard, leaving the original text or object unchanged.
	Pastes the contents of the Clipboard into the current slide.
	Records all attributes (color, font, shadow, pattern, and so on) of the selected object so you can copy all attributes to another object.
	Reverses the most recent action taken. Note that not all actions (commands) can be reversed.
	Embeds a Microsoft Word table of the size (rows and columns) you specify in your presentation.
	Embeds an Excel worksheet of the size (rows and columns) you specify in your presentation.

(continues)

Table 19.2 Continued

Button	Description
	Embeds a graph in your presentation using the data you specify.
	Embeds an organization chart in your presentation.
	Allows you to insert clip art into your presentation from Microsoft's ClipArt Gallery.
	Starts the Pick a Look Wizard, used for creating a presentation for which you define the style or "look."
	Creates an RTF (Rich Text Format) file in Word using the content of the current presentation.
	Lets you zoom in and out of your presentation.
	The mouse pointer changes to a question mark, which you can use to click any PowerPoint menu command, button, or toolbar for which you want help.
 Times New Roman	Displays a drop-down list of available fonts.
 24	Displays a list of available font sizes.
	Increases font size of selected text to the next available size.
	Decreases font size of selected text to the previous available size.
	Adds or removes boldface to and from selected text (this button toggles on and off with each click).
	Adds or removes italics to and from selected text (this button toggles on and off with each click).
	Adds or removes underlining to and from selected text (this button toggles on and off with each click).
	Adds or removes text shadow to and from selected text (this button toggles on and off with each click).

Button	Description
	Displays eight colors for text in a drop-down list. To choose a different color, click the Other Color option, which displays the Other Color dialog box.
	Left-aligns selected text.
	Centers selected text.
	Adds bullets to selected text (this button toggles on and off with each click).
	Moves selected text to next higher level in an outline.
	Moves selected text to next lower level in an outline.

Displaying Rulers and Guides

When you work with text documents in Word, it's helpful to display horizontal and vertical rulers in the Word window. Because presentation slides contain primarily text, rulers can be useful in PowerPoint as well. Rulers give you a reference point within a slide so that you can see at what point (in inches) a text or drawn object appears. They also help you "plan the space" on a slide and ensure that all slide elements fall within reasonable limits of one another and the slides borders.

Tip
To quickly toggle rulers and guides on and off, click the right mouse button to display the shortcut menu, then click the Ruler or Guides command.

To display rulers in the PowerPoint window, choose the **V**iew **R**ulers command. Rulers appear in one of two states—*drawing* or *text*—depending on the objects that are currently selected on the slide. In figure 19.3, rulers are shown in the *drawing state*, which places the zero point at the *center* of each ruler. This allows you to correctly position objects from the center point to the outer edges of a slide. The position of the mouse is indicated on each ruler by a dashed line. In figure 19.3, the mouse position on each ruler is at approximately 2 1/2 inches. You also can see that the slide is 10 inches wide and 7 1/2 inches long.

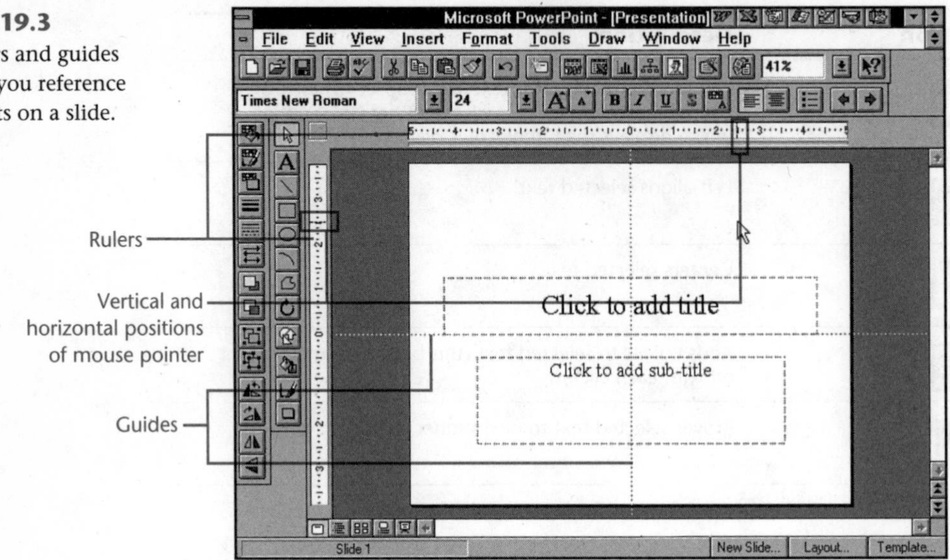

Fig. 19.3
Rulers and guides give you reference points on a slide.

Tip
The View Ruler and View Guides commands toggle on and off. To remove displayed rulers or guides, select the appropriate command again from the View menu.

When it's important to position slide elements precisely or to align certain elements vertically or horizontally, you can choose the **V**iew **G**uides command. This command displays dotted lines vertically and horizontally through the center point of a slide. You use the guides to help you visually align elements on a slide. Guides are shown in figure 19.3. Guides do not appear on printed copies of your slide; they only appear only on-screen while you are working in PowerPoint.

Components of a PowerPoint Presentation

At first you might think that PowerPoint is an application that only lets you create slides for a presentation, but PowerPoint offers much more. It helps you plan, create, and deliver a presentation in a practical way. Think about how a speaker gives a presentation: she might plan the presentation by first creating the outline, then completing the "look" and content of the slides, and, finally, by printing them. While she speaks, the speaker might refer to printed copies of the slides that contain her own handwritten notes. She might also provide copies of her slides to the audience so that they can follow along or take notes.

Slides, *outline*, *speaker's notes*, and *audience handouts* are components of a PowerPoint presentation. To create each of these components without the proper tools could take a great deal of extra time. But PowerPoint makes it easy for you by creating each one automatically. You can use just one component or any combination of the four, depending on your particular requirements.

You can view any of the four components on-screen or print copies. PowerPoint displays slides, as illustrated earlier in figure 19.2, by default. Outline pages look like a typical outline, with main headings aligned at the left margin and lower-level headings indented (see fig. 19.4). Speaker's note pages contain a reduced version of the slide at the top of the page with space at the bottom of the page for the speaker's notes (see fig. 19.5). Audience handouts can contain two, three, or six slides per printed page, as shown in figure 19.6. Notice that when you view audience handouts on-screen, PowerPoint doesn't display the actual slides. Instead, you see dotted frames that outline the location of the slides on the page.

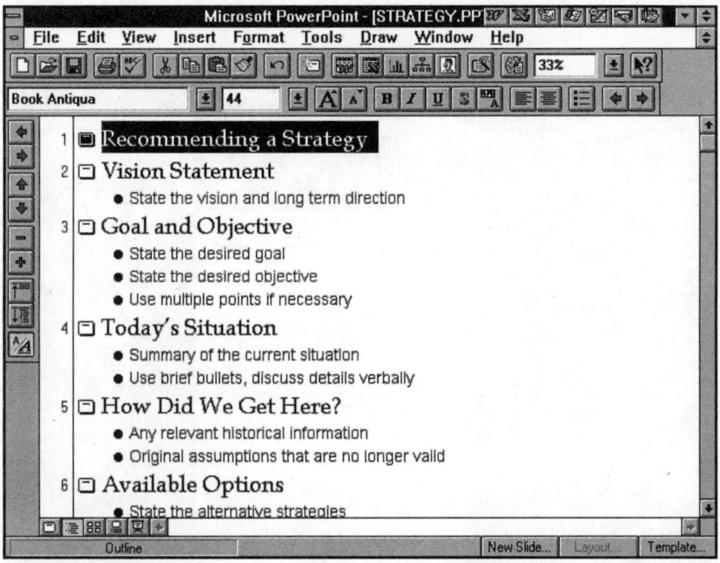

Fig. 19.4 A presentation shown in outline view.

To view slides, the outline, or note pages, choose the **V**iew **S**lides, **V**iew **O**utline, or **V**iew **N**otes Pages command. To view handout pages, choose the **V**iew **M**aster command, then choose Han**d**out Master from the submenu that appears. After you choose a view, the status bar indicates which view is displayed.

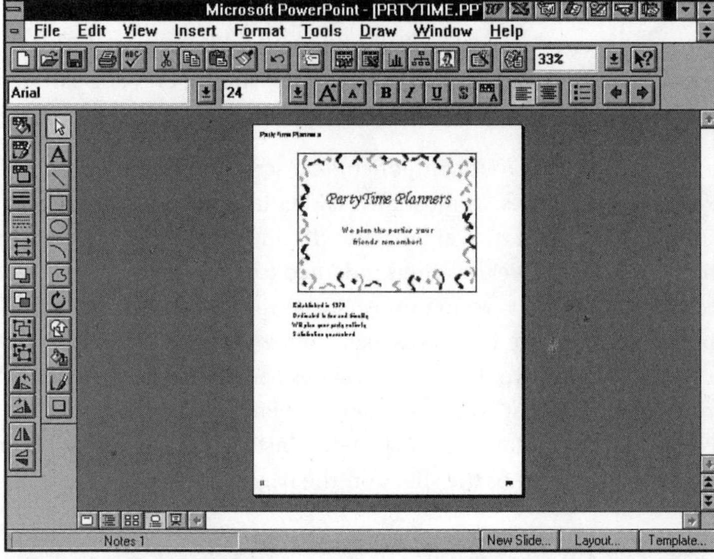

Fig. 19.5
A presentation shown in speaker's notes view.

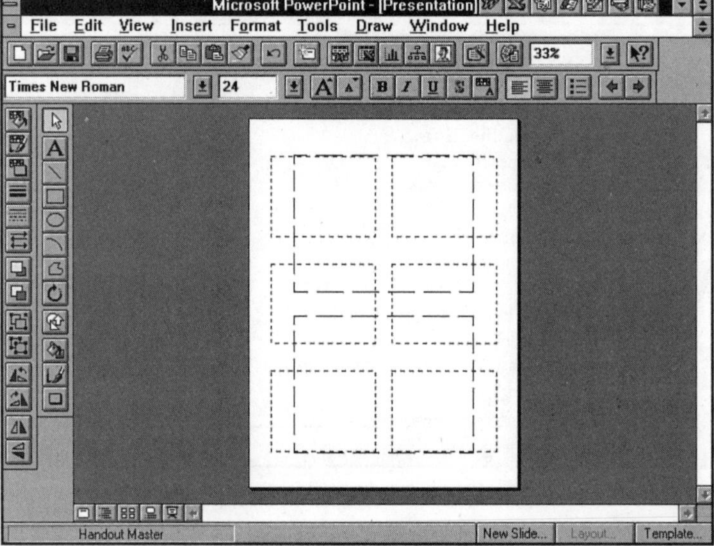

Fig. 19.6
The layout options for audience handout pages are indicated by dotted lines.

▶ "Viewing a Presentation," p. 449

Note

You can quickly display a presentation component by clicking the view buttons at the left end of the horizontal scroll bar. Click the Slide View, Outline View, or Notes View button to display any of these elements. To display handout pages, press and hold the Shift key, then click the Slide Sorter button.

Understanding Masters and Templates

For every presentation you create, PowerPoint creates a set of *masters*: a Slide Master, Outline Master, Notes Master, and Handout Master. Masters correspond directly to the slides, outline, speaker's notes, and handout components of a presentation. Masters contain the elements (text or pictures) that you want to appear on every component page. For instance, if you want your company logo to appear on each of your slides, it isn't necessary to insert the logo on individual slides. You add the logo to the Slide Master and it automatically appears on every slide. Other elements you might add to a master include pictures or clip art, page numbers, the date, the title of the presentation, or reminders such as "Company Confidential."

To display a master, you choose the **V**iew **M**aster command, which displays a submenu. From the submenu, choose **S**lide Master, **O**utline Master, Han**d**out Master, or **N**otes Master. Notice that the left end of the status bar indicates which master is currently displayed. The Slide Master shown in figure 19.7 includes a company name, slide number, and date.

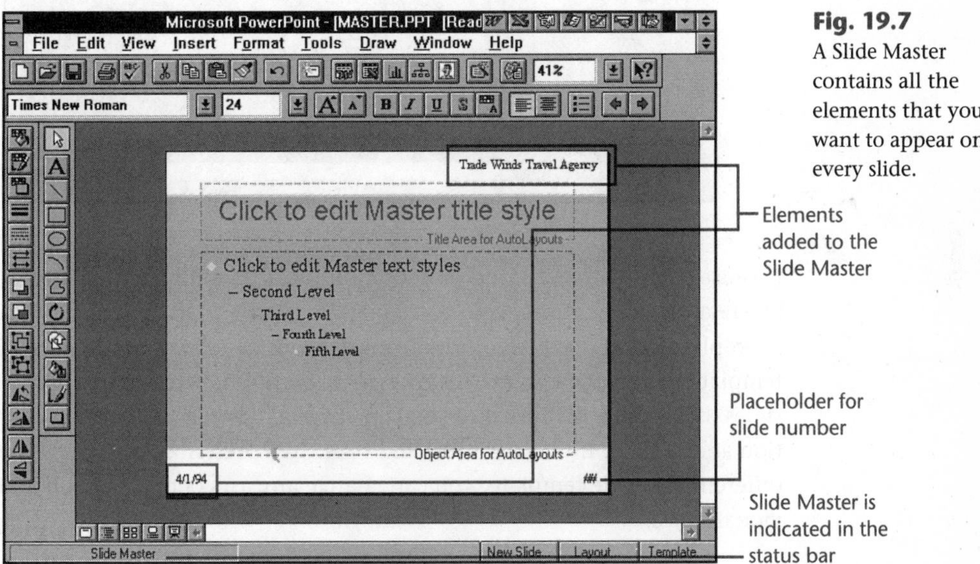

Fig. 19.7
A Slide Master contains all the elements that you want to appear on every slide.

A *template* is a saved presentation file that contains predefined text formatting, color, and graphic elements. Templates are designed by professional graphic artists who understand the use of color, space, and design. Each template is designed to convey a certain look, feel, or attitude. Figure 19.8 shows how the EMBOSSDC.PPT template looks.

Note

You can quickly display a master by using the view buttons at the left end of the horizontal scroll bar. Press and hold the Shift key, then click the slide view (for Slide Master), outline view (for Outline Master), slide sorter view (for Handout Master), or notes view (for Notes Master) button. To return to slide, outline, slide sorter, or notes view, choose the appropriate command from the View menu or click the View button at the lower left corner of the window.

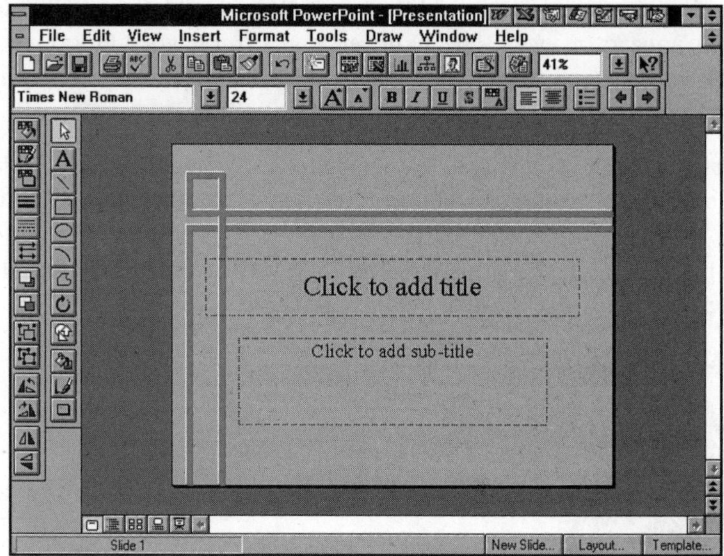

Fig. 19.8 The EMBOSSDC.PPT template conveys a formal image.

Because a template is a saved presentation file, it contains a Slide Master, where all the formatting, color, and graphic elements are defined. You select a template based on the look you want for your presentation, then apply the template to your new or existing presentation file. The template applies to all slides in the presentation, and you can apply a new template to a presentation at any time. If you want selected slides in a presentation to have a look different than the template, you can change any aspect of a slide on an individual basis.

▶ "Creating a New Presentation," p. 439

PowerPoint contains three sets of template files; one for black-and-white overheads, one for color overheads, and one for on-screen slide shows. Each set contains templates of the same style, but the colors are different depending on the output you'll be using. For instance, templates designed for black-and-white overheads make use of many shades of gray. Templates designed for color overheads make use of a wide variety of colors, but seldom use dark backgrounds for a slide. Of the three, the on-screen slide-show templates make the most dramatic use of color, often using dark backgrounds and high-contrast colors for text. Templates are found under the PowerPoint directory in the template subdirectory, under the names BWOVRHD, CLROVRHD, and SLDSHOW.

When you create a new "blank" presentation, you use PowerPoint's default template called DEFAULT.PPT. It appears not to be a template at all because it contains no color (except black and white), no graphic elements, and no stylistic formatting. Figure 19.3, shown earlier in this chapter, illustrates the DEFAULT.PPT template. This is the template you use if you want complete control over your presentation's design, color scheme, and graphic elements because it lets you start as much "from scratch" as possible. You can, however, modify aspects of *any* template, not just the DEFAULT.PPT template.

Understanding Objects and Layouts

PowerPoint slides are made up of *objects*; they are the key elements in any slide. Any time you add text, a graph, a drawing, an organization chart, clip art, a Word table, an Excel spreadsheet, or any other inserted element into a slide, it becomes an object. To work with an object, you select it and then change its content or size, move, copy, or delete it. You also can change *attributes* of an object, such as its color, shadow, border, and so on.

If you don't feel confident positioning or arranging objects on a slide, you can let PowerPoint do the work for you by using AutoLayouts. AutoLayouts save you the time and trouble of creating new objects for a new slide, then arranging, positioning, and aligning them. Each AutoLayout contains placeholders for various kinds of objects such as text, clip art, organization charts, and so on. Placeholders appear as faint dotted lines on the slide and contain identifying text, such as "double-click to add clip art" or "click to add text."

Each AutoLayout contains different object placeholders in different arrangements. For instance, the AutoLayout for a presentation title page contains two text placeholders: one for a slide title and one for a subtitle. The title page AutoLayout is shown earlier in figure 19.3. The AutoLayout in figure 19.9 shows three placeholders: one for a slide title, one for text, and one for clip art.

Whenever you add a new slide to a presentation, PowerPoint automatically displays the New Slide dialog box (see fig. 19.10).

Fig. 19.9
AutoLayouts take the busywork out of arranging objects on a slide.

▶ "Reviewing AutoLayout," p. 457

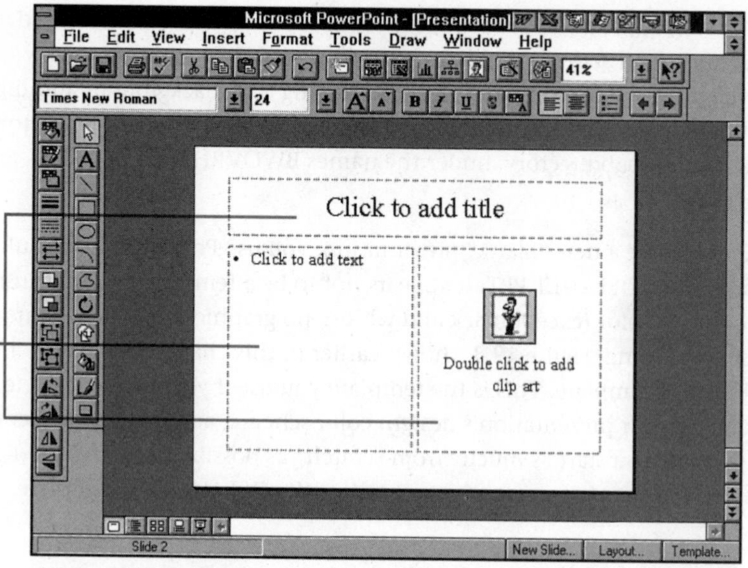

Object placeholders

Fig. 19.10
The New Slide dialog box displays a variety of AutoLayouts.

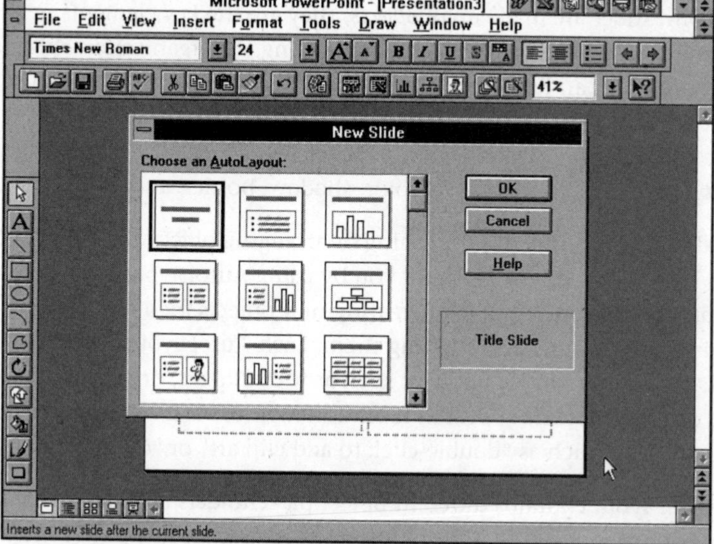

Visuals You Can Add to PowerPoint Slides

There is no reason for a PowerPoint presentation to contain dull slides full of nothing but text. PowerPoint lets you add many different types of objects to your slides to grab an audience's attention, add interest or humor, or to illustrate a particular point. Some objects you can create from within PowerPoint; others you can import from other applications. To insert an object in a PowerPoint slide, you choose an option on the **I**nsert menu or use one of the buttons on the Standard toolbar. Options available on the Insert menu are summarized in Table 19.3. Refer to Chapter 21, "Entering Slide Content," for more information about inserting objects in a presentation.

Table 19.3 Objects You Can Insert in PowerPoint Slides

Object Type	Description
ClipArt	The ClipArt Gallery is a collection of prepared illustrations that depict a wide variety of items and topics. ClipArt is an excellent choice if you don't feel confident about your drawing abilities.
Picture	If you have access to other prepared artwork, such as a bitmap file, you can insert it in a PowerPoint slide. (PowerPoint recognizes 19 different picture file formats.)
Microsoft Word Table	Because Microsoft Word is part of Microsoft Office, you have quick and easy access to Word if you want to insert a table in a slide. The Word table can contain up to 15 columns and up to 4 rows.
Microsoft Graph	Microsoft Graph is an embedded application that lets you create a chart or graph from spreadsheet data. You create the graph similar to the way you create a graph from spreadsheet data in Excel.
Object	The Object option on the Insert menu gives you access to a wide variety of object types such as Microsoft Excel spreadsheets and charts, Microsoft Equation, Word documents, Paintbrush pictures, Microsoft WordArt, Note-It, and OrgCharts. You even can add sound as an object.

From Here...

This chapter has given you a brief overview of PowerPoint, its design, and its capabilities. For in-depth discussions of specific topics, refer to the following chapters:

- Chapter 20, "Creating, Saving, and Opening Presentations," describes the various methods for creating a new presentation file and how to switch your view of a presentation. You also learn how to save, close, and open a PowerPoint presentation file.

- Chapter 21, "Entering Slide Content," describes the basics of entering the content of a presentation and labeling objects. This chapter also describes how to create a Word table, an Excel spreadsheet, and an organization chart in a PowerPoint presentation. You also learn how to insert objects from sources outside PowerPoint.
- Chapter 22, "Working with Objects," describes what objects are, how to select and group them, and how to move, copy, resize, align, rotate, flip, and stack objects.
- Chapter 23, "Drawing Shapes, Curves, and Lines," describes how to use PowerPoints drawing tools to add objects to your slides.
- Chapter 24, "Enhancing a Presentation," describes how to add color, borders, shadows, and other enhancements to your presentation.
- Chapter 25, "Creating Charts," teaches you how to use Microsoft Graph, an embedded application that lets you create a wide variety of graph types from spreadsheet data.
- In Chapter 26, "Creating Output," you learn how to print all the components of a presentation and how to create an on-screen slide show.

Chapter 20

Creating, Saving, and Opening Presentations

by Debbie Walkowski

To work with PowerPoint, you need to understand how to create a new presentation, save a presentation you want to keep, and open an existing presentation when you want to work with it again.

In this chapter, you learn to

- Create a new presentation using a variety of methods
- Change your view of a presentation
- Add, insert, and delete slides
- Save and close a presentation and open an existing one

Creating a New Presentation

To give you the greatest amount of flexibility, PowerPoint offers a variety of ways to create a new presentation. You can create a "blank" presentation that contains no color or style enhancements; you can copy the appearance of an existing presentation; or you can get step-by-step help in creating a presentation by using a wizard (wizards are described in the following section of this chapter).

The options for creating a presentation appear in the New Presentation dialog box, shown in figure 20.1. You display this dialog box by choosing the **F**ile **N**ew command or by pressing Ctrl+N.

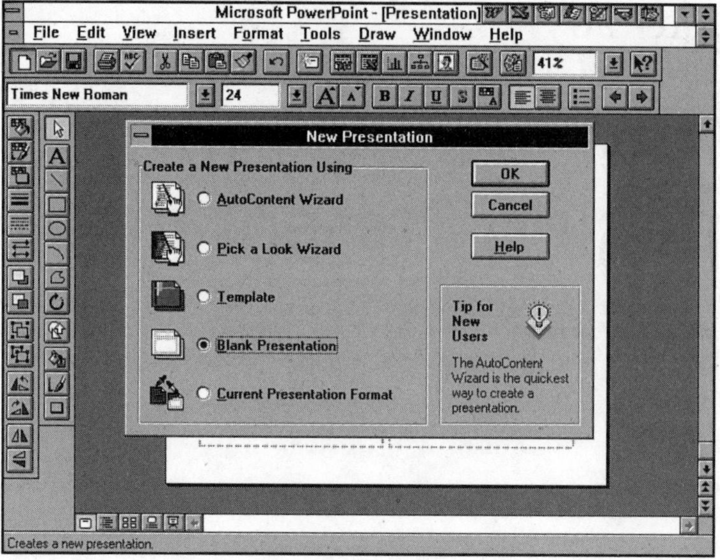

Fig. 20.1
Use the New Presentation dialog box to choose a method of creating a presentation.

Note

The first time you start PowerPoint, the dialog box shown in figure 20.1 has the title PowerPoint. After you begin working with PowerPoint, the name of the dialog box changes to New Presentation.

The following sections describe in greater detail each method of creating a new presentation.

Creating a Presentation Using a Wizard

A *wizard* is a guided on-line script that asks you to respond to questions related to the task you are performing—in this case, creating the framework for a new presentation. Through a series of dialog boxes, you enter your responses to specific questions related to the task. Then, using the information you supply, the wizard creates the new presentation file. Wizards are designed to help you perform unfamiliar tasks and tasks that you feel uncertain about accomplishing without assistance. In PowerPoint, you use a wizard to create a presentation when you want to define all aspects of the presentation at the time you create it; the wizard makes sure you don't forget any steps in the process.

Using the AutoContent Wizard

PowerPoint offers two wizards for creating a new presentation. The first, the AutoContent Wizard, suggests the content and outline of your presentation based on the type of presentation you're creating. For example, if your presentation is designed to introduce or sell a new product, the AutoContent Wizard suggests that you include the following topics:

- Objective
- Customer Requirements
- Features
- Competitive Strengths
- Key Benefits
- Next Steps

You can use the topics exactly as suggested or modify them to suit your needs. Besides helping you sell a new product, AutoContent wizards can help you create presentations for training, recommending a strategy, reporting progress, and communicating bad news (see fig. 20.2). For all other types of presentations, you might choose the General option, which suggests generic contents such as the topic of discussion, main ideas, examples, and summary.

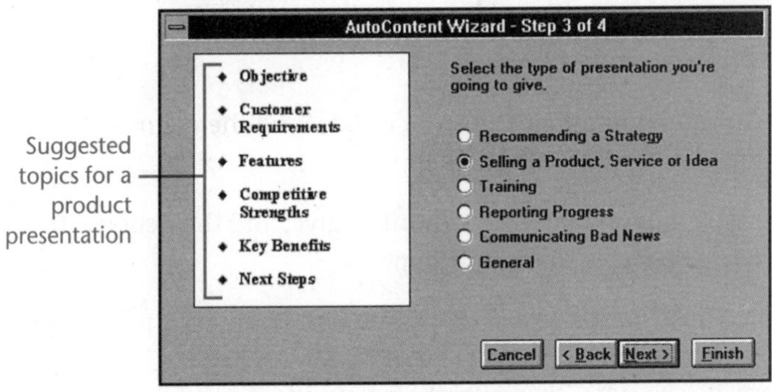

Fig. 20.2
This dialog box lists presentation types and shows suggested topics.

To use the AutoContent Wizard, follow these steps:

1. Choose **F**ile **N**ew or press Ctrl+N. PowerPoint displays the New Presentation dialog box.

2. Select the **A**utoContent Wizard option, and then choose OK. The AutoContent Wizard dialog box appears (see fig. 20.3). Notice that the title bar says `Step 1 of 4`.

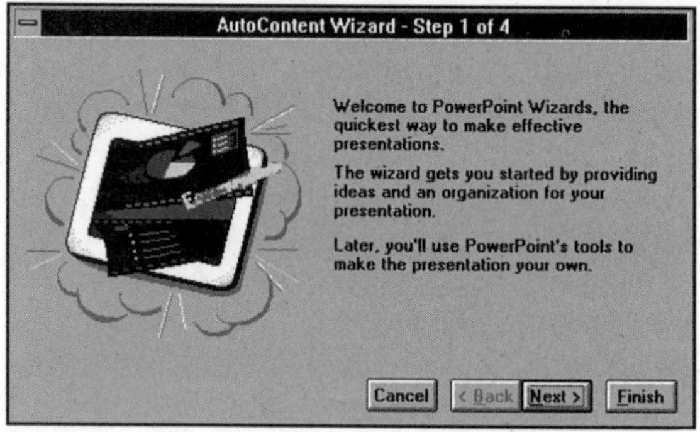

Fig. 20.3
The AutoContent Wizard dialog box.

3. Read the information in the Step 1 dialog box, and then choose the **N**ext button. The Step 2 dialog box appears (see fig. 20.4).

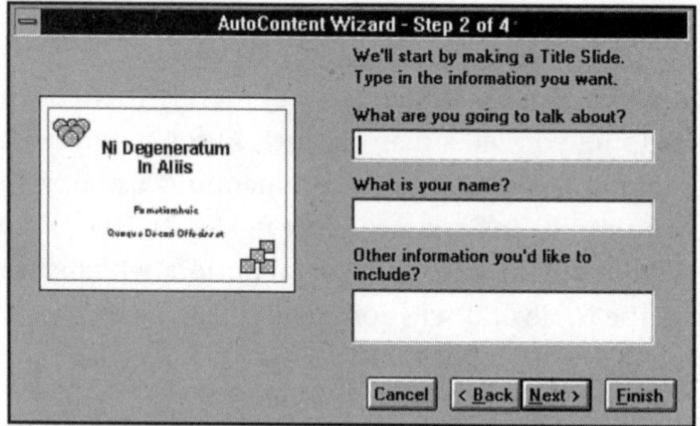

Fig. 20.4
The Step 2 dialog box enables you to specify information for a title page.

4. Enter the information for creating a title slide, and then choose the **N**ext button. The Step 3 dialog box appears (refer to fig. 20.2).

5. Select the type of presentation you want to give, and then choose the **N**ext button. The Step 4 dialog box appears.

6. Choose the **F**inish button to exit the wizard and create your presentation.

When you complete the steps, PowerPoint displays the presentation in outline view. You can use outline view to enter the content of the slides, or you can switch to slide view, whichever you prefer (for information about outline view and slide view, see "Viewing a Presentation" later in this chapter). The presentation contains a title page and a slide for each of the suggested topics. Also displayed on the screen automatically are Cue Cards. To use the Cue Cards, select a topic. If you prefer not to use Cue Cards, close the Cue Cards window by pressing Alt+F4 or choosing the Close command from the Cue Cards Control menu.

Using the Pick A Look Wizard

The second wizard you can use to create a presentation is the Pick a Look Wizard—so named because it enables you to specify the "look" of the presentation. You choose the type of output you want for your presentation (black-and-white slides, color slides, on-screen presentation, or 35mm slides), and a template design. You then specify the information you want to add to the presentation masters (slide master, speaker's notes master, handout master, and outline master).

Tip
To preview a template, place the highlight in the File Name list, then use the up- and down-arrow keys to highlight different templates. A sample of the highlighted template appears in the bottom right corner of the dialog box.

To enable you to choose a template, you can display the Presentation Template dialog box, shown in figure 20.5 (at step 3 in the Wizard, choose the More button to display the Presentation Template dialog box). Templates are stored in the TEMPLATE subdirectory under PWRPNT4 (your PowerPoint directory might have a different name). Templates are divided into subcategories based on the type of output for which the template is designed. The CLROVRHD subdirectory contains templates designed for color overheads; the BWOVRHD subdirectory contains templates for black-and-white overheads; and the SLDSHOW subdirectory contains templates designed for on-screen slide shows. Be sure to choose the correct template subdirectory before selecting a template in the File Name list. When you select a template, a preview of the template appears in the bottom right corner of the Presentation Template dialog box.

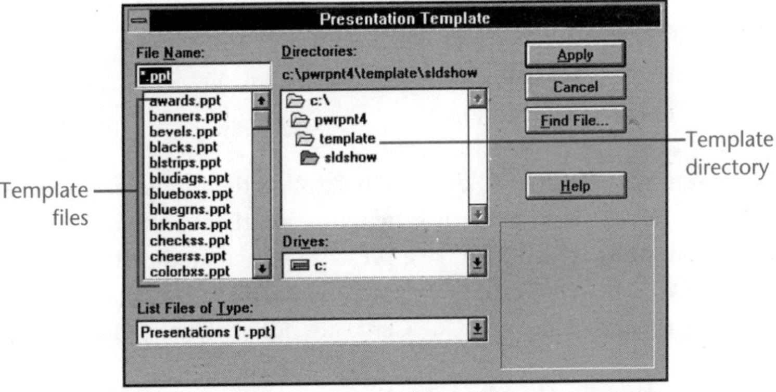

Fig. 20.5
The Presentation Template dialog box lists all available templates.

To use the Pick a Look Wizard, follow these steps:

1. Choose **F**ile **N**ew or press Ctrl+N. The New Presentation dialog box appears.

2. Select the **P**ick a Look Wizard option, and then choose OK. The Pick a Look Wizard dialog box appears. Notice that the title bar says `Step 1 of 9`.

3. Read the information in the Step 1 dialog box, and then choose the **N**ext button. The Step 2 dialog box appears.

4. Select the type of output you want for your presentation: **B**lack and White Overheads, Color Overheads, On-Screen Presentation, or 35mm Slides. Then choose the **N**ext button. The Step 3 dialog box appears.

5. Select one of the four template designs that appear in the dialog box, or choose the More button. When you choose More, PowerPoint displays the Presentation Template dialog box (refer to fig. 20.5).

6. Select a template directory in the **D**irectories list, and then select a template in the File **N**ame list. Choose the **A**pply button to use the selected template. When the Step 3 dialog box reappears, choose the **N**ext button. The Step 4 dialog box appears.

7. Select the printed output options you want: Full-Page Slides, Speaker's Notes, Audience Handout Pages, or Outline Pages. Then choose the **N**ext button.

8. The remaining dialog boxes that appear are determined by the printed output options you select in step 7. For each option, PowerPoint displays a separate dialog box that enables you to add text, the date, or page numbers to masters. When you finish with each dialog box, choose the **N**ext button. The last dialog box to appear is the Step 9 dialog box.

9. In the Step 9 dialog box, choose the **F**inish button to exit the wizard and create your presentation.

When you complete the steps, PowerPoint displays the presentation in slide view. You can remain in slide view or switch to another view to enter the content of your presentation. Unlike a presentation created with the AutoContent Wizard, a presentation created with the Pick a Look Wizard contains only the first slide, and Cue Cards are not automatically displayed.

Creating a Presentation Using a Template

As pointed out in the preceding sections, you use a wizard to create a presentation when you want to take care of all the aspects of the presentation up front. That is, if you want to select a template, specify options for the masters, and use the suggested topics for a presentation, you use a wizard to create the presentation. Sometimes, however, you want to apply only a template to a presentation. In such a case, you choose the Template option in the New Presentation dialog box.

To use a template to create a presentation, follow these steps:

1. Choose **F**ile **N**ew or press Ctrl+N. PowerPoint displays the New Presentation dialog box.

2. Select the **T**emplate option, and then choose OK. PowerPoint displays the Presentation Template dialog box.

3. Select a template directory in the **D**irectories list, and then select a template in the File **N**ame list. Choose the **A**pply button to use the highlighted template. PowerPoint displays slide 1 of the new presentation in slide view.

Creating a Blank Presentation

When you create a blank presentation, PowerPoint uses the DEFAULT.PPT template. The default template uses no color (black and white only) and includes no stylistic enhancements. Creating a blank presentation puts you in complete control of the color scheme, layout, and style characteristics of your slides. You can leave the presentation blank, or you can add a template, colors, and other enhancements selectively at any time by using menu or toolbar commands. Use the blank-presentation method when you want the maximum degree of flexibility.

When you select the Blank Presentation option in the New Presentation dialog box, PowerPoint displays the New Slide dialog box (see fig. 20.6). Use this dialog box to choose the layout you want for the first slide in the new presentation. PowerPoint automatically highlights the first layout, used for the title page of a presentation. You can accept this layout or select a different one.

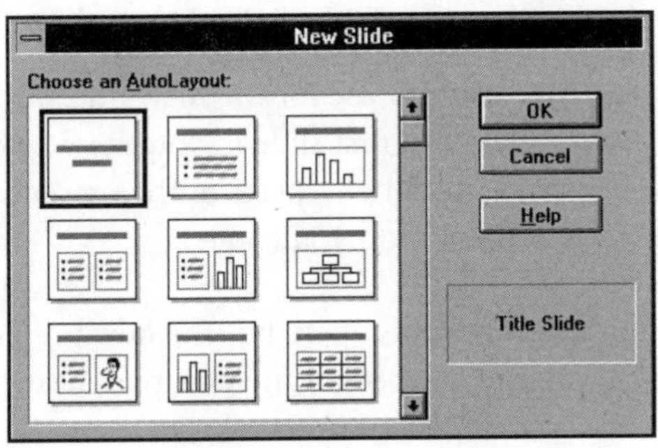

Fig. 20.6
Choose a layout for your slide in the New Slide dialog box.

To create a blank presentation, follow these steps:

1. Choose **F**ile **N**ew or press Ctrl+N. PowerPoint displays the New Presentation dialog box.

2. Select the **B**lank Presentation option, and then choose OK. PowerPoint displays the New Slide dialog box (refer to fig. 20.6).

3. Select the layout you want to use for the first slide, and then choose OK. PowerPoint displays the first slide in your new presentation, using the layout you specify.

Creating a Presentation Using the Current Presentation Format

In subsequent chapters, you learn how to refine your presentations by formatting and aligning text; inserting objects; and adding special enhancements such as color, shadows, and patterns. Sometimes, when you have worked hard to develop a special design for a presentation, you want to use the same design for a new presentation. You can do this simply by copying the style of the existing presentation to a new presentation. PowerPoint uses the template, colors, and features of the presentation masters for the existing presentation and applies them to the new presentation.

To create a new presentation based on an existing presentation, you first must open the existing presentation (to learn how to open an existing presentation, see "Opening an Existing Presentation" later in this chapter). Then follow these steps:

1. Choose **F**ile **O**pen or press Ctrl+O to open the existing presentation.

2. Choose **F**ile **N**ew or press Ctrl+N. PowerPoint displays the New Presentation dialog box.

3. Select the **C**urrent Presentation Format option, and then choose OK. PowerPoint displays the New Slide dialog box (refer to fig. 20.6).

4. Select the layout you want to use for the first slide, and then choose OK. PowerPoint displays the first slide in your new presentation, using the layout you specify. All other aspects of the presentation are identical to those of the presentation you copied.

The original presentation file still is open, but the new presentation is the active file. You can change any aspect of the new presentation after creating the file.

Troubleshooting

The template I chose for my presentation has a background that is much too dark for my overhead slides. I want to use the same template style, but with a lighter background.

Three directories contain templates: BLKOVRHD (black-and-white overhead), CLROVRHD (color overhead), and SLDSHOW (slide show or 35mm slides). Templates in the SLDSHOW directory generally have dark backgrounds; you might have selected a template in this directory by mistake. Look for the corresponding template name in the BLKOVRHD and CLROVRHD directories. Templates in these directories generally have lighter backgrounds than those in the SLDSHOW directory.

You also can consider changing only the background color of the template you chose. Refer to Chapter 24, "Enhancing a Presentation," for an explanation of working with color.

I used a wizard to create a presentation, but I selected the wrong template by mistake. How can I change it?

If you have not yet exited the wizard when you discover the error, choose the **B**ack button to return to the Presentation Template dialog box and correct the error. If you have already exited the wizard, choose F**o**rmat **P**resentation Template, and then select the correct template in the Presentation Template dialog box.

Moving Through a Presentation

When a presentation contains more than one slide, you must be able to display the slide you want easily. The left end of the status bar displays the number of the current slide. To move from one slide to another in slide view or notes pages view, use the vertical scroll bar. To display the preceding slide, click the Previous Slide button (it contains two up arrows). Click the Next Slide button (it contains two down arrows) to display the slide that follows. You can also use the PgUp and PgDn keys to move from one slide to another.

When a presentation contains a large number of slides, the Previous Slide and Next Slide buttons are not efficient for making large jumps—for example, from slide 3 to slide 28. You can move to a specific slide quickly by dragging the scroll box in the vertical scroll bar. As you drag the box up or down, PowerPoint displays a slide number near the scroll bar. When the number of the slide you want to view is displayed, release the mouse button. PowerPoint moves directly to the slide you specify.

Another useful way to quickly move from slide to slide is to switch to slide sorter view, then double-click the slide you want to view. PowerPoint automatically switches back to slide view and displays the slide you select.

Adding, Inserting, and Deleting Slides

After you create your presentation file, you can add, insert, or delete slides whenever necessary. To add a slide after the last slide in a presentation, display the last slide and then click the Insert New Slide button on the toolbar or the New Slide button at the right end of the status bar. You also can add a new slide by choosing the **I**nsert New **S**lide command or by pressing Ctrl+M. When you want to insert a new slide between two existing slides, you use the same method to insert the slide. Be sure to display the slide that you want to precede the new slide before you insert the slide.

Tip
If you are using slide sorter view or outline view, you can delete more than one slide at a time by selecting all slides you want to delete and then choosing the **E**dit Delete Sl**i**de command.

As you work on refining a presentation, you might find that you don't need a slide you created. You can delete a slide at any time by displaying the slide and then choosing the **E**dit Delete Sl**i**de command.

Troubleshooting

Can I insert or add slides in outline, slide sorter, or notes pages view?

Yes, you can, by clicking the Insert New Slide button in the toolbar or the New Slide button at the right end of the status bar, choosing the **I**nsert New **S**lide command, or pressing Ctrl+M. In outline and notes pages views, PowerPoint inserts a new slide after the selected slide. In slide sorter view, PowerPoint also inserts a new slide after the selected slide unless you click the mouse button between slides before you insert a new slide. For more information about working in different views, see "Viewing a Presentation" later in this chapter.

I accidentally deleted a slide from my presentation. How can I restore it?

In any of the views (slide, outline, slide sorter, and notes pages) you can click the Undo button in the toolbar, choose the **E**dit **U**ndo command, or press Ctrl+Z. Remember that you must use Undo *immediately* after deleting the slide. If you take any other actions first, the slide cannot be restored.

I inserted a new slide in the wrong location in my presentation. Can I move it?

Yes. It's best to use slide sorter view to rearrange slides in a presentation. For specific instructions, see "Using Slide Sorter View" later in this chapter.

Viewing a Presentation

PowerPoint offers several ways to view your presentation. Each view has a particular purpose and advantage. The four views are summarized in table 20.1 and described in detail in the sections that follow.

Table 20.1 PowerPoint Views

View	Description
Slide	Displays individual slides in full-slide view, which enables you to see the slide in detail.
Outline	Displays all slides in the presentation, giving you an overview of the content of the presentation.
Slide sorter	Displays a miniature version of every slide in the presentation in proper order. Gives you an overview of the look and flow of the presentation.
Notes Pages	Displays a miniature version of an individual slide at the top of the screen and speaker's notes below the slide. Enables you to review your notes while viewing the slide.
Slide show	Displays slides as they would appear during an on-screen slide show by using the entire screen area. Press PgDn and PgUp to switch from slide to slide. Press Esc to end slide show view.

To switch from one view to another, you can use the commands listed at the top of the **V**iew menu, but the quickest way to switch views is to click the view buttons in the bottom left corner of the PowerPoint window. From left to right, the buttons are Slide View, Outline View, Slide Sorter View, Notes Pages View, and Slide Show (see fig. 20.7). Simply click the button for the view you want to use. Each time you click a view button, PowerPoint changes your view of the current presentation.

By holding down the Shift key when you click a view button, you display the master that corresponds to the selected view. When you hold down the Shift key and click the Slide View button, for example, PowerPoint displays the Slide Master. When you hold down the Shift key and click the Outline View button, PowerPoint displays the Outline Master. Because the Slide Sorter has no corresponding master, holding down the Shift key and clicking the Slide Sorter button displays the Handout Master. To display masters by using a menu command rather than Shift+clicking a view button, choose **V**iew **M**aster, and then choose the appropriate master from the submenu that appears.

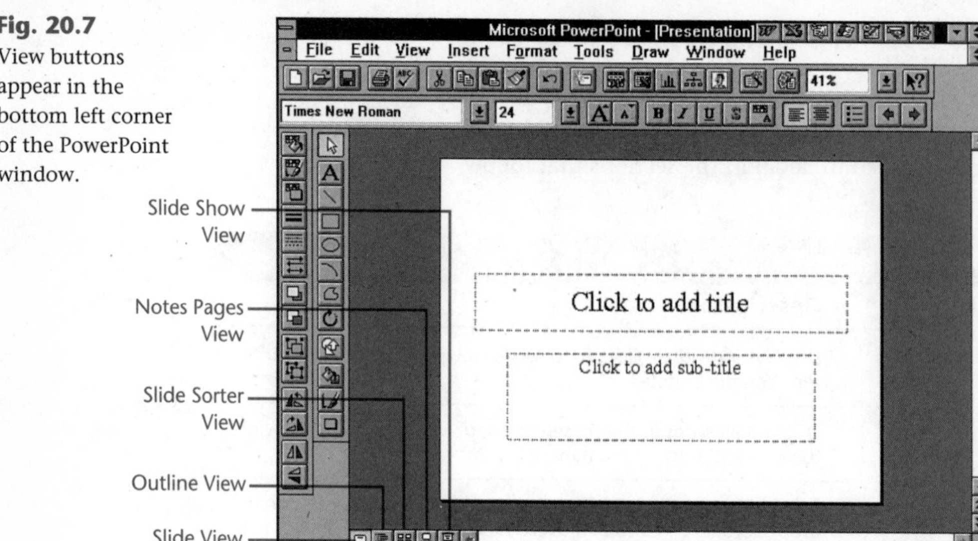

Fig. 20.7
View buttons appear in the bottom left corner of the PowerPoint window.

Zooming In and Out

Regardless of the view you choose, PowerPoint displays your presentation at a preset percentage of its full size, such as 43 percent. The display percentage is the zoom setting that PowerPoint uses. The percentage PowerPoint uses varies, depending on your video driver, the screen resolution you use, and the size of your monitor. If you choose the **V**iew **Z**oom command, the percentage used appears in the Zoom dialog box; other predefined percentages appear as options in the dialog box. The standard PowerPoint toolbar also displays the current zoom percentage.

PowerPoint uses a different zoom percentage in each view. The default percentages are designed to provide an optimized view within the window. If you zoom in closer by setting a higher zoom percentage, you see only a portion of the displayed page.

To change the zoom percentage in any view, select an option from the Zoom Control drop-down list in the toolbar, or type a new percentage in the Zoom Percentage box. To change the percentage by using a menu command, choose the **V**iew **Z**oom command to display the Zoom dialog box; select a zoom option or type a custom percentage in the **P**ercent box, and then choose OK.

Using Slide View

Slide view requires little explanation: it displays individual slides in the current PowerPoint window (see fig. 20.8). This view is the best to use to get a detailed picture of each slide. Slide view also is useful when you are entering or changing slide content. To switch from one slide to another, press the PgUp and PgDn keys or use the scroll bar, as described in "Moving Through a Presentation" earlier in this chapter.

Fig. 20.8 An example of slide view.

Using Outline View

When you are concerned only about the text in a presentation, outline view is the best view to use because it displays only the text of a presentation, without pictures or other objects. Outline view displays the content of multiple slides, each in outline form (see fig. 20.9). A numbered slide icon appears to the left of each slide's title. When a slide contains no pictures or graphical objects, the slide icon is empty except for a narrow line near the top indicating the title. When a slide contains a picture or other object, the slide icon also contains a graphical representation. This difference helps you identify at a glance which slides contain objects and which slides contain only text.

Outline view in PowerPoint is derived from outline view in Microsoft Word, so if you have worked with outline view in Word, you already know how to use outline view in PowerPoint.

Using Slide Sorter View

▶ "Setting Slide Timings and Transitions," p. 565

Slide sorter view gives you an overall perspective of your presentation by displaying a miniature version of each slide on a single screen (see fig. 20.10).

The number of slides you can view at one time depends on your video card, driver, and monitor, as well as on the zoom percentage used. The lower the zoom percentage, the more slides you can view.

Fig. 20.9
Outline view displays only the text of each slide in outline format.

Promote
Demote
Move Up
Move Down
Collapse Selection
Expand Selection
Show Titles
Show All
Show Formatting

Microsoft PowerPoint - [STRATEGY.PP
File Edit View Insert Format Tools Draw Window Help
33%
Book Antiqua
44
1 Recommending a Strategy
2 Vision Statement
• State the vision and long term direction
3 Goal and Objective
• State the desired goal
• State the desired objective
• Use multiple points if necessary
4 Today's Situation
• Summary of the current situation
• Use brief bullets, discuss details verbally
5 How Did We Get Here?
• Any relevant historical information
• Original assumptions that are no longer valid
6 Available Options
• State the alternative strategies
Outline
New Slide...
Layout...
Template...

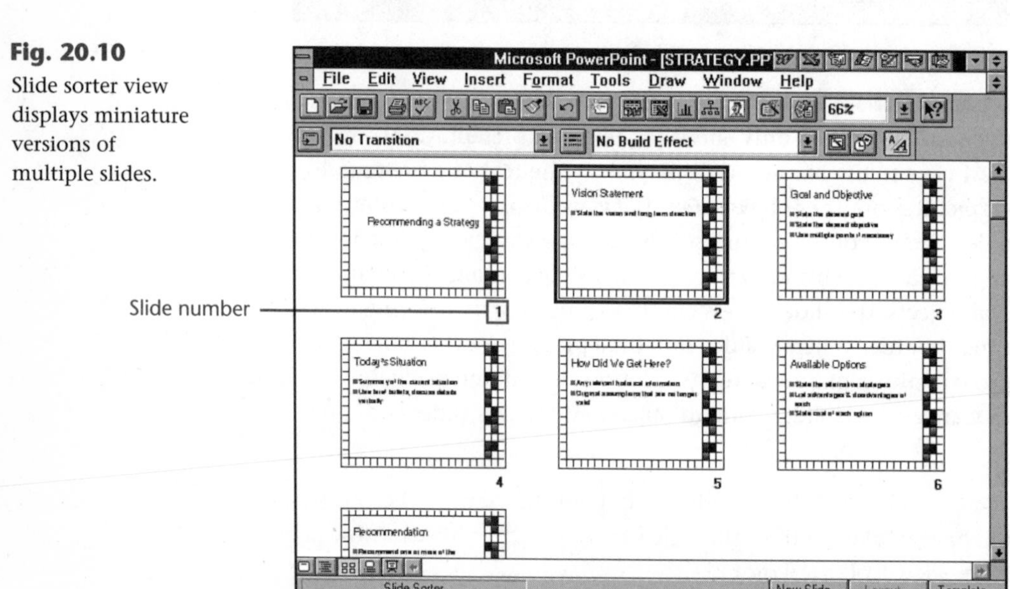

Fig. 20.10
Slide sorter view displays miniature versions of multiple slides.

In slide sorter view, the slide number appears near the bottom right corner of each slide. When your presentation output is intended to be a slide show, the amount of time each slide is displayed during the slide show appears near the bottom left corner of each slide.

You cannot edit slides in slide sorter view; you must return to slide view or outline view to change the content of slides. You can, however, change the order of slides and copy slides in slide sorter view. First, you must select a slide.

To select a slide in slide sorter view, use the arrow keys to highlight a slide or click the slide you want to select. A bold outline surrounds the selected slide. To select multiple slides, press and hold down the Shift key while clicking on all of the slides you want to select. Another way to select multiple slides is to click and hold down the left mouse button as you drag an outline around the slides you want to include. To cancel any selection, click any blank area of the slide sorter view window.

In slide sorter view, rearranging slides is as simple as selecting a slide, then dragging it to a new location. As you drag the mouse, the mouse pointer changes to a miniature slide with a down arrow. When you move the pointer between two slides, a vertical bar appears to mark the location where the slide will be inserted if you release the mouse button. You can move multiple slides using this method as well. Suppose you want to move slides 3 and 4 to the end of your presentation. Select slides 3 and 4; then drag them to the right of the last slide in the presentation and release the mouse button. PowerPoint automatically renumbers rearranged slides.

Slide sorter view is the best view to use when copying slides. Just select the slide (or slides) you want to copy, then press and hold down the Ctrl key as you drag the slide to the copy location. The mouse pointer changes to a miniature slide with a plus symbol (+), and a vertical bar appears between slides to mark the location where the slide will be inserted. When you release the mouse button, a copy of the selected slide is inserted in the new location.

Tip
Press Ctrl+Home to select slide 1; press Ctrl+End to select the last slide.

Using Notes View

When giving a presentation, many presenters prefer to work from prepared speaker's notes. PowerPoint provides a special page on which you can type speaker's notes. The top half of the page displays a reduced version of the slide; the bottom portion of the page contains a text object in which you can type the text of your notes (see fig. 20.11).

At PowerPoint's default zoom percentage, notes view displays an entire page on-screen. When you are typing or editing speaker's notes, however, it's difficult to read the text at the default percentage. If you use a larger percentage (such as 66 or 75), the text you type is more readable, and you still can view part of the slide content as you type.

Fig. 20.11
Use notes view to enter and display speaker's notes.

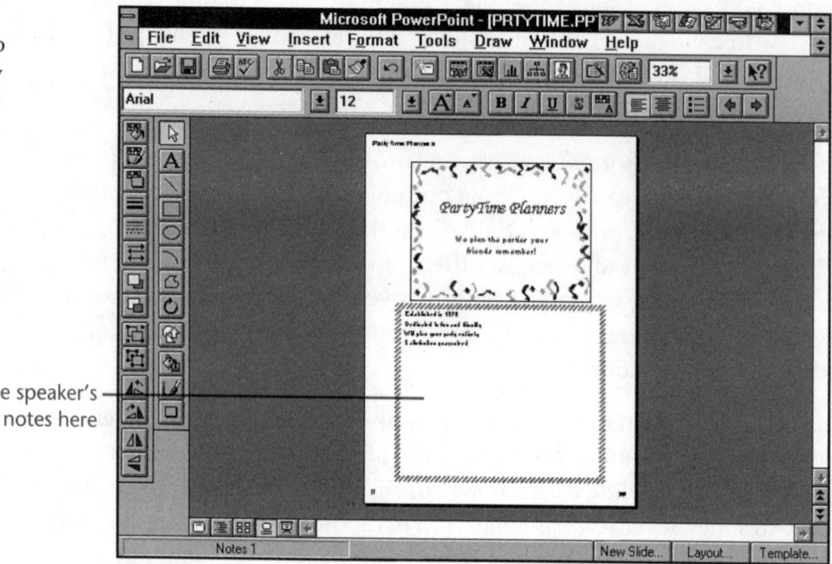

Using Slide Show View

Slide show view enables you see each slide in your presentation at maximum size. When you use this view, the PowerPoint window is not visible; each slide occupies the complete screen area (see fig. 20.12). If your final output is intended to be an on-screen slide show, slide show view is useful for previewing your slides to see how they will look during the actual slide show.

To move from one slide to another, press the PgUp and PgDn keys, or click the left mouse button to move forward and the right mouse button to move backward. You can also use the right- or down-arrow key to move forward, or the left- or up-arrow key to move backward. To exit slide show view and return to the last view you used, press Esc.

Note

Slide show view displays your slides starting with the slide that was displayed before you switched views. If you want the slide show to begin at slide 1, be sure to select slide 1 before switching to slide show view. You can also press Home to move to the first slide and End to move to the last slide in a presentation.

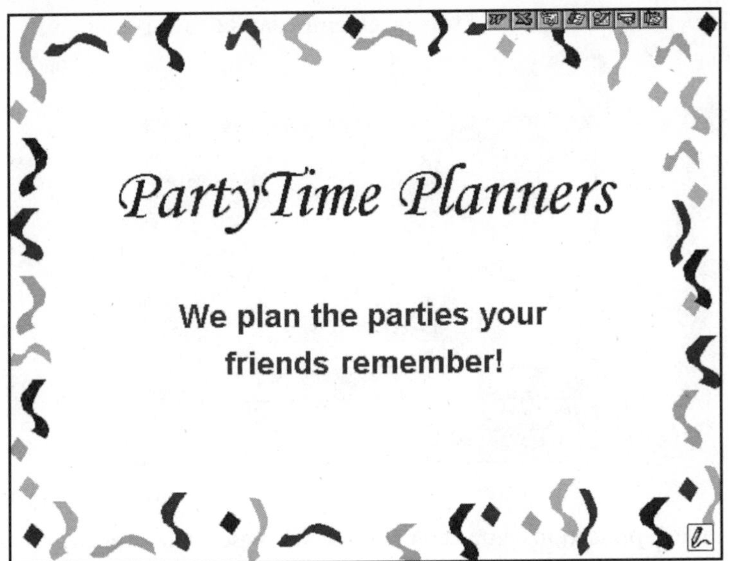

Fig. 20.12
In slide show view, each slide uses the entire screen area.

Saving a Presentation

When you save a presentation, PowerPoint saves *all* components of the presentation (slides, outline, speaker's notes, and handout pages) in one file.

◀ "Saving, Opening, and Closing Files," p. 72

You save a file in PowerPoint the same as you save a file in any other Microsoft Office application. The first time you save a file, PowerPoint displays the Save As dialog box (see fig. 20.13), whether you choose the **F**ile **S**ave or **F**ile Save **A**s command. When you want to save an existing file under a different name, on a different disk or directory, or as a different file type, choose **F**ile Save **A**s.

Tip
Save a file frequently so you don't lose data in case of a power interruption or equipment failure.

PowerPoint saves presentation files with the file extension PPT. When you specify the file name, you don't need to type PPT; PowerPoint adds the file extension to the name automatically.

If you use TrueType fonts anywhere in your presentation, you might want to select the Em**b**ed TrueType Fonts option. Selecting this option ensures that if you run your presentation on someone else's computer, the TrueType fonts will be displayed.

Opening an Existing Presentation

▶ "Enhancing Text," p. 513

You open a PowerPoint presentation using the same method you use to open any file in any of the Microsoft Office Applications. For specific information about opening files, refer to "Saving, Opening, and Closing Files" in Chapter 3.

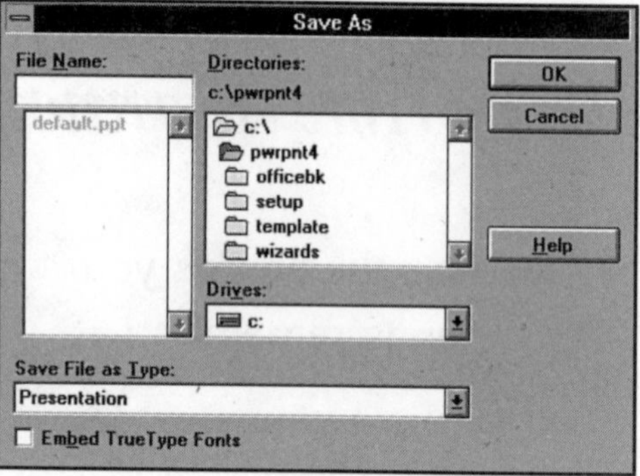

Fig. 20.13
The Save As dialog box enables you to select a drive, directory, and file type.

As in many applications, you can open several presentations at the same time. The active presentation appears on top of the others, and its title bar is highlighted. As with all Windows applications, the names of all open presentation files are listed in the **W**indow menu.

Closing a Presentation

To close an existing presentation, choose **F**ile **C**lose or double-click the presentation window's Control-menu box. If you have made changes in the file since you last saved it, PowerPoint asks whether you want to save those changes. Choose **Y**es to save the changes, **N**o to ignore the changes, or Cancel to return to the presentation without saving the file.

From Here...

In this chapter, you learned how to create, save, and open PowerPoint presentations. For information about related topics and topics referenced in this chapter, see the following chapters:

- Chapter 21, "Entering Slide Content," describes how to insert clip art, pictures, tables, spreadsheets, graphs, organization charts, and many other types of objects into your slides.

- Chapter 24, "Enhancing a Presentation," describes how to add color, borders, shadows, and other enhancements to objects.

- Chapter 26, "Creating Output," describes how to print all the components of a presentation and how to create an on-screen slide show.

Chapter 21

Entering Slide Content

by Debbie Walkowski

PowerPoint slides can contain much more than just text. You can insert clip art, pictures, tables, worksheets, graphs, organization charts, and many other types of objects into your slides. This chapter begins by teaching you how to choose a slide layout and how to enter and edit slide text. You also learn the steps required for entering information other than text (such as pictures, tables, and graphs).

In this chapter, you learn to

- Work with AutoLayout
- Enter and edit text
- Insert clip art, tables, and worksheets
- Insert graphs, organization charts, and other objects

Reviewing AutoLayout

In Chapter 19, "Getting Acquainted with PowerPoint," you were briefly introduced to AutoLayout, a PowerPoint feature that includes 21 prepared slide layouts with different object placeholders and arrangements. Using AutoLayout, you can choose a slide layout that contains the object placeholders you need for your current slide. A title slide, for example, contains two text-object placeholders: one for a title and one for a subtitle. After you select a slide layout, you insert the actual content of your presentation—text, pictures, and graphs—into the placeholders in the slides.

Whenever you add a new slide to a presentation, PowerPoint automatically displays the Slide Layout/New Slide dialog box, which contains the 21 AutoLayouts (see fig. 21.1).

Note

The dialog box shown in figure 21.1 is titled Slide Layout or New Slide, depending on the method you use to display it. The contents of the dialog box are always the same regardless of the name shown in the title bar. To avoid confusion, this chapter refers to the dialog box as the Slide Layout/New Slide dialog box.

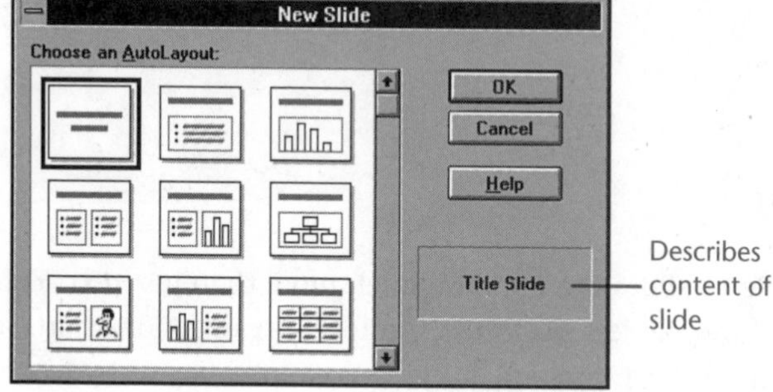

Fig. 21.1 Use the Slide Layout/New Slide dialog box to choose a layout for a new or existing slide.

Take the time to scan the dialog box to see how objects are arranged in each layout. Use the arrow keys to highlight a layout, or click a layout. A description of the highlighted layout appears in the bottom right corner of the dialog box. This description shows the types of objects included in the layout.

The solid gray lines at the top of each slide layout represent the slide title. Other text in a slide layout is represented by faint gray lines. Text nearly always is formatted with bullets. The placeholders that contain vertical bars represent graphs, and those with pictures represent clip art or pictures. The empty boxes represent placeholders for other objects, usually imported from other applications, such as Excel.

Tip

Use the scroll bar, arrow keys, or PgUp/PgDn keys in the Slide Layout/New Slide dialog box to view all AutoLayout options.

Highlight the layout you want to use for your new slide and then choose OK, or double-click the layout you want to use. PowerPoint automatically applies the selected layout to the new slide. After you choose a layout, replace the sample text in each placeholder with actual text or another object, such as a graph or table.

Note

Notice that the last slide layout in the Slide Layout/New Slide dialog box is blank; it contains no placeholder. Use this layout when you want complete control of the objects in a slide.

If you select the wrong layout or change your mind about the layout you want to use for the current slide, you can display the Slide Layout/New Slide dialog box at any time by clicking the Layout button at the bottom of the PowerPoint window or by choosing Format Slide Layout.

After you enter information in a placeholder, be careful about changing the slide layout. The objects that contain information remain in the slide while the placeholders for the new layout are added. PowerPoint tries to rearrange objects so that all of them will fit, but this isn't always possible. The slide can become cluttered with overlapping objects and placeholders, as shown in figure 21.2.

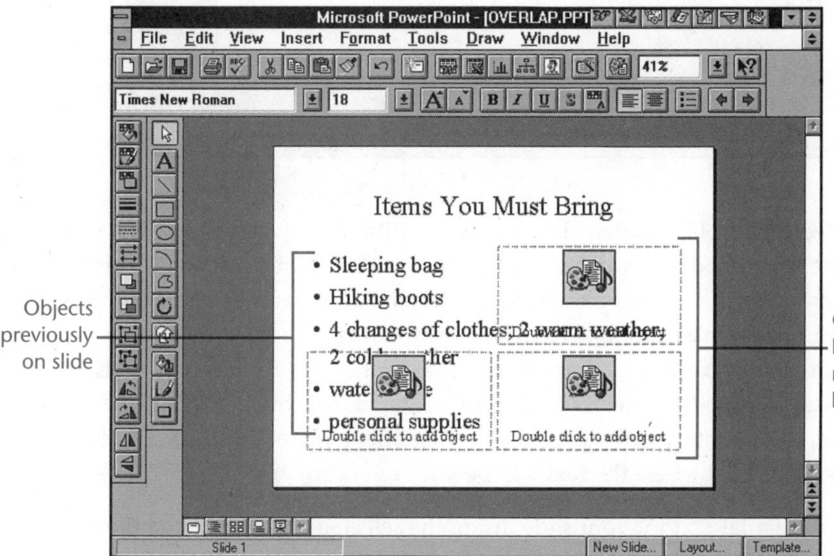

Fig. 21.2
Objects and placeholders can overlap if you change the slide layout after entering information.

Entering and Editing Text

In any slide presentation, text is the most important component. Virtually every slide contains text of some kind, even if it's just a title. The following sections describe how to enter the text content of your slides and how to edit the text when necessary.

Typing the Content for Your Slides

Whenever you choose a slide layout (other than the blank layout), you replace the sample text in a placeholder with real text. The slide shown in figure 21.3, for example, includes two placeholders for text: one that contains a sample title and one that contains a bulleted list. The third placeholder is for clip art. A faint dotted line appears around each placeholder.

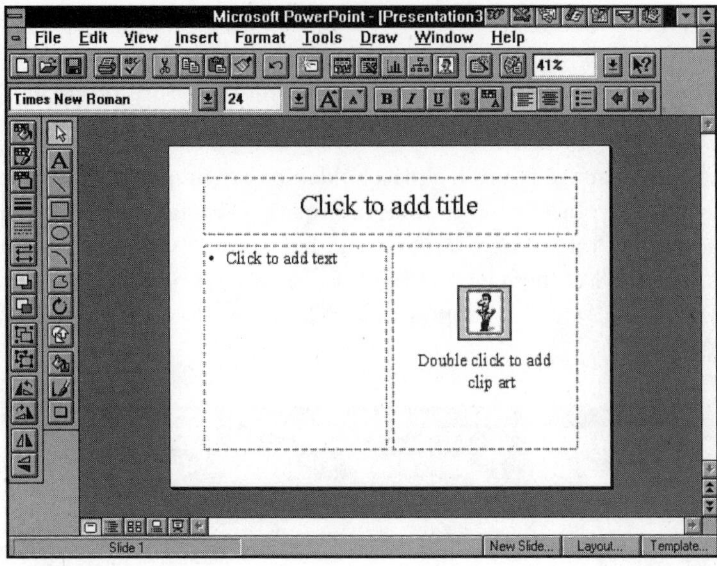

Fig. 21.3
This slide layout contains two placeholders for text and one placeholder for clip art.

To select a text placeholder, click anywhere within the placeholder. The faint outline is replaced by a wide hashed border, as shown in figure 21.4. This line indicates that the current placeholder is selected. The sample text disappears, and an I-beam insertion point appears inside the placeholder, indicating that you can enter text. In a title or subtitle placeholder, the insertion point is centered because titles nearly always are centered. In a bulleted-list placeholder, the sample text disappears and the bullet remains, with the insertion point positioned where the text will begin.

Type the actual text for your slide inside the selected placeholder. In the case of titles and subtitles, press Enter only when you want to begin a new centered line of text. In the case of bullets, press Enter only when you want to begin a new bulleted item. If your bulleted text is too long to fit on one line, PowerPoint automatically wraps the text to the next line and aligns the text appropriately.

When you finish entering text, deselect the object by clicking a blank area of the slide or the gray border around the slide. Notice that the object no longer is defined by the faint dotted line (see fig. 21.5). The absence of the dotted line gives you a more realistic idea of how the completed slide will look. (You can add a border to any object in a slide, however, as you learn in Chapter 24, "Enhancing a Presentation.")

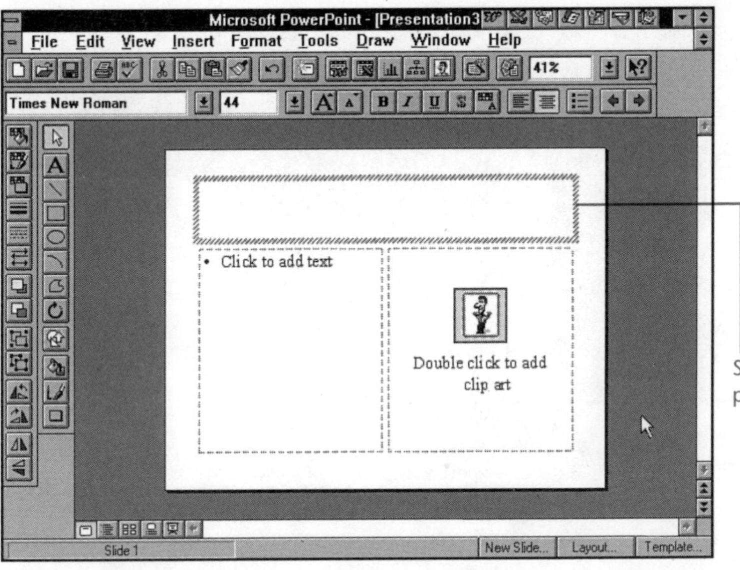

Fig. 21.4
A selected text placeholder is indicated by a wide hashed border; the sample text is removed.

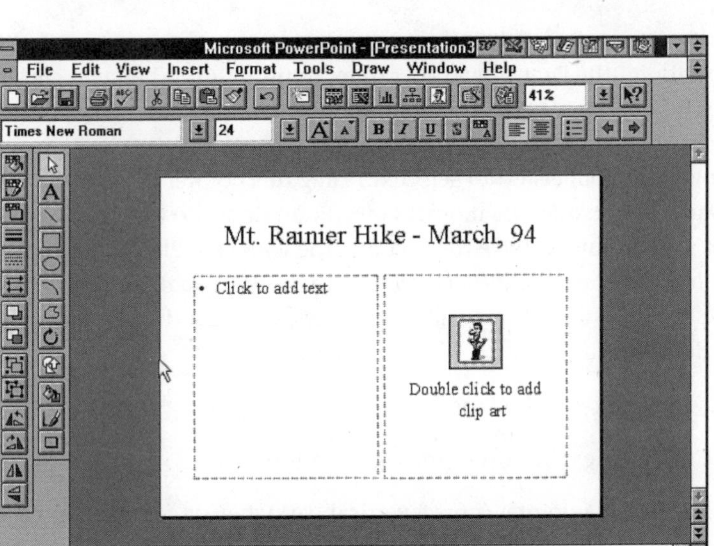

Fig. 21.5
An object no longer is defined by a dotted line when it contains actual text.

Creating New Text Objects

Sometimes you need to add text to a slide. Suppose that your slide contains a title and a bulleted list like the one shown in figure 21.6. You decide to add a note below the bulleted list. To do this, you need to make the note a separate object; otherwise, PowerPoint would format the note text as a bulleted-list item.

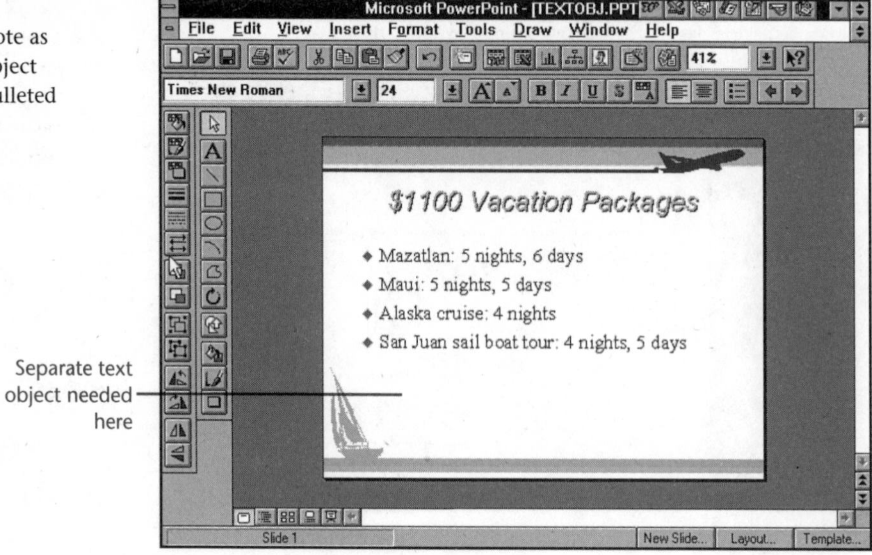

Fig. 21.6
You add a note as a separate object below the bulleted list.

Tip
If you aren't certain what text you want to enter in a new text box, type at least a few characters. Otherwise, the text box is deleted.

To add a note at the bottom of this slide, create a new object by using the Text button in the Drawing toolbar (refer to fig. 21.6). When you click the Text button and move the mouse pointer into the slide area, the pointer changes to a vertical bar with a cross at the bottom. (Be sure that the text object with the bullets is not selected.) Drag this pointer to draw the text box you want. As you drag the mouse, PowerPoint draws an outline for your text box. It's important to make the text box the correct width, but the depth of the box isn't important. Regardless of the depth you draw, PowerPoint shrinks it to one line of text and expands the depth of the box only if you type additional lines of text.

To draw a text box, follow these steps:

1. Click the Text button in the Drawing toolbar.
2. Position the pointer (now a vertical bar) where you want the top left corner of the text box to be.
3. Click and drag the mouse diagonally down and to the right to form a box of the appropriate width.
4. Release the mouse button. The text box you drew is bordered by wide hashed lines, indicating that the box is selected. The I-beam insertion point appears inside the box, ready for you to enter new text.

Figure 21.7 show how the same slide looks with a text object.

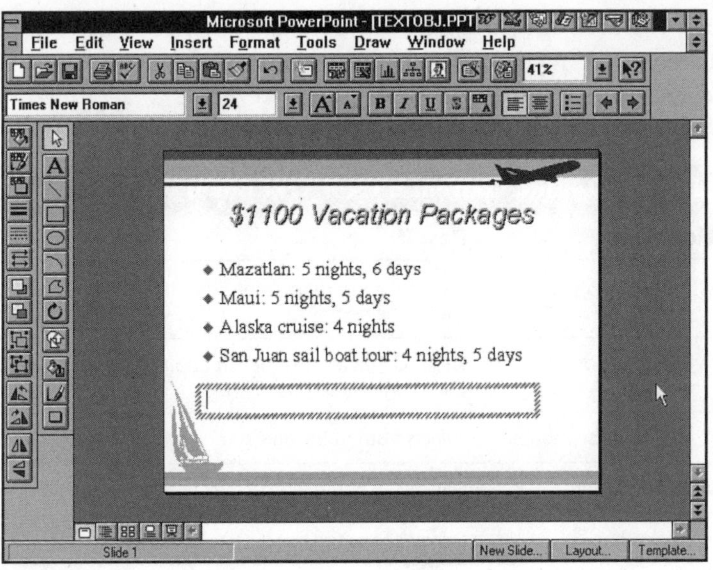

Fig. 21.7
The same slide now contains a text object below the bulleted list.

Labeling Objects

Suppose that your slide contains a clip-art drawing that you want to label. You don't need a large text object, as you might for a note. Your label is likely to contain fewer than 50 characters.

You can quickly create a text box that expands to the required width as you type. The steps are similar to those for creating a larger text box, but with this method, you don't specify the dimensions of the box. Follow these steps:

1. Click the Text button in the Drawing toolbar.

2. Place the mouse pointer where you want to begin typing, and then click and release the mouse button. PowerPoint displays a text box large enough for one character. The text box is selected, as indicated by the wide hashed border.

3. Begin typing the label. With each character you type, the text box expands to the left. To type text on a new line, press Enter and continue typing.

4. When you finish, deselect the box by clicking a blank area of the slide or the gray border surrounding the slide.

Changing Text and Correcting Errors

After you enter text into a text box, you probably will want to change the text or correct errors. Making changes in a text box is as easy as clicking and

◄ "Editing Text," p. 110

retyping. You use standard editing conventions to change text, as summarized in table 21.1. If you are familiar with Microsoft Word, you already know these conventions.

Table 21.1 Editing Conventions for Text Boxes

Action	Result
Press the arrow keys	Moves the insertion point right, left, up, or down within the text
Press Backspace or Del	Erases characters (to the left and right, respectively) of the insertion point
Click and drag the mouse	Selects a string of characters
Double-click a word	Selects the entire word
Triple-click a line	Selects the entire line
Ctrl+A	Selects all text in a text object
Ctrl+click	Selects an entire sentence
Press Del	Clears selected text from the object without placing it in the Clipboard
Press Shift+Del or Ctrl+X	Cuts selected text and places it in the Clipboard
Press Ctrl+C	Copies selected text to the Clipboard
Press Shift+Insert or Ctrl+V	Pastes text from the Clipboard

In addition to the keyboard shortcuts listed in table 21.1, you can use the Cut, Copy, Paste, Clear, and Select All commands (Edit menu) to edit text. When text is selected on a slide, Cut, Copy, and Paste commands also appear in the shortcut menu.

When you finish editing text in a text box, be sure to click any blank area of the slide or the gray area surrounding the slide to deselect the text box.

Checking Your Spelling

It's common to automatically check the spelling in a word processing document before you print it, but you might not have developed the same good habit with PowerPoint. Because presentations contain primarily text, and because slides are highly visible, remember to check your spelling before you print or produce slides for your presentation.

The spelling checker in PowerPoint compares all the words in your document with an on-line dictionary file. When the spelling checker finds a word that's not in the dictionary file, it highlights the word in your slide and displays the word in the Spelling dialog box, shown in figure 21.8.

Note

The spelling checker checks text in all objects in a presentation file *except* those objects that contain text imported from other applications.

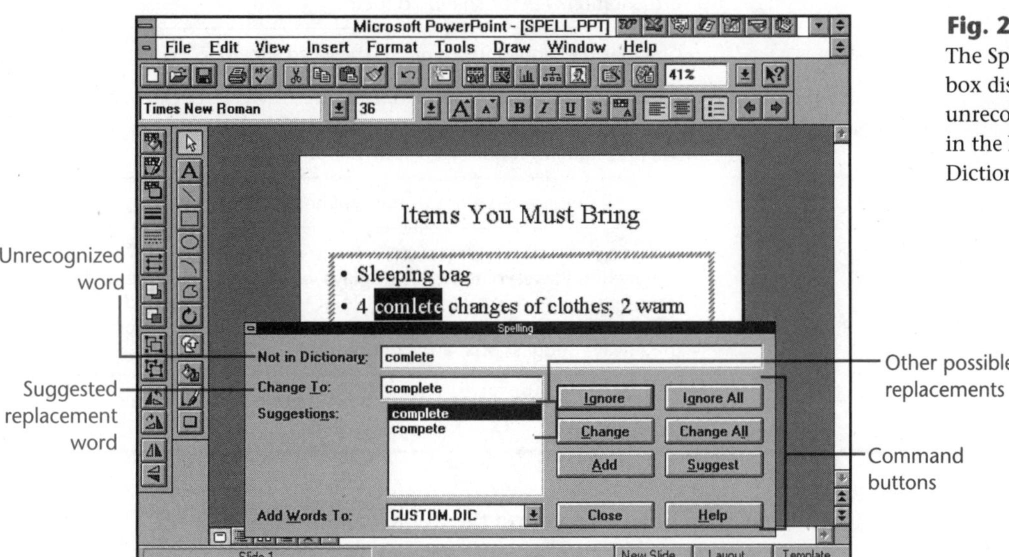

Fig. 21.8
The Spelling dialog box displays the unrecognized word in the Not in Dictionary box.

The spelling checker moves through your presentation one slide at a time, and then checks the speaker's notes (if any) before closing the Spelling dialog box. (If slide 1 is not displayed when you choose the Spelling command, the spelling checker checks all previous slides after the last slide is checked.) You can stop using the spelling checker at any time by clicking the Close button in the Spelling dialog box.

Note

A highlighted word is not necessarily misspelled; it just isn't included in the on-line dictionary. For this reason, the spelling checker occasionally questions correctly spelled words simply because it doesn't recognize them. This situation occurs frequently with technical terms and industry-specific jargon. One of your options is to add these words to the dictionary file so that the spelling checker recognizes them in the future.

Tip
If a word is misspelled and the spelling checker offers no suggested replacement words, you must look up the word in a dictionary, type the correct spelling in the Change To box, and then choose the **C**hange, Change A**l**l, or **A**dd button.

When checking the spelling in a presentation, you have several options for dealing with words that the spelling checker questions. Table 21.2 describes the functions of the command buttons in the Spelling dialog box.

Table 21.2 Spelling Command Buttons

Button	Function
Ignore	Skips the highlighted word without changing it.
I**g**nore All	Skips all occurrences of the highlighted word throughout the presentation without changing them.
Change	Changes the highlighted word to the word shown in the Change To box.
Change A**l**l	Changes all occurrences of the highlighted word throughout the presentation to the word shown in the Change To box.
Add	Adds the highlighted word to the on-line dictionary file.
Suggest	Shows a suggested replacement word in the Suggestions box. (By default, PowerPoint always displays words in the Suggestions box. If you don't want PowerPoint to display suggested words automatically, choose Tools Options, remove the X from the Always Suggest box, and choose OK.)
Close	Closes the Spelling dialog box without checking the remainder of the file.

To check the spelling in a presentation file, follow these steps:

1. Choose **T**ools **S**pelling or press F7 to display the Spelling dialog box. The spelling checker highlights the first unrecognized word in the presentation file and displays the word in the Not in Dictionary box.

2. Choose the appropriate command button (**I**gnore, I**g**nore All, **C**hange, Change A**l**l, or **A**dd). If you want the spelling checker to suggest a replacement word, click the Suggest button, and then choose **I**gnore, I**g**nore All, **C**hange, Change A**l**l, or **A**dd. The spelling checker takes the appropriate action and then highlights the next unrecognized word.

3. Repeat step 2 until the spelling checker displays a message saying that the entire presentation has been checked.

4. Choose OK.

Troubleshooting

I selected an AutoLayout that contains bullets, but I've decided not to use bullets.

Choose the Format Bullet command, or choose Bullet from the shortcut menu. In the Bullet dialog box that appears, remove the X from the Use a Bullet check box, and then choose OK. You also can use this dialog box to change the bullet style, if you want.

I don't understand the difference between drawing a text object and simply creating a label.

A text object has a definite width that PowerPoint uses to automatically wrap text to the next line if your text exceeds that width. A label has no definite width; it expands with each character you type. You can type beyond the bounds of the slide border, and PowerPoint will not wrap the text automatically. To begin a new line in a label, press Enter.

Inserting Clip-Art Pictures

One of the best ways to spice up a slide show is to insert a clip-art drawing. Clip-art drawings are especially appreciated by users who don't feel confident drawing their own pictures. The ClipArt Gallery contains more than 1,000 drawings that cover a wide range of topics.

You can insert clip art into a slide in several ways. In "Reviewing AutoLayout" earlier in this chapter, you saw that some slide layouts include placeholders for clip art. When you use one of these slide layouts, simply double-click the placeholder to choose a clip-art file to insert. The first time you do this, PowerPoint asks whether you want to add clip-art files from Microsoft Office. Responding Yes to this question makes the clip-art files available for you to insert into your slides.

You also can insert clip art by choosing **I**nsert **C**lip Art. Whichever method you use, the next step is to select a file in the ClipArt Gallery dialog box, shown in figure 21.9.

A list of categories appears at the top of the ClipArt Gallery dialog box. The box below the category list displays a sample of each clip-art file in the current category. Use the scroll bar, PgUp/PgDn, or the arrow keys to see each picture in a category. If you prefer to scroll through the entire selection of clip-art files, select the All Categories option in the category list box.

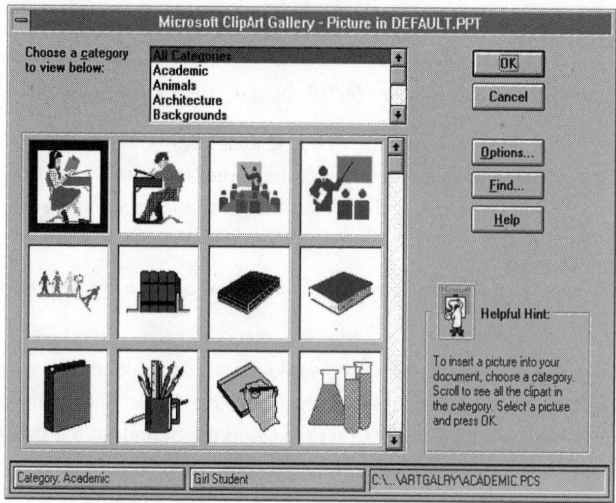

Fig. 21.9 Select a clip-art drawing in the ClipArt Gallery dialog box.

To add a clip-art drawing to your slide, follow these steps:

1. Display the slide into which you want to insert clip art.

2. Choose the **I**nsert **C**lip Art command, or, if your slide contains a clip-art placeholder, double-click it. The Microsoft ClipArt Gallery dialog box appears.

3. Select a category in the category list.

4. Select a picture, and then choose OK. PowerPoint closes the ClipArt Gallery dialog box and inserts the picture into your slide.

Troubleshooting

I want to change the colors in a clip-art picture.

You can change the colors and other attributes of the object as well, such as the line width, fill or line color, shading, and pattern. To do so, first convert the clip-art picture to a group of PowerPoint objects. Select the clip-art picture, and then choose the **D**raw **U**ngroup command. When PowerPoint asks whether you want to convert the picture to PowerPoint objects, choose OK. PowerPoint displays the resize handles of every object that makes up the picture. Select the object you want to change, and then use the appropriate command to change the object's attributes. To learn how to change object attributes such as colors, patterns, shading, shadows, and line styles, see Chapter 24, "Enhancing a Presentation."

I want to add clip-art files from other programs to the ClipArt Gallery dialog box in PowerPoint.

To do this, choose the **O**ptions button in the ClipArt Gallery dialog box. Choose Add from the Options dialog box. The Add Clipart dialog box appears. Select the drive and directory in which the file is located. In the Picture **N**ame list, select the file name; then choose OK. The Add Clipart dialog box changes, asking you to select a category for the new picture. (You also can add a short description, if you want.) To add the picture, choose the Add button.

Inserting a Word Table or Excel Worksheet

In a slide, a table or worksheet can convey useful information as long as it is simple and large enough to read. When you use PowerPoint's text-editing tools, however, you don't have the means to create a table or worksheet, so PowerPoint enables you to use Word and Excel tools.

To create a table or worksheet, choose **I**nsert Microsoft **W**ord Table or click the Insert Microsoft Excel Worksheet button in the Standard toolbar. A drop-down grid of cells appears. This grid enables you to define the size of your table or worksheet, as shown in figure 21.10. Click and drag the mouse pointer across the cells in the grid to indicate how many rows or columns you want in your table or worksheet. The cells you select are highlighted, and the dimensions are listed below the grid. (You can select up to 15 columns and up to 4 rows.)

When you release the mouse button, PowerPoint inserts a special object into your slide. In the case of a Microsoft Word table, the object looks like the one shown in figure 21.11. Notice that PowerPoint's Standard toolbar and menu bar are temporarily replaced by the Word menus and toolbar, so that all Word features and commands are available to you while you create your table. In effect, you are using Word inside a PowerPoint window.

◄ "Editing Text," p. 110

◄ "Formatting Text," p. 124

◄ "Modifying a Table," p. 212

To create the content of your table, click the area in which you want to add text, or press the Tab key to move the insertion point from left to right across the cells in the table. Press the up- and down-arrow keys to move the insertion point from one row to another. Use standard editing conventions to enter and edit text in the table (some of these conventions are listed in table 21.1).

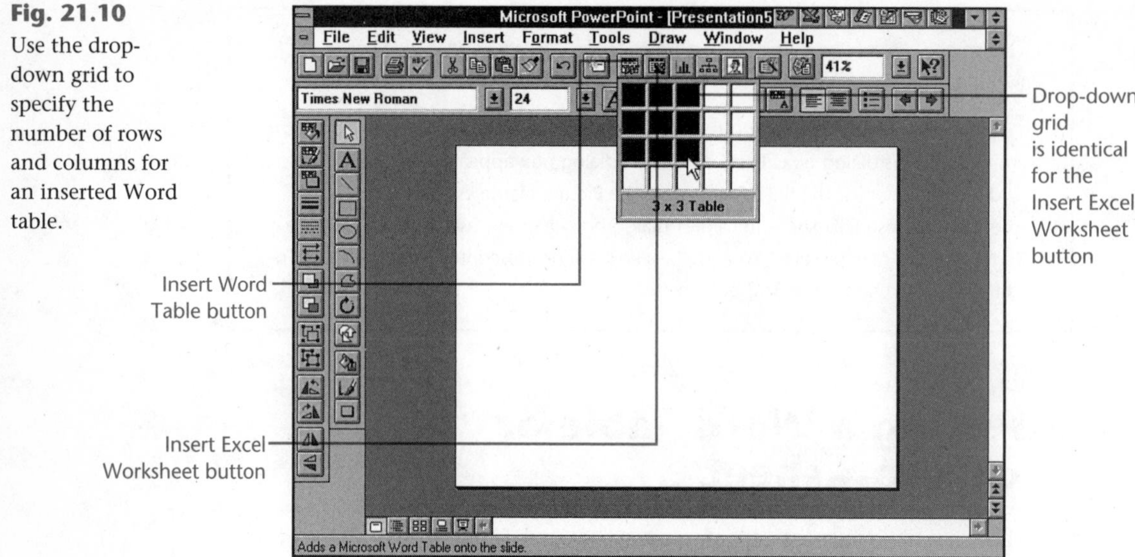

Fig. 21.10
Use the drop-down grid to specify the number of rows and columns for an inserted Word table.

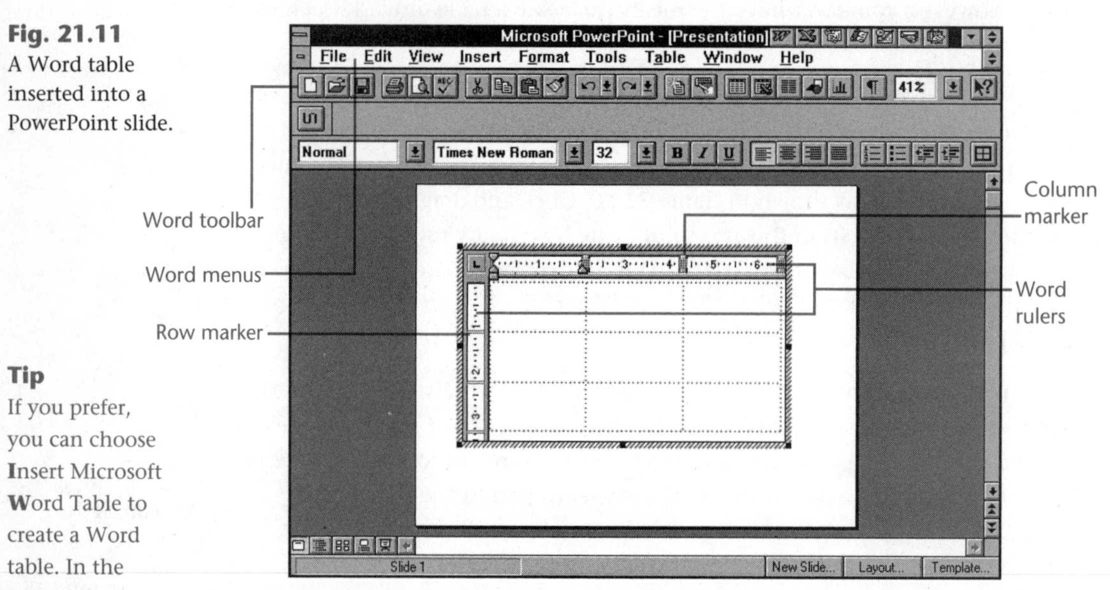

Fig. 21.11
A Word table inserted into a PowerPoint slide.

Tip
If you prefer, you can choose **I**nsert Microsoft **W**ord Table to create a Word table. In the Insert Word Table dialog box, you specify the number of columns and rows for the table.

If you need to adjust the width of rows or columns, add rows or columns, or perform more complex tasks while working with the table, refer to Chapter 10, "Working with Tables, Charts and Graphics."

When your table is complete, deselect it by clicking any blank area outside the table or the gray area that surrounds the slide. When the table no longer is the selected object, the PowerPoint menus and toolbar return. You can make changes in the table at any time by double-clicking inside the table. When the table is selected again, the Word menus and toolbar return automatically.

The same principles that govern Word tables hold true for Excel worksheets. When you click the Insert Excel Worksheet button in the PowerPoint toolbar, a drop-down grid appears. Click and drag the mouse pointer across the cells in the grid to indicate the number of rows and columns for your worksheet. PowerPoint inserts a special worksheet object into your slide, and PowerPoint's standard menus and toolbar are replaced by the Excel menus and toolbar, as shown in figure 21.12. (In the figure, notice that column width and row height are enlarged to a size consistent with other slide content.)

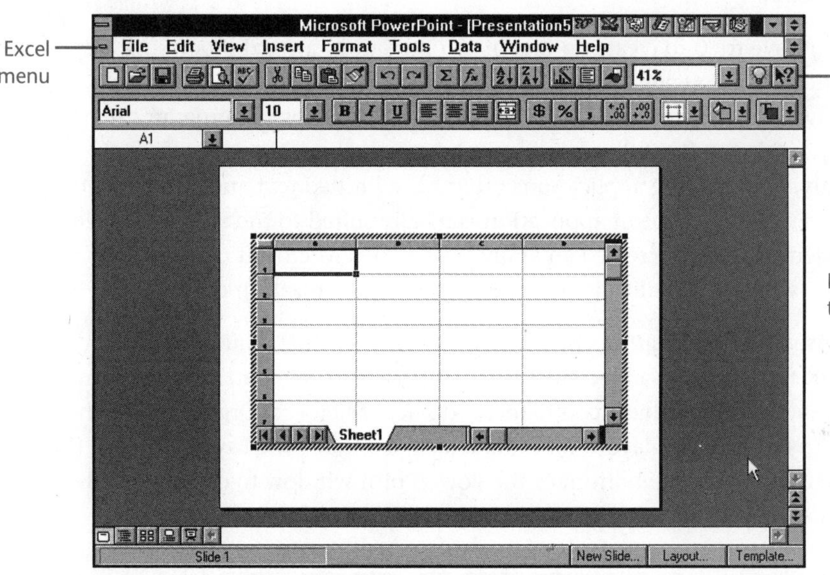

Fig. 21.12
You can insert an Excel worksheet into a PowerPoint slide.

Use Excel's commands and tools to create and edit your worksheet. When the worksheet is complete, deselect it by clicking any blank area of the slide or the border of the slide; the standard PowerPoint menus and toolbar return. If you are not familiar with Excel, refer to Chapter 12, "Creating Worksheets"; Chapter 13, "Editing Worksheets"; and Chapter 14, "Formatting Worksheets."

Inserting a Graph

Graphs, or *charts*, are graphic representations of data in worksheets. In a presentation, a bar, pie, or area chart often can depict data much more clearly than words can. In PowerPoint, you can insert a graph into a slide by using an application called Microsoft Graph. Because Microsoft Graph is an application in itself, Chapter 25, "Creating Charts," is devoted to this subject. Refer to this chapter for instructions on creating data for your graph, charting the data, and enhancing the graph before you insert it into your PowerPoint slide.

Inserting an Organization Chart

Organization charts commonly are included in slide presentations. An organization chart can convey information about new management, a group or department reorganization, or people to contact for specific types of information.

If you have tried to create an organization chart in a word processing program or a drawing application such as Microsoft Draw, you probably discovered how difficult that task can be. Word processing programs may not provide the flexibility you need to draw and connect the boxes uniformly, and drawing applications often have limited text and text-formatting features. Neither type of application is ideally suited to the task. To solve this problem, Microsoft created an application called Microsoft Organization Chart, which is specifically designed to create organization charts.

To insert an organization chart into a PowerPoint slide, you can use a slide layout that includes a placeholder for an organization chart. You also can choose the **I**nsert **O**bject command and select Microsoft Organization Chart 1.0. To use the slide-layout method, choose F**o**rmat Slide Lay**o**ut or click the Layout button at the bottom of the PowerPoint window to display the Slide Layout/New Slide dialog box (see fig. 21.13).

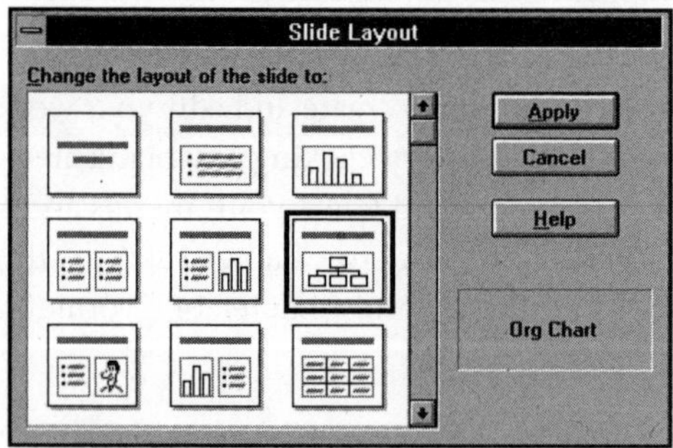

Fig. 21.13
The Org Chart layout is selected in the Slide Layout/New Slide dialog box.

In the dialog box, highlight the layout that include the organization chart, and then choose OK. PowerPoint applies the layout to the current slide, inserting an organization-chart placeholder. To access Microsoft Organization Chart, double-click the placeholder. After a few seconds, the Microsoft Organization Chart window appears. Figure 21.14 shows a sample organization chart.

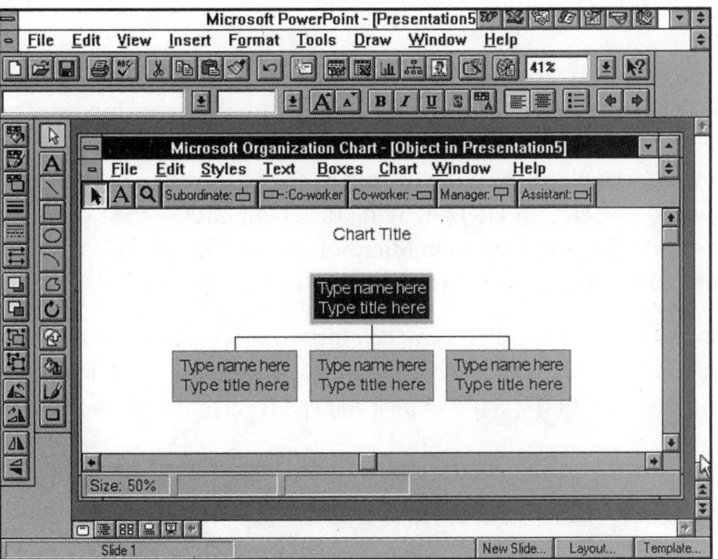

Fig. 21.14
The Microsoft Organization Chart window appears on top of the PowerPoint window.

Enter the appropriate information in the sample organization chart, using Microsoft Organization Chart commands. Because Microsoft Organization Chart is a separate application, it contains its own help files. If you are not familiar with this application, select any of the topics listed in the **H**elp menu or press F1.

When the organization chart is complete and you're ready to return to your PowerPoint presentation, choose the Exit and Return to [File Name] command from the Microsoft Organization Chart File menu. The organization chart is inserted into the current slide. To deselect the organization chart, click any blank area of the slide or the gray area surrounding the slide.

Inserting Other Objects

In this chapter, you have learned how to insert clip art, a Word table, an Excel worksheet, and an organization chart into a PowerPoint slide. You can insert many other types of objects by choosing **I**nsert **O**bject. This command opens another application on top of your PowerPoint window, enabling you to create a new file or open an existing file within that application. When you're ready to return to PowerPoint, choose the Exit command from the other application's File menu. (Sometimes the command is Exit and Return; sometimes it is Exit and Return to Presentation [File Name].) When you choose this command, the open application closes, and the object you created is inserted into your PowerPoint presentation slide.

After you return to PowerPoint, you can change the object you inserted by double-clicking it to redisplay the appropriate application window. If you inserted a chart that you created in Microsoft Works, for example, and want to change it, double-click the chart to start the Microsoft Works application. To return to PowerPoint after changing the chart, choose the Exit and Return command from the File menu in Microsoft Works. Microsoft Works closes, and the chart is updated in your PowerPoint presentation.

To display the types of objects you can insert , choose **I**nsert **O**bject in PowerPoint to display the Insert Object dialog box (see fig. 21.15). The Object Type list displays all the types of files you can insert into a PowerPoint slide.

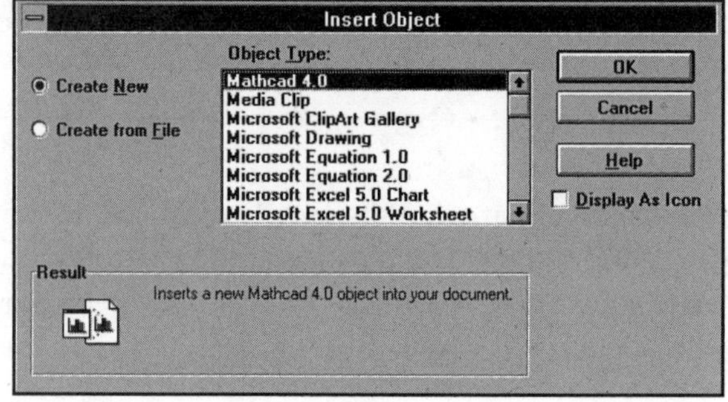

Fig. 21.15
The Insert Object dialog box lists many different types of objects that you can insert into a PowerPoint slide.

Because the Insert Object feature of PowerPoint works by opening another application, you must have that application installed on your computer. If Microsoft Works is installed on your computer, for example, you can select any of the Works options listed in the Insert Object dialog box and then create a new file or insert an existing one. If you don't have Works installed on your computer, you cannot open Works and create or insert a file from that application.

Before selecting the type of object to be inserted, choose Create **N**ew or Create from **F**ile. The Create **N**ew button enables you to create a new file of the object type you selected; the Create from **F**ile button enables you to insert an existing file that was created with the application you selected in the Object **T**ype list. The Result area at the bottom of the dialog box tells you what will be inserted into your PowerPoint slide when you select an item in the Object **T**ype list.

The **D**isplay As Icon check box (located below the command buttons in the Insert Object dialog box) enables you to display the inserted object in the form of an icon rather than as a full-size object. This feature is most useful when your presentation is a slide show, enabling you to conserve space in a slide or to "hide" the inserted object until you're ready to reveal its contents. You also can use this feature to make backup data for an on-screen presentation readily available.

To insert a new file from another application, follow these steps:

1. Display the PowerPoint slide into which you want to insert an object.

2. Choose **I**nsert **O**bject. PowerPoint displays the Insert Object dialog box.

3. Choose the Create **N**ew button.

4. (Optional) Select the **D**isplay As Icon option if you want to display the object as an icon.

5. In the Object **T**ype list, select the object you want to insert, and then choose OK. The Insert Object dialog box closes, and the window for the appropriate application opens on top of the PowerPoint window.

6. Use the application as you normally would—that is, create a new file if necessary, or simply select an item (such as an equation or a clip-art file). For cases in which you select an item, PowerPoint inserts the item and closes the application. For cases in which you create a new file, return to PowerPoint by choosing the Exit and Return to [File Name] command from the open application's File menu. The application window closes, and the file you created is inserted into the current PowerPoint slide.

7. Click any blank area of the slide or the gray area surrounding the slide to deselect the object.

When you insert an existing file from another application, the file is inserted into the PowerPoint slide automatically; PowerPoint does not open the application that you used to create the file. If you want to modify the file, you must open the application by double-clicking the object after it is inserted into your PowerPoint slide.

When you select the Create From **F**ile option in the Insert Object dialog box, PowerPoint modifies the dialog box slightly so that you can select the appropriate file. Figure 21.16 shows this dialog box.

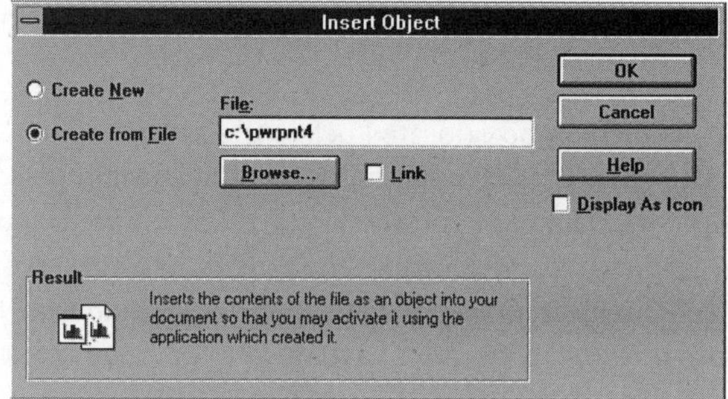

Fig. 21.16
When you are inserting an object from an existing file, the Insert Object dialog box enables you to search for the correct file name.

To insert an existing file from another application, follow these steps:

1. Display the PowerPoint slide into which you want to insert an object.
2. Choose **I**nsert **O**bject. PowerPoint displays the Insert Object dialog box.
3. (Optional) Select the **D**isplay As Icon option if you want to display the object as an icon.
4. Select an item in the Object **T**ype box.
5. Choose the Create from **F**ile button. PowerPoint modifies the Insert Object dialog box to match the one shown in figure 21.16.
6. If you know the name of the file, type the complete path name in the Fil**e** box. If not, choose the **B**rowse button, which displays the Browse dialog box with a directory tree. Select the correct file name, and then choose OK. The Browse dialog box closes, and you return to the Insert Object dialog box, where the file name you selected now appears in the Fil**e** box.
7. Choose OK in the Insert Object dialog box. The file you specified is inserted into your PowerPoint slide *without* opening the application you used to create the file.
8. Click any blank area of the slide or the gray area surrounding the slide to deselect the inserted object.

From Here...

Refer to the following chapters for information related to entering slide content:

- Chapter 22, "Working with Objects," describes how to manipulate objects, including moving, copying, deleting, resizing, grouping, and ungrouping.
- Chapter 23, "Drawing Shapes, Curves, and Lines," describes how to use PowerPoint's drawing tools to add drawn objects to your slides.
- Chapter 24, "Enhancing a Presentation," explains how to add color, borders, shadows, and other enhancements to objects.
- Chapter 25, "Creating Charts," teaches you how to use Microsoft Graph, an embedded application that enables you to create a wide variety of chart types from worksheet data.

Chapter 22

Working with Objects

by Debbie Walkowski

You were introduced to objects in Chapter 19, "Getting Acquainted with PowerPoint," and you learned more about entering content in objects in Chapter 21, "Entering Slide Content." Objects are the building blocks of slides that contain primarily text, graphics, or pictures but also can contain other elements such as tables, spreadsheets, or organization charts. You need to understand how to work with objects because they are the key components of a PowerPoint slide.

In this chapter, you learn to

- Select and group objects
- Move, copy, resize, and delete objects
- Align objects
- Use the grid
- Rotate and flip objects
- Stack objects

Selecting and Grouping Objects

Before you can make any kind of a change to an object—add color, change its size, move, or delete it—you must select the object. Selecting a single object is as simple as clicking it. When you click an object such as a chart, ClipArt drawing, or organization chart, *resize handles* surround the object in a rectangular shape (see fig. 22.1). Resize handles are small boxes that appear at the four corners and on each of the four sides of the rectangle. When you see the resize handles, you know an object is selected. In "Resizing and Scaling Objects" later in this chapter, you learn how to use these handles to change the size of an object.

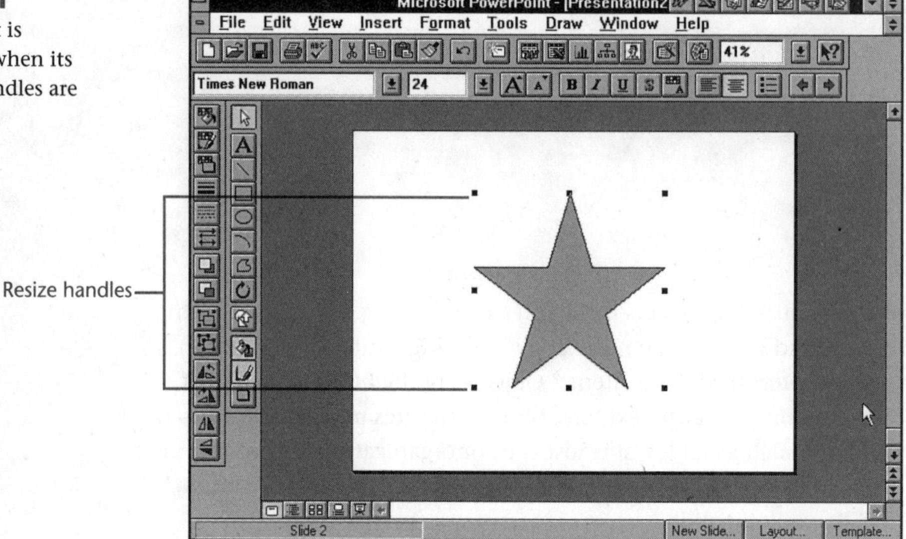

Fig. 22.1 An object is selected when its resize handles are visible.

Selecting Multiple Objects

In PowerPoint, you generally select an object to move, copy, or resize it, or to change one or more of its attributes. An *attribute* is any characteristic that is applied to an object, such as color, border, fill, and shadow. Sometimes you may want to select more than one object at a time. Selecting multiple objects can save you the time of applying the same attribute to several objects individually. When you select multiple objects, any attribute you change is applied to *all* selected objects. To change the color of several objects to blue, for instance, select all objects and then apply the blue fill color.

To select multiple objects at once, press and hold the Shift key and then click each object you want to include in the selection. The resize handles appear around each object you select (see fig. 22.2). If you select an object by mistake and want to remove it from your selection, continue holding the Shift key while you click the object again. PowerPoint removes that object from the selection. Release the Shift key when you have selected all objects.

Another way to select multiple objects at once is to use the Selection tool on the Drawing toolbar (the first button, shaped like a mouse pointer arrow, on the toolbar). Click the Selection tool, and drag the mouse across all objects you want to include in the selection. As you drag the mouse, PowerPoint draws a dashed rectangle that encloses all selected objects. When you release the mouse button, the rectangle disappears and the resize handles of each object in the selection are visible.

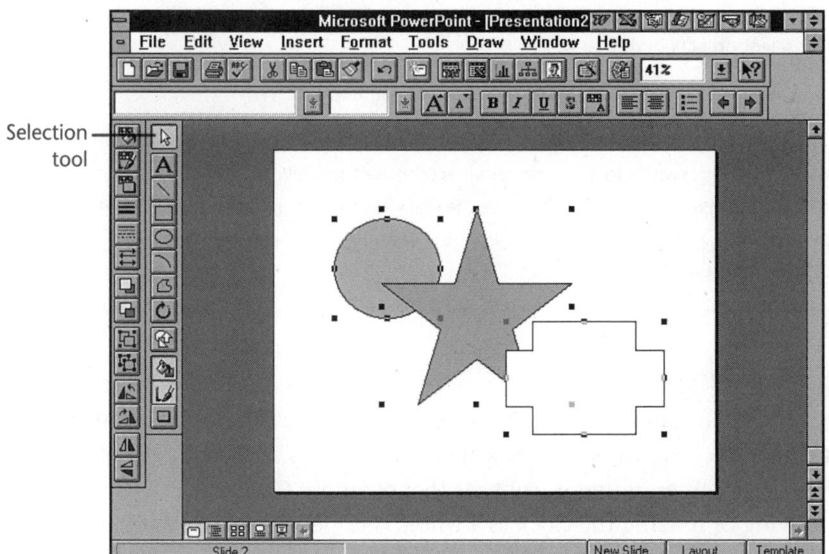

Fig. 22.2
In a multiple selection, resize handles appear around each selected object.

Note

You must *fully enclose* all objects within the selection rectangle you draw. If a portion of any object is not enclosed within the rectangle, that object is excluded from the selection. You can add an object to any selection by holding the Shift key and clicking the object.

Tip
To cancel any multiple selection, click anywhere in a blank area of the slide. To remove one or more objects from a multiple selection, press and hold down the Shift key and then click the object you want to remove.

To quickly select *every* object on a slide, choose the **E**dit Select **A**ll command or press the keyboard shortcut, Ctrl+A. PowerPoint immediately displays the selection handles of all objects on the slide.

Troubleshooting

When I draw a selection box around several objects, some objects are not selected.

(continues)

(continued)

Remember that you must fully enclose all objects you want to select in the selection box. If a portion of an object falls outside the selection box, it isn't selected.

Can I select objects on multiple slides at once?

No. The only way to view multiple slides at once is to use slide sorter view, and you cannot select objects in this view.

I try to select the company logo on my slide, but nothing happens. Why?

The logo probably was inserted into the slide master rather than the individual slide. To select the logo, switch to slide master view (choose the **V**iew **M**aster **S**lide Master command or press Ctrl and click the Slide Master View button in the lower left corner of the window), and then select the object. Any changes you make will affect the object on all slides.

Grouping Objects

Grouping objects enables you to treat several objects as a single object. Suppose, for example, you used PowerPoint's drawing tools to sketch a drawing of a clock. Without grouping the objects that compose the clock (see fig. 22.3), moving or resizing the clock as a whole is impossible. You could inadvertently move or delete a component of the clock or change one of its attributes by mistake. But when you select and group all the objects that make up the clock, the clock is treated as a single object. Any attributes you choose are applied to the entire object as a whole; the object can be moved, copied, resized, scaled, rotated, or flipped as a whole.

To group several objects, select the objects by using one of the methods you just learned (using the Shift key, the Selection tool, or the **E**dit Select A**l**l command). The resize handles for each object are displayed. Now choose the **D**raw **G**roup command. The object is now surrounded by an invisible rectangle, indicated by resize handles at the four corners and along each side of the rectangle. When you select the object in the future, it will appear as a single object with one set of resize handles (see fig. 22.4).

Sometimes you only want to group multiple objects temporarily. Suppose that you have moved or resized your clock drawing, and now you want to apply different attributes to the various components of the clock. To separate objects that are grouped, select the grouped object, then choose the **D**raw **U**ngroup command. PowerPoint separates the objects, and each object's selection handles are visible once again on the slide, as they appeared earlier in figure 22.3.

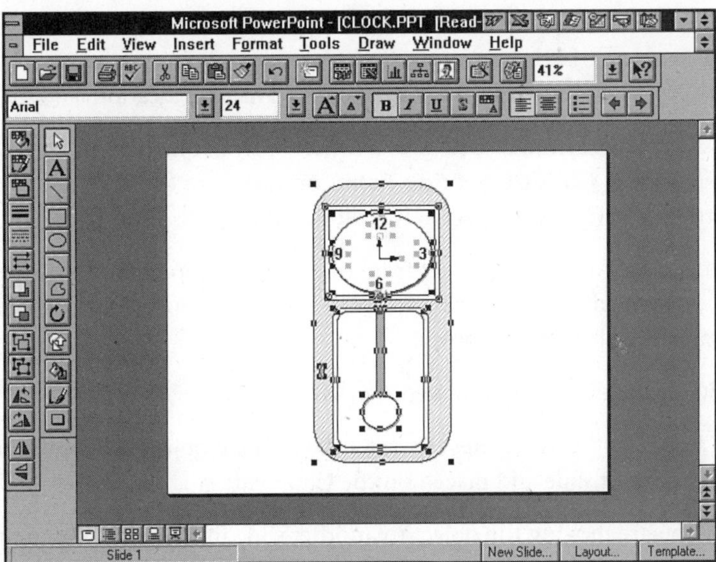

Fig. 22.3
A drawing comprises many individual objects.

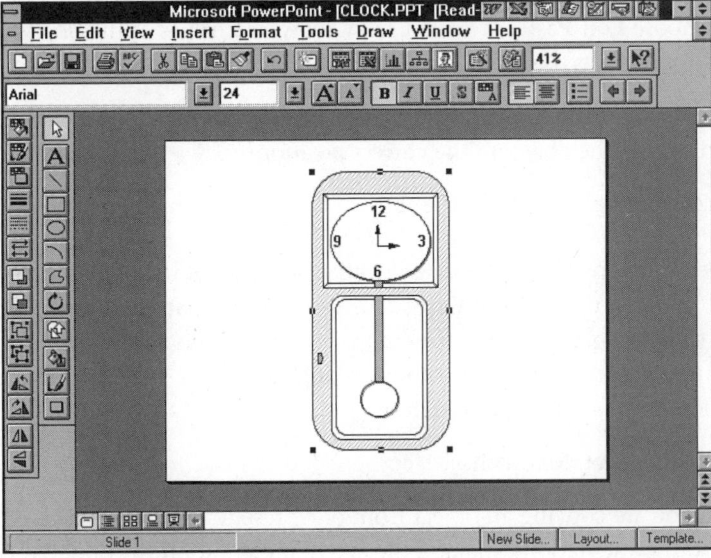

Fig. 22.4
Individual objects are grouped as a whole.

Moving and Copying Objects

Occasionally, you need to move or copy objects in a presentation. Moving an object within a slide is as simple as clicking and dragging the object to a new location. As you drag the mouse to a new location, the original object stays in its current location on the slide while a "ghost" image (a dotted-line silhouette) of the object follows your mouse movements around the screen. Release the mouse button when the silhouette of the object is positioned correctly. PowerPoint then moves the object to its new location.

To move an object from one slide to another or from one presentation to another, use the **E**dit Cu**t** and **E**dit **P**aste commands or the keyboard shortcuts Ctrl+X and Ctrl+V, respectively. Follow these steps:

1. If you are moving an object from one presentation to another, open both presentations, making the active presentation the one that contains the object to be moved.
2. Select the object to be moved.

3. Choose **E**dit Cu**t**, or press Ctrl+X. The selected object is removed from the current slide and placed on the Clipboard.
4. If you are moving the object to another slide in the same presentation, display that slide. If you are moving the object to another presentation, make it the active presentation and display the correct slide.

5. Choose **E**dit **P**aste, or press Ctrl+V. PowerPoint pastes the object on the current slide.
6. Reposition the object appropriately on the current slide by clicking and dragging the object to the correct position.
7. Click any blank area of the slide to deselect the object, or press Esc.

Tip
When moving an object, use the arrow keys to make minor adjustments up, down, right, or left. First select the object, and then press any of the arrow keys. Press Esc when the object is positioned correctly.

The steps for copying an object are similar to those for moving an object except that you use the **E**dit **C**opy command rather than the **E**dit Cu**t** command (the keyboard shortcut for the Copy command is Ctrl+C). As when moving an object, you can also copy an object within a slide, within a presentation, or to another presentation.

To copy an object, follow these steps:

1. If you are copying an object from one presentation to another, open both presentations, making the active presentation the one that contains the object to be copied.
2. Select the object to be copied.

3. Choose **E**dit **C**opy, or press Ctrl+C. The selected object remains unchanged on the current slide and a copy is placed on the Clipboard.

4. If you are copying the object to another slide in the same presentation, display that slide. If you are copying the object to another presentation, make it the active presentation and display the correct slide.

5. Choose **E**dit **P**aste, or press Ctrl+V. PowerPoint pastes the object on the current slide.

6. Reposition the object appropriately on the current slide by clicking and dragging the object to the correct position.

7. Click any blank area of the slide to deselect the object, or press Esc.

Resizing and Scaling Objects

Throughout this chapter you have already seen several examples of the resize handles that become visible when you select an object. To resize an object, you first click the object to select it, and then drag any resize handle to a new position.

The resize handles that appear on the sides of the selection box resize in one dimension only. For instance, if you click the resize handle at the top of the selection box, you can stretch or shrink the height of an object on its top only; the bottom remains anchored. If you click the right resize handle, you can stretch or shrink the width of an object on its right side only; the left side remains anchored. Release the mouse button when the object is the size you want.

The resize handles that appear at the corners of an object enable you to resize an object in two dimensions at once. If you click the resize handle in the upper right corner of an object, for instance, you can change the height or width of the object by dragging the handle in any direction. Whenever you drag a corner handle, the handle in the opposite corner remains anchored while you expand or contract the object's height and width.

When you resize in two dimensions at once, you may want to maintain an object's height-to-width-ratio. To do so, hold the Shift key as you drag any corner resize handle. The handle in the opposite corner remains anchored while you resize the object. Or you might want to resize in two dimensions at once, from the center of the object outward. To do so, hold down the Ctrl key as you drag any corner handle. By holding both the Shift and Ctrl keys as you drag a corner handle, you can maintain an object's height-to-width ratio *and* resize from the center outward, all in one step.

Tip

If you change your mind about an object's new size, choose **E**dit **U**ndo, or press Ctrl+Z.

Another way to resize an object is to scale it. Scaling enables you to specify an object's size by percentage. If you want an object to be half its current size, for example, you scale it by 50 percent. To scale an object, choose the **D**raw **S**cale command, which displays the Scale dialog box shown in figure 22.5.

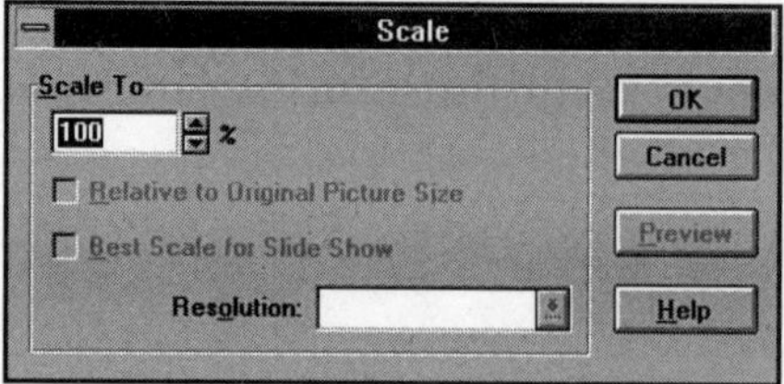

Fig. 22.5 Use the Scale dialog box to size an object precisely.

To scale an object, follow these steps:

1. Select the object.
2. Choose the **D**raw **S**cale command. The Scale dialog box appears.
3. In the % box, enter a number greater than 100 to enlarge the object; type a number smaller than 100 to reduce the object. You can either type a number or click the up or down arrows to change the setting.
4. (Optional) To preview the object, choose the **P**review button. If necessary, repeat step 3 to resize the object.
5. Choose OK.

As an alternative to the steps above, you can have PowerPoint determine a scale for you by selecting the **B**est Scale for Slide Show option in the Scale dialog box. This option automatically chooses the best scale for an object to ensure optimal viewing during an on-screen slide show.

Troubleshooting

My object is a rectangle 1 inch wide by 2 inches high. How can I use the resize handles to add approximately 1/2 inch to the top and bottom of the object uniformly?

Hold down the Ctrl key as you drag either the top or bottom resize handle. You also can use the Ctrl key with a side resize handle to add or subtract width uniformly. When used with a corner resize handle, the Ctrl key enables you to resize in two dimensions from the center of the object outward.

I entered 100% in the Scale dialog box to restore an imported picture to its original size, but the picture is still the wrong size and its dimensions are not correct.

When the original dimensions of an imported picture have been altered, choosing 100% scale will not restore them. You must select the Relative to Original Picture Size option as well. This option restores the picture's original height-to-width ratio to the scale you specify (use 100% for the original picture size). If, for example, you select the Relative to Original Picture Size option and enter 200% for the scale, the original dimensions are restored and the object is twice its original size.

Aligning Objects

Sometimes you may want to align objects in a slide to give the slide a neater, more polished appearance. PowerPoint takes the guesswork out of aligning objects by offering a variety of automatic alignment options. You can use the traditional left-, center-, or right-alignment styles, or you can align the tops, bottoms, or middles of objects. Each of these alignment options is illustrated in the slide sorter view shown in figure 22.6. In the figure, slide 1 shows how the objects were originally arranged. Slides 2, 3, and 4 illustrate how the objects are aligned at the far left, horizontal center, and far right of the slide. Slides 5, 6, and 7 show how the objects are aligned at the top, vertical midpoint, and bottom of the slide.

Tip
You can add any of the six alignment buttons to your toolbar by choosing **View Toolbars**.

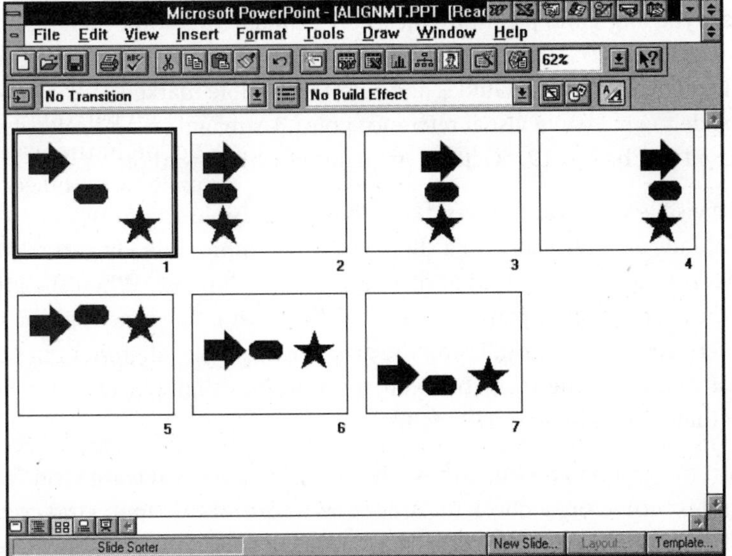

Fig. 22.6
PowerPoint offers six automatic alignment styles.

To use any of PowerPoint's alignment options, follow these steps:

1. Select the objects you want to align.
2. Choose the **D**raw **A**lign command. (You must select two or more objects on the current slide to enable the Draw Align command.) The Align cascading menu shown in figure 22.7 appears.
3. From the cascading menu, choose an alignment option. PowerPoint realigns the selected objects.

Fig. 22.7 Choose an alignment style from the Align cascading menu.

Using the Grid

◀ "Displaying Rulers and Guides," p. 429

To help you align and position objects on a slide, PowerPoint includes three tools—*guides*, *rulers*, and the *grid*—which can be toggled on and off with a simple menu command. Guides and rulers are visible markers that appear on a slide to give you a visual reference point. Using guides and rulers is discussed in Chapter 19, "Getting Acquainted with PowerPoint."

Tip
If you change your mind about the alignment you choose, you can restore the original position of the selected objects by choosing **E**dit **U**ndo or by pressing Ctrl+Z.

Unlike visible guides and rulers, the grid is an invisible set of lines that run horizontally and vertically on a slide. The lines (approximately every 1/8 inch) form a grid similar to that of a very fine graph paper. When the grid is turned on, objects that you draw or move "snap" into alignment at the nearest intersection of the grid. Using the grid helps to make alignment of objects an easier task. Use the grid when you don't need to align objects more precisely than approximately 1/8 inch.

To turn the grid on and off, choose the **D**raw **S**nap to Grid command. When the grid is turned on, a check mark appears next to the Snap to Grid command on the menu (no indicators appear in the PowerPoint window). You also can turn the grid on and off temporarily by holding the Alt key as you drag an object to a new location on a slide. If you experiment with pressing the Alt key on and off as you drag an object, you can see for yourself how the grid works as you watch the object track smoothly across the screen or "snap" into place.

Rotating and Flipping Objects

One way to add visual interest to your slides is to rotate or flip an object. Rotating refers to turning an object around a 360-degree radius. Flipping refers to "turning an object over"—either horizontally or vertically—to create a mirror image of that object. You can rotate or flip any PowerPoint object.

> **Note**
>
> A PowerPoint object is defined as an object created within PowerPoint using a PowerPoint tool (such as the drawing tools) or an object imported from another program and then converted to a PowerPoint object. To convert an object to a PowerPoint object, you must be able to ungroup its components and then regroup them using the **D**raw **G**roup command. If you cannot do this, the object cannot be converted to a PowerPoint object and, therefore, cannot be rotated or flipped.

PowerPoint enables you to rotate an object in either of two ways. You can rotate an object to any position in a 360-degree radius, or you can rotate an object in 90-degree increments to the left or right, which has the effect of turning the object 1/4 turn. When you flip an object, you flip it either horizontally or vertically 180 degrees. These choices are illustrated on the Rotate/Flip cascading menu shown in figure 22.8.

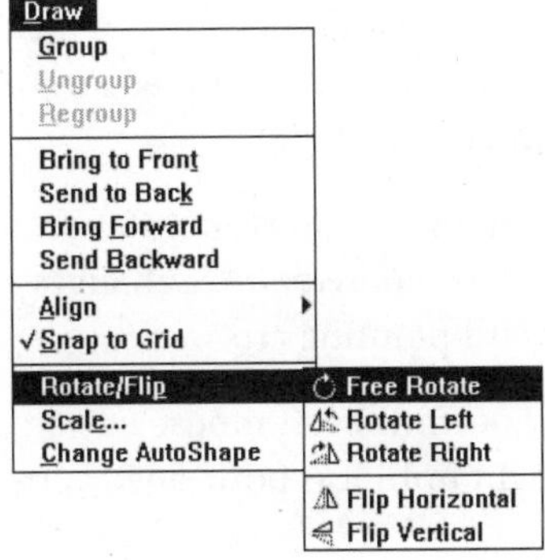

Fig. 22.8
Rotation and flipping options are shown on the Rotate/Flip cascading menu.

To rotate an object by 90 degrees or flip an object 180 degrees, follow these steps:

1. Select the object to rotate.
2. Choose the **D**raw Rotate/Fli**p** command.
3. From the cascading menu, choose the Rotate Left or Rotate Right command to rotate the object, or the Flip Horizontal or Flip Vertical command to flip the object. PowerPoint immediately rotates or flips the object in the direction selected.
4. To rotate the object another 90 degrees, repeat steps 2 and 3.
5. Click any blank area of the slide to deselect the object.

To rotate an object to any angle in a 360-degree radius, you use the Free Rotate tool on the Drawing toolbar or the Free Rotate command on the Rotate/Flip cascading menu. In either case, the mouse pointer changes as shown below:

This mouse pointer indicates that the Free Rotate command or tool is currently selected.

This mouse pointer indicates that the pointer is in position (over a resize handle) for you to begin rotating the selected object.

To rotate an object to any position on a 360-degree radius, follow these steps:

1. Select the object to rotate.

2. Click the Free Rotate Tool on the Drawing toolbar, or choose the **D**raw Rotate/Fli**p** command and then choose the Free Rotate command. The mouse pointer changes to two curved arrows that form a circle with a cross in the center.
3. Position the cross in the mouse pointer on top of any of the object's resize handles. The mouse pointer changes again to a cross in the center with four outward-pointing arrows.
4. Click and hold down the left mouse button as you rotate the object either left or right until it is positioned correctly; then release the mouse button.
5. Click any blank area of the slide to deselect the object.

You can rotate or flip several objects at once, and you can rotate or flip objects that are grouped. When you select multiple objects to rotate or flip, each object rotates or flips independently of the others around its own center point, and each object rotates to the same angle as all others. When you rotate or flip objects that are grouped, however, the individual objects *do not* rotate or flip independently; they rotate or flip *as a whole*. This difference is illustrated in figure 22.9.

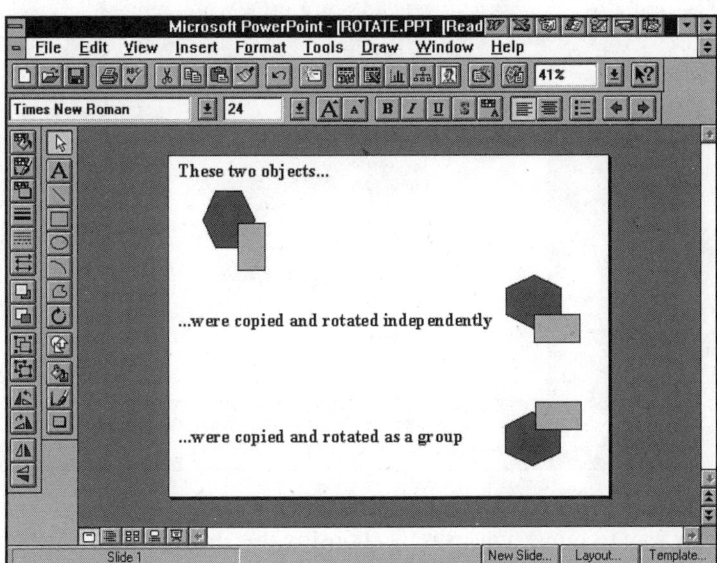

Fig. 22.9 Multiple objects rotate or flip differently depending on their grouping.

Changing the Stacking Order of Objects

As you add objects to a slide and overlap them, you quickly discover that the object drawn first appears underneath and the object drawn most recently appears on top of the others. Think of the objects being "stacked" on the slide as you draw them. The most recently drawn object appears and remains at the top of the stack unless you change the stacking order. In figure 22.10, the circle was drawn first, then the triangle, and then the star. No matter where you move the objects on the slide, the circle is on the bottom, the triangle in the middle, and the star on top.

PowerPoint lets you change the stacking order of objects in several ways. The **D**raw Bring **F**orward and **D**raw Send **B**ackward commands let you move an object one step at a time forward or backward through a stack of objects.

So, if you have six objects stacked on top of one another and the sixth object is selected, that object becomes the fifth object in the stack if you choose the Bring **F**orward command. If you choose the Send **B**ackward command, nothing happens because the selected object is already at the bottom of the stack.

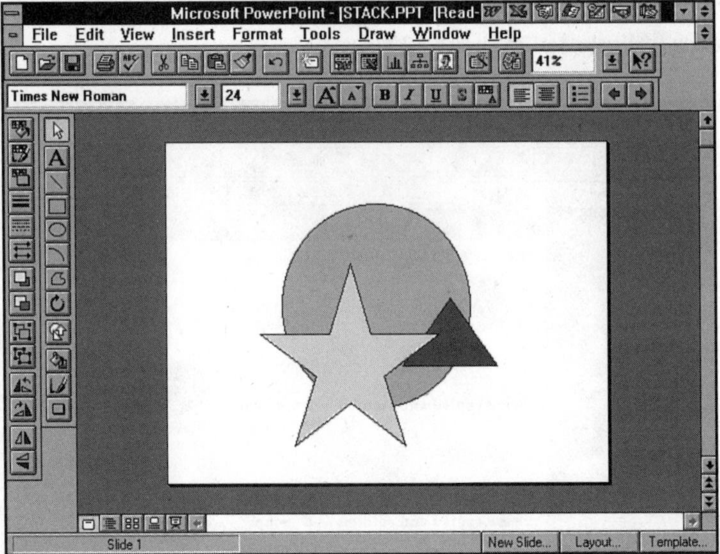

Fig. 22.10
Objects overlap one another in the order they were drawn.

The other way to move objects is by choosing the **D**raw Bring to Fron**t** and Send to Bac**k** commands. These commands move a selected object to the top or to the bottom of the entire stack, regardless of its current position or the total number of objects in the stack. In figure 22.11, all three objects were realigned, and the triangle was selected and brought to the front.

Note

Small objects can easily become completely obscured by others. If you cannot find an object to select it, select any object on the slide, then press the Tab key until the object you want is selected. Each time you press the Tab key, a new object on the current slide is selected.

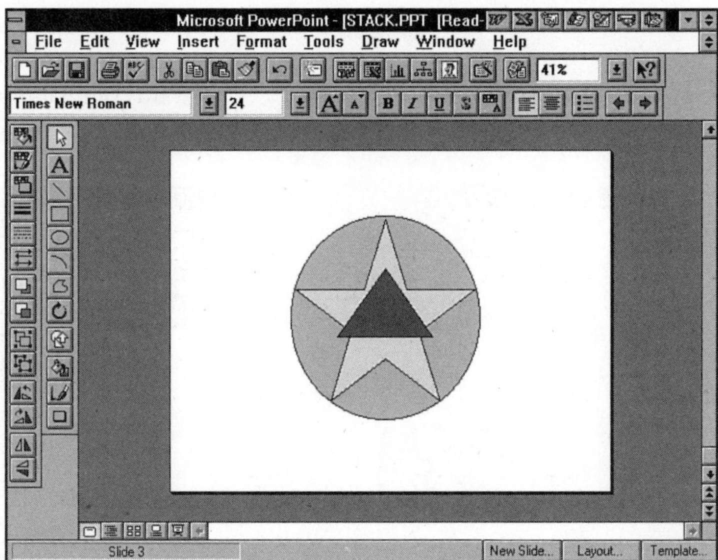

Fig. 22.11
The triangle was brought to the front, and all objects were centered.

From Here...

In this chapter, you learned all the skills you need to know to work with objects, including selecting and grouping, moving and copying, aligning, rotating, flipping, and stacking. For related information about working with objects, refer to the following chapters:

- Chapter 23, "Drawing Shapes, Curves, and Lines," describes how to use PowerPoint's drawing tools to add drawn objects to your slides.
- Chapter 24, "Enhancing a Presentation," describes how to add color, borders, shadows, and other enhancements to objects.

Chapter 23

Drawing Shapes, Curves, and Lines

by Debbie Walkowski

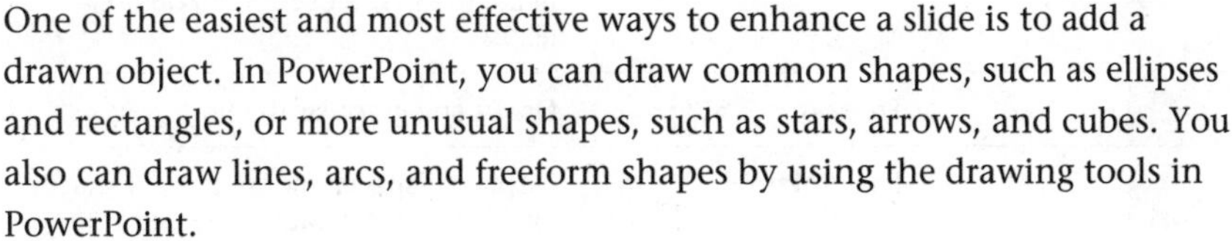

One of the easiest and most effective ways to enhance a slide is to add a drawn object. In PowerPoint, you can draw common shapes, such as ellipses and rectangles, or more unusual shapes, such as stars, arrows, and cubes. You also can draw lines, arcs, and freeform shapes by using the drawing tools in PowerPoint.

In this chapter, you learn to

- Use the drawing tools in PowerPoint
- Draw shapes, AutoShapes, and perfect shapes
- Draw lines, arcs, and freeform shapes
- Modify shapes

Using PowerPoint's Drawing Tools

By now, you should be familiar with the Drawing and Drawing+ toolbars in PowerPoint because they are displayed in the PowerPoint window automatically whenever you start the program. The tools on the Drawing+ toolbar (the leftmost toolbar in the PowerPoint window) are used primarily to change the look of objects on a slide. You learn more about these tools in Chapter 24, "Enhancing a Presentation." In this chapter, you learn how to use the tools in the Drawing toolbar. These tools are described in table 23.1.

Table 23.1 Tools in PowerPoint's Standard Drawing Toolbar

Button	Drawing Tool	Function
	Selection	Displays an arrow-shaped mouse pointer that enables you to select objects in a slide.
	Text	Displays an inverted T-shaped insertion point that enables you to enter text in a slide.
	Line	Draws straight lines in any direction from the point at which you click the mouse.
	Rectangle	Draws rectangles of any dimension.
	Ellipse	Draws curved shapes, including ellipses and circles.
	Arc	Draws arched or curved lines. When filled, the shape becomes a quarter-ellipse.
	Freeform	Draws any irregular shape.
	Free Rotate	Displays a special mouse pointer that enables you to rotate a selected object to any angle on a 360-degree radius.
	AutoShapes	Displays the AutoShapes toolbar, which contains buttons for 24 predefined shapes, including a star, a cube, and an arrow.
	Fill On/Off	Adds or removes the default fill characteristics (color, shade, and pattern) of the selected object.
	Line On/Off	Adds or removes the default line characteristics (color, style, and width) of the selected object.
	Shadow On/Off	Adds or removes the default shadow characteristics (color and offset) of the selected object.

To activate a drawing tool, simply click it. When you click the Text tool, the mouse pointer changes to an inverted T-shaped insertion point. When you click the Line, Rectangle, Ellipse, Arc, Freeform, or AutoShape tool, the mouse pointer changes to a crosshair. To activate any of the remaining tools—Free Rotate, Fill On/Off, Line On/Off, and Shadow On/Off—you must select an object before you click the tool.

Drawing Shapes

In the context of this chapter, a *shaped object*, or *shape*, is defined as a closed object that you draw with a PowerPoint drawing tool, including circles, ellipses, squares, and rectangles. All of the shapes in the AutoShapes toolbar also are considered to be shapes; these are discussed in the next section of this chapter.

To draw a shape, follow these steps:

1. In the Drawing toolbar, click the Rectangle or Ellipse tool to select that shape.
2. Move the mouse pointer to the approximate location in the slide where you want to draw the object. The mouse pointer changes to a crosshair.
3. Click and drag the mouse in any direction. As you drag the mouse, a solid outline of the shape appears in the slide.
4. When the object is the shape and size you want, release the mouse button. The object is selected automatically.
5. Click any blank area of the slide to deselect the object.

Figure 23.1 illustrates what you see on-screen while you draw an object. As you draw, don't feel that you must position your object perfectly the first time; you can move, copy, resize, rotate, flip, or align any object you draw.

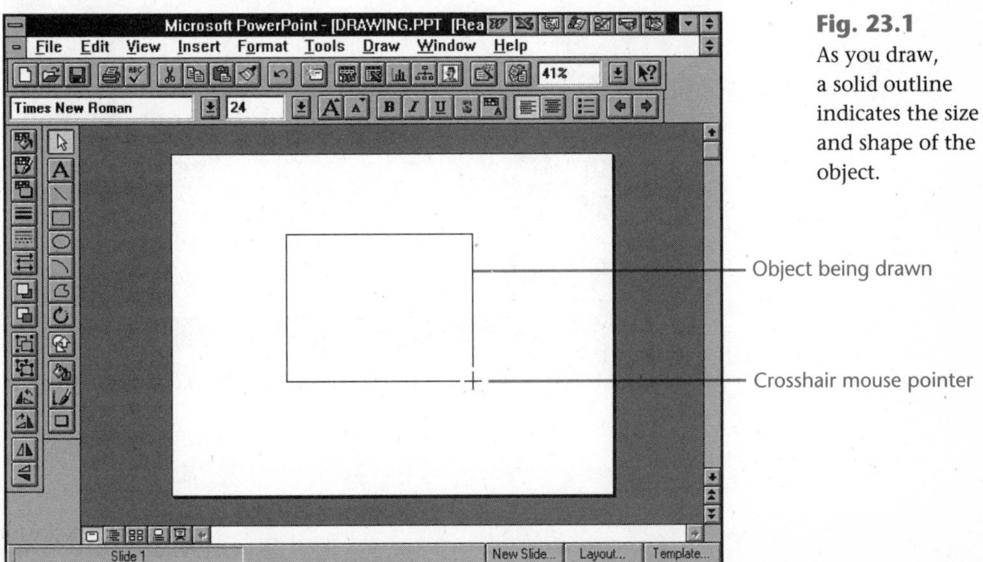

Fig. 23.1
As you draw, a solid outline indicates the size and shape of the object.

Note

Depending on the presentation template you are using when you draw an object, PowerPoint automatically fills the object with a color called the *fill* color (in some templates, the fill color might be white). The fill color is determined automatically by the color scheme of the template you are using. In Chapter 24, "Enhancing a Presentation," you learn how to work with color schemes and change the fill color of an object. For now, don't worry about changing the colors of the objects you draw.

Drawing AutoShapes

The AutoShapes tool is a unique drawing tool in that it displays its own toolbar when you click it. The toolbar contains 24 predefined shapes that you can draw instantly simply by clicking and dragging the mouse. You needn't use the Line tool to draw a perfect star, diamond, or arrow because these shapes are available in the AutoShapes toolbar (see fig. 23.2). Other shapes in this toolbar include the parallelogram, trapezoid, triangle, pentagon, hexagon, octagon, cube, cross, and seal (starburst). The AutoShapes toolbar makes it easy for you to draw shapes that you frequently might include in your slides.

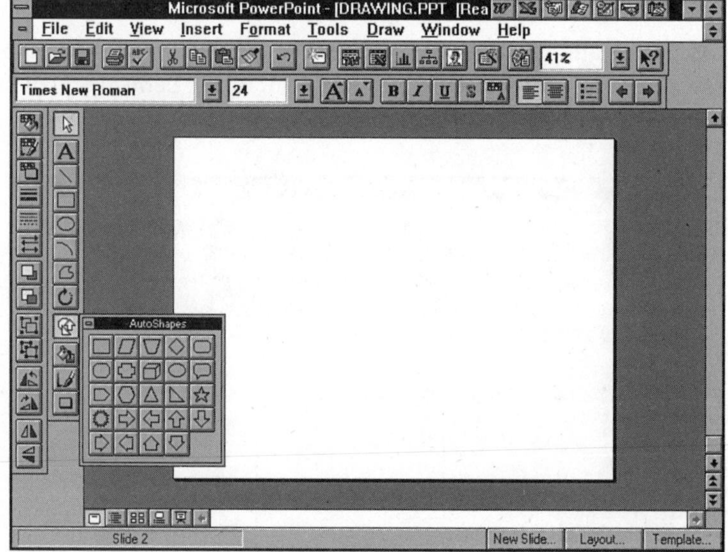

Fig. 23.2 Choose a shape from the AutoShapes toolbar.

To draw an AutoShape, you use the same technique as for an ellipse or rectangle, except that you must select an AutoShape tool before you begin drawing. Follow these steps:

Tip
When you click the AutoShapes tool, the toolbar pops up as shown in figure 23.2. You can move or reconfigure the toolbar simply by dragging it to another location onscreen.

1. Click the AutoShapes tool in the Drawing toolbar. The AutoShapes toolbar appears.
2. Click an AutoShape to activate it.
3. Place the mouse pointer in the slide where you want to draw the object. The mouse pointer changes to a crosshair.
4. Click and drag the mouse in any direction. As you drag, a solid outline of the shape appears.
5. When the object is the shape and size you want, release the mouse button. The object is selected automatically.
6. Click any blank area of the slide to deselect the object.

Drawing Perfect Shapes

To draw a perfect or *uniform* shape, you follow the same basic steps for drawing a shape, except that you use the Shift key as the "constraint" key. Holding down the Shift key maintains the horizontal and vertical distance from the mouse pointer as you draw, so you can use the Ellipse tool, for example, to draw a perfect circle. You can draw a perfect square with the Rectangle, Rounded Rectangle, Cube, or Balloon tool. Figure 23.3 shows several uniform shapes.

To draw a uniform shape, follow these steps:

1. Click the drawing tool you want to use.
2. Place the mouse pointer in the slide where you want to draw the object. The mouse pointer changes to a crosshair.
3. Press and hold down the Shift key.
4. Click and drag the mouse pointer in any direction.
5. When the object is the uniform shape and size you want, release the mouse button. The object is selected automatically.
6. Click any blank area of the slide to deselect the object.

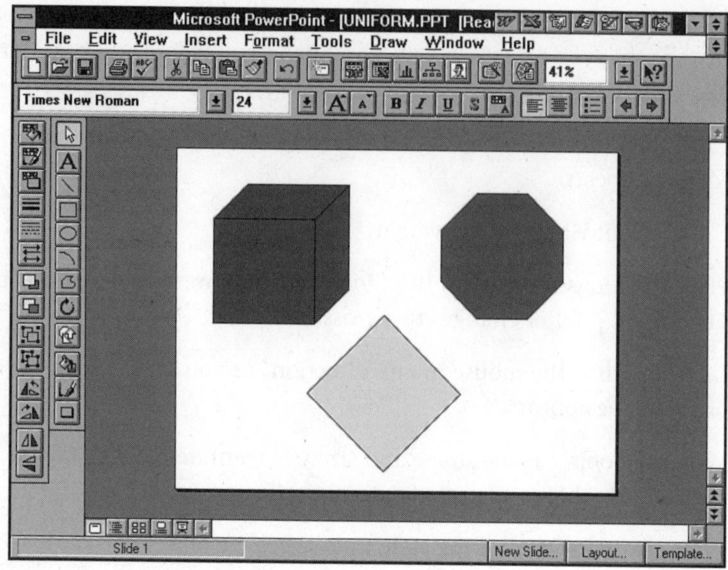

Fig. 23.3 Examples of uniform shapes drawn with the Shift key held down.

Drawing from the Center Outward

You have learned how to draw a shape by starting at one of the corners and drawing in any direction. Sometimes, you might want to draw a shape from the center outward. For example, you might want to center several objects on top of one another. To draw an object from the center outward, you use another constraint key: Ctrl. When you press the Ctrl key as you draw a shape, the center of the object remains anchored at the point where you place the crosshair when you begin drawing.

Tip
You can hold down both constraint keys—Ctrl and Shift—to draw uniform shapes from the center outward.

To draw from the center outward, follow these steps:

1. Click the drawing tool you want to use.
2. Position the crosshair in the slide where you want the center of the object to be located.
3. Press and hold down the Ctrl key.
4. Click and drag the mouse in any direction. As you draw, the center point of the object remains anchored.
5. When the object is the shape and size you want, release the mouse button. The object is selected automatically.
6. Click any blank area of the slide to deselect the object.

Note

To center several objects on a specific point, draw two intersecting lines (one horizontal and one vertical) to mark the point. Then position the crosshair on the point of intersection when you begin to draw the object. You can remove the lines after you draw and center all of your objects.

Switching and Adjusting Shapes

After you draw a shape, you might want to change it to a different shape. You might have enclosed some special information in a star, for example, and then decide to change the star to an octagon. Rather than delete the star and start over, you easily can change it to a different shape. To change a shape, you use the **D**raw **C**hange AutoShape command, which displays the cascade menu shown in figure 23.4.

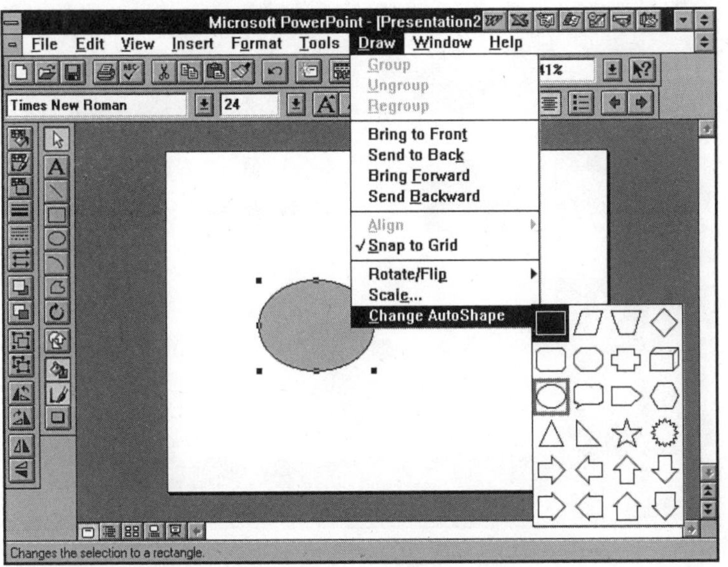

Fig. 23.4
The Change AutoShape cascade menu resembles the AutoShape toolbar.

To change a shape, follow these steps:

1. Select the shape you want to change.

2. Choose **D**raw **C**hange AutoShape. PowerPoint displays a cascade menu similar to the AutoShapes toolbar.

Tip
You can change the shape back again by choosing **E**dit **U**ndo, pressing Ctrl+Z, or clicking the Undo tool in the toolbar. You must undo the change *before* taking any other action.

3. Click the AutoShape you want to use. PowerPoint immediately converts the original shape to the new AutoShape. The object remains selected.

4. Use the resize handles to resize the shape, if necessary.

5. Click any blank area of the screen to deselect the object.

Some objects have unique shape characteristics that you can adjust. For example, you can make the arms of the cross AutoShape thicker or thinner; you can adjust the width of an arrowhead or the length of the sides of an octagon. Objects that can be adjusted display a diamond-shaped *adjustment handle*, as shown in figure 23.5.

Note

Symmetrical objects do not have adjustment handles.

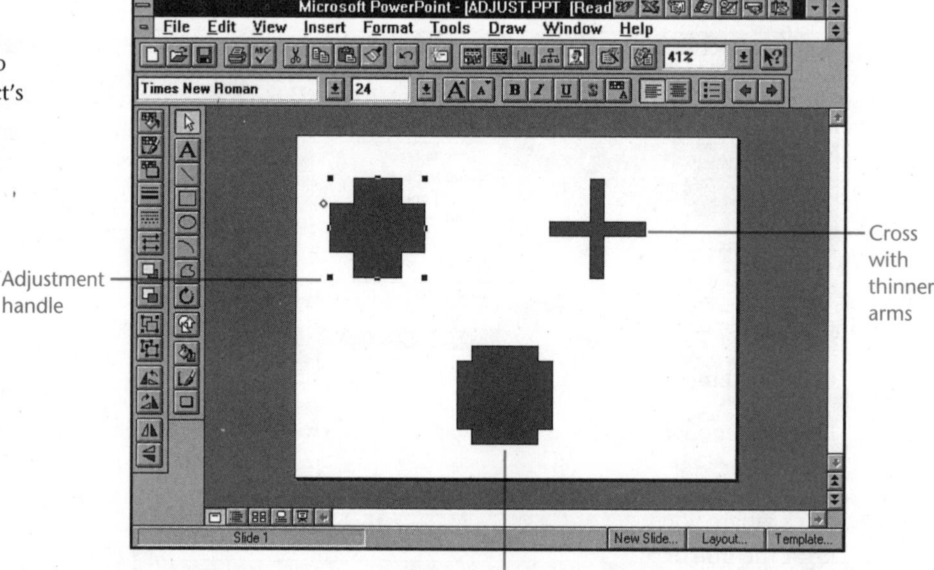

Fig. 23.5
Use the adjustment handle to adjust an object's unique shape characteristics.

To adjust an object, follow these steps:

1. Select the object you want to adjust.

2. Click the adjustment handle and drag it in any direction until you are satisfied with the adjustment. Then release the mouse button. The object remains selected.

3. Click any blank area of the slide to deselect the object.

Drawing Lines and Arcs

The technique for drawing lines and arcs is similar to that used for drawing shapes. The only difference between drawing lines and arcs and drawing other types of shapes is that lines and arcs are not enclosed objects. Lines and arcs have a beginning point and an end point, with resize handles at each of those points. Figure 23.6 shows a drawing made with lines and arcs.

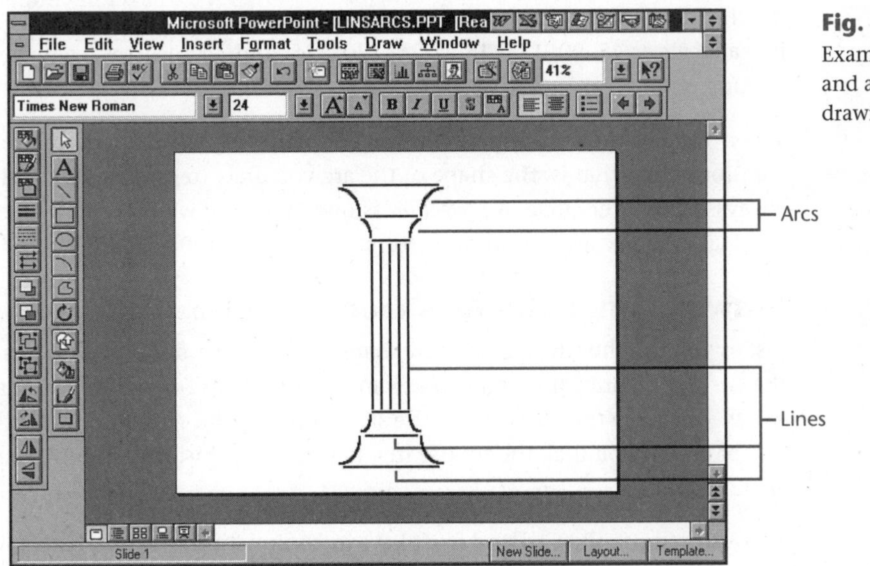

Fig. 23.6
Examples of lines and arcs in a drawing.

To draw a line or arc, follow these steps:

1. Click the Line or Arc tool in the Drawing toolbar.
2. Place the mouse pointer in the slide area. The mouse pointer changes to a crosshair.
3. Click where you want the line or arc to begin, and then drag the mouse until the line or arc is complete.
4. Release the mouse button. The line or arc is selected automatically.
5. Click any area of the slide to deselect the line or arc.

Drawing Perfect Lines and Arcs

In the "Drawing Perfect Shapes" section earlier in this chapter, you learned that the Shift key can be used to draw uniform objects. Used in conjunction with the Line tool, the Shift key enables you to draw vertical lines, horizontal lines, and lines at a 45-degree angle.

To draw a vertical line, press and hold down the Shift key, and then drag the mouse vertically from the starting point of the line. To draw a horizontal line, press and hold down the Shift key, and then drag the mouse horizontally from the starting point. To draw a line at a 45-degree angle, press and hold down the Shift key, and then drag the mouse diagonally in the direction you want to draw the line.

Experiment with the various angles by holding down the Shift key and moving the mouse in a circle around the beginning point of the line. A straight line appears at 45, 90, 135, 180, 225, 270, 315, and 360 degrees from the starting point.

When you use the Shift key in conjunction with the Arc tool, you can draw a uniform arc—that is, the shape of the arc you draw (regardless of the size) always is a quarter-circle. A *perfect arc* is one in which two lines drawn perpendicular to the arc's end points form a right angle (90 degrees).

Drawing Lines and Arcs from a Center Point

Just as you use the Ctrl key to draw shapes from the center outward, you use the Ctrl key to draw lines and arcs from a center point outward. The point at which you place the crosshair in the slide becomes the center point for the line or arc. As you drag the mouse in any direction, this center point remains anchored.

You also can use the Ctrl and Shift keys in conjunction with the Line and Arc tools to draw uniform lines and arcs outward from a center point.

Troubleshooting

I can use the Shift key with the Line tool to draw lines at 45-degree angles, but I want to draw a line at an angle other than 45 degrees.

To draw a line at any angle around a 360-degree radius, press and hold down the Ctrl key as you move the mouse in a circular motion.

I want to change the length or direction of a line and the size or shape of an arc.

Lines contain two resize handles, one at each end of the line. Drag either handle to change the length of a line or its direction. Arcs are defined by eight resize handles, one at each corner plus one on each side of a rectangle. Drag any of the eight handles to change either the size or shape of an arc.

Drawing Freeform Shapes

Using the Freeform tool, you can draw any type of freeform shape or polygon. A freeform shape can consist of curved lines, straight lines, or a combination of the two. You might use the Freeform tool to draw a cartoon, create an unusual shape, or write your name. A freeform shape can be open (that is, the beginning point and end point don't meet) or closed (the beginning point and end point meet to form an object). A closed shape made up of straight lines is called a *polygon*.

To draw a shape (open or closed) consisting of straight lines, click and release the mouse button at each vertex in the shape. A *vertex* is the point at which you click and release the mouse button while drawing a freeform shape. To draw freehand shapes, drag the freeform tool and then double-click where you want the shape to end. The Freeform tool remains active until you complete the shape you're drawing by double-clicking or by pressing Enter. To create a closed object, click near the beginning point of the shape. PowerPoint automatically connects the beginning and end points to create an object.

To draw an open or closed shape consisting of straight lines, follow these steps:

1. Click the Freeform tool in the Drawing toolbar.
2. Place the mouse pointer at the point where you want to begin drawing. The mouse pointer changes to a crosshair.
3. Click the mouse button, and then release it.
4. Place the crosshair where you want the first line to end and the second line to begin, and then click and release the mouse button.
5. Repeat step 4, clicking and releasing the mouse button at each vertex.
6. To make the object an open shape, double-click after you draw the last line. To close the shape, place the mouse pointer near the beginning point, and then click the mouse button. PowerPoint draws a straight line connecting the beginning and end points.

To draw an open or closed freehand shape, follow these steps:

1. Click the Freeform tool in the Drawing toolbar.

2. Place the mouse pointer at the point where you want to begin drawing. The mouse pointer changes to a crosshair.

3. Click and drag the mouse in any direction, drawing the shape you want.

4. To create an open object, double-click when you finish drawing, or press Enter. To create a closed shape, double-click near the point where you began drawing. PowerPoint automatically connects the beginning and end points.

As you draw freehand shapes, you can pause at any point by releasing the mouse button. Before beginning to draw again, place the crosshair where it was located before you paused, and then click and drag to continue drawing. To mix straight and curved lines in the same drawing, alternate between clicking a vertex and dragging the mouse.

Editing Freeform Shapes

When you click a freeform shape to select it, it displays the usual eight resize handles. You can drag any of the resize handles to make a freeform shape larger or smaller. Freeform shapes, unlike other shapes, also contain *control handles* (see fig. 23.7). Control handles enable you to modify the freeform shape in addition to simply resizing it.

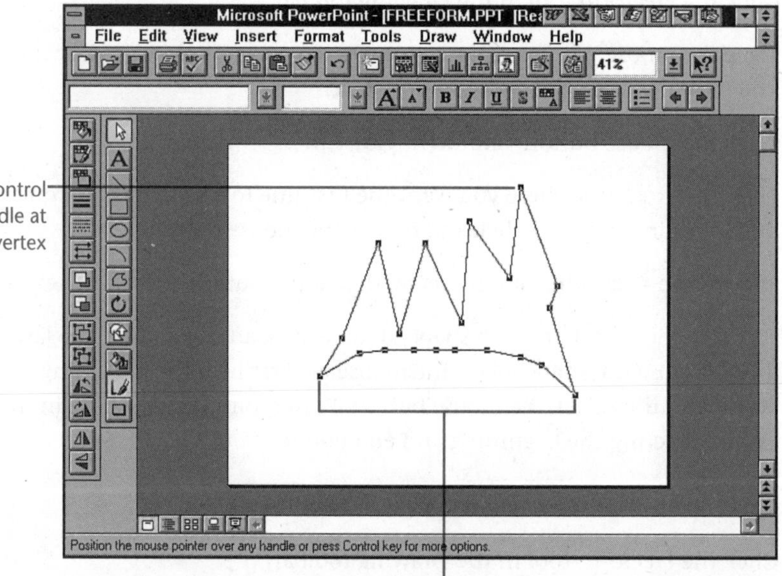

Fig. 23.7
Control handles appear at every vertex and along the curves of a freeform shape.

A control handle appears at each vertex of a freeform shape or polygon. Control handles also appear along the areas where you drag the mouse while drawing a freeform shape. The faster you drag, the fewer control handles appear; the slower you drag, the more control handles appear. If you look closely at the control handles of a freeform shape, you can see that the curves of a shape created by dragging the mouse are not actually curves; they are a series of short lines connected to one another.

You can adjust the shape of a freeform object by dragging an existing control handle to a new position, deleting a control handle, or adding a control handle. Curves that you draw slowly often contain more control handles than are necessary; deleting some handles can make working with the curve easier. If an object contains straight lines that you want to convert to gentle curves, add a few control handles so you can curve the line. In figure 23.8, the bottom edge of the freeform shape shown in figure 23.7 has changed from an upward to a downward curve.

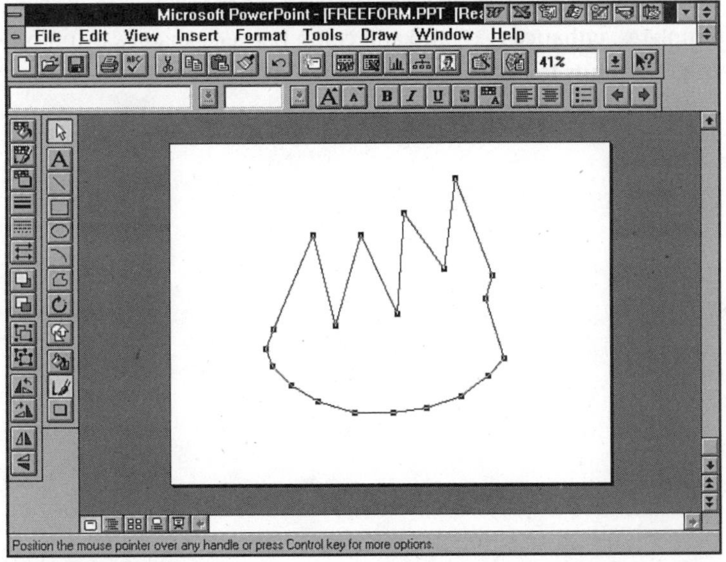

Fig. 23.8
You can move, add, and delete control handles to change the shape of a freeform object.

To display an object's control handles, double-click the object. When you place the mouse pointer on a control handle, the pointer changes to a crosshair. To move a control handle, position the crosshair over the control handle, and then click and drag the handle in any direction. To add a control handle, press and hold down the Shift and Ctrl keys, and then click on the original line where you want to add the handle. To delete a control handle, press and hold down the Ctrl key, and then click the handle.

Tip
To work with small or detailed objects easily, use the Zoom Control button on the toolbar or choose the **V**iew **Z**oom command to zoom in on an object.

Note

When the **D**raw **S**nap to Grid command is turned on, control handles snap into place when you move them. To temporarily turn off the grid so you can move control handles more precisely, hold down the Alt key as you move a control handle.

From Here...

In this chapter, you learned how to create all types of shapes and objects with PowerPoint's drawing tools. Refer to the following chapters for more information about working with objects:

- Chapter 22, "Working with Objects," describes how to manipulate objects by moving, copying, deleting, resizing, grouping, and ungrouping them.
- Chapter 24, "Enhancing a Presentation," describes how to work with templates, enhance text, and add color, borders, shadows, and other enhancements to objects.

Chapter 24

Enhancing a Presentation

by Debbie Walkowski

You can do many things to enhance the appearance of slides in a presentation, whether the slides contain text objects, drawn objects, or inserted objects. When you take the time to add special touches to objects, your slides are easier to read and help hold the attention of your audience. Audiences appreciate interesting slides! Nothing is worse than sitting through a presentation of dull slides that contain no color, patterns, shadows, or special fonts.

In this chapter, you learn the many different techniques you can use to give your slides a powerful presence. You don't have to be a graphic-arts expert; even the simplest touches can make a world of difference in the appearance of a presentation.

In this chapter, you learn to:

- Work with templates
- Enhance text by changing the font, style, and color
- Work with line spacing, bullets, and alignment of text
- Work with colors, fills, and line styles of objects
- Add patterns, shading, borders, and shadows to objects
- Work with color schemes

Working with Templates

In Chapter 19, "Getting Acquainted with PowerPoint," you learned that templates are saved presentation files for which special graphic elements, colors, font sizes, font styles, slide backgrounds, and other special effects have been defined. PowerPoint includes templates specially designed for black-and-white overheads, color overheads, and on-screen slide shows.

Using a template is by far the quickest and easiest way to create professional-looking presentations, because it takes the guesswork and experimentation out of designing a presentation. PowerPoint templates are designed by graphic-arts professionals who understand the elements required to achieve a certain effect and to convey a particular attitude. In Chapter 19, you saw examples of the fiesta (FIESTAC.PPT), world (WORLDC.PPT), and embossed (EMBOSSDC.PPT) templates for color overheads. Figure 24.1 shows the music (MUSICC.PPT) template.

Fig. 24.1
Use this template to convey a musical theme.

In the music template, a musical staff appears across the top of each slide. The notes in the staff are shadowed. Title text is displayed in blue in the 44-point Arial font; subtitle text is displayed in black in the 32-point Arial font. The template's color scheme is shown in the Slide Color Scheme dialog box (see fig. 24.2), displayed by choosing the F**o**rmat Slide **C**olor Scheme command or the Slide Color Scheme command from the shortcut menu.

The MUSICC.PPT template's color scheme is predominately blue, with a light-blue slide background, medium-blue fill for objects, dark-blue title text, and midnight-blue shadows. Red, orange, and white are used as accent colors, and black is used for text and lines. The sample in the lower left corner of the dialog box shows how each of these colors might look on a slide.

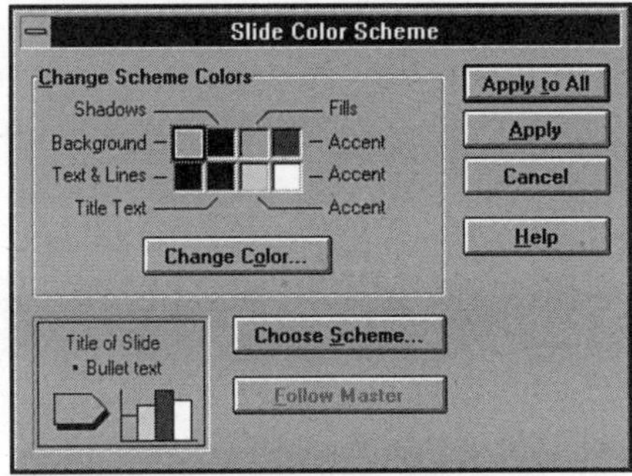

Fig. 24.2
The Slide Color Scheme dialog box displays all colors used in a template.

Choosing a Template

You can specify a template when you create a new presentation; select the **T**emplate option in the PowerPoint dialog box that appears automatically when you start the program.

To change the template of the active presentation, follow these steps:

◄ "Creating a Presentation Using a Template," p. 444

1. Click the Template button in the bottom right corner of the PowerPoint window, or choose the F**o**rmat **P**resentation Template command. The Presentation Template dialog box appears (see fig. 24.3).

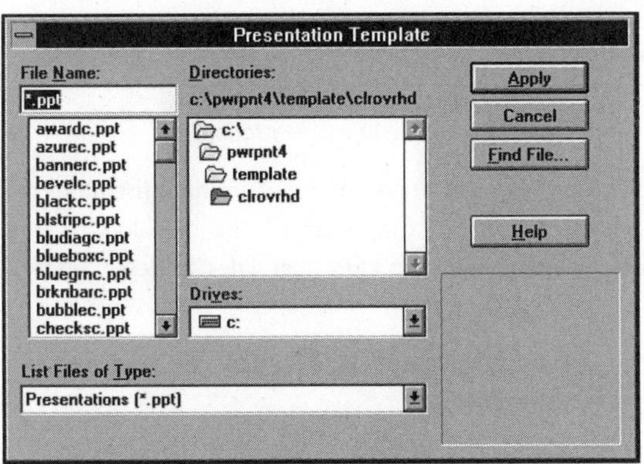

Fig. 24.3
Select a template in the Presentation Template dialog box.

2. Select a template directory in the **D**irectories list, and then highlight a template name in the File **N**ame list.

Note

To preview each template, highlight a template in the File Name list, and then click the up and down arrows in the scroll bar to highlight different templates. A sample of the highlighted template appears in the bottom right corner of the dialog box.

3. Double-click a template name, choose the **A**pply button, or press Enter to select the highlighted template. The dialog box closes, and PowerPoint applies the new template to the active presentation.

Altering a Template

Tip
To identify the template used in a presentation, choose the **F**ile Summary **I**nfo command. The template file name appears in the Summary Infor dialog box.

After you select a template for your presentation, you might want to change several of its characteristics. You might decide to use a different font and larger point size for your slide titles or to add a graphic element (such as your company logo) to the template. To make these changes, which affect all slides in the presentation, you change the slide master after you select a template. Likewise, you might want to change the outline master, handout master, and notes master to make changes that apply to all outline, handout, and notes pages.

You do not have to display the slide master to change colors defined by a template. Instead, choose F**o**rmat Slide **C**olor Scheme command or the Slide Color Scheme command on the shortcut menu to display the Slide Color Scheme dialog box. In this dialog box, you can change individual colors in the current color scheme or specify a different color scheme for the current template. To learn how to change colors, see "Working with Color Schemes" later in this chapter.

Troubleshooting

How can I use more than one template in a presentation?

Templates apply to all slides in a presentation; you cannot use more than one template in a single presentation. You can, however, change colors, fonts, shadows, patterns, and other enhancements in individual slides, as described throughout this chapter.

How can I create a custom template so I don't have to alter a PowerPoint template each time I create a new presentation?

First choose the PowerPoint template on which you want to base your custom template. Then use the Windows File Manager to make a copy of the PowerPoint template file. Give the file a unique file name and store it in the correct template subdirectory (such as c:\pwrpnt4\template\clrovrhd). After the new template file is created, open the file as a presentation and change it for your particular needs, then save and close the file. Now you can apply the custom template to any new or existing presentation.

If I make changes to the slide master in my presentation, how is the PowerPoint template I'm using affected?

Any changes you make to a presentation master affect the current presentation only; the PowerPoint template file you are using is not altered.

Enhancing Text

When you enter text in a slide, the font, style (regular, bold, or italic), size, color, and special effects (underline, shadow, and so on) of the text conform to the settings specified in the current template. Earlier in this chapter, you learned that the MUSICC.PPT template uses the 44-point Arial font in blue for slide titles and the 32-point Arial font in black for slide text. In both cases, the font style is regular (no bold or italic), and no special effects are added. If you want to use a different font, style, size, color, or effect, you can change these settings (collectively called *font settings*) for all slides in a presentation by altering the slide master, or you can change font settings only for selected text objects.

Choosing a Font, Style, and Color for Text

To change font settings, select the text you want to change, then choose the F**o**rmat **F**ont command, or the Font command on the shortcut menu, to display the Font dialog box (see fig. 24.4). The Font, Font Style, Size, and Color settings are self-explanatory; these options appear in most word processing, spreadsheet, and graphics programs. The Effects box, however, contains some options with which you might not be familiar.

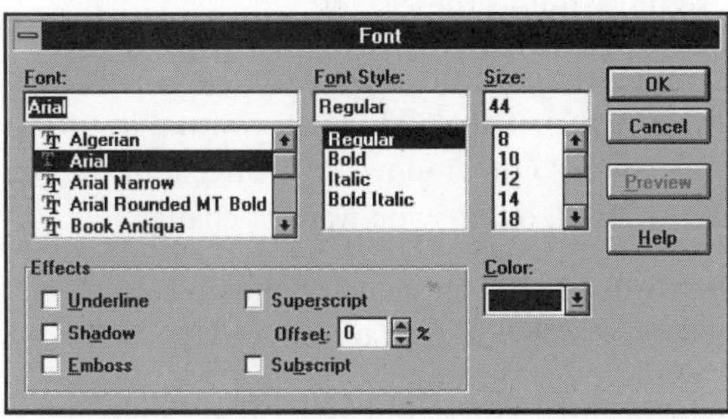

Fig. 24.4
In the Font dialog box, you can select a font, style, size, color, and special effects.

The Shadow option adds a shadow at the bottom and the right side of each character. The Emboss option gives the text the appearance of raised letters by using a light color for the characters and a faint shadow. Figure 24.5 shows an example of each option.

The Subscript option drops a selected character slightly below the normal line level, as in H_20, whereas the Superscript option raises a selected character, as in 10^5. When you choose either of these options, you can specify the Offset percentage—that is, the percentage by which characters are dropped or raised.

Fig. 24.5
The Shadow and Emboss options draw attention to text and make text stand out.

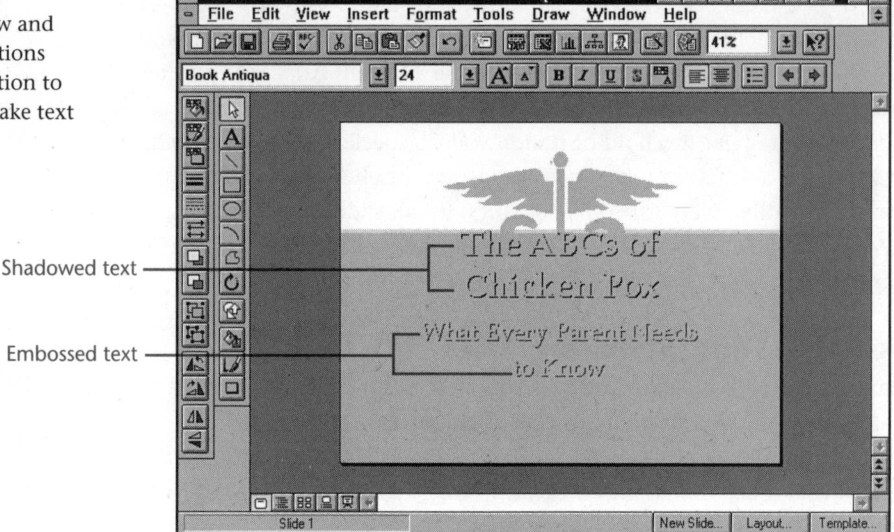

To change font settings, follow these steps:

1. To change font settings in the slide master, press and hold down the Shift key, and then click the Slide Master button in the bottom left corner of the PowerPoint window. To change font settings for selected text objects, select all objects you want to change.

2. Choose the F**o**rmat **F**ont command or choose Font from the shortcut menu. The Font dialog box appears (refer to fig. 24.4).

3. Choose settings in the **F**ont, F**o**nt Style, **S**ize, **C**olor, and Effects boxes. If you choose the Su**b**script or Supe**r**script setting, specify a percentage in the Offse**t** box or use the default setting.

4. Choose OK to apply the changes.

You also can change specific format settings by clicking the following buttons in the Formatting toolbar:

Button	Button Name	Description
Times New Roman	Font	Changes the font of selected text
24	Font Size	Changes the font size of selected text
A	Increase Font Size	Increases the font size
A	Decrease Font Size	Decreases the font size

Changing Line and Paragraph Spacing

Just as the template defines colors, fonts, and other characteristics for a presentation, the template defines the line spacing for text in a text object. PowerPoint enables you to set the spacing between lines, as well as the amount of space before and after paragraphs. In most templates, the default spacing is 1 line, the space after paragraphs is 0, and the space before paragraphs is 0.2 or 0.

You might want to change line or paragraph spacing, depending on the content of your slides. If a slide contains only four bullets, for example, you might want to increase the line spacing so that the bullets fill the slide. If your slide contains several paragraphs of text, you might want to set the space before paragraphs to 0.2 so that each paragraph is distinctly separate from the one before it.

To change line and paragraph spacing, choose the F**o**rmat Line **S**pacing command to display the Line Spacing dialog box (see fig. 24.6). The Line Spacing, Before Paragraph, and After Paragraph options use lines as a unit of measure.

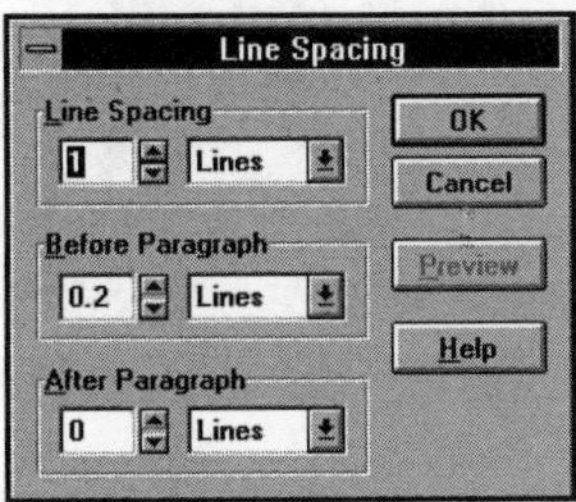

Fig. 24.6
Use the Line Spacing dialog box to set line and paragraph spacing.

If you prefer to use points rather than lines, you can choose the Points option in each of the drop-down lists. (One point equals 1/72 inch.)

To set line or paragraph spacing, follow these steps:

1. Select the text for which you want to adjust line or paragraph spacing.
2. Choose the F**o**rmat Line **S**pacing command. PowerPoint displays the Line Spacing dialog box.
3. In the **L**ine Spacing, **B**efore Paragraph, and **A**fter Paragraph boxes, enter the number of lines or points to be used. If you prefer to use points rather than lines, be sure to choose the Points setting in each drop-down list.
4. Choose OK or press Enter. PowerPoint returns to your slide and reformats the selected text.

Tip
When setting paragraph spacing, specify a setting for **B**efore Paragraph *or* **A**fter Paragraph. If you specify 2 lines for both **B**efore Paragraph *and* **A**fter Paragraph, for example, the net effect is 4 lines.

Aligning Text

Alignment refers to the vertical positioning of text in a text object. In presentation slides, text generally is left-aligned (for paragraphs or bullets) or centered (for titles). However, you also can justify or right-align text (see fig. 24.7). Alignment options appear in a cascading menu when you choose the F**o**rmat **A**lignment command or choose Alignment from the shortcut menu.

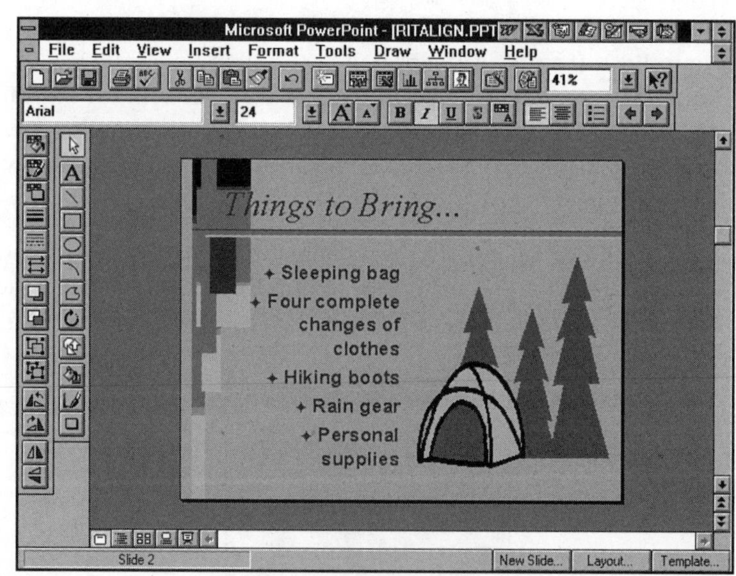

Fig. 24.7
The text to the left of the clip-art picture is right-aligned.

Left alignment aligns text along the left edge of a text object; Right alignment aligns text along the right edge. The Center alignment option aligns text at the center point of the text object so that an equal number of characters appear to the right and left of the center point. The Justify option aligns text along both the right and left edges so that the characters in a line cover the entire width of a text object.

Because alignment involves vertical positioning of text at margins or at the center point, alignment affects entire paragraphs. In other words, you cannot align a single word or line in a paragraph.

You don't have to select any text to align a single paragraph; PowerPoint aligns the entire paragraph in which the insertion point is located. To align several paragraphs, select a portion of text in each paragraph, and then choose an alignment style.

Note

Left Alignment and Center Alignment buttons appear in PowerPoint's Formatting toolbar. You can add Right Alignment and Justify buttons to the Formatting toolbar by customizing it.

Tip

Individual bullet items are separate paragraphs. To realign a set of bullets, select a portion of text in each bullet item.

◄ "Microsoft Applications Toolbars," p. 27

To change the alignment of text, follow these steps:

1. Select the object that contains the text you want to align.
2. Place the insertion point anywhere in the paragraph you want to align, or select a portion of each paragraph you want to align.
3. Choose the F**o**rmat **A**lignment command, or choose **A**lignment from the shortcut menu. The Alignment cascading menu appears.
4. Choose **L**eft, **R**ight, **C**enter, or **J**ustify. PowerPoint immediately realigns the current paragraph or selected paragraphs.

Working with Colors and Line Styles

All objects that you draw in PowerPoint (except lines) have a fill color, a line, and a line style. The *fill color* is the color inside an object; the *line* is the frame that defines the boundaries of an object; and the *line style* defines the width or style of the object's frame.

For any given object, you can turn off the fill color and the line color. Turning both options off makes an object invisible (unless it contains text), so this practice is not as common as turning off one option or the other. In most templates, for example, the line that frames a text object is turned off, because text generally looks better in the slide without a frame. For other objects (such as shapes that you create with the drawing tools), the object's frame usually is visible, and the object has a fill color.

In most templates, an object's line style is a narrow solid line. You can choose any of five wider line styles or any of four double or triple lines. In addition, you can change a solid line to a dashed, dotted, or mixed line by choosing one of the four dashed-line options. If an object is a straight line or arc rather than a shape, you can add arrowheads to either end or to both ends of the line or arc.

Choosing Fill and Line Colors and Line Styles

To set line, fill, and line-style options, use the Colors and Lines dialog box (see fig. 24.8). You display this dialog box by choosing the F**o**rmat Colors and **L**ines command or by choosing Colors and Lines from the shortcut menu.

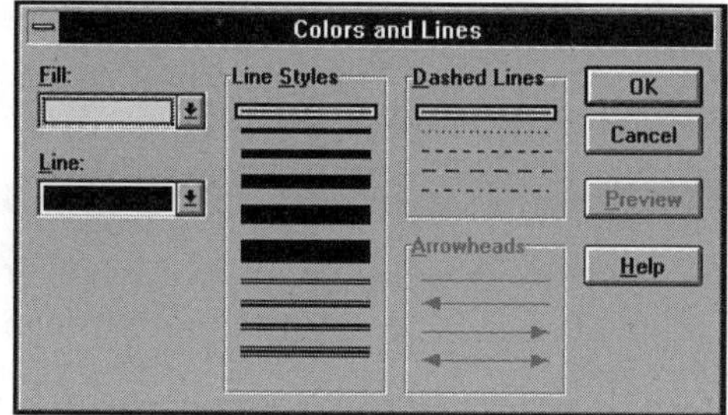

Fig. 24.8
Use the Colors and Lines dialog box to define an object's color and frame style.

To change an object's fill color, follow these steps:

1. Select the object.
2. Choose the F**o**rmat Colors and **L**ines command, or choose Colors and Lines from the shortcut menu. The Colors and Lines dialog box appears, displaying the current fill color in the Fill box.
3. Click the arrow to open the **F**ill drop-down list, which displays the options shown in figure 24.9.

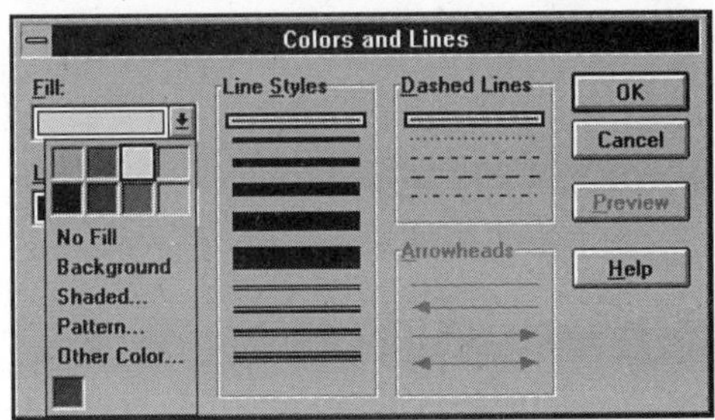

Fig. 24.9
The Fill drop-down list displays fill options.

4. Do one of the following things:

   - Select the No Fill option to remove the fill color from the object.
   - Select one of the colors (derived from the current template).
   - Select the Other Color option, which displays the Other Color dialog box (see fig. 24.10). Select a color in the Color Palette, and then choose OK.

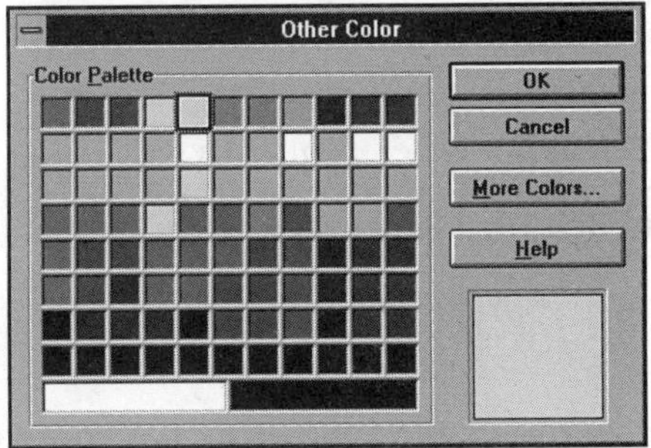

Fig. 24.10
The Other Color dialog box displays a color palette.

5. Choose OK in the Colors and Lines dialog box. PowerPoint returns to your slide and changes the fill color of the selected object.
6. Click any blank area of the screen to deselect the object.

To change an object's line color or line style, or to add dashed lines or arrowheads, follow these steps:

1. Select the object.
2. Choose the F**o**rmat Colors and **L**ines command, or choose Colors and Lines from the shortcut menu. The Colors and Lines dialog box appears, displaying the current line color in the Line box.

3. Click the arrow to open the **L**ine drop-down list, which displays the options shown in figure 24.11.

4. Do one of the following things:

   - Select the No Line option to remove the object's line color.
   - Select one of the colors (derived from the current template).
   - Select the Other Color option, which displays the Other Color dialog box (refer to fig. 24.10). Select a color in the Color Palette, and then choose OK.

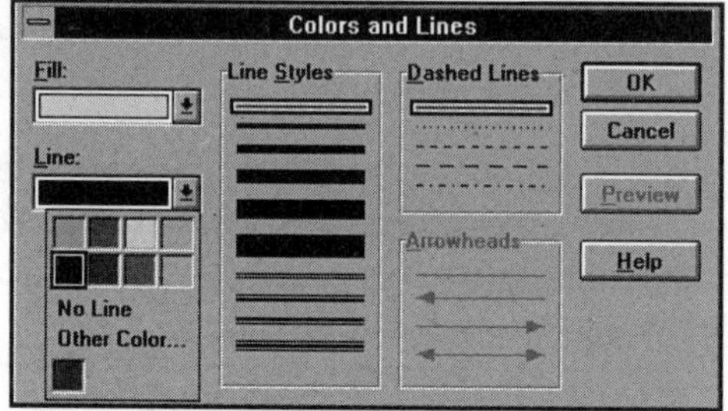

Fig. 24.11
The Line drop-down list displays line color options.

5. To select a different line style, highlight a style in the Line **S**tyles list.

6. To use a dashed line, highlight a style in the **D**ashed Lines list.

7. To add arrowheads to a line or arc, select an option in the **A**rrowheads list.

8. Choose OK in the Colors and Lines dialog box. PowerPoint returns to your slide and changes the line color and style for the selected object.

9. Click any blank area of the screen to deselect the object.

A quick way to change an object's fill, line color, line style, dashed lines, or arrowheads is to use the respective tools in the Drawing+ toolbar. Select the object, and then click any of the tools shown in the following table. In each case, a drop-down list appears, enabling you to select a new color or style.

Tool	Tool Name
	Fill Color
	Line Color
	Line Style
	Dashed Line
	Arrowheads

To turn fill or line options on or off, click either of the following tools in the Drawing toolbar:

Tool	Tool Name
	Fill On/Off
	Line On/Off

Using Shading and Patterns

In a slide presentation, filled objects usually are more interesting than plain ones. Two effective variations for filled objects are the shaded color and the two-color pattern.

A *shaded color* is a dark-to-light or light-to-dark variation of an object's color. This variation can run vertically, horizontally, diagonally, from the center outward, or from any corner. You also can adjust the intensity of the color.

To shade an object, choose the F**o**rmat Colors and **L**ines command or choose Colors and Lines from the shortcut menu. The Colors and Lines dialog box appears, displaying the current fill color in the Fill box. Select the Shaded option to display the Shaded Fill dialog box (see fig. 24.12).

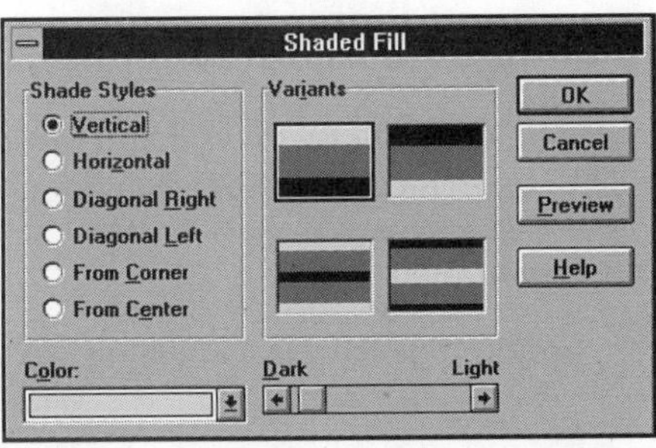

Fig. 24.12
The Shaded Fill dialog box displays many shade variations.

To shade an object, follow these steps:

1. Select the object you want to shade.
2. Choose the F**o**rmat Colors and **L**ines command. The Colors and Lines dialog box appears. The current fill color is shown in the Fill box.
3. Click to open the **F**ill drop-down list, which displays the options shown in figure 24.9.
4. Select the Shaded option. The Shaded Fill dialog box appears (refer to fig. 24.12).
5. Select an option in the Shade Styles list. The Variants box reflects the choice you make.
6. In the Var**i**ants box, highlight one variant.
7. To adjust the brightness, drag the scroll box in the **D**ark/Light scroll bar.
8. Use the C**o**lor option in the Shaded Fill dialog box if you want to change the fill color.
9. If you want, choose the **P**review button to preview the shade in the selected object.
10. Choose OK in the Shaded Fill dialog box. You return to the Colors and Lines dialog box.
11. Choose OK to close the dialog box. PowerPoint applies the shaded color to the selected object.

An alternative to shading an object is patterning. A *pattern* is a design (such as lines, dots, bricks, or checkerboard squares) that contains two colors: a foreground color and a background color.

To add a pattern to a filled object, follow these steps:

1. Select the object to which you want to add a pattern.
2. Choose the F**o**rmat Colors and **L**ines command or Colors and Lines from the shortcut menu. The Colors and Lines dialog box appears.
3. Click to open the **F**ill drop-down list.
4. Select the Pattern option. The Pattern Fill dialog box appears (see fig. 24.13).

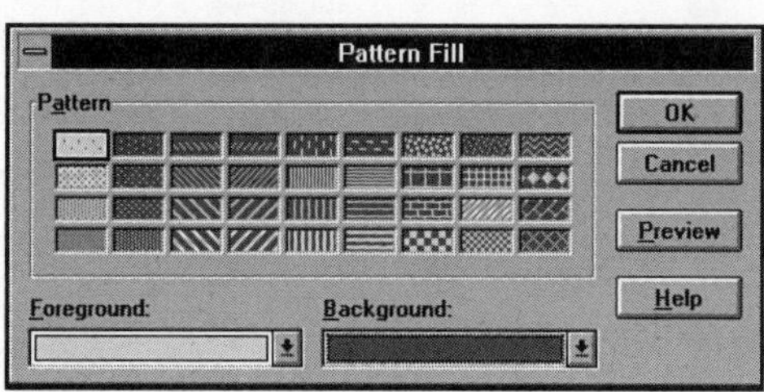

Fig. 24.13
Select a pattern and colors in the Pattern Fill dialog box.

5. In the P**a**ttern box, highlight the pattern you want to use.
6. In the **F**oreground and **B**ackground lists, select the colors for your pattern.
7. If you want, choose the **P**review button to preview the pattern in the selected object.

> **Note**
>
> When you choose the Preview button in the Pattern Fill dialog box, move the Colors and Lines and Pattern Fill dialog boxes if they obscure the selected object.

8. Choose OK to close the Pattern Fill dialog box. You return to the Colors and Lines dialog box.
9. Choose OK to close the dialog box. PowerPoint applies the two-color pattern to the selected object.
10. Click any blank area of the screen to deselect the object.

Adding Shadows to Objects

A final way to enhance objects is to add shadows. You learned earlier in this chapter that shadowed text has shadows at the bottom and the right side of each character. When you shadow an object, you have more flexibility, because you can specify the direction of the shadow and the degree of offset from the original object. For example, you might want the shadow to project up and to the left, as shown in figure 24.14.

To apply a shadow to an object, choose the F**o**rmat S**h**adow command to display the Shadow dialog box (see fig. 24.15). The shadow color that appears in the Color box is determined by the current template. To use a different shadow color, select an option in the drop-down list.

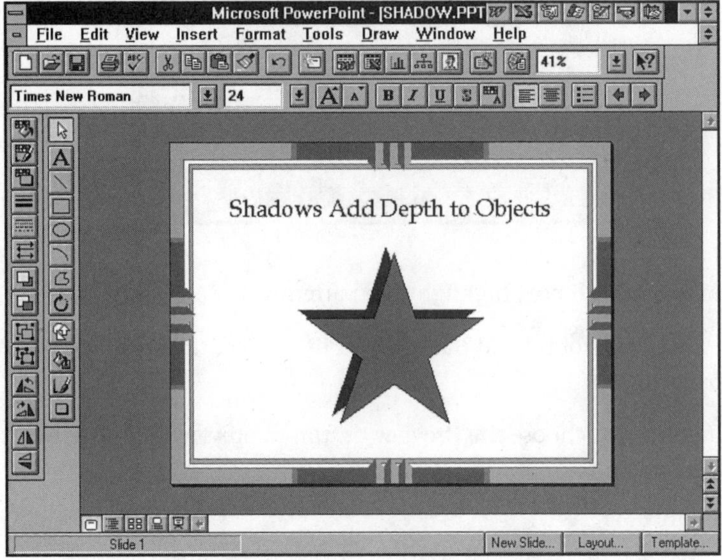

Fig. 24.14
This object's shadow is offset up and to the left.

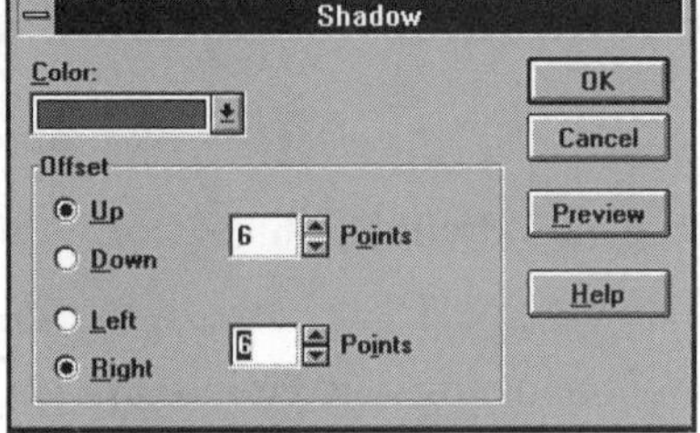

Fig. 24.15
Use the Shadow dialog box to specify shadow direction and offset.

To determine the shadow's offset, select **U**p or **D**own for the horizontal offset, or **L**eft or **R**ight for the vertical offset. You can combine the horizontal and vertical offsets by choosing a combination of these options. The box to the right of each pair of offset options enables you to set the degree of offset in points. The default setting for each offset pair is 6 points; you can specify any number from 0 to 120. Depending on the shape of the object you are shadowing, you may want to choose the Preview button to determine the best offset.

To apply a shadow to an object, follow these steps:

1. Select the object.

2. Choose the F**o**rmat S**h**adow command. The Shadow dialog box appears.

3. To change the color of the shadow, select a color in the **C**olor drop-down list.

4. To set a horizontal shadow offset, select the **U**p or **D**own option, and then enter the number of points in the P**o**ints box.
5. To set a vertical shadow offset, select the **L**eft or **R**ight option, and then enter the number of points in the Po**i**nts box.
6. If you want, choose the **P**review button to preview the shadow on the selected object.
7. Choose OK or press Enter to apply the shadow to the selected object.
8. Click any blank area of the screen to deselect the object.

You can apply a shadow to an object quickly by clicking the Shadow Color tool in the Drawing+ toolbar. Select an object, and then click the Shadow Color tool. A drop-down list appears, displaying eight color options. Select a color in the drop-down list, or select the Other Color option to choose a different color. PowerPoint automatically applies the shadow to the selected object. Be aware that this method does not allow you to specify a shadow's offset.

To turn a shadow on or off quickly, you can click the Shadow On/Off tool in the Drawing toolbar.

Copying Attributes from One Object to Another

Suppose that you have taken care to apply a special color, shade or pattern, line width, line style, and shadow to a particular object. You can apply all these attributes to another object quickly by clicking the Format Painter tool in the Formatting toolbar. When you click this tool after selecting an object, PowerPoint "memorizes" all the attributes of the selected object. The mouse pointer changes to a paintbrush, and the next object you click immediately takes on the same attributes. This process is called *picking up and applying* an object's style to another object.

The Format Painter tool is equivalent to the Format Pick Up Object Style and Format Apply Object Style commands. Using the menu commands requires two steps, however, whereas using the Format Painter tool requires only one step.

To use the menu commands to apply attributes from one object to another, follow these steps:

1. Select the object from which you want to copy attributes.
2. Choose the F**o**rmat Pic**k** Up Object Style command, or choose Pick Up Object Style from the shortcut menu.

3. Select the object to which you want to copy the attributes.

4. Choose the F**o**rmat Appl**y** Object Style command.

Working with Color Schemes

A *color scheme* is a set of colors that are chosen because they complement one another. As you learned earlier in this chapter, every template has a predefined color scheme that consists of specific colors for the slide background, title text, text and lines, fills, shadows, and accent colors. Even the DEFAULT.PPT template, which PowerPoint calls a "blank" presentation, has a predefined color scheme. You can use the colors defined in a template, choose a different color scheme, or change individual colors in a color scheme.

Changing Individual Colors in a Color Scheme

To change individual colors in a color scheme, use the Slide Color Scheme dialog box (see fig. 24.16). You display this dialog box by choosing the F**o**rmat Slide **C**olor Scheme command or by choosing Slide Color Scheme from the shortcut menu (when no objects are selected). The dialog box displays a sample of the background, text and lines, title text, shadows, fills, and accent colors defined by the current template.

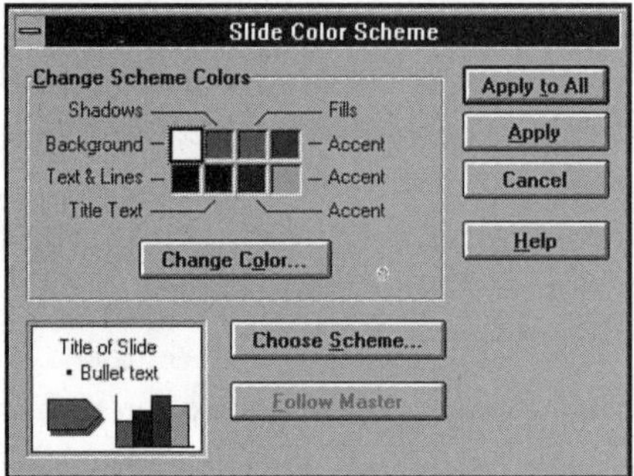

Fig. 24.16
The Slide Color Scheme dialog box displays every color in the current color scheme.

You can change an individual color in the current color scheme and apply the new color to the current slide or to all of the slides in the presentation. Follow these steps:

1. Choose the F**o**rmat Slide **C**olor Scheme command, or choose Slide Color Scheme from the shortcut menu. The Slide Color Scheme dialog box appears (refer to fig. 24.16).

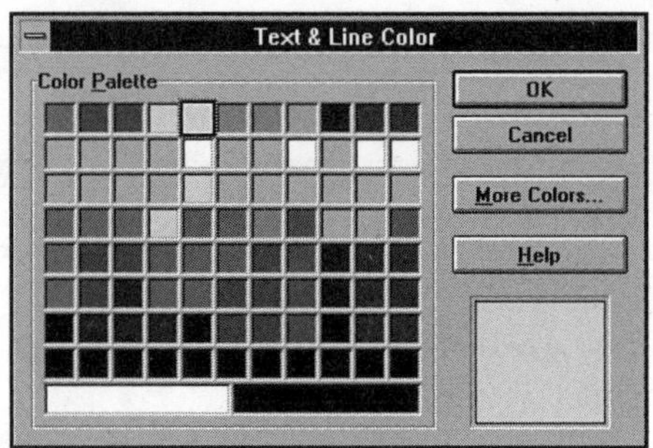

Fig. 24.17
Select a new color in the palette.

2. In the **C**hange Scheme Colors area, highlight the color you want to change.
3. Choose the Change C**o**lor button. PowerPoint displays a dialog box like the one shown in figure 24.17. The title of the dialog box reflects the color you are changing, such as `Background Color` or `Text and Line Color`.
4. In the Color **P**alette area, highlight the color you want to use. Then choose OK. The Slide Color Scheme dialog box returns.
5. Repeat steps 2 and 3 to change other colors in the current color scheme.
6. In the Slide Color Scheme dialog box, choose the **A**pply button to apply the change to the current slide. Choose the Apply **t**o All button to apply the new color to all slides in the current presentation.

Choosing a Different Color Scheme

Suppose that a template contains all the graphic elements you want to use, but the color scheme is not appropriate for the topic you are presenting. Rather than change individual colors in the template's color scheme, you can choose a different color scheme for the current template. When you choose a new color scheme, you are choosing a new set of predefined colors. As always, you can change individual colors in the scheme later if you choose.

To choose a new color scheme for the current template, you use the Choose Scheme dialog box, shown in figure 24.18. To display this dialog box, choose the F**o**rmat Slide **C**olor Scheme command, or choose Slide Color Scheme from the shortcut menu; then choose the Choose **S**cheme button. When the dialog box opens, colors appear in the Background Color list only; the Text & Line Color and Other Scheme Colors lists are blank. The dialog box "fills in" as you make your choices—that is, after you select a background color, color choices appear in the Text & Line Color list, and after you select a Text & Line Color option, color choices appear in the Other Scheme Colors list.

To choose a color scheme, follow these steps:

1. Choose the F**o**rmat Slide **C**olor Scheme command, or choose Slide Color Scheme from the shortcut menu (when no objects are selected). PowerPoint displays the Slide Color Scheme dialog box (refer to fig. 24.16).

2. Choose the Choose **S**cheme button. PowerPoint displays the Choose Scheme dialog box (see fig. 24.18).

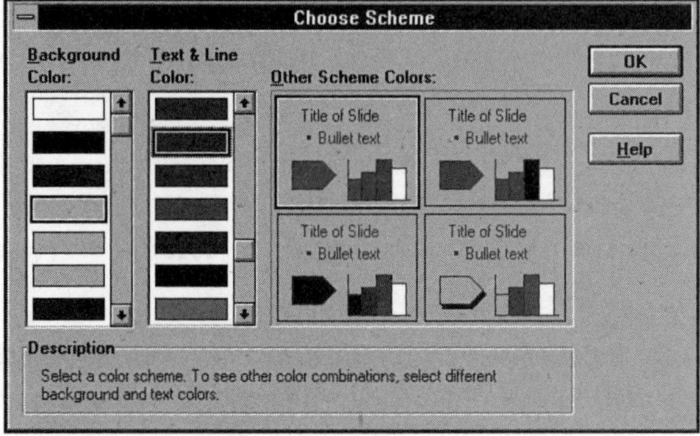

Fig. 24.18
The Choose Scheme dialog box displays color scheme options.

3. Select a color in the **B**ackground Color list. Coordinated colors appear in the **T**ext & Line Color list. Be sure to use the scroll bar to view all possible colors.

Tip
At any time, you can choose a new color scheme by repeating steps 3, 4, and 5.

4. Select a color in the **T**ext & Line Color list. Coordinated colors appear in the **O**ther Scheme Colors box.

5. Select a set of colors in the **O**ther Scheme Colors box.

6. Choose OK to close the Choose Scheme dialog box. The new colors appear in the Slide Color Scheme dialog box.

7. Choose the **A**pply button to apply the new color scheme to the current slide. Choose the Apply **t**o All button to apply the new color scheme to all slides in the current presentation.

Note

To create a custom color scheme, follow the preceding steps, selecting the background color, text color, and line color you want to use. When options appear in the Other Scheme Colors box, select the one that most closely matches what you want in your custom color scheme. Then return to the Slide Color Scheme dialog box and change individual colors, if necessary.

From Here...

This chapter discussed the variety of techniques you can use to enhance objects in a PowerPoint presentation. Refer to the following chapters for more information about working with objects:

- Chapter 23, "Drawing Shapes, Curves, and Lines," describes how to use PowerPoint's drawing tools to add drawn objects to your slides.
- Chapter 25, "Creating Charts," teaches you how to use Microsoft Graph to create, format, and enhance charts that you can insert into your PowerPoint slides.

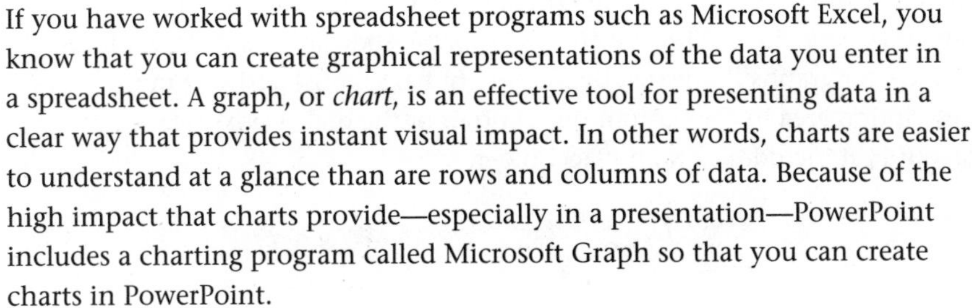

Chapter 25

Creating Charts

by Debbie Walkowski

If you have worked with spreadsheet programs such as Microsoft Excel, you know that you can create graphical representations of the data you enter in a spreadsheet. A graph, or *chart*, is an effective tool for presenting data in a clear way that provides instant visual impact. In other words, charts are easier to understand at a glance than are rows and columns of data. Because of the high impact that charts provide—especially in a presentation—PowerPoint includes a charting program called Microsoft Graph so that you can create charts in PowerPoint.

In this chapter, you learn to

- Start Microsoft Graph
- Enter and edit data in the datasheet window
- Choose a chart type and add chart elements
- Choose colors, patterns, borders, and fonts
- Return to Graph after you exit to edit a chart

Starting Microsoft Graph

Microsoft Graph is a charting application, separate from PowerPoint, that is accessible from within PowerPoint. When you start Graph, a sample chart appears in the current slide of your presentation, and a datasheet appears on top of the chart. The chart appears in the slide as an object; the datasheet appears in a separate window with its own title bar. The datasheet and chart are displayed on-screen simultaneously and are dependent on each other. When you change data in the datasheet, Graph automatically updates the chart to reflect the new data.

Tip
If the datasheet window obstructs the chart, you can drag the datasheet window to a more convenient location.

Note

In PowerPoint and Microsoft Graph, the terms *chart* and *graph* are used interchangeably.

Before accessing Microsoft Graph, you must create a new PowerPoint presentation or open an existing presentation. After opening the presentation, display the slide in which you want to insert a chart, or add a new slide to the presentation. The slide should either be blank or contain a placeholder for a chart.

As you learned in Chapter 20, "Creating, Saving, and Opening Presentations," whenever you add a new slide to a presentation, PowerPoint automatically displays the Slide Layout dialog box, in which you select a slide layout (see fig. 25.1). Three of the 18 available slide layouts include placeholders for graphs (indicated by pictures of bar graphs) and a layout-description area in the bottom right corner of the dialog box. Select a layout that includes a graph placeholder.

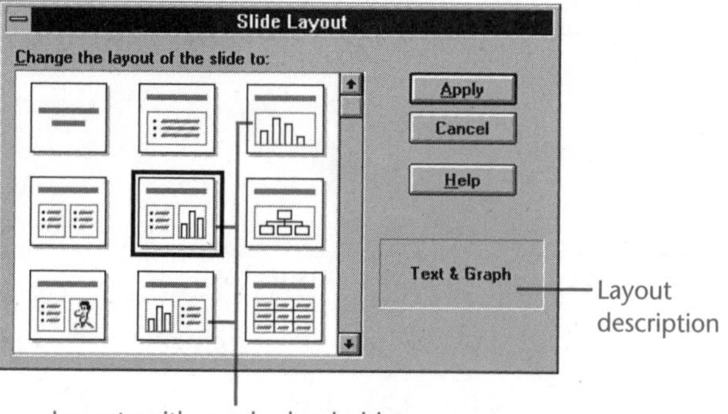

Fig. 25.1
The Slide Layout dialog box includes three layouts that contain graph placeholders.

Note

If you access Microsoft Graph from a slide that contains objects or placeholders other than for a graph, the graph you create will appear on top of other objects (such as text or drawn objects). To avoid obscuring other objects with a graph, select a blank slide layout or a slide layout that contains a graph placeholder before you access Microsoft Graph.

When you select one of the three slide layouts shown in figure 25.1, PowerPoint displays a slide similar to the one shown in figure 25.2. A dotted frame defines the boundaries of the graph placeholder. Inside the placeholder is a small picture of a bar graph with the instruction `Double click to add graph`.

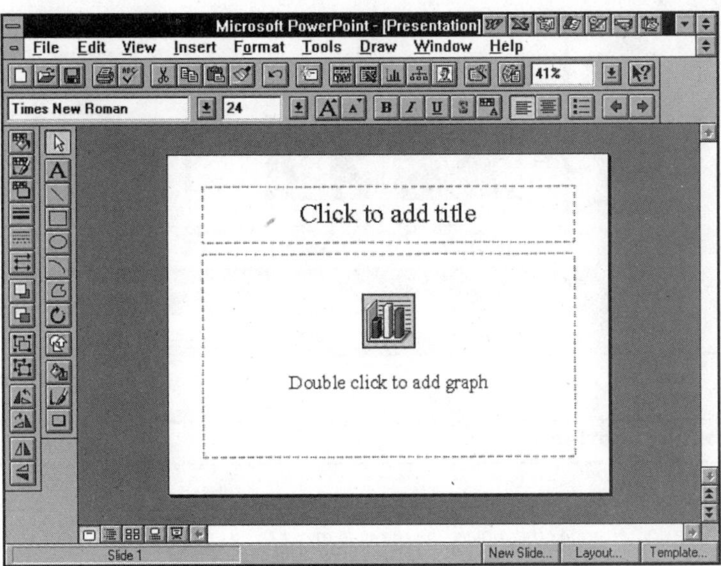

Fig. 25.2
Graph placeholders contain a small picture of a bar graph.

Tip
If the datasheet window obscures the graph, drag the window to a different location. You also can resize the datasheet window.

Starting Microsoft Graph is as easy as the instructions indicate: simply double-click the graph placeholder. After a few seconds, a sample bar chart appears in the graph placeholder in your slide. The datasheet appears on top of the chart, in a separate window (see fig. 25.3). The sample data in the datasheet is used to create the sample bar chart.

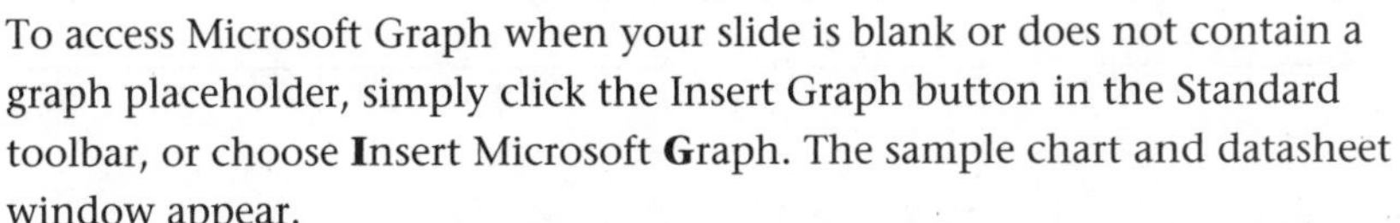

To access Microsoft Graph when your slide is blank or does not contain a graph placeholder, simply click the Insert Graph button in the Standard toolbar, or choose **I**nsert Microsoft **G**raph. The sample chart and datasheet window appear.

Fig. 25.3
Microsoft Graph displays a sample chart in the slide and sample data in the datasheet window.

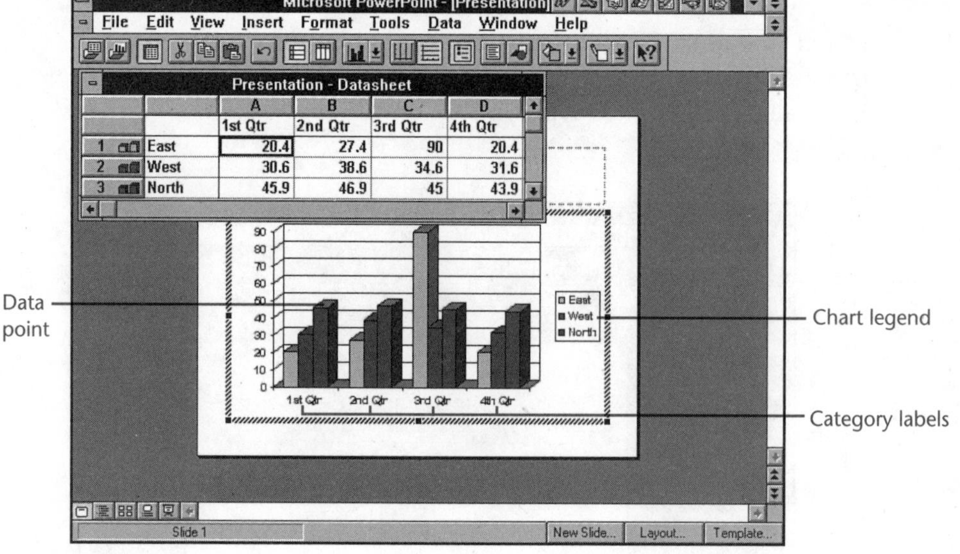

Troubleshooting

I don't want to use any of the Autolayouts that include graphs. How can I add a graph to my slide and arrange other objects on the slide myself?

Choose the blank Autolayout for your slide. When you create a chart using Microsoft Graph, the chart will be centered in the middle of the slide. You can resize the chart object, move it, and add other objects to the slide where you want them.

I closed the datasheet window in Microsoft Graph before I was finished using it. How can I redisplay it?

In Microsoft Graph, choose **V**iew **D**atasheet, or click the View Datasheet button in the Graph toolbar. (This button is indicated in table 25.1.)

Looking at the Microsoft Graph Menus and Toolbar

Notice in figure 25.3 that the Standard PowerPoint toolbar is replaced by the Graph toolbar when Microsoft Graph is active. The menus are identical to those in PowerPoint, except that Graph also includes a **D**ata menu. The commands in each menu, however, are specific to graphs rather than to PowerPoint slides.

The buttons in Graph's Standard toolbar greatly simplify working with charts. For example, you can change the color or pattern of a set of bars in a bar chart by clicking the Color or Pattern button. This chapter emphasizes the use of these buttons, and it also explains menu-command techniques. Table 25.1 explains the functions of the buttons in the Graph Standard toolbar.

Table 25.1 Microsoft Graph's Standard Toolbar

Button	Button Name	Purpose
	Import Data	Used to import data from another application into the Graph datasheet
	Import Chart	Used to import a chart from an Excel worksheet
	View Datasheet	Click to display the datasheet for the current chart
	Cut	Cuts selected objects
	Copy	Copies selected objects to the Clipboard
	Paste	Inserts the contents of the Clipboard
	Undo	Reverses the last action taken
	By Row	Causes Graph to use rows of data as data series
	By Column	Causes Graph to use columns of data as data series
	Chart Type	Displays a drop-down list of chart types
	Vertical Gridlines	Inserts vertical grid lines into the current current chart
	Horizontal Gridlines	Inserts horizontal grid lines into the current chart
	Legend	Turns the chart legend on or off
	Text Box	Inserts a new text box into a chart
	Drawing	Displays or hides a Drawing toolbar for drawing objects in a chart
	Color	Displays a drop-down fill-color palette
	Pattern	Displays a drop-down color and pattern palette

Working with the Datasheet

A Microsoft Graph datasheet, made up of rows and columns, is similar to a Microsoft Excel worksheet. Rows are numbered 1 through 3,999, and columns are labeled A, B, C, AA, AB, AC, and so on, through column EWU. The intersection of each row and column is a *cell*, in which you enter text or a number. Unlike an Excel worksheet, however, a Microsoft Graph datasheet cannot use formulas.

Understanding How Data Is Plotted

In figure 25.3, the sample datasheet shows three rows, or *series*, of data: East, West, and North. A *data series* contains individual *data points* that are plotted along the y-axis (vertical axis) of a chart as columns, lines, or pie slides. From the first column of the datasheet, the row headings—which identify each data series—are translated to the chart's *legend*. The column headings in the first row of the datasheet (the row above row 1) represent *categories* of data. These column headings are translated to the x-axis (horizontal axis) of the chart as category labels. Thus, categories appear as groups in a chart.

Arranging Data by Rows or Columns

By default, Microsoft Graph assumes that data series appear in rows and that categories appear in columns, so Graph plots all charts accordingly. In figure 25.3, this series-in-rows arrangement emphasizes time spans: Qtr 1, Qtr 2, Qtr 3, and Qtr 4.

If you prefer, however, you can reverse the data-series arrangement so that Graph uses columns as data series and rows as categories of data. In figure 25.4, the series-in-columns arrangement emphasizes regions—East, West, and North—rather than time spans. The arrangement you use depends on personal preference and on the data you want to emphasize. Unless otherwise indicated, the examples in this chapter use the series-in-rows arrangement.

By glancing at the datasheet, you can tell whether rows or columns are represented as data series. When rows are plotted as the data series, miniature graphic representations of the chart type (such as bars or lines) appear next to the row numbers. When columns are plotted as the data series, the graphics appear next to the column labels (A, B, C, and so on). You can see examples of these miniature graphics in figures 25.3 and 25.4. The graphics are color-coded to match the colors of each data series in the chart (bars, lines, pie slices, and so on).

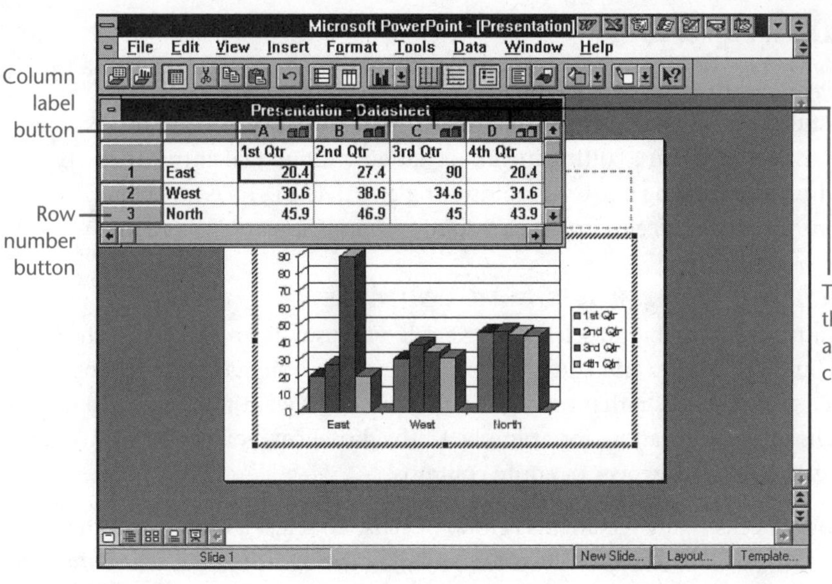

Fig. 25.4
Switching from series in rows to series in columns changes the way a chart is plotted.

To specify the arrangement of data in a chart, click the By Row or By Column button in the Graph toolbar, or choose the Series in Rows or Series in Columns command from the Data menu. You can switch back and forth between the two arrangements to decide which one represents your data most effectively.

Entering Data

When you're ready to enter data in the datasheet, simply type over the existing sample data. You might replace East, West, and North with Sales, Service, and Training, or Qtr 1, Qtr 2, Qtr 3, and Qtr 4 with January, February, March, and April. You can add more data to the datasheet by filling in blank rows and columns.

To highlight a cell in the datasheet, use the arrow keys or click a cell. The *active*, or highlighted, cell is outlined with a bold border. *Overtype mode* always is active in the datasheet, so any entry you type in a cell automatically replaces the current contents of a cell. To complete an entry, press Enter or press any of the arrow keys to move to another cell.

Editing Data

Editing refers to changes that you make in data after it is entered in the datasheet. You change data in a datasheet the same way you do in other spreadsheet programs. Editing includes changing individual entries; cutting, moving, and copying entries; and inserting and deleting rows and columns. Before you can edit cells, however, you must know how to select them.

Selecting Cells, Rows, and Columns

You already know that to select a single cell, you use the arrow keys or click a cell. But as you enter and edit data in the datasheet, you may want to work with a group of cells rather than just one. You might want to move a group of cells to a new location, for example. In the datasheet, you can select a range of cells, entire rows, or entire columns.

A *range* of cells is any rectangular group of cells. To select a range, click the cell in the top left corner of the range and drag the mouse to the cell in the bottom right corner of the range. The entire range is highlighted.

In the datasheet, selecting an entire row or column is as easy as clicking the row number or column label. To select all cells in row 3, for example, click the row number; to select all cells in column D, click the column label. You also can select multiple rows or columns by dragging the mouse across row numbers and column labels. To select rows 1, 2, and 3, for example, click and drag the mouse across the row numbers 1, 2, and 3. All cells in each row are highlighted. You also can press and hold down the Shift key as you highlight cells with the arrow keys.

To cancel any selection, whether you have selected a range of cells or a group of columns or rows, press Esc or click any single cell.

Editing an Entry

Earlier in this chapter, you learned that to enter new data in a datasheet, you actually change the sample data Microsoft Graph provides by typing over it. Overtyping, however, is not the only way to change data in a cell. When an entry that you type contains a minor error, you might consider *editing* the entry rather than overtyping. Editing enables you to change only selected characters in an entry. If a cell contains a part number such as BXN-231-781S and you discover that the *B* should be a *C*, you can simply correct the error rather than retype the entire part number.

To edit an entry, double-click the cell in which it appears. An insertion point appears in the cell. (If the cell contains a text entry, the insertion point appears after the last character. If the cell contains a number, the insertion point appears before the first digit.) Use the arrow keys to position the insertion point, then press Backspace or Del to correct an error. Backspace deletes characters to the left of the insertion point, and Del deletes characters to the right of the insertion point. New characters that you type appear to the left of the insertion point. When you finish editing, press Enter or press any of the arrow keys to move to another cell.

Clearing Cells

Clearing refers to removing the contents, format, or both from cells. You might clear a cell when you realize that you entered the wrong data; you might choose to clear sample data from a datasheet, if you prefer to work with a blank datasheet.

To clear cells, choose the **E**dit Cle**a**r command, or choose Clear from the shortcut menu. This command gives you the option of clearing the contents of a cell, the format of a cell, or both. *Cell contents* refers to the data contained in a cell, such as a number or text character. The *format* of the cell refers to a variety of characteristics, such as the font, font size, and color, as well as to attributes such as number format, underlining, strikethrough, subscript, and superscript.

To clear a cell, follow these steps:

1. Select the cell or cells you want to clear.
2. Choose the **E**dit Cle**a**r command, or choose Clear from the shortcut menu. A cascading menu appears. Select All to clear the contents and formats, Contents to clear only the entries, or Formats to clear only the format assigned to the cell and retain the contents.

Tip
To remove only the contents of a cell and leave the cell blank, select the cell and then press the Del key.

Inserting and Deleting Rows and Columns

As you enter your own data into the datasheet, you may find it necessary to insert a new row or column, or to delete an existing row or column. Suppose that in your columns of monthly data, you inadvertently left out March. You would want to insert a new column between February and April. If you accidentally entered a data series twice, you would want to delete the duplicate row.

You can insert a single row or column, or multiple rows or columns. Before inserting rows or columns, however, you must select the correct row or column. Before inserting a single row, select the row *below* the place where you want a new row. To insert a row before row 4, for example, select row 4. Before inserting a single column, select the column to the *right* of the place where you want the new column. To insert a new column before column D, you would select column D.

To insert a single row or column, select the correct row or column and then choose **I**nsert C**e**lls.

If you select a single cell rather than an entire row or column, Microsoft Graph doesn't know what you want to insert, so the Insert dialog box appears. In the dialog box, choose the Entire **R**ow or Entire **C**olumn option and then choose OK.

To save you time, Microsoft Graph makes it easy for you to insert several rows or columns at once. Highlight the number of rows or columns you want to insert, then choose **I**nsert C**e**lls. Microsoft Graph automatically inserts the number of rows or columns you highlighted. If you highlighted columns B, C, and D, for example, Graph inserts three new columns beginning at column B (see fig. 25.5).

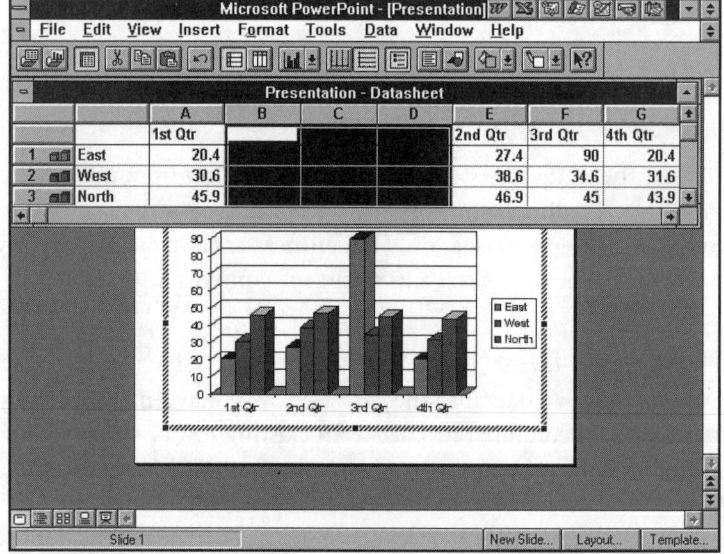

Fig. 25.5
Three new columns were inserted at B, C, and D.

To remove rows or columns from the datasheet, select the appropriate rows or columns; then choose the **E**dit **D**elete command, or choose Delete from the shortcut menu. Notice that the Del key on the keyboard does not have the same function as the **E**dit **D**elete command. The Del key clears the content of cells, but the cells themselves remain part of the datasheet.

Cutting, Moving, and Copying Data

Three common editing tasks are *cutting, moving,* and *copying*. The **E**dit Cu**t** command removes the contents of selected cells and places the data in the Windows Clipboard. (You also can choose Cut from the shortcut menu or press Ctrl+X.) The cells themselves remain intact in the datasheet. You use the cut feature when you want to remove data from the datasheet or to move the selected data within the datasheet.

> **Note**
>
> At first glance, **E**dit Cle**a**r and **E**dit Cu**t** seem to perform the same function: removing data from selected cells. However, the two commands are different. **E**dit Cu**t** removes the data to the Clipboard, whereas **E**dit Cle**a**r permanently removes the data without storing it anywhere. Be sure to use **E**dit Cu**t** if you think you might want to move the data elsewhere in the datasheet.

Follow these steps to cut data from the datasheet:

1. Select the cell or cells from which you want to remove data.

2. Choose the **E**dit Cu**t** command, choose Cut from the shortcut menu, or press Ctrl+X. The data is removed from the worksheet and placed in the Clipboard.

When you want to move data to a new location in the datasheet, cut the selected data, and then choose the **E**dit **P**aste command, choose Paste from the shortcut menu, or press Ctrl+V. The new location you choose should not contain data; if it does, the data you move overwrites the existing data.

To move data within the datasheet, follow these steps:

1. Select the cells from which you want to move data.

2. Choose the **E**dit Cu**t** command, choose Cut from the shortcut menu, or press Ctrl+X. The data is placed in the Clipboard.

3. Select the first cell in the range to which you want to move the data.

4. Choose the **E**dit **P**aste command, choose Paste from the shortcut menu, or press Ctrl+V.

Tip

When cutting, moving, or copying data, you can restore the data to its original location if you click the Undo button in the toolbar, choose **E**dit **U**ndo, or press Ctrl+Z immediately before performing any other action.

A quick way to move a selection is to drag it. Select the cell or cells you want to move, and then point to the border of the selection until the mouse pointer changes to an arrow. Click and drag the selection to a new location, and then release the mouse button. If the new location contains data, PowerPoint asks whether you want to replace the existing data.

Unlike when you cut or move data, when you copy data, the original data remains intact in the datasheet, and a copy of the data is placed in the Clipboard. After the data is in the Clipboard, you can paste the data to any other location in the datasheet. As when you move data, the new location should not contain data; if it does, the original data is overwritten.

To copy data, follow these steps:

1. In the datasheet, select the cells from which you want to copy data.
2. Choose the **E**dit **C**opy command, choose Copy from the shortcut menu, or press Ctrl+C. The data is copied to the Windows Clipboard.
3. Select the first cell in the range to which you want to copy the data.

4. Choose the **E**dit **P**aste command, choose Paste from the shortcut menu, or press Ctrl+V. The data is copied to the new location in the datasheet and remains intact in the original location.

Just as you can move a selection by dragging it, you can copy a selection by dragging it. Select the cell or cells you want to copy, and then point to the border of the selection until the mouse pointer changes to an arrow. Press and hold down the Ctrl key; a plus sign (+) appears next to the mouse pointer, indicating that you are copying a selection. Hold down the Ctrl key as you click and drag the selection to a new location. Then release the mouse button.

Caution

When you drag a selection to copy it, PowerPoint overwrites any data in the new location.

Excluding Rows or Columns

Sometimes, rather than delete rows or columns, you simply want to exclude them from a chart. Suppose that your datasheet contains sales figures for 20 retail departments, but you want to plot the sales performance of only the first 5 departments. To plot this chart, you exclude rows 6 through 20 so that Graph plots only rows 1 through 5.

To exclude rows or columns from a chart, follow these steps:

1. Select the rows or columns that you want to exclude from a chart.
2. Choose **D**ata Exclude **R**ow/Col.

When you exclude cells from a chart, the entries in the cells are grayed, and the buttons for the row numbers or column labels become "flat" (lose their 3-D attributes), as shown in figure 25.6. At the same time, the current chart is updated to reflect the excluded data.

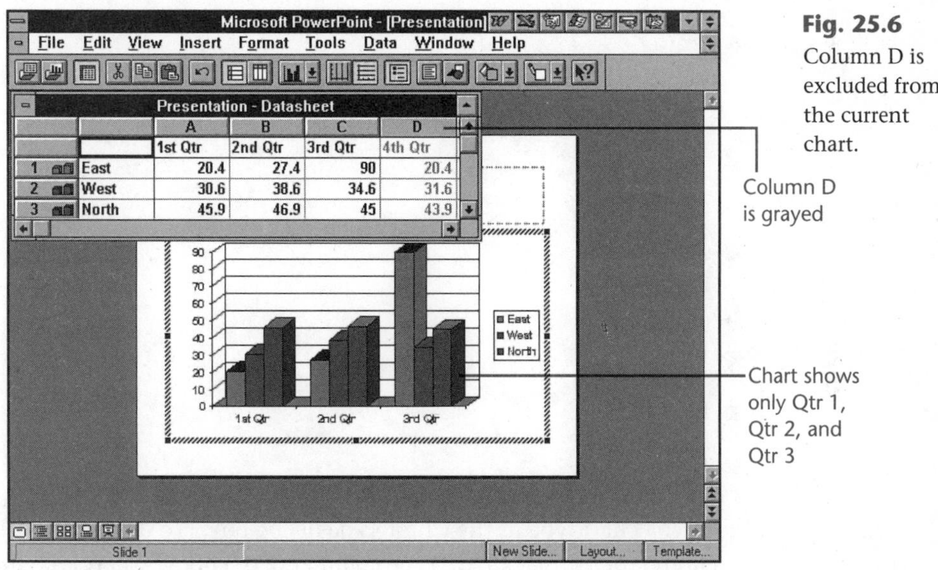

Fig. 25.6
Column D is excluded from the current chart.

To restore excluded cells to a chart, select the appropriate rows or columns, then choose **D**ata **I**nclude Row/Col. The normal attributes return to the entries in the cells, the row numbers, and the column label buttons.

Choosing a Chart Type

When you start Microsoft Graph, a three-dimensional column chart is created from the sample data in the datasheet. A column chart, however, is not the only type of chart you can create in Microsoft Graph. You also can create the following types of two-dimensional charts:

- Area
- Bar
- Column
- Line
- Pie
- Doughnut
- Radar
- Scatter

To create charts with depth, you can select any of the following three-dimensional chart types:

- Area
- Bar
- Column
- Line
- Pie
- Surface

You select a chart type in the Chart Type dialog box. (To display this dialog box, choose the F**o**rmat **C**hart Type command, or choose Chart type from the shortcut menu.) In the dialog box, choose either the 2-D or 3-D option in the Chart Dimension area; then the available chart types appear below the Chart Dimension area.

Figure 25.7 displays 3-D chart types in the Chart Type dialog box.

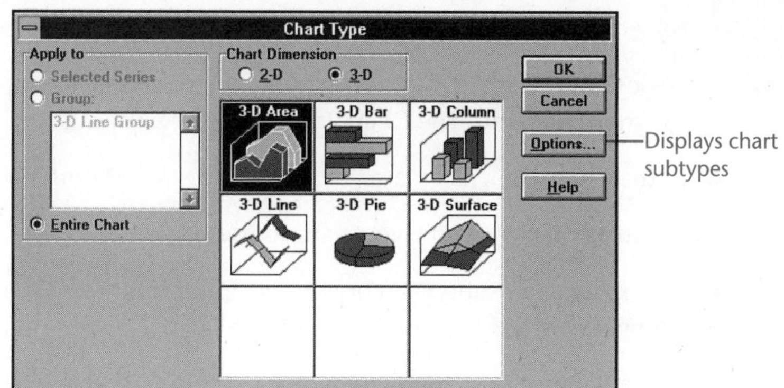

Fig. 25.7
Select a chart type in this dialog box.

For most chart types, Microsoft Graph offers at least one or two variations, or *subtypes*. If you select the 3-D area chart type, for example, you then can select one of three subtypes of that style. In the first 3-D area subtype, data series are stacked on top of one another. In the second subtype, data series are stacked on top of one another, but they fill the entire chart area, showing how each series contributes to the whole. In the third subtype, data series are depicted separately. For each subtype you highlight, the bottom portion of the dialog box displays a sample chart that uses your data.

To display a chart's subtypes, choose the **O**ptions button in the Chart Type dialog box. The Format 3-D area Group dialog box appears (see fig. 25.8).

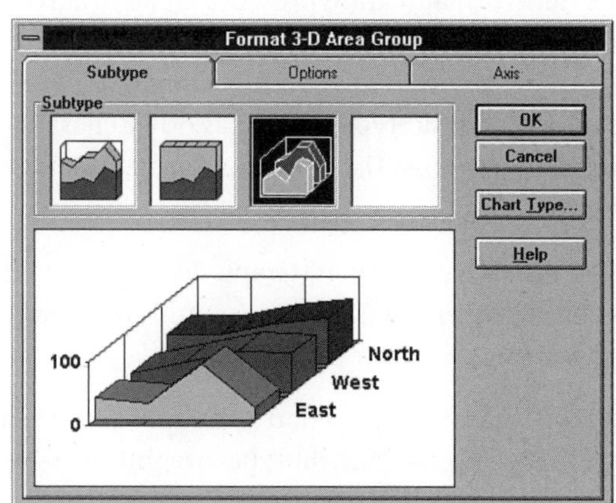

Fig. 25.8
The Format 3-D Area Group dialog box displays subtypes and a sample chart using your data.

To select a chart type, follow these steps:

1. Choose the F**o**rmat **C**hart Type command, or choose Chart Type from the shortcut menu. The Chart Type dialog box appears.
2. In the Chart Dimension area, select the **2**-D or **3**-D option.
3. Highlight the chart type you want to use.
4. To display chart subtypes, choose the **O**ptions button. The Format Group dialog box appears.
5. In the **S**ubtype area, highlight a chart variation, then choose OK. You return to the Chart Type dialog box.
6. Choose OK. The new chart type is applied to the current chart.

When you're not sure what chart type you want to use, experiment by choosing different chart types. To try different chart types, follow the preceding steps, but choose the Chart **T**ype button rather than the OK button in step 6. The Chart Type dialog box appears again, enabling you to select a different chart type.

Using AutoFormats

Microsoft Graph's AutoFormat feature provides an alternative to selecting a chart type in the Chart Type dialog box and specifying chart elements (such as data labels and grid lines) individually. *Autoformats* are predefined formats that specify a chart type and subtype, as well as other chart characteristics, such as color, font, and patterns. Using an autoformat often gives you more chart-subtype choices.

When you choose F**o**rmat **A**utoFormat, Graph displays the AutoFormat dialog box. Select a chart type in the Galleries list, and then select a chart subtype in the Formats area.

Figure 25.9 shows that many 3-D pie-chart variations are available when you use an autoformat, whereas pie-chart subtypes are limited when you use the Chart Type dialog box.

To use an autoformat, follow these steps:

1. Choose the **I**nsert **A**utoFormat command, or choose AutoFormat from the shortcut menu. The AutoFormat dialog box appears.

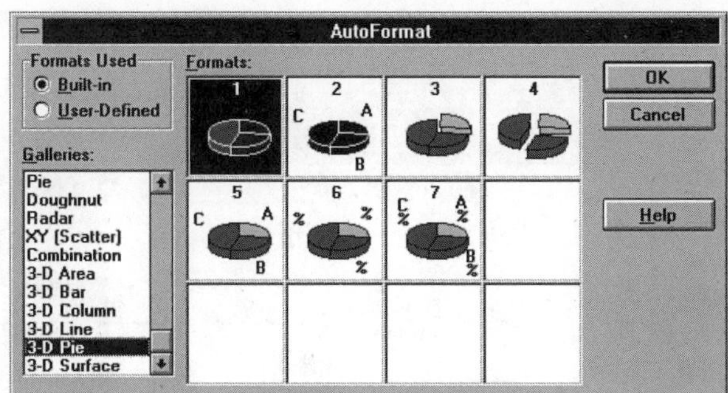

Fig. 25.9
Select a format in the AutoFormat dialog box.

2. In the Formats Used area, select the **B**uilt-in option.
3. In the **G**alleries list, select a chart type.
4. In the **F**ormats area, select a chart subtype.
5. Choose OK. Microsoft Graph applies the autoformat to the current chart.

Adding Visual Elements to a Chart

Aside from the chart itself—that is, the actual bars, lines, slices, or columns—most charts contain additional elements that make the chart easier to read and interpret. For example, you can add a title to describe the purpose of the chart. You also can add titles (such as *Thousands of dollars, Percentage,* or *1994*) to identify the units used in the x-axis (horizontal) and y-axis (vertical). If your chart is self-explanatory and does not require axis labels, you can turn off the x- and y-axes. To identify each data series represented in a chart, you use a legend. You also can add grid lines, which help readers find the values of data points more accurately. Figure 25.10 shows these chart elements.

Adding Titles

To add a chart title, x-axis title, or y-axis title, use the Titles dialog box (see fig. 25.11). You display this dialog box by choosing the **I**nsert **T**itles command, or by choosing Insert Titles from the shortcut menu. In the dialog box, check the boxes that represent the titles you want to add. For each box you check, Graph inserts a text object into the current chart. You edit the text object to add the text of the title.

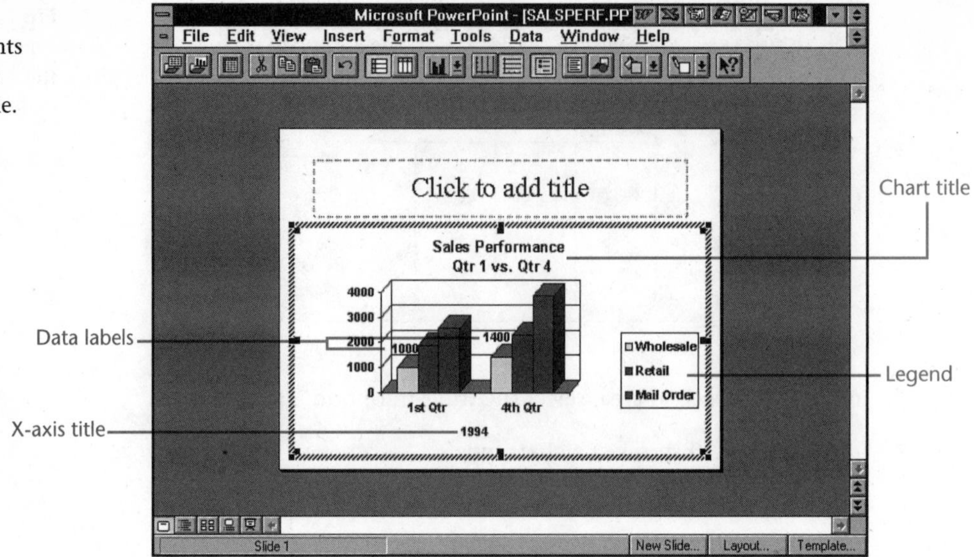

Fig. 25.10 Chart elements make a chart more readable.

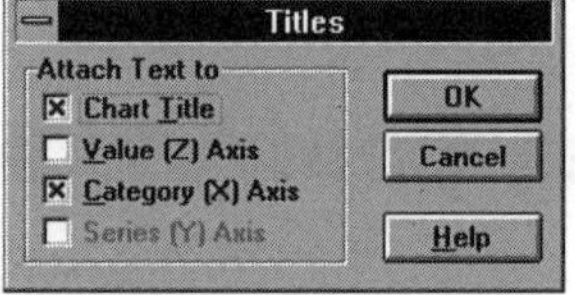

Fig. 25.11 The Titles dialog box enables you to add titles to a chart.

> **Note**
>
> The options in the Titles dialog box vary, depending on the type of chart you are using.

Tip
To change any of the text attributes of a title, double-click the title text. The Format Chart Title dialog box appears. In this dialog box, select a font, style, size, color, and special effects (such as subscript).

To add titles to a chart, follow these steps:

1. Choose the **I**nsert **T**itles command, or choose Insert Titles from the shortcut menu. The Titles dialog box appears.

2. Check all titles you want to add to your chart.

3. Choose OK. Microsoft Graph adds text objects to the chart.

4. Click a text object to select it, then click anywhere inside the text object to produce an insertion point.

5. Enter the correct text for the title.

6. Click any blank area of the chart to deselect the text object.

If necessary, you can resize the title text box, just like any other text box.

If you add a title to a chart and then decide you don't want to use it, you can remove it. Simply select the text object, and then choose the **E**dit Cle**a**r command, choose Clear from the shortcut menu, or press Del.

Adding a Legend

A *legend* uses color-coded boxes to identify the data series in a chart. If the East data series is represented in a bar chart by red bars, for example, the legend shows a small red box next to *East*. Microsoft Graph automatically adds a legend to every new chart, so you don't need to choose a command.

If you prefer not to include a legend in a chart, you can remove the legend. Select the legend, and then choose the **E**dit Cle**a**r command, choose Clear from the shortcut menu, or press Del. To place a legend in the chart again, choose **I**nsert **L**egend.

Adding Data Labels

Data labels mark the exact value or percentage represented by a data point. Data labels often are used in bar or column charts to pinpoint values when data points are close together. These labels also are commonly used in pie charts to identify the exact percentage represented by each pie slide.

Tip
To turn a legend on or off quickly, click the Legend button in the standard Graph toolbar.

To add data labels to a chart, you use the Data Labels dialog box, shown in figure 25.12. Display this dialog box by choosing the **I**nsert **D**ata Labels command, or by choosing Insert Data Labels from the shortcut menu. In the dialog box, you can select more than one data-label option. The Show Value and Show Percent options display numbers, and the Show Label option displays the category label next to the data point. The Show Label and Show Percent options are commonly used in pie charts to identify each pie slide, as well as to pinpoint the percentage.

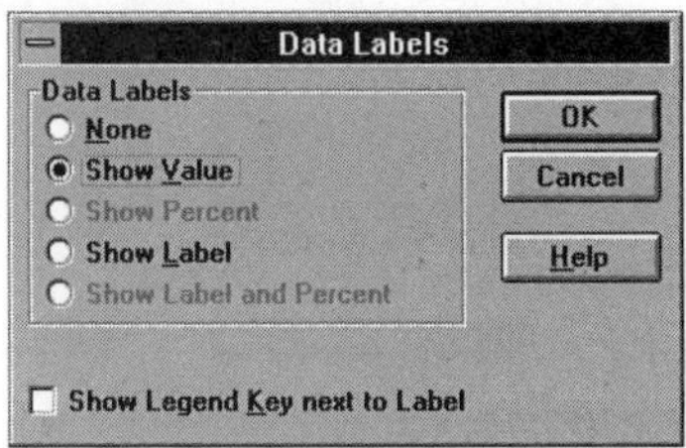

Fig. 25.12
Select one or more options in the Data Labels dialog box.

The Show Legend Key next to Label check box, at the bottom of the Data Labels dialog box, enables you to display a *legend key* (a small color-coded box) alongside each data label. To use this option, click its check box.

To add data labels to a chart, follow these steps:

1. Choose the **I**nsert **D**ata Labels command, or choose Insert Data Labels from the shortcut menu. The Data Labels dialog box appears.
2. Select one or more options.
3. If you want the legend key to appear with the data label, check the Show Legend Key next to Label check box.
4. Choose OK.

Turning the Axes On and Off

All sample column charts that Microsoft Graph creates include an x-axis and a y-axis. Each axis is labeled with the scale (dollars, percentages) or unit of measurement (months, quarters) represented in the axis. For some charts, you might find that the x- and y-axes are unnecessary. When a chart's exact data points for each data series are not important, and when the data markers (bars, lines, columns, and so on) clearly illustrate the differences in values, you might not want to include the x- and y-axes in your chart.

To turn off the x- or y-axis in a chart, follow these steps:

1. Choose the **I**nsert A**x**es command, or choose Insert Axes from the shortcut menu. The Axes dialog box appears (see fig. 25.13).

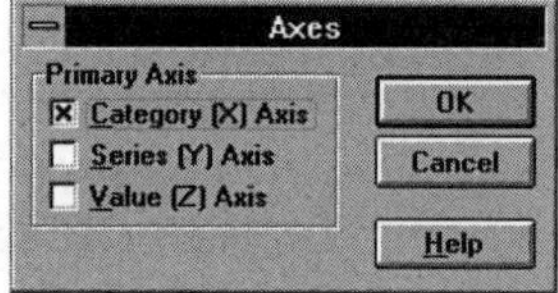

Fig. 25.13
Use the Axes dialog box to add and remove axes in a chart.

2. For each axis you want to remove, deselect the appropriate option.
3. Choose OK. Microsoft Graph removes the axes you specify from the current chart.

To return an axis to a chart, follow the same steps, but select the appropriate axis options.

Adding Grid Lines

Grid lines are horizontal and vertical lines that overlay a chart. These lines help you follow a point from the x- or y-axis to identify a data point's exact value. Grid lines are useful in large charts, charts that contain many data points, and charts in which data points are close together.

The sample column chart that Microsoft Graph creates includes horizontal grid lines. When you choose a new chart type, at least one set of grid lines (horizontal or vertical, depending on the orientation of the chart) is included to make the chart easier to read. You can add the opposite set of grid lines, change from one set to another, or remove all grid lines.

To specify which grid lines to use, you use the Gridlines dialog box, shown in figure 25.14. Display this dialog box by choosing the **I**nsert **G**ridlines command, or by choosing Insert Gridlines from the shortcut menu. Notice that the dialog box contains options for *major* and *minor* grid lines. The grid lines in the sample column chart that Microsoft Graph creates occur at the major intervals on the axis. Using major grid lines helps you pinpoint exact locations in a chart without cluttering the chart. When major grid lines don't provide enough detail, however, you can use minor grid lines as well. Minor grid lines fall between the major intervals on the axis.

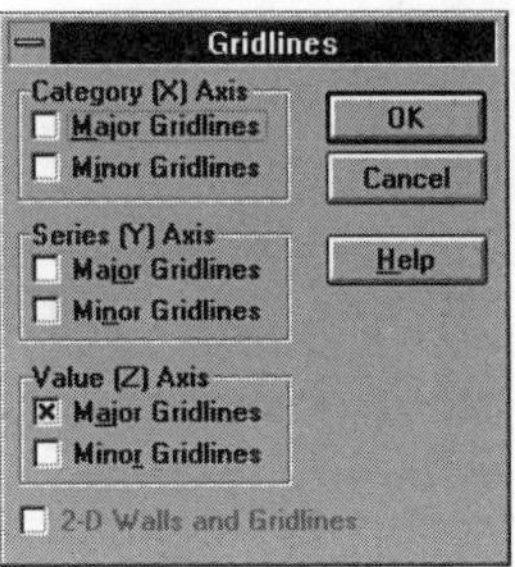

Fig. 25.14
Use the Gridlines dialog box to choose grid-line options.

To turn grid lines on or off in a chart, follow these steps:

1. Choose **I**nsert **G**ridlines, or choose Insert Gridlines from the shortcut menu. The Gridlines dialog box appears.

2. For each axis, turn major and minor grid lines on or off. (Grid lines are on when an X appears in the check box.)

3. Choose OK.

Tip
To turn grid lines on and off quickly, click the Horizontal Gridlines or Vertical Gridlines button in Graph's Standard toolbar.

Specifying Colors, Patterns, Borders, and Fonts in a Chart

Throughout this chapter, you have seen how Microsoft Graph creates a sample chart from sample data. Just as you can change the chart type used for the sample chart, you can change the colors, patterns, borders, and fonts used in the sample chart. Changing these attributes can greatly improve the appearance of a chart.

You can apply colors, patterns, and borders to almost any element in a chart. In the sample column chart shown in figure 25.15, columns that represent the data series are red, green, and blue. Each column is bordered in black. All columns appear in a solid color rather than a two-color pattern. The legend box and the walls of the chart (made visible by the horizontal grid lines) appear in white, and the grid lines themselves appear in black. You can change the colors of all these elements.

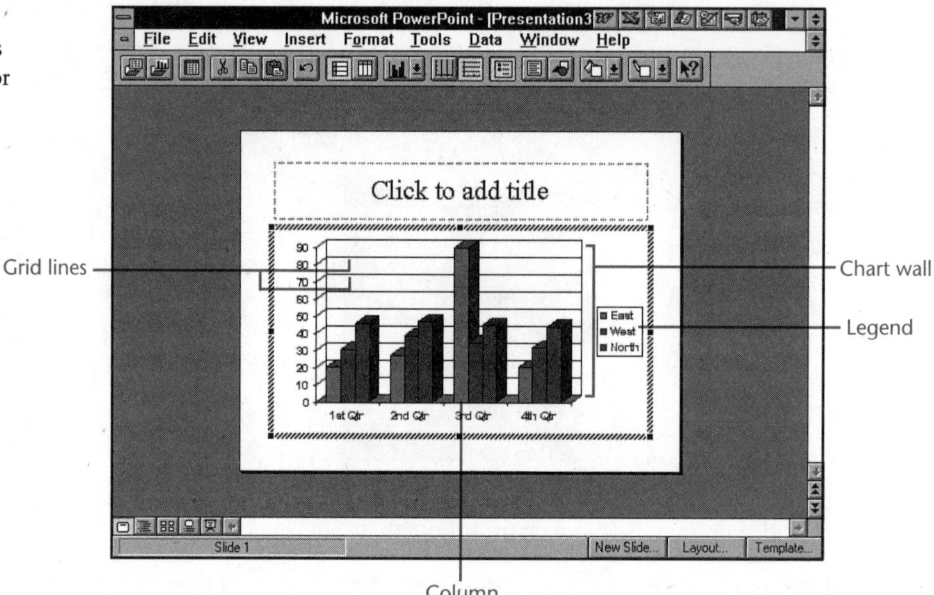

Fig. 25.15
This figure shows chart elements for which you can specify a color, pattern, border, and font.

To change a chart element's color, pattern, or border, begin by selecting the element that you want to change. If you want grid lines to appear in red rather than black, for example, click one of the grid lines. The element's resize handles appear, showing that the element is selected. Then open the F**o**rmat menu, and notice that the first command in the menu reads **Se**lected [Element] (Element refers to the chart element you selected). In this example, the command is **Se**lected Gridlines. If you selected the chart's walls or legend, the command would be **Se**lected Walls or **Se**lected Legend.

When you choose the F**o**rmat S**e**lected [Element] command, Microsoft Graph displays a dialog box like the one shown in figure 25.16. The Patterns tab is selected. (Depending on the element you select, a different tab might be selected in the dialog box.) In the Border area of the dialog box, you can select the border's style, color, and weight, or turn off the border by choosing **N**one. In the Area section, you can select a color and pattern for the element.

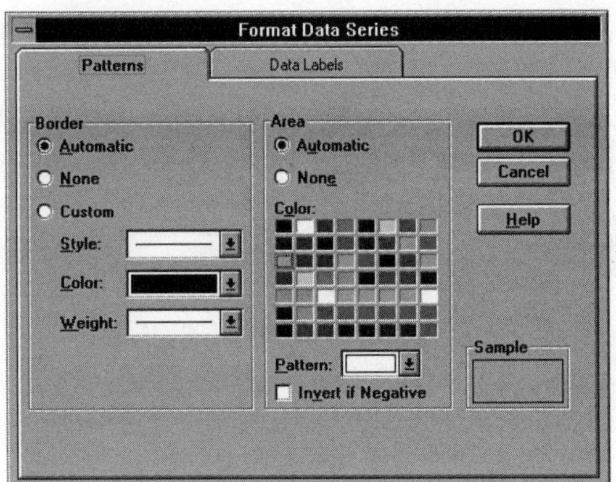

Fig. 25.16
Use the Format [Element] dialog box to change element attributes.

Tip
You can double-click any chart element to display the Format [Element] dialog box.

To change a chart element's color, pattern, or border, follow these steps:

1. Select the element you want to change. The element is selected when its resize handles become visible.

2. Choose the F**o**rmat S**e**lected [Element] command, or choose Selected [Element] from the shortcut menu. The Format [Element] dialog box appears.

3. In the Border area, select the appropriate options. To restore Graph's default style, select **A**utomatic.

4. In the Area section, select the appropriate options. To restore Graph's default color and pattern, select A**u**tomatic.

5. Check the Sample box in the bottom right corner of the dialog box. Repeat steps 3 and 4 to change any colors or styles with which you are not satisfied.

6. When you are satisfied with your choices, choose OK.

For any text object in a chart, you can change the font, size, style, color, and background color. You also can specify underlining or add special effects, such as strikethrough, subscript, and superscript. These attributes are listed on the Font tab of the Format [Element] dialog box (see fig. 25.17). To display this dialog box, select the text object, choose F**o**rmat S**e**lected [Element], or double-click the text object.

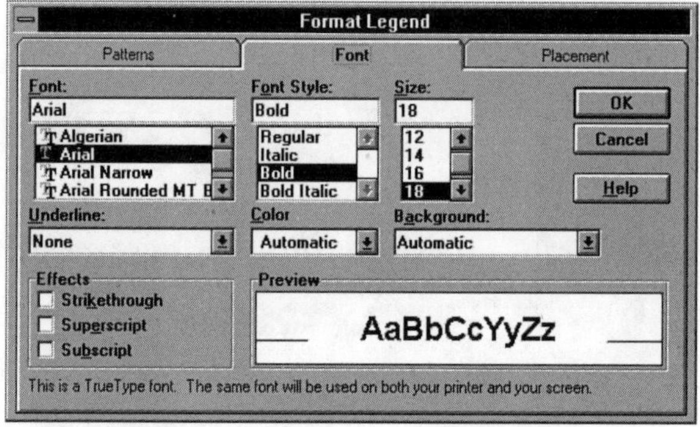

Fig. 25.17 Use the Font tab in the Format [Element] dialog box to change font attributes.

Follow these steps to change the format of text:

1. Select the text object that you want to format, and then choose the F**o**rmat S**e**lected [Element] command, choose Selected [Element] from the shortcut menu, or double-click the text object. The Format [Element] dialog box appears.
2. If the Font tab is not visible, click it or press Ctrl+Tab.
3. Select one item a piece in the **F**ont, F**o**nt Style, and **S**ize list boxes.
4. To change the text color, select a color in the **C**olor drop-down list.
5. (Optional) Select special effects in the **U**nderline and Effects sections.
6. Check the Preview area of the dialog box. If you are not satisfied with any of the changes, repeat steps 3 through 5, selecting different items.
7. When you are satisfied with your choices, choose OK.

Inserting a Chart into a Presentation

While you are working in Microsoft Graph and making changes in your chart, the changes you make are updated in your PowerPoint slide. As long as you continue working in Graph, the Graph menu bar and toolbar remain active. When you are satisfied with your chart and want to return to PowerPoint, click any blank area of the slide outside the chart area. The chart becomes an object in the slide, and PowerPoint's menus and toolbar return.

To save the chart, choose **F**ile **S**ave.

Editing a Chart

After returning to PowerPoint, you might want to edit an existing chart. To start Microsoft Graph again, simply double-click the chart. The Graph menus and toolbar replace the PowerPoint menus and toolbar.

From Here...

In this chapter, you learned how to work with a separate application—Microsoft Graph—to create charts for your presentation slides. Refer to the following chapters for information about other types of objects you can add to slides:

- Chapter 21, "Entering Slide Content," describes the basics of entering the content of a presentation and labeling objects. This chapter also describes all aspects of enhancing text, such as selecting fonts, styles, and colors; aligning text; adding bullets; and checking your spelling.
- Chapter 23, "Drawing Shapes, Curves, and Lines," describes how to use PowerPoint's drawing tools to add drawn objects to your slides.
- Chapter 24, "Enhancing a Presentation," describes how to add color, borders, shadows, and other enhancements to objects.

Chapter 26

Creating Output

by Debbie Walkowski

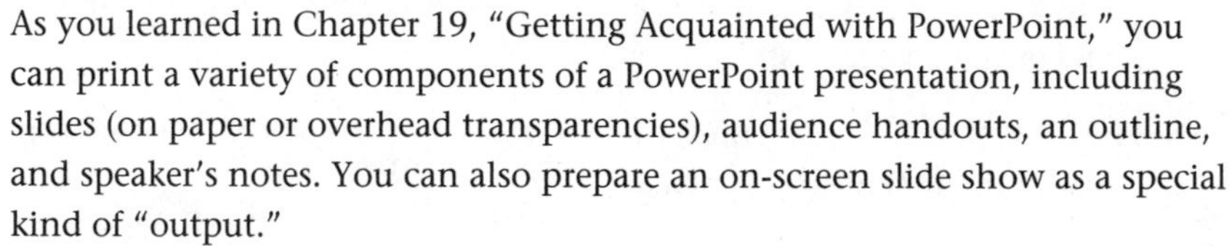

As you learned in Chapter 19, "Getting Acquainted with PowerPoint," you can print a variety of components of a PowerPoint presentation, including slides (on paper or overhead transparencies), audience handouts, an outline, and speaker's notes. You can also prepare an on-screen slide show as a special kind of "output."

In this chapter, you learn to

- Choose a setup for presentation components
- Set up your printer
- Print presentation components (slides, notes, handouts, and an outline)
- Create and run an on-screen slide show

Choosing a Setup for Presentation Components

A *setup* determines the dimensions and orientation to be used for printing each component of a presentation. PowerPoint is set to print slides that are 10 inches wide and 8.5 inches high in landscape orientation. If you want to use different dimensions or portrait orientation, you must choose setup options in the Slide Setup dialog box, shown in figure 26.1. Display this dialog box by choosing the **F**ile Slide Set**u**p command.

In the dialog box, the Slides Sized For drop-down list offers options for different types of paper, on-screen slide shows, and 35mm slides. When you choose an option, the dimensions set for that option appear in the Width and Height boxes.

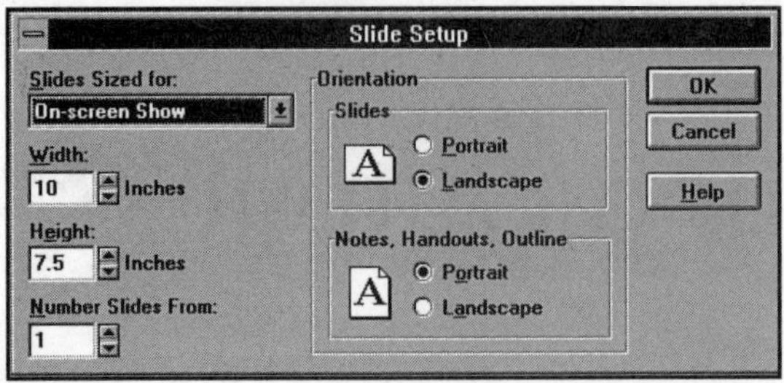

Fig. 26.1
Use the Slide Setup Dialog box to set up all presentation components.

As shown in figure 26.1, the On-Screen Show option uses an area 10 inches wide by 7.5 inches tall so the slides fill the screen. Following are the other Slides Sized For options you may choose:

- The Letter Paper option sets the width to 10 inches and the height to 7.5 inches. Use this option when you are printing on 8 1/2-by-11-inch paper or transparencies.
- The A4 Paper (210 x 297 mm) option sets the width to 10.83 inches (26 cm) and the height to 7.5 inches (18 cm).
- The 35mm Slides option sets the width to 11.25 inches and the height to 7.5 inches so that the content fills the slide area.
- The Custom option allows you to choose the dimensions you want when you are printing on nonstandard paper. Before you specify custom dimensions in the Width and Height boxes, the width and height default to the maximum area your printer is capable of printing.

The Orientation section of the dialog box offers Portrait and Landscape as options. When you choose Portrait, the slide is taller than it is wide. Landscape creates slides that are just the opposite of Portrait—that is, each slide is wider than it is tall. Slides often are printed in landscape orientation, whereas notes, handouts, and outlines are most often printed in portrait orientation. Therefore, PowerPoint offers separate orientation options for slides and notes, handouts, and outlines.

PowerPoint allows you to begin numbering slides with a number other than 1 by entering that number in the Number Slides From box.

To choose a setup for slides, notes, handouts, and outlines, follow these steps:

1. Open the presentation for which you want to specify a setup.
2. Choose the **F**ile Slide Set**u**p command. The Slide Setup dialog box appears.

3. Choose the appropriate option in the **S**lides Sized For drop-down list.

4. To begin numbering slides with a number other than 1, enter a number in the **N**umber Slides From box.

5. To change the print orientation for slides, choose either **P**ortrait or **L**andscape.

6. To change the print orientation for notes, handouts, or an outline, choose either **P**ortrait or **L**andscape.

7. When all settings are correct, choose OK.

Note

It is best to set the slide setup before you create a new presentation. If you change the slide setup after your slides are created, you might need to make adjustments to your slides, depending on the setup dimensions you choose.

Setting Up Your Printer

In most cases, you won't need to change your printer setup before printing PowerPoint slides or other components. Your printer is probably already set up for printing from other Microsoft Office or Windows applications. The only reason you should have to change your printer setup is if you want to use a printer you don't normally use. To change the printer you are using, follow these steps:

1. Open the presentation you want to print.

2. Choose the **F**ile **P**rint command. PowerPoint displays the Print dialog box. The current printer is displayed at the top of the dialog box.

3. Choose the P**r**inter button. PowerPoint displays the Print Setup dialog box shown in figure 26.2. The default printer is listed at the top of the dialog box.

4. To choose a printer for the current printing, highlight an item in the **P**rinters box.

5. To make the printer the default printer, choose the Set As **D**efault Printer button.

6. Choose OK to return to the Print dialog box.

7. Choose OK to close the Print dialog box and return to the active presentation.

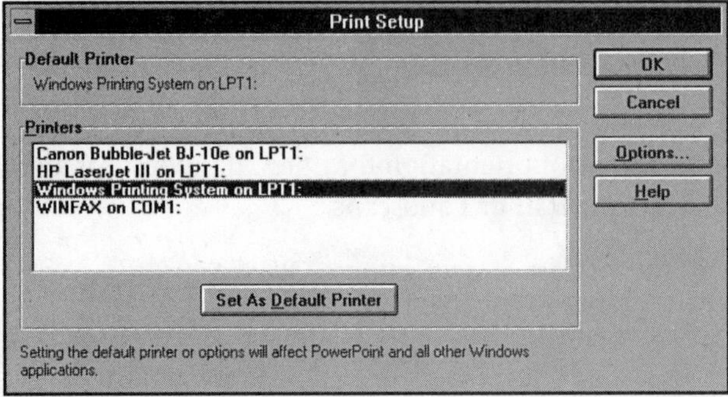

Fig. 26.2
The Print Setup dialog box.

The printer you choose affects the current presentation only. It remains in effect until you change it. If you specified the printer as the default printer, it affects all presentations and remains in effect until you specify a different default printer.

Printing Presentation Components

PowerPoint allows you to print any component of a presentation: slides, notes pages, handouts, and an outline. To print any component, choose the **F**ile **P**rint command. The Print dialog box appears, as shown in figure 26.3. In this dialog box you choose the component you want to print, the number of copies, the specific pages to print, and other printing options. Table 26.1 describes the options in the Print dialog box.

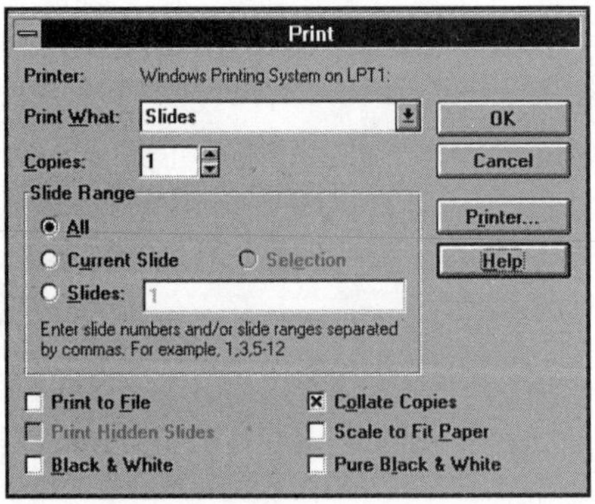

Print
Printer: Windows Printing System on LPT1:
Print What: Slides
Copies: 1
Slide Range
All
Current Slide
Selection
Slides: 1
Enter slide numbers and/or slide ranges separated by commas. For example, 1,3,5-12
OK
Cancel
Printer...
Help
Print to File
Print Hidden Slides
Black & White
Collate Copies
Scale to Fit Paper
Pure Black & White

Fig. 26.3
The Print dialog box.

Table 26.1 Options in the Print Dialog Box

Option	Description
Print **W**hat	Lists the PowerPoint components you can print: slides, notes, handouts, and outline.
Copies	Enables you to specify the number of copies to print.
Slide Range	Gives you the option of printing All slides, only the Current Slide, a Selection of slides, or specific ranges of slides you specify. In the Slides box, use a hyphen, as in 5–8, to specify a continuous range. To specify individual pages, use commas, as in 12, 14, 17. For multiple ranges, use a combination of the two, as in 5–8,12,17–21,25.
Print to **F**ile	Use this option if you want to print to file rather than to a printer. Slides are generally printed to file when they will be produced by a service bureau.
Print H**i**dden Slides	When slides are set to hidden, check this option to include hidden files in the printing.
Black & White	Changes all fill colors to white and adds a thin black border to all objects that are not bordered or do not contain text.
C**o**llate Copies	When printing multiple copies of a presentation, prints collated sets.
Scale to Fit **P**aper	If you choose a different paper size in the Printer Setup dialog box, this option scales each slide to fit the paper.
Pure B**l**ack and White	Changes all fill colors to white and all text and lines to black, adds outlines to filled objects to make them visible, and prints all pictures in shades of gray.

Printing Slides

Using the options in the Slide Range area of the Print dialog box, you can print all slides, only the current slide, the slides that are selected in the presentation, or a range of slides you specify. Be sure to check the Print Hidden Slides check box if your presentation contains slides that are set to hidden and you want to include them in the printed output.

To print slides, complete the following steps:

1. Open the presentation for which you want to print slides.
2. Choose the **F**ile **P**rint command. The Print dialog box appears.
3. In the Print **W**hat drop-down list, choose the component you want to print.

Tip
To bypass the Print dialog box and print all slides in a presentation using the current Print settings, click the Print button on the toolbar.

4. In the **C**opies box, specify the number of copies to print.
5. In the Slide Range box, select the appropriate option, as described in table 26.1.
6. In the lower portion of the dialog box, select any of the check boxes as appropriate.
7. When all settings are correct, choose OK.

Printing Notes Pages

Notes pages contain a reduced slide at the top of the page and speaker's notes at the bottom of the page, as shown in figure 26.4. To print notes pages, you follow the same basic steps you learned for printing slides.

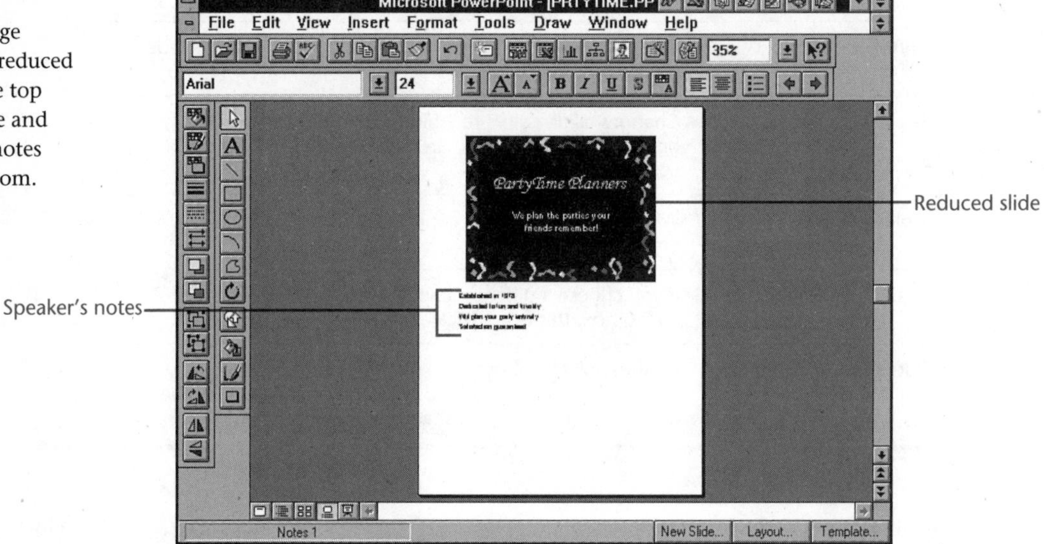

Fig 26.4
A notes page displays a reduced slide at the top of the page and speaker's notes at the bottom.

Because notes pages print one slide per page, specify the slide range for the slides you want to print. If, for example, you want to print notes pages only for slides two through six, enter **2–6** in the Slides text box of the Print dialog box.

Printing Handouts

PowerPoint lets you print handouts using one of three different layout styles. The first layout includes two slides per page. Other layouts let you print three or six slides per page. To see how a handout page looks with each of these layout options, display the Handout Master by holding the Shift key and clicking the Slide Sorter button. Alternatively, select the **V**iew **M**aster command; then choose the Handout Master option. You see a slide like the one shown in figure 26.5. The small dotted lines outline the three- and six-slides-per-page layouts. (If you choose to print three slides per page, the slides are printed on the left slide of the page; the right side is blank. The long dotted lines outline the two-slides-per-page layout.

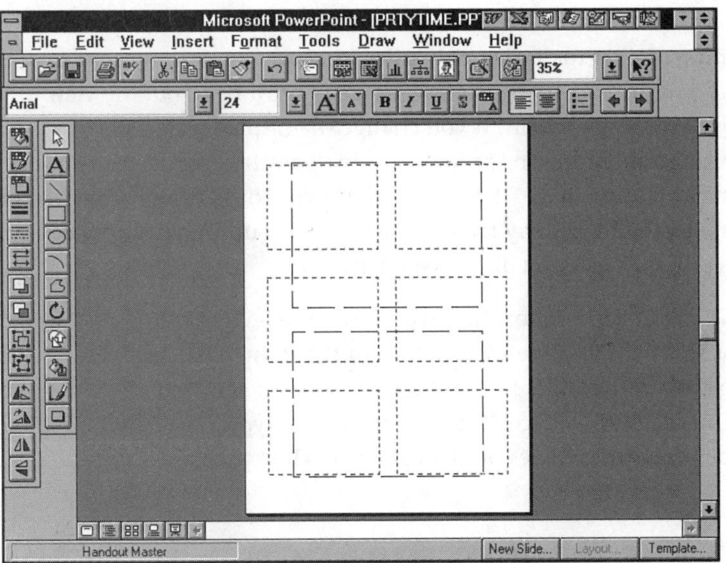

Fig. 26.5
Layout options for handouts include two, three, or six slides per page.

To print handouts, you use the same basic steps for printing slides. In the Print What area of the Print dialog box, choose Handouts (2 Slides Per Page), Handouts (3 Slides Per Page), or Handouts (6 Slides Per Page), as shown in figure 26.6.

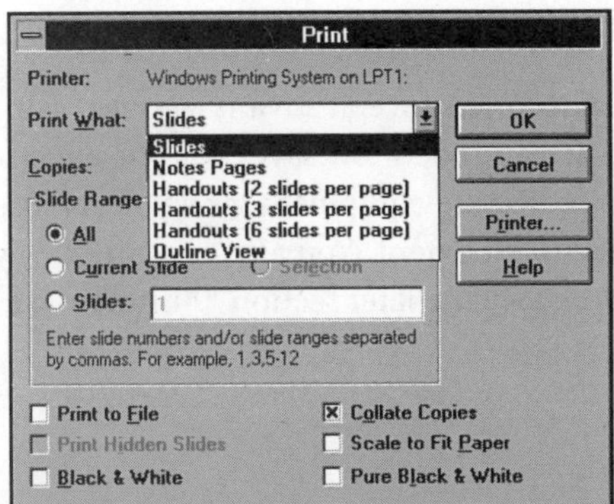

Fig. 26.6
Handout options in the Print dialog box.

To print selected handout pages, it isn't necessary to determine on which page a slide will print. Just specify the *slide numbers* that you want to print in the Slides box. If, for example, you choose 3 slides per page and you want to print slides 4, 5, and 6, enter **4–6** in the Slides text box of the Print dialog box. PowerPoint prints the second handout page.

Printing an Outline

When you print a presentation outline, it is printed just as it was last displayed in outline view. If you clicked the Show Titles button on the Outlining toolbar to display only titles (no body text), for example, PowerPoint prints only the slide titles. (You must be in outline view to see the Outlining toolbar.) If you change the display scale using the Zoom Control button on the Standard toolbar, the outline prints in the current scale percentage. If you click the Show Formatting button on the Outline toolbar to display the outline text without formatting, the outline is printed exactly as displayed on-screen.

To print an outline, follow the steps outlined previously for printing slides, except select the Outline View option in the Print What section of the Print dialog box. In the Slides box, enter the slide numbers that you want to include on the outline page. If, for example, you type **1, 4, 5–9**, PowerPoint includes only those slides on the printed outline page.

Setting Up and Running a Slide Show On-Screen

One of the most effective ways to present your slides is to use your computer screen as an output medium. When you use your computer for an on-screen slide show, the entire screen area is used; PowerPoint's title bar, menu, and toolbars are cleared from the screen, and each slide is displayed using the full screen.

An on-screen slide show offers several advantages over transparencies or 35mm slides. An on-screen slide show saves you the expense of producing slides, it requires no projection equipment, and you can use your computer's color capability to its fullest extent. You also can annotate your slides as you give your presentation. (See the later section "Annotating a Slide Show" for more information.)

You can run a PowerPoint slide show manually (using the mouse or keyboard to advance to the next slide when you're ready); you can set up a slide show to run in a continuous "loop" for demonstration purposes; or you can set up a slide show to advance slides automatically. To learn how to run a slide show manually or in a continuous loop, see the later section "Running a Slide Show."

Setting Slide Timings and Transitions

When you set up a slide show to automatically advance to the next slide, you can set the amount of time each slide remains on-screen, and you can specify a transition style between slides. The transition style determines how one slide is removed from the screen and the next one is presented. *Dissolving* from one slide to the next and *fade through black* are two examples of transition styles. PowerPoint offers 46 transition styles from which to choose.

To set timings and transitions, you use the Transitions dialog box (shown in fig. 26.7). From any of PowerPoint's display views, you can display this dialog box by choosing the **T**ools **T**ransition command. When using Slide Sorter view, you can display the Transition dialog box by clicking the Transition button at the far left end of the toolbar.

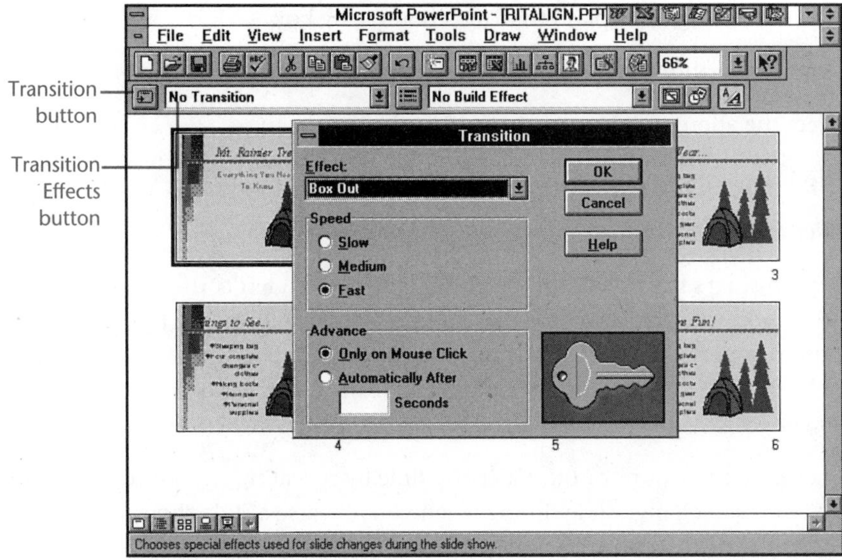

Fig 26.7
Use the Transition dialog box to set slide timings and transitions.

Transition styles are listed in the Effect drop-down list. To see a demonstration of how transitions actually work on-screen, open the Effect drop-down list, and then press the down arrow, highlighting a new transition style. Each time you highlight a new style, the transition is demonstrated on the sample slide in the lower right corner of the dialog box. Try varying the speed (Slow, Medium, or Fast) to see how it affects a transition.

You specify timing options in the Advance section of the Transition dialog box. Select the Only on Mouse Click option to set slides to advance manually whenever you click the mouse. Select Automatically After *N* Seconds to set a specific transition time for the slide; then enter the number of seconds in the box.

Tip
You can quickly set slide transitions using the Transition Effects button on the Slide Sorter toolbar. Select a slide; then select an item from the Transition Effects drop-down list.

To set timing between slides and specify transitions, follow these steps.

1. Display your presentation in slide sorter view.
2. Select the slide for which you want to set timing and transition. If you want to use the same settings for multiple slides, select those slides as a group.
3. Click the Transition button at the far left end of the toolbar, choose the **T**ools **T**ransition command, or choose Transition from the shortcut menu. PowerPoint displays the Transition dialog box.
4. Select a transition style from the **E**ffect drop-down list.
5. Select the appropriate option in the Speed box.
6. Select the appropriate option in the Advance box.
7. Choose OK.

Tip
You can specify more than 60 seconds if you want the slide to remain on-screen longer than one minute.

PowerPoint displays the transition time below the bottom left corner of the slide. When you set a transition for the slide, an icon that looks like the Transition button appears alongside the transition time in the bottom left corner (see fig. 26.8). You can click any transition icon to see a demonstration of the transition effect.

You can change transitions or timing at any time by repeating the above steps. You also can change slide timing when you rehearse a slide show, as described in the next section.

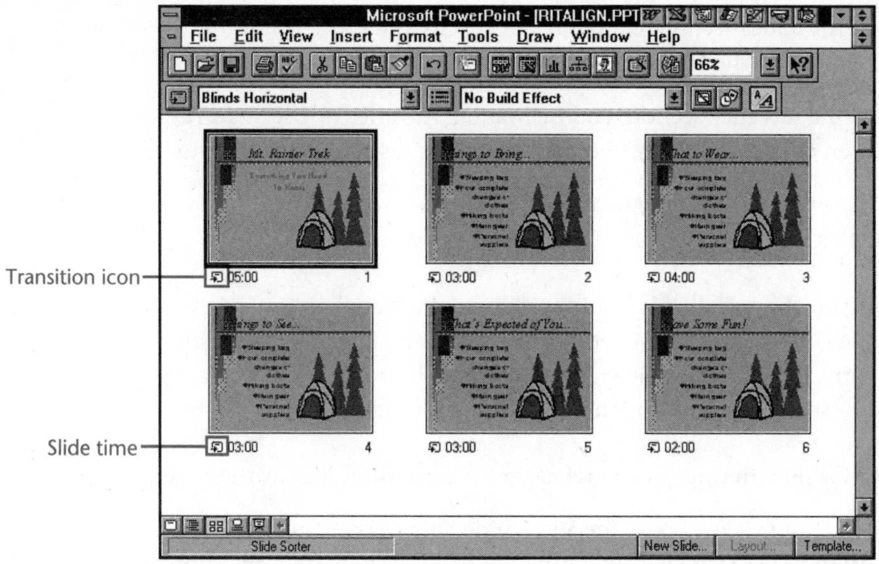

Fig 26.8
Transition symbols and timings appears in the lower left corner of slides.

Rehearsing a Slide Show

Before you actually give your presentation, you'll probably want to rehearse it several times. You can rehearse using manual advance or using the slide timings you set. If you want to set new timings, you can do so as you rehearse.

To rehearse using manual advance or the current slide timings, follow these steps:

1. From any view, choose the **V**iew Slide Sho**w** command. (If you are using slide sorter view, you can choose Slide Show from the shortcut menu.) The Slide Show dialog box shown in figure 26.9 appears.

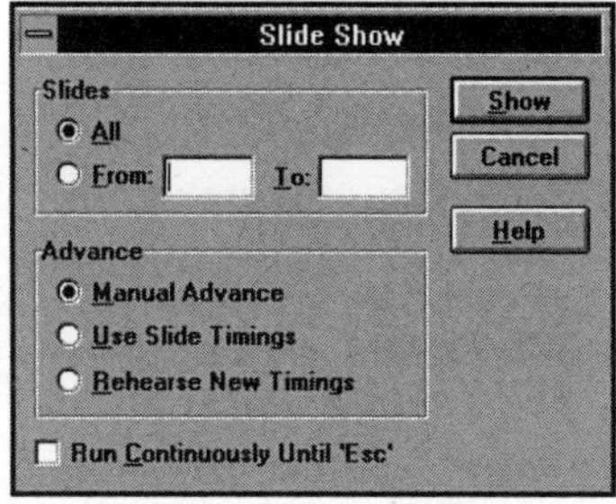

Fig. 26.9
The Slide Show dialog box.

2. In the Slides section, choose **A**ll or specify the slides you want to rehearse in the **F**rom and **T**o boxes.

3. In the Advance section, choose **M**anual Advance or **U**se Slide Timings; then choose the Show button. Your slide presentation begins running.

4. If you chose **M**anual Advance, click the mouse, press Enter, or press PgDn when you're ready to advance to the next slide.

   If you chose **U**se Slide Timings, the slides advance automatically using the current timings. When the last slide is complete, PowerPoint returns to slide sorter view. You can manually advance, however, by pressing Enter, clicking the mouse, or pressing PgDn.

Tip
From slide sorter view, you can start a slide show to rehearse new slide timings by clicking the Rehearse Timings button on the Slide Sorter toolbar.

Tip
If you want to record new timings selectively during a rehearsal, press O to use the original time, press T to use the new time, or press M to hold a slide onscreen until the mouse is clicked.

To set new slide timings as you rehearse a presentation, follow these steps:

1. From any view, choose the **V**iew Slide Sho**w** command. (If you are using slide sorter view, you can choose Slide Show from the shortcut menu.) The Slide Show dialog box appears.

2. In the Slides section, choose **A**ll or specify the slides you want to rehearse in the **F**rom and **T**o boxes.

3. In the Advance section, choose the **R**ehearse New Timings option; then choose the **S**how button. Your slide presentation begins running, and a clock timer appears in the lower-left corner of the screen, counting seconds.

4. Begin rehearsing your presentation. When you are ready to advance to the next slide, click the mouse button, press Enter, or press PgDn.

5. Repeat step 4 until all slides are shown. A message appears telling you the total time for the new slide timings.

   Choose **Y**es to record the new timings; choose **N**o to ignore the new timings and retain the previous timings.

Running a Slide Show

Several ways exist to run a PowerPoint slide show. You can run a slide show from within PowerPoint by first opening the presentation, and then choosing the **V**iew Slide Sho**w** command, or by clicking the Slide Show button in the lower left corner of the PowerPoint window. When you choose the **V**iew Slide Sho**w** command, the Slide Show dialog box appears. Use this dialog box to specify the slides to view and how you want the slide show to run. When you choose the Slide Show button, you bypass the display of the Slide Show dialog box, and PowerPoint uses whatever settings appear in that dialog box.

To run a slide show using the **V**iew Slide Sho**w** command, use these steps:

1. Open the presentation for which you want to run a slide show.
2. Choose any view.
3. Choose the **V**iew Slide Sho**w** command. The Slide Show dialog box appears.
4. In the Slides section of the dialog box, choose **A**ll.
5. In the Advance section, choose **M**anual Advance or **U**se Slide Timings; then choose **S**how. Your slide presentation begins running.

If you chose the **M**anual Advance option in step 5, click the mouse, press Enter, or press PgDn when you're ready to advance to the next slide. If you chose **U**se Slide Timings, the slides advance automatically using the current timings.

Tip
To end a slide show at any time, press Esc. PowerPoint returns to the view that was displayed before you began the slide show.

It's rare that you have an opportunity to run through a slide show completely without interruption. At times, you might want to pause, view a previous slide, or turn a slide "off" by making the screen go black (or white). Table 26.2 lists the methods for controlling your movements through a slide show.

Tip
During a slide show, pressing F1 will show these commands.

Table 26.2 Methods for Controlling a Slide Show

Function	Method
Show the next slide	Click left mouse button or press space bar, N, →, ↓, or PgDn.
Show the preceding slide	Click right mouse button or press Backspace, P, ←, ↑, or PgUp.
Show a specific slide	Type the number and press Enter.
Toggle the mouse pointer on or off (Show or Hide)	Type A or equal sign (=).
Toggle between a black screen and the current slide	Type B or period (.).
Toggle between a white screen and the current slide	Type W or comma (,).

(continues)

Table 26.2 Continued

Function	Method
End the slide show and return to PowerPoint	Press Esc, hyphen (-), or Ctrl+Break.
Pause and resume an automatic slide show	Type S or plus sign (+).

Another method for running a slide show is to simply click the Slide Show button at the lower-left corner of the PowerPoint window. When you click this button, PowerPoint immediately runs the slide show, beginning with the slide that is currently selected. The slide show runs using current slide timings. If there are no timings set, you must advance each slide manually. To run a slide show from the beginning using this method, be sure to select the first slide in the presentation before you click the Slide Show button.

A third method for running a slide show is to use the PowerPoint Viewer, a special program that runs outside PowerPoint. The PowerPoint Viewer lets you run a slide show even if the PowerPoint program itself is not installed on the computer. The PowerPoint Viewer is particularly useful if you need to present a slide show on a computer other than your own (perhaps at a customer's office or at a trade show).

To run a slide show using the PowerPoint Viewer, follow these steps:

1. From the Windows Program Manager, locate and open the Microsoft Office Program Group.

2. Double-click the PowerPoint Viewer program icon. The Microsoft PowerPoint Viewer dialog box appears, as shown in figure 26.10.

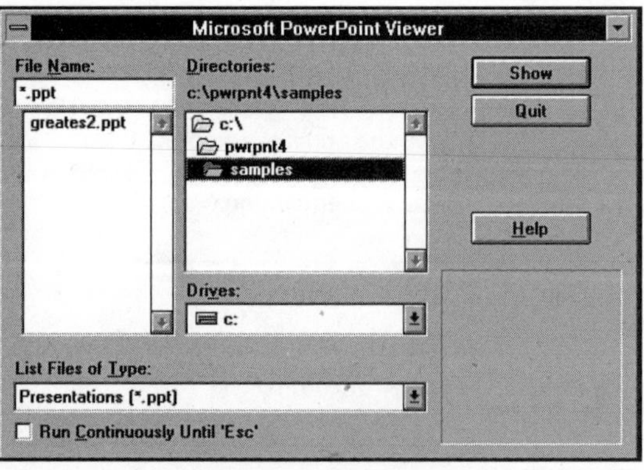

Fig. 26.10
The Microsoft PowerPoint Viewer dialog box.

3. In the **D**irectories list, highlight the directory where the presentation file is located. (Choose a disk drive from the Dri**v**es list, if necessary.)

4. In the File **N**ame list, highlight the presentation file.

5. To run the slide show continuously, choose the Run **C**ontinuously Until 'Esc' check box at the bottom of the dialog box.

6. Choose the **S**how button to begin the slide presentation.

Refer to table 25.2 to control a running slide show.

Annotating a Slide Show

When you deliver a presentation using overhead transparencies, you may often circle or underline a specific point, or write notes on the slide in response to audience questions or comments. If you use a dry-erase marker, you can easily wipe off your annotations so that the transparencies are not permanently marked.

When you run an on-screen slide show, PowerPoint gives you the ability to *electronically* annotate your slides in freehand form using the mouse. For instance, you might want to draw a check mark beside an important point or underline it. As with overhead transparencies and dry-erase markers, electronic annotations are not permanent. They are automatically removed when you move to the next slide in a slide show, or you can remove annotations manually as you present your slides.

To annotate slides during a slide show, follow these steps:

1. Start your slide show either in PowerPoint or in the PowerPoint Viewer.

2. Click the annotation icon, which appears in the lower right corner of your screen. The mouse pointer changes to a pencil.

3. Press and hold the mouse button as you write or draw on-screen, using it as you would a pencil. Release the mouse button to stop drawing or writing. The annotation tool is still active; the annotation icon toggles on and off (see fig. 26.11).

4. Repeat step 3 to write or draw again on the slide.

5. (Optional) Press E to erase all annotations to the current slide.

6. When you are finished annotating the current slide, click the annotation icon again to restore the mouse pointer.

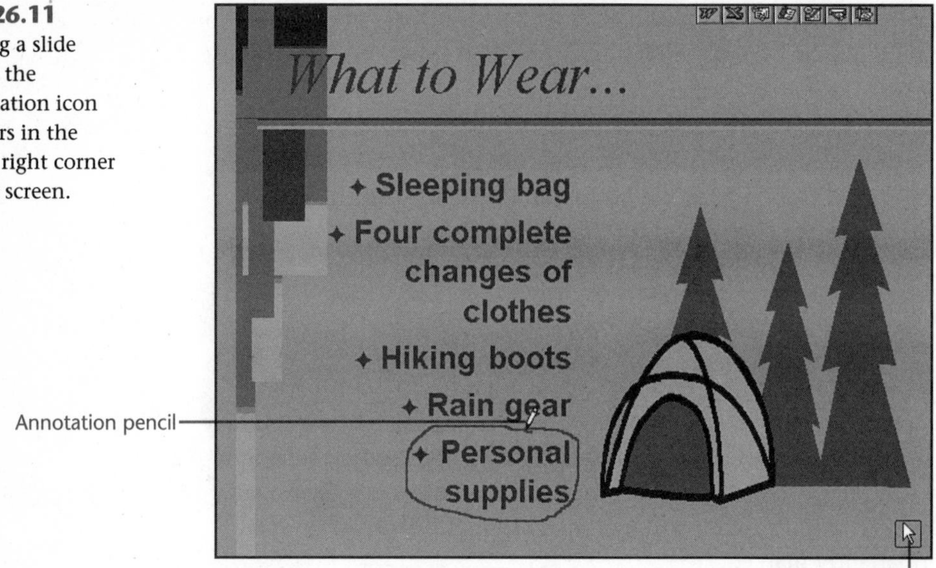

Fig. 26.11 During a slide show, the annotation icon appears in the lower right corner of the screen.

If you don't press E to erase all annotations on the current slide (see step 5 above), PowerPoint erases all annotations automatically when you move to the next slide in the slide show.

From Here...

This chapter, which describes how to prepare your printer, print slide show components, and run a slide show in PowerPoint, concludes the PowerPoint section of *Using Microsoft Office*, Special Edition. To review information about using PowerPoint, refer to any of the chapters listed below:

- Chapter 19, "Getting Acquainted with PowerPoint," describes how to start and exit PowerPoint and describes the PowerPoint window. You also learn about templates, masters, objects, layouts, and visuals that you can add to a PowerPoint presentation.
- Chapter 20, "Creating, Saving, and Opening Presentations," describes the various methods for creating a new presentation file and how to switch your view of a presentation. You also learn how to save, close, and open a PowerPoint presentation file.

- Chapter 21, "Entering Slide Content," describes the basics of entering the content of a presentation and labeling objects. This chapter also describes how to create a Word table, an Excel spreadsheet, and an organization chart in a PowerPoint presentation. You also learn how to insert objects from sources outside PowerPoint.
- Chapter 22, "Working with Objects," describes what objects are, how to select and group them, and how to move, copy, resize, align, rotate, flip, and stack objects.
- Chapter 23, "Drawing Shapes, Curves, and Lines," describes how to use PowerPoint's drawing tools to add objects to your slides.
- Chapter 24, "Enhancing a Presentation," describes how to add color, borders, shadows, and other enhancements to objects.
- Chapter 25, "Creating Charts," describes how to use Microsoft Graph, an embedded application that lets you create a wide variety of chart types from spreadsheet data.

Part V

Using Access

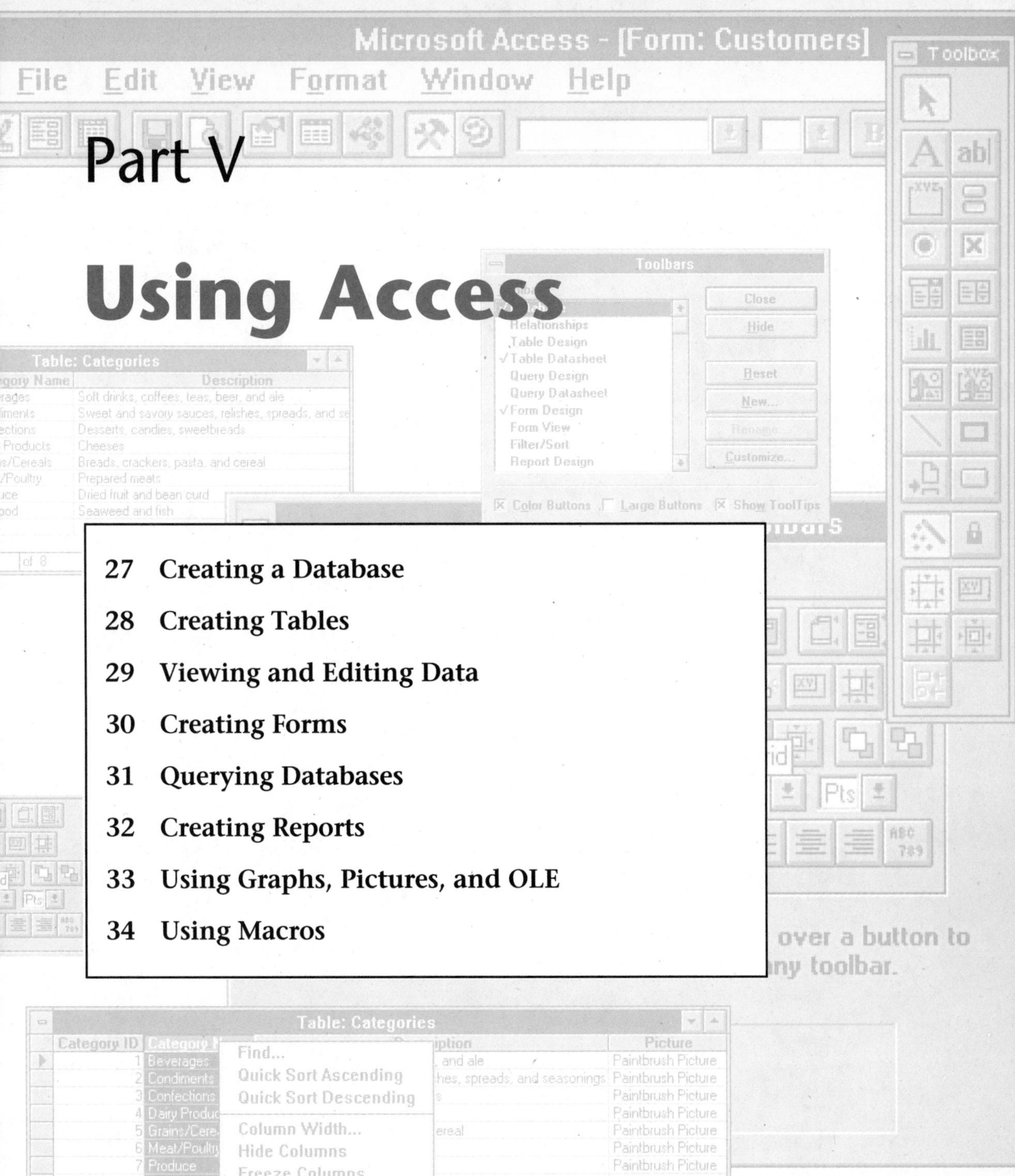

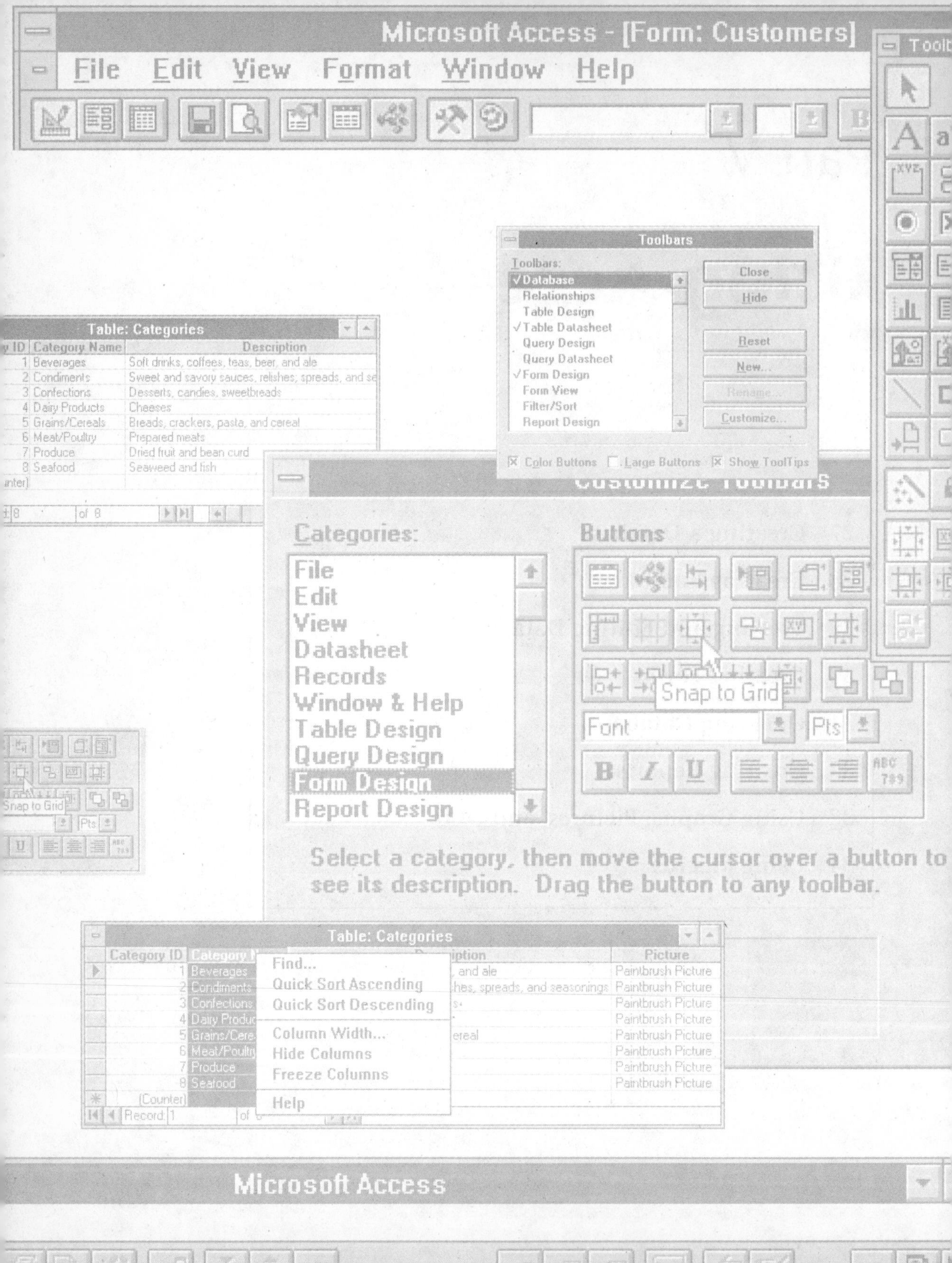
Microsoft Access - [Form: Customers]
File Edit View Format Window Help
Toolbars
Toolbars:
√Database
Relationships
Table Design
√Table Datasheet
Query Design
Query Datasheet
√Form Design
Form View
Filter/Sort
Report Design
Close
Hide
Reset
New...
Rename...
Customize...
Color Buttons
Large Buttons
Show ToolTips
Table: Categories
Category Name
Description
1 Beverages Soft drinks, coffees, teas, beer, and ale
2 Condiments Sweet and savory sauces, relishes, spreads, and se
3 Confections Desserts, candies, sweetbreads
4 Dairy Products Cheeses
5 Grains/Cereals Breads, crackers, pasta, and cereal
6 Meat/Poultry Prepared meats
7 Produce Dried fruit and bean curd
8 Seafood Seaweed and fish
of 8
Customize Toolbars
Categories:
File
Edit
View
Datasheet
Records
Window & Help
Table Design
Query Design
Form Design
Report Design
Buttons
Snap to Grid
Font
Pts
Select a category, then move the cursor over a button to see its description. Drag the button to any toolbar.
Table: Categories
Category ID
Picture
Find...
Quick Sort Ascending
Quick Sort Descending
Column Width...
Hide Columns
Freeze Columns
Help
Paintbrush Picture
(Counter)
Record: 1
Microsoft Access

Chapter 27

Creating a Database

by Diane Tinney

Welcome to Microsoft Access for Windows, the relational database application in Microsoft Office. This chapter is the first of eight chapters on Access. If you are new to databases, this chapter provides a basic foundation in database concepts. If you have worked with other database applications, this chapter builds on those experiences while teaching you how to create a database in Access.

In this chapter, you learn how to

- Design a database
- Navigate Access
- Create a database
- Manipulate a database

What Is a Database?

Before you explore Access, you need to know what a database is, review some basic database concepts, and identify when to use a database.

A *database* is an organized collection of information. A telephone directory is a good example of a database.

A computerized *database management system* (*DBMS*) is a computer application that helps you store, retrieve, sort, analyze, and print information in a database. In a computerized database, data appears in a *table* that looks very similar to a spreadsheet. The column headings are called *field names* and the columns are called *fields*. The rows of data are called *records*. In figure 27.1, `First Name` is a field and `Mary Might 345-9977 345-1112` is one of four records in a telephone table.

First Name	Last Name	Work Phone	Fax Number
Jane	Doe	456-2323	456-9988
John	Smith	567-9834	567-4433
Mary	Might	345-9977	345-1112
Dan	Davis	987-4433	987-2121

Fig. 27.1
A telephone database, called a table, consists of rows called records and columns called fields.

Two types of database management systems exist: file management systems and relational database management systems. *File management systems*, sometimes called *flat file databases,* store data in files without indexing, which means that data is processed sequentially. File management systems lack flexibility in data manipulation. Another drawback of file management systems is the user's tendency toward data redundancy (storing the same data in more than one place) to accomplish common database tasks such as reporting.

Relational database management systems enable users to manipulate data in more sophisticated ways, without data redundancy, by defining relationships between sets of data. The relationship is a common element, such as a customer's name or Social Security number. The data stored in each set can be retrieved and updated based on data in the other set.

Note

Microsoft Access does not provide all the features of a true relational database. However, Access does enable you to relate data from different sources; therefore, Microsoft refers to Access as a relational database system.

For more information on relational database theory and concepts, see *Introduction to Databases* by Que Corporation or *Database Principles for Personal Computers* by Richard F. Walters (Prentice Hall).

To further illustrate the difference between file management systems and relational database systems, consider the database needs of a video rental store, which needs to maintain information on customers, rentals, and movies in stock. In a file management system, every time a customer rents a movie, the customer's name and phone number must be entered along with the movies rented. In a relational database system, the customer name and phone number would be retrieved from the related (linked) customer list automatically and added to the rental invoice without the need for duplicate data entry and storage.

Knowing When To Use a Database

Think of your computer and computer applications as tools you use each day to accomplish your work. Microsoft Office provides a host of tools you can use to automate daily tasks. Knowing when to use the database tool, Access, is important. The purpose of a database is to store a collection of information. Following are a few common examples of information stored in databases:

- Employee data
- Product inventory
- Customer demographics
- Stamp collection
- Home inventory for insurance purposes
- Exercise/workout log
- Sales contacts
- Suppliers
- Invoices
- Video collection
- Tracking investments

Notice that the preceding examples emphasize data collection, not calculation. Although you can perform many financial and statistical calculations in a database, database applications do not calculate as quickly as spreadsheet applications do. For example, a database would not be the proper application to automate the calculation of a single tax return; a spreadsheet application would be a better choice. If you need to track, analyze, and maintain tax data over a period of years, however, a database application would be appropriate for that collection of information.

Exploring Access

Microsoft Access is a relational database management system designed for the graphical environment of Windows. With Access, you can perform the following tasks:

- Organize data into manageable related units
- Enter, modify, and locate data
- Extract subsets of data based on specific criteria
- Create custom forms and reports
- Automate common database tasks
- Graph data relationships
- Add clip art to forms and reports
- Create your own turnkey database application, complete with menus, dialog boxes, and command buttons

In this section, you learn how to perform many of these tasks.

Starting Access

To start Access, double-click the Access icon in the appropriate Program Manager group (the default group is Microsoft Office). If you are part of a workgroup that has set up security permissions, Access prompts you for your user name and password.

> **Note**
>
> To have Access automatically log on for you, select the Access icon in the Program Manager and press Alt+Enter. In the Program Item Properties dialog box, at the end of the command line, add the startup options: **/User** *username* **/Pwd** *password.*

◄ "Using Help," p. 61

The Microsoft Access Startup window contains only two menus: File and Help (see fig. 27.2). The toolbar provides buttons for creating a new database, opening an existing database, accessing Cue Cards, and accessing Help.

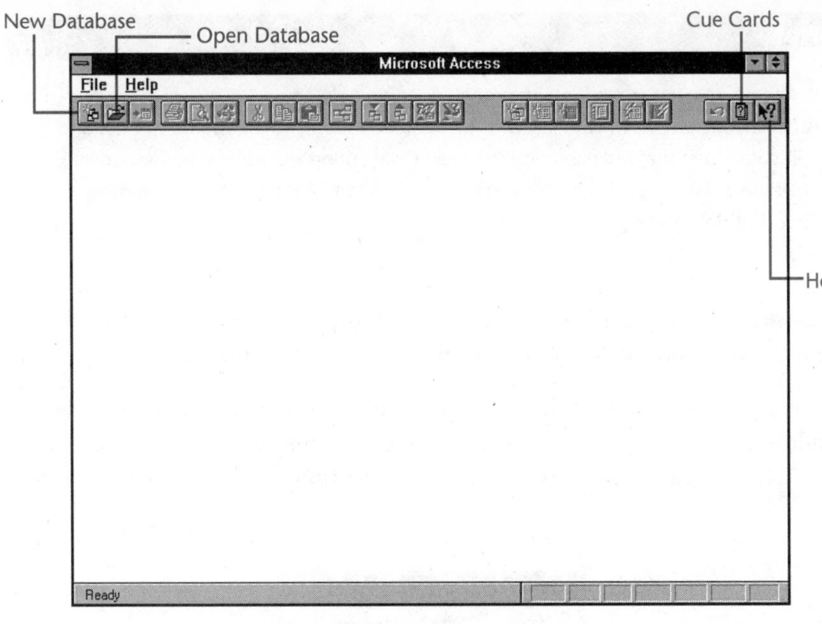

Fig. 27.2
The Microsoft Access Startup window contains only a menu bar, toolbar, and status bar.

Tip
In the Access Startup window, the File menu lists the last four databases you opened. To open one of these databases, click the file name or type its number.

To open an existing database, follow these steps:

1. Choose the **F**ile **O**pen Database command, or press Ctrl+O. The Open Database dialog box appears (see fig. 27.3).
2. Select the desired directory.
3. Select the desired database file name.
4. Choose OK.

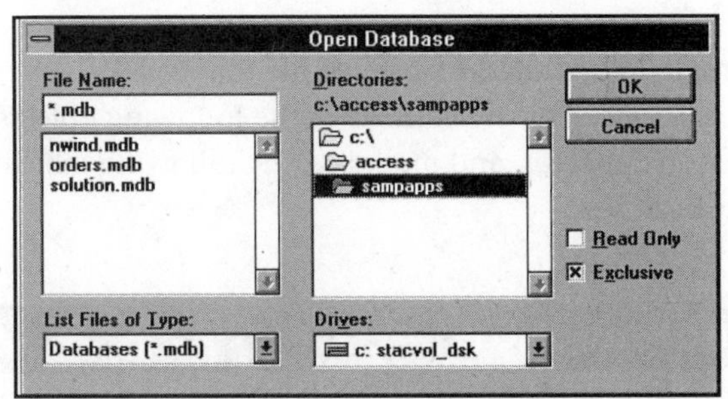

Fig. 27.3
The Open Database dialog box allows you to specify the directory path and file name of the database to open.

V

Using Access

Note

In a multiuser (networked) environment, opening a database for Exclusive use prevents anyone else from working with that database. Also, when you do not need to edit data, open the database with the Read Only option to improve performance. Opening a database with both Exclusive and Read Only options enables all users to view (but not modify) the database.

◀ "Closing Programs," p. 23

To close an open database, choose the **F**ile **C**lose Database command or close the database window by double-clicking its Control-menu box.

When you create a new database or open an existing database, a database window opens, and more menu and toolbar options become available (see fig. 27.4). You can open only one database at a time.

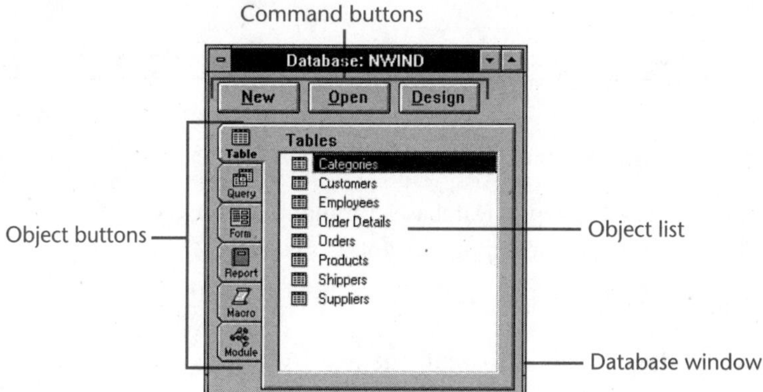

Fig. 27.4
The database window stays open on your desktop until you close the database.

Database Objects

In Access, the term *database* refers to a single file that contains a collection of information. Each Access database consists of the following objects: tables, queries, forms, reports, macros, and modules. The following table describes the major objects in Access.

Table 27.1 Database Objects

Object	Description
Table	Stores data in row-and-column format, similar to a spreadsheet.
Query	Extracts data from table based on user-supplied criteria. Queries enable you to view fields from more than one table in the same record.

Object	Description
Form	Displays data from a table or query based on a user-defined custom format. Forms enable you to view, edit, and print data. A form can display information from more than one table or query.
Report	Displays and prints data from a table or query based on a user-defined custom format. You cannot edit data in a report. Reports can contain information from more than one table or query.
Macro	Automates common database actions based on user-specified commands and events.
Module	Automates complex operations that macros cannot perform. Modules are procedures written in the Access Basic programming language.

Note

In Access, an *object* is something that you can select and manipulate. A table, a field in a table, a form, and a button are examples of objects.

The database window contains a button for each database object. When you select a database object, such as a table, Access lists the existing table names. To open a specific object, double-click the name or select the name and then click the Open button for Tables, Queries, and Forms; the Preview button for Reports; or the Run button for Macros and Modules (see fig. 27.5). Use the New and Design buttons to create new database objects or modify the design of existing database objects.

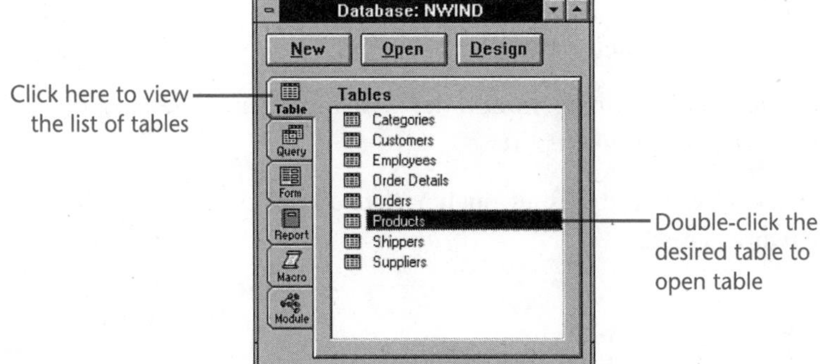

Fig. 27.5
Use the database window to open, preview, or run database objects.

Planning and Designing Your Database

Before you create tables, forms, and reports, you should take the time to plan the database. The time you invest in designing the database will yield productivity gains as you create and maintain the database. Focus your design efforts on the data, the people, and the tasks. Following are some key issues to address as you design your database:

- Start by analyzing the existing database (manual or computerized). Review the current forms and reports being used. Determine the source of the data (if computerized, could the data entry be imported?). Meet with the other people who use the database information, and discuss their needs. Review the database tasks performed (or to be performed), such as weekly reports, data exports, sorting, and analysis.

- After you identify your data storage and retrieval needs, separate the data into groups of common information (for example, separate customer data from invoice data). These groups will become tables.

▶ "Creating a New Table," p. 591

- Determine the type of information to be stored in each table. (A customer table, for example, might store customer names, addresses, and phone numbers.) These categories of information in a table are called *fields*.

▶ "Planning Form Design," p. 638

- Look for common elements among the tables. (A customer name may be the common element between the customer table and the invoice table.) This common element is called the *key field*.

▶ "Creating a New Report," p. 681

- Design forms and reports.

▶ "Exploring Queries," p. 661

- Determine criteria for queries.

- Consider automating common database tasks, such as executing a query and printing a report.

▶ "Creating a Macro," p. 719

- Review data-security issues, such as backup policies, data sharing, and network access.

Troubleshooting

When I start Access, my database does not appear.

The Access Startup window does not automatically open a database. You can achieve this effect by modifying the Access icon's program properties. Select the Access icon in Program Manager, and press Alt+Enter. In the Program Item Properties dialog box, at the end of the command line, add this startup option: /*databasefilename*.

In designing my database, I find that my tables have too many fields. What can I do?

Examine the fields by subject. Do the fields all pertain to the same topic? Consider dividing the large tables into smaller tables based on subtopics. Remember that you can link the separate tables again whenever necessary. "Divide and conquer" is the rule of relational database management.

My database design contains too many tables. I'm afraid that the implementation will be overwhelming.

Look for unnecessary duplication of fields across tables. Also consider reorganizing the tables into one table with additional fields. For example, if you have separate tables for each week's sales, you might want to create one larger table that has the additional fields WEEK BEGIN DATE and WEEK END DATE. Then you can use queries to extract weekly data as needed.

Creating a New Database

After you plan your database design, you are ready to create the database. To create a new database, follow these steps:

1. Choose the **F**ile **N**ew Database command, or select the New Database button in the toolbar. The New Database dialog box appears (see fig. 27.6).

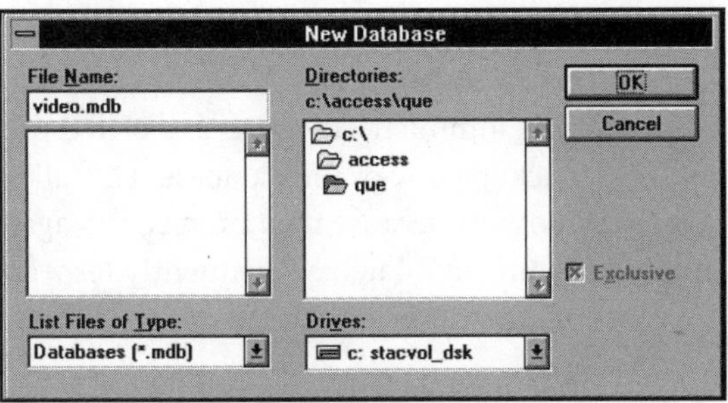

Fig. 27.6
Enter the name of your new database in the New Database dialog box and click OK to create the new database.

2. Select the desired drive and directory.

3. Enter an eight-character name for the new database file. Access automatically assigns the MDB extension to the new database's file name.

4. Choose OK.

After Access creates the new database, an empty database window opens in the Access window, ready for you to create new objects (see fig. 27.7). For information on creating tables, see Chapter 28.

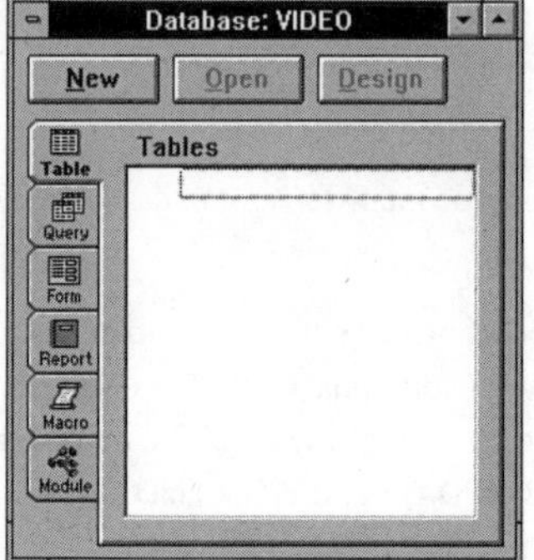

Fig. 27.7
An empty database window appears for the newly created database.

Maintaining an Access Database

As you use your database, you will need to perform various tasks to help protect your database and keep it up to date. You should, for example, back up the database regularly. You might want to compact the database files so that they run more efficiently and take up less storage space, or encrypt the database to prevent unauthorized persons from accessing the data. You also need to know how to recover damaged database files. This section discusses each of these procedures and provides suggestions for why and when you should perform them.

Backing Up Your Database

One of the most important administrative tasks associated with maintaining a database is creating a backup copy of the database. Like all computer data, database backups are important because they protect you against losing critical data. You should back up your database frequently (especially before and after you make major changes to the database).

Backing up an Access database is easy, because all tables, forms, and other objects associated with the database are kept in one file. If you have backup software, simply select your database(s) for backup. Otherwise, from File Manager or DOS, use the Copy command to copy the database(s) to the desired disk/drive/path.

Caution

Make sure that the database is closed (closed across all users on a network) before attempting to copy the database.

Compacting a Database

As you add and delete objects in a database file, the file can become fragmented and inefficient. Compacting the database eliminates the fragmentation and improves performance (speed). Compacting the file also saves storage space. How often you need to compact a database depends on how often the database expands or contracts. For example, a database that is used primarily to look up data will not need compacting, but a database that receives new data each day and new reports each week needs frequent compacting.

To compact a database, follow these steps:

1. Close the database (across all users on a network).
2. In the Access Startup window, choose the **F**ile **C**ompact Database command. The Database to Compact From dialog box appears (see fig. 27.8).

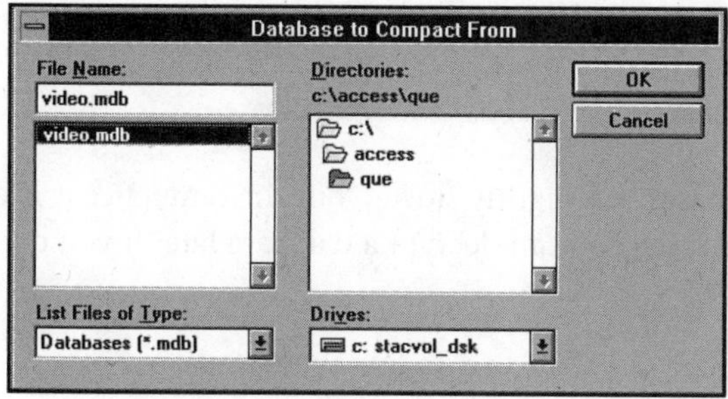

Fig. 27.8 Identify the desired database in the Database to Compact From dialog box.

3. Select or type a database file name and click OK. The Database to Compact Into dialog box appears (see fig. 27.9).
4. Select or type a database file name (the name can be the same as the database being compacted).

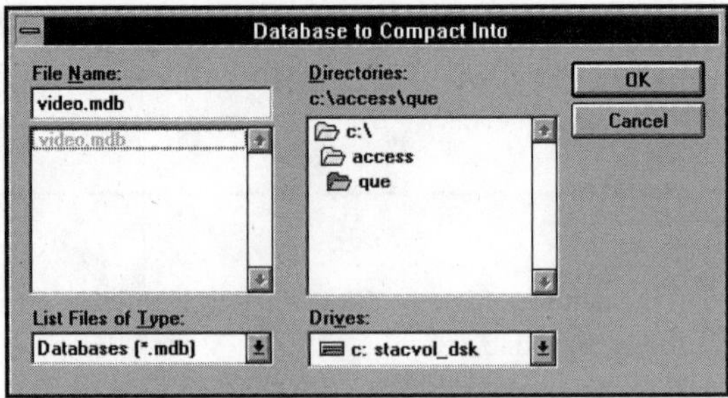

Fig. 27.9
Identify the name of the database to compact into in the Database to Compact Into dialog box.

5. Choose OK.

6. If you are compacting into a file with the same name as the file you are compacting from, a dialog box will prompt you to confirm that you want to replace the existing file. Choose Yes to continue compacting.

Encrypting a Database

If the confidentiality of your data is a concern, consider using the data-encryption feature of Access. Encryption renders a file unreadable by a text editor or utility program. Only Access can read your data. This feature can be important if your confidential data travels over phone lines or other unsecured media.

> **Caution**
>
> Data encryption alone does not provide complete security. Anyone with a copy of Access could decrypt an encrypted database. For better security, use encryption with password protection (from the database window, choose the **S**ecurity **C**hange Password command).

Encrypted databases run slightly slower, but the difference is irrelevant when security is a concern. You can decrypt a database later if you change your mind.

To encrypt or decrypt a database, follow these steps:

1. Close the database (across all users on a network).

2. In the Access Startup window, choose the **F**ile **E**ncrypt/Decrypt Database command. The Encrypt/Decrypt Database dialog box appears (see fig. 27.10).

Fig. 27.10
The Encrypt/Decrypt Database dialog box allows you to protect your database files.

3. Select or type the name of the database to be encrypted and click OK. The Encrypt/Decrypt Database As dialog box appears.

4. Select or type a database file name (the name can be the same as the database being encrypted or decrypted) in which to store the encrypted database.

5. Choose OK.

6. Confirm the overwrite of the existing file, if applicable.

Recovering a Damaged Database

Power outages and other causes of unexpected computer or network shutdowns can corrupt your database. Data corruption means that your data was damaged in some way. When you open a database, Access checks for data corruption and informs you if the database needs to be repaired. Simply choose OK, and Access repairs the damaged file.

If you suspect data corruption because of lost or damaged data, but Access has not detected a problem, choose the **F**ile **R**epair Database command in the Startup window.

> **Caution**
>
> Make sure that the database is closed across all users on the network before attempting a repair.

From Here...

Now that you are familiar with how to create a database, you are ready to begin creating tables and entering data. To learn how to create a table and enter data, refer to the following chapters:

- Chapter 28, "Creating Tables," teaches you how to create tables in which to store your data and how to enter data into a table.
- Chapter 30, "Creating Forms," teaches you how to create forms and how to enter data into a table by using a form.

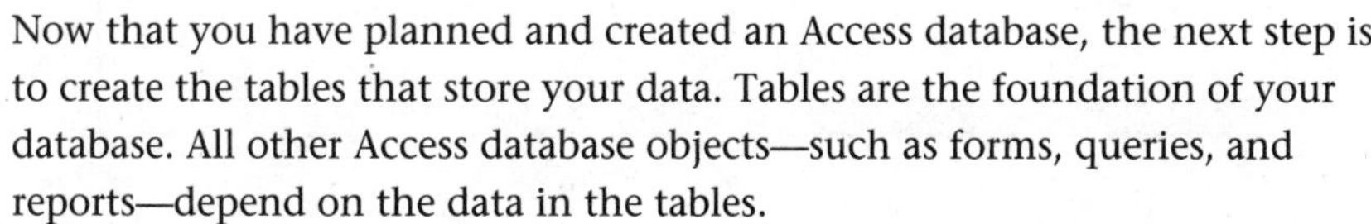

Chapter 28

Creating Tables

by Diane Tinney

Now that you have planned and created an Access database, the next step is to create the tables that store your data. Tables are the foundation of your database. All other Access database objects—such as forms, queries, and reports—depend on the data in the tables.

In this chapter, you learn to

- Create a new table
- Navigate a table
- Use Table Wizards
- Set table properties
- Set field properties

Creating a New Table

To create a new table, first display the database window; then click the Table button, and click the **N**ew button. Access displays the New Table dialog box (see fig. 28.1).

Access provides two methods of table creation: Table Wizard and New Table. Table Wizard helps you create tables quickly from numerous personal and business table types, such as mailing lists, invoices, contacts, recipes, and investments. Each predesigned table comes with sample fields. You can customize Table Wizard by adding your own table designs.

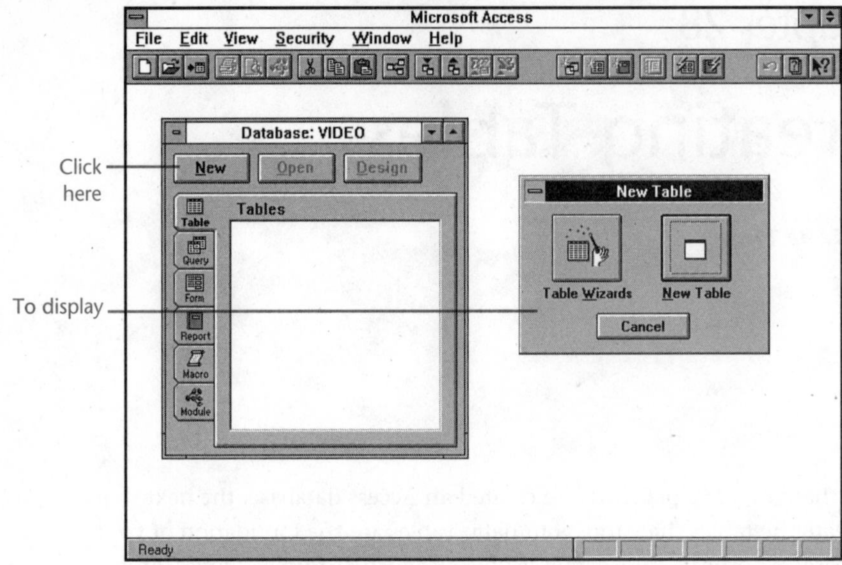

Fig. 28.1 Select Table Wizards for assistance in creating a new table or New Table to display an empty table in design view.

After you select the table type and fields, Access creates the table and enables you to modify the table design (with or without Cue Card help), enter data in the table, or enter data in a form that the wizard creates for you. Wizards are the easiest way to get up and running in Access.

◄ "Using Help," p. 61

Alternatively, you can use the New Table button to display an empty table in design view. You then can define the fields you need in your table.

Creating a Table with Table Wizards

Tip
Click >> to add all fields to your new table list box. Then click < to remove any fields that you don't need in your table.

When you choose Table **W**izards in the New Table dialog box, Access displays the Table Wizard dialog box (see fig. 28.2). Sample tables are listed based on the table option you select: Business or Personal. When you select a sample table, the corresponding predefined sample fields appear in the dialog box. You can use the arrow buttons to add fields to or remove fields from your new table definition. You even can edit the field names in the text edit box below the field list.

When your fields are selected, choose the **N**ext button. Notice that choosing the **F**inish button at this time would abort the wizard process and create the table based on your selections thus far.

When you choose **N**ext, another Table Wizard dialog box appears (see fig. 28.3). The first text box in this dialog box asks you for the name of your table. The names of objects—such as tables, fields, forms, and reports—can contain up to 64 characters; letters, numbers, and spaces are allowed.

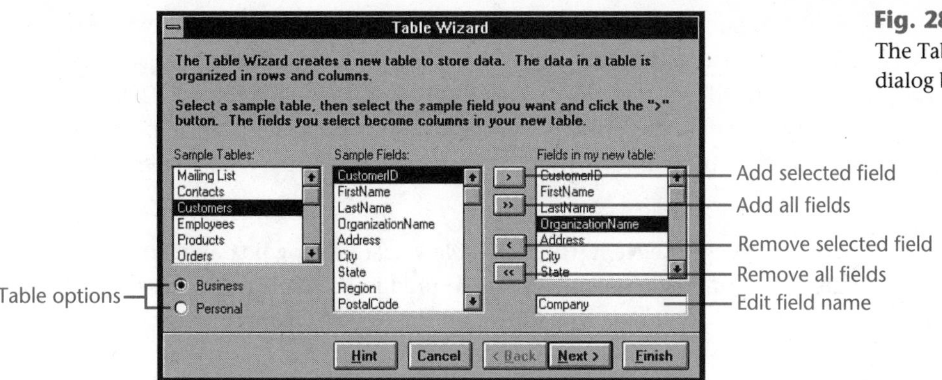

Fig. 28.2
The Table Wizard dialog box.

Fig. 28.3
After you enter the table name, the Table Wizard asks whether you want Access to set a primary key or whether you want to set the key yourself.

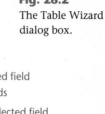

Tip
Let Access automatically increment and enter numerical primary-key field data when you add records. Each time you add a customer record, for example, have Access enter the next sequential number in the CustomerID field.

> **Note**
>
> As a rule of thumb, long, descriptive names are better than short, cryptic names. A table named *Widget Sales USA*, for example, is easier for users to understand than *WIDSLUSA*. But long names that contain spaces can be awkward to use in expressions, SQL statements, and programming code.

The dialog box also explains that each record (row) in a table needs to have a unique tag called a *primary key*. The primary key is the unique element that enables you to link (relate) tables of information. Table Wizard gives you the option of setting the primary key yourself or letting Access set a primary key for you. If you are unsure which field to use as the primary key, let the Table Wizard select one for you. You can change the primary-key field at another time, if you want.

If you decide to set the primary key yourself, the dialog box shown in figure 28.4 appears. In the drop-down list at the top of the dialog box, select the field that will contain the unique information for each record. Then specify the type of data the primary key will contain by clicking the appropriate button. For more information, see "Setting the Primary Key" later in this chapter.

◀ "What Is a Database?" p. 66

When you choose **N**ext, the last Table Wizard dialog box appears (see fig. 28.5). This dialog box enables you to modify the table design, enter data in the table, or enter data in a form that the wizard creates for you. You also can use the Cue Cards for help with table design or data-entry tasks. Choose **F**inish to create the table and display it in the view you selected.

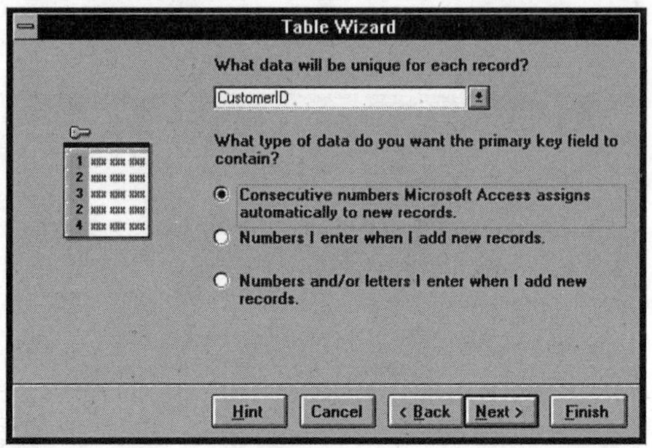

Fig. 28.4
If you decide to set the primary key yourself, the Table Wizard dialog box asks you to select the primary-key field and data type.

◀ "'How To' Windows and Cue Cards," p. 66

You can view tables in datasheet or design view. Datasheet view displays the data in spreadsheet format, ready for data entry and editing (see fig. 28.6).

Fig. 28.5
To complete your Table Wizard design, tell Access what you want to do next: display design view, datasheet view, form view, or Cue Cards.

You can view tables in datasheet or design view. Datasheet view displays the data in spreadsheet format, ready for data entry and editing (see fig. 28.6). Design view enables you to change the structure or appearance of your table (see fig. 28.7). You cannot enter data in design view.

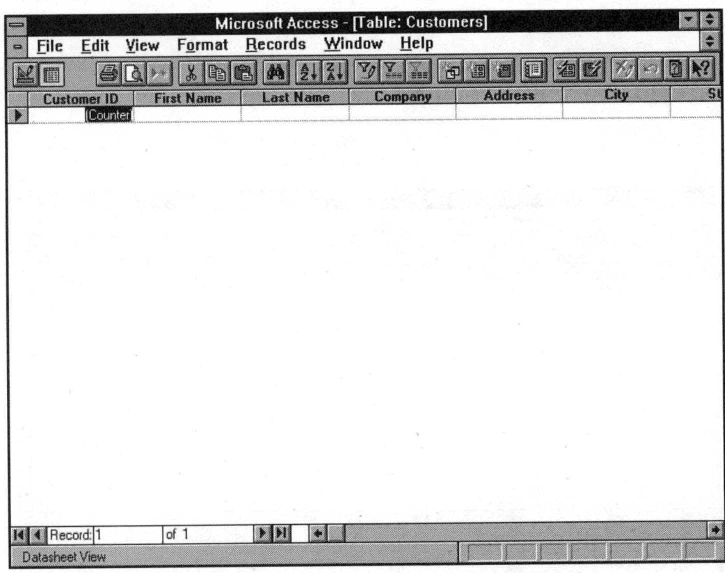

Fig. 28.6
The datasheet view of a new table displays a blank record ready for data entry.

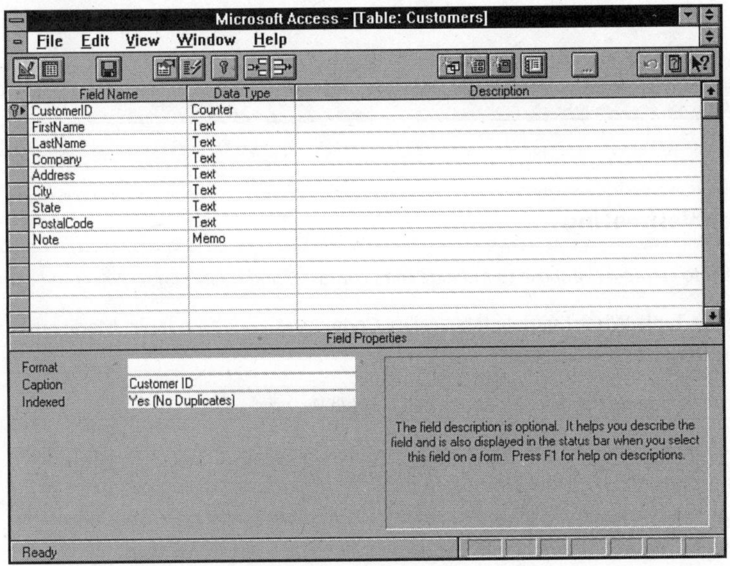

Fig. 28.7
You can switch to design view of a new table to make changes, set field properties, or enter field descriptions at any time.

Tip
Use table design view to further customize a table that you created with Table Wizard.

Creating a Table without Using Table Wizards

To create a table without using the Table Wizards, display the Database window. Choose the New command button to display the New Table dialog box. Choose **N**ew Table in the New Table dialog box. Access displays a blank table in design view (see fig. 28.8). In the top portion of the table design window, specify the field name and data type, and provide an optional description to appear in the status bar. You use the bottom half of the table design window to set field properties, such as format, field size, default value, and validation rules.

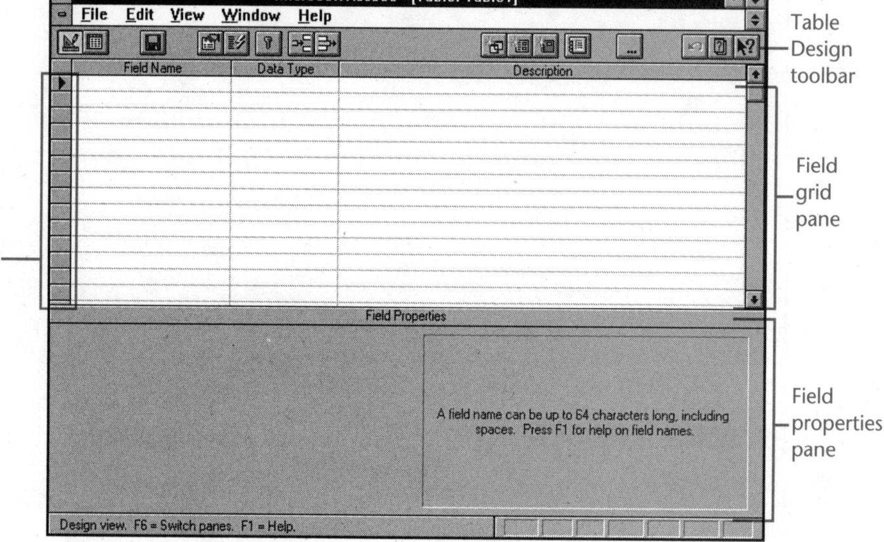

Fig. 28.8 When you create a new table without using Table Wizards, Access displays a blank table in design view.

> **Troubleshooting**
>
> *I need to create a database to manage sales contacts, and I don't know where to begin.*
>
> Use the Table Wizard sample table called Contacts as your base table. Modify the table to meet your needs.
>
> *I want to change the default field names in Table Wizards.*
>
> When using Table Wizards to create a new table, you can change the default field names provided by Table Wizards. In the first Table Wizard dialog box (refer to fig. 28.2), select the sample table and add the desired sample fields to your new table. Select the desired field and edit the name in the Edit Field Name text box.

Navigating Table Design View

You can view a table in datasheet view or design view. Datasheet view is where you enter and modify data in your table; design view is where you add or modify fields. If you created your table using Table Wizards, Access filled out the table design view for you. If you did not use Table Wizards, Access displayed a blank table for you in design view, ready for you to specify the fields to be included in your table. For more information, refer to "Creating a New Table" earlier in this chapter.

▶ "Navigating in Datasheet View," p. 612

To enter design view for an existing table, follow these steps:

1. Open the database.
2. In the Database window, select the desired table.
3. Choose the **D**esign button.

Alternatively, if the table currently is displayed in datasheet view, choose the **V**iew Table **D**esign command.

To enter design view for a new table, follow these steps:

1. Open the database.
2. In the Database window, select the desired table.
3. Choose the **N**ew button.

As shown in earlier in figure 28.8, design view contains the following components:

- *Table Design toolbar.* Contains various tools that help you design and work with your table.
- *Field grid pane.* Contains columns that enable you to define field names, data types, and descriptions.
- *Field properties pane.* Enables you to set various properties for each field.

The next few sections explain how to work with these components.

Working with the Table Design Toolbar

In the table design window, the toolbar contains the buttons listed in table 28.1.

Table 28.1 Buttons in the Table Design Toolbar

Button	Button Name	Description
	Design View	Displays the table in design view.
	Datasheet View	Displays the table in datasheet view.
	Save	Saves the table design.
	Properties	Opens or closes the property sheet for the currently selected object.
	Indexes	Displays the index sheet for the currently selected object.
	Set Primary Key	Enables user to select a column or columns as the primary key.
	Insert Row	Inserts a row above the current row.
	Delete Row	Deletes the selected row(s).
	New Query	Creates a new query based on this table.
	New Form	Creates a new form based on this table.
	New Report	Creates a new report based on this table.
	Database Window	Displays the database window.
 ...	Build	Displays the appropriate wizard or builder. For a field, the Table Wizard sample table and field dialog box appear so that you can select a predefined field.
	Undo	Undoes the most recent change.
	Cue Cards	Displays the on-line tutorial help feature.
	Help	Displays the context-sensitive help feature.

Working in the Field Grid Pane

The field grid pane enables you to define field names, data types, and descriptions. The grid consists of the field row selector column, the Field Name column, and the Description column (refer to fig. 28.8).

Naming Fields

As is true of most objects in an Access database, field names can contain up to 64 characters (letters, numbers, and spaces). Field names must be unique within the table.

Determining the Data Type

A *data type* specifies the kind of information that can be stored in a field. If you define a field as a Date field, for example, Access does not permit you to enter text in that field. When you assign a data type, Access knows not only what kind of data can be stored in the field, but also how much storage space is needed. A date value requires 8 bytes of storage space, whereas text requires 1 byte for each character (a 20-character name needs 20 bytes of storage). Based on the data type, Access also determines the types of calculations or other operations available for that field.

Access provides the following eight basic data types:

- *Text.* Alphanumeric characters, up to 255 bytes (1 byte per character).
- *Memo.* Alphanumeric characters, up to 64,000 bytes.
- *Number.* Any numeric type; see table 28.2 (following this list) for storage sizes and range of values permitted.
- *Date/Time.* Dates and times (8 bytes).
- *Currency.* Rounded numbers accurate to 15 digits on left side of the decimal point and to 4 decimal places.
- *Counter.* Sequential numbering, automatically incremented by Access for each record that you add.
- *Yes/No.* Logical values (Yes/No, True/False, or On/Off).
- *OLE Object.* OLE objects, graphics, or other binary data.

▶ "Using Graphs, Pictures, and OLE," p. 705

▶ "Linking and Embedding within Access To Manage Information," p. 855

Access allows the following range of values for numerical data, depending on the field and data type you select:

Table 28.2 Numeric Values Permitted for the Number Data Type

Field Size	Storage Size	Range
Byte	1 byte	0 to 255; no fractions.
Integer	2 bytes	–32,768 to 32,767; no fractions.
Long Integer	4 bytes	–2,147,483,648 to 2,147,483,647; no fractions.
Single	4 bytes	Numbers with 6 digits of precision. Negatives: –3.402823E38 to –1.401298E–45. Positives: 1.401298E–45 to 3.402823E38.
Double	8 bytes	Numbers with 10 digits of precision. Negatives: –1.79769313486232E308 to – 4.94065645841247E–324. Positives: 4.94065645841247E –324 to 1.79769313486232E308.

By default, Access assigns the data type Text to a new field. To assign a different data type, click the down-arrow button and select one from the Data Type drop-down list (see fig. 28.9).

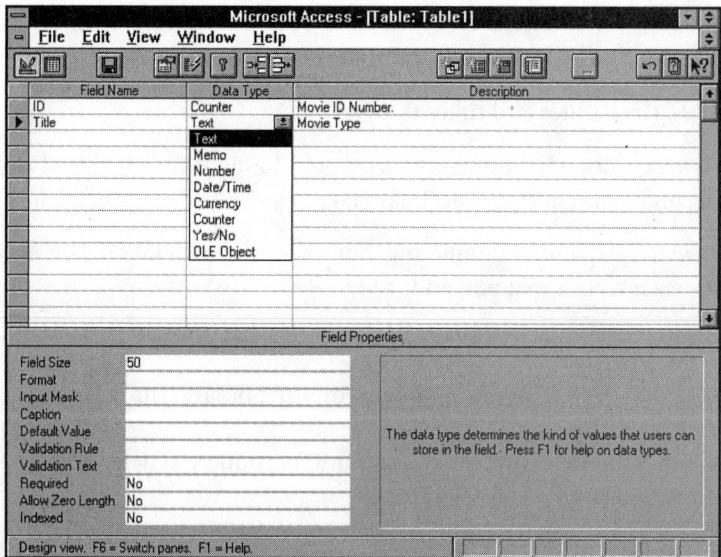

Fig. 28.9
Click the down-arrow button to select a data type from the drop-down list.

Note

For numbers on which you don't need to perform calculations, use the Text data type to save processing time and space.

For numbers containing punctuation (such as hyphens in a Social Security or phone number), you must use the Text data type, because no punctuation is allowed in a Number data type.

Caution

Be careful when choosing between the Number and the Currency data type. Entries in Currency fields are rounded, whereas Number fields use floating-point (the decimal point floats as needed) calculation. Currency uses a faster method of fixed-point (predetermined number of decimal places) calculation that prevents rounding errors.

Describing Fields

Use the Description column to provide further information about a field. The description is optional, but it does appear in the status bar when the insertion point is in that field.

Setting the Primary Key

Although it is not required, every table should have a primary key so that it works efficiently in Access. The primary key identifies a record as being unique. In an employee database, for example, each employee has a unique Social Security number. The Social Security number field would be the primary key.

Tip

To speed selection of data types, type the first letter of the data type, and then press Tab. Access fills in the rest. (Type **co** for Counter and **cu** for Currency, because they both start with *C*.)

The benefits of establishing a primary key include the following:

- *Speed.* Access creates an index based on the primary key, which enables Access to improve processing of queries and other functions.
- *Order.* Access automatically sorts and displays database records in primary-key order.
- *No duplicates.* Access does not permit users to enter data with the same primary key as an existing record.
- *Links.* Access maintains relationships between linked tables based on a common primary key.

Sometimes, the unique fact about a record is a combination of the information kept in several fields. In an invoice table, for example, the primary key may consist of the invoice number and the customer number, because a customer may have more than one invoice number. Access enables you to key more than one field in a table to create a multifield primary key.

To set a primary key, follow these steps:

1. Click the field selector (first column) to select the field that you want to use as the primary key. For a multifield primary key, hold down the Ctrl key and click the field selector for the remaining field(s).

2. Choose the **E**dit **S**et Primary Key command. A key icon appears in the field selector column of each primary-key field (see fig. 28.10).

Fig. 28.10
Access displays a key icon in the field(s) that define the primary key.

Click the Set Primary Key button

Select the field row

Microsoft Access - [Table: Table1]

File Edit View Window Help

Field Name	Data Type	Description
ID	Counter	Movie ID number.
Title	Text	Movie title.
Category	Text	Movie type.
Cost	Currency	Original cost of movie.
Rental Rate	Currency	Rental fee.
Date Purchased	Date/Time	Date of original purchase.
Number of Tapes	Number	Total number of tapes purchased.
Number in Stock	Number	Number of tapes currently in stock.

Field Properties

Format
Caption
Indexed Yes (No Duplicates)

A field name can be up to 64 characters long, including spaces. Press F1 for help on field names.

Design view. F6 = Switch panes. F1 = Help.

Troubleshooting

I want users to be able to enter only Yes or No in a field.

You could use data validation, but a more efficient approach is to define the data type as Yes/No.

I need to know the proper data type to assign to fields named Client Number, Client Name, Phone, Invoice Total, and Notes.

For the Client Number field, use Counter so that Access automatically enters consecutive numbers for you. For the Client Name field, use Text. For the Phone field, you could use Number, but Text is better if you want the phone-number field to contain punctuation, such as dashes. For the Invoice Total field, use Currency to get the proper dollars-and-cents format. For the Notes field, use Memo to get more information into the field than a text field allows.

I want to assign a good primary key for the fields listed above.

Use Client Number as the unique tag for each record.

Setting Field Properties

Fields have properties that define the way data is stored and displayed. By setting field properties, you can provide the following items:

- A default caption
- A default value
- A default format (display layout) for data entry
- Data-entry validation
- An index (for fields that can be indexed)
- Various display qualities, such as field size and formats

The field properties set at the table level are applied automatically to other database objects that use this table, such as forms, reports, and queries.

Following is an overview of the different field properties:

- *Field Size.* Limits Text fields to a specific number of characters; limits Number fields to a range of values, such as 2 for two characters in a State field.
- *Format.* Specifies a specific display format for dates and numbers, such as 2/21/94 or Monday, February 21, 1994.
- *Decimal Places.* Sets the number of decimal places displayed in Number and Currency fields, such as 2.99.

- *Input Mask* (Text and Memo data only). Specifies formatting characters, such as dashes in a phone-number field, to be filled in automatically during data entry.
- *Caption.* Supplies a label to be used in forms and reports instead of the field name, such as Movie Tag instead of MovieID.
- *Default Value.* Specifies a default value to be entered automatically in new records, such as the city and state in which a video-rental store is located.
- *Validation Rule.* Restricts data entry to values that meet specific criteria, such as the return date being greater than today's date.
- *Required.* Specifies that data be entered in the field, such as the member's ID number.
- *Allow Zero Length.* Permits Text and Memo fields to contain zero-length strings (""). By default, Access does not store string values that contain no characters or spaces.
- *Indexed.* Sets up an additional index based on this field. (For more information, see "Setting Index Properties" later in this chapter.)

Tip
For help in entering a validation expression or an input mask, click the Build button in the toolbar while the insertion point is in the field property.

To set field properties in table design view, follow these steps:

1. Select the field for which you want to set properties. The bottom portion of the window displays the properties for that field (see fig. 28.11).
2. Click the specific property you want to set, or press F6 to move to the Field Property pane and then tab to the desired property.
3. Enter the property value, or select it from a drop-down list of values (if available).
4. Continue setting other properties for the field, or select another field for which to set properties.
5. When you finish setting properties, save your table.

Note

If the property box is too small for the value you need to enter, press Shift+F2, or click the right mouse button and choose Zoom from the shortcut menu, to display the Zoom dialog box (see fig. 28.12). The Zoom dialog box is available throughout most of Access.

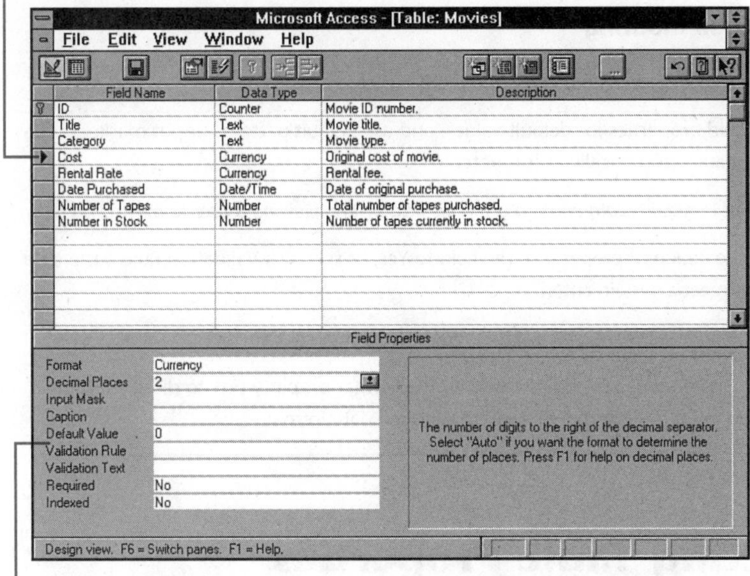

Fig. 28.11
To set field properties, select the desired field, and then set the properties in the Field Property pane.

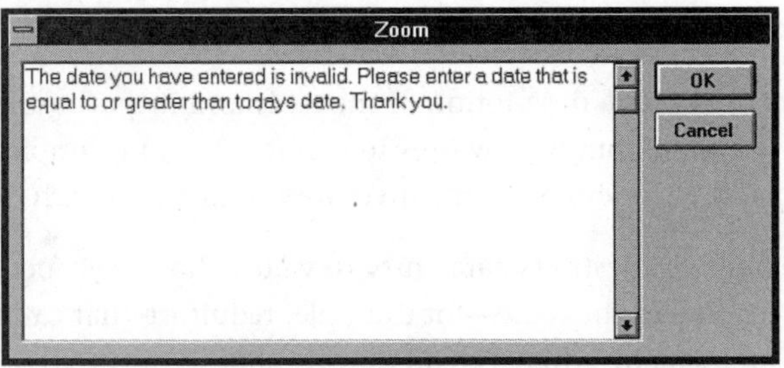

Fig. 28.12
Use the Zoom dialog box to see the entire contents of a field.

Note

Right-clicking a field property displays a pop-up shortcut menu containing the Build, Zoom, Cut, Copy, Paste, and Help commands. (Some commands are disabled, depending on the property or data type.)

> **Troubleshooting**
>
> *I want to automate data entry at the table level.*
>
> Set field properties for default values, and use default patterns (input masks) to format data automatically as it is entered.
>
> *I want to require data entry in a specific field before allowing a user to move off a record.*
>
> Set the Required property of the field to Yes, or specify a Validation Rule if the data must meet a certain criterion.
>
> *I want to select a display format for dates.*
>
> Click the down-arrow button next to the Format property box to display a drop-down list of date formats. Select the desired date format.

Setting Table Properties

Like fields, tables have properties. Table properties apply to the entire table and to all the records that the table contains. You can set the following properties for a table:

- *Description.* Enter a description of the table and its purpose (for more room, use the Zoom box by pressing Shift+F2). For example, the Movies table could be described as the inventory of movies purchased.
- *Validation Rule.* Restricts data entry to values that meet specific criteria for all records in the table—for example, requiring that category and rental-rate data be entered in all new records.
- *Validation Text.* Displays a message when the record-validation rule is violated—for example, describing why the category and rental-rate data is needed.

To set table properties in table design view, follow these steps:

1. Choose the **V**iew Table **P**roperties command. The Table Properties window appears (see fig. 28.13).
2. Enter any desired table properties.
3. Close the Table Properties window.

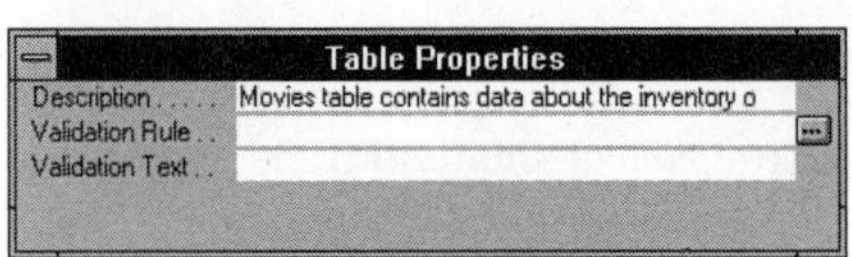

Fig. 28.13
To set table properties, choose the View Table Properties command.

Setting Index Properties

Indexes help Access find values. Access automatically creates and maintains an index for the primary-key fields (see fig. 28.14). You can create additional indexes by setting the field index property.

If you frequently search or sort certain fields, you can increase processing speed by creating an index for those fields. You can set up indexes for all field types except OLE, Memo, and Yes/No.

You can set the following index properties:

- *Yes (Duplicates OK).* Creates an index that includes duplicate field values.
- *Yes (No Duplicates).* Creates an index based on unique field values.
- *No.* Has no index.

Select the field

Select a property from the drop-down list

Click the down-arrow button

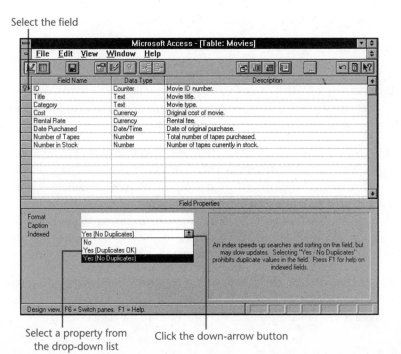

Fig. 28.14
The field index property can be used to create an index that includes duplicates or only unique values.

Tip
Set up indexes for fields in which the data varies. Indexing a field that contains similar data throughout the records does not increase search or sort speed.

To set index properties, follow these steps:

1. In the field grid pane, select the field to be indexed.
2. In the field properties pane, select the indexed property.
3. Click the down-arrow button to display a drop-down list of index property values.
4. Select a type of index (see fig. 28.15).

Note

Although indexes speed searches and sorts, they may slow data processing. Each time a record is added, deleted, or changed, the indexes must be updated.

Modifying a Table

Access makes it easy for you to modify your table to meet changing needs. You can add, rename, delete, and move fields. However, you should always back up your data before modifying the structure of your table. In addition, you should consider the effects of the following actions on dependent database objects, such as forms, queries, and reports:

- *Deleting a field.* Fields deleted from tables also must be deleted from forms, queries, and reports.
- *Renaming a field.* Renamed fields must be renamed in forms, queries, and reports. In addition, you must rename any references to the field in calculations, expressions, macros, and modules.
- *Changing a data type.* Certain data-type conversions are not allowed, such as converting from any data type to the Counter data type. In other cases, if you convert from a larger data type to a smaller data type, data will be truncated (cut off or lost). For example, changing from a Number data type to a Currency data type truncates values beyond the range allowed for currency, and data will be lost. (For more information, refer to "Determining the Data Type" earlier in this chapter.)
- *Changing the field size.* Changes that truncate numbers with decimals are rounded. If a change makes the value too large for the new field, the data is lost (an error message appears before the data is lost).

To insert a field, follow these steps:

1. Position the insertion point in the row before which you want to insert a row.
2. Click the Insert Row toolbar button.

Alternatively, click the field selector (first column) to select the row before which you want to insert a new field row, and press Insert to insert a blank row.

To rename a field, follow these steps:

1. Select the field-name cell.
2. Type the new name.

To delete a field, click the Delete Row toolbar button. Alternatively, click the field selector (first column) to select the field row which you want to delete, and then press Del.

To move a field, follow these steps:

1. Click the field selector (first column) to select the field row that you want to move.
2. Drag the field row to the new position.

Troubleshooting

I want to validate data for all records in a table.

You can validate data for all records in a table by setting the Properties Validation table property. To set table properties, choose the **V**iew Table **P**roperties command and then enter the desired validation.

I need to add a new field to the database I just created.

If you need to add a field at the end of the table, just start defining the field in a blank row. To insert a field between field rows, position the insertion point in the row before which you want to insert a row and then click the Insert Row button.

From Here...

Now that you are familiar with creating a table and working in table design view, you are ready to begin entering data. To learn how to enter data and work with table data, see the following chapters:

- Chapter 29, "Viewing and Editing Data," teaches you how to work in datasheet view, enter and edit data, and manipulate data.
- Chapter 30, "Creating Forms," builds on what you have learned about datasheets and takes you through the process of creating forms.

Chapter 29

Viewing and Editing Data

by Diane Tinney

With your database and table created, you are ready to view and enter data. You can accomplish data-entry and display tasks in datasheet view or form view. Datasheet view enables you to work in a familiar row-and-column format in which you can see many records at the same time. Form view enables you to focus on one record at a time and to replace paper forms with electronic forms that you can view and print. This chapter covers the features of datasheet view. The next chapter shows how to create and use forms for data-entry and display tasks.

In this chapter, you learn to

- Navigate in datasheet view
- Perform basic data-entry tasks
- Locate, sort, and filter data
- Print table data in datasheet format
- Import and export data
- Change the datasheet layout

In the first part of this chapter, you learn to navigate in datasheet view. You also add, edit, and delete records. This chapter teaches you how to cut and paste data and how to customize the layout of the datasheet. By the end of the chapter, you should be able to locate, sort, and filter the data in a table.

Navigating in Datasheet View

After you create your table, you are ready to start entering data. To switch to datasheet view, choose the **V**iew Data**s**heet command. Datasheet view enables you to enter and view data in a table (spreadsheet) format of rows and columns. The intersection of a row and a column is referred to as a *cell*.

Figure 29.1 shows what a new (empty) table looks like.

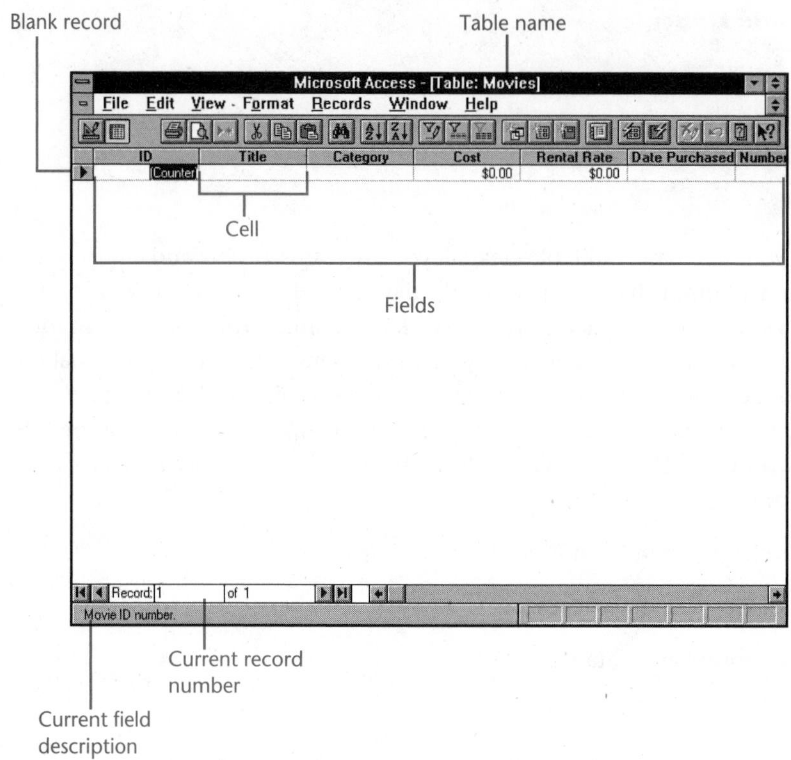

Fig. 29.1
A new table displayed in datasheet view contains only a blank record with the insertion point in the first field, ready for input.

Table 29.1 describes the Datasheet toolbar buttons.

Table 29.1 Datasheet Toolbar Buttons

Button	Button Name	Description
	Design View	Displays the table in design view.
	Datasheet View	Displays the table in datasheet view.

Button	Button Name	Description
	Print	Opens the Print dialog box, which enables you to set up the printer and print the current table in datasheet format.
	Print Preview	Displays the current table in page layout format. Enables you to set up the printer and print the current table in datasheet format.
	New	Moves to a new record at the end of the datasheet.
	Cut	Deletes selected data and copies it to the Clipboard.
	Copy	Copies selected data to the Clipboard.
	Paste	Inserts Clipboard contents.
	Find	Searches the current field for user-specified data.
	Sort Ascending	Sorts data in ascending order.
	Sort Descending	Sorts data in descending order.
	Edit Filter/Sort	Enables you to view and edit the filter and sort criteria.
	Apply Filter/Sort	Applies the filter and sort criteria.
	Show All Records	Removes the filter and sort criteria, and displays all records.
	New Query	Creates a new query based on this table.
	New Form	Creates a new form based on this table.
	New Report	Creates a new report based on this table.
	Database Window	Displays the database window.

(continues)

Table 29.1 Continued

Button	Button Name	Description
	AutoForm	Creates a simple form.
	AutoReport	Creates a simple report.
	Undo Current Field/Record	Undoes last change in the current field or record.
	Undo	Undoes last change.
	Cue Cards	Displays on-screen tutorial.
	Help	Displays context-sensitive help.

Note

You can print the contents of a datasheet view at any time by clicking the Print button in the toolbar or choosing **F**ile **P**rint. To preview the printout on-screen, click the Print Preview button or choose **F**ile Print Pre**v**iew.

Entering and Editing Data

Basic data-entry skills include adding, deleting, and editing table records; copying and moving data; and undoing unwanted data changes. Access provides many keyboard shortcuts to speed up data entry and table navigation. Table 29.2 lists the shortcut keys for data entry, and table 29.3 lists the navigation shortcut keys.

Table 29.2 Data-Entry Shortcut Keys

Shortcut Key	Description
Ctrl+;	Inserts the current date.
Ctrl+:	Inserts the current time.
Ctrl+Alt+Space bar	Enters the default field value.

Shortcut Key	Description
Ctrl+' or Ctrl+"	Enters the value from the same field in the preceding record.
Ctrl+Enter	Inserts a new line in a field, a label, or the zoom box.
Ctrl+ +	Inserts a new blank record.
Ctrl+ –	Deletes the current record.
F2	Toggles between edit and navigation mode.
Shift+Enter	Saves changes in the current record.

Table 29.3 Datasheet-Navigation Shortcut Keys

Shortcut Key	Description
F5	Moves insertion point to record number box above the status bar. Type the number of the record you want to go to, and then press Enter.
Enter+Tab+→	Moves to the following field.
←+Shift+Tab	Moves to the preceding field.
End	Moves to the last field in the current record.
Home	Moves to the first field in the current record.
Ctrl+End	Moves to the last field in the preceding record. Access validates and saves any pending data changes before moving off the current record.
Ctrl+Home	Moves to the first field in the first record.
↑	Moves up one record in the same field.
↓	Move down one record in the same field.
Ctrl+↑	Moves to the current field in the first record.
Ctrl+↓	Moves to the current field in the last record.
PgUp	Moves up one screen.
PgDn	Moves down one screen.
Ctrl+PgUp	Moves left one screen.
Ctrl+PgDn	Moves right one screen.

Tip
Click the scroll bar once to scroll one screen at a time.

You also can use the mouse to select fields, edit fields, and move around the table. Click the navigation buttons to move to the first, preceding, following, or last record (see fig. 29.2). The record number box above the status bar displays the current record number; you also can use this box to go to a specific record. (Click the record number box, enter the number of the record to which you want to go, and press Enter.) You can use the scroll bars to scroll across columns and/or rows that do not appear in the current window.

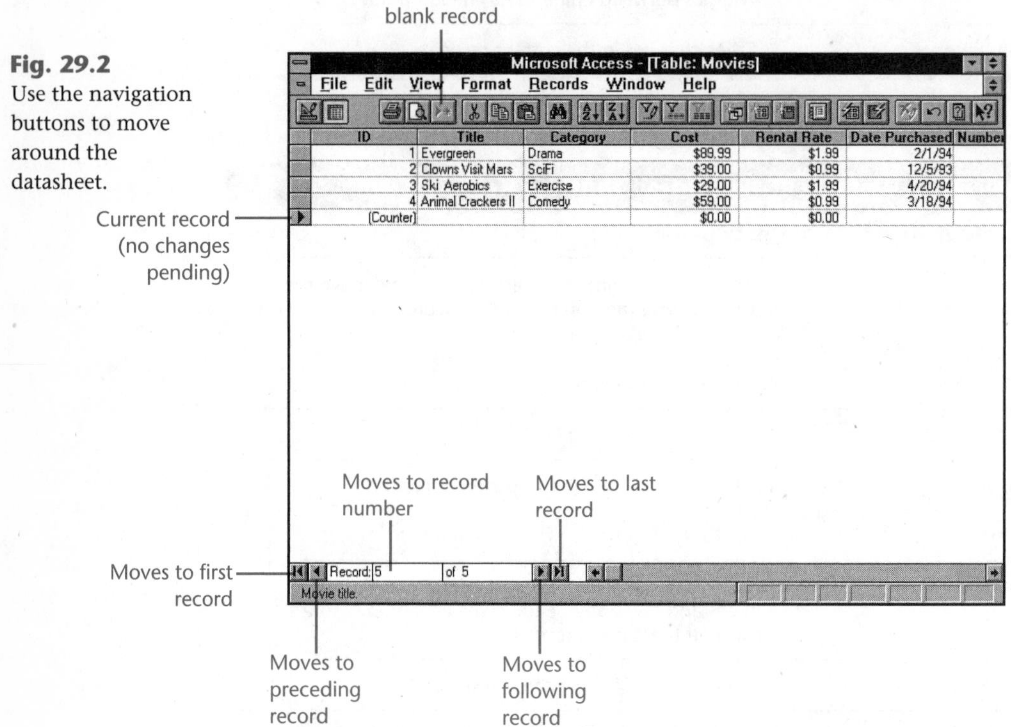

Fig. 29.2
Use the navigation buttons to move around the datasheet.

Note

Navigation keys (and mouse moves) have different results when data has been entered or edited. For example, moving off a field in which data has been entered or edited causes Access to perform certain validations before moving off the field. When you are moving off the last field of a record, Access validates data changes and saves all accepted changes before moving to the first field of the following record. Similarly, moving from a record in which data has been entered or edited causes Access to validate data and save the current record before moving to the new location.

Adding New Records

Access provides two options for adding records: edit mode and data-entry mode.

Edit mode enables you to add new records at the end of a table. Whenever you change data or enter new records, Access automatically places you in edit mode. Data-entry mode hides all existing records in the table and displays a blank table, ready for new records. To activate data-entry mode, choose **R**ecords **D**ata Entry. To deactivate data-entry mode, choose **R**ecords **S**how All Records.

In either case, you use the blank record at the bottom of the datasheet to enter new records in a table. When you begin to enter data in this row, Access moves the blank record down.

The first column on the left side of the datasheet is called the record selector column (see fig. 29.3). By clicking this column, you can select the entire row (record).

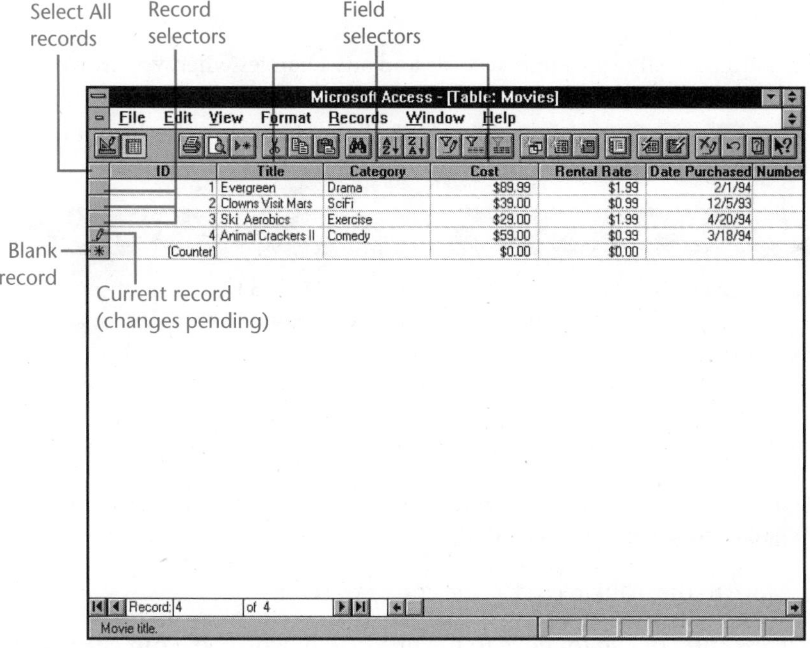

Fig. 29.3
A pencil icon in the record selector column indicates that the current record contains data changes that have not been saved.

Access uses the record selector column to display the following record selector symbols:

The arrowhead indicates the current record (no new data entry or edits pending).

The asterisk marks the blank record that Access keeps at the bottom of the table. When you move to this record, the asterisk changes to an arrowhead, which is the current-record indicator.

The pencil indicates that the current record contains data entries or edits that have not yet been saved.

The record-locked symbol indicates that the record is currently being edited by another user in a multiuser environment. This record is read-only to all users except the one who currently is entering data into it.

As you enter data and move from field to field, Access checks data entry for the proper data type and any special properties (such as validation) that you set. Access notifies you of any invalid entry before you move to the next field or record.

Tip
To move to the blank record at the end of the table quickly, press Ctrl+ +.

Access automatically saves new records and any changes when you move off a record. You can, however, save changes in the current record at any time by choosing **F**ile Save Rec**o**rd or pressing Shift+Enter. You can save the entire table by choosing **F**ile **S**ave Table or by pressing Ctrl+S.

Note

You cannot edit data in counter fields, because Access automatically enters these fields. Press Tab, Enter, or an arrow key to move past these fields. Access will enter the proper value automatically.

◄ "Determining the Data Type," p. 599

◄ "Setting Field Properties," p. 603

To add a new record, follow these steps:

1. If you want to add records without seeing any existing records in the table, choose **R**ecords **D**ata Entry.
2. Move to the blank record at the end of the table.
3. Press Enter or Tab to move to the first field in which you can enter data. The record indicator changes to a pencil, and Access appends a blank record.

4. Continue entering the remaining field data for that record. Access automatically enters data for counter fields.

5. To save changes, press the arrow keys, Tab, or Enter to move off the record, or press Shift+Enter.

6. If in you are in data entry mode, choose **R**ecords **S**how All Records to view the entire table (new and old records).

Editing Data

To edit existing table data, select the field in the record that you need to edit. If no data exists in that cell, simply start typing. If the field does contain data, Access selects the entire cell contents. To replace the cell contents with new data, start typing. To navigate within the cell, press F2. For data that exceeds the width of the cell, use the zoom box (Shift+F2).

Tip

Press F2 to toggle between edit mode and navigation mode.

Note

To edit data in a field, use your mouse. With one click, you can select the record, select the field, and position the insertion point within the cell.

Troubleshooting

I can't add new records.

Check to see whether the Allow Editing option has been deselected. If so, choose **R**ecords Allow **E**diting. Otherwise, you may not have access rights to the table. If that is the case, ask the database manager to grant you editing rights to the table.

I can't edit the text in a field without retyping the entire cell contents.

To edit the data in a cell, click your mouse to insert the insertion point within the data in the cell you want to edit. If you prefer to use the keyboard, move to the desired cell, press F2, and position the insertion point within the data you want to edit.

Undoing Edits

Access enables you to reverse, or *undo*, changes in your data. Depending on what type of editing you have done, the Edit menu provides two types of undo commands: Undo Saved Record or Undo Typing, and Undo Current Record or Undo Saved Record (see table 29.4).

Table 29.4 Edit Menu Undo Commands

Button	Command	Shortcut Key	Description
	Undo Saved Record	Ctrl+Z	Available after saving a record, but before editing another. Reverses changes in the last saved record.
	Undo Typing	Ctrl+Z	Available after typing in a field, but before leaving the field. Reverses most recent typed edits without losing other changes.
	Undo Current Field	Esc	Available after leaving an edited field, but before editing another field. Reverses most recent field edits.
	Undo Current Record	Esc	Available after editing a record, but before leaving the edited record. Reverses all edits in the current record.

Figures 29.4 and 29.5 show how the Edit menu changes to reflect the type of edit reversal you can do.

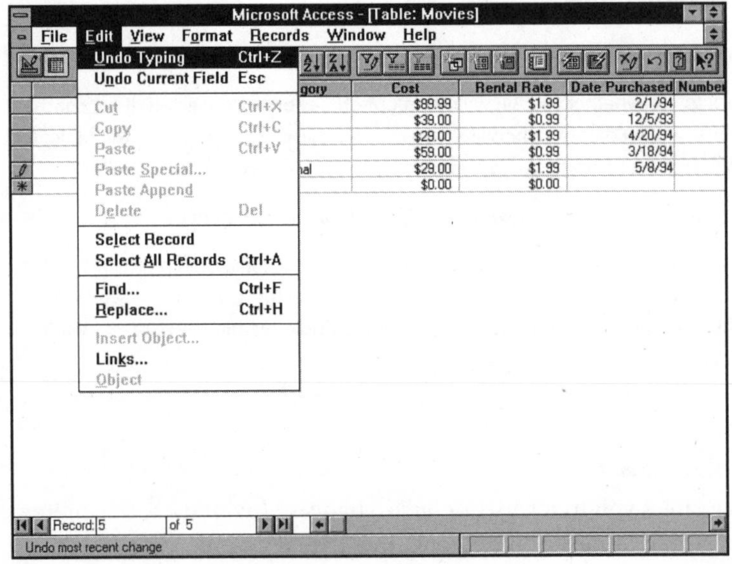

Fig. 29.4
To undo the most recent typing in a field, press Ctrl+Z. To undo all current field edits, press Esc.

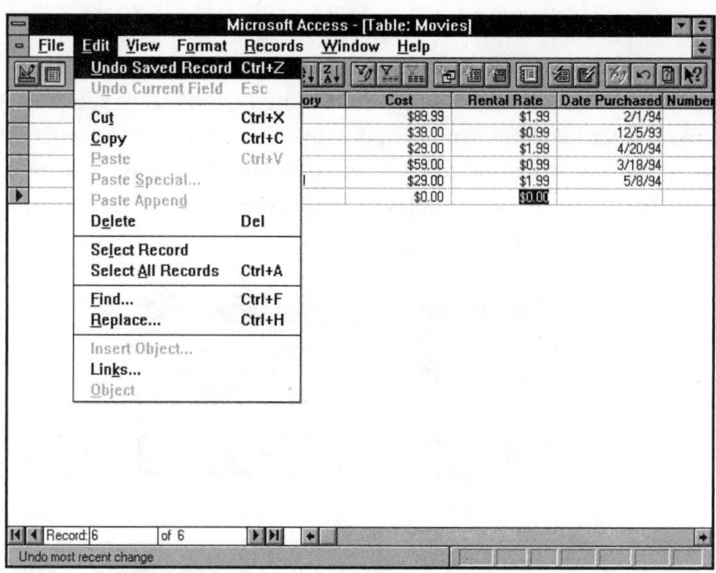

Fig. 29.5
To undo changes in a saved record, press Ctrl+Z.

To discard changes and restore the current field or record, choose **E**dit U**n**do Current Field or press Esc. You can undo an editing change in a field or all changes made in a record. You must undo changes before you start editing another record or switch to a different window.

To reverse your most recent action, choose **E**dit **U**ndo, or press Ctrl+Z or Alt+Backspace. Recent actions that can be undone include the following:

- Last record saved
- Last deletion
- Last cut or paste
- Last characters typed

Even some undo actions can be undone. After you undo a typed entry, for example, the Edit menu contains the command Redo Typing instead of Undo Typing.

Tip
Use Undo or Undo Current Field/Record to reverse errors or unwanted changes.

Note

You cannot undo the most recent paste of a record, a record deletion, or a full replace operation.

Deleting Records

If you need to delete an entire record, click the record selector or use the navigation keys to move to that record, and then choose **E**dit Se**l**ect Record. The current record selector symbol appears in the record selector column, and the entire row is highlighted. Choose **E**dit D**e**lete or press the Del key. Access deletes the record and displays a dialog box asking you to confirm or cancel (undo) the deletion (see fig. 29.6).

Tip
To select a record, click the record selector.

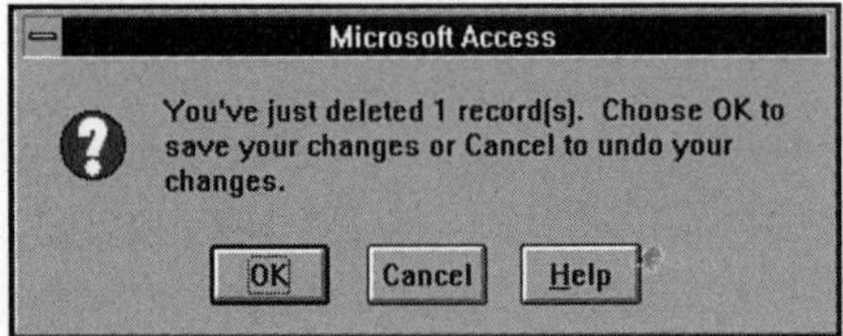

Fig. 29.6
When you delete a record, Access gives you one last chance to undo the deletion.

> **Note**
>
> You do not need to insert records. Access automatically inserts new records where they belong in the table, based on the primary key field.

Manipulating Data

Moving, copying, locating, and sorting data can be overwhelming tasks, unless you are using Access. Data manipulation is one of the database-automation operations at which Access excels.

Most of the program's data-manipulation features can be found in the toolbar:

- Cut
- Copy
- Paste
- Find
- Sort Ascending
- Sort Descending
- Edit Filter/Sort
- Apply Filter/Sort
- Show All Records

Cutting, Copying, and Pasting Data

The standard Windows cut, copy, and paste operations work the same way in Access. You can cut, copy, and paste data from one cell to another or from one table to another.

To cut or copy an entire record, first select the record to be cut or copied. Choose **E**dit Cu**t** or **E**dit **C**opy to place the record on the Clipboard. Then, in the target table, select the records to be replaced and choose **E**dit **P**aste, or **E**dit Paste Appen**d** to add the records to the target table.

Tip
To append records from another table to the end of the current table, choose **E**dit Paste Appen**d**.

Note

To move or copy an entire record to another table, the fields must be the same data types and in the same order in the datasheet. The target datasheet fields must be long enough to receive the data. However, the field names may be different. You cannot paste data into hidden fields.

A paste operation will fail if the data violates a validation property or creates a duplicate primary key (or a duplicate index value for which no duplicates are allowed). Records that cannot be pasted into the target table because of errors (such as validation errors) are placed in the Paste Errors table.

To copy or move records to another datasheet, follow these steps:

1. In the source datasheet, select the record(s) to be copied.

2. Choose **E**dit Cu**t** or **E**dit **C**opy.
3. Open the target datasheet. If necessary, rearrange the field order and properties in the target datasheet to match the source datasheet's field order.
4. To replace target datasheet records, select the records to be replaced and then choose **E**dit **P**aste.

5. To add the source records to the target datasheet, choose **E**dit Paste Appen**d**.

Tip
To undo a cut or paste operation, choose the appropriate undo command before performing any other actions.

Locating Data

A common database task is finding a record based on a field value. Suppose that a customer calls and asks whether you have a certain film in stock. Using the Find feature of Access, you can locate the film based on the film title.

When you choose **E**dit **F**ind, the Find in Field dialog box appears, prompting you for the search data (see fig. 29.7). You can instruct Access to search the current field (the default setting) or all fields, to search forward or backward, and to find exact matches of uppercase and lowercase letters. You also can instruct Access to find matches at the beginning of a field or anywhere in a field, or to find exact matches of the field value. Choose the Find Fir**s**t and **F**ind Next buttons to start and continue your search, respectively.

Fig. 29.7
To find a record quickly, click the Find button in the toolbar, and enter the search text and criteria.

To find a record, follow these steps:

1. Choose **E**dit **F**ind. The Find in Field dialog box appears.
2. Enter the Fi**n**d What data.
3. Select the desired W**h**ere criteria.
4. Specify the scope of the search (Curr**e**nt Field or A**l**l Fields).
5. Specify the search direction (**U**p or **D**own).
6. If desired, select Match **C**ase.
7. If desired, select Search Fields As F**o**rmatted (searches data based on how it is displayed).
8. Choose Find Fir**s**t to start the search. Access displays the first record that matches your search criteria.
9. Choose **F**ind Next to continue the search and display the next match.
10. To end the search, choose Close.

Sorting and Filtering Data

Access enables you to sort and filter data in datasheet view. This feature can be handy for generating a list of records based on some filtering or sorting criteria. Whereas the Find feature operates on only one criterion, the Filter/Sort feature enables you to specify criteria in multiple fields.

> **Note**
>
> The subset of data created by a filter is a temporary view of your table data. This view does not change the underlying table data.

When you choose **R**ecords Edit **F**ilter/Sort, the Filter window appears (see fig. 29.8). Specify the field(s) to be searched, the sort order, and the criteria to be met. The criteria tell Access which records to display. Criteria consist of expressions that you type in, such as the name of a city or an amount. Criteria expressions can include operators, such as = and >, as well as wild-card characters, such as * and ?. For assistance in entering criteria expressions, click the right mouse button in the criteria cell, then choose Build from the shortcut menu.

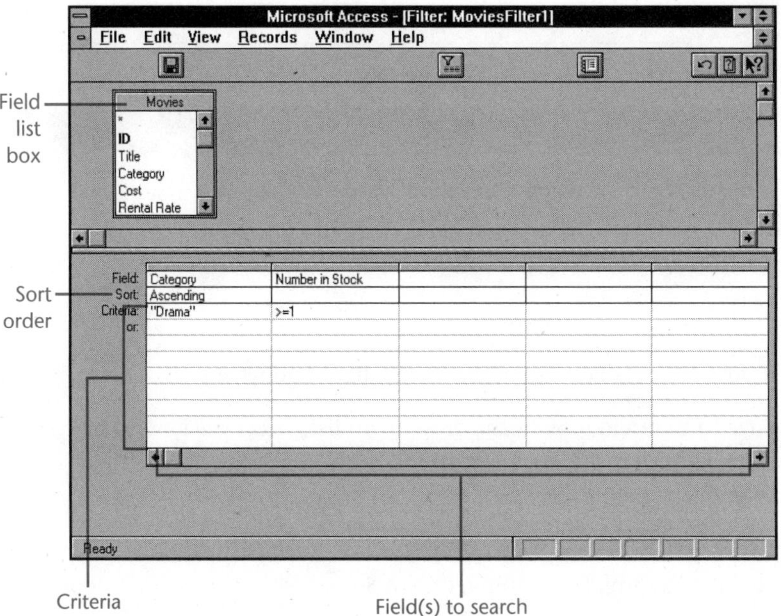

Fig. 29.8
Filters provide a quick, but temporary, subset view of table data.

To apply the filter, choose **R**ecord Appl**y** Filter/Sort. The filter results appear in datasheet view (see fig. 29.9).

To view all records, choose **R**ecord **S**how All Records.

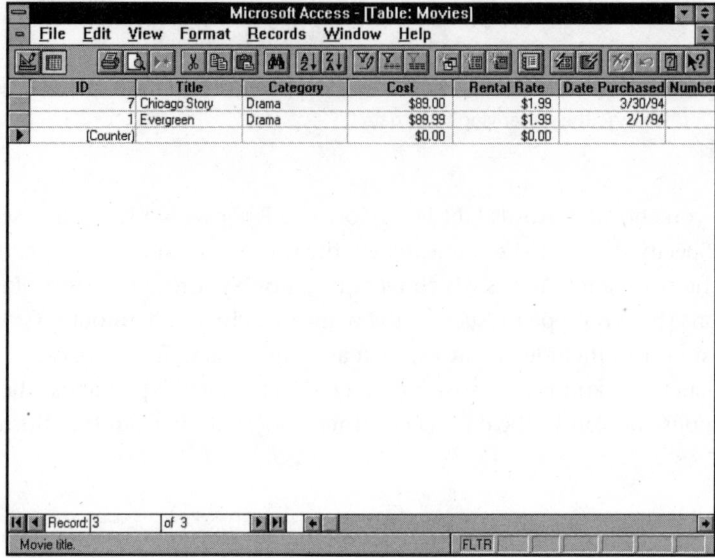

Fig. 29.9
The filter results appear in the datasheet window.

▶ "Adding Calculated Fields," p. 672

> **Note**
>
> You cannot perform calculations in a filter/sort operation. Use a query instead. (See Chapter 31, "Querying Databases.")

To filter data, follow these steps:

1. Choose **R**ecords Edit **F**ilter/Sort. The Filter window appears.
2. Move to the Field row. In the drop-down list, select the field to be searched from the drop-down list, or double-click the desired field name in the field list box.
3. Move to the Sort row. In the drop-down list, select the desired sort order (Ascending, Descending, or Not Sorted).
4. Move to the Criteria row(s), and enter the search criteria.
5. Repeat steps 2–4 for each field to be searched.

6. Choose **R**ecords Apply **F**ilter/Sort to view the desired subset of table data.
7. To save the filter, choose **F**ile Save **A**s Query.
8. To load a saved filter, choose **F**ile **L**oad From Query, or open the filter file as a query (see Chapter 31, "Querying Databases.")

Caution

When saving a filter as a query, be careful not to use the name of an existing table. If you save a filter with the same name as a table, the table and all its data will be overwritten.

Troubleshooting

My filter doesn't list any data.

Return to the filter window. Make sure that you listed the proper field names and criteria. Check the criteria against the table data to see whether at least one record meets your search criteria. If necessary, enter a test record that meets the criteria. Then retest the filter.

My table data is lost. I have only the subset of data from the filter.

Try clicking the Show All Records button. If this does not work, you may have inadvertently saved your filter as a query, using the same table name. Revert to the backup copy of the table.

Importing and Exporting Data

You can transfer data in and out of Access. This capability permits you to use data from another computer system or application, such as from a mainframe computer or from a spreadsheet application. Likewise, you can transfer data that you store in Access to other computer systems or applications. Access provides two methods of data transfer: the Import and Export methods, which enable you to copy data from and to text files, spreadsheets, Access databases, and other database files. The Attach Table method creates a link to a table in another database application so that you can work with the data directly.

Importing and Exporting

Import and Export provide more file-transfer capabilities than the Attach Table method does. Import copies data into an Access table, whereas Export copies data from Access to another file type. The Import and Export features support many different file types. You can import the following file types:

- Text (delimited or fixed)
- Excel

- Lotus 1-2-3 (WKS, .K1, and WK3)
- Paradox 3.x
- FoxPro 2.x
- dBASE III and IV
- Btrieve
- SQL
- Other Access databases

Note

To import or export a fixed-width text file, you must provide an import or export specification. Choose **F**ile **I**mp/Exp Setup, and complete the file specifications.

To import data into an Access table, follow these steps:

1. Open or switch to the database window.

2. Choose **F**ile **I**mport. The Import dialog box appears (see fig. 29.10).

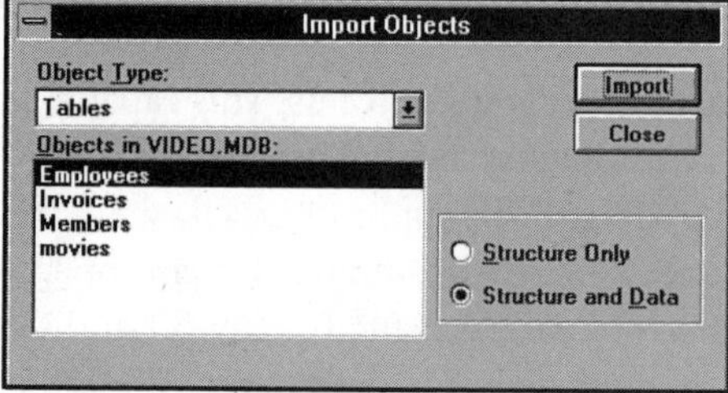

Fig. 29.10
Select the file format of the data that you want to import into Access.

3. Select the file format, and then choose OK. The Select File dialog box appears.

4. Select the file to be imported, and then click the Import button. Access imports the data from the file and creates a new Access table in which to store the data.

5. Access displays a dialog box to inform you that the import was successful. Click OK to close the message dialog box. Click Close to close the Import dialog box.

The Export file types are slightly different. You can export Access data in the following file formats:

- Text (delimited or fixed)
- Word for Windows merge
- Excel 2.0–4.0
- Excel 5.0
- Lotus 1-2-3 (WKS and WK1 only)
- Paradox 3.x
- Paradox 4.x
- FoxPro 2.x
- FoxPro 2.5
- dBASE III and IV
- Btrieve
- SQL
- Other Access databases

To export data from an Access table, follow these steps:

1. Open or switch to the database window.
2. Choose **F**ile **E**xport. The Export dialog box appears (see fig. 29.11).

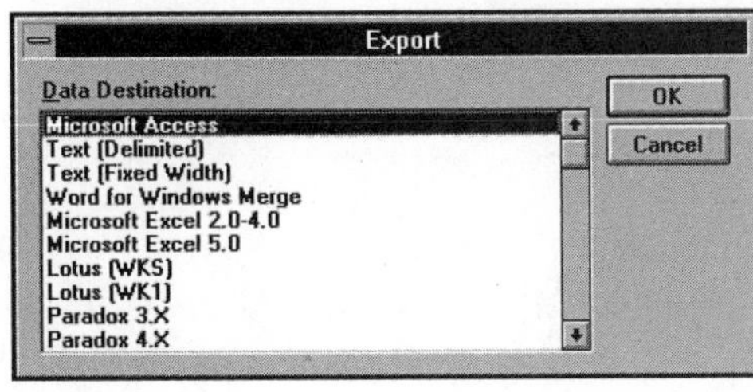

Fig. 29.11
Select the file format of the data that you want to export from Access.

3. Select the export format, and then choose OK. The Select Microsoft Access Object dialog box appears (see fig. 29.12).

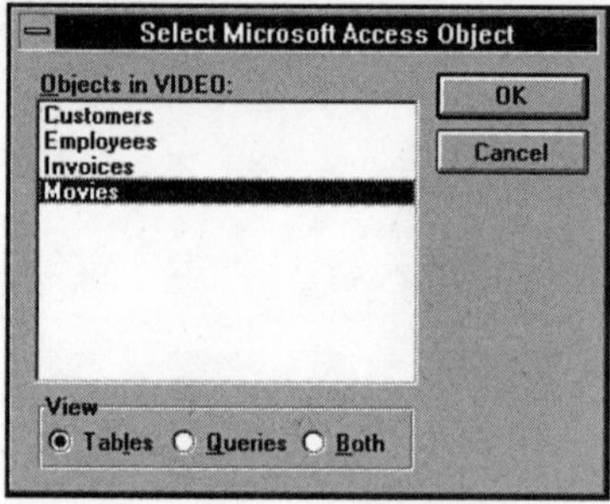

Fig. 29.12
Select the objects in Access that you want to export.

4. Select the object (table or query result) to be exported, and then choose OK. The Export to File dialog box appears.

5. Select the name of the file to which you want to export data, and then choose OK. Access exports the data into the specified file.

Attaching to a Table

Tip
Use the Import feature to transfer data from a system or file format that you are no longer using. Use the Attach feature to access data in another system that you are still using.

Attaching is a more sophisticated method of accessing data outside the current Access database. Attaching a table enables you to view and update data in the other system without making a copy of the data. The attached table is stored outside Access, in its original file. This arrangement eliminates the worry about overwriting updates made within the original application.

You can attach your Access database to tables with the following file formats:

- Paradox 3.x
- FoxPro 2.x
- dBASE III and IV
- Btrieve
- SQL
- Other Access databases

To attach to a table outside your Access database, follow these steps:

1. Open or switch to the database window.

2. Choose **F**ile **A**ttach Table. The Attach dialog box appears (see fig. 29.13).

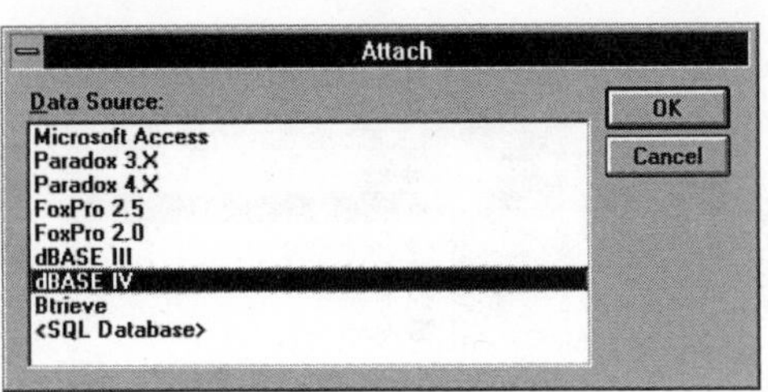

Fig. 29.13
Select the file format of the table that you want to attach to your current Access database.

3. Select the file format, and then choose OK. The Select File dialog box appears.

4. Select the file to be attached, and then click the Attach button. Access displays the Select Index Files dialog box (see fig. 29.14).

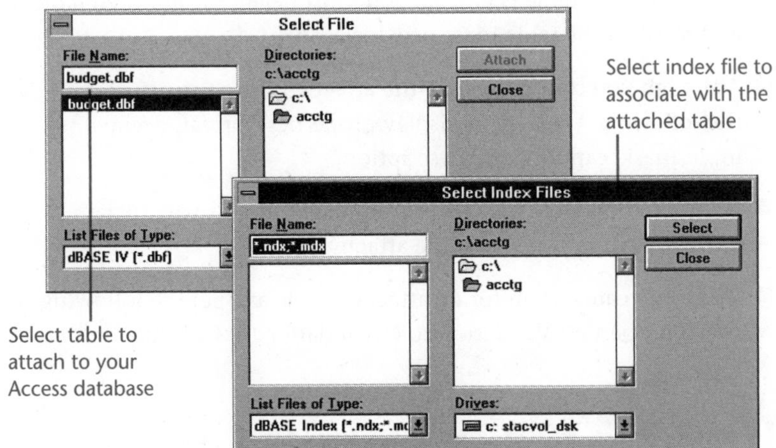

Fig. 29.14
Select the index file(s) that you want to associate with the attached table.

5. Specify the index file you want to associate with the table, and then click the Select button (you can associate more than one index file, or no index files).

6. Click the Close button to exit the Select Index Files dialog box. Access attaches to the specified table.

7. Access displays a dialog box to inform you that the attach was successful. Click OK to close the message dialog box. Click Close to exit the Select File dialog box. The attached table appears in the Database window, below the Tables tab (see fig. 29.15).

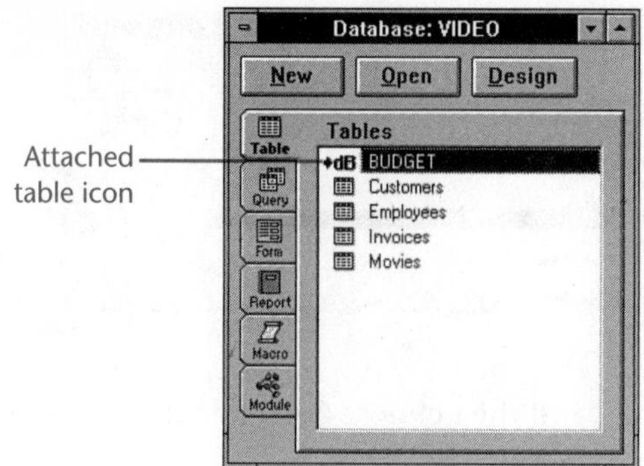

Fig. 29.15
Attached tables appear in the Table section of the Database window, with an attached table icon that signifies the table format.

When attaching tables to your Access database, consider the following issues:

- If the attached table is moved, you must delete the attached table link and reattach the table in its new location.
- Although you cannot change the attached table's structure, you can set the following Access field display properties: format, decimal places, input mask, caption, and description.
- If the external table is password-protected, Access will ask you for the password when you set up the attachment.
- You can create a form for an attached table and set the following additional properties: ValidationRule, ValidationText, and DefaultValue.

Changing the Datasheet Layout

By modifying the datasheet properties, you can customize the layout of your table's datasheet view. Changing the view of the datasheet does not affect the underlying table data. For example, decreasing the width of a column in datasheet view does not truncate data in the table or change the field width of data.

You can use commands in the Format menu to

- Change fonts
- Change row height and column
- Hide or display columns

- Freeze or unfreeze columns (columns to the left stay on-screen while you scroll to the right)
- Turn grid lines on and off

You also can perform many of these tasks by selecting the desired column or row and then clicking the right mouse button to display the shortcut menu (see fig. 29.16). You can change the width of a column or the row height by dragging the grid line in the header or row selector column to the desired position. To change the order of columns, select the column and drag it to the new location.

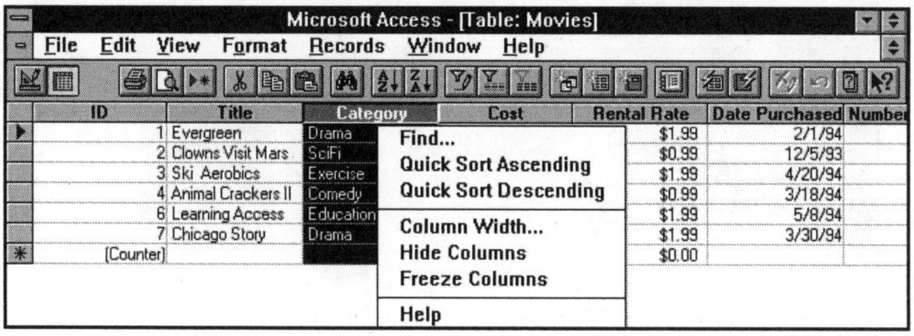

Fig. 29.16
Select the desired column or row and click the right mouse button to display the shortcut menu for that column or row.

When you close the table, Access asks whether you want to save the datasheet layout changes. Choose **Y**es to save the changes, **N**o to discard the changes, or **C**ancel to return to the datasheet.

You can change the datasheet view layout for all datasheets by choosing **V**iew **O**ptions. When Access displays the Options dialog box, select the Datasheet category (see fig. 29.17). Notice that you can set the default grid lines, column width, row height, and font for all datasheets.

Tip
To select a row, click the record selector (leftmost column). To select a column, click the field selector (header with field name).

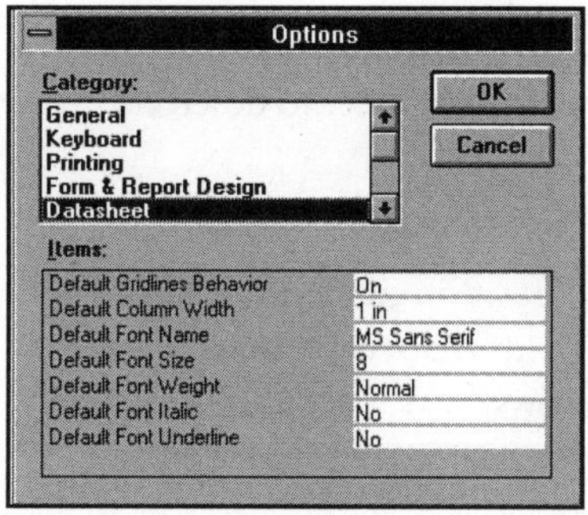

Fig. 29.17
Choose **V**iew **O**ptions to set default datasheet layout options for all datasheets.

To change the location of a field, follow these steps:

1. In datasheet view, click the field selector to select the desired column.
2. Click and hold down the mouse button in the field selector again. Access displays a vertical bar along the left side of the column.
3. Drag the field (column) to its new location. Access moves the vertical bar to show where the column will be inserted and displays a box below the mouse pointer (see fig. 29.18).

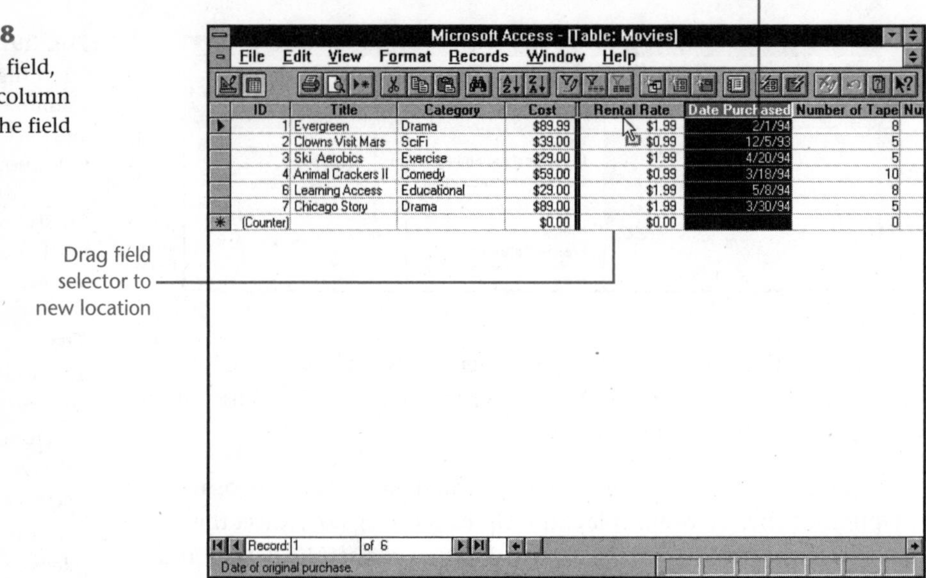

Fig. 29.18 To move a field, select the column and drag the field to its new location.

4. Click to insert the field.
5. Click anywhere in the datasheet to deselect the field.

To resize a field's column width, follow these steps:

1. In datasheet view, position the pointer in the field header row, on the line between the fields that you want to resize. The pointer changes to a line with two arrows.
2. Drag until the column reaches the desired width, and then release the mouse button.

Troubleshooting

I can't import a fixed-width text file.

To import or export a fixed-width text file, you must provide an import or export specification. Choose **F**ile Imp/Exp **S**etup and complete the file specifications.

My table contains more columns than will fit on-screen. Each time I scroll to the right, I lose track of the client record on which I am working.

To keep columns on the left visible as you scroll to the right, use the **F**ormat **F**reeze Columns feature.

From Here...

Now that you are familiar with entering and viewing data, you are ready to create and use forms. To learn how to work with forms, refer to the following chapters:

- Chapter 30, "Creating Forms," builds on what you learned about datasheets in this chapter and takes you through the process of creating forms.
- Chapter 34, "Using Macros," shows you how to automate repetitive tasks by creating macros and how to attach macros to form objects, such as buttons and fields.

Chapter 30

Creating Forms

by Diane Tinney

The key to many information systems (manual and computerized) can be the *form* used to gather and maintain data. Forms seem to be everywhere we go. Some forms, such as employment applications, simply gather information; others, such as computerized tax forms, also perform calculations. And some forms also function as reports (invoices or customer receipts, for example).

In this chapter, you learn to

- Plan a form design
- Use Form Wizards
- Create a blank form
- Navigate in design view
- Modify a form design
- Set control and form properties
- Print forms

In Access, forms provide you alternative ways of viewing table data. Access enables you to create forms that you can use to enter, maintain, view, and print data. This chapter shows you how to create forms by using the Form Wizard. Like Table Wizards, Form Wizards enable you to choose among several generic layouts. This chapter also shows you how to design a custom form and how to modify an existing form in design view.

Planning Form Design

◀ "Determining the Data Type," p. 599

◀ "Setting Field Properties," p. 603

◀ "Setting Table Properties," p. 606

Because forms are just another way to view table data, the first step in designing a form is to create the table(s) or review the design of the table(s). Form problems often can be attributed to an improperly designed table. Remember that table properties and field properties, such as *data validation* and *field type*, help you improve the quality of your data (they are your first line of defense against *GIGO*—garbage in, garbage out).

After table designs have been completed (and tested by end users and data), you are ready to start designing forms. Forms offer several advantages compared to the datasheet view of your table data:

- Forms can display one record at a time, usually in a vertical format.
- Forms can display fields that the user *cannot* edit, as well as fields that the user *can* edit.
- Forms can be designed to resemble paper forms that currently are in use.
- Forms enable you to rearrange fields (to make data entry easier and more accurate).
- Forms can contain fields from more than one table (a datasheet shows the data for only one table).
- Forms provide special field display functions, such as drop-down lists, word wrapping within fields, and calculated fields.
- Forms can contain graphs.
- Forms enable you to automate tasks and display custom menus.

A well-designed form is easy to use. Forms should be designed in ways that facilitate data entry. For example, "busy" forms that contain too many fields crammed into a small screen tend to irritate users and lead to data-entry errors. To prevent these problems, consider using several different forms or spreading data entry over several pages of a single form.

Following are some general guidelines for designing forms:

- Keep the form simple. Use easy-to-read fonts and colors. Use graphics and other objects to enhance the form, but don't clutter the form with too many objects.

- If your form will be printed on a black-and-white printer, adjust the colors and layout as needed to present a clear printout.
- Be careful with colors for on-screen forms. Some monitors with lower graphic resolution or less color capability may not be able to display your form correctly. To prevent this problem, use settings for the lowest-level graphic card and monitor available.
- Be consistent across forms. For example, use the same design for the Customer data-entry form and the Customer order form.
- Clearly show where data is to be entered and what data should be entered.

Access provides several methods for creating forms:

- *AutoForm.* The AutoForm button in the toolbar creates a simple single-column form based on the current table or query and displays the completed form with data in form view (see fig. 30.1).

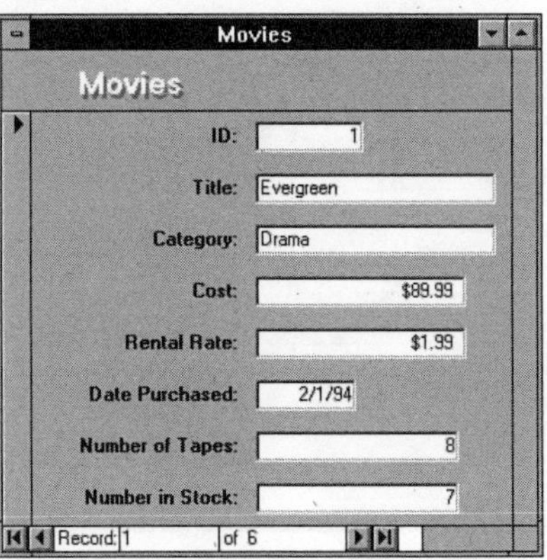

Fig. 30.1
Single-column forms (created with the AutoForm button or Form Wizards) enable you to focus on one record at a time.

- *Form Wizards.* Access provides five generic forms that you can access with Form Wizards. Form Wizards build a form for you, based on your responses to a series of questions (see the following section, "Using Form Wizards").
- *Blank Form.* Access also enables you to design a custom form by using form design view.

Using Form Wizards

Form Wizards generate a form design for you, based on your specifications. Each Form Wizard asks you a series of questions to determine which table you want to use and which type of form you want to create. Access provides the following four Form Wizards:

- *Single-Column.* Displays one record at a time in a vertical format (each field label value on a separate line, in a single column). The resulting forms are similar to those generated by AutoForm (refer to fig. 30.1).

- *Tabular.* Displays multiple records in a row-and-column format, similar to the one used in datasheet view (see fig. 30.2).

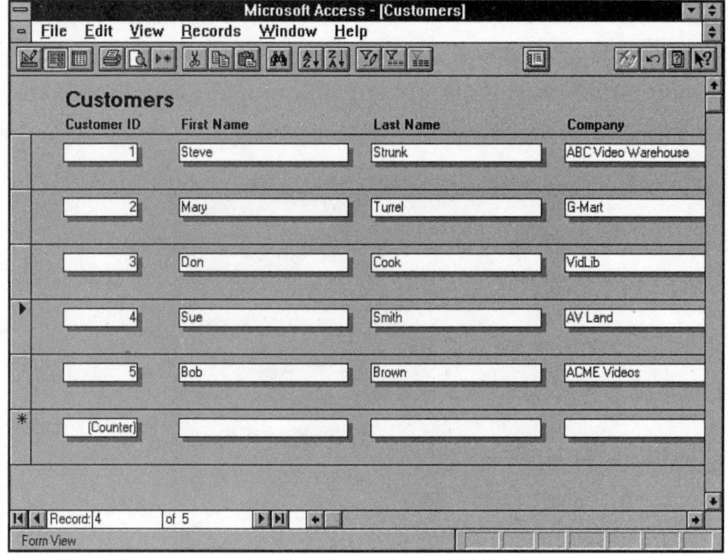

Fig. 30.2
Tabular forms created with the Form Wizard provide all the utility of forms in a familiar datasheet format.

- *Main/Subform.* Combines the single-column and tabular formats in one form (see fig. 30.3). Used to show data from two tables that have a one-to-many relationship. The main (parent) table appears in a single-column format. The subform (child) table appears in a tabular format.

- *Graph.* Displays a graph of the data (see fig. 30.4). This type of form is discussed in Chapter 32, "Creating Reports."

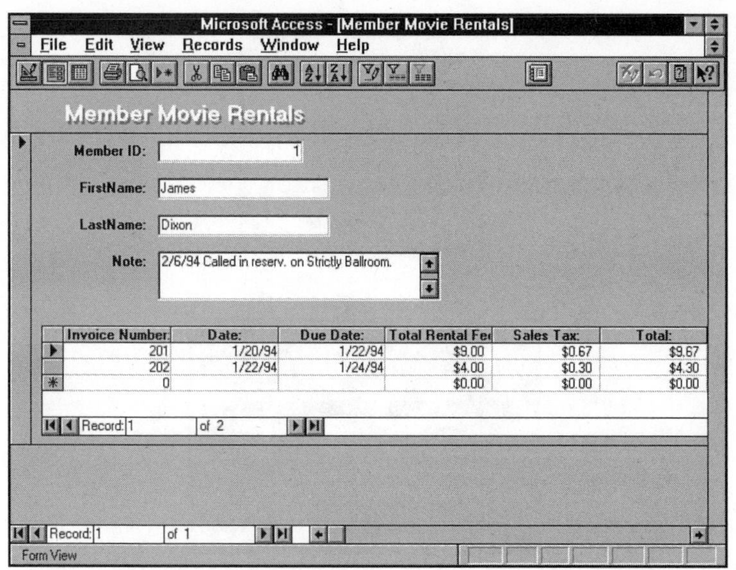

Fig. 30.3
With the Main/Subform design, you can show a one-to-many relationship among tables.

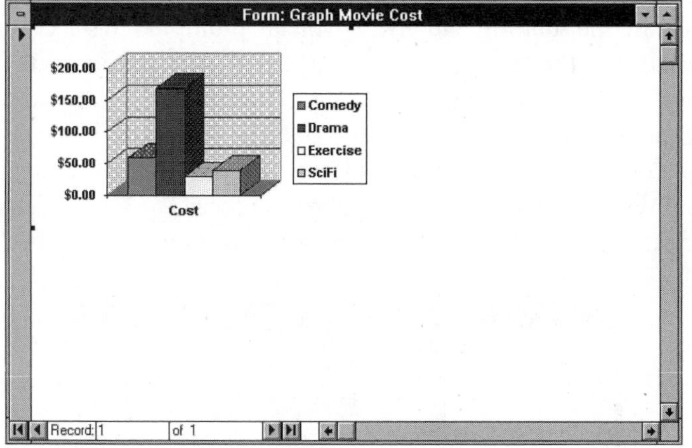

Fig. 30.4
Graph forms enable you to show data in a variety of formats, such as bar graphs, 3-D graphs, and pie charts.

Starting Form Wizards

To start Form Wizards from the Database window, click the Form button and then the **N**ew button, or click the New Form button. Either way, the New Form dialog box appears (see fig. 30.5).

In the New Form dialog box, identify the table or query for which you want to create a form. Then choose Form **W**izards. The first question, `Which Wizard do you want?`, appears in a dialog box (see fig. 30.6). Select the desired Wizard, and then choose OK.

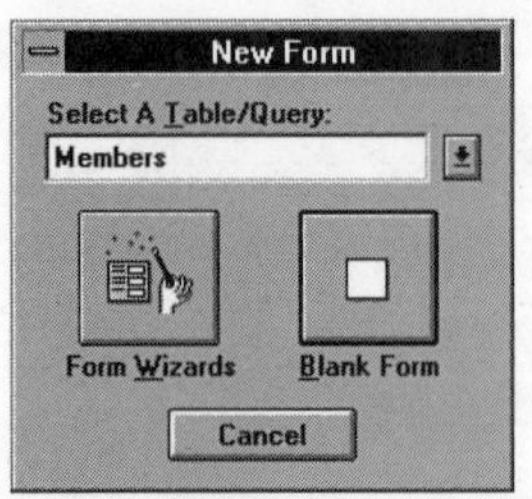

Fig. 30.5
The New Form dialog box asks for the table name and enables you to use Form Wizards.

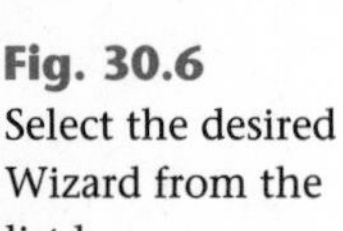

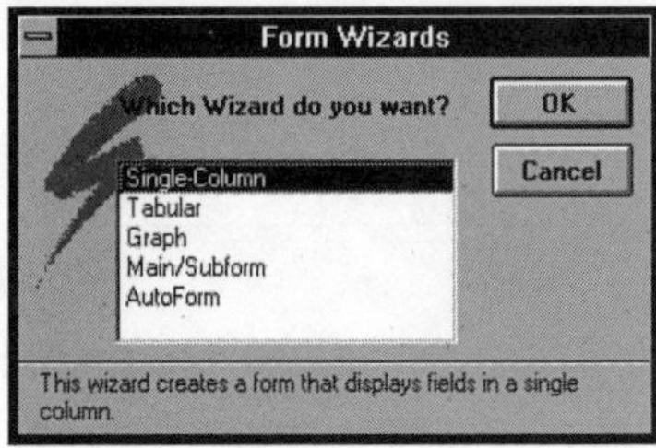

Fig. 30.6
Select the desired Wizard from the list box.

If you select the Main/Subform Wizard, you are prompted to select a table on which to base the subform. Otherwise, you are prompted to select the fields to be included in the form (see fig. 30.7). Click the arrow buttons to add (>) or remove (<) fields from your form design. Click the (>>) button to add all fields or the (<<) button to remove all fields. The **H**int button displays helpful text. The **C**ancel button exits Form Wizard. The <**B**ack button displays the preceding Wizard dialog box. Choose Next to proceed or **F**inish to have Access create the form based on your Wizard selections thus far.

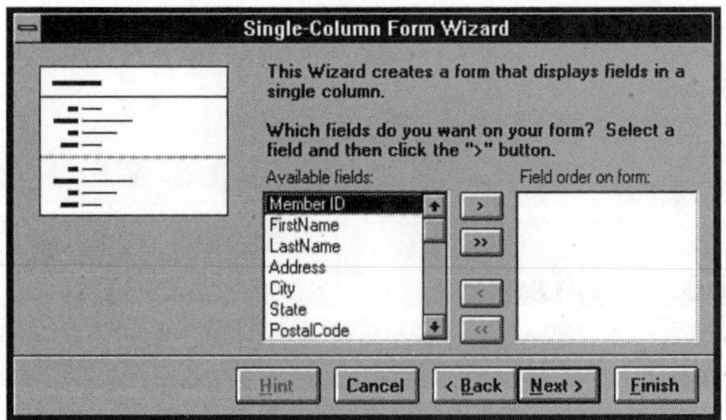

Fig. 30.7
You can select the fields to be included in your form design and control the order of the fields by clicking the arrow buttons.

Selecting Data Display Styles

Next, Access prompts you to select one of the predefined data display styles (see fig. 30.8).

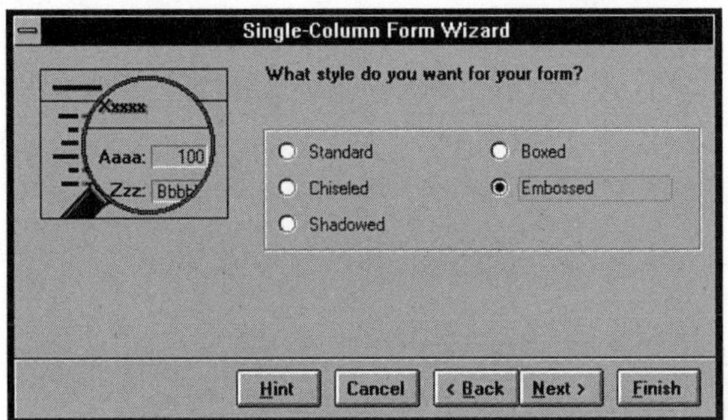

Fig. 30.8
After you click a style option button, Access displays a sample of that style under the magnifying glass on the left side of the dialog box.

The available styles include:

- *Standard.* Displays data in basic border boxes.
- *Chiseled.* Displays data in sunken boxes; the boxes are the same color as the background.
- *Shadowed.* Displays data in basic border boxes, using gray boxes, offset and behind, to produce a shadowed effect.
- *Boxed.* Displays label and data in colored boxes that contrasts with the background.
- *Embossed.* Displays data in sunken boxes of a color that contrasts with the background.

After selecting a style, choose **F**inish to proceed.

The final Form Wizard dialog box prompts you to name your form (see fig. 30.9). If you want to begin using the form immediately, click the Open the Form With Data In It button. If you want to customize the form, click the Modify the Form's Design button. Choose **F**inish to proceed.

To create a new form using Form Wizards, follow these steps:

1. Click the New Form button in the toolbar. The New Form dialog box appears.

2. Type the name of a table or query in the text box, or select a table or query from the drop-down list box.

3. Choose Form **W**izards.
4. Select the form type, and then choose OK.
5. Select the fields to be included in the form, and then choose **N**ext.
6. Select the data display style, and then choose **N**ext.
7. Enter a form name.
8. Select Open, Modify, or Open Cue Cards.
9. Choose **F**inish to complete the form definition and create the form.

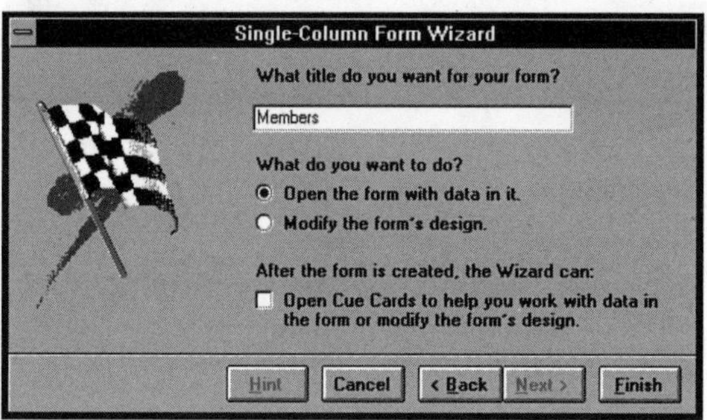

Fig. 30.9
Select Open Cue Cards to get an on-screen tutorial on how to enter data into a form or modify the form's design.

Troubleshooting

I can't create a main/subform Wizard.

You might not have defined the relationship between the two tables. Return to the Database window, and click the Relationships button in the toolbar (or choose **E**dit **R**elationships). Add the appropriate tables to the window, and link the key fields.

The Form Wizard is asking me to select a form style, but I realize that I forgot to select a field to be in the form.

Click the **B**ack button to move back to the preceding screen, where you can add the missing field to your form design.

Using a Blank Form

You can use a blank form to create a custom form that displays data in specific locations, which cannot be achieved by using generic Form Wizards. For example, you may need to create a form that matches a required government form, such as a W-4 form. Or, you may need to create a form that includes pictures in the employee application form.

Tip
To save time, use Form Wizards whenever possible to create the base form. Then enter form design view to modify the predefined form to meet your needs.

To create a blank form, follow these steps:

1. Click the New Form button in the toolbar. The New Form dialog box appears.

2. In the Select A **T**able/Query list box, select the table or query for which you want to create a form.

3. Choose the **B**lank Form button. Access displays a blank form in form design view (see fig. 30.10).

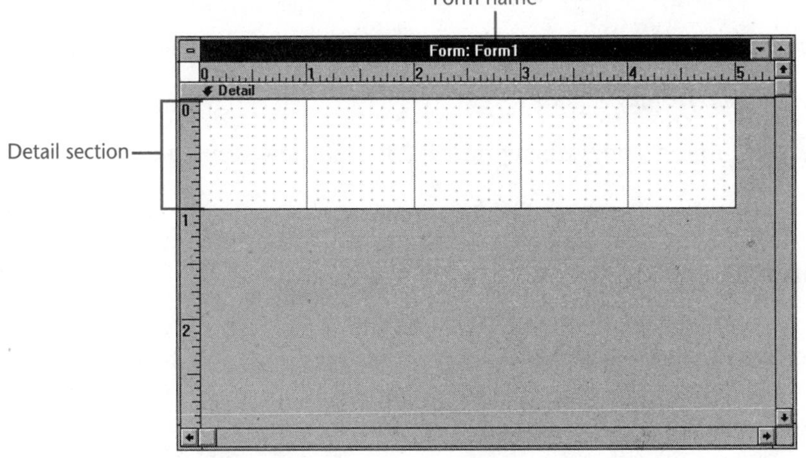

Fig. 30.10
New blank forms contain only a detail section, which is the main body of the form.

Navigating Form Design View

Form design view is where you can create and modify forms. Although new blank forms contain only a detail section, you can add other sections to your form design (see fig. 30.11). To add a form header/footer or page header/footer to your form, choose F**o**rmat Form **H**eader/Footer or F**o**rmat **P**age Header/Footer.

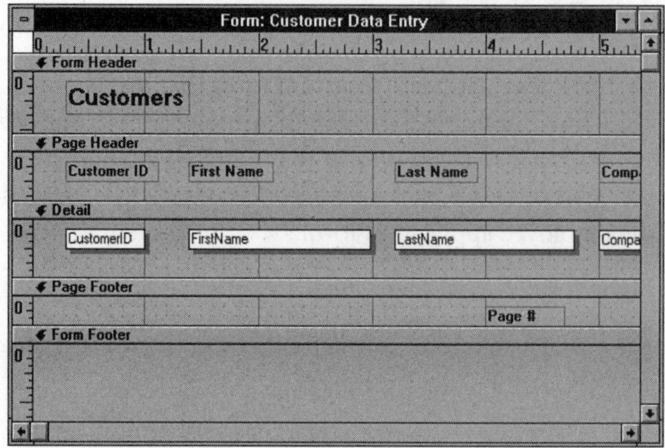

Fig. 30.11
Knowing the sections of a form helps you navigate in form design view.

Following is an overview of each section that can appear in a form:

- *Form header.* Appears at the top of the screen. If the form is printed, prints at the top of the first page.
- *Page header.* Appears only when printed. Prints at the top of each page.
- *Detail section.* Displays data.
- *Page footer.* Appears only when printed. Prints at the bottom of each page.
- *Form footer.* Appears at the bottom of the screen. If the form is printed, prints at the bottom of the last page.

The Design View Toolbar

The Form Design toolbar provides many new buttons to speed up your form design work. Table 30.1 briefly describes these buttons.

Table 30.1 Form Design Toolbar

Button	Button Name	Description
	Design View	Displays form design view
	Form View	Displays form view
	Datasheet View	Displays datasheet view

Button	Button Name	Description
	Save	Saves the form
	Print Preview	Displays the form as it will appear when printed
	Properties	Displays the Properties window
	Field List	Displays the fields linked to the form
	Code	Displays the Module window for the form
	Toolbox	Contains form design objects you can place in a form
	Palette	Opens the palette box
MS Sans Serif	Font Name	Displays current font and provides access to other fonts in a drop-down list
8	Font Size	Displays current font size and provides access to other font sizes in a drop-down list
B	Bold	Boldfaces selection
I	Italic	Italicizes selection
	Left-Align Text	Aligns data to the left
	Center-Align Text	Aligns data to the center
	Right-Align Text	Aligns data to the right
	Database Window	Displays the database window
	Undo	Undoes the last change
	Cue Cards	Displays the Cue Cards (on-screen tutorial)
	Help	Displays context-sensitive help

The Form Design Toolbox

The Form Design toolbox contains all the form design objects (such as fields, text and boxes) that you can place in a form. Objects that you place in a form or a report are called *controls*. Table 30.2 briefly describes each item in the toolbox.

The toolbox is a window that you can move around and resize just like any other window. To display the toolbox, choose **V**iew **T**oolbox. By default, the Select Objects tool is selected. Use this tool to select the object in your form with which you want to work. Access displays handles around the selected object.

To place a new control in the form, select the appropriate tool in the toolbox. The mouse pointer changes to a crosshair and displays the tool's icon (see fig. 30.12). Move the crosshair to the desired location, and then click and drag the control to the desired size.

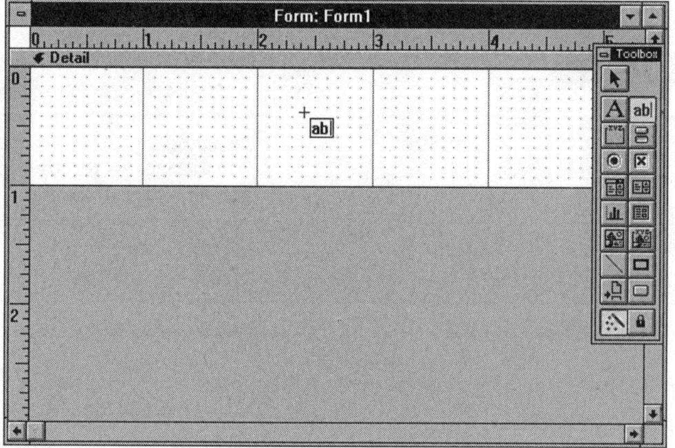

Fig. 30.12 When you select a design tool from the toolbox, Access changes the pointer to a crosshair and displays the tool's icon.

Table 30.2 Form Design Toolbox

Tool	Tool Name	Description
	Select Objects	Selects objects
	Label	Creates a text control
	Option Group	Creates a control for check boxes, option buttons, and toggle buttons
	Option Button	Creates a true/false control

Tool	Tool Name	Description
	Combo Box	Creates a drop-down list of predefined choices, but also enables the user to enter new values
	Graph	Displays data as a graph
	Object Frame	Creates a frame to display pictures, graphs, and OLE objects
	Line	Draws a line
	Page Break	Creates a page break in the form
	Control Wizards	Turns control wizards on and off
ab|	Text Box	Displays field data (label and text box)
	Toggle Button	Creates an on/off button, which in the on position appears depressed
	Check Box	Creates a check box
	List Box	Creates a drop-down list of predefined choices, but unlike Combo Box, does not enable the user to enter new values
	Subform/ Subreport	Displays an embedded form or report
	Bound Object Frame	Creates a frame that is bound to an Access field
	Rectangle	Draws a rectangle
	Command Button	Creates a button that pushes in or pops out when selected; runs a macro or calls an Access function when depressed
	Tool Lock	Keeps the current tool selected until the user selects another tool

Each control tool in the toolbox serves a unique purpose. Following is a brief overview of the tools:

- *Appearance.* Use the Label tool to type text in your form (such as a title for your form). Use the Line tool to draw lines and the Rectangle tool to draw boxes that visually group items or draw attention to an item. The Page Break tool enables you to create multiple-page forms. Sometimes, if a form is getting cluttered, breaking the data entry into separate pages, with fewer items per page, can improve the appearance of a form.

► "Creating Graphs," p. 705

► "Creating a Graph with Form Wizards," p. 706

► "Modifying a Graph," p. 711

- *Data entry and display.* The Text Box tool is used to enter or display data (including pictures). Use the Option Group control when you want to place radio buttons, check boxes, or toggle buttons in the form. Placing an option group in the form displays the Option Group Wizard, which helps you define the option group and set the desired properties. You also can place items individually by selecting the Option Button, Check Box, or Toggle Button tools. The List Box tool enables you to create a drop-down list of values for a field. The Combo Box tool provides the same drop-down list feature and also enables the user to enter a value.

- *Graphing data.* The Graph tool launches the Graph Wizard and Microsoft Graph application, which helps you create a graph object.

► "Understanding OLE Terminology," p. 713

► "Working with Bound and Unbound Objects," p. 714

► "Modifying OLE Objects," p. 717

► "Creating a Macro," p. 719

► "Programming Command Buttons," p. 727

- *Embedding forms.* A common use of the Subform/Subreport tool is to show a one-record-to-many-records relationship between related tables—for example, to show the movie rentals for each customer. When you want to embed a form in another form, use the Subform/Subreport tool in the main form. Before using this tool, you should create the subordinate form to be embedded. You can save time by using Form Wizards to create both the embedded form and the main form.

- *OLE.* The Object Frame and Bound Object Frame tools are used to display OLE (object linking and embedding) objects. The Bound Object Frame tool displays pictures, graphs, or other OLE objects that are stored in an Access database. The Object Frame tool is used to display objects that are not stored in the underlying table.

- *Automating tasks.* The Command Button tool creates a button object on the form. Command buttons are used to run a macro or call an Access Basic function when the button is selected. You could program a button in your form to print a report or open another form.

When the Control Wizards tool is selected, Access will launch any Wizard available for the control being created. The Tool Lock keeps one tool active until you select another. This feature is handy when you are creating many controls of the same type, such as when you are placing several fields in the form.

► "Using the Command Button Wizard," p. 728

The Form Design Palette

Use the Form Design palette (see fig. 30.13) to enhance the appearance of the form and its contents. You can customize the color of text, background, and border for each control you place in a form. To display the palette, choose **V**iew P**a**lette.

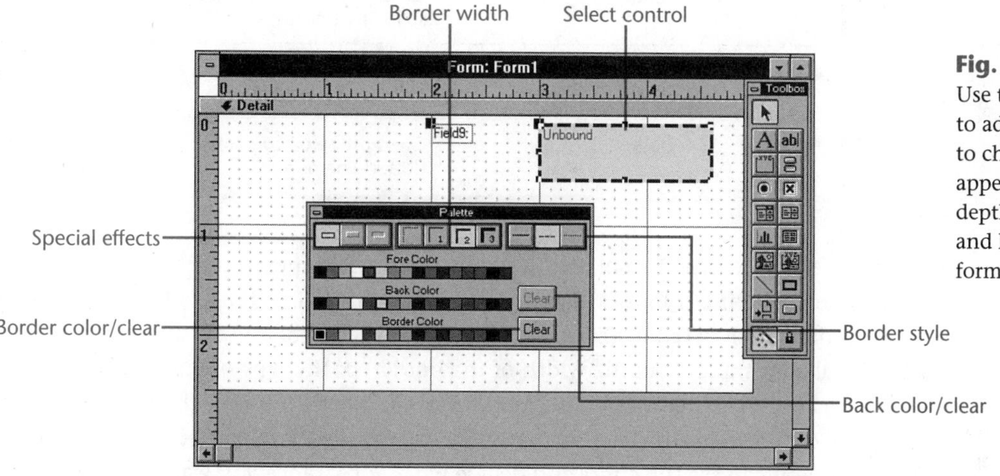

Fig. 30.13
Use the palette to add color and to change the appearance of depth, borders, and lines in your form.

Table 30.3 briefly describes each item in the palette.

Table 30.3 Form Design Palette

Button	Button Name	Description
	Normal Appearance	Gives the selected object a standard appearance
	Raised Appearance	Gives the selected object a raised appearance
	Sunken Appearance	Gives the selected object a sunken appearance

(continues)

Table 30.3 Continued

Button	Button Name	Description
	Hairline Border Width	Sets the selected control's border to the narrowest width possible
	1-pt. Border Width	Sets the width of the selected control's border to 1 point
	2-pt. Border Width	Sets the width of the selected control's border to 2 points
	3-pt. Border Width	Sets the width of the selected control's border to 3 points
	Solid	Gives the selected control a solid-line border
	Dash	Gives the selected control a dashed-line border
	Dots	Gives the selected control a dotted-line border

To use the palette, select an object in the form, or select the form itself. You then can change the color of the foreground, background, or border. Use the buttons described in Table 30.3 to add depth to the control (raised, sunken, or normal appearance), set the width of the border, or the type of border line (solid, dashed, or dotted). As you click the various palette buttons, the appearance of the selected object instantly changes to reflect your selections. This way, you can see the effect and decide what appearance you want to give the object.

Modifying a Form's Design

Changing an existing form design, whether it was created with Form Wizards or a blank form, is a relatively easy task. In most cases, you just need to click and drag, improve appearance with color, or set some properties.

Figure 30.14 shows a single-column form created with Form Wizards (in form view). Although adequate, the form's appearance can be improved. The awkward, extraneous text describing the fields could be modified (or deleted, in some cases). The fields also could be rearranged to create a familiar mailing-label format. You can use the palette buttons to enhance the appearance of the controls.

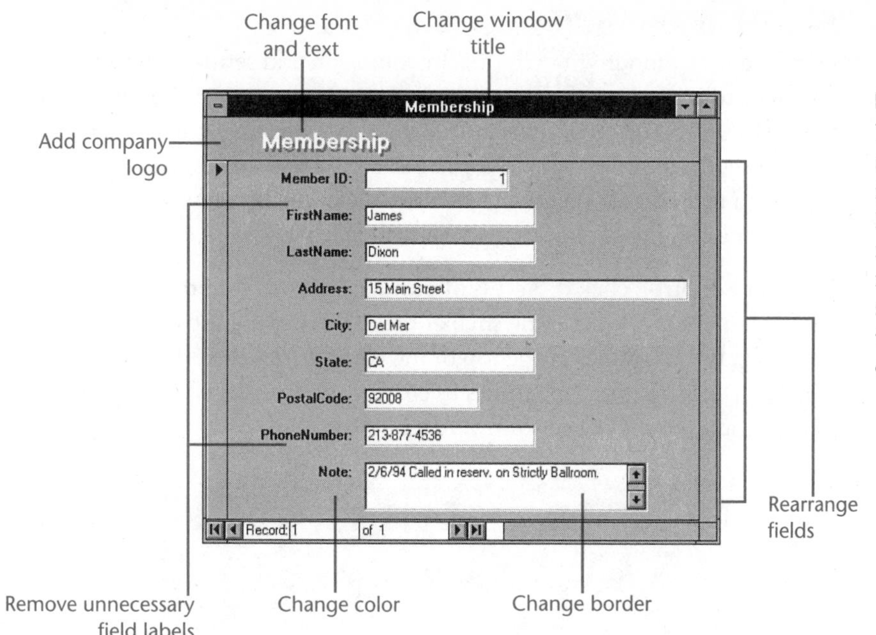

Fig. 30.14
You can enhance a single-column form created with Form Wizards by rearranging fields, removing unnecessary field descriptions, and adding a company logo.

In the next few sections, you learn how to enhance the appearance of this single-column form to produce the enhanced membership form shown in figure 30.15.

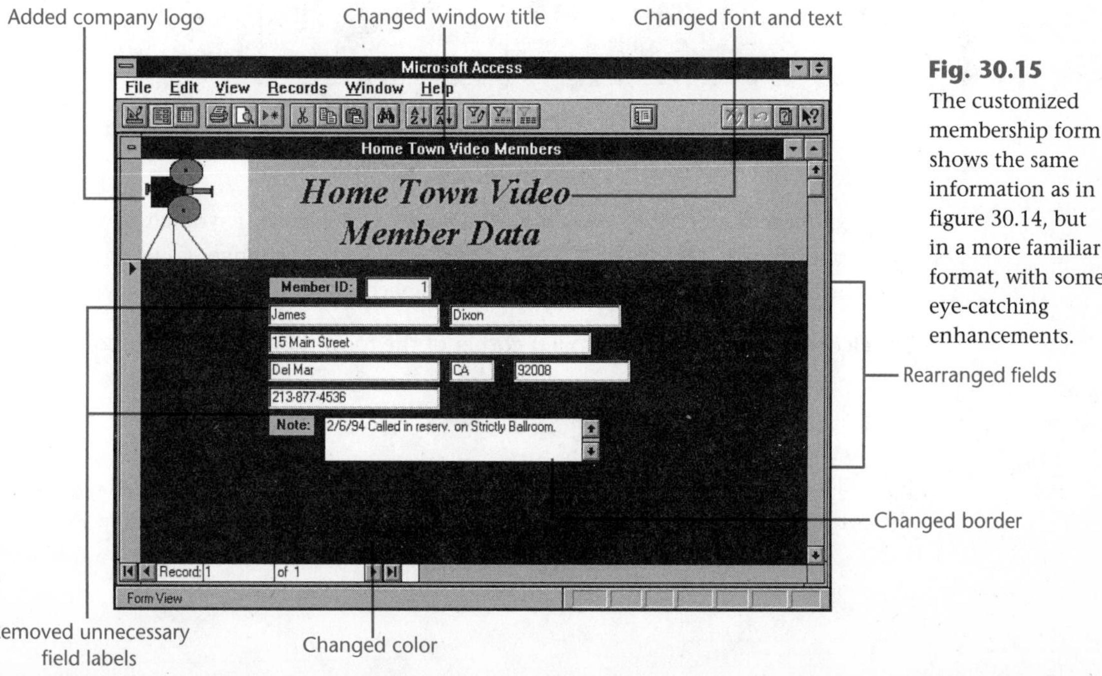

Fig. 30.15
The customized membership form shows the same information as in figure 30.14, but in a more familiar format, with some eye-catching enhancements.

Selecting and Adjusting Controls

Before you start modifying controls in your form and setting form properties, you need to know how to select a control and how to select the form. Figure 30.16 shows the membership form, a single-column form created by Form Wizards, in design view. As you can see, Form Wizards creates a label box and a text box for each field. You can select the text-box control (where data is entered and displayed) or the attached label box.

To select a control, click it. Access displays handles around the control to indicate that it is selected. The smaller black handles are the resizing handles. The larger black handles at the top of the control are called the move handles. Drag the resizing handles to change the size of a control. Drag the move handles to move the control to a new location.

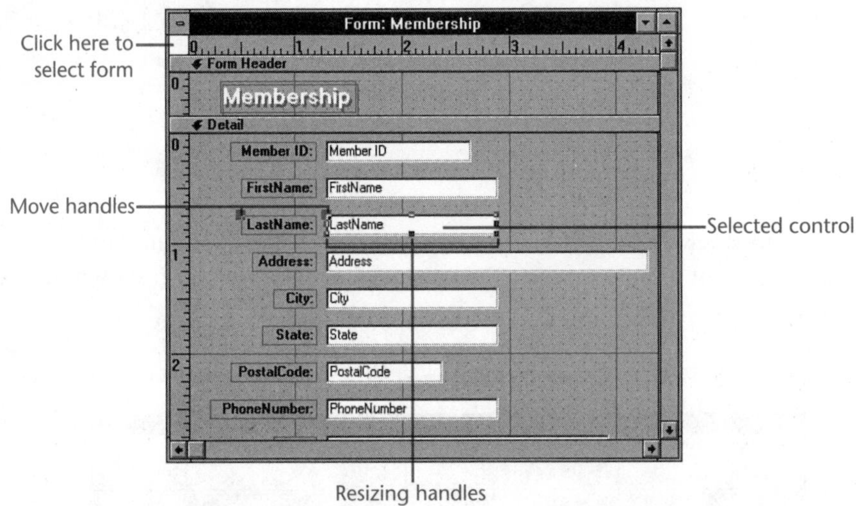

Fig. 30.16 If you click the text box, both the attached label and the text box are selected.

Tip
Working effectively with the various controls takes practice. Create a practice form with Form Wizards and try selecting, resizing, and moving the controls.

To select more than one control, hold the Shift key down while you click each control. After you select all the controls you want to change, you can drag them to a new location or resize them as necessary.

To select the form, click the top left corner of the form (refer to fig. 30.16) or choose **E**dit Select Fo**r**m.

Creating New Controls

To create a new control, select the desired control from the toolbox and place the control in the form. Controls can be classified in three basic categories:

- *Bound controls*, which are linked to a field in a table or query.
- *Unbound controls*, which are not linked to any field in a table or query.
- *Calculated controls*, which are unbound controls that use field data to perform calculations on-screen. The result of the calculation is not stored in any table or query.

Note

You cannot edit data in calculated fields (a control in a form or report that displays the result of an expression, rather than stored data), because Access enters the appropriate value automatically. Press Tab, Enter, or an arrow key to move past these fields. Access automatically enters the proper value.

To assist you in placing bound controls, Access provides a Field List window (see fig. 30.17). To display the Field List, choose **V**iew Field **L**ist. In the Field List, move the highlight bar to the desired field, drag the selected field name to the appropriate position in the form, and release the mouse button.

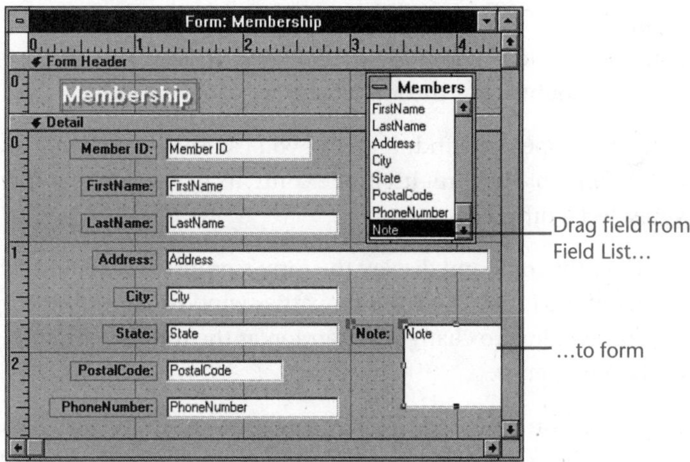

Fig. 30.17
To place bound field controls in the form quickly, drag the field name from the Field List to the form.

To add a control, follow these steps:

1. Display the Toolbox by choosing **V**iew **T**oolbox.
2. Click the desired control tool in the Form Design toolbox.
3. For unbound or calculated controls, position the mouse pointer in the form where you want to add the control. Click to create a default-size control; click and drag to create a custom-size control.

4. For bound controls, display the field list by choosing **V**iew Field **L**ist. Click and drag the desired field name to the appropriate position in the form.

Tip
Use the Control Wizards tool to get help from wizards while you create list boxes and combo boxes.

To create a calculated control, follow these steps:

1. Create the unbound control (one not linked to a field in the table) for the calculated field.

2. Type the expression in the control, or set the control's ControlSource property to the expression, as explained in the next section.

To delete a control, select it and press Del. You also can cut, copy, and paste controls within the same form or across forms. To reverse unwanted changes, use the Undo feature.

Setting Control and Form Properties

Every object in Access has properties. *Properties* determine the appearance and behavior of an object. In form design view, you can view and change the properties of controls and of the form itself.

To display the properties of a control, double-click the control, or select a control and then choose **V**iew **P**roperties. To view the Form's Properties Sheet window, double-click the top-left corner of the form.

After the Properties window opens, you can select different controls, sections of the form, or the form itself; the contents of the window change each time you select a different control.

To select the form and display the form's properties, double-click the top-left corner of the form. The Form Properties window appears (see fig. 30.18). You use this window to change the caption at the top of your form window (the caption property).

Many form property settings are "inherited" from the form's associated table or query. Some properties are set through the toolbox and palette, and some properties have no settings.

For more information on a specific property, place the insertion point in that property's field and press F1.

Fig. 30.18
The Form property Record Source tells Access the name of the underlying table or query for the form.

Displaying Status Bar Text

By default, the status bar in form view displays the field descriptions you entered in the associated table. You may find, however, that the field name is not enough to direct data entry. Instead of changing the field name, you can override this description and enter new text in the StatusBarText property for that control.

Setting Default Values and Validation Rules

Access enables you to set default field values and validation rules, in both tables and their associated forms. Generally, such data parameters should be placed at the table level, but in some cases, the default value or validation rule might apply only to a particular data-entry form. In these cases, you can set default values and validation rules in the property sheet of a control (refer to fig. 30.18).

For assistance in writing expressions, click the Expression Builder button next to the property. The Expression Builder helps you write expressions and offers common validation expressions that you can use.

Changing Tab Order

◄ "Setting Field Properties," p. 603

◄ "Manipulating Data," p. 622

◄ "Entering and Editing Data," p. 614

Tab order refers to the order in which you move from control to control when you press the Tab key. The default tab order of Access forms starts at the top left object and moves from left to right, and then from top to bottom. At times, you may find that the default tab order fails to meet your needs. For example, you may be entering data from a source that displays the information in a different order. Rather than rearrange the field controls in your form, you could rearrange the tab order. You also might want to change tab-order properties when your data-entry task starts in the middle of a form. Rather than tab several times to the desired field, you could assign that field a tab-order index of 1.

To change the default tab order in a form, set the Tab Stop and/or Tab Index. A tab-stop value of Yes enables users to tab to the control; No causes the tab to skip the control. The Tab Index value stipulates the exact numerical tab order (see fig. 30.19).

You also can set the AutoTab property. The AutoTab property controls whether the field automatically tabs to the next field when you type the last allowable character. For example, if a Social Security number field can contain only 11 characters, and the AutoTab property is set to Yes, Access automatically tabs to the next field when the user types the 11th character.

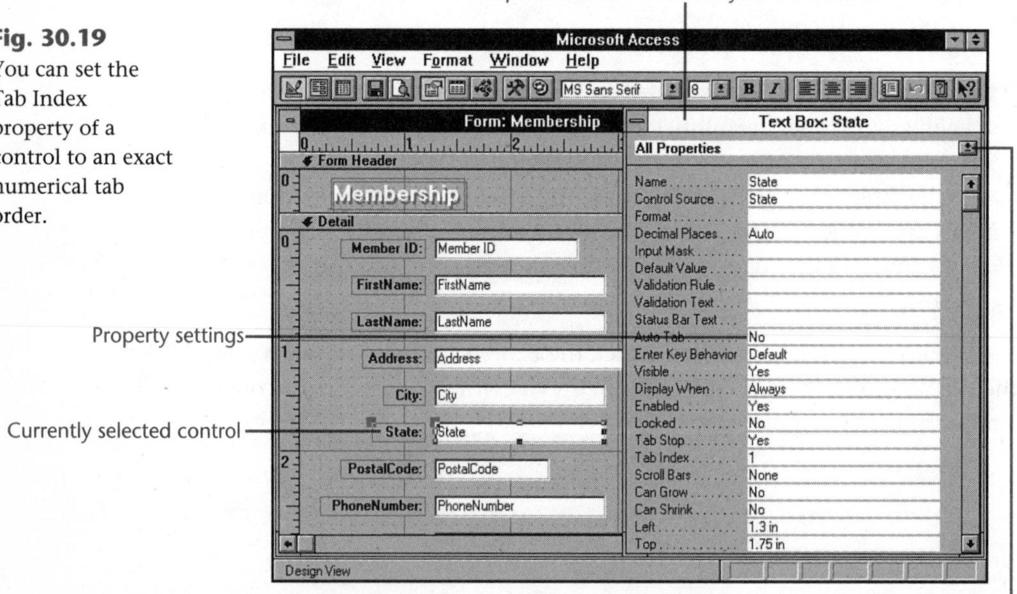

Fig. 30.19
You can set the Tab Index property of a control to an exact numerical tab order.

Navigating Form View

Entering and editing data in form view is the same as in datasheet view. All the data-entry shortcuts and tools, such as Find and Filter/Sort, are available in form view. Using the toolbar, you can easily move between datasheet, form, and design view.

◀ "Navigating in Datasheet View," p. 612

◀ "Entering and Editing Data," p. 614

◀ "Manipulating Data," p. 622

Troubleshooting

I can't access the form's property sheet.

Double-click the top left corner of the form, or choose **E**dit Select Fo**r**m.

One field is not sunken like the others.

Open the palette, select the problem field, and then click the Sunken Appearance button.

When entering a validation expression into a field control's validation property, I keep running out of room.

Press Shift+F2 to open the Zoom box.

The All Properties property list for a text box is too long to view and work with.

You can view the property list by topic. At the top of the Properties window, you can choose a set of properties to view. Click the down arrow to open the drop-down list, and select the type of property you want to view.

From Here...

Now that you are familiar with creating and customizing forms, you are ready to begin creating and using queries. To learn how to use queries, refer to the following chapters:

- Chapter 31, "Querying Databases," builds on what you have learned about tables and forms and takes you through the process of creating queries.
- Chapter 32, "Creating Reports," shows you how to create a report based on the results of a query.
- Chapter 34, "Using Macros," shows you how to automate repetitive tasks, such as executing a query.

Navigating Form View

Chapter 31

Querying Databases

by Diane Tinney

So far, this section of the book has focused on the ways in which you can enter data into your database. Now it's time to explore ways of getting information out of your database. One of the most useful features of modern database applications is the query, which provides you a way to "question" your database. The result of a query (the "answer") then can be printed or viewed on-screen. This chapter explains the query features of Access and shows you how to use queries to extract information from your database.

In this chapter, you learn to

- Create and save a query
- View a dynaset
- Specify query criteria
- Perform query calculations
- Modify field and sort orders

Exploring Queries

A *query* is a statement that tells Access what kind of information you need to extract from one or more tables. A query also can perform an action on the data in the table(s) and summarize data in spreadsheet format.

You can use queries, for example, to accomplish the following tasks:

- Compile a list of employees who live in a certain state.
- Show customer names, demographics, and purchasing information in one report.

- Determine the frequency of movie rentals.
- Calculate the total cost of movies by category.
- Purge the database of customers who have not rented in the past year.
- Add old customer records to a history database.

Queries can be used as a source of information for forms and reports. In such a case, the query enables you to include specific data from more than one table. Access executes the query each time you open the form or report, so you can be sure that the information you see is up to date.

Access enables you to create the following types of queries:

- *Select queries.* Used to extract data from tables based on criteria specified in the query object. This type of query is the most common. A select query could be used to list all customers in New York, for example.
- *Action queries.* Used to perform an action on records that meet criteria specified in the query object. This type of query enables you to change or move data, create new tables, or purge records from a table. You could use an action query to purge inactive customer records.
- *Crosstab queries.* Used to summarize data in a spreadsheet format based on criteria specified in the query object. Crosstab queries most often are used to show data in a graph.
- *Union queries.* Used to combine fields from two or more tables. For example, you could create a query that lists customer data from the customer table and invoice totals from the invoice table.
- *Pass-through queries.* Used to send commands to a Standard Query Language (SQL) database.
- *Data-definition queries.* Used to perform actions on Access databases with SQL statements.

For each query type, you can specify *query parameters* that prompt the user to specify query criteria before the query executes. In the video-store application introduced in Chapter 27, for example, you could create a query that lists movies based on each customer's preferences.

Access places the results of a query or a filter operation in a dynaset. A *dynaset* looks and behaves like a table, but it actually provides a dynamic view of the data in one or more tables. You can enter and update data in a dynaset; after you do so, Access automatically updates the data in the associated table or tables.

◀ "Sorting and Filtering Data," p. 624

Note

In a multiuser environment, changes made by other users are reflected in the dynaset and its associated tables.

Caution

Dynasets seem so much like tables that it is hard to remember that they really are not. Just keep in mind that the data is stored in the primary tables themselves, not in the dynaset.

Creating a New Query

To create a new query, click the New Query button in the toolbar, or switch to the Database window, select the Query tab, and then click the New button. The New Query dialog box appears (see fig. 31.1). As with tables and forms, Access provides two methods of creating queries: Query Wizards and Query New.

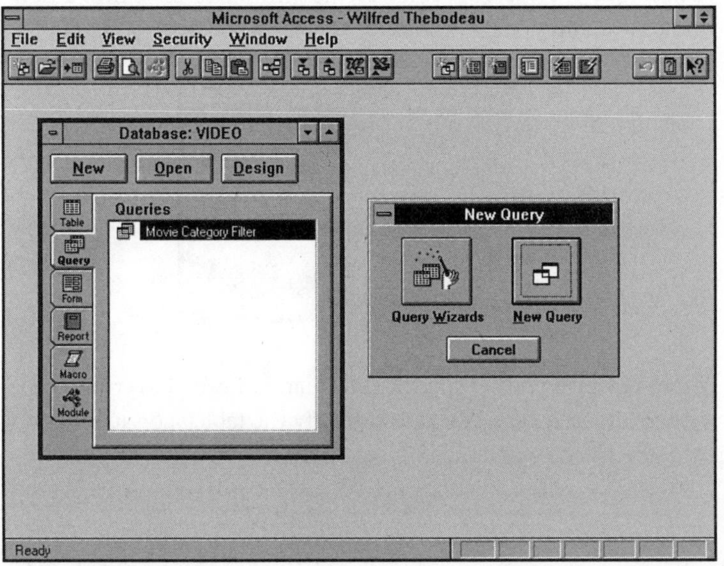

Fig. 31.1 Access provides Query Wizards to assist you in developing your query.

Whichever method you decide to use, it helps to spend some time designing the query before actually creating it. Think about some of the following factors before getting started:

- Which table(s) contain the information you need
- Table relationships (are the tables properly keyed?)
- The type of query you want to perform
- The field conditions and criteria that the records must meet
- Calculations, if desired
- Sort order
- The name under which you want to save the query

Using Query Wizards

The Query Wizards feature provides four basic types of generic queries (see fig. 31.2):

- *Crosstab Query.* Summarizes query data in spreadsheet format.
- *Find Duplicates Query.* Locates duplicate records in a table.
- *Find Unmatched Query.* Locates records in one table that do not have matching records in a related table.
- *Archive Query.* Copies specified records from one table into a new table and (optionally) purges those records from the original table.

Fig. 31.2
Select the type of Query Wizard you want to use.

Each wizard prompts you for specific information needed to create its particular type of query. In each case, you must identify the table(s) or queries on which the new query will be based.

Figures 31.3 through 31.7 show how to use Query Wizards to create a crosstab query—probably the most complicated of the four query types. The completed crosstab shows the total number of tapes, by category and by rental rate (see fig. 31.8), in datasheet view. Crosstab queries often are used to provide summarized data for a graph.

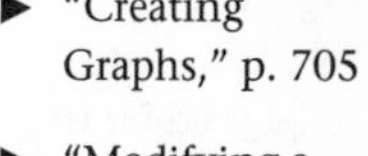

▶ "Creating Graphs," p. 705

▶ "Modifying a Graph," p. 711

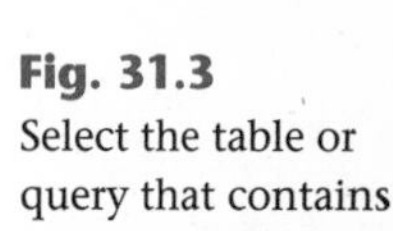

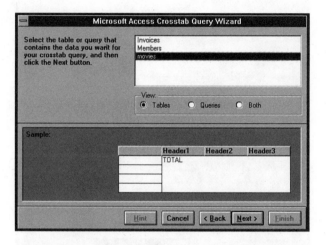

Fig. 31.3
Select the table or query that contains the data needed for the crosstab query.

Fig. 31.4
Select the field(s) to be used for the crosstab row headings.

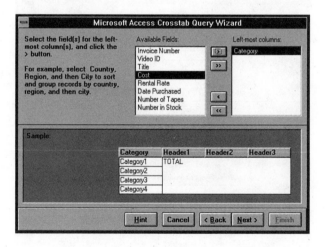

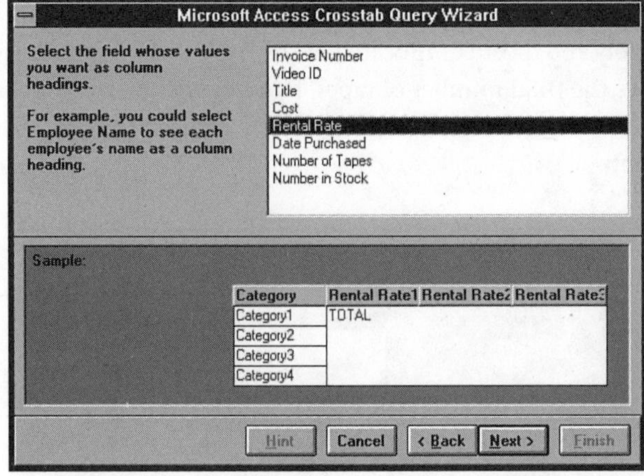

Fig. 31.5
Select the field(s) to be used for the crosstab column headings.

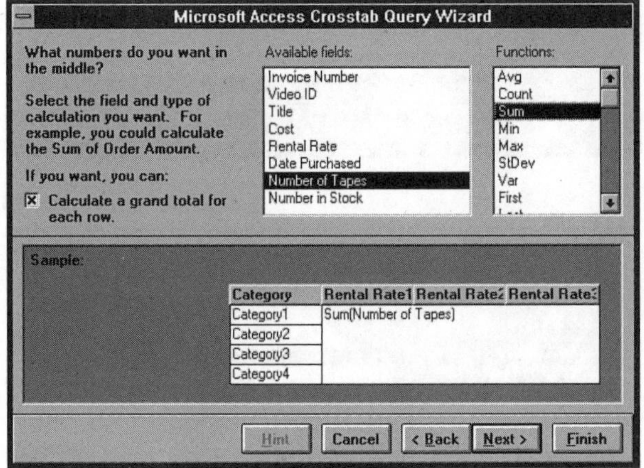

Fig. 31.6
Select the field and type of crosstab calculation needed.

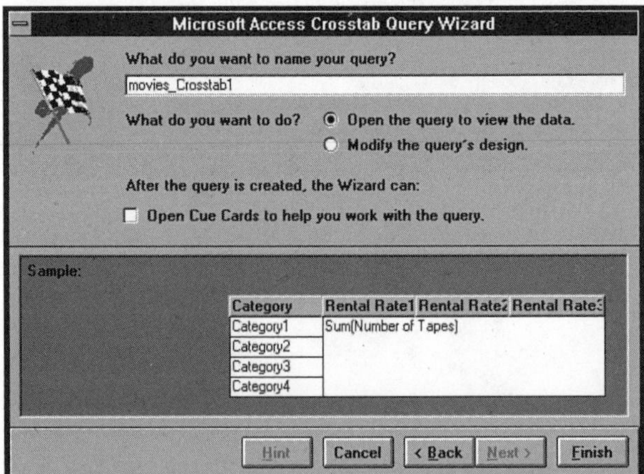

Fig. 31.7
The final Query Wizard dialog box prompts you to name your query.

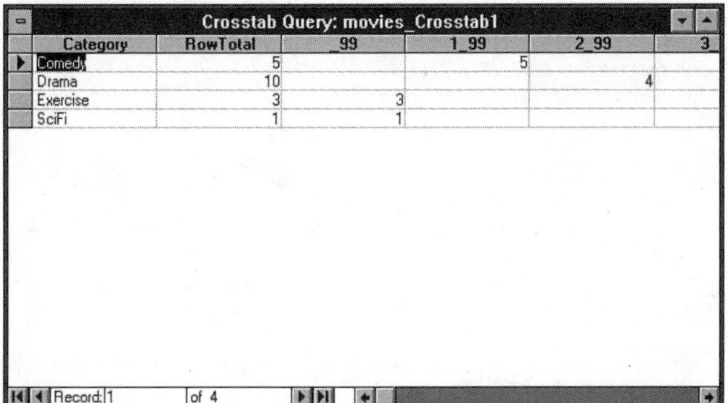

Crosstab Query: movies_Crosstab1
Category | RowTotal | _99 | 1_99 | 2_99 | 3_
Comedy | 5 | | 5 | |
Drama | 10 | | | 4 |
Exercise | 3 | 3 | | |
SciFi | 1 | 1 | | |
Record: 1 of 4

Fig. 31.8
The completed crosstab datasheet shows the total number of movies for each category by rental rate.

Using New Query

To create a query from scratch, click the New Query button in the toolbar, or switch to the Database window, select the Query tab, and then click the **N**ew button. The New Query dialog box appears (refer to fig. 31.1). Choose the **N**ew Query button in the New Query dialog box. Access displays the Select Query: Query1 window and opens the Add Table dialog box (see fig. 31.9). As you select tables, Access places a field list for the table at the top of the Select Query window.

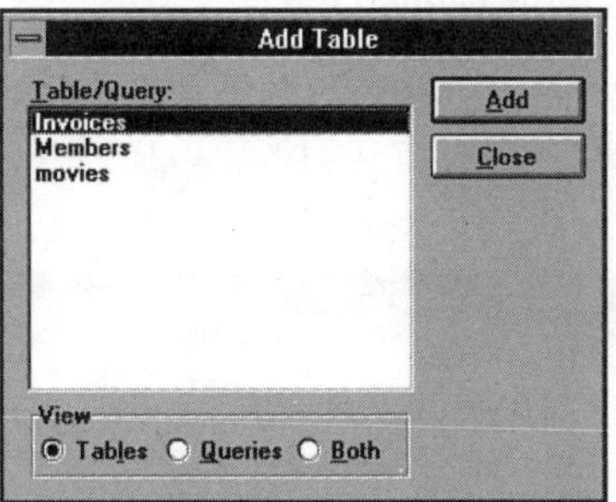

Fig. 31.9
When you create a new (blank) query, Access displays the Add Table dialog box, prompting you to select the tables and/or queries on which to base the query.

To select the table you want to add to your query definition, double-click the table name or highlight the table name and then choose the **A**dd button. Access adds the table to the Select Query: Query1 window; the Add dialog box remains open so that you can add more tables, if necessary. Access automatically finds any relationships among multiple tables added to a query definition and shows those relationships by drawing lines between the related fields (see fig. 31.10).

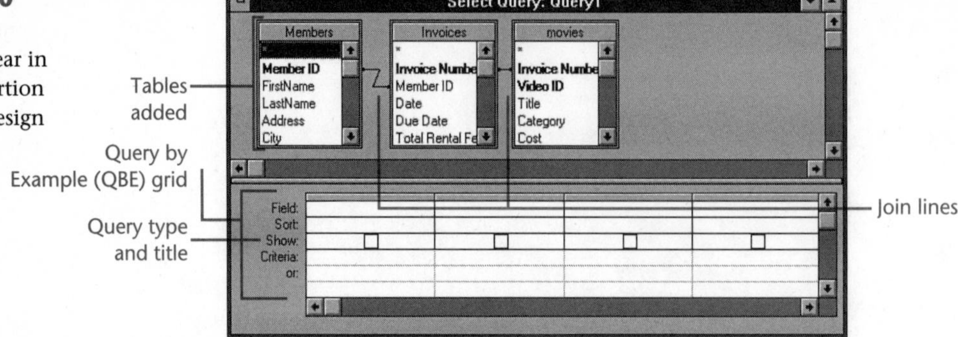

Fig. 31.10
The added tables appear in the top portion of query design view.

Access automatically finds table relationships and draws a line between the matching key fields (same field name and field type). These lines are called join lines. *Join lines* apply only to multitable queries. You can create join lines yourself by dragging and dropping a key field from one table to another.

The bottom half of the window contains the Query-by-Example grid, in which you define the criteria of the query. *Query-by-Example (QBE)* enables you to define query criteria by providing practical examples of the type of data you need. To find all employees in the state of New Jersey, for example, you would type the example element **NJ**.

After you finish adding tables, choose **C**lose. To reopen the Add Tables dialog box, click the Add Table button in the toolbar, or choose the **Q**uery **A**dd Table command.

Note

By default, Access sets the query type to Select Query. You can change the query type by making a different selection from the Query menu.

Exploring the Query Window

Tip
Remember that in addition to these views, query results can be used as the basis for a form or report.

The Query window enables you to see queries in several views (available via the View menu or toolbar):

- *Design view.* Used to define the query.
- *SQL view.* Used to view or modify the SQL query-language definition of your query.
- *Datasheet view.* Used to display the results of your query.

The Query window toolbar provides many buttons that speed your query work. Table 31.1 describes these buttons.

Table 31.1 Query Window Toolbar Buttons

Button	Button Name	Description
	Design View	Displays the query in design view
SQL	SQL View	Displays the query in SQL design view
	Datasheet View	Displays the table in datasheet view
	Save	Saves the query design
!	Run	Executes the query
	Properties	Toggles the Properties window on and off
	Add Table	Displays the Add Table dialog box
Σ	Totals	Displays or hides the total row in the QBE grid
XYZ	Table Names	Displays or hides the table name row in the QBE grid
	Select Query	Changes the query type to Select Query
	Crosstab Query	Changes the query type to Crosstab Query
	Make-Table Query	Changes the query type to Make-Table Query
	Update Query	Changes the query type to Update Query
	Append Query	Changes the query type to Append Query
	Delete Query	Changes the query type to Delete Query
	New Query	Creates a new query based on this query
	New Form	Creates a new form based on this query

(continues)

Table 31.1 Continued

Button	Button Name	Description
	New Report	Creates a new report based on this query
	Database Window	Displays the Database window
	Build	Displays the appropriate wizard or builder
	Undo	Undoes last change
	Cue Cards	Displays on-screen tutorial
	Help	Provides context-sensitive help

Designing a Query

After you start a new query or click the Design button in the Database window for an existing query, Access displays the Query window in design view. Query design view (refer to fig. 31.10) is split into two main sections. The top section contains a field list box for each table being used in the query definition; the bottom section contains the Query-by-Example (QBE) grid, where you define your query. Each column of the QBE grid is a field. For each field, you define the query parameters, such as criteria and sorting, in the rows of the QBE grid.

Selecting Fields

The QBE grid consists of columns and rows. Each column represents one of the fields used in your query. To add a field to the QBE grid, double-click the field in the field list box, or drag the field name to a column. Access fills in the field name and the default selections to total by group and checks the Show check box.

To select all the fields in a field list box, double-click the asterisk (*) or drag the asterisk to the QBE grid. To remove a field, select the field column and press Del, or position the insertion point within the column and choose the **E**dit De**l**ete Column command.

The set of records that results from a query (or a filter) is called a dynaset. You can control which fields are included in the dynaset. To include a field in the dynaset, select the check box in the Show row of the QBE grid (see fig. 31.11). Not all the fields used in the QBE grid must be included in the query results. To exclude a field from the resulting dynaset, deselect the Show check box for that field.

Note

Suppose that you want a list of your friends' names and phone numbers, but not their addresses and birthdays. Even though all that data is stored in your FRIENDS table, you could get a subset of information by creating a query and selecting only the Name and Phone Number fields.

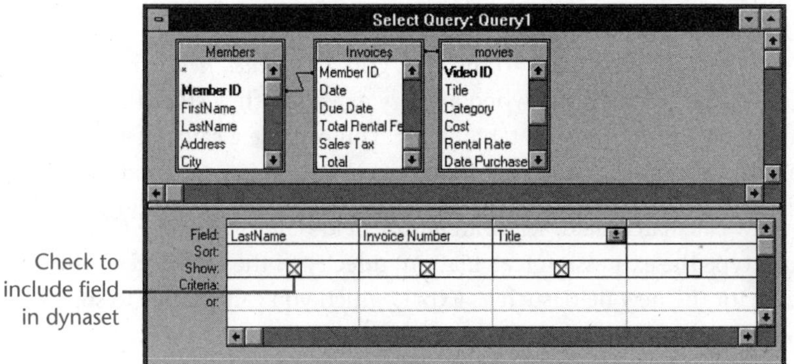

Fig. 31.11
Define your query in the QBE grid by adding fields and setting query parameters for each field.

Tip
To change the order of the field columns, select a field column by clicking the field selector in the QBE grid and then dragging the column to the new location.

The QBE grid contains two more rows that are hidden by default: Table Name and Total. To display these rows, choose the **V**iew **T**otals or **V**iew Table **N**ames command. When selected, the Table Name and Total rows appear below the Field row in the QBE grid.

Troubleshooting

In the results of my crosstab query, the headings are in the wrong order. I used Query Wizards to create the query.

You can correct this problem by moving the field columns in the QBE grid. Open the query in Design view, click the field selector to select the column to be moved, and drag the column to its new location.

I created a select query, but now realize that I should have created an append query.

Rather than re-create the query, you can change the query type in design view and supply the additional information needed. Open the query in design view and click the Append Query button. Access prompts you for the name of the table to which you want to append data and for the database name.

I need to delete a field from the QBE grid.

Select the column by clicking the field selector, and then press Del. Alternatively, with the insertion point in the desired column, choose the **E**dit De**l**ete Column command.

Adding Calculated Fields

You also can add calculated fields to the QBE grid. *Calculated fields* are temporary fields created in the dynaset when a query executes; they store the results of calculations on the contents of table fields. You can use a calculated field, for example, to calculate a markup on products or to concatenate text fields.

To create a new calculated field, select an empty field-name cell in the QBE grid. You can type the expression (calculation) directly in the cell. Access will create a name for the new field, such as Expr1, which you can change to something more meaningful. Alternatively, you can enter a dynaset field name, followed by a colon (:) and the calculation or concatenation expression. Field names used in the calculation must appear in brackets ([ ]), and spaces must be in quotes, but numeric and arithmetic operators do not require any special notation. The new calculated-field name does not need to be entered in brackets. You could create a new field named Total by entering the following:

Tip
To change the width of a column, position the mouse pointer above the Field row, on the vertical grid line. The pointer changes to a set of opposing arrows. Drag the grid line to the desired width.

Total:[Unit Price]*Quantity

For more help on naming fields, search for the help topic "Renaming a Field in a Query." For assistance on writing expressions for calculated fields in a query, search for the help topic "Using a Calculated Field in a Query." You also can use the Build button in the toolbar to launch the Expression Builder, which can help you create the expression. For more information on writing expressions, see Que's *Using Access 2 for Windows,* Special Edition.

Figure 31.12 shows a string concatenation of a member's first and last name and a calculation that computes projected sales based on a price increase of 10 percent.

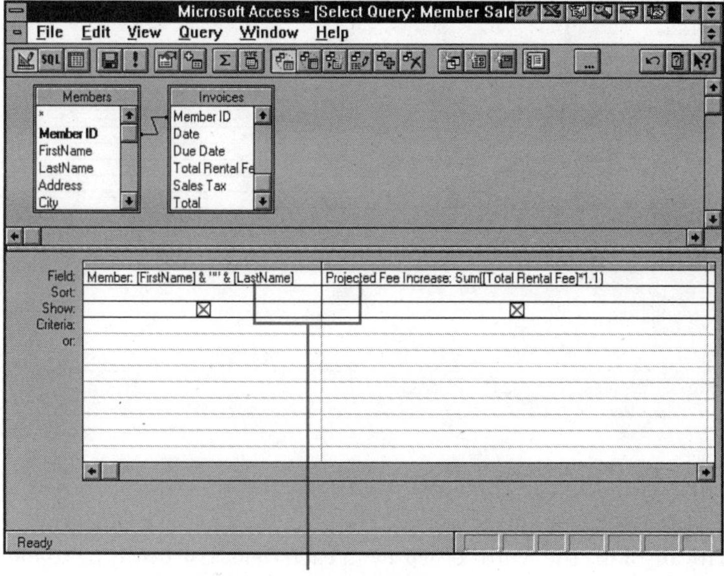

Fig. 31.12
Calculated fields include a dynaset field name, followed by a colon and the calculation.

To create a calculated field, follow these steps:

1. Move to the appropriate column in the QBE grid.
2. Enter a new calculated field name in the Field row, followed by a colon (:).
3. Continue typing in the field-name cell, and enter the desired calculation expression.
4. Save and execute the query.

Adding Group Calculations

Sometimes, query results need to perform calculations for groups of records rather than for each record (see fig. 31.13). You might want to see total sales by state, for example, or advertising cost by product. Access enables you to perform sophisticated calculations on groups of records. For example, you could determine the average salary by department or the maximum hours by job order.

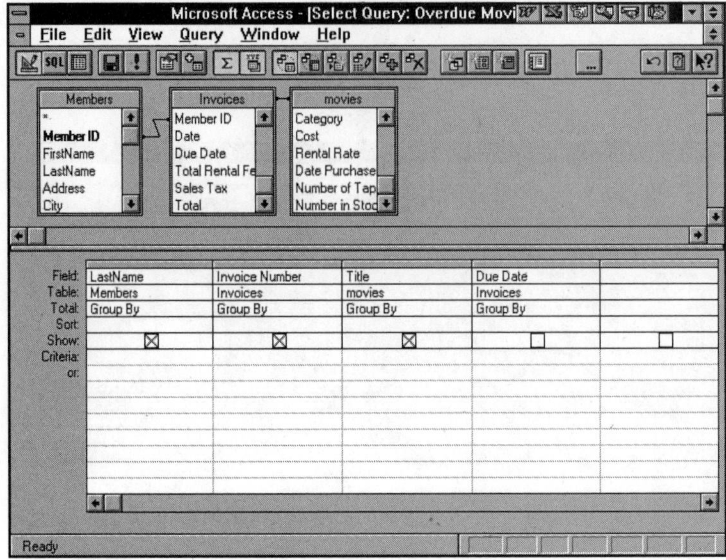

Fig. 31.13
Use the Total row to group query results by records and perform group calculations.

You define groups in the Total row. To display the Total row, choose the **V**iew **T**otals command. After you add the Total row to your QBE grid, Access automatically adds the words `Group By` in each field. Use `Group By` to identify the fields (groups) by which you want to perform the calculation. You can change this selection to any of the following types of calculations:

- *Sum*. Totals the field values.
- *Avg*. Computes an average field value.
- *Min*. Finds the minimum field value.
- *Max*. Finds the maximum field value.
- *Count*. Returns the number of values in a field, disregarding null values.
- *StDev*. Computes the standard deviation (square root of the variance) of the field values.
- *Var*. Computes the variance of the field values.
- *First*. Returns the first value in a field.
- *Last*. Returns the last value in a field.
- *Expression*. Enables you to create a calculated field for a group.
- *Where*. Enables you to specify criteria for a field you are *not* using to define groupings.

Note

Calculation types, such as Count, Avg and Var, that calculate totals can be used only for fields of the following data types: Number, Date/Time, Currency, Counter, and Yes/No. The data type OLE Object also is valid for Count, First, and Last.

To perform group calculations, follow these steps:

1. Create a select or crosstab query.
2. In design view, display the Total row by choosing the **V**iew **T**otals command.

3. In the Total cell for each field, select a total type.
4. If the totals are for all records, no total cells should be of the type `Group By`.
5. If the totals are to be calculated by group, set the total cell of the desired fields to `Group By`.
6. Save the query.
7. Run the query or switch to datasheet view.

Tip
Use multiple Group By total types to calculate totals for several groups.

Specifying Query Criteria

The criteria row of the QBE enables you to include in your query results only records that meet specific conditions. *Criteria* are conditions used to select records. This query feature probably is used more often than any other. You can select records by entering any of the following conditions:

- *Exact Match.* Use a literal value, such as the text string *NJ* or the currency amount *1000*, which the field value (case-insensitive) must match.
- *Wildcard Pattern Match.* Use a combination of literal characters and wild-card characters (see table 31.2, which follows this list), such as *N** or *1###*, which the field value must match.
- *Elimination Match.* Use the NOT operator to eliminate records that meet the criteria (for example, *not NJ*).
- *Date Match.* Use an exact date or the DATE( ) operator, which represents today's date (according to your computer's clock). For example, you could use the criteria *12/1/94* or *DATE( )*.

- *Blank Values.* Use the NULL operator to specify that you want to see only blank values. Conversely, use NOT NULL to specify that you do not want blank values in your query results.
- *Comparison Operators.* Use any of the comparison operators (see table 31.3, which follows this list) to compare record data with a specific condition. For example, you could enter *<DATE( )* to see only records with dates before today's date.
- *Yes/No Values.* Use *Yes, True, On,* or *–1* to specify Yes values. Use *No, False, Off,* or *0* to specify No values.
- *Multiple Criteria.* Use the logic operators (see table 31.4, which follows this list) to establish multiple criteria within the same field.

Table 31.2 Wild-Card Operators

Operator	Description
*	Use in place of any number of characters
?	Use in place of any single character
#	Use in place of any single digit
[]	Use to specify characters within the brackets (e.g., N[JY])
!	Use to match any character not in the list (e.g., N[!JY])
-	Use to match one character in a range of characters (e.g.,N[J-Y])
LIKE	Use to match any characters (e.g., use LIKE "[A-D]*" to see a list of members whose names begin with *A, B, C,* or *D*)

Note

For more information on operators, refer to on-line Help.

Table 31.3 Comparison Operators

Operator	Description
>	Greater than
<	Less than
<=	Less than or equal to
=>	Greater than or equal to
< >	Not equal to
=	Equal to

Table 31.4 Logic Operators

Operator	Description
AND	Requires that all criteria be met
OR	Requires that either criterion be met (either/or)
NOT	Requires that criteria not be met
BETWEEN	Requires that values be within a specified range
IN	Requires that value be within the same field

Note

You can specify multiple rows of criteria for each field (see fig. 31.14). Multiple rows of criteria create an "or" condition. Multiple criteria in the same row create an "and" condition unless the keyword OR is specified.

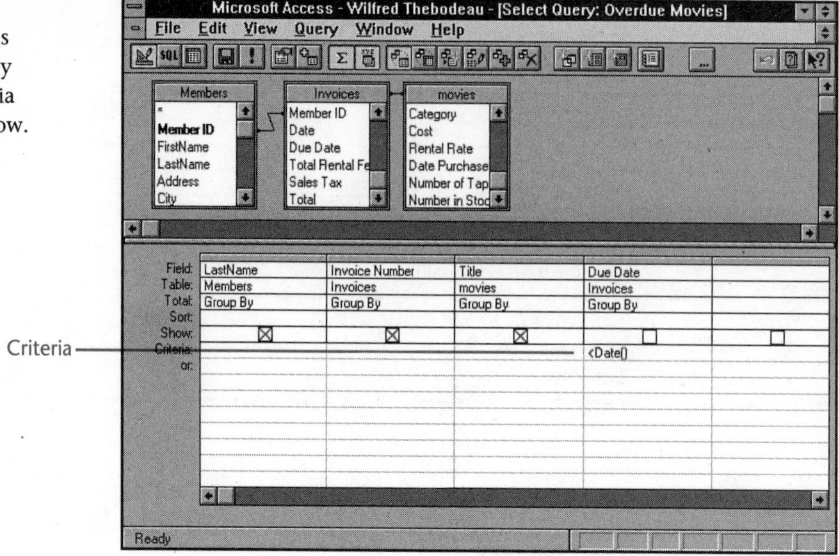

Fig. 31.14
Limit the records in the dynaset by specifying criteria in the Criteria row.

Sorting Query Results

By default, the results of a query appear unsorted, in the order in which query answers were found. You can specify a sort order to organize the query results into a more meaningful list.

The Sort row of the QBE provides a drop-down list that includes the following sort options:

- Ascending
- Descending
- (not sorted)

By default, no sort order is specified. To specify a sort order, select the field and sort order from the drop-down list.

Specifying Query Properties

You can view and modify the properties of a query, of the table field lists that a query uses, or of individual dynaset fields. To view and modify the properties of any of these objects, choose the **V**iew **P**roperties command to open the Properties window. Then click the object for which you want to set properties. The contents of the Properties window change to reflect that object's properties.

You might want to specify the format of a calculated field—for example, to specify the number of decimal places to be displayed.

An important query property is the Unique Values property (see fig. 31.15). By default, this property is set to No, indicating that duplicate records, if they exist and meet your criteria, are listed in the dynaset. To exclude duplicate values, set the Unique Values property to Yes.

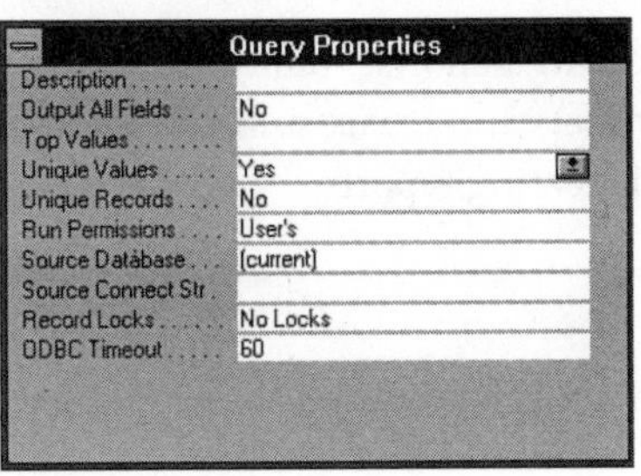

Fig. 31.15
Set the query property Unique Values to Yes to exclude duplicate values from the dynaset.

If the goal of your query is to list movie categories and the rental rate by category, by default your query would list duplicates in each category. To list the categories only once, set the Unique Values property to Yes.

◀ "Setting Field Properties," p. 603

◀ "Setting Table Properties," p. 606

◀ "Setting Index Properties," p. 607

◀ "Setting Control and Form Properties," p. 656

Troubleshooting

I need to combine the data from two text fields into one field in my query results dynaset.

Use a calculated field and string concatenation, as shown in the Member field in figure 31.12. In an empty field cell, type the new field name, followed by a colon. After the colon, type the field names, enclosed in brackets if necessary. Between the field names, type an ampersand (&). If you want to insert a space or text between the fields, use two quotes and another ampersand:

```
([field1]&" and "&[field2])
```

The query takes too long to run.

Within Access, you can improve the efficiency of queries by using Rushmore Technology. Basically, this technology has you create an index for the fields used in your query. For more information on Rushmore Technology, search for the help topic "Optimizing Queries."

I often need to run queries that depend on uncertain criteria, such as partial or incorrect spelling of a name. Which query operator should I use?

When you are working with uncertain data, the best operator to use is the pattern operator LIKE, which searches for all values that are similar to the value you provide. You also can use the wild-card operator * for situations in which the data is partial (for example, LIKE "Smi*").

From Here...

Now that you are familiar with creating and working with queries, you are ready to begin creating reports to print your table and query results. To learn how to work with reports, refer to the following chapter:

- Chapter 32, "Creating Reports," builds on what you have learned about tables, dynasets and forms, and takes you through the process of designing and creating reports.

Chapter 32

Creating Reports

by Diane Tinney

Whereas forms are primarily for input, reports are primarily for output. Reports present data in print better than forms or datasheets do. You have more control of the design layout and print output. For example, you can design a report that prints in landscape orientation on legal paper and that subtotals by page or by group.

In this chapter, you learn to

- Create a new report
- Use Report Wizards
- Set report properties
- Modify report sections
- Use groups and totals
- Insert subreports
- Set print options

Creating a New Report

Before creating a new report, take some time to plan its design. Consider the following items:

- Review the tables, forms, and queries currently used in your database.
- Identify the data components of your report.
- Be sure that all necessary data needed is entered in the appropriate tables.

◀ "Using Form Wizards," p. 640

◀ "Using a Blank Form," p. 645

◀ "Navigating Form Design View," p. 645

◀ "Modifying a Form's Design," p. 652

- Consider using a form instead of a report if you need to perform data entry as well as to report in that particular format. You cannot enter or modify data in a report.

- Review existing printed reports, and get feedback from the people who use the reports on outstanding issues or areas that need improvement.

Report creation is very similar to form creation. To create a new report, display the Database window, click the Report button, and click the **N**ew button. The New Report dialog box appears (see fig. 32.1). The Select A **T**able/Query text box prompts you to select a table or query upon which to base the report.

Note

If you have an Access form that resembles your report design, save the form as a report (in form design view, choose **F**ile Save As Rep**o**rt), and then modify the report to meet your needs.

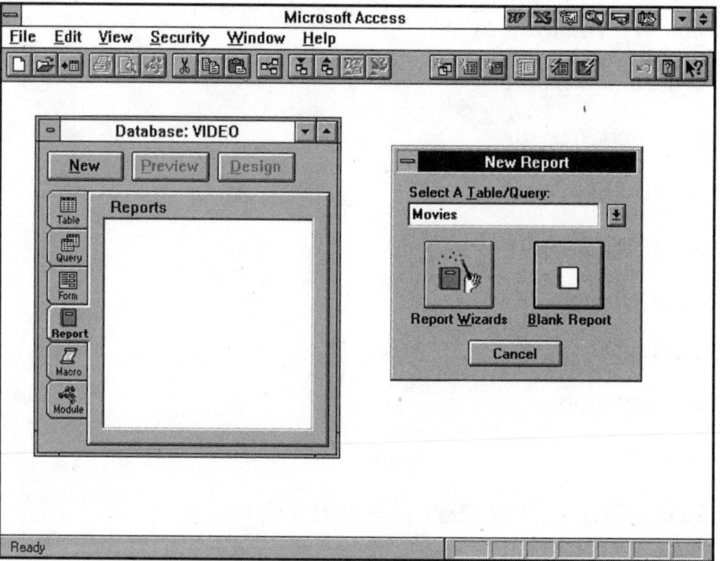

Fig. 32.1
Reports can be based on a table or on a query.

Next, Access provides two methods of creating a new report:

- Report **W**izards

- **B**lank Report

Use Report Wizards to create a report based on one of the predesigned wizard reports. Use the Blank Report to create a report from scratch.

Report Wizards

Report Wizards provide several types of predesigned reports (see fig. 32.2):

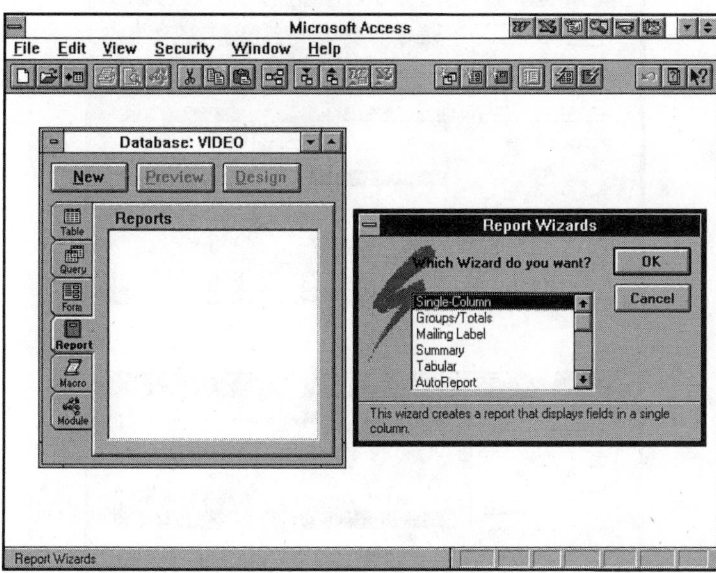

Fig. 32.2
The text at the bottom of the Report Wizards dialog box describes each type of Report Wizard.

- *Single Column.* Lists records vertically, one field per line, one record after another.
- *Groups/Totals.* Enables you to group records and to perform group and grand totals. Records appear in tabular format (horizontal).
- *Mailing Label.* Creates mailing-label reports in a variety of formats.
- *Summary.* Similar to the Group/Totals Wizard, except that the detail records are excluded.
- *Tabular.* Lists records horizontally, one record per row, with field labels as column headings.
- *AutoReport.* Creates a quick report for the selected table or query, using a single-column format.
- *MS Word Mail Merge.* Merges text in a Microsoft Word for Windows document with data from fields in a table or query.

When you select a Report Wizard, Access presents a series of dialog boxes that ask you for the report specifications. The dialog boxes differ for each type of Report Wizard. Figures 32.3 through 32.8 show the dialog boxes displayed for a Group/Totals Report Wizard.

Fig. 32.3
For a Groups/Totals report, the Report Wizard first prompts you for the fields to be included.

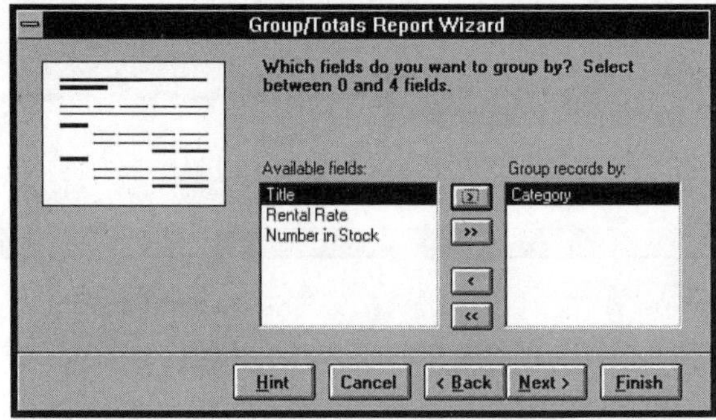

Fig. 32.4
The Groups/Totals Report Wizard prompts you for the fields by which to group.

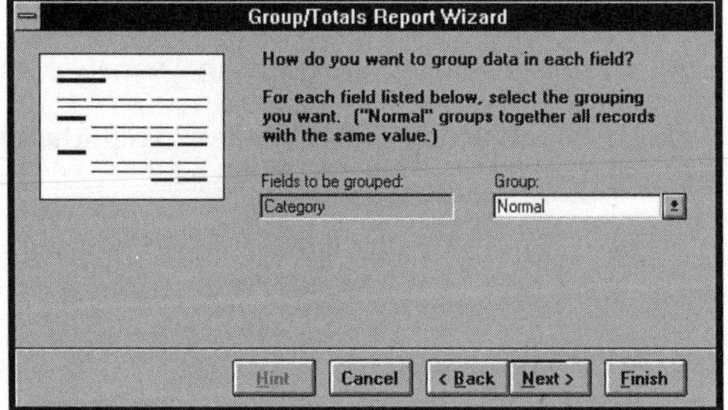

Fig. 32.5
The Groups/Totals Report Wizard asks how you want to group the data within the field.

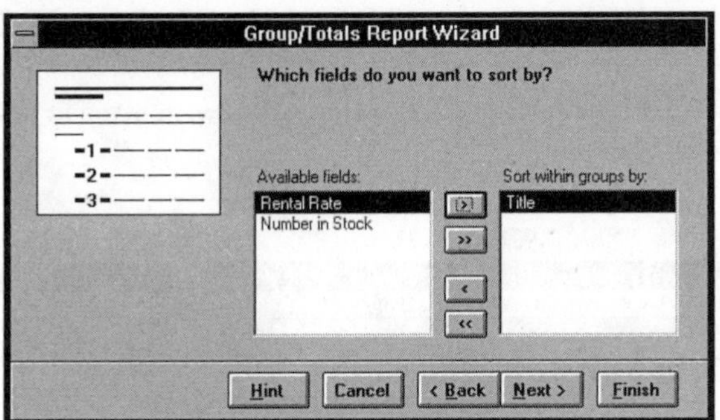

Fig. 32.6
The Groups/Totals Report Wizard asks you to select the field(s) by which to sort the group.

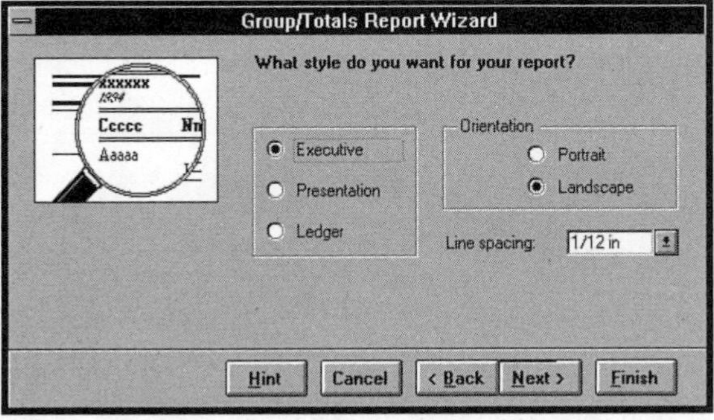

Fig. 32.7
The Groups/Totals Report Wizard asks you to select a report style and page layout.

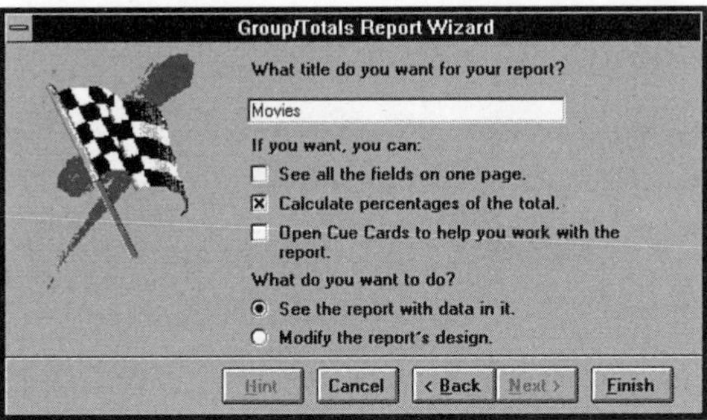

Fig. 32.8
In the last dialog box, the Report Wizard asks you to name the report and also provides additional options.

Print Preview

If you selected the See the Report with Data in It option in the last Report Wizard dialog box, Access displays the print preview view of the report (see fig. 32.9). Print preview shows on-screen how the printed report will look. The mouse pointer resembles a magnifying glass. Clicking the report zooms the view in. Click again to zoom out.

Tip
To control the number of columns and the space between columns, click Print Setup and then click the More button.

> **Note**
>
> You can access print preview from the Database window, from report design view, and from Report Wizards.

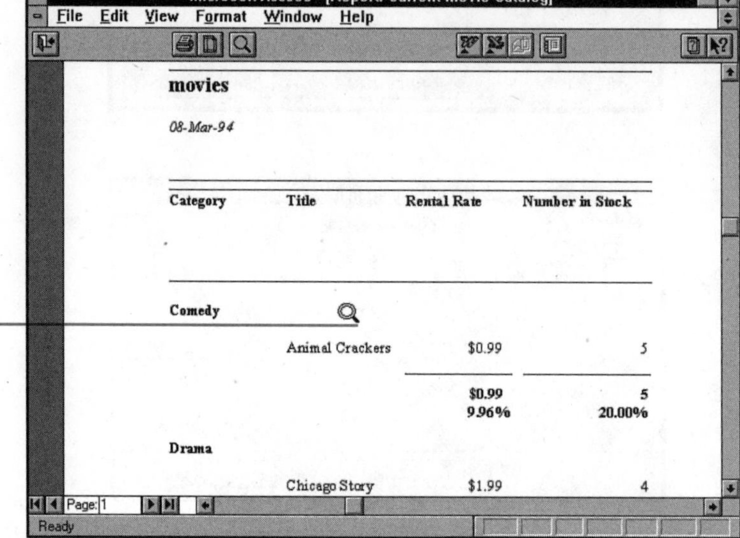

Fig. 32.9 To see the entire page, move the magnifying glass (the mouse pointer) to the page and click. Click again to zoom in on a specific part of the report.

The Print Preview toolbar contains the following buttons:

Table 32.1 Buttons in the Print Preview Toolbar

Button	Button Name	Description
	Close Window	Closes the Print Preview window
	Print	Prints the report
	Print Setup	Enables you to select printers and print settings
	Zoom	Toggles zoom in or out
	Publish It with MS Word	Outputs the report in Microsoft Word format and displays the Word file
	Analyze It with MS Excel	Outputs the report in Microsoft Excel format and displays the Excel file

Button	Button Name	Description
	Mail It	Outputs the report to Mail
	Database Window	Displays the Database window
	Cue Cards	Provides an on-screen tutorial
	Help	Provides context-sensitive help

Blank Report

At times, the generic Report Wizards may not provide the particular report format or layout that you need. In these cases, you can use a blank report to design a report that meets your needs. For example, you may need to create a report that matches a required document format in your business, such as a service contract, or you may need to create a report that includes special effects such as pictures of products.

To create a blank report, follow these steps:

1. Click the New Form button in the toolbar. The New Report dialog box appears.
2. In the Select A **T**able/Query list box, select the table or query for which you want to create a report.
3. Click the **B**lank Report button. Access displays a blank report in design view (see fig. 32.10).

A blank report contains three sections:

- *Page header.* Contains information, such as column headings, that appears at the top of each page in a report.
- *Detail section.* Contains the main body of the report. This area is where you display the data from tables and queries.
- *Page footer.* Contains information, such as page numbers, that appears at the bottom of each page in a report.

You can display the Toolbox window by default or by clicking the Toolbox button in the toolbar. The following section explains how to use the Toolbox to build your report.

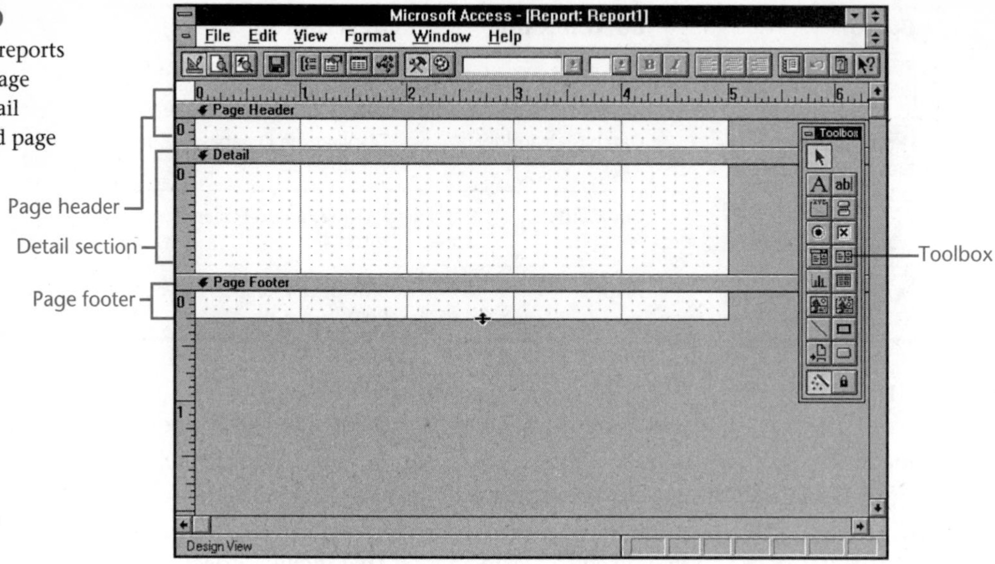

Fig. 32.10
New blank reports contain a page header, detail section, and page footer.

Troubleshooting

I can't create a main/subreport wizard.

You may not have defined the relationship between the two tables. Return to the Database window, and choose **E**dit **R**elationships. Add the appropriate tables to the window, and link the key fields.

The Report Wizard asked me to select a report style, and now I realize that I forgot to select a field to be included in this report.

Click the **B**ack button to move back to the field selection screen, where you can add the missing field to your report definition.

The new report I created for my invoice table contains no fields or data of any kind.

Perhaps you selected **B**lank Report instead of Report **W**izards. If this is the case, you can close the blank report without saving and return to the New Report dialog box to select Report **W**izards. If you meant to create a blank report design, you need to place the fields and build the report yourself, using the tools in design view. For further information on using design view, see "Navigating Report Design View" and "Modifying Report Designs" later in this chapter.

Navigating Report Design View

Report design view is where you can create and modify reports. The tools and features available in report design view are essentially the same tools and features as in form design view. Any new features (or features that work differently) are noted in this section.

◄ "Navigating Form Design View," p. 645

◄ "Modifying a Form's Design," p. 652

Report Sections

Following is an overview of the sections that can be used in a report design:

- *Report header.* Contains information, such as the report title, that appears at the top of the first page in a report.
- *Page header.* Contains information, such as column headings, that appears at the top of each page in a report.
- *Category header.* Contains information, such as a group title, that appears before each group of data.
- *Detail section.* Contains the body of the report. This area is where you display the data from tables and queries.
- *Category footer.* Contains information, such as group totals, that appears after each group of data.
- *Page footer.* Contains information, such as page numbers, that appears at the bottom of each page in a report.
- *Report footer.* Contains information, such as grand totals, that appears at the bottom of the last page in a report.

Although new blank forms contain only a detail section, new reports also have page header and footer sections defined. As with forms, you can add headers and footers to the report. To add a form or page header and footer to your report, choose F**o**rmat Report **H**eader/Footer or F**o**rmat **P**age Header/Footer. In addition, reports can contain two new sections: category headers and footers for groups of data (see fig. 32.11).

The Report Design Toolbar

The Report Design toolbar provides many buttons that speed your report-design work. Table 32.2 briefly describes each button.

Table 32.2 Report Design Toolbar

Button	Button Name	Description
	Design View	Displays report design view.
	Print Preview	Displays the report in print preview view.
	Sample Preview	Displays a quick preview of the report, with sample data.
	Save	Saves the report.
	Sorting and Grouping change	Enables you to add, delete or group levels.
	Properties	Displays the Properties window.
	Field List	Displays the fields linked to the report.
	Code	Displays the report's Module window.
 Toolbox	Toolbox	Contains the report design objects you can place in a report. These objects are called controls. You can move and resize the Toolbox like any window. Table 32.3 describes each item in the Toolbox.
	Palette	Opens the palette box.
 MS Sans Serif	Font Name	Displays current font and provides access to other available fonts in a drop-down list.
 8	Font Size	Displays current font size and provides access to other available font sizes in a drop-down list.

Button	Button Name	Description
	Bold	Boldfaces selection.
	Italic	Italicizes selection.
	Left-align Text	Aligns data to the left.
	Center-align Text	Centers data.
	Right-align Text	Aligns data to the right.
	Database Window	Displays the Database window.
	Undo	Undoes the last change.
	Cue Cards	Displays an on-screen tutorial.
	Help	Displays context-sensitive help.

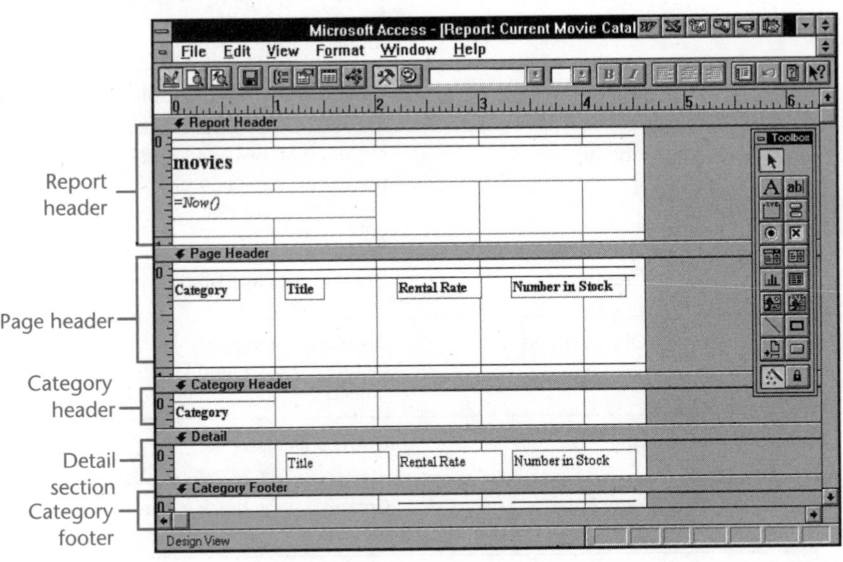

Fig. 32.11 The report header/footer and category header/footer sections can be added to a report design.

The Report Design Toolbox

The Report Design toolbox contains all the report design objects (such as fields, text, and boxes) that you can place in a report. Objects that you place in a report or a form are called *controls*.

The Toolbox is a window that you can move around and resize just like any other window. To display the toolbox, choose **V**iew **T**oolbox. By default, the Select Objects tool is selected. Use this tool to select the object in your report with which you want to work. Access displays moving and sizing handles around the selected object.

◀ "Selecting and Adjusting a Control," p. 654

◀ "Modifying a Form's Design," p. 652

To place a new control in the form, select the appropriate tool in the toolbox. The mouse pointer changes to a crosshair and displays the tool's icon. Move the crosshair to the desired location, and then click and drag the control to the desired size.

Table 32.3 briefly describes each item in the toolbox.

Table 32.3 Report Design Toolbox

Button	Button Name	Description
	Select Objects	Selects objects
	Label	Creates a text control
	Option Group	Creates a control for check boxes, option buttons, and toggle buttons
	Option Button	Creates a true/false control
	Combo Box	Creates a drop-down list of predefined choices, but also enables the user to enter new values
	Graph	Displays data as a graph
	Object Frame	Creates a frame to display pictures, graphs, and OLE objects
	Line	Draws a line
	Page Break	Creates a page break in the report
	Control Wizards	Turns control wizards on and off
	Text Box	Displays field data (label and text box)

Button	Button Name	Description
	Toggle Button	Creates an on/off button, which in the on position appears depressed
	Check Box	Creates a check box
	List Box	Creates a drop-down list of predefined choices, but unlike Combo Box, does not allow the user to enter new values
	Subform/ Subreport	Displays an embedded form or report
	Bound Object	Creates a frame that is bound Frame to an Access field
	Rectangle	Draws a rectangle
	Command Button	Creates a button that pushes in or pops out when selected; runs a macro or calls an Access function when depressed
	Tool Lock	Keeps the current tool selected until you select another tool

Each control tool in the toolbox serves a unique purpose. Following is a brief overview of the purpose of each tool:

- *Appearance*. Use the Label tool to type text in your report (such as a title). Use the Line tool to draw lines and the Rectangle tool to draw boxes to visually group items or draw attention to an item. The Page Break tool enables you to create multiple-page reports. You can use the Page Break tool to mark the start of a new page in a section—for example, before the grand totals in a report footer.

- *Data display*. The Text Box tool is used to display data (including pictures). Use the Option Group tool when you want to place option buttons, check boxes, or toggle buttons in the form. Placing an option group in the report displays the Option Group Wizard, which helps you define the option group and set the desired properties. (You also can place these items individually by using the Option Button, Check Box, and Toggle Button tools.) The List Box tool enables you to create a drop-down list of values for a field. The Combo Box tool combines the features of a text box and a list box.

► "Creating Graphs," p. 705

► "Creating a Graph with Form Wizards," p. 706

- *Graphing data.* The Graph tool launches the Graph Wizard and Microsoft Graph application, which help you create a graph object.

- *Embedding reports.* A common use of the Subform/Subreport tool is to show a one-record-to-many-records relationship between related tables—for example, to show the many movie rentals for one customer. When you want to embed a report in another report, use the Subform/Subreport tool in the main report. Before using this tool, you should create the subordinate report to be embedded. You can save time by letting Report Wizards create and embed the report for you.

► "OLE Terminology," p. 713

► "Working with Bound and Unbound Objects," p. 714

- *OLE.* The Object Frame and Bound Object Frame tools are used to display OLE objects. (*OLE* stands for object linking and embedding.) The Bound Object Frame tool displays pictures, graphs, and other OLE objects that are stored in an Access database. The Object Frame tool is used to display objects that are not stored in the underlying table.

► "Creating a Macro," p. 719

► "Programming Command Buttons," p. 727

► "Using the Command Button Wizard," p. 728

- *Automating tasks.* The Command Button tool creates a button object in the report. Command buttons are used to run a macro or call an Access Basic function when the button is pressed. For example, you could program a button in your report to print a section of the report or open another report.

When the Control Wizards tool is selected, Access launches any wizards that are available for the control you are creating. The Tool Lock tool keeps one tool active until you select another. This feature is handy when you are creating many controls of the same type, such as when you are placing several fields in the form.

The Report Design Palette

Use the Report Design palette to enhance the appearance of the form and its contents. You can customize the color of text, background, and border for each control you place in a report. To display the palette, choose **V**iew P**a**lette. Table 32.4 briefly describes each button in the palette.

◄ "The Form Design Palette," p. 651

Table 32.4 Report Design Palette

Button	Button Name	Description
	Normal Appearance	Gives the selected object a standard appearance
	Raised Appearance	Gives the selected object a raised appearance
	Sunken Appearance	Gives the selected object a sunken appearance
	Hairline Border Width	Sets the selected control's border to the narrowest width possible
	1-pt. Border Width	Sets the width of the selected control's border to 1 point
	2-pt. Border Width	Sets the width of the selected control's border to 2 points
	3-pt. Border Width	Sets the width of the selected control's border to 3 points
	Solid	Gives the selected control a solid-line border
	Dash	Gives the selected control a dashed-line border
	Dots	Gives the selected control a dotted-line border

To use the palette, select an object in the form, or select the form itself. You then can change the color of the foreground, background, or border. Use the buttons described in table 32.4 to add depth to the control (raised, sunken, or normal appearance), set the width of the border or the type of border line (solid, dashed, or dotted). As you click the various palette buttons, the appearance of the selected object changes to reflect your selections. This way, you can see the effect and decide on the appearance that you want to give the object.

◄ "Creating New Controls," p. 654

◄ "Selecting and Adjusting Controls," p. 654

◄ "Setting Control and Form Properties," p. 656

As you can see, the procedures for creating, placing, and defining controls in report design view are essentially the same as those in form design view.

Troubleshooting

I need to move a field and its description to the bottom of the report.

Click the text-box control. This action selects both the label box and the text box. Now you can use the move handles to drag both items to their new location.

After I moved fields around, several fields no longer were lined up on the left.

Hold down the Shift key, and click each field to be aligned. Then choose F**o**rmat **A**lign **L**eft. Access automatically aligns the selected fields under the leftmost object.

The list-box control does not allow me to enter new data.

A list-box control limits users to a drop-down list of predefined choices. You cannot enter new data in a list box. If you need to enter new data and have a drop-down list of options available, use a combo-box control.

Modifying a Report

Tip

A good practice is to date-and time-stamp reports as they are printed. Use a calculated control text box, and enter the expression **=Now()**.

Changing an existing report design, whether you created the design with Report Wizards or a blank report, is relatively easy. In most cases, you can click and drag to improve appearances or set properties.

Figure 32.12 shows a single-column report created with Report Wizards (in print preview view). Although adequate, the report's appearance can be improved. The awkward, extraneous text describing some of the fields could be modified (or eliminated, in some cases). The fields also could be rearranged to create a familiar mailing-label format. The palette buttons enable you to enhance the appearance of this report with color, depth, and borders. In fact, when space is freed in the report, you could enter additional text to transform this single-column report into a form letter.

In the next few sections, you learn how to enhance the appearance of this single-column report to produce the enhanced customer form letter shown in figure 32.13.

Selecting and Adjusting a Control

Before you can start modifying controls in your report and setting form properties, you need to know how to select a control and how to select the report itself. Figure 32.14 shows the Customers report, a single-column report created by Report Wizards, in design view. As you can see, Report Wizards created a label box and a text box for each field. You can select the text-box control (where the data is displayed) or the attached label box.

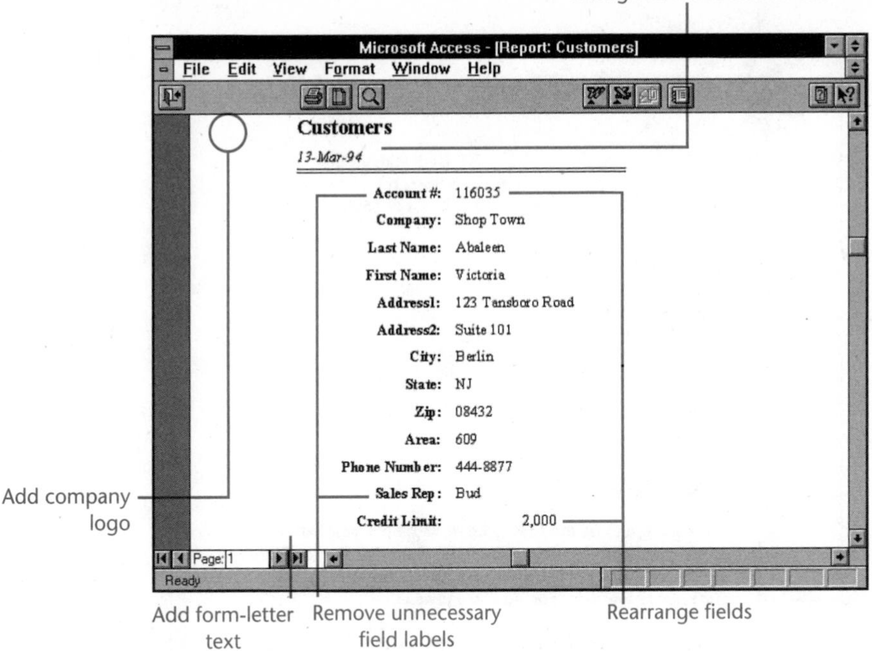

Fig. 32.12
You can enhance a single-column report created by Report Wizards by rearranging the fields, removing unnecessary field descriptions, and adding a company logo.

To select a control, click it. Access displays handles around the control to indicate that it is selected. The small black handles are the resizing handles. The large black handles at the top of the control are the move handles. Drag the resizing handles to change the size of a control. Drag the move handles to move the control to a new location.

To select more than one control, hold down the Shift key while you click each control. After you select all the controls you want to change, you can drag the controls to a new location or resize them as necessary.

To select the form, click the top left corner of the form (refer to fig. 32.14) or choose **E**dit, Select Fo**r**m.

Note

Working efficiently and effectively with the various controls takes practice. Create a practice report with Report Wizards, and try selecting, resizing, and moving the controls.

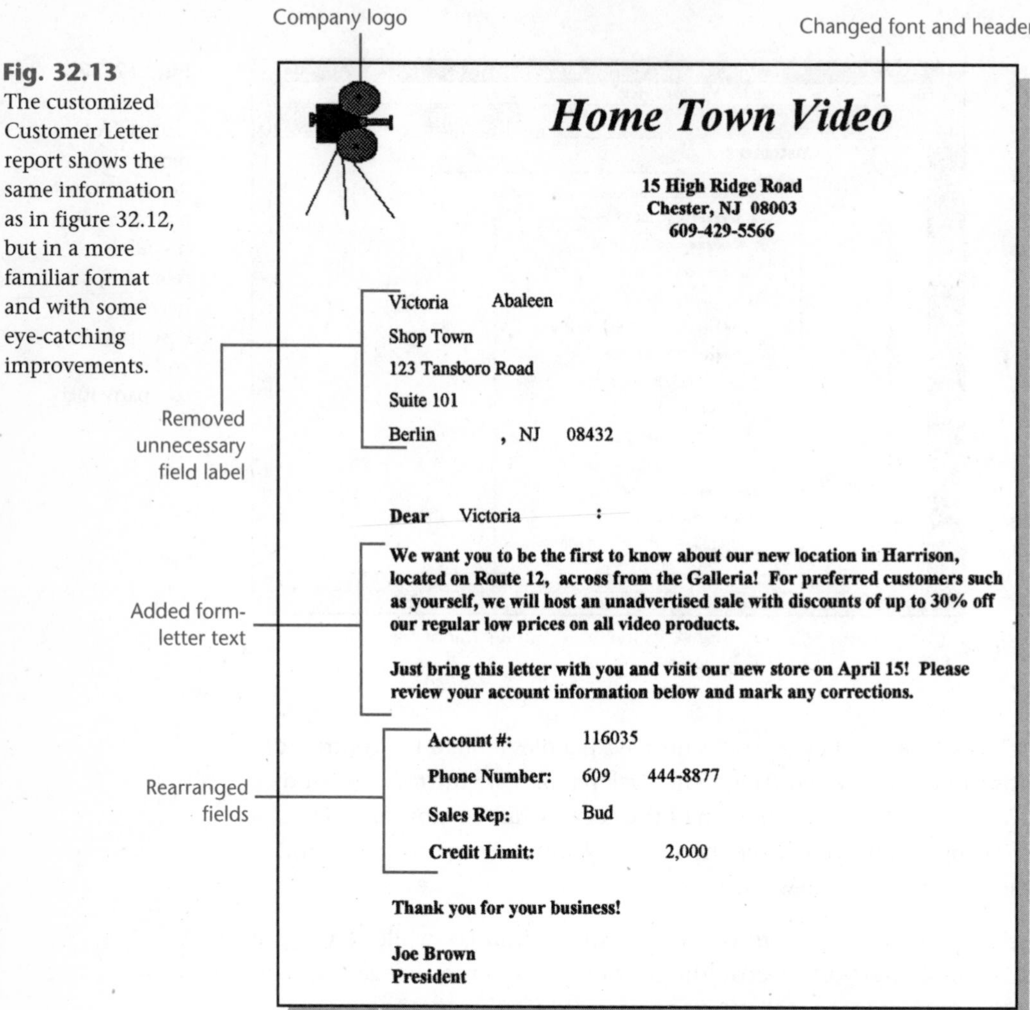

Home Town Video

15 High Ridge Road
Chester, NJ 08003
609-429-5566

Victoria Abaleen
Shop Town
123 Tansboro Road
Suite 101
Berlin , NJ 08432

Dear Victoria :

We want you to be the first to know about our new location in Harrison, located on Route 12, across from the Galleria! For preferred customers such as yourself, we will host an unadvertised sale with discounts of up to 30% off our regular low prices on all video products.

Just bring this letter with you and visit our new store on April 15! Please review your account information below and mark any corrections.

Account #:	116035
Phone Number:	609 444-8877
Sales Rep:	Bud
Credit Limit:	2,000

Thank you for your business!

Joe Brown
President

Fig. 32.13 The customized Customer Letter report shows the same information as in figure 32.12, but in a more familiar format and with some eye-catching improvements.

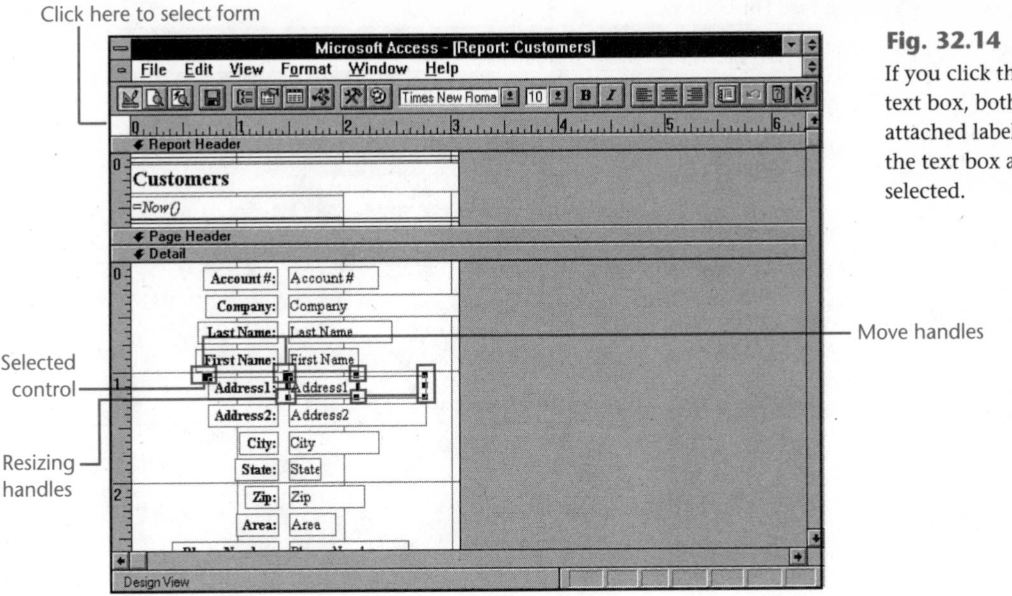

Fig. 32.14
If you click the text box, both the attached label and the text box are selected.

Creating New Controls

To create a new control in the report, select the desired tool in the toolbox, and place the control in the report. Controls can be classified in three basic categories:

- *Bound controls*, which are linked to a field in a table or query.
- *Unbound controls*, which are not linked to any field in a table or query.
- *Calculated controls*, which are unbound controls that use field data to perform calculations on-screen. The result of the calculation is not stored in any table or query.

To help you place bound controls, Access provides a Field List window (see fig. 32.15). To display the Field List, choose **V**iew Field **L**ist. Move the highlight bar to the desired field, drag the selected field name to the appropriate position in the report, and release the mouse button.

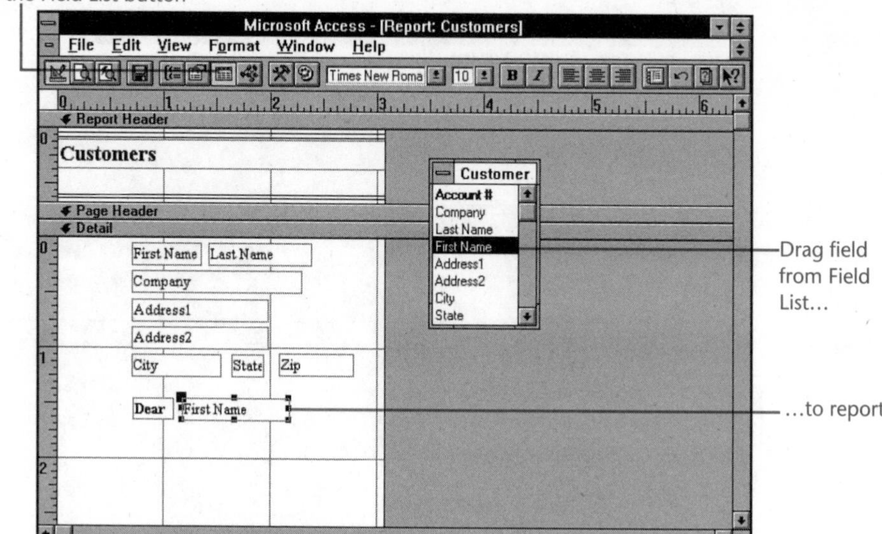

Fig. 32.15
You can place bound field controls in a report quickly by dragging the field name from the Field List to the report.

To add a control, follow these steps:

1. Display the Toolbox by choosing **V**iew **T**oolbox.
2. Click the desired control tool in the Form Design toolbox.
3. For unbound or calculated controls, position the mouse pointer in the form where you want to place the control. Then click to create a default-size control, or click and drag to create a custom-size control.
4. For bound controls, display the field list by choosing **V**iew Field **L**ist. Then click and drag the desired field name to the appropriate position in the form.

To create a calculated control, follow these steps:

1. Create the unbound control (one not linked to a field in the table) for the calculated field.
2. Type the expression in the control, or set the control's ControlSource property to the expression, as explained in the next section.

To delete a control, select it and then press Del. You also can cut, copy, and paste controls within the same form or across forms. To reverse unwanted changes, use the Undo feature.

Setting Control and Report Properties

Properties determine the appearance and behavior of an object. Every object in Access has properties. In report design view, you can view and change the properties of controls and of the report itself.

To display the properties sheet for a control, double-click the control. When the property sheet window is open, the contents of the window change as you select different controls in your report.

To display the report's properties, select the report by clicking the top left corner of the report or by choosing **E**dit Se**l**ect Report (see fig. 32.16). A single click in the top left corner selects the report object. If the property sheet is open, the report properties display in the property sheet window. Double-clicking the top left corner selects the report object and opens the property sheet window.

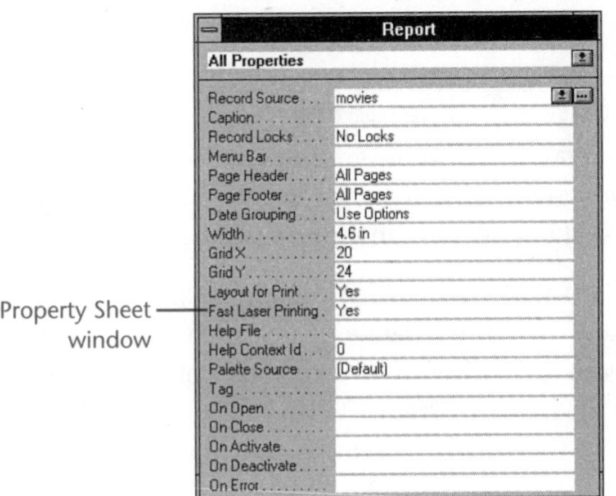

Fig. 32.16
The Record Source property tells Access the name of the underlying table or query for the report.

Many of the property settings are inherited from the underlying table or query. Some properties are set through the toolbox and palette; some other properties have no settings.

Setting Section Properties

Each section of a report has a set of properties that you can view and modify to enhance the appearance of your report. To display the property sheet for a section, open the property sheet window and click a report section. Figure 32.17 shows the properties of the detail section.

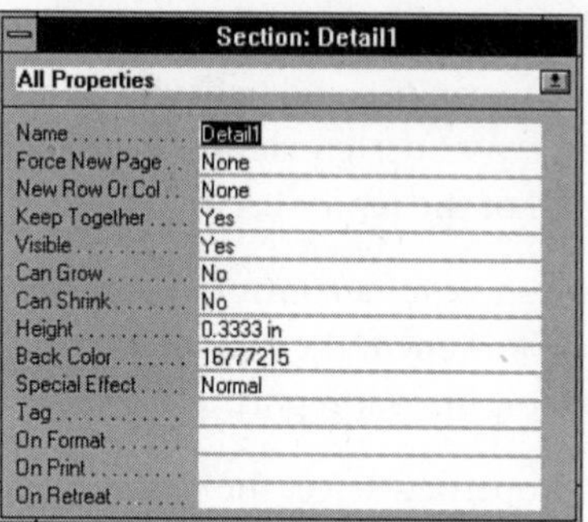

Fig. 32.17
To eliminate blank lines in the detail section, set the Can Shrink property to Yes.

Note

To prevent blank pages, make sure that the width of your report, including the margins, does not exceed the page width.

Sorting and Grouping in Reports

Access enables you to organize report records in a particular order or in specified groups. For a mailing-list report, for example, you can print the labels by ZIP code. For a marketing report, you can group customers by state or region.

The grouping feature is available only when you are designing reports (not forms). Grouping divides data into separate groups and sorts records within the groups based on your specifications. In a company phone-list report, for example, you can use the grouping feature to list employees by department. You also can alphabetize the list by department, and alphabetize the names of employees in each department.

You can group on multiple fields. For example, you could use the grouping feature to create a report that lists all employees' names and phone numbers by division, by department within the division, and by position within the department.

To add grouping to a report, choose **V**iew **S**orting and Grouping. The Sorting and Grouping dialog box appears (see fig. 32.18). In the top section, select the field on which you want to group, and select either ascending or descending sort order. In the bottom section, set the properties for the grouping (such as whether you want a header or footer and what value starts a new group). If you created a report with the Groups/Totals Report Wizard, the appropriate settings were entered for you.

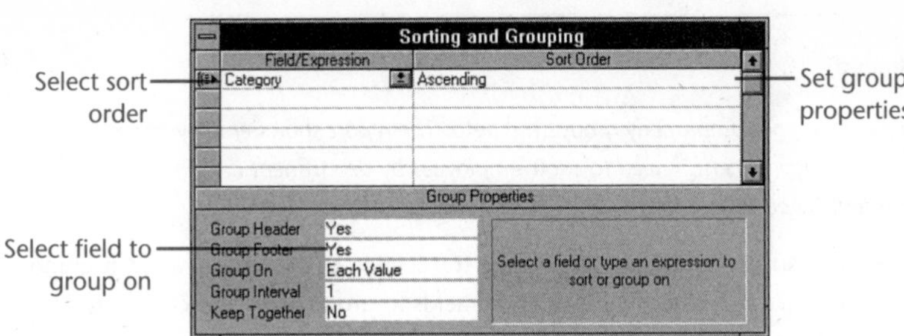

Fig. 32.18
Use the Sorting and Grouping dialog box to divide and sort records in your report into meaningful groups.

Using Subreports

A report within another report is called a *subreport*. You can use subreports to create a multitable report in which detailed subreports display records related to the main report's current record. You also can use subreports to combine two or more unrelated reports in an unbound main report.

To create a subreport, follow these steps:

1. Create the detailed report that you want to use as the subreport.
2. Display the main report in report design view.
3. Display the Database window.
4. Drag the detailed report object icon to the desired section in the main report.
5. If the subreport records are related to the main report, link them by setting the LinkChildFields property in the subreport's property sheet and LinkMasterFields property in the main report's property sheet.
6. Save the report design.

Troubleshooting

I need to add a paragraph of standard text to my report.

Use the Label tool to place a label-box control in the report, and then type your paragraph of text. Use the text-formatting buttons in the toolbar to align the text and select the appropriate font type and size. Use the palette buttons to add color, a border, or depth to your label box.

(continues)

(continued)

The grouping report improperly groups my data. The report shows employees by position and then by department. I need to show employees by department and then within department by position.

Choose **V**iew **S**orting and Grouping. In the top section of the Sorting and Grouping dialog box, make sure that the order of the fields to group by is correct. Access groups based on the order of fields you list in this section.

From Here...

Now that you are familiar with creating and customizing reports, you are ready to begin creating and using graphs, pictures, and OLE. To learn how to use graphs, pictures, and OLE, see the following chapters:

- Chapter 33, "Using Graphs, Pictures, and OLE," builds on what you have learned about designing forms and reports, and takes you through the process of adding graphs, pictures, and OLE to forms and reports.
- Chapter 40, "Linking and Embedding within Access To Manage Information," expands on the basics of OLE to provide a real-world scenario for using OLE.

Chapter 33

Using Graphs, Pictures, and OLE

by Diane Tinney

How does the saying go—"A picture is worth a thousand words"? In Access, graphs and pictures provide more than just visual impact for your database. Graphs show the relationships among data elements. Pictures enable you to file visual images, such as employee photos, in the database along with employee data records. Using a technology known as object linking and embedding (OLE), you can insert objects (such as pictures, graphs, and spreadsheets) created in other applications into your Access database. If you later make changes in the original object, OLE updates the linked object in your database.

In this chapter, you learn to

- Create a graph
- Modify a graph design
- Embed and link unbound objects
- Embed and link bound objects
- Modify OLE links

Creating Graphs

A graphical picture of data can show data relationships and trends that would be difficult to see in a report or datasheet view. You can use graphs to show growth trends and projected versus actual budget amounts, or you can plot sales geographically.

Like forms and reports, graphs are simply another way to view the data contained in a table or query. Often, you must use a query to place the needed data in the proper format to support the graph.

To create a graph in Access, you must use the Graph Wizard. You can start the Graph Wizard in several ways. If you are creating a new form, the easiest way is to use Form Wizards and select the Graph Wizard type. Access then launches the Graph Wizard.

◄ "Using Form Wizards," p. 640

◄ "Starting Form Wizards," p. 641

◄ "Navigating Form Design View," p. 645

◄ "Creating New Controls," p. 654

◄ "Modifying a Report," p. 696

◄ "Selecting and Adjusting a Control," p. 696

If you want to add a graph to an existing form or report, open the form or report in design view, and use the Graph tool (in the Toolbox) to position the graph object and launch Graph Wizard.

Creating a Graph with Form Wizards

The fastest way to create a graph in a form is to use a Form Wizard called Graph Wizard. The Graph Wizard asks you questions and creates a form that contains a single graph (see fig. 33.1).

To launch the Graph Wizard by using Form Wizards, follow these steps:

1. Choose the Form button in the Database window.
2. Choose the New button.
3. Select the table or query to use in the graph.
4. Choose the Form Wizards button.
5. Select the Graph Wizard type, and then choose OK. Access launches the Graph Wizard.

Note

The Graph Wizard functions the same whether you launch it from the Form Wizards or from the Graph tool, except for one item: relating a graph to existing fields in a form.

Because the Form Graph Wizard creates a new form that contains nothing but the graph, no fields exist in the form to relate to the graph. When you create a graph by using the Graph tool in an existing form, however, Graph Wizard asks whether you want to link the graph to related records in a form. If you want to link the graph, Graph Wizard asks you to identify the related field(s). See the following section for a detailed explanation.

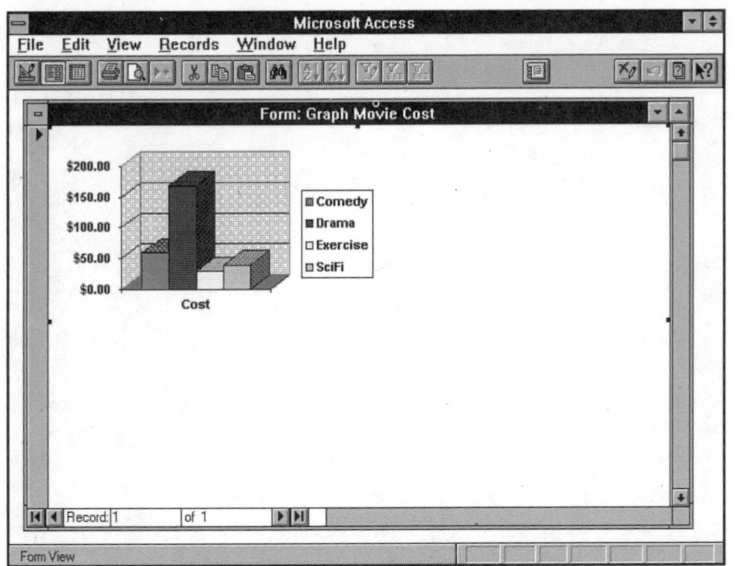

Fig. 33.1
The Graph Form Wizard creates a single graph in the form.

Creating a Graph with the Graph Tool

In both form design view and report design view, the Toolbox contains a Graph tool that you can use to place and size the graph in the form or report.

◄ "Navigating Form Design View," p. 645

◄ "Modifying a Report," p. 696

To create a graph in a form or report by using the Graph tool, follow these steps:

1. Open the existing form or report in design view, or create a new form or report.
2. Open the Toolbox, if it is not already open.
3. Click the Graph tool in the Toolbox. The insertion point changes to a graph icon.

4. Position the crosshair mouse pointer in the form or report, and click and drag the graph object to the desired size (see fig. 33.2). The Access Graph Wizard appears, requesting the table or query for the graph (see fig. 33.3).

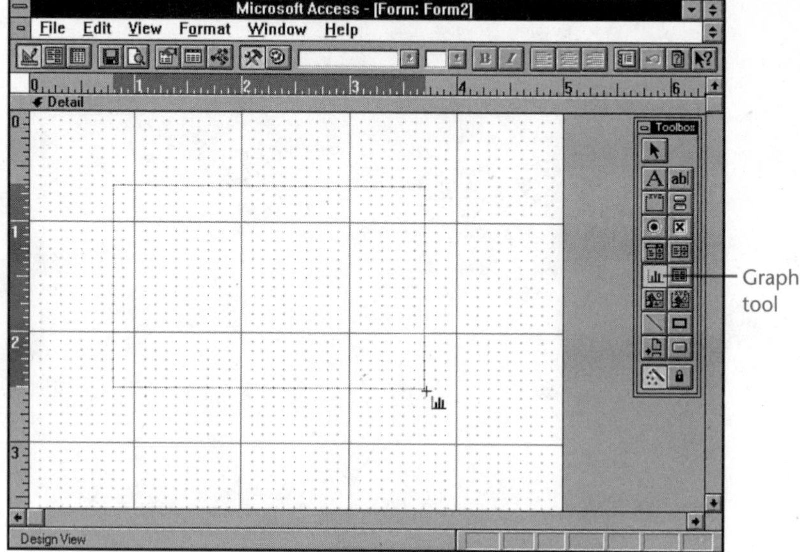

Fig. 33.2 Use the design view Graph tool to create a graph object in a form or report.

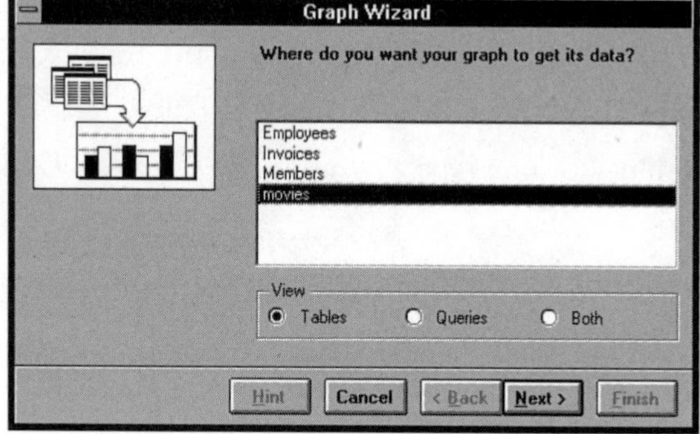

Fig. 33.3 Select the table and/or query on which the graph will be based.

5. Select the table or query (or both) on which to base the graph, and then choose **N**ext to continue.

6. The Access Graph Wizard prompts you for the fields to graph (see fig. 33.4). Choose **N**ext to continue.

7. The Access Graph Wizard asks you to select the categories for the graph's axis (see fig. 33.5). Choose **N**ext to continue.

8. The Access Graph Wizard prompts you for the fields for the graph's legend labels (see fig. 33.6). Choose **N**ext to continue.

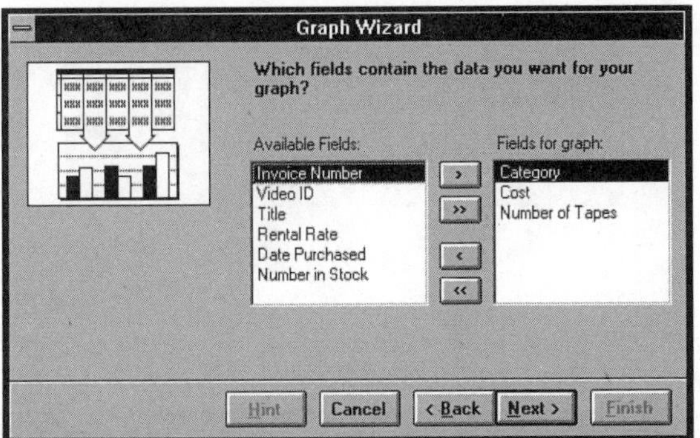

Fig. 33.4
The Graph Wizard prompts you for the fields to graph.

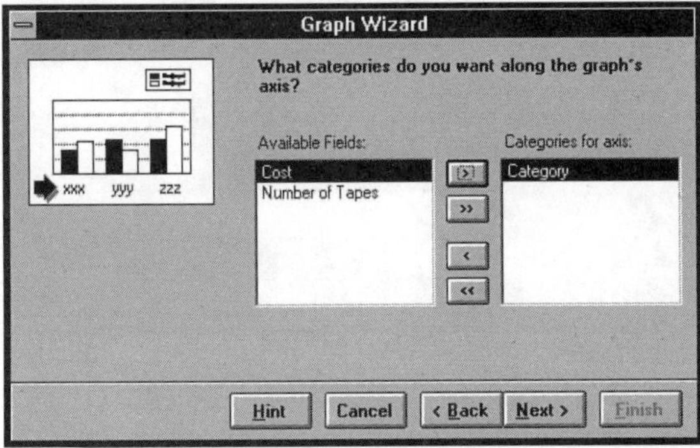

Fig. 33.5
The Graph Wizard prompts you for the graph's axis categories.

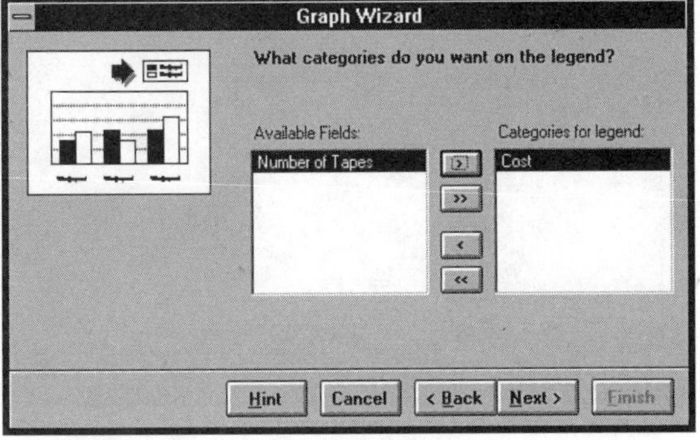

Fig. 33.6
The Graph Wizard prompts you for the legend labels.

9. The Graph Wizard asks whether you want to relate the graph to a field in the form or report (see fig. 33.7). If you choose **Y**es, the Graph Wizard prompts you to identify the fields to link (see fig. 33.8).

Fig. 33.7
When you use the Graph tool to create a graph, the Graph Wizard asks whether you want to link the graph to fields in the form or report.

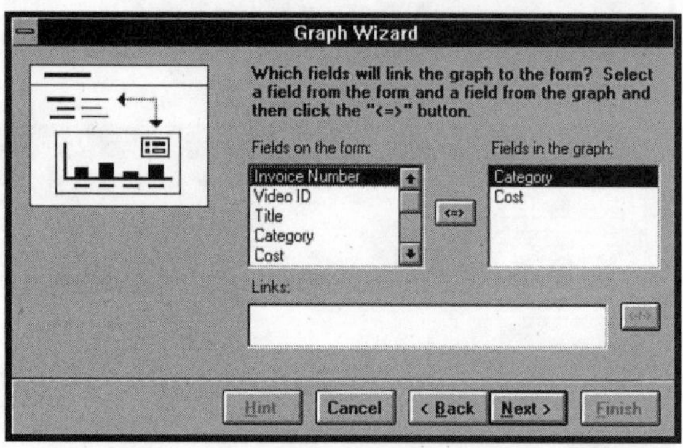

Fig. 33.8
If you decide to link the graph, the Graph Wizard asks you to identify the fields and define the link.

10. The Graph Wizard prompts you to select a graph type (see fig. 33.9).

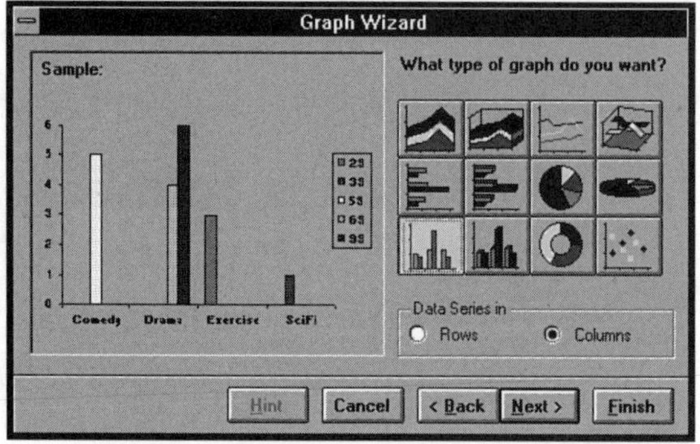

Fig. 33.9
The Graph Wizard shows you a sample of your graph, based on the graph type you selected.

11. The last Graph Wizard dialog box prompts you for a title and asks whether you want to display the legend (see fig. 33.10).

12. Choose the **F**inish button. Access displays the completed graph in design view (see fig. 33.11).

13. Save the form or report.

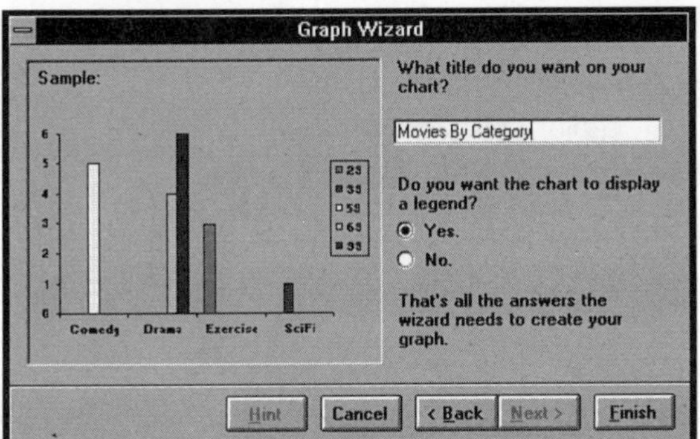

Fig. 33.10
The final Graph Wizard screen asks you to supply a title for your graph.

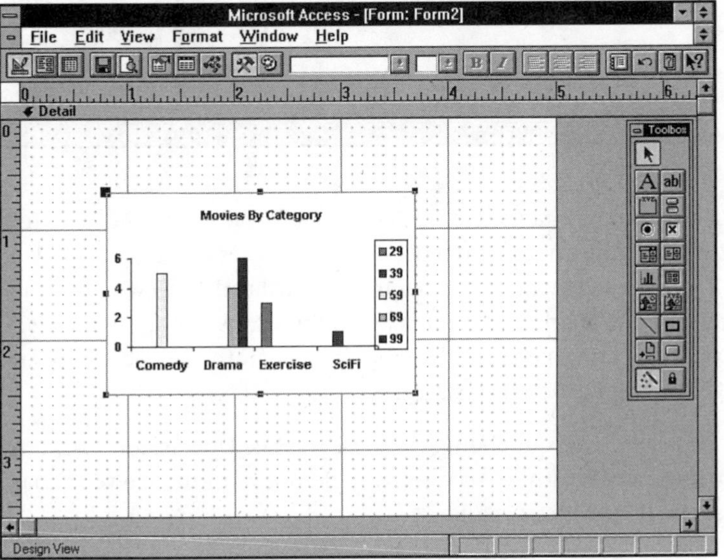

Fig. 33.11
The completed graph appears in design view.

Modifying a Graph

Access uses another Windows application—Microsoft Graph—to create and maintain graphs. Microsoft Graph comes with your copy of Access. The graph in your form or report actually is an OLE object that is linked to Microsoft Graph. When you use the Graph Wizard to create a graph, Access starts Microsoft Graph behind the scenes and presents the completed image in your form or report.

To edit a graph, open the form or report in design view. Then double-click anywhere in the graph to open Microsoft Graph (see fig. 33.12).

Fig. 33.12
Use Microsoft Graph to modify your graph.

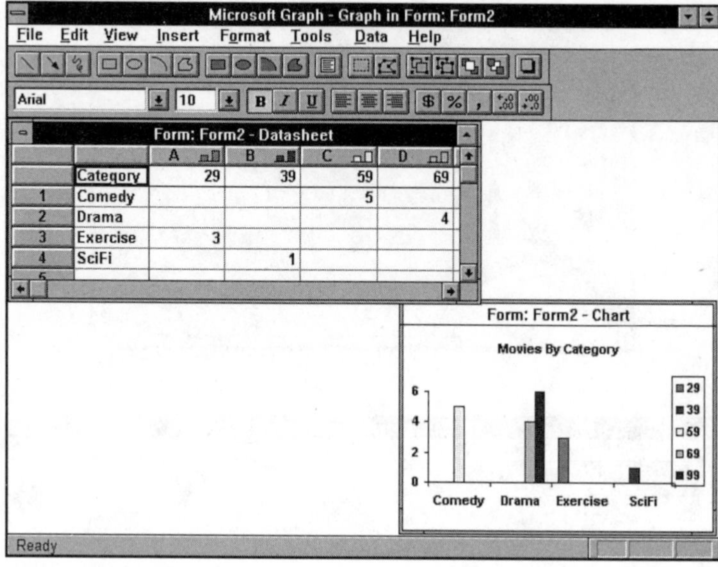

Microsoft Graph contains two windows: Chart and Datasheet (refer to fig. 33.12). The Chart window presents a graphic representation of the datasheet data. The Datasheet window presents a spreadsheetlike view of the data displayed in the chart. You can make modifications in both windows. For example, you can change the graph type, edit the legend labels, and change the graph title's font size.

Tip
Graphs change to reflect changes in the underlying table or query data. To capture a graph at a specific point in time, convert it to a picture (choose **E**dit Chart **O**bject **C**hange to Picture).

After you complete your changes, choose the **F**ile **U**pdate command to save the changes and return to Access. If you do not want to save your changes, choose the **F**ile E**x**it command.

Troubleshooting

I need to relate a graph of product sales to existing fields in the form. Should I use Form Wizards or the design view Graph tool to launch the Graph Wizard?

Use the design view Graph tool to launch the Graph Wizard, which enables you to link the graph to the existing fields in your form.

The legend labels in my graph need to be changed.

Open the graph in design view. Double-click the graph to launch Microsoft Graph. In the Datasheet window, you can edit the labels.

Embedding and Linking Objects

Access supports the Windows feature called OLE, which enables you to add pictures, graphs, charts, and other data created in another application to your current application. OLE adds the features of the other applications to the current application. Whereas the Windows Clipboard provides temporary storage and transfer capability, OLE provides an automated transfer with linkage to the source.

In Access, for example, you can add photos, graphs, or spreadsheet data to your tables, forms, and reports. The preceding section explained how to use OLE to modify a graph object. This section explores using bound and unbound objects to place other OLE objects in a form or report.

Understanding OLE Terminology

Before you use OLE, it is important to review some OLE terms:

- *Server (source) application.* The application used to create the object (such as Microsoft Graph or Paintbrush).
- *Client (user) application.* The application that receives an object from the server application (in this case, Access).
- *Embedding.* Embedded data is stored in the database file in the server application's format. Embedded data is not available for sharing with other applications.
- *Linking.* Linked data is stored in a server-application data file. Linked data is available for sharing with other applications.

One key difference between embedding an object and linking an object is access to that object from other applications. If your word processing, spreadsheet, and database programs need to access the company logo, for example, you can link the object. If only Access uses the object, however, embed it, thus storing the data in the database where it is used.

Another way to differentiate between embedding and linking is that an embedded object is a static copy of information from the source application, which is not updated. Linked objects, however, can be updated from either the server application or client application.

Working with Bound and Unbound Objects

To place an OLE object (such as a picture or chart) in a form or report, use the Object Frame or Bound Object Frame tools in the design view Toolbox. Use the Bound Object Frame tool when the object's value is stored in an Access table. Use the Object Frame tool when the object's value doesn't come from data stored in an Access table.

To embed or link an unbound object, follow these steps:

1. Open the form or report in design view.
2. Open the Toolbox, and click the Object Frame tool.
3. Click and drag the object frame to the desired size. Access displays the Insert Object dialog box (see fig. 33.13).

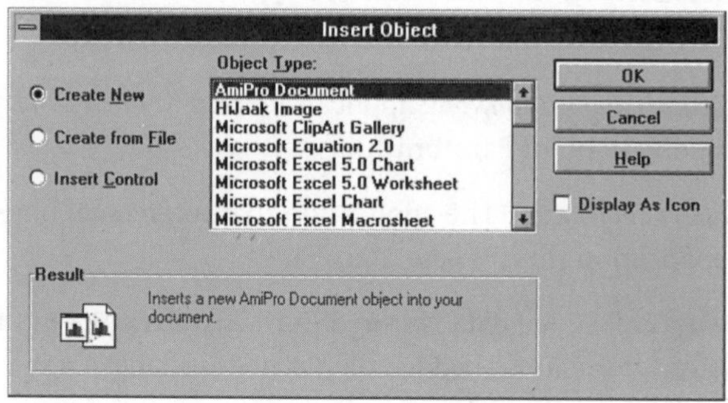

Fig. 33.13
The Insert Object dialog box enables you to insert a new OLE object, an existing OLE object, or an OLE custom control.

◀ "Creating New Controls," p. 654

◀ "The Form Design Toolbox," p. 648

◀ "Navigating Report Design View," p. 689

4. If you are creating a new object, select the desired object type and choose OK. If the object already exists, select Create from **F**ile, and enter the path and file name, or select Insert **C**ontrol to insert a custom control (see fig. 33.14).
5. Check the **L**ink box if you want to link, rather than embed, the object. Then choose OK. If you are creating an object, the source application opens on top of Access so that you can create the object.
6. Create the object, choose the **F**ile **E**xit command in the source application, and choose OK in any message boxes that appear. Access displays the object in the object frame (see fig. 33.15). Notice that the Property sheet window lists the OLE class and type of the embedded unbound object.

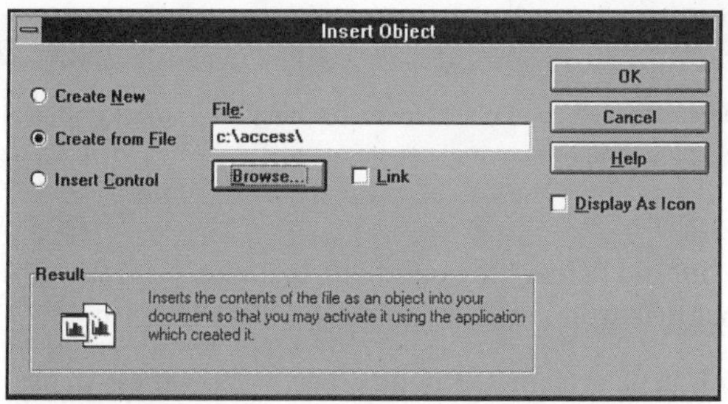

Fig. 33.14
To link or embed a saved file, select the Create from File option.

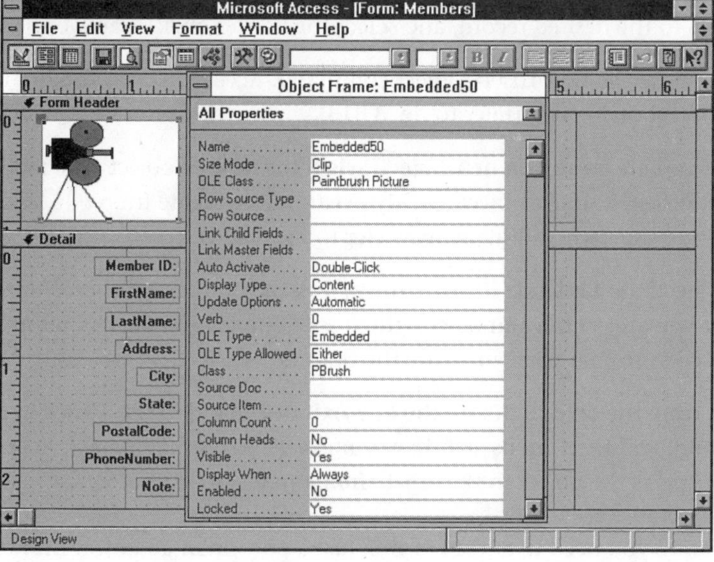

Fig. 33.15
After you create or load the object from a file, Access displays the object in the frame.

To create a bound object, follow these steps:

1. Make sure that the underlying table contains the necessary OLE data-type field(s).
2. Open the form or report in design view.
3. Click the Field List button or choose the View Field List command.
4. Drag the OLE field to the form or report.
5. Adjust the bound object frame as needed.

Note

You also can create the bound object frame by using the Toolbox and then defining the OLE field by setting the ControlSource property of the bound object frame.

After you create and define the bound object frame, you can embed or link objects in that field from form design view or datasheet view.

To embed or link objects into a bound object, follow these steps:

1. Open the desired datasheet or form.
2. Go to the desired record, and select the bound object frame or field cell.
3. Choose the **E**dit **I**nsert Object command. Access displays the Insert Object dialog box (refer to fig. 33.13).
4. If you are creating a new object, select the desired object type and choose OK. If the object already exists, select Create from **F**ile, and enter the path and file name (refer to fig. 33.14).
5. Check the **L**ink box if you want to link the object, and then choose OK. If you are creating an object, the source application opens on top of Access so that you can create the object.
6. Create the object, choose the **F**ile **E**xit command in the source application, and then choose OK in any message boxes that appear. Access displays the object in the object frame (refer to fig. 33.15).

Sometimes, you need to embed or link just a portion of an object—for example, a range in a spreadsheet. To embed or link part of an object, follow these steps:

1. Open the source application that contains the desired object, or create and save the source object.
2. Select the portion of the source object that you want to embed or link.

3. Choose the **E**dit **C**opy command.
4. Switch to Access (press Alt+Tab).
5. Open the bound (in form or datasheet view) or unbound (in design view) Access object into which you want to insert the embedded or linked object.

6. To embed, choose the **E**dit **P**aste command. To link, choose the **E**dit Paste **S**pecial command. Access displays the Paste Special dialog box (see fig. 33.16).

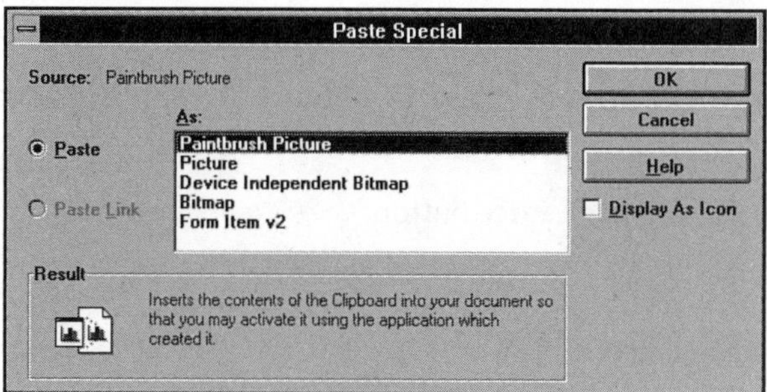

Fig. 33.16
The Paste Special dialog box enables you to link to a source application, based on the source object copied to the Clipboard.

7. Select Paste **L**ink, select a format option, and choose OK.

Modifying OLE Objects

After you create a link or embed an object, you may need to modify object property settings or break a link. Breaking a link severs the connection; consequently, automatic updates no longer occur.

To adjust the frame size, follow these steps:

1. In design view, adjust the object frame by moving the frame handles.
2. If the object still is off-center, open the property sheet for the object, and set the Size Mode property to Clip, Stretch, or Zoom, as needed.
3. To return the object to the original size, choose the Format Size To Fit command.

To break a link, follow these steps:

1. Select the bound object in form or datasheet view, or select an unbound object in design view.
2. Choose the **E**dit **L**inks command.
3. In the Links dialog box, select the link(s) you want to break.
4. Choose the Break Link button.
5. Close the dialog box.

To reconnect or change a link, follow these steps:

1. Select the bound object in form or datasheet view, or select an unbound object in design view.
2. Choose the **E**dit **L**inks command.
3. In the Links dialog box, select the link(s) you want to change or reconnect.
4. Choose the Change Source button.
5. Specify the name of the file to which you want to link.
6. Close the dialog box.

Troubleshooting

The OLE object that I placed in my form no longer appears.

Open the form in design view. Double-click the embedded object to view its property settings. Verify the link. Check to make sure that the path of the source-object file is correct.

I don't need to embed the entire file; I want to embed part of the file.

Copy that section of the file to the Clipboard. In Access, use the Paste Special command to embed the Clipboard contents and create the link.

The bound object frame will not allow me to link an object from Paintbrush.

Use the Bound Object Frame tool only when the object's value is stored in an Access table. Use the Unbound Object Frame tool when the object's value doesn't come from data stored in an Access table.

From Here...

Now that you are familiar with creating tables, forms, reports, and graphs, you are ready to automate your database tasks with macros. To learn how to create macros, see the following chapter:

- Chapter 34, "Using Macros," takes you through the process of creating and running macros to automate common database tasks.

Chapter 34

Using Macros

by Diane Tinney

Access helps you automate common database tasks by providing end-user programming with macros. A macro is an object just like any other Access object, such as tables, forms, and reports. You can use macros to simulate menu choices or perform repetitive tasks. Access macros are so powerful and versatile that you can even use them to create custom database applications, complete with menu bars and command buttons.

In this chapter, you learn to

- Create a macro
- Define macro actions
- Set action arguments
- Save and run a macro
- Debug a macro
- Specify macro conditions
- Program command buttons

Creating a Macro

A *macro* is a set of instructions that tells Access to perform tasks for you. The tasks that you want Access to perform are called *actions*. When you create a macro, you select the actions from a drop-down list. For each action, you can define *arguments*, which tell Access how to perform that action in your database.

Before you create a macro, give some consideration to the actions you want the macro to accomplish. Review how the task to be automated is currently being performed. Write down the tasks and the steps needed to accomplish each task. Then look for common steps and/or tasks. Often, you can use one macro to automate several similar tasks. For example, the steps for automating the task of finding an employee record might be very similar to the steps needed to find a customer record. A generic find routine that asks the user for the table name—or, better yet, extrapolates that information from the current table or form object—is useful and easy to maintain.

To create a macro, follow these steps:

1. Open the Database window.
2. Click the Macro button (see fig. 34.1).

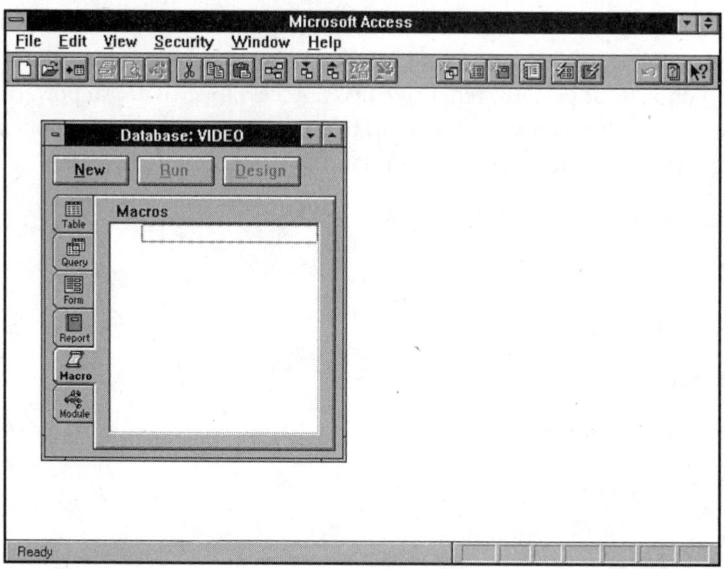

Fig. 34.1 A macro is an object like any other Access object, such as a table, a form, a query, or a report.

3. Click the **N**ew button. Access opens a new Macro window (see fig. 34.2).

The Macro window contains a specialized toolbar to assist you in your automation work. Table 34.1 describes the buttons in this toolbar.

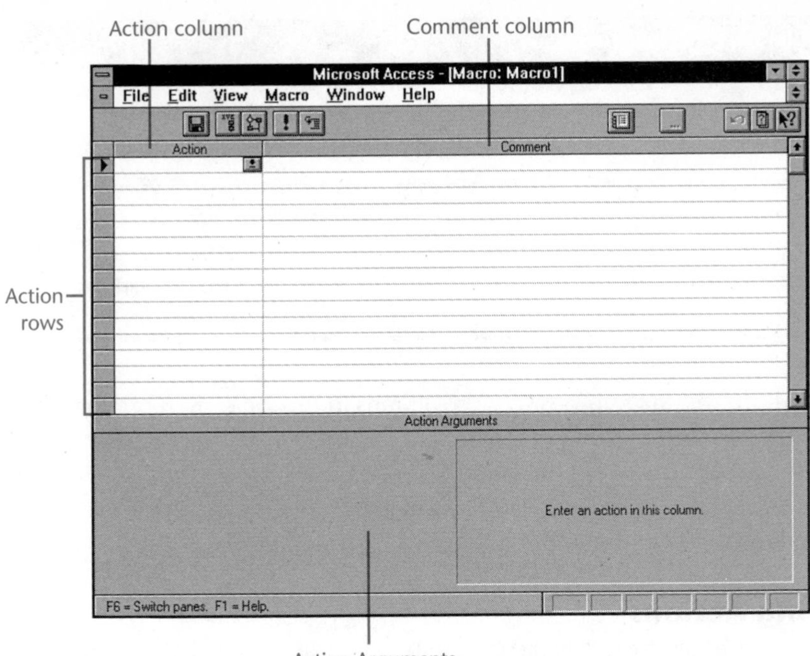

Fig. 34.2
List the actions that you want Access to perform in the Action column.

Table 34.1 The Macro Window Toolbar

Button	Button Name	Description
	Save	Saves the macro
	Macro Names	Shows or hides the Macro Name column
	Conditions	Shows or hides the Condition column
	Run	Executes the macro
	Single Step	Executes the macro one step at a time
	Database Window	Switches to the Database window
	Build	Starts the appropriate wizard or builder

(continues)

Table 34.1 Continued

Button	Button Name	Description
	Undo	Undoes most recent change
	Cue Cards	Displays on-screen tutorial
	Help	Provides context-sensitive help

Tip
To view the Macro and Database windows side by side, choose the **W**indow **T**ile command.

A new Macro window shows only two columns in the top section (Action and Comment) and nothing in the bottom section (Action Arguments). As you enter actions in the Action column, the Action Arguments section displays any available arguments that you can set. Use your mouse to move between the two sections, or press F6 to switch panes.

Adding Actions

You can add actions to your macro definition by selecting an action from the drop-down list, by typing the action directly in the Action cell, or by dragging an object from the Database window into an Action cell. Dragging a Database object has the added advantage of automatically setting some Action Arguments (see fig. 34.3).

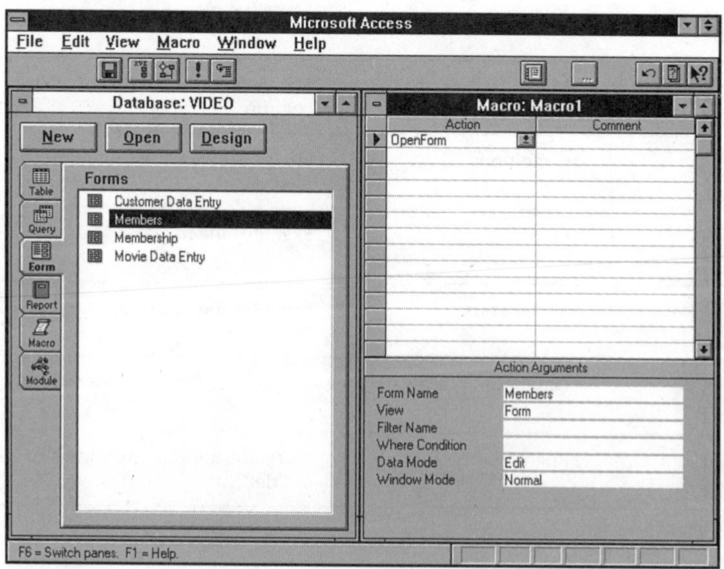

Fig. 34.3
Dragging a form object to an Action cell automatically enters the Action as OpenForm and completes the applicable Action Arguments.

Note

Notice that macros execute line by line. Macros perform actions from top to bottom, one at a time, until complete.

You can move, delete, insert, and copy action rows just as you can Datasheet rows. To move a row, for example, select the row and drag it to its new location.

Tip
Use the first Comment cell to describe what the macro does and to which object the macro is attached.

For each Action, you can enter comments that describe what the macro is doing. Using comments extensively to document your work is considered to be good practice. Comments help you and others understand what the macro does; they also make maintenance easier.

Setting Action Arguments

Tip
To see a list of macro actions and their arguments, open the Help application and search for the topic "Actions Reference."

Most actions have their own set of Action Arguments. Arguments provide additional information to Access on how to perform the action. A GoToControl action, for example, has an argument called *Control Name* that tells Access which control to go to. Notice, in figure 34.4, that the text box in the bottom right corner explains what you need to do as you move around in the Macro window.

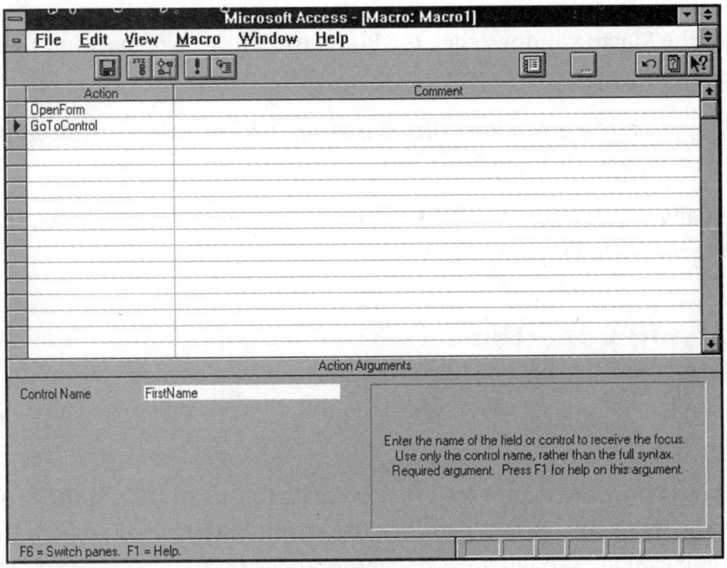

Fig. 34.4
The text box in the bottom right corner explains what you need to do in the current cell.

To add actions and set action arguments, follow these steps:

1. In the Action column of the Macro window, select an action from the drop-down action list, type the name of the action, or drag an object from the Database window to an action cell.

2. Enter a comment, if needed, in the Comment column to describe what the action does.

3. Press F6 or use the mouse to switch to the Action Arguments pane.

4. Complete the required Action Arguments.

5. Repeat steps 1–4 for each step in your macro.

6. Save the macro by choosing the **F**ile **S**ave command.

Note

Macro names follow the same naming conventions as other Access objects, such as tables, forms, queries, and reports.

Running Macros

You can execute a macro in several ways:

- In the Macro window, click the Run button in the toolbar, and then select the macro to execute.

- In the Database window, click the Macro button, select the macro to execute, and click the Run button.

- In any window, choose the **F**ile R**u**n Macro command, and then select the macro to execute.

Specifying Conditions

Macro conditions enable you to control how a macro executes at run time. For example, you can specify a macro to print a record only when all data is entered.

Conditions consist of expressions that evaluate to true or false. If the expression evaluates to true, Access performs the action in that action row. If the expression evaluates to false, Access ignores the action.

Macro conditions are entered in a special column called the Condition column. To display the Condition column, choose the **V**iew **C**onditions command. Access displays the message box shown in figure 34.5 if the user forgot to enter an invoice number. To accomplish this, you need to display the Condition column and enter a conditional expression.

Condition column

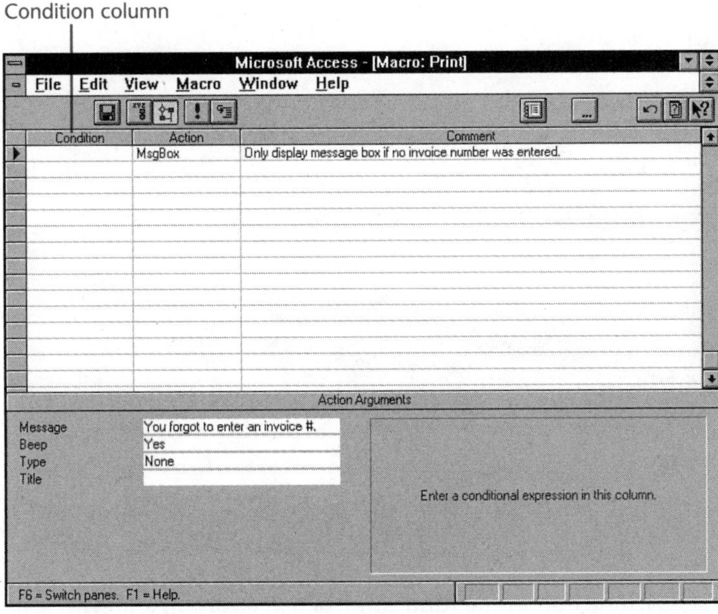

Fig. 34.5
Click the Condition button in the toolbar to display the Condition column.

Conditional expressions follow the same rules as expressions that you write for validity checks, query criteria, and calculated fields. If you need assistance in writing an expression, use the Expression Builder, or search the Help system for the topic "Expressions."

Tip
To get help with writing expressions, use the Expression Builder (click the Build button in the toolbar).

In the example shown in figure 34.6, the expression `[Invoice Number] Is Null` instructs Access to perform the MsgBox action only if the Invoice Number field is blank. If the Invoice Number field contains data, the MsgBox action will not be performed.

If you need to perform several actions when a condition is met, rather than type the condition in each row, you can type three periods (called an ellipsis) in the Condition column of each consecutive row. Access applies the condition until it reaches a blank condition, a macro name, or another condition.

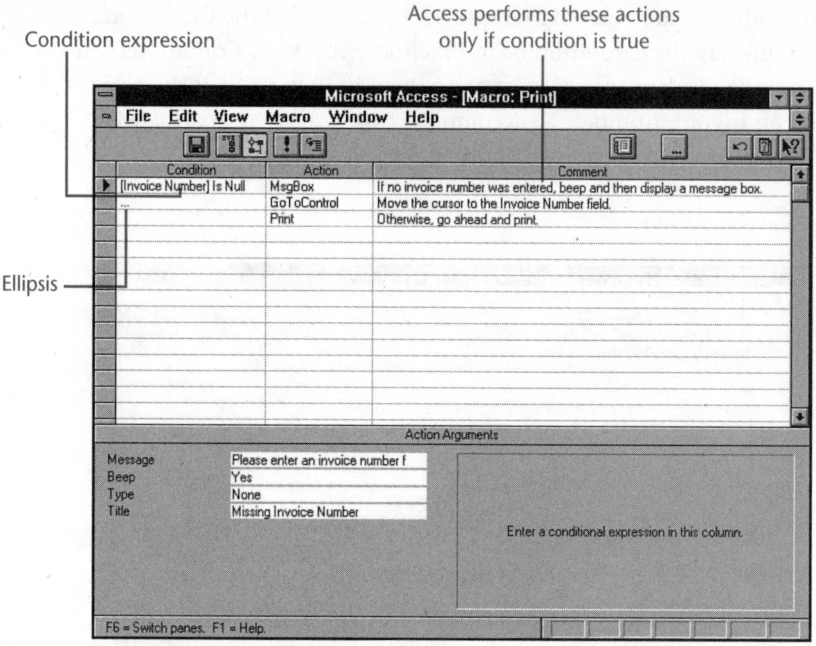

Condition expression

Access performs these actions only if condition is true

Microsoft Access - [Macro: Print]

File Edit View Macro Window Help

Condition	Action	Comment
[Invoice Number] Is Null	MsgBox	If no invoice number was entered, beep and then display a message box.
...	GoToControl	Move the cursor to the Invoice Number field.
	Print	Otherwise, go ahead and print.

Ellipsis

Action Arguments

Message	Please enter an invoice number f
Beep	Yes
Type	None
Title	Missing Invoice Number

Enter a conditional expression in this column.

F6 = Switch panes. F1 = Help.

Fig. 34.6
Conditions enable you to control when and whether macro actions are performed.

In figure 34.6, the ellipsis is used in the second row to tell Access to move to the Invoice Number field only when the Invoice Number field is blank. If the Invoice Number field contains data, Access will not perform the GoToControl action. The Print action in the third row has no condition and will be performed in either case. If you want to block printing until the user enters an Invoice Number, you could enter an ellipsis in the Condition column of the Print action row.

Note

When working with objects such as forms and fields in expressions, you must use the identifier operators. Identifiers begin with the object type, followed by an exclamation point (!) and the name of the object—for example, Forms!Members![Last Name] or Screen.ActiveForm. For more information on identifiers, search for help on "Identifiers in Expressions."

If you do not use the identifier, Access assumes that you are referring to the current object.

Object names that contain spaces must be enclosed in brackets ([ ]).

To enter a condition, follow these steps:

1. In the Macro window, choose the **V**iew **C**onditions command. Access displays the Condition column to the left of the Action column.

2. Enter the conditional expression.

3. To continue the condition in the next action row, type three periods (...) in the next condition cell.

4. Repeat step 3 as needed to complete the condition task.

5. Save and test the macro.

Troubleshooting

During my macro, I need to move to a specific page number.

Use the macro action GoToPage, and provide the Action Argument for the page number.

If a condition test fails, I want to abort the macro processing.

Use the macro action StopMacro to stop the currently running macro.

I need to automate the process of importing data from the mainframe.

Use the macro action TransferDatabase. Set the Action Argument Transfer Type to Import. Select the appropriate database type, and enter the database name. Select the object type Table, and enter the source and destination names.

The Print action in my macro prints all records, not just the current record.

Use DoMenuItem, and set the Action Arguments as follows: Menu Bar: Form, Menu Name: Edit, and Command: Select Record. Then, in the Print action, set the range argument to Selection. This argument tells Access to print only the selected record.

Programming Command Buttons

A command button is an easy-to-use, easy-to-maintain vehicle for automating database tasks. You can program command buttons in two ways:

- Using the Command Button Wizard
- Attaching a macro to the button's OnClick property

Using the Command Button Wizard

Like other wizards, the Command Button Wizard provides predesigned command buttons that you can customize to meet your needs.

The Command Button Wizard provides the following types of buttons:

- *Record Navigation.* Go to a record, create a new record, or find a record.
- *Record Operations.* Save, undo, delete, print, or duplicate the current record.
- *Form Operations.* Open, close, print, filter, edit filter, and refresh forms.
- *Report Operations.* Print reports, preview reports, send reports to a file, or mail reports.
- *Application.* Run or quit applications.
- *Miscellaneous.* Print tables, run queries, run macros, or dial the phone.

Note

Buttons created with the Command Button Wizard usually execute Access Basic functions. If you are interested in learning more about Access Basic, refer to Que's *Using Access 2 for Windows,* Special Edition.

◄ "Navigating Form Design View," p. 645

◄ "Navigating Report Design View," p. 689

To create a button in a form or report, follow these steps:

1. Open the form or report in design view.
2. Display the Toolbox.
3. Select Control Wizards if you want the Command Button Wizard to help you program your button.

4. Click the Command Button tool to select it. The mouse pointer changes to a crosshair with a button icon below it.
5. Position the crosshair in the form or report where you want to add the button.
6. Click and drag the button to the desired shape and size. Access launches the Command Button Wizard (if Control Wizards is selected in the Toolbox).

To program the button using the Command Button Wizard, follow these steps:

1. Select a button action from a list of categories (see fig. 34.7).
2. Select the desired category. Notice that the button-action list changes to reflect the actions available for the selected category.

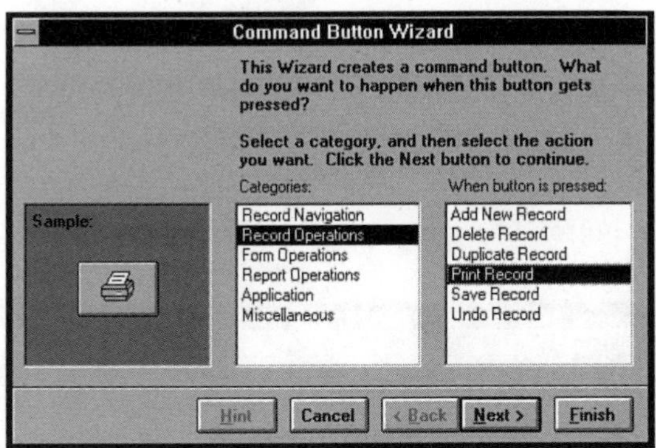

Fig. 34.7
Use the Command Button Wizard to automate common database tasks.

3. Select the desired button action. Notice that the button icon changes to reflect the selected action.
4. Choose the **N**ext button to continue. The Command Button Wizard asks you to specify the text label or picture to be used on the button (see fig. 33.8).
5. Select Text or Picture.

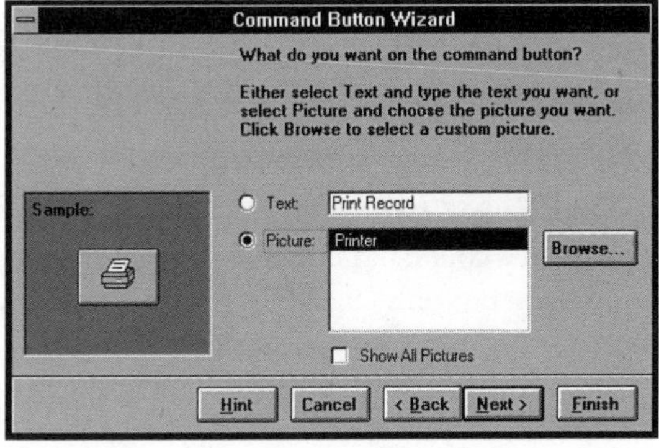

Fig. 34.8
The Command Button Wizard places an appropriate picture on your button.

6. If you selected Text, edit the default label text, or enter your own text label in the text box.

If you selected Picture, select the desired picture from the list, or click the Browse button to select a custom picture.

7. Choose the **N**ext button to continue.

8. The last Command Button Wizard dialog box provides a generic name for the button object and prompts you to supply a more meaningful name.

9. If you want to use Cue Cards to further customize your button, check the Open Cue Cards box.

10. Choose the **F**inish button to create the button. Figure 33.9 shows the completed button in form view.

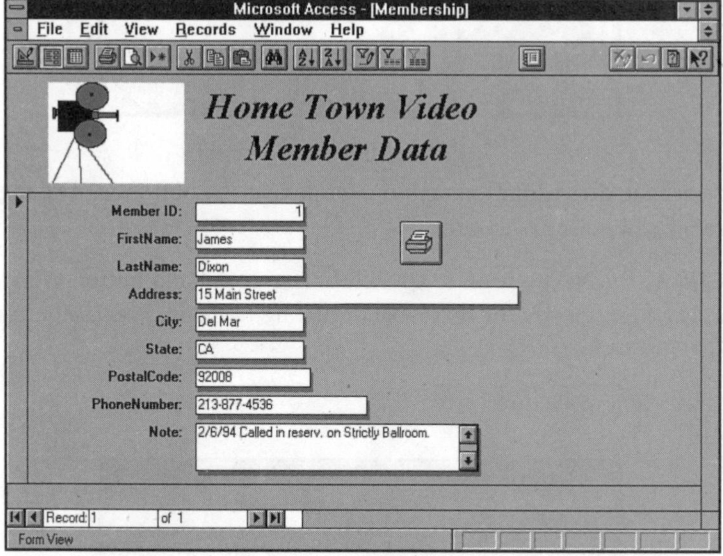

Fig. 34.9
The completed Print button, created with the Command Button Wizard, gives a polished look to your database form or report.

Setting the OnClick Command Button Property

Another way to program a command button is to create a custom macro and attach it to the command button's OnClick property. To set the OnClick property of a command button, follow these steps:

1. Create and save the macro.

2. Open the form or report in design view.

3. Display the Toolbox.

4. Deselect Control Wizards in the Toolbox so that the Command Button Wizard will not launch.

5. Click the Command Button tool to select it. The mouse pointer changes to a crosshair with a button icon below it.

6. Position the crosshair in the form or report where you want to add the button.

7. Click and drag the button to the desired shape and size.

8. With the button selected, display the Property sheet.

9. Select Event Properties from the Property Set drop-down list (see fig. 34.10).

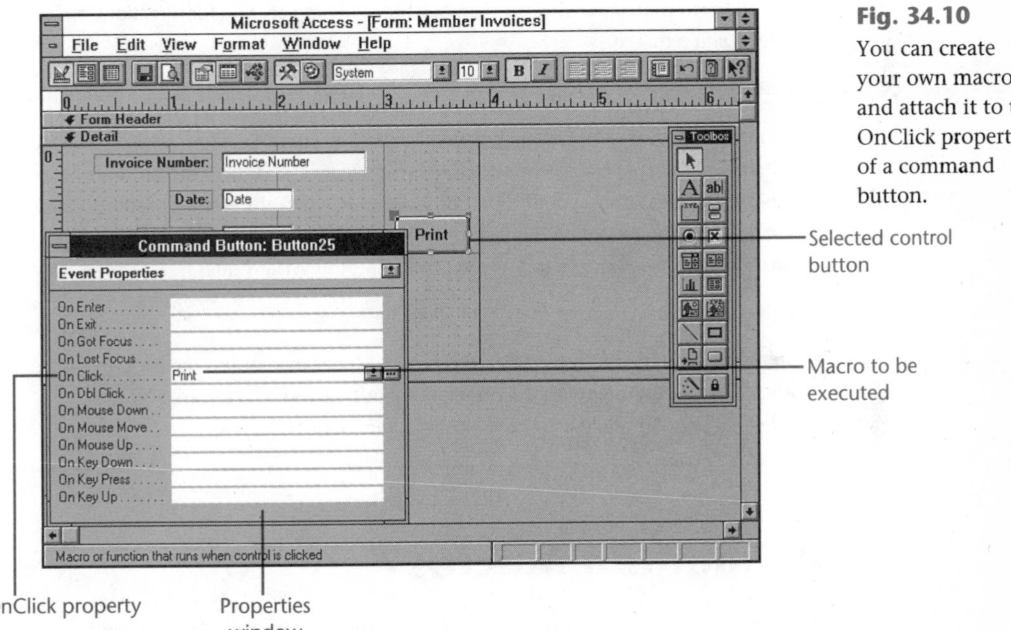

Fig. 34.10 You can create your own macro and attach it to the OnClick property of a command button.

10. Click the OnClick property.

11. Enter the name of the macro, or select the name from the drop-down list. Alternatively, you can use the Build button to launch the Macro Builder, Expression Builder, or Code Builder.

12. Save the form or report, and test your button.

Note

You can attach macros to many types of form and report events. For example, you can create a macro that performs a high-level data validation and attach it to the BeforeUpdate property. This macro enables you to validate data every time you update a record.

Troubleshooting

The command button I created does nothing.

Return to design view, and display the button's property sheet. Check the value of the OnClick property. If the property value is blank, that is the problem. Otherwise, the attached macro may have a bug. See the following section for directions on debugging a macro.

I need to change the picture on the button I created with the Control Button Wizard.

You could re-create the control button and use the Control Button Wizard to select a different picture. Alternatively, switch to design view and display the button's property sheet. Select the Layout Properties section, and click the Picture property. Click the Build button to launch the Picture Builder, which lists all available pictures and provides a Browse button, just as the Control Button Wizard does.

I need to program a button to dial the phone for me.

Select the Command Button Wizard category Miscellaneous and the action AutoDialer. AutoDialer dials the phone number that you select from a control. (The feature works only with Hayes-compatible modems.)

Debugging Macros

If a macro does not work as you expect it to, use the Single Step tool to debug the macro. Single step executes the macro one step at a time. This method enables you to identify which action caused the problem. At any time, you can click any of the following buttons in the Macro Single Step dialog box:

- ***Step***. Runs the action shown in the Macro Single Step dialog box.
- ***Halt***. Stops macro execution.
- ***Continue***. Executes the remaining steps in the macro without pausing (ends single-step mode).

To single-step through a macro, follow these steps:

1. Open the macro in design view.

2. Choose the **M**acro **S**ingle Step command to turn on single-step mode.

3. Run the macro as you normally do. Access displays the Macro Single Step dialog box (see fig. 34.11).

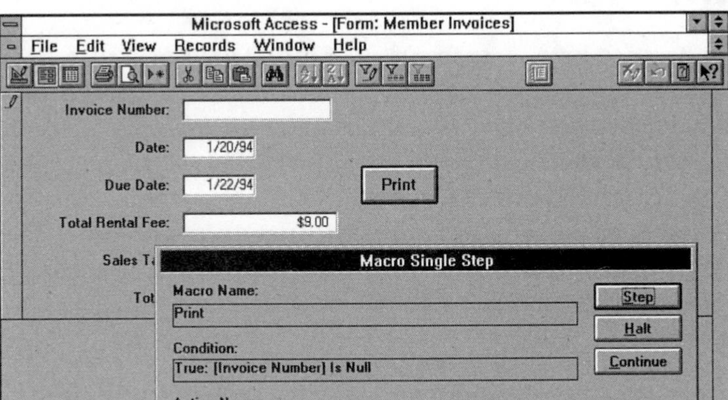

Fig. 34.11 The Macro Single Step dialog box displays each action row in a macro before it executes.

4. Choose **S**tep to run the first action.

5. Choose **S**tep, **H**alt, or **C**ontinue as needed.

Try using the single-step feature to step through the actions of the custom Print button shown in figure 34.10. (The Print button runs the Print macro shown in figure 34.6.) Follow these steps:

1. Open the Print Macro window.

2. Click the Single Step button in the toolbar to turn on single-step mode.

3. Save the macro.

4. Open the Invoice form, and click the Print button. The Macro Single Step dialog box appears, listing the currently executing macro name, condition, action and arguments.

5. Choose the **S**tep button to step through the macro.

To see how single-step mode works when the macro contains a bug, return to the Print Macro window, change the field name from Invoice Number to Invoice #, and save the macro. Return to the Invoice form, and click the Print button. Access informs you that it cannot find the Invoice # field. Choose OK to end macro execution.

From Here...

The best way to learn more about Access is to start using it to manage a simple database, such as your personal or business contacts. Use the Help application, Wizards, Builders, and Cue Cards for assistance. Using these applications in conjunction with Access invariably will teach you something new. Due to space constraints in a book of this type, which covers several applications, many features of Access were not discussed. For a deeper discussion of interactive Access, read Que's *Using Access 2,* Special Edition. For more information on programming Access, see Que's *Access Programming By Example.*

Now that you are familiar with working with Access, you are ready to begin using Microsoft Office applications together. To learn more about using Access with the other Microsoft Office applications, refer to the following chapters:

- Chapter 35, "Viewing and Organizing Files and Working with Windows," builds on what you know about files and shows you how to manage your Microsoft Office files.

- Chapter 36, "Working with Wizards, Multiple Documents, and Cut, Copy, and Paste," shows you how to copy text from a database and pictures from PowerPoint to a Word document.

- Chapter 39, "Sending a Mass Mailing," shows you how to use Access data in your mailings.

- Chapter 40, "Linking and Embedding within Access To Manage Information," builds on what you know about Access and shows you how to link Access to Word, PowerPoint, and Excel.

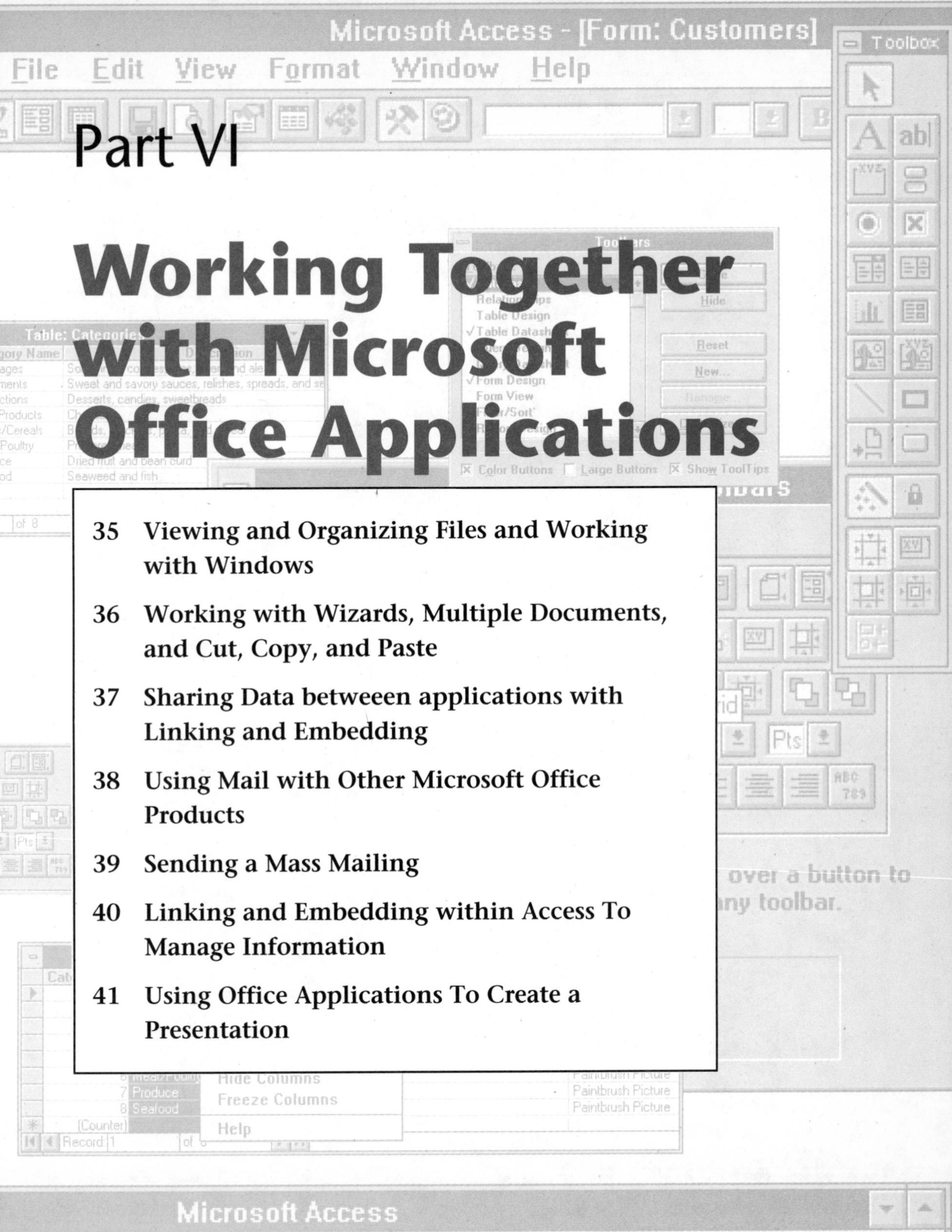

Part VI

Working Together with Microsoft Office Applications

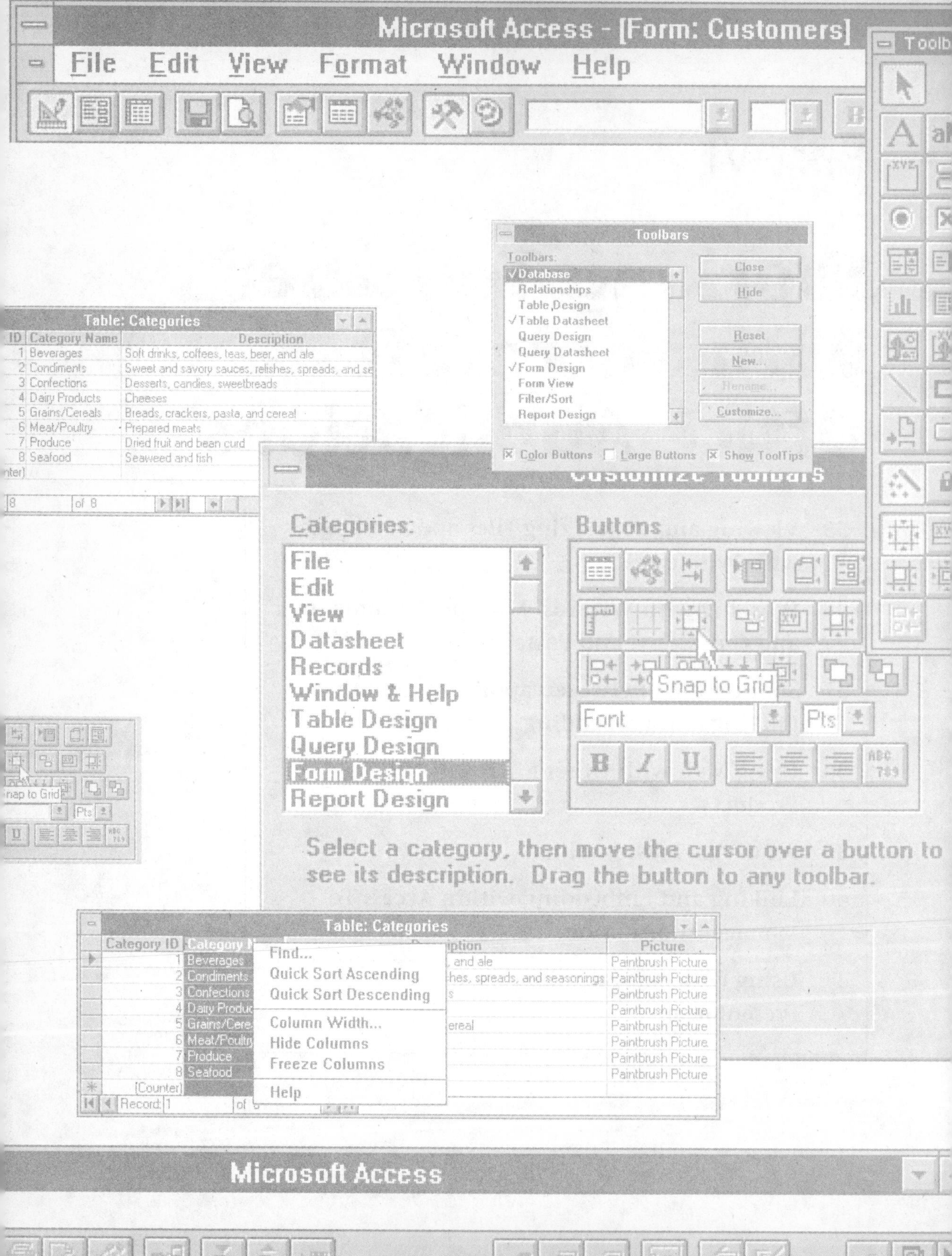

Microsoft Access - [Form: Customers]
File
Edit
View
Format
Window
Help
Toolbars
Toolbars:
Database
Relationships
Table Design
Table Datasheet
Query Design
Query Datasheet
Form Design
Form View
Filter/Sort
Report Design
Close
Hide
Reset
New...
Rename...
Customize...
Color Buttons
Large Buttons
Show ToolTips
Table: Categories
Category Name
Description
Beverages
Soft drinks, coffees, teas, beer, and ale
Condiments
Sweet and savory sauces, relishes, spreads, and se
Confections
Desserts, candies, sweetbreads
Dairy Products
Cheeses
Grains/Cereals
Breads, crackers, pasta, and cereal
Meat/Poultry
Prepared meats
Produce
Dried fruit and bean curd
Seafood
Seaweed and fish
Customize Toolbars
Categories:
File
Edit
View
Datasheet
Records
Window & Help
Table Design
Query Design
Form Design
Report Design
Buttons
Snap to Grid
Font
Pts
Select a category, then move the cursor over a button to see its description. Drag the button to any toolbar.
Table: Categories
Category ID
Picture
Find...
Quick Sort Ascending
Quick Sort Descending
Column Width...
Hide Columns
Freeze Columns
Help
Paintbrush Picture
Record: 1
Microsoft Access

Chapter 35

Viewing and Organizing Files and Working with Windows

by Rick and Patty Winter

Suppose that you are working in a brand new office. The office has new desks and chairs, new computers, and a new copy of Microsoft Office. The organization, Kick Out Gang Violence, Inc., is catching on so fast that it's hard for you to keep up with everything you have to do. And, as the first real employee, you have to do everything—answer the phone, create correspondence, manage volunteers, brainstorm, and even organize the director. Your most basic task is to organize your work.

In this chapter, you learn to

- Make a note in Notepad
- Find and organize files with the File Manager and Find File
- Identify and find files with summary information
- Move between Windows programs
- Create document icons to manage your most used files

Suppose that you receive a phone call requesting more information about the organization, and you take down the questions shown in figure 35.1.

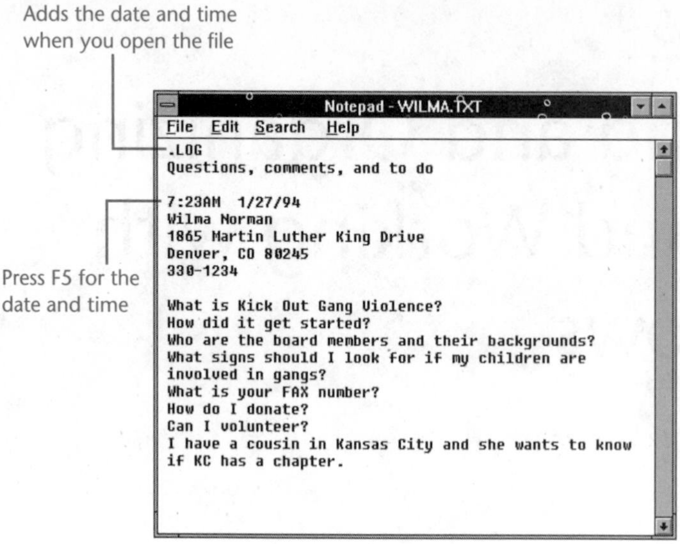

Adds the date and time when you open the file

Fig. 35.1
Choose the Edit WordWrap command to wrap text within the window.

Press F5 for the date and time

```
Notepad - WILMA.TXT
File  Edit  Search  Help
.LOG
Questions, comments, and to do

7:23AM  1/27/94
Wilma Norman
1865 Martin Luther King Drive
Denver, CO 80245
330-1234

What is Kick Out Gang Violence?
How did it get started?
Who are the board members and their backgrounds?
What signs should I look for if my children are
involved in gangs?
What is your FAX number?
How do I donate?
Can I volunteer?
I have a cousin in Kansas City and she wants to know
if KC has a chapter.
```

Making a Quick Note in Notepad

Notepad is an ASCII file editor limited to text files only. It cannot load or display graphic images. You can use Notepad to edit any ASCII file.

To open Notepad, double-click the Accessories group, and then double-click the Notepad icon. As you type in Notepad, your text may keep going past the edge of your window. To have the text word wrap, choose the **E**dit **W**ordWrap command. If you want to add a time and date stamp, press F5. If you want to add the time and date every time you open the file, type **.LOG** at the top of the file.

Note

To make the log date and time stamp work, make sure you type **.LOG** with a period followed by capitalized letters. This entry works only when you type it at the top of the document.

Using File Manager To Organize Files

◄ "Opening Up a File from File Manager," p. 19

Just as you begin setting up an office by labeling file drawers and organizing files in the drawers, you need to organize the files on your hard disk. To find out what files you have on your hard disks and floppy disks, use the File Manager. To start File Manager from Microsoft Office, click the Microsoft

Office button and choose **F**ile Manager from the menu. You also can start File Manager by double-clicking the Main group, and then double-clicking the File Manager icon.

Looking at the Hard Disk

To see how your files are organized, you need to navigate through the File Manager window, shown in figure 35.2. Click each drive icon to see the directories and the files on that drive. On the left (tree) side of the window, click the directory names to see the contents on the right (directory) side of the window. To read a floppy disk, place the disk in the drive and click A or B. If you want to read another floppy disk, place the new disk in the drive and press F5 to refresh the screen.

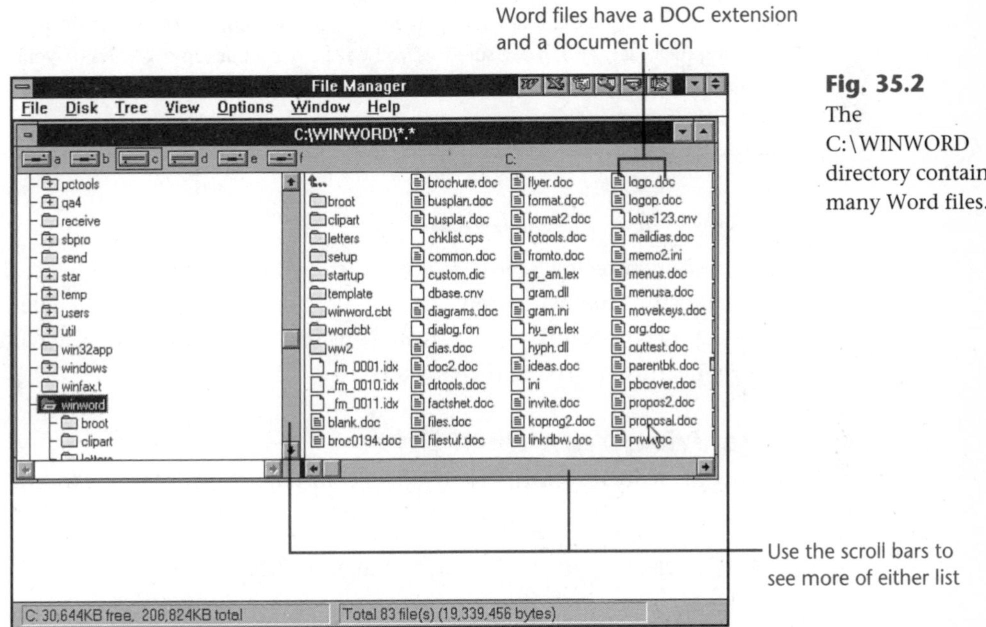

Fig. 35.2
The C:\WINWORD directory contains many Word files.

You can list all the subdirectories on a disk by choosing the **T**ree Expand **A**ll command. If the directory, subdirectory, or the contents list is too large to display in the window, use the scroll bars at the right side and bottom of each list. Click the down arrow to move down one file at a time. Click below the scroll box to see the next screen. To return the tree to one level, go to the top of the list and double-click the first directory name (C:\, A:\, D:\, and so on) to close the list; then double-click the first directory name again to show one level. If you want to see all directories that have subdirectories, choose the **T**ree **I**ndicate Expandable Branches command.

To list only file names on the right side of the window, choose the **V**iew **N**ame command. To see all file information, including the date and time when the file was last saved, choose the **V**iew **A**ll File Details command.

Suppose that you looked in each program directory and noticed that your boss saved all files to the default program directories. (You could tell because there were new XLS files in the EXCEL directory and new DOC files in the WORD directory.) You called your boss, who told you to organize things any way you want, as long as you don't lose any files. You decided to organize the disk drive so that the files would be listed by project.

> **Caution**
>
> Be careful when you move files on your hard disk; you don't want to destroy someone else's organization. Make sure that all users of the computer know where you are putting their files. Also, make sure that you have a good backup of all files on your hard disk before you do any major rearranging. Do not delete files unless you know the files' contents or purpose.

Creating a Subdirectory

To create a subdirectory, move to the left side of the window and select the parent directory that will receive the subdirectory. Then choose the **F**ile Cr**e**ate Directory command. In the Create Directory dialog box, type the name of the subdirectory (up to eight characters).

Organizing Your Hard Drive

When you create directories to organize your hard drive, keep the following questions in mind:

- Who else is going to need access to your files?
- How often will you use files?
- Who else sees your work?
- Will you expect to find your work by date, by person, by project, or by the software that created the files?
- How does your backup procedure work?
- Do your files need to be protected from unauthorized use?

Using the new Find File feature, which is available in most Microsoft Office programs, you can find files based on summary information, such as the date, the project, and the name of the person who created the file. You may want to organize your hard disk anyway, however, to make finding files easier for you and for others who need to view or use your files.

Figure 35.3 shows one way of organizing a directory structure for your hard drive. In the figure, the F:\ drive has three main directories: DATA, PROGRAMS, and TEMP. You may want to backup your data daily and your programs monthly, or whenever you change a program. Therefore, you can create one directory for data and one for programs. If you are on a network or have a security application, you may want to have limited security for programs and tighter security for data. With network programs, you can assign security to a directory, and the security will flow to the subdirectories and files of the directory.

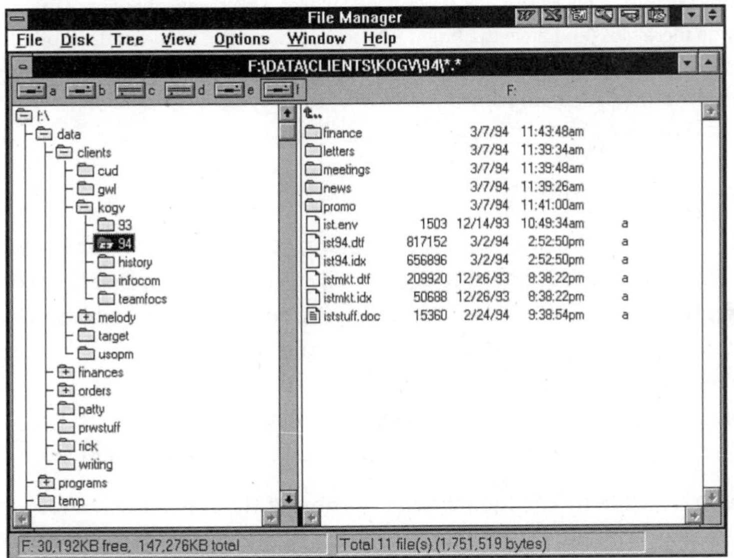

Fig. 35.3
Organize your files so that you and others can find the document you need.

Figure 35.3 also shows subdirectories organized by client, by date, and by project. Below the DATA directory are subdirectories for CLIENTS, FINANCES, WRITING, and for the main partners (RICK and PATTY). The CLIENTS directory is broken down by client name. One of the clients, KOGV, is broken down by date (93, 94, and HISTORY), as well as by project (INFOCOM and TEAMFOCS).

Within the 94 directory, document types are displayed on the right side of the window. The types of documents include FINANCE, LETTERS, MEETINGS, NEWS, and PROMO.

This directory structure contains many levels. When you open or retrieve a file for the first time during a computing session, you may spend a significant amount of time changing to the desired directory and subdirectories (the path). Although Windows will remember this path the next time you open or save the file during the session, you may want to use the Tools Options command to change the default location for files.

Caution

Although File Manager enables you to easily move files and directories associated with programs, be careful when you move them. Not only the location of program files may change, but also the installation of the program, which may change your AUTOEXEC.BAT, CONFIG.SYS, and Windows INI files. Unless you know how to change these files (and have the time to do so), do not move program directories. The best time to plan your directory structure is before you install programs, so you can tell the installation program in which directory to install the programs.

Searching for Files

When you have a directory structure in place, you may forget where you put a file. You can look for a file through the File Manager's Search feature or through the Find File procedure in the applications. The greatest benefit of Search is its capability to move files around and look at your directory structure. The greatest benefit of Find File is its capability to preview the file and the summary information. Search is described in this section; Find File is described in "Using Find File To Organize Files," later in this chapter.

To search for a file by the file name or portion of the file name, choose the **F**ile Searc**h** command. In the Search For text box, type the name of the file, or use wild cards to search for multiple files with the same file pattern. To find Word documents, for example, type ***.DOC**. Type the name of the drive (and a directory, if desired). To see all files on a disk, type the disk name (for example, **C:**\), and make sure that you check the S**e**arch All Subdirectories check box, then choose OK.

After you choose OK, the list of files that matches your criteria appears in a Search Results window, as shown in figure 35.4. If the file details are not listed, choose the **V**iew **A**ll File Details command. When you finish reviewing the results of your search, choose the **F**ile **C**lose command or double-click the Control-menu box.

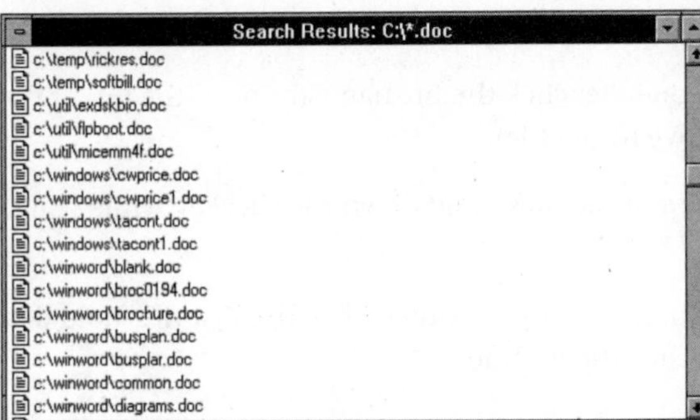

Fig. 35.4
This Search Results window lists the Word document files on the C: drive.

To search for files created by different programs, include the following entries in the **S**earch For text box:

Program	Entry in Search For Text Box
Word	*.DOC
Excel	*.XL*
PowerPoint	*.PPT
Access	*.MDB

Moving and Copying Files

When the file names appear in the Search Results window (or you see the files in a directory window), you can move or copy one or more files. First, select the files, and then use the mouse to drag the files to their new location, or use the menu to indicate the new location. To see where your files are and where they are going, choose the **W**indow **T**ile command to display your source window on one side of the File Manager window and the destination window on the other side.

In this example, the Search Results window is the source window. To open the destination window, complete the following steps:

1. Click the icon in the drive bar for the drive where you want the files to go.

2. On the left side (tree) of the window, select the directory into which the files will go. (You may need to double-click a directory to see which subdirectories are available.)

To select files, do one of the following things:

- To select one file, click the file name (or press the up- or down-arrow key to move to the file).
- To select multiple files, hold down the Ctrl key while you click each of the files.
- To select multiple adjacent files, click the first file, hold down the Shift key, and click the last file.

To move the files, position the mouse pointer on a highlighted file, hold down the Alt key, and drag the file to the desired drive and directory. If the drive and directory are not visible, you can choose the **F**ile **M**ove command and type the drive and directory name. When you copy files, you can hold down the Ctrl key while you drag the files, or you can choose the **F**ile **C**opy command.

Note

To delete a file, highlight it and then press the Del key. To open a file, double-click its document icon (the icon looks like it has small lines of text).

Using Find File To Organize Files

◄ "Finding Files," p. 81

After looking at the long list of files that you found with File Manager, you might decide to use the Find File feature to preview the files and move them in groups to the correct subdirectory. The Find File feature has different options from the File Manager, including the capability to preview files, check their summary information, search across multiple drives, and search for multiple file-name criteria.

Listing Files in Find File

To use the Find File feature, open Word, Excel, or PowerPoint, and choose the **F**ile **F**ind File command. The Search dialog box appears (see fig. 35.5). If you did a previous search, the Find File dialog box appears, as shown in figure 35.6. To return to the Search dialog box, choose the **S**earch button.

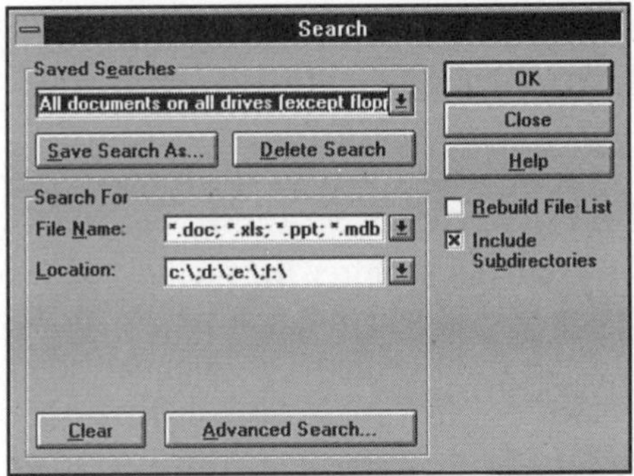

Fig. 35.5
To find all Word, Excel, PowerPoint, and Access files in all directories on all drives, type *.DOC; *.XL*; *.PPT; *.MDB in the File Name text box, all drive letters in the Location text box, and select the Include Subdirectories check box.

	A	B
1	ACCOUNTS:	PERCENTAGE OF DONATION
2	Payroll	6%
3	Marketing	2%
4	Scholarships	85%
5	Supplies	1%
6	Large Equipment (over $500)	1%
7	Travel	1%
8	Lease & Rental	3.50%
9	Petty Cash	0.50%
10	Total	100%
11		

Fig. 35.6
The results of the search criteria in figure 35.5.

To search for a file by its extension, type ***.** and an extension (for example, ***.DOC**) in the File **N**ame text box. If you want to search for more than one extension, type a semicolon (**;**) between the names. To search a hard drive, type the hard drive in the **L**ocation text box (for example, **C:**). If you want to include more than one drive, type semicolons between the drives. You also can include directory names (for example, **C:\WINWORD**) in the **L**ocation text box. If you want to give the search criteria a name, choose the **S**ave Search As command button and type the name in the **S**earch Name text box.

Next, you might want to look at all document files on all drives to see what files didn't get moved. Perhaps you find a few files in the WINDOWS directory that you want to move to the C:\FILES directory. You can use the File

Manager to move those files in one step. If you want to use Find File, you first must copy the files, using the **C**ommands button and **C**opy, and then **C**ommands **D**elete.

Using Find File Advanced Search

To figure out what files should go into what subdirectory, you can use the Advanced Search dialog box, shown in figure 35.7. With Advanced Search, you can search for the file by its contents, its summary information, the user of the file, and the date.

Fig. 35.7
The Advanced Search dialog box contains tabs you can use to specify Location, Summary Info, or Timestamp information for the file.

Tip
When you start a new search, delete from the other tabs any old search criteria that you don't want to use.

To use the Advanced Search feature of File Find, choose the **A**dvanced Search button in the Search dialog box. The Advanced Search dialog box appears. The Advanced Search dialog box has the following three tabs:

- *Location.* This tab enables you to select multiple drives and directories by using buttons, instead of typing, in the Search dialog box.
- *Summary.* This tab enables you to look for summary information and search within the file for words or phrases.
- *Timestamp.* This tab enables you to search for files by user name, or by when they were created or last saved.

Suppose that you want to search for all files that contain the word *gang* and move them to the KOGV (Kick Out Gang Violence) directory. In the Location tab, you would select only files in the C:\FILES directory. In the Summary tab, you would type **Gang** in the Containing Text box.

After moving all the *gang* files to the KOGV directory, you decide to look for all files that a certain person has used since January 1—in this case Gerald

Curry. When you install Microsoft Office or each of the applications, the computer asks for a user name; the name you type at this point is the default user name. Because the user for whom you are searching started working exclusively on this computer for this project on January 1, you would find other files (without the word *gang*) that should be part of the KOGV directory. Enter the date and user name in the Timestamp tab of the Advanced Search dialog box, as shown in figure 35.8. After you finish filling out the dialog box, choose OK. The results appear in the Find File dialog box.

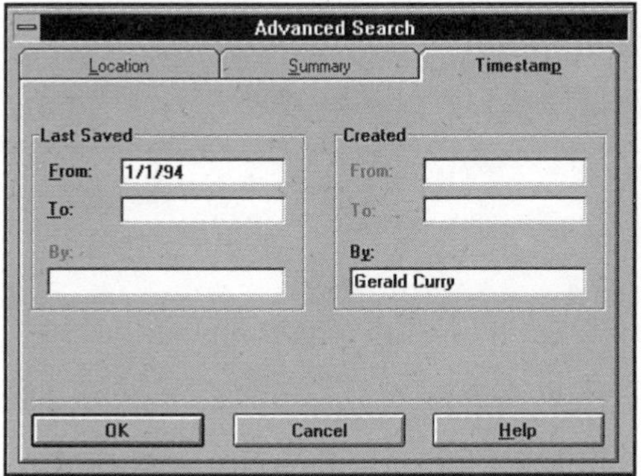

Fig. 35.8
Type date and user information in the Timestamp tab of the Advanced Search dialog box.

Suppose that after you find the KOGV documents, you search for documents created also by Cheryl Curry. This list would only include documents Cheryl created at work and then brought home. You then move these documents to the C:\FILES\CHERYL directory. But you also search for documents containing the text *Cheryl* and move these documents to Cheryl's directory. With the few documents remaining, you preview the documents and move them to their appropriate directory. To preview a file, select Preview from the **V**iew pull-down list in the Find File dialog box (see fig. 35.9).

Opening and Closing Files

To open a file in Find File, double-click the file name, or select the file and choose the **O**pen command button.

◄ "Opening Up a File from File Manager," p. 19

◄ "Saving, Opening, and Closing Files," p. 72

Because you moved all the files, you want anyone else working on Kick Out Gang Violence documents to save them to the C:\FILES\KOGV directory. You decide to show others in the group how to save to different directories, but you want the process to be as easy as possible; therefore, you will change the default to the KOGV directory.

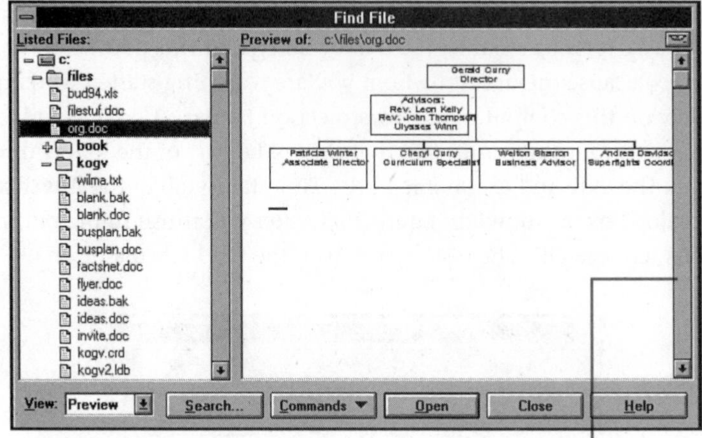

Fig. 35.9
This figure shows a preview of the currently selected file.

To change the default directory in Word, complete the following steps:

1. Choose the **T**ools **O**ptions command. The Options dialog box appears.
2. In the Options dialog box, select the File Locations tab. The location of your files appears in the **F**ile Types list box.
3. Highlight `Documents` and choose **M**odify. The Modify Location dialog box appears (see fig. 35.10).

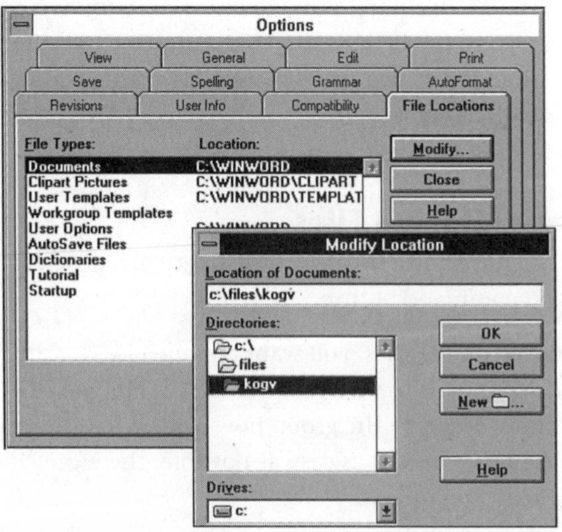

Fig. 35.10
After you enter the Options dialog box, choose the Modify command button to bring up the Modify Location dialog box.

4. In the **L**ocations of Documents text box, type the name of the directory. For this example, **C:\FILES\KOGV** will be the default directory.
5. Choose OK to close the Modify Location dialog box.
6. Choose Close to close the Options dialog box.

To change the default directory in Excel, complete the following steps:

1. Choose the **T**ools **O**ptions command. The Options dialog box appears.
2. Select the General tab. The General information portion of the Option dialog box appears.
3. Type the directory name in the **D**efault File Location text box.
4. When you finish filling in the Options dialog box, choose OK.

Note

You cannot change the default directory in PowerPoint and Access.

Troubleshooting

I tried to search a network drive, but Find File would not search it.

Make sure that you are connected to the network drive. Find File cannot search a network drive to which you are not connected . To connect to a network drive from Find File, choose **S**earch in the Find File dialog box and choose **A**dvanced search in the Search dialog box. Choose **N**etwork. In the Connect Network dialog box, select the drive to connect to, and then choose OK. This connects you to the drive, and Find File will now search this drive if you include it in your search criteria.

I searched for a string of text that I know is in a document, but Find File didn't find the file.

If you save files with the Allow Fast Saves option, Word's Find File cannot search for text in them. You need to turn off Allow Fast Saves. Choose the **T**ools **O**ptions command, and choose the Save tab. Deselect Allow **F**ast Saves, and choose OK. This will not fix your problem for files you have already saved until you open and save them again, but it will fix this problem for any files you save in the future.

Using Summary Info

You may have noticed that it would have been much easier to find and organize files if you had more information about the file. The Summary Info option enables you to add longer titles, the author's name, and other descriptive text to your documents.

Adding Summary Information to Your Document

◀ "Using Summary Info," p. 80

In Word, Excel, and PowerPoint (but not Access), you can add a summary to the document. The Summary Info dialog box contains five text boxes (Title, Subject, Author, Keywords, and Comments), each of which has room for up to 255 characters, including spaces and special characters. In Word, you also can see document statistics, such as total number of pages, words, and paragraphs.

To add summary information, complete the following steps:

1. Choose the **F**ile Summary **I**nfo command. The Summary Info dialog box appears (see fig. 35.11).

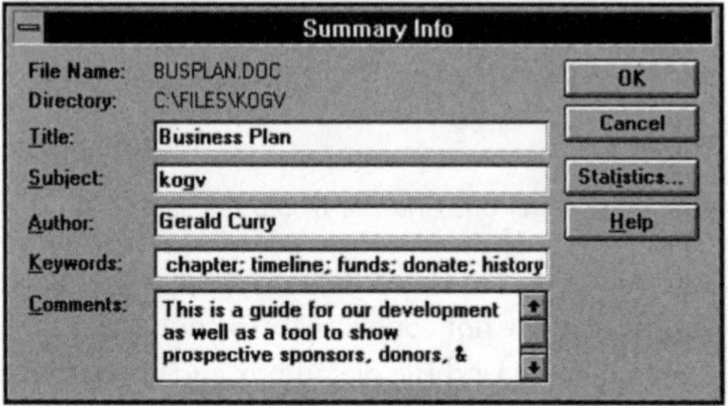

Fig. 35.11 In the Summary Info dialog box, you can enter information that will help you find the file later.

2. In the **T**itle text box, type a description that is longer than the file name of your document.
3. In the **S**ubject text box, type a category.
4. In the **A**uthor text box, type your name.

> **Note**
>
> The user's name—the name entered during installation—is entered in the text box automatically. You can keep this name or change it.

5. In the **K**eywords text box, type words or phrases that describe your document.
6. In the **C**omments text box, type any other notes you have.
7. Choose OK.

Viewing Summary Information in Find File

When you use Find File in Word, Excel, and PowerPoint, you can see a preview of your file and two other views: file info and summary. File info view shows the file name, document title, file size, and the date and time when it was last saved. Summary view shows the information in the Summary Info dialog box, as well as information about the time when the file was created and saved.

To see the Summary Info before you open a file, complete the following steps:

1. Choose the **F**ile **F**ind File command. The Search dialog box or your last Find File dialog box appears, depending on your last use of the Find File command.
2. If the Search dialog box appears, fill in the dialog box and choose OK to do the search and to get to the Find File dialog box.
3. In the Find File dialog box, select Summary from the **V**iew pull-down list.
4. Select the file for which you want to see information. The Find File dialog box displays information similar to that shown in figure 35.12.
5. To see other information about the file, select File Info from the **V**iew pull-down list. The dialog box displays information similar to that shown in figure 35.13.
6. When you finish, choose **O**pen to open the file or Close to close the dialog box.

Note

If you want to open more than one file at a time, you can select multiple files. To select adjacent files, click the first file, hold down the Shift key, and click the last file. To select nonadjacent files, hold down the Ctrl key and click each file. After you select the files, choose **O**pen.

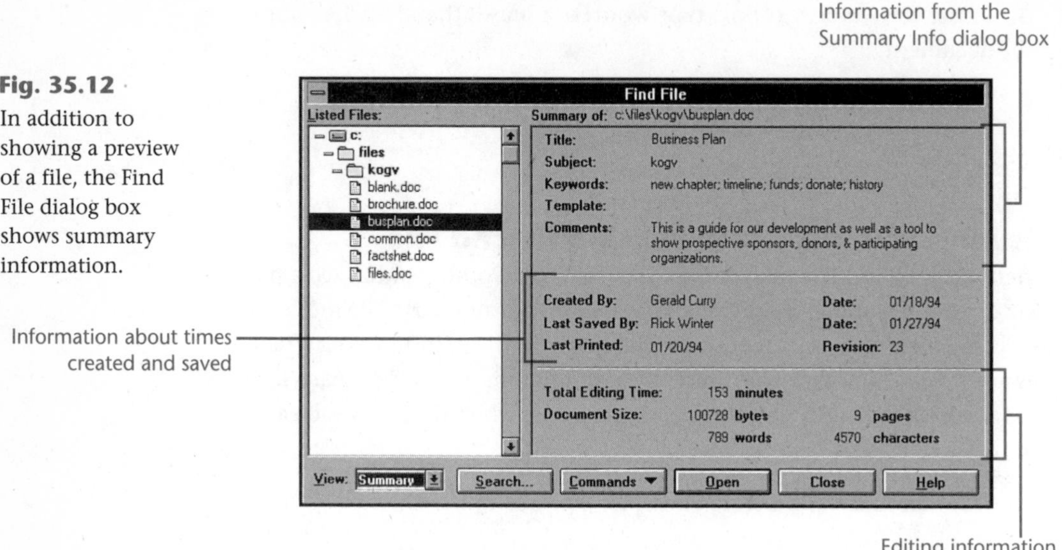

Fig. 35.12
In addition to showing a preview of a file, the Find File dialog box shows summary information.

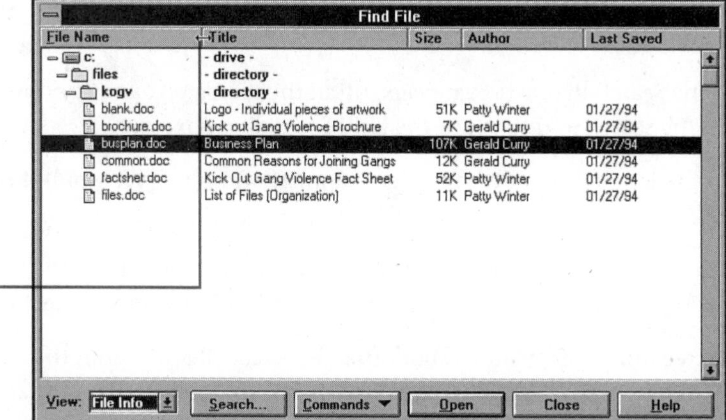

Fig. 35.13
File info view shows some of the same information as summary view and enables you to view more than one file at a time.

Opening Files and Searching for Text

Suppose that you went through the files in the KOGV directory, glanced at the major files, and added summary information. Now that you have the files in the right area, you decide to starting making notes for your phone calls. Choose the Notepad button to open your phone-message file (which grew large as you were answering the phone and organizing your computer). To find out where the answers to the questions are, use Find File and go into the documents that you suspect contain the answers.

In the Find File dialog box, you can double-click the file name, if you are in the right application. You also can click the **O**pen button or choose the **F**ile **O**pen command to open the file.

◄ "Finding and Replacing Worksheet Data," p. 276

◄ "Manipulating Data," p. 622

To search for text when you are in the file, choose the **E**dit **F**ind command. In the Fi**n**d What text box, type the characters you want to find, as shown in figure 35.14. Then choose one of the Find buttons (No Formatting, F**o**rmat, or Sp**e**cial).

Note

In Access, the **E**dit **F**ind command is not available until you select a table. To select a table, click the Table tab, and then double-click a table name.

Fig. 35.14
Type the text for which you want to search in the Find What text box, and click the Find Next button to begin the search.

You remember that a list in the PROPOSAL.DOC file lists your associate Leon Kelly. After you open the PROPOSAL.DOC in Word, you use the Find feature to go to the page.

Moving between Windows Programs

◄ "Switching Between Documents," p. 89

◄ "Switching Between Applications," p. 93

To move to the Word document you have open (PROPOSAL.DOC), click the Word button in the Microsoft Office toolbar. To move back to the phone-message file in Notepad, simply choose the Notepad button. The phone-message file will appear, whether or not it is already open. Using the Microsoft Office toolbar is much easier than using the Program Manager or the Task List. If you don't have the Microsoft Office toolbar, you can press Alt+Tab to scroll through the open applications, or press Ctrl+Esc to bring up the Task List. Double-click the application name to switch to the application. If the application is not open, double-click Program Manager, open the group in which the application is located, and open the application.

Because you are working with several Word documents at once, you decide to open all the important ones. When the documents are open, you can choose a document from the bottom of the **W**indow menu (see fig. 35.15). You also can scroll through open documents by pressing Ctrl+F6.

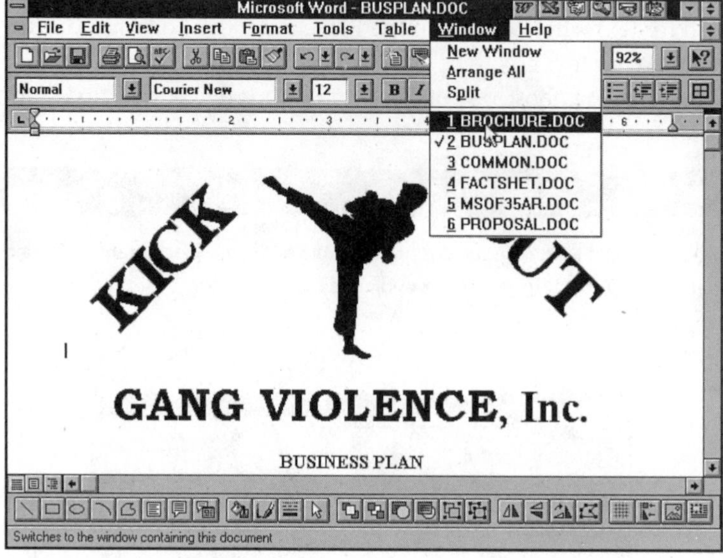

Fig. 35.15
To work with more than one document (to copy information, for example),use the Window menu to switch between documents.

To enter the answers to the questions in your phone-message document, you will switch back and forth between Word and Notepad a lot, writing down the names of the documents and, in some cases, the page numbers, as shown in figure 35.16.

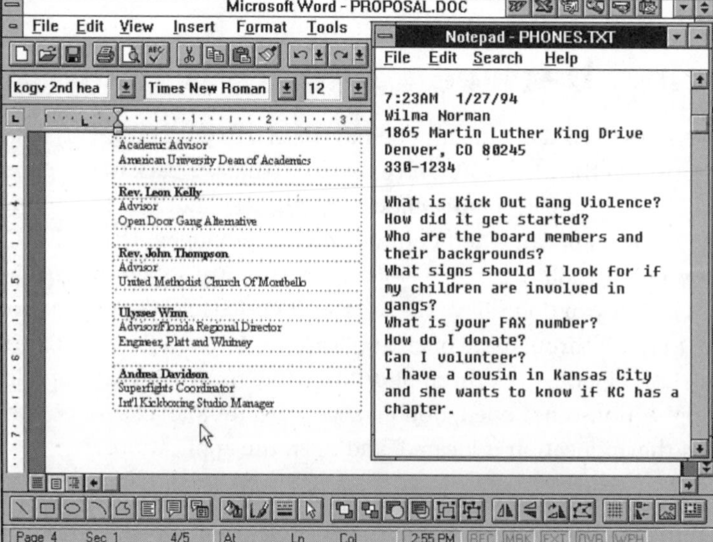

Fig. 35.16
Because the Notepad window does not take up the full screen, you can click anywhere in the Word document to go to the Word window.

Creating Document Icons in a New Group

If you know that you are going to use the same files over and over, you may want to create a separate icon for each file in a group within the Program Manager. The easiest way to create document icons is to open the File Manager and the Program Manager in two windows.

To create a new group, follow these steps:

1. Go to the Program Manager. Click the Microsoft Office button, and choose P**r**ogram Manager from the menu. The Program Manager window appears in front of the other windows.

2. Close all open group windows. (To close a group window, click the Minimize button or double-click the Control-menu box.)

3. Choose the **F**ile **N**ew command. The New Program Object dialog box appears.

4. Make sure that the Program **G**roup option is selected, and choose OK. The Program Group Properties dialog box appears (see fig. 35.17).

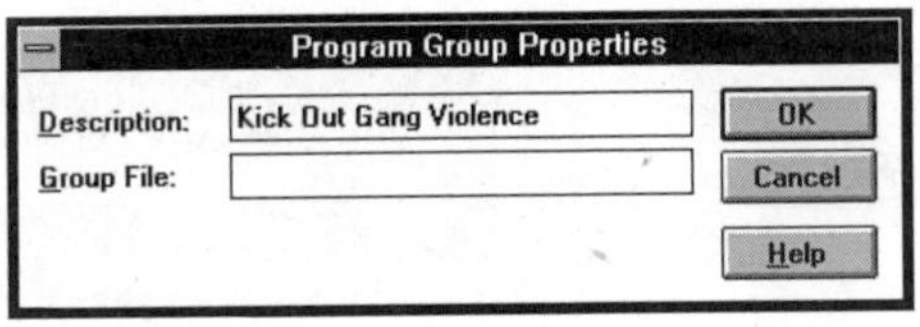

Fig. 35.17
The Program Group Properties dialog box enables you to name your group. The name will appear below the group icon and in the group window's title bar.

5. Type the name of the group in the **D**escription text box, and choose OK. A blank group window appears, displaying the group name in the title bar.

Note

If you previously created a group, you can type the group file name in the **G**roup File text box. Group files generally are located in the WINDOWS directory and have a GRP extension.

You can copy files from the File Manager to your new group. After you open File Manager and arrange the File Manager window and the Program Manager window, complete the following steps:

1. Minimize all programs, and then double-click the Program Manager icon. The Program Manager window opens.
2. Press Ctrl+Esc to bring up the Task List, and double-click File Manager in the list. The File Manager opens.
3. Bring up the Task List again (Ctrl+Esc), and select **T**ile.
4. If necessary, drag the title bar of each window to move the window.
5. If desired, drag the border of a window to size the window.
6. In the File Manager window, select the drive and directory in which the files are located.
7. Select one or more files (Ctrl+click to select more than one file).
8. Drag the file names from the File Manager to the open group window in the Program Manager, as shown in figure 35.18. An icon is created for each file you drag.

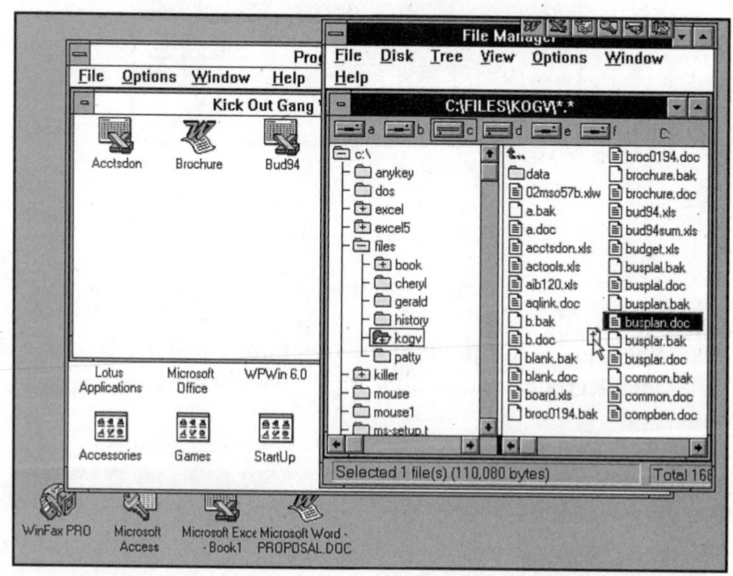

Fig. 35.18
This example shows three icons that will open a document and a program. ACCTSDON and BUD94 will launch Excel and open ACCTSDON.XLS and BUD94.XLS; Brochure will launch Word and open BROCHURE.DOC.

From Here...

This chapter showed you how to become more organized by using the Microsoft Office toolbar, organizing your directory structure, summarizing information in your files, and creating a new program group.

After you organize your files, you may want to create documents. For more information about creating documents, refer to the following chapters:

- Chapter 4, "Creating and Editing Documents," covers the basics of creating a Word document.
- Chapter 12, "Creating Worksheets," covers the fundamentals of creating an Excel worksheet.
- Chapter 20, "Creating, Saving, and Opening Presentations," gives you the basics on how to create a slide presentation.
- Chapter 27, "Creating a Database," explains database terminology and shows you how to start a new database.
- Chapter 36, "Working with Wizards, Multiple Documents, and Cut, Copy, and Paste," shows you how to use multiple open documents and gather information into one document.

Chapter 36

Working with Wizards, Multiple Documents, and Cut, Copy, and Paste

by Rick and Patty Winter

Look at figure 36.1. This Notepad document shows questions from a phone call and the location of the answers in different documents and different applications. Information within your organization probably is scattered throughout your hard drive and everyone else's. Instead of typing the information over and over, you can use the Cut, Copy, and Paste procedures to reuse existing information. To start your documents and save time, try the wizards that come with the Office applications.

This situation calls for you to create a letter in Word and copy information from other Word documents, a PowerPoint slide, an Access query, and an Excel worksheet. In this chapter, you learn how to start a letter with one of Word's wizards and copy information from the other Office applications; then paste this information into your Word document.

In this chapter, you learn to

- Use wizards to start letters
- Switch between programs
- Copy text, data, and pictures between programs

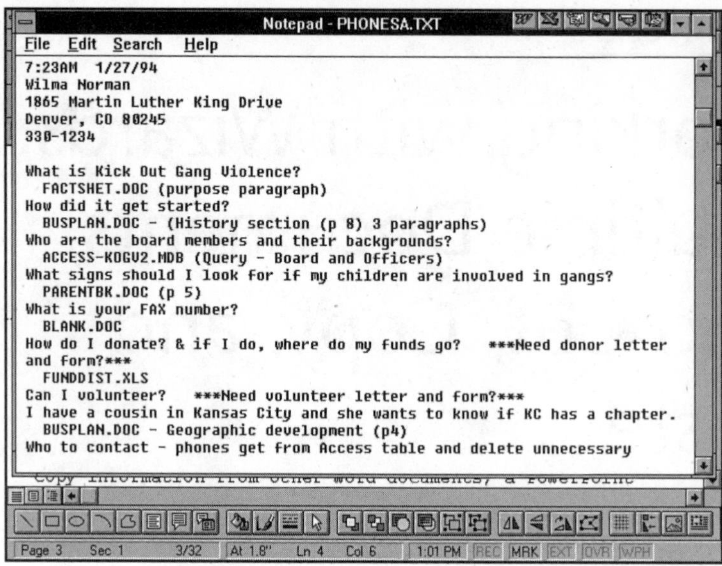

Fig. 36.1
This document shows requested information and potential sources for the answers.

Starting a Letter with Letter Wizard

◀ "Wizards," p. 68

◀ "Using Template Wizards," p. 204

As mentioned in Chapter 2, "Using Common Features," a wizard asks you a series of questions about what you want to do. Through your answers, the wizard creates a format for your document and adds some text to get you started. To begin a wizard in Word, you use the **F**ile **N**ew command.

To start the Letter Wizard, follow these steps:

1. Choose the **F**ile **N**ew command. The New dialog box appears, displaying a list of templates and wizards (see fig. 36.2).

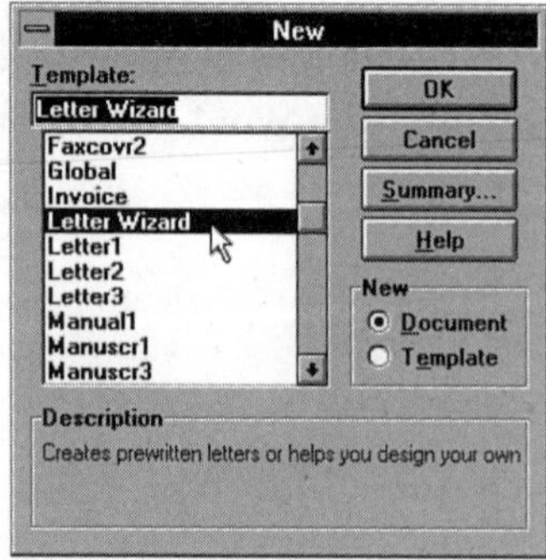

Fig. 36.2
Templates are shown in the New dialog box. Wizards are a subset of templates that walk you through creating a document.

2. Scroll down and select Letter Wizard in the **T**emplate list box.

3. Choose OK.

> **Note**
>
> You can choose **S**ummary in the New dialog box and enter Summary Info for the new document, then enter the first of the wizard dialog boxes.

After you choose OK in the New dialog box, the first dialog box of the Letter Wizard appears, as shown in figure 36.3. The dialog box asks whether you want to select a prewritten business letter, write a business letter, or write a personal letter. If you select prewritten business letter, a list of 15 letters appears. This list, shown in figure 36.4, includes a press release, a collection letter, a résumé cover letter, and various thank-you letters.

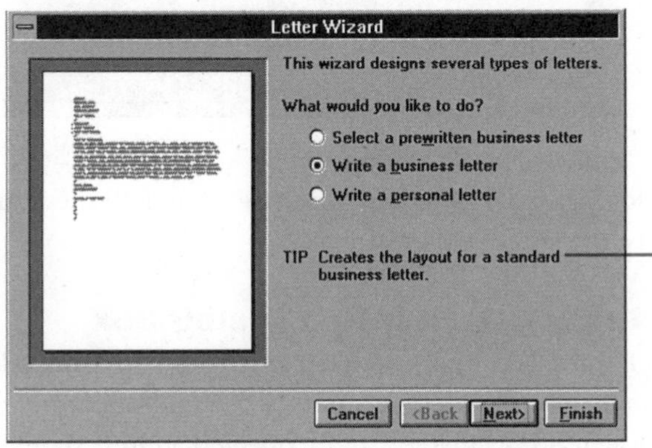

Fig. 36.3
The first Letter Wizard dialog box enables you to select different types of letters.

When you select an option, the tip message changes, giving you more information about your choice

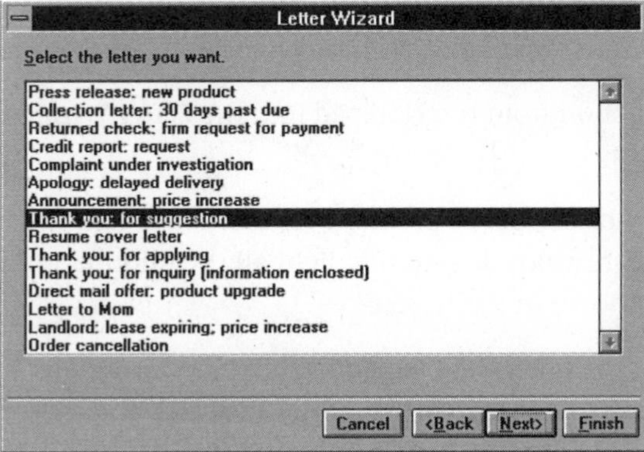

Fig. 36.4
Select a prewritten business letter from the list box.

If none of the prewritten letters is appropriate, choose the **B**ack button to return to the Letter Wizard dialog box shown in figure 36.3. Select the Write a **B**usiness Letter option, and choose the **N**ext button. The next Letter Wizard dialog box, shown in figure 36.5, asks which items you want to appear in your letter, including page numbers and the date. These items are check boxes; turn each item on by putting an X in the box or off by clearing the box.

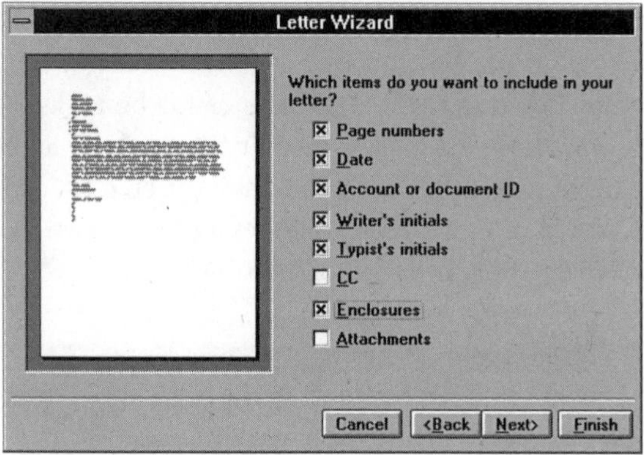

Fig. 36.5
Click a check box to turn the item on (with an X) or off (without an X).

The next dialog boxes ask whether your letter is on letterhead and, if it is, where to place the letterhead on the page.

Copying Information into a Dialog Box

The dialog box shown in figure 36.6 requests your name and address and the recipient's name and address. You can type the information or copy it from somewhere else, if it is available. Your name and address should already be filled in if you created a previous letter with a wizard, or if you entered the information in the Tools, Options, User Info tab of the Options dialog box. The recipient's name and address already appear in your Notepad document.

◄ "Copying and Moving," p. 52

◄ "Switching Between Applications," p. 93

◄ "Moving between Windows Programs," p. 753

To copy information from the Notepad into the Letter Wizard dialog box, follow these steps:

1. Drag the I-beam mouse pointer over the existing information in the recipient's text-box area to highlight all the information you will replace, as shown in figure 36.6.

2. Switch to the open Notepad document by pressing Alt+Tab. Alternatively, press Ctrl+Esc to bring up the Task List, and then double-click the Notepad entry.

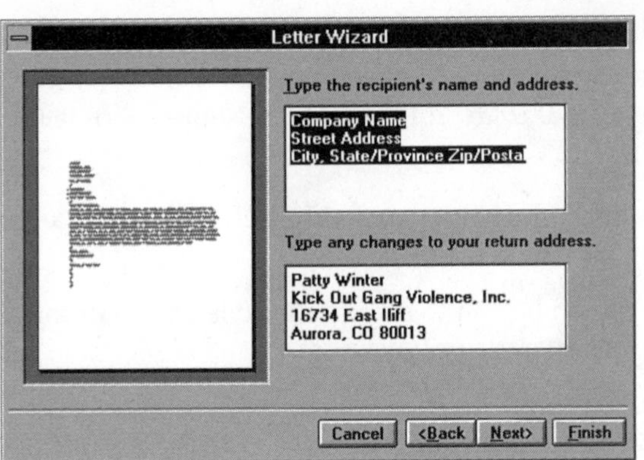

Fig. 36.6
Type or copy the recipient's name and address in the Letter Wizard.

3. In the Notepad window, select the information you want to copy.

4. To copy the highlighted text, choose the **E**dit **C**opy command or press Ctrl+C.

5. Click the Word button in the Microsoft Office toolbar to return to the Letter Wizard dialog box in Word.

6. The old entry in the recipient's text box should still be highlighted. Press Ctrl+V to copy the information from the Clipboard to the text box. Figure 36.7 shows the completed text box.

Note

You cannot use the Edit menu or any button in a toolbar while you are in this dialog box. The only way to copy from the Clipboard is to press Ctrl+V. The same holds true when you are trying to cut or copy from a dialog box. Press Ctrl+X to cut or Ctrl+C to copy highlighted text in a text box.

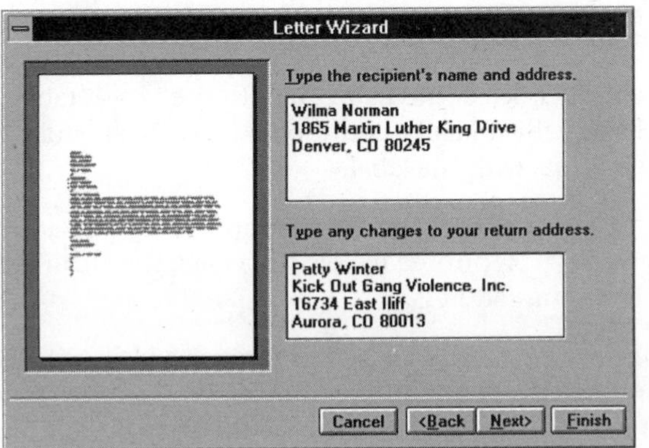

Fig. 36.7
The information from the Clipboard is pasted into the text box.

Finishing the Letter Wizard

To finish the interactive portion of creating a letter, fill out other dialog boxes in the Letter Wizard by following these steps. (Choose the **N**ext button to move to each successive step.)

1. After you insert the names and addresses, choose the **N**ext button to continue to the next dialog box.
2. Select an option button to specify the style you want for your letter: classic, contemporary, or typewriter.
3. The Letter Wizard dialog box, which displays a checkered finish flag (see fig. 36.8), asks whether you want to create an envelope or mailing label, display help, or display the letter. To create a envelope, for example, select the **C**reate an Envelope or Mailing Label option.

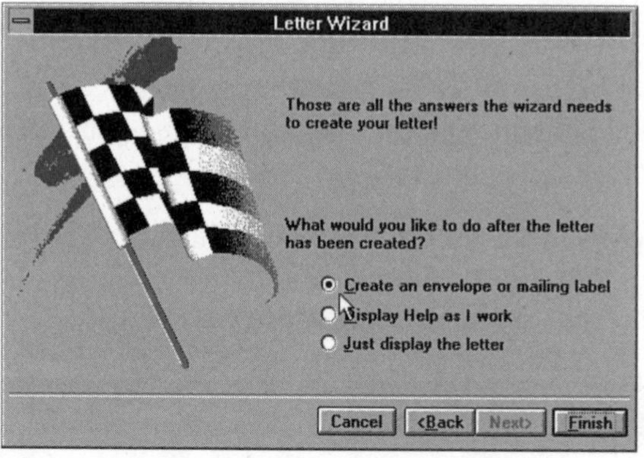

Fig. 36.8
To display a Help window with topics related to your letter, select the Display Help As I Work option.

Tip
You also can enter the Envelopes and Labels dialog box by choosing the **T**ools **E**nvelopes and Labels command.

4. If you select the Create an Envelope or Mailing Label option, the Envelopes and Labels dialog box appears (see fig. 36.9). The name of the recipient appears in the Delivery Address text box, and your address appears in the Return Address text box. If necessary, edit these entries in the dialog box.
5. To create an envelope, select the **E**nvelopes tab.
6. To create a label, select the **L**abels tab. In the Labels tab, you can specify the label size, which label to print on a label sheet, and whether or not a bar code prints with the label.
7. Your name and address automatically appear in the Return Address text box. If you have preprinted envelopes, check the O**m**it check box to remove the return address.
8. To change the envelope size, add or remove a bar code, change the fonts for the delivery or return addresses, or change the placement of the addresses on the envelope, choose the **O**ptions button.

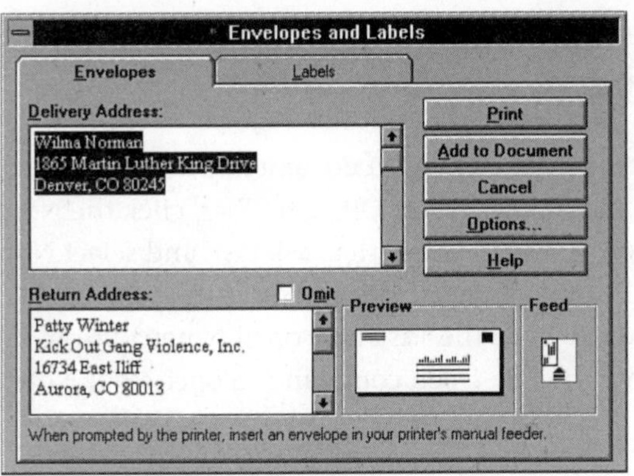

Fig. 36.9
The Wizard takes you to the Envelopes and Labels dialog box, where you can edit addresses.

9. To add the envelope as a separate page in your document, choose the **A**dd to Document button. This option also enables you to preview the envelope before you print it.

10. To go directly to the printer, choose the **P**rint button.

Whether or not you print an envelope, your letter appears with the current date and the recipient's information. Throughout the letter, information that you need to replace is indicated by brackets and italics, as shown in figure 36.10. Highlight the markers, including the brackets, and type your replacement text.

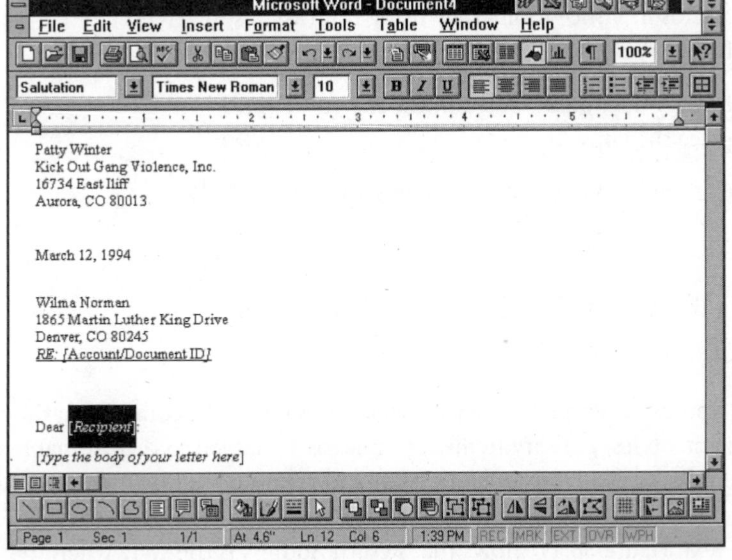

Fig. 36.10
Highlight [Recipient] and type the salutation for the letter.

Copying Information from Notepad to Word

► "Customizing Office Manager," p. 883

You can copy items from a Notepad document into your letter. If you have a Notepad button in your Microsoft Office toolbar, click the Notepad button. Otherwise, press Ctrl+Esc to access the Task List, and select Notepad from the list to move to the open Notepad document. If the program is not open, select Program Manager in the Task List, open Notepad from the Accessories group, and choose the **F**ile **O**pen command to open your Notepad document.

To place the information in the Clipboard, follow these steps:

1. In the Notepad document, select the text you want to copy.

2. Choose the **E**dit **C**opy command or press Ctrl+C.

Note

To remove the information from the Notepad and place it in the Clipboard, choose the **E**dit Cu**t** command or press Ctrl+X.

To copy the information from the Clipboard to your Word document, follow these steps:

1. Return to the Word document by clicking the Word button in the Microsoft Office toolbar, by using the Task List (Ctrl+Esc), or by pressing Alt+Tab.

2. In your document, position the insertion point where you want to place the copy.

3. Choose the **E**dit **P**aste command, or press Ctrl+V.

Using the Styles from the Letter Wizard

◄ "Formatting with Styles," p. 196

When you use a template or wizard, more than just text comes with the document. Styles, glossary items, and macros are added to the normal template entries to give you added flexibility in creating your documents. The first item in the Formatting toolbar shows you the current style for the selected text. Figure 36.11 shows that Return Address is the style when the insertion point is in the letter's return address.

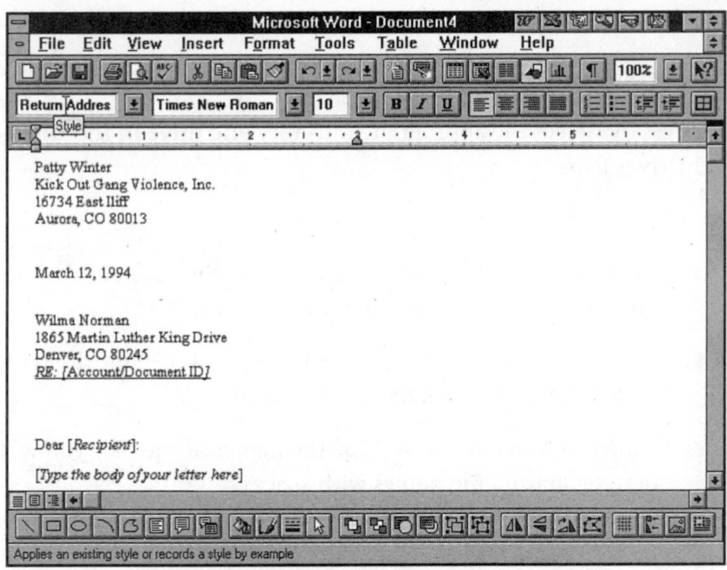

Fig. 36.11
The Letter Wizard adds a return-address style and uses it for the return address.

If you select the date, Wilma's address, or the body of the letter, the style changes to Date, Address, or Body Text, respectively. You can apply a style by selecting the text, clicking the Style pull-down arrow, and selecting the style. In this case, references to the documents and other notes from the Notepad document were first deleted, and then the Lead-in Emphasis style was selected.

In this example, Enter was pressed between each question and changed the style back to Body Text, which is the normal style. To return to the normal style, press Ctrl+space bar.

Copying Text Between Word Documents

The information for your documents may be scattered throughout existing documents. If you dislike typing, especially typing the same thing repeatedly, learning how to copy text between documents is worthwhile.

Opening Word Documents

Part of the process of working with multiple documents in Word is opening those documents. You can open each document separately by choosing the **F**ile **O**pen command. Starting with Version 6, you can open more than one document at a time.

◄ "Working with Files," p. 71

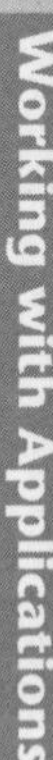

To open more than one document, follow these steps:

1. Choose the **F**ile **O**pen command. The Open dialog box appears.
2. If necessary, select the appropriate directory and drive in the **D**irectories and Dri**v**es lists.
3. Do one of the following:
   - In the File **N**ame list, press Ctrl and then click each of the files you want to open, as shown in figure 36.12.
   - To select adjacent file names, click the first file name, hold down the Shift key, and click the last file name.
   - In the File **N**ame text box, type the names of the files you want to open, separating file names with spaces.

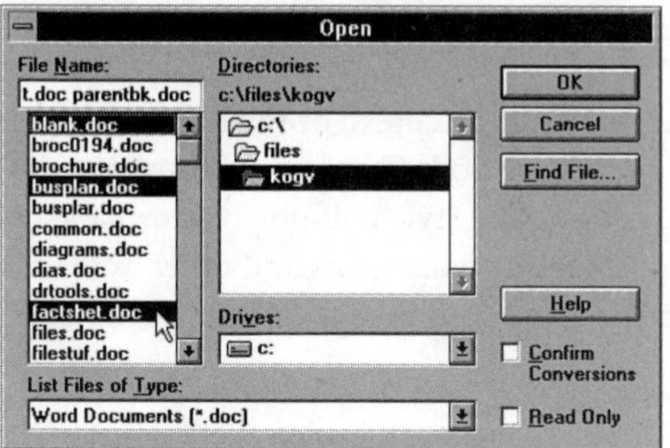

Fig. 36.12 Three files are selected to be opened.

4. Choose OK. All the selected files open.

Switching between Documents

◀ "Switching between Documents," p. 89

When you have several documents open, you need to switch between the documents to copy information between them.

To switch between open documents in Word, do one of the following things:

- Select one of the documents from the bottom of the **W**indow menu, as shown in figure 36.13.
- Press Ctrl+F6 to cycle through the open documents.

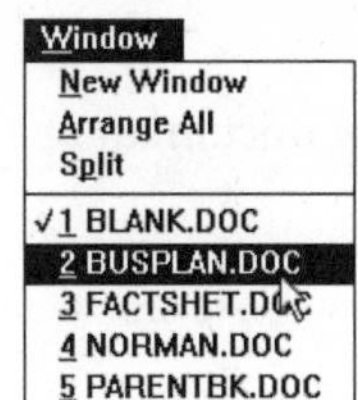

Fig. 36.13
To go to the Business Plan document, type 2 or select BUSPLAN.DOC.

Copying Information from One Word Document to Another

After you open your documents, you can copy information between them. Use the Clipboard method described in this section or the drag-and-drop feature mentioned in the "Using Drag and Drop To Copy Information Between Documents" section, later in this chapter.

To copy information between documents, follow these steps:

◄ "Copying and Moving," p. 52

1. Select the text you want to copy.
2. Choose the **E**dit **C**opy command or press Ctrl+C.

3. Switch to the document that is to receive the copy, and position the insertion point where you want to place the copy.
4. Choose the **E**dit **P**aste command or press Ctrl+V.

After you copy the text into your document, you may have to reformat the text so that it matches the surrounding text.

Note

The Format Painter button is handy for copying formats. Position the insertion point within the text that has the format you want, and click the Format Painter button. Drag the mouse-pointer paintbrush across the text you want to change. When you release the mouse button, the selected text changes format.

◄ "Copying Formats," p. 126

Note

When you use the normal paste procedure in step 4, the text retains some formatting from the original document. If you want the text to assume the formatting of the text at the insertion point in your target document, choose the **E**dit Paste **S**pecial command, and then select the Unformatted Text option in the Paste Special dialog box.

Tip

If you know the page number to move to, double-click the left portion of the status bar to open the Go To dialog box; type that page number and choose Go **T**o.

Arranging Documents

If you want to see more than one document at a time, you can display parts of each document window.

To arrange the documents, follow these steps:

1. Open the documents you want to view.

2. Choose the **W**indow **A**rrange All command. The documents are tiled within the window, as shown in figure 36.14.

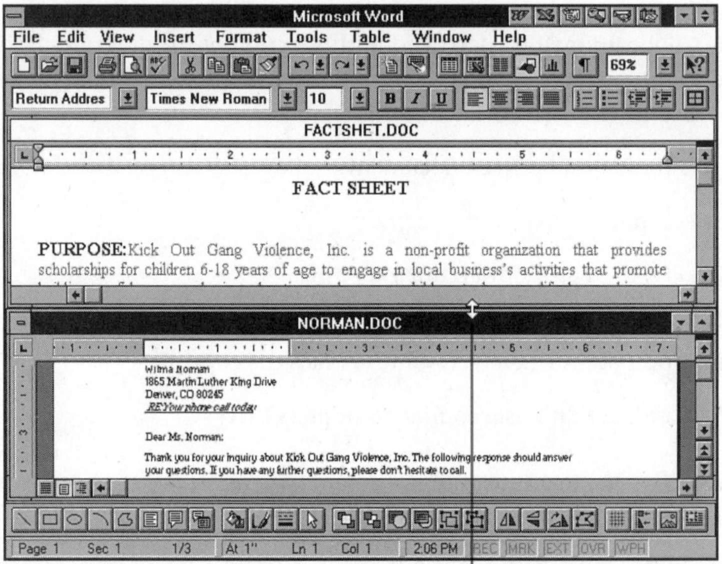

Fig. 36.14
Two documents, FACTSHET.DOC and NORMAN.DOC, are open and visible here.

Position the mouse pointer on the window border to change the window size.

Tip
Close any documents you don't want to view. If you have too many documents open, you will see only a small portion of each document.

3. To change the size or shape of the window, point to a window border and drag the double-headed mouse pointer.

4. To move a window, drag the title bar.

Using Drag and Drop To Copy Information Between Documents

When you have more than one document visible, you can drag text between the two documents.

To move or copy information with drag and drop, follow these steps:

1. Select the text you want to move or copy.

◄ "Moving with Drag and Drop," p. 53

2. Position the mouse pointer in the middle of the selected text.

3. To move the text, drag the mouse pointer.

   To copy text, hold down the Ctrl key and drag the mouse pointer.

   The mouse pointer changes as you drag, as shown in figure 36.15.

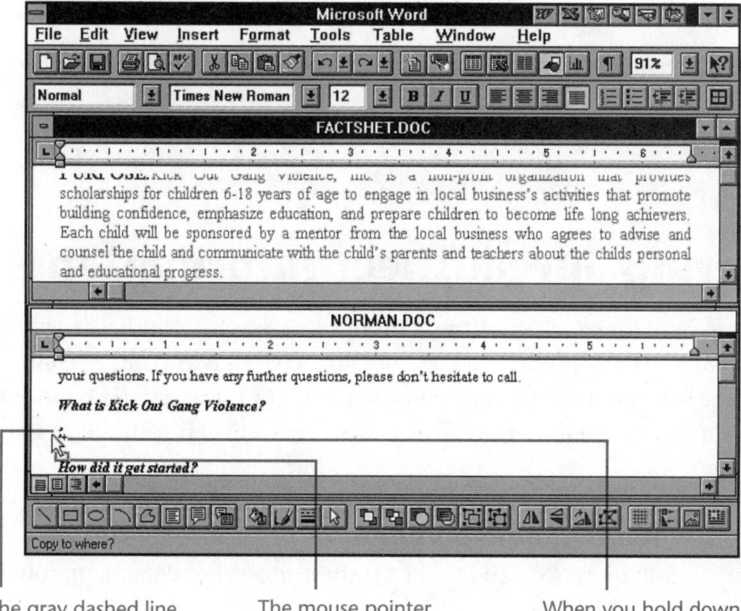

Fig. 36.15
If you want to copy, make sure that the plus sign (+) appears with the mouse pointer.

4. Drag the text into the new window to receive the copy. The gray vertical bar indicates the position of the new text.

5. Release the mouse button to complete the copy procedure.

Note

Use the same drag-and-drop procedure when you move or copy text within the same document.

Troubleshooting

When I copy information with drag and drop, the original document loses its information.

You used the move feature instead. Make sure that you hold down the Ctrl key throughout the process. Release the mouse button first, and then release the Ctrl key.

My copied text appears in the middle of existing text.

Don't forget to watch the gray dashed line that is part of the mouse pointer. This line shows where the copied text will be inserted.

I get a black circle with a slash through it when I try to copy.

When it is on the title bar or status bar, the black circle with the slash indicates that you cannot drop as you drag the mouse with a copy. Make sure you go all the way into the other document before you release the mouse button.

Copying Spreadsheet Information

The procedure for copying information from an Excel spreadsheet to a Word document is essentially the same as copying between two Word documents. Select the area you want to copy, choose the **E**dit **C**opy command, move to the location where you want the copy to appear, and choose the **E**dit **P**aste command.

Copying from Excel to Word

To copy information from an Excel worksheet to a Word document, follow these steps:

1. Click the Excel button in the Microsoft Office toolbar.

2. Choose the **F**ile **O**pen command, or press Ctrl+O.
3. Select the name of the file you want to open, and choose OK.
4. To select the range you want to copy, do one of the following things:
   - With the thick white-cross mouse pointer, drag across the range to copy, as shown in figure 36.16.
   - Hold down the Shift key and use the arrow keys to highlight the range.

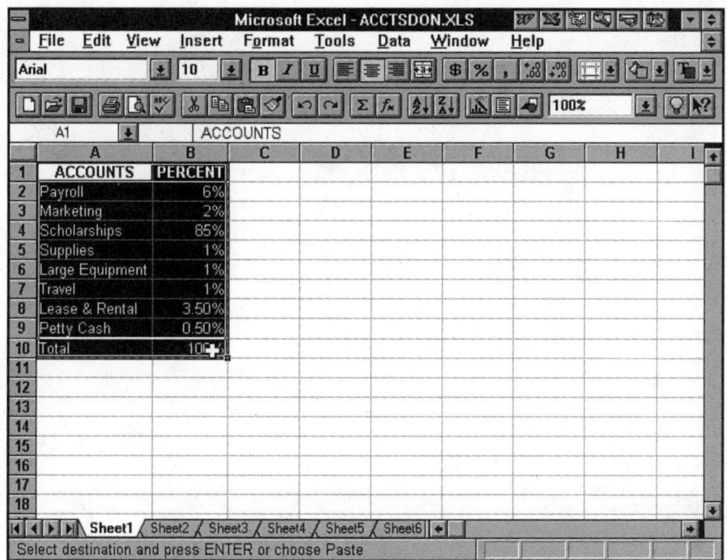

Fig. 36.16
When you choose the Edit Copy command, a marquee surrounds the range to be copied.

5. Choose the **E**dit **C**opy command or press Ctrl+C.

> **Caution**
>
> Be careful when you drag the mouse pointer. Make sure that it is a thick white cross and not an arrow (used for drag-and-drop) or a black plus sign (used for automatic fill).

6. Return to the Word document by using the Word button, the Task List (Ctrl+Esc), or Alt+Tab.

7. Position the insertion point where you want the spreadsheet information to appear.

◄ "Selecting Cells and Ranges," p. 251

8. Choose the **E**dit **P**aste command or press Ctrl+V.

> **Note**
>
> When you perform a normal paste operation in step 8, the information goes into a table in Word, as shown in figure 36.17. The light gray grid lines do not print. If you want additional lines to appear, choose the F**o**rmat **B**orders and Shading command.

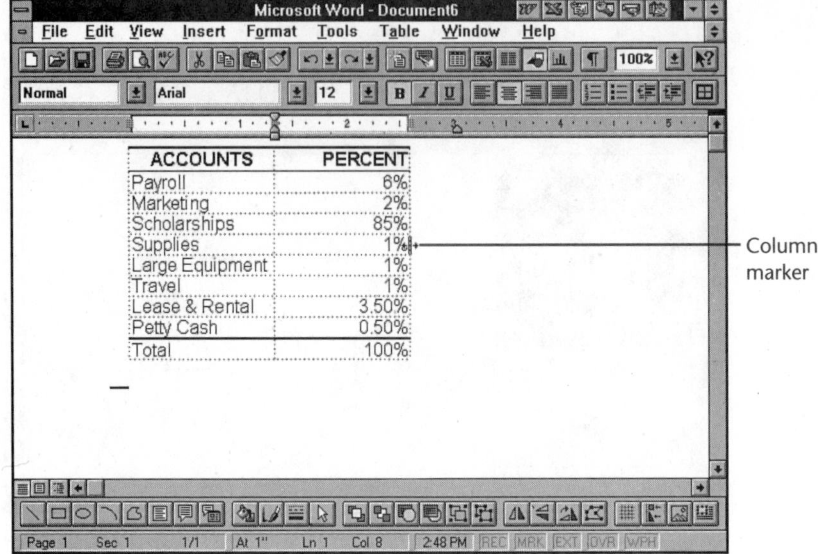

Fig. 36.17
To change your columns in Word, drag the column marker.

◄ "Working with Tables," p. 210

Using Paste Special with a Spreadsheet

If you don't want text to appear in a table in your Word document, you can use the Paste Special option. To use Paste Special with spreadsheet data in the Clipboard, choose the **E**dit Paste **S**pecial command. The Paste Special dialog box appears, as shown in figure 36.18.

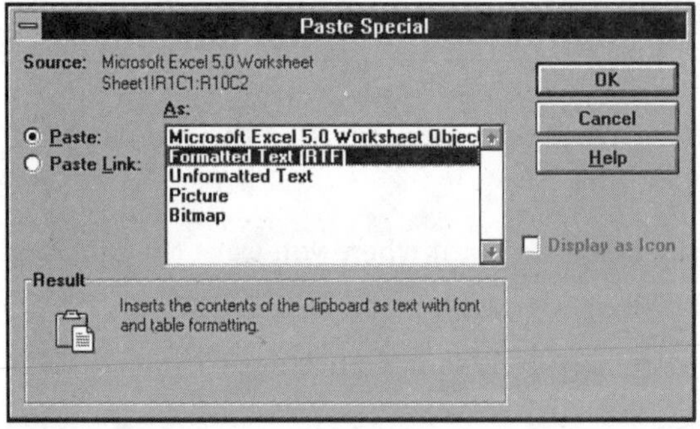

Fig. 36.18
Select one of the options in the Paste Special dialog box to format your text.

► "Linking an Excel Worksheet to a Word Document," p. 795

The options in the Paste Special dialog box enable you to link, embed, or specify a format for the spreadsheet. You can do any of the following things:

- To link information to the spreadsheet, select the Paste **L**ink option.
- To insert the Excel spreadsheet as an object, select Microsoft Excel 5.0 Worksheet Object.

- To insert the spreadsheet as a table in your Word document (the default when you choose the **E**dit **P**aste command), select the Formatted Text (RTF) option.

- To insert the spreadsheet with tabs separating data that was in columns, as shown in figure 36.19, select the Unformatted Text option. If you select this option, you probably will have to select the data and change the tabs if you want the information to align.

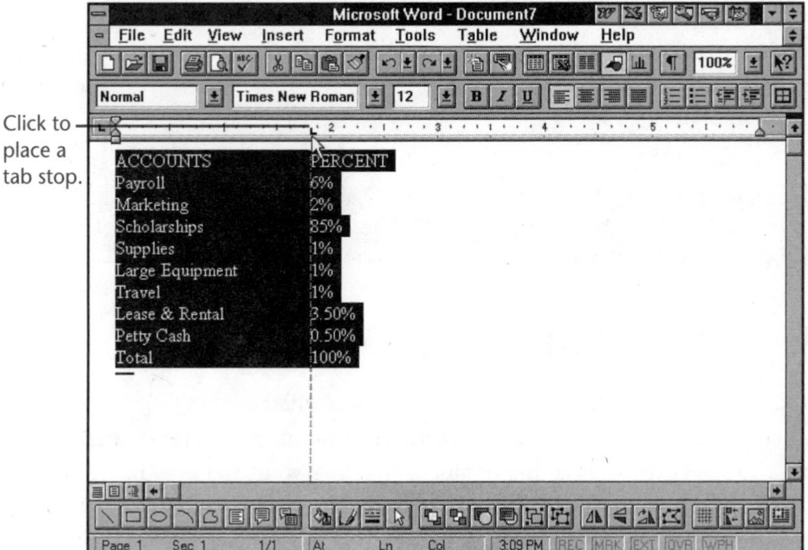

Fig. 36.19
When you copy information from the spreadsheet, set a tab stop to separate the items that were in columns in the worksheet.

◀ "Setting Tabs," p. 130

- To insert the spreadsheet as a graphic, as shown in figure 36.20, select the Picture or Bitmap option in the **A**s list box. Both options insert the spreadsheet as a diagram, but Picture takes up less room in the file and prints faster. To edit the picture, first select the picture to display the small black handles. To resize the picture, point to one of the handles until the mouse pointer changes to a double-headed black arrow, and then drag. To move the picture up or down in the document, drag the drag-and-drop white arrow and rectangle mouse pointer.

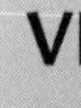

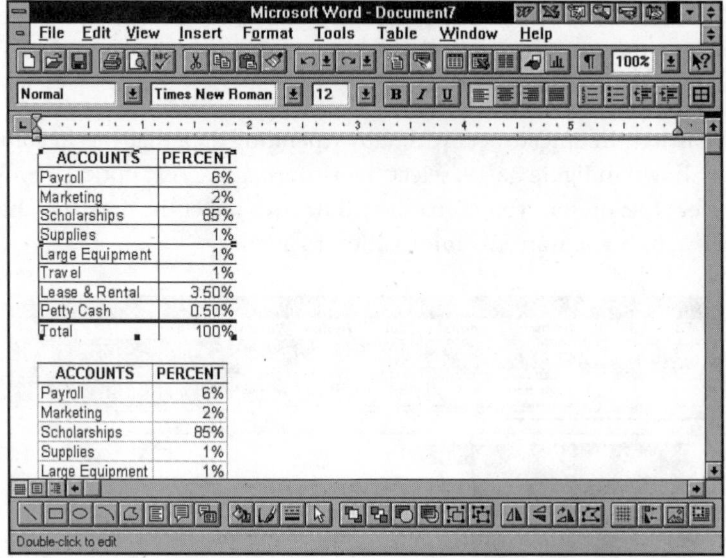

Fig. 36.20 The top table shows the Picture format, and the bottom table shows the Bitmap format.

◄ "Working with Graphics," p. 219

Copying Text from a Database

◄ "Exploring Access," p. 580

Copying information from an Access database is similar to copying a spreadsheet. Because an Access database is organized into many different parts, you first have to select the part of the database that you want to copy. In this section, you need to copy a list of the board members and officers. There is a query with the information you need.

To copy information from a table or query in Access, follow these steps:

1. Click the Access button in the Microsoft Office toolbar.

2. If necessary, choose the **F**ile **O**pen command or press Ctrl+O to open the database. The Database window appears, as shown in figure 36.21.

3. Select an object button. For data in a spreadsheetlike format, select the Table or Query object button.

4. Double-click the name in the object list, or select the name and then click the **O**pen button. The object opens. In this example, the Board and Officers Query opens in a row-and-column format.

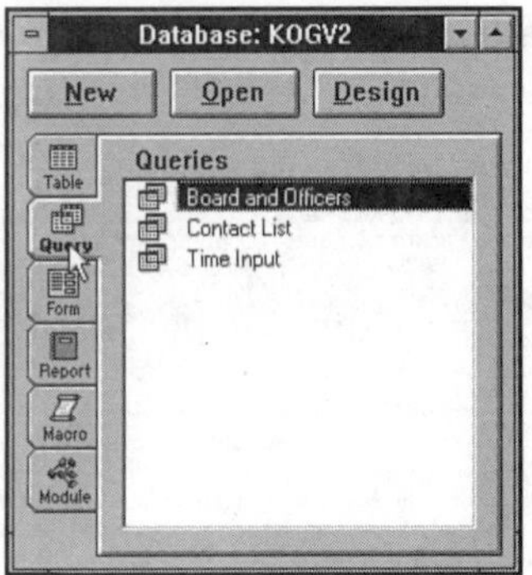

Fig. 36.21
The Database window.

5. Select the items you want to copy. When you move to the field names at the top of the list, the mouse pointer changes to a black down arrow, as shown in figure 36.22. Drag across the field names to select columns. If you position the mouse pointer to the left of the first column, the mouse pointer changes to a black right arrow. Drag the mouse pointer up or down to select an entire row. You also can select adjacent cells with the white arrow within the cells.

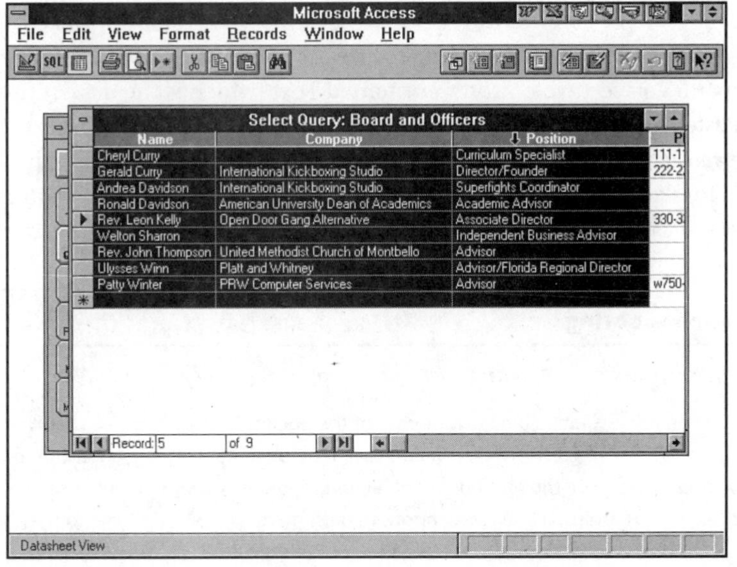

Fig. 36.22
Drag the black down arrow to select columns to copy.

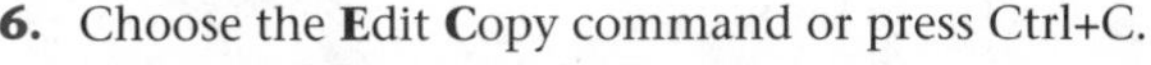
6. Choose the **E**dit **C**opy command or press Ctrl+C.

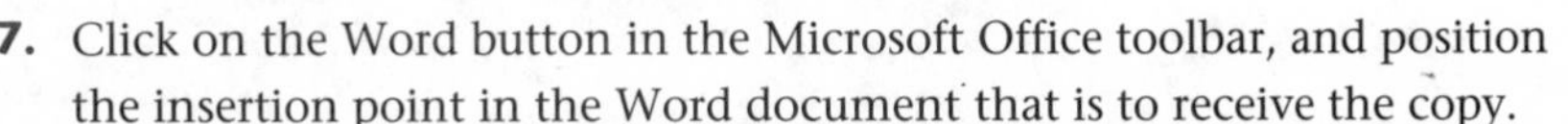
7. Click on the Word button in the Microsoft Office toolbar, and position the insertion point in the Word document that is to receive the copy.

8. Choose the **E**dit **P**aste command or press Ctrl+V. The Access information appears in a table in Word, as shown in figure 36.23.

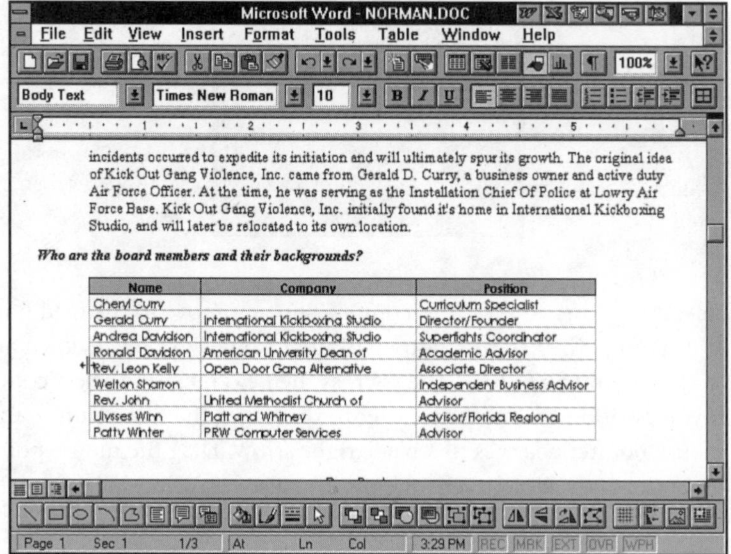

Fig. 36.23 The Access information appears in a formatted table when you paste into Word.

If you choose the **E**dit Paste **S**pecial command with an Access table in the Clipboard, you see two options: Formatted Text (which is the default used for Edit Paste), and Unformatted Text. When you select Unformatted Text, the table translates to tabs between the columns, as shown earlier (in figure 36.19) for Excel. To align the text, you need to set tabs. You cannot link an Access table or query to your Word document.

◄ "Adjusting Column and Cell Width," p. 214

Troubleshooting

I can't see much of my document after I move a table.

When you move a table, the right margin of the document may move so that it no longer is visible. To correct the problem, click the horizontal scroll bar after the scroll box, and then before the scroll box. This action repositions your document so you can see both margins. If you still cannot see both margins, you may have to use the Zoom button (the second button from the right in the Standard toolbar).

Copying Pictures from PowerPoint

In addition to copying text or data, you may want to copy a picture from PowerPoint or a chart from Excel. The procedure is essentially the same: select the object, choose the **E**dit **C**opy command, and then choose the **E**dit **P**aste command.

To copy a PowerPoint picture, follow these steps:

1. Click the PowerPoint button in the Microsoft Office toolbar.
2. If necessary, choose the **F**ile **O**pen command to open the presentation.
3. Go to the slide shown in figure 36.24 by clicking the Next Slide or Preview Slide buttons (double arrows) in the scroll bar, or by using the Slide Sorter View button and double-clicking the slide you want.

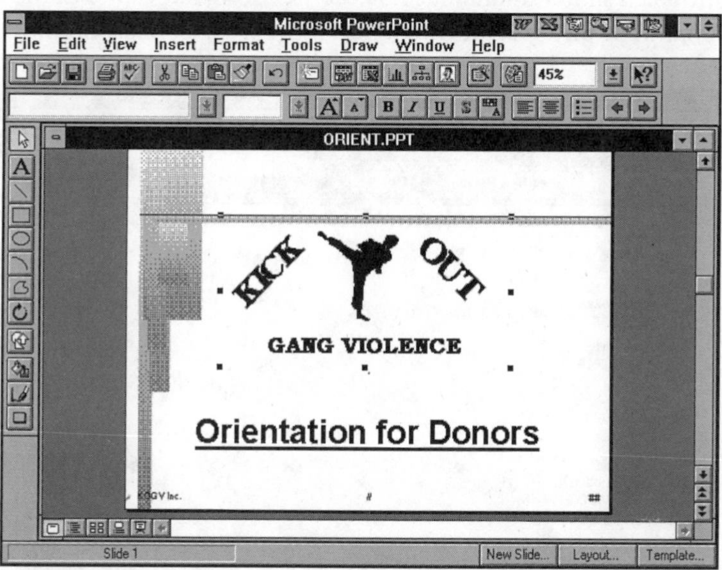

Fig. 36.24
The black handles show that the object is selected and ready to copy.

◄ "Moving Through a Presentation," p. 447

4. Click the object to copy. Black handles surround the object to show that it is selected.
5. Choose the **E**dit **C**opy command or press Ctrl+C.

6. Return to the position in your Word document where you want to place the copy.
7. Choose the **E**dit **P**aste command or press Ctrl+V. The picture appears in your Word document.

The Edit Paste Special option does not do anything different from the Edit Paste command. You cannot link or embed the object with Paste Special.

To select the picture, click the object. To change the size of the picture in Word, drag a handle. To move the picture vertically in the document, drag it to the new position. To move the picture vertically or have text wrap around the object, however, you need to frame the picture first, as described in the following section.

Framing a Picture

When you paste a PowerPoint picture or an Excel chart, or select Picture or Bitmap in the Paste Special dialog box, the graphic is one object in your Word document. For better control in positioning the object, you can frame it. Figure 36.25 shows an unframed object in page layout view. Text does not wrap around the picture, and you cannot move it horizontally on the page.

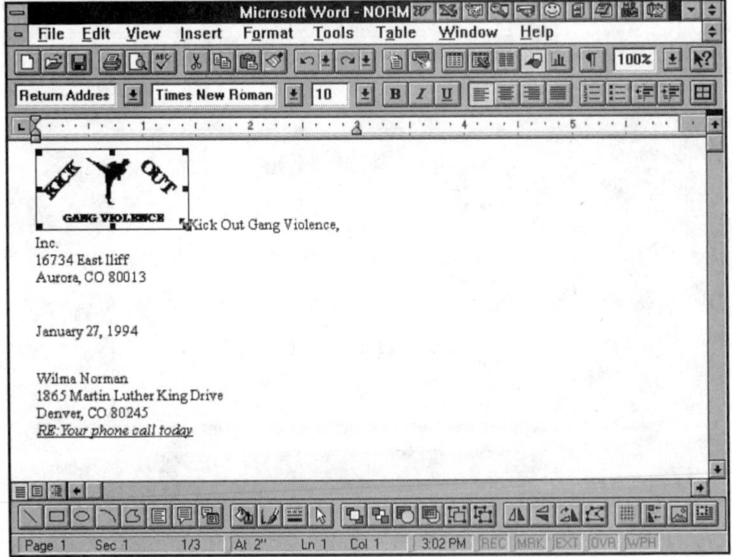

Fig. 36.25 In this example, the picture had to be made smaller. Notice that the text does not wrap around the picture.

To frame a picture, follow these steps:

1. Select the object.

2. Click the Frame button in the Drawing toolbar or choose the **I**nsert **F**rame command.

3. Choose Yes if the program prompts you to go to page layout view.

When the object is framed, you can move it horizontally on the page and position text to the left or right of the object. To edit the properties of the frame, choose the F**o**rmat Fra**m**e command. You can specify whether you want text to wrap around the picture, set the size and location of the picture, and remove the frame. Figures 36.26 and 36.27 show the completed letter.

◄ "Working with Graphics," p. 219

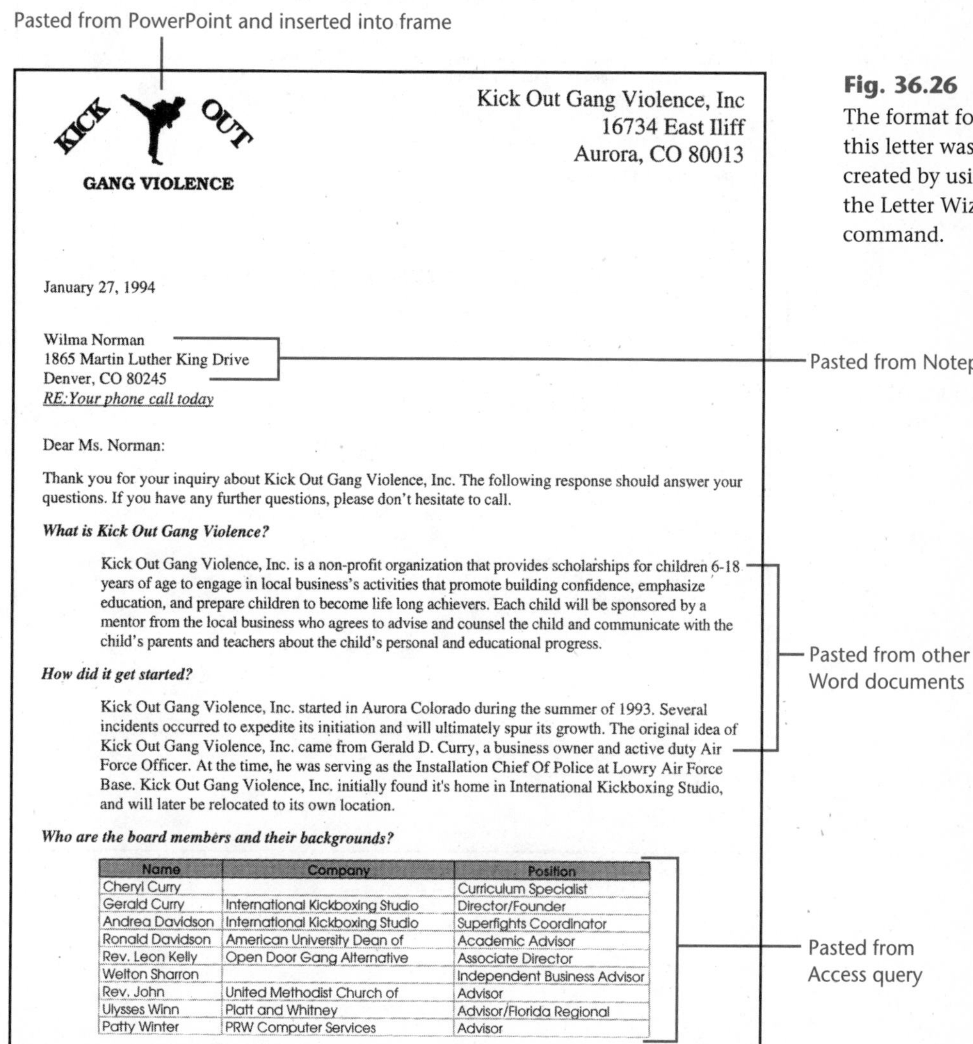

Kick Out Gang Violence, Inc
16734 East Iliff
Aurora, CO 80013

January 27, 1994

Wilma Norman
1865 Martin Luther King Drive
Denver, CO 80245
RE: Your phone call today

Dear Ms. Norman:

Thank you for your inquiry about Kick Out Gang Violence, Inc. The following response should answer your questions. If you have any further questions, please don't hesitate to call.

What is Kick Out Gang Violence?

Kick Out Gang Violence, Inc. is a non-profit organization that provides scholarships for children 6-18 years of age to engage in local business's activities that promote building confidence, emphasize education, and prepare children to become life long achievers. Each child will be sponsored by a mentor from the local business who agrees to advise and counsel the child and communicate with the child's parents and teachers about the child's personal and educational progress.

How did it get started?

Kick Out Gang Violence, Inc. started in Aurora Colorado during the summer of 1993. Several incidents occurred to expedite its initiation and will ultimately spur its growth. The original idea of Kick Out Gang Violence, Inc. came from Gerald D. Curry, a business owner and active duty Air Force Officer. At the time, he was serving as the Installation Chief Of Police at Lowry Air Force Base. Kick Out Gang Violence, Inc. initially found it's home in International Kickboxing Studio, and will later be relocated to its own location.

Who are the board members and their backgrounds?

Name	Company	Position
Cheryl Curry		Curriculum Specialist
Gerald Curry	International Kickboxing Studio	Director/Founder
Andrea Davidson	International Kickboxing Studio	Superfights Coordinator
Ronald Davidson	American University Dean of	Academic Advisor
Rev. Leon Kelly	Open Door Gang Alternative	Associate Director
Welton Sharron		Independent Business Advisor
Rev. John	United Methodist Church of	Advisor
Ulysses Winn	Platt and Whitney	Advisor/Florida Regional
Patty Winter	PRW Computer Services	Advisor

Fig. 36.26
The format for this letter was created by using the Letter Wizard command.

Fig. 36.27
The second page of the letter shown in figure 36.26.

Pasted from other Word document

Pasted from Excel spreadsheet

What signs should I look for if my children are involved in gangs?

Be aware if your child:

1. Wants to buy an excessive amount of blue and red for his or her wardrobe.
2. Wears sagging pants on hips or waist.
3. Wears an excessive amount of gold jewelry.
4. Uses excessive amounts of gang language.
5. Withdraws from family members.
6. Associates with undesirables.
7. Stays out later than usual.
8. Desires too much privacy.
9. Develops major attitude problems with parents, teachers or those in authority.
10. Starts to use drugs and alcohol.
11. Uses hand signs.
12. Receives money or articles without your permission or awareness.
13. Suddenly using racial slurs or hateful comments about other religions.
14. Wants to wear boots, shave his/her head, wear suspenders of a specific color.
15. Lacks identification or has false identification.
16. Wears beepers and begins using cellular phones.

What is your FAX number?

750-3317

How do I donate? & if I do, where do my funds go?

ACCOUNTS:	PERCENTAGE OF DONATION
Payroll	6%
Marketing	2%
Scholarships	85%
Supplies	1%
Large Equipment (over $500)	1%
Travel	1%
Lease & Rental	3.50%
Petty Cash	0.50%
Total	100%

Can I volunteer?

Certainly, we need office workers and volunteers to recruit sponsors, participating organizations, and scholarship candidates. Call us at (303)745-3646. Thank you for your interest in our organization and for your concern about our children and violence.

Sincerely,

Patricia L. Winter

PW/rw

Enclosures: 1

From Here...

This chapter focused on copying information from different sources into a Word document. In some cases, you may want to link information instead. This added capability means that when the source document changes, the link automatically updates the target document. For more information, refer to the following chapters:

- Chapter 37, "Sharing Data Between Applications with Linking and Embedding," focuses on linking information so that the document remains updated.
- Chapter 38, "Using Mail with Other Microsoft Office Products," shows you how to pass documents among different users on your network.
- Chapter 39, "Sending a Mass Mailing," shows how you can avoid typing the name and address in every letter by using your existing Excel spreadsheet or Access database.
- Chapter 40, "Linking and Embedding within Access To Manage Information," shows you how to use Access with other Office applications.

Chapter 37

Sharing Data between Applications with Linking and Embedding

by Rick and Patty Winter

Earlier chapters in this part of the book showcased the nonprofit organization Kick Out Gang Violence and suggested ways that you can use Microsoft Office. Many parts of the existing documents could be useful for requests for information and for other reports and documents that may need to be created. Those who would need the information include prospective donors, sponsors, participating organizations, the press, parents, schools, prospective scholarship recipients, event attendees, paid staff, volunteers, the director, and the board of directors. Trying to provide information to everyone is a huge task. By using Microsoft Offices capabilities to link and embed information, you can streamline the task of supplying information to a diverse audience.

In this chapter, you learn to

- Link information between documents
- Update links
- Edit links
- Embed information within documents

Moving beyond Copy and Paste To Link Information

◀ "Copying Text between Word Documents," p. 767

You also may have documents or portions of documents that you need to use over and over. With Microsoft Office applications, you have different options to accomplish the same task. The first option is a simple copy and paste. Whenever you need information from one document, open the document, and select and copy the information. Then open the second document and paste the information at the appropriate point.

Although the copy and paste procedure is the easiest to master, there are two drawbacks. First, if the original information changes, you have to continually repeat the procedure if you want to keep your documents current. The second drawback is that you have to remember the application that created the information and where you put the files. If you want to edit the data, you may have to return to the original application.

To overcome these drawbacks, you have additional options for sharing data between files (and applications). One option is to create a link between two files. Whenever the data in the source file changes, the destination file will receive the update. The technical term for this is *dynamic date exchange* or *DDE*.

Note

This chapter references the *source* application and document as the application and file on disk that supplies data. The *destination* or target application and document is the application and file on disk that receives the data.

Using Embedding To Link Information

◀ "Embedding the Chart," p. 218

◀ "Embedding and Linking Objects," p. 713

Another option is to embed the information into your destination document. When you embed the information, you can use the source application to update the information. You have two ways to get to the tools (menus and toolbars) of the source application. You can launch the source application from within the destination document, and a window appears with the source application showing the information to edit. The other possibility is new for Microsoft Office 4 applications. This is called *in-place editing*. When you select the object to edit, your menu and toolbar change to the source application, but you remain in the document and can see the surrounding text or data. The technical term for this kind of sharing is *object linking and embedding (OLE)*. If the source application starts when you edit the data, it is OLE 1.0 compliant. If you can edit the data without leaving the destination, the source application is OLE 2.0 compliant.

Note

This chapter mentions objects. An *object* can be text, a chart, table, picture, equation or any other form of information that you create and edit, usually with an application different from your source application.

One difference between linking and embedding is where the information is stored. Linked information is stored in the source document. The destination contains only a code that supplies the name of the source application, document, and the portion of the document. Embedded information is stored in the destination document.

In some cases, you cannot launch the source application by itself; you have to use your destination application to start the application. These applications are called *applets* (small applications) and include WordArt, Microsoft Graph, and others.

You may want to look at your existing documents and see if you will continually use different portions in other documents. Table 37.1 shows lists of the existing available documents for Kick Out Gang Violence. Suppose as office manager you use Excel to list the original document and divide the document into parts that might be used in multiple documents. You decide it would be better to create separate documents for each frequently used part of a larger document. You also include a column for which application might be best for the subdocuments.

Table 37.1 Portions of Documents That Can Be Linked with Other Applications

Portion of Document That Can Be Used Elsewhere	Proposed Application	Where Else Needed
BUSPLAN.DOC		
Logo	PowerPoint	Will this change in many documents?
Purpose	Word	Queries, brochure, many documents
New-chapter networking	Word	Also instruct new chapters
Timeline for development	Word	Goals, manage timeline, board notes
Geographic development	Word	Goals, board notes
Distribution of funds	Excel	Goals, board notes
Reasons to donate	Word	Donors, sponsors presentations, brochure
Benefits to your company	Word	Sponsors presentation, brochure
History	Word	Queries, press release, brochure
Equipment needed for startup	Excel	Need to update as new numbers, info received
Orgchart	Organization Chart	Will change; board notes
Budget	Excel	Summary, internal management, board notes
Board of directors	Access	Queries, phone list, mailing, board notes
FACTSHET.DOC		
Logo	PowerPoint	Will this change in many documents?
Purpose	Word	Queries, brochure, many documents
Eligibility	Word	New-chapter notices, scholarship queries
Scholarship amount	Word	New-chapter notices, scholarship queries
Submission process	Word	New-chapter notices, scholarship queries

Using Common Steps To Link Documents

The procedure for linking any kind of application to any other application is essentially the same regardless of the source or destination application. You copy the source into the Clipboard and then use the Link option in the Paste Special dialog box to create the link. In the Paste Special dialog box, you also can specify the type of format in which the information is presented.

In some cases, you may not be able to use the Paste Special dialog box to create the link. To link a PowerPoint slide to a Word document, for example, you may have to use the Insert Object dialog box to create the link. This procedure is described in "Linking a PowerPoint Picture to a Word Document" later in this chapter.

To copy an item to the Clipboard and link the item to another document, follow these steps:

1. Select the item in the source document.
2. Choose the **E**dit **C**opy command or press Ctrl+C.

3. Move to the target application and document. Position the insertion point where you want the link to appear.
4. Choose the **E**dit Paste **S**pecial command. A Paste Special dialog box appears, as shown in figure 37.1.

   Several format types may be available, depending on the source application. Two options usually are available: Paste and Paste Link. The Link option is grayed if the source document for the selected format cannot be linked.

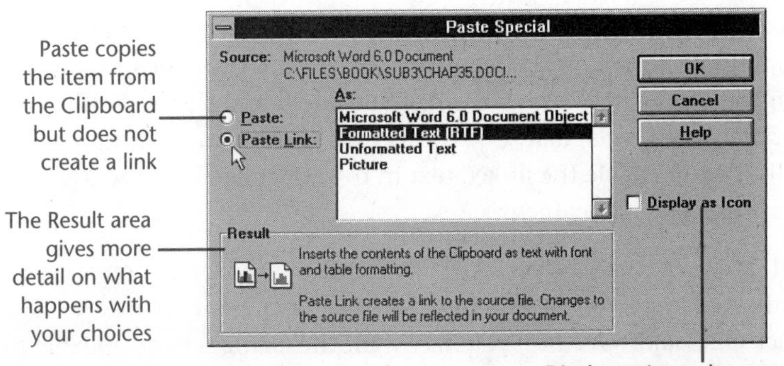

Fig. 37.1
In the Paste Special dialog box, you can choose Paste and Paste Link.

5. Select a format option in the **A**s list box.

6. Select Paste **L**ink.

7. Choose OK.

The As list box shows different formats. These formats change, depending on the source and target applications. In general, four different formats appear in most links. One of the formats usually is Object. In figure 37.1, the specific format is Microsoft Word 6.0 Document Object. When you insert, or embed, an object, you can double-click the object or its icon (if the Display as Icon option is active) and then edit the object with the source application.

Another format option is Formatted Text. This option means that the object appears in your target document with most of the formatting (fonts, borders, and so on) from the source document. This option is different from Unformatted Text, in which the text takes on the format of the target document.

The last option is to add a picture of the document. Picture and Bitmap both create a picture of the object. Whether the original document is a picture or text, the link becomes a picture, and you can size and move the picture as one item.

Linking Two Word Documents

When you want to link two Word documents, you can use Paste Special to create the link, or you can use the Insert File feature. To insert a portion of a file, use the Paste Special feature, which is helpful if the source document is not a complete paragraph. To insert an entire document, use the Insert File feature.

To link two Word documents, follow the steps in the preceding section, "Using Common Steps To Link Documents." Select and copy the text you want to link, and then move to your target document and choose **E**dit Paste **S**pecial. In the Paste Special dialog box, select the Unformatted Text option in the **A**s list box to enable the linked text in the target document to assume the format of the target document.

Figure 37.1 shows that the purpose for Kick Out Gang Violence is mentioned in the business plan, fact sheet, and in most other documents. As office manager for Kick Out Gang Violence, you may want the changes to be updated in all documents containing the purpose. Therefore, you might create the separate document PURPOSE.DOC to describe the purpose of Kick Out Gang Violence. Because the text is formatted differently in the documents, you would link the text using the Unformatted Text option in the **A**s list box of the Paste Special dialog box.

Displaying the Link

When you move within the linked section, as shown in figure 37.2, the link is highlighted in gray. Although you can edit the linked text, the editing changes disappear when the link is updated (when you open the file again; print the file; or press F9, the Update Field shortcut key). The gray highlight reminds you not to edit this part of the document. If the link is not highlighted, choose the **T**ools **O**ptions command and then select the View tab. In the Fi**e**ld Shading drop-down list, select When Selected or Always.

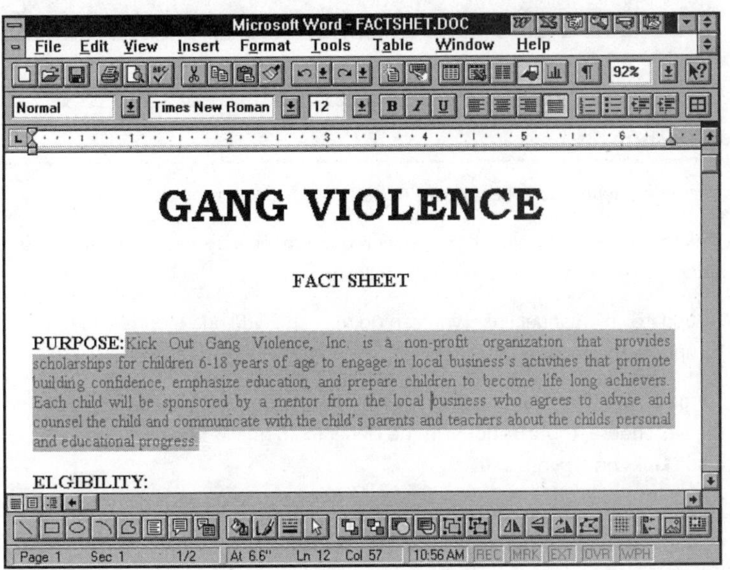

Fig. 37.2
The linked area in the document is highlighted in gray.

If you want to see the name of the source document, you can display the field name codes rather than the actual text. Choose the **T**ools **O**ptions command. In the View tab, select the **F**ield Codes option. (To display the text, deselect **F**ield Codes.) Figure 37.3 shows field code used in place of text.

Fig. 37.3
Field code used in place of text.

The file is linked to PURPOSE.DOC, and Word 6 is the source application

The file is linked to LOGO.PPT, and PowerPoint is the source application

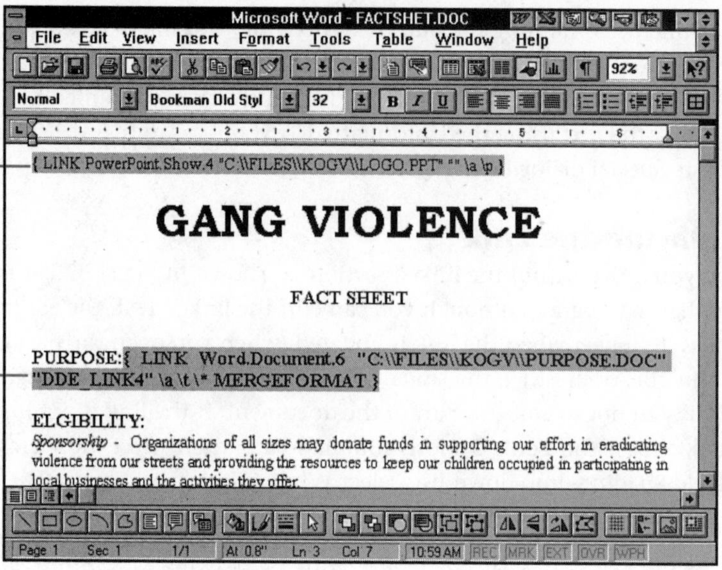

> **Troubleshooting**
>
> *Changes in my source document aren't reflected in my destination document.*
>
> The link may be an automatic link or may require manual updating (see the section on updating links). You can also do the following things:
>
> To update any manual links, you can go to each field code by pressing F11. To update the code or link, press F9.
>
> To make sure that your document updates any automatic links when you open the file, choose **T**ools **O**ptions. In the General tab, make sure that Update Automatic **L**inks on Open is active.
>
> To make sure that your document prints with the latest information, choose **T**ools **O**ptions. In the Print tab, make sure that Update **L**inks is active.

Editing Links

When you link a document, you must keep both the document name and the document in the same location (drive and directory). If you rename, delete, or move a document, the link is broken, and you get an error in your destination document. In some cases, you can break the link so that the source document is inserted into the target document without a link; in other cases, you can change the name of the source document.

To change links, follow these steps:

1. In Word, choose the **E**dit Lin**k**s command. The Links dialog box appears, as shown in figure 37.4.

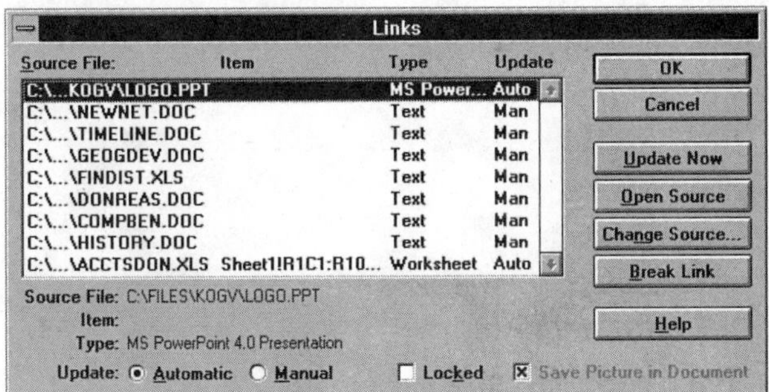

Fig. 37.4
The Links dialog box allows you to update, change, or break links.

2. Select the files in the **S**ource file list box.

3. Do one or more of the following things:

   - Choose the **U**pdate Now button to update the link with any changes in the source file.

   - Choose the Cha**n**ge Source button to change the file name or location of the linked file in the Change Source dialog box.

   - Choose the **B**reak Link button to insert the object into the document and unlink it. When Word displays a message box, asking whether you are sure you want to break the selected links, choose Yes.

4. Choose OK when you finish.

Inserting a File into a Document

You also can link documents by using the Insert File feature, which enables you to insert the entire file. When you use Paste Special to link a file, you can insert text before or after the source-document information, so the target document does not include the entire text. Insert File alleviates this problem. The file that you insert can be from the same application or a different application.

To insert a file into a document, follow these steps:

1. Move to the position in the target document where you want to insert the file.

◄ "Using File Dialog Boxes," p. 73

2. Choose the **I**nsert Fi**l**e command. The File dialog box appears, as shown in figure 37.5.

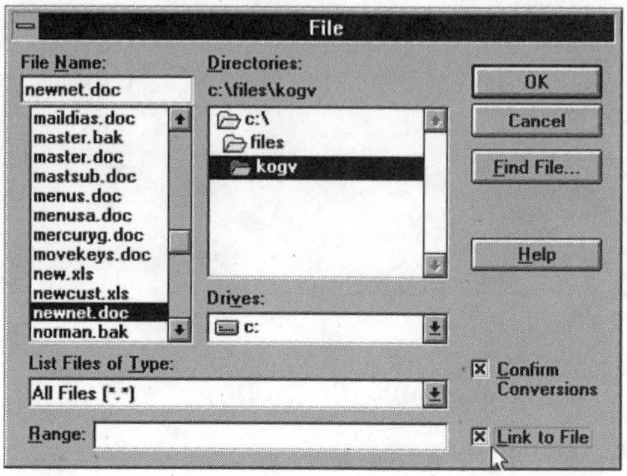

Fig. 37.5
Select the Link to File option to create the link between the files.

3. Identify the file you want to insert, including the drive and directory if necessary.

4. Select the **L**ink to File option.

5. Choose OK.

As in the Paste Special example earlier in this chapter, you can display the linked document with a gray highlight or how the field codes. In figure 37.6, the revised business-plan document shows field codes for the linked documents.

Note

If you want to insert several documents into a single larger document, give your documents a consistent appearance by using the same formats for each one. You also can use templates and styles to help ensure consistency among documents. For more information, see "Formatting with Styles" in Chapter 9, "Working with Large Documents."

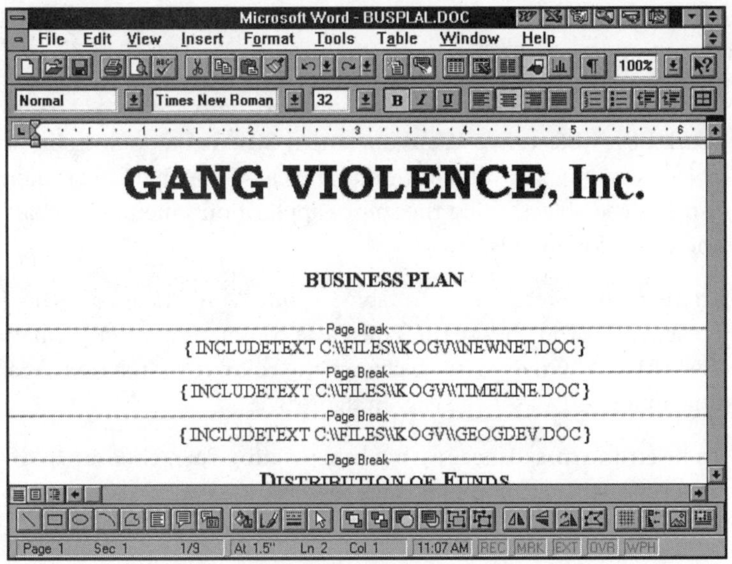

Fig. 37.6
The field code INCLUDETEXT appears for the Word documents NEWNET.DOC, TIMELINE.DOC, and GEOGDEV.DOC.

Linking an Excel Worksheet to a Word Document

The procedure for linking a range or an entire Excel worksheet to a Word document is the same as for linking Word documents. You can use either the Paste Special command or the Insert File command, although it's easier to format a document when you use the Paste Special command. When you use the Insert File command, the resulting table sometimes is hard to center on the page because of extra space for the last column or extra cells. In the Paste Special dialog box, you have the same formatting choices when you Paste Link as when you Paste (see fig. 37.7).

◄ "Copying Text Between Word Documents," p. 767

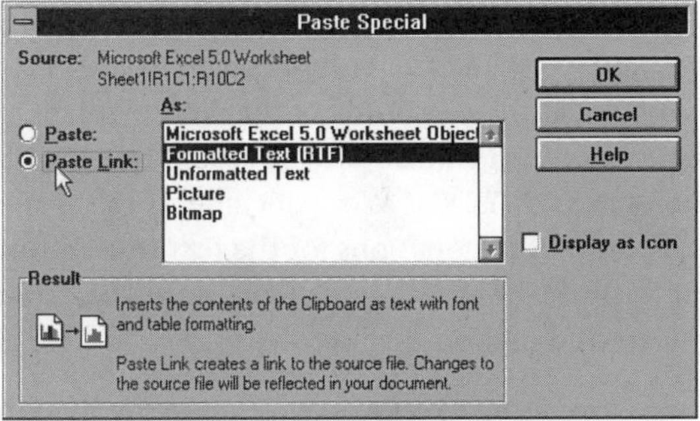

Fig. 37.7
Choose the Paste Link option to link the spreadsheet to the Word document.

The following list describes the formatting options in the Paste Special dialog box shown in figure 37.7. The results appear in figure 37.8.

- To insert the Excel spreadsheet as an object, select Microsoft Excel 5.0 Worksheet Object. In a Word document, when you double-click the object, you enter the application that created the object. You then can edit the object, using the source application's menus, toolbars, and other commands.

- To insert the spreadsheet as a table in your Word document (the default choice when you choose the **E**dit **P**aste command), select Formatted Text (RTF). You may need to change the column widths for the table to line up properly, as is the case in figure 37.8.

- To insert the spreadsheet with tabs separating data, choose Unformatted Text. You may have to select the data and change the tabs for the selection if you want the information to align.

◄ "Working with Graphics," p. 219

- To insert the spreadsheet as a graphic, select Picture or Bitmap. Both options insert the spreadsheet as a diagram, but Picture generally takes up less room in the file and prints faster. In figure 37.8, however, there is almost no discernible difference between Microsoft Excel 5.0 Worksheet Object, Picture, and Bitmap. In fact, these three options do the same thing. They all insert a picture into the Word document, and you can double-click all three options to go to Excel to edit the object. To edit the picture, first select the picture to show the small square handles. To resize the picture, point to one of the handles until the mouse pointer changes to a small double-headed black arrow; then drag. To move the picture up or down in the document, drag the drag-and-drop white arrow and rectangle mouse pointer. To go to Excel to change the data, double-click the picture.

Suppose that now you need to create a quarterly report which contains text, Excel worksheets, and Excel charts. To do this, you would begin by inserting some introductory text at the beginning of the report which includes the purpose and history of the organization. You would then link the PURPOSE.DOC and HISTORY.DOC Word documents to the quarterly report file. In order to report on the donations for the first three months, you probably might want to show the amount in a table, a pie chart by type of donation, and a bar chart of donations by month.

Figure 37.9 shows a formatted Excel worksheet. Because the numbers will change, you will want to link rather than paste the worksheet and the charts.

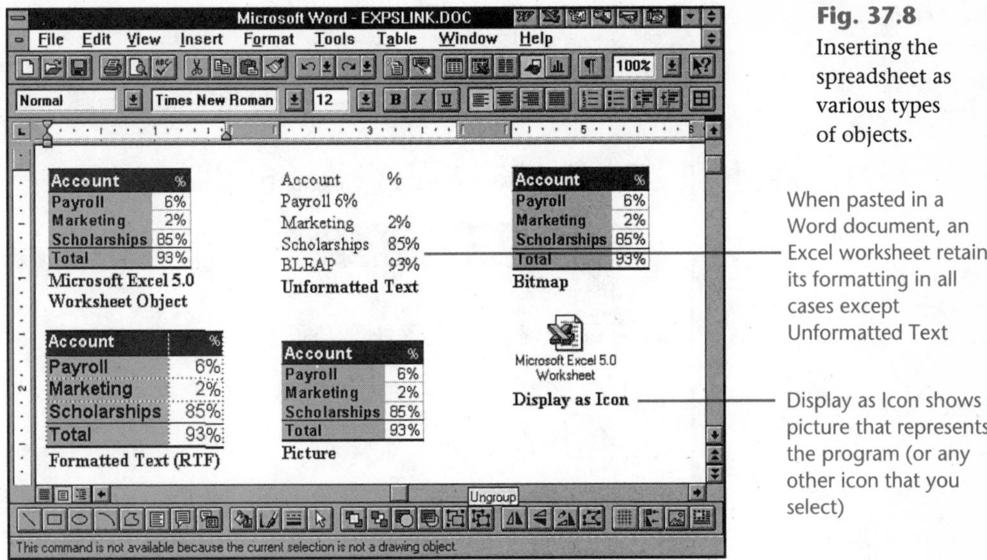

Fig. 37.8 Inserting the spreadsheet as various types of objects.

When pasted in a Word document, an Excel worksheet retains its formatting in all cases except Unformatted Text

Display as Icon shows a picture that represents the program (or any other icon that you select)

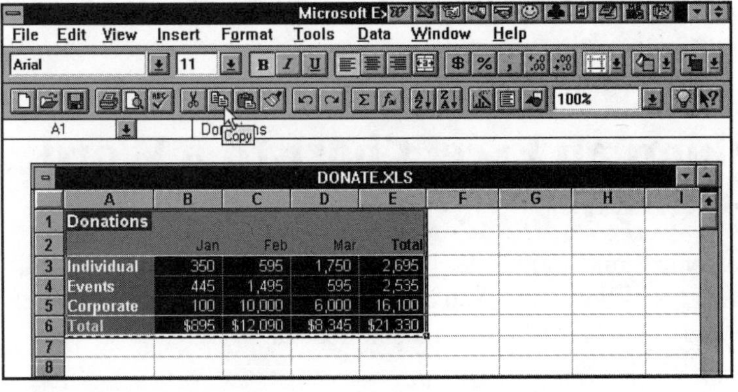

	A	B	C	D	E
1	Donations				
2		Jan	Feb	Mar	Total
3	Individual	350	595	1,750	2,695
4	Events	445	1,495	595	2,535
5	Corporate	100	10,000	6,000	16,100
6	Total	$895	$12,090	$8,345	$21,330

Fig. 37.9 Highlight the range in Excel, and choose Edit Copy.

To copy this worksheet into a Word document, follow these steps:

1. In Excel, highlight the range to be linked (A1:E6).
2. Choose **E**dit **C**opy or press Ctrl+C.
3. Switch to Word.
4. Choose **E**dit Paste **S**pecial. The Paste Special dialog box appears.
5. Select Paste **L**ink and **A**s Picture. Choose OK. The result appears in figure 37.10. Notice that the picture is left-justified.

◄ "Switching between Applications," p. 93

◄ "Moving between Windows Programs," p. 753

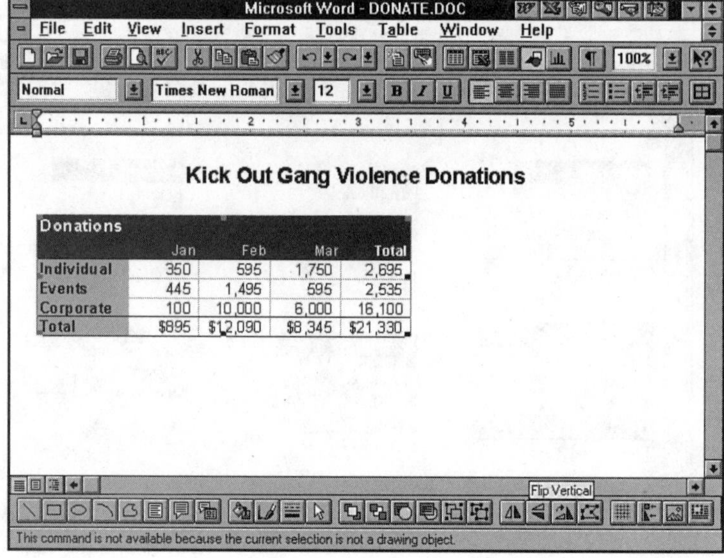

Fig. 37.10
The worksheet picture appears left-justified in the Word document.

6. If you want to center the worksheet, select the picture and then click the Center button.

Linking an Excel Chart to a Word Document

◄ "Creating a Chart with the ChartWizard," p. 348

Suppose you want to add a pie chart and bar chart to this page in your quarterly report document. You can create charts quickly by clicking the ChartWizard button in Excel's Standard toolbar.

Creating a Pie Chart

To create a pie chart, follow these steps:

1. Drag the white-cross mouse pointer to highlight the titles in A3 to A5.

2. Hold down the Ctrl button and drag to highlight E3 to E5.

3. Click the ChartWizard button. The mouse pointer changes to a graph and a plus sign, as shown in figure 37.11.

4. Click Sheet2 to draw the chart there.

5. Drag from the top-left corner to the bottom-right corner of the range where you want the chart to appear. The ChartWizard dialog box appears, displaying five steps.

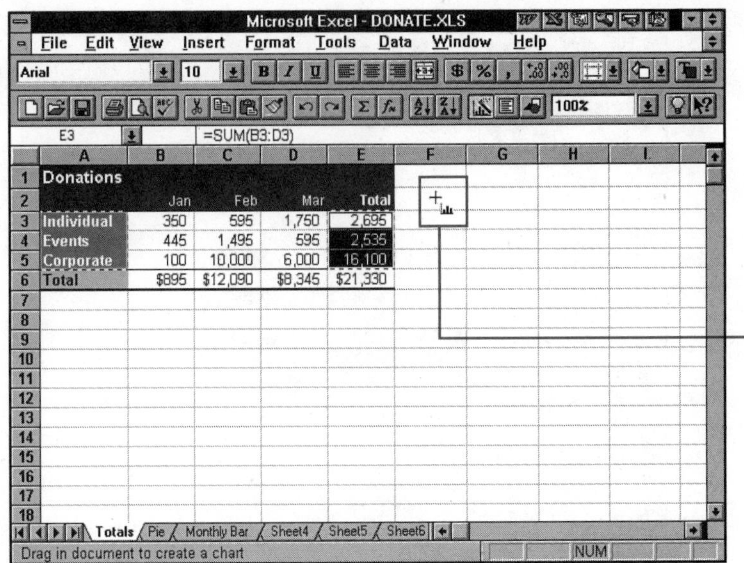

Fig. 37.11
After you select the ranges for your chart and click the ChartWizard button, the mouse pointer changes to a graph-and-plus-sign icon.

6. Choose **N**ext to go to the Step 2 ChartWizard dialog box.

7. Select 3-D Pie, and then choose the **N**ext button, as shown in figure 37.12.

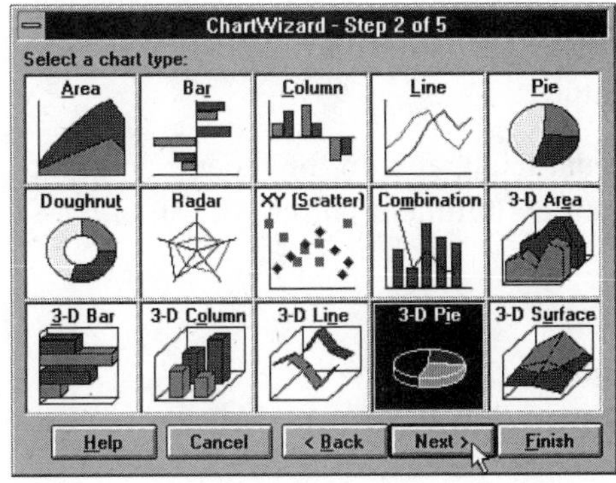

Fig. 37.12
The ChartWizard dialog boxes enable you to select chart types and other settings.

8. Choose **N**ext until you get to the Step 5 ChartWizard dialog box. Type **Donations YTD** in the **C**hart Title text box, and then choose **F**inish. The chart appears in the second sheet of the workbook, as shown in figure 37.13.

9. You can copy the chart the same way you do a range. Because the chart already is selected (handles surround the chart), choose the **E**dit **C**opy command or press Ctrl+C.

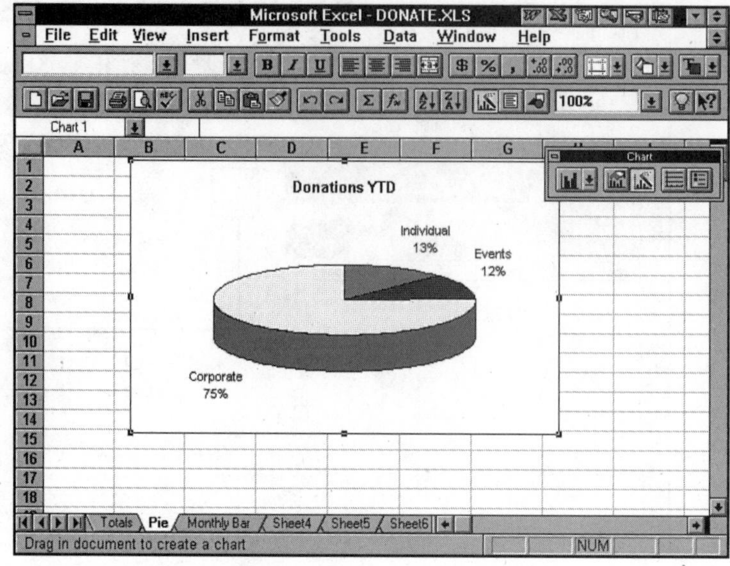

Fig. 37.13
The chart appears in Sheet2, surrounded by handles.

10. Return to the quarterly report document.
11. Choose the **E**dit Paste **S**pecial command. The Paste Special dialog box appears.
12. Select Picture and Paste **L**ink. Choose OK. The chart appears in the Word document, surrounded by handles. If the handles do not appear, click the picture.

13. Choose F**o**rmat **P**aragraph. In the Indents and Spacing Tab, select Center from the Ali**g**nment pull-down list, or press Ctrl+E to center the picture.

Creating a Bar Chart

To create a bar chart, follow these steps:

1. Drag the white-cross mouse pointer to highlight the range A2 through D5.

2. Click the ChartWizard button.
3. Move to Sheet3, and highlight the range where the chart will appear.
4. Fill in the ChartWizard dialog boxes, including the 3-D column chart in Step 2 and format 4 in Step 3, and type **Donations by Month** in the **C**hart Title text box in Step 5. After you finish the ChartWizard dialog boxes, the chart is selected, with handles.

5. Choose the **E**dit **C**opy command, or press Ctrl+C.

6. Return to the quarterly report document.

7. Choose the **E**dit Paste **S**pecial command. The Paste Special dialog box appears.

8. In the **A**s list box, select Picture, and select the Paste **L**ink option. Choose OK. The chart appears in the Word document, with handles.

The third diagram on the page from the quarterly report is shown in figure 37.14. When the final numbers come in, simply go to the Excel range and edit them. Figure 37.15 shows an updated Word document with the new number (15,000) for March corporate donations.

Kick Out Gang Violence Donations

Donations	Jan	Feb	Mar	Total
Individual	350	595	1,750	2,695
Events	445	1,495	595	2,535
Corporate	100	10,000	6,000	16,100
Total	$895	$12,090	$8,345	$21,330

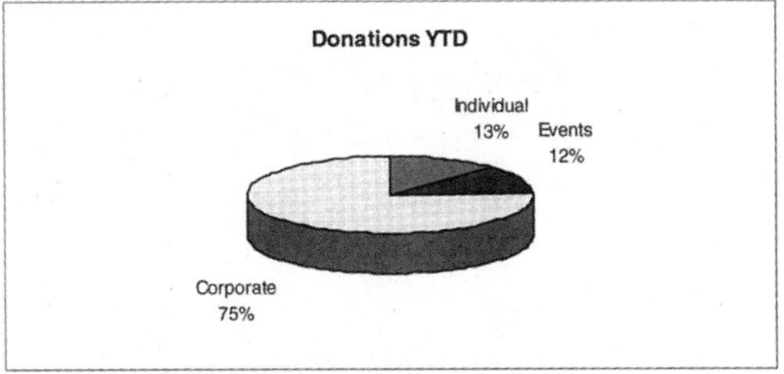

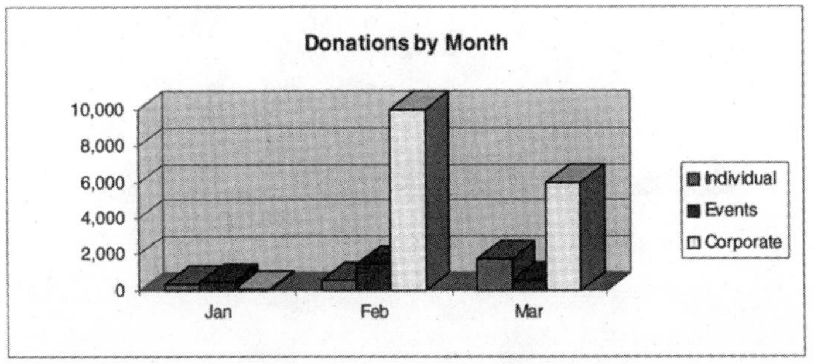

Fig. 37.14
The Excel range and two charts appear in the Word document.

> **Note**
>
> To remove the border surrounding the charts, change the charts in Excel rather than Word. In Excel, click to select the chart. In the middle of the chart, click the right mouse button and choose Format Object from the shortcut menu. In the Patterns tab, select **N**one in the Border section.

Kick Out Gang Violence Donations

Donations	Jan	Feb	Mar	Total
Individual	350	595	1,750	2,695
Events	445	1,495	595	2,535
Corporate	100	10,000	15,000	25,100
Total	$895	$12,090	$17,345	$30,330

New number in March (15,000)

Donations YTD

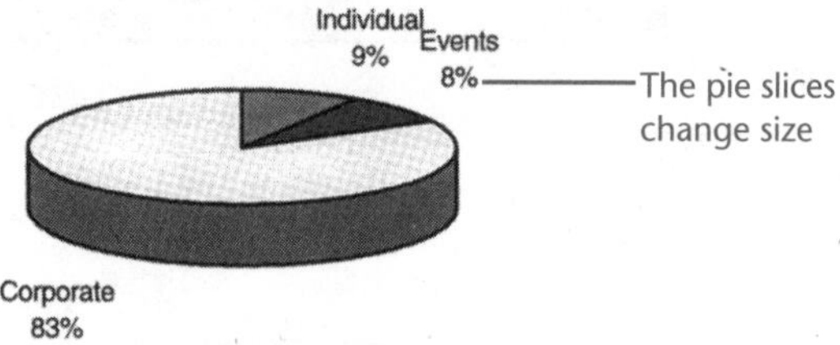

Donations by Month

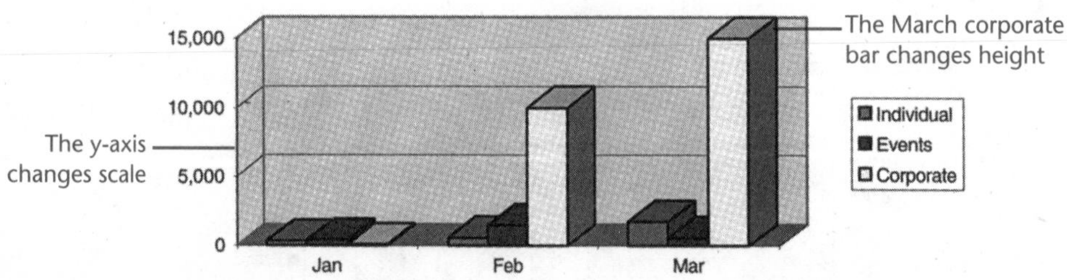

Fig. 37.15 After you update the Excel worksheet, the changes occur in the Word document.

Linking a PowerPoint Picture to a Word Document

Suppose that you went through your documents and noticed that the organization logo was on almost every document. If this was an established organization, simply pasting the logo would be appropriate. However, linking the logo may be inappropriate if there is a chance that the logo might change. If you want to link a PowerPoint slide to a Word document, the Paste Special command does not allow you to choose the Paste Link option. Insert File also does not have a PowerPoint option. To do the link you need to use the Insert Object command, and the first slide of the presentation must be the picture you want to link.

◄ "Adding, Inserting, and Deleting Slides," p. 448

To create your PowerPoint slide, follow these steps:

1. Go to PowerPoint.
2. To insert pictures into your slide, choose the **I**nsert **C**lip Art command (if the picture is part of Microsoft ClipArt Gallery) or the I**n**sert Picture command (if you got the picture from another source).
3. To type text, click the Text tool. Then click the location in the document where you want to add text, and type.

4. To create rotated text, click the Free Rotate tool, and drag the mouse pointer as shown in figure 37.16.

5. Save the document.

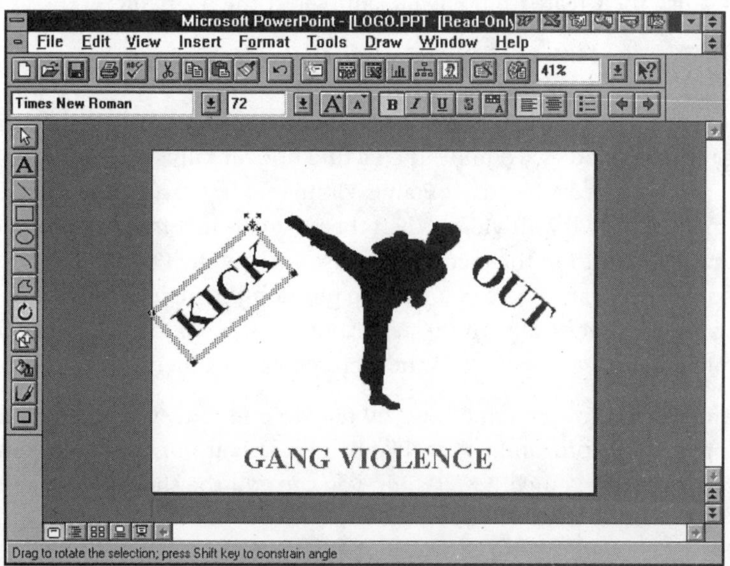

Fig. 37.16
Click the Free Rotate Tool, and drag the top-right handle to change the orientation of the text.

To link a PowerPoint slide to Word, follow these steps:

1. Create a PowerPoint slide with a picture and/or text you want to link to your Word document.

2. Save the PowerPoint presentation.

3. Go to the location in your Word document where you want to position the picture.

4. Choose the **I**nsert **O**bject command. The Object dialog box appears, as shown in figure 37.17.

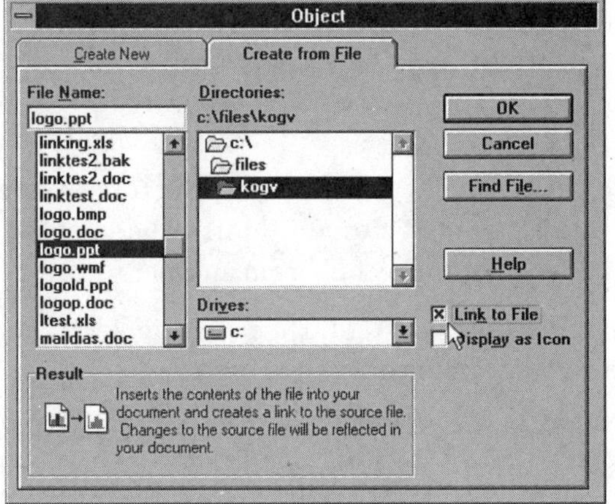

Fig. 37.17
You use the Object dialog box to select the type of information you want to insert.

5. Click the Create from **F**ile tab, and select the file name.

6. Select the Lin**k** to File option, and then choose OK.

The picture appears in your Word document. You can resize the picture by dragging the handles. To move the picture horizontally, you need to frame the picture. Choose the **I**nsert **F**rame command. If you are prompted, choose Yes to go to page layout view. When the picture is in a frame, you can drag the frame to position the picture. You also can use the F**o**rmat Fra**m**e command, and indicate where you want to position the picture (such as centered horizontally or vertically on the page) and whether text should wrap around the picture. Figure 37.18 shows the picture in a document.

If your PowerPoint presentation is more than one slide, you can double-click the picture in Word, and you will launch PowerPoint or the PowerPoint presentation. If you launch PowerPoint, you can edit the slide. If you launch the presentation, you can play the presentation by clicking each slide to move to the next slide.

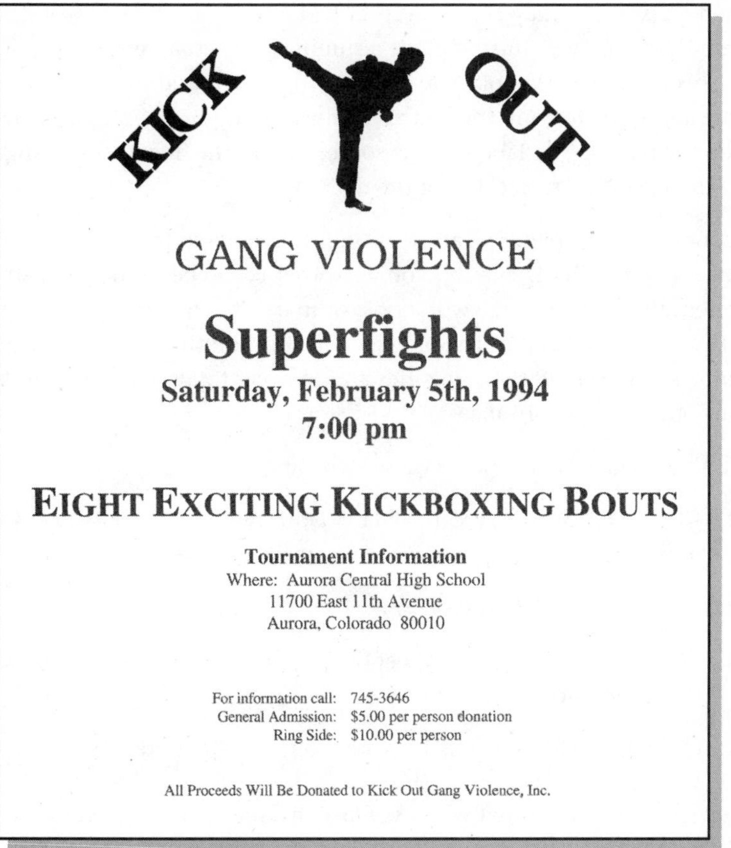

Fig. 37.18
The PowerPoint slide inserted into a Word document.

To change the object to a PowerPoint presentation within Word, follow these steps:

1. Select the PowerPoint object.
2. Choose **E**dit.
3. Choose MS PowerPoint 4.0 Slide **O**bject.
4. Choose Con**v**ert. The Convert Object dialog box appears.
5. Select the **C**overt To option, select MS PowerPoint 4.0 Presentation, and choose OK.

Linking Data between Excel Worksheets

◀ "Linking Formulas," p. 323

In some cases, you may want to repeat text or data in an Excel worksheet. For example, you may want to include a summary of actual numbers on a separate sheet of the workbook. You can copy the labels and numbers, or you can create a formula to copy the text and values. If you link through a formula, when the numbers or labels in the source part of the document change, they also change in the target part of the document.

The formula is simple: type an equal sign (=), move to the cell you want to copy, and press Enter. The cell you want to link can be in the same sheet, in a different sheet of the same workbook, or in a different workbook file. Figure 37.19 shows an example. The budget worksheet on the left contains monthly numbers. To see only the categories and the year totals, you could hide columns or create the formula.

To link the worksheets, follow these steps:

1. Choose **F**ile **N**ew to create a blank worksheet, and type **Budget 1994** in cell A1.
2. Move to cell A3, and type **=**.
3. Move to the source worksheet (identified as BUD94.XLS in the Kick Out Gang Violence example).
4. Click A3 in the BUD94.XLS worksheet, and then press Enter.

◀ "Creating Formulas," p. 309

Notice in figure 37.19 that when you use this method, the reference to the cells includes the file name (BUD94.XLS), the sheet name (Budget!), and an absolute reference to the cell (A3). If you want to copy the information, as in this example, remove the dollar signs to make the reference absolute. Then you can copy cell A3 from A4 through A11 to link the other cells. Notice in figure 37.20 that the cell reference has no dollar signs (N3).

Note

To arrange your worksheets side by side, as shown in figure 37.19, choose the **W**indow **A**rrange command, and then select the **T**iled option in the Arrange Window dialog box. You don't have to arrange your worksheets this way, however; you could move to the other worksheet by choosing the document name from the bottom of the Window menu.

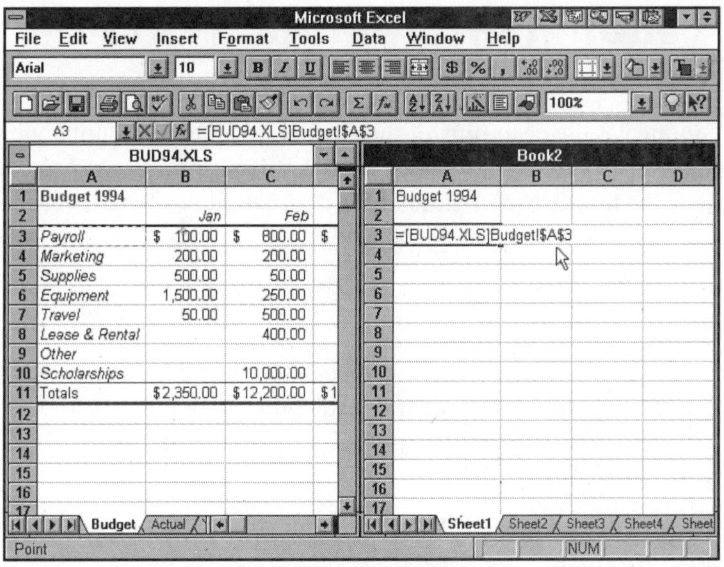

Fig. 37.19
After you link the cell, the reference contains the file name, the sheet name, and an absolute reference to the cell (A3).

Fig. 37.20
To copy the cell information, change the reference so that no dollar signs appear, as shown in the edit line (A3).

The formula automatically contains the file name (if the reference is to a cell in a different workbook), the sheet name (if the reference is to another sheet), and the cell name. The default formula includes dollar signs; this means that if you copy the formula, the reference does not change. In the example, `Payroll` would be in every cell in column A. Delete the dollar signs so the copy will work correctly.

Embedding Information in Your Documents

As mentioned at the beginning of the chapter, in addition to linking information, you can embed information within a document. When you embed an object, the information resides in the destination document, but the source application's tools are available for use in editing.

You can use any of the following methods to embed information in a document:

- Copy the information to the Clipboard, choose **E**dit Paste **S**pecial, and select an object format. (This method was discussed earlier in the section "Using Common Steps To Link Documents," along with other Paste Special formats.)

◀ "Moving with Drag and Drop," p. 53

- Arrange two windows side by side, and use drag-and-drop to copy information between the applications.
- Choose **I**nsert **O**bject, and open an existing file. (This method was discussed in "Inserting a File into a Document" earlier in this chapter.)
- Choose **I**nsert **O**bject, and create a new object. This section will describe this method.

Inserting a New Object into Your Document

If you want to use the features of another application in your document, you can choose the **I**nsert **O**bject command and select an application from a list. In addition to the standard Microsoft Office applications, the list contains applets and other Windows applications. *Applets* are small applications that cannot be run by themselves. When you purchase an application, one or more applets may be available.

Following is a list of applets that come with Microsoft Office. If you purchased your applications separately, you may not have all the applications.

Applet	Use
Microsoft WordArt	To create logos and other special text effects
Microsoft Equation	To create mathematical expressions
Microsoft Graph	To insert charts from data in a Word table
Microsoft ClipArt Gallery	To insert clip-art pictures
Microsoft Organization Chart	To create organization charts

To use the tools from another application or applet within your document to create a new object, follow these steps:

1. Position the insertion point in the destination document.
2. Choose **I**nsert **O**bject. The Object dialog box appears, as shown in figure 37.21.

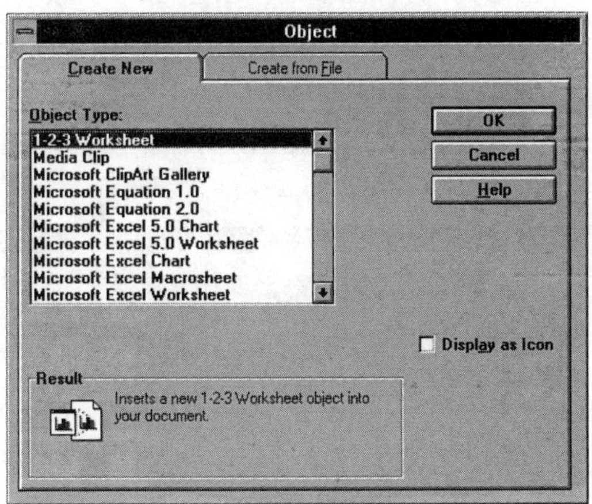

Fig. 37.21
The Insert Object dialog box lists applets as well as Windows applications.

3. In the **C**reate New tab, select an application or applet from the **O**bject Type list.
4. If you want to only see an icon for the object, select the Displ**a**y as Icon option.
5. When you finish with the Object dialog box, choose OK.

After you complete these steps, one of two things will occur. You may enter a separate window for the application or the applet, as shown in figure 37.22. The other possibility is that you will remain in your destination document window, but the menu bar and toolbar will change to reflect the source application, as shown in figure 37.23.

Complete the object, using the application's toolbar and menus.

When you finish creating the object, you can exit the object in either of two ways. If you launched a separate window for the application or applet, choose **F**ile **E**xit. If you stayed in your destination document, click outside the object.

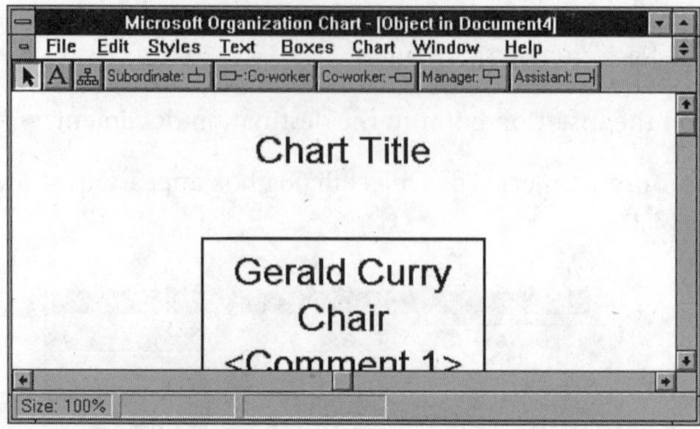

Fig. 37.22 When you choose Microsoft Organization Chart, a separate window opens. After you finish with the chart program, choose File Exit to return to the Word document.

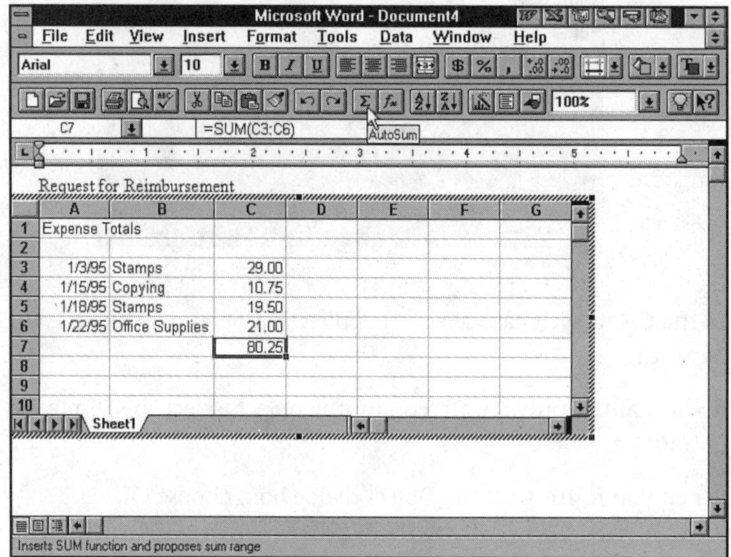

Fig. 37.23 When you choose Microsoft Excel 5.0, you get in-place editing. The menu bar and toolbar change to Microsoft Excel, enabling you to use Excel features such as the AutoSum button.

Editing an Embedded Object

Regardless of which of the four methods you use to embed information into your document, you can edit the embedded object with the tools of the source application.

To edit the object, follow these steps:

1. Click the object. Handles appear around the object, and the status bar tells you to double-click the object (see fig. 37.24).

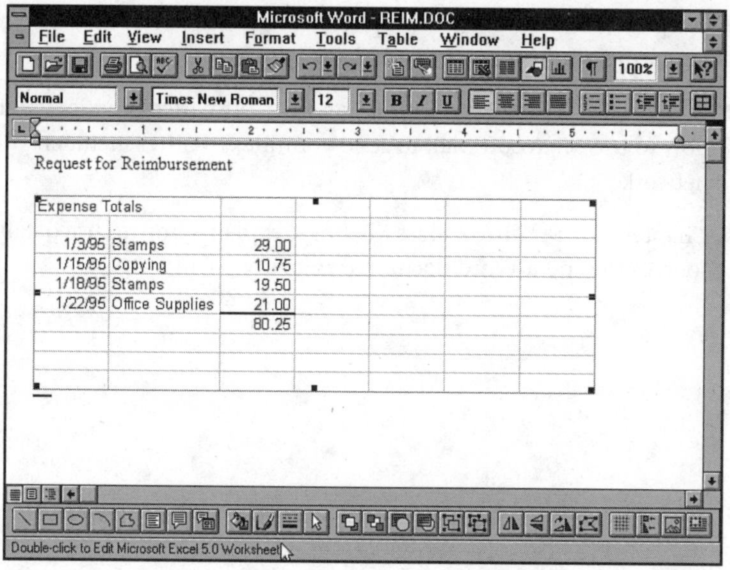

Fig. 37.24
The status bar displays instructions on how to get to the source-application tools.

2. Double-click the object. Depending on the source and destination applications, a separate window for the program appears, or the current window's toolbar and menu bar change to those of the source application.

3. Complete the object, using the application's toolbar and menus.

4. When you finish creating the object, exit the object. If you launched a separate window for the application or applet, choose **F**ile **E**xit. If you stayed in your destination document, click outside the object.

From Here...

This chapter showed you how to create links and embed information between different source applications and Word. Because you may need to know the basics of the other Microsoft Office applications, you may want to review the following chapters or continue with other sharing-information chapters:

- Chapter 12, "Creating Worksheets," covers the fundamentals of creating an Excel worksheet.

- Chapter 20, "Creating, Saving, and Opening Presentations," shows you how to create a slide presentation.

- Chapter 27, "Creating a Database," explains database terminology and teaches you how to start a new database.
- Chapter 38, "Using Mail with Other Micrsoft Office Products," tells you how to use Microsoft Mail to send your files to other members of your network.
- Chapter 39, "Sending a Mass Mailing," explains how to use database sources to send a Word document to many people.

Chapter 38

Using Mail with Other Microsoft Office Products

by Rick and Patty Winter

Microsoft Mail enables you to send messages to people connected to your network. You don't have to use any paper; your message appears on the recipients' computer screens, addressed to them. If you have another Microsoft Office product, you also can send or route documents to selected people on the network. In addition, you can copy portions of a document or attach entire documents to a Mail message.

When you purchase Microsoft Office, software for Microsoft Mail is not included; however, you get an additional license to use Mail on your network (assuming, of course, that you have a network). Microsoft Mail is a tool that enables you to communicate with other people in your company. If you don't have a network, this chapter may not be relevant to you unless you want to get an overview of what Mail does.

Note

The figures in this chapter reflect the use of Microsoft Mail used on a system running Windows for Workgroups. Your figures may vary slightly if you run Windows 3.1 or Windows NT.

In this chapter, you learn to

- Start Mail and create a message
- Copy information from a Word document to Mail

- Send a document through Mail or through the Routing commands in your File menu
- Attach other Office files to your Mail message

Starting Mail and Addressing the Message

Starting Mail is similar to starting any other Office program. When you load Office, the Microsoft Office toolbar appears at the top of your screen. Click the Microsoft Mail button to start Mail, or switch to Mail if it is already open. To begin with, you have at least two message view windows in the Mail program, as shown in figure 38.1. One window stores messages that you receive or send. The Outbox window stores messages that are waiting to be sent. You can save messages in default folders (Deleted Mail, Inbox, and Sent Mail) or in private folders that you create. The title bar of the first window changes to indicate the open folder. In this case, the title is Inbox because of the open Inbox folder.

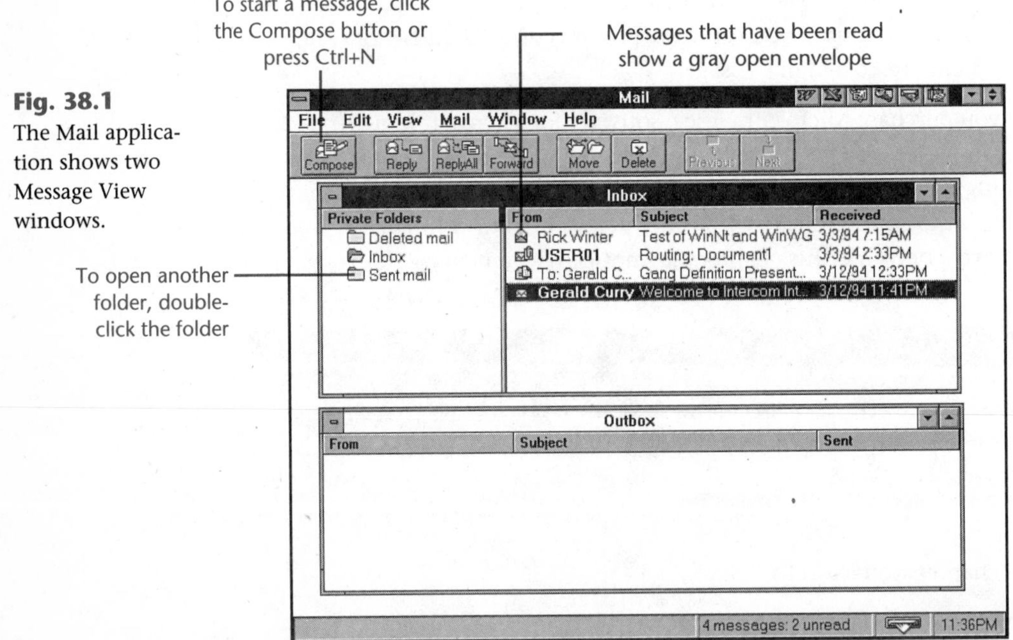

Fig. 38.1 The Mail application shows two Message View windows.

Like all other Office applications, the Mail window has a menu bar and toolbar. You can use the toolbar to compose, reply to, read, move, or delete a message.

Note

If you cannot see the Outbox window, it may be hidden behind the other window. Choose **W**indow Outbox. In figure 38.1, for example, choose the **W**indow **T**ile command to arrange both windows and then size them with the Window border.

Creating a Personal Group

Suppose as office manager of the Kick Out Gang Violence nonprofit organization, you have access to the Mail system where some of the board members worked. You want to be able to send messages to the board as a group as well as to individual members. You decide to create a personal group for the Kick Out Gang Violence board so that you don't have to include multiple names when you address a message.

To create a personal group, follow these steps:

1. Choose the **M**ail Personal **G**roups command. The Personal Groups dialog box appears, showing a list of the current groups.

2. To create a new group, choose the **N**ew command button.

3. In the New Group Name text box, type the group name and click the **C**reate command button, as shown in figure 38.2. The Personal Groups dialog box appears, as shown in figure 38.3.

4. Select the name you want to add. Hold down the Shift key and click to select adjacent names, or hold down the Ctrl key and click to select nonadjacent names.

5. Choose the **A**dd command button, or double-click the name.

6. Repeat steps 4 and 5 for all the names you want to add to your group.

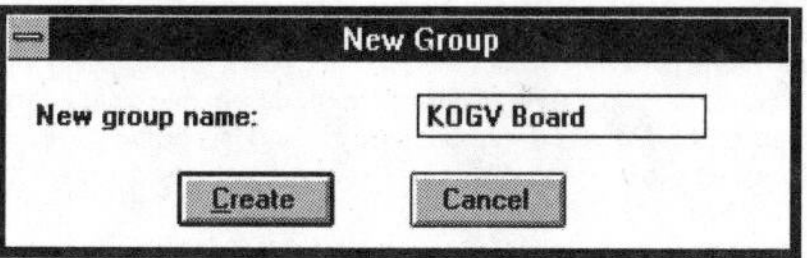

Fig. 38.2
The new group will be KOGV Board.

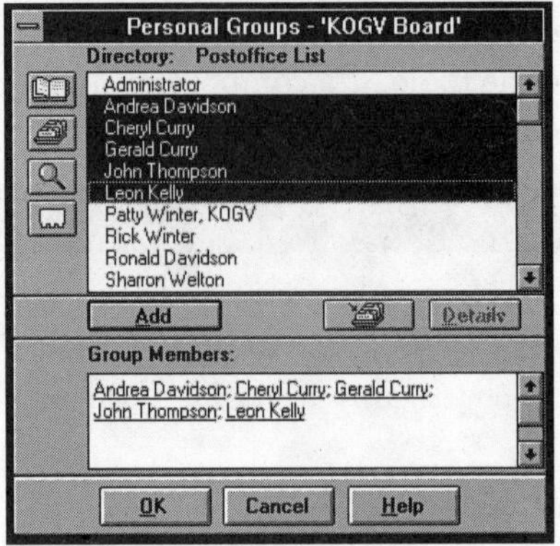

Fig. 38.3
Select names for the group in the Address List box.

7. When you finish adding names, choose OK. You return to the Personal Groups dialog box.

8. Choose Cl**o**se.

Creating a Message

To create a message, click the Compose button in the toolbar. The Compose window appears, with an input box for the recipients' names, an input box for the recipients you want to copy the letter to, an input box for the subject of the message, and an input box for the message.

To create and address the message, follow these steps:

1. Choose the **M**ail Compose **N**ote command, or press Ctrl+N. The Send Note window appears, as shown in figure 38.4.

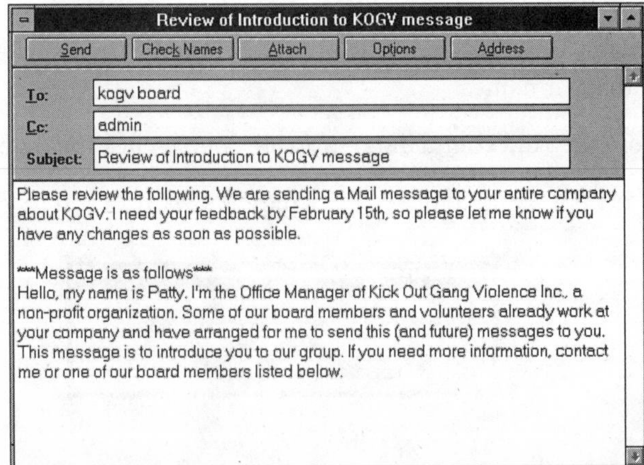

Fig. 38.4
The Send Note window adds its own buttons and places for text.

2. To address the message, move to the **T**o input box and do one of the following things:

   - Type the names of the individuals or groups.

   - Choose **M**ail A**d**dress, select a name in the Address text box, and select the **T**o or **C**c button.

3. If necessary, move to the **C**c text box and repeat step 2 for other recipients.

4. If you want to check the names to see whether they are spelled correctly or are part of the current address list, press Alt+K.

5. Click the message input area, or press Tab to get to the message input area. Then type your message.

6. When you finish and are ready to send the message, press Alt+S.

Copying Information from a Document to a Mail Message

Suppose that you want to use text from existing documents in your introduction to Kick Out Gang Violence. To copy information into a Mail message, you would follow the same procedures as in any Office application. The following sections explain how to use the Paste command to copy text without retaining any formatting from the source application, and how to maintain formatting from other applications with the Paste Special command.

Copying Text Only Without Formatting

To copy information from an existing document, follow these steps:

1. Address the Mail message and type any desired text in the Mail text window (refer to fig. 38.4).

2. Click the appropriate application icon in the Microsoft Office toolbar, and open the document.

3. Select the information you want to copy, as shown in figure 38.5.

4. Choose the **E**dit **C**opy command, or press Ctrl+C.

5. Click the Microsoft Mail button in the Microsoft Office toolbar.

6. Move the insertion point to the place in the Mail message where you want to insert the text.

7. Choose the **E**dit **P**aste command, or press Ctrl+V. The text or diagram appears in the message, as shown in figure 38.6.

Fig. 38.5
Move to the file you want to copy, and select the portion of the text or graphics you want to copy.

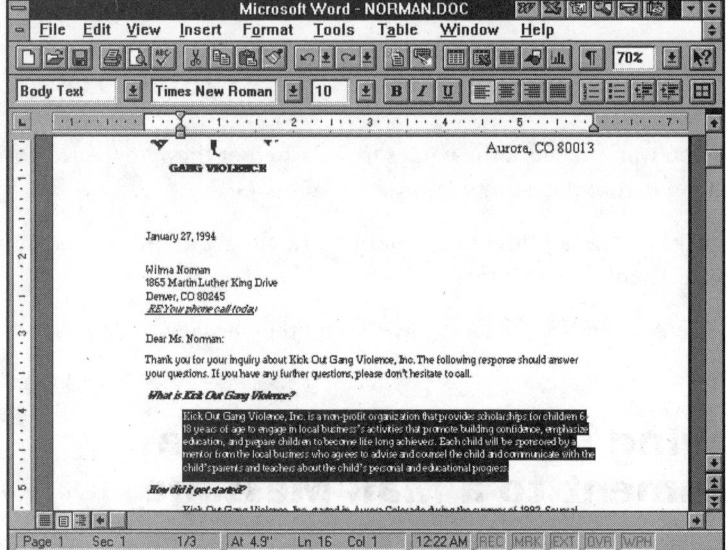

Fig. 38.6
Text pasted from a Word document and Excel worksheet.

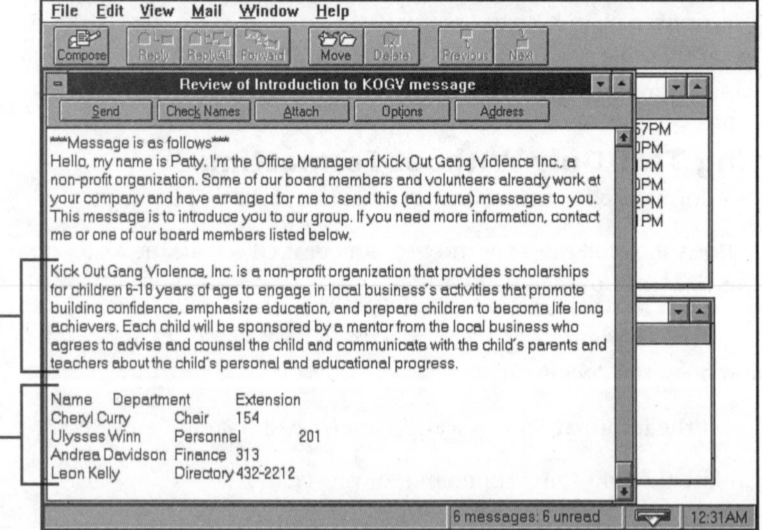

This paragraph was pasted from a Word document.

This section was pasted from an Excel worksheet. Notice that the columns do not align.

Note

You may have to add tabs to align columns for normal text.

Using Paste Special To Maintain Formatting

In figure 38.6, notice that the text in the Word document takes on the formatting of the rest of the Mail message and that the data from the Excel worksheet is not aligned. To maintain formatting from other applications, use the Paste Special command instead of the normal Paste command.

In step 7 in the preceding section, choose the **E**dit Paste **S**pecial command. The Paste Special dialog box appears, displaying formatting options for the source application, as shown in figure 38.7.

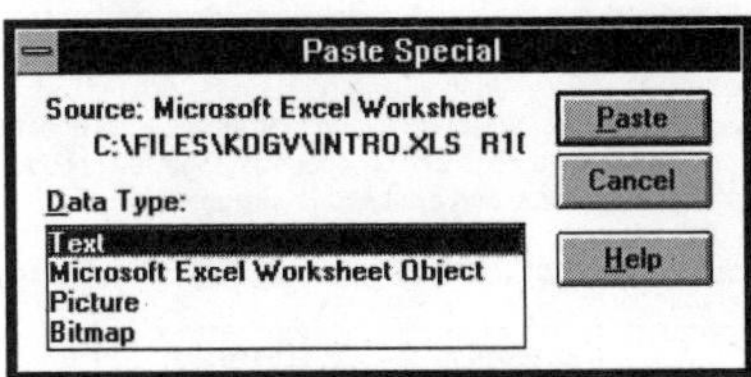

Fig. 38.7
In this example, the Paste Special dialog box contains Excel formatting options.

Select one of the formats, as described in the following list:

- To insert the selection without formatting, choose Text. If the selected text was an Excel worksheet or Access table, tabs will separate the data but may not align. If you select Text, you probably will have to add tabs for the selection if you want the information to align.

- To insert the copy into the Clipboard as an object, select the choice that identifies the object. In figure 38.7, the list box indicates Microsoft Excel 5.0 Worksheet Object. When you double-click the object, you enter the application that created the object; you then can edit the object, using the source application's menu, toolbar, and other commands.

- To insert the selection as a graphic, choose Picture or Bitmap. Both options insert the selection as a diagram, but Picture generally takes less room in the file and prints faster.

Note

For information on linking to a file, see "Attaching Word, Excel, or PowerPoint Files to Your Message" later in this chapter. The options available depend on your source application.

In figure 38.8, a formatted spreadsheet is inserted as a picture into the Mail message.

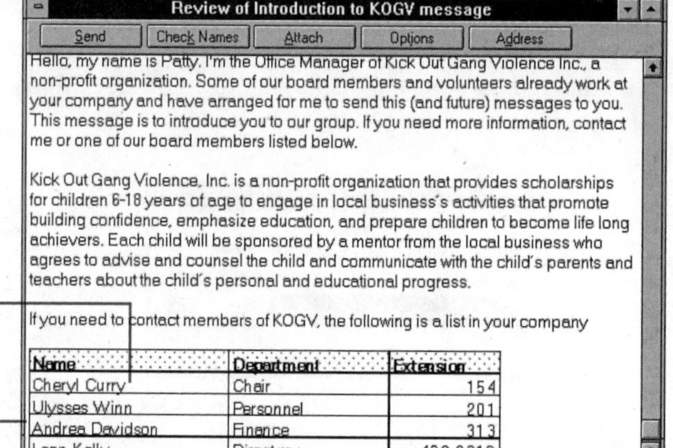

Fig. 38.8
A formatted spreadsheet is inserted into the message.

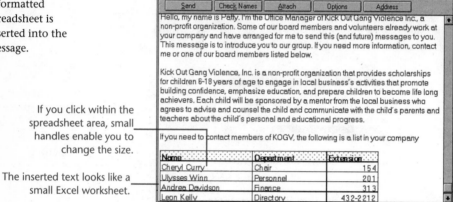

If you click within the spreadsheet area, small handles enable you to change the size.

The inserted text looks like a small Excel worksheet.

Note

Choosing the **E**dit Paste **S**pecial command in a Word document gives you two formatting choices: text and picture. Figure 38.9 shows the picture format.

Caution

If you use the Edit Insert Object command, you must select a file in the text format. If you try to insert another file type (such as Word, Excel, PowerPoint, or Access), you may get a message that the file is too large or get garbage in your message text area.

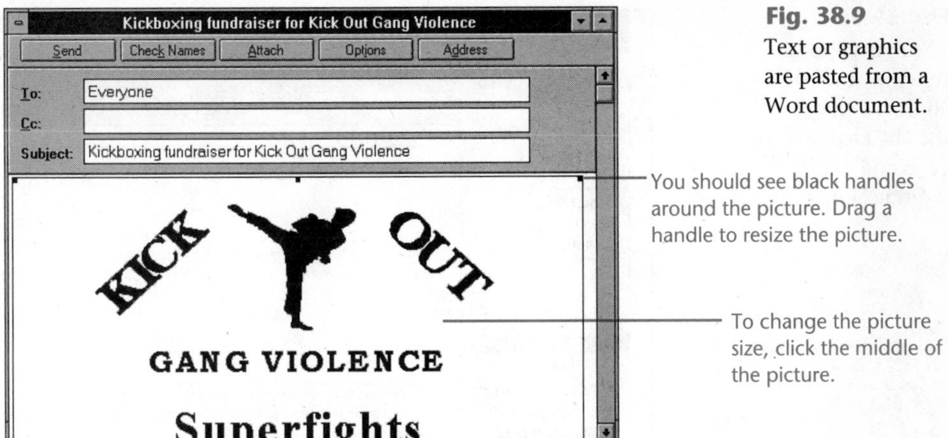

Fig. 38.9
Text or graphics are pasted from a Word document.

Sending a Document

You may have difficulty pasting documents or parts of documents within a Mail message, especially if the document is large or complex. You may have better luck if you send the document as an attachment within the application rather than directly through Mail. You have this choice in your Office applications if you also have Microsoft Mail. When you send a document from within an Office application, you are asked for the recipients' names, the subject of the message, and additional text.

To send a document from Word or Excel to a Mail recipient, follow these steps:

1. Open the application and the file you want to send.
2. Choose the **F**ile Sen**d** command as shown in figure 38.10.

> **Note**
>
> If the Send option is not in the File menu, choose **T**ools **O**ptions. In the General tab, select Mail as A**t**tachment.

3. In the Send Note dialog box, fill in the **T**o and **C**c text boxes and the subject box, and type a message if desired, as shown in figure 38.11.
4. Choose the **S**end button or press Alt+S to send the file. After sending the file, you return to the source application.

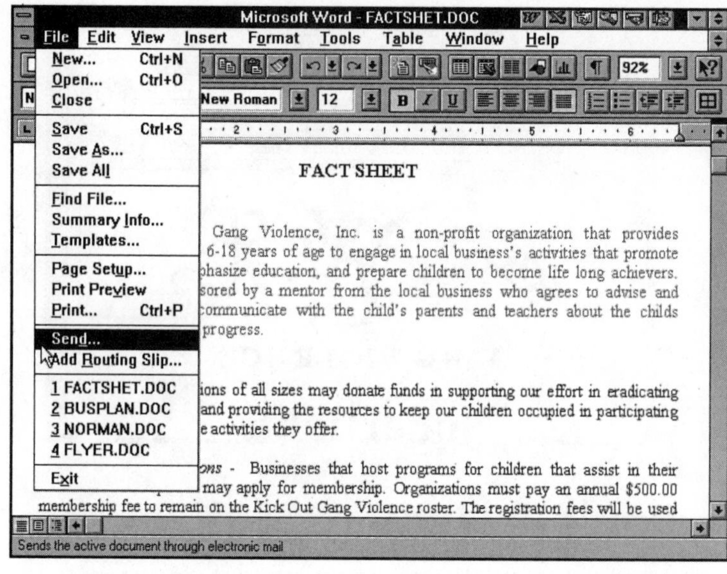

Fig. 38.10
The Mail application provides two additional items in the File menu: Send and Add Routing Slip.

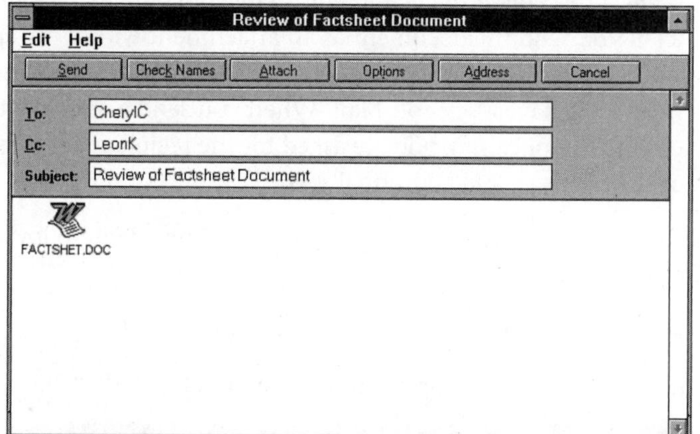

Fig. 38.11
After you choose the **File Send** command, you enter a Compose Mail window, which enables you to identify the recipients and type a subject, and which shows an icon of your document.

Troubleshooting

My File menu does not show Send or Add Routing Slip.

You probably don't have Mail loaded correctly, or you may be missing the [MAIL]MAP1=1 entry in your WIN.INI file. See your administrator.

Reading a Sent Document

To read any message, including one with a sent document, follow these steps:

1. Start or switch to the Mail program by clicking the Microsoft Mail button in the Microsoft Office toolbar.

2. Go to your messages window.
3. If necessary, double-click the Inbox folder.
4. Double-click the message you want to read, as shown in figure 38.12. When you open the message, you see an icon for the attached file, as shown in figure 38.13.

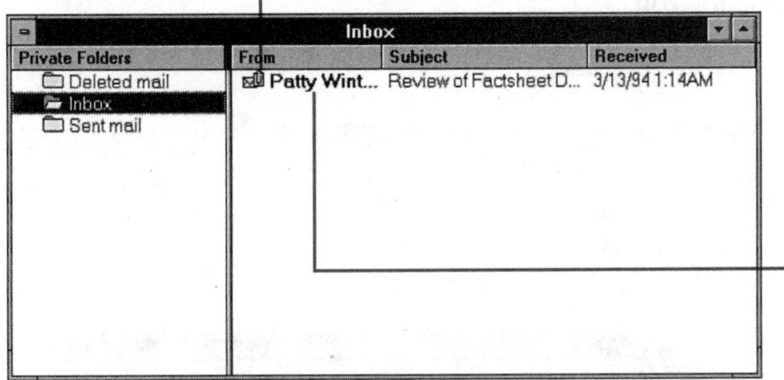

Fig. 38.12
An unread message with an attached file.

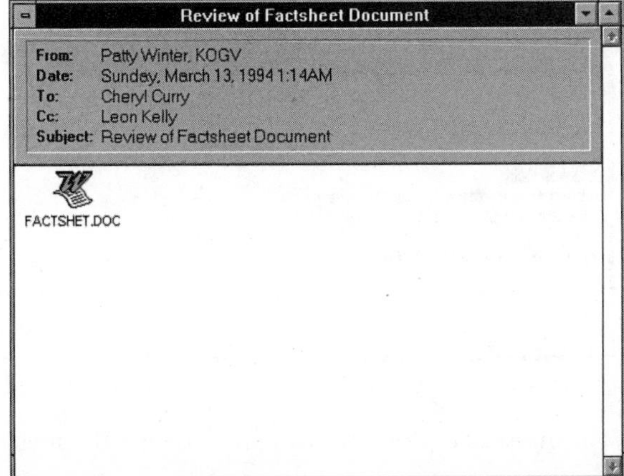

Fig. 38.13
The message shows an attached file icon.

5. Double-click the file icon to open the application that is associated with the file type. When you double-click the file icon within Mail, the application opens, and then the file opens.

6. Read or edit the document. Close the document when you finish.

7. To return to the Mail message, click the Microsoft Mail button in the Microsoft Office toolbar.

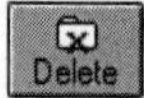

8. When you finish reading the message, choose **F**ile **D**elete, or press Ctrl+D. If you want to save and close your message, double-click the Control-menu box.

If you want to reply to the message, you have two options: you can send a normal message, or you can choose the Reply button to show the original sender a copy of the original message and provide room for a reply. When you use the Reply button, you don't have to address the message; it is already addressed for you.

To reply to the message, follow these steps:

1. With the message open, choose **M**ail **R**eply, or press Ctrl+R. The message and address change, as shown in figure 38.14.

The To box automatically fills in the name of the original message sender.

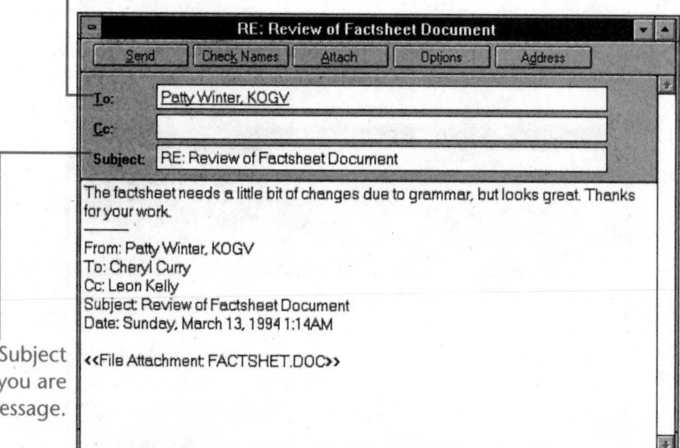

The RE in the title bar and Subject text box indicates that you are replying to the message.

Fig. 38.14
When you choose the Reply button, an extra line appears before the message, enabling you to insert your response.

2. Type your message at the insertion point before the message.

3. When you finish your reply, click the **S**end button, or press Alt+S.

Routing a Document

As an alternative to sending a document, you can route it to selected parties if you have this option enabled through Excel and/or Word. With routing, you can track the document's location; you also can send it simultaneously to all recipients or to one recipient after the other.

Creating a Routed Mail Message

To route a document from an Office application, follow these steps:

1. Choose the **F**ile Add **R**outing Slip command. The Routing Slip dialog box appears.
2. Choose A**d**dress, and select the names of the people to whom you want to send your document, as shown in figure 38.15.

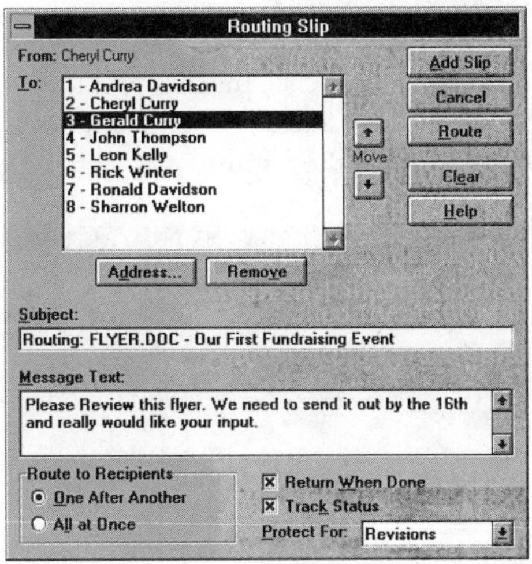

Fig. 38.15
The Routing Slip adds more options than **F**ile Sen**d**.

3. To change the order of the list, select a name and use the Move up or down arrow beside the list box.
4. To remove a name from the list, click the Remo**v**e button.
5. The **S**ubject text box automatically includes Routing and the name of the document. To change what appears in the recipient mail folder, edit the text in this box.
6. In the **M**essage Text box, add any information that appears in the message text area before the document.

7. In the Route to Recipients area, specify whether you want to route this file simultaneously to every recipient or to one after the other.

8. If you want to be notified via your Mail Inbox of the status every time someone reads the document, select Trac**k** Status.

9. If you want the final document returned to you at the end of the routing, select Return **W**hen Done.

10. In the **P**rotect For drop-down list box, specify whether you want to protect part or all of your document so that recipients cannot make any changes.

11. When you finish, click the **R**oute button to begin routing the document.

Working with Routed Mail

When the recipients open their mail, they see a message indicating that they have new mail. When they double-click the message, they see your correspondence, with the attached file and any instructions you include, as well as instructions on how to continue the routing, as shown in figure 38.16.

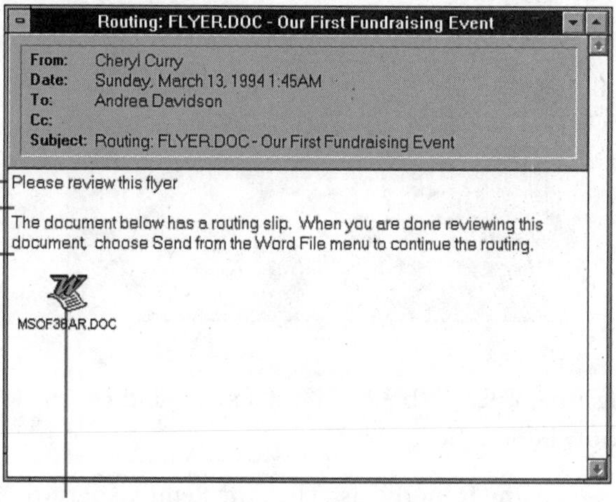

Fig. 38.16
The recipient sees the message and attached file.

Routing: FLYER.DOC - Our First Fundraising Event
From: Cheryl Curry
Date: Sunday, March 13, 1994 1:45AM
To: Andrea Davidson

Subject: Routing: FLYER.DOC - Our First Fundraising Event
Please review this flyer
MSOF38AR.DOC
The content of your message appears above the document icon.

Mail instructs you to choose Send from the Word menu to continue the routing.

To go to the application and file, double-click the document icon.

Note

Unless you add a message in the message or subject area, the recipients of a sequential routing (except the first one in the list) won't know who originally routed the document. Make sure that you include a message informing recipients that you sent the document if it's important for them to know that.

Each recipient can make notes in the document. When you get the document, you see different colors for the annotations and editing changes, as shown in figure 38.17. To see annotation marks, click the Show/Hide button in the toolbar. To see the annotations themselves, choose **V**iew **A**nnotations, or double-click one of the annotation marks.

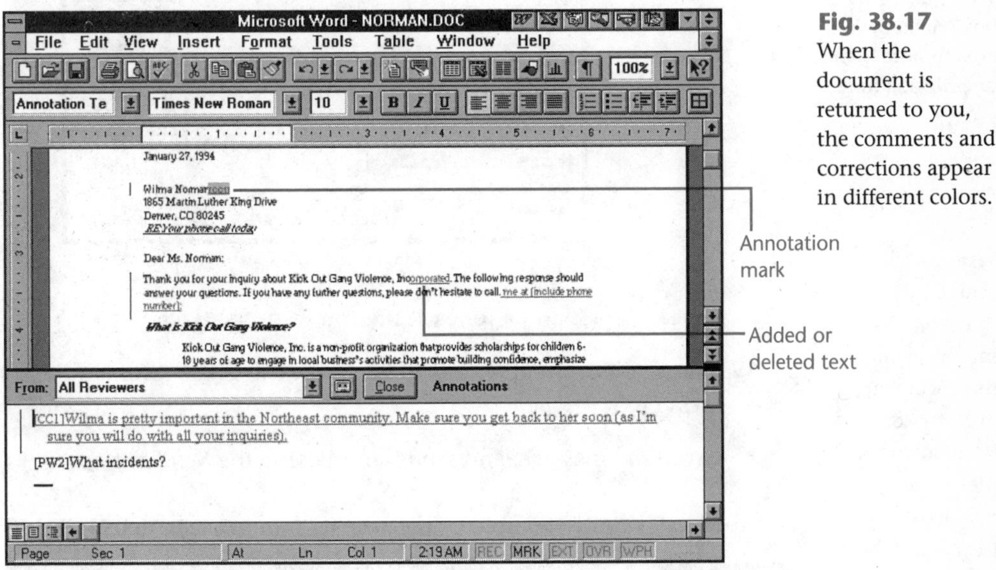

Fig. 38.17
When the document is returned to you, the comments and corrections appear in different colors.

Attaching Word, Excel, or PowerPoint Files to Your Message

When you send or route a document, you start in the document's application. If you are creating a Mail message, you can add a document to your message with the Attach button. By using the Attach button, you can attach more than one document to each message. With the Send or Route buttons, you can attach only one document to the message.

To attach a document to your message, follow these steps:

1. In the Mail message, move to where you want to attach the document.
2. Click the **A**ttach command button, or press Alt+A. The Attach dialog box appears.
3. Identify the name and location of the file.
4. If you want to attach more than one file, choose the **A**ttach command button. A document icon appears in your message, showing the file name and icon of the application that created the file, as shown in figure 38.18.

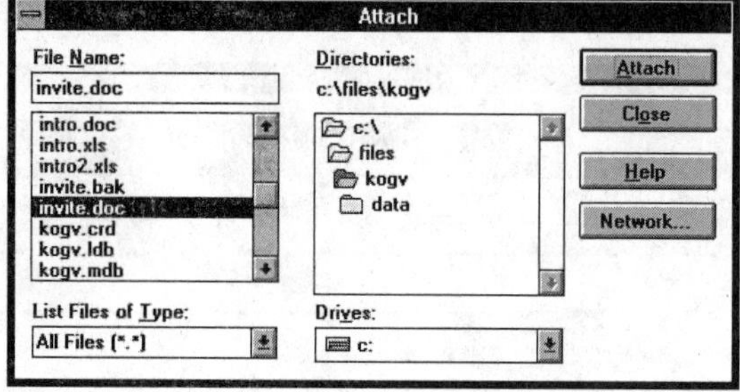

Fig. 38.18
The Attach dialog box enables you to attach more than one file at a time.

Tip
If no association exists, you can bring up the document in Notepad. Hold down the Alt key and double-click the icon. If the document is in a compatible format, you will be able to read the text.

5. Repeat steps 3 and 4 for each file you want to attach.
6. When you finish attaching files, choose the Cl**o**se command button, or press Esc.
7. Finish the message, and send it by clicking the **S**end button.

Figure 38.19 shows a completed message with multiple attached files.

Note

If Windows does not recognize the extension, no application is associated with the file, and a blank icon appears with the file name.

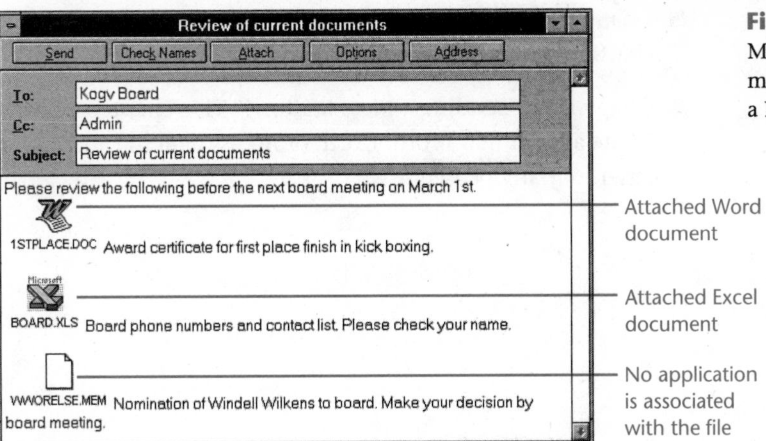

Fig. 38.19 Multiple documents attached to a Mail message.

> **Troubleshooting**
>
> *I try double-clicking an icon, and I get the message that no application is associated with the file.*
>
> If you include extensions (up three characters after a period) when you name files, Windows may not know what application created the file, and the recipient cannot double-click the icon to open the file. Avoid including extensions in file names; let your Windows application add its own extension (DOC for Word documents, XLS for Excel worksheets, and so on).

From Here...

This chapter showed you how to work with Mail and other Office applications to send electronic messages to people on your computer network. If you want to send information to people or to present information, you will want to master the mail merge in Word, charting in Excel, and PowerPoint presentations. See the following chapters:

- Chapter 16, "Creating and Printing Reports and Charts." This chapter introduces larger Excel documents and shows you how to create charts in Excel.
- Chapter 20, "Creating, Saving, and Opening Presentations." This chapter shows you the basics of creating a PowerPoint presentation.

- Chapter 25, "Creating Graphs." This chapter introduces the elements of charting with PowerPoint.
- Chapter 39, "Sending a Mass Mailing." This chapter shows you how to create a letter in a Word, Excel, or Access data file and address that letter to many people.

Chapter 39

Sending a Mass Mailing

by Rick and Patty Winter

When you have one letter you want to send to many people, you can edit and print the letter for each person. Even if you use copy and paste, the process can be long and drawn out when you have more than a few names. When you have a personalized letter that you want to send out to many people, you should consider a mail merge. You may already have your names and addresses in a file. If that file is a Word table, an Excel spreadsheet, or an Access database, the merge process is much easier than it is when you use the mail merge feature of Word 6.

For Kick Out Gang Violence to pay for scholarships and operating expenses, the organization needs money. Many of the board members and volunteers have lists of potential donors. The problem is that these lists are all in different places. The lists are in Access, Excel, Word, dBASE III, Lotus 1-2-3, and in address books and Rolodex files. Your directive is to get out the fund-raising letter immediately. Ideally, you should combine all your sources into one file, but you may not have time for that now. Luckily, you have some resources at your disposal—the new tools in Microsoft Office.

In this chapter, you learn to

- Begin a mail merge with the Mail Merge Helper
- Create, edit, and use Word, Excel, and Access data files to address the letter
- Make envelopes and labels from the data files
- Create a list of the contents of the data file

Creating a Letter

You can start the fund-raising form letter as you would any other letter in Word. You can choose the **F**ile **N**ew command and then select the Letter Wizard. When you create the letter, leave off the name and address. Save the file before you continue and position the insertion point where you want to insert name and address information. Figure 39.1 shows a portion of the letter before placeholders for the name and address are added.

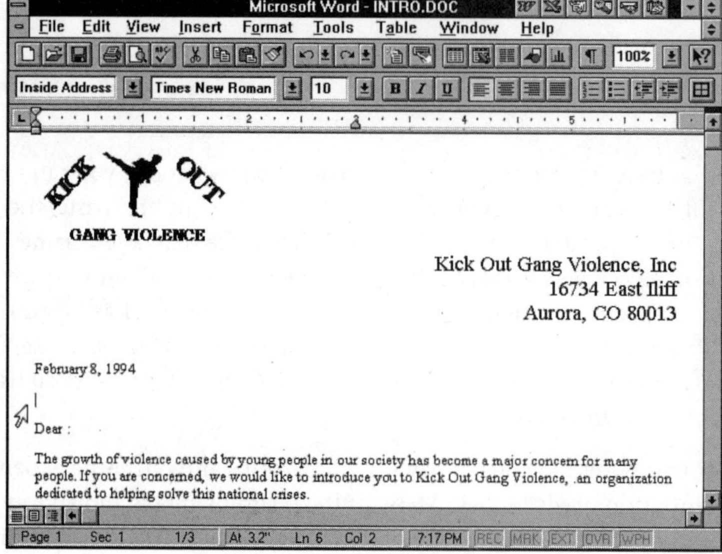

Fig. 39.1
Create a letter as you normally would, and position your insertion point where the name will go.

Using the Mail Merge Helper

◄ "Entering Text," p. 106

◄ "Editing Text," p. 110

◄ "Starting a Letter with Letter Wizard," p. 760

Word 6 has added a Mail Merge Helper dialog box to step you through the merge process. You need to identify this letter as a merge document, attach your data file, and then merge the letter and the data file.

To get to the merge helper, choose the **T**ools Mail Me**r**ge command. The Mail Merge Helper dialog box appears, as shown in figure 39.2.

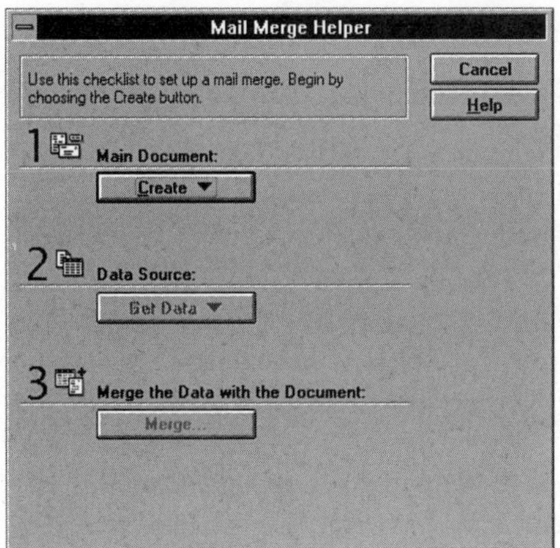

Fig. 39.2
The Mail Merge Helper dialog box asks you for the letter (main document) and the name-and-address file (data source).

During the merge process, you may need to return to the Mail Merge Helper. To do so, choose the **T**ools Mail Me**r**ge command again. If you are editing the letter, you can click the Mail Merge Helper button in the Mail Merge toolbar, as shown in figure 39.3.

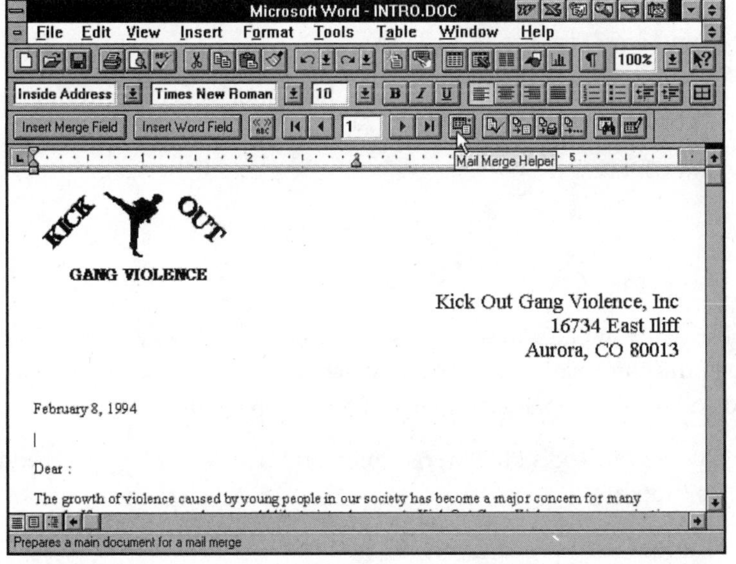

Fig. 39.3
The Mail Merge toolbar appears after you identify your letter as a merge document.

Identifying the Letter as a Merge Document

After you enter the Mail Merge Helper dialog box, the first step is to identify your letter as a letter you want to use for the merge.

◄ "Identifying the Document," p. 234

To identify the letter you are working on as a merge letter, follow these steps:

1. Choose the **T**ools Mail Me**r**ge command. The Mail Merge Helper dialog box appears.

2. In the Main Document section, choose **C**reate.

3. In the drop-down-list, select Form **L**etters.

4. You are asked whether you want to use the active window or a new window. Because you already have opened the letter you want to use, click the **A**ctive Window button.

You return to the Mail Merge Helper dialog box, and need to identify where you will get the names and addresses for your letter. You have a number of options:

- If you want to create or use an existing table in Word, see "Using a Data File in Word" later in this chapter.

- If you want to use names from an Excel spreadsheet, see "Using Data from Excel" later in this chapter.

- If you want to use names from an Access database, see "Using Data from Access" later in this chapter.

- If your data is from another spreadsheet or database application, see "Using Data from Other Databases and Spreadsheets" later in this chapter.

Using a Data File in Word

◄ "Choosing a Data Source," p. 234

Suppose that you had a number of sources for your names and addresses but some of this information was not in the computer yet. To create a data file in Word and to add the names and addresses, complete the following steps:

1. Choose the **T**ools Mail Me**r**ge command. The Mail Merge Helper dialog box appears.

2. Choose the **G**et Data command button.

3. In the pull-down list, select **C**reate Data Source. The Create Data Source dialog box appears, as shown in figure 39.4.

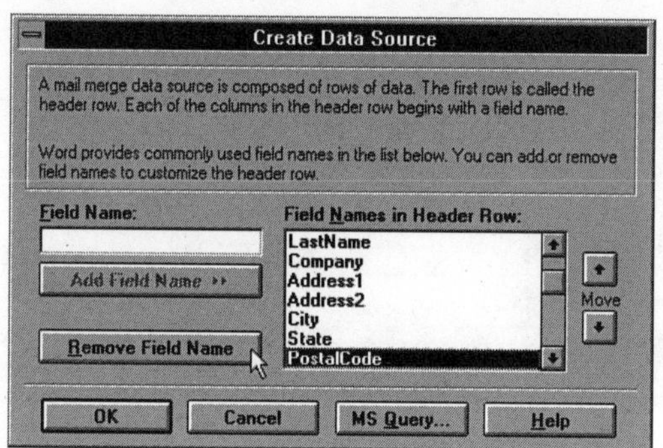

Fig. 39.4
The Create Data Source dialog box shows a list of common field names for merges.

4. Change the field in the Create Data Source dialog box as shown in figure 39.4 by doing any of the following things:

   - Type a new field name in the **F**ield Name text box, and click the **A**dd Field Name button.

   - Remove a field name from the suggested list by selecting a name in the Field **N**ames in Header Row list box and then choosing the **R**emove Field Name button.

   - Change the order of the field names in the list by selecting a name and then choosing the Move up or down button.

5. When you finish in the Create Data Source dialog box, choose OK.

6. Identify the File Name and location of the file for your data in the Save Data Source dialog box. This dialog box is the same as the File Save As dialog box.

7. After you name the file, Word asks you whether you want to add records to the data file or edit the main document. Choose Edit **D**ata Source to add your records now. A Data Form dialog box appears, showing the fields you identified in step 4 (see fig. 39.5).

Fig. 39.5
Your field names appear in the Data Form dialog box.

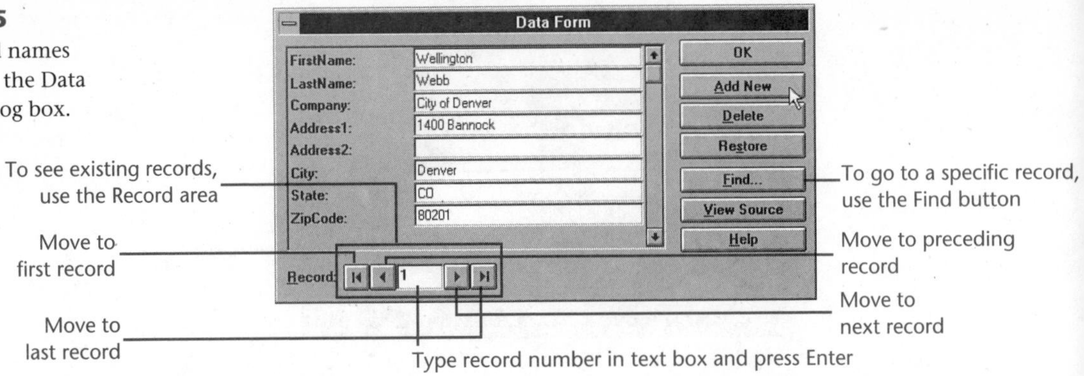

Data Form

FirstName: Wellington
LastName: Webb
Company: City of Denver
Address1: 1400 Bannock
Address2:
City: Denver
State: CO
ZipCode: 80201
Record: 1

OK
Add New
Delete
Restore
Find...
View Source
Help

To see existing records, use the Record area

Move to first record

Move to last record

To go to a specific record, use the Find button

Move to preceding record

Move to next record

Type record number in text box and press Enter

8. Type the information in each field. Press Tab to go to the next field; press Shift+Tab to go to the preceding field. Choose the **A**dd New button to add someone else's information. Then choose OK.

After you create the data file, choose OK to return to your letter. If you need to make changes to the data, click the Edit Data Source button.

Adding Field Names to Your Letter

◀ "Creating a Data Source," p. 235

After you identify your letter as a main document and create or attach your data file, you need to tell Word where each field name appears in the main document. From your letter, click the Insert Merge Field button in the Mail Merge toolbar and select the field name to insert, as shown in figure 39.6.

Fig. 39.6
The Insert Merge Field Button in the Mail Merge toolbar shows you a list of field names in your data file.

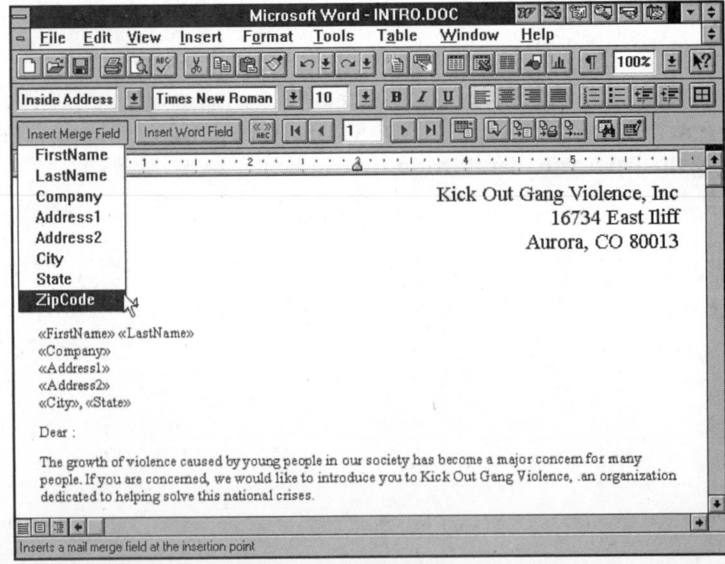

Each field name appears in the letter in chevrons (<< >>). Don't forget to add spaces between field names and any necessary punctuation (such as a comma between the city and state). If you need to delete a field, you can highlight the field name, including the chevrons, and press Del.

Completing the Merge

After you identify the main document and the data source, and insert the merge fields, you are ready to merge the names and addresses with the letter. You can merge through the Mail Merge toolbar or through the Mail Merge Helper dialog box. The Mail Merge Helper dialog box gives you more options, such as selecting some of the names and addresses and sorting the names. For more information on selecting whom you want to send to, see "Selecting Who Receives the Document" later in this chapter. For more information on sorting, see "Sorting the Mailing" later in this chapter.

You can merge and create a new document, or go directly to the printer. Unless you are certain that the merge will turn out correctly, you should merge to a new document so you can preview the merged document before you print it. You can do any of the following things at this point:

◀ "Merging the Data and the Document," p. 238

- To merge to a new document from the main document, click the Merge to New Document button in the Mail Merge toolbar.

- To see whether you have the wrong field names or other problems, click the Check for Errors button.

- To merge the letter and data into a new window, click the Merge to New Document button.

- To go directly to the printer, click the Merge to Printer button.

- To return to the Mail Merge Helper dialog box, click the Mail Merge Helper button.

In addition to using the buttons in the Mail Merge toolbar, you can use the Mail Merge Helper so you have more options during the merge. To merge to a new document from the Mail Merge Helper, complete the following steps:

1. Choose the **T**ools Mail Me**r**ge command. The Mail Merge Helper dialog box appears.

2. Choose the **M**erge button in section 3, as shown in figure 39.7. The Merge dialog box appears, as shown in figure 39.8.

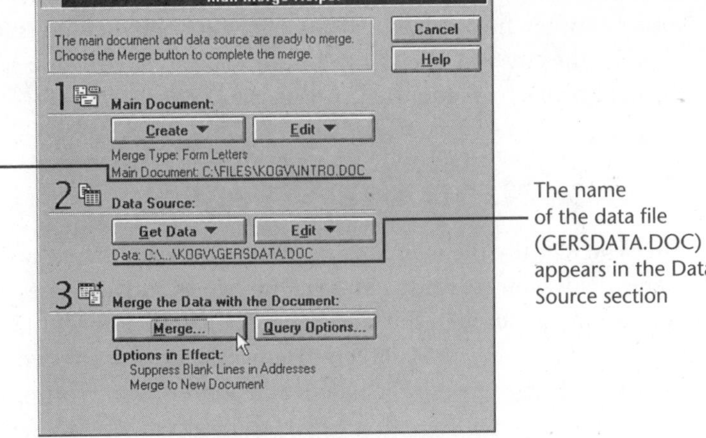

Fig. 39.7
The Mail Merge Helper dialog box identifies your letter and data file.

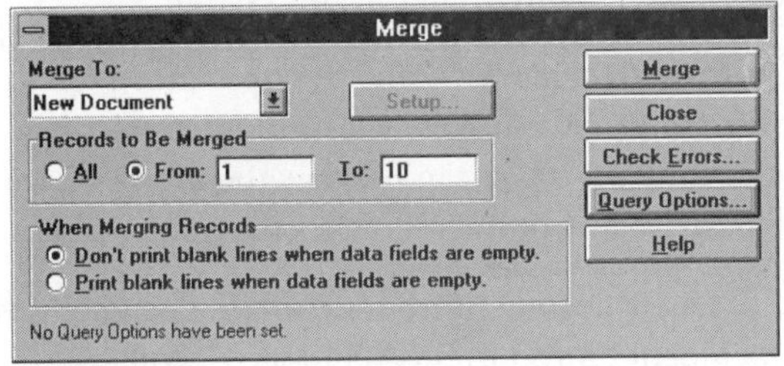

Fig. 39.8
The Merge dialog box enables you to select records, query the data file, and perform other tasks.

3. In the Merge To drop-down list, select New Document.

4. If your source is particularly long, you can select the first few records to test the merge. In the Records To Be Merged section, choose **A**ll to merge all the data, or type in the **F**rom and **T**o text boxes. Figure 39.8 identifies the first 10 records.

5. Choose the **M**erge command button to perform the merge.

If you use the Merge to New Document button or the Mail Merge Helper, the results appear in a new document, as shown in figure 39.9.

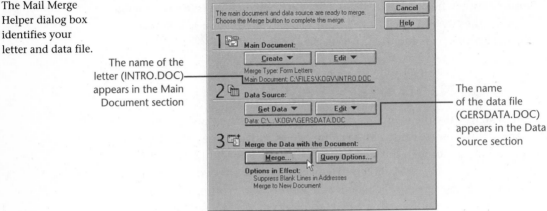

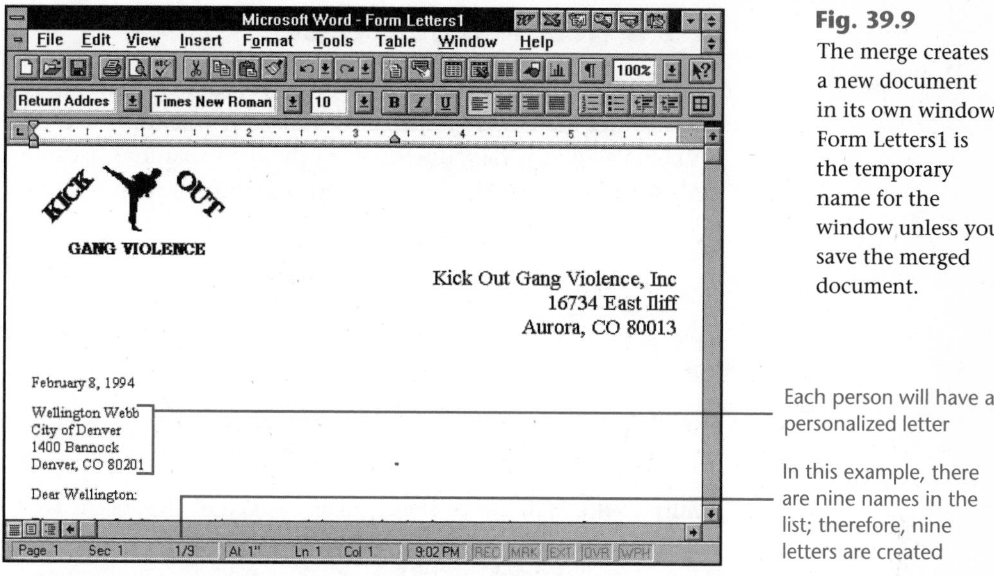

Fig. 39.9
The merge creates a new document in its own window. Form Letters1 is the temporary name for the window unless you save the merged document.

> **Note**
>
> Generally, it is not recommended that you save a merged document, especially when you have a large data file. The merged document can take a lot of space. If you need to regenerate the merged document, simply complete the merge again.

After scrolling through the document to check for problems, print the document as you would any other by choosing the **F**ile **P**rint command. If you want to print specific pages of the merge (and therefore to selected letters addressed to individuals), fill in the Pages text box in the Print dialog box.

◄ "Printing a Document," p. 150

To print directly to the printer instead creating a new document on-screen, select one of the following options:

- Click the Merge to Printer button.
- In the Merge dialog box (refer to fig. 39.8), select Printer in the Me**r**ge To drop-down list, and then choose **M**erge.

Using Data from Excel

One of the advantages of Word 6 is how easily you can perform merges with data sources other than Word documents. In fact, if you know Excel or Access, it is better to do the data file in one of those applications because you have more search, calculation, and reporting capabilities than in a Word data file.

To merge your letter with an Excel spreadsheet, follow these steps:

◄ "Using Mail Merge," p. 233

1. Choose the **T**ools Mail Me**r**ge command. The Mail Merge Helper dialog box appears.

2. Identify your letter as a main document, as described in "Identifying the Letter as a Merge Document" earlier in this chapter.

3. Return to the Mail Merge Helper dialog box, and choose the **G**et Data button in the Data Source section.

4. Select **O**pen Data Source in the pull-down list. The Open Data Source dialog box appears, as shown in figure 39.10.

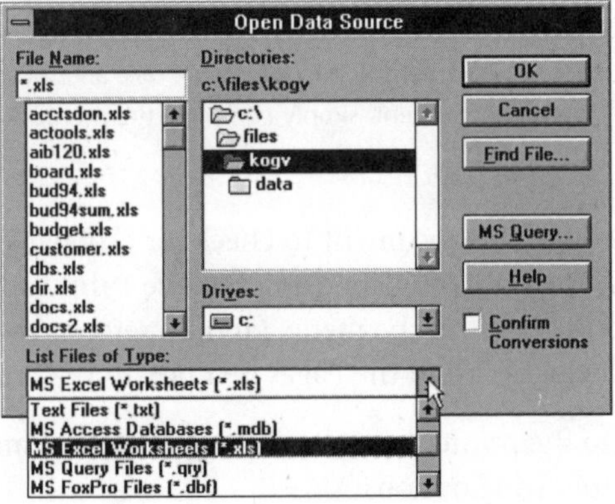

Fig. 39.10
In the Open Data Source dialog box, select MS Excel Worksheets to list Excel files.

5. Pull down the List Files of Type list, and select `MS Excel Worksheets (*.xls)`.

6. If necessary, change the location information in the Dri**v**e and **D**irectories list boxes, and then select the file name in the File **N**ame list box. Choose OK to continue.

Note

Before you link to Excel or Access, that application must be available to be loaded. You cannot link to a source file without having its native application available.

7. Another dialog box prompts you to enter the name or the cell range. Leave the **N**amed or Cell Range entry as Entire Spreadsheet, as shown in figure 39.11, and choose OK to use all of sheet 1 in the workbook file. The Mail Merge Helper reappears, as shown in figure 39.12.

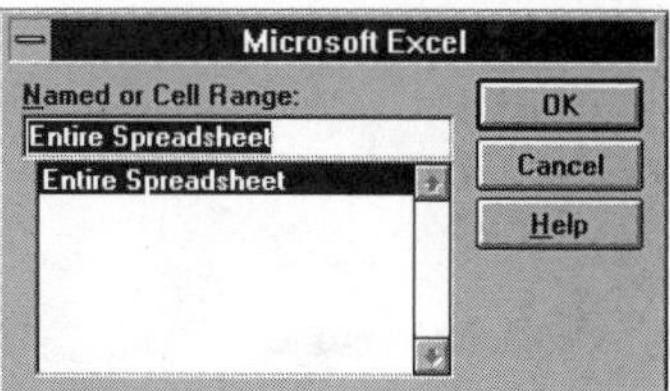

Fig. 39.11
Leave Entire Spreadsheet selected to include all data in the spreadsheet.

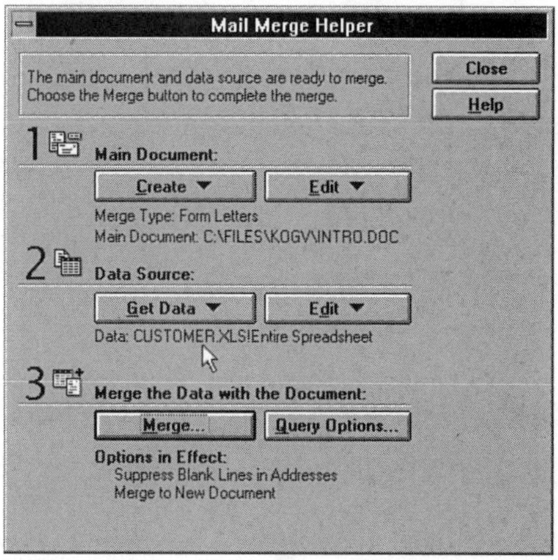

Fig. 39.12
The Data Source area now shows the CUSTOMER.XLS worksheet.

8. If necessary, change the field names, as described in "Adding Field Names to Your Letter" earlier in this chapter.

9. Complete the merge, as described in "Completing the Merge" earlier in this chapter.

Using Data from Access

Using Access is almost identical to using Excel in the preceding section. With Access, however, you can choose among multiple tables as well as multiple queries for your data source. Perform the same steps as in "Using Data from Excel," but in step 5, select `MS Access Databases (*.mdb)` (refer to fig. 39.10).

◀ "Exploring Access," p. 580

After you specify the file name and location, as mentioned in step 6, a Microsoft Access dialog box appears, with two tabs: Tables and Queries. You can specify whether the data is from a table or a query, as shown in figure 39.13. Select the name of the table or query in the list box, and choose OK. Then continue with steps 8 and 9 in "Using Data from Excel."

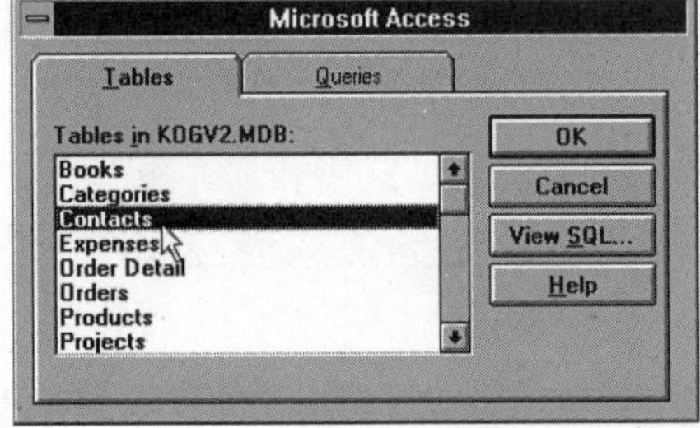

Fig. 39.13
When you use Access as a data source, you can choose among a list of tables or queries in the Access database.

After you save your Word main document, the last data source you selected in the Mail Merge Helper is linked with the letter. If you update your data source in Access, for example, and then open the Word document, the next time you merge, any changes in the source are reflected in the merged documents.

Using Data from Other Databases and Spreadsheets

If your data is in another database source, Word may be able to use that file directly. For example, you can use FoxPro, dBASE, and Paradox files as a data source. If your worksheet is in a spreadsheet file format, try opening the spreadsheet in Excel. Save the spreadsheet in Excel format, using the **F**ile Save **A**s command. In the List Files of Type pull-down list, change the type to Microsoft Excel. After you convert the file, perform the steps in "Using Data from Excel" earlier in this chapter.

If you cannot open your spreadsheet file, you may need to return to that application and save the spreadsheet in another format. If, for example, you use Lotus 1-2-3 Release 4, you can save the worksheet with a WK1 or WK3 extension in Lotus 1-2-3 and then open the file in Excel.

Sorting the Mailing

You can sort the letters on one to three fields in the data source. To sort the letters (or labels, or envelopes), follow these steps:

1. Choose the **T**ools Mail Me**r**ge command. The Mail Merge Helper dialog box appears.

2. Choose **Q**uery Options. (You also can choose the **Q**uery Options button in the Merge dialog box.) The Query Options dialog box appears.

3. Select the S**o**rt Records tab. The Query Options dialog box appears, as shown in figure 38.14.

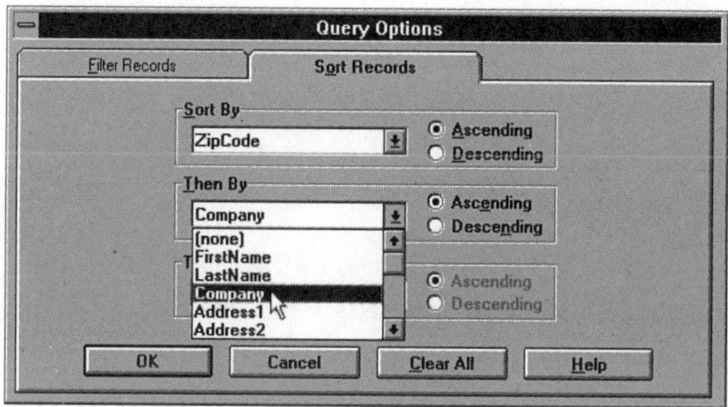

Fig. 39.14
You can select specific records in the Filter Records tab or order records in the Sort Records tab of the Query Options dialog box.

4. You can sort on up to three fields. In the **S**ort By drop-down list, select one of your fields. The example in figure 39.14 shows `ZipCode`.

5. If you want to sort from lowest to highest (A to Z or 1 to 9), select **A**scending. If you want to sort from highest to lowest, select **D**escending.

   If your list is long, you may want to sort by another field. In figure 39.14, your list is sorted first by ZIP code. For all names with the same ZIP code, the sort is then organized by company name.

6. When you finish using the Sort Records tab, choose OK. You return to the Mail Merge Helper dialog box.

7. Finish your sort by choosing the **M**erge button in the Mail Merge Helper dialog box, as described in "Completing the Merge" earlier in this chapter.

Selecting Who Receives the Document

You may not want to send the letter to everyone in the data source. If you want to send only to selected people, you can complete the merge and choose Curr**e**nt Page or fill in the Pa**g**es area in the Print dialog box, as described in "Completing the Merge" earlier in this chapter. You also can use the Mail Merge toolbar and Query Options dialog box to select specific records.

Sending to One Person

If you want to send the letter to only one person in the data source, you can use the Mail Merge toolbar to find the person and then print the letter like a normal document.

To show the merge for one person, follow these steps:

1. After identifying the main document and the data source, return to the main document.
2. Click the View Merged Data button in the Mail Merge toolbar. The first name in the data source shows where the field codes were in the letter, as shown in figure 39.15.
3. You can choose the record by scrolling through the list with the same buttons that are in the Data Form dialog box (refer to fig. 39.5). Go to the first record or last record, and scroll through the records to find the name you want. Figure 39.15 shows the selection buttons in the Mail Merge toolbar.

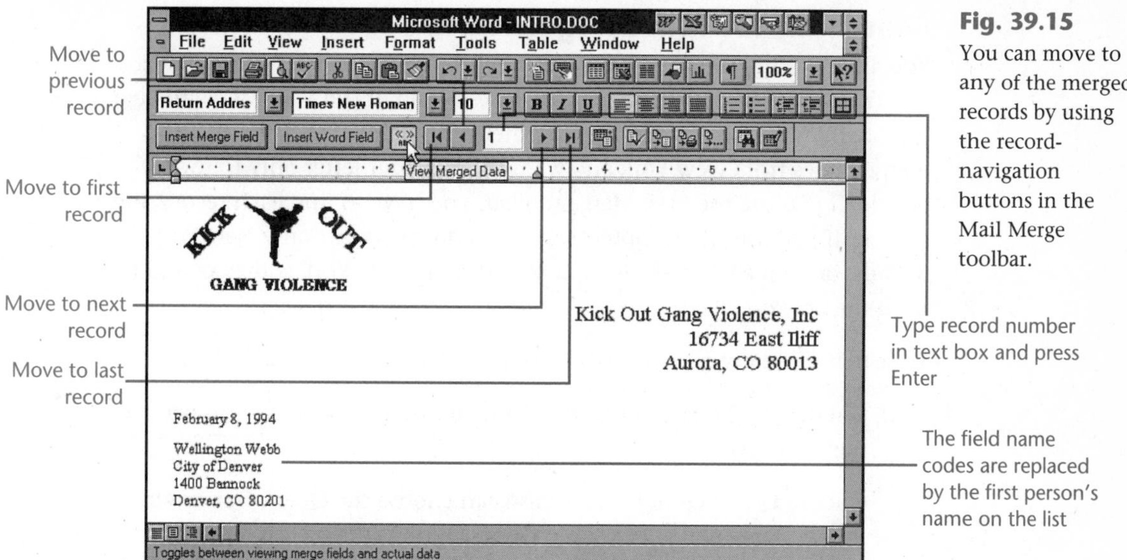

Fig. 39.15 You can move to any of the merged records by using the record-navigation buttons in the Mail Merge toolbar.

4. You can find a name by clicking the Find Record button and then filling out the Find in Field dialog box, shown in figure 39.16.

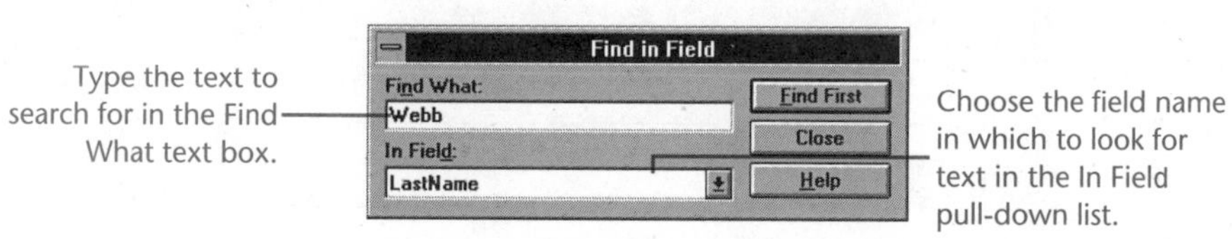

Fig. 39.16 Choose the **F**ind First button to find the first occurrence in the database. The button changes to Find Next. Click the button to search for each occurrence of the text.

5. After the name appears in the letter, click the Print button to print the letter.

Troubleshooting

When I try to find a record, the program does not find one that I know exists.

Make sure that you select the right field from the In Field drop-down list box in the Find in Field dialog box. If the program prompts you to search from the beginning of the file, choose **Y**es.

Searching for Matching Criteria

You also can find the record you want by using the Query Options dialog box. You may want to use this dialog box instead of the Mail Merge toolbar if more than one record meets your criteria. You may, for example, have many names from New York and want to send your letter only to those people. If you use the Mail Merge toolbar, you have to find each record and print it. If you use Query Options, you can directly print only New York records, or merge to a new document with only New York addresses and then print the new document.

To search for many records with the same text, follow these steps:

1. Choose the **T**ools Mail Me**r**ge command. The Mail Merge Helper dialog box appears.

2. Choose **Q**uery Options. (You also can choose the **Q**uery Options button in the Merge dialog box.) The Query Options dialog box appears.

3. Select the **F**ilter Records tab, as shown in figure 39.17.

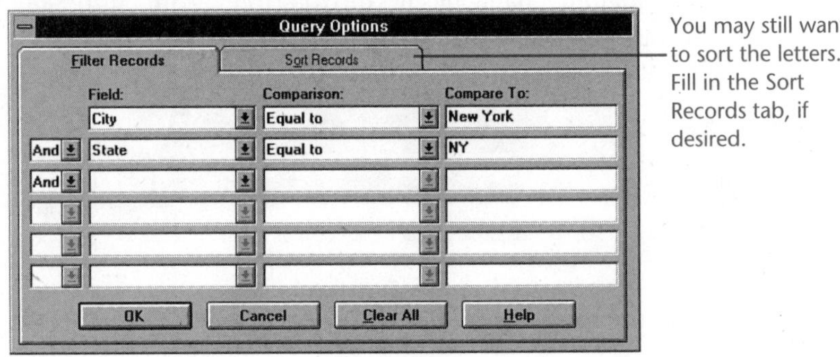

You may still want to sort the letters. Fill in the Sort Records tab, if desired.

Fig. 39.17
Select the Filter Records tab to find specific records in your data-source file.

4. In the Field drop-down list, select the name of the field. You can have up to six fields.

5. In the Comparison drop-down list, you can select Equal to match the text you type in the next column. You also can select options such as Is Blank, Is Not Blank, and Greater Than.

6. In the Compare To text box, type the text or value that you want to match for the field. If, for example, you want to find Atlanta in the city field, type **Atlanta** here. If you want salaries above $50,000, type **50000** here (and select Greater Than in the Comparison list).

7. If you have more than one line of criteria, you can indicate that you want every record that meets all criteria by choosing And or every record that meets any of the criteria by choosing Or.

8. When you complete the **F**ilter Records tab, choose OK.

9. Finish your sort by choosing the **M**erge button in the Mail Merge Helper dialog box, as described in "Completing the Merge" earlier in this chapter.

Marking Records for Selection

If not all the letters you want to print have the same criteria, it may be easier to create an extra column or field in the source file and then perform the merge. For example, you can go to Excel, create an extra column (such as Send), and place an X in each row for data that you want, as shown in figure 39.18.

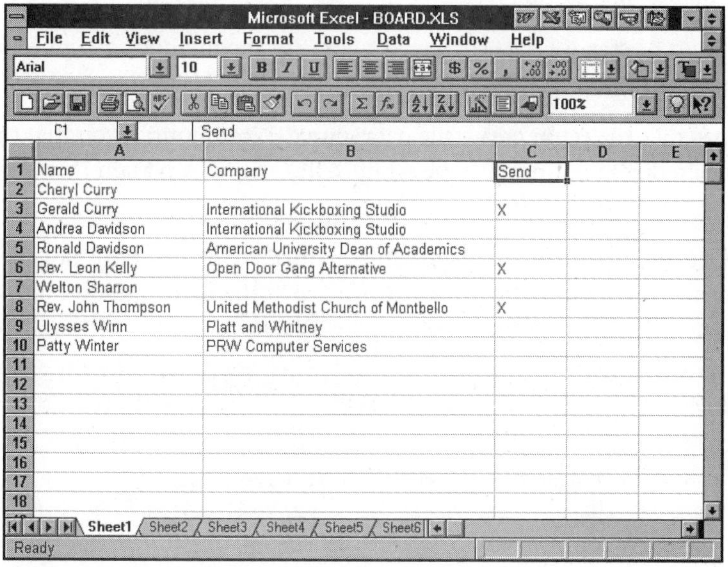

Microsoft Excel - BOARD.XLS

File Edit View Insert Format Tools Data Window Help

C1 Send

	A	B	C	D	E
1	Name	Company	Send		
2	Cheryl Curry				
3	Gerald Curry	International Kickboxing Studio	X		
4	Andrea Davidson	International Kickboxing Studio			
5	Ronald Davidson	American University Dean of Academics			
6	Rev. Leon Kelly	Open Door Gang Alternative	X		
7	Welton Sharron				
8	Rev. John Thompson	United Methodist Church of Montbello	X		
9	Ulysses Winn	Platt and Whitney			
10	Patty Winter	PRW Computer Services			

Sheet1 Sheet2 Sheet3 Sheet4 Sheet5 Sheet6

Ready

Fig. 39.18
The Xs in the Send column designate the people to whom you want to send the letter.

When you return to Word, return to the **F**ilter Records tab of the Query Options dialog box, and put Send in the Field column, Equal To in the Comparison column, and X in the Compare To column.

Addressing Envelopes and Mailing Labels

After you merge a letter, you probably will want to address envelopes or mailing labels for each letter. The process is essentially the same as creating the letter.

To create envelopes or mailing labels, follow these steps:

1. Choose the **T**ools Mail Me**r**ge command. The Mail Merge Helper dialog box appears.

2. In the Main Document section, choose **C**reate.

3. In the pull-down list, select either **E**nvelopes or **M**ailing Labels.

4. You are prompted to use the existing active document or a new document. Choose **N**ew Main Document. The Mail Merge Helper dialog box reappears.

5. Select or create a data source, using one of the methods described in the sections for Word, Excel, and Access earlier in this chapter.

6. After you select or create the data source, Word notifies you that the main document needs to be set up. Click the **S**et Up Main Document button.

   Depending on your choice in step 3, the Envelope Options or Label Options dialog box appears. See "Filling in the Envelope Options Dialog Box" or "Filling in the Label Options Dialog Box" later in this chapter.

   > **Note**
   >
   > If you later want to edit the Label or Envelope settings, from the main document, choose the **T**ools **E**nvelopes and Labels command.

7. When you finish creating the address, you return to the Mail Merge Helper dialog box. Choose **M**erge to merge the addresses with the envelope or label form. Figure 39.19 shows a completed envelope.

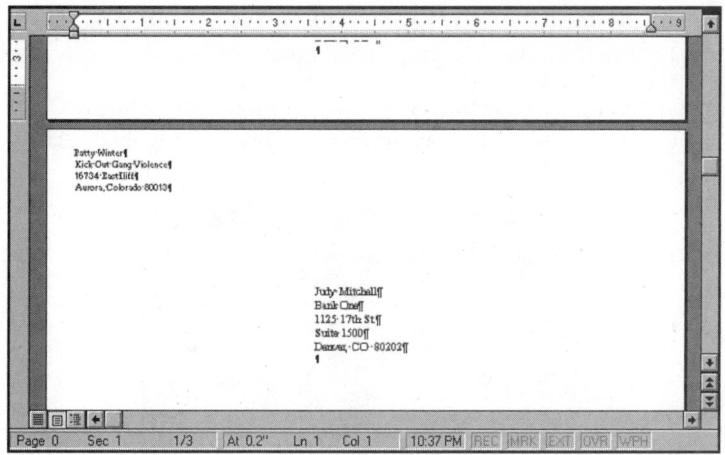

Fig. 39.19 Merging the addresses with the envelope form results in completed envelopes.

Filling in the Label Options Dialog Box

To set up labels after step 6 in the preceding section, follow these steps:

1. In the Label Options dialog box, select the type of printer and the location of the paper tray to which you want to print (see fig. 39.20).

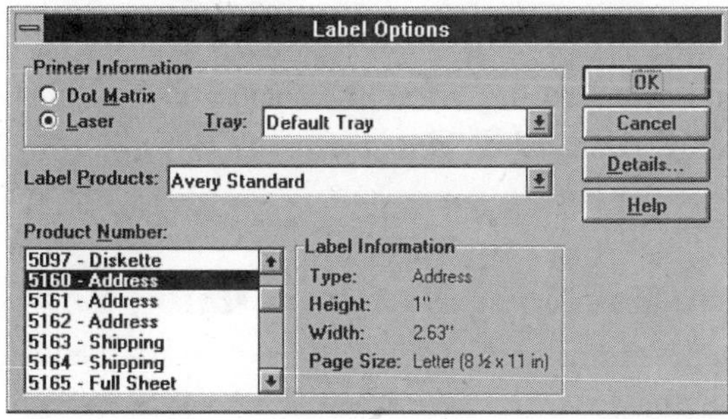

Fig. 39.20 The Label Options dialog box enables you to specify the type of label and printer you have.

2. The Label **P**roducts pull-down list gives you a choice of Avery Standard labels or other types of labels. Most labels have an equivalent Avery number. This example shows Avery Standard.

3. In the Product **N**umber list box, select the label type by its Avery number.

4. Verify that the label information is correct for your label.

5. If you want to customize the size or spacing for the label, choose the **D**etails command button.

6. When you finish with the Custom Information dialog box, choose OK to return to the Label Options dialog box.

7. When you finish with the Label Options dialog box, choose OK. The Create Labels dialog box appears, as shown in figure 39.21.

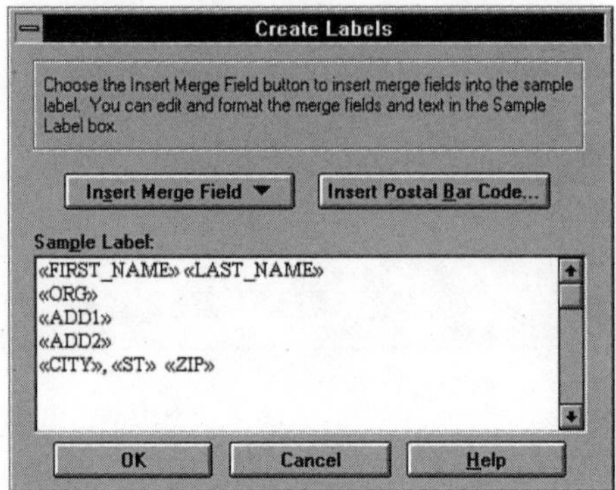

Fig. 39.21
The Create Labels dialog box is like a small document, enabling you to enter merge fields for the label.

8. Choose Insert Merge Field, and select a field from the list. Make sure that you add spaces and punctuation as necessary to create your label.

9. When you finish with the label, choose OK.

10. When you finish creating the address, you return to the Mail Merge Helper dialog box. Choose **M**erge to merge the addresses with the label form.

Filling in the Envelope Options Dialog Box

To set up envelopes after step 6 of the process of creating envelopes or mailing labels, follow these steps:

1. In the **E**nvelope Options tab of the Envelope Options dialog box, select an envelope size in the Envelope **S**ize drop-down list box (see fig. 39.22).

2. In the Delivery Address and Return Address area, you can change the fonts or placement of the addresses.

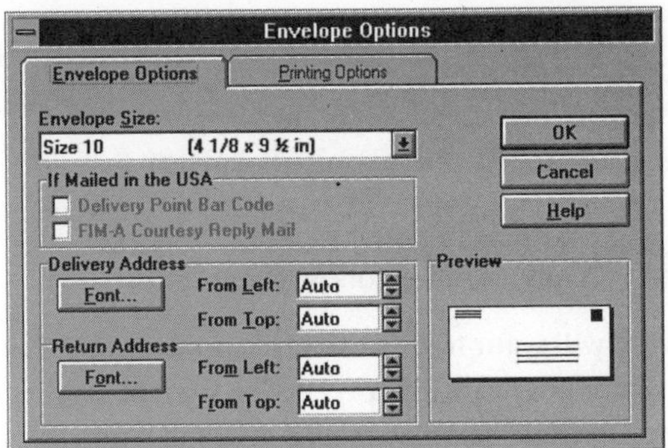

Fig. 39.22
The Envelope Options dialog box enables you to change the size and font of the envelope as well as the orientation of the envelope in the printer.

3. In the **P**rinting Options tab, you can select the orientation for the envelope and placement for the addresses.

4. After you finish filling out the Envelope Options dialog box, choose OK. The Envelope Address dialog box appears, as shown in figure 39.23.

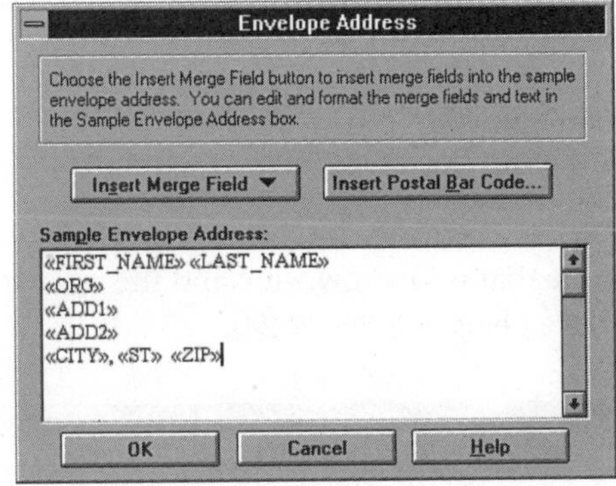

Fig. 39.23
The Envelope Address dialog box is just like the Create Labels dialog box, shown in figure 39.21.

5. Choose In**s**ert Merge Field, and select a field from the list of fields. Make sure that you add spaces and punctuation as necessary to create your envelope.

6. When you finish with the envelope, choose OK.

7. When you finish creating the address, you return to the Mail Merge Helper dialog box. Choose **M**erge to merge the addresses with the envelope form.

Creating a List of What You Mailed

If you mailed many different letters, you may want to create a log of each of the data sources. You can use the log to compare the lists and remove duplicates.

To create a list of each data source, follow these steps:

1. You probably will want to print the list in landscape (horizontal) mode. Therefore, start a new document; choose the **F**ile Page Set**u**p command; and then select the Paper **S**ize tab, Lands**c**ape, and OK to return to the document.

2. Choose the **T**ools Mail Me**r**ge command. The Mail Merge Helper dialog box appears.

3. In the Main Document section, choose the **C**reate button, and then select **C**atalog.

◄ "Working with Tables," p. 210

4. Answer the prompt to edit the active window, and select the data source to use data from Word, Excel, or Access.

5. After you select your data source, Word reports that it found no fields. Choose the Edit **M**ain document button to return to your document.

6. When you return to the main document, choose T**a**ble **I**nsert Table, and create a table that is one row wide and the same number of columns as you have fields (see fig. 39.24).

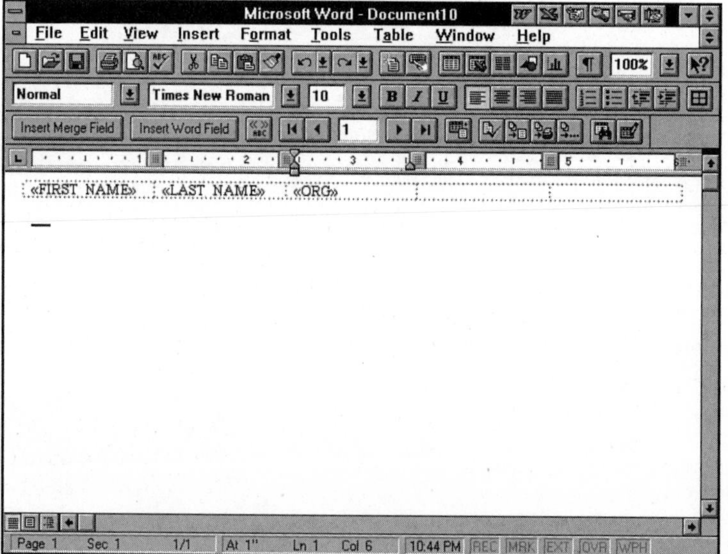

Fig. 39.24
In the table's only row, you use the Insert Merge Field button to add the names of the fields in the table cells.

7. Use the Insert Merge Field button to add field names in each cell of the table.

> **Note**
>
> Because you may have several lists, make sure that you sort them the same way by choosing the **Q**uery Options button in the Mail Merge Helper dialog box and by filling in the S**o**rt Records tab, as discussed in "Sorting the Mailing" earlier in this chapter.

8. Complete the merge by clicking the Merge to New Document button in the Mail Merge toolbar. Each record of your database now appears in a row of your new table.

In some cases, it may make sense to combine all data sources into one file. This probably would be true if you were using the list for one purpose. In other cases, you may want to keep the data sources in separate files if you use the lists for different purposes, such as mailing, accounting, and reporting. The hardest part of maintaining multiple sources of data is getting rid of duplicate information (or, more exactly, conflicting information). What do you do when you have two different addresses for the same person from different sources? Which one is correct? Because of this problem, you should include in all your records a field that shows the date when the record is created or updated. You then can go by the latest date when you have a conflict.

From Here...

This chapter showed you how to create a Word document and merge the document with a data source. The Word document could be a letter, an envelope, or a label form. The data source could be a Word data file, Excel spreadsheet, or Access table or query. You merge through the automated process of the Mail Merge Helper. If you want to merge different kinds of information, you may want to read the following chapters:

- Chapter 38, "Using Mail with Other Microsoft Office Products," shows you how to send one mail message to multiple network users.
- Chapter 40, "Linking and Embedding within Access To Manage Information," shows you how to create a database that enables you to link to Word documents, Excel spreadsheets and charts, and PowerPoint slides.

Chapter 40

Linking and Embedding within Access To Manage Information

by Rick and Patty Winter

Because Access is a database program, you can quickly find the information that you're looking for. As a database program, Access also enables you to manage that information. When you use Access in conjunction with other Office products, you have a powerful information-handling tool. You can use Access to hold information from different sources. With the new OLE (object linking and embedding) field, you can link to PowerPoint slides, Word documents, and Excel spreadsheets and charts.

In this chapter, you learn to

- Link a presentation to Access
- Line a Word document to Access
- Link an Excel spreadsheet and chart to Access
- Create a query and form to manage information from other sources

Importing Excel Spreadsheet Information into Access

If you have entered information in Excel, you can easily import it into Access. To do so, reorganize your Excel spreadsheet if necessary and create a range name if desired. Go to your Access database, and select a new or existing table. Choose the File Import command, and then identify your file format, file name, and range name if necessary. After you import the spreadsheet, you may need to add fields, edit information, or add records.

◄ "Modifying a Table," p. 608

◄ "Entering and Editing Data," p. 614

◄ "Importing and Exporting Data," p. 627

Linking a Presentation, Word Document, and Excel Spreadsheet to an Access Database

Originally, you may not need to manage your documents. You could look for a file by using the File Manager or the Find File feature in most of the Office applications. After you start getting a large number of files, however, you may want to list the files and organize them in Excel, as shown in figure 40.1.

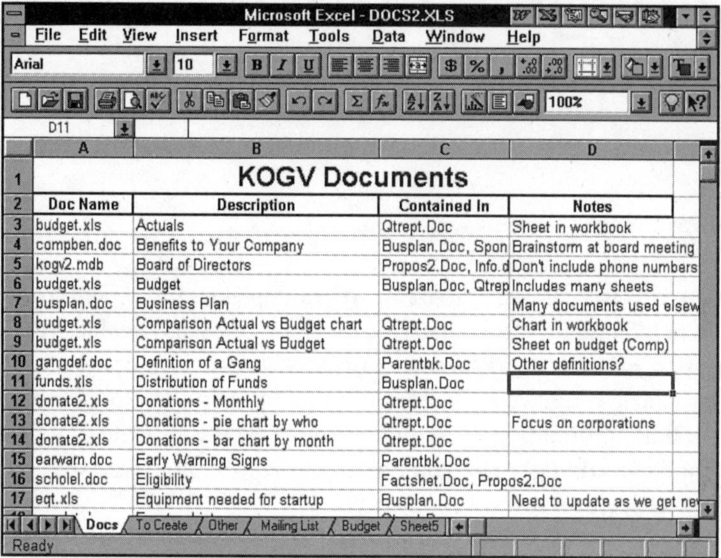

KOGV Documents

Doc Name	Description	Contained In	Notes
budget.xls	Actuals	Qtrept.Doc	Sheet in workbook
compben.doc	Benefits to Your Company	Busplan.Doc, Spon	Brainstorm at board meeting
kogv2.mdb	Board of Directors	Propos2.Doc, Info.d	Don't include phone numbers
budget.xls	Budget	Busplan.Doc, Qtrep	Includes many sheets
busplan.doc	Business Plan		Many documents used elsew
budget.xls	Comparison Actual vs Budget chart	Qtrept.Doc	Chart in workbook
budget.xls	Comparison Actual vs Budget	Qtrept.Doc	Sheet on budget (Comp)
gangdef.doc	Definition of a Gang	Parentbk.Doc	Other definitions?
funds.xls	Distribution of Funds	Busplan.Doc	
donate2.xls	Donations - Monthly	Qtrept.Doc	
donate2.xls	Donations - pie chart by who	Qtrept.Doc	Focus on corporations
donate2.xls	Donations - bar chart by month	Qtrept.Doc	
earwarn.doc	Early Warning Signs	Parentbk.Doc	
scholel.doc	Eligibility	Factshet.Doc, Propos2.Doc	
eqt.xls	Equipment needed for startup	Busplan.Doc	Need to update as we get ne

Fig. 40.1
You can organize your files in an Excel table.

◀ "Finding Files," p. 81

◀ "Working in Find File," p. 168

◀ "Using File Manager To Organize Files," p. 738

◀ "Creating a New Database," p. 585

Such a list of files may work for a while, but when the list starts to grow exceptionally large, you may need something more. You then can use Access to link the information from Excel, Word, and PowerPoint, and use the query and reporting capabilities of Access to manage your documents. For example, you may want to show slides from a PowerPoint presentation to senior management. If you change the presentation, you will want management to see those changes.

To link a presentation to the database, follow these steps:

1. Go to your Access database, and open the table containing information about your documents.

2. Move to an empty OLE field (in this example, a field called Object).

Note

An OLE field is a special field that can accept information from other sources. The information can be text, a picture, or even sound.

3. Choose **E**dit Insert Ob**j**ect. The Insert Object dialog box appears, displaying a list of new objects that you can insert.

4. To insert information from an existing file, select Create From **F**ile. The Insert Object dialog box changes to prompt you for the file name (see fig. 40.2).

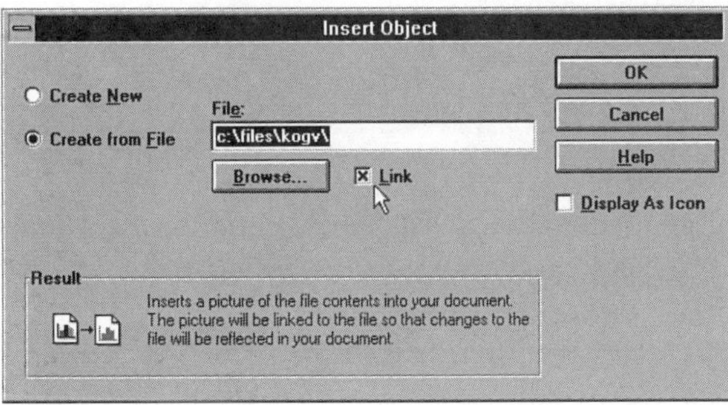

Fig. 40.2
The Insert Object dialog box enables you to identify a file and link it to the Access OLE field.

5. Type the file name and location in the Fil**e** text box (or choose the **B**rowse button and then select the file name and location).

6. To link the file so that you always see the latest changes, check the **L**ink box.

Note

If you do not check the Link box, the file will be embedded. This means that you can edit the information, using the source application's tools, but if you update the information in the source file, changes will not appear in the Access database.

Note

If you want to see an icon representing the link in your forms rather than an actual view of the document, check the Display As Icon check box.

7. Choose OK. The name of the application appears in the field (see fig. 40.3).

Table: Projects

	Doc Name	Description	Notes	Object
	flyer.doc	Superfights	Use in presentation	
	funds.xls	Distribution of Fund		
	gangdef.doc	Definition of a Gang	Other definitions?	
	ganglev.doc	Levels of Gang Inv		
	gangwhy.doc	Why Kids Join Gan		
	geogra.doc	Geographic Dev't		
	history.doc	History	Use for press releas	
	invite.doc	Invitation to Superfi	Need to update	
	karinfo.doc	General karate info		
	kbrules.doc	Kickboxing Rules	Use also for training	
	kogv2.mdb	Board of Directors	Don't include phon	
	kogvdef.doc	Overview (what is K		
	loc.doc	Location		
	logo.ppt	Logo		
	mission.doc	Our Goal (mission)		
	newnet.doc	New Chapter Netw		
	org.doc	Orgchart		
✎	orient.ppt	Orientation Present	needs a lot more w	MS PowerPoint 4.0
	parsug.doc	Suggestions for Par		
	po.doc	Participating Organ		
	purpose.doc	Purpose		
	qrdef.doc	Quarterly Reporting		

Record: 35 of 46

Fig. 40.3
The name of the application that created the file appears in the Object field (in this case, `MS PowerPoint 4.0`).

To show the presentation, double-click the appropriate field name. A full-screen view of the presentation appears (see fig. 40.4).

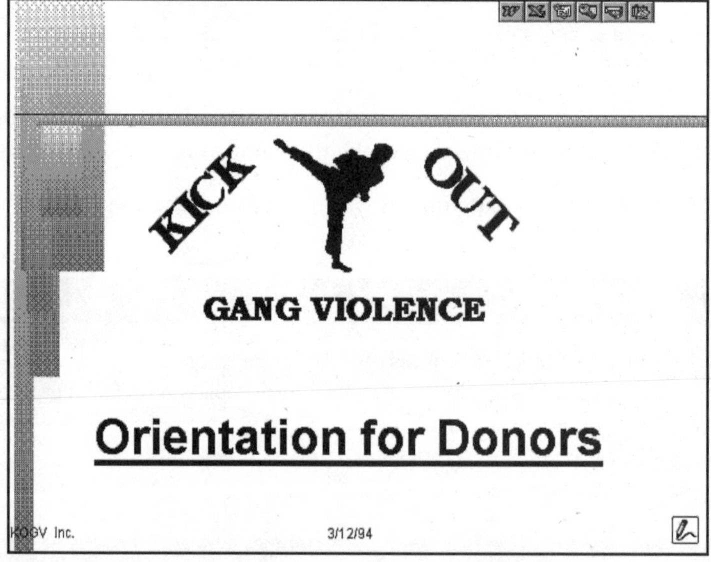

Fig. 40.4
The first slide of the presentation appears when you double-click the OLE object.

◄ "Setting Up and Running a Slide Show On-Screen," p. 564

After the presentation starts, click the middle of the slide to see the next slide (see fig. 40.5).

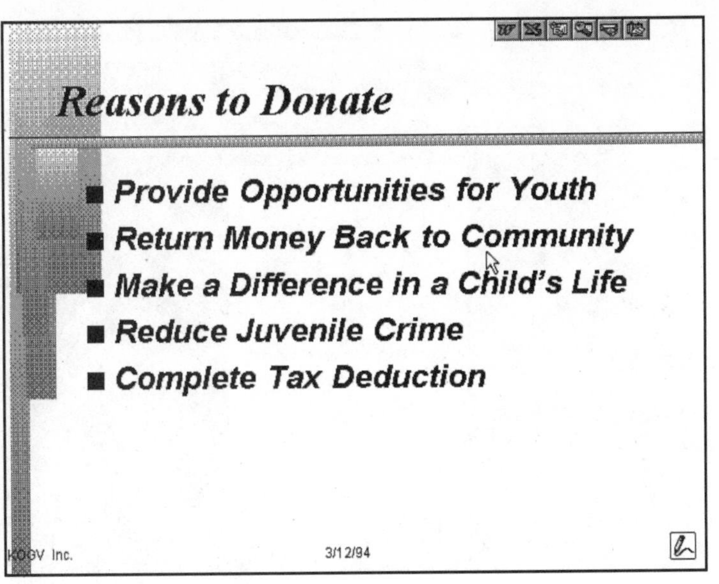

Fig. 40.5 When you click the first slide, the next slide of the presentation appears.

You can link a Word document or Excel workbook to your Access database in essentially the same way that you link a PowerPoint presentation. Figure 40.6 shows different applications linked to the database.

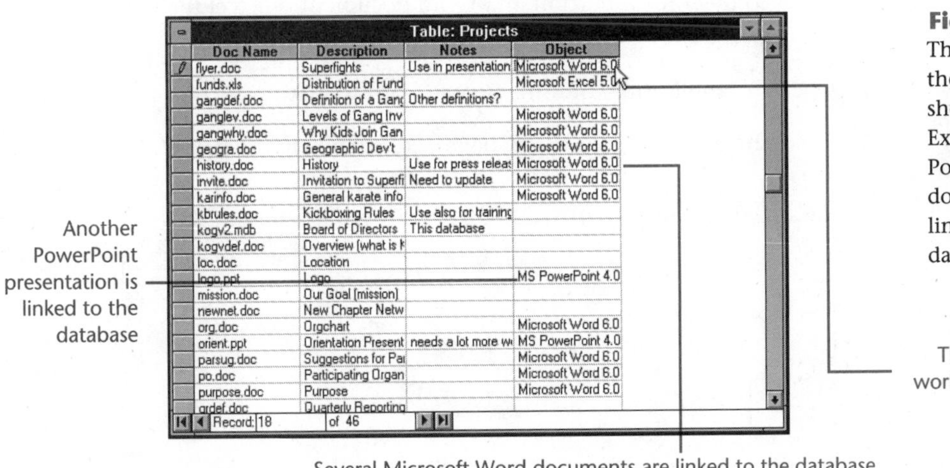
Table: Projects

Doc Name	Description	Notes	Object
flyer.doc	Superfights	Use in presentation	Microsoft Word 6.0
funds.xls	Distribution of Fund		Microsoft Excel 5.0
gangdef.doc	Definition of a Gang	Other definitions?	
ganglev.doc	Levels of Gang Inv		Microsoft Word 6.0
gangwhy.doc	Why Kids Join Gan		Microsoft Word 6.0
geogra.doc	Geographic Dev't		Microsoft Word 6.0
history.doc	History	Use for press releas	Microsoft Word 6.0
invite.doc	Invitation to Superfi	Need to update	Microsoft Word 6.0
karinfo.doc	General karate info		Microsoft Word 6.0
kbrules.doc	Kickboxing Rules	Use also for training	
kogv2.mdb	Board of Directors	This database	
kogvdef.doc	Overview (what is K		
loc.doc	Location		
logo.ppt	Logo		MS PowerPoint 4.0
mission.doc	Our Goal (mission)		
newnet.doc	New Chapter Netw		
org.doc	Orgchart		Microsoft Word 6.0
orient.ppt	Orientation Present	needs a lot more wo	MS PowerPoint 4.0
parsug.doc	Suggestions for Par		Microsoft Word 6.0
po.doc	Participating Organ		Microsoft Word 6.0
purpose.doc	Purpose		Microsoft Word 6.0
qrdef.doc	Quarterly Reporting		

Record: 18 of 46

Fig. 40.6 The Object field in the Projects table shows that Word, Excel, and PowerPoint documents are linked to this database.

If you double-click a Word or Excel object, the application opens, and you can edit the file. For example, figure 40.7 shows FLYER.DOC open in Word and displayed in Whole Page zoom mode for viewing. After you finish editing or viewing the file, double-click the document's Control-menu box or choose **F**ile E**x**it.

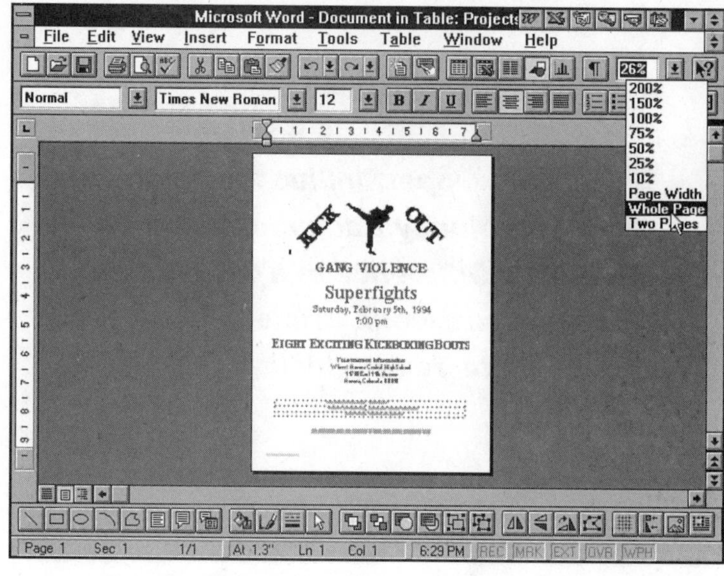

Fig. 40.7
The FLYER.DOC document is shown in Whole Page zoom mode. To get out of the application, double-click the application's Control-menu box.

Linking a Portion of a Document to an Access Database

◄ "Selecting Text," p. 49

◄ "Selecting Text," p. 108

◄ "Selecting Cells and Ranges," p. 251

If you want to link only a portion of a Word document or Excel file to your Access database, follow these steps:

1. Open the application and the file you want to link.

2. Select the portion of the file to be linked, as shown in figure 40.8.

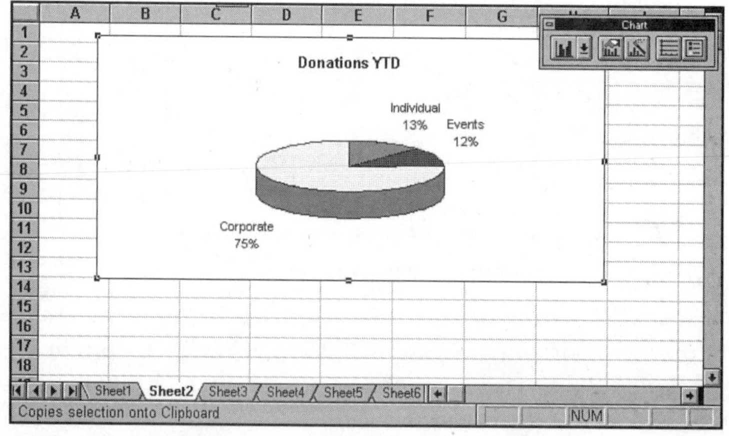

Fig. 40.8
In this figure, the black handles indicate that the Excel chart is selected. This portion of the file will be linked to Access.

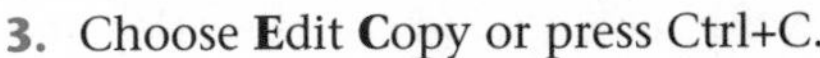

3. Choose **E**dit **C**opy or press Ctrl+C.

4. Return to the Object field of the Access database, and choose **E**dit Paste **S**pecial. The Paste Special dialog box appears (see fig. 40.9).

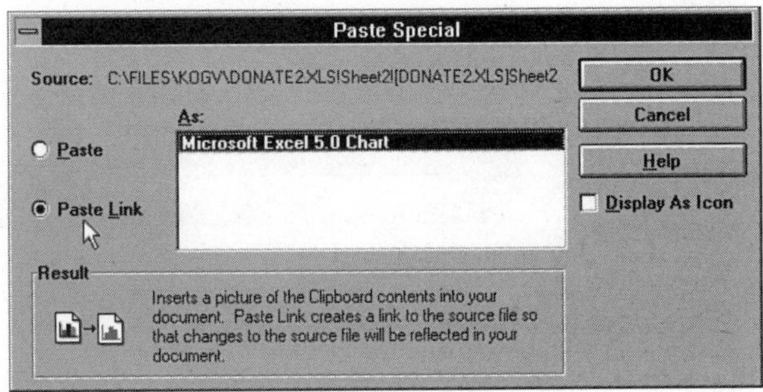

Fig. 40.9
In the Paste Special dialog box, the file name, sheet reference, and chart reference appear in the Source information area.

5. To link the object, select the Paste **L**ink option.

6. Select the correct format for the link. In figure 40.9, only Microsoft 5.0 Excel Chart is available. But depending on the object you are linking, you may be able to choose among various format types. (For more information on format types, see Chapter 37, "Sharing Data between Applications with Linking and Embedding.")

7. When you finish with the dialog box, choose OK.

When you return to the Access table, the field reference shows `Microsoft Excel 5.0` or `Microsoft Word 6.0`, as it would if you were linking an entire file (refer to fig. 40.6). But when you double-click the field, you see the selected object within the file.

◄ "Creating a New Query," p. 663

With queries, you can limit the view to items of interest only. Figure 40.10 shows a query designed to show only items that are of interest to a manager.

Select Query: Items for Management Review

Description	Object	Who	When	Notes
Purpose	Microsoft Word 6.0	Curry, G.	2/15/94	
Comparison Actual	Microsoft Excel 5.0	Welton, S.	4/1/94	Chart in workbook
Comparison Actual	Microsoft Excel 5.0	Welton, S.	4/1/94	Sheet on budget (C
Actuals	Microsoft Excel 5.0	Welton, S.	4/1/94	Sheet in workbook
Donations - Monthl	Microsoft Excel 5.0	Winter.P.	4/1/94	
Donations - pie cha	Microsoft Excel 5.0	Winter, P.	4/1/94	Focus on corporatic
Donations - bar cha	Microsoft Excel 5.0	Winter, P.	4/1/94	
Logo	MS PowerPoint 4.0	Curry, G.	2/15/94	
Orientation Present	MS PowerPoint 4.0	Kelly, L.	3/1/94	needs a lot more w
Orgchart	Microsoft Word 6.0	Curry, G.	3/1/94	
Equipment needed	Microsoft Excel 5.0	Winter, R.	2/15/94	Need to update as
Events - List	Microsoft Word 6.0	Curry, C.	2/15/94	

Record: 1 of 12

Fig. 40.10
Query showing only items that are of interest to a manager.

◄ "Modifying a Form's Design," p. 652

When you look at an OLE field in the table view, all you can see is the reference to the source application. If you want to see the document or a portion of the document, you can create a form to show the OLE field. Figures 40.11 and 40.12 show a form record for a Word document and an Excel spreadsheet.

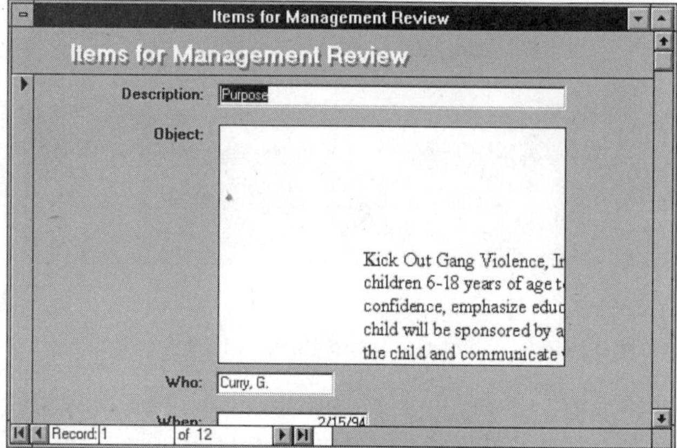

Fig. 40.11
This form shows a portion of a Word document.

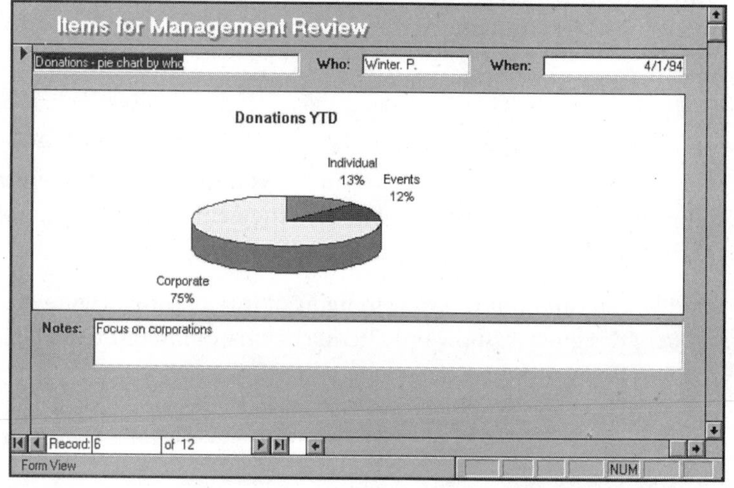

Fig. 40.12
This form, which was redesigned to display more information, shows an Excel chart in the OLE field.

From Here...

This chapter showed how you can use Access to manage your information. You can link Word, Excel, PowerPoint, and other files or portions of files into an object field of your database. When you work with the different Office applications, a central application generally is the focus of your work. For more information on working with multiple applications, see the following chapters:

- Chapter 36, "Working with Wizards, Multiple Documents, and Cut, Copy, and Paste," shows you how to use multiple open documents and gather information into one document.
- Chapter 37, "Sharing Data between Applications with Linking and Embedding," also focuses on a Word document, but the information is linked, so information in the document is updated constantly.
- Chapter 38, "Using Mail with Other Microsoft Office Products," focuses on a mail message and shows you how to pass documents among different users on your network.
- Chapter 39, "Sending a Mass Mailing," focuses on a Word document but enables you to use your existing Excel spreadsheet or Access database to personalize many letters.
- Chapter 41, "Using Office Applications To Create a Presentation," focuses on a PowerPoint presentation and explains how you can pull information from different sources to create and organize your slide show.

Chapter 41

Using Office Applications To Create a Presentation

by Rick and Patty Winter

The focus of the last chapter was on integrating Microsoft Office applications with Access. This chapter focuses on integrating Microsoft Office applications with PowerPoint. If you need overhead transparencies, 35mm slides, a graphical report, or a computer-driven presentation, use PowerPoint to create the presentation. If you have information in other sources, such as Word or Excel, you can copy or link the information from the source application to PowerPoint.

In this chapter, you learn to

- Organize a presentation
- Use Word Outline to create slides
- Copy or link information to PowerPoint
- Embed a presentation in a Mail message

Organizing the Presentation with a Word Outline

If you are accustomed to using Word, you can create an outline of your presentation in Word and use the outline to create slides in PowerPoint. Suppose that you need to create a presentation for community groups about gangs.

◄ "Formatting with Styles," p. 196

◄ "Outlining a Document," p. 190

You have the basics of the presentation in a Word document. PowerPoint uses Word's heading styles for the title and bullets of slides. Therefore, you first reformat the Word document to include Heading 1 for the planned title of the slide, Heading 2 for each major bullet item, and Heading 3 for each minor bullet item.

If you use Heading 1, Heading 2, and Heading 3 styles, you also can use the outline feature of Word to organize and view your slides. To change the view, choose the **V**iew **O**utline command, or the Outline View button in the horizontal scroll bar directly above the status bar. The view changes to show your indents for each heading level (see fig. 41.1).

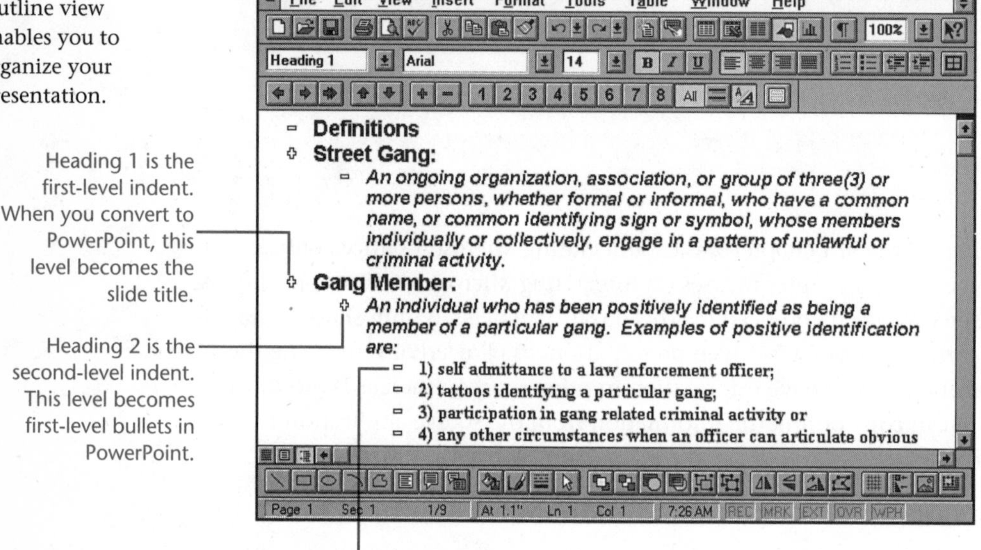

Fig. 41.1
Outline view enables you to organize your presentation.

When you choose the **V**iew **O**utline command, the document changes to show different levels, and the Outlining toolbar becomes available. You can use the Outlining toolbar to show one or more levels in the outline. The numbers 1 through 8 in the toolbar enable you to show one level, two levels, or up to eight levels of your outline. The 1 corresponds to Heading 1 style, 2 corresponds to Heading 2 style, and so on. When you show Heading 2, Heading 1 also appears, and so on. Figure 41.2 shows the outline when you click the Show Heading 1 button. Click the All button to show your entire document. You also can use the Outlining toolbar to promote or demote levels in the outline.

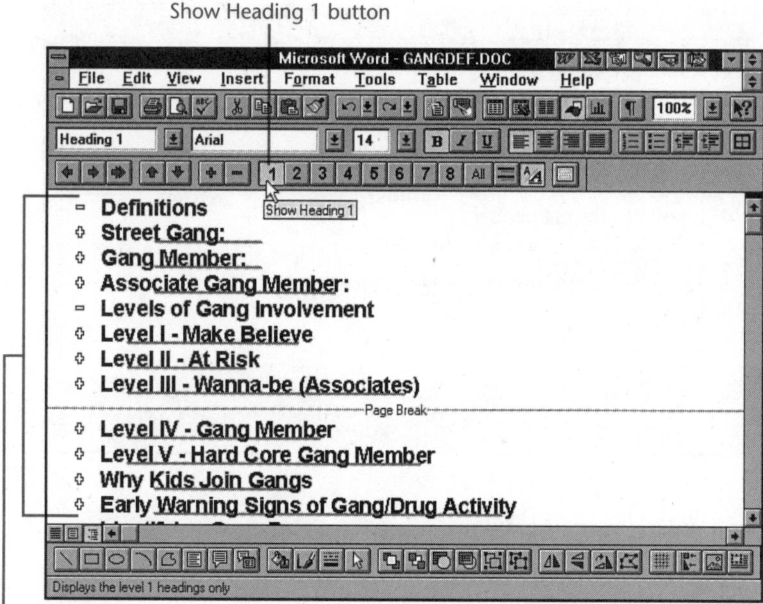

Fig. 41.2
The numbered Outlining toolbar buttons enable you to see one or more heading styles.

If a Heading 1 contains no supporting text (Heading 2, and so on), a minus sign appears to the left of the text. If a Heading 1 contains supporting text, a plus sign appears to the left of the text. Double-click the plus sign to show other headings and body text. Double-click the plus sign again to compress the text.

◀ "Editing a Style," p. 199

To move a heading (and all text below the heading), place the mouse pointer on the plus or minus sign before the text. The mouse pointer changes to a black four-headed arrow (see fig. 41.3). Drag the mouse up or down to the new position. You also can use the Move Up or Move Down button in the Outlining toolbar. The Move Up button moves the selected text up in the outline. The Move Down button moves the text down in the outline. To change a level in the outline, use the Promote and Demote buttons in the toolbar, or change the style to a different heading. The Promote button changes the selection to a higher level (from Heading to Heading 1). The Demote button changes the selection to a lower level.

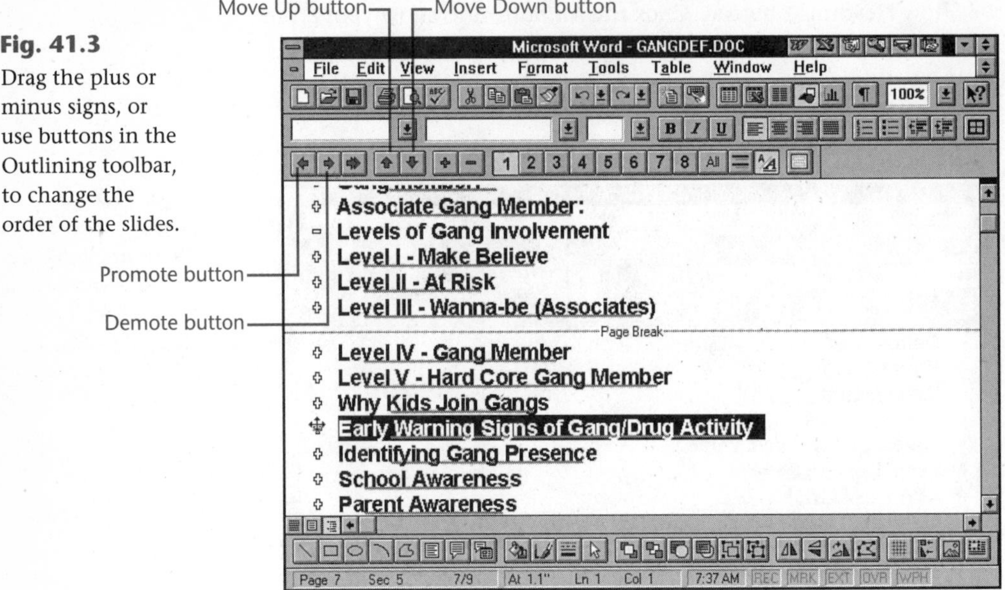

Fig. 41.3
Drag the plus or minus signs, or use buttons in the Outlining toolbar, to change the order of the slides.

When you finish organizing your outline, save and close the document.

Using a Word Outline To Create Slides

When you want to use the Word document in PowerPoint, you can create a new presentation or add to an existing presentation. Heading 1 becomes the title of each slide. Heading 2 becomes the first-level bullet for each slide.

To start a new presentation, follow these steps:

1. Within PowerPoint, choose the **F**ile **O**pen command or press Ctrl+O.
2. Change the drive and directory, if necessary.
3. In the pull-down List Files of **T**ype list, select Outlines to display Word documents.

> **Note**
>
> You also can use Excel worksheets and Write documents to create slides.

4. Type the file name in the File **N**ame text box, or scroll the list box to select the file.

5. Choose OK.

Tip
In place of steps 4 and 5, you can double-click the file name in the File **N**ame list box.

Figure 41.4 shows the outline view of the presentation. The number 3 slide shows Gang Member. To switch between views, click the buttons in the bottom-left corner of the presentation window, or use the **V**iew menu. Figure 41.5 shows the slide view of the Gang Member definition slide. Compare this slide with figure 41.1. Heading 1 style became the title of the slide, Heading 2 became the first bullet, and Heading 3 items became subpoints of the bullet. Figure 41.5 also shows that editing text for a slide presentation may be necessary if there is too much text for the slide.

◄ "Viewing a Presentation," p. 449

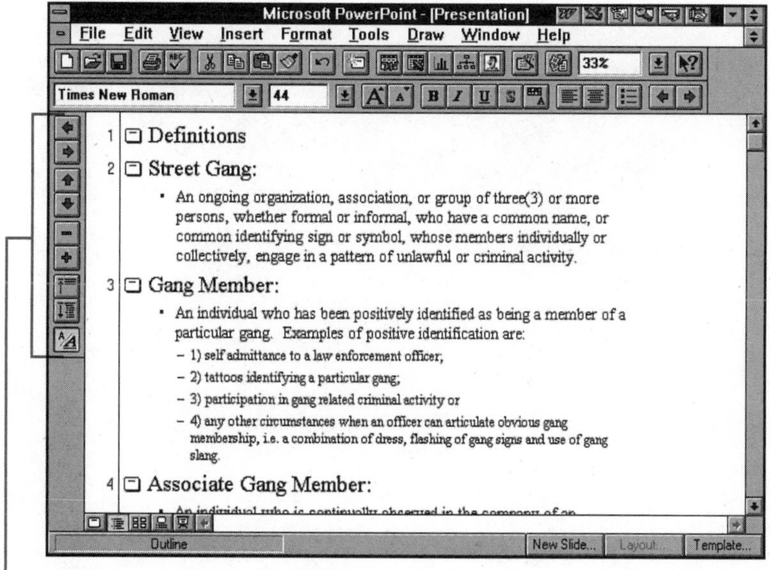

The Outlining toolbar for the presentation works the same way as it does in Word

Fig. 41.4
Opening a Word document brings you into a PowerPoint outline.

Tip
If you want to add a level or change a level, use the Outlining toolbar in outline view.

After you open a Word file to create a PowerPoint presentation, you can select a more interesting format than simple black text on a white background. To change the format, click the Pick a Look Wizard button (see fig. 41.6), or use the F**o**rmat Pick a Look **W**izard command. Follow the steps in the Wizard dialog box to select the formatting for the slide, notes pages, outline, and handout pages. To accept all the default choices or choices you made for the last wizard, choose the Finish button. Figure 41.7 shows the formatted and edited slide from figure 41.5.

◄ "Creating a Presentation Using a Wizard," p. 440

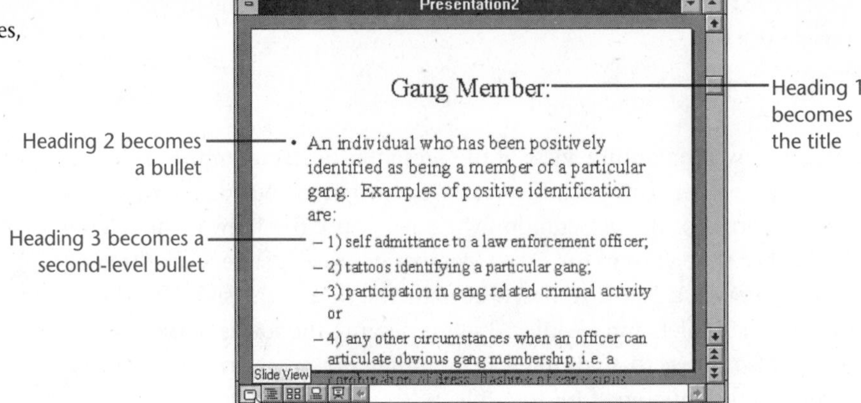

Fig. 41.5
The heading styles, shown in figure 41.1, create each slide.

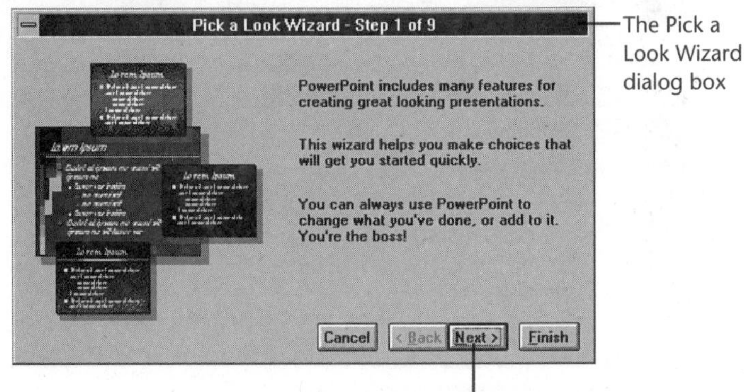

Fig. 41.6
Use the Pick a Look Wizard to change the formatting of your presentation.

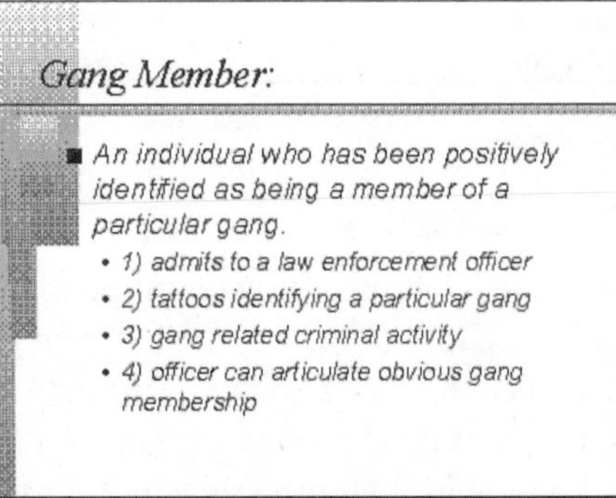

Fig. 41.7
The original slide in figure 41.5 is edited and formatted.

Note

You can insert the Word outline into an existing presentation. The Word outline assumes the format of the existing PowerPoint presentation. To insert a file into the presentation, choose the **I**nsert Slides from Out**l**ine command, and identify the file name and location.

Troubleshooting

I cannot open my file.

You may not have closed the Word document before you returned to PowerPoint. Click the Word button in the Microsoft Office toolbar. If necessary, choose the **W**indow command and select the document name. Choose the **F**ile **C**lose command to close the document. Click the PowerPoint button to return to PowerPoint.

Automating the Process from Word to PowerPoint

Buried within Word is a wonderful macro and button that can automate the process of going from a Word outline to Presentation slides. The Present It macro and button are in the CONVERT.DOT template (in the WINWORD\MACROS subdirectory). You can attach the template to your current document with the **F**ile **T**emplates **A**ttach command. If you create many presentations, however, you may want to add the Present It macro and button to your NORMAL.DOT template so that the button is available whenever you need it.

◄ "Choosing Macro Templates," p. 226

◄ "Using Template Wizards," p. 204

To add the Present It button to your normal template, follow these steps:

1. Go to Word and choose the **F**ile **O**pen command. The Open dialog box appears.

2. In the File **N**ame text box, type the following and choose OK:

   C:\WINWORD\MACROS\CONVERT.DOT

   If your Word program is in a different drive or directory, change the drive and directory.

3. Choose **F**ile **T**emplates. The Templates and Add-Ins dialog box appears.

4. Choose the **O**rganizer command button. The Organizer dialog box appears, as shown in figure 41.8.

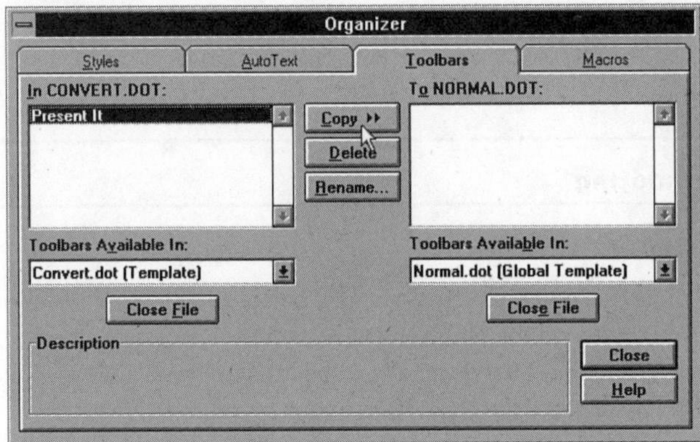

Fig. 41.8
Select Present It in the CONVERT.DOT list box, and copy it to the NORMAL.DOT list box.

5. In the **T**oolbars tab, select Present It from the In CONVERT.DOT list box, and then choose the **C**opy command button. Present It appears in the **T**o NORMAL.DOT list box.

6. In the **M**acros tab, select Present It from the In CONVERT.DOT list box, and then choose the **C**opy command button. Present It appears in the **T**o NORMAL.DOT list box.

7. Choose the Close button to finish copying the toolbar and macro.

8. Close the CONVERT.DOT document, and return to your Word outline document.

When you want to display the Present It toolbar and button, follow these steps:

1. Open the Word outline document that you want to convert.

2. If the Present It toolbar does not appear, place the mouse pointer on any toolbar, click the right mouse button, and then select Present It, as shown in figure 41.9.

3. Click the Present It button. After a few moments, PowerPoint opens, and the document converts from the Word outline to a PowerPoint presentation.

Tip
You also can run the Present It macro by choosing the **T**ools **M**acro Run command.

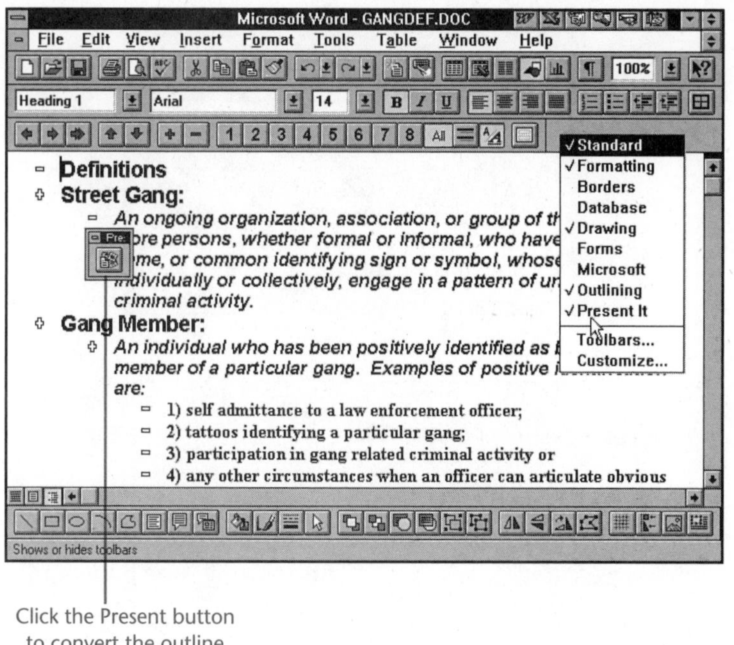

Fig. 41.9
The Present It toolbar has only one button—the Present It button.

Summarizing Data in Excel and Linking a Range to PowerPoint

If you have information in Excel that you want to bring to the presentation, you can copy and paste the information or link the information. If you want the data in the presentation to be updated every time the Excel worksheet changes, link the information from Excel.

◄ "Adding, Inserting, and Deleting Slides," p. 448

◄ "Inserting a Graph," p. 471

You first must create a new slide to accept the data. To create a new slide that accepts data from Excel, follow these steps:

1. Choose the **I**nsert New **S**lide command, or press Ctrl+M.

2. Select the graph layout, and then choose OK (see fig. 41.10). A new slide appears, with instructions on where to add the title and graph, as shown in figure 41.11.

3. Click the middle of the area (where the slide tells you to double-click), and press the Del key to remove the graph.

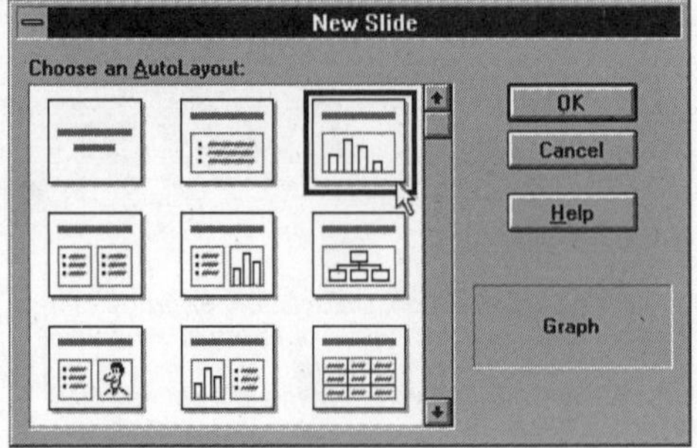

Fig. 41.10
Select the graph style.

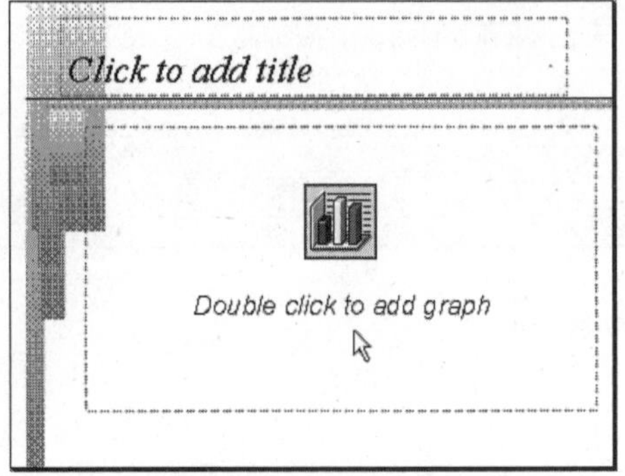

Fig. 41.11
Click the graph area and press Del to remove the instruction to add a graph.

◀ "Copying and Moving," p. 52

◀ "Copying Spreadsheet Information," p. 772

Now you are ready to copy information from Excel into the slide. To copy or link the information from Excel, follow these steps:

1. From the PowerPoint presentation, click the Excel button in the Microsoft Office toolbar.
2. Open the file containing the information that you want to copy or link.
3. Drag the mouse pointer (a white cross) to select the range in Excel (see fig. 41.12).

4. Choose the **E**dit **C**opy command or press Ctrl+C.

5. Click the PowerPoint button in the Microsoft Office toolbar to return to PowerPoint.

Note

If both applications are windowed and tiled, just click the slide you want, or use Alt+Tab to switch applications.

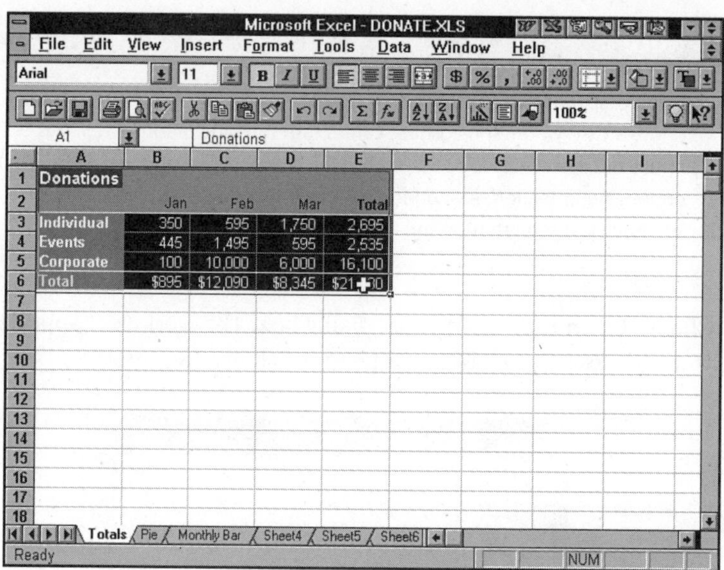

Fig. 41.12
Highlight the range you want to copy in Excel.

6. Choose the **E**dit Paste **S**pecial command. The Paste Special dialog box appears (see fig. 41.13).

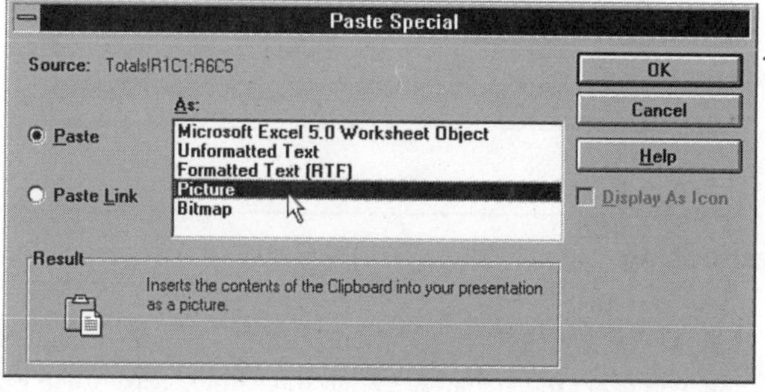

Fig. 41.13
The Paste Special dialog box enables you to paste or link information from Excel.

7. Do one of the following things:

- To paste a picture of the Excel chart, choose the **P**aste command, and then select Picture in the **A**s list box.

- To link the information so that the slide updates when the Excel worksheet updates, choose the Paste **L**ink command. Select the only option in the **A**s list box when you link: Microsoft Excel 5.0 Worksheet Object. When you use this option, you can double-click the worksheet data to enter Excel and edit the worksheet.

◀ "Entering and Editing Text," p. 459

◀ "Resizing and Scaling Objects," p. 485

Note

If you click the Paste button in the toolbar, choose the **E**dit **P**aste command, or press Ctrl+V. The spreadsheet comes into the slide unformatted. It is better to use the Paste Special options. The Unformatted Text and Formatted Text options bring the information from the worksheet as text; the columns are not lined up. You can reformat the text, if you want.

8. Choose OK in the Paste Special dialog box. The worksheet appears in your slide (see fig. 41.14). Complete the slide as necessary.

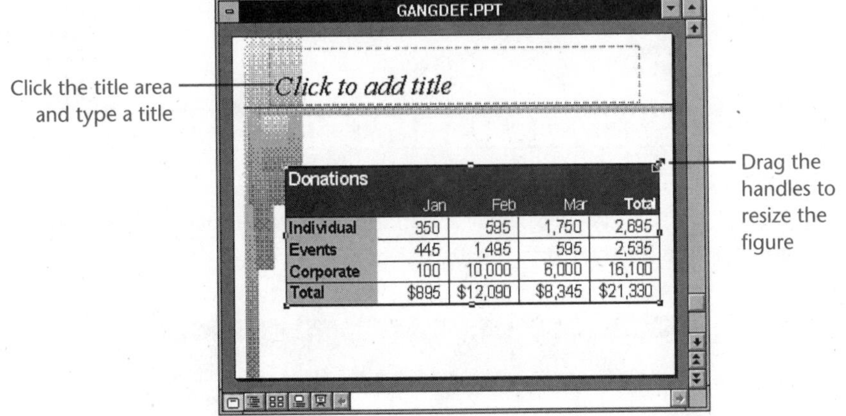

Fig. 41.14
The worksheet appears in the slide.

Troubleshooting

When I copy to PowerPoint, the data from my Excel spreadsheet is not lined up.

Make sure that you select the Picture option in the Paste Special dialog box. Do not choose the **E**dit **P**aste command, click the Paste button, or press Ctrl+V to bring in your copy.

The Excel worksheet is too big for my PowerPoint slide.

Try simplifying the worksheet before you copy it into PowerPoint. You also can change the size of the worksheet in PowerPoint by dragging the picture handles, but remember that your viewers have to be able to read the slide.

Creating Charts in Excel and Copying to PowerPoint

Adding an Excel chart to the presentation is essentially the same as adding a worksheet.

To add an Excel chart to a slide, follow these steps:

1. Click the middle of a chart in a worksheet to display handles on the chart (see fig. 41.15).

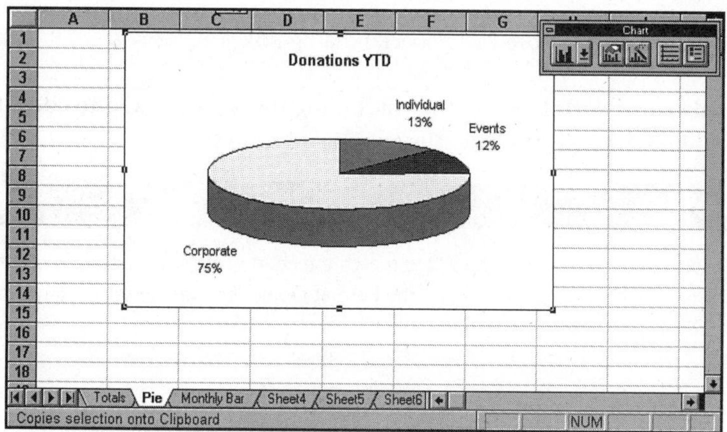

Fig. 41.15
Select the chart you want to copy.

2. Choose the **E**dit **C**opy command or press Ctrl+C.

3. Return to the PowerPoint slide.
4. Choose the **E**dit Paste **S**pecial command. The Paste Special dialog box appears (see fig. 41.16).

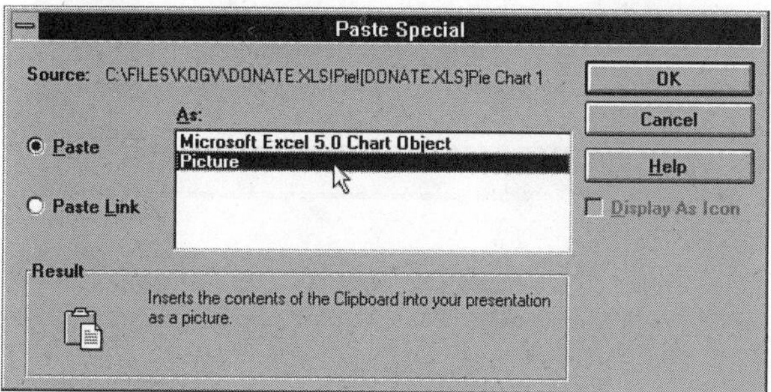

Fig. 41.16
Fill out the Paste Special dialog box to display the chart in the slide.

5. Do one of the following things:

   - Choose the **P**aste command, and in the **A**s list box, select the Microsoft Excel 5.0 Chart Object command. The object choice enables you to double-click the chart to return to Excel and edit the object.
   - Choose the **P**aste and Picture command to see only the chart.
   - Choose the Paste **L**ink command, and select the Microsoft Excel 5.0 Chart Object item (in the **A**s list box) to link and embed the slide with the Excel worksheet.

6. Choose OK in the Paste Special dialog box.

You also may need to resize the chart (drag the handles) and to add a title to the slide. Figure 41.17 shows the completed slide.

Note

If you want the slide background to match the chart background, make sure that you format the chart in Excel by using the F**o**rmat Obj**e**ct command; select **N**one for Borders and Non**e** for Fill.

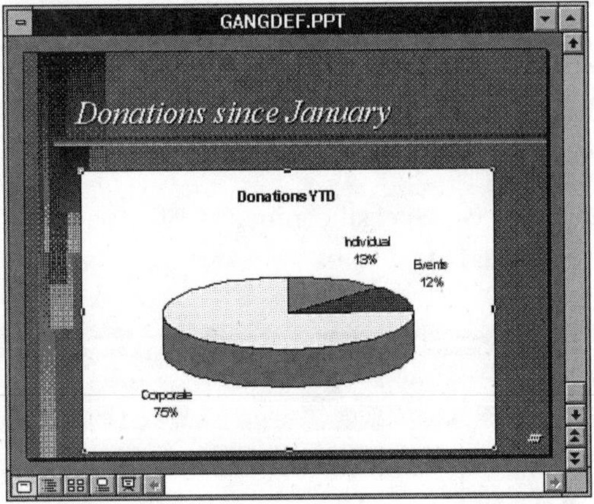

Fig. 41.17
The edited slide appears with the Excel chart.

Embedding the Presentation in a Mail Message

As with any document, continually save your presentation so that your updates are protected. When you finish the presentation, make sure that you save it. If you want to send the presentation to others on your network for review, embed the presentation in a Mail message.

To create a message with the presentation, follow these steps:

1. Click the Mail button in the Microsoft Office toolbar.

2. Click the Compose button in the Mail toolbar.
3. Address the message in the **T**o and **C**c text boxes.
4. Type a short summary in the Subject text box.
5. Type any message you want in the message area.
6. Choose the **A**ttach button.
7. Identify the file name and location in the Attach dialog box, and then choose the **A**ttach button. The presentation appears as an icon in the message window (see fig. 41.18).

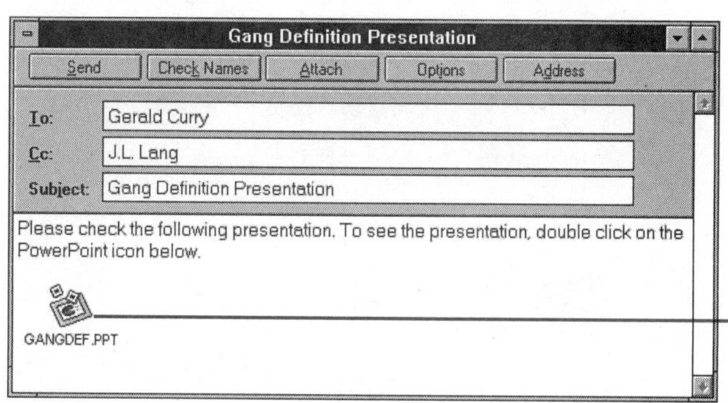

Fig. 41.18
The PowerPoint presentation appears as an icon in the message text area.

8. Click the **S**end button to send the message.

When the recipients get the message, they can double-click the PowerPoint icon to see the presentation on their computers.

From Here...

This chapter showed you how to work with the different applications in Microsoft Office to create documents and presentations. If you want more detail about how to create a presentation and work with graphics, refer to the following chapters:

- Chapter 10, "Working with Tables, Charts, and Graphics." This chapter helps you with these Word features.
- Chapter 16, "Creating and Printing Reports and Charts." This chapter shows you how to create and enhance a chart in Excel.
- Chapter 23, "Drawing Shapes, Curves, and Lines." This chapter explains how to add additional drawing items to your PowerPoint slides.
- Chapter 26, "Creating Output." This chapter shows you how to print your slides or run your PowerPoint presentation on-screen.

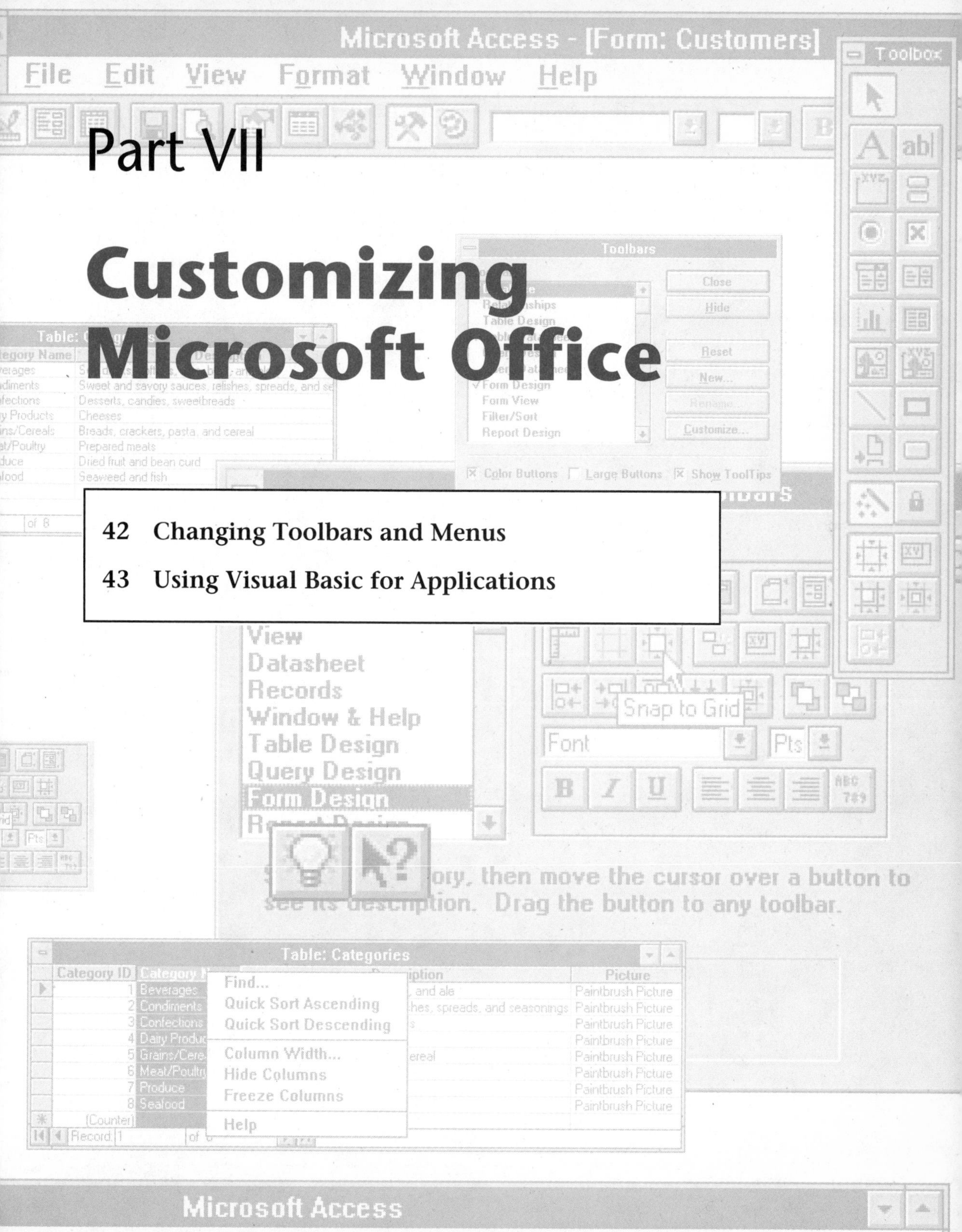

Part VII

Customizing Microsoft Office

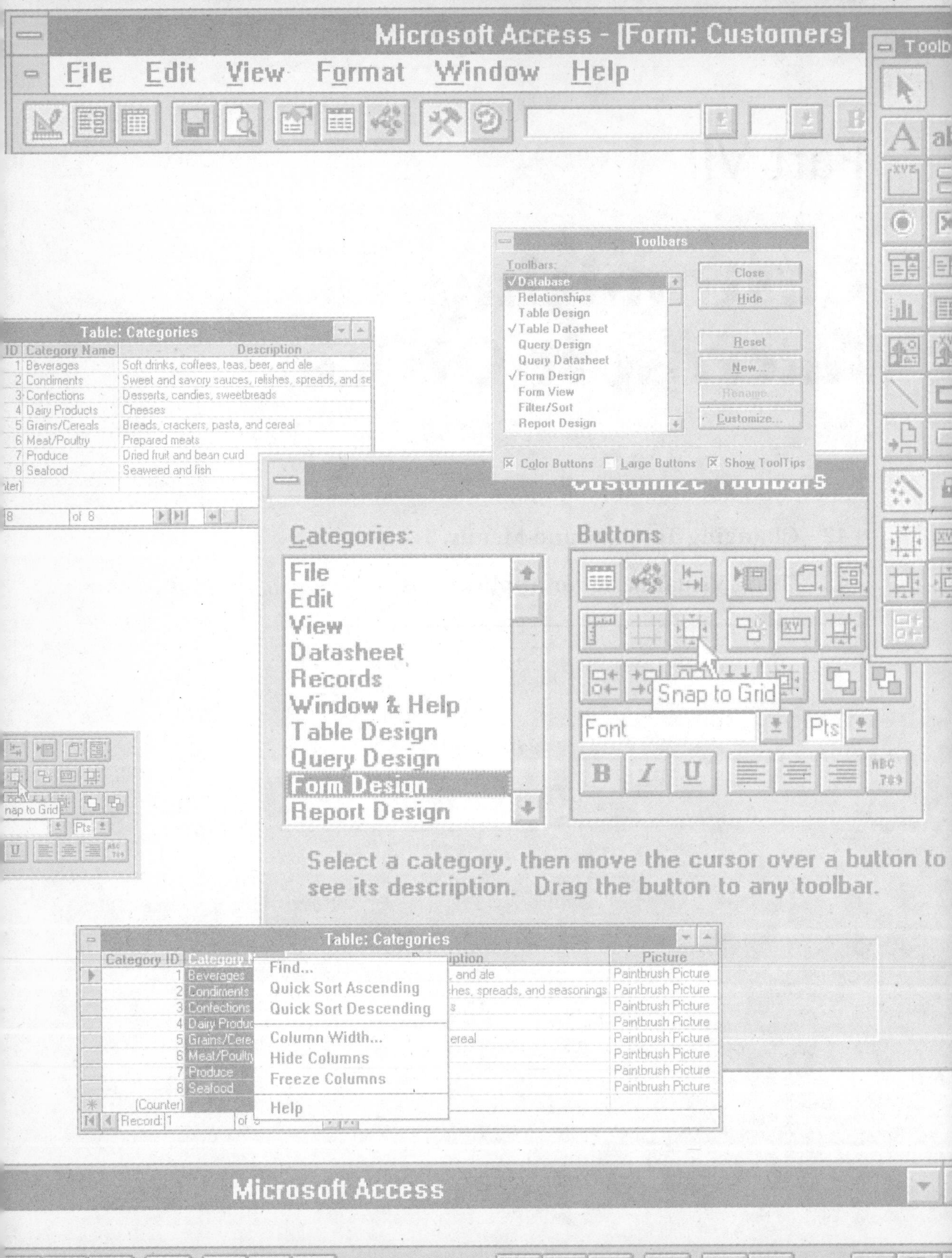

Microsoft Access - [Form: Customers]
File Edit View Format Window Help
Toolbars
Toolbars:
√Database
Relationships
Table Design
√Table Datasheet
Query Design
Query Datasheet
√Form Design
Form View
Filter/Sort
Report Design
Close
Hide
Reset
New...
Rename...
Customize...
Color Buttons
Large Buttons
Show ToolTips
Table: Categories
ID
Category Name
Description
1 Beverages
Soft drinks, coffees, teas, beer, and ale
2 Condiments
Sweet and savory sauces, relishes, spreads, and se
3 Confections
Desserts, candies, sweetbreads
4 Dairy Products
Cheeses
5 Grains/Cereals
Breads, crackers, pasta, and cereal
6 Meat/Poultry
Prepared meats
7 Produce
Dried fruit and bean curd
8 Seafood
Seaweed and fish
of 8
Customize Toolbars
Categories:
File
Edit
View
Datasheet
Records
Window & Help
Table Design
Query Design
Form Design
Report Design
Buttons
Snap to Grid
Font
Pts
Select a category, then move the cursor over a button to see its description. Drag the button to any toolbar.
Table: Categories
Category ID
Picture
Find...
Quick Sort Ascending
Quick Sort Descending
Column Width...
Hide Columns
Freeze Columns
Help
Paintbrush Picture
(Counter)
Record: 1
Microsoft Access

Chapter 42

Changing Toolbars and Menus

by Diane Tinney

Microsoft Office makes it easy for you to customize application toolbars and menus to meet your needs. You can add, remove, or change the order of the application features in the menus and toolbars. You even can create your own toolbars. Better yet, when you know how to customize toolbars and menus in one application, you can do so in all applications.

In this chapter, you learn to

- Customize Office Manager
- Customize application toolbars
- Customize application menus

Customizing Office Manager

You can customize the Office Manager toolbar and menu to meet your needs. You can add buttons to the toolbar, add applications to the menu bar, and change the display of the toolbar. To customize Office Manager, click the Office Manager button and choose **C**ustomize from the drop-down menu. Office Manager displays the Customize dialog box (see fig. 42.1).

◄ "Looking at Microsoft Office," p. 21

◄ "Using Dialog Boxes," p. 40

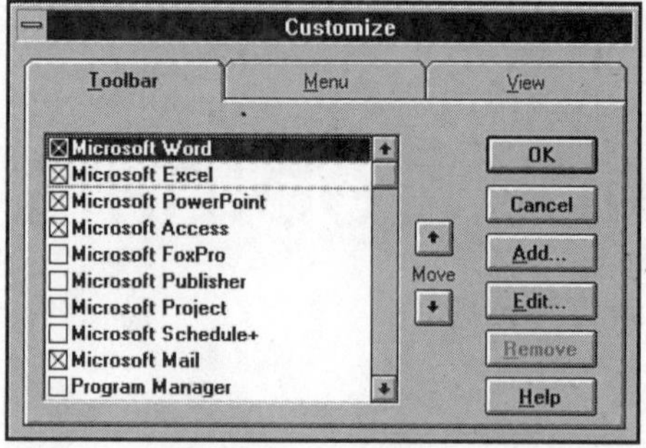

Fig. 42.1 The Customize dialog box consists of three tabs: Toolbar, Menu, and View.

Customizing the Toolbar and Menu

The Toolbar and Menu tabs operate the same and contain the same command buttons. By default, they list the Microsoft Office programs and many of the Microsoft Windows programs (refer to fig. 42.1). Select the check boxes to include or exclude an application.

Tip
Use the Move buttons to change the order of toolbar buttons or menu items.

The Add button enables you to add your own menu and toolbar items. When you click the **A**dd button in the **M**enu tab, the Add Program to Menu dialog box appears (see fig. 42.2).

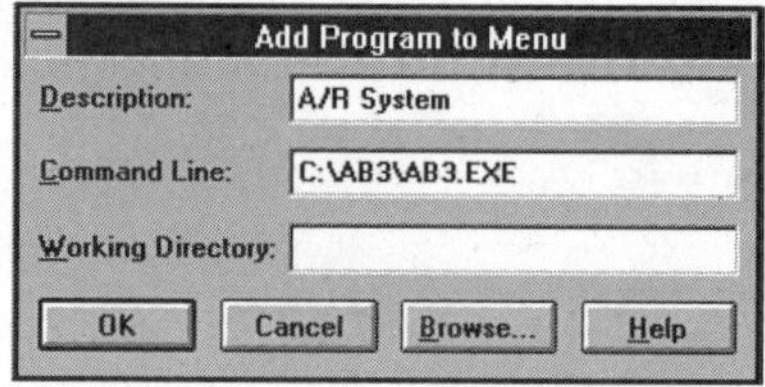

Fig. 42.2 The Add Program to Menu dialog box enables you to add any program to the Office Manager menu.

To add menu items, follow these steps:

Tip
Add the MS-DOS prompt to the toolbar for quick access to the command prompt from any application.

1. Choose **C**ustomize from the Microsoft Office menu.
2. Select the **M**enu tab.
3. Choose the **A**dd button.
4. Enter a **D**escription of the menu item.
5. In the **C**ommand Line text box, enter the path and name of the program, along with any command-line parameters needed. (If necessary, choose the **B**rowse button to find the program.)
6. (Optional) In the **W**orking Directory text box, enter the directory path where the program files and documents are located.

7. Choose OK to close the Add Program to Menu dialog box.

8. Choose OK to close the Customize dialog box and add the program item to the Microsoft Office menu.

To edit the settings for an existing item, select the item and choose the **E**dit button (or press Alt+E). The **R**emove button enables you to remove toolbar and menu items that you add. When you complete your selections, choose OK to save your settings and close the Customize dialog box.

Note

When you add a program to the Microsoft Office menu, you can specify a letter in the description to be the shortcut key. To assign a shortcut key, type an ampersand (&) in front of the desired letter in the description. If you enter the description **&A/R System**, for example, you can choose that menu item by typing **A**. You cannot edit the description of the default Microsoft Office menu items, however.

Note

You do not need to add programs to both the toolbar and the menu; you can add programs to one or the other.

Tip

Create your own separator line for the menu list by typing a dash (—) in the Description text box of the Add Program to Menu dialog box.

When adding a program to the toolbar (see fig. 42.3), you also must select a button in bit-map format (BMP). Several stock button images, such as a smiley face and a heart, are provided in the MS-BTTNS subdirectory.

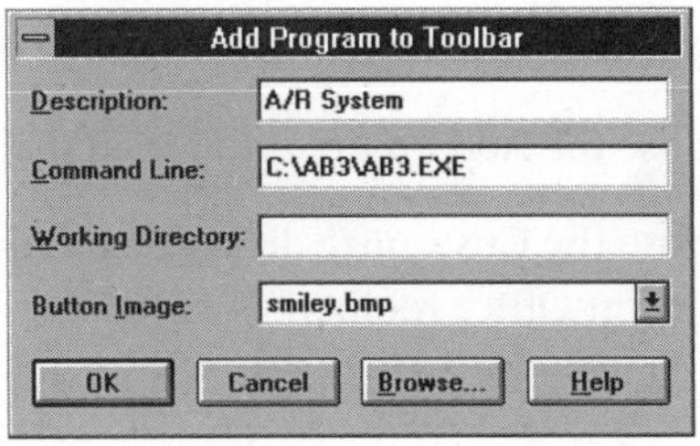

Fig. 42.3
Adding a program icon to the toolbar.

To create your own button images, edit a button bit map in Windows Paintbrush and save it in the MS-BTTNS directory under a new file name. Microsoft cautions against changing the button image's background color.

Figure 42.4 shows a new toolbar button (smiley face) and menu choice (A/R System).

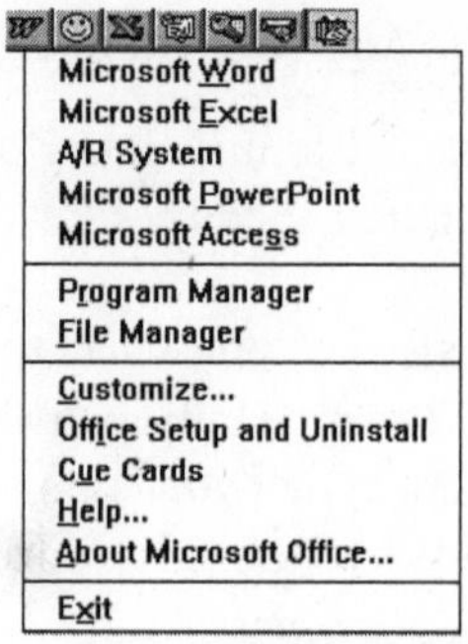

Microsoft Word
Microsoft Excel
A/R System
Microsoft PowerPoint
Microsoft Access
Program Manager
File Manager
Customize...
Office Setup and Uninstall
Cue Cards
Help...
About Microsoft Office...
Exit

Fig. 42.4
The new toolbar button (smiley face) and menu choice (A/R System) appear in the specified order.

To add toolbar items, follow these steps:

1. Choose **C**ustomize from the Microsoft Office menu. The Customize dialog box appears.

2. Select the **T**oolbar tab.

3. Choose the **A**dd button.

4. Enter a **D**escription of the toolbar button.

5. In the **C**ommand Line text box, enter the path and name of the program, along with any command-line parameters needed. (If necessary, choose the **B**rowse button to find the program.)

6. (Optional) In the **W**orking Directory text box, enter the directory path where the program files and documents are located.

7. Select a bit-map image for your button from the drop-down Button **I**mage list. (If necessary, choose the **B**rowse button to find the desired bit-map file; remember to change the browse file extension to *.BMP.)

8. Choose OK to close the Add Program to Menu dialog box.

9. Choose OK to close the Customize dialog box and add the program item to the Microsoft Office toolbar.

Tip
Add frequently used spreadsheets, documents, or databases to the Office Manager toolbar or menu for quick access to your data and application. Simply enter the data file's name to the command-line path for example, c:\access\clients.db.

Customizing the View

The View tab of the Customize dialog box enables you to control the display of the Office Manager toolbar (see fig. 42.5). By default, the toolbar buttons are set to a small size. You can change the size to regular or large by clicking the appropriate radio button, or by pressing Alt with the appropriate shortcut key.

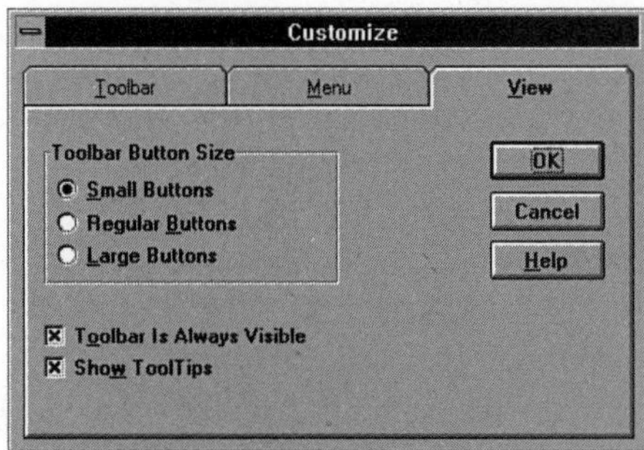

Fig. 42.5
Customize the display of the toolbar by changing settings in the View tab.

Note

You also can change the position of the toolbar. Regular and large buttons appear in their own window, which you can click and drag to any position on the desktop. Small buttons appear in the application title bar. You cannot move these buttons by clicking and dragging. To change the position of a small toolbar, you must use an editor, such as Notepad, to edit the MSOFFICE.INI file in the Windows directory. In the [OPTIONS] section, change the `RightPos` = line to a number higher than the default, which is 48 pixels in from the right.

To make the Office Manager toolbar available to all applications, check the T**o**olbar Is Always Visible check box. The Sho**w** ToolTips check box controls whether descriptive text appears when the mouse pointer rests on an Office Manager button. ToolTips appear when Office Manager is the current application (press Alt+Tab to switch to Office Manager).

Tip
Place the mouse pointer on the Office Manager toolbar and click the right mouse button to access the shortcut menu, which enables you to **C**ustomize, change button size, **M**inimize, and access C**u**e Cards or **H**elp.

Customizing Application Toolbars

The process of customizing toolbars in Microsoft Office applications is much the same as customizing the toolbars in the Office Manager. In most applications, however, you have even more options.

Customizing Predefined Toolbars

Each application comes with several built-in toolbars, some of which display automatically. For example, by default, Microsoft Word displays the Standard and Formatting toolbars. In addition to these, you can display the following predefined toolbars:

- Borders
- Database

- Drawing
- Forms
- Microsoft
- Word for Windows 2.0

Access, Excel, and PowerPoint provide sets of predefined toolbars. Access has 18 built-in toolbars, whereas, Excel has 13, and PowerPoint has 7. You can customize any of the built-in toolbars to better meet your needs, or you can create your own toolbar. You could have a toolbar for every type of task you perform (for example, one for mail merges and one for desktop publishing) or for each user of a computer.

To customize a built-in toolbar, follow these steps:

1. Choose the **V**iew Tool**b**ars command. The Toolbars dialog box appears (see fig. 42.6).

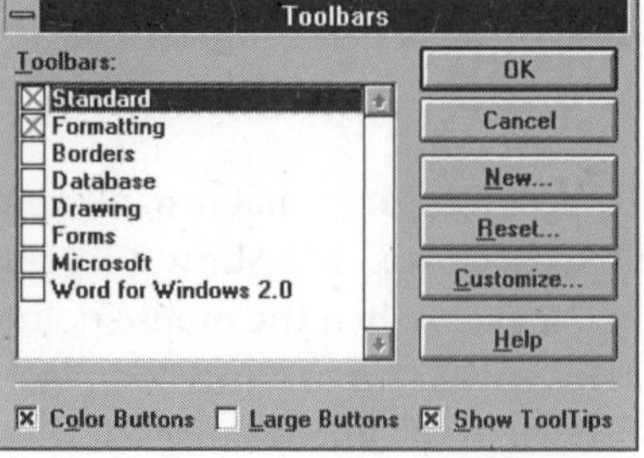

Fig. 42.6
The Toolbars dialog box enables you to customize the view and contents of toolbars.

2. Choose the **C**ustomize button. The Customize dialog box appears (see fig. 42.7).

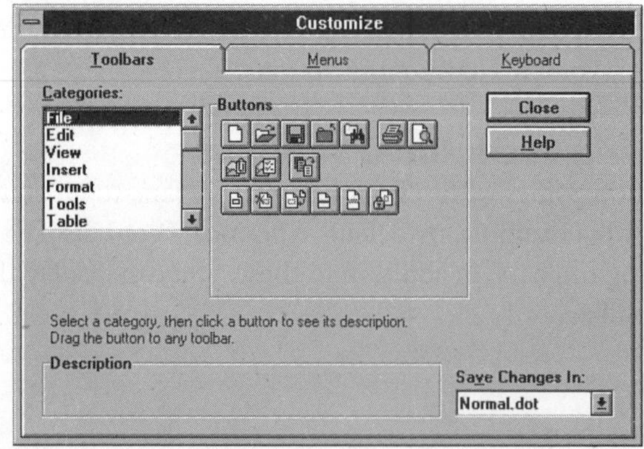

Fig. 42.7
The Toolbars tab of the Customize dialog box enables you to drag buttons and other items to any toolbar displayed on the desktop.

3. To add items to a built-in toolbar, select the category that contains the buttons or other items that you want to add.

4. Drag the desired buttons or items from the Buttons section to the built-in toolbar.

5. To remove items from the built-in toolbar, drag the buttons or items from the toolbar to the Customize Toolbars dialog box.

6. To move buttons or items, drag them to a new location or a different toolbar.

7. To copy buttons or items, press Ctrl while dragging them to the destination toolbar.

8. Choose Close to close the Customize Toolbars dialog box.

Creating a Custom Toolbar

In addition to modifying the default toolbars of Microsoft Office applications, you can create your own custom toolbar (except in PowerPoint, which does not allow you to create new toolbars). For example, you could have a toolbar for every type of task you do, such as one for mail merge and one for desktop publishing.

To create a custom toolbar, follow these steps:

1. Choose the **V**iew **T**oolbars command to display the Toolbars dialog box.

> **Note**
>
> For information about each application's Standard toolbar, see Chapter 2, "Using Common Features," or see the chapters pertaining to the individual application.

2. Choose the **N**ew button. (In Excel, the **N**ew button is not available until you enter a name for the toolbar in the Tool**b**ar Name text box.) In Word and Access, the New Toolbar dialog box appears (see fig. 42.8).

3. Enter a name for the toolbar in the **T**oolbar Name text box.

4. In Word, select the template in which you want to store the toolbar from the **M**ake Toolbar Available To drop-down list.

◄ "Formatting with Styles," p. 196

◄ "Using AutoFormat," p. 200

◄ "Using Template Wizards," p. 204

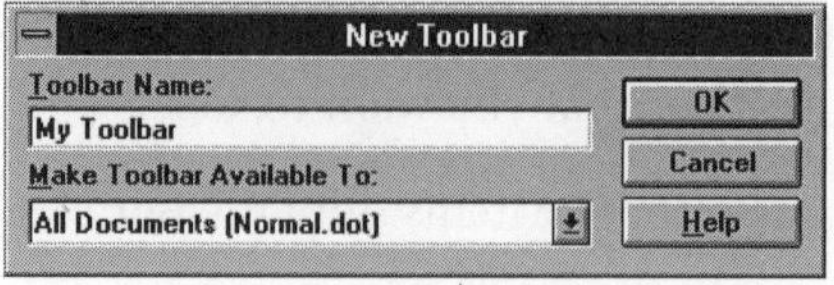

Fig. 42.8
In Word, Excel, and Access, new toolbars must be named and stored in a file.

5. Choose OK. The Customize dialog box appears, along with the new (empty) toolbar.
6. Select the category that contains the buttons or other items that you want to add to the new toolbar.
7. Drag the desired buttons or items from the Buttons section shown in figure 42.9 to the new toolbar.

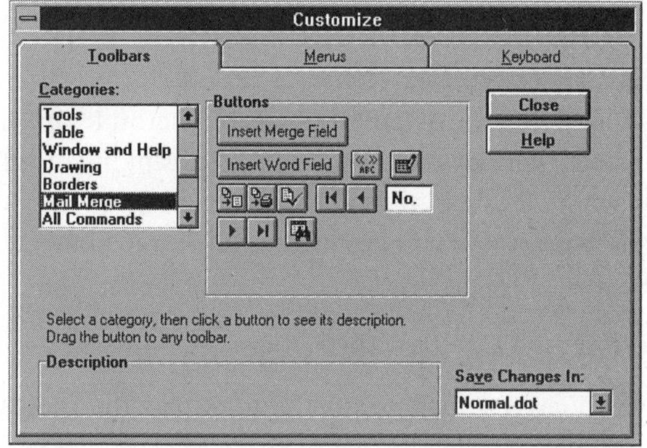

Fig. 42.9
You can drag buttons from the buttons area to the new toolbar.

8. Repeat steps 6 and 7 until you fill your custom toolbar with the desired features (the toolbar expands to accommodate your selections).
9. Click the Close button to close the Customize dialog box.

Note

Although Word screens are used in this section to illustrate the process of creating custom toolbars, the screens in Excel and Access are similar. Any exceptions are noted.

Troubleshooting

The new toolbar I created contains no buttons.

A new toolbar is empty until you add buttons. With the new toolbar visible on-screen, return to the Customize dialog box. Select the category containing the buttons you want to use, and drag the button images to your custom toolbar.

Someone customized the default toolbar. I need to get the standard toolbar back.

Choose the **V**iew **T**oolbars command, select a toolbar, and click the **R**eset button to return to the built-in version of the selected toolbar.

The colored toolbars are hard to see on my black-and-white monitor.

Choose the **V**iew **T**oolbars command, and deselect the C**o**lor Toolbars check box at the bottom of the Toolbars dialog box. Deselecting this option gives the toolbar buttons better contrast.

Customizing Application Menus

Consistency among products is not as good when it comes to customizing the application menus. No interactive method of modifying the application menus exists in Access, Excel, or PowerPoint. Access requires you to use macros to create custom menus and then attach the macros to a form or report. Excel requires you to use Visual Basic, Application Edition. Currently, only Word provides an interactive method of customizing built-in menus and creating custom menus.

Customizing Word Menus

You can change the organization, position, and content of default Word menus. To do so, follow these steps:

1. Choose the **T**ools **C**ustomize command. Alternatively, place the mouse pointer on the toolbar, click the right mouse button, and choose Customize from the shortcut menu. The Customize dialog box appears (see fig. 42.10).

2. Select the **M**enus tab.

3. Select the category that contains the command you want to use.

4. In the C**o**mmands list, select the command.

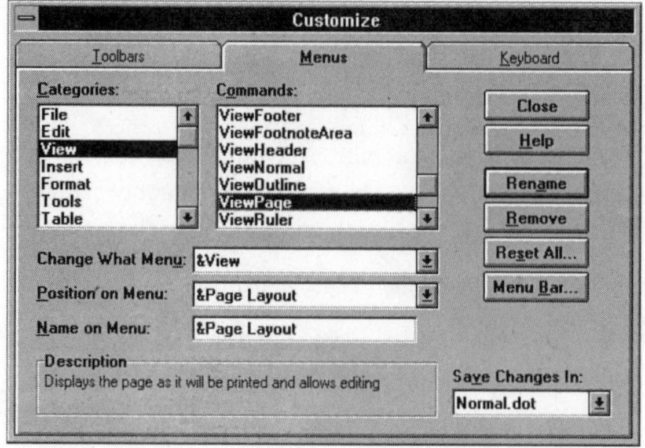

Fig. 42.10
Word enables you to customize its built-in menus.

5. To assign a command to another menu, select the menu name from the Change What Men**u** drop-down list.

6. To change the position, select the desired position from the **P**osition on Menu drop-down list. (Select Auto if you want Word to position the menu item for you.)

7. To change the name of the menu item or the shortcut key, edit the text in the **N**ame on Menu text box.

8. In the Sa**v**e Changes In drop-down list, select the template in which you want to save the customized menu.

◀ "Using Template Wizards," p. 204

9. Click the Close button when you complete your changes.

Creating Custom Menus

In addition to modifying the built-in menus, you can add your own custom menus to Word's built-in menu bar. The Menus tab of the Customize dialog box provides easy access to this helpful feature.

To create custom menus, follow these steps:

1. Choose the **T**ools **C**ustomize command. Alternatively, place the mouse pointer on the toolbar, click the right mouse button, and choose Customize from the shortcut menu. The Customize dialog box appears.

2. Select the **M**enus tab.

3. Choose the Menu **B**ar button. The Menu Bar dialog box appears (see fig. 42.11).

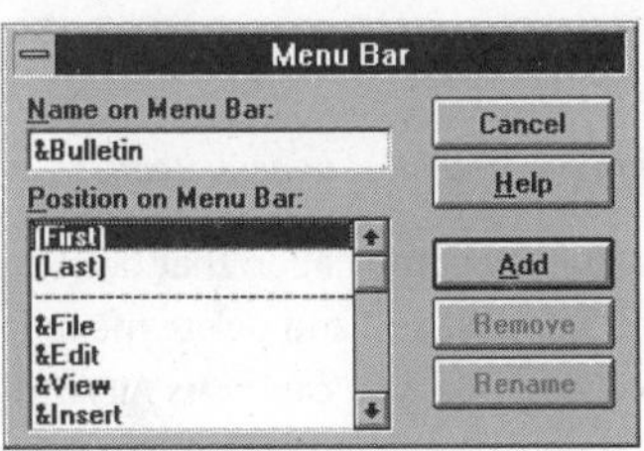

Fig. 42.11
Use the Menu Bar dialog box to create custom menus.

4. In the **N**ame on Menu Bar text box, enter the name of the first menu item. To assign a shortcut key, enter an ampersand (&) in front of the letter you want to be underlined.

5. Select a position from the **P**osition on Menu list.

6. Choose the **A**dd button.

7. Repeat steps 4–6 until you finish creating your menu.

8. Click Close to exit the Menu Bar dialog box. You return to the Customize dialog box.

9. Close the Customize dialog box. The new menu should appear on-screen (see fig. 42.12).

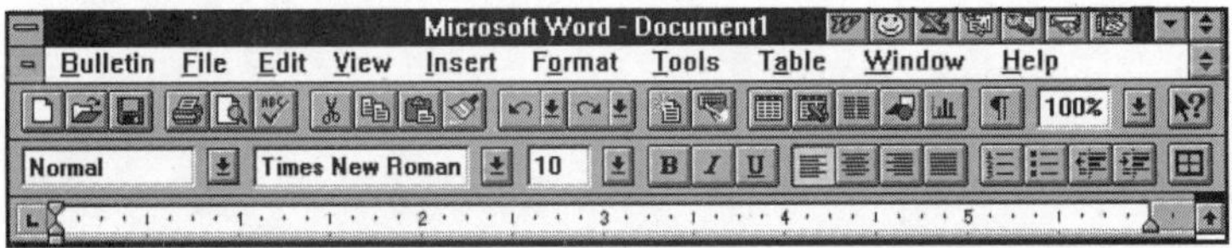

Fig. 42.12
The custom menu bar now lists Bulletin as the first menu item, with B as the shortcut key.

Troubleshooting

I find the default Edit Links menu description misleading. I need to change it to something more meaningful.

Choose the **T**ools **C**ustomize command, and select the **M**enus tab. Select the Edit category and the EditLinks menu item. In the **N**ame on Menu text box, enter a name for the new menu item. Choose the Ren**a**me button to save your change.

Someone customized the default menus. I need to get the standard menus back.

Choose the **T**ools **C**ustomize command. Select the desired template (.DOC file). Choose the Re**s**et All button to return to the built-in versions of all menus in the selected template.

(continues)

(continued)

I pressed Alt+Ctrl+minus sign (–), and I lost a menu item.

You pressed a special shortcut-key combination that deletes menu items. Word provides shortcut keys that help you add and delete menu items as you work. Rather than open the Customize dialog box, you can press Alt+Ctrl+minus sign (–) to delete an item from the selected menu, or Alt+Ctrl+equal sign (=) to add a menu item to the selected menu. See the preceding troubleshooting item for directions on resetting the menus.

From Here...

Now that you are familiar with customizing toolbars and menus, you are ready to begin automating with Visual Basic, Application Edition (VBA), and working with other applications. To learn more about working with Microsoft Office applications, refer to the following chapters:

- Chapter 43, "Using Visual Basic for Applications," shows you how to use VBA to automate common tasks.

Chapter 43

Using Visual Basic for Applications

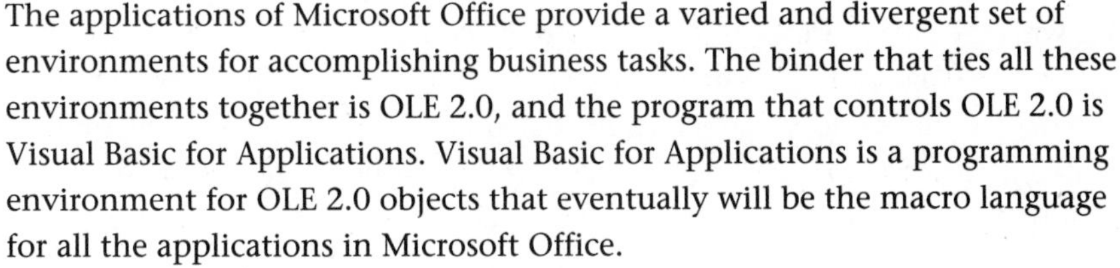

The applications of Microsoft Office provide a varied and divergent set of environments for accomplishing business tasks. The binder that ties all these environments together is OLE 2.0, and the program that controls OLE 2.0 is Visual Basic for Applications. Visual Basic for Applications is a programming environment for OLE 2.0 objects that eventually will be the macro language for all the applications in Microsoft Office.

In this chapter, you learn

- What Visual Basic for Applications is all about
- What makes Visual Basic for Applications different from other Basics
- How to use Visual Basic for Applications to automate tasks
- How to program in the Visual Basic for Applications language

Understanding Visual Basic for Applications

Visual Basic for Applications is a programming environment based on the Visual Basic for Windows programming language. Currently, Visual Basic for Applications is fully developed only in Excel, but it is nearly fully developed in Microsoft Project, which lacks only the elaborate Visual Basic for Applications Forms Designer for creating custom forms. Project does have custom-forms capability, but it is very limited in scope. Project is not part of Microsoft Office.

The two most recent versions of Word have Basic programming capability, but not with Visual Basic for Applications. Word is, however, compatible with Visual Basic for Applications and can be controlled by another application, such as Excel. PowerPoint, on the other hand, has no programming capability of any kind in the current version.

Access has nearly the full capabilities of Visual Basic (not Visual Basic for Applications), in the form of Access Basic. Access Basic is a language that is similar to Visual Basic but does not register that capability for other applications to use. Applications that are fully compliant with Visual Basic for Applications register their capabilities with the Windows operating system so that Visual Basic for Applications, running in other applications, can access those capabilities and control the compliant application.

Eventually, Microsoft plans to make all its mainstream applications compliant with Visual Basic for Applications; Microsoft has made a very credible start with the current releases of its products. Because Excel has the most developed Visual Basic for Applications capability, most of the examples in this chapter are developed in Excel. As Visual Basic for Applications is implemented in other applications, the procedures developed here can be moved to those other applications with few, if any, changes.

Understanding Why Objects Are Special

The difference between Visual Basic for Applications and other Basic programming languages is that Visual Basic for Applications is object-oriented. You already have seen objects in action in Microsoft Office. In Chapter 36, "Working with Wizards, Multiple Documents, and Cut, Copy, and Paste," you embedded graphics (Graphic objects), Excel ranges (Range objects), and Access database reports (Report objects) into Word documents. All these objects know how to manipulate and display themselves, even when they are embedded in another application's document. Visual Basic for Applications takes advantage of this capability to control those objects. This capability to control another application, using the other application's objects, is known as *OLE automation.*

Understanding Objects in Visual Basic for Applications

The objects of Visual Basic can be visualized as a series of containers (see fig. 43.1). The largest container is the Application object, which is the current program you are running, such as Excel. In Excel, the Application object contains Menu objects, Control objects, Workbook objects, and so forth. Within the Workbook objects are Sheet objects (worksheets, macro sheets, modules, dialog sheets, and so on), and within the Sheet objects are Range objects (cell ranges.) Other applications have similar objects to cover their particular needs. See the documentation and the on-line help for the different applications of Microsoft Office for a list of the objects in each application.

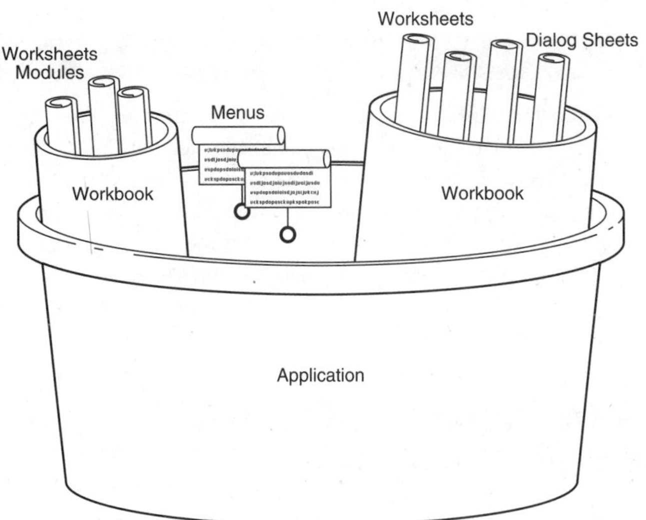

Fig. 43.1
The Visual Basic for Applications object model: containers within containers.

> **Note**
>
> Individual cells are not objects in Excel but are accessed as Range objects, which contain a cell or cell range.

Learning More with On-Line Help

Visual Basic for Applications has many more features than this chapter describes, especially the unique syntaxes and special options of all the commands and functions, as well as all the programming objects in the different applications. To learn about the details of all these features, use the on-line help system within each application. Choose the **H**elp **C**ontents command or press F1, and then look for the "Programming with Visual Basic" section in Excel or Project, the "Language and Technical Reference" section in Access, or the "Programming with Microsoft Word" section in Word. When you are in the language section of on-line help, you can list all the language elements or select one of the individual language elements' sections to display an alphabetical list of those elements. You also can use the application's search capability to locate specific topics.

Note

You can switch to the help files of other applications without having to start the other application and then choose the help command. Start help in one application, and then use the **F**ile **O**pen command in help to switch to some other application's directory, where you can open that application's help file. Most applications have a separate help file for Visual Basic for Applications, and you must be in that help file for help's search capability to locate terms related to Visual Basic.

Creating Procedures with the Macro Recorder

The best way to learn to use Visual Basic for Applications is to create procedures with it, by using the Macro Recorder as you did in Chapter 18, "Automating with Excel Macros." When you turn on the Macro Recorder and create a worksheet, the recorder writes the Visual Basic code that performs the same actions you are performing by hand. By examining that code, you learn how to use Visual Basic for Applications to access and change an application's objects.

In the following sections, you create a simple worksheet that calculates the tax on the cost of an item and then calculates the total cost. The worksheet has an input cell and two calculated output cells. The input cell accepts a cost, and the output cells display the tax and the total cost.

Starting the Recorder

To prepare the worksheet and display the Record New Macro dialog box, follow these steps:

1. Open a new workbook by choosing **F**ile **N**ew.

2. Choose **T**ools **R**ecord Macro **R**ecord New Macro, and then choose the **O**ptions button. The Record New Macro dialog box appears (see fig. 43.2).

3. In the **M**acro Name field, type **FigureTax**.

◄ "Recording a Macro," p. 406

4. In the **D**escription field, type **Create a worksheet to calculate the tax on an item**.

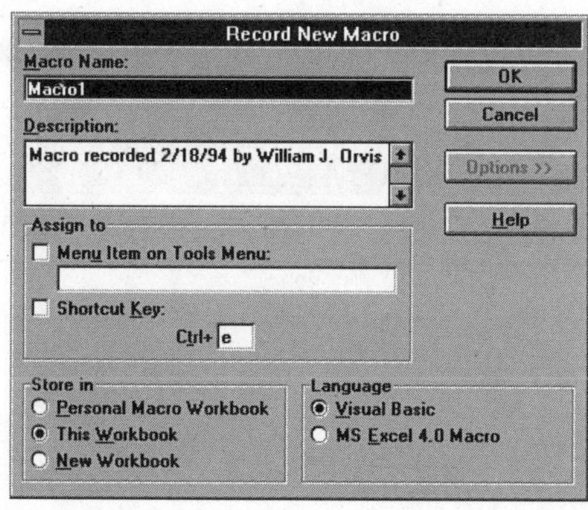

Fig. 43.2
The Record New Macro dialog box enables you to set the name and other options for a new procedure.

5. Leave the other fields at the default values shown in figure 43.2, and choose OK.

The Stop Recording button appears in a floating toolbar, and the Macro Recorder records what you do, recording all your keystrokes and mouse clicks until you click the Stop Recording button.

Recording a Procedure

You can create the procedure simply by creating the worksheet as you normally do. To create the worksheet, follow these steps:

1. Select cell B4, and type **Cost**.

2. Select cell B5, and type **Tax**.

3. Select cell B6, and type **Total**.

◄ "Entering Data," p. 247

◄ "Selecting Cells and Ranges," p. 251

◄ "Formatting Numbers," p. 281

4. Select cell C4, and type **12.43**.
5. Select cell C5, and type = **C4*0.0825**.
6. Select cell C6, and type = **C4 + C5**.
7. Select cells C4:C6, choose F**o**rmat C**e**lls, and select the Number tab. Select the Currency format type, select the `#,##0.00);(#,##0.00)` format, and choose OK.
8. Select cell C5, choose the F**o**rmat C**e**lls command, and select the Border tab.
9. In the Borders dialog box, click the **B**ottom box and choose OK.

The worksheet now should look like figure 43.3.

Fig. 43.3
The completed worksheet before the Macro Recorder is turned off. Notice the Stop Recording button on the right side.

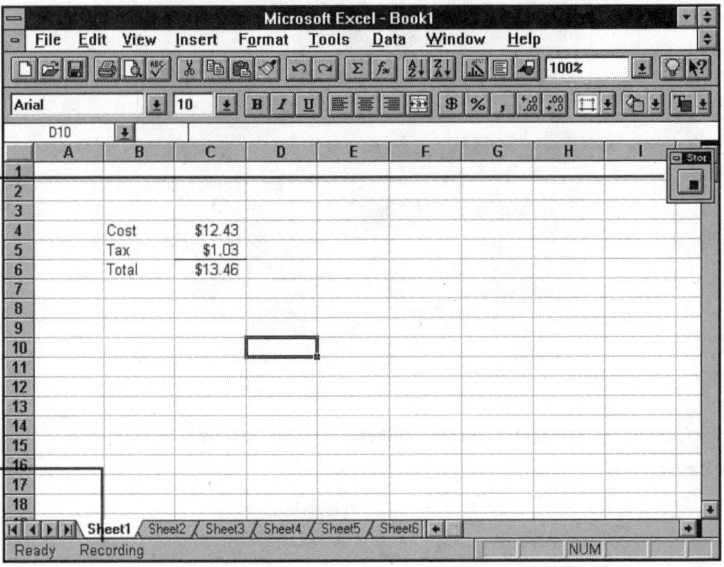

Stop Recording button

Status bar indicates that macro is recording

Stopping the Recorder

Stopping the recorder is easy; simply click the Stop Recording button.

Examining the Procedure

To examine your newly created procedure, find the Module1 tab at the bottom of the screen and click it. Your procedure appears on-screen and looks like figure 43.4.

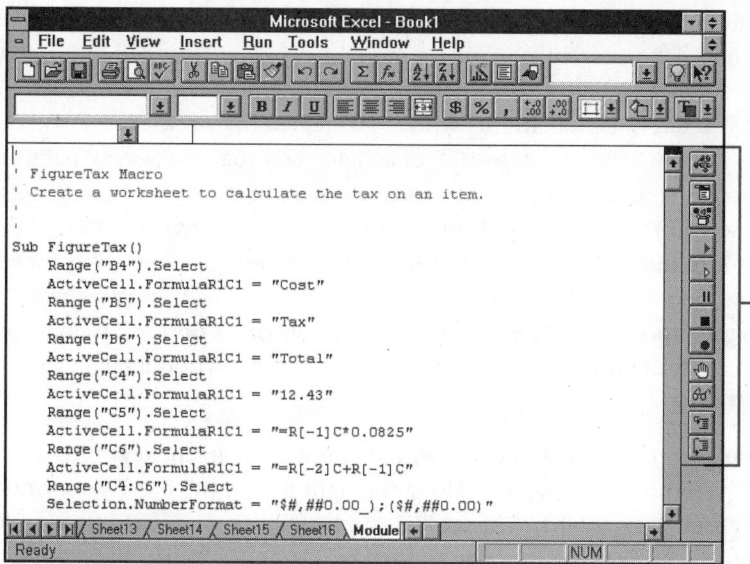

Fig. 43.4
The Excel Macro Recorder places the recorded commands in a module, as shown here for the FigureTax procedure.

The listing of the procedure is:

```
'
' FigureTax Macro
' Create a worksheet to calculate the tax on an item.
'
'
Sub FigureTax()
    Range("B4").Select
    ActiveCell.FormulaR1C1 = "Cost"
    Range("B5").Select
    ActiveCell.FormulaR1C1 = "Tax"
    Range("B6").Select
    ActiveCell.FormulaR1C1 = "Total"
    Range("C4").Select
    ActiveCell.FormulaR1C1 = "12.43"
    Range("C5").Select
    ActiveCell.FormulaR1C1 = "=R[-1]C*0.0825"
    Range("C6").Select
    ActiveCell.FormulaR1C1 = "=R[-2]C+R[-1]C"
    Range("C4:C6").Select
    Selection.NumberFormat = "$#,##0.00_);($#,##0.00)"
    Range("C5").Select
    Selection.Borders(xlLeft).LineStyle = xlNone
    Selection.Borders(xlRight).LineStyle = xlNone
    Selection.Borders(xlTop).LineStyle = xlNone
    With Selection.Borders(xlBottom)
        .Weight = xlThin
        .ColorIndex = xlAutomatic
    End With
    Selection.BorderAround LineStyle:=xlNone
End Sub
```

If you examine this listing and compare it with the steps you just took, you see that each step results in one or more lines of code inserted into the procedure. Many extra lines also are in the procedure; these lines set parameters that you did not explicitly set when you created the worksheet. These extra lines result when you choose OK in a dialog box that sets several parameters. Although you may change only one parameter in the dialog box, closing the box sets all the parameters displayed in that box and inserts corresponding lines into the procedure being recorded. In the Borders dialog box, for example, you set only the Bottom option (step 9), but eight lines were inserted into the procedure, setting the values of all the other options. In many cases, you can delete these extra lines from the procedure without changing its results.

The procedure appears in color, with comments in green, keywords in blue, and everything else in black. Along the right side of the procedure window is the Visual Basic toolbar. The toolbar can be floating or docked on any side. Figure 43.5 shows the function of each button in the Visual Basic toolbar.

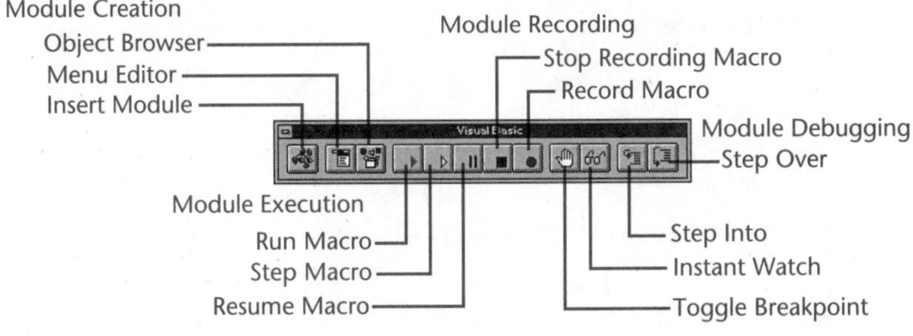

Fig. 43.5 The Visual Basic toolbar contains controls for executing and debugging a program.

Running the Procedure

To run this procedure, first select an unused worksheet. Make sure that the sheet is unused or has nothing useful in the B4:C6 range because the procedure overwrites that area. Choose the **T**ools **M**acro command. The Macro dialog box shown in figure 43.6 appears, showing all procedures available in this sheet and in the global sheet (currently, none). In the dialog box, select the `FigureTax` procedure and choose **R**un. The worksheet appears and the procedure runs, setting the contents and formatting the worksheet cells. The completed worksheet is identical to the one that you created by hand.

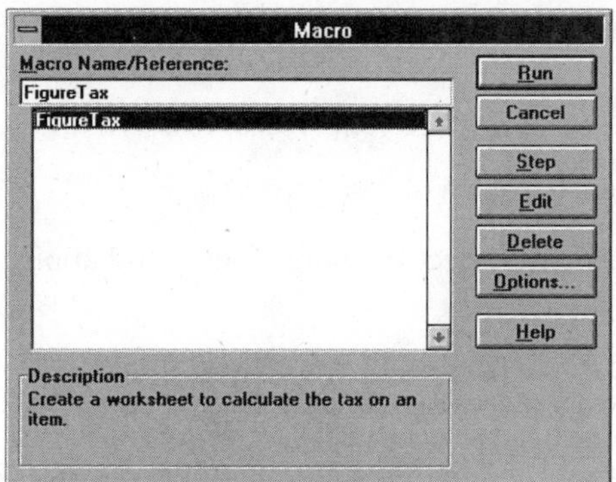

Fig. 43.6
The Macro dialog box enables you to select and execute procedures. The dialog box also provides an easy way to locate, edit, or delete procedures.

Understanding the Procedure

Now go back and take a closer look at the listing of the procedure by selecting the Module1 tab. The first few lines of the procedure are comments. Comments are ignored by an executing procedure and can contain any text. Any text following a single quotation mark is a comment. Comments can appear at the beginning of a line or to the right of any valid Visual Basic for Applications statement.

```
'
' FigureTax Macro
' Create a worksheet to calculate the tax on an item.
'
'
```

Following the comments is the procedure header, which names the procedure.

```
Sub FigureTax()
```

Following the procedure header are 12 statements that alternately select each cell in the range B4:C6 and insert a label or a formula. The last four lines insert formulas, but they are written in the R1C1 style instead of the A1 style of cell addressing. This is the default method for saving inserted formulas, no matter what method was used to create the worksheet while the recorder was running. When this procedure is played back, the formulas are automatically converted into whatever style is the default in the active worksheet.

```
Range("B4").Select
ActiveCell.FormulaR1C1 = "Cost"
Range("B5").Select
ActiveCell.FormulaR1C1 = "Tax"
Range("B6").Select
ActiveCell.FormulaR1C1 = "Total"
```

```
Range("C4").Select
ActiveCell.FormulaR1C1 = "12.43"
Range("C5").Select
ActiveCell.FormulaR1C1 = "=R[-1]C*0.0825"
Range("C6").Select
ActiveCell.FormulaR1C1 = "=R[-2]C+R[-1]C"
```

The next two statements select the range C4:C6 and apply the currency format to those cells.

```
Range("C4:C6").Select
Selection.NumberFormat = "$#,##0.00_);($#,##0.00)"
```

The last nine lines of the procedure are the result of selecting cell C5 and making changes in the Borders dialog box. Notice that you selected only the Bottom box, but the procedure set values for all the options in the dialog box. The values `xlNone`, `xlBottom`, `xlThin`, and so on are built-in Excel constants. See on-line help for a list of the constants available for use with different properties and methods.

```
Range("C5").Select
Selection.Borders(xlLeft).LineStyle = xlNone
Selection.Borders(xlRight).LineStyle = xlNone
Selection.Borders(xlTop).LineStyle = xlNone
With Selection.Borders(xlBottom)
     .Weight = xlThin
     .ColorIndex = xlAutomatic
End With
Selection.BorderAround LineStyle:=xlNone
```

Note

The With, End With structure in the procedure is a method of decreasing the size of a procedure and arranging together all statements that apply to a specific object. The With statement works by inserting the object that follows the word *With* just before the period in each line below it. Thus, the following two blocks of code are equivalent:

```
With Selection.Borders(xlBottom)
  .Weight = xlThin
  .ColorIndex = xlAutomatic
End With
Selection.Borders(xlBottom).Weight = xlThin
Selection.Borders(xlBottom).ColorIndex = xlAutomatic
```

The last statement in the procedure is the procedure footer, which marks the end of the procedure.

```
End Sub
```

Understanding Objects

Visual Basic for Applications uses an object-oriented programming model. If you understand object-oriented programming (OOP), understanding Visual Basic for Application's implementation of it is easy. If you don't, don't worry—it is not as complicated as it sounds.

Visual Basic for Applications' *objects* are just a convenient way of storing and hiding data and code in a program. Instead of writing a program to manipulate some data values, you encapsulate the data and the code that manipulates that data in an object. From then on, you have only to access the object to use or display its data. You don't write code to manipulate the data; you send the object a message, and the object does the work for you.

You see this capability in action when you embed an object from one application into another. The embedded object takes care of itself, and the embedding object has only to give the embedded object a place to display itself. When you attach a Visual Basic button to a worksheet, for example, the worksheet does not have to know how to make the button work when you click it—the button handles that. In code, you do much the same thing. You don't try to manipulate an object's data directly, you send messages to the object and let it do the work.

◄ "Linking an Excel Worksheet to a Word Document" p. 795

◄ "Linking Data between Excel Worksheets," p. 806

◄ "Adding Macros to Sheet Buttons and Toolbars," p. 415

Visual Basic for Applications' objects include such things as buttons, menu items, ranges of worksheet cells, and even a worksheet itself. Almost everything you can see on-screen while an application is running is an object.

Accessing Objects

To access a specific object in Visual Basic for Applications, you start with the outermost container object, followed by a period, followed by the next inner container object, followed by a period, and so on until you reach the object you want. To access cell B5 in an Excel worksheet named Sheet3 in a workbook named Book2, for example, you could use the following reference:

```
Application.Workbooks("Book2").Worksheets("Sheet3").Range("B5")
```

Because Visual Basic for Applications deals with objects, any application that registers its objects with the Windows operating system makes those objects available to Visual Basic for Applications. Thus, even if you are running Visual Basic for Applications in another application, you still can access an object in Excel in much the same way as you would if you were in Excel itself. The only difference is that you must include the name that the other application used when registering itself, to specify which Application object to use. For example, you could use the following reference in Project to access a cell in Excel:

```
Excel.Application.Workbooks("Book2").Worksheets("Sheet3").Range("B5")
```

This reference is somewhat cumbersome, so Visual Basic for Applications makes an assumption that enables you to leave out some of these containers. For each container not included on the left side of a reference to an object (such as the workbook or worksheet reference), Visual Basic for Applications assumes that the currently active object of that type is the one being referenced.

Thus, you almost always can leave out the application, as well as the workbook. Be careful, though—make sure you know what objects are active before you leave them out of the specification. Leaving out the containers has the positive effect of making your procedures more portable. If you leave out all but the Range object, your code always applies to the currently active sheet, so you don't have to change the sheet name to apply your code to a different sheet. In addition to the named sheets and workbooks, you can use the objects `ActiveWorkbook`, `ActiveSheet`, `ActiveCell` to reference the currently active objects without having to know their names.

Note

Keep in mind that if you use specific workbook and sheet names in your procedures, the procedures will work only in those named workbooks and procedures. By leaving out parts of an object's specification, you make your code applicable to all objects of the class you left out.

Understanding Classes and Collections

A *class* of objects is a reference to a general type or classification of objects. In Visual Basic for Applications, for example, each cell or cell range in a worksheet is a Range object, which is an example of the Range class.

If you combine all the objects of a specific class into a group, that group is known as a *collection*. Thus, all the workbooks in the Application object are in the collection Workbooks, and all the worksheets in a workbook are in the collection Worksheets. All the worksheets also are in the collection Sheets, which includes all types of sheets (worksheet, chart, module, and dialog) in a workbook.

Accessing Collections

Collections are how you access most objects. To access a specific member of a collection, follow the collection name with either a string containing the object name or an integer in parentheses. Thus, `Worksheets("Sheet1")` refers to the sheet named Sheet1, and `Worksheets(2)` refers to the second worksheet in the collection of all worksheets in the active workbook. If you want to access cell B5 in the third worksheet in a workbook named Book2, you could use the following reference:

```
Workbooks("Book2").Worksheets(3).Range("B5")
```

If you leave out the number and parentheses in the reference to a collection, the reference is to all the members of the collection.

Caution

Be careful when using numbers to select objects in a collection. If you add or delete members of a collection, the numbering of all the other members of that collection can change, and your number may select a different object.

Understanding Properties

An object contains data, and data that you can access from outside an object is a *property* of that object. Most properties are readable, but not all can be written or changed. See the Visual Basic for Applications section of on-line help for a description of each of the properties. In the description of each object is a list of the properties that apply to it.

For a Range object (one or more worksheet cells), the font, color, font size, contents, and so on are read/write properties, but the location is read-only (cells don't move.) Properties can refer to the direct data contained in an object, such as the value of a cell, or to data values that control how an object looks and behaves, such as color.

Property values can be strings of text, numbers, logicals (`True` or `False`), or enumerated lists. An *enumerated list* is a numbered list of options, where the number is used to select a specific option. For example, the `Color` property of most objects is an enumerated list in which 0 is none, 1 is black, 2 is white, 3 is red, 4 is green, 5 is blue, and so on. For the enumerated lists, Visual Basic for Applications and the other compliant applications in Microsoft Office contain lists of predefined constants to use in place of the numbers. Using the constants is much more informative than using the numbers. The constants that are applicable to a property are listed in the description of the property in on-line help. You can see a list of constants by searching for *constants* or *variables* in on-line help and selecting the "Variables and Constants Keywords Summary" and "Visual Basic Constants" topics. You also can use the Object Browser (described later in this chapter) to search the Excel and VBA libraries for the Constants object.

Accessing Properties

The easiest way to see what properties to set, and what values to set them to, is to start the Macro Recorder, perform whatever changes you want to perform, turn off the recorder, and then copy the recorded property changes into your program. Both Excel and Word currently have macro recorders.

Following is the syntax for accessing an object's properties:

```
object.property
```

In this example, *object* is the object whose properties you want to change or view, and *property* is the name of the property. If the preceding construct is on the right side of a statement, you are reading the value of the property from the object. If the construct is on the left side of a statement, you are setting the value of the property. To set the value of the `Formula` property (the contents of the cell) of cell B5 to `=ABS(B4)` when cell B5 is in the `Sheet1` worksheet (which is in the `Book2` workbook), you could use the following statement:

```
Workbooks("Book2").WorkSheets("Sheet1").Range("B5").Formula = "=ABS(B4)"
```

To read the same property from the same cell and store it in the variable `myFormula`, you could use this statement:

```
myFormula = Workbooks("Book2").WorkSheets("Sheet1").Range("B5").Formula
```

The rules concerning omitting container objects (described in "Accessing Objects" earlier in this chapter) apply here. Because you must include an object with the property, you cannot leave off the `Range` object to get the formula in whatever cell is the active cell. For these and similar cases involving other objects, some special properties return the currently active or selected object. Table 43.1 lists these special properties.

Table 43.1 Special Properties That Return the Active Objects

Property	Description
ActiveCell	The active cell in the active window
ActiveChart	The active chart in a workbook
ActiveDialog	The active dialog sheet in a workbook
ActiveSheet	The active worksheet, chart, module, or dialog sheet in a workbook
ActiveWorkbook	The active workbook in an application
Selection	The currently selected object in the currently selected sheet

Caution

Be sure that an object of the expected type is the active object before you try to use the active properties, such as ActiveSheet, in a procedure. If an object of the specified type is not the active object, these properties return nothing, and a procedure that uses them is likely to crash.

To get the formula contained in the active cell of the `Sheet3` worksheet, for example, you could use the following statement:

```
myFormula = Workbooks("Book2").WorkSheets("Sheet3").ActiveCell.Formula
```

If `Book2` and `Sheet3` are the currently active workbook and worksheet, you could use this statement:

```
myFormula = ActiveCell.Formula
```

If `Book2` is the active workbook, but `Sheet3` is not necessarily the active worksheet, you could use this statement:

```
myFormula = WorkSheets("Sheet3").ActiveCell.Formula
```

If you wanted to access cell B5 in whatever worksheet is active in `Book2`, you could use this statement:

```
myFormula = WorkBooks("Book2").ActiveSheet.Range("B5").Formula
```

Everything to the left of the last period must evaluate to an object or a collection of objects.

Understanding Methods

Visual Basic for Applications *methods* are the blocks of code stored in an object that know how to manipulate the object's data. For the `Range` object, for example, the `Calculate` method causes the formulas in the selected cells to be recalculated, and the `Clear` method clears the cell's contents. Methods do things to objects and the data they contain, as opposed to properties, which set values. To learn more about the specifics of different methods, and to find out what methods apply to what objects, see the Visual Basic for Applications section of on-line help. You also can use the Object Browser to see what methods are available for certain objects (see "Finding Objects with the Object Browser" later in this chapter).

Accessing Methods

You access or execute an object's methods in nearly the same way that you access an object's properties. The main difference is that a property always is accessed as part of a formula, but a method must be part of a formula only if it returns a value. The `Rows` method, for example, returns a collection containing all the rows in the range. To use this method to set the `RowHeight` property of all the rows in the currently selected range to 20, use a formula like the following:

```
Selection.Rows.RowHeight = 20
```

To get the number of rows in the current selection, you could use the `Rows` method to return a collection and the `Count` property to return the number of items in the collection, as follows:

```
numRows = Selection.Rows.Count
```

Some methods require arguments to make them work. For example, the `Insert` method, when applied to a range object, needs an argument to tell it how to move the cells that are already in the selection; the `Rows` method needs an index number to select a single row in the collection of rows. If the method is part of a formula, the arguments must go in parentheses. To get the `RowHeight` of the second row in the collection of rows, you could use the following statement:

```
theHeight = Selection.Rows(2).RowHeight
```

If the method is only being executed and is not part of a formula, place the arguments to the right of the reference to the method. To use the `Insert` method to insert blank cells for the current selection and to move the current selection down to make room, you could use this statement:

```
Selection.Insert xlDown
```

The argument actually is an integer, but the built-in constant is used here to make the code more readable. You can get the built-in constants that apply to a method in the description of the method in on-line help, or you can search for *constants* or *variables* in on-line help and then select the "Variables and Constants Keywords Summary" or "Visual Basic Constants" topic. To see the Excel constants, use the Object Browser, described in the following section, to search the Excel library for the Constants object.

Finding Objects with the Object Browser

With all these objects floating around, keeping track of all the names, what properties go with what methods, and what objects are contained in what applications becomes difficult and confusing. On-line help is a good reference for the objects and methods in the current application, but to see what applications have made their objects available by registering them with the Windows operating system, use the Object Browser in Excel.

Before you can use the Object Browser, you must register any external object libraries (other OLE-compliant applications) with Excel. To register the external libraries, first open a new module sheet; choose the **I**nsert **M**acro **M**odule command, or switch to a module by clicking its tab. When you choose the **T**ools Re**f**erences command, the dialog box shown in figure 43.7 appears. In the dialog box, mark the check boxes for the object libraries you want to register with Excel, and then choose OK. As more applications support OLE automation, they also will appear in the References list.

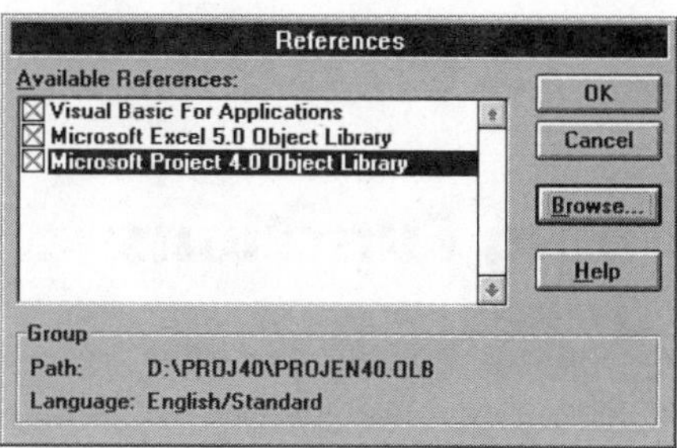

Fig. 43.7
Use the References dialog box to register other object libraries with Excel.

To use the Object Browser, choose the **V**iew **O**bject Browser command. The Object Browser dialog box appears, as shown in figure 43.8. In the **L**ibraries/ Workbooks field at the top, you select the object library, such as Excel, VBA (Visual Basic for Applications), external libraries, or other modules in open worksheets. You must register external libraries with Excel by using the References dialog box.

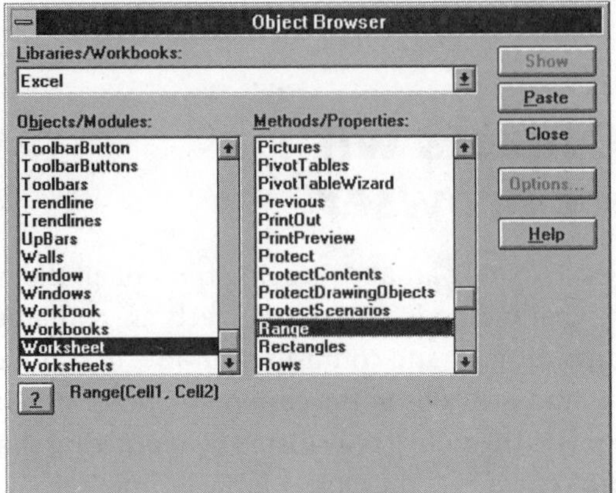

Fig. 43.8
The Object Browser, with the Excel object library selected. Within the library, the Worksheet object and its Range method also are selected. The syntax of the Range method appears at the bottom.

If you select Excel, as shown in the figure, all the objects and modules contained in Excel appear in the O**b**jects/Modules list on the left side of the dialog box. If you select one of the objects, such as the `Worksheet` object, all the properties and methods appear in the Methods/Properties window on the right. If you select one of the methods or properties, such as `Range`, the method—along with its syntax—appears at the bottom. If you click the question-mark button in the bottom left corner of the dialog box, you go directly to the on-line help topic that explains that method or property. If you choose the **P**aste button, the selected object or method is inserted into the active module at the current insertion-point location.

Understanding Functions and Procedures

A *procedure* is the smallest programming object in Visual Basic for Applications. Visual Basic for Applications uses two types of procedures: Sub procedures and Function procedures.

Sub Procedures

Sub procedures generally are called procedures. Sub procedures can be sent arguments and can make changes to those arguments. The syntax of a procedure is as follows:

```
Sub procedurename()
.
' Procedure Body
.
End Sub
```

Sub procedures always start with a procedure header that begins with the keyword `Sub`, followed by the procedure name and parentheses. The names of any arguments to be passed to the procedure are placed between the parentheses. *Arguments* are the data values that a calling procedure is passing to this procedure to work on; they also can contain the values that a procedure is passing back to the procedure that called it. Sub procedures must end with the `End Sub` procedure footer. Between the procedure header and footer is the procedure body, which can contain declarations, statements, and commands that the procedure executes. To execute a Sub procedure, select it in the Macro dialog box, call it from another procedure, or click a button or other object to which the procedure is attached.

For example, a simple procedure to calculate the tax on an item could be written as follows:

```
'
' Calculate the tax on an item.
'
Sub GetTax(Cost, Tax)
  Const TaxRate = 0.0825
  Tax = Cost * TaxRate
End Sub
```

This procedure is passed the cost of an item, and it calculates the tax by multiplying the cost by the tax rate. The calculated tax is then passed back to the calling program in the second argument.

Note

In the `GetTax` procedure, the constant `TaxRate` is defined in the procedure by the `Const` declaration, and then the constant is used in place of the actual number. Although this step may seem to be unnecessary, it makes the procedure much more readable.

User-Defined Functions

Function procedures are similar to Sub procedures, except that the function's name returns a value. These functions are identical in operation to worksheet functions—you can define new functions with Visual Basic for Applications and then use them in the worksheet. The main restriction on functions that are used in the worksheet is that they can only do calculations. These functions cannot access and change other cells in the worksheet, nor can they execute menu commands.

Functions have a procedure header and footer similar to that used for Sub procedures, and they must assign a value to the procedure name before completing.

```
Function functionname()

'  function body

  functionname = value
End Function
```

After you define a function, you can use it in the worksheet.

The following example performs the same calculation as the preceding example, but does it as a function. The function accepts the cost of an item as an argument, and then calculates and returns the tax on that cost in the function's name.

```
'
' Calculate the tax on an item.
'
Function theTax(Cost)
  Const TaxRate = 0.0825
  theTax = Cost * TaxRate
End Function
```

You can use this type of function in another procedure or in a worksheet as a user-defined function.

To use the preceding function in a worksheet, switch to the workbook used for the Macro Recorder example shown in figure 43.3. Create a module by choosing the **I**nsert **M**acro **M**odule command. Type the preceding listing into the module as shown in figure 43.9.

Select Sheet1 by clicking the tab at the bottom, and insert the following formula into cell C5:

```
=theTax(C4)
```

The new function now can be used in the worksheet like any of the built-in functions.

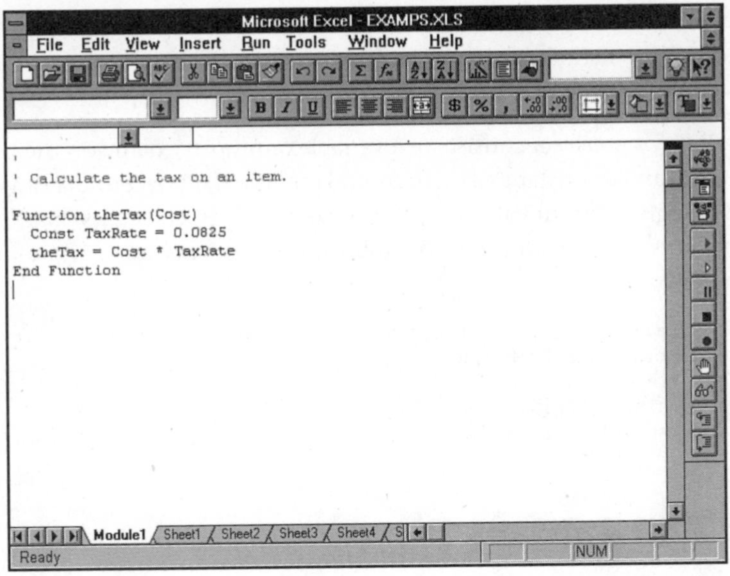

Fig. 43.9
A user-defined function named "theTax" defined in a module.

The worksheet returns the same result as the one shown in figure 43.3, but now the tax is calculated with a user-defined function.

Event Procedures

Event procedures are regular Sub procedures that are attached to specific events. Events that are attachable to procedures include buttons being clicked, worksheets opening or closing, or values being changed in cells. See the documentation for the specific objects for a list of the events to which procedures can be attached. An object's events that can cause a procedure to be executed are listed as properties of that object. Procedures are attached to an object's events by storing the procedure's name in the property. For example, most objects have an `OnAction` property. Depending on the object, if the object is clicked (button or graphic) or changed (text box or list box), the procedure whose name is stored in the `OnAction` property is executed.

Understanding Variables and Assignment Statements

Variables are named places in memory for storing data. Like naming cells in a worksheet, using variables to name storage locations in memory makes a program much more readable. You don't have to explicitly name a specific location in memory to use a variable; Visual Basic for Applications takes care of that for you. Simply using a name in a formula causes Visual Basic for Applications to define storage for it. After defining a variable, you can use it in assignment statements to store data.

An *assignment statement* consists of a variable or property name on the left, an equal sign, and a constant value or formula on the right. A formula can consist of a single constant value or a mixture of variables, constants, mathematical operators, and functions. All the following statements are assignment statements:

```
myFormula = ActiveSheet.Range("B5").Formula
Selection.Rows.RowHeight = 20
myVariable = 17
someThing = Log(3.5)
yourVariable = myVariable * 33
```

Creating an Application

Now that you know about objects, properties, and methods, you can start putting some of that information together to create an application. The application you are going to create is a receipt maker, such as you might use at a checkout stand where you don't have a regular cash register. The program inputs data with a dialog box, inserts the data into a form in an Excel worksheet, and prints the form.

The basic structure of this program—input data; store it; do something with it—forms the basis of many programs, such as an inventory program or a personal organizer. You should be able to adapt the methods shown here for many different applications.

The program uses a worksheet and a module. The worksheet contains the receipt form that stores the data until you are ready to print it. The module contains the code that gets the data, stores it in the sheet, and prints it. First, create the worksheet. Don't worry if you don't understand what the code does; it will be explained in the next few sections.

To create the worksheet, follow these steps:

1. Select an unused worksheet. Choose F**o**rmat S**h**eet **R**ename, or double-click the tab at the bottom of the sheet and change the sheet's name to **Receipt** in the dialog box.

2. Select cell A2, and type **The XYZ Stationers**.

3. Select cell A3, and type **1127 Somewhere St.**

4. Select cell A4, and type **RightHere, CA 12345**.
5. Select cell B6, and type **Item**.
6. Select cell C6, and type **Cost**.
7. Select cell A7, and type **1**.
8. Select cell A8, and type **2**.
9. Select cells A7:A8, select the fill handle at the bottom right corner, and drag it down to A16 to create the series of numbers from 1 to 10.
10. Select C16, choose F**o**rmat C**e**lls, select the Border tab, select a thick line style, click the Bottom box, and choose OK.
11. Select cells C7:C19, choose F**o**rmat C**e**lls, select the Number tab, select the Currency type, select the format `X,XX0.00);(X,X00.00)`, and choose OK.
12. Select the bar between the B and C column headings, and drag it until the column width is 27 characters.
13. Select cell B7 and name it **TopOfList**, using the **I**nsert **N**ame **D**efine command or the name box at the left end of the edit bar.
14. Select cells A1:D20, and name them **PrintRange**.
15. Choose the **F**ile Page Set**u**p command, select the Header/Footer tab, and set both the header and footer to none. Select the Sheet tab, uncheck all the check boxes, and choose OK.

The worksheet should look like figure 43.10, without the two buttons on the right side.

The next step is to create the procedures in a module and attach those procedures to two buttons in the form.

To create the procedures, perform the following steps.

1. Choose the **I**nsert **M**acro **M**odule command to insert a new module.
2. Select the module, and rename it **ReceiptMaker** by choosing the **E**dit **S**heet **R**ename command or by double-clicking the module's name tab.
3. Type the procedures shown in listing 43.1 into the module.

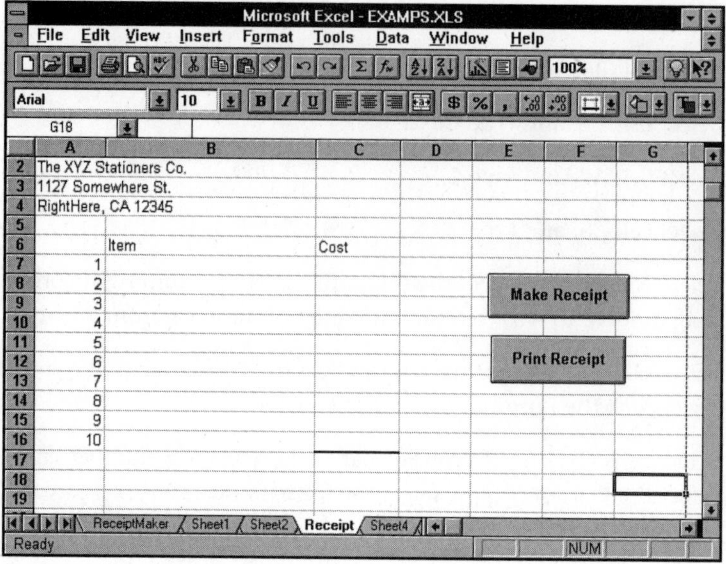

Fig. 43.10 Layout of the Receipt Maker worksheet.

Listing 43.1 The Receipt Maker program

```
'
' Receipt Maker
' A program to make receipts.
'
Option Explicit   'Force the declaration of all variables.
Dim theSheet As Object     'Pointer to the worksheet.
Dim OutputRange As Object 'Pointer to the list of items.
Const MaxNumItems = 10     'Maximum number of items allowed.
'
' Get entries.
'
Sub GetEntries()
  Dim theItem As String, theCost As Currency
  Dim theRow As Integer, NumItems As Integer
  'Define the pointer to the worksheet.
  Set theSheet = Application.Workbooks("Examps.xls"). _
      Worksheets("Receipt")
  'Define the pointer to the top of the table of items.
  Set OutputRange = theSheet.Range("TopOfList")
  ClearRange OutputRange     'Clear the table of items.
  NumItems = 1
  'Ask for the name and cost for up to 10 items.
  Do While NumItems <= MaxNumItems
    'Get the name.
    theItem = InputBox("Item Name:", "Make Receipt")
    'If the user didn't enter anything, _
        he must be done, so quit.
    If theItem = "" Then Exit Do
    'Get the cost.
```

```
    theCost = Val(InputBox("Item Cost:", "Make Receipt"))
    'Insert the items name and cost on the worksheet.
    OutputRange.Cells(NumItems, 1).Formula = theItem
    OutputRange.Cells(NumItems, 2).Formula = Str(theCost)
    NumItems = NumItems + 1  'Increment the number of items.
  Loop
  TotalIt   'Calculate and print the totals.
  'Make the TotalIt procedure an event procedure
  'attached to the worksheet.
  theSheet.OnEntry = "TotalIt"  'Retotal it if the user
     makes changes.
End Sub
'
' Calculate subtotal and total.
'
Sub TotalIt()
  Dim theRow As Integer
  Dim SubTotal As Currency, ItemTax As Currency
  Dim theTotal As Currency
  SubTotal = 0
  'Calculate the total by extracting the values from the worksheet.
  For theRow = 1 To MaxNumItems
    SubTotal = SubTotal + Val(OutputRange.Cells(theRow, 2).Value)
  Next theRow
  'Insert the subtotal, tax, and total on the worksheet.
  With OutputRange
    .Cells(MaxNumItems + 1, 1).Formula = "Subtotal"
    .Cells(MaxNumItems + 1, 2).Formula = Str(SubTotal)
    .Cells(MaxNumItems + 2, 1).Formula = "Tax"
    ItemTax = theTax(SubTotal)  'Calculate the tax.
    .Cells(MaxNumItems + 2, 2).Formula = Str(ItemTax)
    theTotal = SubTotal + ItemTax
    .Cells(MaxNumItems + 3, 1).Formula = "Total"
    .Cells(MaxNumItems + 3, 2).Formula = Str(theTotal)
  End With
End Sub
'
' Clear the output range.
'
Sub ClearRange(theRange As Object)
  Dim theRow As Integer
  For theRow = 1 To MaxNumItems + 3
    'Clear the cells. Use ClearContents to only clear the values
    'and not the formatting.
    theRange.Cells(theRow, 1).ClearContents
    theRange.Cells(theRow, 2).ClearContents
  Next theRow
End Sub
'
' Print the receipt.
'
Sub PrintReceipt()
  theSheet.OnEntry = ""  'Turn off the automatic retotaling.
  theSheet.Range("PrintRange").PrintOut  'Print the worksheet.
End Sub
```

(continues)

Listing 43.1 Continued

```
'
' Calculate the tax on an item.
'
Function theTax(Cost As Currency) As Currency
  Const TaxRate = 0.0825
  theTax = Cost * TaxRate
End Function
```

4. Switch to the worksheet, and display the Drawing toolbar by choosing the **V**iew **T**oolbars command.

5. Click the Button tool in the Drawing toolbar, and draw the Make Receipt button as shown in figure 43.10. When the Assign To dialog box appears, select `GetEntries` for the macro and choose OK.

6. The button should still be selected; if not, click the Selection tool in the Drawing toolbar and select the button. Select the text on top of the button, and change it to **Make Receipt**.

7. Create the Print Receipt button, attach it to the macro PrintReceipt, and make the title **Print Receipt**.

8. Save the workbook as EXAMPS.XLS.

The worksheet should look like figure 43.10. If you did everything correctly, you can use the program to create a receipt. Switch to the Receipt worksheet, and click the Make Receipt button. In the first dialog box that appears, type the name of an item and press Enter. In the second dialog box, type the cost of the item and press Enter. Continue typing names and costs until you have entered all the items you want to use in this receipt. To end the list, press Enter, or click the Cancel button in the Item Name dialog box. The totals are calculated and displayed in the receipt, as shown in figure 43.11. Click the Print Receipt button to print the receipt.

Using Declarations and Visual Basic for Applications Data Types

Not all data values are the same type in Visual Basic for Applications. If you don't declare any variables, all variables have a data type of `Variant`. The `Variant` type is useful because it can store anything from strings to pictures to floating-point numbers. The problem with a `Variant`-type variable is that to

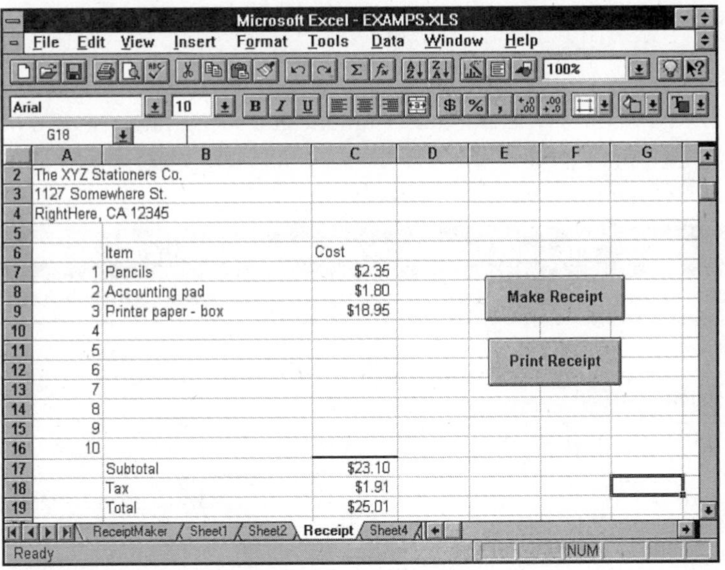

Fig. 43.11
The Receipt Maker worksheet after inputting a receipt.

hold anything, it must check every time to see what kind of data is being stored in it—and must have a lot of memory available to store that data. Thus, a variable of the `Variant` data type wastes time and memory. For a few small items, this waste won't matter, but it becomes important if you are storing many data items.

If you declare the type of a variable before you use the variable, Visual Basic for Applications does not have to check every time to see what the variable's data type is and then reserve space for it. If the variable is declared, the type is known and the space is reserved ahead of time.

Another reason to declare all variables is to help ensure that you did not misspell something, creating a program *bug*. Visual Basic for Applications does not force you to declare everything, but you can do it yourself by placing `Option Explicit` at the top of a module (see the start of listing 43.1). If you do this, Visual Basic for Applications forces you to explicitly declare the data type of every variable in that module before you use it.

Note

If you have not yet encountered a program bug, you are living a charmed life. But never fear—you undoubtedly will see many in the near future. A bug in a program actually is an error of some sort caused by using improper syntax (syntax errors), improper calculations or assignments (run-time errors), or improper program logic (logical errors).

Visual Basic for Applications has several built-in data types, which are listed in table 43.2. Of these, `Variant` is the most general but the least conservative in terms of resources. A few things, such as pictures, must be stored in variables with a `Variant` type, but most numeric and string values should be stored in the appropriate type of variable to save time and space.

Table 43.2 The Built-in Data Types in Visual Basic for Applications

Data Type	Size (bytes)	Digits	Approximate Range
`Boolean`	2	1	`True` or `False`
`Integer`	2	5	–32,768 to 32,767
`Long`	4	10	–2.15E9 to 2.15E9
`Single`	4	7	–3.402E38 to 3.402E38
`Double`	8	15	–1.797E308 to 1.797E308
`Currency`	8	19	–9.22E14 to 9.22E14
`Date`	8		1/1/100 to 12/31/9999
`String`	number of characters + 1		
`Object`	4		
`Array`	Depends on type and number of elements		

To declare the type of a variable, use the `Dim` statement. At the top of a procedure or module, type the keyword **Dim**, followed by a variable name, and then type the keyword **As**, followed by the variable's data type. If the type is not specified, the variable is the `Variant` type. You can put multiple variable-type declarations in a single line, separating the declarations with commas. All the following statements are variable declaration statements.

```
Dim theSheet As Object
Dim OutputRange As Object
Dim theItem As String, theCost As Currency
Dim theRow As Integer, NumItems As Integer
```

Variables passed as arguments to a procedure are declared in the procedure header. The following procedure header defines the arguments being passed to a procedure as an integer and a string:

```
Sub myProcedure(aVariable As Integer, AnotherVariable As String)
```

The type of value returned by a function procedure is declared by placing the type at the right side of the function header. The following function takes a `Single` type value as an argument and returns a `Double` type value:

```
Function myFunction(aVariable As Single) As Double
```

Arrays

Arrays are not really a new data type; they are lists of one of the existing types, such as Integer or String. An *array* is an indexed list of data values, where the array name is followed by one or more integers in parentheses. The integer selects the specific *element* (data value) of the array. The number of integers in the parentheses determines the *dimension* of the array.

A one-dimensional array has a single-integer index and is a sequential list of values. The index selects which element of the list to use, counting from the beginning. For example, the statement

```
Dim myArray(10) As Integer
```

declares a list of 11 memory elements for storing integers (elements 0 through 10). In a formula, the value `myArray(3)` selects the fourth integer in that list, and `myArray(7)` selects the eighth.

Note

When you examine array indices, everything may seem to be off by one. This occurs because the default starting point in Visual Basic for Applications for an array index is 0, which makes the number of elements in an array one more than the value of the upper limit specified in the `Dim` statement. You can modify the default property by placing an `Option Base 1` statement at the top of a module, which changes the default starting point to 1. You also can use constructions like `Dim anArray(5 to 7)` to force the index to range between specific limits

A two-dimensional array uses two integers in the parentheses and is a two-dimensional table of numbers, with the first index selecting the row and the second index selecting the column. Higher-order arrays are allowed, but arrays are a little difficult to imagine when the dimensions exceed three. Following are declarations for arrays:

```
Dim anArray(5) As Single, thedigits(50,2) As Integer
Dim anOther(5,3,10) As Long
```

User-Defined Types

In addition to the built-in data types, you can define your own data types to make storing data more convenient. Suppose that you want to store five strings and an integer in a personal organizer. You could store these elements in five different variables, but it makes sense to create a new data type that combines them in a single user-defined type. A *user-defined* type is a data type that you create to fit the specific circumstances of whatever program you are creating. A user-defined type can be nearly any combination of the existing data types, including other user-defined types.

To create a user-defined data type, place a `Type` statement at the top of the module that needs the type. The `Type` statement consists of a `Type` header containing the keyword `Type`, followed by the new type name, one or more named subvariables with `As`-type clauses, and an `End Type` statement. An address-book program, for example, stores the names and addresses of a large number of people. It would be confusing to store the Name, Address, City, State, ZIP, and Telephone data in four separate variables, so create a compound variable type that stores all this data in a single variable. Following is a user-defined data type that can accomplish this task:

```
Type myType
   Name As String
   Address As String
   City As String
   State As String
   Zip As Integer
   Phone As String
End Type
```

To use this type, you must declare a variable in a `Dim` statement and use the new type name as the type. For example,

```
Dim theData(100) As myType
```

creates an array of 101 elements of `myType` variables (remember that array indices start at 0). To access the parts of a user-defined type, follow the variable name with a period and the part name. To get the ZIP-code part from element number 34, for example, you would use the following variable:

```
theData(34).Zip
```

The Scope of Variables

In listing 43.1, some of the variable declarations are placed at the top of the module outside the procedures. The type definitions and variable declarations placed here are available to all the procedures within the module. If the declarations were placed within a procedure, the values stored in the variables would be available only within that procedure. The same variable could be defined in each of the five procedures, and each of those variables would be independent of the other four, even though they have the same name. If you have more than one module in a program, and you want a variable to be available to all the procedures in all the modules, you must declare that variable at the module level and use `Public` instead of `Dim` in the declaration.

Constants

One more declaration appears at the top of the module:

```
Const MaxNumItems = 10
```

An entry of this type declares a constant. When a constant is declared at the top of a module, it is available to all the procedures in that module. If the keyword `Public` precedes the `Const` in the constant declaration, the constant is available to all procedures in all open modules. A constant is not a variable, so you cannot change its value in a running program. When you use a constant, it behaves exactly as if you had typed the value of the constant everywhere the name is used. Using constants makes programs easier to understand and easier to change. In the Receipt Maker program, if you want to increase the maximum number of items allowed in a single receipt, you need only change the value of the constant. If you didn't use the constant, you would have to change the code everywhere the maximum value is used.

Branching and Decision-Making

As you read down the listing of the Receipt Maker program, you come across the following line:

```
If theItem = "" Then Exit Do
```

The line is an `If` statement that tests the value of `theItem` to see whether it contains an empty string. The variable `theItem` contains the text name of the item to be added to the receipt. If it is empty, the user is finished entering data, and you execute the `Exit Do` statement to exit from the `Do-Loop` structure. Thus, the `If` statement controls a branch in the structure of the program.

Block If Structures

A block `If` structure enables you to use a logical condition equation to decide which block of code to execute. The block `If` structure follows:

```
If condition1 Then
   statements1
ElseIf condition2
   statements2
Else
   statements3
End If
```

When the `If` statement is executed, ***condition1*** is tested, and if the result is `True`, the block ***statements1*** is executed. If ***condition1*** is `False`, ***condition2*** is tested, and if the result is `True`, the block ***statements2*** is executed. There can be multiple `ElseIf` clauses, and each is tested in turn, looking for one whose condition is `True`. If none of the conditions is `True`, the statements following the `Else` clause are executed. Only the block of statements following the first condition that returns `True` is executed; all the others are skipped, even if their conditions would have returned `True`.

Logical Formulas

The conditions used in the `If` statements are logical values, formulas that result in a logical value, or numeric formulas that result in a value of zero (`False`) or nonzero (`True`). Logical formulas usually are created by comparing two values, using one of the comparison operators shown in table 43.3. Logical expressions also can be combined with the Boolean operators listed in table 43.4. For more information, search for *comparison operators* and *logical* in the Visual Basic for Applications section of on-line help.

Table 43.3 The Comparison Operators

Operator	Description
=	Equal to
<>	Not equal to
>	Greater than
<	Less than
>=	Greater than or equal to
<=	Less than or equal to

Table 43.4 The Logical Operators

Operator	Description
`And`	Logical and
`Eqv`	Logical equivalence
`Imp`	Logical implies
`Not`	Logical negation
`Or`	Logical or
`Xor`	Logical exclusive or

Select Case

The `Select Case` structure performs a function similar to that of the block `If` structure, in that an expression is used to select a particular block of statements. In `Select Case`, the expression returns a value, and that value is used to determine which block of statements to execute. The syntax of the `Select Case` structure follows:

```
Select Case expression
Case list1
   statements1
Case Else
   statements2
End Select
```

When the `Select Case` statement is executed, *`expression`* is evaluated. Following the `Select Case` statement are one or more `Case` statements. The value of *`expression`* is compared with the comma-delimited list of values in *`list1`*. If one of the values matches, the block *`statements1`* is executed. Otherwise, that block is skipped, and the next `Case` statement is checked for a match. If none of the `Case` statements results in a match, the block *`statements2`* following the `Case Else` statement is executed. As with the block `If` structure, only one of the blocks of statements is executed.

Accessing Worksheet Cells

In the example, after the user provides an item's name and cost, that information is inserted into cells in the worksheet. Following is the code that performs the insertion:

```
Set theSheet = Application.Workbooks("Examps.xls"). _
   Worksheets("Receipt")
'Define the pointer to the top of the table of items.
Set OutputRange = theSheet.Range("TopOfList")
.
.
.
   'Insert the items name and cost on the worksheet.
   OutputRange.Cells(NumItems, 1).Formula = theItem
   OutputRange.Cells(NumItems, 2).Formula = Str(theCost)
```

You use a range reference and a `Set` statement to define an object variable that points to the cell named `TopOfList` in the worksheet. That range reference is used with the `Cells` method to select worksheet cells in positions relative to the cell `TopOfList`. After obtaining a range reference to a cell, use the `Value` and `Formula` properties to get or set the value of a cell. Notice that the `Value` property contains the value of a cell—that is, the number displayed in the worksheet—whereas the `Formula` property contains what was typed in the cell. In this case, because none of the cells contains a formula, the `Value` and `Formula` properties are the same.

The range reference in the `OutputRange` variable refers to a named cell. This reference is preferable to referencing an explicit cell because you can rearrange the worksheet and the code still will get the value from the correct cell. You can reference the cells by using a cell reference, or reference a cell by row and column by using `Cell`, which also returns a Range object. The following three statements reference the contents of cell C7 in the example:

```
theCost = theSheet.Range("C7").Value
theCost = theSheet.Range("TopOfList"). Cells(1, 2).Value
theCost = theSheet.Cells(7, 3).Value
```

The `TotalIt` procedure demonstrates both reading and changing the values of worksheet cells. The first part of the procedure gets the value in each cell in column C that contains a value and calculates a subtotal.

```
SubTotal = 0
  'Calculate the total by extracting the values from the worksheet.
  For theRow = 1 To MaxNumItems
    SubTotal = SubTotal + Val(OutputRange.Cells(theRow, 2).Value)
  Next theRow
```

The `For` and `Next` statements form a loop that executes the `SubTotal` statement one time for each row in the data range of the receipt. The value of the cell is obtained and totaled in the variable `SubTotal`.

Note

Notice how the `Val()` function is applied to the contents of the cell, to ensure that a number is passed to the variable. Without the `Val()` function, the user could type into a cell a string that would crash your code if you attempted to store it in a numeric variable. The `Val()` function converts a string to a number and prevents that potential problem.

The second half of the procedure writes the labels and values for the subtotal, the tax, and the total in the worksheet:

```
With OutputRange
    .Cells(MaxNumItems + 1, 1).Formula = "Subtotal"
    .Cells(MaxNumItems + 1, 2).Formula = Str(SubTotal)
    .Cells(MaxNumItems + 2, 1).Formula = "Tax"
    ItemTax = theTax(SubTotal)  'Calculatethe tax.
    .Cells(MaxNumItems + 2, 2).Formula = Str(ItemTax)
    theTotal = SubTotal + ItemTax
    .Cells(MaxNumItems + 3, 1).Formula = "Total"
    .Cells(MaxNumItems + 3, 2).Formula = Str(theTotal)
  End With
```

This block of statements also demonstrates the use of the `With` statement to block cells together and to save some typing. The statements are logically blocked together because they refer to the same object, and they save some typing because you have to type the first object only once. The object following the `With` clause (`OutputRange`) is assumed to attach before the period to all the statements between the `With` and `End With` statements.

Calling Procedures

The `TotalIt` procedure is an example of a Sub procedure that is called by other procedures. The `GetEntries` procedure needs to be able to calculate and display the totals in the worksheet, and it calls the `TotalIt` procedure to do so.

At the beginning of the `GetEntries` procedure, any old entries must be cleared from the receipt. The `ClearRange` procedure is called to perform that action.

```
Sub ClearRange(theRange As Object)
  Dim theRow As Integer
  For theRow = 1 To MaxNumItems + 3
    'Clear the cells. Use ClearContents to only clear
    'the values and not the formatting.
    theRange.Cells(theRow, 1).ClearContents
    theRange.Cells(theRow, 2).ClearContents
  Next theRow
End Sub
```

The procedure needs one object for an argument named `theRange` in the `ClearRange` procedure. In the `GetEntries` procedure, the `ClearRange` procedure is called with the following statement:

```
ClearRange OutputRange      'Clear the table of items.
```

Because this procedure call is not part of a formula, no parentheses around the argument are required.

The function procedure `theTax` is another procedure that is called from elsewhere in the program.

```
'
' Calculate the tax on an item.
'
Function theTax(Cost As Currency) As Currency
  Const TaxRate = 0.0825
  theTax = Cost * TaxRate
End Function
```

Notice that in this procedure, the argument is a `Currency`-type variable named `Cost`. The function is called as part of a formula in `TotalIt`.

```
ItemTax = theTax(SubTotal)  'Calculate the tax.
```

In `TotalIt`, the function `theTax` is passed the variable `SubTotal` as an argument. This variable points to a memory location, and that memory location is passed to the `theTax` function, where it is named `Cost`. Both names point to the same memory location, so if the value of `Cost` were changed in `theTax`, the value of `SubTotal` would be changed in `TotalIt` when the function completes executing.

In some cases, you want to make sure that a procedure does not change an argument, so you must pass the argument as a value instead of a memory address. You can do this in the procedure heading or in the calling program. In a procedure heading, for example, precede the argument with the keyword `ByVal`, as follows:

```
Function theTax(ByVal Cost As Currency) As Currency
```

The other way is to turn the argument in the calling program into a formula. Instead of the addresses of any of the variables, the address where the result of the formula is stored is sent to the procedure. You make a variable into a formula simply by enclosing the variable name in parentheses, as follows:

```
ItemTax = theTax((SubTotal))  'Calculate the tax.
```

The TotalIt procedure also is an event procedure attached to the worksheet. This attachment is done at the end of the GetReceipt procedure, as follows:

```
'Make the TotalIt procedure an event procedure attached
'to the worksheet.
  theSheet.OnEntry = "TotalIt"  'Retotal it if the user makes changes.
```

Later in the program, the TotalIt procedure is unattached from the worksheet in the PrintReceipt procedure, as follows:

```
theSheet.OnEntry = ""  'Turn off the automatic retotaling.
```

The OnEntry property of a worksheet contains the name of a procedure to be executed whenever the user changes the contents of a worksheet cell. By making the TotalIt procedure an event procedure, the user can make changes in the receipt before printing, and those changes will immediately be included in the totals at the bottom of the receipt.

Using Loops

The TotalIt procedure has to search through the cells in the worksheet and add the contents to calculate the subtotal. If you were to write range references to all 10 of the cells in the worksheet, you could add them up that way, but you probably don't want to spend your time typing the same statement over and over. To handle cases like this, you use loops.

For/Next

The most common loop is the For/Next loop, which executes a block of statements a specified number of times. The syntax of the For/Next loop is as follows:

```
For loopvariable = start To end Step stepval
.
.statements
.
Next loopvariable
```

In the For/Next loop, *loopvariable* is a standard variable. The first time the loop executes, *loopvariable* has the value *start*, and all the statements down to the Next statement are executed. The second time the loop executes, *stepval* is added to *loopvariable*, and that value is compared with *end*. If *loopvariable* is greater than *end*, the loop terminates; otherwise, the statements within the loop are executed again. The Step *stepval* clause can be omitted, in which case the *stepval* is 1. If *stepval* is negative, the loop counts down instead of up until *loopvariable* is less than *end*.

The TotalIt procedure uses a For/Next loop to select all the cells that might contain values in the worksheet, and calculates a total for all the values found.

```
For theRow = 1 To MaxNumItems
  SubTotal = SubTotal + Val(OutputRange.Cells(theRow, 2).Value)
Next theRow
```

In this example, theRow is the loop variable, and it ranges from 1 to MaxNumEntries. Each time the loop executes, a different worksheet cell is selected, using the Cells method.

Do/Loop

The Do/Loop loop uses a condition to determine how many times to execute the loop. The condition can be tested at the beginning or the end of the loop, and the loop can continue While the condition is True or Until the condition becomes True (while it is False.) Thus, there are four variations of the syntax, as follows:

```
Do While condition
.
.statements
.
Loop
```

```
Do Until condition
.
.statements
.
Loop
```

```
Do
.
.statements
.
Loop While condition
```

```
Do
.
.statements
.
Loop Until condition
```

The GetEntries procedure uses a Do/Loop structure to loop over the 10 allowed lines of input in the receipt. In this case, the Do While construction is used with a condition that remains True until the value of NumItems is less than or equal to MaxNumItems.

```
Do While NumItems <= MaxNumItems
    'Get the name.
    theItem = InputBox("Item Name:", "Make Receipt")
    'If the user didn't enter anything, he must be done, so quit.
    If theItem = "" Then Exit Do
    'Get the cost.
    theCost = Val(InputBox("Item Cost:", "Make Receipt"))
    'Insert the items name and cost on the worksheet.
    OutputRange.Cells(NumItems, 1).Formula = theItem
    OutputRange.Cells(NumItems, 2).Formula = Str(theCost)
    NumItems = NumItems + 1  'Increment the number of items.
  Loop
```

All the statements between the `Do` statement and the `Loop` statement are executed until the condition becomes `False`. An exception occurs if the user presses Cancel and the `If` statement within the loop has a `True` condition.

```
If theItem = "" Then Exit Do
```

If the condition is `True`, the `Exit Do` statement is executed, immediately terminating the loop and starting execution at the statement following the `Loop` statement. An `Exit For` statement also exists for exiting a `For/Next` loop early.

For Each

The `For Each` loop is used to perform some action for all the elements of an array or collection. The syntax is as follows:

```
For Each element In group
  statements
Next element
```

The `For Each` loop applies to arrays and collections only. The loop executes once for each element in the array or collection. This loop is useful when you don't know (or don't care) how many elements are in a collection. The loop variable *element* is of the data type of the elements in the *group* collection. Each time the loop is calculated, *element* takes on the value of another member of the collection.

Accessing Disk Files

If you have been playing with the example, you may have noticed that each time you create a new receipt, all the data values go away. What is missing is a way to save the data so that it can be retrieved and used. You might want to know how many items of what type were sold, or you might want to calculate the total receipts for the day to compare with receipts in the cash box.

You have a couple of options: you could store the data in another worksheet so that the data is saved with the workbook, or you can open a disk file and store the data immediately. These methods have different advantages, depending on what you plan to do with the data. If you save the data in a worksheet, you can apply all Excel database functions to it. If you save the data in a disk file, other programs could open it directly. In this example, you are going to save the data in a disk file. Add code to the `PrintRange` procedure to add the data to the end of a data file, as shown here (the added lines are in bold):

```
'
' Print the receipt.
'
Sub PrintReceipt()
  Dim theRow As Integer
  theSheet.OnEntry = ""  'Turn off the automatic retotaling.
  theSheet.Range("PrintRange").PrintOut  'Print the worksheet.
  'Save the data from the receipt.
  Open "c:\examps.dat" For Append As #1
  For theRow = 1 To MaxNumItems
    Write #1, OutputRange.Cells(theRow, 1).Value,
    Write #1, OutputRange.Cells(theRow, 2).Value
  Next theRow
  'Write the subtotal, tax, and total.
  With OutputRange
    Write #1, "Subtotal",
    Write #1, .Cells(MaxNumItems + 1, 2).Value
    Write #1, "Tax",
    Write #1, .Cells(MaxNumItems + 2, 2).Value
    Write #1, "Total",
    Write #1, .Cells(MaxNumItems + 3, 2).Value
  End With
  Close #1
End Sub
```

In the added lines, the file is opened for appending, using a file number of 1. Appending places each new entry at the end of the file. The loop then copies the data from the worksheet and writes it to the file. The program still appears to work the same, but now the data is saved every time the Print Receipt button is clicked. After you enter the data shown in figure 43.11, the following text is in EXAMPS.DAT:

```
"Pencils",2.35
"Accounting pad",1.8
"Printer paper - box",18.95
,
,
,
,
,
,
,
"Subtotal",23.1
"Tax",1.9058
"Total",25.0058
```

Notice that the `Write` statement delimits the data in the file by placing quotation marks around the strings of text and placing commas between items written to disk. These delimiters make it easy for the `Input` statement to be used to read the data back into a program for further processing. If you use `Print` instead of `Write`, the text and strings are written to the file without delimiters, creating a text file suitable for printing rather than for reading back into another program.

For more information about reading and writing files, search for *input* in the Visual Basic for Applications section of on-line help, and select the topic "Input and Output Keyword Summary."

Using Built-in Dialog Boxes

Visual Basic for Applications has two built-in dialog boxes that you can use in your programs to send data to the user and to get data from the user. The two dialog boxes are created with the `MsgBox()` and `InputBox()` functions. You already have used the `InputBox()` function to get data from the user in the Receipt Maker program. The `MsgBox()` function displays a dialog box containing a message and one or more buttons to be clicked to close the dialog box. Both functions take one or more arguments to set the prompt text, box title, number and type of buttons, and so on. See on-line help for a complete list of arguments.

In addition to these two dialog boxes, you can use two Excel dialog boxes to enhance your programs when opening and saving files. The two dialog boxes are displayed with the `GetSaveAsFilename` and `GetOpenFilename` methods.

The `GetSaveAsFilename` method displays the standard File Save As dialog box and gets a file name from the user. The dialog box does not really save anything; it only gets you a path and file name to use. You then must use the `Open` statement to actually create the file and save something in it. The `GetOpenFilename` method operates in the same way, but it displays the standard File Open dialog box instead.

Creating Custom Dialog Boxes

In addition to the built-in dialog boxes, you can create your own custom dialog boxes and attach them to a Visual Basic for Applications program. The Receipt Maker program could use a data-entry form to replace the two dialog boxes necessary to input a single entry.

To make this change, perform the following steps:

1. Open the EXAMPS.XLS workbook, and save it as EXAMPS2.XLS.

2. Choose the **I**nsert **M**acro **D**ialog command. Your worksheet should look like figure 43.12, with a blank custom dialog box, and the Forms toolbar. The Forms toolbar can be floating or can be docked at the top or bottom of the page, as shown in the figure. The tools in the Forms toolbar are listed in table 43.5.

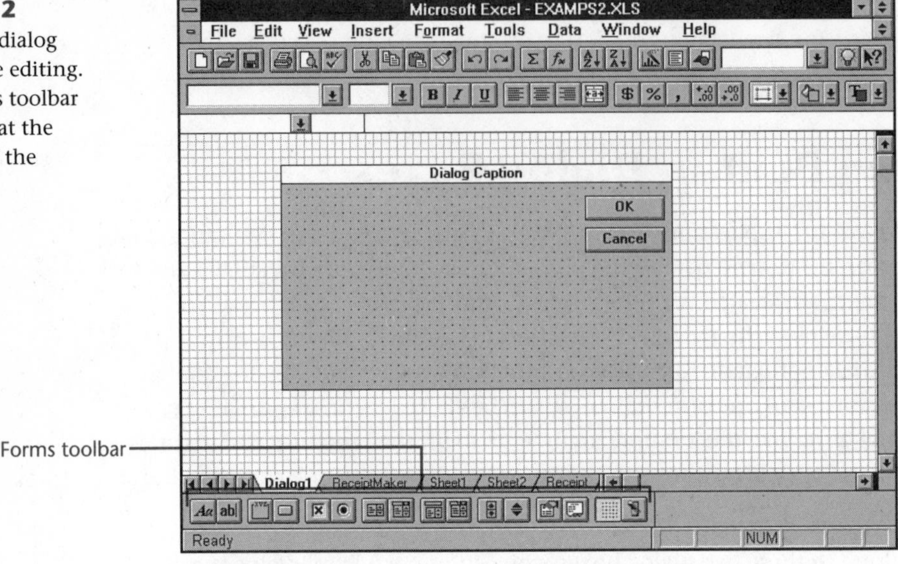

Fig. 43.12
A custom dialog box before editing. The Forms toolbar is docked at the bottom of the screen.

Table 43.5 Tools in the Forms Toolbar

Tool	Tool Name	Description
	Label	Creates a text label.
	Edit Box	Creates an edit box for inputting data.
	Group	Creates a group frame to visually group other controls and to functionally group option buttons.
	Button	Creates a command button that can execute a procedure.
	Check Box	Creates a check box with a label for selecting nonexclusive options.
	Option Button	Creates an option button with a label for setting exclusive options. (Create an option-button group with the Group frame.)
	List Box	Creates a list box for selecting a value from a list of values in a scrollable box.
	Drop-Down	Creates a drop-down list box for selecting a value.
	List–Edit	Creates a list–edit box (a combination of a list box and an edit box).

Tool	Tool Name	Description
	Drop-Down Edit	Creates a drop-down edit box (a combination of a drop-down list box and an edit box).
	Scroll Bar	Creates a scroll bar for inputting a value by sliding a slider, or for using as an indicator of a value.
	Spinner	Creates a spinner for quickly stepping through a list of integer values.
	Properties	Displays the Properties dialog box for setting the properties of the selected control.
	Edit Code	Jumps to the procedure attached to the selected control.
	Toggle Grid	Turns on or off a grid to simplify the alignment of controls in a dialog box.
	Run Dialog	Activates the dialog box so that changing values or clicking buttons executes the attached procedures.

3. Select the dialog caption, type **Receipt Maker**, and click a blank portion of the dialog sheet.

4. Choose the Format Sheet Rename command, and change the dialog sheet name to **ItemDialog**.

5. Using the Label button in the Forms toolbar, draw two labels in the dialog box, as shown in figure 43.13. Select the caption of the first and type **Item Name:**. Select the caption of the second and type **ItemCost:**.

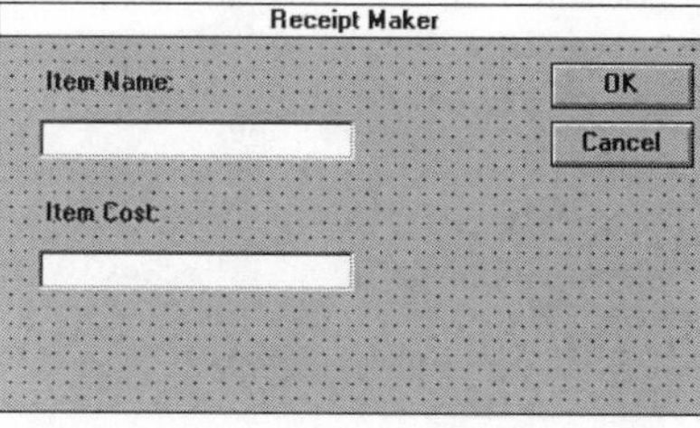

Fig. 43.13
Layout of the Receipt Maker dialog box.

6. Using the Edit box button, draw two edit boxes in the dialog box, as shown in figure 43.13.

7. Select the edit box next to the Item Name label, and change its name to **ItemNameBox**.

> **Note**
>
> To change the name of a control in a dialog sheet, select the control; then click the name box on the left side of the edit bar, type the new name, and press Enter.

8. Select the edit box next to the Item Cost label and name it **ItemCostBox**.

9. Choose the Format Object command, and select the Control tab. In the dialog box, choose the Number button in the Edit Validation group, and choose OK. This procedure forces the user to type a number in this box before the dialog box will close.

10. Choose the Tools Tab Order command. Select the `ItemNameBox` and move it to the top of the list; select the `ItemCostBox`, and move it just below the `ItemNameBox`. This procedure makes `ItemNameBox` the first thing selected when the dialog box appears; `ItemCostBox` is selected second, when the user presses the Tab key. Choose OK to complete the change in tab order.

11. Switch to the `ReceiptMaker` module and make the following changes in the `GetEntries` procedure (the changes are in bold):

```
'
' Get entries.
'
Sub GetEntries()
  Dim theItem As String, theCost As Currency
  Dim theRow As Integer, NumItems As Integer
  Dim theDialog As Object
  'Define the pointer to the worksheet.
  Set theSheet = Application.Workbooks("Examps2.xls"). us
     Worksheets("Receipt")
  'Define the pointer to the top of the table of items.
  Set OutputRange = theSheet.Range("TopOfList")
  Set theDialog = Application.Workbooks("Examps2.xls"). us
     DialogSheets("ItemDialog")
    ClearRange OutputRange     'Clear the table of items.
  NumItems = 1
  'Ask for the name and cost for up to 10 items.
```

```
    Do While NumItems <= MaxNumItems
      'Clear the edit boxes.
      theDialog.EditBoxes("ItemNameBox").Text = ""
      theDialog.EditBoxes("ItemCostBox").Text = ""
      theDialog.Show
      'Get the name.
      theItem = theDialog.EditBoxes("ItemNameBox").Text
      'If the user didn't enter anything, he must be done, so quit.
      If theItem = "" Then Exit Do
      'Get the cost.
      theCost = Val(theDialog.EditBoxes("ItemCostBox").Text)
      'Insert the items name and cost on the worksheet.
      OutputRange.Cells(NumItems, 1).Formula = theItem
      OutputRange.Cells(NumItems, 2).Formula = Str(theCost)
      NumItems = NumItems + 1  'Increment the number of items.
    Loop
    TotalIt   'Calculate and print the totals.
    'Retotal it if the user makes changes.
    theSheet.OnEntry = "TotalIt"
End Sub
```

12. Save the workbook.

The first change in the procedure defines a new object named `theDialog` that references the dialog sheet. That object then is used with the `EditBoxes` collection to clear the two edit boxes. The `Show` method is used to display the dialog box. After the user chooses the OK button, the contents of the two edit boxes are returned to the procedure and processed as before.

When you run the program by clicking the Make Receipt button in the worksheet, the dialog box appears, as shown in figure 43.14. Type the item's name, press Tab, type the item's cost, and press Enter. The first item is inserted into the receipt, and the dialog box appears again. To end entry, press Enter without typing anything in the dialog box. The totals are calculated.

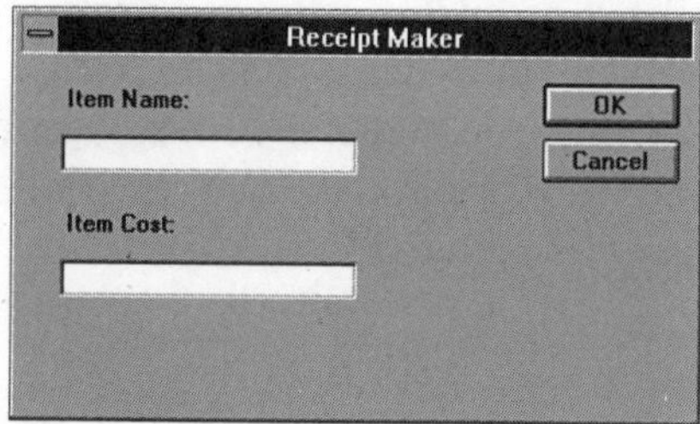

Fig. 43.14
The Receipt Maker dialog box.

Using the Debugging Tools

Program bugs are a fact of life for computer programmers. No matter how careful you are, bugs almost always appear; you must find them and remove them from your codes. The simplest bugs are *syntax errors*, in which you put a comma in the wrong place or used a keyword improperly. Syntax errors normally are found by Visual Basic for Applications as soon as you type them. Next are *run-time errors*, which are caused by using the wrong type of variable or by performing an improper numeric calculation (for example, taking the square root of –1). These errors also are found by Visual Basic for Applications as soon as the improper statement is executed. Last are *logical errors*, in which a program does not do what you want it to. Logical errors are the most difficult to find because everything seems to work; it just works wrong.

Visual Basic for Applications has a set of powerful debugging tools to help you find and correct program bugs. You can set breakpoints anywhere in your programs to force them to stop executing at that point. After you stop your program, choose **T**ools **I**nstant Watch to view the value of any variable or expression. You then can continue executing a program or step through it one statement at a time until you find your problem. You also can set watchpoints that automatically break a program when a variable or expression reaches a certain value.

Break Mode

Break mode is where an executing program is halted with all its variables still intact. Normally, when you end a program, the contents of all the variables are lost. However, break mode actually is a pausing of the executing program, so the contents of the variables that have been assigned values during program execution still are available. A running program enters break mode when you press Ctrl+Break, when it encounters an error, or when it encounters a breakpoint or watchpoint. When a program enters break mode by encountering an error, or when you press Ctrl+Break, the Macro Error dialog box appears (see fig. 43.15), giving you the choice to quit, continue, or open the Debug window.

Breakpoints

Breakpoints and watchpoints also put a program into break mode. A *breakpoint* is a marker in a line of code that forces a program to stop executing when Visual Basic for Applications attempts to execute the marked line. A *watchpoint* is a marker in the value of a variable or a simple formula. When the value of a watchpoint changes in some specific way, the program is stopped and placed in break mode.

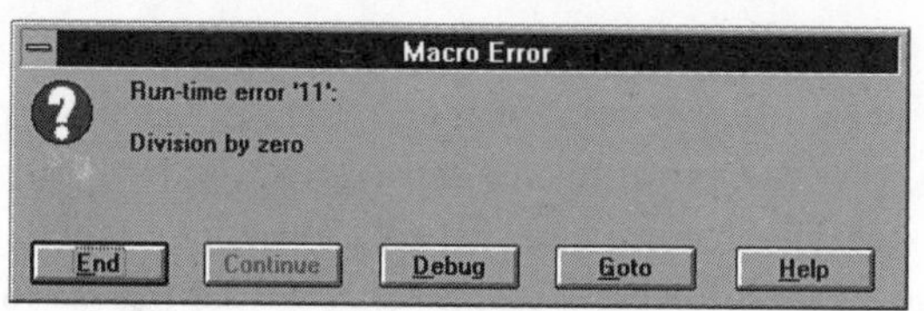

Fig. 43.15
The Macro Error dialog box.

To set a breakpoint, open the module containing your procedure, and select the line of code where you want the program to stop. Choose the **R**un Toggle **B**reakpoint command to set a breakpoint. Choose the command again to remove a selected breakpoint, or choose the **R**un **C**lear All Breakpoints command to remove all breakpoints. Then run your code. When it reaches a breakpoint, it stops and enters break mode. When a program enters break mode by encountering a breakpoint or watchpoint, it goes directly to the debug window, which is discussed in the following section.

The Debug Window

If you choose **D**ebug in the Macro Error dialog box, or encounter a breakpoint or watchpoint, the Debug window appears (see fig. 43.16). The Debug window is a split window, with the currently executing procedure in the bottom half and the Immediate pane or the Watch pane at the top. In the bottom half of the window, you can select lines of code, add or remove breakpoints, and select code for watchpoints.

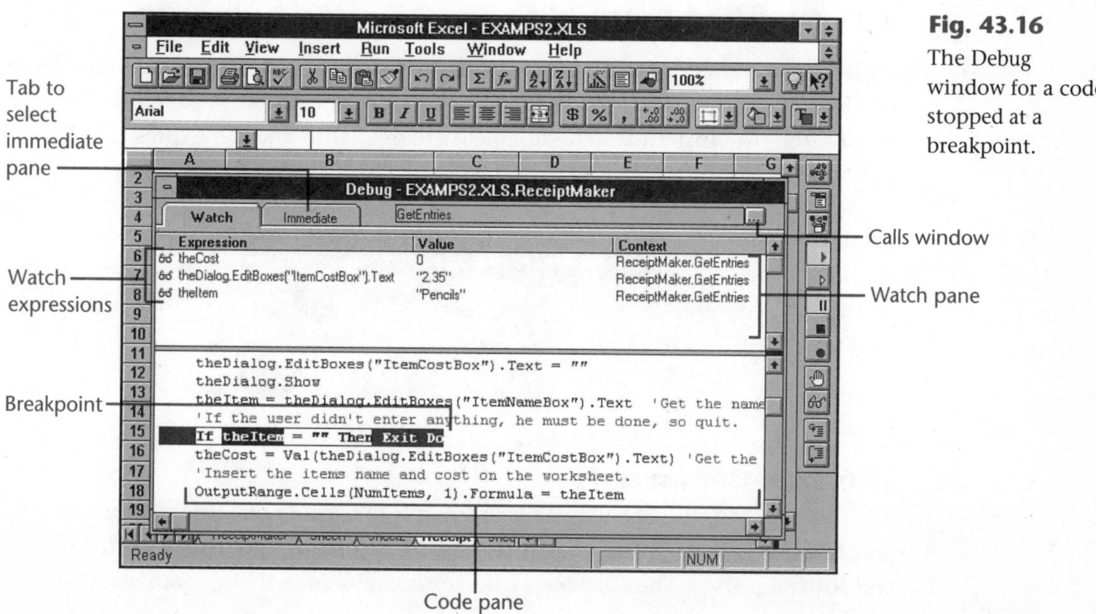

Fig. 43.16
The Debug window for a code stopped at a breakpoint.

The Debug window shown in figure 43.16 shows the code stopped at a breakpoint set in the `If` statement highlighted in the Code pane. The Watch pane shows the current value of `theItem`, `theCost`, and `theDialog.EditBoxes("ItemCostBox").Text` as watch variables. Notice that `theCost` has no value yet because it has not yet been passed the value in `theDialog.EditBoxes("ItemCostBox").Text`. At this point, you can continue execution of a procedure, set or delete more watchpoints, examine the value of variables, or step through the procedure one statement at a time.

The Immediate Pane

In the Immediate pane of the Debug window, you can type and execute almost any Visual Basic for Applications command. The only restriction is that the command must be only one line long. The Immediate pane also receives any printed values caused by the `Debug.Print` statement, used to print values from a running program.

The Watch Pane and Watch Expressions

The Watch pane displays the current value of watchpoints and watch expressions. Watchpoints, and watch expressions displayed in the Watch pane, continuously show the current value of the variables and expressions. The difference between these two is that although both show a value, a watchpoint can stop your code if the selected value changes in some specified way. The Instant watch is used to show the current value of a variable or expression without placing it in the Watch pane.

Figure 43.17 shows the result of selecting the variable `theItem` in the Debug window and choosing the **T**ools Instant **W**atch command. If you choose the **A**dd button, the Instant watch variable is changed into a watch expression and added to the Watch pane.

Fig. 43.17
An Instant watch dialog box.

The Step Commands

At this point, you can use two step commands to execute one line of your program and stop again in break mode. Those commands are **R**un Step **I**nto and **R**un Step **O**ver. The **R**un Step **I**nto command makes the program execute one line at a time. If the program reaches a procedure call, the next step occurs in that called procedure.

The **R**un Step **O**ver command is similar, but when it reaches a procedure call, it executes the procedure completely before stopping and going into break mode again. Thus, the Step Over command appears to step over procedure calls in the procedure you are executing.

The Calls Window

The Calls window is on the top right side of the Debug window shown in figure 43.16. The Calls window shows the name of the procedure that contains the current point of execution. If you select the Calls window, it expands and lists all the active procedures in this program. Active procedures are those that have not finished running, either because they contain the current execution point or because they are among the calling procedures that eventually called the procedure containing the execution point.

From Here...

Now that you understand the basics of Visual Basic for Applications, you are ready to begin building programs of your own. To build your own programs efficiently, you need the details of the syntax for all the Visual Basic objects and statements. On-line help is one of the best sources of information about the syntax and usage of the Visual Basic for Applications commands and functions. Select the Visual Basic for Applications section; then explore all the different functions and methods.

The Object Browser is another helpful feature because it looks at the actual library files and extracts the real procedure names and properties directly from the procedures themselves.

Other chapters that relate to Visual Basic for Applications include the following:

- Chapter 18, "Automating with Excel Macros." See this chapter for several examples of working code that you can examine and run.
- Chapter 11, "Automating with Macros and Mail Merge." See this chapter for examples of Word Basic code that can be accessed by Visual Basic for Applications.

Part VIII

Appendixes

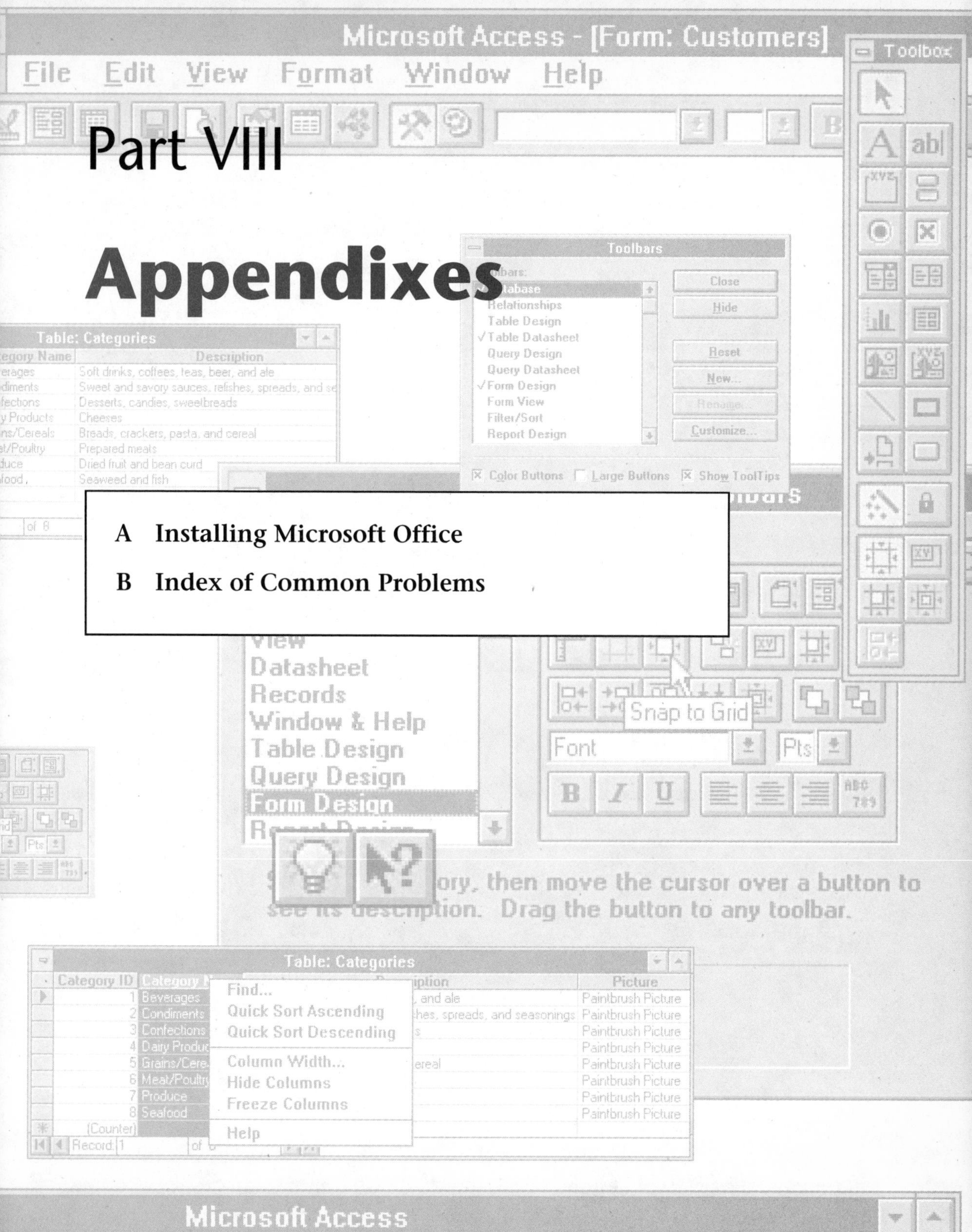

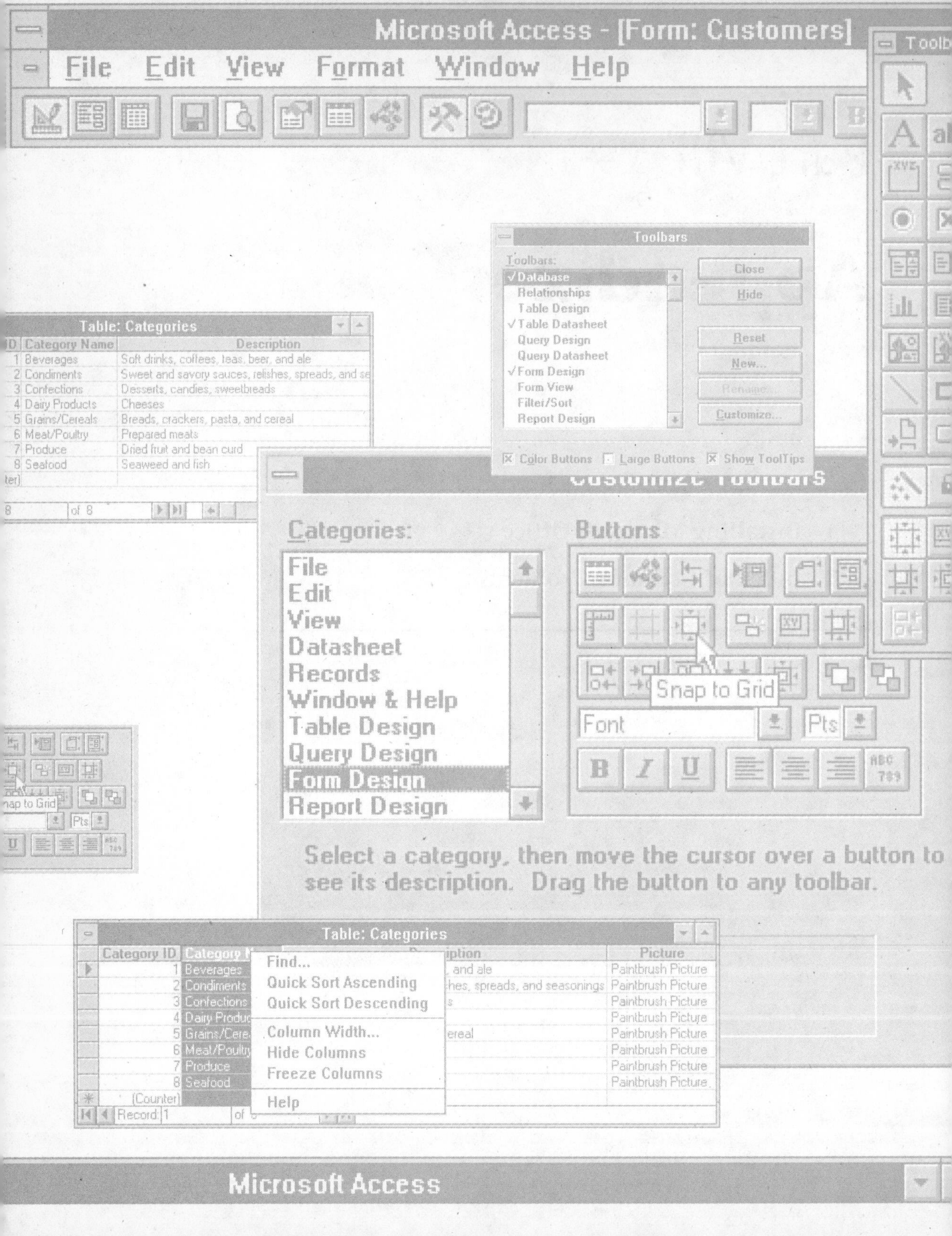
Microsoft Access - [Form: Customers]
File Edit View Format Window Help
Toolbars
Toolbars:
Database
Relationships
Table Design
Table Datasheet
Query Design
Query Datasheet
Form Design
Form View
Filter/Sort
Report Design
Close
Hide
Reset
New...
Rename...
Customize...
Color Buttons
Large Buttons
Show ToolTips
Customize Toolbars
Categories:
File
Edit
View
Datasheet
Records
Window & Help
Table Design
Query Design
Form Design
Report Design
Buttons
Snap to Grid
Font
Pts
Select a category, then move the cursor over a button to see its description. Drag the button to any toolbar.
Table: Categories
Category ID
Category Name
Description
Picture
Beverages
Condiments
Confections
Dairy Products
Grains/Cereals
Meat/Poultry
Produce
Seafood
Soft drinks, coffees, teas, beer, and ale
Sweet and savory sauces, relishes, spreads, and seasonings
Desserts, candies, sweetbreads
Cheeses
Breads, crackers, pasta, and cereal
Prepared meats
Dried fruit and bean curd
Seaweed and fish
Paintbrush Picture
(Counter)
Record: 1
of 8
Find...
Quick Sort Ascending
Quick Sort Descending
Column Width...
Hide Columns
Freeze Columns
Help
Microsoft Access

Appendix A

Installing Microsoft Office

by Stephen A. Swope

The standard edition of Microsoft Office 4 consists of Word for Windows, Excel, and PowerPoint.

The Professional edition of Microsoft Office includes all of these programs and adds the relational database program, Microsoft Access.

If you've already installed an older version of Office, but need to update an individual application (from Excel 4.0 to 5.0, for instance, or PowerPoint 3.0 to 4.0), refer to the later section in this appendix, "Updating an Existing Installation."

In this appendix, you learn how to

- Install Microsoft Office for the first time
- Install Microsoft Office on a network
- Update an existing installation of Microsoft Office

Preparing To Install Office

Before you install Microsoft Office, you should take a few minutes to check your system and backup important system files. Hints for preparing to install Office are described in the sections that follow.

Checking Your System Requirements

Verify that your system can run Microsoft Office.

Microsoft Office requires Microsoft Windows 3.1, which should already be installed on your computer. The computer should have at least an 80386 CPU and 4M of RAM. (Access 2.0 requires at least 6M of RAM.) If you want faster processing, increase your RAM to at least 8M.

You'll especially notice the difference that more RAM can make if you run multiple applications simultaneously. If it needs more RAM than you have available, Windows uses a swap file on your disk as virtual memory. Since disk access is so much slower than RAM access, however, this results in noticeable sluggishness. Everything still runs, but it runs much more slowly than if actual RAM were available.

If you notice lots of drive accesses (and delays) when shifting from one application to another, consider installing additional RAM so that you're less dependent upon your hard disk for virtual memory.

Verifying Your Hard Disk Space

The amount of space you need depends upon how much of the suite you choose to install. If you install everything in the standard package, you need about 57M of disk space. A full installation of Microsoft Access consumes another 12M.

If you don't have that much disk space free, you can select a portion of Microsoft Office to install now and install the rest later. You'll have to make room for it, of course, by deleting files from your hard drive. If you don't already use a disk compression utility, you can also gain space by installing one.

Deactivating Other Programs

To be on the safe side, Microsoft Office should be the only program active in your Windows session (with the exception of the Windows Program Manager). Deactivate all other programs before you begin the installation.

Even if you just began your Windows session and haven't started any other programs, remember that you may have active programs from your Startup program group. Press Ctrl+Esc to see whether any program other than Program Manager is active. If another program is active, choose the End Task button to deactivate it.

Backing Up System Files

The Office Setup program makes changes to two of your system files. The files it modifies are WIN.INI (in the Windows directory) and AUTOEXEC.BAT (in the root directory). Before beginning the installation, make a backup copy of each of these with a different extension (such as .BAK or .OFF). If you encounter problems with your system (such as your system not running or Windows not starting correctly) after installing Office, you can undo any changes Office Setup made by restoring WIN.INI and AUTOEXEC.BAT from these backups.

Installing Office for the First Time

After you have verified that you have enough space and no other programs are running, you are ready to run Microsoft's Setup program to install Office onto your hard drive.

Running the Setup Program

The Setup program for Office installs Word, Excel, PowerPoint, and the Microsoft Office Manager. If you have the Professional version of Office, Access is installed through a separate installation, which will be covered later in this appendix. To start the Office installation, insert Microsoft Office Setup Disk #1 into the appropriate floppy drive (for example, drive A). If your installation disks are for B instead, you should substitute B for A.

From the Program Manager main menu, choose the **F**ile **R**un command. In the Run dialog box, type **a:setup** and press Enter.

After a few moments, you will see the initial Microsoft Office installation screen. The installation screen provides some brief copyright information, as well as options to continue the installation (**O**K), exit the installation, or get help. Be prepared to wait while Setup prepares your system for installation.

Entering Your Name, Organization, and Serial Number

When Setup finishes preparing your system, the Welcome to Setup screen appears. The first time you run the Office Setup program, you are prompted to enter the name and organization to use for the installation. You can't install Office unless you enter a name here, but the organization name is optional.

This information is written to the installation disk, where it is stored in the SETUP.INI file. This file is read on subsequent passes through the Setup program, so that you don't have to enter the information again. The name and organization you enter will be displayed on the opening screens when you start a Microsoft Office program.

After you have entered the name and organization, your Microsoft Office serial number appears.

Tip
You can select Help from the main menu of any Microsoft Office program to retrieve your serial number. Just click on the About button.

Selecting Directories

You will be prompted for a directory in which to store your Microsoft Office program files. The default is C:\MSOFFICE. You can accept the default directory or choose another one.

You can choose the Change **D**irectory button if you want the files to be installed somewhere else. When you choose this button, the Change Directory dialog box appears. You change a default directory by typing the new path in the **P**ath text box, or clicking the path in the tree in the **D**irectories box. If the directory you want doesn't exist, Setup will create it for you, after confirming in a dialog box that this is what you want to do.

Similarly, you will next be prompted to create the directories for the primary Office programs: PowerPoint, Word for Windows, and Excel. By default, these directories are placed directly beneath C:\MSOFFICE, as in the following list:

C:\MSOFFICE\POWERPNT

C:\MSOFFICE\WINWORD

C:\MSOFFICE\EXCEL

Note

Remember that the Office Setup program doesn't install Access for you. You need to install it separately, as described in the section "Installing Microsoft Access."

Choosing the Installation Type

Office lets you choose how much of each program you want to install. The choices are for Typical, Complete/Custom, or Laptop (Minimum) configurations. Choose an installation type based on the space available on your hard drive and how much of the programs you need installed. As you proceed with the installation, Setup informs you of how much disk space your selections require.

By default, the Complete/Custom installation installs everything. It gives you the option to deselect portions of each program, though, so you can omit selected example files, for instance. If you don't want to install part of a program's files, select the category of optional files in the **O**ptions list box, and then choose Chan**g**e Option. A dialog box listing files in that category appears. Deselect any files you don't want to install, then choose OK. This will return you to the previous dialog box. Repeat this procedure for any other categories for which you want to install only part of the files. When you have only the files you want to install for all the categories, choose **C**ontinue. Once you complete this process, you will be ready to move on to the next phase of installation, described in the section "Choosing a Program Group."

The Laptop (Minimum) configuration installs only those files that are absolutely necessary to run the programs. No examples or help files are included. Bare-bones installation of Word requires 6.5M, Excel needs 5.3M, and PowerPoint needs 6.2M.

The Typical installation falls somewhere in between. You get all of the files that are minimally sufficient to run the programs, of course, but you also get the Help files and the Microsoft Office Manager. Total disk space needed: about 40M.

You can return to Setup anytime to modify your installation; you don't have to do everything at one sitting (and, with as many as 23 high-density disks, you may not want to).

If an option is grayed out on the menu and cannot be chosen, Setup has determined that you don't have enough disk space for it. If this happens and you want to install Office according to an option that isn't available, you don't necessarily have to cancel the installation. Instead, you could do one of the following:

- Try installing on a different drive that may have more space. Choose the Change **D**irectory button; it also permits you to choose another drive.

- Switch to another application (for example, Windows File Manager) to free more space on the drive. Press Alt+Tab to access Program Manager, or press Ctrl+Esc and choose Program Manager from the menu. Then use your disk management utility to delete files until you have enough space. Remember to close the application before you return to Office Setup.

If these options don't work, then you may have to consider another installation type, or exit and wait until you can consider your options more completely.

While the custom installation provides the greatest flexibility, each option gives you some control over what is installed. The minimum configuration lets you decide only which applications to install. Note that Change Option is grayed out; there is nothing left to pare away from the minimum installations of any of the programs.

Depending upon your installation strategy, Setup has a few more questions for you. If you choose a Typical or Complete/Custom installation, and Excel is on your list, then you have the option to install Lotus 1-2-3 support for Excel. This option lets you use the slash (/) key to display Help on Excel equivalents for 1-2-3 commands.

If you choose a Typical or Complete/Custom installation that includes Word for Windows, then you can install a special Help for WordPerfect users. If Help is installed, choosing a WordPerfect command key automatically summons Help to explain how Word handles the equivalent function.

Choosing a Program Group

After you have chosen your configuration, Setup prompts you to select a program group. The default program group is Microsoft Office, but you can change it if you want.

After you select the program group, Setup checks for disk space once again and begins to install the programs you chose. While you change disks, the Windows background displays "billboards" about registration, OLE 2.0, sharing data, wizards, autoformatting, and other features of the Microsoft Office suite.

When the installation is complete, you are notified of its success.

After all of the files are installed, Setup will prompt you to restart Windows so that its changes to WIN.INI can take effect. Office programs may not run properly until Windows is restarted.

> **Note**
>
> Windows will also add the line
>
> ```
> C:\DOS\SHARE /L:500 /F:5100
> ```
>
> to your AUTOEXEC.BAT file, if the Share is not already in that file. For this change to take effect, you will need to reboot your computer. Share is required for proper functioning of OLE features.

If you have installed all the programs into a single program group, you will see the program group box (e.g., Microsoft Office) displayed in Program Manager, after you restart Windows.

Setup will also add the Office Manager to your Startup group. When Windows restarts, so will the Office Manager. If you don't want Office Manager running whenever you start windows, delete its icon from the Startup group.

Installing Microsoft Access

In addition to Word, Excel, and PowerPoint, the professional edition of Microsoft Office includes a separate set of disks to install Microsoft Access. The Office Setup program doesn't install Access for you, so you need to install it separately.

You install Access the same way you installed the rest of Office; no other applications should be active. Put the first Access disk in your drive. Choose the **F**ile **R**un command (from the Program Manager's menu), and enter **a:setup.** If your disk is in drive A, for example, type **a:setup** and press Enter.

Setup again prompts you for your name and organization (a name is required). When you are prompted for a directory, you see that the Access default is the following:

C:\ACCESS

You can install Access in that directory, if you like. You may want to change the directory to the following, however, if you want to keep all of your Office programs together under a single directory:

C:\MSOFFICE\ACCESS

This is purely a matter of personal preference; Access doesn't care where you install it, and neither does the rest of Office.

You will also have options for Typical, Complete/Custom, or Laptop installations. You choose these options the same way you did in the Office Setup, as described earlier in this appendix.

Insert each disk as prompted, until the installation is complete.

Installing Office on a Network

Microsoft Office can be installed on a network using the Setup program that comes with the software. However, before doing so, you must consult Microsoft and obtain a license agreement that allows you to do so.

Installing Office on the Network Server

The Setup program for networks is very similar to the standalone installation. Some key differences are described in this section. The Setup program can be started with a command-line switch to permit network administrators to install a shared copy of Microsoft Office for multiple users on a network. In the Run dialog box, type **a:setup /a**.

If you are a network administrator installing Office on a LAN, Windows should already be installed there. The network copy of Windows can be used either to facilitate local installations, or as a workstation server.

All that matters is that Office's Setup should use the same copy of Windows that will be used by the end users who will share the Office installation. Setup modifies various Windows system files, and your users need to have access to those files. If you install Setup using a copy of Windows other than the one they use, your users' copy won't be updated.

Note

Network administrators can install Access to the network using these same techniques.

Naturally, you need to have write access to the Windows directory. No one else should have access to the network during the installation process.

You will need to choose a network drive path for the installation. You do this in the Change Directory dialog box, which is used in the same manner that it was in the standalone installation, except that you choose a network drive. You will also be prompted, in the next dialog box, for the path for shared files. Before proceeding, you are required to confirm these choices in the next dialog box.

After this, you need to determine where the shared files will be installed. In the next dialog box, choose where workstation users should be allowed to install the shared files. Depending on your network and workstation resources and performance requirements, you need to decide whether shared files should be installed only on the server, on the local workstations, or left up to the user to decide when installing to individual workstations. If space on the local workstation hard drives is limited, select **S**erver. If you select **L**ocal Hard Drive for users to install shared files to their hard drives, Performance (speed) will be better, and there will be fewer demands on the network server. If you want to leave the choice up to each user that installs Office on their workstation, select **U**ser's Choice.

After this, the installation will proceed in the same fashion as a standalone installation.

Installing Office from the Network to Workstations

After the network administrator installs Office on the network server, each user that will use Office needs to run the Setup program to install it on the workstation. The network administrator needs to contact Microsoft to secure a license for the appropriate number of workstation installations.

Note

Access can be installed from the network to workstations in the same manner, except it uses the Setup program in the \ACCESS\SETUP directory on the network.

The workstation installation will be very similar to the standalone installation. You choose the Program Manager's **F**ile **R**un command and type ***p:\path\setup***, where *p:\path* is the path where Office is installed on the network. The installation will proceed just like the standalone installation, until you get to the point where you choose the installation type. You can choose one of the standard installation types discussed earlier in the appendix. Or you have one additional option—**W**orkstation. This installation option does not copy all of the files from the network to your local drive. Instead, it only copies a few files and the rest will be accessed from the network when you run any Office program. You can also choose any of the other installation options (Typical, Complete/Custom, or Laptop), and proceed as in the standalone installation.

If you choose a Workstation installation, you will not need to choose which programs to set up. Since all of the program files are already on the network, Office will set up your local hard drive to run all of the applications.

During the installation, you will see a progress message box. The title bar in the progress message box indicates that you are running the network installation. When the installation is done, you will be prompted to restart Windows.

Updating an Existing Installation

Microsoft Office provides for maintenance of existing installations. You can use this to add or remove parts of Office in your installation. If you run Setup again after an earlier Office installation, you will see the maintenance screen. From this screen, you can choose to add or remove components of Office.

Choosing Installation Options

If you choose the **A**dd/Remove button in the installation maintenance screen, you see a selection menu just like the one used for a custom installation of Microsoft Office. You just select the boxes corresponding to the files you want to add (or remove), and Setup handles the rest. The Chan**g**e Option button gives you substantial control over your selections. If you choose Chan**g**e Option while Microsoft Excel is highlighted, for example, you can select which components of Excel to install.

If you want even finer control, you can choose Chan**g**e Option again, while an item at the component level is selected, to determine which of its subcomponents to install. If you select Microsoft Excel, you can see how Excel's main program files are subdivided.

If an option is not installed, its check box will be blank. To install new options, select the box and choose OK. Setup then prompts you for the installation disks as needed.

Removing Programs and Installing New Versions

Each program in Microsoft Office has its own development schedule, so version upgrades of individual programs are not likely to be issued simultaneously. This makes the purchase of the suite somewhat vexing, since you may not get all of the most current versions of each program packaged together. You might have Version 4.0a of Excel or Version 5.0 of Excel, for example, depending on when you purchased Office.

Many people purchased or upgraded to Microsoft Office 4.0 with the understanding that automatic upgrades (for example, Excel 5.0 and PowerPoint 4.0) would be forthcoming. Others may eventually want to upgrade only various modules of the suite. Managing changing versions of individual Office modules is simplified by the maintenance menu's **A**dd/Remove option.

If you want to remove an older version of a single program before installing an upgrade, choose **A**dd/Remove from the maintenance menu. You will see which programs are installed on your system. If an item is currently installed, an *X* is marked in its check box. Otherwise, the box is blank.

However, you may not need to remove older programs before upgrading them. Setup typically lets you install over older installations. If you have Excel 4.0, PowerPoint 3.0, or Access 1.1, run the Setup program that comes with your new version of Excel 5.0, PowerPoint 4.0, or Access 2.0. These setup programs function similarly to the Office Setup earlier in this appendix.

At the highest level, you can deselect the single box corresponding to any program in the suite and completely remove it from your system. If you are ready to install the newest version of Excel and want to delete the older one to avoid any possible conflicts between the two versions, for example, deselect the Excel box and choose OK. Setup will remove all the Excel files you previously installed with Office.

If you want to remove only certain elements of a program, choose Chan**g**e Options while that program is highlighted on the menu list. You will see the currently installed options for each program. To delete items, remove their marks. When you choose OK, the items you have changed will be removed.

Caution

The Re**m**ove All option on the installation maintenance screen wipes out all your Microsoft Office installation!

If, for any reason, you want to reinstall all of your Microsoft Office programs (you may have had a problem with your hard drive, for example, and some files were corrupted), choose **R**einstall. Setup determines what programs you originally installed, and will reinstall any files that have been lost or damaged.

Appendix B

Index of Common Problems

B

VIII

Appendixes

All Office Applications and Application Integration	
If you have this problem...	**You'll find help here...**
Association with application does not exist for a file icon	p. 829
Copy cuts instead of copying with drag-and-drop	p. 772
Copy of unwanted material appears when you paste	p. 53
Copy with drag-and-drop does not leave the original	p. 54
Copying with drag-and-drop puts text in the wrong position	p. 772
Display doesn't show enough of document after moving table	p. 778
Drag-and-drop won't work and black circle with slash through it appears	p. 772
Excel data doesn't line up properly in PowerPoint	p. 876
Excel worksheet too big to fit in PowerPoint	p. 876
File won't open when embedding Word file in PowerPoint	p. 871
Find File doesn't find documents with specified text	p. 749
Find File doesn't search specified network drive	p. 749
Formatted with wrong format	p. 58

(continues)

Application Integration (continued)	
If you have this problem...	**You'll find help here...**
Menu description needs to be edited	p. 893
Menu items lost	p. 894
Menus have been customized	p. 893
Record is not found in Mail Merge search	p. 845
Send and Add Routing commands not on File menu	p. 822
Source document changes not reflected in destination document	p. 792
Standard toolbar has been modified	p. 891
Toolbar contains no buttons	p. 891
Toolbars hard to see on monochrome monitor	p. 891

Word	
If you have this problem...	**You'll find help here...**
AutoCorrect additions without running Spelling Checker	p. 143
AutoFormat doesn't change document's formatting	p. 203
Autoformating only part of a document	p. 203
Column is missing on-screen when text is formatted in two columns	p. 123
Deleted or cleared text accidentally	p. 113
Drag-and-drop pointer appears when you do not want it	p. 114
File format for saving not listed in file types	p. 117
Files: Copy, delete, or print multiple files	p. 168
Find File cannot find desired file with search criteria	p. 163
Find File dialog box has unusual icon in it	p. 168
Find File: Searching for text in a file	p. 163
Formatted text with fonts and alignment changes needs to be changed to original formatting	p. 127

If you have this problem...	You'll find help here...
Formatting quickly in more than one place in document	p. 127
Grammar checker stops on spelling errors	p. 147
Grammar checker: Undoing changes	p. 147
Justified text has large gaps between words	p. 134
Line spacing needs to change without changing paragraph spacing	p. 133
Lines of text need to be prevented from flowing to next page	p. 149
Macro directory cannot be found	p. 233
Macro recording doesn't record mouse steps	p. 233
Macro: Moving from Normal template to another template	p. 233
Margins cannot be set accurately with ruler in Print Preview	p. 149
Outline doesn't display body text when outline is collapsed	p. 195
Outline levels: Printing only certain levels	p. 196
Pasted selected text in wrong place	p. 114
Printing an 8 1/2- by 14-inch document	p. 137
Printing leaves off edges of text	p. 137
Printing tables without printing lines and fills	p. 151
Printing to a different printer	p. 151
Saving a document that was created in another file format	p. 117
Screen doesn't display enough of document to edit	p. 123
Screen redraws slowly with many fonts and graphics	p. 123
Selecting text difficult with mouse	p. 110
Spell checker cannot find words with numbers	p. 143
Spelling dictionary needs words edited	p. 143
Summary Info has title even though you didn't add a title	p. 158
Summary Info limit on number of keywords	p. 158

(continues)

If you have this problem...	You'll find help here...
Data Form command generates error message that no list was found	p. 370
Date converted to a number	p. 250
Drag-and-drop copies cells instead of moving them	p. 270
Drag-and-drop won't copy data	p. 270
Error in a formula	p. 316
Filtered list doesn't display any records	p. 379
Formula appears in a cell as a label instead of being calculated	p. 250
Formula used to calculate a Range doesn't calculate properly	p. 250
Formula with name treated as a text entry	p. 316
International currency symbol used without changing the symbol for all currency formats	p. 288
Macro changes data but changes are undone	p. 411
Macro commands start with an equal sign	p. 415
Macro Error dialog box appears when macro runs	p. 414
Macro needs steps added	p. 411
Macro recording mistakes are repeated when the macro runs	p. 411
Macro shortcut key doesn't work	p. 414
Page break cannot be removed because Remove Page Break isn't on Insert menu	p. 344
Page breaks: Only some removed	p. 344
Parentheses do not match in formula	p. 316
Paste won't paste a second copy of copied cells	p. 270
Pasting pastes only a portion of data selected to be pasted	p. 272
Printing selected embedded chart instead of the entire worksheet	p. 363

(continues)

Excel (continued)	
If you have this problem...	**You'll find help here...**
Record can't be added to list	p. 370
Report cannot be created because the Print Report command does not appear in the File menu	p. 348
Report printed with all pages numbered 1	p. 348

PowerPoint	
If you have this problem...	**You'll find help here...**
Background is too dark in template	p. 447
Bullets: Deleting from an AutoLayout containing bullets	p. 467
Clip-art picture: Changing colors	p. 468
ClipArt Gallery: Adding clip art from other programs	p. 469
Deleted a slide from presentation	p. 448
Graph: Adding a graph on a slide that doesn't include a graph in AutoLayout	p. 534
Lines and arcs: Changing the length or direction	p. 504
Lines: Drawing at angle other than 45 degrees	p. 504
Microsoft Graph: Closed MS Graph before you were finished with it	p. 534
Resizing an object by the same amount on opposite sides	p. 486
Selecting objects on multiple slides at once cannot be done	p. 482
Selecting the company logo on a slide doesn't work	p. 482
Selection box doesn't select all objects it should	p. 482
Size and scale of imported picture are wrong	p. 486-487
Slide inserted in the wrong location	p. 448
Slide master changes in a presentation affecting the template	p. 513
Slides: Inserting and adding	p. 448

If you have this problem...	You'll find help here...
Template: Can't use more than one template in a presentation	p. 512
Template: Creating a custom template	p. 512
Template: Selected wrong template when creating presentation with Wizard	p. 447
Text object and label differences	p. 467

Access

If you have this problem...	You'll find help here...
Adding a field to database	p. 609
Adding new records	p. 619
All Properties property list for a text box is too long to view and work with	p. 659
Crosstab query results headings are in wrong order	p. 672
Data type: Don't know proper type to assign to fields	p. 603
Database design has too many tables	p. 585
Database doesn't appear when Access opens	p. 585
Database tables have too many fields	p. 585
Database: Where to begin creating a database	p. 596
Dates: Selecting a display format for dates	p. 606
Deleting a field from the QBE grid	p. 672
Embedding part of a file	p. 718
Field and description need to be moved to bottom of the report	p. 696
Field control's validation property out of room	p. 659
Field forgotten in selecting fields for a form	p. 644
Field forgotten in selecting fields for a report	p. 688
Field is not sunken like the others	p. 659

(continues)

Access (continued)	
If you have this problem...	**You'll find help here...**
Fields don't line up on left	p. 696
Filter doesn't list any data	p. 627
Fixed-width text file cannot be imported	p. 635
Form's property sheet cannot be accessed	p. 659
Graph: Changing legend labels a graph	p. 712
Graphing existing fields on the form	p. 712
Grouping report improperly groups data	p. 704
List-box control does not allow new data entry	p. 696
Macro command button does nothing	p. 732
Macro processing: Aborting macro processing if a condition test fails	p. 727
Macro: Changing the picture on a button	p. 732
Macro: Moving to a specific page in a macro	p. 727
Macro: Programming a button to dial the phone	p. 732
Main/subform Wizard can't be created	p. 644, 688
Mainframe data import automation	p. 727
Need to require data entry in a field	p. 606
OLE object on form is missing	p. 718
Paintbrush object can't be linked in a bound frame	p. 718
Primary key for fields	p. 603
Print action in macro prints all records, not just the current record	p. 727
Queries that depend on uncertain criteria	p. 679
Query results dynaset: Combining data from two text fields	p. 679
Query takes too long to run	p. 679
Report contains no fields or data	p. 688

Index

Symbols

A

B

C

D

E

F

G

H

I

J-K

L

M

N

O

Q

R

S

T

U

V

X–Y–Z